Contemporary Authors®

NEW REVISION SERIES

Contemporary

Authors®

**A Bio-Bibliographical Guide to
Current Writers in Fiction, General Nonfiction,
Poetry, Journalism, Drama, Motion Pictures,
Television, and Other Fields**

NEW REVISION SERIES *volume* 140

THOMSON

GALE™

Detroit • New York • San Francisco • San Diego • New Haven, Conn. • Waterville, Maine • London • Munich

THOMSON
GALE

Contemporary Authors, New Revision Series, Vol. 140

Project Editor
Tracey L. Matthews

Editorial
Katy Balcer, Michelle Kazensky, Julie Mellors, Joshua Kondek, Lisa Kumar, Mary Ruby, Maikue Vang

Permissions
Emma Hull, Jacqueline Key, Sue Rudolph

Imaging and Multimedia
Lezlie Light, Michael Logusz

Composition and Electronic Capture
Carolyn Roney

Manufacturing
Drew Kalasky

LIBRARY OF CONGRESS CATALOG CARD NUMBER 81-640179

ISBN 0-7876-7894-5
ISSN 0275-7176

Printed in the United States of America
10 9 8 7 6 5 4 3 2 1

Contents

Preface vii

Product Advisory Board xi

International Advisory Board xii

CA Numbering System and
Volume Update Chart xiii

Authors and Media People
Featured in This Volume xv

Acknowledgments xvii

Author Listings 1

Indexing note: All *Contemporary Authors* entries are indexed in the *Contemporary Authors* cumulative index, which is published separately and distributed twice a year.

As always, the most recent Contemporary Authors cumulative index continues to be the user's guide to the location of an individual author's listing.

Preface

Contemporary Authors (*CA*) provides information on approximately 120,000 writers in a wide range of media, including:

- Current writers of fiction, nonfiction, poetry, and drama whose works have been issued by commercial publishers, risk publishers, or university presses (authors whose books have been published only by known vanity or author-subsidized firms are ordinarily not included)

- Prominent print and broadcast journalists, editors, photojournalists, syndicated cartoonists, graphic novelists, screenwriters, television scriptwriters, and other media people

- Notable international authors

- Literary greats of the early twentieth century whose works are popular in today's high school and college curriculums and continue to elicit critical attention

A *CA* listing entails no charge or obligation. Authors are included on the basis of the above criteria and their interest to *CA* users. Sources of potential listees include trade periodicals, publishers' catalogs, librarians, and other users.

How to Get the Most out of *CA*: Use the Index

The key to locating an author's most recent entry is the *CA* cumulative index, which is published separately and distributed twice a year. It provides access to *all* entries in *CA* and *Contemporary Authors New Revision Series* (*CANR*). Always consult the latest index to find an author's most recent entry.

For the convenience of users, the *CA* cumulative index also includes references to all entries in these Thomson Gale literary series: *African-American Writers, African Writers, American Nature Writers, American Writers, American Writers: The Classics, American Writers Retrospective Supplement, American Writers Supplement, Ancient Writers, Asian American Literature, Authors and Artists for Young Adults, Authors in the News, Beacham's Encyclopedia of Popular Fiction: Analyses, Beacham's Encyclopedia of Popular Fiction: Biography and Resources, Beacham's Guide to Literature for Young Adults, Beat Generation: A Gale Critical Companion, Bestsellers, Black Literature Criticism, Black Literature Criticism Supplement, Black Writers, British Writers, British Writers: The Classics, British Writers Retrospective Supplement, British Writers Supplement, Children's Literature Review, Classical and Medieval Literature Criticism, Concise Dictionary of American Literary Biography, Concise Dictionary of American Literary Biography Supplement, Concise Dictionary of British Literary Biography, Concise Dictionary of World Literary Biography, Contemporary American Dramatists, Contemporary Authors Autobiography Series, Contemporary Authors Bibliographical Series, Contemporary British Dramatists, Contemporary Canadian Authors, Contemporary Dramatists, Contemporary Literary Criticism, Contemporary Novelists, Contemporary Poets, Contemporary Popular Writers, Contemporary Southern Writers, Contemporary Women Dramatists, Contemporary Women Poets, Contemporary World Writers, Dictionary of Literary Biography, Dictionary of Literary Biography Documentary Series, Dictionary of Literary Biography Yearbook, DISCovering Authors, DISCovering Authors 3.0, DISCovering Authors: British Edition, DISCovering Authors: Canadian Edition, DISCovering Authors Modules, Drama Criticism, Drama for Students, Encyclopedia of World Literature in the 20th Century, Epics for Students, European Writers, Exploring Novels, Exploring Poetry, Exploring Short Stories, Feminism in Literature, Feminist Writers, Gay & Lesbian Literature, Guide to French Literature, Harlem Renaissance: A Gale Critical Companion, Hispanic Literature Criticism, Hispanic Literature Criticism Supplement, Hispanic Writers, International Dictionary of Films and Filmmakers: Writers and Production Artists, International Dictionary of Theatre: Playwrights, Junior DISCovering Authors, Latin American Writers, Latin American Writers Supplement, Latino and Latina Writers, Literature and Its Times, Literature and Its Times Supplement, Literature Criticism from 1400-1800, Literature of Developing Nations for Students, Major Authors and Illustrators for Children and Young Adults, Major Authors and Illustrators for Children and Young Adults Supplement, Major 21st Century Writers* (eBook version), *Major 20th-Century Writers, Modern American Women Writers, Modern Arts Criticism, Modern Japanese Writers, Mystery and Suspense Writers, Native North American Literature, Nineteenth-Century Literature Criticism, Nonfiction Classics for Students, Novels for Students, Poetry Criticism, Poetry for Students, Poets: American and British, Reference Guide to American Literature, Reference Guide to English Literature, Reference Guide to Short Fiction, Reference Guide to World Literature, Science Fiction Writers, Shakespearean Criticism, Shakespeare for Students, Shakespeare's Characters for Students, Short Stories for Students, Short Story Criticism, Something About the Author, Something About the Author Autobiography Series, St. James Guide to Children's Writers, St. James Guide to Crime & Mystery Writers, St. James Guide to Fantasy Writers, St. James Guide to Horror, Ghost & Gothic Writers, St. James Guide to Science Fiction Writers, St. James Guide to Young Adult Writers, Supernatural Fiction*

Writers, Twayne Companion to Contemporary Literature in English, Twayne's English Authors, Twayne's United States Authors, Twayne's World Authors, Twentieth-Century Literary Criticism, Twentieth-Century Romance and Historical Writers, Twentieth-Century Western Writers, William Shakespeare, World Literature and Its Times, World Literature Criticism, World Literature Criticism Supplement, World Poets, World Writing in English, Writers for Children, Writers for Young Adults, and *Yesterday's Authors of Books for Children.*

A Sample Index Entry:

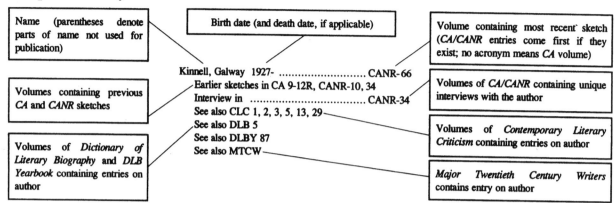

How Are Entries Compiled?

The editors make every effort to secure new information directly from the authors; listees' responses to our questionnaires and query letters provide most of the information featured in *CA*. For deceased writers, or those who fail to reply to requests for data, we consult other reliable biographical sources, such as those indexed in Thomson Gale's *Biography and Genealogy Master Index,* and bibliographical sources, including *National Union Catalog, LC MARC,* and *British National Bibliography.* Further details come from published interviews, feature stories, and book reviews, as well as information supplied by the authors' publishers and agents.

An asterisk (*) at the end of a sketch indicates that the listing has been compiled from secondary sources believed to be reliable but has not been personally verified for this edition by the author sketched.

What Kinds of Information Does An Entry Provide?

Sketches in *CA* contain the following biographical and bibliographical information:

- **Entry heading:** the most complete form of author's name, plus any pseudonyms or name variations used for writing

- **Personal information:** author's date and place of birth, family data, ethnicity, educational background, political and religious affiliations, and hobbies and leisure interests

- **Addresses:** author's home, office, or agent's addresses, plus e-mail and fax numbers, as available

- **Career summary:** name of employer, position, and dates held for each career post; resume of other vocational achievements; military service

- **Membership information:** professional, civic, and other association memberships and any official posts held

- **Awards and honors:** military and civic citations, major prizes and nominations, fellowships, grants, and honorary degrees

- **Writings:** a comprehensive, chronological list of titles, publishers, dates of original publication and revised editions, and production information for plays, television scripts, and screenplays

- **Adaptations:** a list of films, plays, and other media which have been adapted from the author's work

- **Work in progress:** current or planned projects, with dates of completion and/or publication, and expected publisher, when known

- **Sidelights:** a biographical portrait of the author's development; information about the critical reception of the author's works; revealing comments, often by the author, on personal interests, aspirations, motivations, and thoughts on writing

- **Interview:** a one-on-one discussion with authors conducted especially for *CA*, offering insight into authors' thoughts about their craft

- **Autobiographical essay:** an original essay written by noted authors for *CA*, a forum in which writers may present themselves, on their own terms, to their audience

- **Photographs:** portraits and personal photographs of notable authors

- **Biographical and critical sources:** a list of books and periodicals in which additional information on an author's life and/or writings appears

- **Obituary Notices** in *CA* provide date and place of birth as well as death information about authors whose full-length sketches appeared in the series before their deaths. The entries also summarize the authors' careers and writings and list other sources of biographical and death information.

Related Titles in the *CA* Series

Contemporary Authors Autobiography Series complements *CA* original and revised volumes with specially commissioned autobiographical essays by important current authors, illustrated with personal photographs they provide. Common topics include their motivations for writing, the people and experiences that shaped their careers, the rewards they derive from their work, and their impressions of the current literary scene.

Contemporary Authors Bibliographical Series surveys writings by and about important American authors since World War II. Each volume concentrates on a specific genre and features approximately ten writers; entries list works written by and about the author and contain a bibliographical essay discussing the merits and deficiencies of major critical and scholarly studies in detail.

Available in Electronic Formats

GaleNet. *CA* is available on a subscription basis through GaleNet, an online information resource that features an easy-to-use end-user interface, powerful search capabilities, and ease of access through the World-Wide Web. For more information, call 1-800-877-GALE.

Licensing. *CA* is available for licensing. The complete database is provided in a fielded format and is deliverable on such media as disk, CD-ROM, or tape. For more information, contact Thomson Gale's Business Development Group at 1-800-877-GALE, or visit us on our website at www.galegroup.com/bizdev.

Suggestions Are Welcome

The editors welcome comments and suggestions from users on any aspect of the *CA* series. If readers would like to recommend authors for inclusion in future volumes of the series, they are cordially invited to write the Editors at *Contemporary Authors*, Thomson Gale, 27500 Drake Rd., Farmington Hills, MI 48331-3535; or call at 1-248-699-4253; or fax at 1-248-699-8054.

Contemporary Authors Product Advisory Board

The editors of *Contemporary Authors* are dedicated to maintaining a high standard of excellence by publishing comprehensive, accurate, and highly readable entries on a wide array of writers. In addition to the quality of the content, the editors take pride in the graphic design of the series, which is intended to be orderly yet inviting, allowing readers to utilize the pages of *CA* easily and with efficiency. Despite the longevity of the *CA* print series, and the success of its format, we are mindful that the vitality of a literary reference product is dependent on its ability to serve its users over time. As literature, and attitudes about literature, constantly evolve, so do the reference needs of students, teachers, scholars, journalists, researchers, and book club members. To be certain that we continue to keep pace with the expectations of our customers, the editors of *CA* listen carefully to their comments regarding the value, utility, and quality of the series. Librarians, who have firsthand knowledge of the needs of library users, are a valuable resource for us. The *Contemporary Authors* Product Advisory Board, made up of school, public, and academic librarians, is a forum to promote focused feedback about *CA* on a regular basis. The seven-member advisory board includes the following individuals, whom the editors wish to thank for sharing their expertise:

- **Anne M. Christensen,** Librarian II, Phoenix Public Library, Phoenix, Arizona.

- **Barbara C. Chumard,** Reference/Adult Services Librarian, Middletown Thrall Library, Middletown, New York.

- **Eva M. Davis,** Youth Department Manager, Ann Arbor District Library, Ann Arbor, Michigan.

- **Adam Janowski, Jr.,** Library Media Specialist, Naples High School Library Media Center, Naples, Florida.

- **Robert Reginald,** Head of Technical Services and Collection Development, California State University, San Bernadino, California.

- **Stephen Weiner,** Director, Maynard Public Library, Maynard, Massachusetts.

International Advisory Board

Well-represented among the 120,000 author entries published in *Contemporary Authors* are sketches on notable writers from many non-English-speaking countries. The primary criteria for inclusion of such authors has traditionally been the publication of at least one title in English, either as an original work or as a translation. However, the editors of *Contemporary Authors* came to observe that many important international writers were being overlooked due to a strict adherence to our inclusion criteria. In addition, writers who were publishing in languages other than English were not being covered in the traditional sources we used for identifying new listees. Intent on increasing our coverage of international authors, including those who write only in their native language and have not been translated into English, the editors enlisted the aid of a board of advisors, each of whom is an expert on the literature of a particular country or region. Among the countries we focused attention on are Mexico, Puerto Rico, Spain, Italy, France, Germany, Luxembourg, Belgium, the Netherlands, Norway, Sweden, Denmark, Finland, Taiwan, Singapore, Malaysia, Thailand, South Africa, Israel, and Japan, as well as England, Scotland, Wales, Ireland, Australia, and New Zealand. The sixteen-member advisory board includes the following individuals, whom the editors wish to thank for sharing their expertise:

- **Lowell A. Bangerter,** Professor of German, University of Wyoming, Laramie, Wyoming.

- **Nancy E. Berg,** Associate Professor of Hebrew and Comparative Literature, Washington University, St. Louis, Missouri.

- **Frances Devlin-Glass,** Associate Professor, School of Literary and Communication Studies, Deakin University, Burwood, Victoria, Australia.

- **David William Foster,** Regent's Professor of Spanish, Interdisciplinary Humanities, and Women's Studies, Arizona State University, Tempe, Arizona.

- **Hosea Hirata,** Director of the Japanese Program, Associate Professor of Japanese, Tufts University, Medford, Massachusetts.

- **Jack Kolbert,** Professor Emeritus of French Literature, Susquehanna University, Selinsgrove, Pennsylvania.

- **Mark Libin,** Professor, University of Manitoba, Winnipeg, Manitoba, Canada.

- **C. S. Lim,** Professor, University of Malaya, Kuala Lumpur, Malaysia.

- **Eloy E. Merino,** Assistant Professor of Spanish, Northern Illinois University, DeKalb, Illinois.

- **Linda M. Rodríguez Guglielmoni,** Associate Professor, University of Puerto Rico—Mayagüez, Puerto Rico.

- **Sven Hakon Rossel,** Professor and Chair of Scandinavian Studies, University of Vienna, Vienna, Austria.

- **Steven R. Serafin,** Director, Writing Center, Hunter College of the City University of New York, New York City.

- **David Smyth,** Lecturer in Thai, School of Oriental and African Studies, University of London, England.

- **Ismail S. Talib,** Senior Lecturer, Department of English Language and Literature, National University of Singapore, Singapore.

- **Dionisio Viscarri,** Assistant Professor, Ohio State University, Columbus, Ohio.

- **Mark Williams,** Associate Professor, English Department, University of Canterbury, Christchurch, New Zealand.

CA Numbering System and Volume Update Chart

Occasionally questions arise about the *CA* numbering system and which volumes, if any, can be discarded. Despite numbers like "29-32R," "97-100" and "233," the entire *CA* print series consists of 301 physical volumes with the publication of *CA* Volume 234. The following charts note changes in the numbering system and cover design, and indicate which volumes are essential for the most complete, up-to-date coverage.

CA First Revision

- 1-4R through 41-44R (11 books)
  Cover: Brown with black and gold trim.
  There will be no further First Revision volumes because revised entries are now being handled exclusively through the more efficient *New Revision Series* mentioned below.

CA Original Volumes

- 45-48 through 97-100 (14 books)
  Cover: Brown with black and gold trim.
  101 through 234 (134 books)
  Cover: Blue and black with orange bands.
  The same as previous *CA* original volumes but with a new, simplified numbering system and new cover design.

CA Permanent Series

- *CAP*-1 and *CAP*-2 (2 books)
  Cover: Brown with red and gold trim.
  There will be no further Permanent Series volumes because revised entries are now being handled exclusively through the more efficient *New Revision Series* mentioned below.

CA New Revision Series

- CANR-1 through CANR-140 (140 books)
  Cover: Blue and black with green bands.
  Includes only sketches requiring significant changes; **sketches are taken from any previously published CA, CAP, or CANR volume.**

If You Have:	You May Discard:
CA First Revision Volumes 1-4R through 41-44R and *CA Permanent Series* Volumes 1 and 2	*CA* Original Volumes 1, 2, 3, 4 and Volumes 5-6 through 41-44
CA Original Volumes 45-48 through 97-100 and 101 through 234	**NONE:** These volumes will not be superseded by corresponding revised volumes. Individual entries from these and all other volumes appearing in the left column of this chart may be revised and included in the various volumes of the *New Revision Series*.
CA New Revision Series Volumes *CANR*-1 through *CANR*-140	**NONE:** The *New Revision Series* does not replace any single volume of *CA*. Instead, volumes of *CANR* include entries from many previous *CA* series volumes. All *New Revision Series* volumes must be retained for full coverage.

A Sampling of Authors and Media People
Featured in This Volume

Evan S. Connell Jr.

Connell, the award-winning author of both fiction and nonfiction, is best known for the critically acclaimed best-seller *Son of the Morning Star: Custer and the Little Bighorn.* Lauded by critics for their consummate craftsmanship, his works range widely in scope and theme, from domestic dramas of the modern middle class to fictitious historical treatises on the Crusades and alchemy. His most recent book is *Francisco Goya: A Life,* published in 2004.

Maureen Howard

Howard is an accomplished literary critic and editor whose novels are often compared to the writings of Henry James and Virginia Woolf. Praised for their clarity, linguistic precision, and character development, her works, including novels like *Grace Abounding* and *Expensive Habits* as well as the award-winning autobiography *Facts of Life,* have been described as brilliantly sensitive commentaries on contemporary American society. She explores the complexities of communication and disconnection in her most recent novel, *The Silver Screen,* published in 2004.

Maxine Kumin

Kumin, the Pulitzer Prize-winning author of *Up Country: Poems of New England,* is known for poetry and fiction that is deeply rooted in her native New England. Often likened to Robert Frost or Henry David Thoreau, Kumin deals with subjects ranging from the relation of man to nature and the fragility of human life to religious and cultural identity and and the ever-present threat of loss. In 2003, she published her most recent book, *Bringing Together: Uncollected Early Poems, 1958-1988.*

Steve Martin

Martin, known to audiences worldwide as a stand-up comedian-turned-screen actor, is less widely known as an accomplished writer of screenplays (like *Dead Men Don't Wear Black* and *L. A. Story*), stage plays (*Picasso at the Lapin Agile* and *WASP*), essays (*Pure Drivel*), and fiction (*Shop Girl*). Critics applaud Martin's literary development from a humorist in the tradition of James Thurber and S. J. Perelman to a writer of serious fiction. His most recent book is the 2003 novella *The Pleasure of My Company.*

James Alan McPherson

McPherson, a Pulitzer Prize winner and recipient of the prestigious MacArthur Fellowship, is the author of stories that portray ordinary, working-class people, often African Americans, as they confront universal human problems. Critics praise his story collections like *Hue and Cry* and *Elbow Room* for McPherson's ability to create believable characters, both black and white, and to focus on their underlying humanity. His most recent publication is the 2000 book *A Region Not Home: Reflections from Exile.*

M. S. Merwin

Merwin—an acclaimed writer of poetry, prose, and transalations—is noted for his spare, hard verse which decries man's separation from nature. Poetry collections like *The Lice* declare Merwin's despair over man's desecration of nature. Noting his obsession with the meaning of America and its values, critics often compare Merwin to Walt Whitman, while his surrealistic style echoes that of Theodore Roethke and Robert Bly. Merwin's most recent books are *Migration: New and Selected Poems* and *Present Company,* both published in 2005.

Frederik Pohl

Pohl is a preeminent figure in the field of science fiction, with a host of awards and an international reputation as a writer, editor, literary agent, and enthusiastic promoter of the genre. According to critics, the prolific Pohl may be at his best in a novel like *Starburst,* blending science, speculation, and satire, or in *JEM: The Making of a Utopia,* giving free rein to his poetic imagination. Pohl's most recent book is *The Boy Who Would Live Forever: A Novel of Gateway,* published in 2004.

Sam Shepard

Shepard, well known for his roles in major feature films, is considered the preeminent literary playwright of his generation. Among his accolades are eleven Obie Awards for best Off-Broadway plays, a Pulitzer Prize for *Buried Child,* and a New York Drama Critics' Circle Award for *A Lie of the Mind.* Critics admire his exploration of American popular culture, in the nation's own eccentric vernacular. Shepard's most recent literary efforts include *Great Dream of Heaven: Stories,* published in 2002, and his play *The God of Hell,* produced in 2004.

Acknowledgments

Grateful acknowledgment is made to those publishers, photographers, and artists whose work appear with these authors' essays. Following is a list of the copyright holders who have granted us permission to reproduce material in this volume of *CA*. Every effort has been made to trace copyright, but if omissions have been made, please let us know.

Photographs/Art

Bernard Ashley: Ashley, photograph. Reproduced by permission.

Bernard Bailyn: Bailyn, February 26, 2003, photograph by Julia Malakie. AP/Wide World Photos. Reproduced by permission.

Edward Bloor: Bloor, photograph by Pamela Bloor. Reproduced by permission of Edward Bloor.

Nicole Brossard: Brossard, photograph by John Reeves. Reproduced by permission.

Austin Clarke: Clarke, photograph by John Reeves. Reproduced by permission.

Betty Comden: Comden, October 10, 2003, photograph by Gino Domenico. AP/Wide World Photos. Reproduced by permission.

Evan S. Connell Jr.: Connell, photograph. © Jerry Bauer. Reproduced by permission.

Catherine Cookson: Cookson, receiving an honorary doctorate of letters from Sunderland University in Newcastle, England, July 1991, photograph by John Giles. AP/Wide World Photos. Reproduced by permission.

Will Eisner: Eisner, photograph. Reproduced by permission of Will Eisner Studios, Inc.

Howard Fast: Fast, photograph. Reproduced by permission.

Alasdair Gray: Gray, photograph by Eric Thorburn. Reproduced by permission of the Estate of Eric Thorburn.

Romesh Gunesekera: Gunesekera, photograph. © Jerry Bauer. Reproduced by permission.

Beth Henley: Henley, 1984, photograph. AP/Wide World Photos. Reproduced by permission.

Michel Houellebecq: Houellebecq, photograph by P. Ferbos. AP/Wide World Photos. Reproduced by permission.

Maureen Howard: Howard, 1979, photograph. AP/Wide World Photos. Reproduced by permission.

Catherine Jinks: Jinks, photograph by Peter Dockrill. Reproduced by permission of Peter Dockrill.

Maxine Kumin: Kumin, 1973, photograph. AP/Wide World Photos. Reproduced by permission.

Joanne Kyger: Kyger, photograph. © Chris Felver. Reproduced by permission.

Barry Levinson: Levinson, 1998, photograph by Greg Nelson. AP/Wide World Photos. Reproduced by permission.

A

ABBEY, Lynn
    See ABBEY, Marilyn Lorraine

*   *   *

ABBEY, Marilyn Lorraine 1948-
  (Lynn Abbey)

PERSONAL: Born September 18, 1948, in Peekskill, NY; daughter of Ronald Lionel (an insurance manager) and Doris Lorraine (a homemaker; maiden name, De Wees) Abbey; married Ralph Dressler, July 14, 1969 (divorced October 31, 1972); married Robert Asprin (a writer), August 28, 1982 (divorced, 1993). *Education:* University of Rochester, A.B., 1969; New York University, M.A., 1971. *Hobbies and other interests:* "History (particularly eleventh century and the Normans), embroidery."

ADDRESSES: Home—FL. *Agent*—Spectrum Literary Agency, 432 Park Ave. S., Suite 1205, New York, NY 10016. *E-mail*—labbey@iag.net.

CAREER: Metropolitan Life Insurance Company, New York, NY, actuarial assistant, 1969-76; Citizens Hanover Insurance, Howell, MI, systems analyst, 1976-80; community resources teacher at public schools in Ann Arbor, MI, 1980-82; American Automobile Association, Dearborn, MI, systems analyst, 1982-84. Writer.

MEMBER: Science Fiction Writers of America.

WRITINGS:

FANTASY NOVELS; UNDER NAME LYNN ABBEY

The Guardians, Ace Books (New York, NY), 1982.
(With C. J. Cherry and Janet Morris) *The Soul of the City,* Ace Books (New York, NY), 1986.
(With Robert Asprin) *Catwoman,* Warner (New York, NY), 1992, published as *Catwoman: Tiger Hunt,* Millennium (London, England), 1992.
Siege of Shadows, Ace Books (New York, NY), 1996.
Aquitania, TSR (Lake Geneva, WI), 1997.
The Simbul's Gift, TSR (Lake Geneva, WI), 1997.
Planeswalker, TSR (Lake Geneva, WI), 1998.
Jerlayne, Penguin USA (New York, NY), 1999.
The Nether Scroll: Lost Empires, Wizards Publishing, 2000.

"RIFKIND SAGA"; UNDER NAME LYNN ABBEY

Daughter of the Bright Moon, Ace Books (New York, NY), 1979.
The Black Flame, Ace Books (New York, NY), 1980.

"UNICORN AND DRAGON" SERIES; UNDER NAME LYNN ABBEY

Unicorn & Dragon, Avon (New York, NY), 1987.
Conquest, Avon (New York, NY), 1988, published as *The Green Man,* Hodder Headline (London, England), 1989.

"ULTIMA SAGA"; UNDER NAME LYNN ABBEY

The Forge of Virtue, Warner (New York, NY), 1991.
The Temper of Wisdom, Warner (New York, NY), 1992.

1

"WALENSOR SAGA"; UNDER NAME LYNN ABBEY

The Wooden Sword, Ace Books (New York, NY), 1991.
Beneath the Web, Ace Books (New York, NY), 1994.

"DARK SUN" TRILOGY; UNDER NAME LYNN ABBEY

The Brazen Gambit, TSR (Lake Geneva, WI), 1994.
Cinnabar Shadows, TSR (Lake Geneva, WI), 1995.
The Rise and Fall of a Dragonking, TSR (Lake Geneva, WI), 1996.

"EMMA MERRIGAN" SERIES; UNDER NAME LYNN ABBEY

Out of Time, Ace Books (New York, NY), 2000.
Behind Time, Ace Books (New York, NY), 2001.
Taking Time, Ace Books (New York, NY), 2004.
Down Time, Ace Books (New York, NY), 2005.

"THIEVES' WORLD" SERIES; UNDER NAME LYNN ABBEY

(Editor, with Robert Asprin) *The Face of Chaos* (also see below), Ace Books (New York, NY), 1983.
(Editor, with Robert Asprin) *Wings of Omen* (also see below), Ace Books (New York, NY), 1984.
(Editor, with Robert Asprin) *Cross-Currents* (omnibus; includes *Storm Season, The Face of Chaos,* and *Wings of Omen*), Doubleday (New York, NY), 1984.
(Editor, with Robert Asprin) *The Dead of Winter* (also see below), Ace Books (New York, NY), 1985.
(Editor, with Robert Asprin) *Soul of the City* (also see below), Ace Books (New York, NY), 1986.
(Editor, with Robert Asprin) *Blood Ties* (also see below), Ace Books (New York, NY), 1986.
(Editor, with Robert Asprin) *The Shattered Sphere* (omnibus; includes *The Dead of Winter, Soul of the City,* and *Blood Ties*), Doubleday (New York, NY), 1986.
(Editor, with Robert Asprin) *Aftermath* (also see below), Ace Books (New York, NY), 1987.
(Editor, with Robert Asprin) *Uneasy Alliances* (also see below), Ace Books (New York, NY), 1988.
(Editor, with Robert Asprin) *Stealer's Sky* (also see below), Ace Books (New York, NY), 1989.

(Editor, with Robert Asprin) *The Price of Victory* (omnibus; includes *Aftermath, Uneasy Alliances,* and *Stealer's Sky*), Doubleday (New York, NY), 1990.
(Editor) *Turning Points,* Tor (New York, NY), 2002.
Sanctuary: An Epic Novel of Thieves' World, Tor (New York, NY), 2002.
(Editor, with Robert Asprin) *First Blood* (anthology), Tor (New York, NY), 2003.
(Editor) *Enemies of Fortune,* Tor (New York, NY), 2004.

Also adaptor of "Thieves' World" as a graphic-novel series, Starblaze Graphics (Norfolk, VA), 1985-87, and Donning Co. (Norfolk, VA), beginning 1986.

"ELFQUEST" SERIES; EDITOR, WITH ROBERT ASPRIN AND RICHARD PINI; UNDER NAME LYNN ABBEY

The Blood of Ten Chiefs, Tor (New York, NY), 1986.
Wolfsong: The Blood of Ten Chiefs, Tor (New York, NY), 1988.

ADAPTATIONS: "Thieves' World" was licensed as a board game and a fantasy role-playing game.

SIDELIGHTS: Writing under the name Lynn Abbey, Marilyn Lorraine Abbey is noted for her creation and coeditorship of the long-running "Thieves' World" fiction anthology series, as well as for her many fantasy novels. According to *St. James Guide to Fantasy Writers* essayist Mary Corran, "Abbey's talent is unmistakable . . . , most particularly in the creation of cheerless terrains peopled by sinister creatures of every type. She has constructed her own type of fantasy, where the endings are not always happy nor the heroes and heroines noble or fulfilled by their quests. . . . Abbey possesses the ability to create dark nightmares, where motives for valour are more complex than simple virtue. Her characters reflect the worlds they inhabit, filled with unsettling, malign emotions. The dismal settings may occasionally irritate; but they are very well drawn, and filled with a rare depth of detail which is formidably imagined."

Abbey came to her career as a fiction writer after working for several years as a systems programmer for New York and Midwest-based insurance companies. Always interested in science fiction, she was eventually inspired to write her first sci-fi story while recovering from an automobile accident in 1977. Since her first book, *Daughter of the Bright Moon,* was published in 1979, she has gone on to write numerous other fantasy novels set in widely varying worlds. Both *Daughter of the Bright Moon* and its sequel, *The Black Flame,* focus on Rifkind, a warrior, priestess, healer, and witch who, while also finding love with Domnhall, ultimately loses him to her ultimate destiny: battling evil in a hostile world of deserts and dangerous swamps. Abbey's "Ultima Saga," which includes *The Forge of Virtue* and *The Temper of Wisdom,* is set in a more conventional, near-medieval world.

Abbey's complex, detailed settings are a key ingredient in her work. As Corran noted, "Whether the plot involves a quest, or a conflict of good versus evil, each world displays dirt and squalor and constant perils, both human and magical. These settings are designed to repel, not appeal to, the senses, and the major characters are similarly contrived to lack attractive or sympathetic qualities." In *The Wooden Sword,* for example, Abbey casts as protagonist a shepherdess named Berika, who avoids marriage to a deformed and mentally stunted man by running away with a mysterious stranger, who is ultimately killed. Although avoiding an ill-fated marriage, Berika ultimately is drawn into a tangle of political rivalries and revenge, and it is questionable whether her lot has improved by story's end.

The "Emma Merrigan" series is something of a change of pace for Abbey in that the setting is not as gritty as those featured in much of the author's fiction. A forty-something librarian, Merrigan is introduced in the 2000 novel *Out of Time,* when she discovers that she has inherited magical powers from a mother she has not seen in years. In *Behind Time,* Merrigan is called upon to rescue her mother from the underworld, battling demons at every turn, and when Mom is recovered and attempts to help Emma master her time-travel abilities—in *Taking Time*—she turns out to look and act like a twenty-year-old. In a review of *Taking Time, Kliatt* contributor Lesley Farmer wrote that Abbey's fantasy world in the "Emma Merrigan" books is "believable and fun, her characters "generally well developed," and her plot full of "interesting twists to sustain the reader's interest." Praising *Behind Time* as "compact and literate," Roland Green noted in a *Booklist* review that Abbey has created a "carefully

and intelligently worked out system" of magic that "skillfully curb[s] . . . the bloating tendency of most fantasy fiction."

Together with former husband and fellow novelist Robert Asprin, Abbey created a unique body of work within the fantasy-sci-fi genre with their shared-world concept known as "Thieves' World." The series, which began in the late 1970s, assembles fiction by a number of well-known writers, each story based on characters and plots centered in the imaginary town of Sanctuary, founded by runaway slaves and described by a *Kirkus Reviews* writer as a "lawless, cynical, pun-filled, sometimes satiric and always-atmospheric pseudo-medieval fantasy realm." As Abbey once explained the "shared-world" concept: "Certain settings and characters were provided by us at the beginning of the project; each author is responsible for developing new characters. These settings and characters are 'shared' to the extent that, while retaining the author's individual style and outlook in a particular story, each volume of the series presents unified themes and advances along a single, predetermined chronology."

With the success of "Thieves' World," other publishers began to experiment with the shared-world concept, and similar projects have been published that collect not only science-fiction and fantasy, but also horror and mystery short fiction. Although Abbey's own series went into a hiatus after 1990, it was restarted in 2002 with *Turning Points,* which contains stories by Abbey, Jody Lynn Nye, Jeff Grubb, Andrew Offutt, and Diana L. Paxton, among others. *Enemies of Fortune* further extends the popular series, and features characters that a *Kirkus Reviews* contributor described as "magical malcontents, scheming underlings, and charming criminal lowlifes" within its thirteen interrelated stories. Offutt, Nye, and Grubb are joined by C. J. Cherryh, Jane Fancher, and other respected writers in the fantasy genre, their stories interwoven by Abbey "so deftly that the book reads like a novel," according to *Booklist* contributor Frieda Murray. The "Thieves' World" books have also inspired a series of role-playing games, and have been the basis for a graphic-novel series. In addition, Abbey has authored an entire novel based on the series. Appropriately titled *Sanctuary,* the book features many of the characters that series fans have come to know. Containing much of the history of the town of Sanctuary, the novel provides a refresher course for those out of touch with the two-decade-old series; according to Green in *Booklist,* "coming from Abbey's capable pen," this well-crafted introduction for Thieves' World neophytes "is good news for all heroic fantasy fans."

BIOGRAPHICAL AND CRITICAL SOURCES:

BOOKS

St. James Guide to Fantasy Writers, St. James Press (Detroit, MI), 1996.

PERIODICALS

Booklist, August, 1994, p. 2029; June 1, 2001, Roland Green, review of *Behind Time,* p. 1855; April 15, 2002, Roland Green, review of *Sanctuary,* p. 1386; November 15, 2002, Roland Green, review of *Thieves' World: Turning Points,* p. 584; November 15, 2004, Frieda Murray, review of *Thieves' World: Enemies of Fortune,* p. 571.
Kirkus Reviews, October 1, 2002, review of *Thieves' World: Turning Points,* p. 1433; July, 2004, Lesley Farmer, review of *Taking Time,* p. 26.
Library Journal, June 15, 2002, Jackie Cassada, review of *Sanctuary,* p. 99l November 15, 2002, Jackie Cassada, review of *Thieves World: Turning Points,* p. 106; November 15, 2004, Jackie Cassada, review of *Thieves' World: Enemies of Fortune,* p. 54.
Publishers Weekly, August 16, 1991, review of *The Wooden Sword,* p. 55.

ONLINE

Lynn Abbey Web site, http://www.lynnabbey.com/ (January 5, 2004).*

*   *   *

AGHILL, Gordon
    See SILVERBERG, Robert

*   *   *

ALOFSIN, Anthony 1949-

PERSONAL: Born 1949, in Memphis, TN; married Patricia Tierney (a policy analyst and energy expert), June 5, 1993. *Education:* Harvard University, A.B.

(magna cum laude), 1971, M.Arch. (with distinction), 1981; Columbia University, M.Phil., 1983, Ph.D., 1987.

ADDRESSES: Home—110 W. 33rd St., Austin, TX 78705. *Office*—School of Architecture, WMB4 102B, Goldsmith Hall, University of Texas at Austin, Austin, TX 78712. *E-mail*—alofsin@mail.utexas.edu.

CAREER: University of Texas at Austin, professor of art and art history, 1987—, Sid Richardson Centennial Teaching Fellow, 1987-91, Sid Richardson Centennial Professor, 1991-97, Martin S. Kermacy Centennial Professor, 1998-99, Roland Gommel Roessner Centennial Professor, 1999—. Academy of Fine Arts (Vienna, Austria), guest professor, 1989-90. Designer and exhibition curator. Lecturer at colleges and universities in the United States and abroad. Featured author at Texas Book Festival, 1999.

MEMBER: American Institute of Architects, College Art Association, Frank Lloyd Wright Building Conservatory, Historians of German and Central European Art and Architecture, Society of Architectural Historians, Society of Historians of East European and Russian Art and Architecture, United States International Council on Monuments and Sites.

AWARDS, HONORS: Vasari Award, Dallas Museum of Art, 1989; Fulbright Professorship for Research and Lectures; International Architecture Book Award, American Institute of Architects, 1993, for *Frank Lloyd Wright: The Lost Years, 1910-1922;* winner in monograph category, International Architecture Book Awards, American Institution of Architects, 1994; Faculty Research Award, University Research Institute; fellow, International Research Center for Cultural Sciences (Vienna, Austria), 1995; Mike Hogg Scholars Grant, 2000-01; Outstanding Scholarship Award, University of Texas—Austin School of Architecture, 2000-01; Alisa Mellon Bruce Senior Fellow, Center for Advanced Studies in the Visual Arts, National Gallery of Art, 2003-04.

WRITINGS:

(With John P. Conron) *Socorro: A Historic Survey,* University of New Mexico Press (Albuquerque, NM), 1980.

(Editor and author of introduction) *Frank Lloyd Wright: An Index to the Taliesin Correspondence*, Garland Publishing (New York, NY), 1988.

(Editor) *Center: Modernist Visions and the Contemporary American City*, Rizzoli (New York, NY), 1989.

(Coauthor) *Center: The Final Decade: Architectural Issues for the 1990s and Beyond*, Rizzoli (New York, NY), 1992.

Frank Lloyd Wright: The Lost Years, 1910-1922, University of Chicago Press (Chicago, IL), 1993.

(Editor and contributor) *Center 8: Social Life, Buildings, and the Spaces between Them*, Center for American Architecture and Design (Austin, TX), 1993.

(Editor) *Frank Lloyd Wright: Europe and Beyond*, University of California Press (Berkeley, CA), 1999.

The Struggle for Modernism: Architecture, Landscape Architecture, and City Planning at Harvard, Norton (New York, NY), 2002.

Contributor to books, including *Frank Lloyd Wright, Architect*, Abrams (New York, NY), 1994; *The History of History in American Schools of Architecture, 1865-1975*, Princeton Architectural Press (Princeton, NJ), 1990; and *Shifting Boundaries of the Real: Making the Invisible Visible*, edited by Helga Nowotny and Martina Weiss, VDF Hochschulverlag (Zurich, Switzerland) 2000. Contributor of articles and reviews to art and architecture journals, including *Times Literary Supplement, Platform, Studies in the Decorative Arts, Journal of the Society of Architectural Historians*, and *L'Architettura cronache e storia*.

WORK IN PROGRESS: A book on central European architecture from 1868 to 1933, for the University of Chicago Press.

SIDELIGHTS: Anthony Alofsin has written, edited, and contributed to many books about the renowned architect Frank Lloyd Wright, including *Frank Lloyd Wright: An Index to the Taliesin Correspondence, Frank Lloyd Wright: The Lost Years, 1910-1922*, and *Frank Lloyd Wright: Europe and Beyond*. The essays in *Frank Lloyd Wright: Europe and Beyond*, edited by Alofsin, were deemed "groundbreaking" by *Library Journal* contributor David Soltesz. Nine scholars, called "international experts" by Soltesz, throw light on Wright's considerable influence on architectural trends outside of the United States, especially in Europe, South America, Iraq, and Japan.

Alofsin's immersion in the world of Frank Lloyd Wright even led him to take the legendary architect's work as the starting point for his own home design. Reed Kroloff, a writer for *Architecture*, mused that while Alofsin's home in Austin, Texas, does not have an obvious echo of Wright's style, on closer examination one can see the great architect's influence in the design. "The plan is rich with subtle shifts and alignments, an homage to Wright's mastery of symmetry and asymmetry," noted Kroloff. He also observed that it owes much to Wright in the way it defines "height and volume with familiar pitched and hipped forms." Pointing out the Japanese restraint and influences from other cultures as well, Kroloff concluded: "Rome, Asia, and the American heartland are all at play in this house. It is in the seemingly effortless amalgamation of the three that Alofsin comes closest to Wright's distinctive and inclusive spirit."

BIOGRAPHICAL AND CRITICAL SOURCES:

PERIODICALS

Architecture, December, 1996, Reed Kroloff, "Building on Wright," p. 82.

Globe and Mail (Toronto, Ontario, Canada), February 26, 1994.

Journal of Architectural Education, winter, 1990, p. 54.

Journal of the Society of Architectural Historians, Volume 48, number 3, 1989, p. 200.

Library Journal, February 15, 2000, David Soltesz, review of *Frank Lloyd Wright: Europe and Beyond*, p. 156.

London Review of Books, April 7, 1994.

New York Review of Books, January 13, 1994, Martin Filler, review of *Frank Lloyd Wright: The Lost Years, 1910-1922*, p. 28.

New York Times Book Review, February 20, 1994, D. J. R. Bruckner, review of *Frank Lloyd Wright: The Lost Years, 1910-1922*, p. 20.

Times Literary Supplement, May 16, 1994, Joseph Ryckwert, "Towards a Well-Distributed World," review of *Frank Lloyd Wright: The Lost Years, 1910-1922*, pp. 16-17; November, 2002, Jules Lubbock, "No Place Like Home," review of *The Struggle for Modernism: Architecture, Landscape Architecture, and City Planning at Harvard*, pp. 8-9.

Urban Explorer, April, 1994, p. 9.
Wilson Quarterly, spring, 1994, p. 36.

*   *   *

ANDREWS, Elton V.
   See POHL, Frederik

*   *   *

ARNETTE, Robert
   See SILVERBERG, Robert

*   *   *

ASCHERSON, (Charles) Neal 1932-

PERSONAL: Born October 5, 1932, in Edinburgh, Scotland; son of Stephen Romer (a sailor) and Evelyn (Gilbertson) Ascherson; married Corinna Adam (a journalist), November 20, 1958 (divorced); married Isabel Hilton (a journalist), August, 1984; children: (first marriage) Marina, Isobel; (current marriage) Alexander, Iona. *Education:* King's College, Cambridge, M.A. (honorary fellow; degree with distinction), 1955. *Politics:* Socialist

ADDRESSES: Home—27 Corsica St., London N5, England.

CAREER: East African Institute of Social Research, Kampala, East Africa, researcher, 1955-56; *Guardian,* Manchester, England, journalist, 1956-58, *Scotsman,* London, England, Commonwealth correspondent, 1958-59, Scottish politics correspondent, 1975-79; *Observer,* London, journalist, 1960-75, associate editor, 1985-89; *The Independent on Sunday,* London, assistant editor, 1989-98; Institute of Archaeology, UCL, London, lecturer, 1998—. *Military service:* Royal Marines; served in Malaya.

MEMBER: Society of Antiquaries of Scotland (fellow).

AWARDS, HONORS: Granada Awards for Reporter of the Year, 1982, and Journalist of the Year, 1987; James Cameron Award, 1988; George Orwell Prize for Politi-

cal Journalism, 1993; Golden Insignia of Polish Order of Merit, 1993; Saltire Award for Literature (joint award), 1995; *Los Angeles Times* Book Award for History, 1996, for *Black Sea.* Honorary degrees: D.Litt., Strathclyde, 1988; D.Sc. (Social Science), Edinburgh, 1990; L.L.D., St. Andrews, 1999.

WRITINGS:

The King Incorporated: Leopold in the Age of Trusts, Allen & Unwin (London, England), 1963, Doubleday (New York, NY), 1964.
(Editor and author of introduction) *"The Times" Reports the French Revolution: Extracts from "The Times," 1789-1794,* Times Books (London, England), 1975.
(Author of introduction) *The Book of Lech Walesa,* Simon & Schuster (New York, NY), 1982.
The Polish August: The Self-Limiting Revolution, Viking (New York, NY), 1982.
(With others) *The Fourth Reich: Klaus Barbie and the Neo-Fascist Connection,* Hodder & Stoughton (London, England), 1984, published as *The Nazi Legacy: Klaus Barbie and the International Fascist Connection,* Holt (New York, NY), 1985.
The Struggles for Poland, M. Joseph (London, England), 1987, Random House (New York, NY), 1988.
Games with Shadows, Radius (London, England), 1988.
Black Sea, Hill & Wang (New York, NY), 1995.
(Author of foreword) Hubert Butler, *In the Land of Nod,* Lilliput Press (Dublin, Ireland), 1996.
The Yes Road: A Reflection on Two Devolution Campaigns, The National Library of Wales (Aberystwyth, Wales), 1999.
(With others) *Berlin: A Century of Change = Die Gesichter des Jahrhunderts,* Prestel (New York, NY), 2000.
Stone Voices: The Search for Scotland, Hill & Wang (New York, NY), 2003.

Also author of *New Europe!,* 1990. Author of scripts for Thames TV's "World at War" series, 1973-76, and BBC's "Cold War" television program, 1998. Contributor to the *New Statesman, New York Review of Books,* and other periodicals.

SIDELIGHTS: Neal Ascherson has served as a journalist, reporter, and columnist for several British publications, most notably the *Observer.* His work as a foreign correspondent has taken him all over the world, but especially to Eastern Europe. Ascherson's writing is characterized by a deep grasp of history and an ability to apply its lessons to contemporary social and political situations. In the *Times Literary Supplement,* John Dunn wrote of the author: "A person's views are always a blend of sentiments and beliefs. On the page Ascherson is a marvellous companion. His sentiments are consistently engaging, his beliefs invariably intelligent, and the experience on which he draws, both vicariously and directly, is impressively wide and intense."

In the late 1970s and early 1980s Ascherson worked as a foreign correspondent in Poland. He was present on many of the occasions that marked the founding and rise to power of the Solidarity movement. His books on the movement and its leadership include *The Polish August: The Self-Limiting Revolution* and the introduction to *The Book of Lech Walesa.* Additionally he has published a wider-ranging history of Poland in conjunction with a British Broadcasting Corporation television series, *The Struggles for Poland.* These books draw not only upon Ascherson's own experiences as a reporter in that nation, but also upon his knowledge of several hundred years of Polish history. "Neal Ascherson has a matchless ability to evoke periods of intense experience with a few strokes of his pen," observed Timothy Garton Ash in the *Observer.* "*The Polish August* is repeatedly illuminated by such flashes of evocative brilliance." *New York Times Book Review* correspondent Richard M. Watt noted that Ascherson's work "contributes mightily to understanding . . . Poland," adding that *The Polish August* "is a major work by an author who is at once a political scientist, a historian and a very good writer, indeed."

Between 1985 and 1989 Ascherson wrote a political column for the *Observer.* Some of this column work is collected in *Games with Shadows,* published in 1988. In his review of the book for the *Observer,* Michael Frayn wrote: "Journalism is about the here and now; but Ascherson approaches these two familiar points from everywhere in space and time except here and now; and very strange he makes them look." The critic concluded that Ascherson "writes with a wonderful sinewy expressiveness, always colloquial but always elegant. . . . His idiosyncratic intelligence and shameless erudition give me hope each week; hope for newspapers, hope for all of us."

Another well-received Ascherson title is *Black Sea,* a wide-ranging meditation on the countries and states,

past and present, that fringe the Black Sea. Traveling through Turkey, Georgia, Ukraine, Russia, and Abkhazia, Ascherson pondered the legacy the region has given the world in its perhaps unparalleled blending of divergent cultures. In a review of the work for the *Spectator,* Dominic Lieven contended that the author "understands both classical and modern history. He uses both to illuminate issues which haunt contemporary mankind. Because he combines interests and approaches which are not usually found in one head he can make connections which most authors would miss." Lieven concluded: "Ascherson's book has sweep and style. It makes one ponder the transience of civilisations, our own included. Above all, it simply encourages its readers to think. It is a glorious antidote to a contemporary university education in the social sciences." In the *New York Times,* Richard Bernstein called *Black Sea* "a fascinating hodgepodge with something to learn on almost every page. With ethnic conflicts much in the headlines, Mr. Ascherson's portrait of a place whose chief characteristic is the durability of its many ethnic identities comes at the right moment, providing perspective on a primordial element in human history."

Ascherson continues to examine the fascinating people, histories, and politics of Europe's less publicized nations in *Stone Voices: The Search for Scotland.* One of Ascherson's most acclaimed works, it's spirit flows from the author's abiding love and concern for Scotland, his homeland. It is not a direct history of the country or its citizens, but instead a compelling patchwork of that author's insights on varied topics, including archaeology, demography, geography, and nationalism. Some of its highlights include Ascherson's own experiences during Scotland's recent bid for independence. June Sawyers wrote in *Booklist* that one of the book's finest offerings is the tale of "the sometimes amusing, often illuminating, back-country bus expedition that Ascherson and other Scots took during the 1997 referendum campaign that eventuated in the new parliament. In Scotland, Ascherson points out, love of country is, more often than not, a private affair." In the *London Review of Books,* Andrew O'Hagan wrote that the book is "one man's attempt to map his feelings about his own country, to send his affections through the prism of history and then through the mincer." The end result, O'Hagan continued, is "a story about what it's like to spend your life married to a scenic fiction: Scotland the Brave." Similarly, one *Economist* contributor noted that Ascherson "is a subtle and insightful writer" who has written a "tough, closely woven book" which is "much more a reflections, or a series of them, in the continental manner, than it is a history or a piece of reportage."

BIOGRAPHICAL AND CRITICAL SOURCES:

PERIODICALS

American Book Review, March, 1985, p. 19.
Booklist, April 15, 2003, June Sawyers, review of *Stone Voices: The Search for Scotland,* p. 1444.
Bookseller, March 28, 2003, "Orwell Prize." p. 26.
Contemporary Review, November 1, 1995, Leo Muray, review of *Black Sea,* pp. 274-275; October, 1999, review of *The King Incorporated: Leopold in the Age of Trusts,* p. 219; May, 2003, R.D. Kernohan, review of *Stone Voices,* p. 309.
Economist (U.S.), January 4, 2003, "Puzzles of Patriotism: Scottish Nationalism," review of *Stone Voices,* p. NA.
Foreign Affairs, March-April, 1996, Robert Legvold, review of *Black Sea,* p. 162.
History: Reviews of New Books, spring, 1997, Mari A. Firkatian, review of *Black Sea,* p. 133; September, 1997, review of *Black Sea,* p. 133.
Kirkus Reviews, February 15, 2003, review of *Stone Voices,* pp. 280-281.
Library Journal, October 1, 1995, Melinda Stivers, review of *Black Sea,* p. 107; May 1, 2003, Jo-Anne Mary Benson, review of *Stone Voices,* pp. 132-133.
London Review of Books, November 24, 1988, p. 7; May 9, 1996, p. 19; October 31, 2002, Andrew O'Hagan, "Beast of a Nation," review of *Stone Voices,* pp. 11-12.
Los Angeles Times, February 13, 2000, Neal Ascherson, review of T. M. Devine's *The Scottish Nation A History: 1700-2000,* p. E-1.
National Review, October 4, 1985, Curtis Carroll Davis, review of *The Nazi Legacy: Klaus Barbie and the International Fascist Connection,* p. 53.
New Republic, December 18, 1995, Nader Mousavizadeh, review of *Black Sea,* pp. 42-45.
New Statesman, September 25, 1998, Andrew Billen, television program review of "Cold War," p. 68.
New Statesman & Society, July 7, 1995, p. 40.
New York Review of Books, February 4, 1982, p. 3; September 29, 1983, pp. 18-27; April 18, 1996, article by Norman Davies, pp. 50-54.

New York Times, December 6, 1995, p. C21.
New York Times Book Review, April 25, 1982, pp. 11, 19; November 26, 1995, p. 17.
Observer, December 6, 1981; August 16, 1987, p. 23; May 15, 1988, p. 23.
Publishers Weekly, August 14, 1995, review of *Black Sea,* p. 63.
Slavic Review, summer, 1996, Dianne E. Farrel, review of *Black Sea,* pp. 477-478.
Spectator, February 6, 1982, pp. 20-21; June 20, 1987, pp. 23-24; July 15, 1995, pp. 29-30; January 17, 1998, Stephen Glover, "So This Is How Serious the Sindie Now Is: Neal Ascherson 'Released' by the *Independent on Sunday,*" p. 28.
Sunday Telegraph (London, England), October 6, 2002, James Campbell, "Yes for Scotland; James Campbell on a Rich, Politically Partial Scots History and Memoir," review of *Stone Voices.*
Times Literary Supplement, June 11, 1982, p. 640; July 1, 1988, p. 724; July 28, 1995, p. 4; November 1, 2002, Keith M. Brown, "Blame England," review of *Stone Voices,* p. 30.
World Today, November, 1995, Anthony Hyman, review of *Black Sea,* pp. 223-224.

ONLINE

Granta Web site, http://www.granta.com/ (June 30, 2004), "Neal Ascherson."
Guardian Unlimited Web site, http://www.guardian.co.uk/ (June 30, 2004), Neal Ascherson, "End the Exile."
London Review of Books Web site, http://www.lrb.co.uk/ (June 30, 2004), "Contributor: Neal Ascherson: Articles Available Online."
Radio Prague Web site, http://www.radio.cz/en/ (June 30, 2004), Ian Willoughby, "Neal Ascherson: Fascinating Memories of the Soviet Invasion and Much More."

*   *   *

ASHLEY, Bernard 1935-

PERSONAL: Born April 2, 1935, in London, England; son of Alfred Walter (an assistant company secretary) and Vera (a store proprietor; maiden name, Powell) Ashley; married Iris Holbrook (a head teacher), August 2, 1958; children: Christopher, David, Jonathan. *Edu-*

Bernard Ashley

cation: Trent Park College of Education, certificate, 1957; Cambridge Institute of Education, Associate Diploma, 1971. *Hobbies and other interests:* Theater, music, football (soccer), travel.

ADDRESSES: Home—128 Heathwood Gardens, London SE7 8ER, England. *E-mail*—bernardashley@ talktalk.net.

CAREER: King's Farm Primary School, Gravesend, England, teacher, 1957-65; Hertford Heath Primary School, Hertford Heath, England, head teacher, 1965-71; Hartley Junior School, London, England, head teacher, 1971-76; Charlton Manor Junior School, London, head teacher, beginning 1977, retired, 1995. Ashley Chappel Productions (professional theatre company), producer. Member, British Academy of Film and Television Arts children's awards committee; member of board of Greenwich Theatre. *Military service:* Royal Air Force, 1953-55; became senior aircraftman.

MEMBER: National Association of Headteachers, Writers Guild, BAPTA.

AWARDS, HONORS: Other Award, Children's Rights Workshop, 1976, for *The Trouble with Donovan Croft;* Carnegie Medal commendation, 1979, for *A Kind of Wild Justice,* and 1987, for *Running Scared;* best entertainment series for children citation, Royal Television Society, 1992, for *Dodgem; Guardian* Children's Fiction Prize shortlist, and Carnegie Medal shortlist, both 2000, both for *Little Soldier;* honorary D.Ed., University of Greenwich; honorary D. Lit., University of Leicester.

WRITINGS:

JUVENILE FICTION

The Trouble with Donovan Croft, illustrated by Fermin Rocker, Oxford University Press (Oxford, England), 1974, reprinted, 2002.

Terry on the Fence, illustrated by Charles Keeping, Oxford University Press (Oxford, England), 1975.

All My Men, Oxford University Press (Oxford, England), 1977.

A Kind of Wild Justice, illustrated by Charles Keeping, Oxford University Press (Oxford, England), 1978, reprinted, 2002.

Break in the Sun, illustrated by Charles Keeping, S. G. Phillips, 1980.

I'm Trying to Tell You (short stories), illustrated by Lyn Jones, Kestrel (London, England), 1981.

Dinner Ladies Don't Count, illustrated by Janet Duchesne, F. Watts (London, England), 1981.

Dodgem (also see below), Julia MacRae Books (London, England), 1982.

Linda's Lie, illustrated by Janet Duchesne, F. Watts (London, England), 1982.

High Pavement Blues, F. Watts (London, England), 1983.

Your Guess Is As Good As Mine, illustrated by Steven Cain, Barn Owl (London, England), 1983, illustrated by David Parkins, F. Watts (London, England), 1987.

A Bit of Give and Take, illustrated by Trevor Stubley, Hamish Hamilton (London, England), 1984.

Janey, Julia MacRae Books (London, England), 1985.

Running Scared (novelization of British Broadcasting Corporation television series of the same title), Julia MacRae Books (London, England), 1986.

Bad Blood, Julia MacRae Books (London, England), 1988.

The Country Boy (novelization of Ashley's television series), Julia MacRae Books (London, England), 1989.

The Secret of Theodore Brown, 1989.

Boat Girl, and Other Dockside School Stories, 1990.

Getting In, 1990.

The Caretaker's Cat, 1990.

The Ghost of Dockside School, 1990.

Cleversticks, illustrated by Derek Brazell, Crown (New York, NY), 1991.

Dockside School Stories, 1992.

More Stories from Dockside School, 1992.

Seeing Off Uncle Jack, Viking (London, England), 1992.

(With son Christopher Ashley) *Three Seven Eleven* (based on the television series; also see below), Puffin (Harmondsworth, England), 1993.

Johnnie's Blitz, illustrated by Paul Hunt, Viking (London, England), 1995, Barn Owl Books, 2003.

I Forgot! Said Troy, illustrated by Derek Brazell, Viking (London, England), 1996.

A Present for Paul, illustrated by David Mitchell, Collins (London, England), 1996.

Justin and the Demon Drop-kick, illustrated by Nick Ward, Viking (London, England), 1997, Happy Cat Books (Essex, England), 2005.

Flash ("Pen Pals" series), Orchard (London, England), 1997.

King Rat, illustrated by Mark Robertson, Collins (London, England), 1998.

Tiger without Teeth, Orchard (London, England), 1998.

Justin and the Big Fight, illustrated by Nick Ward, Viking (London, England), 1999.

Little Soldier, Orchard (London, England), 1999, Scholastic (New York, NY), 2002.

Growing Good, illustrated by Anne Wilson, Bloomsbury Children's Books (London, England), 1999.

Who Loves You, Billy?, illustrated by Philip Hopman, Collins (London, England), 2000.

Playing against the Odds, illustrated by Derek Brazell, Barrington Stoke (Edinburgh, Scotland), 2000.

Justin Strikes Again, illustrated by Nick Ward, Viking (London, England), 2001.

Double the Love, illustrated by Carol Thompson, Orchard (London, England), 2002.

Revenge House, Orchard (London, England), 2002.

Freedom Flight, Orchard (London, England), 2003.

The Bush, illustrated by Lynne Willey, Tamarind (Camberley, England), 2003.

Torrent, Barrington Stoke (Edinburgh, Scotland), 2004.

Ten Days to Zero, Orchard (London, England), 2005.

A Present for Paul has been published in bilingual editions, including Turkish, Chinese, Somali, Yoruba, Bengali, Gujarati, and Arabic translations. Other books by Ashley have been translated into Welsh.

"CLIPPER STREET STORIES" SERIES

Calling for Sam, illustrated by Jane Cope, Orchard House (Concord, MA), 1987.

Taller Than Before, illustrated by Jane Cope, Orchard House (Concord, MA), 1987.

Down-and-Out, illustrated by Jane Cope, Orchard House (Concord, MA), 1988.

The Royal Visit, illustrated by Judith Lawton, Orchard House (Concord, MA), 1988.

All I Ever Ask . . . , illustrated by Judith Lawton, Orchard House (Concord, MA), 1988.

Sally Cinderella, illustrated by Jane Cope, Orchard House (Concord, MA), 1989.

"GRAFFIX" SERIES

Roller Madonnas, illustrated by Kim Harley, A & C Black (London, England), 1997.

Rapid, illustrated by Kim Harley, A & C Black (London, England), 1999.

Respect, illustrated by Kim Harley, A & C Black (London, England), 2000.

"CITY LIMITS" SERIES

Stitch Up, Orchard (London, England), 1997.

The Scam, Orchard (London, England), 1997.

Framed, Orchard (London, England), 1997.

Mean Streets, Orchard (London, England), 1997.

OTHER

Don't Run Away (reader), illustrated by Ray Whittaker, Allman, 1966.

Wall of Death (reader), illustrated by Ray Whittaker, Allman, 1966.

Space Shot (reader), illustrated by Laszlo Acs, Allman, 1967.

The Big Escape (reader), illustrated by James Hunt, Allman, 1967.

The Men and the Boats: Britain's Life-Boat Service (nonfiction), Allman, 1968.

Weather Men (nonfiction), Allman, 1970, revised edition, 1974.

Running Scared (television screenplay), British Broadcasting Corporation (BBC), 1986.

(Editor) *The Puffin Book of School Stories,* Puffin (Harmondsworth, England), 1992.

Dodgem (television screenplay; based on Ashley's novel), BBC, 1993.

(With Christopher Ashley) *Three Seven Eleven* (television series), Granada, 1993.

Author of plays *The Old Woman Who Lived in a Cola Can,* produced 1988; and *The Secret of Theodore Brown,* produced 1989. Also author of children's television serial, "The Country Boy," BBC-TV. Contributor to various educational and literary journals.

SIDELIGHTS: While most of Bernard Ashley's stories are set in the Charlton area of London where he himself grew up, teenagers everywhere can identify with the protagonists he creates in novels such as *Running Scared, Little Soldier,* and *Break in the Sun.* Mistreated and misunderstood, victims of child abuse, crime, or racism, the multiracial or otherwise marginalized protagonists in Ashley's books attempt to understand themselves as they learn to cope in a world that is sometimes harsh and unforgiving.

Running Scared, a novelized version of a popular television series Ashley wrote for the British Broadcasting Corporation (BBC), is a typical example of Ashley's work. In this novel, Paula, a white teenager, and her best friend Narinder, a Sikh girl born in India, find themselves involved in a fight against crime when Paula's grandfather becomes an inadvertent witness to a robbery. Reviewing the book for the *Times Literary Supplement,* Tony Bradman commented: "In the similarities in the way the two girls feel about the pressures on their respective families, the novel reveals the common humanity of two communities who live uneasily together." Bradman also praised Ashley for writing a "novel around the subject of racism" that "avoids preaching."

Prior to writing books, Ashley gained years of experience teaching school and guiding children as a head teacher in England, and his background has allowed

him to make observations and create plots, characters, and dialogue that is realistic to younger readers. As he explained in an interview posted on his Web site, he began writing at age thirty while teaching a class of students with reading problems. They "had nothing to read that grabbed them," Ashley recalled. "The stories I wrote for them weren't much good—but a publisher saw them and treated me as an author, and I responded by becoming one." Additionally, he views reading as an antidote to the results-driven system in which children are educated. As he wrote in *Books for Your Children,* "The educational system contains a high proportion of built-in stresses of one sort and another—the whole business of examination and the awaiting of results, the changing of schools and classes, the pressure to read and to compute—and we must constantly ask ourselves how unacceptable stresses can be relieved."

Ashley explores some of these stresses in his first novel, *The Trouble with Donovan Croft.* In this book, a Jamaican boy named Donovan loses his ability to speak when he finds out that his mother has deserted him and that his father is sending him to a foster home. Keith Chapman, Donovan's foster brother, gradually learns to attune himself to Donovan's moods and stands up to those who make fun of his brother. Although Keith is ostracized by his own friends for protecting Donovan, he gains in maturity through the experience, while also forging a strong relationship with Donovan. Writing in the *Children's Book Review,* Barbara Sherrard-Smith declared that *The Trouble with Donovan Croft* has "rare quality," and Ashley "has a keen ear for dialogue." Especially appreciative of the realistic language used by Ashley, the critic went on to say that "it is tempting to quote at length . . . to give the flavour of this book . . . but it is more sensible to urge others to read it."

In *Terry on the Fence,* Ashley tells the story of an eleven-year-old who runs away only to find himself being threatened at knife-point by a gang of youths. Terry is forced to participate as gang members break into his school and steal two radios. As the gang makes its escape, its leader, Les, prevents Terry's capture by helping him over a fence. Later, after Terry's school principal persuades the boy to admit his involvement in the theft of the radios, and the police catch the gang's leader, Terry is stuck on another "fence." Should he testify against Les and save himself, or refuse to turn on Les and face punishment? A reviewer for *School Library Journal* concluded that Ashley's "skillful characterizations and well-constructed plot should find an audience among good readers."

According to Helen Gregory writing in *School Library Journal,* the world Ashley creates in *Break in the Sun* is "convincing in its detail as well as interesting in its novelty." In this novel, thirteen-year-old Patsy Bligh runs away from her abusive stepfather, Eddie, and the bedwetting problem she has had since Eddie's marriage to her mother. As she tours on a showboat, she is pursued by Eddie and a young neighbor named Kenny. According to a reviewer for the *Bulletin of the Center for Children's Books,* the rapid scene shifts between Patsy's experiences and Kenny and Eddie's chase serve to make *Break in the Sun* "a dramatic story." Also impressed with the novel, a *Times Educational Supplement* reviewer wrote that "Ashley understands how children work," and *Break in the Sun* possesses "a throbbing immediacy which undeniably grips the reader."

Ashley's highly praised novel *A Kind of Wild Justice* was characterized as a "tense thriller" by a reviewer for *Publishers Weekly.* Ronnie, who lives in a London slum, fears for his life because his parents are involved with criminals. After his mother runs away with one of these ne'er-do-wells and his father is arrested, Ronnie finds out about the criminals' plans. As Kathy Piehl reported in *School Library Journal,* the boy manages, in the end, "to get his father out of jail and to take revenge" on the criminals. A reviewer for the *Bulletin of the Center for Children's Books* appreciated the novel's "good pace and suspense" as well as the "vivid picture" it paints "of a poor, multiethnic community."

Shortlisted for the prestigious Carnegie Medal and *Guardian* Children's Fiction Prize, Ashley's 2002 novel *Little Soldier* focuses on Kaninda, an African boy who is orphaned during a time of civil war, joins a rebel force to avenge his family's murder at the hands of the Yusulu tribe, and then is brought by the Red Cross to live with a London family. Resentful of the family who has taken him in, steeped in the violence of the African war, and still wishing to avenge the death of his parents and baby sister, Kaninda gradually finds himself drawn into a local gang as an outlet for his own aggression. Meanwhile, his new foster sister, Laura, is battling demons of her own, and looks to Kaninda's turmoil as a way to find redemption for her involvement in a tragic car accident. As

Kliatt contributor Claire Rosser noted, in a complex but "well written" novel, "Ashley presents the London [gang] world through the eyes of Kaninda, and that is quite amazing." In *Publishers Weekly* a reviewer also had praise for *Little Soldier,* calling it "timely" and "meticulously orchestrated," and noting that Ashley forces readers to examine "the tragic consequences and effects of violence before judging the characters' actions."

In addition to writing novels for middle-grade and older readers, Ashley has also penned stories for elementary-aged children, all of which reflect his characteristic concern for the problems of minorities and outsiders. In *Cleversticks,* for example, young Ling Sung believes he is the only student in his class who does not have a special talent: He cannot yet tie his shoelaces, button his jacket, or write his name. However, at snack-time, when the resourceful Ling Sung uses two paintbrushes as chopsticks, the other children in the class are impressed with his ability. After Ling Sung teaches them how to use chopsticks, his fellow students help him learn other skills they have acquired. As Diane S. Marton noted in her *School Library Journal* review, the "strength" of Ashley's book "lies in the ethnic diversity of the children and teachers."

Ashley remains enthusiastic about the prospect of assisting children and young adults through literature. He once wrote in *Books for Your Children,* "I very much hope books *can* help children with problems. But let's make no mistake about it, whatever value literature may have in this sort of way, the most important thing about books must always be the pleasure they can give."

BIOGRAPHICAL AND CRITICAL SOURCES:

BOOKS

Ashley, Bernard, *Cleversticks,* Crown (New York, NY), 1991.
Children's Literature Review, Volume 4, Thomson Gale (Detroit, MI), 1984.

PERIODICALS

Booklist, May 1, 2002, Hazel Rochman, review of *Little Soldier,* p. 1518.

Books for Your Children, summer, 1976, Bernard Ashley, "Children under Stress," pp. 10-11.

Bulletin of the Center for Children's Books, July, 1977, p. 170; April, 1979, review of *All My Men,* pp. 129-130; June, 1979, review of *A Kind of Wild Justice,* p. 169; February 2, 1981, review of *Break in the Sun,* p. 106; September, 1982, review of *Dodgem,* p. 2; September, 1991, p. 4; July, 1992, p. 288.

Children's Book Review, summer, 1974, Barbara Sherrard-Smith, review of *The Trouble with Donovan Croft,* pp. 61-62.

Kliatt, May, 2002, Claire Rosser, review of *Little Soldier,* p. 5.

Los Angeles Times Book Review, December 6, 1992.

Publishers Weekly, March 19, 1979, review of *A Kind of Wild Justice,* p. 94; January 21, 2002, review of *Little Soldier,* p. 91.

School Library Journal, May, 1977, review of *Terry on the Fence,* p. 77; April, 1979, Kathy Piehl, review of *A Kind of Wild Justice,* pp. 65-66; March, 1981, Helen Gregory, review of *Break in the Sun,* p. 154; January, 1982, Anna Biagioni Hart, review of *Dinner Ladies Don't Count,* p. 60; September, 1982, Karen Harris, review of *Dodgem;* March, 1993, Diane S. Marton, review of *Cleversticks,* p. 170; October, 2003, review of *Little Soldier,* p. 68.

Times Educational Supplement, August 15, 1980, review of *Break in the Sun,* p. 20.

Times Literary Supplement, October 21, 1977, p. 1247; June 20, 1986, Tony Bradman, review of *Running Scared.*

ONLINE

Bernard Ashley Web site, http://www.bashley.com/ (October 23, 2004).

B

BAILYN, Bernard 1922-

PERSONAL: Born September 10, 1922, in Hartford, CT; son of Charles Manuel and Esther (Schloss) Bailyn; married Lotte Lazarsfeld, June 18, 1952; children: Charles David, John Frederick. *Education:* Williams College, A.B., 1945; Harvard University, M.A., 1947, Ph.D., 1953.

ADDRESSES: Home—170 Clifton St., Belmont, MA 02478. *Office*—Harvard University, 35 Quincy Street, Robinson Hall, Cambridge, MA 02138.

CAREER: Harvard University, Cambridge, MA, joined faculty in 1949, instructor in education, 1953-54, assistant professor, 1954-58, associate professor, 1958-61, professor of history, 1961-66, Winthrop Professor of History, 1966-81, Adams University Professor, 1981-93, James Duncan Phillips Professor of Early American History, 1991-93, professor emeritus, 1993—, director of Charles Warren Center for Studies in American History, 1983-94. Colver Lecturer, Brown University, 1965; Phelps Lecturer, New York University, 1969; Trevelyan Lecturer, Cambridge University, 1971; Becker Lecturer, Cornell University, 1975; Walker-Ames Lecturer, University of Washington, 1983; Curti Lecturer, University of Wisconsin, 1984; Lewin Visiting Professor, Washington University (St. Louis, MO), 1985; Pitt Professor of American History, Cambridge University, 1986-87; Thompson Lecturer, Pomona College, 1991; Jefferson Lecturer, National Endowment for the Humanities, 1998; first millennium lecturer, White House, 1998; trustee, Institute of Advanced Study, Princeton, 1984-

Bernard Bailyn

94. International Seminar on the History of the Atlantic World, director, 1995. *Military service:* U.S. Army, 1943-46; served in Army Signal Corps and Army Security Agency.

MEMBER: National Academy of Education, American Historical Association (president, 1981), American

Academy of Arts and Sciences, American Philosophical Society, Royal Historical Society, Mexican Academy of History and Geography, Russian Academy of Sciences, Massachusetts Historical Society, Academia Europaea.

AWARDS, HONORS: Harvard Faculty Prize, 1965, for Volume 1 of *Pamphlets of the American Revolution;* Pulitzer Prizes in history, 1967, for *The Ideological Origins of the American Revolution,* and 1986, for *Voyagers to the West: A Passage in the Peopling of America on the Eve of the Revolution;* Bancroft Prize, Columbia University, 1967, for *The Ideological Origins of the American Revolution;* recipient of first Robert H. Lord Award, Emmanuel College, 1967; L.H.D., Lawrence University, 1967, Bard College, 1968, Clark University, 1975, Yale University, 1976, Grinnell College, 1979, Trinity College, 1984, Manhattanville College, 1991, Dartmouth College, 1991, University of Chicago, 1991, and William and Mary College, 1994; Litt.D., Williams College, 1969, Rutgers University, 1976, Fordham University, 1976, and Washington University (St. Louis, MO), 1988; National Book Award in history, 1975, for *The Ordeal of Thomas Hutchinson;* Saloutos Award, Immigration History Society, 1986, Triennial Book Award, and nomination for National Book Critics Circle Award, 1986, all for *Voyagers to the West;* fellow, British Academy, and Christ's College, Cambridge University, and Montgomery fellow, Dartmouth College, 1991; Thomas Jefferson Medal of the American Philosophical Society, 1993; Henry Allen Moe Prize, American Philosophical Society, 1994; Medal of the Foreign Policy Association, 1998; Catton Prize, Society of American Historians, 2000.

WRITINGS:

The New England Merchants in the Seventeenth Century, Harvard University Press (Cambridge, MA), 1955.

(With wife, Lotte Bailyn) *Massachusetts Shipping, 1697-1714: A Statistical Study,* Belknap Press of Harvard University Press (Cambridge, MA), 1959.

Education in the Forming of American Society: Needs and Opportunities for Study, University of North Carolina Press (Chapel Hill, NC), 1960.

(Editor, with Jane N. Garrett, and author of introduction) *Pamphlets of the American Revolution, 1750-1776,* Volume 1, Belknap Press of Harvard University Press (Cambridge, MA), 1965.

(Editor) *The Apologia of Robert Keayne: The Self-Portrait of a Puritan Merchant,* Harper & Row (New York, NY), 1965.

The Ideological Origins of the American Revolution, Belknap Press of Harvard University Press (Cambridge, MA), 1967, enlarged edition, 1992.

The Origins of American Politics, Knopf (New York, NY), 1968.

(Editor, with Donald Fleming) *The Intellectual Migration: Europe and America, 1930-1960,* Belknap Press of Harvard University Press (Cambridge, MA), 1969.

(Editor, with Donald Fleming) *Law in American History,* Little, Brown (Boston, MA), 1972.

The Ordeal of Thomas Hutchinson, Belknap Press of Harvard University Press (Cambridge, MA), 1974.

(With others) *The Great Republic: A History of the American People,* Heath (Lexington, MA), 1977, 4th edition, 1992.

(Editor, with John B. Hench) *The Press and the American Revolution,* American Antiquarian Society (Worcester, MA), 1980.

History and the Creative Imagination, Washington University (St. Louis, MO), 1985.

The Peopling of British North America: An Introduction, Knopf (New York, NY), 1986.

Voyagers to the West: A Passage in the Peopling of America on the Eve of the Revolution, Knopf (New York, NY), 1986.

From Protestant Peasants to Jewish Intellectuals: The Germans in the Peopling of America (published together with *Causes and Consequences of the German Catastrophe,* by Heinrich August Winkler), Berg for the German Historical Institute (New York, NY), 1988.

Faces of Revolution: Personalities and Themes in the Struggle for American Independence, Knopf (New York, NY), 1990.

(Editor, with Philip D. Morgan) *Strangers within the Realm: Cultural Margins of the First British Empire,* University of North Carolina Press (Chapel Hill, NC), 1991.

(Editor) *The Debate on the Constitution: Federalist and Antifederalist Speeches, Articles, and Letters during the Struggle over Ratification,* two volumes, Library of America (New York, NY), 1993.

The Great Republic: Nineteenth and Early Twentieth-Century America, 1820-1920, D. C. Heath (Lexington, MA), 1993.

On the Teaching and Writing of History: Responses to a Series of Questions, edited by Edward Connery Lathem, Montgomery Endowment (Hanover, NH), 1994.

The Federalist Papers (Bradley Lecture Series Publication), Library of Congress (Washington, DC), 1998.

To Begin the World Anew: The Genius and Ambiguities of the American Founders, Knopf (New York, NY), 2003.

Also author of *Religion and Revolution: Three Biographical Studies,* 1970. Contributor to books including *A Lyme Miscellany, 1776-1976,* edited by George J. Willauer, Jr., Wesleyan University (Middletown, CT), 1977; and *Glimpses of the Harvard Past,* Harvard University Press (Cambridge, MA), 1986.

Editor-in-chief, "John Harvard Library," 1962-70. Editor with Donald Fleming, *Perspectives in American History,* annual of Charles Warren Center for Studies in American History, Harvard University, 1967-77, 1984-86. Contributor to symposia and proceedings of professional organizations. Contributor to professional journals, including *American Historical Review* and *William and Mary Quarterly.*

SIDELIGHTS: Historian Bernard Bailyn has earned critical accolades for his writings about and interpretation of American history, particularly involving the American Revolution. The winner of two Pulitzer Prizes and numerous other prestigious awards, Bailyn has been described in the *Washington Post Book World* as "arguably the pre-eminent historian of the thirteen colonies' break with Britain." Robert V. Remini of Chicago's *Tribune Books* labeled Bailyn "the foremost historian of the American Revolution," while Stephen Presser, also of *Tribune Books,* identified him as the "dean of American colonial historians." Another *Washington Post Book World* critic remarked that "any book by Bailyn . . . is an event."

In the foreword to his Pulitzer Prize-winning *The Ideological Origins of the American Revolution,* Bailyn writes that the book attempts to "trace back into the early eighteenth century—and back into the European sources, wherever possible—the specific attitudes, conceptions, formulations, even in certain cases particular phrases, which together form the ideology of the American Revolution." According to a reviewer from the *New York Times Book Review,* what the author has contributed "is not so much a new viewpoint as a brilliantly persuasive analysis of the

current viewpoint, bolstered by a thorough knowledge of the sources and an impressive grasp of the intellectual setting in which they were produced." *Book Week* reviewer Staughton Lynd noted the value of the book to both historians and casual readers and mentioned that it "avoids the stereotypes and clichés and allows us to see more clearly the real nature of the American Revolution." Lynd also believed that "apart from the fullness of its documentation, the excellence of Bailyn's argument lies in its painstaking effort to grasp eighteenth-century political rhetoric."

Bailyn's *The Ordeal of Thomas Hutchinson,* a 1975 National Book Award winner, achieved distinction for the generally charitable portrayal of the Royalist governor of Massachusetts, Thomas Hutchinson (1771-1774), a well-known target of many statesmen of the day, including Samuel Adams, John Adams, and John Quincy Adams. D. B. Little, in a *Christian Science Monitor* review, explained Bailyn's position: "[Hutchinson] was a loyal British subject devoted to the welfare of the empire and believed firmly that America's well-being depended upon close ties with a strong Great Britain." In the *New York Review of Books,* E. S. Morgan observed, "In the concluding pages of [the book] Bailyn points out that Hutchinson never understood the forces that destroyed him. . . . And in the opening pages he tells us that his own instinctive sympathies remain with the revolutionists, that he is simply showing us how it was possible for a good man to take the other side. But in between the opening and closing pages he succeeds so well that he leaves the American Revolution looking a pretty shabby affair." *New Republic* reviewer Steven Kelman pointed out that Bailyn based the book, to a large extent, on Hutchinson's own papers "(which no doubt introduces an inevitable bias), and the author, while aware of the limitations of Hutchinson's political thought, is unsympathetic to most of the imputations of malice his contemporaries made against him." Still, Kelman found that "Bailyn's approach—history written from the viewpoint of the losers—challenges us to imagine ourselves in Hutchinson's position and to ask ourselves how we would have acted in the America of the 1770s."

In *Voyagers to the West: A Passage in the Peopling of America on the Eve of the Revolution,* the first of a projected multivolume work, Bailyn examines in detail the historical register kept by the customs officials in England and Scotland from 1773-76 which lists particulars about English migrants to the Colonies. The directory indexes the names and addresses of citizens embarking for America, their reasons for departure, their occupations, and their planned destination. "Although Mr. Bailyn makes no claim to have discovered the register," observed John Gross of the *New York Times,* "he is the first historian to have analyzed it systematically—taking into account its defects, making use of a computer and drawing on a wide range of secondary sources to amplify his findings." Patrick Reardon noted in the *Chicago Tribune* that *Voyagers to the West* "is an astonishingly rich book, filled with insights and detail, scholarly yet fascinating in the human dimensions it gives to a broad social movement. In a way, *Voyagers to the West* is four or five books in one handsomely prepared volume."

In *Faces of Revolution: Personalities and Themes in the Struggle for American Independence,* a collection of essays on the ideologies and leaders of the American Revolution, Bailyn "has stitched together . . . a series of previously written personality sketches and interpretive essays and added a concluding commentary on the Constitution to provide an extraordinarily lucid and informative representation of the revolutionary age out of which the American nation emerged," claimed Remini in Chicago's *Tribune Books.* The reviewer added, "In elegant and persuasive language, Bailyn seeks to convey several basic ideas about the age, all of them exciting, important and provocative." Forrest McDonald wrote in the *New York Times Book Review,* "Rarely has a single book stimulated such a burst of productive scholarship, though the new works often presented alternative formulations of the argument. Mr. Bailyn has little patience with revisionist positions, and while in the present essays he corrects and enlarges his original thesis, he essentially adheres to it."

About *The Debate on the Constitution: Federalist and Antifederalist Speeches, Articles, and Letters during the Struggle over Ratification,* Theodore Draper commented in the *New York Times Book Review,* "For anyone, European or American, interested in what the genesis of the Constitution may teach us, help has providentially appeared. It is *The Debate on the Constitution,* handsomely published in two volumes by the Library of America and masterfully edited by Bernard Bailyn of Harvard University." The book chronicles the procedure whereby the Constitution and its articles were debated and discussed prior to ratification: in speeches, newspaper commentaries, rebuttals, personal correspondence. Draper continued, "A reader of these pages is ennobled and inspired by the dignity and grandeur of this debate. Not all the contributions were on the loftiest level, but so many were that they made reading these volumes a proud and exalting experience." The reviewer mentioned Bailyn's ability to involve and virtually absorb the reader in the ratifying process, so that "with a little effort of imagination we can take part in it as if we were present and engaged." Although Draper would have preferred that Bailyn include an introduction outlining the historical framework of the time, he nevertheless concluded, "The very idea of putting this debate in the Library of America was inspired. Both it and Mr. Bailyn can be proud of how they have carried it out."

Presser admired the scope of *The Debate on the Constitution,* stating, "Here, after more than 200 years, is an easily accessible set of sacred writings for America's civil religion—the adoration and veneration of the United States Constitution. In these roughly 2,400 pages is to be found virtually every major writing from the pamphlet and newspaper wars over ratification of the Constitution, in addition to a sampling from the private correspondence and the state constitutional convention debates regarding the document." Presser also observed that "there is no helpful introductory essay to ease in the uninitiated," yet appreciated the brief biographies and "astonishingly detailed notes" provided. He further mentioned, "Preparing this set must have been a labor of love for its editor, Bernard Bailyn." In the *Washington Post Book World,* Gary Jeffrey Jacobsohn praised *The Debate on the Constitution,* "which, as chronologically arranged by Bernard Bailyn, permits the reader to appreciate that defining historical moment in the illuminating context of an unfolding drama whose lessons speak directly to us today."

In *On the Teaching and Writing of History: Responses to a Series of Questions,* Bailyn discusses what it's like to be a historian and write about history. According to Edward Shapiro of the *World and I,* "Bailyn emphasized in the classroom that the true historian is not so much concerned with what the past was like but with why one part of the past had supplanted another." Bailyn teaches "invaluable lessons" as he provides "his own opinions and reflections regarding the meaning of history, how history is taught and how history should be taught, conducting historical research, and writing and communicating historical subject matter," wrote *Booklist*'s Margaret Flanagan. A *Publishers Weekly* reviewer observed that *On the Teaching and Writing of History* demonstrates Bailyn's "passion for teaching history" and "his belief that knowledge of the past is crucial to understanding the present."

Focusing once again on the time period after the American Revolution, Bailyn wrote *To Begin the World Anew: The Genius and Ambiguities of the American Founders,* in which he argues, according to Michael Zuckert in *First Things: A Monthly Journal of Religion and Public Life,* that eighteenth-century Americans and America's founding fathers were "able to question the truisms that dominated British political thought, and thus set out in astonishingly new directions." Five essays comprise this volume that "endeavors to portray the likes of [Thomas] Jefferson, [John] Adams, and [Benjamin] Franklin in all their ambiguities, inconsistencies, and ability to think freely," wrote a *Kirkus Reviews* contributor. Bailyn, according to a *Publishers Weekly* critic, believes that the founding fathers were "idealists as much as realists." The critic remarked that after reading the book "one comes away with a rounded appreciation of the founders' limitations, failures and moral failings as well as their extraordinary achievements."

"Bailyn's distinctive voice, as level-headed and acute as ever, works as both a stimulant and a balm, wrapped in an umbra of intellectual integrity," wrote a *Kirkus Reviews* critic. The *Boston Herald*'s Rob Mitchell observed that the "brief but discerning" essays capture the "thoughts, struggles, and dilemmas of the Revolutionary generation." *Los Angeles Times* reviewer Anthony Day called Bailyn's thinking "subtle," his style "forceful," and noted, "he is not afraid to look ambiguities square in the eye." For example, Bailyn points out the inconsistencies in Jefferson's way of thinking. In an essay from *To Begin the World Anew* titled "Jefferson and the Ambiguities of Freedom," Bailyn wrote that Jefferson was "simultaneously a radical utopian idealist and a hardheaded, adroit, at times cunning politician; a rhetorician, whose elegant phrases had propulsive power, and a no-nonsense administrator. . . . In [his] double role—ideologist and practical politician, theorist and pragmatist—he sought to realize the Revolution's most glittering promise, and as he did so he discovered the inner

complexities and ambiguities of those ideals as well as their strengths, and left a legacy of compromise and incompleteness which his critics would forever assail."

According to Zuckert, *To Begin the World Anew* is benefited not only by "beautifully written" essays, but also by "delicious" pictures of prominent eighteenth-century people and homes. Zuckert dubbed Bailyn "an author who wears his immense learning lightly, and conveys it with grace . . . a master of the essay form and of the period of which he writes." Zuckert concluded, "If he has any shortcoming it is that he leaves us wanting more."

BIOGRAPHICAL AND CRITICAL SOURCES:

BOOKS

Bailyn, Bernard, *The Ideological Origins of the American Revolution,* Belknap Press of Harvard University Press (Cambridge, MA), 1967.
Bailyn, Bernard, *To Begin the World Anew: The Genius and Ambiguities of the American Founders,* Knopf (New York, NY), 2003.
Dictionary of Literary Biography, Volume 17: *Twentieth-Century American Historians,* Thomson Gale (Detroit, MI), 1983.
Directory of American Scholars, 10th edition, Thomson Gale (Detroit, MI), 2001.
Global Encyclopedia of Historical Writing, Garland, 1998.
Oxford Companion to American Literature, 6th edition, Oxford Press, 1995.

PERIODICALS

Biography: An Interdisciplinary Quarterly, fall, 1996, review of *On the Teaching and Writing of History: Responses to a Series of Questions,* p. 429.
Booklist, May 1, 1995, Margaret Flanagan, review of *On the Teaching and Writing of History,* p. 1548; December 1, 2002, Gilbert Taylor, review of *To Begin the World Anew,* p. 643.
Book Week, May 7, 1967.
Boston Herald, January 12, 2003, Rob Mitchell, "New Nonfiction: Founders' Ambiguity Made America Strong," review of *To Begin the World Anew,* p. 48.

Chicago Tribune, December 1, 1986; July 4, 1993, p. 1.

Christian Science Monitor, April 17, 1974.

Commentary, February, 2003, Adam Schulman, "These Truths," review of *To Begin the World Anew,* p. 68.

First Things: A Monthly Journal of Religion and Public Life, June-July, 2003, Michael Zuckert, "Revolutionary Perspectives," review of *To Begin the World Anew,* p. 36.

Journal of American History, March, 1995, Thomas C. Holt, review of *The Great Republic: A History of the American People,* p. 1641.

Kirkus Reviews, November 1, 2002, review of *To Begin the World Anew,* p. 1581.

Kliatt Young Adult Paperback Book Guide, July, 1996, review of *On the Teaching and Writing of History,* p. 31.

Library Journal, April 1, 1995, Anthony O. Edmonds, review of *On the Teaching and Writing of History,* p. 107.

Los Angeles Times, April 17, 1987; January 17, 2003, Anthony Day, review of *To Begin the World Anew,* p. E-38.

National Review, June 7, 1974.

New Republic, May 4, 1974.

Newsweek, April 27, 1987.

New York Review of Books, March 21, 1974; February 13, 2003, Gordon S. Wood, "Creating the Revolution," review of *To Begin the World Anew,* p. 38.

New York Times, November 11, 1986; April 17, 1987; January 9, 1988.

New York Times Book Review, June 25, 1967; June 2, 1974; August 17, 1986, p. 6; June 19, 1988, p. 32; September 9, 1990, p. 10; October 10, 1993, p. 3.

Poets & Writers, March-April, 1987.

Publishers Weekly, February 13, 1995, review of *On the Teaching and Writing of History,* p. 69; November 18, 2002, review of *To Begin the World Anew,* p. 50.

Times Literary Supplement, October 12, 1967; June 13, 1975; September 4, 1987, p. 959; January 24, 1992, p. 24; September 1, 1995, John Kenyon, review of *On the Teaching and Writing of History,* p. 28.

Tribune Books (Chicago, IL), August 19, 1990, p. 1.

Virginia Quarterly Review, summer, 1995, review of *On the Teaching and Writing of History,* p. 81.

Washington Post, January 13, 1987.

Washington Post Book World, November 30, 1986, p. 6; May 29, 1988, p. 12; September 23, 1990, p. 13; September 5, 1993, p. 6.

William and Mary Quarterly, January, 1995, review of *The Debate on the Constitution: Federalist and Antifederalist Speeches, Articles, and Letters during the Struggle over Ratification,* p. 209.

World and I, July, 2003, Edward Shapiro, "A Historian's Historian: Bernard Bailyn Demonstrates Once Again Why He Is America's Most Trenchant Historian," review of *To Begin the World Anew,* p. 224.

Yale Review, October, 1995, *On the Teaching and Writing of History,* p. 95.

ONLINE

Harvard University Directory Web site, http://www.directory.harvard.edu/ (June 4, 2004), "Bernard Bailyn."

Harvard University Faculty and Staff Web site, http://www.fas.harvard.edu/~atlantic/bailyn.html/ (February 3, 2003), brief biography of Bernard Bailyn.*

*   *   *

BAKER, Kevin (Breen) 1958-

PERSONAL: Born August 20, 1958, in Englewood, NJ; son of Charles Kenneth (an actor) and Claire (a social worker; maiden name, Slade) Baker; married Ellen J. Abrams (a writer), October 11, 1992. *Education:* Columbia University, B.A., 1980. *Politics:* Democrat. *Religion:* Quaker. *Hobbies and other interests:* Baseball, American history.

ADDRESSES: Home—New York, NY. *Agent*—Philip G. Spitzer Literary Agency, 50 Talmage Farm Lane, East Hampton, NY 11937.

CAREER: Gloucester Daily Times, Gloucester, MA, staff writer, 1971-80; Foundation Center, New York, NY, compiler of entries for reference books, 1980-85; Public Securities Association, New York, NY, freelance writer on municipal bonds papers, 1986-87; letter writer for mayor's office, New York, NY, 1987-88; freelance writer, 1988—.

MEMBER: American Civil Liberties Union, Amnesty International.

AWARDS, HONORS: Today Show Book Club Selection, 2002, for *Paradise Alley.*

WRITINGS:

Sometimes You See It Coming (novel), Crown (New York, NY), 1993.
(Contributor) Harold Evans and Gail Buckland, *The American Century,* Knopf (New York, NY), 1998.
Dreamland, HarperCollins (New York, NY), 1999.
Paradise Alley, HarperCollins (New York, NY), 2002.

Contributor to *In a Word,* edited by Jack Hitt, Dell (New York, NY), 1992.

SIDELIGHTS: Published in 1993, Kevin Baker's first novel, *Sometimes You See It Coming,* tells the story of a great baseball player's career. In an article in *Publishers Weekly,* Crown editor Dick Marek explained that *Sometimes You See It Coming* "is a book we bought for a modest advance. It's a first novel by a young writer and we bought it because we fell in love with it." *Publishers Weekly* went on to elaborate, however: "But did Marek really see *this* coming: 100,000 first printing and $100,000 in promotion budget?" These figures are impressive for a first novel, and they came about because several editors at Crown continued to read the manuscript and urge its promotion.

Although *Sometimes You See It Coming* reminded many of Bernard Malamud's classic baseball novel *The Natural,* the story in *Sometimes You See It Coming* holds its own, according to critics. After noting that "this one ends the way a baseball story should: three and two, two out in the ninth, legend at bat," John Skow in *Time* urged readers to "put this one on the shelf with *The Natural.*" *Chicago Tribune* writer Kerry Luft acknowledged *Sometimes You See It Coming* "is almost ideal for a student of baseball history. Baker is clearly a dedicated fan, and he has based many of the characters on real players."

Dreamland, set in New York at the turn of the twentieth century, stars "Gyp the Blood," a strong-arm man who would kill a man who defaulted on a two-dollar bet. His associates, "Kid Twist" and "Trick the Dwarf," are also seedy characters in the New York underworld. *Book Page* reviewer Alden Mudge wrote

that the book effectively portrays the "anger and anguish" of immigrants to the United States, as well as their children's rebellion against Old World cultures. Baker told Mudge, "One of the interesting dilemmas of historical fiction is how much room a writer has to make things up. I think you can create composite characters and change chronologies just as long as you get the essence of the thing right. That's pretty much the trick in any kind of fiction—to reach for that greater truth."

Published in 2002, *Paradise Alley* is set during the Draft Riots of 1863. It is told from the point of view of Herbert Willis Robinson, a New York reporter who travels undercover among the poor people of New York, and reports their rage at being drafted when they are unable to pay a fee to avoid it. During the three days of the riots, working men tried to burn the city down. Baker depicts the riots, and tells the stories of many of those who participated in them or were affected by them. A *Kirkus Reviews* writer commented that the book is frequently "grisly," but noted that it was "deftly plotted."

BIOGRAPHICAL AND CRITICAL SOURCES:

PERIODICALS

American Heritage, February-March, 2003, review of *Paradise Alley,* p. 17.
Atlanta Journal-Constitution, March 14, 1999, Eileen M. Drennen, review of *Dreamland,* p. L12.
Booklist, January 1, 1999, p. 79; September 15, 1999, review of *Dreamland,* p. 277; December 15, 1999, p. 797; July, 2002, p. 1795.
Chicago Tribune, April 5, 1993, section 5, p. 3.
Christian Science Monitor, March 11, 1999, Ron Charles, review of *Dreamland,* p. 20.
Esquire, March, 1999, p. 38.
Kirkus Reviews, January 1, 1999, review of *Dreamland,* p. 4; August 15, 2002, review of *Paradise Alley,* p. 1155.
Library Journal, October 1, 1998, p. 110; January, 1999, review of *Dreamland,* p. 146; September 15, 1999, review of *Dreamland,* p. 130; August, 2002, Andrea Kempf, review of *Paradise Alley,* p. 138.
Los Angeles Times Book Review, April 4, 1993, pp. 2, 13; March 7, 1999, review of *Dreamland,* p. 4.
New Republic, May 24, 1999, p. 46.

New York Times Book Review, October 11, 1998, David
    S. Reynolds, review of *The American Century,*
    p. 8; February 28, 1999, Thomas Mallon, review
    of *Dreamland,* p. 10.
Publishers Weekly, February 1, 1993, pp. 61-62;
    September 14, 1998, p. 55; September 9, 2002,
    review of *Paradise Alley,* p. 40.
St. Louis Post-Dispatch, February 28, 1999, Harry
    Levins, review of *Dreamland,* p. C5.
San Francisco Chronicle, April 4, 1999, Adam
    Mazmanian, review of *Dreamland,* p. 9.
Time, March 22, 1993, p. 70; November 23, 1998,
    p. 56.
Times Literary Supplement, August 6, 1999, Jonathan
    Fasland, review of *Dreamland,* p. 21.
Wall Street Journal, February 26, 1999, Emily R.
    Sendler, review of *Dreamland,* p. W11.

ONLINE

BookPage, http://www.bookpage.com/ (March, 1999)
    interview by Alden Mudge, "On Coney Island with
    Kevin Baker, in Search of the American Dream."*

* * *

BARTON, (Samuel) Wayne 1944-

PERSONAL: Born May 23, 1944, in Odessa, TX; son
of John Samuel (an oil field worker) and Alene (a
homemaker; maiden name, Gurley) Barton; married
Margaret Whisenand (a homemaker), April 4, 1966;
children: Charles, Kristin. *Education:* Texas Tech
University, B.S., 1967. *Religion:* Presbyterian.

ADDRESSES: Home—2509 Emerson, Midland, TX
79705. *Agent*—Charles Neighbors, Inc., 7600 Blanco
Rd., Suite 3607, San Antonio, TX 78216.

CAREER: Arco Oil and Gas Co., began as engineer,
became senior engineer in Roswell, NM, Casper, WY,
and Midland, TX, 1967-94; writer, 1994—. Also works
as woodcarver, with work represented in private collections in the United States and abroad; guest on
media programs, including the television series *The
American Woodshop* and *The Woodwright Shop.*
Writer's Digest School of Short Fiction, editorial
associate, 1987-94.

MEMBER: Society of Petroleum Engineers, Western
Writers of America (member of board of directors,
1985-87).

AWARDS, HONORS: Spur Award, Western Writers of
America, 1981, for magazine article "One Man's
Code"; Medicine Pipe Bearer Award, 1982, for *Ride
down the Wind;* additional awards for wood chip
carving.

WRITINGS:

WESTERN NOVELS

Ride down the Wind, Doubleday (New York, NY),
    1982.
Return to Phantom Hill, Doubleday (New York, NY),
    1984.
(With Stan Williams) *Warhorse,* Pocket Books (New
    York, NY), 1988.
(With Stan Williams) *Live by the Gun,* Pocket Books
    (New York, NY), 1989.
(With Stan Williams) *Manhunt,* Pocket Books (New
    York, NY), 1992.
(With Stan Williams) *High Country,* Pocket Books
    (New York, NY), 1993.
(With Stan Williams) *Shadow of Doubt,* Pocket Books
    (New York, NY), 1994.
(With Stan Williams) *Wildcat,* Pocket Books (New
    York, NY), 1995.
(With Stan Williams) *Fairchild's Passage,* Forge (New
    York, NY), 1997.
(With Stan Williams) *Lockhart's Nightmare,* Forge
    (New York, NY), 1998.

OTHER

Chip Carving: Techniques and Patterns, Sterling (New
    York, NY), 1984.
Chip Carving Patterns, Sterling (New York, NY),
    1990.
*New and Traditional Styles of Chip Carving: From
    Classic to Positive Imaging,* Sterling (New York,
    NY), 1994.
The Art of Chip Carving: Award-Winning Designs,
    Sterling (New York, NY), 1998.

(Coeditor and contributor) *What Western Do I Read Next? A Reader's Guide to Recent Western Fiction,* Thomson Gale (Detroit, MI), 1998, 2nd edition, 1999.

Chip Carving: Design and Pattern Sourcebook, Sterling (New York, NY), 2002.

Author of "Bookmarks for Westerns," a monthly column in *Roundup,* 1985-88; also columnist for *Chip Chats.* Contributor of stories to anthologies, including *Roundup,* edited by Stephen Overholser, Doubleday (New York, NY), 1982; and *The Texans,* edited by Bill Pronzini and Martin H. Greenberg, Fawcett (New York, NY), 1988. Contributor of articles and stories to magazines, including *Far West, Western Fiction, Analog,* and *Empire.*

SIDELIGHTS: Wayne Barton traces his interest in Western history to his childhood, when he frequently listened to his parents tell stories of their early years in central Texas. By the time he was twelve years old, he was an avid reader and felt sure he wanted to be a writer some day. Yet his first attempts at writing left him discouraged, and he enrolled in engineering school. "Graduation, marriage, and an engineer's position with a major oil company never quite killed the urge to write," he reminisced in *Twentieth-Century Western Writers,* "and finally I learned enough to do something about it." His first published short story, a western, was nominated for the American Spur award for best short western fiction. Barton went on to sell many short stories in various genres, and eventually to write novels as well. Writing remains a part-time activity, and as David Whitehead commented in *Twentieth-Century Western Writers,* "it is indicative of the quality of Wayne Barton's work that the most common complaint levelled against him is simply that he has not produced enough to satisfy his many admirers."

In one of his best-known books, *Ride down the Wind,* Barton tells the tale of two army scouts, one white, one Indian, who eventually become adversaries. It is "a thrilling western," according to a *Booklist* writer. "Barton introduces many of his recurring themes and trademarks in this book," mused Whitehead. "His use of solitary, introspective men as heroes; strong, intelligent women who guide or enlighten them; an atmosphere of suspicion, where few men can be trusted or relied upon until the last shot has been fired; and a solid understanding of how ordinary people react to extraordinary situations."

BIOGRAPHICAL AND CRITICAL SOURCES:

BOOKS

Twentieth-Century Western Writers, St. James Press (Detroit, MI), 1991.

PERIODICALS

American Reference Books Annual, 1999, review of *What Western Do I Read Next? A Reader's Guide to Recent Western Fiction,* p. 427.
Booklist, January 1, 1982, review of *Ride down the Wind,* p. 585; February 15, 1998, review of *What Western Do I Read Next?,* p. 1038; May 15, 1998, Budd Arthur, review of *Lockhart's Nightmare,* p. 1593.
Books of the Southwest, May, 1989, p. 13.
Knowledge Quest, March, 1998, review of *What Western Do I Read Next?,* p. 54.
Library Journal, June 1, 2002, Jonathan Hershey, review of *Chip Carving: Design and Pattern Book,* pp. 187-188.
Publishers Weekly, April 6, 1998, review of *Lockhart's Nightmare,* p. 56.
Roundup Monthly, January, 1994, p. 24; March, 1995, p. 27; February, 1996, p. 28; August, 1998, review of *Lockhart's Nightmare,* p. 28.
School Library Journal, August, 1998, Herman Sutter, review of *What Western Do I Read Next?,* p. 188.*

*   *   *

BATTLE-LAVERT, Gwendolyn 1951-

PERSONAL: Born October 28, 1951, in Paris, TX; daughter of Charles Edward (a Campbell's Soup employee) and Ozie Mae (a Campbell's Soup employee; maiden name, Dangerfield) Battle; married Donald Rae Lavert (a teacher), February 28, 1975; children: Leslie Lynn, Lance Lamont. *Ethnicity:* "African-American." *Education:* Paris Junior College, A.S., 1972; East Texas State University, B.S. (elementary/kindergarten endorsement), 1974, M.Ed. (reading specialist certification), 1976; also attended Texarkana Community College, 1990, and the Institute of Children's Literature, 1992. *Politics:* Democrat. *Religion:* Baptist. *Hobbies and other interests:* Writing, sewing, speaking, drawing.

ADDRESSES: Home—842 Ross Dr., Marion, IN, 46953. *Office*—Indiana Wesleyan University, 4201 S. Washington St., Marion, IN 46953. *E-mail*—gwen. lavert@indwes.edu.

CAREER: Texarkana Independent School District, Texarkana, TX, elementary classroom teacher, 1974-87, reading specialist, 1981-87, reading/writing coordinator, 1987-91; Harcourt Brace School Publishers, Southwest regional consultant, beginning 1991; Indiana Wesleyan University, Marion, IN, assistant professor of education, 1999—. Consultant and lecturer for writing workshops; former dean-assistant principal, DeSoto Schools. Member, Black Chamber of Commerce, Girl Scouts, St. Paul Baptist Church Prayer Group.

MEMBER: International Reading Association, Society of Children's Book Writers and Illustrators, Parent-Teacher Association (lifetime member), TSTA (president), National Education Association, Association for Supervision and Curriculum Development, ATLAS, Classroom Teachers Association, Texas State Reading Association, Texas Publishers Association, Iota Sorority.

AWARDS, HONORS: Teacher of the Year, 1979; recipient of local teacher grant, 1982, John Hindman Fellowship, International Paper Mill Foundation, 1986-87, and Open Community Grant, 1990.

WRITINGS:

The Barber's Cutting Edge, illustrated by Raymond Holbert, Children's Book Press (Emeryville, CA), 1994.
Off to School, Holiday House (New York, NY), 1995.
The Music in Derrick's Heart, Holiday House (New York, NY), 2000.
The Shaking Bag, A. Whitman (Morton Grove, IL), 2000.
Papa's Mark, Holiday House (New York, NY), 2002.

Also author of "Poetic Scribblers," published in *Reading Education in Texas,* 1989.

WORK IN PROGRESS: Tabias Leads the Way, Eddie Ray and His Rocking Chair, The Harmonica Man, Daisy's Christmas Wish.

SIDELIGHTS: An educator and storyteller, Gwendolyn Battle-Lavert has been publishing books for children since 1994. Her warm, simple stories feature African-American characters and impart gentle messages about the values that make families and individuals strong. Some of her tales take young readers into the past, to show a time when African Americans did not have the right to vote and many struggled to attend school.

Battle-Lavert's first book, *The Barber's Cutting Edge,* follows a young boy on a trip to the barber shop. Not only is Mr. Bigalow the best barber in town, he also loves words and, dictionary in hand, helps Rashaad with his school vocabulary list. A *Publishers Weekly* reviewer called it an "unremarkable but likeable tale." Another little boy is being taught to play the harmonica by an elderly uncle in *The Music in Derrick's Heart.* In the process, he learns that he too has a special power to help others through his music. A *Publishers Weekly* critic judged that the story had "some lyrical moments" but proved to be "little more than a one-note story." According to Nancy Menaldi-Scanlan in *School Library Journal,* however, it was "an appealing look at the sense of community the music fosters throughout [Derrick's] black neighborhood." In a *Booklist* review, Shelle Rosenfeld called it a "charming, uplifting story" in which "the easy-flowing rhythmic prose beautifully echoes and conveys the messages."

Other stories by Battle-Lavert consider the events and living conditions of decades past. The monumental importance of gaining the right to vote is dramatized in *Papa's Mark,* in which a boy watches his father learn to write his name so that he doesn't have to place an X on his first ballot. The author's sensitive treatment creates "the gentle ambience of this powerful story," according to GraceAnne A. DeCandido in *Booklist.* In *Off to School,* the author shows the difficult life of the daughter of a black sharecropper, Wezielee, who longs to go to school but must work on the farm, or worse in her mind, cook for the family. *Booklist*'s Susan Dove Lempke credited the story with showing "a warm family atmosphere . . . and a sense of the simplicity and anxiety of the sharecroppers' life."

Another book by Battle-Lavert that evokes an old-fashioned, rural existence is *The Shaking Bag,* a myth-like story about a poor old woman who is rewarded for her joy in sharing with others. Annie Mae is as generous with the birds as she is with a stranger named Raven Reed who comes to her door. Offering him her only chair and the last of her food, he turns an empty sack into a magical bag that produces wood, food, and furniture and will insure that Annie Mae is never hungry again. Writing in *School Library Journal,* Donna L. Scanlon said that the author "spins a brilliant, beautifully written original tale" that is "elegant in its sheer simplicity." The story prompted Shelley Townsend-Hudson to say in *Booklist* that the "goodness of the soul has never looked so fresh."

Commenting on the roots of her stories, Gwendolyn Battle-Lavert commented: "Every family has a recorder. I happen to be the one for my family. Hearing my Mama tell about her life has strengthened me. Her stories have given me the self-esteem, pride, and love that tells me who I am and sustains me as I strive to be the best I can be.

"Writing is not easy. But the more I read, the better my writing becomes. I enter my first draft into the computer, then go back and rework the words I wrote days, weeks, even months before. The stories become better, and better, and better.

"So as a writer, I've taken my mother's stories, reworked them, and submitted them. . . . As a final quest, I would like to go into classrooms and read my stories to children all over the world. I want students to know that reading opens up the world to them. It's a journey that will last them a lifetime."

BIOGRAPHICAL AND CRITICAL SOURCES:

PERIODICALS

Booklist, October 15, 1995, Susan Dove Lempke, review of *Off to School,* p. 410; February 15, 2000, Shelle Rosenfeld, review of *The Music in Derrick's Heart;* April 1, 2000, Shelley Townsend-Hudson, review of *The Shaking Bag,* p. 1466; November 1, 2003, Shelle Rosenfeld, review of *Papa's Mark,* p. 500.
Publishers Weekly, November 14, 1994, review of *The Barber's Cutting Edge,* p. 68; January 24, 2000, review of *The Music in Derrick's Heart,* p. 310.
School Library Journal, March, 2000, Nancy Menaldi-Scanlan, review of *The Music in Derrick's Heart,* p. 178; April, 2000, Donna L. Scanlon, review of *The Shaking Bag,* p. 90.*

BAUMBACH, Jonathan 1933-

PERSONAL: Born July 5, 1933 in New York, NY; son of Harold M. (an artist) and Ida Helen (Zackheim) Baumbach; married Elinor Berkman, September 10, 1956 (divorced, 1967); married Georgia A. Brown, June 10, 1969 (divorced, May, 1991); children: (first marriage) David, Nina; (second marriage) Noah, Nicholas. *Education:* Brooklyn College (now of the City University of New York), A.B., 1955; Columbia University, M.F.A., 1956; Stanford University, Ph.D., 1961.

ADDRESSES: Office—Department of English, Brooklyn College of the City University of New York, Brooklyn, NY 11210. *E-mail*—jquarte@panix.com.

CAREER: Fiction writer and educator in English and creative writing. Stanford University, Stanford, CA, instructor in English, 1958-60; Ohio State University, Columbus, instructor in English, 1961-62, assistant professor of English, 1962-64; New York University, New York, NY, assistant professor of English and director of freshman English, 1964-66; Brooklyn College of the City University of New York, Brooklyn, NY, associate professor, 1966-70, professor of English, beginning 1970, director of MFA in creative writing, beginning 1975, professor emeritus; The New School University, New York, NY, faculty member, 2004. Member of board of directors, Teachers and Writers Collaborative, NY, 1966—. Fiction Collective, cofounder, 1974, codirector, 1974-78, currently member of board of directors. Visiting professor, Tufts University, 1970-71, University of Washington, 1978-79 and 1985-86, Princeton University, 1990-91, Brown University, 1994. *Military service:* U. S. Army, 1956-58.

MEMBER: National Society of Film Critics (chair, 1982-84).

AWARDS, HONORS: Young Writers Award, *New Republic,* 1958; Yaddo fellowship, summers, 1963, 1964, and 1965; National Endowment for the Arts creative writing fellowship, 1969; Guggenheim fellowship, 1978; Ingram-Merrill fellowship, 1983.

WRITINGS:

The One-Eyed Man Is King (play), first produced at Theater East, New York, NY, 1956.

The Landscape of Nightmare: Studies in the Contemporary American Novel, New York University Press (New York, NY), 1965.

(Contributor) W. R. Robinson, editor, *Man and the Movies,* Louisiana State University Press (Baton Rouge, LA), 1967.

(Editor, with Arthur Edelstein) *Moderns and Contemporaries: Nine Masters of the Short Story,* Random House (New York, NY), 1968, republished as *Moderns and Contemporaries: Twelve Masters of the Short Story,* Random House (New York, NY), 1977.

(Editor and author of introduction) *Writers As Teachers/Teachers As Writers,* Holt (New York, NY), 1970.

(Editor) *Statements: New Fiction from the Fiction Collective,* Braziller (New York, NY), 1975.

(Editor, with Peter Spielberg) *Statements 2: New Fiction,* Fiction Collective (New York, NY), 1977.

The Return of Service: Stories, University of Illinois Press (Urbana, IL), 1979.

The Life and Times of Major Fiction: Stories, Fiction Collective (New York, NY), 1986.

NOVELS

A Man to Conjure With, Random House (New York, NY), 1965.

What Comes Next, Harper (New York, NY), 1968.

Reruns, Fiction Collective (New York, NY), 1974.

Babble, Fiction Collective (New York, NY), 1976.

Chez Charlotte and Emily, Fiction Collective (New York, NY), 1979.

My Father More or Less, Fiction Collective (New York, NY), 1982.

Separate Hours, Fiction Collective Two (Boulder, CO), 1990.

Seven Wives: A Romance, Fiction Collective Two (Boulder, CO), 1994.

D-Tours, FC2 (Normal, IL), 1998.

B, Low Fidelity Press (New York, NY), 2002.

Contributor of over eighty short stories and numerous articles to periodicals, including *Esquire, Iowa Review, Kenyon Review, Partisan Review, Chicago Review, TriQuarterly,* and *Nation.* Movie reviewer, *Partisan Review,* 1973-82. Contributor to anthologies, including *O. Henry Prize Stories, Best American Short Stories,* and *Best of Esquire.* Manuscript collection resides at the Boston University Library.

SIDELIGHTS: In his first book, *The Landscape of Nightmare: Studies in the Contemporary American Novel,* experimental writer Jonathan Baumbach examines the works of a number of postwar American novelists. "Baumbach explored each novel," wrote Larry McCaffery of the *Dictionary of Literary Biography,* "in terms of how it portrays the nightmarish conditions of contemporary society and how each individual protagonist attempts to carve his own niche, or openly rebels against these conditions." In contrast to the novelists of an earlier generation, who expressed the nightmarish quality of society "in terms of social defeats and victories," Bernard McCabe explained in *Commonweal,* the contemporary novelists Baumbach studies express it "in terms of the Self." It is this psychological approach that especially interests Baumbach. The novels he examines, Baumbach clarifies in his study, are concerned with "the confrontation of man with the objectification of his primordial self and his exemplary spiritual passage from innocence to guilt to redemption." Of particular importance to Baumbach, McCaffery reported, is "the way in which [these novels] make manifest the inner worlds and secret lives of their protagonists."

In his own novels, Baumbach also explores "inner worlds and secret lives," but does so through innovative narrative structures. Baumbach's narratives have "placed him in the company of our most serious experimentalists," Jerome Klinkowitz explained in *The Life of Fiction.* The similarities and interrelationships between memories, dreams, our perceptions of the real world, and the images of popular culture are constant concerns in all of Baumbach's fiction. With his first novel, *A Man to Conjure With,* Baumbach "immediately established the shifting terrain of dream, memory, imagination, and public nightmare that his fiction would explore," wrote McCaffery. Ironically, it is the most conventional of Baumbach's novels. As Klinkowitz explained, "There is experimentation [in *A Man to Conjure With*], but within traditional bounds; there is nothing unrealistic in the book except the character's dreams, which are clearly identified as such."

In the novel, Peter Becker tries to restore his marriage after being separated from his wife for many years. By piecing his life back together, Becker also hopes to reestablish a sense of personal identity. Speaking of Becker, Baumbach told John Graham in *The Writer's Voice: Conversations with Contemporary Writers,* "It's as if all the details will add up to a picture of himself. And then, he can look at himself as he was. He has the idea, perhaps, that the man he was at twenty is still somewhere there, all the potentiality that was there at twenty and forgotten and lost. To look at himself at twenty is to come back there and start again, to recoup what he's lost."

"Much of the action," observed Klinkowitz, "takes place in Peter [Becker's] dreams, and his character is defined by them." Klinkowitz noted that Baumbach uses dreams in this novel to study the workings of the human imagination and to determine how dreams are expressed in language. While Haskel Frankel of the *New York Times Book Review* admitted that "there is no question as to the author's talent, sensitivity, control, and intelligence," she also maintained that *A Man to Conjure With* "adds up to nothing. We are introduced to a man by someone we respect, asked to study the man carefully—and then are never told the point of our studies." However, S. L. Bellman of the *Saturday Review* stressed the importance of the protagonist's dreams. This novel, he wrote, "has the character of a weird Freudian nightmare that involves no stage effects or supernaturalism whatever." Also writing in the *Saturday Review,* Henry S. Rasnik found the novel to be "an ingenious portrait of a schlemiel-Everyman cracking up," while Emile Capouya of *Book Week* related that "Baumbach writes with great elegance and wit. . . . He is inventive and amusing."

The dreams found in Baumbach's next novel, titled *What Comes Next,* "are indistinguishable from life," Klinkowitz wrote, since the protagonist, a college student named Christopher Steiner, is going mad. There is no specific catalyst for his madness. He is simply reacting to his society. "Too much violence in the street. Sex, bombing, suffocation, rape. Too much madness," as Baumbach describes it in the novel. The narrative is structured to reflect Steiner's deteriorating state of mind, interweaving his dreams and hallucinations with the real events around him. "Baumbach's short-jabbing prose, skirting the necessary edge of hysteria thrusts the violent city at us. . . . Throughout the novel Baumbach works to dissolve ugly fact into fantasy, fantasy into fact, so that the nightmare and the reality are convincingly one," explained McCabe.

C. D. B. Bryan of the *New York Times Book Review* compared Baumbach's handling of *What Comes Next* to the work of Nathanael West. "Baumbach's writing,"

Bryan stated, "like West's, is finely chiseled, keen and tough; his images are violent and garish; his hero, like [West's character] Miss Lonelyhearts, is obsessed by nightmares. . . . [But] Baumbach's value as a writer is that he makes the insanity of his hero seem appallingly sane."

In *Reruns,* Baumbach's narrator is again concerned with reassembling his life into a meaningful pattern. The narrator describes himself as "a hostage to the habit of rerunning the dead past in the cause of waking from the dream." Organized into a series of thirty-three short chapters—each a "dream-exorcism," as John Ager remarked in the *Carolina Quarterly*—the book presents the record of a man's life as a month's worth of short films at a cinema. Some experiences are redone several times in different ways, as if the narrator were attempting to change the past through the power of his imagination. "These 'reruns,'" McCaffery explained, "are nightmarish, frantic, often violent episodes . . . whose characters and events are generated from a wide variety of cultural clichés, fairy tales, stories, and movies. This is a world of terror, loneliness, and absurdity." Irving Malin of the *New Republic* expressed a similar opinion: "Usual routines are destroyed; only explosive energy remains. . . . The confusion, violence, humor, and madness are mixed so quickly that we . . . are overwhelmed."

By using cinematic techniques in *Reruns,* wrote Michael Mewshaw in the *New York Times Book Review,* Baumbach attempts to capture in prose "the kind of simultaneous vision a movie or painting can express. He wants to show us objects and characters from mutually exclusive perspectives, to stretch our understanding of time and expand our comprehension of emotions so that contrary feelings will spring from the same experiences." Malin also saw the cinematic presentation as important to the novel's theme. "Baumbach," Malin observed, "asks important questions: does the individual gain self-knowledge by confronting his popular culture? What exactly is the value of dream (fantasy) in creating identity?" In *Reruns,* and the following novels, *Babble* and *Chez Charlotte and Emily,* McCaffery reported, Baumbach explores "the role of the media (especially cinema) in creating societal norms and the individual's notion of self."

The characters and situations of popular culture form an important part of *Babble,* the adventures of a baby-hero. Because the novel is narrated by a three-year-old, the conventions of fairy tales, comic books, and television are often used to tell the story; these, after all, are the storytelling techniques most familiar to a small child. In this way, McCaffery thought, Baumbach investigates "the process whereby language is discovered and narrative patterns are imposed."

In contrast to Baumbach's previous novels, the distinctions between dream and reality are irrelevant in *Babble* since the baby narrator can make no such distinctions when relating his adventures. Fact, fantasy, and dream are intertwined into "a kind of surreal Bildungsroman," as McCaffery described the book. Although the novel uses "the episodic form of *Reruns* and the beleaguered protagonists of [the] earlier novels," Thalia Selz wrote in *fiction international*, "a transformation takes place in attitude. *Baby,* whom we seem prepared to label a clown, manages through patience and stratagem, to remain a hero in a dangerous world."

Like *Reruns* and *Babble, Chez Charlotte and Emily* is a fragmented narrative constructed much like a film montage. As Irving Malin wrote in the *Hollins Critic,* it is a series of "stories within stories, boxes within boxes. The narrator writes about a couple; the couple write or fantasize about another couple; the third couple in turn have novelistic tendencies." All of the stories thus related are strongly reminiscent of the cinema, partly because the characters restage and reshoot scenes in varying ways, as might be done while making a movie. Other characters have the names of famous movie stars, while certain plot elements have their parallels in old movie scripts. The importance of these cinematic references, McCaffery pointed out, lies in the characters' abilities to use their imaginations to restructure their world. "All these stories," McCaffery stated, "are evidently metaphorical reflections of inner tensions, desires, and personality traits. . . . Through the agency of imagination and metaphor, . . . Joshua and Genevieve perpetuate themselves and their relationship, make love, and communicate."

In the 1982 novel *My Father More or Less,* Baumbach explores the complicated relationship between a long-separated father and son. According to McCaffery, writing this time for the *American Book Review,* the author seeks to develop "a fictional structure which can probe beneath the surface of our waking lives and awaken the intuition." Baumbach's next work of long

fiction, *Separate Hours,* describes another muddled relationship—that of husband and wife psychotherapists who analyze the deterioration of their ill-starred marriage. Using a variety of literary techniques, including multiple narrative voices and a simulated cinematic recreation of the couple's conflicts, Baumbach creates "a curiously bracing novel of dissolution," noted Steven G. Kellman in the *New York Times Book Review.*

Seven Wives: A Romance features the narrator of *Reruns* conducting a cynical review of his seven failed marriages and fearing that he is the target of a murderous plot by one or more of his ex-wives. Catherine Bush, reviewing the work in the *New York Times Book Review,* suggested that Baumbach's female characters "never breathe with the suggestiveness of life beyond the page. . . . Nor does [the narrator's] obsession with them ever quiver with a sensuality that would allow us to feel him saturated by their presence." In the end, the reader is left wondering whether the protagonist has "learned anything from his misadventures." Bush concluded, however, that this may be just "what Mr. Baumbach intends."

In his 1998 novel *D-Tours,* protagonist Max Million tries to find his way back to the Paradise Hotel where he last left his dying lover years ago. As another of Baumbach's characters wanders through a variety of movie genres—science fiction, kung-fu, horror, film noir, and even slapstick—Max becomes involved in several different plots whose only common thread is his presence within them, making the novel almost appear as a collection of short stories. The novel was inspired by photographer David Axel Baumbach's series *Stills from Imaginary Movies.* A *Publishers Weekly* critic described *D-Tours* as "painfully postmodern," maintaining, "As Max declares from the outset, clichés are what make up his existence. Instead of reinventing and illuminating them, however, Max is doomed—as no character should be—to repeat them." Similarly, Steve Tomasula commented on Baumbach's use of movie genres in the *Review of Contemporary Fiction,* stating that "[the novel's] weakness is that in episodically taking on all of these genres, the point to which the gags are put isn't so much developed by the book as used as a framing device." However, Tomasula concluded, "When the story does come out the other end of its murder and chase scenes . . . it borders on the profound . . . [and] forces the reader to reconsider the episodes as cultural consciousness, autobiography, memory—the constituent components of self."

Baumbach's fictionalized memoir *B* is the failed attempt of the writer B to record the story of his life in a memoir. Sexual relationships and literary mishaps permeate the novel, which is more a collection of fourteen individual stories than a fluid novel in the traditional sense. In *B*'s prologue, the author wrote, "When I reached fifty, turned that mortal corner, I decided it was time to tell my own story unmediated by metaphorical disguise. Mainly I was blocked on a novel I had started two years ago and needed to try something else to get out of my funk. I imagined in telling the story of my life I would rediscover pieces of myself I had lost, which might have some interest to readers who had a similar sense of incompleteness and dislocation. . . . If not exceptionally unusual, my life at least had been eventful. I had been married three times and in love (in the illusion of) at least seven others; I had four children; I had lived passionately (some of the time, much of it in the imagination); I had served in the army (between wars); I had written a number of books. And if not that eventful, at least my life had been substantial and serious. Or so I believed or mostly believed or aspired to believe. It was possible that the memoir I was positioned to write was a story of self-deception. . . . My failures were what gave my life the shape and dazzle of fiction. I continually found new ways to deceive myself into making what turned out to be a mistake."

Critics reacted strongly—in both positive and negative lights—to Baumbach's tenth novel. "*B* is a book of blurred boundaries and self-negation," wrote Matthew Flaming in a review of the book on the *Word Riot* Web site. While Flaming describe B's character as "likeable and fallible and convincing," Flaming found it to be problematic that "over the course of the book, B learns nothing, nothing changes. And the stories that he imagines or wanders through—often the distinction is unclear—seem to be a kind of atrophied realism; revolving around the narrator's self-centered blundering through a string of failed romances, they dissolve into unreconciled alternatives, stop mid-sentence, and do not even imagine that resolution is possible." However, Flaming did point out that some of the chapters were "lovely pieces of work" and that some "come very close to telling something genuinely true and moving about the human condition." One *Publishers Weekly* reviewer described *B* as a "sly, diverting read," while a *Kirkus Reviews* contributor termed it "amusing but short of hilarity." While likely meant to be funny, but probably not hilarious, other critics felt that the novel was no less brilliant than Baumbach's previous works. James Browning of the *Village Voice,* revealed to readers, "*B* is the book to read if you're sick of other books, something to beat the worst case of reader's block." Browning felt that the premise and construction of the novel worked. He wrote, "Every sentence . . . works against itself, resulting in stories torn beautifully at the seams."

BIOGRAPHICAL AND CRITICAL SOURCES:

BOOKS

Baumbach, Jonathan, *The Landscape of Nightmare: Studies in the Contemporary American Novel,* New York University Press (New York, NY), 1965.

Baumbach, Jonathan, *What Comes Next,* Harper (New York, NY), 1968.

Baumbach, Jonathan, *Reruns,* Fiction Collective (New York, NY), 1974.

Baumbach, Jonathan, *B,* Low Fidelity Press (New York, NY), 2002.

Contemporary Literary Criticism, Thomson Gale (Detroit, MI), Volume 6, 1976, Volume 23, 1983.

Contemporary Novelists, 7th edition, Thomson Gale (Detroit, MI), 2001.

Dictionary of Literary Biography Yearbook: 1980, Thomson Gale (Detroit, MI), 1981.

Directory of American Poets and Fiction Writers, 2001-2002, Thomson Gale (Detroit, MI), 2002.

Directory of American Scholars, 10th edition, Thomson Gale (Detroit, MI), 2001.

Graham, John, *The Writer's Voice: Conversations with Contemporary Writers,* Morrow (New York, NY), 1973.

Klinkowitz, Jerome, *The Life of Fiction,* University of Illinois Press (Urbana, IL), 1977.

PERIODICALS

American Book Review, March-April, 1981; January, 1984, p. 7; January, 1988, p. 12; July, 1999, review of *D-Tours,* p. 27.

Book Week, October 3, 1965.

Carolina Quarterly, winter, 1975.

Chicago Review, autumn, 1978.

Commonweal, September 24, 1965; December 13, 1968.

Contemporary Literature, winter, 1978.

fiction international, numbers 6-7, 1976.

Film Comment, May-June, 1991, pp. 62,64; March-April, 1996, p. 7.

Hollins Critic, February, 1980.

Hudson Review, winter, 1976-77.

Kenyon Review, January, 1966.

Kirkus Reviews, March 15, 1987; March 1, 1994, p. 223; October 15, 2002, review of *B,* p. 1490.

Nation, December 7, 1974.

New Republic, October 19, 1974.

New York Times Book Review, November 21, 1965; October 13, 1968; October 13, 1974; January 13, 1980; July 27, 1980; June 7, 1987, p. 22; July 15, 1990, p. 10; May 22, 1994, p. 10.

Publishers Weekly, March 12, 1982, p. 76; April 3, 1987, p. 65; July 13, 1990, p. 50; March 28, 1994, p. 91; March 2, 1998, review of *D-Tours,* p. 60; January 13, 2003, review of *B,* p. 44.

Review of Contemporary Fiction, September 22, 1998, Steve Tomasula, review of *D-Tours,* p. 249.

Saturday Review, April 17, 1965; October 26, 1968.

Sewanee Review, July, 1980.

Village Voice, October 31, 1974.

Washington Post Book World, March 30, 1980; May 30, 1982, p. 9.

ONLINE

Euphorbus Arts Publication of Princeton University, http://www.princeton.edu/~euphorb/ (spring, 1991), Jonathan Baumbach, "The Reading."

Frigate Online Magazine, http://www.frigatezine.com/ (April 30, 2004), "Biography: Jonathan Baumbach," and Jonathan Baumbach, "The Pleasures of the Difficult."

Lofi Press Web Site, http://www.lofipress.com/ (April 30, 2004), description of *B.*

New School University Web Site, http://www.nsu.newschool.edu/ (May 3, 2004), "Faculty."

Village Voice, http://www.villagevoice.com/ (December 16, 2002), James Browning, review of *B.*

Word Riot, http://www.wordriot.org/ (April 30, 2004), Matthew Flaming, review of *B.*

Writing Site, http://www.writingsite.com/ (May 3, 2004), excerpt from *B.**

BELL, Anthea 1936-

PERSONAL: Born May 10, 1936, in Sudbury, Suffolk, England; daughter of Adrian (a writer) and Marjorie (Gibson) Bell; married Antony Kamm (a publisher), 1957 (divorced, 1973); children: Richard, Oliver. *Education:* Somerville College, Oxford University, B.A., 1957; Oxford University, M.A., 1962. *Hobbies and other interests:* Breeding Birman cats, gardening, cooking.

ADDRESSES: Home and office—9 Saffron Rd., Histon, Cambridge CB4 4LJ, England.

CAREER: Freelance translator, adapter, and writer, 1958—. Judge, annual Schlegel-Tieck German translation prize in England.

MEMBER: Translators Association (England).

AWARDS, HONORS: Mildred L. Batchelder Award nomination, 1970, for *Storm over the Caucasus,* 1971, for *Hunters of Siberia,* 1975, for *There, Far beyond the River; The Satanic Mill* by Otfried Preussler was a *New York Times* Notable Book, 1973; Mildred L. Batchelder Award, 1976, for *The Cat and Mouse Who Shared a House,* 1979, for *Konrad,* 1990, for *Buster's World,* and 1995, for *The Boys from St. Petri;* translator's prize, German Academy of Literature for Children and Young People, 1976; International Board on Books for Young People (IBBY) award for translation, 1978, for *The Cucumber King: A Story with a Beginning, a Middle and an End,* and 1982, for *The Big Janosch Book of Fun and Verse;* Schlegel-Tieck Prize, 1987, for *The Stone and the Flute;* Astrid Lindgren Prize, Federation Internationale des Traducteurs (FIT), 1990, for translation of children's books; two-time recipient, Hans Christian Andersen Award certificate of honor for translation; Helen and Kurt Wolff Translator's Prize for outstanding translation from German into English, the Goethe-Institut of Chicago, 2002, for *Austerlitz;* Marsh Award for children's literature in translation, for *A Dog's Life,* and 2003, for *Where Were You Robert?*

WRITINGS:

TRANSLATOR

Traudl and Walter Reiner, with Simone Stein, *Astrology for Cats,* Gollancz (London, England), 1992.

Maguelonne Toussaint-Samat, *History of Food,* Blackwell Publishers (London, England), 1994.

Akif Pirincci, *Felidae on the Road,* Fourth Estate (London, England), 1995.

Birger Sellin, *I Don't Want to Be Inside Me Anymore: Messages from an Autistic Mind,* illustrated by Michael Klonovsky, Basic Books (New York, NY), 1995 (originally published as *Ich will kein in mich mehr sein*).

E.T.A. Hoffmann, annotator, *The Life and Opinions of the Tomcat Murr: Together with a Fragmentary Biography of Kapellmeister Johannes Kreisler on Random Sheets of Waste Paper,* introduction by Jeremy Adler, Penguin (London, England), 1999.

Wladyslaw Szpilman, *The Pianist: The Extraordinary Story of One Man's Survival in Warsaw, 1939-45,* (with extracts from the diary of Wilm Hosenfeld), foreword by Andrzej Szpilman, epilogue by Wolf Biermann, Chivers Press (Bath, England), Picador (New York, NY), 1999.

W. G. Sebald, *Austerlitz,* Hamish Hamilton (London, England), 2001, Modern Library (New York, NY), 2002.

Sybille Knauss, *Eva's Cousin,* Ballantine (New York, NY), 2002.

W. G. Sebald, *On The Natural History of Destruction,* Random House (New York, NY), 2003.

Stefan Zweig, *Confusion: The Private Papers of Privy Councillor R. Von D,* Pushkin Press (London, England), 2003.

Martin Geck, *Beethoven,* Haus Publishing (London, England), 2003.

Martin Geck, *Bach,* Haus Publishing (London, England), 2003.

Karen Duve, *Rain,* Bloomsbury (London, England), 2003.

Sigmund Freud, *The Psychopathology of Everyday Life,* Penguin (New York, NY), 2003.

Stefan Zweig, *Twenty-four Hours in the Life of a Woman,* Pushkin Press (London, England), 2003.

Michael Kumpfmueller, *The Adventures of a Bed Salesman,* Picador (New York, NY), 2003.

Also translator of numerous fiction and nonfiction books for adults. These include, from the German: *World Armament and World Hunger,* by Willy Brandt, Gollancz; *My Life in Politics,* by Willy Brandt, Hamish Hamilton; *The Baader-Meinhof Group,* by Stefan Aust, Bodley Head; *Offside,* by Gisela Elsner, Virago; *After Midnight,* by Irmgard Keun, Gollancz; *The Stone and the Flute,* by Hans Bemmann, Viking; *Reading*

Psychosis, by Evelyne Keitel, Basil Blackwell; and *Cat Sense,* by Akif Pirincci, Fourth Estate.

Translations from the French include several novels by Henri Troyat, including the trilogy beginning with *Sylvie,* Aidan Ellis; Francoise Sagan's *Painting in Blood,* Aidan Ellis; Jose Luis de Vilallonga's *The King,* Weidenfeld & Nicolson. Translator of material from both the French and German, including articles for encyclopedic books, musicological essays for Grove Dictionaries (Macmillan), contributions to encyclopedic works on art, archaeology and urban development for Blackwell's, and contributions from the German to *FMR* art magazine (Milan).

NOVELS

A London Season, St. Martin's Press (New York, NY), 1983.

The Floral Companion, St. Martin's Press (New York, NY), 1988.

Also author of a monograph about E. Nesbit, Walck (New York, NY), 1964.

FOR CHILDREN AND YOUNG ADULTS

(Adapter) *The Great Menagerie,* Kestrel (London, England), 1979 (originally published in German by J. F. Schreiber).

(Adapter) Hans Christian Andersen, *The Little Mermaid,* illustrated by Chihiro Iwasaki, Picture Book Studio (Natick, MA), 1984.

(Reteller) Hans Christian Andersen, *The Emperor's New Clothes,* illustrated by Dorothee Duntze, North-South Books (New York, NY), 1986 (originally published as *Des Kaisers neue Kleider*).

(Reteller) *Swan Lake: A Traditional Folktale* (adaptation of Tchaikovsky's *Lebedinoe ozero*), illustrated by Chihiro Iwasaki, Picture Book Studio (Natick, MA), 1986.

(Reteller) *The Wise Queen,* illustrated by Chihiro Iwasaki, Picture Book Studio (Natick, MA), 1986.

(Adapter) George MacDonald, *Little Daylight,* illustrated by Dorothee Duntze, North-South Books (New York, NY), 1987.

(Adapter) Jacob and Wilhelm Grimm, *The Golden Goose,* illustrated by Dorothee Duntze, North-South Books (New York, NY), 1988 (originally published as *Die golden Gans*).

(Adapter) Jacob and Wilhelm Grimm, *The Goose Girl,* illustrated by Sabine Bruntjen, North-South Books (New York, NY), 1988.

(Reteller) Jacob and Wilhelm Grimm, *Jack in Luck,* illustrated by Tharlet, Picture Book Studio (Natick, MA), 1992.

(Editor) Charles Dickens, *David Copperfield,* illustrated by Alan Marks, North-South Books (New York, NY), 1995.

(Adapter) Joseph Cundall, *Goldilocks and the Three Bears,* illustrated by Noelle Prinz, Kingfisher (New York, NY), 1995.

(Reteller) *Jack and the Beanstalk: An English Fairy Tale,* illustrated by Aljoscha Blau, North-South Books (New York, NY), 2000.

FOR CHILDREN AND YOUNG ADULTS; TRANSLATOR

Otfried Preussler, *Robber Hotzenplotz,* Abelard-Schuman (New York, NY), 1965 (originally published in Germany).

B. Bartos-Hoeppner, *Avalanche Dog,* Walck (New York, NY), 1967.

B. Bartos-Hoeppner, *Storm over the Caucasus,* Walck (New York, NY), 1968.

Wilhelm Hauff, *Fairy Tales of Wilhelm Hauff,* illustrated by Ulrik Schramm, Abelard-Schuman (New York, NY), 1969 (originally published as *Maerchen*).

Ludwig Bechstein, *Fairy Tales of Ludwig Bechstein,* Abelard-Schuman (New York, NY), 1969 (originally published in Germany).

(And adapter) Rudi Strahl, *Sandman in the Lighthouse,* illustrated by Eberhard Binder, Children's Press (New York, NY), 1969 (originally published as *Sandmaennchen auf der Leuchtturminsel*).

B. Bartos-Hoeppner, *Hunters of Siberia,* Walck (New York, NY), 1969.

Otfried Preussler, *The Satanic Mill,* Abelard-Schuman (New York, NY), 1972.

Yuri Korinetz, *There, Far beyond the River,* O'Hara, 1973 (originally published in Germany).

Ruth Huerlimann, *The Cat and Mouse Who Shared a House,* illustrated by Ruth Huerlimann, Walck (New York, NY), 1974 (originally published as *Katze und Maus in Gesellschaft,* Atlantis Verlag, 1973).

Christine Noestlinger, *The Cucumber King: A Story with a Beginning, a Middle and an End,* illustrated by Werner Maurer, Abelard-Schuman (New York, NY), 1975.

Jacob and Wilhelm Grimm, *The Brave Little Tailor,* illustrated by Svend Otto S., Larousse (New York, NY), 1979, illustrated by Eve Tharlet, Picture Book Studio (Natick, MA), (originally published as *Das tapfere Schneiderlein*).

(With Anne Rogers) Jacob and Wilhelm Grimm, *The Best of Grimm's Fairy Tales* (selected from *Kinder- und Hausmaerchen*), illustrated by Svend Otto S., Larousse (New York, NY), 1979.

Janosch, *The Big Janosch Book of Fun and Verse,* Andersen Press (London, England), 1980 (originally published as *Die Maus hat rote Strumpfe an*).

Leo Tolstoy, *The Fool,* Schocken Books (New York, NY), 1981 (originally published as *Duren'*).

Voltaire, *The Dog and the Horse,* Schocken Books (New York, NY), 1981 (originally published as *Chien et le cheval*).

Hans Christian Andersen, *The Swineherd,* illustrated by Lisbeth Zwerger, Morrow (New York, NY), 1982 (originally published as *Svinedrengen*).

(And adapter) E. T. A. Hoffman, *The Nutcracker and the Mouse-King* (based on *Nussknacker und Mausekoenig*), illustrated by Lisbeth Zwerger, Picture Book Studio (Natick, MA), 1983, published as *The Nutcracker,* Picture Book Studio (Natick, MA), 1987.

Hans Christian Andersen, *The Red Shoes,* illustrated by Chihiro Iwasaki, Neugebauer (Boston, MA) Press, 1983 (originally published as *De rode sko*).

Stories of the Arabian Nights, illustrated by Giannini, Bedrick Books (New York, NY), 1983.

Hans Christian Andersen, *The Nightingale,* illustrated by Lisbeth Zwerger, Picture Book Studio (Natick, MA), 1984 (originally published as *Nattergalen*).

(And adapter) E. T. A. Hoffman, *The Strange Child,* illustrated by Lisbeth Zwerger, Picture Book Studio (Natick, MA), 1984 (originally published as *Das fremde Kind*).

A. A. Milne, *Winnie-the-Pooh and the Blustery Day,* Scholastic (New York, NY), 1985 (originally published as *Die Heffalumps*).

(And adapter) Jacob and Wilhelm Grimm, *Snow White and the Seven Dwarves,* illustrated by Chihiro Iwasaki, Picture Book Studio (Natick, MA), 1985 (originally published as *Schneewittchen*).

(And adapter) Hans Christian Andersen, *The Old House,* illustrated by Jean Claverie, North-South Books (New York, NY), 1986 (originally published as *Das alte Haus*).

(And adapter) Hans Christian Andersen, *The Snow Queen,* illustrated by Bernadette Watts, North-

South Books (New York, NY), 1987 (originally published as *Die Schneekoenigin*).

Anneliese Lussert, *The Farmer and the Moon,* illustrated by Josef Wilkon, North-South Books (New York, NY), 1987 (originally published as *Sieben Mondthaler*).

Max Velthuijs, *Frog in Love,* illustrated by Max Velthuijs, Farrar, Straus (New York, NY), 1989.

Hans Christian Andersen, *The Ugly Duckling,* illustrated by Alan Marks, Picture Book Studio (Natick, MA), 1989 (originally published as *Grimme aelling*).

Jacob and Wilhelm Grimm, *Fisherman and His Wife,* illustrated by Alan Marks, Picture Book Studio (Natick, MA), 1989 (originally published as *Von dem Fischer und seiner Frau*).

Marcus Pfister, *Penguin Pete's New Friends,* Scholastic (New York, NY), 1989 (originally published as *Pits neue Freunde*).

Heinz Janisch, *The Merry Pranks of Till Eulenspiegel,* illustrated by Lisbeth Zwerger, Picture Book Studio (Natick, MA), 1990 (originally published as *Till Eulenspiegel*).

Gert Loschtz, *The Penny-Mark,* illustrated by Friedrich Karl Waechter, Turton & Chambers, 1990 (originally published as *Das Pfennig-Mal*).

Marcus Pfister, *Penguin Pete and Pat,* illustrated by Marcus Pfister, Hippo Books, 1990 (originally published as *Pit und Pat*).

Hans Christian Andersen, *Hans Christian Andersen Fairy Tales,* selected and illustrated by Lisbeth Zwerger, Picture Book Studio (Natick, MA), 1991 (originally published as *Hans Christian Andersen Maerchen*).

Jacob and Wilhelm Grimm, *Mother Holle,* illustrated by Kirsten Hcker, Neugebauer (Boston, MA), 1991.

Bjarne B. Reuter, *The Boys from St. Petri,* Dutton Children's Books (New York, NY), 1994 (originally published as *Drengene fra Sankt Petri,* Gyldendal, 1991).

Hans Christian Andersen, *The Sandman,* illustrated by Lisbeth Zwerger, Picture Book Studio (Natick, MA), 1992.

August Kopisch, *The Elves of Cologne,* illustrated by Eve Tharlet, Picture Book Studio (Natick, MA), 1992.

Jacob and Wilhelm Grimm, *The Bremen Town Musicians,* illustrated by Bernadette Watts, North-South Books (New York, NY), 1992 (originally published as *Die Bremer Stadtmusikanten*).

Gabrielle Vincent, *Mr. Bingley's Bears,* Hutchinson (London, England), 1993.

Jacob and Wilhelm Grimm, *Little Red Cap: A Fairy Tale,* illustrated by Monika Laimgruber, North-South Books (New York, NY), 1993 (originally published as *Rotkaeppchen*).

Jacob and Wilhelm Grimm, *Rumpelstiltskin: A Fairy Tale,* illustrated by Bernadette Watts, North-South Books (New York, NY), 1993 (originally published as *Rumpelstilzchen*).

Hans Bemmann, *The Broken Goddess,* Penguin (London, England), 1993 (originally published *Beschaedigte Goettin*).

Jacob and Wilhelm Grimm, *The Seven Ravens: A Fairy Tale,* illustrated by Lisbeth Zwerger, Picture Book Studio (Natick, MA), 1993, illustrated by Henriette Sauvant, North-South Books (New York, NY), 1995 (originally published as *Sieben Raben*).

Werner Thuswalder, *Aesop's Fables,* illustrated by Gisela Duerr, North-South Books (New York, NY), 1994.

Wilhelm Hauff, *Dwarf Nose,* illustrated by Lisbeth Zwerger, North-South Books (New York, NY), 1994 (originally published as *Zwerg Nase*).

Christian Morgenstern, *Lullabies, Lyrics & Gallows Songs,* illustrated by Lisbeth Zwerger, North-South Books (New York, NY), 1995 (originally published as *Kindergedichte & Galgenlieder*).

Pierro Vainio, *The Christmas Angel,* illustrated by Pierro Vainio, North-South Books (New York, NY), 1995 (originally published as *Weihnachtsengel*).

Clemens Brentano, *The Legend of Rosepetal,* illustrated by Lisbeth Zwerger, North-South Books (New York, NY), 1995 (originally published as *Maerchen von Rosenblattchen*).

Theodor Storm, *Little Hobbin,* illustrated by Lisbeth Zwerger, North-South Books (New York, NY), 1995 (originally published as *Kleine Haewelmann*).

Jacob and Wilhelm Grimm, *The Sleeping Beauty: A Fairy Tale,* illustrated by Monika Laimgruber, North-South Books (New York, NY), 1995 (originally published as *Dornroeschen*).

Jacob and Wilhelm Grimm, *The Twelve Dancing Princesses,* illustrated by Dorothee Duntze, North-South Books (New York, NY), 1995 (originally published as *Zertanzten Schuhe*).

Jacob and Wilhelm Grimm, *The Wolf & the Seven Kids,* illustrated by Bernadette Watts, North-South Books (New York, NY), 1995 (originally published as *Wolf und die sieben jungen Geisslein*).

Didier Levy, *Albert,* illustrated by Coralie Gallibour, Kingfisher (New York, NY), 1995.

Rafik Schami, *The Crow Who Stood on His Beak,* illustrated by Els Cools and Oliver Streich, North-South Books (New York, NY), 1996.

Rafik Schami, *Fatima and the Dream Thief,* illustrated by Els Cools and Oliver Streich, North-South Books (New York, NY), 1996.

Jacob and Wilhelm Grimm, *Little Brother and Little Sister: A Fairy Tale,* illustrated by Bernadette Watts, North-South Books (New York, NY), 1996.

Charles Perrault, *Puss in Boots: A Fairy Tale,* retold and illustrated by Hans Fischer, afterword by Hans ten Doornkaat, North-South Books (New York, NY), 1996.

Jacob and Wilhelm Grimm, *The Six Servants,* illustrated by Sergei Goloshapov, North-South Books (New York, NY), 1996.

Brigitte Weninger, *Lumina: A Story for the Dark Time of the Year,* illustrated by Julie Wintz-Litty, North-South Books (New York, NY), 1997.

Kemal Kurt, *The Five Fingers and the Moon,* illustrated by Aljoscha Blau, North-South Books (New York, NY), 1997.

Wolfram Hnel, *The Gold at the End of the Rainbow,* illustrated by Loek Koopmans, North-South Books (New York, NY), 1997.

Jacob and Wilhelm Grimm, *Rapunzel: A Fairy Tale* (collected), illustrated by Maja Dusikova, North-South Books (New York, NY), 1997.

Jacob and Wilhelm Grimm, *The Six Swans: A Fairy Tale,* illustrated by Dorothee Duntze, North-South Books (New York, NY), 1998.

Rafik Schami, *Albert & Lila,* illustrated by Els Cools and Oliver Streich, North-South Books (New York, NY), 1999.

Charles Perrault, *Cinderella: A Fairy Tale,* illustrated by Loek Koopmans, North-South Books (New York, NY), 1999.

Sergei Prokofiev, *Peter and the Wolf,* illustrated by Julia Gukova, adapted by Gerlinde Wiencirz, North-South Books (New York, NY), 1999.

Hans Christian Andersen, *Thumbeline,* illustrated by Lisbeth Zwerger, North-South Books (New York, NY), 2000.

Hans Christian Andersen, *Hans Christian Andersen's Fairy Tales,* illustrated by Lisbeth Zwerger, North-South Books (New York, NY), 2001.

Mischa Damjan, *The Clown Said No,* illustrated by Christa Unzner, North-South Books (New York, NY), 2002.

Friedrich Recknagel, *Sarah's Willow,* illustrated by Maja Dusikova, North-South Books (New York, NY), 2002.

Karl Ruehmann, *The Fox and the Stork: A Fable by Aesop,* North-South Books (New York, NY), 2003.

Cornelia Caroline Funke, *Inkheart,* Scholastic (New York, NY), 2003.

Reinhardt Jung, *Dreaming in Black and White,* Phyllis Fogelman (New York, NY), 2003.

Hans Magnus Enzensberger, *Where Were You Robert?,* Pearson Schools (London, England), 2003.

Also translator (with Derek Hockridge) of "Asterix the Gaul" series by Rene Goscinny, illustrated by Albert Uderzo, Hodder & Stoughton (London, England), 1969—.

Translator of other books for children, including almost all the works of Otfried Preussler and over a dozen titles by Christine Noestlinger (including *A Dog's Life* and *But Jasper Came Instead*); Willi Faehrmann, *The Long Journey of Lukas B.;* Rene Goscinny's "Little Nicholas" series; two novels in Claude Gutman's French trilogy, *The Empty House* and *Fighting Back; The Selfish Giant* and *Hansel and Gretel,* both illustrated by Lisbeth Zwerger; and Bjarne Reuter's *Buster's World* and *The Sheikh of Hope Street.*

SIDELIGHTS: Anthea Bell is best known for her work as a translator and adapter of novels and stories for both adults and children, an oeuvre that is over 200 titles strong. Her award-winning work has allowed English-speaking readers access to traditional stories, contemporary picture books, classic novels, and even cartoon strips originally written in German, French, and Danish. For adults, she has translated books by diverse authors, including politician Willy Brandt; translations of the works of German author W. G. Sebald have also won her awards and critical acclaim. Her work for children includes stories and books by the Brothers Grimm, Clemens Brentano, Ludwig Bechstein, Wilhelm Hauff, and Hans Christian Andersen. Bell has won several awards for her translations of contemporary original works or retellings, including a Hans Christian Andersen Award for her translation of a Christine Noestlinger novel, and Mildred L. Batchelder awards for her translations of books like *The Cat and Mouse Who Shared a House* and *The Boys from St. Petri,* the Helen and Kurt Wolff Translator's Prize, and the Marsh Award for children's literature in translation.

Bell recalls how much she enjoyed reading books like *The Story of Babar* (written in French by Jean de Brunhoff), which had been translated into English when she was a child. Yet she believes translated books do more than entertain children. First, they encourage children to understand other languages: "The avid child reader just *has* to know what is inside a book, and if it happens to be in a foreign language, it may impel the child to learn the language," she wrote in *Horn Book* in 1978. Second, as Bell suggested in a speech published in *Top of the News*, translated books allow ideas to be shared despite the barriers language can impose. It is the role of the translator "to give authors from other countries a voice as like their own as possible in which to address English-speaking children, so that their ideas can be passed on."

Then again, as Bell suggested in *Bookbird*, there is something to be said for a book that entertains because it is funny. Humorous books, like *Asterix the Gaul* by Rene Goscinny and Albert Uderzo or Christine Noestlinger's novels, are Bell's favorite books to translate. "Humour is a most peculiar thing, when you stop to think of it: universal, easily recognizable, extraordinarily hard to define. But a wonderful builder of bridges and crosser of frontiers, and thus surely of special value to growing young people the world over."

After earning a degree in English language and literature from Oxford University in the late 1950s, Bell had the opportunity to read and report on some German books that a London publisher was considering for translation and publication. As she wrote in *Horn Book*, her "curious if mentally rewarding job snowballed from there." Bell continued to read and report on German and French books selected for possible publication in English, and she began to translate some of these.

Many of Bell's works are new translations or adaptations of familiar favorites. According to a critic for *Publishers Weekly*, Bell's translation of the beloved story *The Golden Goose* brings readers the "full flavor" of the original work by the Brothers Grimm. *Booklist* critic Ilene Cooper described Bell's translation of Hans Christian Andersen's *The Nightingale* as "lyrical." Although it is a somewhat condensed version, Bell's adaptation of Andersen's *The Little Mermaid* "retains the beauty of the language," in the words of Jean Bennetts in *School Library Journal*.

Bell has also brought English-speaking children works that aren't well known outside Europe. Andersen's *The Old House* tells the story of a boy who gives an elderly man a tin soldier; after the man dies and his home is rebuilt, the boy (a man now) moves into the home and finds the toy. According to Karen Radtke, writing in *School Library Journal*, Bell's "judicial pruning of some visual details moves the action along." *The Wise Queen*, a traditional European tale, features a clever courtier's daughter who beats a king at his own game by solving his riddles. The king decides to marry her, but he makes her promise not to make decisions in the court. When she does exercise her own judgment, she is exiled from the palace. Yet the Queen then asks the king for permission to take with her what she loves most: she selects the king himself to take away from the castle to her old home. *School Library Journal* contributor Cathy Woodward asserted that the story is "aptly retold," and "is as straightforward and direct as the queen herself."

For adults, Bell has introduced a disparate cast of Central European writers—many of them German and many of them writing of the horrors of World War II and the Holocaust—to readers of English. Going farther afield linguistically, she translated the 1999 reprint of Wladyslaw Szpilman's memoir written in Polish, *The Pianist: The Extraordinary True Story of One Man's Survival in Warsaw, 1939-1945*. Later made into an award-winning film, the book is a "significant contribution to the literature of remembrance, a document of lasting historical and human value," according to Michael Frank, writing in the *Los Angeles Times*. Bell has also translated works by the German author W. G. Sebald, including *Austerlitz* and *On the Natural History of Destruction*. For the former title, Bell was awarded the 2002 Helen and Kurt Wolff Translator's Prize. The prize jury commended Bell for her ability to "bring the richness of the German text into a correspondingly rich English," as was reported on the Goethe Institut Web site. Barbara Walden, writing in *Library Journal*, found Bell's translation of *On the Natural History of Destruction* to be "felicitous."

Bell has additionally introduced the works of German writers Michael Kumpfmueller, Reinhardt Jung, Cornelia Funke, Karen Duve, and Sybille Knauss to the English-speaking world. Jung's novella *Dreaming in Black and White* explores the Holocaust via the dream world of a contemporary young boy. A work for young adults as well as adults, the book and its translation won praise from Betsy Hearne in the *Bulletin of the Center for Children's Books*. Hearne noted that the "clean minimalist style that delivers this complex tale-within-a-tale is well supported by veteran translator Bell's practiced clarity." In a review of Duve's *Rain*, a contributor for *Publishers Weekly* felt that this "deftly translated dark comedy is a razor-edged treat." And writing on Knauss's *Eva's Cousin*, a critic for *Publishers Weekly* found that the "narrative is adeptly translated by prize-winning Anthea Bell."

Bell has provided aspiring translators with advice. In her *Horn Book* article, she explained that translators must have "a good command of English" as well as of the book's original language. "Dictionary knowledge . . . is far from enough." Also, a translator must "keep his or her mind as clear and as neutral as possible." The resulting translation, according to Bell, "should faithfully reflect the author's intentions without ever sounding like a translation, clumsy or stilted." As *Top of the News* reported in 1976 when Bell received the Batchelder Award, Bell believes that "ideally translators ought to be entirely invisible. If a reviewer ignores the fact that a book is a translation, one takes it as a compliment, because bad translation will always call forth a comment." According to Bell in the same speech, "A translator is merely middleman or go-between, craftsman or interpreter." That Bell has accomplished this task is proven by the comments of the award committee for the 2002 Helen and Kurt Wolff Translator's Prize, which declared she had done the "impossible" with her translation of Sebald's *Austerlitz:* she had created the illusion that "while we are reading English—real English—we are also reading German."

BIOGRAPHICAL AND CRITICAL SOURCES:

PERIODICALS

Bookbird, February 2, 1985, pp. 8-13.
Booklist, December 15, 1984, Ilene Cooper, review of *The Nightingale,* p. 585; May 15, 2003, Carolyn Phelan, review of *Dreaming in Black and White,* pp. 1665-1666.
Bookseller, February 21, 2003, "Marsh Award Winner," p. 34.
Boston Globe, September 21, 1999, Richard Dyer, review of *The Pianist,* p. D3.
Bulletin of the Center for Children's Books, September, 2003, Betsy Hearne, review of *Dreaming in Black and White,* pp. 19-20.

Horn Book, October, 1978, pp. 548-553; September-October, 2003, Joanna Rudge Long, review of *Dreaming in Black and White,* p. 612.
Kirkus Reviews, June 15, 2002, review of *Eva's Cousin,* p. 830.
Library Journal, August, 1999, Marie Marmo Mullaney, review of *The Pianist,* p. 116; January, 2003, Barbara Walden, review of *On the Natural History of Destruction,* p. 134.
Los Angeles Times, January 16, 2000, Michael Frank, review of *The Pianist,* p. BR5.
Publishers Weekly, September 9, 1988, review of *The Golden Goose,* p. 134; June 28, 1999, review of *The Pianist,* p. 60; July 1, 2002, review of *Eva's Cousin,* p. 51; March 17, 2003, review of *Rain,* p. 55; July 7, 2003, review of *Dreaming in Black and White,* p. 73; July 21, 2003, review of *Inkheart,* p. 196.
School Library Journal, February, 1985, Jean Bennetts, review of *The Little Mermaid,* p. 70; November, 1986, Karen Radtke, review of *The Old House,* pp. 71-72; March, 1987, Cathy Woodward, review of *The Wise Queen,* p. 139; May, 2002, Gay Lynn Van Vleck, review of *Sarah's Willow,* p. 125; July, 2002, Amy Lilien-Harper, review of *The Clown Said No,* p. 87; August, 2003, Delia Fritz, review of *Dreaming in Black and White,* p. 161.
Times Literary Supplement, April 23, 1999, David Pryce-Jones, review of *The Pianist,* p. 30; November 29, 2002, Lesley Chamberlain, review of *The Adventures of a Bed Salesman.*
Top of the News, June, 1976.

ONLINE

Goethe-Institut Web site, http://www.goethe.de/uk/chi/ (October 27, 2003), "Anthea Bell Recipient of the 2002 Helen and Kurt Wolff Translator's Prize for Outstanding Translation from German into English."*

*   *   *

BELTING, Hans 1935-

PERSONAL: Born 1935 in Andernach, Germany.

ADDRESSES: Office—c/o University of Chicago Press, 1427 East 60th St., Chicago, IL 60637.

CAREER: School for New Media, Karlsruhe, Germany, professor of art history and new media.

WRITINGS:

Die Oberkirche von San Francesco in Assisi: ihre Dekoration als Aufgabe u.d. Genese e. neuen Wandmalerei, Mann (Berlin, Germany), 1977.

Der serbische Psalter: Faksimile-Ausgabe des Cod. slav. 4 der Bayerischen Staatsbibliothek Munchen, L. Reichert (Wiesbaden, Germany), 1978.

(With Cyril A. Mango and Doula Mouriki) *The Mosaics and Frescoes of St. Mary Pammakaristos (Fethiye Camii) at Istanbul,* Dumbarton Oaks Center for Byzantine Studies (Locust Valley, NY), 1978.

(With Guglielmo Cavallo) *Die Bibel des Niketas: ein Werk der hofischen Buchkunst in Byzanz und sein antikes Vorbild,* L. Reichert (Wiesbaden, Germany), 1979.

Das Bild und sein Publikum im Mittelalter: Form und Funktion fruher Bildtafeln der Passion, Mann (Berlin, Germany), 1981, translation by Mark Bartusis and Raymond Meyer published as *The Image and Its Public in the Middle Ages: Form and Function of Early Paintings of the Passion,* Caratzas (New Rochelle, NY), 1990.

(With Dagmar Eichberger) *Jan van Eyck als Erzahler: fruhe Tafelbilder im Umkreis der New Yorker Doppeltafel,* Werner'sche Verlagsgesellschaft (Worms, Germany), 1983.

Das Ende der Kunstgeschichte?, Deutscher Kunstverlag (Munich, Germany), 1983, translation by Christopher S. Wood published as *The End of the History of Art?,* University of Chicago Press (Chicago, IL), 1987, republished as *Art History after Modernism,* University of Chicago Press (Chicago, IL), 2003.

Max Beckmann: die Tradition als Problem in der Kunst der Moderne, Deutscher Kunstverlag (Berlin), 1984, translation by Peter Wortsman published as *Max Beckmann: Tradition As a Problem in Modern Art,* Timken (New York, NY), 1989.

(With others) *Der Mensch und seine Gefuhle: Beitrage,* EOS Verlag (St. Ottilien, Germany), 1985.

Giovanni Bellini, Pieta: Ikone und Bilderzahlung in der venezianischen Malerei, Fischer Taschenbuch (Frankfurt am Main, Germany), 1985.

(With Dieter Blume) *Malerei und Stadtkultur in der Dantezeit: die Argumentation der Bilder,* Hirmer (Munich, Germany), 1989.

Bild und Kult: eine Geschichte des Bildes vor dem Zeitalter der Kunst, Beck (Munich, Germany), 1990, translation by Edmund Jephcott, published as *Likeness and Presence: A History of the Image before the Era of Art,* University of Chicago Press, 1994.

Die Deutschen und ihre Kunst: ein schwieriges Erbe, Beck (Munich, Germany), 1992.

(Contributor) *Thomas Struth: Museum Photographs,* Schirmer/Mosel (Munich, Germany), c. 1993.

(Contributor) *Sigmar Polke: The Three Lies of Painting,* Distributed Art Publishers (New York, NY), 1997.

The Germans and Their Art: A Troublesome Relationship, translated by Scott Kleager, Yale University Press (New Haven, CT), 1998.

Das Unsichtbare Meisterwerk: Die Modernen Mythen der Kunst, C. H. Beck (Munich, Germany), 1998, translation by Helen Atkins, published as *The Invisible Masterpiece: The Modern Myth of Art,* University of Chicago Press (Chicago, IL), 2001.

Identität im Zweifel: Ansichten der deutschen Kunst, DuMont (Koln, Germany), 1999.

Der zweite Blick: Bildgeschichte und Bildreflexion Herausgegeben von Hans Belting und Dietmar Kamper, W. Fink (Munich, Germany), 2000.

(With others) *Qu'est-ce qu'un chef-d'oeuvre?,* Gallimard (Paris, France), 2000.

Andrea Pozzo und die Videokunst: Neue Uberlegungen zum Barocken Illusionismus, Mann (Berlin, Germany), 2001.

Bild-Anthropologie: Entwürfe für eine Bildwissenschaft, W. Fink (Munich, Germany), 2001.

Hieronymus Bosch: Garden of Earthly Delights, Prestel Publishing (New York, NY), 2002.

(Contributor) Bill Viola, *Bill Viola: The Passions,* J. Paul Getty Museum (Los Angeles, CA), 2003.

SIDELIGHTS: Hans Belting is a renowned professor of art history and media theory on the faculty of the School for New Media in Karlsruhe, Germany. He is the author of numerous books on the history of art, among which *The End of the History of Art?,* *A History of the Image before the Era of Art,* and *The Invisible Masterpiece: The Modern Myth of Art* have been translated into English.

In the twenty chapters that make up *History of the Image before the Era of Art* (published in German as *Bild und Kult: eine Geschichte des Bildes vor dem*

Zeitalter der Kunst), Belting traces the use of holy images—icons—from antiquity to the Middle Ages. In doing so, he also explores the development of icons in Byzantine art and considers their impact and use in the West during the twelfth through sixteenth centuries. He discusses the emergence of icons featuring Christian images and their espousal and use by the Roman Catholic Church, considering them within their original context and function in religious rites. "It remains a long, hard read, lightened by the extremely helpful choice of illustrations, yet leaving the impression that one is but a dizzy Ben Hur whirling round and round the hippodrome, regularly passing the same landmarks," observed Robin Cormack in the *New York Times Book Review.* Jean Michel Massing, writing for the *Times Literary Supplement,* stated that "*Bild und Kult* is an important contribution to the study of medieval culture."

The End of the History of Art? contains a pair of essays in which Belting discusses the divergence of art criticism in modern times from its traditional form. He proposes that the disciplines of art history and art criticism should be combined in a single method that emphasizes a historical and anthropological approach. To quote Belting: "Art history, obviously, is not yet finished as a discipline . . . [but it is perhaps] more appropriate to regard the interrogation of the medium of art, of historical man and his images of the world, as a permanent experiment."

In *The Germans and Their Art,* Belting considers what makes German art German by examining German artistic attitudes from the Romantic period to the present. Belting observes that German artists were perceived unfavorably throughout the world and believes that this influenced the style of their art and made them fearful of being replaced with artists from abroad. Belting also explains why German artists adopted a Gothic art style, first during the Romantic period and again after World War I. He notes the drastically different art styles of the two "Germanies" and discusses how unification has spurred new conflicts.

According to Balzac, the "invisible masterpiece" is an unattainable ideal, a work of art into which a dream of absolute art is incorporated but can never be realized. Belting borrows the metaphor from Balzac and uses it as the basis for his book, *The Invisible Masterpiece: The Modern Myth of Art.* In the book, Belting presents

the history of art beginning in the late eighteenth century, a time when he believes artists began to abandon standards constituting what is and is not a masterpiece. In the *New Republic,* Christopher S. Wood described the book as "a forceful and highly original history of nineteenth-century and twentieth-century art." Wood went on to explain, "Belting's thesis in his new book is simple, and he frequently repeats it: since 1800, new works of art have failed again and again to live up to the idea of 'absolute' art represented by the concept of the 'masterpiece.'" Writing in *American Prospect,* Julie Ardery praised the book's wide appeal, noting, "Even those well versed in modern-art history will encounter surprising anecdotes." She added, "One of my favorites, in Belting's chapter about *Les Demoiselles of Avignon,* reveals that Picasso bought his first primitive masks from the poet 'Apollinaire's secretary, but without knowing that the secretary had stolen them from—of all places—the Louvre, whose stale museum atmosphere Picasso thought he was so determinedly leaving behind.'" A contributor writing in the *Economist* expressed similar sentiments about *The Invisible Masterpiece,* noting that Belting's "material is rich and always rewarding" although this reviewer also felt that Belting's interpretations "often fail to convince."

In *Hieronymus Bosch: Garden of Earthly Delights,* "Belting argues persuasively for an interpretation of the enigmatic central panel as a representation of the earthly paradise that would have existed, if Adam and Eve's fall had never taken place," observed Kathryn Wekselman in *Library Journal.* Wekselman felt that the book was "more philosophical and less comprehensive" than some other books about Bosch, but concluded that Belting's book is valuable "for its novel view of a much-discussed painting."

Belting has also contributed to books by other authors. In *Thomas Struth: Museum Photographs,* Belting penned an essay that Doug McClemont of *Library Journal* termed "outstanding." Struth is an artist from the esteemed Dusseldorf School who studied under conceptualists Bernd and Hilla Becher. McClemont explained, "Struth's work excavates the nature of photography itself." Belting also contributed to *Sigman Polke: The Three Lies of Painting,* which *Library Journal*'s Eric Bryant considered the "catalog to the largest Polke retrospective ever undertaken. . ." that "reproduces more than 250 works spanning thirty-five years output in many media."

BIOGRAPHICAL AND CRITICAL SOURCES:

BOOKS

The Invisible Masterpiece: The Modern Myth of Art, translated by Helen Atkins, University of Chicago Press (Chicago, IL), 2001.

PERIODICALS

American Prospect, March 11, 2002, Julie Ardery, review of *The Invisible Masterpiece: The Modern Myth of Art,* pp. 35-38.
Central European History, January, 2001, review of *The Germans and Their Art: A Troublesome Relationship,* p. 83.
Economist, September 22, 2001, review of *The Invisible Masterpiece,* p. 98.
German Studies Review, May, 2000, David Ehrenpreis, review of *The Germans and Their Art,* pp. 395-397.
Library Journal, April 15, 1987, p. 76; September 15, 1993, p. 39; February 1, 1998, Eric Bryant, review of *Sigmar Polke: The Three Lies of Painting,* p. 83; July, 2001, Doug McClemont, review of *Thomas Struth: Museum Photographs,* p. 82; December, 2002, Kathryn Wekselman, review of *Hieronymus Bosch: Garden of Earthly Delights,* p. 115.
New Republic, March 25, 2002, Christopher S. Wood, review of "Not Yet the End," p. 40.
New York Times Book Review, August 7, 1994, p. 23.
Parachute: Contemporary Art Magazine, April, 2002, Stephen Wright, review of *The Invisible Masterpiece and the Madonna of the Future,* pp. 123-125.
Reference and Research Book News, February, 2002, review of *The Invisible Masterpiece,* p. 187.
Sunday Times, June 17, 2001, Frank Whitford, "Art; At a Glance," p. 38.
Times, June 27, 2001, Ian Brunskill, "Portrait of Modern Art," p. 12.
Times Literary Supplement, September 18-24, 1987, p. 1015; August 3-9, 1990, p. 826.
The Wall Street Journal, December 6, 2002, Eric Gibson, review of *Garden of Earthly Delights,* p. W12.*

* * *

BETHLEN, T. D.
See SILVERBERG, Robert

BINYON, T(imothy) J(ohn) 1936-2004

PERSONAL: Born February 18, 1936, in Leeds, Yorkshire, England; died of heart failure, October 7, 2004, in Witney, Oxfordshire, England; son of Denis Edmund Fynes-Clinton (a university lecturer) and Nancy (Emmerson) Binyon; married Felicity Antonia Roberts (a stenciller), September 11, 1974; children: Polly Charlotte. *Education:* Exeter College, Oxford, M.A., 1963, D.Phil., 1968.

CAREER: University of Leeds, Leeds, Yorkshire, England, lecturer in Russian, 1962-65; Oxford University, Oxford, England, lecturer in Russian, 1965-2004, senior research fellow of Wadham College, 1968-2004.

AWARDS, HONORS: Samuel Johnson Prize for Nonfiction, BBC-4, 2003, for *Pushkin: A Biography.*

WRITINGS:

(Editor) *A Soviet Verse Reader,* Pitman (New York, NY), 1964.
Swan Song (novel), Hamish Hamilton (London, England), 1982.
Greek Gifts (novel), Hamish Hamilton (London, England), 1988.
Murder Will Out: The Detective in Fiction, Oxford University Press (New York, NY), 1989.
Pushkin: A Biography, HarperCollins (London, England), 2002.

Contributor of articles and reviews to periodicals, including *Modern Language Review, Times Literary Supplement, Literary Review, Oxford Slavonic Papers,* and *Slavonic Review.* Also contributor to *The World of Raymond Chandler,* edited by Miriam Gross, Weidenfeld and Nicolson, 1977.

SIDELIGHTS: Writing in the *Literary Review,* Peter Levi considered T. J. Binyon to be "an heir worth watching" to the traditions of the English thriller novel. *Swan Song,* Binyon's first novel, drew upon his knowledge of Russian life and culture, while his second, *Greek Gifts,* "shows his powers of invention and suspense at full throttle," according to John Coleman in the *Sunday Times.* "In fact," stated Levi, "he offers all you can expect from a thriller, and a good deal more."

After writing two thriller novels and an examination of the role of the mystery detective titled *Murder Will Out: The Detective in Fiction,* Binyon turned from mystery to biography with *Pushkin,* a biographical investigation of the life of the famed and tragic Russian poet Alexander Pushkin. Binyon traces Pushkin's life in great detail, from his eclectic heritage all the way to his untimely and foolish death. It also highlights along the way those personality traits that made Pushkin such an unforgettable historical figure. *Spectator* reviewer Jonathan Sumption described Pushkin's personality as "rude, crude, dissolute, scurrilous, mendacious . . . affected . . . quarrelsome, snobbish, feckless and arrogant. . . . [He] offended large numbers of people, ogling their wives and mistresses, spreading unpleasant gossip, thrusting his atheism in their faces, and generally making a nuisance of himself." At the age of twenty, Pushkin was exiled by Russian Tsar Alexander I, who invited him back to St. Petersburg after four years, but kept him under careful scrutiny.

The examination of Pushkin's character is built up until it reaches a crescendo on the fateful day of the poet's death. Natalia Goncharova, Pushkin's wife, was admired by many, and though she was known for her flirtations, Binyon asserts that she was faithful to the poet in her affections. Pushkin exhibited jealousy nonetheless, and after learning that Guards officer Baron Georges d'Anthes was stalking his beautiful wife, Pushkin challenged the man to a duel. Though Pushkin had previously won many duels, this would be his last, as d'Anthes shot and killed him at the age of thirty-seven. Binyon went as far to assert, however, that Pushkin's challenge was a death wish ultimately fulfilled.

Many reviewers commented on the detail with which Binyon chronicles the poet's life, which was the main reason many felt that this biography stood above other biographies in its attempts to explain the vast life experiences of Alexander Pushkin. "Producing such a detailed yet absorbing chronicle of Pushkin's life is a remarkable achievement," stated Catriona Kelly in the *Guardian Unlimited.* "A weighty biography in every sense, Binyon's book is poignant, brisk, and at times downright funny: the best possible tribute to the changeable and elusively fascinating character of its subject," Kelly continued. One *Economist* reviewer wrote that the book "doesn't lazily pretend to put us inside Pushkin's head or explain his writings but sits so close to the man and his times that by the time Pushkin is dead . . . you almost feel you have lived his life."

While some readers enjoyed the book's expansive detail, others thought that it made the biography too weighty for general readership. Orlando Figes, fellow Russian scholar and contributor to the London *Times,* wrote that while Binyon's *Pushkin* is "by far the most important [biography of Pushkin] to appear in years," he concluded that "one really needs to be a specialist to get the most from this deeply learned book. . . . There are just too many details for the general reader to cut through. . . . There are many instances where Binyon does not give sufficient explanation of the historical or cultural context for the non-specialist to find his way." Figes also commented on the biography's lack of attention to Pushkin's work itself, a sentiment expressed by many reviewers. "He never really stops to analyse the qualities of Pushkin's verse," Figes wrote, "nor to explain why the use of the language was so original." In the *Spectator,* Sumption wrote that "apart from giving exact translations of the many four-letter words in Pushkin's writings instead of the euphemisms preferred by earlier biographers, Binyon cannot claim to have advanced the frontiers of modern science." Sumption went on to comment, however, that "to write such a readable, perceptive, and witty biography, based on a careful study of the known sources and a synthesis of current, largely Russian scholarship, is as valuable an achievement." Similarly, George Walden wrote in London's *Sunday Telegraph* that "'scholarly' and 'engrossing' are often antonyms, yet such is Binyon's skill in presenting his phenomenal research, and so patiently does he build up the reader's interest in the man and his era that he ends by captivating us. . . . Reading this book is like breathing clean air, unpolluted by loaded or emotive commentary. The myths evaporate under Binyon's scrutiny, leaving a far more complex portrait of the poet than we are used to."

BIOGRAPHICAL AND CRITICAL SOURCES:

PERIODICALS

Armchair Detective, winter, 1991, review of *Murder Will Out: The Detective in Fiction,* p. 108; summer, 1992, review of *Murder Will Out,* p. 352.

Bookseller, December 5, 2003, Caroline Sanderson, "Samuel Johnson Prize," p. S9.

Choice, January, 1990, review of *Murder Will Out,* p. 794.

Contemporary Review, January, 1990, James Morton, review of *Murder Will Out,* pp. 54-55; January, 2003, review of *Pushkin: A Biography,* p. 63.

Daily Telegraph (London, England), September 28, 2002, Alan Marshall, "The Philandering Poet: Alan Marshall Enjoys the Tempestuous Life of Pushkin," review of *Pushkin.*

Economist (U.S.), September 14, 2002, "A Small Man of Great Stature: Literary Biography," review of *Pushkin;* December 14, 2002, "Seriousness, the New Black: Books of the Year 2002," review of *Pushkin.*

Library Journal, October 1, 2003, Ron Ratliff, review of *Pushkin,* p. 75.

Literary Review, January, 1988.

Michigan Quarterly Review, spring, 1991, James Gindin, review of *Murder Will Out,* p. 343.

Modern Fiction Studies, summer, 1990, Edward S. Lauterbach, review of *Murder Will Out,* pp. 285-287.

New Leader, September-October, 2003, Rebecca Reich, "Russia's Don Juan Darling," review of *Pushkin,* pp. 21-22.

New Republic, January 19, 2004, Joseph Frank, "Liberties," review of *Pushkin,* p. 29.

New Statesman, September 30, 2002, Julian Evans, "Slave to Passion," review of *Pushkin,* pp. 78-79.

Publishers Weekly, September 15, 2003, review of *Pushkin,* pp. 55-56.

Spectator, September 21, 2002, Jonathan Sumption, "Bankrupt in All But Talent," review of *Pushkin,* p. 48.

Sunday Telegraph (London, England), September 8, 2002, George Walden, "The Poet Who Was Russia: George Walden Praises a Masterful Biography of Alexander Pushkin," review of *Pushkin,* p. 14.

Sunday Times, January 10, 1988.

Times Literary Supplement, October 22, 1982; September 27, 2002, Clive James, "Master of Paradise: The Libertine Pushkin, Mythologized by Liberals, Fans and Lovers," review of *Pushkin,* pp. 3-4.

Times (London, England), September 25, 2002, Orlando Figes, "A Crime against Rhyme," review of *Pushkin,* p. 20.

Wilson Quarterly, winter, 2004, Andrew Reynolds, review of *Pushkin,* pp. 130-132.

ONLINE

Baronage Press Web site, http://www.baronage.co.uk/ (May-August, 2003), *The Feudal Herald* online newsletter.

BBC Web site, http://www.bbc.co.uk/ (March 22, 2004), "*Pushkin,* by T. J. Binyon."

Better Living Web site, http://www.betterliving.co.nz/ (March 22, 2004), Bob Williams, review of *Pushkin.*

Guardian Unlimited Web site, http://books.guardian.co.uk/ (October 5, 2002), Catriona Kelly, "Turbulent Poet and Femme Fatale," review of *Pushkin.**

*   *   *

BLADE, Alexander
    See SILVERBERG, Robert

*   *   *

BLAKEMORE, Colin (Brian) 1944-

PERSONAL: Born June 1, 1944, in Stratford-on-Avon, England; son of Cedric Norman and Beryl (Smith) Blakemore; married Andrée Elizabeth Washbourne, August 28, 1965; children: Sarah Jayne, Sophie Ann, Jessica Katy. *Education:* Corpus Christi College, Cambridge, B.A., 1965, M.A., 1969; University of California—Berkeley, Ph.D., 1968. *Hobbies and other interests:* Running marathons, the arts.

ADDRESSES: Office—University Lab of Physiology, Parks Rd., Oxford OX1 3PT, England. *E-mail*—blakemore@physiol.ox.ac.uk.

CAREER: Cambridge University, Cambridge, England, demonstrator at Physiological Laboratory, 1968-72, lecturer, beginning 1972, fellow and director of medical studies at Downing College, 1977-79; Oxford University, Oxford, England, Waynflete Professor of Physiology, 1979—, and director of Centre for Cognitive Neuroscience, 1990-2003; Medical Research Council, London, England, Chief Executive, 2003—. Visiting professor at New York University, 1970, and Massachusetts Institute of Technology, 1971; visiting scientist, Salk Institute, San Diego, CA, 1982, 1983,

1992; McLaughlin visiting professor, McMaster University, Hamilton, Ontario, Canada, 1992; Regents' professor, University of California—Davis, 1995-96; member of British Broadcasting Corp. Science Consultative Group, 1975-79 and Reith Lecturer for BBC, 1976; Lethaby Professor at Royal College of Art, 1978. Member of several advisory committees, including Schizophrenia: A National Emergency (SANE), 1983-2003, Dana Alliance for Brain Initiatives, 1996—, European Dana Alliance for the Brain, 1996—, UK Forum for Genetics and Insurance, 1998—, Independent Expert Group on Mobile Phones, 1999-2000, Royal Society Science in Society Committee, 2001—, Sense about Science, 2002—.

MEMBER: International Brain Research Organization (member of governing council, 1973—; member of executive committee, 1979-91), International Society on Infant Studies, Council of Federation of European Neuroscience Societies (member of council, 1998-2000), European Biomedical Research Association (founding member), European Neuroscience Association, Society for Neuroscience, European Brain and Behaviour Society (member of committee, 1974-76), National Conference of University Professors, British Association for the Advancement of Science (vice president, 1990-97 and 1998-2001; treasurer, 1993; president, 1997-98; chair, 2000—), British Neuroscience Association (formerly Brain Research Association; member of national committee, 1973-77, and 1997-2003; president, 1997-2000), Physiological Society (president, 2001—), Experimental Psychology Society, Oxford Medical Society, Cambridge Philosophical Society (member of council, 1975—), Child Vision Resource Society, Sigma Xi, Biosciences Federation (president, 2003—).

AWARDS, HONORS: Robert Bing Prize for Research in Neurology, Swiss Academy of Medical Sciences, 1975; Locke Research Fellowship, Royal Society, 1976-79; Copeman Medal for Medical Research, Corpus Christi College, Cambridge, 1977; Richardson Cross Medal, Southwestern Ophthalmological Society, 1978; named Man of the Year by Royal Association for Disability and Rehabilitation, 1978; Phi Beta Kappa Award in Science, 1978; Honorary President, World Cultural Council, 1983—; Netter Prize, Academie Nationale de Medecine (France), 1984; Michael Faraday Award and Medal, 1989; G. L. Brown Prize, Physiological Society, 1990; John P. McGovern Science and Society Medal, Sigma Xi, 1990; Fellow of the Royal Society, 1992; Osler Medal, 1993; Ellison-Cliffe Medal, 1993; Foreign Member, Royal Netherlands Academy of Arts and Sciences, 1993; Charles F. Prentice Award, 1994; Annual Review Prize, Physiological Society, 1995; member of the Academia Europaea, 1995; Honorary Member, Alpha Omega Honor Medical Society, 1996; Alcon Prize, Alcon Research Institute, 1996; fellow of the Institute of Biology, 1996; Memorial Medal, Charles University (Prague, Czechoslovakia), 1998; Alfred Meyer Award, British Neuropathological Society 2001; Institute of Biology Charter Award and Medal, 2001; Baly Medal for distinction in the science of physiology, Royal College of Physicians, 2001; Outstanding Contribution to Neuroscience Award, British Neuroscience Association, 2001. Fellowships from several universities; D.Sc., Aston University, 1992; D.SC., Salford University, 1994; honorary fellowship, Cardiff University, 1993.

WRITINGS:

(Editor, with M. S. Gazzaniga) *Handbook of Psychobiology,* Academic Press (San Diego, CA), 1975.
Mechanics of the Mind, Cambridge University Press (New York, NY), 1977.
Mindwaves: Thoughts on Intelligence, Identity and Consciousness, Blackwell (Malden, MA), 1989.
(Editor) *Vision: Coding and Efficiency,* Cambridge University Press (New York, NY), 1990.
The Mind Machine, BBC Consumer Publishing (London, England), 1990.
(Editor, with Horace Barlow and Miranda Weston-Smith) *Images and Understanding: Thoughts about Images, Ideas about Understanding,* Cambridge University Press (New York, NY), 1990.
(Editor, with Susan Iversen) *Gender and Society: Essays Based on Herbert Spencer Lectures Given in the University of Oxford,* Oxford University Press (New York, NY), 2000.
(Editor, with Sheila Jennett) *The Oxford Companion to the Body,* Oxford University Press (New York, NY), 2001.
(Editor, with Andrew Parker and Andrew Derrington) *The Physiology of Cognitive Processes,* Oxford University Press (New York, NY), 2003.

Writer and broadcaster for British Broadcasting Corp. Series editor, *Perspectives in Vision Research,* Plenum (New York, NY), 1981—; editor in chief, *IBRO News,*

1986—. Contributor to learned journals and popular magazines, including *Sciences* and *Nature*. Member of several editorial boards, including *Perception, Trends in Neurosciences, Behavioural and Brain Sciences, Experimental Brain Research,* 1979-89, *Reviews in the Neurosciences,* 1984—, *Language and Communication,* 1979-90, *International Review of Neurobiology,* 1996—, and *Eurobrain,* 1998—.

SIDELIGHTS: A highly respected neuroscientist and communicator, Colin Blakemore is one of England's most recognized science professionals. He has also been the subject of controversy, targeted by certain animal-rights activists for his research on the causes of childhood blindness, which involves experiments on cats. "He has sewn [cats'] eyelids shut—precisely the technique that is used on babies with eye injuries," explained Arlene Judith Klotzko in an article for the *Scientist* online. "He later recorded with microelectrodes from nerve cells in the visual parts of the brain to assess the effects of the early disturbance of vision. The animals were anaesthetized at the beginning of the experiment and did not suffer." Blakemore, however, did suffer at the hands of some activists. In addition to being the center of an orchestrated campaign, said Klotzko, the scientist was the target of death threats: "Bombs were delivered to his home, his daughters were threatened with kidnap. And the terrorism continued for years."

Blakemore's case made headlines in England when Gillian Reynolds, a writer for the *Daily Telegraph,* focused on this kind of animal-rights action in the light of the terrorist events of September 11, 2001. Regarding the letter-bombs sent to the scientist's home, Reynolds was quoted in *AnimalRights.net:* "His children had picked it up, looked at it. Had they opened it, at least one of them might have died, the others showered with [HIV-infected] needles with which the explosive was said to be packed." For his part, Blakemore has attempted to engage in dialogue with his critics, and told Klotzko that he has been torn between "the crucial importance of scientific research and the safety of my family."

Among the books Blakemore has edited or coedited is *The Oxford Companion to the Body,* a general-interest volume that, according to *Lancet* reviewer Graham Farmelo, "[unleashes] not only scientists, but writers, artists, and poets on a subject that obsesses almost all

of us." This work covers topics in not only the mechanics of the body but also the emotional, psychological, and cultural forces that shape human behavior. *Times Literary Supplement* reviewer W. F. Bynum admitted expecting to find dull a book that boasted "two distinguished physiologists as editors [with] information on the dust jacket that the book has been supported by the Physiology Society." Instead, Bynum deemed *Oxford Companion* a book that "succeeds brilliantly. It combines the palatable essence of the historical, anthropological and gender-based insights of social approaches to the body with accessible and full accounts of contemporary scientific understanding of the way our bodies work." Bynum went on to praise the editors' "eclectic and sometimes wacky coverage, everything from *Codpiece* to *Coitus,* from *Brain Stem* to *Brassière.*" Tim Radford of the *Guardian* found the book a "rare thing, an encyclopaedia you want to go on reading." He added that while some entries seemed "terse and functional," most "celebrate the intimacy between physiology and achievement."

BIOGRAPHICAL AND CRITICAL SOURCES:

PERIODICALS

Books, October, 1988, review of *The Mind Machine,* p. 20.

British Book News, September, 1987, review of *Mindwaves: Thoughts on Intelligence, Identity and Consciousness,* p. 589.

British Journal of Psychology, February, 1993, Ian Gordon, review of *Vision: Coding and Efficiency,* p. 134.

Choice, February, 1988, review of *Mindwaves,* p. 974; February, 1992, R. H. Cormack, review of *Vision,* p. 919; November, 1995, review of *Mindwaves,* p. 411.

Daily Telegraph, October 23, 2002, Gillian Reynolds, "Conscience and the Call to Arms."

Endeavor, summer, 1991, D. Perrett, review of *Vision,* p. 144.

Financial Times, May 13, 2003, Clive Cookson, "Oxford Neuroscientist to Lead Research Council."

Guardian (London, England), January 22, 1995, review of *The Mind Machine,* p. 29; December 22, 2001, Tim Radford, review of *The Oxford Companion to the Body,* p. 9.

Lancet, May 11, 2002, Graham Farmelo, "Serendipitous Discoveries," p. 1705.

Los Angeles Times, March 11, 2002, Jane Allen, "Media Mix," p. S2.

Medical Research Council, May 23, 2003, Jocelyn Kaiser, "Out of the Frying Pan into the MRC," p. 1230.

Nature, November 19, 1987, review of *Mindwaves,* p. 297; December 1, 1988, Geoffrey Hall, review of *The Mind Machine,* p. 431; May 2, 1991, J. Anthony Movshon, review of *Vision,* p. 24.

New Scientist, August 25, 1988, Susan Blackmore, review of *Mindwaves,* p. 58; March 25, 1989, Jennifer Altman, review of *The Mind Machine,* p. 60; November 24, 2001, Maggie McDonald, "Body Amazing," p. 45.

Quarterly Review of Biology, March, 1994, review of *Vision,* p. 125.

Science, May 3, 2002, Steven Vogel, "Habeas Corpus," p. 854.

Science Books & Films, September, 1988, review of *Mindwaves,* p. 3.

Scientist, May 13, 2003, Pat Hagan, "New MRC Head Named."

SciTech Book News, March, 1988, review of *Mindwaves,* p. 2.

Times (London, England), February 26, 2000, Valerie Grove, "'Cruelty? They Just Have No Idea'" (interview), p. 21.

Times Literary Supplement, April 8, 1988, Stuart Sutherland, review of *Mindwaves,* p. 403; February 15, 2002, W. F. Bynum, "Cherries and Cobwebs," p. 10.

Washington Post Book World, December 27, 1987, review of *Mindwaves,* p. 4.

ONLINE

AnimalRights.net, http://www.animalrights.net/ (September 17, 2002), Brian Carnell "Eloquent Commentary on Animal Rights Terrorism."

Scientist, http://www.the-scientist.com/ (April 15, 2002), Arlene Judith Klotzko, "Profile."

* * *

BLAYNE, Diana
  See KYLE, Susan (Spaeth)

BLOOR, Edward (William) 1950-

PERSONAL: Born October 12, 1950, in Trenton, NJ; son of Edward William and Mary (Cowley) Bloor; married Pamela Dixon (a teacher), August 4, 1984; children: Amanda Kristin, Spencer Dixon. *Education:* Fordham University, B.A., 1973.

ADDRESSES: Home—12021 Windstone St., Winter Garden, FL 34787. *E-mail*—ebloor@harcourtbrace.com.

CAREER: Novelist and editor. English teacher in Florida public high schools, 1983-86; Harcourt Brace School Publishers, Orlando, FL, senior editor, beginning 1986.

AWARDS, HONORS: Named among Books in the Middle Outstanding Titles of 1997, named on *Voice of Youth Advocates* and *Horn Book* honor lists, named to Pick of the List, American Booksellers Association, and among 100 Titles for Reading and Sharing, New York Public Library, all 1997, and Top Ten Best Books for Young Adults and Best Books for Young Adults citations, American Library Association, and Edgar Allan Poe Award nomination for Best Young Adult Novel, all 1998, all for *Tangerine.*

WRITINGS:

Tangerine, Harcourt Brace (San Diego, CA), 1997.
Crusader, Harcourt Brace (San Diego, CA), 1999.
Story Time, Harcourt (Orlando, FL), 2004.
London Calling, Harcourt (Orlando, FL), 2005.

ADAPTATIONS: Tangerine was adapted as an audiobook, Recorded Books, 2001.

SIDELIGHTS: A former high school English teacher, Edward Bloor has managed to find time while working as a book editor at a major publishing house and helping to raise his two children to pen four well-received novels for teen readers: *Crusader, Story Time,* the award-winning debut novel *Tangerine,* and *London Calling.* As Bloor once commented: "My teaching job

Edward Bloor

led to a job in educational publishing, where I was actually required to sit and read young adult novels all day long. So I decided to try it myself."

Born in 1950, Bloor was raised in Trenton, New Jersey, and recalled that, during his childhood, soccer reigned supreme. "Different ethnic communities— Poles, Italians, Germans, Ukrainians—all had their kids' soccer clubs. Parents of the children on these teams raged and howled at the games as if their national pride was at stake. I was one of those little kids trying desperately to kick a soccer ball amidst the multilingual howling. I continued my soccer playing through high school, on a really good team, and into college, on a really bad team." Bloor's memories of the game eventually found their way into his fiction.

In the meantime, Bloor graduated from college, then worked for three years as a teacher. He began his career in children's publishing in 1986, and came up with the idea for his first novel while commuting to work on Florida's back roads west of Orlando. As he once recalled: "To my dismay, I watched the daily destruction of the citrus groves along this route. This is how it happens: The citrus trees are uprooted and bulldozed into piles; the piles are set on fire; the

charred remains of the trees are buried, and tons of white sand are dumped over their graves. After that, a completely different place is created, a place as fictional as any novel. A developer erects a wall, thinks of a theme, and gives the place a name. Then the place fills up with large houses and with people whose only common bond is that they qualified for the same amount of mortgage money." Upset by the changing landscape, Bloor asked himself: "Who are the people who used to make a go of it here? Who are the people now making their exit while we're making our entrance? And how do they feel about all this?"

Bloor addresses such questions in his debut novel, 1997's *Tangerine*. Set in the tangerine-growing region of Florida, the novel touches on environmental and social issues while exploring the trials of its legally blind, soccer-playing protagonist, Paul Fisher. As Bloor once explained: "Paul lives in constant fear of his evil older brother, Erik. Paul also struggles mightily to lead a normal life and to see things as they really are despite the thick-framed glasses that cover his injured eyes. Playing goalie in soccer is at the core of Paul's life, and he gets to do it on two teams, one of which is a mixture of boys and girls. It is the clash of these two teams, these two schools, and these two worlds that brings about the climactic scenes of the novel." *Bulletin of the Center for Children's Books* reviewer Deborah Stevenson praised *Tangerine* as "a richly imagined read about an underdog coming into his own," while a *Kirkus Reviews* critic cited "a series of gripping climaxes and revelations" as among the book's strengths. Noting that well-rounded characterization and a humorous edge add to the appeal of the book, *Booklist* reviewer Kathleen Squires asserted that "this dark, debut novel proves that Bloor is a writer to watch."

Bloor also draws readers to southern Florida in his second novel, *Crusader*. Here he focuses on fifteen-year-old Roberta, who works in her uncle's virtual-reality arcade in a seedy suburban strip mall. Roberta has felt helpless since her mother's murder seven years ago, and the strangeness of her home life and the virulent atmosphere at the arcade make her loneliness and adolescent growing pains even more painful. When a brutal new racist video game called Crusader taps into the ethnic hatreds of the arcade's clientele and brings in an even more violent clientele, Roberta begins to see how distorted her world is. She breaks from her family's traditions, and begins to take action to track down her mother's murderer, in addition to furthering her own career as a journalist.

While some reviewers noted that the novel's multiple plot lines sometimes tangle, Frances Bradburn wrote in *Booklist* that Bloor's message—that life holds "no easy answers"—makes *Crusader* "a stretch book in the truest sense." Praising the novel as "ambitious," a *Publishers Weekly* reviewer added that the book's "characters are sharply drawn" and that Bloor's story line is "deeper, denser, and more complex than most YA fare." Echoing the praise of these reviewers, a *Horn Book* contributor noted that the novel's "situations and characters are both intriguing and unsettling," and that Bloor successfully supplies readers with "palpable atmosphere and a fascinating range of undeniable human characters."

Published in 2004, *Story Time* draws on Bloor's quirky sense of humor as well as his short tenure as a public school teacher. In this darkly comic, quasi-ghost story, eighth-grader Kate Melvil and her very bright, slightly younger uncle George are unexpectedly transferred into the Whittaker Magnet School, where they expect to be challenged by advanced classwork in the county's "Leave No High-Scoring Child Behind" program. Instead, they spend much of the time in the school's basement, where they are barraged with an endless stream of practice tests, horrid health-food concoctions and exercise designed to keep them in top testing shape, administrative mumbo jumbo from a controlling principal who plays favorites, and a malevolent presence emanating from a collection of old books in the school's upper regions. Large vocabulary words are memorized, but their meanings are never understood; the principal's quest is for higher test scores, not education. As Bloor noted in an interview posted on the Harcourt Books Web site, the message behind *Story Time* is that "standardized testing is not really about [students] . . . at all. It is about real estate and politics and money, but not about them. Therefore, they should not let such tests upset them. They should concentrate on discovering and developing their God-given talents."

Story Time was praised by several reviewers, *Kliatt* critic Paula Rohrlick describing the novel as "a funny, offbeat, often Gothic tale." While, as a *Kirkus Reviews* contributor noted, adult readers "will relish this wild satire on modern education," Bloor's novel addresses readers on more than one level; the engaging characters, bizarre plot twists, and haunted library setting balance what a *Publishers Weekly* contributor dubbed as "a no-holds-barred, deeply subversive tale about modern education." While Mary R. Hofmann wrote in her *School Library Journal* review that *Story Time* is "overly ambitious" in its attempt to combine "social satire, black comedy, fantasy/humor, and extreme situations," she added that Bloor nonetheless creates an "expansive and engrossing tale" on the order of works by writers Roald Dahl and *Peter Pan* author J. M. Barrie.

BIOGRAPHICAL AND CRITICAL SOURCES:

PERIODICALS

Booklist, May 15, 1997, Kathleen Squires, review of *Tangerine,* p. 1573; November 15, 1999, Frances Bradburn, review of *Crusader,* p. 614; March 15, 2004, Jennifer Mattson, review of *Story Time,* p. 1306.

Bulletin of the Center for Children's Books, March, 1997, Deborah Stevenson, review of *Tangerine,* p. 241.

Horn Book, July-August, 1997, review of *Tangerine,* p. 449; January, 2000, review of *Crusader,* p. 70.

Kirkus Reviews, February 1, 1997, review of *Tangerine,* p. 219; February 15, 2004, review of *Story Time,* p. 174.

Kliatt, March, 2004, Paula Rohrlick, review of *Story Time,* p. 6.

Publishers Weekly, March 24, 1997, review of *Tangerine,* p. 84; June 30, 1997, p. 27; November 8, 1999, review of *Crusader,* p. 69; February 16, 2004, review of *Story Time,* p. 174.

St. Petersburg Times, February 18, 2002, Holly Atkins, interview with Bloor.

School Library Journal, April, 1997, review of *Tangerine,* p. 1334; March, 2002, Sarah Flowers, review of *Tangerine,* p. 87; April, 2004, Mary R. Hofmann, review of *Story Time,* p. 148.

ONLINE

Harcourt Books Web site, http://www.harcourtbooks. com/ (July 2, 2004), interview with Bloor.

BROCHU, André 1942-

PERSONAL: Born March 3, 1942, in St. Eustache, Quebec, Canada; son of Edouard (a microbiologist) and Jeanne (Lacroix) Brochu; married Celine Cadieux (a musician), June 24, 1962; children: Hugo, Xavier. *Ethnicity:* "Québécoise." *Education:* College of St. Marie, B.A., 1960; University of Montreal, M.A., 1961; University of Vincennes, doctorate, 1971. *Politics:* Independent.

ADDRESSES: Home—53 Avenue Wicksteed, Mont-Royal, Quebec H3P 1P9, Canada. *Office*—University of Montreal, Montreal, Quebec, Canada. *E-mail*—andrebroc@hotmail.com.

CAREER: Educator and writer. University of Montreal, Montreal, Quebec, Canada, professor of literature, 1963-97; full-time writer, 1997—.

MEMBER: Quebec Writers Union, Academy des lettres du Quebec.

AWARDS, HONORS: Prix Gabrielle-Roy, l'Association des littératures canadienne et québécoise, 1989, for *La visée critique: essais autobiographiques et littéraires;* Deuxième Prix, Radio Canada, 1990, for a short story, "L'esprit ailleurs"; Governor-General's Prize, 1991, for *La croix du Nord;* Grand Prix, *Journal de Montréal,* 1993, for *La vie aux trousses;* Grand Prix, Festival international de poesis, 1995, for *Delà.*

WRITINGS:

POETRY

(With J.-André Constant and Yves Dube) *Étranges domaines,* foreword by Germaine Guevremont, Editions de la Cascade (Montreal, Quebec, Canada), 1957.
Privilèges de l'ombre, Éditions de l'Hexagone (Montreal, Quebec, Canada), 1961.
Délit contre délit, Association générale des étudiants de l'Université de Montréal (Montreal, Quebec, Canada), 1965.
Les matins nus, le vent, Éditions Trois (Laval, Quebec, Canada), 1989.

Dans les chances de l'air, Éditions de l'Hexagone (Montreal, Quebec, Canada), 1990.
Particulièrement la vie change, Noroît (Montreal, Quebec, Canada), 1990.
Delà, Éditions de l'Hexagone (Montreal, Quebec, Canada), 1994.
L'inconcevable, Éditions Trois (Montreal, Quebec, Canada), 1998.
Je t'aime, je t'écris: poèmes, précédé de, Le corps de l'amoureuse, Québec Amérique (Montreal, Quebec, Canada), 2001.

NOVELS

Adéodat I, Éditions du Jour (Montreal, Quebec, Canada), 1973.
La croix du Nord (novella), XYZ Éditeur (Montreal, Quebec, Canada), 1991.
La vie aux trousses, XYZ Éditeur (Montreal, Quebec, Canada), 1993.
Fièvres blanches (novella), XYZ Éditeur (Montreal, Quebec, Canada), 1994.
Adele intime (novella), XYZ Éditeur (Montreal, Quebec, Canada), 1996.
Les épervières, XYZ Éditeur (Montreal, Quebec, Canada), 1996.
Le maître rêveur: la vie aux trousses II, XYZ Éditeur (Montreal, Quebec, Canada), 1997.
Matamore premier: roman-farce, XYZ Éditeur (Montreal, Quebec, Canada), 2000.
The Devil's Paintbrush, translated by Alison Newall, Dundarn Press (Tonawanda, NY), 2003.

OTHER

(Editor) *La littérature par elle-même* (essays), Association générale des étudiants de l'Université de Montréal (Montreal, Quebec, Canada), 1962.
(With Jacques Brault and André Major) *Nouvelles* (short stories), Association générale des étudiants de l'Université de Montréal (Montreal, Quebec, Canada), 1963.
Hugo: amour, crime, révolution; essai sur "Les Misérables" (essays), Presses de l'Université de Montréal (Montreal, Quebec, Canada), 1974.
(With Laurent Mailhot and Albert Le Grand) *Le reel, le réalisme et la littérature québécoise* (essays), Libraire de l'Université de Montréal (Montreal, Quebec, Canada), 1974.

L'instance critique: 1961-1973 (collected articles), Leméac (Montreal, Quebec, Canada), 1974.

(With Gilles Marcotte) *La littérature et le reste: livre de lettres* (essays), Quinze (Montreal, Quebec, Canada), 1980.

L'évasion tragique—essai sur les romans d'André Langevin (essay), Hurtubise (Montreal, Quebec, Canada), 1985.

La visée critique: essais autobiographiques et littéraires (essays), Boréal (Montreal, Quebec, Canada), 1988.

L'esprit ailleurs (short stories), XYZ Éditeur (Montreal, Quebec, Canada), 1992.

Le singulier pluriel (essays), Éditions de l'Hexagone (Montreal, Quebec, Canada), 1992.

La grande langue: éloge de l'anglais (essay), XYZ Éditeur (Montreal, Quebec, Canada), 1993.

Tableau du poème, XYZ Éditeur (Montreal, Quebec, Canada), 1994.

Roman et énumération de Flaubert à Perec (essays), Université de Montréal (Montreal, Quebec, Canada), 1996.

Anne Hébert: Le secret de vie et de mort (essay), University of Ottawa Press (Ottawa, Ontario, Canada), 1998.

Saint-Denys Garneau: le poète en sursis, XYZ Éditeur (Montreal, Quebec, Canada), 1999.

Rêver la lune: l'imaginaire de Michel Tremblay dans les Chroniques du plateau Mont-Royal, Hurtubise (Montreal, Quebec, Canada), 2002.

Les jours à vif, Éditions Trois (Laval, Quebec, Canada), 2004.

Contributor to periodicals, including *La Crue, Quartier Latin, Lettres québécoises, Voix et Images du Pays,* and *Voix et Images.*

SIDELIGHTS: André Brochu is a prominent French-Canadian writer who has distinguished himself as a poet, novelist, and literary critic. Brochu was born in 1942 in St. Eustache, Quebec. In 1957, while he was still in his mid-teens, Brochu collaborated with J.-André Constant and Yves Dube on the verse collection *Étranges domaines.* He received his undergraduate degree from the College of St. Marie in 1960 and obtained a master's degree from the University of Montreal in 1961, the same year that he published the poetry volume *Privilèges de l'ombre,* which focuses on the sufferings of a rebellious adolescent. The following year he served as editor of *La littérature par elle-même,* a collection of essays by writers described by *Dictionary of Literary Biography* essayist Camille R. La Bossiere as "optimistic secular humanists."

In 1963 Brochu teamed with Jacques Brault and André Major on *Nouvelles,* a collection of short stories. Among the tales in this volume is Brochu's "Quand je serai grand," in which a rebellious youth rejects his family's Catholicism only to plunge into despair when he fails to find a worthy replacement for his forsaken religion. Eventually the youth realizes a measure of consolation by reading French poet Arthur Rimbaud's *A Season in Hell.*

Like his rebellious protagonists, Brochu found it necessary to reconcile the often contradictory aspects of life and art. He began to approach his own reconciliation by exploring the Hegelian dialectic, in which the clash of thesis and antithesis leads to synthesis. Brochu's embracing of the Hegelian dialectic is visible in his *Délit contre délit,* a volume of autobiographical poetry described by La Bossiere as expressions of "a voice at once nostalgic and ironic." These poems, La Bossiere observed, "review Brochu's suspension in paradox, between nihilism and hope, joy and despair." *Délit contre délit* culminates in a brace of poems in which rebellion is likened to the synthesis of inseparable opposites. For Brochu, the ambiguity of these inseparable opposites is itself an affirmation of life, according to La Bossiere.

Brochu's notion of affirmative paradox is exemplified in *Adéodat I,* his 1973 novel that lampoons contemporary critical theories—including structuralism and deconstructuralism—and culminates in the advocacy of scatology as a principle means of authentic expression. A succeeding volume, the essay collection *L'instance critique: 1961-1973,* also serves as an examination of synthesized opposites. For Brochu, according to La Bossiere, unity is essential and positive, while the lack of synthesis or reconciliation—even with regard to seemingly disparate objects or subjects—constitutes a sickness.

Throughout much of the 1980s, in works such as *L'évasion tragique—essai sur les romans d'André Langevin* and *La visée critique: essais autobiographiques et littéraires,* Brochu collected his essays on a range of subjects, from his own childhood to his achievements as a literary critic, and from French-Canadian culture to socio-political issues imbedded in Quebec's drive for separatism from Canada. In 1989, however, Brochu broke from this stream of nonfiction to publish the poetry collection, *Les matins nus, le vent.* He then published *La croix du Nord,* a novella about a husband whose marriage declines when his wife enters into sexual relations with his best friend. Much of the novel concerns the husband's recollection of the friendship that resulted in betrayal. Critic Norman J. Lamoureux, writing in the *French Review,* found the protagonist's plight both moving and disturbing, and he called *La croix du Nord* "a beautifully written, compact work well worth pondering."

Among Brochu's works of the 1990s is *Particulière-ment la vie change,* a volume of surreal, wide-ranging poems. Here the author again examines life's reconcili-ations and extols the virtues of acceptance and understanding, particularly with regard to his own experiences. Reviewer Adele Sullivan noted in the *French Review* that *Particulièrement la vie change* constitutes a "poetic odyssey," one that is "vividly articulated."

Brochu once told *CA:* "A very important event for me happened during the 1980s. A medication, lithium, al-lowed me to defeat a terrible illness and to finally realize my ambitions as a writer by giving me access to my imagination. Since then, I have tried to explore my interior reality—in connection with simple reality, which is not so different—and to give a literary existence, even a dimension of universality, to this secret flaw which is my destiny and that of many others. Those in the minority (the insane, homosexuals, the infirm, etc.) know as much and often more of hu-man nature than those who can repose in the comfort of the majority."

BIOGRAPHICAL AND CRITICAL SOURCES:

BOOKS

Dictionary of Literary Biography, Volume 53: *Cana-dian Writers since 1960,* First Series, Thomson Gale (Detroit), 1986.

PERIODICALS

Booklist, September 1, 1993, Norman J. Lemoureux, review of *La croix du Nord,* p. 43; March 1, 1996, Adele Sullivan, review of *Particulièrement la vie change,* p. 1126.

Canadian Literature, spring, 1991, pp. 157-159; summer, 1998, Cedric May, review of *Particulière-ment la vie change,* p. 125; summer, 2000, Paul Raymond Cote, review of *Le maître rêveur: la vie aux trousses II,* p. 94.
French Review, October, 1992, pp. 171-172; May, 1994, pp. 1102-1103; October, 1996, pp. 139-140; March, 1999, Paul Raymond Cote, review of *Le maître rêveur,* p. 772.
University of Toronto Quarterly, winter, 1999, Roger Chamberland, review of *L'inconcevable,* p. 401; winter, 2001, Pierre Karch, review of *Matamore premier: roman-farce,* p. 409; winter, 2001, Nicole Cote, review of *Saint-Denys Garneau: le poète en sursis,* p. 499; winter, 2001, Janet Paterson, review of *Anne Hébert: Le secret de vie et de mort,* p. 513.
World Literature Today, summer, 1998, Steven Daniell, review of *Le maître rêveur,* p. 575.

*   *   *

BROOKS, Bruce 1950-

PERSONAL: Born September 23, 1950, in Washington, DC; son of Donald D. Brooks and Lelia Colleen Col-lins; married Penelope Winslow, June 17, 1978; children: Alexander. *Education:* University of North Carolina at Chapel Hill, B.A., 1972; University of Iowa, M.F.A, 1982 *Politics:* "Certainly." *Religion:* "Lapsed Baptist." *Hobbies and other interests:* Music, nature study, sports, reading.

ADDRESSES: Home and office—11208 Legato Way, Silver Spring, MD 20901.

CAREER: Writer. Has worked variously as a let-terpress printer, newspaper and magazine reporter, and teacher.

AWARDS, HONORS: School Library Journal Best Book, American Library Association (ALA) Notable Children's Book, and *New York Times* Notable Book of the Year designations, all 1984, and *Boston Globe/ Horn Book* Award, and Newbery Honor Book, both 1985, all for *The Moves That Make the Man; School Library Journal* Best Book, and ALA Best Book for Young Adults designations, both 1986, *Horn Book* Fanfare Honor List book, and National Council of

Teachers of English Teachers' Choice, both 1987, International Reading Association Young Adult Choice, 1988, and ALA Best of the 1980s Book for Young Adults designations, all for *Midnight Hour Encores;* ALA Best Book for Young Adults and Young Adult Editor's Choice, *School Library Journal* Best Book, and Notable Children's Trade Book in social studies designation, all 1989, all for *No Kidding;* ALA Notable Children's Book, and *School Library Journal* Best Book designations, both 1990, both for *Everywhere;* John Burroughs List choice, 1991, for *Nature by Design,* 1994, and for *Making Sense;* Newbery Honor Book designation, ALA Best Book for Young Adults and Notable Children's Book Award, and *Horn Book* Fanfare Book, all 1993, all for *What Hearts;* Orbus Pictus Award, 1994, for *Making Sense.*

WRITINGS:

FICTION

The Moves Make the Man, Harper (New York, NY), 1984.
Midnight Hour Encores, Harper (New York, NY), 1986.
No Kidding, Harper (New York, NY), 1989.
Everywhere, HarperCollins (New York, NY), 1990.
What Hearts, HarperCollins (New York, NY), 1992.
Each a Piece (picture book), illustrated by Elena Pavlov, Harper Collins (New York, NY), 1996, hardcover edition, 1998.
Asylum for Nightface, Laura Geringer Book (New York, NY), 1996.
Vanishing, Laura Geringer Book (New York, NY), 1999.
Throwing Smoke, HarperCollins (New York, NY), 2000.
All That Remains, Atheneum Books for Young Readers (New York, NY), 2001.
Dolores: Seven Stories about Her, HarperCollins (New York, NY), 2002.

"WOLFBAY WINGS" SERIES; YOUNG-ADULT FICTION

Woodsie, Laura Geringer Books (New York, NY), 1997.
Zip, HarperCollins (New York, NY), 1997.
Cody, HarperCollins (New York, NY), 1997.
Boot, Laura Geringer Book (New York, NY), 1998.

Prince, Laura Geringer Book (New York, NY), 1998.
Shark, Laura Geringer Book (New York, NY), 1998.
Billy, Laura Geringer Book (New York, NY), 1998.
Dooby, Laura Geringer Book (New York, NY), 1998.
Reed, Laura Geringer Book (New York, NY), 1998.
Subtle, Laura Geringer Book (New York, NY), 1999.
Barry, Laura Geringer Book (New York, NY), 1999.
Woodsie, Again, Harper Trophy (New York, NY), 1999.

NONFICTION

On the Wing: The Life of Birds from Feathers to Flight, Scribner (New York, NY), 1989.
Predator, Farrar, Straus (New York, NY), 1991.
Nature by Design, Farrar, Straus (New York, NY), 1991.
(With Glenn Rivers) *Those Who Love the Game: Glenn "Doc" Rivers on Life in the NBA and Elsewhere,* Henry Holt (New York, NY), 1993.
Making Sense: Animal Perception and Communication, Farrar, Straus (New York, NY), 1993.
NBA by the Numbers, photographs from the National Basketball Association, Scholastic Press (New York, NY), 1997.

ESSAYS

Boys Will Be, Hyperion (New York, NY), 1995.
(Editor) *The Red Wasteland: A Personal Selection of Writings about Nature for Young Readers,* Henry Holt (New York, NY), 1998.

Author of introductions to reprinted sports fiction of John R. Tunis, including *The Kid from Tomkinsville, Rookie of the Year, World Series,* and *Keystone Kids.* Contributor to *Horn Book.*

SIDELIGHTS: Bruce Brooks is an award-winning and versatile writer of nonfiction, novels, and stories. Brooks's novels, which include *The Moves Make the Man, Midnight Hour Encores, No Kidding,* and *Everywhere,* have been described by reviewers as intelligent and thought-provoking. Christine McDonnell, writing in *Horn Book,* praised the "strong voice, unusual characters, and powerful emotional ties" exhibited in Brooks's stories. *Publishers Weekly* contributor Leonard Marcus was equally enthusiastic, deeming the author's works "impassioned, [and] often psychologically complex." Critical attention to these aspects of his work pleases Brooks who, in an interview with *Authors and Artists for Young Adults* (*AAYA*), remarked, "We are capable as readers of a wild and intricate world of thought and response and feeling—things going on in different layers at the same time. I hope to write books that involve all those layers of the thinking and feeling in my reader."

Brooks's first book, *The Moves Make the Man,* is set in 1950s North Carolina and chronicles the budding interracial friendship of two boys, Jerome and Bix. The boys discover that their racial differences prove less important than their common personality traits. Both loners, they frequent a secluded basketball court where Jerome teaches Bix how to play the game. Through this activity, Jerome learns about his new friend's unfortunate domestic situation. Bix's confidence and happiness has eroded since his mother suffered a nervous breakdown and entered the hospital. In addition, his stepfather refuses to take Bix to see her. Determined to visit his mother, Bix proposes a deal to his stepfather. If Bix beats him at a game of one-on-one, they will go to the hospital. Although Bix wins and invites Jerome along for the ensuing trip, the reunion is not what Bix had expected and he runs away from home, leaving Jerome alone to sort out the jarring events.

The Moves Make the Man earned enthusiastic critical response; it was named a Newbery honor book and won a *Boston Globe/Horn Book* Award. Yet, Brooks confessed that such praise was not as heady as might be expected for a first-time novelist. At the times the awards were bestowed, the author explained to *AAYA,* "I hadn't written a word of fiction in three years. I'd been working out the story on my second book, *Midnight Hour Encores,* for three years mentally, but I had not written anything because I was too busy earning a living and I had a new child. So when the awards came, I felt like a hypocrite." Nonetheless, Brooks's success afforded him new career opportunities. He decided to quit his job and write full-time.

For Brooks's next, and equally successful venture, he produced *Midnight Hour Encores,* a story narrated by Sibilance (Sib for short), a sixteen-year-old musical prodigy. Sib, whose parents separated after her birth, lives with her father, Taxi, in Washington, D.C., and has never met her mother. The self-absorbed Sib, one

of the top-ranked cello players in the world, is wrapped up in her practices, competitions, and concerts, and is preparing to attend the prestigious Juilliard School of Music in New York City. While searching for a mentor after her cello teacher dies, Sib discovers that a brilliant but reclusive player may accept a teaching post at a new music school in California. Under the guise of visiting her mother who also lives in the state, Sib travels to California to audition for the institution. Taxi drives her there, afraid all the while that his daughter will leave him. After an enjoyable and educational stay with her mother, Sib gradually becomes aware of what her parents mean to her. *Midnight Hour Encores* ends as Sib decides what school to attend and, consequently, which parent to live with.

Midnight Hour Encores was favorably received by critics. Deeming the work "another terrific book" for Brooks, *Washington Post Book World* contributor Katherine Paterson acknowledged the welcome complexity of the novel. "This is a book the reader will have to fool around with, poke into, and tell in his own accents," Paterson insisted. Although several reviews of the book focused on the novel's coming-of-age slant, Brooks remarked in *AAYA* that "to me *Midnight Hour Encores* is about being a father. I wrote that book in the year after my son was born. The most important thing in my life was being a father. . . . My curiosity about the future—of what you get when you invest certain things in the very early days of your child's life—inspired my imagination to come up with those characters and that story."

Brooks's 1989 literary enterprise, *No Kidding,* again tackles a sophisticated topic. Set in twenty-first century Washington, D.C., *No Kidding* presents a bleak environment in which alcoholics comprise the majority of the population. Society is overwhelmed by this problem and schools have curriculum geared specifically toward alcoholics' offspring, more commonly referred to as "AOs." The fourteen-year-old protagonist, an AO named Sam, has been forced to assume adult-level responsibility in his fatherless home. He previously committed his mother to a rehabilitation program and placed his younger brother, Ollie, with foster parents. Now that his mother's stint is completed, Sam must decide whether to reunite the family. At the book's end, however, Sam's mother manipulates events to generate the outcome, giving Sam the chance to assume the role of a child once again. Elizabeth S. Watson, writing in *Horn Book*, remarked that "Brooks is a fine writer," and although she found some of the issues perplexing for young readers, she conceded that "Brooks has created a wonderful vehicle for discussion."

In 1990 Brooks published a short novel titled *Everywhere*. In this book, a nameless young protagonist frets about his beloved grandfather who has suffered a heart attack and is near death. As the boy keeps a vigil, a local nurse arrives with her nephew, Dooley, who suggests killing an animal in a soul-switching ceremony to save the grandfather. During the course of the story, the boy ponders his grandfather's fate, his own mortality, and the ethics of taking one life to save another. Recognizing both the accessibility and complex issues in *Everywhere, Horn Book* contributor Nancy Vasilakis deemed the work a "masterly novella" and added that "Brooks's precise use of language is a tour de force."

Brooks won his second Newbery Honor for *What Heart* in 1992. This book presents four short stories about seven-year-old Asa and his efforts to deal with life-changing events. As he grows, Asa experiences the break up of his home, conflicts with Dave, his new stepfather, falling in love for the first time, and beginning a new life with his mother without Dave. The stories are held together by the common element of love—within the family, among friends, between boy and girl, between mother and son. Vasilakis said, "The book defies category and asks much of the reader." A *Publishers Weekly* reviewer described this book as "honest and intense from beginning to end." Vasilakis called it "original in structure and subtle in scope."

Patsy Campbell, writing for *Horn Book*, described Brooks's career as "notable for audacious undertakings and unexpected shifts to new styles and genres, as well as memorable characters and distinguished writing." In *Asylum for Nightface, Vanishing*, and *All That Remains*, Brooks lives up to this reputation, taking on "philosophical and theological questions" that, according to Deborah Stevenson in the *Bulletin of the Center for Children's Books*, "are rarely raised in children's literature."

Asylum tells the story of Zim, a religious fourteen-year-old whose "party-happy" parents transform their zeal for self-indulgence and drug abuse into a cult-like

zest for religion. Zim's initial pleasure in his parents' religious awakening turns to concern as they attempt to force their religion on him in much the same way they had previously tried to force their drugs on him. The story is told by Zim as a narrator "beset by feelings of alienation and confusion. Many young adult readers will have similar emotions," said Kirk Beetz, editor of *Beacham's Guide to Literature for Young Adults*. "How [Zim] manifests his rebellious nature and copes . . . makes the book attractive and stimulating," Beetz concluded. The conflict reaches critical mass when Zim's parents decide that he is "marked by God for a holy purpose" and proclaim him the perfect "living Saint," ideal to serve as poster boy for their sect. Zim resolves a difficult moral choice by deciding to prove himself to be human, not saint.

Vanishing is a compelling glimpse into the reality of two eleven-year-olds sharing a hospital room. Rex is dying of cancer. Alice is in and out of hallucination while dying of self-inflicted starvation—a choice deemed preferable to life with an alcoholic mother and racist stepfather. A *Horn Book* reviewer called *Vanishing* "a trenchant and powerful fable" with characters "preternaturally precocious for eleven-year-olds" yet whose "dialogue is so inventive and witty that it achieves a . . . hyper-reality [revealing] truths too cruel to express more directly."

Of the three novellas that comprise *All That Remains*, "any one rates discussion," according to a reviewer in *Horn Book*, and "together they are . . . provocative." Each of this trio of novellas is concerned with teenagers encountering and dealing with death—some more effectively and maturely than others. According to a *Booklist* critic, "There is nothing ghoulish or creepy here . . . clever wordplay and gallows humor bring a new dimension to death and how we deal with it." In the (rather bizarre) title story, cousins conspire against AIDS prejudice and the law to keep their aunt from a pauper's burial by cremating her remains in a potter's kiln and substituting the body of a deer for delivery to the State. In the second story, *Playing the Creeps*, a decidedly cool teen mentors his decidedly un-cool cousin to fulfill a promise made to a dying uncle. The final story, *Teeing Up*, features a young girl laden with a backpack who joins a trio of boys in a round of golf. As the story progresses, the relationship between golfers transforms from antagonism to friendship, culminating as the boys convince her to leave the contents of her backpack, the ashes of her father, in the course's sand traps. In these macabre and poignant stories, "Brooks challenges readers with an assortment of themes, including loyalty, acceptance, friendship, and defiance of stereotypes," said Tim Rausch in *School Library Journal.* Despite the serious nature of death as the central theme, a *Publishers Weekly* critic called these tales "surprisingly life-affirming as they reveal the many faces of grief," joining three mood pieces "to create a unified requiem."

In a brisk change of pace for Brooks, *Throwing Smoke* is a lighthearted fantasy that exalts the value of playing sports for fun before glory. Whiz is the pitcher and co-captain of a baseball team with more love of the game and each other than sports talent. In what a *Horn Book* reviewer called a "delectably unnerving fantasy element," Whiz introduces magic into "this cerebral sports novel," by creating baseball cards first for his teammates and then for his "dream" players—players who magically come to life on the baseball field. Not all critics were immediately taken with this book. A *Publishers Weekly* reviewer described the characterization as "sketchy" and lacking dynamics, pointing out that "the immediacy and involvement . . . conveyed so compellingly in Brooks's 'Wolfbay Wings' series goes missing here." Shelle Rosenfeld of *Booklist* had a more positive opinion, saying that "readers will be drawn by the witty, edgy prose, great dialogue, dimensional, diverse characters, and abundant baseball lingo."

Upon first glance, *Dolores: Seven Stories about Her* might be considered similar to *What Hearts* in that both are short stories about a child growing up through adversity. Yet, the similarities end here. In the first story, seven-year-old Dolores is abducted, then rescued by her brother. In the last story, sixteen-year-old Dolores is again abducted, then rescued by her own actions. In the five stories in between, Brooks presents the free-spirited Dolores through the dynamic interactions of her family, her peers, her enemies, and her friends. A *Kirkus Reviews* critic described Dolores as "articulate and opinionated . . . a winning heroine, gifted with a fierce intelligence, combative personality, and an unconventional turn of mind." A *Kirkus Reviews* writer felt that Dolores as a character may be too good to be true, saying, "a fetching and fascinating creation . . . she doesn't seem to be quite of this earth." However, the same reviewer concluded that despite any perceived negatives, "Brooks wows the reader with his finely honed craft, piercing dry wit, and clever turn of phrase."

Ably demonstrating his versatility as a writer of fiction, Brooks created the "Wolfbay Wings" series of hockey books and the picture book *Each a Piece,* two vastly dissimilar endeavors yet equally thoughtful literature for young adults. Each book in the "Wolfbay Wings" series focuses on a different member of the team, beginning with Dixon "Woodsie" Woods as he begins his rookie year with the team. Typical of Brooks, the series comes full circle with the twelfth and final book revisiting Woodsie and the team two seasons later. A *Kirkus* reviewer called the series "thoughtful though action-oriented" and noted that the "intelligence that informs the book is every bit as sharp as the action."

Brooks's first picture book received mixed reviews. *Each a Piece,* according to a reviewer for the *Encyclopedia of Children's Literature,* was "admired for its memorable characters and stimulating scenes." However, a *Publishers Weekly* reviewer criticized it for its "disjointed text which is overwhelmed by . . . nostalgic collages of Victorian illustrations." A *Publishers Weekly* reviewer concluded that the book may appeal to "collectors of Victoriana, but for others, it will be a conundrum."

With each of his literary endeavors Brooks has shown his versatility. The opportunity for variety pleases the author, who concluded in *AAYA:* "One of the nice things about being a writer is also the biggest challenge about being a writer: you're always going to be a beginner as soon as you finish something. You wrap up one book and immediately you are a rookie again because you've never written your next book. You start all over and you're fresh and you're challenged and you're green, and you don't yet know how to solve all the problems that are going to come up. You're going to have to gain wisdom and technique as you write, so that you can take care of these new challenges."

BIOGRAPHICAL AND CRITICAL SOURCES:

BOOKS

Authors and Artists for Young Adults, Volume 8, Thomson Gale (Detroit, MI), 1992, pp. 17-24.
Beetz, Kirk H., editor, *Beacham's Guide to Literature for Young Adults,* Volume 9, Thomson Gale (Detroit, MI), 1999, pp. 4444-4451.

Cullinan, Bernice E., and Diane G. Person, editors, *Continuum Encyclopedia of Children's Literature,* Continuum (New York, NY), 2001, pp. 115-117.

Drew, Bernard A., editor, *The 100 Most Popular Young-Adult Authors: Biographical Sketches and Bibliographies,* Libraries Unlimited (Englewood, CO), 1996, pp. 62-64.

Gallo, Donald R., editor, *Speaking for Ourselves,* National Council of Teachers of English (Urbana, IL), 1988, pp. 33-35.

Helbig, Alethea, and Agnes Regan Perkins, cditors, in *Dictionary of American Children's Fiction, 1985-1989,* Greenwood Press (Westport, CT), 1993, p. 35.

Pendergast, Tom, and Sara Pendergast, editors, *St. James Guide to Young Adult Writers,* St. James Press (Detroit, MI), 1988, pp. 102-104.

Senick, Gerard J., editor, *Children's Literature Review,* Volume 25, Thomson Gale (Detroit, MI), 1991, pp. 16-26.

Silvey, Anita, editor, *Children's Books and Their Creators,* Houghton Mifflin (Boston, MA), 1995, p. 95.

PERIODICALS

ALAN Review, fall, 1988, "The Difference between Reading and Reading," p. 1.

Appraisal, summer, 1992, review of *Nature by Design,* p. 71; summer, 1992, review of *Predator!,* p. 71.

Booklist, October 15, 1990, Carolyn Phelan, review of *Everywhere,* p. 441; January 1, 1992, Chris Sherman, review of *Predator!* and *Nature by Design,* p. 82; March 15, 1992, review of *Predator!,* p. 1362; September 1, 1992, Hazel Rochman, review of *What Hearts,* p. 53; March 15, 1993, review of *What Hearts,* p. 1334; July 1, 1993, review of *The Moves Make the Man,* p. 1864; October 1, 1993, review of *The Moves Make the Man,* p. 334; December 1, 1993, Carolyn Phelan, review of *Making Sense: Animal Perception and Communication,* p. 687; December 1, 1993, Hazel Rochman, review of *Boys Will Be,* p. 697; April 15, 1994, Bill Ott, review of *Those Who Love the Game: Glenn "Doc" Rivers on Life in the NBA and Elsewhere,* p. 1524; October 15, 1994, review of *The Moves Make the Man,* p. 413; February 1, 1985, Denise M. Wilms, review of *The Moves Make the Man,* p. 782-783; June 1, 1996, Michael Cart, review of *Asylum for Night-face,* p. 1696; March 1, 1997, Carolyn Phelan, review of *NBA by the Numbers,* p. 1168; May 15, 1997, A. James, audio book review of *The Moves Make the Man,* p. 1595; January 1, 1998, Lauren Peterson, review of *Zip,* p. 809; January 1, 1998, Lauren Peterson, review of *Woodsie,* p. 809; April 15, 1998, review of *Everywhere,* p. 1445; June 1, 1998, review of *Asylum for Nightface,* p. 1696; August, 1998, Hazel Rochman, review of *The Red Wasteland: A Personal Selection of Writings about Nature for Young Readers,* p. 1987; September 15, 1998, Sally Estes and Hazel Rochman, review of *No Kidding,* p. 219; May 15, 1999, GraceAnne A. DeCandido, review of *Vanishing,* p. 1696; May, 2000, Shelle Rosenfeld, review of *Throwing Smoke,* p. 1743; May, 2001, Debbie Carton, review of *All That Remains,* p. 1682; July, 2001, Jennifer Hubert and Patrick Jones, review of *Boys Will Be,* p. 1998; September 1, 2001, Jean Hatfield, review of *Vanishing,* p. 128; May 15, 2002, Ilene Cooper, review of *Dolores: Seven Stories about Her,* p. 1590.

Book Report, May-June, 1994, Clyde Hofflund, review of *Boys Will Be,* p. 59; September-October, 1996, William McLoughlin, review of *Asylum for Nightface,* p. 36; January-February, 1999, Corine H. Smith, review of *The Red Wasteland,* p. 70.

Bulletin of the Center for Children's Books, January, 1992, review of *Nature by Design,* p. 119; January, 1992, review of *Predator!,* p. 119; December, 1992, review of *What Hearts,* p. 106; December, 1993, review of *Boys Will Be,* p. 116; January, 1994, Roger Sutton, review of *Making Sense,* pp. 148-149; June, 1996, Deborah Stevenson, review of *Asylum for Nightface,* p. 328; November, 1998, review of *Each a Piece,* p. 90; May, 1999, review of *Vanishing,* p. 309; June, 2001, review of *All That Remains,* p. 367.

Canadian Materials, October 31, 1997, Dave Jenkinson, review of *NBA by the Numbers.*

Children's Book Review Service, February, 1992, review of *Nature by Design,* p. 79; November, 1993, review of *Boys Will Be,* p. 33; July, 1996, review of *Asylum for Nightface,* p. 154; December, 1998, review of *A Piece of Each,* p. 37; spring, 1999, review of *Vanishing,* p. 141.

Children's Bookwatch, January, 1992, review of "Knowing Nature" Series, p. 4; January, 1992, review of *Nature by Design,* p. 4; January, 1992, review of *Predator!,* p. 4; March, 1993, review of *What Hearts,* p. 4; September, 1999, review of *Vanishing,* p. 4.

Children's Literature Association Quarterly, winter, 1994, review of *Nature by Design,* p. 148.

Children's Literature in Education, June, 1992, review of *Midnight Hour Encores,* p. 101.

Emergency Librarian, May, 1993, review of *What Hearts,* p. 52; May, 1996, review of *Asylum for Nightface,* p. 43.

Horn Book, March-April, 1987, Christine McDonnell, "New Voices, New Visions: Bruce Brooks" (interview), pp. 188-190; July, 1989, Elizabeth S., Watson, review of *No Kidding,* p. 486; January, 1991, Nancy Vasilakis, review of *Everywhere,* pp. 72-73; January, 1992, review of *Nature by Design,* p. 96; January, 1992, review of *Predator!,* p. 96; January-February, 1993, Nancy Vasilakis, review of *What Hearts,* p. 89; January-February, 1994, Peter D. Sieruta, review of *Boys Will Be,* p. 86; November, 1995, review of *The Moves Make the Man,* p. 777; July-August, 1996, Patsy Campbell, review of *Asylum for Nightface,* p. 492; September-October, 1996, Maria B. Salvadore, review of *Asylum for Nightface,* p. 601; May-June, 1998, C. Heppermann, "Bruce Brooks on Ice"; May, 1999, review of *Vanishing,* p. 327; May, 2000, C.M.H., review of *Throwing Smoke,* p. 308; May, 2001, Kristi Beavin, audiobook review of *Vanishing,* p. 358; July, 2001 review of *All That Remains,* p. 447.

Hungry Mind Review, fall, 1996, review of *Asylum for Nightface,* p. 36; fall, 1998, review of *The Red Wasteland,* p. 33.

Journal of Adolescent and Adult Literacy, December, 1996, review of *The Moves Make the Man,* p. 318; September, 1999, review of *Billy,* p. 92; September, 1999, review of *Cody,* p. 92; September, 1999, review of *Shark,* p. 92; September, 1999, review of *Zip,* p. 92; September, 1999, review of *Woodsie,* p. 92.

Journal of Reading, November, 1993, review of *Predator!,* p. 225; May, 1994, review of *Boys Will Be,* p. 704.

Kirkus Reviews, October 15, 1992, review of *What Hearts,* p. 1307; October 1, 1993, review of *Boys Will Be,* p. 1270; October 1, 1993, review of *Shark,* p. 1270; November 15, 1993, review of *Making Sense,* p. 1458; May 1, 1996, review of *Asylum for Nightface,* p. 685; October 1, 1997, review of *Woodsie,* p. 1270; April 1, 1998, review of *Shark,* p. 493; April 1, 1998, review of *Each a Piece,* p. 1381; June 1, 1998, review of *The Red Wasteland,* p. 808; September 15, 1998, review of *Each a Piece,* p. 1381; May 1, 1999, review of

Vanishing, p. 119; June 1, 1999, review of *Vanishing;* April 1, 2001, review of *All That Remains,* p. 495; March 1, 2002, review of *Dolores,* p. 329.

Kliatt, March, 1995, review of *What Hearts,* p. 4; September, 1996, review of *Asylum for Nightface,* p. 72; January, 1998, audiobook review of *What Hearts,* p. 46; June 20, 1999, review of *Vanishing,* p. 20; July, 1999, review of *Vanishing,* p. 6; May, 2001, review of *All That Remains,* p. 8.

Language Arts, November, 1992, review of *Nature by Design,* p. 516; January, 1993, review of *The Moves Make the Man,* p. 64; October, 1994, review of *Making Sense,* p. 454.

Library Talk, May, 1992, review of *Nature by Design,* p. 44; May, 1992, review of *Predator!,* p. 44; September, 1994, review of *Making Sense,* p. 54.

Los Angeles Times Book Review, February 13, 1994, review of *Boys Will Be,* p. 12; September 12, 1999, review of *Vanishing,* p. 4.

New Advocate, winter, 1993, review of *What Hearts,* p. 84; spring, 1992, "The Creative Process: Imagination, the Source of Reading," pp. 79-85.

New York Times Book Review, November 11, 1984, Mel Watkins, "A Trickster and His Upright Friends," p. 54; April 6, 1986, "Playing Fields of Fiction," p. 20; January 4, 1987, p. 33; June 25, 1989, p. 30; September 8, 1991, p. 40; November 8, 1992, review of *What Hearts,* p. 40; November 9, 1992; June 20, 1999, review of *Vanishing,* p. 20; July 15, 2001, review of *All That Remains,* p. 24.

Publishers Weekly, July 29, 1990, Marcus Leonard, "Interview with Brooks," pp. 214-215; November 16, 1992, review of *What Hearts,* p. 65; September 27, 1993, review of *Boys Will Be,* p. 65; February 20, 1995, review of *What Hearts,* p. 207; May 1, 1995, review of *Boys Will Be,* p. 60; June, 1996, review of *Asylum for Nightface,* p. 84; September 1, 1997, review of *Woodsie,* p. 105; July 6, 1998, review of *The Red Wasteland,* p. 27; October 26, 1998, review of *Each a Piece,* p. 64; April 19, 1999, review of *Vanishing,* p. 74; November 1, 1999, review of *Asylum for Nightface,* p. 86; February 14, 2000, Leonard S. Marcus, interview with Brooks, p. 98; July 3, 2000, review of *Throwing Smoke,* p. 72; April 16, 2001, review of *All That Remains,* p. 66; February 18, 2002, review of *Dolores,* p. 97; November 18, 2002, Gerry Larson, review of *Dolores,* p. 142.

Reading Teacher, May, 1993, review of *What Hearts,* p. 695; November, 1993, review of *What Hearts,* p. 238.

San Francisco Review of Books, September, 1995, review of *Boys Will Be,* p. 47; September, 1995, review of *Midnight Hour Encores,* p. 47.

School Library Journal, December, 1984, Robert E. Unsworth, review of *The Moves Make the Man*, p. 103; February, 1992, Amy Nunley, review of *Predator!*, p. 112; February, 1992, Amy Nunley, review of *Nature by Design*, p. 112; July, 1992, review of *The Moves Make the Man*, p. 30; November, 1992, Jacqueline Rose, review of *What Hearts*, p. 116; December, 1993, Tom S. Hurlburt, review of *Boys Will Be*, p. 142; January, 1994, Cynthia M. Sturgis, review of *Making Sense*, p. 118; April, 1994, Tom S. Hurlburt, review of *Those Who Love the Game*, p. 164; June, 1996, Luann Toth, review of *Asylum for Nightface*, p. 150; December, 1997, Jana R. Fine, review of *Zip*, p. 123; December, 1997, Jana R. Fine, review of *Woodsie*, p. 123; December, 1997, Jana R. Fine, review of *Cody*, p. 123; November, 1997, audio book review of *What Hearts*, p. 70; March, 1998, Blair Christolon, review of *Boot*, p. 208; June, 1998, Blair Christolon, review of *Shark*, p. 143; June, 1998, Michele Snyder, review of *The Red Wasteland*, p. 143; June, 1998, Blair Christolon, review of *Prince*, p. 140; July, 1998, Barb Lawler, review of *Billy*, p. 92; September, 1998, review of *Everywhere*, p. 120; October, 1998, Pam Gosner, review of *Each a Piece*, p. 87; February, 1999, Todd Morning, review of *Reed*, p. 104; February, 1999, Todd Morning, review of *Dooby*, p. 104; June, 1999, Lauralyn Persson, review of *Vanishing*, p. 126; June, 2000, Todd Morning, review of *Throwing Smoke*, p. 142; September, 2000, Marcus Loenards, "Song of Myself" (interview), p. 50; March, 2001, Nicole A. Cooke, audio book review of *Vanishing*, p. 88; May 2001, Tim Rausch, review of *All That Remains*, p. 148; April, 2002, review of *All That Remains*, p. 63.

Science Books and Films, January, 1992, review of *Nature by Design*, p. 17; March, 1992, review of *Predator!*, p. 44.

Tribune Books (Chicago, IL), August 12, 1990, p. 5.

Village Voice, June 21, 1990, "Pulling Proof," pp. S22-S25.

Village Voice Literary Supplement, February, 1994, review of *Boys Will Be*, p. 26.

Voice of Youth Advocates, February, 1983, Allan A. Cuseo, review of *The Moves Make the Man*, p. 322; June, 1993, review of *What Hearts*, p. 86; February, 1994, review of *Boys Will Be*, p. 390; October, 1996, review of *Asylum for Nightface*, p. 206; June, 1998, review of *Asylum for Nightface*, p. 103; August, 1998, review of *The Red Wasteland*, p. 226; June, 2001, review of *All That Remains*, p. 119.

Washington Post Book World, November 9, 1986, Katherine Paterson, "Heart Strings and Other Attachments," p. 17; November 14, 1993, review of *Boys Will Be*, p. 8; November 14, 1993, review of *Making Sense*, p. 8.

Wilson Library Bulletin, June, 1993, Frances Bradburn, review of *What Hearts*, p. 102; February, 1994, Frances Bradburn, review of *Making Sense*, p. 89; June, 1986, Linda Perkins, review of *Those Who Love the Game*, p. 42.*

* * *

BROSSARD, Nicole 1943-

PERSONAL: Born November 27, 1943, in Montréal, Québec, Canada; daughter of Guillaume (an accountant) and Marguerite (a homemaker; maiden name, Matte) Brossard; married Robert Soubliere, 1966 (divorced); children; Julie-Capucine Brossard-Soubliere. *Education:* Attended College Marguerite Bourgeoys, 1955-60; Universite de Montréal, B.A., 1965, Licencie en lettres, 1968, Scolarite de maitrise en lettres, 1972; Universite du Québec a Montréal, B.A. (education), 1971. *Politics:* Radical feminist.

ADDRESSES: Home and office—34 avenue Robert, Outremont, Québec H3S 2P2, Canada.

CAREER: Poet and novelist. *La Barre du jour* (literary magazine), Montréal, Québec, Canada, cofounder and codirector, 1965-75; *Les Tetes de pioche* (feminist editorial collective), Montréal, cofounder, 1976-79; *La Nouvelle Barre du jour* (magazine), Montréal, cofounder, coeditor, and codirector, 1977-79; Integrale (publishing house), Montréal, founder and director, 1982—. Teacher in Montréal, 1969-70, 1971-72; Queen's University at Kingston, visiting professor of French, 1982-84; Princeton University, short-term fellow, 1991. *Some American Feminists* (film), codirector and co-researcher, 1976. Pavillon de la jeunesse, Expo '67, organizer of jazz and poetry events; co-organizer of "Celebrations" (event about women's texts); "Recontre Québecoise internationale des ecrivains," member of organization committee. Participant in colloquiums, conferences, and meetings on Québecois and feminist literary topics. Member, Conseil des Arts de la Communaute urbaine de Montréal.

Nicole Brossard

MEMBER: Québec Writers Union (member of board of directors, 1977-79; vice president, 1983-85).

AWARDS, HONORS: Governor-General's Award for poetry, Canada Council, 1974, for *Mécanique jongleuse,* and 1984, for *Double Impression;* Grand Prize for poetry, Forges Foundation, 1989, for *A tout regard* and *Installations;* Athanase-David prize, 1991; Harbourfront Festival Prize, 1991.

WRITINGS:

POETRY

Aube a la saison (title means "Dawning Season"), published in *Trois,* A.G.E.U.M., 1965.

Mordre en sa chair (title means "Bite the Flesh"), Esterel (Montréal, Québec, Canada), 1966.

L'écho bouge beau (title means "The Echo Moves Beautifully"), Esterel (Montréal, Québec, Canada), 1968.

Suite logique (title means "Logical Suite/Sequence"), Hexagone (Montréal, Québec, Canada), 1970.

Le centre blanc, Orphee (Montréal, Québec, Canada), 1970.

Mécanique jongleuse, Generation (Paris, France), 1973, published as *Mécanique jongleuse; Masculin grammaticale,* Hexagone (Montréal, Québec, Canada), 1974, translation by Larry Shouldice published as *Daydream Mechanics,* Coach House Press (Toronto, Ontario, Canada), 1980.

La partie pour le tout, Aurore (Montréal, Québec, Canada), 1975.

Le Centre blanc (collected poems; includes "Le centre blanc"), Hexagone (Montréal, Québec, Canada) 1978.

D'Arcs de cycle la derive, etchings by Francine Simonin, Maison (St.-Jacques-le-Mineur, Québec, Canada), 1979.

Amantes, Quinze (Montréal, Québec, Canada), 1980, translation by Barbara Godard published as *Lovhers,* Guernica Editions (Montréal, Québec, Canada), 1986.

Double Impression: Poèmes et textes 1967-1984 (collected poems), Hexagone (Montréal, Québec, Canada) 1985.

L'aviva, NBJ (Montréal, Québec, Canada), 1985.

(With Daphne Marlatt), *Mauve,* NBJ (Montréal, Québec, Canada), 1985.

Domaine d'écriture, NBJ (Montréal, Québec, Québec, Canada) 1985.

(With Daphne Marlatt) *Character/Jeu de lettres,* NBJ (Montréal, Québec, Canada) 1986.

Sous la langue/Under the Tongue, translation by Susanne de Lotbimier-Harwood, Essentielle (Montréal, Québec, Canada), 1987.

(With Daphne Marlatt) *A tout regard,* BQ (Montréal, Québec, Canada) 1989.

Installations: avec et sans pronoms, Forges (Trois-Rivières, Québec, Canada), 1989, translated by Erin Moure and Robert Majzels, 2000.

Langues obscures: poésie, Hexagone (Montréal, Québec, Canada), 1992.

Typhon dru, Generation (Paris, France), c. 1990.

Langues Obscures, Hexagone (Montréal, Québec, Canada), 1992.

Baroque at Dawn, McClellan & Stewart (Toronto, Ontario, Canada), 1997.

Vertige de l'avant-scène, Forges/L'Orange bleue, (Trois-Rivières, Québec, Canada), 1997.

She Would be the First Sentence of My Next Novel, translated by Susanne de Lotbiniére-Harwood, Mercury Press (Toronto, Ontario, Canada), 1998.

Amantes; suivi de, Le sens apparent; et de, Sous la langue, Hexagone (Montréal, Québec, Canada), 1998.

Musée de l'os et de l'eau, Cadex Editions, Saint-Hippolyte (Québec, Canada), 1999.

Au présent des veines, Forges (Trois-Rivières, Québec, Canada), 1999.

PROSE

Un livre, Éditions du Jour (Montréal, Québec, Canada), 1970, translation by Larry Shouldice published as *A Book,* Coach House Press (Toronto, Ontario, Canada), 1976.

Sold-out: étreinte/illustration (novel), Jour (Montréal, Québec, Canada), 1973, translation by Patricia Claxton published as *Turn of a Pang,* Coach House Press (Toronto, Ontario, Canada), 1976.

French Kiss: étreinte/exploration (novel), Jour (Montréal, Québec, Canada), 1974, translation by Patricia Claxton published as *French Kiss; or, A Pang's Progress,* Coach House Press (Toronto, Ontario, Canada), 1986.

L'Amèr ou, Le chapitre effrité: fiction theorique, Quinze (Montréal, Québec, Canada), 1977, revised edition, Hexagone (Montréal, Québec, Canada), 1988, translation by Barbara Godard published as *These Our Mothers; or, The Disintegrating Chapter,* Coach House Press (Toronto, Ontario, Canada), 1983.

Journal intime, ou voilà donc un manuscrit (novel), Les herbes rouges (Montréal, Québec, Canada), 1984.

Le Sens apparent, Flammarion (Paris, France), 1980, translation published as *Surfaces of Sense,* Coach House Press (Toronto, Ontario, Canada), 1989.

Picture Theory (fiction), Nouvelle Optique (Montréal, Québec, Canada), 1982, translated by Barbara Godard, Roof (New York, NY), Guernica (Montréal, Canada), 1991.

La Lettre aérienne (essays), Editions Remue-Menage, 1985, translation by Marlene Wilderman published as *The Aerial Letter,* Women's Press (Toronto, Ontario, Canada), 1988.

Le désert mauve, Hexagone (Montréal, Québec, Canada), 1987, published as *Mauve Desert,* Coach House Press (Toronto, Ontario, Canada), 1990.

La nuit verte du parc labyrinthe, Trois Rivieres (Laval, Québec, Canada), 1992, translation by Lou Nelson and Marina Fe published as *Green Night of Labyrinth Park.*

Hier: Roman, Québec Amerique (Montréal, Québec, Canada), 2001.

OTHER

Narrateur et personnages (play), first aired by Radio Canada, 1971.

L'Ecrivain (monologue; produced in Montréal, 1976), published in *La nef des sorcières,* Quinze, 1976, translation by Linda Gaborian published as *The Writer* in *A Clash of Symbols,* Coach House Press (Toronto, Ontario, Canada), 1979.

Une Impression de fiction dans le retroviseur, first aired by Radio Canada, 1978

(Editor) *The Story so Far: Les strategiés du réel* (anthology), Coach House Press (Toronto, Ontario, Canada), 1979.

Journal intimes; ou, voilà donc un manuscrit (radio play based on her book), first aired by Radio Canada, 1983.

La falaise, first aired by Radio Canada, 1985.

(Contributor) *Emergence d'une culture au feminin,* Editions Saint-Martin (Montréal, Québec, Canada), 1987.

(Editor, with Lisette Girouard) *Anthologie de la poésie des femmes au Québec,* Remue-Menage (Montréal, Québec, Canada), 1991.

Also author of *Baroque d'aube.* Work represented in anthologies, including *La poésie contemporaine de langue française,* St.-Germain-des-Pres, 1973; *Québec mai francia kolteszete,* Europa, 1978; *The Poets of Canada,* Hurtig Publishers, 1978; *Antologia de la poesia francesa actual, 1960-1976,* Editora nacional, 1979; *Anthologie '80,* Editions le Castor astral, 1981; *La poésie Québecoise: des origines a nos jours,* Editions Ripostes, 1981; *Poesia des Québec,* Editions Ripostes, 1985; *Sp/elles,* Black Moss Press, 1986; and *Poésie du monde francophone,* Le castor astral/Le Monde, 1986; *Deep Down,* 1988; and *Cradle and All,* 1989. Contributor to periodicals, including *Opus International, Etudes Françaises, La Nouvelle Barre du Jour, Liberte, Possibles, Protee, Cross Country, Contemporary Literature, Exile, Room of One's Own, Journal of Canadian Fiction, Essays on Canadian Writing, Fireweed, Prism International, Island Ethos, Resources for Feminist Research, Cistre, Journal des Poètes, Masques, Actuels, Action Poetique, Fem, Lisaon, Les Herbes Rouges, Trois, La Vie en Rose, Dalhousie French Studies, Tessera, How(ever), Writing, Between C and D, Notus, Estuaire, Die Horen Vlasta, Oracl, Jungle, Chemin de Ronde, Les Cahiers Bleus,* and *Trivia.* Also associated with *Reelles,* Quinze, 1980.

Work has been translated into English, German, Italian, and Spanish.

Brossard's papers are housed in The Library and Archives of Canada.

SIDELIGHTS: Nicole Brossard, famous in the arena of contemporary Québecois literature and internationally acclaimed as a leader in feminist theory, was recognized for the totality of her work in 1991 when she received Québec's Athanase-David prize. Brossard's writing is described as having "developed in the margins—in the avant-garde—as a critique of received practices and of the text as commodity," according to a reviewer for *Feminist Writer.* Brossard's work is commonly categorized in three distinct phases or periods. In the 1960s, her poetry was strongly influenced by surrealism. She used her writings to explore "sexuality as a mode of consciousness in an associative flux of images with surprising juxtapositions."

Brossard's first volume of poetry, *Aube a la saison,* which means "Dawning Season," was published when she was twenty-two years old. This early work, along with Brossard's second book of poems, *Mordre en sa chair* ("Bite the Flesh"), followed in the path of the 1950s and 1960s Québecois tradition of *appartenance.* Taken from the French word *appartenance,* meaning "to belong to," *appartenance* was adopted as a literary term referring to mapping out spatial territory; Québecois writers believed that by describing their land's physical features they could define its essence. While Brossard's work in her first two volumes has been compared to that of poets Paul-Marie Lapointe, Gaston Miron, Fernand Ouellette, and Paul Chamberland, Brossard's "appartenance" is different. As Caroline Bayard observed in *Essays of Canadian Writing* about *Mordre en sa chair,* "What she sets out to map in 1966 is not Québec's territory but the human body. . . . History or time takes on physiological features, it is made flesh, given corporeal pleasure, pain, veins, blood, hair and muscles." And Barbara Godard remarked in *Contemporary World Writers* that Brossard's focus on the female body "attempted to undermine the symbolic Woman to examine women's desires."

Unlike *Aube a la saison,* which adheres to conventional linguistic forms, *Mordre en sa chair* is more experimental. Beginning with *Mordre en sa chair* and

increasing with each following set of poems, Brossard deviates from traditional syntax and semantics, challenging readers through experimentation with punctuation, spacing, and typography. Her work between 1966 and 1975 was shaped by a literary view which condemns the idea of poetry or prose as a reflection of objective reality. Important from this critical perspective are, in Bayard's words, "the linguistic tensions among [the literary text's] visual, graphic, and sonic elements, and the way these are resolved." In Brossard's native Québec, this way of looking at literature led to writing as a form of subversion. Confusing syntax and grammar became a way of overthrowing traditional logic, which seemed analogous to the desire of the Québec separatists of the 1960s to rid themselves of English-speaking Canadian rule. Of Brossard's *Daydream Mechanics* and *La Partie pour le tout,* Bayard remarked, Brossard "stylistically remains on the offensive. Syntax, grammar, layout, punctuation, spelling, omissions, all concur, to different degrees, to upset the rules and give us a provocative text, lashed by blanks and typographical variations, ambiguous hyphens, brackets and parentheses."

Brossard uses similar techniques in her novels *A Book, The Turn of a Pang,* and *French Kiss; or, A Pang's Progress. French Kiss* is set in Montréal, but its landscape is not intended to reflect reality. This novel marked the beginning of the second phase of Brossard's career during which time she continued to write poetry, but turned her primary focus toward experimentation with the structure of novel writing. *French Kiss* focuses on the experiences of Marielle, and also includes her brother Alexandre, his friend Georges, and two women named Lucy and Camomille. Brossard is more concerned with detailing the physical qualities of these characters—their movements, their smells, their textures—than with exploring their inner psychologies. In Bayard's words, "The novel's focus is upon objects, sensations, and the way they hit the eye or start chain reactions of varying orders and intensities in all five senses."

Beginning in the mid-1970s, Brossard's poetry collections and novels became concerned with making strong feminist and lesbian statements. *These Our Mothers* stemmed from Brossard's realization that patriarchal society had stifled women's voices and that she needed to break this imposed silence by giving voice to women's previously censored desires. If examined casually, this need to speak from a lesbian-feminist viewpoint might seem contradictory to the literary perspective she embraced earlier, which devalued the meaning of a text in favor of its stylistic features, leaving little room for social statements. Brossard resolves the apparent conflict with the argument that traditional syntax and punctuation were established by a patriarchal society. In this way, her continued subversion of textual expectation is also a subversion of male dominance. As Barbara Godard explained in *Profiles in Canadian Literature 6,* "Women's writing, according to Brossard, must inevitably be fiction and Utopia, visionary, posturing, feigning. By remaining self-conscious, and [using] deliberate artifice, it avoids the trap of naturalization, of pretending to be reality, that has made traditional writing a weapon for the subjugation of women and reality." Thus Brossard explores feminist ideas with elusive syntax and meaning in *These Our Mothers:* "The figure is real like a political intent to subject her to the plural before our eyes, or, singularly to power. The realistic figure is thus the most submissive there is. Quite simply, she agrees. She can be reduced then to the general (to the house) by using the singular: woman or image of milk women, 'lait figures'," observed Godard.

Godard also noted in *Contemporary World Writers* that during the 1970s Brossard "entered a formalist phase stimulated by French post-structuralism, especially the work of Roland Barthes which, following Ferdinand de Saussure, stressed the non-referentiality of signs (words) articulated as a system of differences. Brossard realized that words could never capture the private life of her body: they could however, combine in an infinite number of ways to create multiple networks."

Brossard's involvement with literary and feminist magazines, such as *La Barre du jour* and *Les Tetes de pioche,* both of which she cofounded, provided a forum for discussing the theory behind her experimental writing. Between 1968 and 1970 Brossard published articles in *La Barre du jour* and *La Presse* about the meaning expressed by her writing style. As her writing career entered its third phase, Brossard's focus and primary interest moved in the direction of feminism, she helped establish the feminist newspaper *Les Tetes de pioche* and introduced feminist viewpoints into *La Barre du jour.*

Working, as always, through her writing and the strong experimental voice it provides her, Brossard pursues a call to "make the difference" in the arena of poetics, politics, and sexuality. Like other Québecois writers of the 1970s and 1980s, Brossard, especially in *Amantes* and *Le Sens apparent,* often associates the writing and/or reading process with sexuality. She differs from many of her peers, however, by adding a lesbian, feminist perspective to the sexual imagery that she weaves into her textual stylistics. Speaking of this practice, Bayard suggested, "There is a complicity, but also an ironic sense of defiance, between the two movements, as if they were almost bent on similar ends and yet wanted to destroy each other at the same time. . . . Stylistic figures and sexual movements occasionally—but only occasionally—become one." Godard noted in *Contemporary World Writers* that the third phase of Brossard's career is concerned with taking "up [the] call to 'make the difference' and [in it she] develops a poetics and politics of sexual difference. Influenced by French feminist philosophers such as Luce Irigaray and Hélène Cixous, Brossard developed a mode of writing she calls 'fiction/theory,' fiction as a hypothesis forming potential worlds."

This third phase, and its focus on the connection between sexuality and textuality, is reflected in *Amantes* (translated and published in English as *Lovhers*), "a set of love poems written for another woman . . . richly erotic in language and theme," according to Louise H. Forsyth's review in *Canadian Literature.* Forsyth noted that in the book, the two lovers "have been brought into the world by their love, their awareness, their language and the exchange of their experience. The result is dazzling, with the poet's voice stating in the end that her 'body is enraptured.'"

According to Forsyth, *Picture Theory* "picked up in narrative form major images and expressions from *Amantes.*" Eileen Manion called the book "a relentlessly postmodern text" that departs from two classics of modernist literature: Djuna Barnes's *Nightwood* and James Joyce's *Ulysses.* Godard called it Brossard's "major work to date. . . . [a] book of light" which "rewrites the great modernist books of the night, especially the works of James Joyce." While a *Publishers Weekly* review found the language of the book "flat and dull, and Brossard's interpretation of the relationship between language and desire . . . narcissistic," Manion found that the female characters of the book "always interact intensely, exuberantly, ecstatically." Using the metaphor of the hologram, Brossard is able, for Manion, to "develop a new way of seeing, in order to explore a new way of being." *Picture Theory* is considered to be "Brossard's major work to date," according to a reviewer for *Feminist Writers.* Brossard reworks major motifs from her previous works, the reviewer added, "in a complex theoretical fiction based on Wittgenstein's statement that a 'proposition is a picture of reality'[;] a superimposition of Monique Wittig's Amazonian island on anecdotes of the family. . . ." Brossard draws upon science and a "mathematics of the imaginary" to create a model for text as a process of transformation, a concept central to her sense of aesthetic reality.

Surfaces of Sense further explores the French feminist philosophy of writing the body and the intersection of theory and fiction, as, in the words of Charlene Diehl-Jones's review for *Books in Canada,* Brossard's work "finger[s] the surfaces of experience" and continues her experimentation with language, syntax, and narrative. *Mauve Desert,* however, is probably Brossard's most popular work, according to Godard. While a *Publishers Weekly* reviewer believed that the book "functions well as a literary game," but is ultimately unable "to support the meta-literature" it aspires to, Godard noted that it is probably "her most accessible" work.

Mauve Desert is set in the Arizona desert and is structured in three parts: a journal written by a young girl, the story of another girl's (Laure Angstell) finding, reading, and gradually becoming enthralled with the journal, and Laure's translation of the journal, with minor changes. Elizabeth Anthony, writing for *Books in Canada,* did find that the "philosophical abstractions" did sometimes "dematerialize the real," but concluded that the volume "glitters as one of these rarefied reals, condensed from the genetics of language recoded."

Forsyth compared *Mauve Desert* with *Amantes/ Lovhers:* "Brossard writes with the assumption that both the both the personal and the poetic are political. *Lovhers* and *Le désert mauve.* . . . both . . . contain characters who write, read and appreciate the texts of others: words have unlimited power to move the imagination." In other words, for Brossard, as Forsyth claimed, "Love known is love expressed. The taste of lips is inseparable from the taste of words, however hard the right ones are to find."

Installations also reflects Brossard's major preoccupations with writing, feminism, sexuality, and subjectivity. Neil B. Bishop called it "excellent

Brossard," "a joy," adding that "Feminism goes hand in hand with linguistic transgression" in one of the book's poems, "Chapitre." But what he found "most interesting is the tone of euphoric contemplation . . . with which these themes are treated."

Green Night of Labyrinth Park is a prose poem which, according to Charlene Diehl-Jones in another review for *Books in Canada,* "tracks real and imagined landscapes." Like many of Brossard's other works, it is in part, wrote Diehl-Jones, concerned with the "politics of subjectivity and representation" and has moments of "great loveliness."

Brossard's book *Hier: Roman* weaves in and out of character. Beginning as a novel, it tells the story of four women. As in much of Brossard's work since the early 1980s, structure is as much a part of the book as characterization, plot, or thematic elements. Partway through, the book transforms into a play. The shift in form from novel to play reinforces the "notion that character is defined largely through dialogue," reported Geoff McMaster in Alberta's *Express News.* "You don't know a character unless you hear her speak," said Brossard in the McMaster interview.

Brossard once told *CA:* "I write to understand the process of writing, words, words traveling back and forth between reality and fiction. The mind is too fast for words. Fiction is a very old-fashioned word to express a holographic body spiralling into space."

This sense of movement or motion between poles is also reflected in her comments in an interview with *Books in Canada:* "In feminist writing. . . .You have to write two kinds of pages almost at the same time: one on which you try to understand and uncover the patriarchal lies; and another on which you try to give your new values, your utopias, and everything you find positive about yourself and about women. You have to write an unedited version, something that is totally new, to shape it. You bring in thoughts that have never been thought, use words in ways they have never been used. You want to bring your anger but also your utopia and your connection and solidarity with other women."

BIOGRAPHICAL AND CRITICAL SOURCES:

BOOKS

Benson, Eugene, and William Toye, editors, *The Oxford Companion to Canadian Literature,* 2nd edition, Oxford University Press (Oxford, England), 1997.

Brossard, Nicole, *These Our Mothers,* translation by Barbara Godard, Coach House Press (Toronto, Ontario, Canada), 1983.

Buck, Claire, editor, *The Bloomsbury Guide to Women's Literature,* Prentice Hall (New York, NY), 1992.

Chevalier, Tracy, editor, *Contemporary World Writers,* 2nd edition, St. James Press (Detroit, MI), 1993.

Dictionary of Literary Biography, Volume 53: *Canadian Writers since 1960, First Series,* Thomson Gale (Detroit, MI), 1986.

Dupre, Louise, *Strategies du vertige: trois poètes, Nicole Brossard, Madeleine Gagnon, France Theoret,* Editions du Remue-Ménage, 1989.

Heath, Jeffery M., *Profiles in Canadian Literature 6,* Dundurn Press (Toronto, Ontario, Canada), 1986.

Hunter, Jeffrey W., and Timothy J. White, editors, *Contemporary Literary Criticism,* Volume 115, Thomson Gale (Detroit, MI), 1999.

Jay, Karla, and Joanne Glasgow, editors, *Lesbian Texts and Contexts: Radical Revisions,* University Press (New York, NY), 1990.

Kester-Shelton, Pamela, editor, *Feminist Writers,* St. James Press (Detroit, MI), 1996.

Lewis, Paula Gilbert, editor, *Traditionalism, Nationalism, and Feminism: Women Writers of Québec,* Greenwood Press (Westport, CT), 1985.

Longspoon, Shirley Neuman, editor, *A Mazing Space: Writing Canadian Women Writing,* [Edmonton, Alberta, Canada] 1986, p. 335.

Parker, Alice A., *Liminal Visions of Nicole Brossard,* P. Lang (New York, NY), 1997.

Pendergast, Tom, and Sara Pendergast, editors, *Gay and Lesbian Literature,* Volume 2, St. James Press (Detroit, MI), 1998.

Perkins, George, Barbara Perkins, and Phillip Leininger, editors, *Benet's Reader's Encyclopedia of American Literature,* HarperCollins (New York, NY), 1991.

Robinson, Lillian S., editor, *Modern Women Writers,* St. James Press (Detroit, MI), 1996.

Royer, Jean, *Ecrivains contemporains, entretiens 2,* Hexagone (Montréal, Quebec, Canada) 1983.

Siemerling, Winfried, *Discoveries of the Other: Alterity in the Work of Leonard Cohen, Hubert Aquin, Michael Ondaatje, and Nicole Brossard,* University of Toronto Press, (Toronto, Ontario, Canada) 1994.

Wolfe, Susan J., and Julia Penelope, editors, *Sexual Practice/Textual Theory: Lesbian Cultural Criticism,* Blackwell (New York, NY), 1993.

PERIODICALS

Advocate, May 21, 1991, Sarah Schulman, "The Surprise of the New: Five Women Writers Who Are Making a Difference," p. 90.

American Book Review, May-June, 1988, Barbara Godard, "Feminism and Postmodernism," p. 8; spring, 1994, review of *Mauve Desert,* p. 6.

Belles Lettres, spring, 1994, Alice A. Parket, review of *Picture Theory* and *Mauve Desert,* p. 6.

Booklist, February 1, 1992, review of *Desert Mauve,* p. 1012.

Books in Canada, November, 1990, Elizabeth Anthony, review of *Mauve Desert,* p. 47; June-July, 1990, p. 41-2; December, 1991, p. 49; March, 1991, pp. 19-21; summer, 1993, Charlene Diehl-Jones, review of *Green Night of Labyrinth Park,* pp. 38-40; spring, 1994, review of *Mauve Desert,* p. 6.

Brechs, fall, 1973.

Broadside, June, 1981.

Canadian Book Review Annual, 1998, review of *Baroque at Dawn,* p. 174; 2000, review of *Installations,* p. 186.

Canadian Fiction, 1983, "Interview with Nicole Brossard on *Picture Theory,*" pp. 122-135.

Canadian Forum, January, 1990, Louise H. Forsyth, review of *Surfaces of Sense,* p. 26.

Canadian Journal of Fiction, numbers 25-26, 1979.

Canadian Literature, autumn, 1989; Louise H. Forsyth, review of *Lovhers* and *Le désert mauve,* pp. 190-193; summer, 1991, Kenneth W. Meadwell, review of *Le Québec en Poésie,* p. 218; spring, 1992, Aline Baehler, "Traversee du Desert," review of *A Tout Regard,* pp. 177-179; winter, 1992, Neil B. Bishop, review of *Installations,* p. 158; fall, 1993, Jane Tilley, review of *Anthologie de la poésie des femmes au Québec,* p. 166-167.

English Studies in Canada, June, 1995, review of *Un livre,* pp. 111-112; June, 1995, Barbara Godard, "Producing Visibility for Lesbians: Nicole Brossard's Quantum Poetics," pp. 125-137.

Essays on Canadian Writing, fall, 1977, Caroline Bayard, "Subversion Is the Order of the Day," pp. 17-25; spring, 1997, Kimberly Verwaayen, "Religion/Body: In? Of? And? Or? (Alter/Native): Separatism in the Politics of Nicole Brossard," pp. 1-16; spring, 2000, Lianne Moyes, "Nothing Sacred: Nicole Brossard's Baroque at Dawn at the Limits of Lesbian Feminist Discourses of Sexuality" (critical essay), p. xii.

Etudes litteraires, April, 1981, Irene Duranleau, review of *Un Livre,* pp. 111-112.

French Review, December, 1993, "L'anthologie de la poésie des femmes au Québec," p. 382; April, 1997, Andrea Moorhead, review of *Baroque d'aube,* p. 746.

Globe and Mail (Toronto, Ontario, Canada), May 2, 1976; February 24, 2001, review of *Installations,* p. D14.

Hobo-Québec, January, 1974.

Incidences, January-April, 1979, May-December, 1980.

La Nouvelle Barre du jour, November-December, 1982.

La Presse, September 28, 1974.

Le Devoir, December 19, 1970; April 14, 1973; July 13, 1974; May 7, 1975; May 23, 1975; June 21, 1975; December 15, 1978; October 30, 1982.

Les Cahiers de la femme, spring, 1979.

Le Soleil, April 28, 1973, September 28, 1974.

Lettres Québecoises, November, 1976; winter, 1980; spring, 1990, article by Gerald Gaudet, p. 11.

Livres et auteurs Québecois, 1970; 1973; 1974; 1975; 1980.

MultiCultural Review, April, 1992, review of *Mauve Desert,* p. 68.

Present, October, 1978.

Publishers Weekly, April 12, 1991, Penny Kaganoff, review of *Picture Theory,* p. 53; November 1, 1991, review of *Mauve Desert,* p. 77; April 12, 1992, p. 53.

Quill & Quire, May, 1997, review of *Baroque at Dawn,* p. 36.

Review of Contemporary Fiction, spring, 1992, Irving Malin, review of *Mauve Desert,* p. 158.

Room of One's Own, Volume 4, numbers 1 and 2, 1978.

Sortie, October, 1982.

Studies in Canadian Literature, 1991, Christian Bok, "i, a mother / i am other: *L'Amèr* and the *Mater,*" pp. 17-38.

University of Toronto Quarterly, fall, 1988, Barbara Godard, review of *Under Tongue,* p. 97; fall, 1989, Anne-Marie Picard, "La Theorie un Dimanche," p. 206; fall, 1989, Linda Hutcheon, "Gynocritics / La Gynocritique: Feminist Approaches to Writing by Canadian and Québecoise Women," p. 144; fall, 1989, Barbara Godard, review of *The Aerial Letter,* p. 108; fall, 1990, Andre Marquis, review of *Installations,* p. 50; fall, 1992, Jane Koustas, review of *Le désert mauve,* p. 109; spring, 2000, Jane Koustas, review of *Translations,* review of

Letters in Canada, p. 104; winter, 2000, Roger Chamberland, "Poésie" review of *Lettres Canadiennes,* 1999, p. 39.

Unomi e libri (Milan, Italy), September-October, 1983.

Vlasta (Paris, France), spring, 1983.

Voix et images du pays, number 9, 1975; September, 1977; fall, 1979; fall, 1985, article by Louis Milot, pp. 58-59; fall, 1985, article by Jean Fisette, pp. 63-64.

Women's Review of Books, January 4, 1987, Marguerite Andersen, "Women of Skin and Thought," p. 16.

World Literature Today, fall, 1996, Maria Green, "Baroque d'aube," review of *Baroque at Dawn,* p. 905.

Yale French Studies, 1995, Lynne Huffer, "An Interview with Nicole Brossard: Montréal, October, 1993," pp. 115-121; June, 1996, Lynne Huffer, "From Lesbos to Montréal: Nicole Brossard's Urban Fictions," pp. 95-114.

ONLINE

Express News Web site, http://www.expressnews.ualberta.ca/ (October 1, 2001), Geoff McMaster, "Canadian Literary Star Kicks Off Lecture Series."

Nicole Brossard Web site, http://epc.buffalo.edu/authors/brossard (November 12, 2003).*

*   *   *

BROWN, Elaine 1943-

PERSONAL: Born March 2, 1943, in Philadelphia, PA; daughter of Dorothy Clark (a factory worker); children: Ericka Suzanne Brown. *Education:* Attended Temple University, 1961.

ADDRESSES: Home—Atlanta, GA. *Office*—c/o Author Mail, Beacon Press, 25 Beacon St., Boston, MA 02108.

CAREER: Author, songwriter, lecturer, and activist. Los Angeles Black Congress, Los Angeles, CA, staff member of newspaper, beginning 1967; Black Panther Party, Deputy Minister of Information, 1970s, party chair, 1974-77; delegate to 1976 Democratic convention; lobbied for job-creating projects in Oakland, CA. President, Fields of Flowers (nonprofit educational corporation); vice-president, Dr. Huey P. Newton Foundation; director of political affairs, National Alliance of Radical Prison Reform; board member, Mothers Advocating Juvenile Justice. Songwriter and recording artist for *Seize the Time*, Vanguard Records, 1969, and *Elaine Brown*, Motown, 1973.

WRITINGS:

A Taste of Power: A Black Woman's Story, Pantheon (New York, NY), 1992.
The Condemnation of Little B, Beacon Press (Boston, MA), 2002.

Also author of *A Light Shines*, Tyndale.

ADAPTATIONS: A Taste of Power has been optioned for an HBO film by producer Suzanne de Passe.

SIDELIGHTS: The first woman ever to head the Black Panther Party, Elaine Brown has written about the turbulent times of her life in the memoir *A Taste of Power: A Black Woman's Story*. Raised in a poor Philadelphia neighborhood, Brown was able to attend the best schools in the city due to the hard work of her mother. Brown excelled academically, although she left Temple University after two semesters in order to pursue a songwriting career. Moving to Los Angeles, she was introduced to black literature and politics, and she joined the Black Panther Party (BPP) in 1967. She became party chair in 1974 after BPP cofounder Huey Newton was charged with murder and fled the country. Under Brown's leadership, the BPP began important voter registration and education initiatives, although she found that many men in the party did not want to accept her leadership. After Newton returned to the United States and cleared his name, Brown found there was little room for a woman to hold power in the party leadership. The book concludes in 1977, with Brown leaving the party and taking her daughter to live in France.

Reviewers praised *A Taste of Power* not only as memoir but as a new perspective on the history of the Black Panther Party. *Nation* contributor Ellen DuBois noted that in providing an account of female roles in the BPP, Brown makes "a signal contribution" to its history: "Brown tells her own story with power and

distinction, and greatly expands the party's history by doing so." "Brown is such an engaging storyteller, and her life is so full of extraordinary experiences, that one becomes attached to *A Taste of Power*," Alice A. Deck observed in *African American Review*. In *ETC.: A Review of General Semantics*, Philip Vassallo observed that while Brown's book is filled with "riveting moments," it "transcends biography and is at its most disturbing when characterizing the seemingly unbridgeable chasm between blacks and whites in America." The critic concluded: "Because of this exceptional woman's remarkable insight into two strikingly different worlds, both worlds can benefit from a reading of *A Taste of Power*."

Brown returned to the United States in the 1990s, moving to Atlanta. There she was intrigued by the case against a thirteen-year-old black youth who was vilified and eventually convicted for the murder of a black father of two. Disturbed by how a boy abandoned by his drug-addicted mother and the state social system could end up being tried and convicted as an adult with no physical evidence, she penned the investigative account *The Condemnation of Little B* in 2002. Not only does Brown trace the personal background and legal trial of Michael "Little B" Lewis, she explores the history of race and politics in America that has led to the demonization of a whole generation of black youth. *Choice* contributor P. J. Venturelli found Brown's inclusion of historical information "very comprehensive and instructive" and praised her "very strong opinions" for providing "perspectives and analyses that beg for further discussion and debate." *Washington Post* contributor Brian Gilmore, however, believed these details "sometimes bog down her excellent prose." A *Publishers Weekly* critic praised her journalistic and historical detail and called the work a "damning, often excruciating account of racism in contemporary American society." The critic concluded: "Packed with detail, strong arguments and flashes of brilliance, Brown's book is extraordinarily powerful."

Brown lectures around the country and remains involved in several causes, including Lewis's retrial and prison policy and juvenile justice reform. As she told *Atlanta Journal-Constitution* reporter Teresa K. Weaver: "I get angry when people are pushing these kids off the cliff. That's just who I am. . . . It's not that I'm an especially good person. I just identify with being someone who nobody cares about."

BIOGRAPHICAL AND CRITICAL SOURCES:

BOOKS

Brown, Elaine, *A Taste of Power: A Black Woman's Story,* Pantheon, 1992.
Contemporary Black Biography, Volume 8, Thomson Gale (Detroit, MI), 1994, pp. 30-33.
Notable Black American Women, Book II, Thomson Gale (Detroit, MI), 1996, pp. 65-67.

PERIODICALS

African American Review, summer, 1997, Alice A. Deck, review of *A Taste of Power: A Black Woman's Story,* p. 367.
Atlanta Journal-Constitution, March 3, 2002, Teresa K. Weaver, "Little B Revisited: Author Decries Tarring of Suspect," p. E1.
Black Issues Book Review, May-June, 2002, Robert Fleming, review of *The Condemnation of Little B,* p. 63.
Choice, October, 2002, P. J. Venturelli, review of *The Condemnation of Little B,* p. 361.
ETC.: A Review of General Semantics, spring, 1994, Philip Vassallo, review of *A Taste of Power,* p. 100.
Los Angeles Times, March 7, 2002, Kai Maristed, "Tracing History's Links to Bigotry in America through 'Little B,'" p. E3.
Nation, September 6, 1993, Ellen DuBois, review of *A Taste of Power,* p. 251.
New York Times Magazine, January 31, 1993, Rosemary L. Bray, "A Black Panther's Long Journey," p. 20.
Publishers Weekly, November 9, 1992, review of *A Taste of Power,* p. 65; January 28, 2002, review of *The Condemnation of Little B,* p. 283.
Social Justice, spring-summer, 1993, Roxanne Dunbar Ortiz, review of *A Taste of Power,* p. 176.
Virginia Quarterly Review, spring, 1994, Tucker Carrington, "A Deeper Place in Themselves," p. 366.
Washington Post, March 10, 2002, Brian Gilmore, "The Dispossessed," p. T4.*

*   *   *

BURKE, Ralph
    See SILVERBERG, Robert

BYRNE, John Keyes 1926-
    (Hugh Leonard)

PERSONAL: Born November 9, 1926, near Dublin, Ireland; son of Nicholas Keyes (a gardener) and Margaret (Doyle) Byrne; married Paule Jacquet, May 28, 1955; children: Danielle. *Education:* Attended Presentation Colllege, Dun Laoghaire, Ireland, 1941-45. *Religion:* "Lapsed Catholic."

ADDRESSES: Home—Theros, Coliemore Rd., Dalkey County, Dublin, Ireland. *Office*—6 Rossaun, Pilot View, Dalkey County, Dublin, Ireland. *Agent*—Harvey Unna, 14 Beaumont Mews, Marylebone High St., London W1N 4HE, England.

CAREER: Author, playwright, and screenwriter. Department of Lands, Dublin, Ireland, civil servant, 1945-59; Granada Television, Manchester, England, script editor, 1961-63; freelance writer in London, England, 1963-70; *Plays and Players,* drama critic, 1964-72; *Hibernia,* weekly columnist, 1973-76; Abbey Theatre, Dublin, literary editor, 1976-77; *Sunday Independent Ireland,* weekly columnist, 1977—; Dublin Theatre Festival, program director, 1978-80.

MEMBER: Dramatists' Club (London, England), Players (New York, NY).

AWARDS, HONORS: Italia Prize, International Concourse for Radio and Television, and Writers Guild of Great Britain award of merit, both 1967, both for *Silent Song;* Antoinette Perry ("Tony") Award nominee for best play, 1974, for *The Au Pair Man;* Tony Award for best play, New York Drama Critics' Circle Award for best play, Drama Desk Award for outstanding new play, and Outer Critics Circle Award for outstanding play, all 1978, all for *Da;* Harvey Award for *A Life.*

WRITINGS:

UNDER PSEUDONYM HUGH LEONARD

Leonard's Last Book (essays), Egotist Press (Enniskerry, Ireland), 1978.
A Peculiar People (essays), Tansy Books (Enniskerry, Ireland), 1979.

Home before Night: Memoirs of an Irish Time and Place (autobiography), Deutsch (London, England), 1979, Atheneum (New York, NY), 1980.

Suburb of Babylon, S. French (New York, NY), 1983.

Leonard's Year (journalism), Canavaun (Dublin, Ireland), 1985.

Leonard's Log, illustrated by Jim Cogan, Brophy Books (Dublin, Ireland), 1987.

Out after Dark (memoirs), Deutsch (London, England), 1989.

Parnell and the Englishwoman, Atheneum (New York, NY), 1991.

Selected Plays of Hugh Leonard, chosen, and with an introduction by S. F. Gallagher, Catholic University of America Press (Washington, DC), 1992.

Rover and other Cats (essays), Deutsch (London, England), 1992.

Dear Paule (letters), Mercier Press (Cork, Ireland), 2001.

A Wild People (novel), Methuen (London, England), 2001.

Also author of *The Off-Off-Shore Island,* 1993.

PLAYS

The Italian Road (two-act play), produced in Dublin, 1954.

The Big Birthday, produced in Dublin at Abbey Theatre, 1956.

A Leap in the Dark (two-act play), produced in Dublin at Abbey Theatre, 1957.

Madigan's Lock (two-act play; produced in Dublin at Globe Theatre, 1958; produced in London, 1963; produced in Olney, MD, 1970), Brophy Books (Dublin, Ireland), 1987.

A Walk on the Water, produced in Dublin at Eblana Theatre, 1960.

The Passion of Peter McGinty (two-act play; adaptation of *Peer Gynt* by Henrik Ibsen), produced in Dublin at Gate Theatre, 1961.

Stephen D. (two-act play; adaptation of *A Portrait of the Artist As a Young Man* and *Stephen Hero* by James Joyce; produced in Dublin at Gate Theatre, 1962; produced in London at St. Martin's Theatre, 1963; produced in New York, NY, 1967), M. Evans (New York, NY), 1962.

Dublin One (two-act play; adaptation of *Dubliners* by James Joyce), produced in Dublin at the Dublin Theatre Festival, 1963.

The Poker Session (produced in Dublin at Gate Theatre, 1963; produced in London at Globe Theatre, 1964; produced in New York, NY, 1967), M. Evans (New York, NY), 1964.

The Family Way (two-act play; adaptation of Eugene Marin Labiche's play), produced in Dublin, 1964, produced in London, 1966.

The Late Arrival of the Incoming Aircraft (one-act play; adaptation of Leonard's television play), M. Evans (New York, NY), 1968.

The Saints Go Cycling In (two-act play; adaptation of *The Dalkey Archives* by Flann O'Brien), produced in Dublin at Dublin Theatre Festival, 1965.

Mick and Mick (two-act play; produced in Dublin at Dublin Theatre Festival, 1966; produced as *All the Nice People* in Olney, MD, 1976), S. French (New York, NY), 1966.

The Quick, and the Dead (two-act play), produced in Dublin, 1967.

The Au Pair Man (three-act play; produced in Dublin at Dublin Theatre Festival, 1968; produced in London, 1969; produced in New York, NY, 1973), S. French (London, England), 1974.

The Barracks (two-act; adaptation of novel by John McGahern), produced in Dublin, 1969.

The Patrick Pearse Motel (two-act play; produced in Dublin at Olympia Theatre, 1971; produced in London, 1971; produced in Washington, DC, 1972), S. French (London, England), 1971.

Da (two-act play; produced in Olney, MD, 1973; produced in Dublin at Olympia Theatre, 1973; produced on Broadway, 1978), Proscenium Press (Newark, DE), 1975.

Summer (two-act play; produced in Olney, MD, 1974; produced in Dublin at Olympia Theatre, 1974; produced in London at Watford Palace Theatre, 1979; produced Off-Broadway, 1980), S. French (New York, NY), 1979.

Suburb of Babylon (contains *A Time of Wolves and Tigers, Nothing Personal,* and *The Last of the Last Mohicans;* produced as *Irishmen* in Olney, MD, 1975; produced in Dublin, 1975), S. French (New York, NY), 1983.

Some of My Best Friends Are Husbands (two-act play; adaptation of play by Eugene Marin Labiche), produced in London, 1976.

Liam Liar (two-act play; adaptation of *Billy Liar* by Keith Waterhouse and Willis Hall), produced in Dublin, 1976.

Time Was (two-act play; produced in Dublin at Abbey Theatre, December 21, 1976), Penguin (New York, NY), 1981.

A Life (two-act play; produced in Dublin at Abbey Theatre, 1979; produced on Broadway, 1980; produced Off-Broadway at the Irish Repertory Theatre, 2001), Atheneum (New York, NY), 1981.

Kill, produced in Dublin at the Dublin Theatre Festival, 1982; produced in New York, NY, 1986.

Scorpions (contains *A View from the Obelisk, Roman Fever,* and *Pizzazz*; also see below), produced in Dublin at the Dublin Theatre Festival, 1983.

Pizzazz, S. French (New York, NY), 1986.

The Mask of Moriarty (based on characters by Sir Arthur Conan Doyle; produced in Dublin at the Dublin Theatre Festival, 1985), Brophy Books (Dublin, Ireland), 1987.

Moving (produced in Dublin at Abbey Theatre, 1992), S. French (New York, NY), 1994.

Love in the Title: A Play (produced in Dublin at Abbey Theatre, 1999), S. French (London, England), 2000.

Also author of plays *Moving Days,* 1981; *Good Behavior,* 1983; *O'Neill,* 1983; *Senna for Sonny,* 1994; *The Lily Lally Show,* 1994; and *Magic,* 1997.

SCREENPLAYS

Great Catherine (adaptation of play by George Bernard Shaw), Warner Brothers, 1968.

(With Lee Langley) *Interlude,* Columbia, 1968.

Whirligig, 1970.

(With Terence Feely) *Percy* (adaptation of novel by Raymond Hitchcock), Metro-Goldwyn-Mayer, 1971.

Our Miss Fred, EMI, 1972.

Herself Surprised, 1977.

Widows' Peak, 1986.

Da, FilmDallas, 1988.

Mattie, 1998.

RADIO PLAYS

The Kennedys of Castleross (series).

Ending It, 1976.

TELEVISION PLAYS

The Irish Boys (trilogy), 1962.

A Kind of Kingdom, 1963.

The Second Wall, 1964.

A Triple Irish, 1964.

Realm of Error, 1964.

My One True Love, 1964.

The Late Arrival of the Incoming Aircraft, 1964.

Do You Play Requests?, 1964.

A View from the Obelisk, 1964.

I Loved You Last Summer, 1965.

Great Big Blond, 1965.

The Lodger [and] *The Judge,* 1966.

Insurrection, 1966.

Second Childhood, 1966.

The Retreat, 1966.

Silent Song (adapted from a story by Frank O'Connor), 1966.

A Time of Wolves and Tigers, 1967.

Love Life, 1967.

Great Expectations (adaptation of the novel by Charles Dickens), 1967.

Wuthering Heights (adaptation of the novel by Emily Brontë), 1967.

No Such Thing As a Vampire, 1968.

The Egg on the Face of the Tiger, Independent (ITV), 1968.

The Corpse Can't Play, 1968.

A Man and His Mother-in-Law, 1968.

Assassin, 1968.

Nicholas Nickleby (adaptation of the novel by Charles Dickens), 1968.

A Study in Scarlet (adaptation of a story by Arthur Conan Doyle), 1968.

The Hound of the Baskervilles (adaptation of a story by Arthur Conan Doyle), 1968.

(With H. R. Keating) *Hunt the Peacock,* 1969.

Talk of Angels, 1969.

The Possessed (adaptation of the novel by Fyodor Dostoevsky), 1969.

Dombey and Son (adaptation of the novel by Charles Dickens), British Broadcasting Corp (BBC-TV), 1969.

P and O (adaptation of a story by Somerset Maugham), 1969.

Jane (adaptation of a story by Somerset Maugham), 1970.

A Sentimental Education (adaptation of a story by Gustave Flaubert), 1970.

White Walls and Olive Green Carpets, 1971.

The Removal Person, 1971.

Pandora, Granada Television, 1971.

The Virgins, 1972.

The Ghost of Christmas Present, 1972.

The Truth Game, 1972.

The Moonstone (adaptation of the novel by Wilkie Collins), 1972.

The Sullen Sisters, 1972.

The Watercress Girl (adaptation of a story by H. E. Bates), 1972.

The Higgler, 1973.

High Kampf, 1973.

Milo O'Shea, 1973.

Stone Cold Sober, 1973.

The Bitter Pill, 1973.

Another Fine Mess, 1973.

Judgment Day, 1973.

The Traveling Woman, 1973.

The Hammer of God, 1974.

The Actor and the Alibi, 1974.

The Eye of Apollo, 1974.

The Forbidden Garden, 1974.

The Three Tools of Death, 1974.

The Quick One, 1974.

London Belongs to Me (adaptation of the novel by Norman Collins), 1977.

Bitter Suite, 1977.

Teresa, The Fur Coat, and *Two of a Kind* (adaptations of stories by Sean O'Faolain), 1977.

The Last Campaign (adaptation of the novel *The Captains and the Kings,* by Jennifer Johnston), 1978.

The Ring and the Rose, 1978.

Strumpet City (adaptation of the novel by James Plunkett), 1980.

The Little World of Don Camillo (adaptation of the novel by Giovanni Guareschi), BBC-TV, 1980.

The Slab Boys, Scottish Society of Playwrights (Glasgow, Scotland), 1981.

Kill, 1982.

Good Behavior (adaptation of work by Molly Keane), 1982.

O'Neill, 1983.

Beyond the Pale, 1984.

The Irish RM, 1985.

Hunted Down (adaptation of a story by Charles Dickens), 1985.

Troubles, 1987.

Parnell and the Englishwoman, 1991.

The Celadon Cup, 1993.

Writer for television series *Saki, Jezebel Ex-UK, The Hidden Truth, Undermine, Blackmail, Public Eye, The Liars, The Informer, Out of the Unknown, Conan Doyle,* *Somerset Maugham, The Sinners, Me Mammy, Tales from the Lazy Acre, Sweeney, Country Matters,* and *Father Brown.*

SIDELIGHTS: Irish playwright, screenwriter, and novelist John Keyes Byrne, who writes under the name Hugh Leonard, is known for his wickedly humorous story lines that focus on humanity's dark nature. At his birth in Dublin, he was named John Byrne; following his adoption by a working-class family, he began using his adoptive father's name, "Keyes," as his middle name. Byrne began his writing career as a civil servant in the Department of Lands. While with the department, he became involved with amateur theater and began writing for and about the stage. Byrne's pseudonym, Hugh Leonard, is the name of a character in his first play, *The Italian Road,* which was originally rejected by the Abbey Theatre. After three of his plays were staged in Dublin, he became a professional writer, drafting serious dramas as well as scripts for television and films.

Since 1960 Byrne's plays have been staged nearly every year at the Dublin Theatre Festival. Among Byrne's numerous plays are *The Au Pair Man, The Patrick Pearce Motel, Da, A Life,* and *Love in the Title.* Jeremy Kingston called Byrne's play, *The Au Pair Man,* a "witty social parable" in which the author pokes fun at the British. The comedy revolves around Mrs. Elizabeth Rogers, whose initials indicate she is a parody of Queen Elizabeth (Elizabeth Regina). Her poverty-stricken but royal residence is soon invaded by a gauche young Irish debt collector endeavoring to reclaim a wall-unit. Considering how valuable this unit is to her, Mrs. Rogers seduces the young man and gradually transforms him into a personage possessing social grace. A *Variety* critic noted that the play "shows the British Empire crumbling but defiantly clinging to its outworn past, arrogant, broke, but still loftily trying to ignore the new world and control 'the peasants.'" He added: "Some of [Byrne's] dialog has the air of secondhand Oscar Wilde, but he provides . . . many splendid flights of fancy and airy persiflage."

A more recent play, *The Patrick Pearce Motel,* met with an enthusiastic reception. Critics praised the work for its artful combination of farce and satire. A *Plays and Players* critic observed that the play "is both an act of conscious homage to Feydeau and a pungent, witty, acerbic attack on the Irish *nouveau riche*—in particular on their exploitation of their country's political and folk heritage as a tourist attraction." The two principal characters are prosperous Irish business partners whose new venture, a motel, has recently been constructed. In an effort to attract customers, the entrepreneurs name each room after a famed Irish hero. The story begins at the celebration of the motel's opening and rapidly becomes a farcical comedy of misunderstanding and sexual innuendo involving the businessmen, their discontented wives, a rambunctious television personality, the nymphomaniac motel manager, and the night watchman. *Stage*'s R. B. Marriott hailed Byrne's efforts, asserting that while he "creates vivid personalities among his bizarre characters, he also creates strong, smoothly progressive farcical situations with rich trimmings." Marriott continued that Byrne's "wit can be sharp, his humour splendidly" rowdy.

The author's next play received rave reviews and won several drama awards. *Da* is an autobiographical comedy-drama about a bereaved son, Charlie, on his return to Ireland and the scene of his boyhood. Charlie's father, Da, has recently died and the son tries to exorcise himself of the painful memory of his parent while sitting in his father's vacant cottage discarding old papers. Da returns, however, in the form of a ghost, and the father and son remember the past together. "*Da* is a beguiling play about a son's need to come to terms with his father—and with himself," disclosed Mel Gussow of the *New York Times*. "Warmly but unsentimentally, it concerns itself with paternity, adolescence, the varieties of familial love and the tricks and distortions of memory." He concluded that "*Da* is a humane and honest memory play in which, with great affection and humor, we are invited to share the life of a family." Similarly complimentary, John Simon of *New York* remarked: "A charming, mellow, saucy, and bittersweet boulevard comedy, but from a boulevard whose dreams are not entirely housebroken and have a bit of untamable Hibernian wilderness left fluttering in them." Byrne later wrote the screenplay for a film version of *Da,* starring Martin Sheen as Charlie.

Love in the Title, is the story of Katie, a thirty-seven-year-old Irish novelist, who, while enjoying a picnic in a meadow, is joined by her mother and grandmother in earlier stages of their lives. Cat, Katie's grandmother, is a twenty-year-old, free-spirited girl in 1932. Triona, Katie's mother, is an uptight, conservative woman

from the 1960s. Together, the three women compare the Ireland of the present to the Ireland of the past. Steve Winn of the *San Francisco Chronicle* observed: Byrne's "fanciful meeting of mother, daughter, and granddaughter in an Irish meadow takes a beguiling look at how both past and future exert a powerful hold." In the *Guardian,* Mic Moroney noted that while the play is "uneven," it is "by far the most probing and perhaps honest of Leonard's plays in many years."

In addition to his plays and screenplays, Byrne has written several books. In *Home before Night,* Byrne rehashes some of the incidents he already covered in *Da.* Richard Eder stated in the *New York Times Book Review:* "The book's sketches, touching or comical though many of them are, lack the vitality that they had when dramatized onstage." Susan von Hoffmann of the *New Republic* also spotted annoying similarities between the play and book; however, she asserted that "a three-character play by nature lacks the richer texture of the memoir and these rough spots melt away in the larger view of Ireland and of a boy's slow and often painful discovery that his life is in the end a journey home." A *New Yorker* reviewer called *Home before Night* an "eloquent little book of merry and bitter reminisce," noting that Byrne "has led a life of classic Irish disarray."

Out after Dark, the sequel to *Home before Night,* continues Byrne's autobiographical account of his boyhood in Ireland. This second volume tells the story of his adolescence in the 1940s and 1950s and his first experiences as a writer.

A Wild People, Byrne's first novel, is the story of TJ Quill, a film critic chosen as the archivist for his favorite Western filmmaker, Sean O'Fearna. Karen Traynor wrote in the *Library Journal,* "The authenticity of [Byrne's] characters captures the essence of Irish culture." A reviewer in *Publishers Weekly* said the plot was "haphazard" at first, but it "gradually grows into a complex social comedy."

Byrne's book *Dear Paule* is a collection of letters that appeared in his weekly column in the London *Sunday Independent.* The letters, addressed to his wife, Paule, helped Byrne work through his grief over her sudden death. A compilation of memories of their life together, the column expresses how the smallest things in life remind him of her. Pauline Ferrie, a reviewer for *Book-view Ireland,* wrote that Byrne's letters are a "realization that he cannot fulfill his promise to remember his wife without first facing up to her absence."

Byrne once told *CA:* "I am not an Irish writer, but a writer who happens to be Irish. This is not hair-splitting: I find that the former is usually categorized as someone who writes quaint, charming, witty, idiomatic dialogue, but whose work has no real validity outside of Ireland. The people I write about are those in the small seaside town I was born in and in which I now live, ten miles from Dublin. I use them as a means of exploring myself, which is what I believe writing is about. I usually pick an emotional or biological crossroads: the realization of middle age (*Summer*), the death of a parent (*Da*), or the onset of death (*A Life*). The themes are weighty, but I treat them in terms of comedy—serious comedy, that is. I write without knowing where I am going; it is a journey for me as well as the audience, and I write about recognizable human beings. If a play of mine does not evoke recognition in Buffalo, Liverpool, Lille, or Melbourne, then it is an utter failure. I try not to repeat myself; life is too short to chew the same cabbage twice. I think that basically I am that unfashionable thing: an optimist. My work says that life may be bad, but we can change it by changing ourselves, and of course my best play is always the next one."

BIOGRAPHICAL AND CRITICAL SOURCES:

BOOKS

Contemporary Dramatists, 6th edition, St. James Press (Detroit, MI), 1999.
Contemporary Literary Criticism, Volume 19, Thomson Gale (Detroit, MI), 1981.
Contemporary Theatre, Film, and Television, Volume 6, Thomson Gale (Detroit, MI), 1988.
Dictionary of Literary Biography, Volume 13: *British Dramatists since World War II,* Thomson Gale (Detroit, MI), 1982.
Drama for Students, Volume 13, Thomson Gale (Detroit, MI), 2001.
International Dictionary of Theatre, Volume 2: *Playwrights,* St. James Press (Detroit, MI), 1993.
King, Kimball, *Ten Modern Irish Playwrights,* Garland (New York, NY), 1979.
New York Theatre Annual, Volume 2, Thomson Gale (Detroit, MI), 1978.

PERIODICALS

Back Stage, July 27, 2001, Irene Backalenick, theater review of *A Life,* p. 44.
Back Stage West, March 23, 2000, Judy Richter, theater review of *Love in the Title,* p. 19.
Booklist, June 1, 2002, Patricia Monaghan, review of *A Wild People,* p. 1686.
Canadian Journal of Irish Studies, July 1989, Thomas B. O'Grady, "Insubstantial Fathers and Consubstantial Sons: A Note on Patrimony and Patricide in Friel and Leonard," pp. 71-79.
Guardian, Mic Moroney, theatre review of *Love in the Title,* p. 8.
Irish Literary Supplement, spring, 1990, S. F. Gallagher, "Q. and A. with Hugh Leonard," pp. 13-14.
Kirkus Reviews, May 15, 2002, review of *A Wild People,* p. 689.
Library Journal, July 2002, Karen Traynor, review of *A Wild People,* p. 120; April 1, 2003, Ming-ming Shen Kuo, review of *Leonard, Hugh and Others, New Plays from the Abbey Theatre, 1999-2001,* p. 98.
New Republic, June 7, 1980, p. 39; May 16, 1988, Stanley Kauffmann, movie review of *Da,* p. 20; June 20, 1994, Stanley Kauffmann, movie review of *Widows' Peak,* p. 26.
New York, April 10, 1978.
New Yorker, July 28, 1980, p. 102.
New York Times, March 14, 1978; May 2, 1978; May 14, 1978; November 10, 1978; March 25, 1979; April 23, 1980.
New York Times Book Review, June 1, 1980, p. 11.
Observer Review, June 20, 1971.
Plays and Players, August, 1971.
Publishers Weekly, March 15, 1991, Sybil Steinberg, review of *Parnell and the Englishwoman,* p. 45; June 21, 1991, review of *Out after Dark,* p. 47; June 17, 2002, review of *A Wild People,* p. 43.
Punch, April 30, 1969.
San Francisco Chronicle, March 21, 2000, Steven Winn, "*Love,* Family and Time in an Irish Meadow," p. B1.
Stage, June 10, 1971; June 24, 1971.
Sunday Times (London, England), March 14, 1999, Gerry McCarthy, "Hugh Scores with His Three Ladies," p. 2.
Times (London, England), March 12, 1999, Luke Clancy, "Time Travelers," p. 35.

Variety, April 30, 1969.
Washington Post, June 6, 1978.

ONLINE

Bookview Ireland, http://bookviewireland.ie/ (October 17, 2003), Pauline Ferrie, review of *Dear Paule.*

Irish Writers Online, http://www.irishwriters-online. com/ (October 20, 2003).
Mercier Press Web site, http://www.mercierpress.ie/ (October 17, 2003).
Methuen Publishing Web site, http://www.methuen.co. uk/ (October 20, 2003).*

C

CHAFFEE, Wilber Albert

PERSONAL: Born in Los Angeles, CA; married Alice Blake (marriage ended); married Edivanir Fontanelli; children: Graham S., Lyman B. *Ethnicity:* "Caucasian." *Education:* Occidental College, B.A.; University of Texas at Austin, M.A., 1970, Ph.D., 1975. *Religion:* Presbyterian.

ADDRESSES: Agent—c/o Author Mail, Lynne Rienner Publishers, 1800 30th St., Ste. 314, Boulder, CO 80301. *E-mail*—wchaffee@stmarys-ca.edu.

CAREER: University of Texas at Austin, assistant professor, 1975-77; St. Mary's College of California, Moraga, professor of politics, 1978-99, professor emeritus, 1999—. Iuperj, Rio de Janeiro, Brazil, senior researcher, 1999-2000; University of California, Berkeley, visiting professor, 2003. *Military service:* U.S. Army; became sergeant.

MEMBER: American Political Science Association, Latin American Studies Association.

WRITINGS:

(With Honor M. Griffin) *Dissertations on Latin America by U.S. Historians, 1960-1970: A Bibliography,* Institute of Latin American Studies, University of Texas (Austin, TX), 1973.
(Editor, with Stanley R. Ross) *Guide to the Hispanic American Historical Review, 1956-1975,* Duke University Press (Durham, NC), 1980.

(With Gary Prevost) *Cuba: A Different America,* Rowman & Littlefield (Totowa, NJ), 1989.
The Economics of Violence in Latin America, Praeger (New York, NY), 1992.
Desenvolvimento: Politics and Economy in Brazil, Lynne Rienner Publishers (Boulder, CO), 1998.

Contributor to books, including *Politics in Latin America,* Oxford University Press (New York, NY), 2005.

* * *

CHAPMAN, Walker
See SILVERBERG, Robert

* * *

CHERNOW, Burt 1933-1997

PERSONAL: Born July 28, 1933, in New York, NY; died of a heart attack, June 9, 1997, in Deerfield Park, FL; son of Abe and Selma (Schneider) Chernow; married Tamara Sackman, January 1, 1957 (divorced, July, 1970); married Ann Levy, December 12, 1970; children: (first marriage) Perrin, Paul, Paige. *Education:* New York University, B.S., 1958, M.A., 1960.

CAREER: Educator, sculptor, art historian, author. Art teacher at public schools in Valley Stream, NY, 1958-60, and Westport, CT, 1960-66; Housatonic Community College, Bridgeport, CT, assistant professor,

1966-70, associate professor, 1970-74, chairman of department of art, professor of art history, 1974—; founder and director of Housatonic Museum of Art, 1974-85. Member of teaching staff of Museum of Modern Art, New York, NY, 1966-71; member of faculty at Silvermine School of the Arts, 1969-77, Stamford Museum, Greenwich Art Center, local Center for Continuing Education, and Higher Education Center for Urban Studies, 1968-71. Member of board of directors of Westport Weston Arts Council, 1969-97, Bridgeport Commission on the Arts, 1972-97, Art Resources of Connecticut, 1976-79, and ABCD Art Center, Bridgeport, 1983-86. Work exhibited in group shows, including in the 1964-65 World's Fair and in permanent and private collections. *Military service:* U.S. Army, 1953-55.

AWARDS, HONORS: First prizes from Barnum Festival, 1966, for sculpture; the Burt Chernow Galleries of the Housatonic Museum of Art were named in Chernow's honor.

WRITINGS:

Paper, Paint, and Stuff, two volumes, Technifax and Educational Directions, 1969.
Lester Johnson Paintings: The Kaleidoscopic Crowd, David Anderson, 1975.
Gabor Peterdi: Paintings, Taplinger (New York, NY), 1982.
The Drawings of Milton Avery, Taplinger (New York, NY), 1984.
Christo and Jeanne-Claude: A Biography, epilogue by Wolfgang Volz, St. Martin's Press (New York, NY), 2002.

Author of exhibition catalogs. Art critic for *Fairpress, Westport News,* and *Stratford News,* 1972-73, 1978-79. Contributor of essays and reviews to newspapers and periodicals, including *Arts, Art News, Art New England, Four Winds, Intellect, Craft Horizons, County,* and *Instructor.*

SIDELIGHTS: Burt Chernow gained acclaim in the art world, winning the Barnum Festival's prize for sculpture in 1966, and for his work as the founding director of the Housatonic Museum of Art. He began teaching art in public schools in Connecticut and New York after serving in the U.S. Army in the mid-1950s.

In 1966, he accepted a position at Housatonic Community College in Bridgeport, Connecticut, and in 1974, founded the art museum there. Chernow authored many exhibition catalogs, as well as articles for art journals. His artwork is seen in private collections and was on display at the 1964-65 New York World's Fair.

Among his books is *Christo and Jeanne-Claude: A Biography,* published posthumously. He follows the careers of his friends, Bulgarian Christo Javacheff and his wife and artistic partner, Jeanne-Claude de Guillebon, born in French-controlled Casablanca. The couple—who share the same birthday, June 13, 1935—came from very different backgrounds. When they met in Paris in 1959, he was a poor exile from Communism, while she came from a wealthy French family. Christo's avant-garde minimalist style became popular, first in Paris, and then in New York, and he is best known for his "wrapped" works. Chernow's narrative ends in 1983, but Christo/Jeanne-Claude collaborator Wolfgang Volz adds to the biography with an epilogue about the couple who declared their "artistic interdependence" in 1994. *Booklist*'s Donna Seaman wrote that *Christo and Jeanne-Claude* "will stand as the keystone biography of a truly revolutionary artist and his soul mate."

Chernow once commented: "Few areas attract as much irrelevant writing as the visual arts. People who read the text that appears with art images deserve thoughtful discussion and insight and some degree of intelligent analysis. The artists deserve no less."

BIOGRAPHICAL AND CRITICAL SOURCES:

PERIODICALS

Booklist, February 15, 2002, Donna Seaman, review of *Christo and Jeanne-Claude: A Biography,* p. 980.
Library Journal, May 1, 2002, Martin R. Kalfatovic, review of *Christo and Jeanne-Claude,* p. 96.

OBITUARIES

PERIODICALS

New York Times, June 15, 1997, p. 31.*

CHESLER, Phyllis 1940-

PERSONAL: Born October 1, 1940, in Brooklyn, NY; daughter of Leon and Lillian (Hammer) Chesler; children: Ariel David (son). *Education:* Bard College, B.A., 1962; New School for Social Research, M.A., 1967, Ph.D., 1969; New York Medical College, graduate study, 1968-69. *Religion:* Jewish.

ADDRESSES: Office—Department of Psychology, College of Staten Island of the City University of New York, Staten Island, NY 10301. *Agent*—Lois de la Haba, 133 Broadway, Suite 810, New York, NY 10010.

CAREER: New York University, New York, NY, intern in psychotherapy at Washington Square Institute for Psychotherapy and Mental Health, 1968-69; Metropolitan Hospital, New York, NY, clinical research associate, 1968-69; College of Staten Island of the City University of New York, Staten Island, NY, assistant professor of psychology, 1969-98, emerita professor, 1998—; Research Associate, International Research Institute on Jewish Women (founded by Hadassah), Brandeis University, Waltham, MA, 1997—. Lecturer at institutions, including Institute for Developmental Studies and New School for Social Research, City University of New York; psychotherapist in private practice. Cofounder, Association for Women in Psychology, 1970; cofounder, National Women's Health Network, 1976. Member of board of directors of Women's Action Alliance, 1972—, and Center for the Study of Psychiatry, 1974—.

MEMBER: American Association for the Abolition of Involuntary Mental Hospitalization, American Association for the Advancement of Science, American Psychological Association, Association for Women in Psychology (founder), American Association of University Professors, National Organization for Women, Eastern Psychological Association, New York State Psychological Association.

AWARDS, HONORS: Positive Image of Women Award, National Organization of Women, 1978; Feminist Book Fortnight Award (London, England), 1990, for *Sacred Bond: Motherhood under Siege;* Medal of Honor Award, Veteran Feminists of America, 1993; Nike Prize, International Book Fair, 1998, for "distinguished achievement, in recognition of work to promote the rights of women."

WRITINGS:

Women and Madness, Doubleday (Garden City, NY), 1972, twenty-fifth anniversary edition, Four Walls Eight Windows Press (New York, NY), 1997.

(Author of interpretive essay) *Wonder Woman,* introduction by Gloria Steinem, Holt (New York, NY), 1972.

(With Emily Jane Goodman) *Women, Money and Power,* Morrow (New York, NY), 1976.

About Men, Simon & Schuster (New York, NY), 1978.

With Child: A Diary of Motherhood, Lippincott-Crowell (New York, NY), 1979, revised edition, including a new introduction by son, Ariel Chesler, Four Walls Eight Windows Press (New York, NY), 1998.

Mothers on Trial: The Battle for Children and Custody, McGraw-Hill (New York, NY), 1986, revised edition, Four Walls Eight Windows Press (New York, NY), 1998.

Sacred Bond: The Legacy of Baby M, Times Books (New York, NY), 1988, published as *Sacred Bond: Motherhood under Siege,* introduction by Ann Oakley, Virago (London, England), 1990.

Patriarchy: Notes of an Expert Witness, Common Courage Press (Monroe, ME), 1994.

(Editor, with Esther D. Rothblum and Ellen Cole) *Feminist Foremothers in Women's Studies, Psychology, and Mental Health,* Haworth Press (New York, NY), 1995.

Letters to a Young Feminist, Four Walls Eight Windows Press (New York, NY), 1997.

Woman's Inhumanity to Woman, Thunder's Mouth Press/Nation Books (New York, NY), 2001.

(Editor, with Rivka Haut) *Women of the Wall: Claiming Sacred Ground at Judaism's Holy Site,* Jewish Lights (Woodstock, VT), 2002.

The New Anti-Semitism: The Current Crisis and What We Must Do about It, Jossey-Bass (San Francisco, CA), 2003.

Contributor to numerous publications, including *The Radical Therapist Collective Anthology,* edited by Jerome Agel, Ballantine (New York, NY), 1971; *Women in Sexist Society: Studies in Power and Powerlessness,* edited by Vivian Gornick and Barbara K. Moran, Basic Books (New York, NY), 1971; *Psychology for Our Times: Readings,* edited by Philip Zimbardo and Christina Maslach, Scott, Foresman (Glenview, IL), 1973; *Psychology of Adjustment,* edited by James F.

Adams, Holbrook, 1973; *The Encyclopedia of the Future,* edited by George Thomas Kurian and Graham T. T. Molitor, Simon & Schuster (New York, NY), 1996; and *For Women Only,* edited by Gary Null and Barbara Seaman, Seven Stories Press (New York, NY), 2000.

Also contributor to periodicals, including *New York Magazine, Ms., Psychology Today, Radical Therapist,* and *Village Voice.* Contributor to professional journals, including *Journal of Feminism and Psychology, Journal of Mind and Behavior, Criminal Practice Law Report,* and *New York Law Journal.* Past editor-at-large and columnist for *On the Issues* magazine.

SIDELIGHTS: Radical feminist Phyllis Chesler has been "an articulate and consistent critic of American culture for over twenty-seven years," according to *Feminist Writers* contributor Mary A. Hess. "Her candor and incisive prose style have [provided her with] a reputation as one of America's most articulate and thoughtful feminist writers, while her activism in representing women who are marginalized by illness, poverty, and exploitation has not diminished despite personal hardship." In her writings, Chesler has sought to expose what she believes to be the unfair and unequal treatment of women in the health care and criminal justice systems; her 1972 book *Women and Madness* was "instrumental in initiating reforms in the mental health establishment," stated Hess. In other books, she has focused on motherhood and society's changing attitudes toward women and children. In addition, she has written books and essays in defense of controversial female figures such as Mary Beth Whitehead—the surrogate mother in the Baby M case—and Aileen Wuolnos, a prostitute who killed four men in self-defense.

Chesler documents her mixed feelings about pregnancy and motherhood in *With Child: A Diary of Motherhood.* Linda B. Osborne wrote in the *Washington Post Book World:* "At thirty-seven, Phyllis Chesler gave birth to a son, and *With Child* is a diary of her pregnancy, the birth and her first year of motherhood. It is an informal, very personal narrative, charged with nervous energy, enthusiasm and anxiety, and marked by the ambivalence towards motherhood that grew out of the feminist movement over the last fifteen years." Chesler's pregnancy also led her to write *Mothers on Trial: The Battle for Children and Custody.* While

awaiting the birth of her child, she began exploring the assault on women's custody rights. Because of that book, related Hess, Chesler is now "often approached by women seeking her advocacy, as she was by numerous mothers whose experiences as both traditional and non-traditional mothers were challenged on the basis of their fitness as caregivers and as a result of the non-custodial parent claiming rights to the child." Hess further reported that whenever possible, Chesler uses "oral histories to grant silenced women their own voice, believing strongly in their power to persuade the reader."

Chesler continues her exploration of the oppression of women in *Patriarchy: Notes of an Expert Witness.* In this collection of previously published essays, she documents the effects of what she sees as the patriarchal bias in the health care and criminal justice systems. Included are stories of women in custody battles, women on trial, and women imprisoned in psychiatric institutions. Reviewing the book in the *New York Times Book Review,* Anndee Hochman rated it "provocative but uneven" and explained that the essays are bound together by Chesler's contention that the media, the court systems, and the mental health system "all operate on a sexist double standard that punishes women." Therese Stanton, a reviewer for *Ms.,* called *Patriarchy* "thrilling and devastating reading—thrilling because of the explosion created when truth is spoken, and devastating because of the harshness of that truth."

In 1997, Chesler published a book written in a series of twenty-two letters to young girls titled *Letters to a Young Feminist.* The book is part memoir in that Chesler reflects on her participation in the feminist movement and seeks to share what she learned with young women of today. She also uncovers what she calls the "failings" of her movement, such as the concept of women hating women. Kim France, a critic for the *New York Times Book Review,* suggested that Chesler may be a bit "out of touch with the ways that feminism has evolved." France claimed that the author may offend the modern young woman by implying that she is "far from free," while she believes that she has only ever known complete freedom. However, Meg Daly of *Tikkun* noted that "Chesler's heartfelt and unflinching letters come as a welcome antidote to young women," and "addresses real empowerment and tells the truth about the continued injustices rampant in women's lives."

Chesler expanded on an idea she referred to in *Letters to a Young Feminist* in her 2001 book *Women's Inhumanity to Women.* Using twenty years of research on women and feminism, Chesler seems to come to some realizations about her gender, which are backed by scientific and historical evidence. She begins by explaining how even primate females were extremely competitive, often attempting to damage the reproductive organs of other females. They also were known to kill the babies of potential competitors. Chesler sites other historical examples of Chinese and Indian mothers-in-law abusing their sons' wives, and examines rituals such as female genital mutilation in Africa and dowry disputes in India. These rites of passage are all supported by other women. More modern examples of women on women aggression include gossip, manipulation, and backstabbing. Chesler uses many anecdotes from her own life, and Kay S. Hymowitz from *Commentary* suggested that the stories are a bit "self-serving." However, as the author writes, "Only recently have I been able to acknowledge that my own bold ideas and my passionate, direct style are probably very threatening to other women." Eleanor J. Bader of *Library Journal* called this book a "groundbreaking look at how women perpetuate oppression."

In 2003, Chesler published *The New Anti-Semitism: The Current Crisis and What We Must Do about It,* a book that surmises that anti-Jewish hatred has reemerged in the guise of being politically correct among "many liberal feminists, intellectuals, and Jewish leftists," stated a reviewer for *Publishers Weekly.*

BIOGRAPHICAL AND CRITICAL SOURCES:

BOOKS

Bailey, Martha J., *American Women in Science,* ABC-Clio (Santa Barbara, CA).
Feminist Writers, St. James Press (Detroit, MI), 1996.

PERIODICALS

Booklist, February 1, 1998, Mary Carroll, review of *Letters to a Young Feminist,* p. 882.
Chicago Tribune Book World, October 28, 1979.
Commentary, May, 2002, Kay S. Hymowitz, "Femme Fatale," p. 79.
Library Journal, October 15, 1994, p. 75; March 15, 2002, Eleanor J. Bader, review of *Women's Inhumanity to Women,* p. 98; December, 2002, Marcia Welsh, review of *Women of the Wall: Claiming Sacred Ground at Judaism's Holy Site,* p. 137.
Ms., January, 1995, p. 72.
New York Times, March 9, 1978.
New York Times Book Review, October 21, 1979; February 26, 1995, p. 16; April 26, 1998, Kim France, "Passing the Torch," p. 10.
off our backs, February, 1998, Carol Anne Douglas, review of *Letters to a Young Feminist,* p. 8.
Publishers Weekly, April 3, 1978; February 25, 2002; November 25, 2002, review of *Women of the Wall,* p. 60; June 23, 2003, review of *The New Anti-Semitism: The Current Crisis and What We Must Do about It,* p. 58.
Signs: Journal of Women and Culture in Society, Volume 14, number 1, 1988.
Tikkun, July-August, 1998, Meg Daly, review of *Letters to a Young Feminist,* p. 75; May, 2002, Miriam Greenspan, "When Women Injure Women," p. 77.
Washington Post Book World, December 23, 1979.

ONLINE

Jewish Lights Publishing, http://www.jewishlights.com/ (July 24, 2002).

*   *   *

Chichester CLARK, Emma 1955-

PERSONAL: Born October 15, 1955, in London, England; daughter of Robin Chichester Clark (a company director) and Jane Helen (Goddard; present surname, Falloon); married Lucas van Praag (a management consultant). *Education:* Chelsea School of Art, B.A. (with honors), 1978; Royal College of Art, M.A. (with honors), 1983.

ADDRESSES: Home—47 Richford St., London W12 8BU, England. *Agent*—Laura Cecil, 17 Alwyne Villas, London N1, England.

CAREER: Author, illustrator, and editor of children's books, 1983–. Worked in a design studio and as a freelance illustrator of newspapers, periodicals, and book jackets. Visiting lecturer at Middlesex Polytechnic and City and Guilds School of Art, 1984-86. *Exhibitions:* Exhibitor at the Thumb Gallery, England, 1984 and 1987.

MEMBER: Chelsea Arts Club.

AWARDS, HONORS: Mother Goose Award, 1988, for *Listen to This;* Golden Duck Award, 1999, for *Noah and the Space Ark;* Kate Greenaway Medal shortlist, 1999, for *I Love You, Blue Kangaroo!;* Kurt Maschler Award shortlist, 1999, for *Elf Hill: Tales from Hans Christian Andersen.*

WRITINGS:

SELF-ILLUSTRATED PICTURE BOOKS

Catch That Hat!, Bodley Head (London, England), 1988, Little, Brown (Boston, MA), 1990.
The Story of Horrible Hilda and Henry, Little, Brown (Boston, MA), 1988.
Myrtle, Tertle, and Gertle, Bodley Head (London, England), 1989.
The Bouncing Dinosaur, Farrar, Straus (New York, NY), 1990.
Tea with Aunt Augusta, Methuen (London, England), 1991, published as *Lunch with Aunt Augusta,* Dial (New York), 1992.
Miss Bilberry's New House, Methuen (London, England), 1993, published as *Across the Blue Mountains,* Harcourt (San Diego, CA), 1993.
Little Miss Muffet Counts to Ten, Andersen (London, England), 1997, published as *Little Miss Muffet's Count-Along Surprise,* Bantam (New York, NY), 1997.
More!, Andersen (London, England), 1998, Bantam (New York, NY), 1999.
I Love You, Blue Kangaroo!, Bantam (New York, NY), 1999.
Follow My Leader, Andersen (London, England), 1999.
Where Are You, Blue Kangaroo?, Andersen (London, England), 2000, Random House (New York, NY), 2001.
It Was You, Blue Kangaroo!, Andersen (London, England), 2001, Random House (New York, NY), 2002.
No More Kissing!, Doubleday (New York, NY), 2002.

What Shall We Do, Blue Kangaroo?, Random House (New York, NY), 2003.
Mimi's Book of Opposites, Charlesbridge (Watertown, MA), 2003.
Mimi's Book of Counting, Charlesbridge (Watertown, MA), 2003.
Follow the Leader!, Margaret K. McElderry Books (New York, NY), 2003.
Up in Heaven, Andersen (London, England), 2003, Random House (New York, NY), 2004.
Merry Christmas to You, Blue Kangaroo!, Random House (New York, NY), 2004.
No More Teasing, Andersen (London, England), 2005.

Several of Chichester Clark's books have been translated into Spanish.

ILLUSTRATOR

Laura Cecil, compiler, *Listen to This,* Greenwillow (New York, NY), 1987.
Janet Lunn, *Shadow in Hawthorn Bay,* Walker (London, England), 1988.
Laura Cecil, compiler, *Stuff and Nonsense,* Greenwillow (New York, NY), 1989.
Primrose Lockwood, *Cissy Lavender,* Little, Brown (Boston, MA), 1989.
James Reeves, *Ragged Robin: Poems from A to Z,* Little, Brown (Boston, MA), 1990.
Margaret Ryan, *Fat Witch Rides Again,* Methuen (London, England), 1990.
Laura Cecil, compiler, *Boo! Stories to Make You Jump,* Greenwillow (New York, NY), 1990.
Jane Rohmer, *Rock-a-Bye Baby,* 1990.
Roald Dahl, *James and the Giant Peach,* Unwin Hyman (London, England), 1990.
(And compiler) *I Never Saw a Purple Cow, and Other Nonsense Rhymes* (anthology), Little, Brown (Boston, MA), 1990.
Pat Thomson, *Beware of the Aunts!,* Margaret K. McElderry Books (New York), 1991.
Margaret Mahy, *The Queen's Goat,* Dial (New York, NY), 1991.
Diana Wynne Jones, *Wild Robert,* Mammoth (London, England), 1991, Chivers North America, 1992.
Diana Wynne Jones, *Castle in the Air,* Mammoth (London, England), 1991.
Jenny Nimmo, *Delilah and the Dogspell,* Methuen (London, England), 1991.

Laura Cecil, compiler, *A Thousand Yards of the Sea,* Methuen (London, England), 1992, published as *A Thousand Yards of Sea,* Greenwillow (New York, NY), 1993.

D. J. Enright, *The Way of the Cat,* HarperCollins (New York, NY), 1992.

Anne Fine, *The Haunting of Pip Parker,* Walker (London, England), 1992.

Ben Frankel, *Tertius and Plinty,* Harcourt (San Diego, CA), 1992.

Geraldine McCaughrean, reteller, *The Orchard Book of Greek Myths,* Orchard (London, England), 1992, published as *Greek Myths,* Margaret K. McElderry Books (New York, NY), 1993.

Peter Dickinson, *Time and the Clockmice, et cetera,* Doubleday (London, England), 1993, Delacorte (New York, NY), 1994.

Rosemary Sutcliff, *The Princess and the Dragon Pup,* Walker (London, England), 1993, Candlewick (Cambridge, MA), 1996.

Ann Turnbull, *Too Tired,* Hamish Hamilton (London, England), 1993, Harcourt (San Diego, CA), 1994.

Laura Cecil, *The Frog Princess,* Jonathan Cape (London, England), 1994, Greenwillow (New York, NY), 1995.

Laura Cecil, compiler, *Preposterous Pets,* Hamish Hamilton (London, England), 1994, Greenwillow (New York, NY), 1995.

Charles Ashton, *Ruth and the Blue Horse,* Walker (London, England), 1994.

Kate McMullan, *Good Night, Stella,* Candlewick (Cambridge, MA), 1994.

William S. Gilbert and Arthur Sullivan, *I Have a Song to Sing, O!: An Introduction to the Songs of Gilbert and Sullivan,* selected and edited by John Langstaff, Margaret K. McElderry Books (New York, NY), 1994.

Laura Cecil, *Piper,* Jonathan Cape (London, England), 1995.

Something Rich and Strange: A Treasury of Shakespeare's Verse, compiled by Gina Pollinger, Larousse Kingfisher Chambers (New York, NY), 1995, published as *A Treasury of Shakespeare's Verse,* Kingfisher (New York, NY), 2000.

Allan Ahlberg, *Mrs. Vole the Vet,* Puffin (London, England), 1996.

(And editor, with Catherine Asholt and Quentin Blake) *The Candlewick Book of First Rhymes* (anthology), Candlewick (Cambridge, MA), 1996.

Henrietta Branford, *Dimanche Diller at Sea,* Collins (London, England), 1996.

Ian Whybrow, *Miss Wire and the Three Kind Mice,* Kingfisher (London, England), 1996.

Sam McBratney, editor, *Little Red Riding Hood,* 1996.

Emma Alcock, *Sinan,* 1996.

Laura Mare, *Mehmet the Conqueror,* 1997.

Laura Cecil, *Noah and the Space Ark,* Hamish Hamilton (London, England), 1997, Lerner (New York, NY), 1998.

Geraldine McCaughrean, reteller, *The Orchard Book of Greek Gods and Goddesses,* Orchard (London, England), 1997.

Jane Falloon, reteller, *Thumbelina,* Pavilion (London, England), 1997.

The Little Book of Shakespeare, compiled by Gina Pollinger, Kingfisher (London, England), 1997.

John Yeoman, *The Glove Puppet Man,* Collins (London, England), 1997.

Adrian Mitchell, reteller, *The Adventures of Robin Hood and Marian,* Orchard (London, England), 1998.

Mathew Price, *Where's Alfie?,* Orchard (London, England), 1999.

Mathew Price, *Don't Worry, Alfie,* Orchard (London, England), 1999.

Naomi Lewis, *Elf Hill: Tales from Hans Christian Andersen,* Star Bright Books, 1999.

Mathew Price, *Patch and the Rabbits,* Orchard (London, England), 1999, Orchard (New York, NY), 2000.

Mathew Price, *Patch Finds a Friend,* Orchard (New York, NY), 2000.

Laura Cecil, compiler, *The Kingfisher Book of Toy Stories,* Kingfisher (New York, NY), 2000.

Geraldine McCaughrean, reteller, *Roman Myths,* Margaret K. McElderry Books (New York, NY), 2001.

Michael Morpurgo, *The McElderry Book of Aesop's Fables,* Margaret K. McElderry Books (New York, NY), 2005.

Contributor of illustrations to *Tom's Pirate Ship and Other Stories* and *Mostly Animal Poetry,* both Heinemann (London, England), 1997, and *Alphabet Gallery,* Mammoth (London, England), 1999. Illustrations have also appeared in newspapers and periodicals, including the London *Sunday Times, Cosmopolitan,* and *New Scientist.*

SIDELIGHTS: A popular and prolific author, illustrator, and anthologist, Emma Chichester Clark is considered one of England's most distinguished picture-book creators. Cited alongside noted illustrators Beatrix Potter, Edward Ardizzone, Tony Ross, and Quentin Blake—her former teacher—she has written and illustrated many of her own picture books while also creating accompanying artwork for numerous stories, picture books, anthologies, and retellings by other writers, including Roald Dahl, Anne Fine, Peter Dickinson, Allan Ahlberg, Rosemary Sutcliff, Sam McBratney, Diana Wynne Jones, John Yeoman, Naomi Lewis, Matthew Price, Janet Lunn, Jenny Nimmo, and Geraldine McCaughrean. In her own books, which include *Up in Heaven, The Story of Horrible Hilda and Henry,* and the award-winning *I Love You, Blue Kangaroo!,* she features child, adult, and animal characters in situations that, although usually humorous and fantastic, provide realistic portrayals of human feelings and foibles. Gwyneth Evans noted in an essay for the *St. James Guide to Children's Writers* that Chichester Clark's original stories "are reassuring, but have an underlying toughness." Their protagonists—boys and girls, older women, and anthropomorphized animals ranging from donkeys to lemurs—are not perfect: they fight, tease, overeat, and are greedy and absentminded. However, they ultimately make positive choices and, at the end of their adventures, return home, satisfied with their situation.

As an artist, Chichester Clark is praised for her distinctive, easily recognizable style, as well as for her use of color and her ability to evoke action and emotion. She often works in watercolor and pen, and her pictures range from bucolic scenes in gentle pastels to luminous, vivid paintings teeming with activity. "While her illustrations often suggest the serenity and charm of a timeless world," stated Evans, "her work has a vitality and a multicultural perspective which also makes it contemporary."

Born in London, England, Chichester Clark was brought to Ireland at the age of three and grew up in an old white farmhouse surrounded by fields. Her family kept many pets, including dogs, roosters, mice, rabbits, and, as the artist wrote in *Ladybug,* "a very old pony who was pretty vicious." Because she lived a long way from any other children, Chichester Clark and her siblings "had to entertain ourselves, which was easy there. I used to draw a lot, houses with windows jammed into the four corners and people with no necks." She also made her own small books, "with proper spines that my mother sewed up for me." "All the way through school," she added, "it didn't

ever occur to me that I would do anything other than illustrate books when I was 'grown up.'"

In 1975, Chichester Clark left Ireland to attend the Chelsea School of Art in London. After graduating with honors, she began to submit original picture books to publishers. When two of them were rejected, she suspended her quest to work in a design studio. Instead, she designed book jackets and submitted illustrations to newspapers and magazines. A few years later, she enrolled at the Royal College of Art, where she was taught by Quentin Blake and prominent author/illustrator Michael Foreman. After receiving her master's degree, again with honors, she received a phone call from an editor at London publisher Bodley Head, who had found copies of the drawings Chichester Clark had submitted several years previously. She was asked to illustrate the story anthology *Listen to This,* which began her fruitful collaboration with the book's editor, Laura Cecil.

Listen to This contains thirteen stories, including works by Rudyard Kipling, Philippa Pearce, Virginia Hamilton, Margaret Mahy, and the Brothers Grimm. Writing in the *Times Educational Supplement,* Jenny Marshall noted that Chichester Clark's colorful illustrations "have verve and wit," while Lesley Chamberlain concluded in the *Times Literary Supplement* that the artist "has brought an energetic and unsentimental streak to very varied material." In response to her work the illustrator received the Mother Goose Award in 1988, acknowledging her position as the most exciting newcomer to British children's book illustration.

Chichester Clark and Cecil have continued their collaboration on several well-received compilations, as well as original stories by Cecil. *Noah and the Space Ark,* Cecil's picture book with an environmental theme, places the Biblical character in a future in which Earth is so polluted that people and animals are in danger of extinction. Noah builds a rocket ship and takes the small animals—the larger ones have already died out—into space to find a new home. After they find a planet that resembles Earth, they disembark and vow to take better care of it than the stewards of Earth had done.

Chichester Clark serves as compiler and illustrator of *I Never Saw a Purple Cow, and Other Nonsense Rhymes,* which includes over one hundred poems by such writers as Edward Lear, Lewis Carroll, and Hilaire Belloc. Filled out by an additional selection of traditional rhymes, riddles, limericks, and ballads, the book is arranged according to animal species and behavior. A *Kirkus Review* critic dubbed Chichester Clark's witty illustrations "just right" and called *I Never Saw a Purple Cow* a "delightful compilation, handsomely presented." Writing in *School Librarian,* Joan Nellist claimed that Chichester Clark matches the rhymes and poems "with a beautiful simplicity which is sure to please young and old alike."

While she has illustrated many works by others, Chichester Clark has gained much of her following for her original stories. She began her writing career with the picture book *Catch That Hat!,* published in 1988. In this work, which is written in rhyme, Rose loses her pink hat to the wind as she chases a cat. As she retrieves and then again loses her hat, Rose is aided by animals such as a cow, a rabbit, and a kangaroo, as well as by a boy. Her hat finally lands in a monkey puzzle tree that no one can climb. A cockatoo lands on the hat and makes a nest, which pleases Rose even as she sheds a tear for her lost chapeau. At the end of the story, Rose's friends give her a new hat, complete with a ribbon to tie under her chin, that is even better than the old one. *Booklist* contributor Barbara Elleman predicted that children "will enjoy the whimsy of this airy, light-as-a-breeze tale."

Called "bibliotherapy at its best" by *School Library Journal* reviewer Rosalyn Pierini, *Up in Heaven* tackles a subject that almost every child has to face at some point: the death of a beloved pet. Arthur spends much of his play time with the family dog, Daisy, but eventually the elderly Daisy starts to sit out the most rambunctious games on the sidelines. When Daisy finally passes away, she looks down from Doggy Heaven and sees how sad Arthur is, so sends the young boy a dream to let him know that she is happy and that it is okay to give his affection to a new puppy. Martha V. Parravano praised the story in *Horn Book* as "comforting and uplifting but not in the least saccharine," while in *Booklist* Hazel Rochman noted that in her "joyful fantasy" Chichester Clark presents a forthright way to view the loss of a loved one; because *Up in Heaven* "never denies the child's sorrow and loss, the hopeful, loving scenes will help preschoolers move on," Rochman added.

The Story of Horrible Hilda and Henry is a cautionary tale in picture-book form about a brother and sister who like to misbehave: They trash their house, squirt their parents with a hose, have food fights, and tease each other unmercifully. Finally, the children's parents send them to the zoo. After annoying the animals, Hilda and Henry are placed in a cage with Brian, a bad-tempered lion who frightens the siblings so much that they become model children. Their parents take Brian home along with Hilda and Henry, hoping that the lion will act as insurance; however, Chichester Clark's last picture shows the children reverting back to their former disobedient ways. Writing in *Booklist,* Ilene Cooper noted that Chichester Clarks's use of "comic-book strips, full-page pictures, and two-page spreads" all work to relay her humorous story "to good effect," while a *Kirkus Reviews* critic claimed that young readers will enjoy the "gleefully exaggerated pranks here, which [Chichester] Clark illustrates with her usual zest."

Tea with Aunt Augusta—published in the United States as *Lunch with Aunt Augusta*—is one of Chichester Clark's most popular works. The story outlines what happens when Jemima, a ring-tailed lemur who is the youngest in her family, goes with her two older brothers to visit their beloved Aunt Augusta. After Jemima gorges herself on the lavish variety of mixed fruits provided by Aunt Augusta, the little lemur cannot keep up with her older brothers on their way home. Lost in the dark, she is rescued by a group of friendly fruit bats, who carry her home in a leaf sling. Jemima is lectured by her parents on overeating, but they welcome her with hugs and kisses. Her brothers, on the other hand, are sent to bed without supper for abandoning their sister in the jungle. Calling Chichester Clark's illustrations "delightfully vivid, witty, and tender," *Times Educational Supplement* reviewer Andrew Davies concluded, "I've never given ring-tailed lemurs much thought before. Now I wish I owned one. In fact I wish I was one." A *Publishers Weekly* reviewer noted the book's "unique and captivating cast" and "playful artwork," while in *Booklist* Hazel Rochman concluded that, "with all its nonsense . . . this satisfying story combines the small child's fear of being lost with the dream of adventure."

With *Little Miss Muffet Counts to Ten*—published in the United States as *Little Miss Muffet's Count-Along Surprise*—Chichester Clark extends the traditional nursery rhyme in a concept book that teaches basic mathematics. Instead of frightening Miss Muffet away, the spider asks her politely to stay. The arachnid is pleased when her animal friends—including bears with chairs and puffins with muffins—arrive to give her a surprise birthday party. When two crocodiles with greedy smiles show up, things get tense; however, they are just bringing the cake. Writing in *School Librarian,* Sarah Reed termed the book a "successful combination of a counting book, traditional rhyme, repetition, a chain story, all beautifully illustrated," while *FamilyFun* reviewer Sandy MacDonald wrote, "The rhymes are tightly sprung, the imagery deliciously imaginative." A critic for *Kirkus Reviews* concluded by calling *Little Miss Muffet's Count-Along Surprise* "a wonderful variation on the nursery rhyme that for once will frighten no one away."

In *More!* little Billy stalls, demanding one more story, one more ice cream, one more game to avoid the dreaded bedtime. When his mother refuses, Billy stomps off to his room, gathers his stuffed toys and the life-size lion that lives behind the curtain, and goes off to the center of the Earth, where he gets more rides, more spins, and more lollipops than he could ever want. Billy becomes over-saturated and finally realizes that all he wants to do is to go home to bed, which he does. *School Librarian* critic Jane Doonan raved that, with *More!,* "she succeeds in picturing the indescribable."

Shortlisted for the coveted Kate Greenaway Medal for illustration, *I Love You, Blue Kangaroo!* begins a series that includes some of Chichester Clark's most popular books. Lily loves her stuffed blue kangaroo more than any of her other toys, but when she receives new stuffed animals, Blue Kangaroo is pushed to the side. The toy eventually makes his way to the crib of Lily's baby brother, where he is welcomed joyfully. Not surprisingly, when Lily sees Blue Kangaroo in her brother's arms, she realizes that she still loves him and wants him back. Ultimately, Lily comes up with a mutually beneficial plan: she trades all of her new stuffed toys to her baby brother in exchange for her beloved Blue Kangaroo. Writing in the *Times Educational Supplement,* William Feaver stated that Chichester Clark "has perfect pitch as an author/illustrator" and hailed *Blue Kangaroo* as "a winner." Stephanie Zvirin, writing in *Booklist,* praised the book's illustrations, noting that they "can open the way to parent-child discussions of selfishness and generosity." A reviewer for *School Library Journal* called *I Love You, Blue Kangaroo!* a "heartwarming story . . . wholly satisfactory."

Other books featuring Blue Kangaroo include *Where Are You, Blue Kangaroo?, It Was You, Blue Kangaroo!,* and *What Shall We Do, Blue Kangaroo?,* the last which finds Lily and her favorite toy thinking about ways to pass some free time, and ultimately host a garden tea party to which all of the household toys are invited. Noting that Chichester Clark's technique of depicting the kangaroo's face close up "pulls [readers] . . . into his perspective" and presents a view of childhood from the toy's perspective, *Horn Book* contributor Christine M. Heppermann praised the author/illustrator's use of an "appealingly repetitive text and joyful spring-like colors" throughout the "Blue Kangaroo" series. Citing the "can-do message" of *What Shall We Do, Blue Kangaroo?,* Lisa Dennis added in her *School Library Journal* review that the illustrations "show a cozy, idealized domestic setting. . .—the perfect place for a preschooler to develop a bit of independence."

A pair of young monkeys are the focus of several books by Chichester Clark. In *No More Kissing!* Momo ducks the kisses of relatives, and decides that even among his own affectionate family, there's just too much smooching going on. Realizing that not only monkeys but also lion, snake, and even crocodile families engage in this off-putting practice, Momo goes to the extreme of wearing a sign pronouncing "No More Kissing" when he walks through the jungle, as a way to make his point. However, his attitude starts to change when a new baby brother enters the family, causing *School Library Journal* contributor Linda M. Kenton to note that *No More Kissing!* provides parents with "a fresh approach to introducing a new baby in a family." In the board books *Mimi's Book of Opposites* and *Mimi's Book of Counting,* Momo's older cousin is introduced, presenting basic concepts to toddlers with the help of several family members. Momo returns to share center stage with his cousin in the picture-book *No More Teasing!,* as Mimi becomes exasperated by Momo's constant joking and just plain pestering. Fortunately, Grandma comes to the rescue and together the two hatch a plot that the impish Momo will not forget. Although their solution involves a cape and a scary mask, Chichester Clark's art "with its happy colors and exotic locale, is not so terrifying as to curdle young readers' blood," concluded a *Kirkus Reviews* contributor.

BIOGRAPHICAL AND CRITICAL SOURCES:

BOOKS

St. James Guide to Children's Writers, edited by Sara and Tom Pendergast, St. James Press (Detroit, MI), 1999, pp. 230-232.

PERIODICALS

Booklist, April 15, 1989, Ilene Cooper, review of *The Story of Horrible Hilda and Henry,* p. 1464; May 15, 1990, Barbara Elleman, review of *Catch That Hat!,* pp. 1797-1798; May 1, 1992, Hazel Rochman, review of *Lunch with Aunt Augusta,* p. 1606; January 1, 1999, Stephanie Zvirin, review of *I Love You, Blue Kangaroo!,* p. 886; November 1, 2002, Hazel Rochman, review of *It Was You, Blue Kangaroo!,* p. 504; May 15, 2003, Gillian Engberg, review of *What Shall We Do, Blue Kangaroo?,* p. 1669; February 1, 2004, Hazel Rochman, review of *Up in Heaven,* p. 979.

Books for Keeps, January, 1998, p. 18.

FamilyFun, November, 1997, Sandy MacDonald, review of *Little Miss Muffet's Count-Along Surprise.*

Horn Book, March-April, 2002, Martha V. Parravano, review of *No More Kissing!,* p. 201; March-April, 2004, Martha V. Parravano, review of *Up in Heaven,* p. 169; September-October, 2003, Christine M. Heppermann, review of *What Shall We Do, Blue Kangaroo?,* p. 492.

Independent (London, England), May 14, 1998, Sally Williams, review of *More!*

Junior Bookshelf, April, 1996, p. 56.

Kirkus Reviews, April 15, 1989, review of *The Story of Horrible Hilda and Henry,* p. 622; April 15, 1991, review of *I Never Saw a Purple Cow, and Other Nonsense Rhymes;* September 15, 1997, review of *Little Miss Muffet's Count-Along Surprise,* p. 1454; December 15, 2001, review of *No More Kissing!,* p. 1755; February 14, 2004, review of *Up in Heaven,* p. 175; January 1, 2005, review of *No More Teasing!,* p. 50; June 1, 2002, review of *It Was You, Blue Kangaroo!,* p. 802.

Ladybug, March, 1997, "Meet the Artist: Emma Chichester Clark," p. 39.

Magpies, September, 1998, p. 28; November, 1998, p. 26.

Publishers Weekly, January 6, 1992, review of *Lunch with Aunt Augusta,* p. 65; January 20, 2003, review of *Follow the Leader!,* p. 80.

School Librarian, August, 1987, Sarah Reed, review of *Little Miss Muffet Counts to Ten,* p. 130; May, 1991, Joan Nellist, review of *I Never Saw a Purple Cow, and Other Nonsense Rhymes,* pp. 681-682; autumn, 1998, Jane Doonan, review of *More!,* p. 129.

School Library Journal, April, 1999, review of *I Love You, Blue Kangaroo!;* January, 2002, Linda M.

Kenton, review of *No More Kissing!,* p. 96; May, 2003, Rosalyn Pierini, review of *Follow the Leader!,* p. 110; July, 2003, Lisa Dennis, review of *What Shall We Do, Blue Kangaroo?,* p. 88; November, 2003, Olga R. Kuharets, review of *Mimi's Book of Counting,* p. 90; March, 2004, Rosalyn Pierini, review of *Up in Heaven,* p. 155.

Times Educational Supplement, November 6, 1987, Jenny Marshall, "Storybook Worlds," p. 27; February 14, 1992, Andrew Davies, "Having a Good Time," p. 27; December 11, 1998, William Feaver, "Leap of Imagination," p. 37.

Times Literary Supplement, December 4, 1989, Lesley Chamberlain, "Igniting the Imagination," p. 1361.

ONLINE

Andersen Press Web site, http://www.andersenpress.co.uk/ (December 2, 2004).*

*　　*　　*

CLARKE, Austin C(hesterfield) 1934-

PERSONAL: Born July 26, 1934, in St. James, Barbados; son of Kenneth Trothan (an artist) and Gladys (a hotel maid) Clarke; married Betty Joyce Reynolds, 1957 (divorced); children: Janice, Loretta, Jordan (also known as Mphahlele). *Education:* Attended secondary school at Harrison College in Barbados; studied economics and politics at Trinity College, University of Toronto, beginning in 1955.

ADDRESSES: Home—62 McGill St., Toronto, Ontario M5B 1H2, Canada. *Agent*—Phyllis Westberg, Harold Ober Associates, 425 Madison Ave., New York, NY 10017.

CAREER: Coleridge-Parry Primary School, St. Peter, Barbados, teacher, 1952-55; newspaper reporter in Timmins and Kirkland Lake, Ontario, Canada, 1959-60; Canadian Broadcasting Corp., Toronto, Ontario, Canada, producer and freelance broadcaster, beginning 1963; Barbados Embassy, Washington, DC, cultural and press attaché, 1974-76; Caribbean Broadcasting Corp., St. Michael, Barbados, general manager, 1975-76. Also has worked as a freelance journalist for *Toronto Globe and Mail* and Canadian Broadcasting Corp.

Austin C. Clarke

Yale University, New Haven, CT, Hoyt fellow, 1968, visiting professor of Afro-American literature and creative writing, 1968-71; Brandeis University, Waltham, MA, Jacob Ziskind Professor of Literature, 1968-69; Williams College, Williamstown, MA, Margaret Bundy Scott Visiting Professor of Literature, 1971; Duke University, Durham, NC, lecturer, 1971-72; University of Texas, Austin, visiting professor, 1973-74; Concordia University, Montreal, Quebec, writer in residence, 1977; University of Western Ontario, writer in residence, 1978. Rhode Island School of Design, Providence, member of board of trustees, 1970-75; Ontario Board of Censors, vice-chairperson, 1983-85; Immigration and Refugee Board of Canada, member, 1988-93.

MEMBER: Writers Guild, Writers' Union of Canada (founding member), Yale Club (New Haven).

AWARDS, HONORS: President's Medal for best story, University of Western Ontario, 1966; Belmont Short Story Award, 1965, for "Four Stations in His Circle";

Canada Council, senior arts fellowships, 1968, 1970, 1974, grant, 1977; Indiana University School of Letters, Bloomington, fellow, 1969; Cuba's Casa de las Americas Literary Prize, 1980; Toronto Arts Award for lifetime achievement in literature, 1993; Toronto Pride Achievement Award, 1995; Rogers Writers Trust Prize, 1997, for _The Origin of Waves;_ Lifetime Achievement Award, Frontier College, Toronto, 1997; Order of Canada, 1998; W. O. Mitchell Literary Prize, 1999; Writer's Trust of Canada, 1999; Martin Luther King, Jr. Award for excellence in writing, 1999; Giller Prize, 2002, Commonwealth Writers Prize for the best overall book, 2003, Trillium Prize, and Regional Commonwealth Writers Prize for the best book in Canada and the Caribbean, all for _The Polished Hoe._ Also received honorary doctorates from Brock University, 1998, and University of Toronto, 1999.

WRITINGS:

NOVELS

The Survivors of the Crossing, McClelland & Stewart (Toronto, Ontario, Canada), 1964.
Amongst Thistles and Thorns, McClelland & Stewart (Toronto, Ontario, Canada), 1965.
The Prime Minister, General Publishing (Don Mills, Ontario, Canada), 1977.
Proud Empires, Gollancz (London, England), 1986, Viking-Penguin (Markham, Ontario, Canada), 1988.
The Origin of Waves, McClelland & Stewart (Toronto, Ontario, Canada), 1997.
The Question, McClelland & Stewart (Toronto, Ontario, Canada), 1999.
The Polished Hoe, Thomas Allen (Toronto, Ontario, Canada), 2002, Amistad (New York, NY), 2003.

NOVELS; "THE TORONTO TRILOGY"

The Meeting Point, Macmillan (Toronto, Ontario, Canada), 1967, Little, Brown (Boston, MA), 1972.
Storm of Fortune, Little, Brown (Boston, MA), 1973.
The Bigger Light, Little, Brown (Boston, MA), 1975.

SHORT STORY COLLECTIONS

When He Was Free and Young and He Used to Wear Silks, Anansi (Toronto, Ontario, Canada), 1971, revised edition, Little, Brown (Boston, MA), 1973.

When Women Rule, McClelland & Stewart (Toronto, Ontario, Canada), 1985.

Nine Men Who Laughed, Penguin (New York, NY), 1986.

In This City, Exile Editions (Toronto, Ontario, Canada), 1992.

There Are No Elders, Exile Editions (Toronto, Ontario, Canada), 1993.

Choosing His Coffin: The Best Stories of Austin Clarke, Thomas Allen (Toronto, Ontario, Canada), 2003.

Author of *Short Stories of Austin Clarke,* 1984.

OTHER

(Contributor) Lloyd W. Brown, editor, *The Black Writer in Africa and the Americas,* Hennessey & Ingalls (Los Angeles, CA), 1973.

The Confused Bewilderment of Martin Luther King & the Idea of Non-Violence As a Political Tactic, Watkins (Burlington, Ontario, Canada), 1986.

Growing up Stupid under the Union Jack: A Memoir, McClelland & Stewart (Toronto, Ontario, Canada), 1980.

Charlotte Stewart, compiler, *The Austin Clarke Collection,* Mills Memorial Library, McMaster University (Hamilton, Ontario, Canada), 1982.

A Passage Back Home: A Personal Reminiscence of Samuel Selvon, Exile Editions (Toronto, Ontario, Canada), 1994.

Barry Callaghan, editor, *The Austin Clarke Reader,* Exile Editions (Toronto, Ontario, Canada), 1996.

Pigtails 'n Breadfruit: The Rituals of Slave Food: A Barbadian Memoir, Random House Canada (Toronto, Ontario, Canada), 1999, published as *Pig Tails 'n Breadfruit: A Culinary Memoir,* New Press (New York, NY), 1999.

Also author of *Myths and Memories, African Literature,* and other film scripts for Educational Television (ETV), Toronto, beginning in 1968. Managing editor of *Contrast,* a newspaper devoted to Toronto's black community. Launched *McGill Street,* a literary journal. Contributor to periodicals, including *Studies in Black Literature* and *Canadian Literature.* Manuscript collection held at McMaster University, Hamilton, Ontario.

SIDELIGHTS: Austin C. Clarke's childhood in colonial Barbados and his experiences as a black immigrant to Canada have provided him with the background for most of his fiction. His writing is almost exclusively concerned with the cultural contradictions that arise when blacks struggle for success in a predominantly white society. Clarke's "one very great gift," in the words of a *New Yorker* critic, is the ability to see "unerringly into his characters' hearts," and this ability is what makes his stories memorable. Martin Levin wrote in the *New York Times Book Review,* "Mr. Clarke is plugged into the fixations, hopes, loves and dreams of his characters. He converts them into stories that are charged with life." In the *Reference Guide to Short Fiction,* Allan Weiss labeled Clarke "unquestionably the most important black Canadian writer." Whether writing novels, short stories, or memoirs, Clarke has a knack for capturing the dialect, the troubles, the emotions, and the thoughts of his individual characters, and through them relays a larger picture to his readers.

Among Clarke's short-story collections are *When He Was Free and Young and He Used to Wear Silks, When Women Rule, Nine Men Who Laughed,* and *In This City.* According to a *Short Story Criticism* contributor, "Clarke's short stories are fueled by his experience of cultural alienation as a West Indian and his analysis of how racism and colonialism impact the daily lives of Caribbean immigrants. Clarke's frequently anthologized short stories are populated by portraits of complex individuals navigating the difficult terrain of cultural adjustment and assimilation." The stories in the collection *When Women Rule* are about immigrants, both white and black, from a variety of cultural origins, who share similar anxieties and fears for the future. Lloyd Brown remarked in *Contemporary Novelists,* "It is the central irony of this collection that the very idea of a Canadian mosaic, with its implicit promise of social harmony and individual success, binds Clarke's diverse Canadians together by virtue of its failure, rather than its fulfillment." In his introduction to the collection *Nine Men Who Laughed,* according to Victor J. Ramraj in the *Dictionary of Literary Biography,* the author "rails against the Canadian system that perpetually perceives the West Indian immigrant as an outsider," and he also criticizes the immigrant who finally succeeds, then "becomes tolerant of abuses." These stories, Ramraj concluded, "show Clarke honing his skills as a short-story writer. Most of the stories achieve an ironic control, discipline, and aesthetic distance not evident in [his] earlier work." The *Short Story Criticism* contributor commented, "Clarke is often criticized for letting his political agenda interfere with the narrative of his later works, thereby alienating the reader. Many scholars, however, emphasize that while these stories present a world rife with despair, they are ultimately underpinned by an idealized vision of a more equitable society."

Clarke's memoir, *Growing up Stupid under the Union Jack,* is an example of the author's typical theme and style. The narrator, Tom, is a young man from a poor village in Barbados. Everyone in the village is proud that Tom is able to attend the Combermere School, for it is run by a "real, true-true Englishman"—an ex-British army officer who calls his students "boy" and "darky" and who flogs them publicly. The students eagerly imitate this headmaster's morals and manners, for to them he represents "Mother England"; they are unaware that in England he would be looked down upon as a mere working-class soldier. The book is "a personal, captivating, provoking, and often humorous record of ignorance, inhumanity and lowly existence under colonial imperialism in World War II Barbados. . . . With its major emphasis on education and childhood, *Growing up Stupid under the Union Jack* continues to draw attention to one of the chief preoccupations of the anticolonial Anglo-Caribbean novel," wrote Robert P. Smith in *World Literature Today.* "The colonial situation is the essence of the absurd because it both causes and symbolizes the condition of being isolated from one's self, one's cultural and personal roots," explained Brown, who maintained, "the most central, and universal, of all [Clarke's] themes [is] alienation." The theme is well rendered in what Darryl Pinckney called in the *New York Review of Books* Clarke's "tender, funny, unpolemical style." This style emphasizes what Ramraj described as "his immense talent for capturing the feel and flow of Barbadian speech and his adeptness at creating hilariously comic scenes."

Some of Clarke's novels are also "set in Barbados and they explore the twin evils of colonial self-hatred and Caribbean poverty," Brown commented. *The Survivors of the Crossing* describes the attempts of Rufus, a worker at a white-owned sugar plantation, to lead a labor strike. He fails because the powerful white owners and the middle-class black islanders ally themselves against him, and even the poor working-class laborers eventually thrust him from their midst. Rufus's inspiration to incite rebellion came from his perception of the American dream, in this case, the power of the working class in Canada. *Amongst Thistles and Thorns* is the story of a nine-year-old runaway who finds his

birth father, spends a weekend with him, then returns home still alienated from his current lot in life, but filled with stories about the American land of opportunity, in particularly New York City's Harlem. As Ramraj summarized, "What North America, in particular Canada, actually holds for the black migrant is not so pleasant, however, which is the concern of Clarke's next three novels, the Toronto trilogy."

The trilogy, which is perhaps Clarke's best-known work, details the lives of the Barbadian blacks who immigrate to Toronto hoping to better their lot. In these novels, *The Meeting Point, Storm of Fortune,* and *The Bigger Light,* "it is as if the flat characters of a Dickensian world have come into their own at last, playing their tragicomic roles in a manner which owes much to Clarke's extraordinary facility with the Barbadian dialect," commented Diane Bessai in *Canadian Literature.* Bessai also expressed eagerness for Clarke to "continue to create his Brueghel-like canvasses with their rich and contrasting detail and mood." "The sense of defeat among the poor islanders is enlivened by the humour of the characters and their glowing fantasies about the presumed wealth of relatives and friends who make it big in the fatlands of the United States or Canada," remarked John Ayre in *Saturday Night.* The reality for such immigrants, according to Brown, is that "West Indians must choose between being integrated into a strange culture—at the cost of their cultural uniqueness and racial integrity—or being so dedicated to maintaining their black, West Indian identity that they risk being cultural and economic outsiders in their adopted homeland."

The first two novels dwell mostly on Bernice Leach, a live-in maid at a wealthy Toronto home, and her small circle of fellow immigrants. The *New York Times Book Review*'s Martin Levin praised, "Mr. Clarke is masterful at delineating the oppressive insecurities of Bernice and her friends, and the claustrophobic atmosphere that envelops such a mini-minority" as the Caribbean blacks in Toronto. In *The Meeting Point,* Ramraj wrote, "these characters have to contend with inner as well as outer conflicts as they try to retain their black pride and identity and come to grips with self-hatred and beckoning materialism." In *Storm of Fortune,* he continued, some of the group have increased their "measure of economic success and feel they deserve acceptance into the system [but] now have to cope with more sharply felt social alienation."

The third novel, *The Bigger Light,* explores the life of Boysie, the most successful of this immigrant group, and his wife, Dots. Boysie has at last realized the dream that compelled him to leave Barbados; he owns a prosperous business and his own home. However, in the process of realizing his goals, he has become alienated from his wife and his community. "His economic successes have not protected him from emotional failure," explained Brown. Now he searches for a greater meaning to his life—a "bigger light." "*The Bigger Light* is a painful book to read," claimed David Rosenthal in the *Nation.* It is "a story of two people with many things to say and no one to say them to, who hate themselves and bitterly resent the society around them. . . . Certain African novelists have also dealt with the isolation of self-made blacks, but none with Clarke's bleak intensity." A *New Yorker* writer praised the book further, citing Clarke's strong writing skill as the element that lifts the book beyond social comment: "The universal longings of ordinary human beings are depicted with a simplicity and power that make us grateful for all three volumes of this long and honest record."

Clarke has also written works that attack political corruption in his native Barbados. These include the novel *The Prime Minister* which, according to some critics, bears striking comparisons to Clarke's own experiences and observations in Barbados in 1975, when he served briefly as the general manager of the Caribbean Broadcasting Corporation. The novel *Proud Empire,* set in the 1950s, examines political corruption and middle-class values from the perspective of a teenaged boy not yet tainted by the reality of island politics. It follows Boy through graduation, a period of study in Canada, and a return to Barbados, after which he enters politics himself, though now reluctant and with open eyes. "The novel confirms," Ramraj explained, "that Clarke's strength as a novelist lies not so much in his probing the psyche and inner development of his protagonists as in capturing the subtleties of the social and political behavior of his Barbadian characters, whether at home or abroad."

In 1997 Clarke published the novel *The Origin of Waves* which, according to John Bemrose in *Maclean's,* "contains some of Clarke's best writing ever." It follows a chance reunion of two old friends, of an age similar to that of the author, who have not seen each other since childhood. The two reminisce for hours in a local bar, enabling Clarke, through their stories, to express what Bemrose called "a gentle melancholy and, finally, a spark of hopefulness" about the lot of the immigrant in Canadian society.

Pig Tails 'n Breadfruit: Rituals of Slave Food: A Barbadian Memoir, also published as *Pig Tails 'n Breadfruit: A Culinary Memoir,* is Clarke's remembrance of the classic Barbadian cuisine of his youth, mixed with a dash of family tales, a hint of island culture, and a sprinkle of his own cooking stories. The book explains how to prepare traditional Barbadian dishes, such as Breadfruit Cou-Cou with Braising Beef, Pepperpot, Souse, Bakes, and other "slave food." In addition, the reader is offered a heaping spoonful of insights on the culture of Barbados. *Library Journal*'s John Charles reported, "The colorful cuisine of Barbados is the star of this book, and readers will find themselves immersed in the food and culture of that vibrant country." *Booklist*'s Mark Knoblauch noted, "Clarke's marvelous ability to set down the unique Barbadian dialect and make it accessible sparkles throughout these essays." Knoblauch continued, "Clarke's recipes for ham hocks and lima beans and split pea soup illustrate how slave cooks drew the most flavor out of the simplest staples." One complaint critics had about *Pig Tails 'n Breadfruit* is the lack of measurements in the recipes, but as Clarke points out in the book, "To be caught reading a cookbook would suggest that the wife, daughter, or maid does not know how to cook, does not know how to take care of her man." Charles explained, "Cooks there are expected to rely more on taste and touch." *Kola*'s Anthony Joyette dubbed *Pig Tails 'n Breadfruit* "a masterpiece," and noted that Clarke is "humorous, witty, and direct."

Clarke's next novel, *The Question,* focuses on a West Indian judge in Toronto who attends a party and meets a young white woman with whom he eventually goes home, even though his girlfriend intends to pick him up at the end of the party. The judge, who was taught by his mother never to discuss his personal problems in public, is intensely private with his thoughts and feelings. The result, according to Neil Querengesser of the *Canadian Ethnic Studies Journal,* is that "he has throughout his adult life construed as public . . . virtually everything and everyone outside himself. Consequently he carries on an intense and very revealing monologue only within his own mind, which Clarke adroitly relays to the reader." The judge's relationship with the new woman, explained Querengesser, provides "deeper and deeper insight into his psychosexual makeup." Readers soon realize that, though the judge has attained a prestigious place in society, his insecurities with women and inability to communicate effectively with them have robbed him of any form of prestige or power.

"Clarke develops his central character master-fully. . . . The judge draws us into his thoughts, almost effortlessly it seems, so interesting are his insights and so effective his means of expression," wrote Querengesser. The critic praised Clarke for his "vivid and insightful portrayals" of the characters in the novel, writing, "His fictional characters inhabit a compellingly realistic world, their lives shaped by a complex mixture of racial, cultural, sexual, political, geographic, linguistic, and economic influences." Querengesser remarked, "Clarke skillfully weaves an absorbing tale of a man impelled by these influences of his past into a strange and uncertain future."

Clarke's *The Polished Hoe,* published first in Canada and then in the United States, has received much praise from critics and has won several awards. The novel is set in the 1940s on the island of Bimshire (a nickname for Barbados). "In a twenty-four-hour time span," noted Denolyn Carroll of the *Black Issues Book Review,* "the novel's main character, Mary Mathilda, giving a statement to authorities about a crime she has committed, unwittingly dissects the evils of slavery and its legacy of colonialism." Mary Mathilda, former field worker and mistress of Mr. Bellfeels, a plantation owner, and the mother of Bellfeels's only son, exacted revenge on the man that dominated her life for so many years, killing him with a hoe she spent years obsessively polishing. *Library Journal*'s Faye A. Chadwell explained, "The twenty-four-hour saga begins after Mary has murdered Mr. Bellfeels and [police sergeant Percy Stuart] must record her all-night confession, an obligation complicated by his lifelong love for Mary."

A *Publishers Weekly* critic praised the work, saying "Most of the story . . . unfolds through brilliantly written dialogue, a rich, dancing patois that fills out the dimensions of the island's painful history and its complex caste system." *Kola*'s H. Nigel Thomas commented, "[The Polished Hoe] focuses our gaze on an ugly aspect of Caribbean reality which many of us have been unwilling to examine." Donna Bailey Nurse of *Publishers Weekly* reflected, "Through horror and humor, and this dazzling vernacular, Clarke conjures an idiosyncratic people clinging doggedly to their humanity." *Booklist*'s Brad Hooper felt the novel was "creatively executed" and Chadwell called it "a tragic, complex story" that "deftly reveals an abominable state of sexual oppression and racist tyranny and the revenge both can invoke." A *Kirkus Reviews* contribu-

tor dubbed the novel "a scorching indictment of the island's power elite" that is "warmed and softened by Clarke's celebration of Bimshire life: its foods, plants, rum shops, and the fortitude of its regular folks as they laugh and curse in cadences that Clarke catches so expertly."

Clarke has been writing in one form or another for several decades, but when asked by Linda Richards of *January Magazine Online* why he chose to write *The Polished Hoe,* he responded, "I felt the freedom for the first time that I needed as an author to deal with this subject. I did not know the subject was going to be this. But I felt the freedom and the liberation from all of the things that could influence the writing of a book negatively. I was not anxious for anything. I was in a very good mood. I was healthy. I was cheerful. And I had retained my sense of humor. And I thought, if not at the time, certainly now reflecting on it because of your question, that they are the ingredients that an author must experience and realize if he or she is going to write something that is great and good."

BIOGRAPHICAL AND CRITICAL SOURCES:

BOOKS

Algoo-Baksh, Stella, *Austin C. Clarke: A Biography,* Press of the University of West Indies [Barbados], 1994.
Brown, Lloyd, *El Dorado and Paradise: A Critical Study of the Works of Austin Clarke,* Center for Social and Humanistic Studies, University of Western Ontario (London, Ontario, Canada), 1989.
Clarke, Austin C., *Pig Tails 'n Bread Fruit: A Barbadian Memoir,* Random House Canada (Toronto, Ontario, Canada), 1999, published as *Pig Tails 'n Breadfruit: A Culinary Memoir,* New Press (New York, NY), 1999.
Contemporary Authors Autobiography Series, Volume 16, Thomson Gale (Detroit, MI), 1992.
Contemporary Black Biography, Volume 32, Thomson Gale (Detroit, MI), 2002.
Contemporary Literary Criticism, Thomson Gale (Detroit, MI), Volume 8, 1978, Volume 53, 1989.
Contemporary Novelists, 7th edition, St. James Press (Detroit, MI), 2001.
Dictionary of Literary Biography, Thomson Gale (Detroit, MI), Volume 53: *Canadian Writers since 1960, First Series,* 1986, Volume 125: *Twentieth-Century Caribbean and Black African Writers, Second Series,* 1993.

Gibson, Graeme, *Eleven Canadian Novelists,* Anansi (Toronto, Ontario, Canada), 1973, pp. 33-54.

Modern Black Writers, 2nd edition, Thomson Gale (Detroit, MI), 2000.

Reference Guide to Short Fiction, 2nd edition, St. James Press (Detroit, MI), 1998.

Short Story Criticism, Volume 45, Thomson Gale (Detroit, MI), 2001.

PERIODICALS

Black Issues Book Review, November-December, 2003, Denolyn Carroll, "Austin Clarke on Honing His Craft: An Island Epic Is a Capstone on a Distinguished Literary Career," review of *The Polished Hoe,* p. 64.

Booklist, February 15, 2000, Mark Knoblauch, review of *Pig Tails 'n Breadfruit: A Culinary Memoir,* p. 1067; May 15, 2003, Brad Hooper, review of *The Polished Hoe,* p. 1637.

Bookseller, February 20, 2004, "Austin Clarke," p. 27.

Books in Canada, October, 1986, pp. 20-21.

Canadian Book Review Annual, 1999, review of *Pig Tails 'n Breadfruit,* p. 140; 2000, review of *The Question,* p. 141.

Canadian Ethnic Studies Journal, summer, 2000, Neil Querengesser, review of *The Question,* p. 164.

Canadian Forum, August, 1999, Judy Schultz, "A Barbadian Memoir Centered in the Kitchen," review of *Pig Tails 'n Breadfruit,* p. 39.

Canadian Literature, summer, 1974; autumn, 1981, pp. 136-38; winter, 1982, pp. 181-85; spring, 2000, Dorothy Lane, review of *The Origin of Waves,* p. 150; autumn-winter, 2001, Maureen Moynagh, review of *Pig Tails 'n Breadfruit,* p. 193.

College Language Association Journal, September, 1985, pp. 9-32; December, 1992, pp. 123-33.

Essence, July, 2003, Diane Patrick, "Take Note," review of *The Polished Hoe,* p. 106.

Globe and Mail (Toronto, Ontario, Canada), April 24, 1999, review of *Pig Tails 'n Breadfruit,* p. E10; October 30, 1999, review of *The Question,* p. D22; November 27, 1999, review of *The Question,* p. D49.

Journal of Caribbean Studies, fall, 1985-spring, 1986, pp. 71-78.

Journal of Commonwealth Literature (Leeds, England), July, 1970.

Kirkus Reviews, May 1, 2003, review of *The Polished Hoe,* p. 624.

Kola, fall, 1999, Anthony Joyette, review of *Pig Tails 'n Breadfruit,* p. 73; winter, 2003, H. Nigel Thomas, review of *The Polished Hoe,* p. 47, and "The Montreal Black Community Congratulates," p. 53.

Library Journal, February 1, 2000, John Charles, review of *Pig Tails 'n Breadfruit,* p. 96; May 15, 2003, Faye A. Chadwell, review of *The Polished Hoe,* p. 122.

Listener, June 15, 1978.

M2 Best Books, November 8, 2002, "Austin Clarke Awarded Canada's Giller Book Prize"; May 12, 2003, "Commonwealth Writers Prizes Awarded."

Maclean's, April 21, 1997, p. 62; November 18, 2002, "Passages," p. 17, "ScoreCard," p. 13; July 1, 2003, Brian Bethune, "Austin Clarke: 'I Feel That My Feet Are Planted Here in This Landscape,'" brief biography of Austin Clarke.

Nation, November 1, 1975.

New Yorker, February 24, 1975.

New York Review of Books, May 27, 1982.

New York Times Book Review, April 9, 1972; December 9, 1973; February 16, 1975; August 23, 1987; April 9, 2000, Laura Shapiro and Michael Sragow, "Cover-She-Down," review of *Pig Tails 'n Breadfruit,* p. 38.

Publishers Weekly, March 6, 2000, review of *Pig Tails 'n Breadfruit,* p. 92; April 21, 2003, review of *The Polished Hoe,* p. 36; August 11, 2003, Donna Bailey Nurse, "Austin Clarke: A Barbadian Abroad," interview with Austin Clarke, p. 250.

Quill & Quire, December, 1999, review of *The Question,* p. 32.

Saturday Night, October, 1971; June, 1975.

Times Literary Supplement, May 11, 1967, p. 404.

World Literature Today, winter, 1982.

World Literature Written in English, spring, 1986, pp. 115-127.

ONLINE

Athabasca University Canadian Writers Web site, http://www.athabascau.ca/writers/ (June 21, 2004), "Austin Clarke," brief biography.

Bukowski Agency Web site, http://www.thebukowski agency.com/ (February 7, 2003), description of *Pig Tails 'n Breadfruit.*

January Magazine Online, http://www.january magazine.com/ (November, 2002), Linda Richards, interview with Austin Clarke.

Northwest Passages Web site, http://www.nwpassages. com/ (June 21, 2004), "Author Profiles: Austin Clarke," brief biography.*

*   *   *

CLEVELAND, Ceil 1940-

PERSONAL: Born January 10, 1940, in Olton, TX; daughter of Joe Donaldson Cleveland Slack (a rancher and teacher) and Margaret Ellen (an artist and teacher; maiden name, Gowdy) Slack; married Donald R. Waldrip (marriage ended); married Jerrold K. Footlick, 1984; children: Wendy, Tim, Jay. *Education:* Whitworth College, B.A. (cum laude), 1968; Midwestern University, M.A. (with honors), 1971; attended writing program at Columbia University, 1977-79; attended University of Cincinnati, 1974-76. *Hobbies and other interests:* Music, theater, travel, gardening.

ADDRESSES: Home—4010 Wynford Place, Durham, NC 27707. *Office*—Shimkin Hall, Room 228, New York University, NY, 10012. *E-mail*—ceilc@nc.rr.com.

CAREER: Scriptwriter for educational television, Spokane, WA, 1966-69, and Dallas, TX, 1970-72; Cincinnati Arts and Humanities Consortium, Cincinnati, OH, director of curriculum, 1972-74; University Press, University of Cincinnati, associate editor, 1974-76; *Columbia—The Magazine of Columbia University,* New York, NY, founder and editor-in-chief, 1976-86; Cleveland Communications, Inc. (marketing and editorial projects organization), founder and president, 1986—; Queens College of the City University of New York, vice president for university relations, 1991-95; State University of New York at Stony Brook, vice president for university affairs and associate professor of English and women's studies, 1995-98, currently adjunct professor. Cofounder, *Syzygy: A Journal of Short Fiction,* 1976; founder, Cincinnati Women's Press, and *Brook* (magazine), c. 1996. Lecturer at colleges, including University of Cincinnati and Xavier University, c. 1972-74, Washington College, Rhodes College, Goucher College, and Austin College. Lonesome Dove Inn, Archer City, TX, proprietor.

MEMBER: American Council on Education (coordinator of women's program, NY metro area, 1994—); Council for Advancement and Support of Education (trustee).

AWARDS, HONORS: Gold Award, Educational Publishers, and Magazine of the Decade Award, Council for Advancement and Support of Education (CASE), both for *Columbia—The Magazine of Columbia University.* Ohio Arts Council grant; Woodrow Wilson teaching fellow; Outstanding Alumnus Award, Midwestern University, 2003; named Redmond Reader, Whitworth College, 2002; Virginia Center for Creative Arts grant, 2002.

WRITINGS:

NONFICTION

Whatever Happened to Jacy Farrow? (memoir), University of North Texas Press (Denton, TX), 1997.
Better Punctuation in 30 Minutes a Day (reference book), Career Press (Franklin Lakes, NJ), 2003.
For Better and for Words (reference book), McGraw-Hill (New York, NY), 2005.

Author of *Iron, Gold, and Bronze Women, and a Few Made of Steel: Three Generations of Women and Their Relationship to Work,* a research study for Queens College of the City University of New York, 1994, and *In the World of Literature,* a literary quiz book. Contributor to *New York Times, Working Woman, New York Woman, Houston Post, Chronicle of Higher Education, Cincinnati Enquirer, Gannet Center Journal,* and *Information Age,* among many other periodicals, journals, and newspapers.

NOVELS

The Bluebook Solution, America House (Baltimore, MD), 2001.

EDITOR

Asa Briggs, Lord Briggs, *English Musical Culture, 1776-1976,* University of Cincinnati Press (Cincinnati, OH), 1977.
Mauk Mulder, *Managing with Power,* Elsevier Focus (Amsterdam, Netherlands), 1979.

Editor of *Syzygy: A Journal of Short Fiction,* 1976-79; editor of *We Have Something to Say: Arts Consortium Review,* 1974.

WORK IN PROGRESS: The novels *Against the Setting Sun,* 2005, and *The Blue Pig Solution,* 2007.

SIDELIGHTS: In the 1950s Ceil Cleveland and author Larry McMurtry were teenagers and friends in Archer City, a small, dusty west Texas town that later became the real-life setting for the town of Thalia in McMurtry's 1966 novel, *The Last Picture Show.* The book was made into a 1971 film by Peter Bogdanovich, and actress Cybill Shepherd, in her first role, would become indelibly associated with the work for her portrayal of the cool, daring, blonde, Jacy Farrow. Many residents back in Archer City theorized that Cleveland had been the basis for McMurtry's memorable character, but by then Cleveland had long departed.

After attending college in Spokane, Washington, and earning an M.A. from Wichita Falls' Midwestern University, Cleveland began a long and diversified career, beginning as a Cincinnati newspaper journalist, segueing into arts-foundation administration, and then graduate work at Columbia University. In 1976 she founded *Columbia—The Magazine of Columbia University,* which won several journalism awards. By the mid-1980s Cleveland had started her own marketing and editorial communications firm, but she continued to write articles for an array of magazines. In 1991 she took a job as vice president for university relations at Queens College in New York City and four years later became an associate professor of English and women's studies at the State University of New York at Stony Brook, as well as the school's vice president for university affairs. Today she is adjunct professor of English at New York University.

Cleveland left the academic world behind not long after the publication of her autobiographical *Whatever Happened to Jacy Farrow?* in 1997. In her book Cleveland chose the unorthodox strategy of letting "Jacy" narrate the story of her life, beginning with her high-school days and concluding with Cleveland's commencement address at her Archer City alma mater. "This is one of those currently trendy memories where the reader has to figure what's true and what has been fictionalized," according to reviewer Mike Cox in the *Lubbock Avalanche-Journal,* but he termed it "an engaging read, particularly for women who were teenagers in the 1950s and McMurtry fans in general." *Entertainment Weekly* contributor Don Graham echoed

that endorsement, noting that the memoir is noteworthy for revealing "what it was like to grow up female, pretty, and smart" in the era of limited, small-town possibilities.

Cleveland told *CA:* "When I was a girl in a Texas town of 1,600 on the High Plains, I couldn't wait to get out of there. After traveling all over the world, and living in New York City for twenty years—and especially going through the agony and ecstasy of writing a memoir—I went back to the little town of my girlhood and built the Lonesome Dove Inn as a retreat for writers. I grew up in a town without a library, or anyone except for my mother, who cared about books. Now the town has McMurtry's half million books and a retreat for people who want to read, write, or talk about books. I visit there, but I write better overlooking the lake behind my new home in North Carolina.

"Both the strength and the weakness of my writing career is that I select a variety of subjects and genres to work in: memoir, mystery novel series, stand-alone novel, academic texts, and reference books. I do the novels for fun and the texts for profit; with luck and assiduous application of backside to desk chair, maybe I can move my novels into the second category. Strengths of this variety: I am versatile, have many interests, and can shift voice and style easily. Weakness: I'm hard for publishers to pidgeon-hole."

BIOGRAPHICAL AND CRITICAL SOURCES:

PERIODICALS

Entertainment Weekly, December 12, 1997, p. 80.
HR Magazine, January, 2003, review of *Better Punctuation in 30 Minutes a Day,* p. 83.
Lubbock Avalanche-Journal, December 14, 1997.
Publishers Weekly, October 20, 1997, p. 68.
San Antonio Express-News, March 8, 1998.

*   *   *

CLINTON, Dirk
See SILVERBERG, Robert

COLLIGNON, Rick 1948-

PERSONAL: Born 1948; children: three.

ADDRESSES: Home—Taos, NM. *Agent*—c/o Mac-Adam/Cage Publicity, 820 16th St., Ste. 331, Denver, CO 80231.

CAREER: Novelist. Has worked as a roofer for over twenty years.

WRITINGS:

The Journal of Antonio Montoya: A Novel, MacMurray & Beck (Denver, CO), 1996.
Perdido: A Novel, MacMurray & Beck (Denver, CO), 1997.
A Santo in the Image of Cristóbal García, BlueHen Books (New York, NY), 2002.

The Journal of Antonio Montoya has been translated into twelve languages, and *A Santo in the Image of Cristóbal García* has been translated into ten languages.

SIDELIGHTS: Rick Collignon burst upon the literary scene with the widely reviewed and well-received novel *The Journal of Antonio Montoya.* The novel concerns a series of supernatural events occurring in the town of Guadalupe, New Mexico, after an accident that leaves a young boy orphaned. Custody of José Montoya is left to his father's brother, but after the funeral, the boy's dead mother rises in her coffin to request a change. She asks Ramona Montoya, her husband's unmarried sister, to take the boy in. On Ramona's return home with the boy, she is awaited by her long-dead grandparents, who, between fixing dinner and running errands in her car, bequeath to her the journal of her great-uncle, her grandfather's cousin. Ramona reads the journal, which is spliced into the action of the novel. Like Ramona, who has given years of her life to try to establish a career in painting, Antonio Montoya was an artist, a sculptor of santos (small figures of the saints). The novel weaves parallels between Antonio's and Ramona's lives, and between all the living and the dead.

A number of critics, including Lawrence Olszewski, who reviewed the novel for *Library Journal,* linked Collignon's surreal situations to the writing of Gabriel

García Márquez, the renowned South American author. But critics were mixed in their appreciation for the novel as a whole. Olszewski called the book an "enchanting work," and Wendy Cavenett of *Between the Lines* maintained that "in *The Journal of Antonio Montoya,* Collignon beckons us to drink from the cup of divine omniscience, to believe that the world is a vast realm of the improbable and that life, in its many guises, exists concurrently, each effecting the other." She also called the book "an astonishing debut, one that heralds a clear, imaginative voice from the contemporary chasm of post-modernism." Others, however, though finding much to like in the novel, had criticisms as well. A *Publishers Weekly* reviewer praised Collignon's "spare style" and "bracingly fresh descriptions," but requested more plot line. Andy Solomon, writing for the *New York Times Book Review,* commented that "the problem . . . is less that the novel's dead characters are still living than that its living ones are half dead."

Collignon worked as a roofer for twenty years before publishing his first novel, but published his second novel, *Perdido,* only a year after the first. Like *The Journal of Antonio Montoya, Perdido* is also set in Guadalupe, New Mexico, which is inhabited almost exclusively by Mexican Americans. The protagonist is Will Sawyer, an Anglo who drifted into Guadalupe nearly twenty years prior to the beginning of the novel. Sawyer's sense of belonging in the community is challenged, however, after he discovers that a mysterious death has occurred—the hanging of a young Anglo woman at a bridge—shortly before his arrival in town. When he starts asking questions, it is not long before tensions bloom into violence, revealing just how tentatively accepted Will is in the town.

Nancy Pearl of *Booklist* praised *Perdido.* Although she thought some readers might be distracted by the author's habit of "dropping the reader into the middle of the story," she admired the novel's style and its "simple and direct narrative." In a review of the book for *Library Journal,* Faye A. Chadwell expressed appreciation for Collignon's ability to explore the connections between ethnic and racial groups "while delving into the concept of identity." An *Atlantic Monthly* reviewer believed Collignon "created a distinct and meaningful world," while *New York Times Book Review* critic Denise Gess concluded, "Driven by Collignon's decisive prose, his strong characters and his deep knowledge of New Mexico folklore, *Perdido* is a one-sitting read, a novel that captivates and surprises all the way to its chilling end."

In the final installment of the Guadalupe trilogy, *A Santo in the Image of Cristóbal García,* an elderly Flavio Montoya, Ramona's brother, is the protagonist. Ramona has long since been dead, and Flavio continues to tend the fields of his family, of which he is the only remaining member. Magic realism returns when Flavio sees his childhood friend Felix García—who has been incapacitated since he suffered a stroke years ago—walking through the fields. A terrible fire threatens to consume the entire town, and when Felix speaks for the first time in years, he accuses Flavio of starting the blaze. Reality and imagination blur as many of the story's events are told through flashbacks and Flavio's dreams. Using these devices, Collignon provides readers with the history of the town and its founder, Cristóbal García, answering many questions readers may have had from the first and second novels.

Critical reception of this book, like that of the first, was varied. "Though it situates itself squarely in a tired genre, Collignon's book is not without merit," wrote one *Publishers Weekly* contributor. "Dreamlike and melancholy," the reviewer continued, *A Santo in the Image of Cristóbal García* "is a worthy read, if slow-paced and often painfully—though not tritely—sentimental." Olszewski, reviewing *A Santo in the Image of Cristóbal García* in *Library Journal,* maintained, "As in the earlier works, the narrative carries strong strains of oral tradition." Olszewski also thought, however, that since Collignon reintroduces characters from *The Journal of Antonio Montoya* and *Perdido,* "this new book won't mean much outside of their context." Dan Wickett, however, in a review of the book for the *Emerging Writers Forum* Web site, thought that *A Santo in the Image of Cristóbal García* "works by itself," but encouraged readers to start with the first two books, explaining that "it would be a shame to not enjoy the town as it was meant to be." Wickett praised the author's efforts in writing the final book of the trilogy, stating, "Collignon is hitting on all cylinders with this effort—the writing is fantastic and further develops the dancing use of the English language established in the first two novels." Writing for *Booklist,* Brendan Dowling also had much praise to offer Collignon. Claiming the author "deftly blends history and magic realism," Dowling found *A Santo in the Image of Cristóbal García* "a fitting and evocative end to his trilogy."

In an interview with Kathryn Eastburn for the *Colorado Springs Independent,* Collignon admitted, "I dropped out of two colleges and never took any writing classes. My training was reading, which I did and still do voraciously." Collignon explained to Eastburn that his brother, who is also a writer, encouraged him to pursue his neglected passion. The author confessed, "Writing for me is a struggle. . . . I wouldn't do it if I didn't thrive on it. I think if you're going to write you're going to write, no matter what else is going on in your life."

BIOGRAPHICAL AND CRITICAL SOURCES:

PERIODICALS

Atlantic Monthly, August, 1997, review of *Perdido,* p. 98.
Booklist, July, 1997, Nancy Pearl, review of *Perdido,* p. 1794; October 15, 2002, Brendan Dowling, review of *A Santo in the Image of Cristóbal García,* p. 385.
Library Journal, May 1, 1996, Lawrence Olszewski, review of *The Journal of Antonio Montoya,* p. 129; June 15, 1997, Faye A. Chadwell, review of *Perdido,* p. 94; November 15, 2002, Lawrence Olszewski, review of *A Santo in the Image of Cristóbal García,* p. 99.
New York Times Book Review, August 25, 1996, Andy Solomon, review of *The Journal of Antonio Montoya,* p. 19; February 14, 1999, review of *Perdido,* p. 32.
Publishers Weekly, April 29, 1996, review of *The Journal of Antonio Montoya,* p. 53; October 28, 2002, review of *A Santo in the Image of Cristóbal García,* p. 50.
Western American Literature, spring, 1997, p. 88.

ONLINE

Between the Lines, http://www.thei.aust.com/isite/btl/btlrvmontoya.html/ (1998), Wendy Cavenett, review of *The Journal of Antonio Montoya.*
Colorado Springs Independent Web site, http://www.csindy.com/ (November 14-20, 2002), Kathryn Eastburn, "Fine Print, The Journal of Rick Collignon: On Writing, Roofing, and His New Mexico Trilogy."

Emerging Writers Forum Web site, http://www.break tech.net/EmergingWritersForum/View_Review. aspx?id=33/ (September 13, 2002), Dan Wickett, review of *A Santo in the Image of Cristóbal García.*

San Francisco Chronicle Web site, http://www.sfgate. com/ (December 29, 2002), Jules Siegel, review of *A Santo in the Image of Cristóbal García.**

*   *   *

COMDEN, Betty 1917-

PERSONAL: Born Basya Cohen, on May 3, 1917, in Brooklyn, NY; daughter of Leo (a lawyer) and Rebecca (a school teacher; maiden name, Sadvoransky) Comden; married Steven Kyle (a designer and businessperson), January 4, 1942; children: Susanna, Alan. *Ethnicity:* "White." *Education:* New York University, B.S., 1938. *Politics:* Democrat. *Religion:* Jewish.

ADDRESSES: Office—c/o The Dramatists Guild, 234 West 44th St., New York, NY 10036. *Agent*—Ronald S. Konecky, 1 Dag Hammarskjold Plaza, New York, NY 10017. *E-mail*—bcomden@aol.com.

CAREER: Author of musical comedies and screenplays, collaborating with Adolph Green, 1915-2002. Actress, performing in night club act "The Revuers," in Broadway musicals *On the Town,* 1944, *A Party with Betty Comden and Adolph Green,* 1958 and 1977, and *Isn't It Romantic,* 1983, and in films *The Band Wagon,* 1953, and *Garbo Talks,* 1985.

MEMBER: Writers Guild of America (East and West), American Federation of Television and Radio Artists, Screenwriters Guild, American Guild of Variety Artists, American Society of Composers, Authors, and Publishers, Dramatists Guild (member of council, 1948—), Authors League of America.

AWARDS, HONORS: Screenwriters Guild of America Award, 1949, for *On the Town,* 1952, for *Singin' in the Rain,* and 1955, for *It's Always Fair Weather;* Donaldson Award for lyrics, 1953, for *Wonderful Town;* Antoinette Perry ("Tony") Award for lyrics, 1953, for *Wonderful Town,* for best book of a musical (nomination), 1957, for *Bells Are Ringing,* for best score, 1968, for

Betty Comden

Hallelujah, Baby, for best book for musical, 1970, for *Applause,* for best book and lyrics, 1978, for *On the Twentieth Century,* for best book and lyrics (nomination), 1983, for *A Doll's Life,* and for best book of a musical (nomination), 1986, for *Singin' in the Rain; Village Voice* Off-Broadway (Obie) Award, 1959, for *A Party with Betty Comden and Adolph Green;* Woman of Achievement Award, New York University Alumnae Association, 1978; New York City Mayor's Award for Art and Culture, 1978; named to Songwriters Hall of Fame, 1980; elected to Theatre Hall of Fame; Kennedy Center Honors, 1991; New York University Musical Theater Hall of Fame Award, 1994; Governor Cuomo Award, 1994; Laurel Award for Screen, 2001.

WRITINGS:

MUSICALS; WITH ADOLPH GREEN

(Book and lyrics) *On the Town,* music by Leonard Bernstein, first produced on Broadway, 1944.

(Book and lyrics) *Billion Dollar Baby,* first produced on Broadway, 1945.

(Book and lyrics) *Bonanza Bound,* music by Saul Chaplin, first produced in Philadelphia at Shubert Theatre, 1947.

(Sketches and lyrics) *Two on the Aisle,* music by Jule Styne, first produced on Broadway, 1951.

(Lyrics) *Wonderful Town,* music by Leonard Bernstein, first produced on Broadway, 1953.

(Additional lyrics) *Peter Pan,* music by Jule Styne, first produced on Broadway, 1954.

(Book and lyrics) *Bells Are Ringing* (first produced on Broadway, 1956, revived on Broadway at the Plymouth Theatre, 2001), music by Jule Styne, Random House (New York, NY), 1957.

Say, Darling, music by Jule Styne, first produced on Broadway, 1958.

A Party (revue based on collection of their previously written songs and sketches), first produced Off-Broadway, 1958, expanded version produced on Broadway as *A Party with Betty Comden and Adolph Green,* 1958, new version produced on Broadway, 1977.

(Lyrics) *Do Re Mi,* music by Jule Styne, first produced on Broadway, 1960.

(Book and lyrics) *Fade Out—Fade In* (first produced on Broadway, 1964), music by Jule Styne, Random House (New York, NY), 1965.

(With others) *Leonard Bernstein's Theatre Songs,* produced at Theatre de Lys in New York, NY, 1965.

(Lyrics) *Hallelujah, Baby,* music by Jule Styne, first produced on Broadway, 1967.

(Book) *Applause,* lyrics by Lee Adams, music by Charles Strouse (based on film *All about Eve,* original story by Mary Orr; first produced on Broadway, 1970), Random House (New York, NY), 1971.

Lorelei (based on *Gentlemen Prefer Blondes*), first produced on Broadway, 1974.

(With others) *By Bernstein,* produced at Chelsea Theater Center Westside in New York, NY, 1975.

(Lyrics and music, with others) *The Madwoman of Central Park West* (one-woman show), produced at 22 Steps Theatre, New York, NY, 1979.

(Book and lyrics) *On the Twentieth Century* (based on plays by Ben Hecht, Charles MacArthur, and Bruce Millholland; first produced on Broadway, 1978), music by Cy Coleman, S. French (New York, NY), 1980.

(Book and lyrics) *A Doll's Life,* (based on play *A Doll's House,* by Henrik Ibsen; first produced on Broadway, 1982), music by Larry Grossman, S. French (New York, NY), 1983.

(Lyrics, with others) *Diamonds* (two acts), produced at Circle in the Square Downtown, New York, NY, 1984–85.

The Will Rogers Follies, music by Cy Coleman, produced at Palace Theatre, New York, NY, 1991.

(With Adolph Green and Mike Nichols) *The New York Musicals of Comden & Green: On the Town, Wonderful Town, Bells Are Ringing,* Applause Books (New York, NY), 1997.

SCREENPLAYS; WITH ADOLPH GREEN

Good News, Metro-Goldwyn-Mayer, 1947.

The Barkleys of Broadway, Metro-Goldwyn-Mayer, 1949.

(And lyrics) *On the Town,* Metro-Goldwyn-Mayer, 1949.

(Lyrics) *Take Me out to the Ballgame,* Metro-Goldwyn-Mayer, 1949.

(And lyrics) *Singin' in the Rain* (Metro-Goldwyn-Mayer, 1952), Viking (New York, NY), 1972.

(And lyrics) *The Band Wagon,* Metro-Goldwyn-Mayer, 1953.

(And lyrics) *It's Always Fair Weather,* Metro-Goldwyn-Mayer, 1955.

Auntie Mame, Warner Bros., 1958.

(And lyrics) *Bells Are Ringing,* Metro-Goldwyn-Mayer, 1960.

(And lyrics) *What a Way to Go,* Twentieth Century-Fox, 1964.

OTHER

(With Adolph Green) *Good Morning, Good Night,* Holt, Rinehart & Winston (New York, NY), 1967.

Off Stage (memoir), Simon & Schuster (New York, NY), 1995.

Also author, with Adolph Green, of music, book, and lyrics for night club act, "The Revuers," 1939-43; musical television comedy specials for the American Broadcasting Company; and of book, *Comden and Green on Broadway.* Contributor to magazines, including *Esquire* and *Vogue.*

SIDELIGHTS: Together with her collaborator, Adolph Green, Betty Comden has written the lyrics, and often the librettos, for some of the most memorable musicals of all time. Cited by the *New Yorker*'s Brendan Gill as being "among the most gifted people on Broadway," Comden and Green have had successes through the years that include *On the Town, Singin' in the Rain, Applause, On the Twentieth Century,* and *Hallelujah, Baby.*

Singin' in the Rain, which starred Gene Kelly, was described by *New York Times* reviewer Frank Rich as "the happiest movie musical ever made." *Chicago Tribune* reviewer Howard Reich said: "Ask any film buff to name the greatest movie musical of all time, and odds are he will cite *Singin' in the Rain* or *The Band Wagon,* both of which Comden and Green wrote." Of the 1985 Broadway stage version, however, Rich declared: "It says much about the stage version of the film that it doesn't send us home with the image of a joyous man singing and dancing. What is most likely to be remembered about this *Singin' in the Rain* is the rain." Rich attributed the play's shortcomings to a fundamental difference in genre which director Twyla Tharp was unable to overcome. "*Singin' in the Rain* was a fantasy movie about the dream factory of the movies," Rich said. "Once transposed to the stage in realistic terms, the fantasy evaporates even as the rain pours down. No matter how much Miss Tharp recreates specific gestures from the film, they play differently in the theater. Watching her Don Lockwood splash about, we aren't carried away into never-never Hollywoodland. . . . We're still in the humdrum everyday world, wondering how stage technicians achieve the effect and watching an actor get very, very wet."

One of Comden and Green's biggest hits was not a conventional Broadway show. *A Party with Betty Comden and Adolph Green,* originally produced in 1958 and revived in 1977, presents an overview of the pair's best material, performed by the authors themselves. Some portions of the show date back to their nightclub revue days of the late 1930s; although much of the satire contained in the skits was topical when first produced, audiences and reviewers found it no less entertaining the second time around. Said Gill in the *New Yorker,* "Comden and Green's acute, affectionately bantering view of human frailty covers a period of four decades and manages to end up looking little worse for the wear. And no more do they; in their eager determination to win all hearts, they might be charming young folk at the very beginning of their careers. . . . [They] have never lost their freshness,

and it is plainly their intention, growing older, never to grow old. I salute them with respect and envy."

The *Nation*'s Harold Clurman praised Comden and Green's singing, noting that while they are not professional singers, "they deliver [their lyrics] with gusto in unaffected good humor. . . . Their intelligent and spirited joshing is infectious. They strike one as part of our family, a family of citizens aware of the absurdities and peccadilloes we enjoy poking fun at. There is something 'clean' and fresh about them (Betty Comden possesses a natural dignity) and, without being in the least condescending about it, one can honestly call their 'party' nice home revelry."

A *Time* critic agreed with these assessments, concluding that "a party, according to Webster's, is a social gathering for pleasure, and by the definition—or any other—an evening with Betty Comden and Adolph Green is an invitation into high society. . . . Rarely has so much wit and fun been packed into two hours. To cop a line from another songwriter, Cole Porter, what a swellegant, elegant party this is."

Despite numerous Tony awards and household-name shows, Comden and Green are best known for their longevity as a team. Said the *Chicago Tribune*'s Reich in 1990, "No one . . . has written more hit songs over the decades than Comden and Green, who, after fifty triumphant and oft-tumultuous years together, remain unchallenged as the longest-running act on Broadway." Citing standard tunes such as "New York, New York (It's a Hell of a Town)," "Make Someone Happy," and "Never Never Land," Reich described Comden and Green as "the wordsmiths who have helped define—and energize—the great American musical."

In 1999 performers including Nathan Lane, Faith Prince, Brian Stokes Mitchell, and Amanda Green came together in *Carnegie Hall Celebrates Betty Comden and Adolph Green,* to sing the duo's famous show tunes. *Variety* reviewer Charles Isherwood concluded that "one of the hallmarks of their works is energy, a zest that infuses both their funniest songs and their most reflective ballads." The show included performances of "Perfect Relationship" from the musical *Bells Are Ringing,* "Captain Hook's Waltz" from *Peter Pan,* and "100 Ways to Lose a Man," from *Wonderful Town.* Isherwood noted that the duo's "witty words have shaped some of the century's most cherished musicals and movies."

In addition to their works for stage and screen, Comden and Green wrote *The New York Musicals of Comden and Green: On the Town, Wonderful Town, Bells Are Ringing* with Mike Nichols. The work includes the complete book and lyrics for all three musicals, as well as more than a hundred photographs.

While most of her creative energy was spent working as one half of a team, Comden's autobiography, *Off Stage,* focuses on her life apart from Green. *Off Stage* chronicles Comden's life as a young girl growing up in Brooklyn, to the death of her husband, Kyle, to her son's losing battle with drug addiction. Some reviewers criticized the book for not covering more of her career and what inspires her talent, but J. D. Reed of *People* declared the book "an engaging portrait of a woman of the theater away from the theater."

BIOGRAPHICAL AND CRITICAL SOURCES:

BOOKS

Contemporary Theatre, Film, and Television, Volume 39, Thomson Gale (Detroit, MI), 2002.
Dictionary of Literary Biography, Volume 265: *American Song Lyricists, 1920-1960,* Thomson Gale (Detroit, MI), 2002.
International Dictionary of Films and Filmmakers, Volume 4: Writers and Production Artists, St. James Press (Detroit, MI), 1996.
Robinson, Alice M., *Betty Comden and Adolph Green: A Bio-Bibliography,* Greenwood Press (Westport, CT), 1994.
Women Filmmakers and Their Films, St. James Press (Detroit, MI), 1998.

PERIODICALS

America, March 11, 1978.
American Theatre, September 1998, Rachel Shteir, "Betty Comden: That Ol' Zappo Punch," p. 76.
Booklist, February 15, 1995, Jack Helbig, review of *Off Stage,* p. 1050.
Chicago Tribune, August 10, 1990.
Christian Science Monitor, November 21, 1996, Merle Rubin, review of *The New York Musicals of Comden and Green: On the Town, Wonderful Town, Bells Are Ringing,* p. B3.

Insight, June 5, 1989.
Life, April 3, 1970.
Michigan Quarterly Review, William Baer, "*Singin' in the Rain:* A Conversation with Betty Comden and Adolph Green," p. 1.
Nation, April 20, 1970; May 7, 1977; March 11, 1978; October 16, 1982, pp. 378-379.
New Leader, March 27, 1978.
New Republic, May 23, 1970; March 18, 1978.
Newsweek, April 13, 1970; February 21, 1977; March 6, 1978.
New York, October 4, 1982, pp. 91-92.
New Yorker, April 11, 1970; May 12, 1975; February 21, 1977; March 6, 1978; October 4, 1982, p. 122.
New York Times, July 27, 1971; November 1, 1971; November 7, 1971; September 24, 1982; November 4, 1984; June 9, 1985, pp. 1-24; August 3, 1985; June 20, 1993, David Zippel, "Together Again—and Again—and Again," p. H8; June 7, 1998, Nora Sayre, "Orchestrating the Show Within; In Their Hollywood Musicals, the Writers Adolph Green and Betty Comden Didn't Dance around their Emotional Conflict," p. AR14; December 25, 1998, Peter Applebone, "Still Fancy Free? Of Course!," p. E1; September 5, 1999, Terry Teachout, "That Tune You're Humming? These Two Probably Wrote It," p. AR23; April 12, 2001, Jesse McKinley, "Comden and Green's Office. They're on Broadway. Any Message?," p. B1.
New York Times Book Review, David Kaufman, review of *Off Stage,* p. 14.
People, April 3, 1995, J. D. Reed, review of *Off Stage,* p. 32.
Publishers Weekly, January 16, 1995, review of *Off Stage,* p. 448.
Saturday Review, April 18, 1970; April 22, 1972; April 15, 1978.
Stereo Review, April, 1973.
Time, April 13, 1970; February 21, 1977; March 6, 1978.
Variety, June 21, 1999, Markland Taylor, theater review of *On the Twentieth Century,* p. 88; September 27, 1999, Charles Isherwood, theater review of *Carnegie Hall Celebrates Betty Comden and Adolph Green,* p. 160.
Wall Street Journal, Joanne Kaufman, "Comden without Green in Lyrical Memoir *Off Stage,*" p. A16.

ONLINE

Leonard Bernstein Web site, http://www.leonard bernstein.com/ (October 31, 2003), "Comden and Green."

Writers Guild Awards Web site, http://www.wga.org/ (October 31, 2003).

*   *   *

CONNELL, Evan S(helby) Jr. 1924-

PERSONAL: Born August 17, 1924, in Kansas City, MO; son of Evan Shelby (a surgeon) and Elton (Williamson) Connell. *Education:* Attended Dartmouth College, 1941-43; University of Kansas, A.B., 1947; graduate study at Stanford University, 1947-48, Columbia University, 1948-49, and San Francisco State College (now University).

ADDRESSES: Home—Fort Marcy 13, 320 Artist Rd., Santa Fe, NM 87501. *Agent*—Don Congdon, 156 Fifth Ave., Suite 625, New York, NY 10010-7002.

CAREER: Writer. Editor, *Contact* magazine, Sausalito, CA, 1960-65. *Military service:* U.S. Navy, pilot, 1943-45; served as flight instructor.

AWARDS, HONORS: Eugene F. Saxton fellow, 1953; Guggenheim fellow, 1963; Rockefeller Foundation grant, 1967; California Literature silver medal, 1974, for *The Connoisseur;* nomination for award for general nonfiction from National Book Critics Circle, 1984, and *Los Angeles Times* Book Award, 1985, both for *Son of the Morning Star: Custer and the Little Big-horn;* American Academy and Institute of Arts and Letters award, 1987; Lifetime Achievement Award, Lannan Foundation, 2000.

WRITINGS:

FICTION

The Anatomy Lesson, and Other Stories, Viking (New York, NY), 1957.

Mrs. Bridge, Viking, (New York NY), 1959.

Evan S. Connell, Jr.

The Patriot, Viking (New York NY), 1960.

At the Crossroads: Stories, Simon & Schuster (New York, NY), 1965.

The Diary of a Rapist, Simon & Schuster (New York NY), 1966.

Mr. Bridge, Knopf (New York, NY), 1969.

The Connoisseur, Knopf (New York NY), 1974.

Double Honeymoon, Putnam (New York, NY), 1976.

St. Augustine's Pigeon (stories), North Point Press (Berkeley, CA), 1980.

The Alchymist's Journal, North Point Press (Berkeley, CA), 1991.

The Collected Stories of Evan S. Connell, Counterpoint Press (Washington, DC), 1995.

Deus Lo Volt!: A Chronicle of the Crusades, Counterpoint (Washington, DC), 2000.

OTHER

(Editor) Jerry Stoll, *I Am a Lover,* Angel Island Publications, 1961.

Notes from a Bottle Found on the Beach at Carmel (epic poem), Viking (New York NY), 1963.

(Editor) *Woman by Three,* Pacific Coast Publishers, 1969.

Points for a Compass Rose (epic poem), Knopf (New York NY), 1973.

A Long Desire (nonfiction), Holt (New York, NY), 1979.

The White Lantern (nonfiction), Holt (New York, NY), 1980.

Son of the Morning Star: Custer and the Little Bighorn (nonfiction), North Point Press (Berkeley, CA), 1984.

Mesa Verde (nonfiction), Whitney Museum, 1992.

The Aztec Treasure House: New and Selected Essays, Counterpoint Press (New York, NY), 2001.

Francisco Goya: A Life, Counterpoint (New York, NY), 2004.

Contributor of short stories and reviews to periodicals, including *New York Times, Washington Post, Chicago Sun-Times, New York, San Francisco Chronicle, Carolina Quarterly, Paris Review,* and *Esquire.* Editor of *Contact* (literary magazine), 1960-65.

ADAPTATIONS: The novels *Mrs. Bridge* and *Mr. Bridge* were adapted as the film *Mr. and Mrs. Bridge* by Merchant-Ivory Productions in 1990, starring Paul Newman and Joanne Woodward. *Son of the Morning Star* was adapted for American Broadcasting Companies, Inc. (ABC) by Republic Pictures in 1991.

SIDELIGHTS: The works of Evan S. Connell, Jr. range widely in scope and theme, from domestic dramas of the modern middle class to fictitious historical treatises on the Crusades and alchemy. While his fiction has been widely reviewed, and adapted to film, it was his nonfiction work, *Son of the Morning Star: Custer and the Little Bighorn,* that placed him on the best-seller lists. According to William H. Nolte in the *Dictionary of Literary Biography,* Connell "would probably rank today as the most important American novelist if critical reception were the sole criterion for determining the reputation of a writer." Brooks Landon, in the *Dictionary of Literary Biography Yearbook: 1981,* explained that "Connell's works have been successful with critics and have enjoyed respectable sales, but his impressive writing still remains one of America's best-kept literary secrets." A *Publishers Weekly* critic noted that while Connell "never developed a clear literary profile," he is nonetheless "a consummate craftsman who has enjoyed some remarkable successes." In 2000,

Connell received the Lifetime Achievement Award of the Lannan Foundation. With the exception of *Francisco Goya: A Life,* which received lackluster praise, Connell has generally drawn high praise among literary critics.

The critical acclaim for Connell's work began with his first collection, *The Anatomy Lesson, and Other Stories.* At the time of the book's publication in 1957, Anne Chamberlain of the *New York Herald Tribune Book Review* wrote: "With a virtuoso's dexterity [Connell] explores theme and treatment, subject matter and attack, darting from the precious and the esoteric to almost legendary folk tales, laid in his native Midwest and in distant corners of America. This is a many-faceted writer." *New York Times* reviewer Siegfried Mandel called him "a craftsman who can evoke, sustain and dignify the 'small' tragedy that is often hidden from view." And William Hogan, writing for the *San Francisco Chronicle,* said that the stories in *The Anatomy Lesson* are "well-observed, well-worked slices of life that exhibit craftsmanship, discipline and maturity. Connell is obviously a serious writer of promise and I look forward with great expectations to the publication of his first novel."

That first novel, *Mrs. Bridge,* published in 1959, is probably Connell's best-known work, as well as the one to which his subsequent books are most often compared. In it the author tells the story of India Bridge, an upper-class Midwestern woman, wife of a lawyer, mother of three children, who comes to personify Connell's concept of the idle rich. She is easily confused, she is bored with her leisure-class existence, and she is dominated by materialism and the need to be "socially correct." India Bridge, according to some critics, may be the most fully developed character in any post-World War II American novel. In her *New York Herald Tribune Book Review* assessment, Chamberlain said that Connell had achieved "a triumph of ironic characterization. In his heroine, who appears at first meeting the acme of mediocrity, he manages to create an interesting, a pathetically comic, a tragically lonely figure. . . . It is sad, somewhat terrifying to reflect upon the numberless Mrs. Bridges trotting befuddledly through this urgent age."

In the decade following the publication of *Mrs. Bridge,* Connell published two more novels, *The Patriot* and *The Diary of a Rapist,* one book-length poem, *Notes from a Bottle Found on the Beach at Carmel,* and a collection of short stories, *At the Crossroads.* Most of these were generously accepted by reviewers. He then returned to the Bridge family for his fourth novel, *Mr. Bridge,* which tells the story from the husband's point of view. A *Playboy* critic called the book "a brilliant dissection of the quintessential small-town WASP—performed under the light of high art, with irony, insight, and a bleak pity." Webster Schott wrote in the *Washington Post Book World:* "Had Sinclair Lewis possessed compassion equal to his anger, discipline to complement his energy, he might have written *Mr. Bridge.* Evan Connell looks at his world straight. No artifice. But with full awareness of the quiet comedy, tenderness and tight-lipped waste. This job need not be done again. *Mr. Bridge* is a tour de force of contemporary American realism, a beautiful work of fiction." Some reviewers felt that the novel fell short of Connell's work in *Mrs. Bridge,* commenting that the characterization is somewhat weaker in the newer book. However, as John Gross of the *New York Review of Books* explained: "If *Mr. Bridge* is a less engaging work than its predecessor, it is chiefly because Walter Bridge himself has little of his wife's pathos. Where she was vulnerable in her innocence, funny and touching in her hapless cultural aspirations, he is rigid, efficient, proud of knowing his own mind. Not an especially likable man; but then Mr. Connell's purpose in writing about him is not to draw up a brief for the defense, but simply to restore a cliché-figure to humanity."

Connell's 1991 novel, *The Alchymist's Journal,* is a demanding work that features the journal entries of seven sixteenth-century men, all of them attempting alchemy: the transformation of basic metals into gold. Only one of the men is named—Paracelsus, who is based on the actual physician who experimented with new methods of treatment in the 1500s. The other men reflect readily identifiable types, such as a skeptic, a revolutionary, and a philosopher. As with many other Connell works, reviewers of this novel expressed admiration for the author's obvious painstaking research, experimental form, and intellectual daring. Bettina L. Knapp, writing in *World Literature Today,* praised the "highly cerebral and wisdom-filled work" as a "tour de force." *Hudson Review* critic William H. Pritchard, while calling the novel "erudite," admitted that "most of the entries were impenetrable to this uninformed sensibility." *New York Times Book Review* correspondent Sven Birkerts likewise contended that Connell "has here dared the unfashionable—a work that concedes nothing to the reader's appetite for dramatic structure or vivid historical tableaux."

In an interview with Melody Sumner for the *San Francisco Review of Books,* Connell brushed aside questions about the inaccessibility of *The Alchymist's Journal.* "I don't write to an audience," he said. "I wanted all seven of the journals to create a unity, but I was trying to avoid repetition. I went over it several times, just to make sure I wasn't using the same words again and again." Birkerts concluded of the novel: "If we are willing to read with sustained attentiveness, facing the otherness and letting the indecipherable elements burn against our demand for clarity, we may at times feel as though we have stepped into a new place. We may get an inkling of what the world felt like some centuries before it assumed its modern contours." Sybil Steinberg, writing in *Publishers Weekly,* likewise felt that the book "commands thoughtful attention, its surface resplendent with forgotten lore of alchemy, science and love."

In 1995, many of Connell's short stories were collected and published as *The Collected Stories of Evan S. Connell.* Many of the collection's fifty-six stories were written in the 1950s and 1960s, while most of the remainder were products of the 1990s. All of the stories feature Connell's trademark minimalist prose; many offer wry commentaries on contemporary American life. The character of Koerner, a writer who in some ways resembles Connell, reappears in several of the stories, works that, to quote a *Kirkus Reviews* critic, "[sparkle] with Connell's learnedness, sharp wit, and spare, concise prose."

If *The Alchymist's Journal* deals with the Middle Ages in an interior and cerebral manner, *Deus Lo Volt!: A Chronicle of the Crusades* embraces the panoramic view of the age. A fictitious first-hand account of the European conquest of the Holy Land from 1095 through 1290, the book not only gives a history of the Crusades but also imparts that history from the perspective of a participant—with the enormous differences between the modern and the Medieval mind everywhere incorporated. Calling the novel "a massive, determinedly archaic history of the crusades from the point of view of a French knight," a *Publishers Weekly* reviewer commended it as "a great feat of historic empathy." In *Booklist,* Michael Spinella maintained that Connell "researches with the eye of an expert historical scholar and writes with the hand of an expert novelist."

Aside from his works of fiction, Connell's most notable work is *Son of the Morning Star,* his account of the Battle of the Little Bighorn, where Sioux Indian warriors, led by Sitting Bull, overwhelmed and slaughtered General George Armstrong Custer's band of American troops. A classic story of American history, "Custer's Last Stand" has been the subject of numerous books and articles since the 1880s. But despite the story's familiarity, Connell's account of the battle became a best-seller as well as a critical success. Besides winning a National Book Critics Circle nomination and the *Los Angeles Times* Book Award in history, *Son of the Morning Star* sold over 80,000 copies in hardcover, and paperback rights were sold for over 200,000 dollars. The book's success did not surprise Connell. He told the *New York Times:* "I always thought it was a pretty wild story. I had a feeling that since I found it so intensely interesting, other people would, too."

Research and writing for the book took Connell four years and involved reading dozens of books on the battle, the diaries of soldiers who participated in the campaign, and accounts by the Indians themselves. He visited the battle site in Montana on four occasions. The resulting manuscript was difficult to sell. Holt, publisher of some of his earlier fiction, declined *Son of the Morning Star.* They wanted Connell to rewrite the book as a straight biography of Custer or as an overview of the Indian Wars. Connell refused. Eventually North Point Press, a relatively small publisher in California, accepted the book as it was written.

Critical reception to *Son of the Morning Star* was enthusiastic. Ralph E. Sipper of the *Los Angeles Times* called it "a monumental study of the philosophical and cultural differences between red and white men that instigated so much mutual animosity and destruction. . . . In a masterly display of literary structure, Connell has drawn from hundreds of pertinent historical accounts and created the modern equivalent of a biblical work of witness." Writing in the *New York Times Book Review,* Page Stegner stated that "Connell's narrative of the life and times of General Custer becomes a narrative of the conflict between two cultures, and the battle Custer fought at the Little Bighorn [becomes] a metaphor for all the self-righteous hypocrisy that characterizes Indian-white negotiations to this day." Kenneth Turan, in *Time,* concluded that *Son of the Morning Star* is "a new American classic."

BIOGRAPHICAL AND CRITICAL SOURCES:

BOOKS

Contemporary Authors Autobiography Series, Volume 2, Thomson Gale (Detroit, MI), 1985.
Contemporary Literary Criticism, Thomson Gale (Detroit, MI), Volume 4, 1975, Volume 6, 1976, Volume 45, 1987.
Dictionary of Literary Biography, Volume 2: *American Novelists since World War II,* Thomson Gale (Detroit, MI), 1978.
Dictionary of Literary Biography Yearbook: 1981, Thomson Gale (Detroit, MI), 1982.

PERIODICALS

Art in America, April, 2004, Janis Tomlinson, "Reimagining Goya," pp. 33-34.
Atlantic, February, 2002, review of *The Aztec Treasure House: New and Selected Essays,* pp. 102-103.
Best Sellers, April 15, 1969; June 15, 1973.
Bloomsbury Review, June, 1991.
Booklist, January 1, 2000, Michael Spinella, review of *Deus Lo Volt!: A Chronicle of the Crusades,* p. 833; February 1, 2004, Donna Seaman, review of *Francisco Goya: A Life,* p. 941.
Boston Review, June, 1991.
Catholic World, March, 1959.
Christian Science Monitor, May 22, 1969.
Commentary, March, 1985.
Commonweal, February 13, 1959; August 23, 1963.
Detroit News, March 10, 1985.
Harper's, January, 1974.
Hudson Review, summer, 1986; autumn, 1991, William H. Pritchard, review of *The Alchymist's Journal,* p. 507.
Interview, November, 1990.
Kenyon Review, September, 1966.
Kirkus Reviews, March 1, 1957; July 15, 1960; August 15, 1995, review of *The Collected Stories of Evan S. Connell,* p. 1126; December 1, 2003, review of *Francisco Goya: A Life,* p. 1388; July 1, 2004, "Anniversaries . . . Battle of Little Bighorn."
Library Journal, April 15, 1957; January 1, 1959; September 1, 1960; March 15, 1973; August, 1974; April 15, 1991; November 1, 1991; October 1, 1995, p. 122; March 1, 2000, David Keymer, review of *Deus Lo Volt!,* p. 123; November 15, 2003, Nathan Ward, review of *Francisco Goya,* p. 60.

Life, April 25, 1969.

Los Angeles Times, November 21, 1980; October 3, 1984, Ralph E. Sipper; review of *Son of the Morning Star: Custer and the Little Bighorn.*

Los Angeles Times Book Review, August 3, 1986; April 19, 1987; July 14, 1991.

Nation, June 15, 1963; June 30, 1969.

National Review, February 28, 1975; August 9, 1985.

New Mexico Quarterly, summer, 1966.

New Republic, October 14, 1957; June 7, 1969; October 22, 1990.

New Statesman, February 13, 1960.

Newsweek, May 12, 1969; February 4, 1991.

New Yorker, October 14, 1974; June 3, 1985; July 1, 1991.

New York Herald Tribune Book Review, May 26, 1957, Anne Chamberlain, review of *The Anatomy Lesson, and Other Stories;* January 18, 1959, Anne Chamberlain, review of *Mrs. Bridge;* September 25, 1960; May 26, 1963.

New York Review, April 24, 1969.

New York Review of Books, June 23, 1966; May 17, 1973, John Gross, review of *Mr. Bridge;* November 28, 1974.

New York Times, May 19, 1957, Siegfried Mandel, review of *The Anatomy Lesson, and Other Stories;* February 1, 1959; April 23, 1969; February 13, 1985; February 18, 1990; May 13, 1990.

New York Times Book Review, February 1, 1959; September 25, 1960; April 20, 1969; April 29, 1973; September 1, 1974; May 23, 1976; June 24, 1979; July 20, 1980; December 7, 1980; March 29, 1981; May 30, 1982; January 20, 1985, Page Stegner, review of *Son of the Morning Star;* April 30, 1989; May 12, 1991, Sven Birkerts, "A World Ripe with Magic"; September 13, 1992, p. 40.

People, December 10, 1990.

Playboy, June, 1969, review of *Mr. Bridge.*

Publishers Weekly, November 20, 1981, Patricia Holt, interview with Evan S. Connell, p. 12; February 22, 1991, Sybil Steinberg, review of *The Alchymist's Journal,* p. 208; August 21, 1995, review of *The Collected Stories of Evan S. Connell,* p. 47; February 21, 2000, review of *Deus Lo Volt!,* p. 61; October 2, 2000, "Nine Writers Win Lannan Awards," p. 12; July 2, 2001, review of *The Aztec Treasure House,* p. 59; December 1, 2003, review of *Francisco Goya,* p. 50.

San Francisco Chronicle, May 28, 1957, William Hogan, review of *The Anatomy Lesson, and Other Stories;* January 19, 1959; September 19, 1960.

San Francisco Review of Books, February, 1991, Melody Sumner, interview with Evan S. Connell, p. 26.

Saturday Review, May 18, 1957; January 31, 1959; September 24, 1960; July 17, 1965; May 3, 1969; April 17, 1976.

Time, May 27, 1957; January 19, 1959; June 20, 1969; September 2, 1974; June 21, 1976; November 5, 1984, Kenneth Turan, review of *Son of the Morning Star.*

Times Literary Supplement, July 29, 1983; August 18, 2000, Emily Wilson, review of *Dues Lo Volt!,* p. 24.

Tribune Books (Chicago, IL), April 5, 1981; October 14, 1984.

Village Voice, June 18, 1991.

Virginia Quarterly Review, autumn, 1965; summer, 1969; spring, 1991; winter, 1992, p. 23.

Voice Literary Supplement, March, 1985; November, 1991.

Washington Post, July 17, 1979; November 11, 1981.

Washington Post Book World, April 20, 1969, Webster Schott, review of *Mr. Bridge;* May 27, 1973; September 1, 1974; July 13, 1980; March 15, 1981; November 18, 1984; September 22, 1985; October 27, 1985; May 3, 1987; September 4, 1988; May 7, 1989; May 19, 1991.

Wisconsin Studies in Contemporary Literature, summer, 1967.

World Literature Today, summer, 1992, Bettina L. Knapp, review of *The Alchymist's Journal,* p. 526.

Yale Review, winter, 1985.

ONLINE

Ploughshares Online, http://www.pshares.org/ (August 2, 2004), Gerald Shapiro, "Evan S. Connell: A Profile."

Salon.com, http://www.salon.com/ (July 18, 2000), Greg Bottoms, "Evan S. Connell."*

*   *   *

CONNERS, Bernard F. 1926-

PERSONAL: Born September 14, 1926, in Albany, NY; married Catherine Connors, November 30, 1957; children: Christopher, Sarah, Jane. *Education:* St. Lawrence University, B.A., 1951. *Hobbies and other interests:* Tennis, skiing, football.

ADDRESSES: Home—60 Old Niskayuna Rd., Loudonville, NY 12211. *Agent*—Oscar Collier, 280 Madison Ave., New York, NY 10016.

CAREER: Federal Bureau of Investigation, Washington, DC, special agent, 1951-60; former owner of soft drink and real estate businesses in New York and New England; publisher for *Paris Review;* creator of British American Publishing. *Military service:* U.S. Army, 1945-47, 1951; became lieutenant.

WRITINGS:

Don't Embarrass the Bureau, Bobbs-Merrill (Indianapolis, IN), 1972.
Dancehall, Bobbs-Merrill (Indianapolis, IN), 1983.
The Hampton Sisters, D. I. Fine (New York, NY), 1987.
Tailspin: The Strange Case of Major Call, British American Publishing (Latham, NY), 2001.

Contributor to magazines and newspapers.

SIDELIGHTS: Bernard F. Conners has worked in various fields of employment, from business, to government, to publishing. He began writing in his early teens and has published four books. He is also a former FBI special agent and draws on personal knowledge and expert research skills in his nonfiction book *Tailspin: The Strange Case of Major Call.* In this work, Conners determines to prove that Dr. Sam Sheppard, who was convicted of his wife's murder in the infamous Marilyn Sheppard murder case of 1954, was not the culprit. Instead, the author has collected nearly 150 pages of circumstantial evidence pointing to Air Force Major James Arlon Call. The successful Major's life began to spin out of control after the death of his own wife. He started gambling and embarked on a life of crime, which culminated in a shootout with four police officers. He was pursued through the Adirondacks on a 106-day manhunt, supposedly committing other crimes along the way. Conners's book contains forensic results, fingerprint records, and photographs, which help convince readers that Call was the "bushy-haired stranger" who murdered Marilyn Sheppard. As quoted by Marc Schogol in the *Knight-Ridder/Tribune News Service,* a former executive director of the National District Attorneys Association called this book "one of the best written on the subject" and also noted that the book delivers a "theory that will hold the reader spellbound from start to finish." A *Publishers Weekly* critic thought that the book had some problems with narration and Conners's "liberal dramatization based on the facts garnished with re-created conversation." But a writer for the *Hutton Book Review* called *Tailspin* "excellent reading," and a critic for the *Midwest Book Review* stated that the book is "gripping" and "persuasive."

BIOGRAPHICAL AND CRITICAL SOURCES:

PERIODICALS

Hutton Book Review, April 16, 2002.
Knight-Ridder/Tribune News Service, July 3, 2002, Marc Schogol, review of *Tailspin: The Strange Case of Major Call,* p. K6443.
Library Journal, May 1, 2002, review of *Tailspin,* p. 118.
Midwest Book Review. June 8, 2002.
Publishers Weekly, April 13, 1990, Joseph Barbato, "British American: Responding to Authors," p. 45; February 25, 2002, review of *Tailspin,* p. 49.
Washington Post Book World, July 14, 2002.*

* * *

COOK, Roy
　See SILVERBERG, Robert

* * *

COOKSON, Catherine (McMullen) 1906-1998
　(Catherine Marchant)

PERSONAL: Born June 20, 1906, in Tyne Dock, South Shields, England; died June 11, 1998, in Jesmond Dene, England; mother's name, Catherine Fawcett; married Thomas H. Cookson (a schoolmaster), June 1, 1940.

CAREER: Novelist and author of children's books.

MEMBER: Society of Authors, PEN (England), Authors Guild, Authors League of America, Women's Press Club (London, England).

Catherine Cookson

AWARDS, HONORS: Winifred Holtby Award for best regional novel from Royal Society of Literature, 1968, for *The Round Tower;* Order of the British Empire, 1985; Freedom of the County Borough of South Shields in recognition of services to the city; honorary master's and doctorate degrees from University of Newcastle, 1983.

WRITINGS:

Kate Hannigan, Macdonald (London, England), 1950, Simon & Schuster (New York, NY), 2004.

Fifteen Streets (also see below), Macdonald (London, England), 1952, Simon & Schuster (New York, NY), 2002.

Colour Blind, Macdonald (London, England), 1953, published as *Color Blind,* New American Library (New York, NY), 1977.

Maggie Rowan, Macdonald (London, England), 1954, New American Library (New York, NY), 1975.

Rooney, Macdonald (London, England), 1957, reprinted, 1974.

The Menagerie, Macdonald (London, England), 1958, reprinted, Macdonald & Jane's (London, England), 1974.

Slinky Jane, Macdonald (London, England), 1959, reprinted, Macdonald & Jane's (London, England), 1979.

Fenwick Houses, Macdonald (London, England), 1960, reprinted, Macdonald & Jane's (London, England), 1979.

The Garment, Macdonald (London, England), 1962, New American Library (New York, NY), 1974.

The Blind Miller (also see below), Macdonald (London, England), 1963, reprinted, Heinemann (London, England), 1979.

Hannah Massey, Macdonald (London, England), 1964, New American Library (New York, NY), 1973.

The Long Corridor, Macdonald (London, England), 1965, New American Library (New York, NY), 1976.

The Unbaited Trap, Macdonald (London, England), 1966, New American Library (New York, NY), 1974.

Katie Mulholland, Macdonald (London, England), 1967, reprinted, Macdonald & Jane's (London, England), 1980.

The Round Tower (also see below), Macdonald (London, England), 1968, New American Library (New York, NY), 1975.

The Nice Bloke, Macdonald (London, England), 1969, published as *The Husband,* New American Library (New York, NY), 1976.

Our Kate: An Autobiography, Macdonald (London, England), 1969, Bobbs-Merrill, 1971, published as *Our Kate: Catherine Cookson—Her Personal Story,* Macdonald & Jane's (London, England), 1974.

The Glass Virgin, Macdonald (London, England), 1970, Bantam (New York, NY), 1981.

The Invitation, Macdonald (London, England), 1970, New American Library (New York, NY), 1974.

The Dwelling Place, Macdonald & Jane's (London, England), 1971.

Fanny McBride, Corgi Books (London, England), 1971.

Feathers in the Fire (also see below), Macdonald (London, England), 1971, Bobbs-Merrill, 1972.

Pure As the Lily, Macdonald (London, England), 1972, Bobbs-Merrill, 1973.

The Invisible Cord (also see below), Dutton (New York, NY), 1975.

The Gambling Man (also see below), Morrow (New York, NY), 1975.

The Tide of Life, Morrow (New York, NY), 1976.

The Girl (also see below), Morrow (New York, NY), 1977.

The Cinder Path (also see below), Morrow (New York, NY), 1978.

Tilly Trotter, Heinemann (London, England), 1978, published as *Tilly*, Morrow (New York, NY), 1980.

Selected Works, Heinemann/Octopus (London, England), Volume 1 (contains *Fifteen Streets, The Blind Miller, The Round Tower, Feathers in the Fire*, and *A Grand Man;* also see below), 1978, Volume 2 (contains *The Mallen Streak, The Invisible Cord, The Gambling Man, The Girl*, and *The Cinder Path*), 1980.

The Man Who Cried, Morrow (New York, NY), 1979.

Tilly Wed, Morrow (New York, NY), 1981, published as *Tilly Trotter Wed*, Heinemann (London, England), 1981.

Tilly Alone, Morrow (New York, NY), 1982, published as *Tilly Widowed*, Heinemann (London, England), 1982.

The Whip, Summit Books (New York, NY), 1982.

Hamilton (comic), Heinemann (London, England), 1983.

The Black Velvet Gown, Summit Books (New York, NY), 1984.

Goodbye Hamilton, Heinemann (London, England), 1984.

The Bannaman Legacy, Summit Books (New York, NY), 1985, published as *A Dinner of Herbs*, Heinemann (London, England), 1985.

Harold, Heinemann (London, England), 1985.

The Moth, Summit Books (New York, NY), 1986, published as *The Thorman Inheritance*, 1986.

Bill Bailey, Heinemann, 1986.

Catherine Cookson Country, Heinemann, 1986.

The Parson's Daughter, Summit Books (New York, NY), 1987.

The Baily Chronicles, Summit Books (New York, NY), 1988.

The Harrogate Secret, Summit Books (New York, NY), 1988.

Let Me Make Myself Plain, Bantam (New York, NY), 1988.

The Black Candle, Summit Books (New York, NY), 1989.

The Spaniard's Gift, Summit Books (New York, NY), 1989.

The Gillyvors, Bantam (New York, NY), 1990.

The Wingless Bird, Summit (New York, NY), 1990.

Bill Bailey's Lot, G. K. Hall (Boston, MA), 1990.

Bill Bailey's Daughter, G. K. Hall (Boston, MA), 1990.

The Love Child, Summit Books (New York, NY), 1990.

My Beloved Son, Bantam (New York, NY), 1991.

The Iron Facade, Bantam (New York, NY), 1991.

The Rag Nymph, Bantam (New York, NY), 1991.

The House of Women, Bantam (New York, NY), 1992.

The Maltese Angel, Simon & Schuster (New York, NY), 1992.

The Forester Girl, Simon & Schuster (New York, NY), 1993.

The Golden Straw, Simon & Schuster (New York, NY), 1993.

The Year of the Virgins, Simon & Schuster (New York, NY), 1993.

Maggie Rowan, Corgi (London, England), 1993.

Justice Is a Woman, Bantam (New York, NY), 1995.

The Obsession, Bantam (New York, NY), 1995.

Plainer Still, Bantam (New York, NY), 1995.

A Ruthless Need, Bantam (New York, NY), 1995.

Plainer Still: A New Personal Anthology, Bantam (New York, NY), 1995.

Three Complete Novels (includes *The Love Child, The Maltese Angel*, and *The Year of the Virgins*), Wings (New York, NY), 1996.

Tinker's Girl, Bantam (New York, NY), 1996.

The Bonny Dawn, Bantam (New York, NY), 1996.

The Upstart, Bantam (New York, NY), 1996.

The Bondage of Love, Bantam (New York, NY), 1997.

The Lady on My Left, Bantam (New York, NY), 1997.

Riley, Bantam (New York, NY), 1998.

The Solace of Sin, Bantam (New York, NY), 1998.

A House Divided, Simon & Schuster, 1999.

Kate Hannigan's Girl, Bantam (New York, NY), 2000.

The Silent Lady, Bantam (New York, NY), 2001.

The Simple Soul, and Other Stories, Bantam (New York, NY), 2001.

Cookson's books have been translated into over fifteen languages.

"MARY ANN" SERIES

A Grand Man, Macdonald (London, England), 1954, Macmillan (New York, NY), 1955, reprinted, Morrow (New York, NY), 1975.

The Lord and Mary Ann, Macdonald (London, England), 1956, reprinted, Macdonald & Jane's (London, England), 1974, Morrow (New York, NY), 1975.

The Devil and Mary Ann, Macdonald (London, England), 1958, Morrow (New York, NY), 1976.

Love and Mary Ann, Macdonald (London, England), 1961, Morrow (New York, NY), 1976.

Life and Mary Ann, Macdonald (London, England), 1962, Morrow (New York, NY), 1977.

Marriage and Mary Ann, Macdonald (London, England), 1964, Morrow (New York, NY), 1978.

Mary Ann's Angels, Macdonald (London, England), 1965, Morrow (New York, NY), 1978.

Mary Ann and Bill, Macdonald (London, England), 1966, Morrow (New York, NY), 1979.

Mary Ann Omnibus (contains all novels in "Mary Ann" series), Macdonald & Jane's (London, England), 1981.

"MALLEN NOVELS" TRILOGY

The Mallen Streak (also see below), Heinemann (London, England), 1973.

The Mallen Girl (also see below), Heinemann (London, England), 1974.

The Mallen Lot, Dutton (New York, NY), 1974, published as *The Mallen Litter,* Heinemann (London, England), 1974.

The Mallen Novels (contains *The Mallen Streak, The Mallen Girl,* and *The Mallen Litter*), Heinemann (London, England), 1979.

CHILDREN'S NOVELS

Matty Doolin, Macdonald (London, England), 1965, New American Library (New York, NY), 1976.

Joe and the Gladiator, Macdonald (London, England), 1968.

The Nipper, Bobbs-Merrill, 1970.

Blue Baccy, Macdonald & Jane's (London, England), 1972, Bobbs-Merrill, 1973.

Our John Willie, Morrow (New York, NY), 1974.

Mrs. Flanagan's Trumpet, Macdonald & Jane's (London, England), 1977, Lothrop (New York, NY), 1980.

Go Tell It to Mrs. Golightly, Macdonald & Jane's (London, England), 1977, Lothrop (New York, NY), 1980.

Lanky Jones, Lothrop (New York, NY), 1981.

UNDER PSEUDONYM CATHERINE MARCHANT

Heritage of Folly, Macdonald (London, England), 1963, reprinted, Macdonald & Jane's (London, England), 1980, reprinted, Corgi Books (London, England), 1994.

The Fen Tiger, Macdonald (London, England), 1963, Morrow (New York, NY), 1979.

House of Men, Macdonald (London, England), 1964, reprinted, Macdonald & Jane's (London, England), 1980.

Evil at Roger's Cross, Lancer Books (London, England), 1965, revised edition published as *The Iron Facade,* Heinemann (London, England), 1976, Morrow (New York, NY), 1980.

Miss Martha Mary Crawford, Heinemann (London, England), 1975, Morrow (New York, NY), 1976.

The Slow Awakening, Heinemann, 1976, Morrow (New York, NY), 1977.

Also author of *The Cultured Handmaiden,* 1988, and the children's books *Rory's Fortune, Nancy Nutall and the Mongrel,* and *Bill and the Mary Ann Shaughnessy.*

SIDELIGHTS: Catherine Cookson was a prolific British author who enjoyed a large following. Her family sagas, for which she is most noted, are still read in some thirty countries. A frequent name on the bestseller list, in the early 1980s, Cookson was commemorated by Corgi Books for exceeding the 27,000,000 mark in paperback sales alone. According to Anne Duchene in the *Times Literary Supplement,* "These days there are never fewer than fifty Cookson titles in print in English at any time . . . translated into fifteen languages." In a London *Times* interview with Caroline Moorehead, Cookson once emphasized that she never had trouble coming up with ideas for her historical novels: "I've always been a jabberer. I just talked. I see everything in images. The plot sort of unfolds. Even the dialogue. In the morning, it's all there to put down." As Duchene observed: "Cookson writes stories in which her readers can gratefully recognize experiences and emotions of their own— heightened, to be sure, by greater comedy or greater violence than their own lives normally vouchsafe, but based on all their own affections, furies, aspirations and reactions."

Born the illegitimate daughter of an alcoholic mother, Cookson lived with her mother in her grandparents' strict Catholic household during most of her childhood. By the age of eighteen, Cookson had been working as a laundry checker, although she longed for an education. Her success in overcoming her disadvantaged childhood, critics noted, was one source of her broad appeal. Anita Brookner commented in the *Ob-*

server that "Cookson brings comfort to millions and one can see the reason why: she represents the strong woman of various mythologies, a Mother Courage with no children but more than fifty-seven titles. She is an entirely remarkable person." Published in 1969, Cookson's autobiography *Our Kate* documents the difficulties she experienced during her childhood; the book quickly became a popular and critical success. A later autobiographical work, *Let Me Make Myself Plain,* presents essays, poetry, and paintings, each of which draw upon the author's personal reflections and experiences.

Cookson's experience of life in the working-class, industrial environment of Tyneside also provided material for her numerous novels. Autobiographical elements strongly inform the narrative of *The Love Child,* for example, which portrays a nineteenth-century girl who is tormented by the hostility of villagers and the disapproval of the church pastor due to her illegitimate status. An example of Cookson's use of the "family saga" form, *The House of Women,* focuses on four generations of women living in the same house in Tyneside and chronicles their experience of hypochondria, an unhappy marriage, and teenaged pregnancy, among other trials. Along with their treatment of northern English settings and British class structures, Cookson's novels are noted for their portrayal of appealing female characters. *The Wingless Bird,* for instance, depicts Agnes Conway, the daughter of an English shopkeeper, who must choose between an unhappy marriage or spinsterhood. Her life changes unexpectedly, however, when she falls in love with an upper-class man and subsequently finds the courage and the means to escape her family's oppressive treatment.

The character Mary Ann Shaughnessy has reappeared in eight of Cookson's novels, which have been published together in a single volume titled *The Mary Ann Omnibus.* Mary Ann is eight years old in *A Grand Man,* the first novel of the series, and the twenty-seven-year-old mother of twins in *Mary Ann and Bill,* the final story. "In the earlier books Mary Ann bounces through her own and other people's lives like a cross between a deus (or dea) ex machina and a gremlin, interfering in situations and people with blithe impartiality, generally for the benefit of her beloved, drunken father Mike Shaughnessy," noted Judith Rhodes in *Romance and Historical Writers.* "Few of Cookson's other novels demonstrate her capacity for comedy as this series does; not only does Mary Ann herself create a number of amusing situations, but her grannie McMullen . . . is a wonderful comic character."

Cookson was also well established as an author of children's books, several of which draw upon historical and autobiographical themes. Set in England during the 1850s, her children's novel *Our John Willie,* for example, portrays two brothers who manage to survive poverty and exploitation at the hands of mine-owners. While some critics objected to the extreme sentimentality of the story, others commented favorably on Cookson's treatment of her historical subject. Like many of her novels for adults, Cookson's children's stories often draw upon her experience of the English community of Tyneside. *Joe and the Gladiator,* for example, is set in the Tyneside shipyards and depicts a hard-working young man who is plagued with financial and family problems that grow worse when an elderly man dies, leaving an old horse in Joe's care.

Although bedridden and disabled by seriously declining eyesight, Cookson continued to create fiction until her death in 1998, dictating her stories to a tape-recorder, and working in collaboration with her husband during the editing process.

BIOGRAPHICAL AND CRITICAL SOURCES:

BOOKS

Cookson, Catherine, *Our Kate: An Autobiography,* Macdonald (London, England), 1969, Bobbs-Merrill, 1971, published as *Our Kate: Catherine Cookson—Her Personal Story,* Macdonald & Jane's (London, England), 1974.

PERIODICALS

Booklist, February 1, 1984, p. 769; January 15, 1991, p. 979; September 1, 1991, p. 28; November 1, 1992, p. 466.
Books, November, 1990; July, 1991, p. 10.
Catholic World, June, 1955.
Chicago Tribune, November 27, 1994, p. 9.

Kirkus Reviews, August 1, 1969, p. 793; May 15, 1978, p. 562; February 1, 1981, p. 140; October 1, 1992, p. 1203; October 1, 1993, p. 1219; September 1, 1994, p. 1148; February 1, 1995, p. 86.
Kliatt, September, 1990, p. 6.
Library Journal, June 1, 1975, p. 1152; May 15, 1985, p. 78; March 15, 1987, p. 400; April 15, 1987, p. 96; April 15, 1990, p. 141; September 1, 1991; October 1, 1994, p. 112, 228.
London Review of Books, June 27, 1991, p. 22.
New York Times, January 7, 1955.
New York Times Book Review, October 20, 1974, p. 41; April 2, 1984, p. 25; June 30, 1985, p. 20.
Observer (London, England), April 1, 1984; November 27, 1988.
Publishers Weekly, July 21, 1969, p. 53; November 17, 1975, p. 95; August 16, 1976, p. 118; March 22, 1985, p. 51; March 28, 1986, p. 52; March 27, 1987, p. 37; February 10, 1989, p. 53; March 16, 1990, p. 60; January 25, 1991, p. 48; August 9, 1991, p. 44; October 12, 1992, p. 64; October 11, 1993, p. 70; October 3, 1994, p. 52; February 20, 1995, p. 195.
School Library Journal, August, 1990, p. 174.
Spectator, July 6, 1991, p. 26; October 12, 1991, p. 39.
Times (London, England), August 15, 1983.
Times Literary Supplement, January 7, 1955; June 6, 1968; June 19, 1969; March 29, 1974; July 24, 1981, p. 830.
Washington Post Book World, April 1, 1990.

OBITUARIES

PERIODICALS

Chicago Tribune, June 12, 1998, section 1, p. 12.
Los Angeles Times, June 12, 1998, p. A22.
New York Times, June 12, 1998, p. A19.
Times (London, England), June 12, 1998.
Washington Post, June 12, 1998, p. C9.*

*   *   *

COPELAND, Lori 1941-

PERSONAL: Born June 12, 1941, in Springfield, MO; daughter of John Seneca and Josephine Alice (Pottenger) Smart; married Lance Eldon Copeland (a planner), June 14, 1958; children: Randall, Richard, Russell. *Religion:* Methodist.

ADDRESSES: Home—4881 S. Jewell, Springfield, MO 65810. *Office*—1340 W. Battlefield, Ste. 106, Springfield, MO 65807-4102. *Agent*—Evan Marshall Agency, 22 South Park St., Montclair, NJ 07042.

CAREER: Romance novelist, 1982—.

MEMBER: Romance Writers of America, Novelists Ink, and Ozark Romance Authors.

AWARDS, HONORS: Career Achievement Award from *Romantic Times,* 1991; Affaire de Couer Conference, Silver Certificate, 1987, Gold Certificate, 1988, for *Passion's Captive;* inducted into the Missouri Writers' Hall of Fame, 2000; Reviewers' Choice award, *Romantic Times,* 2002, for the "Heavenly Daze" series.

WRITINGS:

ROMANCE NOVELS

Playing for Keeps, Dell (New York, NY), 1983.
A Tempting Stranger, Dell (New York, NY, 1983.
All or Nothing, Dell (New York, NY), 1984.
Rainbow's End, Dell (New York, NY), 1984.
Out of Control, Dell (New York, NY), 1984.
A Winning Combination, Dell (New York, NY), 1984.
Two of a Kind, Dell (New York, NY), 1984.
Only the Best, Dell (New York, NY), 1984.
High Voltage, Dell (New York, NY), 1985.
More Than She Bargained For, Dell (New York, NY), 1985.
Spitfire, Dell (New York, NY), 1985.
Forever After, Dell (New York, NY), 1985.
Tug of War, Dell (New York, NY), 1986.
Hot on His Trail, Dell (New York, NY), 1986.
When Lightning Strikes, Dell (New York, NY), 1986.
A Love of Our Own, Dell (New York, NY), 1986.
Passion's Folly, Dell (New York, NY), 1987.
Avenging Angel, Dell (New York, NY), 1987.
Tale of Love, Dell (New York, NY), 1988.
Passion's Captive, Dell (New York, NY), 1988.
The Trouble with Thorny, Harlequin (New York, NY), 1988.
Sweet Talkin' Stranger, Dell (New York, NY), 1989.
Dancy's Woman, Pageant (New York, NY), 1989.
Tall Cotton, Harlequin (New York, NY), 1990.
Darling Deceiver, Loveswept (New York, NY), 1990.
Fool Me Once, Dell (New York, NY), 1990.

Tiz the Season, Loveswept (New York, NY, 1990.

Sweet Hannah Rose, Dell (New York, NY), 1991.

Squeeze Play, Loveswept (New York, NY), 1991.

Melancholy Baby, Loveswept (New York, NY), 1991.

Forever, Ashley, Dell (New York, NY), 1992.

Taste of Temptation, Loveswept (New York, NY), 1992.

Built to Last, Loveswept (New York, NY), 1992.

Timeless Love, Avon (New York, NY), 1993.

Three Complete Novels (contains *Avenging Angel, Passion's Captive,* and *Sweet Talkin' Stranger*), Wings Books (New York, NY), 1994.

The Courtship of Cade Kolby, Avon (New York, NY), 1997.

(With others) *With This Ring: A Quartet of Charming Stories about Four Very Special Weddings,* Tyndale House (Wheaton, IL), 1998.

Child of Grace, Tyndale House (Wheaton, IL), 2001.

Christmas Vows: $5.00 Extra, Tyndale House (Wheaton, IL), 2001.

Roses Will Bloom Again, Tyndale House (Wheaton, IL), 2002.

Stranded in Paradise: A Story of Letting Go, Word Publishing (Nashville, TN), 2002.

"SISTERS OF MERCY FLATS" TRILOGY

Promise Me Today, Fawcett (New York, NY), 1992.

Promise Me Tomorrow, Fawcett (New York, NY), 1993.

Promise Me Forever, Fawcett (New York, NY), 1994.

"BRIDES OF THE WEST" SERIES

Faith, Tyndale House (Wheaton, IL), 1998.

Hope, Tyndale House (Wheaton, IL), 1999.

June, Tyndale House (Wheaton, IL), 1999.

Glory, Tyndale House (Wheaton, IL), 2000.

Ruth, Tyndale House (Wheaton, IL), 2002.

Patience, Heart Quest (Wheaton, IL), 2004.

WITH ANGELA HUNT; "HEAVENLY DAZE" SERIES

The Island of Heavenly Daze, Word Publishing (Nashville, TN), 2000.

Grace in Autumn, Word Publishing (Nashville, TN), 2001.

A Warmth in Winter, Word Publishing (Nashville, TN), 2001.

A Perfect Love, Word Publishing (Nashville, TN), 2002.

Hearts at Home, Word Publishing (Nashville, TN), 2003.

"MORNING SHADE MYSTERY" SERIES

A Case of Bad Taste, Tyndale House (Wheaton, IL), 2003.

A Case of Crooked Letters, Tyndale House (Wheaton, IL), 2004.

A Case of Nosy Neighbors, Tyndale House (Wheaton, IL), 2004.

SIDELIGHTS: Since Dell published her first novel in 1983, Lori Copeland has written dozens of Christian romance novels and created several series, including the popular "Brides of the West" series. The first three books in the series are named for sisters Faith, June, and Hope Kallahan, whose pastor father has died, leaving them with no means of support. Faith, the eldest at nineteen, and her younger sisters answer an ad for mail-order brides, then in 1872, set out from their home in Michigan for Western adventures. The second three titles are named for other young women who follow in their footsteps. In *Faith,* the first sister travels to Texas to meet her intended, Nicholas, a rancher who then has second thoughts. When she turns her attention to teaching Braille to the son of a local widower, Nicholas realizes he may lose her. *Library Journal's* Melissa Hudak felt that the characters are endowed "with enough liveliness to make the book a fun light read."

June finds the sister in Seattle to marry Eli Messenger, the assistant of a well-known evangelist. When she arrives, however, she finds Eli ill, and after he dies, she stays to help with the local orphanage. She soon discovers that the evangelist, Isaac Inman, has been funneling funds intended for the orphans to build a fancy tabernacle. June does find romance with Eli's friend, Parker Sentell, and together they try to show Inman the error of his ways. Hudak noted that the character of the flawed clergyman is "an intriguing twist in a genre that usually demands perfect behavior from its religious characters."

Unknown to the residents of Heavenly Daze, an island off the coast of Maine, they share their idyllic setting with seven angels who have safeguarded the residents for more than two centuries, and six of the angels have taken human forms and live among them. *Library Journal*'s Shawna Saavedra Thorup reviewed *A Perfect Love,* the fourth book in the "Heavenly Daze" series, the plot of which involves a couple having marital problems. "Amusing incidents . . . keep the pace brisk," noted Thorup, "and the angelic assistance is low-key but powerful."

Copeland began her "Morning Shade Mystery" series with *A Case of Bad Taste,* which features novelist Maude Diamond, her widowed daughter, and her mother-in-law, Stella, who has moved in with Maude. Maude is suffering writer's block but becomes inspired when Stella and her card-playing friends talk about neighborhood break-ins in which the culprit doesn't take anything, just redecorates. With this series, Copeland heads in a new direction with a multigenerational cast of women who solve mysteries in their town of Morning Shade.

BIOGRAPHICAL AND CRITICAL SOURCES:

PERIODICALS

Library Journal, November 1, 1998, Melissa Hudak, review of *Faith,* p. 64; April 1, 1999, Melissa Hudak, review of *June,* p. 79; September 1, 2002, Shawn Saavedra Thorup, review of *A Perfect Love,* p. 156; April 1, 2004, Tamara Butler, review of *A Case of Crooked Letters,* p. 78.
Today's Christian Woman, March-April, 2004, review of *A Case of Crooked Letters,* p. 8.

ONLINE

Lori Copeland Home Page, http://www.loricopeland. com (April 12, 2004).*

*   *   *

COPPER, Basil 1924-
(Lee Falk)

PERSONAL: Born February 5, 1924, in London, England; married Annie Renee Guerin. *Education:* Attended Glasgow Wireless College. *Hobbies and other interests:* Old films.

ADDRESSES: Home—Stockdoves, South Park, Sevenoaks, Kent TN13 1EN, England.

CAREER: Journalist and author. News editor with Kent county, England, newspaper for thirty years; freelance writer, 1970—. *Military service:* Royal British Navy, served four years; Light Costal Forces.

MEMBER: Society of Authors, Crime Writers Association, British Film Institute, Tunbridge Wells Vintage Film Society (founder), Vintage Film Circle.

AWARDS, HONORS: Runner up for year's best book, First World Fantasy Convention, for *From Evil's Pillow;* elected Knight of Mark Twain, for "contribution to modern fiction."

WRITINGS:

NOVELS

The Great White Space, R. Hale (London, England), 1974, St. Martin's Press (New York, NY), 1975.
The Curse of the Fleers, Harwood Smart (London, England), 1976, St. Martin's Press (New York, NY), 1977.
Necropolis, illustrated by Stephen E. Fabian, Arkham House (Sauk City, WI), 1980.
The House of the Wolf, illustrated by Stephen E. Fabian, Arkham House, 1983, reprinted, Sarob Press (Carmarthenshire, Wales), 2003.
Into the Silence, Sphere Books (London, England), 1983.
The Black Death, illustrated by Stefanie K. Hawks, Fedogan & Bremer (Minneapolis, MN), 1991.
Solar Pons versus the Devil's Claw, Sarob Press (Carmarthenshire, Wales), 2004.

STORY COLLECTIONS

Not after Nightfall: Stories of the Strange and Terrible, New English Library (London, England), 1967.
From Evil's Pillow, Arkham House (Sauk City, WI), 1973.
When Footsteps Echo: Tales of Terror and the Unknown, St. Martin's Press (New York, NY), 1975.

And Afterward, the Dark: Seven Tales, Arkham House (Sauk City, WI), 1977.

Here Be Daemons: Tales of Horror and the Uneasy, St. Martin's Press (New York, NY), 1978.

The Dossier of Solar Pons, Pinnacle Books (New York, NY), 1979.

The Further Adventure of Solar Pons, Pinnacle Books (New York, NY), 1979.

The Secret Files of Solar Pons, Pinnacle Books (New York, NY), 1979.

Some Uncollected Cases of Solar Pons, Pinnacle Books (New York, NY), 1980.

Voices of Doom: Tales of Terror and the Uncanny, St. Martin's Press (New York, NY), 1980.

(Editor) August Derleth, *The Solar Pons Omnibus,* two volumes, Arkham House (Sauk City, WI), 1982.

The Exploits of Solar Pons, illustrated by Stefanie K. Hawks, Fedogan & Bremer, 1993.

The Recollections of Solar Pons, illustrated by Stefanie K. Hawks, Fedogan & Bremer, 1996.

Whispers in the Night, Fedogan & Bremer (Minneapolis, MN), 1999.

Cold Hand on My Shoulder: Tales of Terror and Suspense, Sarob Press (Carmarthenshire, Wales), 2002.

"MIKE FARADAY" PRIVATE EYE NOVELS

The Dark Mirror, R. Hale, 1966.
Night Frost, R. Hale, 1966.
No Flowers for the General, R. Hale, 1967.
Scratch on the Dark, R. Hale, 1967.
Die Now, Live Later, R. Hale, 1968.
Don't Bleed on Me, R. Hale, 1968.
The Marble Orchard, R. Hale, 1969.
Dead File, R. Hale, 1970.
No Letters from the Grave, R. Hale, 1971.
The Big Chill, R. Hale, 1972.
Strong-Arm, R. Hale, 1972.
A Great Year for Dying, R. Hale, 1973.
Shock-Wave, R. Hale, 1973.
The Breaking Point, R. Hale, 1973.
A Voice from the Dead, R. Hale, 1974.
Feedback, R. Hale, 1974.
Ricochet, R. Hale, 1974.
The High Wall, R. Hale, 1975.
Impact, R. Hale, 1975.
A Good Place to Die, R. Hale, 1975.
The Lonely Place, R. Hale, 1976.

Crack in the Sidewalk, R. Hale, 1976.
Tight Corner, R. Hale, 1976.
The Year of the Dragon, R. Hale, 1977.
Death Squad, R. Hale, 1977.
Murder One, R. Hale, 1978.
A Quiet Room in Hell, R. Hale, 1979.
The Big Rip-Off, R. Hale, 1979.
The Caligari Complex, R. Hale, 1980.
Flip-Side, R. Hale, 1980.
The Long Rest, R. Hale, 1981.
The Empty Silence, R. Hale, 1981.
Dark Entry, R. Hale, 1981.
Hang Loose, R. Hale, 1982.
Shoot-Out, R. Hale, 1982.
The Far Horizon, R. Hale, 1982.
Trigger-Man, R. Hale, 1983.
Pressure-Point, R. Hale, 1983.
Hard Contract, R. Hale, 1983.
The Narrow Corner, R. Hale, 1983.
The Hook, R. Hale, 1984.
You Only Die Once, R. Hale, 1984.
Tuxedo Park, R. Hale, 1984.
The Far Side of Fear, R. Hale, 1984.
Snow-Job, R. Hale, 1986.
Jet-Lag, R. Hale, 1986.
Blood on the Moon, R. Hale, 1986.
Heavy Iron, R. Hale, 1987.
Turn down an Empty Glass, R. Hale, 1987.
Bad Scene, R. Hale, 1987.
House-Dick, R. Hale, 1988.
Print-Out, R. Hale, 1988.

NOVELS; UNDER PSEUDONYM LEE FALK

The Phantom, Avon (New York, NY), 1972.
The Phantom and the Scorpia Menace, Avon (New York, NY), 1972.
The Phantom and the Slave Market of Mucar, Avon (New York, NY), 1972.

OTHER

The Vampire: In Legend, Fact, and Art (nonfiction), R. Hale, 1973, Citadel (New York, NY), 1974.
The Werewolf: In Legend, Fact, and Art (nonfiction), St. Martin's Press (New York, NY), 1977.

Also author of a film script of M. R. James's novel *Count Magnus.*

ADAPTATIONS: Copper's novel *Camera Obscura* was made into a film.

WORK IN PROGRESS: Knife in the Back, for Nightshade Press, and *Solar Pons Companion.*

SIDELIGHTS: British-based writer Basil Copper has written prolifically in the mystery and horror genres, including over fifty novels featuring Los Angeles private eye Mike Faraday and several collections of short stories featuring 1920s detective Solar Pons. Copper is best known for his horror fiction. As Mike Ashley explained in the *St. James Guide to Horror, Ghost, and Gothic Writers,* Copper "remains the most complete traditionalist working in the field of horror fiction today."

Ashley noted that Copper's "soul is in the mist-enshrouded age of the late Victorian and Edwardian era, or a timeless 1920s that nostalgia has created. Copper is a great emulator, rather in the vein of his mentor August Derleth. He is able to reproduce accurately the pace, mood and approach of the work of authors he admires, particularly H. P. Lovecraft, Mickey Spillane, Arthur Conan Doyle, and Derleth himself. This is not to detract from Copper's creative abilities—he can produce excellent original material—rather it is a demonstration of his flexibility within the field. . . . In the horror field, Copper's work falls loosely into three categories. There are his stories which emulate the work of H. P. Lovecraft, there are those which are Victorian gothics, and there are his own individual stories."

Copper's Lovecraftian fiction includes his novels *The Great White Space* and *Into the Silence* which, according to Ashley, are both "similar in structure and development to Lovecraft's major works such as *At the Mountains of Madness.* Copper superbly captures the timelessness of Lovecraft's 1920s and 1930s when individuals, usually university professors, explored little-known parts of the globe. The books start with that apprehension and excitement of entering the unknown checked to some degree by a more leisurely academic pace and reserve until events begin to snowball out of control and menaces from Earth's distant past are unearthed."

Copper's more Victorian fiction is, according to Ashley, "best exemplified by *Necropolis,* a wonderful emporium of a novel in which a private investigator,

looking into the death of a client's father, unearths foul deeds in the depths of the massive Brookwood Cemetery. The novel is set in the same atmospheric London as Sherlock Holmes inhabited: in fact Inspector Lestrade is one of the characters and there are several cross-references to Holmes's cases. Copper succeeds in recreating this atmosphere in his more recent novels, *The House of the Wolf* and *The Black Death,* though neither of these has the gothic extravagance of *Necropolis.*"

Copper's more individualistic stories, those drawing upon his vast knowledge of the ghost and horror genre to create wholly original effects, include those works in which the author "likes to bring the reader into the narrator's mind and follow the gradual mental degradation amidst rising fright," as Ashley explained. Among his best works, and "arguably Copper's best short story," Ashley noted, is "The Janissaries of Emilion," a tale in which "a visionary is killed by a product of his own dreams." Other stand-out stories include "The Grey House," "a vivid haunted-house story which presages Stephen King's *The Shining* in its evocation of possession. Another powerful story . . . , one which demonstrates Copper's interest in and knowledge of the cinema, [is] 'Amber Print' in which two collectors discover an unknown and, it transpires, haunted print of [F. W. Murnau's classic silent film] *The Cabinet of Dr. Caligari.*"Ashley believed the story "Wish You Were Here," another haunted-house tale, to be among Copper's finest works "because he is able to bring to the story his wide experience of horror fiction and his ability to create an almost Victorian atmosphere . . . to produce a modern-day ghost story which packs the punch of a century of supernatural fiction."

Copper told *CA:* "I usually go to bed at around one a.m. after watching movies, of which I have a vast collection; rise around eight a.m. and am at the desk in my study at nine a.m. and work a normal office day, answering mail and working on fresh projects, sometimes two or three at a time. My wife is French and we spend a couple of months at the family home in Burgundy each year (i.e., a month around May and another month in October), and I do a lot of writing in my spare time.

"People often ask, 'Where do you get your inspiration?' Well, of course, the professional author simply sits down at the typewriter and starts writing;

in my case it is like water from a tap and fresh ideas evolve as one progresses. It was a great pleasure to me last year when Professor Howard Gotlieb, the distinguished Archivist at Boston University established the Basil Cooper Archive there. My great idols in the macabre field are, of course, Edgar Allan Poe, H. P. Lovecraft, M. R. James and E. F. Benson; two American and two British."

BIOGRAPHICAL AND CRITICAL SOURCES:

BOOKS

St. James Guide to Horror, Ghost, and Gothic Writers, St. James Press (Detroit, MI), 1998.

PERIODICALS

Book and Magazine Collector, February, 1999, Richard Dalby "Basil Cooper: Crimewriter and Master of Macabre," p. 82.
Publishers Weekly, September 25, 1995, p. 47.

*   *   *

CUNNINGHAM, E. V.
   See FAST, Howard (Melvin)

*   *   *

CURRIE, Katy
   See KYLE, Susan (Spaeth)

D

DAHEIM, Mary 1937-

PERSONAL: Surname is pronounced "*day*-hime"; born November 7, 1937, in Seattle, WA; daughter of Hugh E. (a marine engineer) and Monica (a legal secretary; maiden name, Dawson) Richardson; married David C. Daheim (a professor of humanities), December 18, 1965; children: Barbara, Katherine, Magdalen. *Education:* University of Washington, Seattle, B.A., 1960. *Politics:* Democrat. *Religion:* Roman Catholic.

ADDRESSES: Office—Ballantine Books, c/o Random House, 1745 Broadway, New York, NY 10019.

CAREER: Author and communications consultant. Pacific Northwest Bell, Seattle, WA, public relations manager and communications consultant, 1960—. Consultant to banks and telecommunications companies.

MEMBER: Romance Writers of America, Mystery Writers of America, Authors Guild.

AWARDS, HONORS: Pacific Northwest Writers Association Achievement Award, 2000.

WRITINGS:

HISTORICAL ROMANCE NOVELS

Love's Pirate, Avon (New York, NY) 1983.
Destiny's Pawn, Avon (New York, NY), 1984.
Passion's Triumph, Avon (New York, NY), 1988.

"BED AND BREAKFAST" SERIES

Just Desserts, Avon (New York, NY), 1991.
Fowl Prey, Avon (New York, NY), 1991.
Holy Terrors, Avon (New York, NY), 1992.
Dune to Death, Avon (New York, NY), 1993.
Bantam of the Opera, Avon (New York, NY), 1993.
A Fit of Tempera, Avon (New York, NY), 1994.
Major Vices, Avon (New York, NY), 1995, Beeler Large Print (Hampton Falls, NH), 2002.
Murder, My Suite, Avon (New York, NY), 1995.
Auntie Mayhem, Avon (New York, NY), 1996.
Nutty As a Fruitcake, Avon (New York, NY), 1996.
September Mourn, Avon (New York, NY), 1997.
Wed and Buried, Avon (New York, NY), 1998.
Snow Place to Die, Avon (New York, NY), 1998.
Legs Benedict, Avon (New York, NY), 1999.
Creeps Suzette, Avon (New York, NY), 2000.
A Streetcar Named Expire, Avon (New York, NY), 2001.
Suture Self, William Morrow (New York, NY), 2001.
Silver Scream, William Morrow (New York, NY), 2002.
Hocus Croakus, William Morrow (New York, NY), 2003.
This Old Souse, William Morrow (New York, NY), 2004.

"ALPINE" SERIES

The Alpine Advocate, Ballantine (New York, NY), 1992.
The Alpine Betrayal, Ballantine (New York, NY), 1993.

The Alpine Christmas, Ballantine (New York, NY), 1993.

The Alpine Decoy, Ballantine (New York, NY), 1994.

The Alpine Escape, Ballantine (New York, NY), 1995.

The Alpine Fury, Ballantine (New York, NY), 1996.

The Alpine Gamble, Ballantine (New York, NY), 1996, Beeler Large Print (Hampton Falls, NH), 1999.

The Alpine Hero, Ballantine (New York, NY), 1996, Beeler Large Print (Hampton Falls, NH), 1999.

The Alpine Icon, Ballantine (New York, NY), 1998.

The Alpine Journey, Ballantine (New York, NY), 1998.

The Alpine Kindred, Ballantine (New York, NY), 1998.

The Alpine Legacy, Ballantine (New York, NY), 1999.

The Alpine Menace, Ballantine (New York, NY), 2000.

The Alpine Nemesis, Ballantine (New York, NY), 2001.

The Alpine Obituary, Ballantine (New York, NY), 2002.

The Alpine Pursuit, Ballantine (New York, NY), 2004.

OTHER

(With Carolyn Hart, Jane Isenberg, and Shirley Rousseau Murphy) *Motherhood Is Murder* (mystery collection), Avon (New York, NY), 2003.

Also author of *Sound of Surrender,* Avon (New York, NY), and other historical romance novels. Managing editor of *Anacortes American Bulletin,* 1960; reporter and columnist for *Port Angeles Daily News,* 1966-69; former staff member of *Pacific Search* (now *Northwest* magazine). Contributor to magazines and newspapers.

SIDELIGHTS: As a child in the Pacific Northwest, Mary Daheim aspired to a career as a sports reporter. Friends and relatives told her that women do not become sports reporters. When she asked her grandmother why, she was told, "Because those boys don't want you to see them with their clothes off." Daheim turned to writing novels instead and became the author of the popular "Bed and Breakfast" and "Alpine" mystery series.

After penning a number of historical romances, Daheim realized she was working in a field that did not reflect her interests as a reader. She was actually a fan of mystery novels, and proceeded to launch two successful mystery series. Both series are set in the Pacific Northwest, and feature casts of characters drawn from her own experiences. The "Bed and Breakfast" series

takes place on the coastal island of Chavez where its protagonist, Judith McMonigle Flynn, runs the only B & B when she is not too busy solving crimes. The "Alpine" series is based in Alpine, Washington, which a reviewer from *Publishers Weekly* characterized as a "soap-opera small town." It features amateur sleuth Emma Lord, editor of the *Alpine Advocate.*

Daheim's mysteries have received a mixed critical response. In the sixth novel of the Alpine series, *The Alpine Fury,* the town is suffering the economic effects of a failed logging industry when rumors begin to circulate that its only bank is headed for a merger. Emma Lord begins to investigate in her capacity as a journalist. However, when the bank's bookkeeper turns up murdered, her role soon switches to that of detective. A reviewer for *Publishers Weekly* stated, "The book's small town ambience makes a good contrast to this high-finance very 1980s mystery. The town's quirky characters . . . add a nice, honest feel to the tale." However, another *Publishers Weekly* reviewer found nothing to praise in the seventh novel in the series, *The Alpine Gamble,* describing it as a "predictable, mundane book."

Despite some harsh criticism, Daheim has had considerable success with the "Alpine" series. The author made her hardcover debut with the sixteenth novel in the series, *The Alpine Pursuit,* in which Emma investigates the shooting death of an actor killed onstage during the performance of a play. *Library Journal*'s Rex Klett said the novel contains "solid prose, remarkable characters, and [an] entertaining plot."

Daheim's "Bed & Breakfast" series has also established itself as a popular mystery series. In *Holy Terrors,* the third book in the series, investigator Judith McMonigle falls in love with homicide detective (and future husband) Joe Flynn as the two search for the murderer of a local woman. A *Publishers Weekly* reviewer observed that "Daheim creates a credible and sympathetic character in McMonigle." In *Wed and Buried,* the twelfth installment in the "Bed and Breakfast" series, Judith believes she has seen a murder outside of her hotel's reception area. To the consternation of her husband, Judith investigates. According to a *Publishers Weekly* reviewer, "Luckily clues contrive to drop into Judith's lap because, generally speaking, she doesn't seem competent enough to find them herself. . . . All in all, neither the characters nor the construction of the plot seems believable or coherent." In contrast, another *Publishers Weekly* reviewer credited *September Mourn,* the eleventh book in the series, with "inventive plot twists," while also praising Daheim's portrayal of the book's "picturesque backdrop."

Daheim added installations to her "Bed & Breakfast" series including *Creeps Suzette, Silver Scream,* and *Hocus Croakus.* In *Creeps Suzette,* Judith and her cousin look after an elderly woman who is convinced that someone is trying to kill her. A *Publishers Weekly* critic felt that Daheim's "acerbic wit and sarcasm propel the dialogue" in this mystery. *Silver Scream* finds Judith's B & B overrun by Hollywood, as actors, directors, and producers descend upon Hillside Manor on Halloween weekend. When a famous producer turns up dead, Judith begins a murder investigation. A contributor to *Publishers Weekly* wrote, "The fog, mist, and rain of a Pacific Northwest October add to the Halloween atmosphere" as Judith searches for clues among the strange cast of characters. The critic concluded, "Fans will be enthralled." While *Silver Scream* contains many Halloween tricks and treats, *Hocus Croakus* offers only tricks. Judith, on vacation from her beloved B & B, investigates the murder of a magician's assistant who turns up dead at a casino. A *Publishers Weekly* reviewer deemed *Hocus Croakus* a "winning addition."

In addition to writing solo, Daheim contributed to a mystery collection titled *Motherhood Is Murder* with mystery authors Carolyn Hart, Jane Isenberger, and Shirley Rousseau Murphy. Daheim's contribution, *Dial M for Mom,* finds Cousin Renie, from the "Bed & Breakfast" series, preparing for the weddings of her three children, all on the same day. When the photographer is found dead, things become even more complicated.

Prior to her mystery writing career, Daheim once told *CA:* "I've always written, never wanted to do anything else. I use the historical romance to inform, entertain, and amuse. I like research and do a lot of it. I consider myself a storyteller, not a novelist. While the genre isn't exactly suited to one-liners, I try to inject at least a hint of humor. I have as much fun writing the books as I hope readers will have reading them.

"I try to create characters that fit the romantic novel genre without being clichés. I also use historical personages as much as possible to give authenticity while presenting their characters with what I term interpretive accuracy. Stories with a strong historical background suit my style best, using the actual events as a springboard for my characters, real and imagined.

"The personal views I present tend to deal with my own interpretation of historical events, though I know that the historian must, by definition, deal in hindsight. To compensate I try to show how characters reacted to events within the context of their time and personal experiences. For me, history is not a grand, faceless panorama, but the meshing of individual personalities, needs, ambitions, and every other human emotion that eventually becomes what we later call 'history.'"

BIOGRAPHICAL AND CRITICAL SOURCES:

BOOKS

Detecting Women, Purple Moon Press (Dearborn, MI)1994.

PERIODICALS

Booklist, January 1, 2001, Jenny McLarin, review of *Suture Self,* p. 924.
Kirkus Reviews, July 15, 2003, review of *Hocus Croakus,* p. 938.
Library Journal, February 1, 2004, Rex Klett, review of *The Alpine Pursuit,* p. 128.
Publishers Weekly, February 24, 1992, review of *Holy Terrors,* p. 50; November 2, 1992, review of *The Alpine Advocate,* p. 67; November 13, 1995, review of *The Alpine Fury,* p. 58; June 17, 1996, review of *The Alpine Gamble,* p. 62; September 30, 1996, review of *Nutty As a Fruitcake,* p. 80; July 7, 1997, review of *September Mourn,* p. 66; January 12, 1998, review of *Wed and Buried,* p. 57; December 14, 1998, review of *The Alpine Kindred,* p. 72; December 13, 1999, review of *Creeps Suzette,* p. 69; April 29, 2002, review of *Silver Scream,* p. 46; January 1, 2001, review of *Suture Self,* p. 71; April 29, 2002, review of *Silver Scream,* p. 46; August 26, 2002, review of *The Alpine Obituary,* p. 50; June 16, 2003, review of *Hocus Croakus,* p. 54.

ONLINE

Ballantine Books Web site, http://www.randomhouse.com/BB/ (February 16, 2004), list of Mary Daheim books.

Killing Time Mystery Books Web site, Mary Daheim page, http://members.aol.com/ktbooks/daheim. htm/ (March 11, 2003), "Northwest Mystery Writers: Mary Daheim."

What You Need to Know about Bed and Breakfasts Web site, http://bandb.about.com/ (March 11, 2003), Elizabeth Arneson, "Interview with Mary Daheim; This Author Writes about B&B-Themed Mysteries."*

* * *

DEFANT, Marc J. 1951-

PERSONAL: Born August 28, 1951, in Niles, MI; son of John P. (a director of a university press) and Martha J. (Harper) Defant; married Susan Robertson, June 21, 1986; children: Jack, Colin, Juliette. *Ethnicity:* "White." *Education:* University of Alabama, B.S. (geology), 1973, B.S. (chemistry), 1977, M.S., 1980; Florida State University, Ph.D., 1985. *Religion:* "Atheist."

ADDRESSES: Home—18309 Cypress Stand Circle, Tampa, FL 33647. *Office*—Deans Office, University of South Florida, Tampa, FL 33620; fax 813-907-8107. *E-mail*—defant@tampabay.rr.com.

CAREER: Schlumberger Well Services, New Iberia, LA, logging engineer, 1977-78; Shell Oil Co., Houston, TX, production engineer, 1978-79, geological engineer, 1979-80; Florida State University, Tallahassee, instructor, 1983-84; University of South Florida, Tampa, visiting assistant professor, 1984-85, assistant professor, 1985-89, professor of geology, 1994, member of research board of directors and chairperson of university research council, both 1993-94. Geoprospects International (consulting firm), owner; Aurcana Corp., past director.

MEMBER: American Geophysical Union, Geological Society of America.

AWARDS, HONORS: Grants from Geological Survey of Alabama, 1975, Electrical Company of Panama, 1986-88, American Chemical Society Petroleum Research Fund, 1987, National Science Foundation,

beginning 1988, National Geographic Society, 1989, Academy of Sciences of the USSR, 1991, and National Academy of Sciences, 1993.

WRITINGS:

A Voyage of Discovery from the Big Bang to the Ice Age, Mancorp Publishing (Tampa, FL), 1998.

Contributor to scientific journals and popular magazines, including *Nature, Earth Planetary Science Letters, Journal of Geophysical Research, Journal of Geology, Journal of Petrology, Mineralogy and Petrology, Geochemica, Cosmochemica, ACTA, World and I, Popular Science,* and *Precambrian Geology.*

WORK IN PROGRESS: A book; research on diamonds in subduction zones; research on the metamorphic evolution of the Ganal Terrane, Central Kamchatka, Russia, particularly on partial melting and fluid-rock interaction in a paleo-subduction zone.

* * *

DeFREES, Madeline 1919-
(Sister Mary Gilbert)

PERSONAL: Born November 18, 1919, in Ontario, OR; daughter of Clarence C. and Mary Teresa (McCoy) DeFrees. *Education:* Marylhurst College, B.A., 1948; University of Oregon, M.A., 1951. *Politics:* Democrat. *Religion:* Roman Catholic. *Hobbies and other interests:* Reading, walking, exercising.

ADDRESSES: Home—7548 11th Ave. NW, Seattle, WA 98117.

CAREER: Entered Roman Catholic order of Sisters of the Holy Names of Jesus and Mary as Sister Mary Gilbert, 1937; released from religious vows, 1973. Elementary school teacher in Bend, OR, 1938-39, St. Monica's School, Coos Bay, OR, 1939-40, and St. Francis School, Portland, OR, 1940-42; St. Mary's Academy, Medford, OR, teacher, 1942-44, 1946-49; St. Mary's, The Dalles, OR, teacher, 1944-46; Holy Names College (now Fort Wright College), Spokane, WA, instructor, 1950-55, assistant professor, 1955-63, associate professor of English and journalism, 1963-67; University of Montana, Missoula, visiting associate professor, 1967-69, associate professor, 1969-72, professor of English, 1972-79; University of Massachusetts—Amherst, professor of English, 1979-85, director of M.F.A. program in creative writing, 1980-83, professor emeritus, 1985—; full-time writer, 1985—. Visiting professor at Seattle University, 1965-66, 1972, Marylhurst College, 1969, University of Washington, 1970, and University of Victoria, 1974; poet-in-residence, Bucknell University, 1988; distinguished visiting writer, Eastern Washington University, 1988; distinguished visiting poet-in-residence, Wichita State University, 1993; creative writing teacher, Richard Hugo House, Seattle, WA, 1998-99.

MEMBER: Associated Writing Programs, Academy of American Poets.

AWARDS, HONORS: T. Neil Taylor award, University of Oregon, 1950, for journalism research; D.Litt., Gonzaga University, 1959; Indiana University Writer's Conference Poetry Prize, 1961; Abbie M. Copps Poetry Prize (corecipient), Olivet College, 1973; Hohenberg Prize, *Memphis Review*, 1979, for poetry; poetry fellowship, Guggenheim Foundation, 1980-81; poetry grant, National Endowment for the Arts, 1981-82; Consuelo Ford award (corecipient), Poetry Society of America, 1982; Carolyn Kizer Prize, *Calapooya Collage*, 1994; Ann Stanford Poetry Prize, Southern California Anthology, 1998; Lenore Marshall Award, Academy of American Poets, 2002.

WRITINGS:

(As Sister Mary Gilbert) *The Springs of Silence* (autobiography), Prentice-Hall (Englewood Cliffs, NJ), 1953.

(As Sister Mary Gilbert) *Later Thought from the Springs of Silence* (autobiography), Bobbs-Merrill (Indianapolis, IN), 1962.

(As Sister Mary Gilbert) *From the Darkroom* (poetry), Bobbs-Merrill (Indianapolis, IN), 1964.

Black Box 11 (sound recording), Watershed, 1976.

When Sky Lets Go (poetry), Braziller (New York, NY), 1978.

Imaginary Ancestors (poetry chapbook), Cutbank/Smoke Root Press (Missoula, MT), 1978, revised edition, Broken Moon (Seattle, WA), 1990.

Existing Light (sound recording), Watershed, 1980.

Magpie on the Gallows, Copper Canyon Press (Port Townsend, WA), 1982.

The Light Station on Tillamook Rock, illustrated by Rosalyn Richards, Arrowood Books (Corvallis, OR), 1990.

Possible Sibyls: New Poems, Lynx House Press (Amherst, MA), 1991.

Double Dutch, Red Wing Press (West Sacramento, CA), 1999.

Blue Dusk: New and Selected Poems, 1951-2001, Copper Canyon Press (Port Townsend, WA), 2001.

Works anthologized in *Best Poems of 1960* and *Best Poems of 1965* (Borestone Mountain Poetry Awards), Pacific Books, 1962, 1966; *Best American Short Stories, 1962,* edited by Martha Foley and David Burnett, Houghton Mifflin, 1962; and other anthologies. Regular contributor to *San Diego Weekly Reader,* 1994-96; contributor to journals and magazines, including *America, New American Review, Poetry Northwest, Sewanee Review, Northwest Review, New Republic, Writer's N.W., Nation, New Letters, Sisters Today, Yale Review, Paris Review, Atlantic Monthly, Massachusetts Review,* and *Iowa Review.* Contributor of essays to *Spectrum: A Reader,* Harcourt, Brace, and Jovanovich, 1987; *Northwest Variety: Personal Essays by Fourteen Regional Authors,* edited by Lex Runciman and Steven Sher, Arrowood Books (Corvallis, OR), 1987; and *Anonymous Was a Woman,* California Institute for the Arts (Valencia, CA), 1974.

WORK IN PROGRESS: A new poetry collection; a chapbook for Pudding House Press "Greatest Hits" series.

SIDELIGHTS: Madeline DeFrees is an American poet whose verses often reflect the tension between the religious and secular worlds. As a former nun, DeFrees knows both worlds well, yet she reveals her private side very reluctantly in her work, having gradually opened the door only after years of writing. A shy person, DeFrees entered the order of Sisters of the Holy Names of Jesus and Mary immediately after finishing high school and took the name Sister Mary Gilbert. Being a nun and working within the Church seemed well suited to her quiet and sensitive personality, and DeFrees served as a teacher while completing her college degrees in English and journalism. Not long after graduating, she published her first book, *The Springs of Silence,* an autobiographical work about her experiences upon entering her convent. This was later followed by *Later Thoughts from the Springs of Silence,* which focuses on a time when Holy Names College was moving to a new location. Although these are prose works, DeFrees was also privately writing verses, which she rarely showed to anyone and did not publish in book form until 1964's *From the Darkroom.*

"The self-effacement of the individual in religious life is reflected in DeFrees's first book of poetry, *From the Darkroom,*" according to Barbara Drake in the *Dictionary of Literary Biography,* "which is more traditional in form and voice than her later work, though original." Although DeFrees wrote these poems as a means of expressing the inner life she had been hiding, her poems are nonetheless obscure and difficult to understand at times. Still, themes such as a search for enlightenment and the tension between good and evil can be seen. Writing the poems, however, posed a personal problem for DeFrees. "I lived for a long time in terror of some kind of mental breakdown," she admitted to Carol Ann Russell in the *Massachusetts Review.* "The poems were, in a sense, my lifeline because they provided a measure of release for my feelings. At the same time they compounded the problems because I felt guilty about my absolute need for writing."

DeFrees did not publish another poetry collection until 1978's *When Sky Lets Go,* which was released five years after she was dispensed from her vows. As DeFrees told *CA:* "The Montana move triggered new work, and in 1967, Stanley Moss, poetry editor of *New American Review,* included a poem in the magazine's first number. He hoped to persuade New American Library, the publisher, to do my book, but changes (from New American Library to Simon and Schuster to Bantam Books) kept the manuscript bouncing from Missoula to New York and back. Finally, Richard Howard volunteered to do the book in his 'Braziller' series if I was willing to wait two years. Two lengthened into four as 'Braziller' poets produced second volumes and bumped everyone on the list back by six months. In 1978, *When Sky Lets Go* finally appeared." Reviewing *When Sky Lets Go* for *Poetry,* Robert Holland commented, "For nearly thirty years a nun known as Sister Mary Gilbert, DeFrees now writes, from outside the convent, a series of 'Holy Sonnets' which turn Donne inside out. . . . These

poems are like Donne's . . . mostly in their refusal to allow the speaker (or the reader) any rest, any false resolution of the unrelenting struggle she is locked in." In the poems, the reader can see DeFrees struggling toward her own identity after leaving her order. "Several of the poems," explained Drake, also "deal with feelings of isolation and repressed sexuality," which can be seen in the section "The Blue Nun" in which the narrative voice takes a "defiant walk on the wild side."

"The tension between repression and expression led, for DeFrees, to the development of a complex poetry that must be read with attention to all the various levels of meaning in language," wrote Drake. The poet uses such devices as double meaning, puns, allusions, and line breaks to obscure any direct insights into her feelings. At the same time, this type of abstruse writing makes her verses more open to interpretation, thus leading some readers to come to their own conclusions about what they mean. "The final section of the book, 'Pictures on the Shifting Wall,' focuses on poems of acceptance and resolution, dealing with death, hope, and despair," wrote Drake.

With *Imaginary Ancestors* DeFrees continues her course of self-reconciliation as she "mourns an ancestry she never knew and religious vows abandoned," as *Literary Review* contributor Fran Thomas put it. *Imaginary Ancestors* is a chapbook containing poems that are republished in *Magpie on the Gallows* and subsequently expanded in a 1990 revised edition of the original collection. Pointing out the feminist point of view in the new edition, Thomas commented that the verses display a "faith in womankind [that] supplements her faith in God. Though Ms. DeFrees's world is not easily accessible to the reader, the poems are strong and courageous, public but personal, universal and private." The poet continues to write about women and faith in her more recent collections, including *Blue Dusk: New and Selected Poems, 1951-2001.*

DeFrees once told *CA:* "Writing is for me both an instrument of discovery and a way of organizing and understanding experience. I get along best when I am writing every day—preferably the first thing in the morning—because under those conditions I am less likely to lose my nerve, and I make fewer false starts, can trust my judgment. Because writing is a physical act, I use anything to get going, usually writing in a kind of diary-journal first. I will allow anything here, not putting myself under any constraint to be brilliant: a mood, something I've been thinking about, what happened since I last wrote in this book. I next move to my notebook looking for snippets that might take fire. I often work on several poems at once, and if one of them fails to engage me, a totally different one may interpose itself. When I feel myself becoming involved, it is as recognizable as the motor turning over on a cold morning as I try to start my car.

"My favorite book is the dictionary in all its forms, including the *Oxford English Dictionary*. I refer to it often whenever I am writing. I have even been known to buy a fourth collegiate dictionary when on vacation at the beach because I couldn't exist without one. I like to revive former senses of words, to use their derivations, and, above all, to be as precise as possible while, at the same time, drawing on the richness of language, its connotative values.

"My working methods were profoundly affected by having to do much of my writing in odd minutes through the tightly-scheduled convent days. As a consequence, I developed my memory and could revise quite lengthy passages in my head while walking to school or waxing the hallway floor. I also like to write my way through a pile of scratch paper and, on typing a completed draft, tearing up the trail that led me to it. In my early writing career, I was strongly influenced by Gerard Manley Hopkins, Edwin Arlington Robinson, and Emily Dickinson. What I retain from them, I think, is: Hopkins—a fondness for juxtaposed stresses and for the sounds of hard *c* and *k;* Robinson—an innate preference for 'dark' poems, a kind of brooding melancholy; Dickinson—a metaphysical cast. My sensibility has sometimes been compared to that of Donne, and I admit that I find the roughness of his rhythms enormously attractive. In fiction, I am drawn to the work of J. F. Powers and Flannery O'Connor among recent writers. Among earlier models, some favorites are George Eliot, Henry James, and Thomas Hardy."

DeFrees more recently told *CA:* "I wrote my first verse at age eleven when the seventh-grade teacher assigned a Mother's Day poem. Mine was proclaimed the best, and from that time one, I wrote regularly. I read the Untermeyer anthologies and taught myself the elements of versification. When I found a poem I liked well enough, I modeled one on it, trying to duplicate the rhythmic structure exactly.

"Probably the reason I continued to write was that I felt like an outsider in Hillsboro, Oregon, a community of Dutch farmers. I lived in town. My mother insisted (wrongly, as it turned out) that we were not Dutch.

"My poems often begin with a new experience: a visit to the zoo, a tour of a newspaper plant, a foot reconstruction, or cataract surgery. Sometimes the 'trigger' is a phrase or sentence or sign: some language fragment that registers with particular intensity. If the poem is to succeed, regardless of which way it started, both language and experience must come together.

"Among my books so far, *Blue Dusk* is my favorite—partly because it contains the best from all my collections—and because it is so beautifully produced."

BIOGRAPHICAL AND CRITICAL SOURCES:

BOOKS

Contemporary Poets, 7th edition, St. James Press (Detroit, MI), 2001.
Dictionary of Literary Biography, Volume 105: *American Poets since World War II, Second Series,* Thomson Gale (Detroit, MI), 1991.
Woman Poet, Volume 1: *The West,* Regional Editions (Reno, NV), 1980, pp. 42-44, 45-47.

PERIODICALS

American Poetry Review, May-June, 1979.
Georgia Review, winter, 2002, Judith Kitchen, review of *Blue Dusk.*
Literary Review, winter, 1993, Fran Thomas, review of *Imaginary Ancestors,* p. 253.
Massachusetts Review, summer, 1982, Carol Ann Russell, "An Interview with Madeline DeFrees," pp. 265-269.
Ploughshares, fall, 1991, Joyce Peseroff, review of *Imaginary Ancestors,* p. 282.
Poetry, March, 1979, Robert Holland, "Lost and Found," pp. 348-349; October, 1983, Peter Stitt, review of *Magpie on the Gallows,* p. 42.
Prairie Schooner, summer, 1983, Carolyne Wright, "Courage, Honesty, and a Sense of Humor," pp. 90-94.

Quarterly West, spring, 1978.
Southwest Review, autumn, 1980, Fredrick Zydek, "Smorgasbord or Bread and Water?" pp. 425-430.

*   *   *

DICKEY, Glenn (Ernest, Jr.) 1936-

PERSONAL: Born February 16, 1936, in Virginia, MN; son of Glenn Ernest and Madlyn Marie (a homemaker; maiden name, Emmert) Dickey; married Nancy Jo McDaniel (an artist and homemaker), February 25, 1967; children: Kevin Scott. *Education:* University of California, Berkeley, B.A., 1958. *Politics:* Democrat. *Religion:* Presbyterian.

ADDRESSES: Home—120 Florence Ave., Oakland, CA 94618. *Office*—San Francisco Chronicle, 901 Mission St., San Francisco, CA 94103. *Agent*—Mitchell J. Hamilburg Agency, 292 South La Cienega Blvd., Ste. 212, Beverly Hills, CA 90211. *E-mail*—gdickey@sfchronicle.com.

CAREER: Watsonville Register-Pajaronian, Watsonville, CA, sports editor, 1958-63; *San Francisco Chronicle,* San Francisco, CA, sports writer, 1963-71, sports columnist, 1971—.

MEMBER: Newspaper Guild, Baseball Writers Association of America.

AWARDS, HONORS: "Best Sports Stories" award, 1963, 1968, 1971, and 1977.

WRITINGS:

The Jock Empire: Its Rise and Deserved Fall, Chilton (Radnor, PA), 1974.
The Great No-Hitters, Chilton (Radnor, PA), 1976.
Champs and Chumps: An Insider's Look at American Sports Heroes, Chronicle Books (San Francisco, CA), 1976.
The History of National League Baseball since 1876, Stein & Day (New York, NY), 1979, updated edition, 1982.
The History of American League Baseball since 1901, Stein & Day (New York, NY), 1980.

America Has a Better Team: The Story of Bill Walsh and San Francisco's World Champion 49ers, Harbor (San Francisco, CA), 1982.
The History of Professional Basketball since 1896, Stein & Day (New York, NY), 1982.
The History of the World Series since 1903, Stein & Day (New York, NY), 1984.
(With Jim Tunney) *Impartial Judgment: The "Dean of NFL Referees" Calls Pro Football As He Sees It,* F. Watts (New York, NY), 1988.
San Francisco 49ers: The Super Years, Chronicle Books (San Francisco, CA), 1989.
(With Bill Walsh) *Building a Champion: On Football and the Making of the 49ers,* St. Martin's Press (New York, NY), 1990.
Just Win, Baby: Al Davis and His Raiders, Harcourt (New York, NY), 1991.
Sports Great Jerry Rice (juvenile), Enslow Publishers (Hillside, NJ), 1993.
Sports Great Kevin Mitchell (juvenile), Enslow Publishers (Hillside, NJ), 1993.
The San Francisco 49ers: The First Fifty Years, Andrews & McMeel (Kansas City, MO), 1995.
The San Francisco Giants: A Forty-Year Anniversary, Woodford Press (San Francisco, CA), 1997.
Glenn Dickey's 49ers: The Rise, Fall, and Rebirth of the NFL's Greatest Dynasty, Prima Publications (Roseville, CA), 2000.
Champions: The Story of the First Two Oakland A's Dynasties—and the Building of the Third, Triumph Books (Chicago, IL), 2002.

Author, with Dick Berg, of *Eavesdropping America,* 1980; also author of a television script for a pilot children's sports program. Contributor to magazines, including *TV Guide, Argosy, Sport, Women Sports,* and *Pro Quarterback.*

SIDELIGHTS: Veteran sports journalist Glenn Dickey has been covering major league sports in the San Francisco area for over forty years, most of that time for the *San Francisco Chronicle.* During that time he has written books on several championship teams, as well as several broad examinations of sports history. In his 1980 survey *The History of the American League since 1901,* Dickey manages to cover eighty years of baseball history in a "well-organized, clear treatment," according to *Library Journal* contributor G. S. Schwartz. Similarly, Dickey's 1983 survey *The History of the World Series since 1903* is "a lively, interpretive history," Morey Berger noted in *Library Journal.* Dickey has also written histories of baseball's National League and of professional American basketball.

With his long experience in sports, Dickey has written biographies both about and with prominent sports figures. He collaborated with National Football League referee Jim Tunney on the latter's autobiography, *Impartial Judgment,* as well as with Super Bowl-winning coach Bill Walsh of the San Francisco 49ers. The latter book, *Building a Champion: On Football and the Making of the 49ers,* was termed "a notch above the usual sports autobiography" by *Library Journal* contributor Ron Chepesiuk.

Dickey's works also include several volumes on individual teams, including football's San Francisco 49ers and Oakland Raiders, and baseball's San Francisco Giants and Oakland A's. In his 2002 book *Champions: The Story of the First Two Oakland A's Dynasties—and the Building of the Third,* Dickey explores the reasons for the success of the team, which won three World Series in the 1970s and played in three World Series in the 1980s, winning in 1989. The author "effectively mixes a straight narrative approach with oral history," Wes Lukowsky noted in *Booklist;* as a result he "conveys a vivid sense" of each dynasty's workings. *Champions* is "a solid, telling, and delightful account of the A's," Robert C. Cotrell and Paul Kaplan remarked in *Library Journal,* "with many insightful portraits."

BIOGRAPHICAL AND CRITICAL SOURCES:

PERIODICALS

Booklist, March 1, 2002, Wes Lukowsky, review of *Champions: The Story of the First Two Oakland A's Dynasties—and the Building of the Third,* p. 1078.
Library Journal, April 15, 1980, G. S. Schwartz, review of *The History of the American League since 1901,* p. 997; September 15, 1984, Morey Berger, review of *The History of the World Series since 1903,* p. 1768; October 15, 1990, Ron Chepesiuk, review of *Building a Champion: On Football and the Making of the 49ers,* p. 91; February 1, 2002, Robert C. Cottrell and Paul Kaplan, review of *Champions,* p. 103.

New York Times Book Review, November 17, 1991, Mark Goodman, review of *Just Win, Baby: Al Davis and His Raiders,* p. 22.*

*　　*　　*

DOSS, James D(aniel) 1939-

PERSONAL: Born March 9, 1939, in Reading, PA. *Education:* Kentucky Wesleyan College, B.S., 1964; University of New Mexico, M.S., 1969. *Religion:* Episcopalian.

ADDRESSES: Office—Los Alamos National Laboratory, N15-B B-230, 905 Tewa Loop, Los Alamos, NM 87544-3210. *E-mail*—jddoss@earthlink.net.

CAREER: Electrical engineer and mystery novelist. Los Alamos National Laboratory, Los Alamos, NM, staff member, beginning 1964; University of New Mexico School of Medicine, adjunct instructor in radiology and surgery. Holder of fourteen patents in fields of electronics, biomedical engineering, and automotive engineering. Developed radio-frequency electric current method for thermal treatment of tumors, and superconductor characterization.

MEMBER: Mystery Writers of America.

AWARDS, HONORS: IR-100 Award for product development, *Industrial Research* magazine, 1978; engineer of the year, Los Alamos Institute of Electrical and Electronics Engineers, 1980; distinguished performance award, Los Alamos National Laboratory, 1982; distinguished patent award, Los Alamos National Laboratory, 1983.

WRITINGS:

"CHARLIE MOON" MYSTERY SERIES

The Shaman Sings, St. Martin's Press (New York, NY), 1994.
The Shaman Laughs, St. Martin's Press (New York, NY), 1995.
The Shaman's Bones, Avon (New York, NY), 1997.

The Shaman's Game, Avon (New York, NY), 1998.
The Night Visitor, Avon (New York, NY), 1999.
Grandmother Spider, Morrow (New York, NY), 2001.
White Shell Woman, Morrow (New York, NY), 2002.
Dead Soul, St. Martin's Press (New York, NY), 2003.
The Witch's Tongue, St. Martin's Minotaur (New York, NY), 2004.
Shadow Man, St. Martin's Minotaur (New York, NY), 2005.

OTHER

Engineers' Guide to High-Temperature Superconductivity, Wiley (New York, NY), 1989.

Contributor to professional journals.

SIDELIGHTS: James D. Doss spent a distinguished career in the field of electrical engineering, where he specialized in superconductivity and biomedical technology, and then became a successful mystery novelist at the age of fifty-five, when he published his debut book, *The Shaman Sings.* Doss's popular series is set on a Ute Indian reservation in Colorado and features police detective Charlie Moon, Moon's aunt Daisy Perika, a Native American shaman, and Scott Parris, another detective on the force. Rex E. Klett, reviewing the "Charlie Moon" books for *Library Journal,* called them "an excellent series," while Bill Ott maintained in *Booklist* that Doss's novels provide "the most complete treatment of Native American spirituality in the genre."

The initial novel in the "Charlie Moon" series, *The Shaman Sings,* is set on and near a Ute reservation in Colorado and profits from Doss's intimacy with the Southwest as a longtime staffer at New Mexico's Los Alamos National Laboratory. Superconductivity—another area of the author's expertise—also enters the plot; the murder victim, a graduate student, was working on potentially world-changing research in that field when he met his untimely death. Many critics found Doss to be an exciting new talent in the mystery genre. A *Publishers Weekly* reviewer called *The Shaman Sings* one of the best mysteries of 1994, while *Washington Post Book World* contributor Pat Dowell dubbed the novel "a fantastic read."

The Shaman Sings features detective Scott Parris, a big-city police officer who has taken a job as a small-town Colorado police chief in order to recover from the death of his wife in an accident. Joining Parris in the murder investigation is the shaman of the title, Daisy Perika, a Ute who communicates with the unseen world. The narrative switches through the points of view of many characters, including several suspects and, in Dowell's opinion, keeps the reader guessing even when the narration comes from within the murderer's head. According to Dowell, "*The Shaman Sings* has a high page-turning quotient, thanks in large part to Doss's vivid characters." The *Publishers Weekly* reviewer also called the novel "stunning" and an "ambitious, successful debut." A *Library Journal* contributor voiced similar opinions, concluding that *The Shaman Sings* is "a finely written first novel."

Doss continues the adventures of Scott Parris and Daisy Perika in several novels, including *The Shaman Laughs* and *The Shaman's Bones.* In *The Shaman Laughs,* Perika's nephew, Ute police officer Charlie Moon, joins Parris and Perika in the investigation of the murder and mutilation of sheep and prize bulls, as well as the equally gruesome murder and dismemberment of a local insurance agent. Aiding Parris, Perika, and Moon are the "pitukupf," Daisy's invisible dwarf spirit-helpers, as well as two agents from the Federal Bureau of Investigation: an eccentric profiler named Oswald Oakes and the ultraconservative James Hoover. In *The Shaman's Game* participants in the reservation's sun dance begin to die mysteriously, moving detective Charlie Moon to investigate.

According to a critic for *Publishers Weekly, The Shaman Laughs* combines "top-notch procedural drama with Indian spirituality" in a "multilayered" work which Doss executes with "grace and suspense." A *Kirkus Reviews* contributor expressed a preference for the "dazzling" *The Shaman Sings,* but called its successor "a remarkably well-crafted portrait of a fascinating corner of America." Marilyn Stasio, writing in the *New York Times Book Review,* remarked that Doss "writes with a naturalist's scientific precision when he describes the desert" and called the plot of *The Shaman Laughs* "harrowing."

Grandmother Spider finds a frightening figure from Native American mythology seemingly stalking the reservation and scaring the locals. Moon and Parris are called upon to quell rumors and calm fears while also unraveling the mystery of the strange sightings. According to Ott, "the interplay of characters here . . . is thoroughly entertaining, a spot-on mix of realism and humor." A *Kirkus* reviewer called *Grandmother Spider* "every bit as dazzling" as Doss's fiction debut. Praising the novel as a "mysterious and ethereal tale," *School Library Journal* contributor Trudy Williams added that Doss's "descriptive powers as well as his storyteller's skills and sharp wit make readers feel as if they are there."

In his seventh mystery outing, *White Shell Woman,* Moon turns to moonlighting as a special tribal investigator as a way to pay the expenses of his second career as a cattle rancher. Taking on a job involving ancient tribal artifacts, he soon finds himself involved in murder when an archeology student is found dead at a controversial dig. In a *Booklist* review, Bill Ott praised Doss for his "fine comic touch," particularly when pitting Moon's "laconic wit" and rational approach against "flamboyant" Aunt Daisy, who "functions as a kind of cantankerous Greek chorus" by consistently interpreting unexpected occurrences as supernatural phenomena.

Dead Soul finds Moon drawn once more away from his ranching duties when his responsibilities as a special tribal investigator lead him to murder. This time he must sift through the evidence in the murder of a fellow Ute named Billy Smoke, while Aunt Daisy has visions of a missing redheaded co-ed in trouble. Smoke's death somehow involves his job as chauffeur to a U.S. senator, and as espionage and ties to the young woman of Daisy's visions begin to involve themselves, Moon starts to question his own sense of reality. Ranking Doss's series with the works of novelist Tony Hillerman, *Booklist* reviewer Bill Ott praised *Dead Soul* as a "potent brew of crime and Native American spirituality."

BIOGRAPHICAL AND CRITICAL SOURCES:

PERIODICALS

Booklist, August, 1998, John Rowen, review of *The Shaman's Game,* p. 1974; August, 1999, John Rowen, review of *The Night Visitor,* p. 2032; May 1, 2000, Bill Ott, review of *The Shaman's Game,* p. 1594; January 1, 2001, Bill Ott, review of *Grandmother Spider,* p. 924; January 1, 2002, Bill Ott, review of *White Shell Woman,* p. 816; September 15, 2003, Bill Ott, review of *Dead Soul,* p. 214.

Kirkus Reviews, October 15, 1995, review of *The Shaman Laughs,* p. 1458; August 15, 1998, review of *The Shaman's Game,* p. 1156; September 15, 1999,

review of *The Night Visitor,* p. 1448; December 1, 2000, review of *Grandmother Spider,* p. 1645; November 15, 2001, review of *White Shell Woman,* p. 1581; August 1, 2003, review of *Dead Soul,* p. 995.

Library Journal, February 1, 1994, review of *The Shaman Sings,* p. 115; August, 1998, Rex E. Klett, review of *The Shaman's Game,* p. 139; September 1, 1999, Rex E. Klett, review of *The Night Visitor,* p. 237; April 1, 2000, Dean James, review of *The Night Visitor,* p. 160; January, 2002, Rex Klett, review of *White Shell Woman,* p. 158; August, 2003, Rex Klett, review of *Dead Soul* p. 140.

New York Times Book Review, December 24, 1995, Marilyn Stasio, review of *The Shaman Laughs,* p. 18; October 3, 1999, Marilyn Stasio, review of *The Night Visitor,* p. 24.

Publishers Weekly, December 20, 1993, review of *The Shaman Sings,* p. 53; October 23, 1995, review of *The Shaman Laughs,* p. 60; June 29, 1998, review of *The Shaman's Game,* p. 38; August 2, 1999, review of *The Night Visitor,* p. 76; November 27, 2000, review of *Grandmother Spider,* p. 57; December 3, 2001, review of *White Shell Woman,* p. 43.

School Library Journal, August, 2001, Trudy Williams, review of *Grandmother Spider,* p. 209.

Washington Post Book World, February 20, 1994, Pat Dowell, review of *The Shaman Sings,* p. 8.*

*   *   *

DOYLE, Brian 1935-

PERSONAL: Born August 12, 1935, in Ottawa, Ontario, Canada; son of Hulbert (a government worker and customs broker) and Charlotte (a homemaker and poet; maiden name, Duff) Doyle; married Jacqueline Aronson (a homemaker and government worker), December 26, 1960; children: Megan, Ryan. *Ethnicity:* "Canadian; Irish." *Education:* Carleton University, B.J. and B.A. (journalism), 1957; also completed coursework for M.A. at Ottawa University. *Hobbies and other interests:* Camping, fishing, wood cutting.

ADDRESSES: Home—118 Ossington Ave., Ottawa, Ontario K1S 3B8, Canada. *Agent*—c/o Author Mail, Groundwood/Douglas & McIntyre, Children's Books, 2nd Fl., 585 Bloor St. W., 2nd Fl., Toronto, Ontario M6G 1K5, Canada.

CAREER: Full-time children's author and playwright. High-school English teacher at Glebe Collegiate, Ottawa, Ontario, Canada (also former head of English Department), and Ottawa Technical High School, Ottawa, beginning in 1969; retired from teaching, 1991; served on the Ottawa Board of Education and the faculty of Queen's University, Kingston, Ontario, Canada. Worked variously as a journalist (Toronto *Telegram*), waiter, taxi driver, driving instructor, office worker, bricklayer, and jazz singer. *Military service:* Canadian Naval Reserve, 1955-56.

MEMBER: James Joyce Society of Ottawa (chairman).

AWARDS, HONORS: Book of the Year awards, Canadian Library Association, 1983, for *Up to Low,* 1989, for *Easy Avenue,* and 1997, for *Uncle Ronald;* International Board on Books for Young People award, 1984, for *J'Attends a Peggy's Cove;* Mr. Christie's Book of the Year Award, Canadian Children's Book Center and Communications Jeunesse, 1990, for *Covered Bridge,* and 1996, for *Uncle Ronald;* Vicky Metcalf Body of Work Award, Canadian Authors Association, 1991, for the body of his work; Blue Ribbons, Center for Children's Books, 1996, for *Spud Sweetgrass* and *Spud in Winter;* New York Public Library Best Book for the Teenage, 1997, for *Spud in Winter,* and 1999, for *Easy Avenue;* Hans Christian Andersen Author Award, International Board on Books for Young People, honorable mention, 1998; Jugendliteraturpreis (Germany's national award for children's literature), 2001, for *Angel Square;* Horn Book Fanfare Selection, 2002, for *Mary Ann Alice; Mary Ann Alice* has also won an IODE National Chapter Award and the Leishman Prize, and was nominated for the Ruth Schwartz Award and the Geoffrey Bilson Award. Ruth Schwartz Children's Book Award for Best Book for Young Adults/Middle Readers, 2004, for *Boy O'Boy;* Laureate designation, NSK Neustadt Prize for Children's Literature, 2005. Other honors include three-time runner-up, Governor-General's Award, Canadian Authors Association, and a YALSA Popular Paperback Selection.

WRITINGS:

(Editor and compiler) *Who's Who of Boy's Writers and Illustrators, 1964,* The Author (London, England), 1964.

(Editor and compiler) *The Who's Who of Children's Literature,* Evelyn (London, England), 1968, Schocken Books (New York, NY), 1968.
Hey Dad!, Groundwood Books (Toronto, Ontario, Canada), 1978.
You Can Pick Me up at Peggy's Cove, Groundwood Books (Toronto, Ontario, Canada), 1979.
Up to Low, Groundwood Books (Toronto, Ontario, Canada), 1982.
Angel Square, Groundwood Books (Toronto, Ontario, Canada), 1984.
Easy Avenue, Groundwood Books (Toronto, Ontario, Canada), 1988.
Covered Bridge, Groundwood Books (Toronto, Ontario, Canada), 1990.
Spud Sweetgrass, Groundwood Books (Toronto, Ontario, Canada), 1992.
Spud in Winter, Groundwood Books (Toronto, Ontario, Canada), 1995.
Uncle Ronald, Douglas & McIntyre (Buffalo, NY), 1997.
Dam Lies, Groundwood Books (Toronto, Ontario, Canada), 1998.
The Low Life: Five Great Tales from Up and Down the River (omnibus), Douglas & McIntyre (Toronto, Canada), 1999.
Mary Ann Alice, Groundwood Books (Toronto, Ontario, Canada), 2001.
Boy O'Boy, Groundwood Books (Toronto, Ontario, Canada), 2003.

Also author of children's plays. Contributor of articles and short stories to newspapers and magazines, including the Toronto *Globe and Mail* and *Fiddlehead.* Contributor to *Children's Literature Review,* Volume 22, Thomson Gale (Detroit, MI), 1991; and *Something about the Author Autobiography Series,* Thomson Gale (Detroit, MI), 1993. CNIB released sound recordings of *You Can Pick Me up at Peggy's Cove* (1984), *Angel Square* (1985), *Easy Avenue* (1994), and *Covered Bridge* (1995). Doyle's works have been translated into French and published in Braille editions. Doyle's books have been published in France, Italy, Germany, Scandinavia, and South America.

ADAPTATIONS: You Can Pick Me Up at Peggy's Cove was adapted into a film directed by Don McBrearty and into a video released by Beacon Films, 1982; *Meet the Author: Brian Doyle* was released as a short film in 1987; *Angel Square* was adapted into a film directed by Ann Wheeler, adapted for stage at the National Performing Arts Centre (1987), and released by the National Film Board of Canada, Edmonton, Alberta (1990).

WORK IN PROGRESS: A book about a soda truck.

SIDELIGHTS: Brian Doyle is an award-winning writer for young adults whose respect for the clarity of children's insight radiates throughout his novels, inspiring him, according to many critics, to "write up" rather than to "write down" to his readers. Doyle's works turn on timeless coming-of-age themes and feature poetically crafted prose, hefty doses of tragedy and comedy, and realistic representations that acknowledge the imperfections of contemporary human life without overlooking its goodness. His books often incorporate a physical journey as a parallel to the emotional growth of the characters. Critics celebrate his writing, explaining that it doesn't patronize young people. Humor also plays a key role in Doyle's books, with scenes that are both dark and slapstick. Set largely in Ottawa, Ontario, where Doyle spent his youth and where he still lives, his stories benefit from an atmosphere that sidesteps regionalism for universality.

Many critics have praised the knowledge of the inner workings of children's minds reflected in Doyle's novels. Although the author taught high school students for thirty-three years, it was his own children who originally inspired his fiction. His first two books, *Hey Dad!* and *You Can Pick Me Up at Peggy's Cove,* were each written for his children, Megan and Ryan. "I never could have gotten started without my own kids," Doyle commented in a interview with Sonia Benson for *Something about the Author (SATA).* "I don't think I ever knew anybody as well as I did my daughter when she was that age. I felt like I was right inside her skin. So writing *Hey Dad!* and *You Can Pick Me Up at Peggy's Cove* was an attempt to capture that knowledge before it went away. I did the same thing for my son a couple years later, when he got to be that age."

Doyle's first novel, *Hey Dad!,* is the story of how Megan begins the process of growing up. On a family trip from Ottawa to Vancouver she abandons her childhood self-centeredness and begins to look at the world around her. She also comes to terms with her feelings toward her unconventional father. Drawn largely from

diaries that Doyle and his daughter kept during the trip, *Hey, Dad!* is, according to *In Review: Canadian Books for Children* contributor Irma McDonough, both a "subliminally educational" rendering of Canada's geography and a vivid journey through some of the psychological pathways to maturity. Doyle observes in his interview with Agnes Nieuwenhuizen of *Magpies,* "I made it funny, but included stuff she had been grappling with. Stuff about time and mortality. I read bits to the neighborhood kids and when they started asking about what was going to happen NEXT, I realized the story went beyond family interest." Doyle conveys a rather heroic struggle to grasp and cope with a confusing world.

In *You Can Pick Me Up at Peggy's Cove,* the teenage narrator Ryan hopes to lure his father to a vacation resort by getting himself into trouble and needing to be rescued. As a means to this end he keeps a record of these dangers in a long letter to his father. By the end of the summer, when his father does in fact return, Ryan has confronted punishment, loss, and death, finally reaching a new understanding of himself and his father. Wendy R. Katz noted in *Canadian Children's Literature* that "Doyle's emphasis is not on the adventures the children have but on their psychological states of being," an idea echoed by Adele Ashby, who deemed the book "sensitive, insightful, funny, sad, and true," in a review for *Quill & Quire.*

While the first two novels are contemporary, Doyle's next four novels go back in time to the mid-twentieth century, when the author himself was young. *Up to Low* takes place in the Gatineau Hills, where the author spent his summers as a child. "This is a world ripe with story," commented Sarah Ellis in a review for *Horn Book,* "with anecdote and rumor, scandal and tall tale, sentimental ballads that have passed down four generations, and a running gag we can see approaching from a mile away." In creating the protagonist Tommy, Doyle reverses the usual order of adult authority and teenage alienation, *Maclean's* reviewer Anne Collins commented, presenting "a sane and loving teenager who helps a slapstick and misfit world find its feet." Tommy reprises his role as narrator in *Angel Square,* where he tells a tale of ethnic conflict (in which he becomes reluctantly involved) in the Lowertown section of Ottawa in 1945. *Angel Square* is "a poignant message of tolerance and love," declared a reviewer in *Children's Book News.* Todd Morning, writing in the *School Library Journal,* noted that

"Doyle is best at capturing the feel of postwar Ottawa. . . . Tommy is an appealing hero—resourceful and courageous."

Easy Avenue keeps *Angel Square*'s Lowertown setting and introduces orphan Hubbo O'Driscoll as narrator. With its contrasts of rich and poor, its characters either ashamed by their poverty or snobbishly attached to their wealth, and its between-two-worlds protagonist, the book is often compared by reviewers to Charles Dickens's novel *Great Expectations*. In *Canadian Children's Literature,* Lionel Adey also noted this similarity, but added that "the hero's laid-back ridicule of fools in office" recalls J. D. Salinger's *The Catcher in the Rye*. Writing in *Maclean's,* Pamela Young celebrated the "delightful mix of comedy, irony and sentiment" in the story, concluding that "*Easy Avenue* offers ample cause for rejoicing."

The idea for Doyle's next book, *Covered Bridge,* came from one of the author's very first jobs, which was to help tear down a covered bridge near Low, "my first real job doing adult work," Doyle commented in *Something about the Author Autobiography Series* (*SAAS*). In the novel, Doyle brings back Hubbo O'Driscoll, but his mission this time is to save the covered bridge slated for razing. Hubbo sets himself the task of keeping the bridge intact despite the plans to destroy it, resulting in what Nieuwenhuizen calls a "hauntingly beautiful tribute to conserving and respecting old things." Sandra Martin, writing in *Quill & Quire,* took the book to task for being "a short story started up as a novel," but acknowledged that Doyle had "cleverly and amusingly" drawn a wide-ranging cast of characters.

Spud Sweetgrass is the seventh of Doyle's novels and, like his previous works, tells about a young boy's journey toward the maturity and independence that lie at the end of the road. Along the way, John Sweetgrass, named "Spud" because he sells chips (French fries), discovers his boss's shady business dealings—the possibly environmentally damaging arrangement he's made for dumping the old grease from his fleet of vans—and finally comes to terms with his father's death. Despite the seriousness of its subject matter, *Booklist* contributor Susan Dove Lempke wrote that the book is enlivened by "many wryly humorous touches."

Spud returns in *Spud in Winter,* also set in Ottawa. Spud and his friend Connie Pan, who appeared in the previous novel, track down those involved in a murder that Spud witnessed, including "B. Faroni," the getaway car driver. "The short sentences used so effectively in the first book are overused" in the sequel, maintained *Booklist* contributor Susan Dove Lempke, who also noted that Doyle "enriches his story with plays on names," and that "alert readers will catch some Shakespearean references." On the *CM Magazine* Web site, Elaine Seepish wrote that the book "rolls along playfully . . . culminating with lots of action." Seepish also described its characters as "well-rounded" and "textured."

Doyle confronts the difficult issue of child abuse in his next children's novel, *Uncle Ronald*. Mickey, the 112-year-old narrator, recalls the summer of 1895, when he was twelve. Mickey suffers physical and emotional abuse at the hands of his alcoholic father, who Mickey believes likes him more than his wife because she is hit with the buckle end of the belt while Mickey is only hit with the other end. When Mickey experiences dizzy spells and bedwetting, his mother sends him to spend the summer with her brother and twin cousins, the O'Malley girls, on Ronald's farm just outside the town of Low. Uncle Ronald is tender and kind, and under his care, Mickey's troubles recede. After being brutally beaten by her husband, Mickey's mother joins them in Low. Soon after, federal troops encroach on the town and demand payment of back taxes, threatening violence. Mickey's extended family finds a way to deal with the troops and with the turmoil within their family, so that they are all at peace in the end. While Irene Gordon wrote on the *CM Magazine* Web site that she enjoyed the book, she expressed concern that "the device by which the novel is introduced (Mickey at age 112 recalling the events of his twelfth year) may put off a lot of young readers and some of the humor may appeal more to adults than to children." However, Gordon concluded, "Undoubtedly it is a book that will be enjoyed by a certain group of young readers." *Horn Book*'s Martha V. Parravano dubbed the book a "darkly comic, occasionally earthy, yet tender novel," commenting that readers will not want to pass over this book "for the evocation of setting, for the genuine feel of the lively local stories, and for the sheer joy of Doyle's prose."

Uncle Ronald, along with four other novels set in Low—*Angel Square, Easy Avenue, The Covered Bridge,* and *Up to Low,*—was republished in a 1999 omnibus titled *The Low Life: Five Great Tales from Up and Down the River.* Though *Uncle Ronald* was the last book to be published, its plot is chronologically the first, and so the book organizes the stories in order from 1895 to about 1950. *CM Magazine* Web site's Mary Thomas had the following to say about *The Low Life:* "It makes for quite a feast of Doyle, but, while his first-person style of tongue-tied adolescent-boy narrators gets a little wearing, I did not get the sort of literary indigestion that frequently results from a gathering of independent works between one set of covers." Thomas is not the first reviewer to compare Doyle's writings to a satisfying helping of food. In an article in *Horn Book,* Tim Wynne-Jones wrote that Doyle's novels "are more like Widow Kealey's stew. . . . Stir the pot and there's another tasty spoonful. . . . Stir in a pinch of cornstarch; the plot thickens. . . . Every passage adds another taste to the plot. And Doyle knew how to stir the whole thing up in a most appetizing and satisfactory manner."

"Widow Kealey" is just one character in the small town of Doyle's next novel, *Mary Ann Alice.* Published in 2001, the book is the story of seventh-grader Mary Ann Alice McCrank, a young poet who is deeply connected to the soul of her hometown, Martindale, located on the Gatineau River. Set in 1926, the town is serene until a dam-building project rouses its residents, including Mary Ann Alice and her teacher, Patchy Drizzle, who stirs his students with his love of geology. Mary Ann Alice is not a typical twelve-year-old. She is a "bluntly spoken protagonist"—as described by *School Library Journal's* Robyn Ryan Vandenbroek—with what Parravano described as a "conversational, idiosyncratic voice" and, according to *Resource Link's* Joan Marshall, a "cheeky, irreverent attitude." Mary Ann Alice learns a lot about life, loss, and love as the townspeople work furiously to complete the dam while the river steadily rises. So does Patchy, who hides out and pretends to be dead after a dam explosion to escape his unhappy marriage, only to return after his grieving wife leaves town. "Readers will come away with a powerful message about what's important in life," wrote Vandenbroek, adding that the book provides "a good dose of Canadian with a generous mixture of humor and expressive language." Parravano praised the author's work in her review: "Doyle is a fearless writer, and he negotiates this novel as one would a changeable river, shifting pace and focus and tone with unerring control." Marshall proffered similar praise to the author, stating, "Doyle's lyrical style paints lilting pictures as sentences go on and on with no stopping

for breath," and that his "wry, observant wit shines in every corner of this marvelous story."

Doyle's next novel, *Boy O'Boy,* deals with the sexual abuse of Martin O'Boy, an already troubled boy dealing with the loss of his grandmother, the turbulent relationship between his pregnant mother and alcoholic father, and the mental illness of his twin brother, Phil, all against the backdrop of Ottawa at the end of World War II. Perhaps it is this loaded plot that led *Kliatt's* Rebecca Rabinowitz to suggest that though the book is a "clear, well-written novel," it appears to be "the type of child's-eye-view piece usually marketed to adults." Martin and his good friend, Billy Batson, sing in the church choir, accompanied by the organist, Mr. George. This seems like a good way for the boys to pass the summer, until Mr. George takes Martin for ice cream, laces it with liquor, and molests him in a scene that one *Publishers Weekly* reviewer described as "devastating in its minimalism."

Martin can't tell anyone his demoralizing secret until he realizes that Billy has also fallen victim to Mr. George. The two boys plot his ruin, and despite the unfortunate circumstances of Martin's life, his friendship with Billy, his cat Cheap, his newspapers and National Geographic magazines, his soldier neighbor Buz, and the wise voice of his grandmother echoing in his head help Martin persevere. "As usual, Doyle tempers the grimmer aspects of his novel with a sly sense of humor and colorful, memorably named characters," wrote Christine M. Heppermann in *Horn Book. Booklist's* Todd Morning observed that the scenes of sexual abuse, "described graphically from a child's viewpoint, are unsettling," and explained that readers may be "frustrated" with the mild retribution that serves as Mr. George's punishment. The aforementioned *Publishers Weekly* reviewer reported, "Although Doyle's narrative occasionally hits a false note . . . overall, it comes across honestly and effectively," and Morning concluded that Martin's mindset is "authentic" and that the book is "a rich historical portrait with a winning young character at its center."

Doyle once commented: "There is a perception that young people are worried about menstruation, divorce, masturbation, hitchhiking—subjects that just carloads of kids' books are written about. These are not the concerns of young people at all as far as I'm concerned. They are the concerns of adults who have young people. Kids' concerns are the classic concerns:

Am I brave? Am I a hero? Am I honest? Do I love this person? Am I afraid? Am I admired? Am I weak? Am I strong? These are their concerns, and that's what I write about."

More recently, Doyle told *CA:* "Writing is like shoveling now in your laneway—steady as she goes, and it'll get done. My books do what I'd hoped they'd do: they create readers."

BIOGRAPHICAL AND CRITICAL SOURCES:

BOOKS

Oxford Companion to Canadian Literature, 2nd edition, Oxford University Press (New York, NY), 1997.
St. James Guide to Young Adult Writers, 2nd edition, St. James Press (Detroit, MI), 1999.

PERIODICALS

Booklist, June, 1996, Susan Dove Lempke, reviews of *Spud Sweetgrass* and *Spud in Winter,* pp. 1696-1697; December 1, 1998, Kathleen Squires, review of *Easy Avenue,* p. 661; April 1, 2004, Todd Morning, review of *Boy O'Boy,* p. 1360.
Books for Young People, October, 1988, pp. 12, 18.
Books in Canada, February, 1983, Mary Ainslie Smith, review of *Up to Low,* pp. 32-33; June, 1997, review of *Uncle Ronald,* p. 34; November, 2001, review of *Mary Ann Alice,* p. 46.
Bulletin of the Center for Children's Books, February, 1997, review of *Uncle Ronald,* p. 203.
Canadian Book Review Annual, 1999, review of *The Low Life: Five Great Tales from Up and Down the River,* p. 490.
Canadian Children's Books, Authors, and Illustrators, 1985-86.
Canadian Children's Literature, number 22, 1981, pp. 47-50; number 37, 1985, pp. 67-70; number 54, 1989, pp. 71-72.
Children's Book News, December, 1984, p. 3; winter, 1997, review of *Uncle Ronald,* p. 30.
Children's Book Review Services, winter, 1999, review of *Easy Avenue,* p. 68.
Emergency Librarian, March, 1997, review of *Uncle Ronald,* p. 28.

Globe and Mail, December 4, 1999, review of *The Low Life,* p. D37; August 25, 2001, review of *Mary Ann Alice,* p. D11.
Horn Book, February, 1984, pp. 99-103; May-June, 1997, Martha V. Parravano, review of *Uncle Ronald,* pp. 318-319; March-April, 2002, Tim Wynne-Jones, "The Widow Kealey's Stew: A Look at the Novels of Brian Doyle," pp. 181-186; May-June, 2002, Martha V. Parravano, review of *Mary Ann Alice,* pp. 327-328; March-April, 2004, Christine M. Heppermann, review of *Boy O'Boy,* p. 181.
Horn Book Guide, fall, 1997, review of *Uncle Ronald,* p. 312.
In Review: Canadian Books for Children, autumn, 1978, p. 57; August, 1980, p. 45.
Kirkus Reviews, February 1, 1997, review of *Uncle Ronald,* p. 221.
Kliatt, March, 2004, Rebecca Rabinowitz, review of *Boy O'Boy,* p. 18.
Maclean's, December 13, 1982, pp. 56-58; December 26, 1988, p. 60.
Magpies, November, 1994, pp. 11-13.
Publishers Weekly, January 16, 1987, p. 74; April 5, 2004, review of *Boy O'Boy,* p. 63.
Quill & Quire, August 1980, p. 30; November, 1982, p. 26; December, 1982, p. 27; November, 1984, p. 18; October, 1990, p. 16; September, 1992, p. 72; March, 1995, p. 75; February, 1997, review of *Uncle Ronald,* p. 51; September, 2001, review of *Mary Ann Alice,* p. 53.
Resource Links, February, 1997, review of *Uncle Ronald,* p. 136; February, 2002, Joan Marshall, review of *Mary Ann Alice,* pp. 26-27.
School Library Journal, May, 1987, p. 97; May, 1997, Cindy Darling Codell, review of *Uncle Ronald,* p. 132; November, 1998, Lisa Denton, review of *Easy Avenue,* p. 121; June, 2002, Robyn Ryan Vandenbroek, review of *Mary Ann Alice,* p. 137.
Voice of Youth Advocates, April, 1998, review of *Spud Sweetgrass,* p. 42; June, 1999, review of *Easy Avenue,* p. 112.
World of Children's Books, 1981, pp. 27-33.

ONLINE

CM Magazine Web site, http://www.umanitoba.ca/outreach/cm/ (October 6, 1995), Elaine Seepish, review of *Spud in Winter;* (January 17, 1997), Irene Gordon, review of *Uncle Ronald;* (October 20, 2000), Mary Thomas, review of *The Low Life.*

Groundwood Books Web site, http://www.groundwood books.com/ (June 14, 2004), "Brian Doyle."

Ottawa International Writers Festival Web site, http://www.writersfest.com/ (June 14, 2004), "Brian Doyle."

The Writers' Union of Canada Web site, http://www.writersunion.ca/d/doyle_b.htm/ (June 14, 2004), "Brian Doyle."*

*   *   *

DRUMMOND, Walter
  See SILVERBERG, Robert

*   *   *

DUGGAN, Joseph J(ohn) 1938-

PERSONAL: Born September 8, 1938, in Philadelphia, PA; son of Bart J. (a mechanic) and Mary (Boyce) Duggan; married Mary Kay Conyers (a musicologist), March 3, 1962; children: Marie Christine, Kathleen. *Education:* Attended Sorbonne, University of Paris, 1958-59; Fordham University, B.A., 1960; Ohio State University, Ph.D., 1964.

ADDRESSES: Home—2229 Marin Ave., Berkeley, CA 94707. *Office*—Department of Comparative Literature, University of California—Berkeley, Berkeley, CA 94720-2510. *E-mail*—roland@socrates.berkeley.edu.

CAREER: University of California—Berkeley, instructor, 1964-65, assistant professor, 1965-71, associate professor of French and comparative literature, beginning 1971, currently professor of French, Bernie S. Williams Professor of Comparative Literature, and associate dean of Graduate Division.

MEMBER: Modern Language Association of America, Mediaeval Academy of America.

AWARDS, HONORS: National Humanities Foundation fellowship, 1968-69.

WRITINGS:

(Editor) *A Concordance of the "Chanson de Roland,"* Ohio State University Press (Columbus, OH), 1970.

"The Song of Roland": Formulaic Style and Poetic Craft, University of California Press (Berkeley, CA), 1973.

Oral Literature: Seven Essays, Barnes & Noble (New York, NY), 1975.

A Guide to Studies on the "Chanson de Roland," Grant & Cutler (London, England), 1976.

A Fragment of "Les Enfances Vivien," University of California Press (Berkeley, CA), 1985.

The "Cantar de mio Cid:" Poetic Creation in Its Economic and Social Contexts, Cambridge University Press (New York, NY), 1989.

The Romances of Chrétien de Troyes, Yale University Press (New Haven, CT), 2001.

Contributor to periodicals, including *Romania, Orbis Literarum, University of Southern California Studies in Comparative Literature, Revue,* and *Romance Philology.* Member of editorial board, *Forum for Modern Language Studies.*

WORK IN PROGRESS: Editing additional manuscripts of the *Chanson de Roland;* research on the medieval epic in the Romance languages.

BIOGRAPHICAL AND CRITICAL SOURCES:

PERIODICALS

Medium Aevum, spring, 1991, D. G. Pattison, review of *The "Cantar de mio Cid:" Poetic Creation in Its Economic and Social Contexts,* p. 140.
Modern Language Review, October, 1991, Milija N. Pavlovic, "Oralist Vision and Neo-traditionalist Revision: A Review Article," p. 866.
Romance Philology, May, 1991, Brigitte Cazelles, review of *A Fragment of "Les Enfances Vivien,"* p. 479; February, 1993, Maria Eugenia Lacarra, review of *The "Cantar de mio Cid,"* p. 302.
Speculum: Journal of Medieval Studies, April, 1987, Jan A. Nelson, review of *A Fragment of "Les Enfances Vivien,"* p. 499; January, 1992, Maria Rosa Menocal, review of *The "Cantar de mio Cid,"* p. 138.

Times Literary Supplement, April 13, 1990, Richard Fletcher, review of *The "Cantar de mio Cid,"* p. 400; July 19, 2002, A. D. Putter, review of *The Romances of Chrétien de Troyes,* p. 26.

ONLINE

Joseph J. Duggan Home Page, http://www.grad.berkeley.edu/deans/duggan (October 20, 2004).*

E

EDWARDS, Louis 1962-

PERSONAL: Born 1962.

ADDRESSES: Home—New Orleans, LA. *Agent*—c/o Author Mail, Dutton, 375 Hudson St., New York, NY 10014.

CAREER: Writer. Has worked in public relations for the New Orleans Jazz and Heritage Festival and the New York JVC Jazz Festival, beginning 1986.

AWARDS, HONORS: PEN Oakland/Josephine Miles Award for excellence in literature, 1991, for *Ten Seconds; Ten Seconds* was named one of the best books of 1991 by *Publishers Weekly.*

WRITINGS:

NOVELS

Ten Seconds, Graywolf Press (St. Paul, MN), 1991.
N: A Romantic Mystery, Dutton (New York, NY), 1997.
Oscar Wilde Discovers America, Scribner (New York, NY), 2003.

SIDELIGHTS: Louis Edwards has penned three notable novels: the critically acclaimed *Ten Seconds,* the ambitious *N: A Romantic Mystery,* and the complex *Oscar Wilde Discovers America. Ten Seconds* recounts the life of Eddie, an African-American male, former high-school track star, refinery worker, and young husband. While Eddie watches a one hundred-yard-dash event at a high-school track meet in his small Louisiana hometown, Edwards takes the reader on a journey through Eddie's past, present, and future.

Edwards plays with the element of time in *Ten Seconds.* The ten chapters of the book are structured around the ten seconds that it takes a fast runner to finish the one-hundred-yard dash. The story skips forward and backward through Eddie's life, a technique that, according to Mason Buck of the *New York Times Book Review,* "allows the events of the future to illuminate those of the past." For instance, newlywed Eddie pledges to take care of his wife, but this scene does not occur until after the reader has witnessed Eddie's wife threatening to leave him because of his philandering and drug use.

Edwards paints a vivid picture of African-American culture and class with Eddie's inner monologue. Eddie ruminates on his inner self, his friends, and his family; his thoughts and recollections guide the reader through topics such as love, sex, friendship, youth, parenting, and liberty. Called "a strikingly poignant and polished debut" by *Booklist* contributor Donna Seaman, *Ten Seconds* was named by *Publishers Weekly* as one of the best books of 1991.

Edwards followed *Ten Seconds* with *N: A Romantic Mystery.* In this novel, protagonist Aimee DuBois investigates the murder of a teenager in a New Orleans, Louisiana, housing project. DuBois, an intellectual Creole woman who runs an alternative newspaper, must explore the hidden world of black society, and her investigation gives Edwards room to comment on race and class. The search for the teenager's killer leads DuBois to a variety of colorful characters, including a bookstore owner, an alluring drug dealer, a drug-dealing mother, a malicious minister, and a pregnant niece. Edwards shifts the point of view from third-person to first-person in a story that closely examines New Orleans.

Contrary to its title, the protagonist in *Oscar Wilde Discovers America* is William Traquair, a young black man who has recently graduated from college. Traquair is intelligent, charismatic, and handsome, but disheartened by the limited opportunities available to him as an African-American male in 1882. When his father suggests that he accept a job as a valet for a visiting writer, Traquair is at first aghast and dispels the idea of being anyone's servant. When Traquair learns that the writer is Oscar Wilde, however, he has a change of heart. Already familiar with Wilde's work, the young man is certain he can learn a great deal from Wilde, and the two set off on a one-year trek across America. Traquair comes of age during the trip—he falls in love, loses his virginity, gains insight into his family, and realizes that establishing an identity will be difficult in a society rife with racial and sexual prejudice. He learns from Wilde, but Wilde also learns from him, and the two become close friends.

Oscar Wilde Discovers America is mostly fictional, except that Edwards allows the characters to follow Wilde's historical route. Edwards's inspiration for Traquair stemmed from two newspaper references to Oscar Wilde's African-American valet. "This young, handsome, well-educated black American male seems to be the ultimate outsider in the world of wealth, social pretense, cultural ambition and moral hypocrisy to which he is admitted in the company of his celebrated employer," observed William S. Doan in the *Lambda Book Report*. Doan also noted that "Edwards develops their relationship with subtlety and skill."

Oscar Wilde Discovers America was generally well received by critics, although a *Publishers Weekly* reviewer felt that the novel was "slowed by awkward prose with a false, old-timey stiffness." A *Kirkus Reviewer* dubbed the book "a marvelous story animated with just the right savvy, melodrama, wit, and fantasy." According to *Library Journal* critic Rebecca Stuhr, "This complex novel requires—and deserves—multiple readings to be understood and appreciated fully."

BIOGRAPHICAL AND CRITICAL SOURCES:

PERIODICALS

Booklist, May 15, 1991, Donna Seaman, review of *Ten Seconds,* p. 1779; February 15, 1994, p. 1043; May 15, 1997, p. 1566; January 1, 2003, Margaret Flanagan, review of *Oscar Wilde Discovers America,* p. 844.

Book World, June 30, 1991, p. 10.

Choice, December, 1991, p. 591.

Essence, September, 1991, p. 50.

Kirkus Reviews, November 1, 2002, review of *Oscar Wilde Discovers America,* p. 1551.

Lambda Book Report, August-September, 2003, William S. Doan, "Wilde, Wilde, World," pp. 21-23.

Library Journal, May 1, 1991, p. 105; October 1, 1991, p. 55; April 1, 1997, p. 133; November 15, 2002, Rebecca Stuhr, review of *Oscar Wilde Discovers America,* pp. 99-101.

Los Angeles Times Book Review, June 23, 1991, p. 5; September 8, 1991, p. 10.

Multicultural Review, January, 1992, p. 45.

New York Times Book Review, August 11, 1991, Mason Buck, review of *Ten Seconds,* p. 20.

Publishers Weekly, May 3, 1991, p. 69; November 1, 1991, p. 21; January 20, 1992, p. 11; March 3, 1997, p. 67; November 11, 2002, review of *Oscar Wilde Discovers America,* p. 39.

San Francisco Review of Books, Volume 16, number 2, 1991, p. 43.*

*   *   *

EHRLICH, H. M.
See ZIEFERT, Harriet

*   *   *

EISNER, Will(iam Erwin) 1917-2005
(Will Erwin, Willis Rensie)

PERSONAL: Born March 6, 1917, in New York, NY; died January 3, 2005, in Fort Lauderdale, FL; son of Samuel (a furrier) and Fannie (maiden name, Ingber) Eisner; married Ann Louise Weingarten (a director of

Will Eisner

volunteer hospital services), June 15, 1950; children: John David, Alice Carol (deceased). *Education:* Attended Art Students League, New York, NY, 1935.

CAREER: Author, cartoonist, publisher. *New York American,* New York, NY, staff artist, 1936; Eisner & Iger, New York, NY, founder, partner, 1937-40; Eisner-Arnold Comic Group, New York, NY, founder, publisher, 1940-46; author and cartoonist of syndicated newspaper feature, "The Spirit," 1940-52; founder and president of American Visuals Corp., beginning in 1949; president of Bell McClure North American Newspaper Alliance, 1962-64; executive vice-president of Koster-Dana Corp., 1962-64; president of Educational Supplements Corp., 1965-72; chair of the board of Croft Educational Services Corp., 1972-73; member of faculty of School of Visual Arts, New York, NY, beginning 1973. President of IPD Publishing Co., Inc. Member of board of directors of Westchester Philharmonic. *Military service:* U.S. Army, Ordnance, 1942-45.

MEMBER: Princeton Club (New York, NY).

AWARDS, HONORS: Comic book artist of the year, National Cartoonists Society, 1967; best artist, National Cartoonists Society, 1968-69; award for qual-

ity of art in comic books, Society of Comic Art Research, 1968; International Cartoonist Award, 1974; named to Hall of Fame of the Comic Book Academy; Eisner Award for Best Archival Collection, 2001, for *The Spirit Archives.*

WRITINGS:

A Pictorial Arsenal of America's Combat Weapons, Sterling (New York, NY), 1960.

America's Space Vehicles: A Pictorial Review, edited by Charles Kramer, Sterling (New York, NY), 1962.

A Contract with God, and Other Tenement Stories, Baronet (New York, NY), 1978.

(With P. R. Garriock and others) *Masters of Comic Book Art,* Images Graphiques (New York, NY), 1978.

Odd Facts, Ace Books (New York, NY), 1978.

Dating and Hanging Out (for young adults), Baronet (New York, NY), 1979.

Funny Jokes and Foxy Riddles, Baronet (New York, NY), 1979.

Ghostly Jokes and Ghastly Riddles, Baronet (New York, NY), 1979.

One Hundred and One Half Wild and Crazy Jokes, Baronet (New York, NY), 1979.

Spaced-Out Jokes, Baronet (New York, NY), 1979.

The City (narrative portfolio), Hollygraphic, 1981.

Life on Another Planet (graphic novel), Kitchen Sink (Princeton, WI), 1981.

Will Eisner Color Treasury, text by Catherine Yronwode, Kitchen Sink (Princeton, WI), 1981.

Illustrated Roberts Rules of Order, Bantam (New York, NY), 1983.

Spirit: Color Album, Kitchen Sink (Princeton, WI), 1981–1983.

(Catherine Yronwode, with Denis Kitchen) *The Art of Will Eisner,* introduction by Jules Feiffer, Kitchen Sink (Princeton, WI), 1982.

(Coauthor, with Jules Feiffer and Wallace Wood) *Outer Space Spirit, 1952,* edited by Denis Kitchen, Kitchen Sink (Princeton, WI), 1983.

Signal from Space, Kitchen Sink (Princeton, WI), 1983.

Will Eisner's Quarterly, Kitchen Sink (Princeton, WI), 1983–86.

Will Eisner's 3-D Classics Featuring. . ., Kitchen Sink (Princeton, WI), 1985.

Comics and Sequential Art, Poorhouse (Tamarac, FL), 1985.

Will Eisner's Hawks of the Seas, 1936-1938, edited by Dave Schreiner, Kitchen Sink (Princeton, WI), 1986.

Will Eisner's New York, the Big City, Kitchen Sink (Princeton, WI), 1986.

Will Eisner's The Dreamer, Kitchen Sink (Princeton, WI), 1986.

The Building, Kitchen Sink (Princeton, WI), 1987.

A Life Force, Kitchen Sink (Princeton, WI), 1988.

City People Notebook, Kitchen Sink (Princeton, WI), 1989.

Will Eisner's Spirit Casebook, Kitchen Sink (Princeton, WI), 1990–98.

Will Eisner Reader: Seven Graphic Stories by a Comics Master, Kitchen Sink (Princeton, WI), 1991.

To the Heart of the Storm, Kitchen Sink (Princeton, WI), 1991.

The White Whale: An Introduction to "Moby Dick," Story Shop (Tamarac, FL), 1991.

The Spirit: The Origin Years, Kitchen Sink (Princeton, WI), 1992.

Invisible People, Kitchen Sink (Northampton, MA), 1993.

The Christmas Spirit, Kitchen Sink (Northampton, MA), 1994.

Sketchbook, Kitchen Sink (Northampton, MA), 1995.

Dropsie Avenue: The Neighborhood, Kitchen Sink (Northampton, MA), 1995.

Graphic Storytelling, Poorhouse (Tamarac, FL), 1996.

(Adapter) *Moby Dick by Herman Melville,* NBM (New York, NY), 1998.

A Family Matter, Kitchen Sink (Northampton, MA), 1998.

(Reteller) *The Princess and the Frog by the Grimm Brothers,* NBM (New York, NY), 1999.

Minor Miracles: Long Ago and Once upon a Time, Back when Uncles Were Heroic, Cousins Were Clever, and Miracles Happened on Every Block, DC Comics (New York, NY), 2000.

The Last Knight: An Introduction to "Don Quixote" by Miguel de Cervantes, NBM (New York, NY), 2000.

Last Day in Vietnam: A Memory, Dark Horse (Milwaukie, OR), 2000.

Will Eisner's The Spirit Archives, DC Comics (New York, NY), 2000.

The Name of the Game, DC Comics (New York, NY), 2001.

Will Eisner's Shop Talk, Dark Horse (Milwaukie, OR), 2001.

(With Dick French, Bill Woolfolk, and others) *The Blackhawk Archives,* DC Comics (New York, NY), 2001.

Fagin the Jew, Doubleday (New York, NY), 2003.

(Adapter) *Sundiata: A Legend of Africa,* NMB (New York, NY), 2003.

For U.S. Department of Defense, creator of comic strip instructional aid, *P. S. Magazine,* 1950, and for U.S. Department of Labor, creator of career guidance series of comic booklets, *Job Scene,* 1967. Also creator of comic strips, sometimes under pseudonyms Will Erwin and Willis Rensie, including "Uncle Sam," "Muss 'em Up Donovan," "Sheena," "The Three Brothers," "Blackhawk," "K-51," and "Hawk of the Seas." Author of newspaper feature, "Odd Facts." Also contributor to *Artwork for "9-11 Emergency Relief,"* issued by Alternative Comics, 2001.

SIDELIGHTS: Cartoonist Will Eisner, the creator of many popular comic strips, was also well known as a pioneer in the educational applications of this medium. Throughout his fifty-plus-year career, he created a host of comic-book characters to guide young people in their choice of a career, to instruct military personnel, and simply to entertain children of all ages. Eisner has also produced a series of comic-book training manuals for developing nations, which teach modern farming techniques and the maintenance of military equipment. These booklets are used by the Agency for International Development, the United Nations, and the U.S. Department of Defense.

Eisner's career began in the mid-1930s, when he sold his first comic feature, "Scott Dalton," to *Wow!* magazine. He went on to create more comic strips, including "Sheena, Queen of the Jungle" and his best-known work, "The Spirit," a weekly adventure series published as an insert in Sunday papers from 1940 to 1951. This strip featured protagonist Denny Colt, a private investigator who is seriously injured, and presumed dead, after an explosion in the laboratory of evil scientist Dr. Cobra. Once Colt recovers, he vows to exploit his new anonymity to enhance his ability to bring hardened criminals to justice. The strip, renowned for its social satire, also featured the first African-American character to make ongoing appearances in an American comic feature.

In 1942, Eisner was drafted into the U.S. Army, where he was put to work designing safety posters. He also used cartoon-strip techniques to simplify the military's training manual for equipment maintenance, *Army*

Motors. After his discharge in 1946, Eisner continued to write and illustrate "The Spirit," but decided to discontinue the strip in 1951. He then founded the American Visuals Corporation, a company that produced comic books for schools and businesses. In 1967, the U.S. Department of Labor asked Eisner to create a comic book that would appeal to potential school dropouts. The result was *Job Scene,* a series of booklets designed to introduce career choices to young people in the hope that they would see the need for further education. *Job Scene* proved so successful that several national publishers have issued similar series.

Eisner also developed *P.S. Magazine,* an instructional manual for the U.S. Department of Defense designed to replace the verbose, unwieldy technical manuals formerly used by military trainers. Eisner wrote in a 1974 article for *Library Journal:* "The significance of comics as a training device is perhaps not so much the use of time-honored sequential art as the language accompanying the pictures. For example, *P.S. Magazine* . . . employed the soldier's argot, rendering militarese into common language. The magazine said 'Clean away the crud from the flywheel' instead of 'All foreign matter should be removed from the surface of the flywheel and the rubber belt which it supports.'" Eisner's version reduced the original one-hundred-word section describing that procedure to a sequence of three panels which quickly and simply presented the necessary instruction.

The immediate visual impact and simple language used in *P.S. Magazine* are assets which Eisner believes make comics desirable in more traditional classroom situations. Critics, however, complain that while teachers are trying to instill a healthy respect for proper language, comic books and strips violate every rule of grammar. In his *Publishers Weekly* article, Eisner responded: "This is an understandable criticism, but it is based on the assumption that cartoons are designed primarily to teach language. *Comics are a message in themselves!* . . . To readers living in the ghetto and playing in the street and school yard, comic books, with their inventive language, argot, and slang, serve as no other literature does."

Eisner believes it is remarkable that many reading teachers are still reluctant to adapt this "inviting material." He praises those educators who have recognized the merit in his art form. Eisner concluded his *Publishers Weekly* article with a commentary on the improv-

ing status of comics in the schools: "In schools, comic strip reprints are reaching reluctant readers who are either unresponsive or hostile to traditional books. . . . Certain qualities distinctive to comic books support their educational importance. Perhaps their most singular characteristic is *timeliness.* Comics appeal to readers when they deal with 'now' situations, or treat them in a 'now' manner. Working in a high-speed transmission, the author faces instant acceptance or rejection. He or she is writing for a transient audience who are in a hurry to savor vicarious experiences. Loyalties are to the characters themselves, so the need for imaginative storytelling is great. Equally vital is the choice of terms. The reader's instant recognition of symbols and concepts challenges the ingenuity and empathy of comic-book creators."

Satisfying as his educational-and-vocational-based work had been, Eisner was drawn back to narrative forms again in the mid-1970s, after he attended a comic-book convention and was inspired by the innovative work he saw there, in particular that of underground cartoonist R. Crumb. In 1975 he began work on what he called a "graphic novel," published three years later as *A Contract with God and Other Tenement Stories.* Unlike his earlier adventure comics, this work is a serious treatment of such serious themes as religious faith, sexual betrayal, and prejudice. Other graphic novels, which depicted the lives of Jewish immigrants in America, followed, including *Life on Another Planet, Big City, A Life Force,* and *Minor Miracles.* Eisner's 2001 graphic novel, *The Name of the Game,* is a multigenerational family saga about the Arnheim family, who expand their businesses from corset manufacturing to stock brokering. Though *Booklist* reviewer Gordon Flagg found the book melodramatic and predictable, the critic appreciated Eisner's "expressive" artwork and noted that the book reflects "a sensibility somehow appropriate to the period and subject."

Eisner has also used the comic-strip medium to adapt literary classics, including *Don Quixote* and *Moby Dick* as well as fairy tales by the Brothers Grimm. These projects have received mixed reviews. Susan Weitz of *School Library Journal* found Eisner's version of *Moby Dick* "simplistic" and disappointing; *Booklist* contributor Francisca Goldsmith, however, considered it highly successful in conveying the original work's plot, characterizations, and mood. Similar differences marked critical reception to *The*

Last Knight: An Introduction to "Don Quixote" by Miguel de Cervantes. Marian Drabkin commented in *School Library Journal* that, in Eisner's hands, Don Quixote becomes merely a "clownish madman whose escapades are slapstick and pointless," while Cervantes depicted him as a much more complex character. *Booklist* critic Roger Leslie, on the other hand, felt that Eisner's book is "faithful to the spirit of the original" and an excellent introduction to the great classic.

In *Comics and Sequential Art,* Eisner explains the unique aspects of sequential art: imagery, frames, timing, and the relationship between written word and visual design. Ken Marantz, reviewing the book's twenty-first printing for *School Arts,* praised its clarity, creativity, and detailed descriptions, and concluded that the book is a valuable introduction to an innovative medium for creative expression.

Despite being an octogenarian, Eisner has continued to work vigorously. In *Fagin the Jew,* published in 2003, Eisner takes the famous character from Charles Dickens's *Oliver Twist* and tells his personal story, one in which Fagin comes out in a much better light. As told by Eisner, Fagin was virtually forced into crime as a youth because of circumstances, not the least of which was the general prejudice against his family as Ashkenazi Jews. "As written by Eisner, Fagin gains depth and humanity, and he could have found success on the right side of the law had not persecution, poverty, and bad luck hindered him," wrote Steve Raiteri in *Library Journal.* The graphic novel includes a foreword explaining the probable historical antecedents of the tale and how they related to Dickens's portrayal of Jews. While noting that Eisner's depiction of nineteenth-century London is "wholly convincing," a *Publishers Weekly* reviewer felt that "the story errs on the side of extreme coincidence and melodrama." *Library Journal* contributor Steve Weiner commented that "Eisner masterfully weaves a Dickensian story of his own focusing on racism and stereotypes." Francisca Goldsmith, writing in *School Library Journal* noted that the book would appeal to readers looking for another view of the Dickens classic but was "also for those concerned with media influence on stereotypes and the history of immigration issues."

In another 2003 publication, Eisner adapted an African story set in the thirteenth century for the graphic novel, *Sundiata: A Legend of Africa.* The story revolves around the death of the Mali peoples' leader and their subsequent conquest by a tyrant, who can control the elements. Sundiata, son of the former Mali leader, eventually leads his people in victory against their oppressor. *Booklist* contributor Carlos Orellana felt that the ending was unsatisfying but noted that "the plot flows smoothly; the telling never feels rushed; and the sequential art, which is full of movement and expression, gives the familiar good-versus-evil theme extra depth." Steve Raiteri, writing in *Library Journal,* commented that the book would interest not only children but that teens and adults as well would "appreciate Eisner's concise and clear storytelling and his dramatic artwork, distinctively colored in grays and earth tones."

BIOGRAPHICAL AND CRITICAL SOURCES:

PERIODICALS

Booklist, August, 1998, Gordon Flagg, review of *A Family Matter,* p. 1948; December 15, 1999, Stephanie Zvirin, review of *The Princess and the Frog by the Grimm Brothers,* p. 780; June 1, 2000, Roger Leslie, review of *The Last Knight: An Introduction to "Don Quixote" by Miguel de Cervantes,* p. 1884; August, 2000, Gordon Flagg, review of *The Spirit Archives,* p. 2094; September 15, 2000, Gordon Flagg, review of *Minor Miracles,* p. 200; November 15, 2001, Francisca Goldsmith, review of *Moby Dick by Herman Melville,* p. 568, and "Sequential Art Meets the White Whale," p. 569; February 1, 2002, Gordon Flagg, review of *The Name of the Game,* p. 914; February 1, 2003, Carlos Orellana, review of *Sundiata: A Legend of Africa,* p. 984; September 1, 2003, Gordon Flagg, review of *Fagin the Jew,* p. 76.
College English, February, 1995, George Dardess, review of *Comics and Sequential Art,* p. 213.
Library Journal, October 15, 1974, Will Eisner, "Comic Books in the Library"; June 1, 1991, Keith R. A. DeCandido, review of *To the Heart of the Storm,* p. 134; October 15, 1974; September 15, 2000, Stephen Weiner, review of *Minor Miracles,* p. 66; March 1, 2003, Steve Raiteri, review of *Sundiata: A Legend of Africa,* p. 74; November 1, 2003, Steve Raiteri, review of *Fagin the Jew,* p. 60.
New York Review of Books, June 21, 2001, David Hajdu, "The Spirit of the Spirit," p. 48.

Philadelphia Magazine, August, 1984, Jack Curtin, "Signals from Space," p. 70.

Publishers Weekly, October 4, 1985, review of *Comics and Sequential Art,* p. 75; March 25, 1988, review of *A Life Force,* p. 61; March 22, 1991, review of *To the Heart of the Storm,* p. 76; June 21, 1991, review of *Will Eisner Reader: Seven Graphic Stories by a Comics Master,* p. 58; May 8, 1995, review of *Dropsie Avenue: The Neighborhood,* p. 293; January 3, 2000, review of *The Princess and the Frog,* p. 78; November 17, 2003, review of *Fagin the Jew,* p. 46.

School Arts, April, 2002, Ken Marantz, review of *Comics and Sequential Art,* p. 58.

School Library Journal, July, 2000, Marian Drabkin, review of *The Last Knight,* p. 115; January, 2002, Susan Weitz, review of *Moby Dick by Herman Melville,* p. 138; February, 2003, John Peters, review of *Sundiata,* p. 129; January, 2004, Francisca Goldsmith, review of *Fagin the Jew,* p. 166.

Variety, September 28, 1988, "Comic Book Confidential," p. 30.

Whole Earth, spring, 1998, review of *The Spirit,* p. 25.

ONLINE

Will Eisner Web site, http://willeisner.tripod.com (July 22, 2002).*

ELIOT, Dan
    See SILVERBERG, Robert

*   *   *

ELLIOTT, Don
    See SILVERBERG, Robert

*   *   *

ERICKSON, Walter
    See FAST, Howard (Melvin)

*   *   *

ERICSON, Walter
    See FAST, Howard (Melvin)

*   *   *

ERWIN, Will
    See EISNER, Will(iam Erwin)

F

FALK, Lee
   See COPPER, Basil

*   *   *

FAST, Howard (Melvin) 1914-2003
   (E. V. Cunningham, Walter Erickson, Walter Ericson)

PERSONAL: Born November 11, 1914, in New York, NY; died March 12, 2003, in Old Greenwich, CT; son of Barney (an ironworker, cable car gripper, tin factory worker, and dress factory cutter) and Ida (a homemaker; maiden name, Miller) Fast; married Bette Cohen (a painter and sculptor), June 6, 1937 (died November, 1994); married Mimi O'Connor, June 17, 1999; children: (first marriage) Rachel, Jonathan; stepchildren: three. *Education:* Attended National Academy of Design. *Religion:* Jewish. *Hobbies and other interests:* "Home, my family, the theater, the film, and the proper study of ancient history. And the follies of mankind."

CAREER: Worked at several odd jobs and as a page in the New York Public Library prior to 1932; writer, beginning 1932. Foreign correspondent for *Esquire* and *Coronet,* 1945. Taught at Indiana University, 1947; member of World Peace Council, 1950-55; American Labor Party candidate for U.S. Congress, 23rd New York District, 1952; owner, Blue Heron Press, New York, 1952-57; film writer, 1958-67; chief news writer, Voice of America, 1982-84. Gave numerous lectures and made numerous appearances on radio and television programs. *Military service:* Affiliated with U.S.

Howard Fast

Office of War Information, 1942-44; correspondent with special Signal Corps unit and war correspondent in China-India-Burma theater, 1945.

MEMBER: Century Club, Fellowship of Reconciliation.

AWARDS, HONORS: Bread Loaf Literary Award, 1937; Schomberg Award for Race Relations, 1944, for *Freedom Road;* Newspaper Guild award, 1947; National Jewish Book Award, Jewish Book Council, 1949, for *My Glorious Brothers;* International Peace Prize from the Soviet Union, 1954; Screenwriters annual award, 1960; annual book award, National Association of Independent Schools, 1962; American Library Association notable book citation, 1972, for *The Hessian;* Emmy Award for outstanding writing in a drama series, American Academy of Television Arts and Sciences, 1975, for episode "The Ambassador," *Benjamin Franklin;* Literary Lions Award, New York Public Library, 1985; Prix de la Policia (France), for books under name E. V. Cunningham.

WRITINGS:

Two Valleys, Dial (New York, NY), 1933.

Strange Yesterday, Dodd (New York, NY), 1934.

Place in the City, Harcourt (New York, NY), 1937.

Conceived in Liberty: A Novel of Valley Forge, Simon & Schuster (New York, NY), 1939.

The Last Frontier, Duell, Sloan & Pearce (New York, NY), 1941, reprinted, North Castle Books (Armonk, NY), 1997.

The Romance of a People, Hebrew Publishing (New York, NY), 1941.

Lord Baden-Powell of the Boy Scouts, Messner (New York, NY), 1941.

Haym Salomon, Son of Liberty, Messner (New York, NY), 1941.

The Unvanquished, Duell, Sloan & Pearce (New York, NY), 1942, reprinted, M. E. Sharpe (Armonk, NY), 1997.

The Tall Hunter, Harper (New York, NY), 1942.

(With wife, Bette Fast) *The Picture-Book History of the Jews,* Hebrew Publishing (New York, NY), 1942.

Goethals and the Panama Canal, Messner (New York, NY), 1942.

Citizen Tom Paine, Duell, Sloan & Pearce (New York, NY), 1943.

The Incredible Tito, Magazine House (New York, NY), 1944.

Tito and His People, Contemporary Publishers (Winnipeg, Manitoba, Canada), 1944.

Freedom Road, Duell, Sloan & Pearce (New York, NY), 1944, new edition with foreword by W. E. B. DuBois, introduction by Eric Foner, M. E. Sharpe (Armonk, NY), 1995.

Patrick Henry and the Frigate's Keel, and Other Stories of a Young Nation, Duell, Sloan & Pearce (New York, NY), 1945.

The American: A Middle Western Legend, Duell, Sloan & Pearce (New York, NY), 1946.

(With William Gropper) *Never Forget: The Story of the Warsaw Ghetto,* Book League of the Jewish Fraternal Order, 1946.

(Editor) Thomas Paine, *Selected Works,* Modern Library (New York, NY), 1946.

The Children, Duell, Sloan & Pearce (New York, NY), 1947.

(Editor) Theodore Dreiser, *Best Short Stories,* World Publishing (New York, NY), 1947.

Clarkton, Duell, Sloan & Pearce (New York, NY), 1947.

My Glorious Brothers, Little, Brown (Boston, MA), 1948, new edition, Hebrew Publications (New York, NY), 1977.

Departure and Other Stories, Little, Brown (Boston, MA), 1949.

Intellectuals in the Fight for Peace, Masses & Mainstream (New York, NY), 1949.

The Proud and the Free, Little, Brown (Boston, MA), 1950.

Literature and Reality, International Publishers (New York, NY), 1950.

Spartacus, Blue Heron (New York, NY), 1951, reprinted with new introduction, North Castle Books (Armonk, NY), 1996.

Peekskill, U.S.A.: A Personal Experience, Civil Rights Congress (New York, NY), 1951.

(Under pseudonym Walter Erickson) *Fallen Angel,* Little, Brown (Boston, MA), 1951.

Tony and the Wonderful Door, Blue Heron (New York, NY), 1952.

Spain and Peace, Joint Anti-Fascist Refugee Committee, 1952.

The Passion of Sacco and Vanzetti: A New England Legend, Blue Heron (New York, NY), 1953.

Silas Timberman, Blue Heron (New York, NY), 1954.

The Last Supper, and Other Stories, Blue Heron (New York, NY), 1955.

The Story of Lola Gregg, Blue Heron (New York, NY), 1956.

The Naked God: The Writer and the Communist Party (memoir), Praeger (New York, NY), 1957.

Moses, Prince of Egypt, Crown (New York, NY), 1958, with new introduction by the author, Pocket Books (New York, NY), 2000.

The Winston Affair, Crown (New York, NY), 1959.

The Howard Fast Reader, Crown (New York, NY), 1960.

April Morning, Crown (New York, NY), 1961.

The Edge of Tomorrow (stories), Bantam (New York, NY), 1961.

Power, Doubleday (New York, NY), 1962.

Agrippa's Daughter, Doubleday (New York, NY), 1964.

The Hill, Doubleday (New York, NY), 1964.

Torquemada, Doubleday (New York, NY), 1966.

The Hunter and the Trap, Dial (New York, NY), 1967.

The Jews: Story of a People, Dial (New York, NY), 1968, Cassell (London, England), 1960.

The General Zapped an Angel, Morrow (New York, NY), 1970.

The Crossing (based on his play of the same title), Morrow (New York, NY), 1971, New Jersey Historical Society, 1985.

The Hessian, Morrow (New York, NY), 1972, reprinted with new foreword, M. E. Sharpe (Armonk, NY), 1996.

A Touch of Infinity: Thirteen Stories of Fantasy and Science Fiction, Morrow (New York, NY), 1973.

Mohawk (screenplay; short film), Paulist Productions, 1974.

Time and the Riddle: Thirty-one Zen Stories, Ward Richie Press (Pasadena, CA), 1975.

The Immigrants, Houghton Mifflin (Boston, MA), 1977.

The Art of Zen Meditation, Peace Press (Culver City, CA), 1977.

The Second Generation, Houghton Mifflin (Boston, MA), 1978.

The Establishment, Houghton Mifflin (Boston, MA), 1979.

The Legacy, Houghton Mifflin (Boston, MA), 1980.

The Magic Door (juvenile), Avon (New York, NY), 1980.

Max, Houghton Mifflin (Boston, MA), 1982.

The Outsider, Houghton Mifflin (Boston, MA), 1984.

The Immigrant's Daughter, Houghton Mifflin (Boston, MA), 1985.

The Dinner Party, Houghton Mifflin (Boston, MA), 1987.

The Call of Fife and Drum: Three Novels of the Revolution (contains *The Unvanquished,Conceived in Liberty,* and *The Proud and the Free*), Citadel, 1987.

The Pledge, Houghton Mifflin (Boston, MA), 1988.

The Confession of Joe Cullen, Houghton Mifflin (Boston, MA), 1989.

Being Red: A Memoir, Houghton Mifflin (Boston, MA), 1990.

The Trial of Abigail Goodman: A Novel, Crown (New York, NY), 1993.

War and Peace: Observations on Our Times, M. E. Sharpe (Armonk, NY), 1993.

Seven Days in June: A Novel of the American Revolution, Carol (Secaucus, NJ), 1994.

The Bridge Builder's Story, M. E. Sharpe (Armonk, NY), 1995.

An Independent Woman, Harcourt (New York, NY), 1997.

Redemption, Harcourt (New York, NY), 1999.

Greenwich, Harcourt (New York, NY), 2000.

Masuto Investigates (contains *Samantha* and *The Case of the One-Penny Orange;* also see below), ibooks (New York, NY), 2000.

Author of weekly column, *New York Observer,* 1989-92; also columnist for *Greenwich Time* and *Stamford Advocate.*

PLAYS

The Hammer, produced in New York, NY, 1950.

Thirty Pieces of Silver (produced in Melbourne, 1951), Blue Heron (New York, NY), 1954.

George Washington and the Water Witch, Bodley Head (London, England), 1956.

The Crossing, produced in Dallas, TX, 1962.

The Hill (screenplay; produced for television by A&E, 1999), Doubleday (New York, NY), 1964.

The Hessian, 1971.

David and Paula, produced in New York at American Jewish Theater, November 20, 1982.

Citizen Tom Paine: A Play in Two Acts (produced in Williamstown, MA, then in Washington, DC, at the John F. Kennedy Center for the Performing Arts, 1987), Houghton Mifflin (Boston, MA), 1986.

The Novelist (produced in Williamstown, MA, then Mamaroneck, NY, 1991), published as *The Novelist: A Romantic Portrait of Jane Austen,* Samuel French (New York, NY), 1992.

Also wrote for television series *Benjamin Franklin,* Columbia Broadcasting System (CBS), 1974 and *How the West Was Won,* American Broadcasting Companies (ABC), 1978-79.

NOVELS; UNDER PSEUDONYM E. V. CUNNINGHAM

Sylvia, Doubleday (New York, NY), 1960, published under name Howard Fast, Carol, 1992.

Phyllis, Doubleday (New York, NY), 1962.

Alice, Doubleday (New York, NY), 1963.

Shirley, Doubleday (New York, NY), 1963.

Lydia, Doubleday (New York, NY), 1964.

Penelope, Doubleday (New York, NY), 1965.

Helen, Doubleday (New York, NY), 1966.

Margie, Morrow (New York, NY), 1966.

Sally, Morrow (New York, NY), 1967, published under name Howard Fast, Chivers, 1994.

Samantha, Morrow (New York, NY), 1967.

Cynthia, Morrow (New York, NY), 1968.

The Assassin Who Gave Up His Gun, Morrow (New York, NY), 1969.

Millie, Morrow (New York, NY), 1973.

The Case of the One-Penny Orange, Holt (New York, NY), 1977.

The Case of the Russian Diplomat, Holt (New York, NY), 1978.

The Case of the Poisoned Eclairs, Holt (New York, NY), 1979.

The Case of the Sliding Pool, Delacorte (New York, NY), 1981.

The Case of the Kidnapped Angel, Delacorte (New York, NY), 1982.

The Case of the Angry Actress, Delacorte (New York, NY), 1984.

The Case of the Murdered Mackenzie, Delacorte (New York, NY), 1984.

The Wabash Factor, Doubleday (New York, NY), 1986.

Author of introduction for *Saving the Fragments: From Auschwitz to New York,* by Isabella Leitner and Irving A. Leitner, New American Library (New York, NY), 1985; *Red Scare in Court: New York versus the International Workers Order,* by Arthur J. Sabin, University of Pennsylvania Press (Philadelphia, PA), 1993; and *The Sculpture of Bette Fast,* M. E. Sharpe (Armonk, NY), 1995.

ADAPTATIONS: The film *Rachel and the Stranger,* RKO Radio Pictures, 1948, was based on the novels *Rachel* and *Neighbor Sam; Spartacus* was filmed in 1960 by Universal Pictures, directed by Stanley Kubrick and Anthony Mann, and starred Kirk Douglas, Laurence Olivier, Tony Curtis, Jean Simmons, Charles Laughton, and Peter Ustinov. Other works by Fast have been adapted to film, including *Man in the Middle,* Twentieth Century-Fox, 1964, based on his novel *The Winston Affair; Mirage,* based on a story he wrote under the pseudonym Walter Ericson, Universal, 1965; *Fallen Angel,* based on his novel of the same title; *Sylvia,* Paramount, 1965, based on the novel of the same title; *Penelope,* Metro-Goldwyn-Mayer (MGM), 1966, based on the novel of the same title

written under the pseudonym E. V. Cunningham; and *Jigsaw,* Universal, 1968, based on the screenplay for *Mirage* which was based on Fast's novel *Fallen Angel.* Writings by Fast have also been adapted for television, including *The Face of Fear,* CBS, 1971, based on the novel *Sally,* written under the pseudonym E. V. Cunningham; *What's a Nice Girl Like You. . . ?,* ABC, 1971, based on his novel *Shirley; 21 Hours at Munich,* ABC, 1976, based on a story by Fast; *The Immigrants,* syndicated, 1978, based on his novel of the same title; *Freedom Road,* National Broadcasting Corporation (NBC), 1979, based on the novel of the same title; *April Morning,* broadcast as a *Hallmark Hall of Fame* movie, CBS, 1988, based on the novel of the same title; and *The Crossing,* Arts and Entertainment (A&E), 2000, based on the novel of the same name. *The Crossing* was recorded on cassette, narrated by Norman Dietz, Recorded Books, 1988; *The Immigrant's Daughter* was recorded on cassette, narrated by Sandra Burr, Brilliance Corporation, 1991; *Spartacus* was adapted for a miniseries, USA cable network, 2002.

SIDELIGHTS: A prolific writer, Howard Fast published novels, plays, screenplays, stories, historical fiction, and biographies in a career that dated from the early days of the Great Depression until his death in 2003. Fast's works have been translated into eighty-two languages and have sold millions of copies worldwide. Some observers have ranked him as the most widely read writer of the twentieth century. *Los Angeles Times* contributor Elaine Kendall wrote: "For half a century, Fast's novels, histories, and biographies have appeared at frequent intervals, a moveable feast with a distinct political flavor." *Washington Post* correspondent Joseph McLellan found Fast's work "easy to read and relatively nourishing," adding that the author "demands little of the reader, beyond a willingness to keep turning the pages, and he supplies enough activity and suspense to make this exercise worthwhile."

The grandson of Ukrainian immigrants and son of a British mother, Fast was raised in New York City. His family struggled to make ends meet, so Fast went to work as a teen and found time to indulge his passion—writing—in his spare moments. His first published novel, *Two Valleys,* was released in 1933 when he was only eighteen. Thereafter Fast began writing full time, and within a decade he had earned a considerable reputation as an historical novelist with his realistic tales of American frontier life. *Dictionary of Literary Biography* contributor Anthony Manousos commented, "As a storyteller, Fast has his greatest appeal: his knack for sketching lifelike characters and creating brisk, action-packed narratives has always insured him a wide readership, despite occasionally slipshod writing."

Fast found himself drawn to the downtrodden peoples in America's history—the Cheyenne Indians and their tragic attempt to regain their homeland (*The Last Frontier*), the starving soldiers at Valley Forge (*Conceived in Liberty: A Novel of Valley Forge*), and African Americans trying to survive the Reconstruction era in the South (*Freedom Road*). In *Publishers Weekly,* John F. Baker called these works "books on which a whole generation of radicals was brought up." A *Christian Science Monitor* contributor likewise noted: "Human nature rather than history is Howard Fast's field. In presenting these harassed human beings without any heroics he makes us all the more respectful of the price paid for American liberty." *Freedom Road* in particular was praised by the nation's black leaders for its depiction of one race's struggle for liberation; the book became a best-seller and won the Schomberg Award for Race Relations in 1944.

During the World War II, Fast worked as a correspondent for several periodicals and for the Office of War Information. After the conflict ended he found himself at odds with the Cold War mentality developing in the United States. At the time Fast was a member of the Communist Party and a contributor of time and money to a number of antifascist causes. His writing during the period addressed such issues as the abuse of power, the suppression of labor unions, and communism as the basis for a utopian future. Works such as *Clarkton, My Glorious Brothers,* and *The Proud and the Free* were widely translated behind the Iron Curtain and earned Fast the International Peace Prize in 1954.

Baker noted that Fast's political views "made him for a time in the 1950s a pariah of the publishing world." The author was jailed for three months on a contempt of Congress charge for refusing to testify before the House Committee on Un-American Activities about his political views. Worse, he found himself blacklisted to such an extent that no publishing house would accept his manuscripts. Fast's persecution seemed ironic to some observers, because in the historical and biographical novels he had already published—like *Conceived in Liberty: A Novel of Valley Forge* and

The Unvanquished—as well as in his work for the Office of War Information, Fast emphasized the importance of freedom and illuminated the heroic acts that had built American society. As a correspondent for the radio program that would become the Voice of America, he was entrusted with the job of assuring millions of foreigners of the country's greatness and benevolence during World War II.

Fast makes the relatively unknown or forgotten history of the United States accessible to millions of Americans in books like *The Last Frontier,* in which he writes a fictional account of the real-life 1878 rebellion by a tribe of northern Cheyenne Indians. According to *Twentieth-Century Western Writers* contributor David Marion Holman, "Starved and denuded of pride, the small group of 300 men, women, and children illegally leave the reservation to return to their ancestral homeland. After eluding the U.S. cavalry for weeks . . . part of the tribe is eventually captured. As a result of their unwavering determination not to return to the Oklahoma reservation, the imprisoned Indians suffer from starvation and exposure, and are eventually massacred when they attempt a desperate escape." Because of this tragedy, the Secretary of the Interior eventually grants the rest of the tribe its freedom. Holman concluded, "Throughout the novel, Fast impresses upon the reader the inherent racism of American settlers' treatment of the Indian and points out the irony of double standards of freedom in a democracy."

Fast subsequently learned of Stalin's atrocities and broke his ties with the Communist Party in 1956; but he did not regret the decision he had made in 1944. His experience as the target of political persecution evoked some of his best and most popular works. It also led Fast to establish his own publishing house, the Blue Heron Press. In a discussion of Fast's fiction from 1944 through 1959, *Nation* correspondent Stanley Meisler contended that the "older writings must not be ignored. They document a unique political record, a depressing American waste. They describe a man who distorted his vision of America to fit a vision of communism, and then lost both." Fast published *Spartacus* under the Blue Heron imprint in 1951. A fictional account of a slave revolt in ancient Rome, *Spartacus* became a best-seller after it was made into a feature film in 1960.

Fast went on to publish five books chronicling the fictional Lavette family, beginning with *The Immigrants* in 1977. *The Immigrants* and its sequels represent some of his most popular work. The first book of the series is set mostly in San Francisco, where Dan Lavette, the son of an Italian fisherman, lives through the great earthquake in that city and goes on to build a fortune in the shipping business. The fates of an Irish family and a Chinese family are also entwined with those of the Lavettes. *The Immigrant's Daughter* relates the story of Barbara Lavette—Dan Lavette's daughter—and her political aspirations. Denise Gess in the *New York Times Book Review* called *The Immigrant's Daughter* "satisfying, old-fashioned storytelling" despite finding the novel occasionally "soap-operatic and uneven." Barbara Conaty, reviewing the novel in *Library Journal*, called Fast a "smooth and assured writer." A reviewer for *Publishers Weekly* commented that, "smoothly written, fast-paced, alive with plots and subplots, the story reads easily." With the publication of *The Immigrant's Daughter,* the series appeared to reach its conclusion, but in 1997, Fast surprised readers with a sixth installment in the saga, *An Independent Woman.* This book relates the final years of Barbara Lavette's life. Barbara has some things in common with her creator: like him, she is a reporter, a victim of McCarthyism, and a worker for civil rights. The twilight years of her life continue to be dynamic. She battles injustice and cancer, finds romance, and astonishes her family by marrying again. A *Kirkus Reviews* writer called *An Independent Woman* "a muted, somewhat puzzling, addenda to a lively (and successful) series."

Fast published another politically charged novel in 1989, with *The Confession of Joe Cullen.* Focusing on U.S. military involvement in Central America, *The Confession of Joe Cullen* is the story of a C.I.A. pilot who confesses to New York City police that, among other things, he murdered a priest in Honduras, and has been smuggling cocaine into the United States. Arguing that the conspiracy theory that implicates the federal government in drug trafficking and gun running has never been proved, Morton Kondracke in the *New York Times Book Review* had reservations about the "political propaganda" involved in *The Confession of Joe Cullen.* Robert H. Donahugh, however, highly recommended the novel in *Library Journal,* calling it "unexpected and welcome," and lauding both the "fast-moving" storyline and the philosophical probing into Catholicism. Denise Perry Donavin, in *Booklist,* found the politics suiting the characters "without lessening the pace of a powerful tale."

Fast focuses on another controversial subject, the issue of abortion, in his 1993 novel, *The Trial of Abigail Goodman.* As a *Publishers Weekly* critic noted, Fast views America's attitude toward abortion as "parochial," and is sympathetic to his protagonist, a college professor who has an abortion during the third trimester in a southern state with a retroactive law forbidding such acts. Critical reaction to the novel was mixed. Ray Olson in *Booklist* argued that "every anti-abortion character" is stereotyped, and that Fast "undermines . . . any pretensions to evenhandedness," and called the novel "an execrable work." A *Publishers Weekly* critic, on the other hand, found *The Trial of Abigail Goodman* "electrifying" and considered Fast "a master of courtroom pyrotechnics." Many critics, including Susan Dooley in the *Washington Post,* viewed the novel as too polemical, failing to flesh out the characters and the story. Dooley argued that Fast "has not really written a novel; his book is a tract for a cause, and like other similar endeavors, it concentrates more on making converts than creating characters." A reviewer for *Armchair Detective* concluded that the novel would have been much stronger if "there were some real sincerity and some well-expressed arguments from the antagonists." A *Rapport* reviewer commented, "Fast is more than capable of compelling character studies. There's a kernel of a powerful trial novel here, but this prestigious writer chooses not to flesh it out."

Fast returns to the topic of the American Revolution in *Seven Days in June: A Novel of the American Revolution.* A *Publishers Weekly* critic summarized: "Fictionalizing the experiences of British commanders, loyalists to the crown and a motley collection of American revolutionaries, Fast . . . fashions this dramatic look at a week of profound tension that will erupt [into] the battle of Bunker Hill." Some critics saw *Seven Days in June* as inferior to Fast's *April Morning,* also a novel about the American Revolution, which was considered by some to be a minor masterpiece. Charles Michaud in *Library Journal* found that *Seven Days* "is very readable pop history, but as a novel it is not as involving as . . . *April Morning.*" A *Kirkus Reviews* critic faulted the novel for repetitiveness and a disproportionate amount of focus on the sexual exploits of the British commanders, concluding that *Seven Days* "has a slipshod, slapdash feel, cluttered with hurried, lazy characterizations." The critic for *Publishers Weekly,* however, argued that the novel "ekes genuine suspense" and lauded Fast's "accomplished storytelling."

The Bridge Builder's Story tells of Scott Waring and his young bride, Martha, who honeymoon in Europe during the Nazi era and find themselves persecuted by Hitler's thuggish minions. After Martha is killed by the Gestapo, Scott makes his way to New York, where his ensuing sessions with a psychiatrist provide much of the narrative. Albert Wilheim, writing in *Library Journal,* thought that the novel tested "the limits of credibility," but praised Fast's "skillful narration." And Alice Joyce, in *Booklist,* opined that in *The Bridge Builder's Story* "Fast's remarkable prowess for story-telling" results in a "riveting tale, sure to satisfy readers."

Fast's time as a communist in Cold War America provided him with an extraordinary story to share in his autobiographical works, which included *Being Red: A Memoir.* Charles C. Nash of *Library Journal* called *Being Red* "indispensable to the . . . literature on America's terrifying postwar Red Scare." Fast once told *CA:* "There is no way to imagine war or to imagine jail or to imagine being a father or a mother. These things can only be understood if you live through them. Maybe that's a price that a writer should pay." Fast told Ken Gross in *People* that he wrote the book at the request of his son Jonathan, who wanted to share the story with his own children. Rhoda Koenig of *New York* magazine remarked that Fast's story is "a lively and gripping one," and that he "brings alive the days of parochial-school children carrying signs that read 'KILL A COMMIE FOR CHRIST.'"

With a critical eye, Ronald Radosh claimed in *Commentary* that *Being Red* contains information and perspectives that contradict portions of Fast's 1957 memoir, *The Naked God: The Writer and the Communist Party.* In Radosh's opinion, *Being Red* was the author's attempt to "rehabilitate" the Communist Party he had admonished in *The Naked God.* "Now, nearly thirty-five years later, it almost sounds as though Fast wants to end his days winning back the admiration of those unreconstructed Communists," Radosh asserted, even calling them "some of the noblest human beings I have ever known."

In 1999 Fast published *Redemption,* a suspense novel featuring Ike Goldman, a character who seems to be the author's alter ego. Goldman is a retired professor, highly intelligent, and the veteran of numerous political and social struggles. Driving through New York City one night, he sees a woman, Elizabeth, about to jump from a bridge. He talks Elizabeth out of her desperate act and, in the weeks that follow, finds himself falling in love with her. The two are planning to wed, when Elizabeth's ex-husband is found dead in suspicious circumstances, making her a suspect. Goldman does all he can to aid in her defense, but as the evidence against her mounts, his own doubts about her innocence increase. "The story moves along sedately in Fast's most relaxed style ever, with the author . . . plainly enjoying and indulging himself in this smoked salmon of romantic fantasy, adding plot dollops to keep the reader alert. . . . Fast's followers won't be disappointed," advised a contributor to *Kirkus Reviews.* The following year, Fast published *Greenwich,* a tale of eight people invited to a high-society dinner party in Greenwich, Connecticut. The comfortable life they enjoy masks an evil undercurrent; Fast suggests that guilt is widespread, and redemption is vital. Although faulting the book as stylistically "bland," a *Kirkus Reviews* writer nevertheless added: "It doesn't have to be a classic if it comes from the heart."

Fast also published a number of detective novels under the pseudonym E. V. Cunningham, for which he was awarded with a Prix de la Policia. Many of these novels feature a fictional Japanese-American detective named Masao Masuto, who works with the Beverly Hills Police Department. Fast told *Publishers Weekly,* "Critics can't stand my mainline books, maybe because they sell so well, [but] they love Cunningham. Even the *New Yorker* has reviewed him, and they've never reviewed me." In the *New York Times Book Review,* Newgate Callendar called detective Masuto "a well-conceived character whose further exploits should gain him a wide audience." *Toronto Globe and Mail* contributor Derrick Murdoch also found Masuto "a welcome addition to the lighter side of crime fiction." "Functional and efficient, Fast's prose is a machine in which plot and ideals mesh, turn and clash," *Los Angeles Times* contributor Elaine Kendall concluded, adding, "The reader is constantly being instructed, but the manner is so disarming and the hectic activity so absorbing that the didacticism seldom intrudes upon the entertainment."

Fast's voice interpreted America's past and present and helped shape its reputation at home and abroad. One of his own favorites among his novels, *April Morning,* has been standard reading in public schools for generations. The film *Spartacus* has become a popular classic, and *Being Red* offers an account of American history that Americans may never want to forget, whether or not they agree with Fast's perspectives. As Victor Howes commented in *Christian Science Monitor,* if Howard Fast "is a chronicler of some of mankind's most glorious moments, he is also a register of some of our more senseless deeds."

Upon Fast's death in 2003, Holly J. Morris wrote an obituary in the *U.S. News & World Report* recounting a story demonstrating that readers did not have to agree with Fast's politics. At a 1987 party, Pat Buckley, wife of William Buckley, told Fast she read all of his books. Fast was doubtful, noting that his beliefs were diametrically opposite to the staunch conservative couple. According to Morris, Buckley replied, "'Oh, I don't care about that—I love your books.'" In a *Knight-Ridder/Tribune News Service* obituary appearing in the *Chicago Tribune,* Ron Grossman noted that Fast never enjoyed the same popularity he did as a young writer, but his books will survive. Grossman opined, "Years from now, some young person, trapped in the poverty Fast knew, will find his books, preserved in those heavy library bindings, on a shelf somewhere. He or she will realize that others have made life's difficulty journey before them, while reading that remarkable passage in *Freedom Road* where those anxious women, who had so recently been slaves, see a distant sign of a better world to come." Brad Hooper perhaps summed up Fast's popularity best in *Booklist,* commenting, "The bottom line is that when it comes to reading Howard Fast, we continue to understand and appreciate that, simply, he could tell a darn good story."

BIOGRAPHICAL AND CRITICAL SOURCES:

BOOKS

Authors and Artists for Young Adults, Volume 16, Thomson Gale (Detroit, MI), 1995.
Contemporary Authors Autobiography Series, Volume 18, Thomson Gale (Detroit, MI), 1994.
Contemporary Literary Criticism, Thomson Gale (Detroit, MI), Volume 23, 1983, Volume 131, 2000.
Contemporary Novelists, 6th edition, St. James Press (Detroit, MI), 1996.
Contemporary Popular Writers, St. James Press (Detroit, MI), 1997.
Dictionary of Literary Biography, Volume 9: *American Novelists, 1910-1945,* Thomson Gale (Detroit, MI), 1981.

MacDonald, Andrew, *Howard Fast: A Critical Companion,* Greenwood (Westport, CT), 1996.
Meyer, Hershel, D., *History and Conscience: The Case of Howard Fast,* Anvil-Atlas (New York, NY), 1958.
St. James Guide to Crime and Mystery Writers, 4th edition, St. James Press (Detroit, MI), 1996.
St. James Guide to Young Adult Writers, 2nd edition, St. James Press (Detroit, MI), 1999.
Twentieth-Century Romance and Historical Writers, 3rd edition, St. James Press (Detroit, MI), 1994.
Twentieth-Century Western Writers, St. James Press (Detroit, MI), 1991.

PERIODICALS

Antioch Review, winter, 1993, review of *Sylvia,* p. 156.
Armchair Detective, spring, 1994, review of *The Trial of Abigail Goodman,* p. 218.
Atlantic Monthly, September, 1944; June, 1970.
Best Sellers, February 1, 1971; September 1, 1973; January, 1979; November, 1979.
Booklist, June 15, 1989, p. 1739; July, 1993, review of *The Trial of Abigail Goodman,* p. 1916; October 1, 1995, review of *The Bridge Builder's Story,* p. 252; May 1, 1997, review of *An Independent Woman,* p. 1460; February 15, 1999, review of *Redemption,* p. 1003; February 1, 2000, review of *Greenwich,* p. 996.
Book Week, May 9, 1943.
Chicago Tribune, April 21, 1987; January 20, 1991, section 14, p. 7.
Christian Science Monitor, July 8, 1939; August 23, 1972, p. 11; November 7, 1977, p. 18; November 1, 1991, p. 12; August 12, 1999, review of *Redemption,* p. 20.
Commentary, March, 1991, pp. 62-64.
Detroit News, October 31, 1982.
Entertainment Weekly, August 1, 1997, review of *An Independent Woman,* p. 69; July 30, 1999, review of *Redemption,* p. 66.
Globe and Mail (Toronto, Ontario, Canada), September 15, 1984; March 1, 1986; July 17, 1999, review of *Redemption,* p. D14.
Kirkus Reviews, June 15, 1993, review of *The Trial of Abigail Goodman,* p. 739; June 15, 1994, review of *Seven Days in June,* p. 793; July 15, 1995, review of *The Bridge Builder's Story,* p. 968; June 15, 1997, review of *An Independent Woman,* p. 909; May 1, 1999, review of *Redemption,* p. 650.

Library Journal, November 15, 1978; September 15, 1985, p. 92; May 15, 1989, p. 88; October 1, 1990, p. 96; August, 1991, p. 162; July, 1994, review of *Seven Days in June,* p. 126; September 1, 1995, review of *The Bridge Builder's Story,* p. 206; February 1, 1997, p. 112; June 15, 1997, review of *An Independent Woman,* p. 96; May 15, 1999, review of *Redemption,* p. 125.

Los Angeles Times, November 11, 1982; November 11, 1985; November 21, 1988.

Los Angeles Times Book Review, December 9, 1990.

Nation, April 5, 1952; May 30, 1959.

New Republic, August 17, 1942, p. 203; August 14, 1944; November 4, 1978; May 27, 1992.

New Statesman, August 8, 1959.

New York, November 5, 1990, pp. 124-125.

New Yorker, July 1, 1939; May 1, 1943.

New York Herald Tribune Book Review, July 21, 1963.

New York Herald Tribune Books, July 27, 1941, p. 3.

New York Times, October 15, 1933; June 25, 1939; April 25, 1943; February 3, 1952; September 24, 1984; February 9, 1987, p. C16; March 10, 1987; April 21, 1991, pp. 20-21; October 23, 1991, p. C19; November 19, 1993, p. A2.

New York Times Book Review, October 13, 1933; April 25, 1943; February 3, 1952; March 4, 1962; July 14, 1963; February 6, 1966; October 2, 1977, p. 24; October 30, 1977; May 14, 1978; June 10, 1979; September 15, 1985, p. 24; March 29, 1987, p. 22; August 20, 1989, p. 23; February 28, 1993, review of *The Jews: Story of a People,* p. 32; October 22, 1995, review of *The Bridge Builder's Story,* p. 37.

People, January 28, 1991, pp. 75-79.

Publishers Weekly, August 6, 1979; April 1, 1983; July 19, 1985, p. 48; November 28, 1986, p. 66; July 22, 1988, p. 41; June 30, 1989, p. 84; June 21, 1993, review of *The Trial of Abigail Goodman,* p. 83; July 11, 1994, review of *Seven Days in June,* p. 66; September 4, 1995, review of *The Bridge Builder's Story,* p. 49; May 26, 1997, review of *An Independent Woman,* p. 64; May 17, 1999, review of *Redemption,* p. 54.

Rapport, number 1, 1994, review of *The Trial of Abigail Goodman,* p. 38.

Reference and Research Book News, November, 1995, review of *Freedom Road,* p. 69; February, 1998, review of *The Unvanquished,* p. 150.

Saturday Review, March 8, 1952; January 22, 1966; September 17, 1977.

Saturday Review of Literature, July 1, 1939; July 26, 1941, p. 5; May 1, 1943; December 24, 1949.

Science and Society, spring, 1993, review of *Being Red,* p. 86.

Time, November 6, 1977.

Times Literary Supplement, November 11, 1939.

Tribune Books (Chicago, IL), February 8, 1987, pp. 6-7.

Washington Post, October 4, 1979; September 26, 1981; September 25, 1982; September 3, 1985; February 9, 1987; March 3, 1987; September 6, 1993, p. C2.

Washington Post Book World, October 23, 1988; November 25, 1990; November 17, 1996, p. 12; August 8, 1999, review of *Redemption,* p. 4.

ONLINE

New York Times, http://www.nytimes.com/ (March 13, 2003).

OBITUARIES, AND OTHER SOURCES:

PERIODICALS

Booklist, May 15, 2003, Brad Hooper, "A Tribute to Howard Fast," p. 1639.*

Chicago Tribune (Knight-Ridder/Tribune News Service), March 18, 2003, Ron Grossman, "Howard Fast, The Last of the Proletarian Writers."

Los Angeles Times, March 14, 2003, p. B13.

New York Times, March 13, 2003, p. C12.

Times (London, England), March 20, 2003.

U.S. News & World Report, March 24, 2003, Holly J. Morris, "The Steadfast Howard Fast," p. 8.*

*   *   *

FINE, Jane
   See ZIEFERT, Harriet

*   *   *

FITCH, Noel Riley 1937-

PERSONAL: Born December 24, 1937, in New Haven, CT; daughter of John Eckel (a college president) and Dorcas Tarr Riley (a homemaker); married Philip Arthur Fitch (an educator), May 29, 1958 (divorced May 6, 1986); married Albert Sonnenfeld, August 23,

1987; children: (first marriage) Gailyn. *Education:* Northwest Nazarene College, B.A., 1959; Washington State University, M.A., 1965, Ph.D., 1969.

ADDRESSES: Home and office—11829 Mayfield Ave., Los Angeles, CA 90049. *Agent*—Kris Dahl, ICM, 40 West 57th St., New York, NY 10019. *E-mail*—noelriley@aol.com.

CAREER: Moscow Junior High School, Moscow, ID, teacher of language arts, 1959-62; Moscow Senior High School, Moscow, teacher of English, 1962-63; Washington State University, teaching assistant, 1963-66, part-time instructor, 1967-68; Eastern Nazarene College, assistant professor, 1966-67, 1968-71; California State University, San Diego, part-time associate professor, 1976-78; Point Loma College, professor of literature, 1971-87, chair of department of literature and modern languages, 1982-85. University of Southern California, lecturer, 1986—; American University of Paris, lecturer, beginning 1987. *Los Angeles Times* Book Awards, member of biography selection committee, 1990-92; cofounder of Professional Biographers Group, 1993.

MEMBER: PEN, Authors Guild, Authors League of America, American Association of University Professors (chapter president, 1970-71), Modern Language Association, American Studies Association, California Teachers Association (member of executive board and faculty affairs chairperson, 1973-75), Phi Delta Lambda (international president, 1970-72).

AWARDS, HONORS: Award from Outstanding Young Women of America, 1968; WHO Award, California Teachers Association, 1975; National Endowment for the Humanities senior fellowship, 1980-81; American Philosophical Society research grant, 1981; nominee, award for best history published in 1983, *Los Angeles Times,* for *Sylvia Beach and the Lost Generation: A History of Literary Paris in the Twenties and Thirties;* American Council of Learned Societies grant, 1984; National Endowment for the Humanities travel grants, 1985, 1986; named Alumna of the Year, Northwest Nazarene College, 1985; Grand Prix des Lectrices de Elle, 1995, for *Anaïs;* finalist, Literary Food Writing, International Association of Culinary Professionals, 1997, for *Appetite for Life.*

WRITINGS:

Sylvia Beach and the Lost Generation: A History of Literary Paris in the Twenties and Thirties, Norton (New York, NY), 1983.

(Editor, with Richard W. Etulain) *Faith and Imagination: Essays on Evangelicals and Literature,* Far West Books (Albuquerque, NM), 1985.
Literary Cafés of Paris, Starrhill Press, 1989.
(Author of introduction) *In Transition: A Paris Anthology,* Doubleday (New York, NY), 1990.
Walks in Hemingway's Paris: A Guide to Paris for the Literary Traveler, St. Martin's Press (New York, NY), 1990.
Anaïs: The Erotic Life of Anaïs Nin, Little, Brown (Boston, MA), 1993.
Appetite for Life: The Biography of Julia Child, Doubleday (New York, NY), 1997.

Contributor of chapters to books, including *Dictionary of Literary Biography,* Volume 4: *Americans in Paris, 1920-1939,* Thomson Gale (Detroit, MI), 1980; *Faith and Imagination,* Far West Books (Albuquerque, NM), 1985; *James Joyce: The Augmented Ninth,* edited by Bernard Benstock, Syracuse University Press (Syracuse, NY), 1988; *Lesbian Texts and Contexts: Radical Revisions,* edited by Karla Jay and Joanne Glasgow, New York University Press (New York, NY), 1990; *American Writers Supplement III,* Scribner (New York, NY), 1993; *Significant Others: Creativity and Intimate Partnership,* edited by Whitney Chadwick and Isabelle de Courtivron, Thames & Hudson (London, England), 1993; *A Living of Words: American Women in Print Culture,* edited by Susan Albertine and Elizabeth Horan, University of Tennessee Press (Knoxville, TN), 1995; and *Anaïs Nin: A Book of Mirrors,* edited by Paul Herron, Sky Blue Press, 1996. Contributor of articles to journals and periodicals, including *Michigan Quarterly Review, Areté, James Joyce Literary Supplement, Journal of Library Science,* and *Research Studies.*

Author's works have been translated into Japanese, French, Italian, Portuguese, German, Italian, Polish, and Spanish.

WORK IN PROGRESS: Grand Literary Cafés of Europe, New Holland (London, England), 2006; *Paris Café: The Select Café,* illustrated by Rick Tulka; and a biography of Louison O'Morphi.

SIDELIGHTS: Noel Riley Fitch once told *CA:* "My abiding interest is in the English-speaking artist in Paris during the first fifty years of the twentieth century." Fitch has written several books that bear witness to this abiding interest. When *Sylvia Beach and the Lost Generation,* her study of the influence of an American bookseller and publisher on the most significant writers of the early twentieth century, appeared in 1983, reviewers agreed that the author had made a major contribution to literary history. Most scholars were well aware of American expatriate writers in Paris in the 1920s and 1930s, writers whose numbers included such major figures as Sherwood Anderson, John Dos Passos, T. S. Eliot, F. Scott Fitzgerald, Ernest Hemingway, Ezra Pound, Gertrude Stein, and William Carlos Williams, among others. Few, however, had been aware of the importance of Sylvia Beach, the owner of the English-language bookstore Shakespeare and Company. In telling Beach's story, Fitch cast a new perspective on Paris literary life as a whole. As Fiona MacCarthy, writing in the London *Times,* put it, "We have seen them all before, and actually pretty often, as in a favourite and rather faded home movie. But Sylvia Beach is new, and as the centre of Professor Fitch's copiously researched narrative, she gives that whole familiar scene an unexpected sharpness." *New York Times* contributor Anatole Broyard went one step further, claiming that *Sylvia Beach and the Lost Generation* "is probably the best and most complete history of that important period."

Fitch relates the story of Beach, a remarkable woman who escaped the constraints of her Victorian upbringing to live among writers and intellectuals in Paris. Beach's English-language bookstore was a particularly important home for literary women such as Katherine Anne Porter, Anaïs Nin, H. D., and Djuna Barnes, who, with Beach, participated in the salon life of Paris. Broyard calls Shakespeare and Company "perhaps the most famous and influential bookstore in history."

Beach was also a friend and supporter of Irish writer James Joyce, whose major novel *Ulysses* she published when others found it obscene and unpublishable. When *Sylvia Beach* appeared, reviewers were particularly appreciative of the new light Fitch shed on that aspect of Joyce's literary history. Besides being a portrait of an unusual woman and of a seminal time in literary history, Fitch's book, according to Broyard, is "a lively collection of anecdotes" that is, in addition to its other virtues, simply a pleasure to read.

Fitch continued her exploration of American literary life in Paris with a number of other books on that period, including the well-received *Walks in Hemingway's Paris.* A reviewer for the *Los Angeles Times Book Review* found the book a useful guide to all who have ever wondered about where Hemingway and his friends lived, ate, and socialized. Another prominent Paris personality is investigated in Fitch's 1993 work, *Anaïs: The Erotic Life of Anaïs Nin.* The volume analyzes the novelist and diarist's own writings to create an in-depth look at the woman known for her numerous and unconventional love affairs as well as for her work. John Peter Applebranch, reviewing *Anaïs* in the *San Diego Weekly Reader,* praised Fitch's detailed research, calling it "detective work of the first order, carried out with relentless skill."

Fitch is also the author of *Appetite for Life: The Biography of Julia Child,* a departure from her usual subject matter and a work that engendered some heated commentary from critics. For this work, Fitch drew upon interviews with Julia Child, who has often been cited as the most influential culinary expert on the American scene in the second half of the twentieth century, as well as diaries, letters exchanged by Child and her husband of many years, Paul Child, countless magazine articles and reviews, and reminiscences supplied by Child's friends and colleagues. The story Fitch tells is one of American enterprise triumphing over what at first appears to be inauspicious material. Born Julia McWilliams to wealthy parents in California, the 6'2" young woman was in danger of spending her life as a partygoer when she was galvanized by the onset of World War II into joining the British Office of Strategic Services (OSS), which stationed her in China. There she met Paul Child, an epicure ten years her senior; the two married after the war, and when they traveled to France, Julia Child found the inspiration of her life in the gustatory delights to be savored there. She enrolled in the famed Cordon Bleu cooking school in Paris and within a few years had started her own school and ventured upon the research for the first volume of her pivotal series of books on French cooking for American cooks. Child's rise to fame, cast as a by-product of her Public Television series, which seemed to prove that if someone as awkward as Child could master the techniques of French cooking then anyone could, as well as the continuing success of her marriage, are detailed in a "meticulously researched and satisfying biography," according to Thomas Fields-Meyer writing in *People.*

Fitch told *CA:* "Writing biography involves a very personal journey with your subject. It is like living with a person for years. And the biography has many tensions: the struggle of judging someone's life and actions, but not sitting in judgment; respecting the dead and yet telling the truth; invading people's privacy yet knowing I am the keeper of the record; getting inside someone's skin yet retaining my own mind; having empathy and yet, as much as possible, remaining uninvolved and objective. Transcending my own being in order to capture another's life and illuminate it from within and yet maintaining my own emotional identity. This tension was most difficult with Julia Child, whom I knew."

BIOGRAPHICAL AND CRITICAL SOURCES:

PERIODICALS

Booklist, August, 1997, p. 1843.
Chicago Tribune, October 24, 1993.
Economist, December 13, 1997, p. S13.
Entertainment Weekly, October 17, 1997, p. 68.
Idaho Statesman, September 30, 1993, p. D1.
Library Journal, September 13, 1997, p. 82.
Los Angeles Times Book Review, July 10, 1983, p. 1; October 23, 1983; December 9, 1990, p. 6; December 26, 1993, p. 6; November 9, 1997, p. 10.
Nation, December 15, 1997, pp. 30-34.
New Yorker, October 13, 1997, pp. 86, 88-91.
New York Times, June 18, 1983.
New York Times Book Review, July 31, 1983; October 17, 1993; October 26, 1997, p. 13.
People, November 3, 1997, p. 31.
Publishers Weekly, April 22, 1983, p. 90; June 28, 1993, p. 61; August 25, 1997, p. 51.
San Diego Weekly Reader, September 30, 1993, p. 53.
Times (London, England), March 15, 1984.
Times Literary Supplement, May 25, 1984, p. 590.
Washington Post Book World, June 12, 1983, p. 3; October 26, 1997, p. 1.

ONLINE

Noel Riley Fitch Web site, http://www.noelrileyfitch. com (February 15, 2005).

* * *

FLEUR, Paul
    See POHL, Frederik

FLEW, Antony G(arrard) N(ewton) 1923-

PERSONAL: Born February 11, 1923, in London, England; son of Robert Newton (a minister) and Alice Winifred (Garrard) Flew; married Annis Ruth Harty Donnison (a school teacher); children: Harriet Rebecca, Joanna Naomi. *Education:* St. John's College, Oxford, M.A. (with first-class honors), 1948. *Politics:* Conservative. *Hobbies and other interests:* Travel, walking, house maintenance.

ADDRESSES: Home—26 Alexandra Rd., Reading RG1 5PD, England.

CAREER: Oxford University, Christ Church, Oxford, England, lecturer in philosophy, 1949-50; University of Aberdeen, Aberdeen, Scotland, lecturer in moral philosophy, 1950-54; University of Keele, Keele, England, professor of philosophy, 1954-71; University of Calgary, Calgary, Alberta, Canada, professor of philosophy, 1972-73; University of Reading, Reading, England, professor of philosophy, 1973-82, professor emeritus, 1982—. Visiting professor at New York University, 1958, Swarthmore College, 1961, University of Pittsburgh, 1965, University of Malawi, 1967, University of Maryland, 1970, State University of New York at Buffalo, 1971, and University of California—San Diego, 1978-79; York University (Toronto, Ontario, Canada), 1983, 1986, and 1985; Gavin David Young Lecturer, University of Adelaide, 1963. Distinguished research fellow, Social Philosophy and Policy Center, Bowling Green State University, part-time, 1983-91. Has participated in talks and discussions on radio and television in England, Zambia, Australia, Canada, and United States. *Military service:* Royal Air Force, Intelligence, 1943-45.

MEMBER: Mind Association, Aristotelian Society, Rationalist Press Association (vice-president, 1972-88), Freedom Association (member of council), Voluntary Euthanasia Society (chairman of executive committee, 1976-79).

AWARDS, HONORS: John Locke Prize, Oxford University, 1948; D.Litt., University of Keele, 1974; Laureate of the Academy of Humanism, 1983; In Praise of Reason Award, 1985; Richard M. Weaver Award, 1998; James Wilbur Award, 1999; Schlarbaum Laureate, 2001.

WRITINGS:

A New Approach to Psychical Research, C. A. Watts (London, England), 1953.

Hume's Philosophy of Belief, Humanities Press (New York, NY), 1961.

God and Philosophy, Hutchinson (London, England), 1966, Harcourt (New York, NY), 1967, revised edition published as *God: A Philosophical Critique,* Open Court (La Salle, IL), 1984.

Evolutionary Ethics, St. Martin's Press (New York, NY), 1967.

An Introduction to Western Philosophy, Bobbs-Merrill (Indianapolis, IN), 1971.

Crime Punishment and Disease?, Barnes & Noble (New York, NY), 1973, with a new introduction, Transaction Publishers (New Brunswick, NJ), 2002.

Thinking about Thinking, Collins, 1975, published as *Thinking Straight,* Prometheus Books (Buffalo, NY), 1977.

The Presumption of Atheism (philosophical essays), Barnes & Noble (New York, NY), 1976, published as *God, Freedom and Immortality,* Prometheus Books (Buffalo, NY), 1984.

Sociology, Equality and Education (philosophical essays), Barnes & Noble (New York, NY), 1976.

(With T. B. Warren) *The Warren-Flew Debate on the Existence of God,* National Christian Press (Jonesboro, AR), 1977.

A Rational Animal (philosophical essays), Clarendon Press (London, England), 1978.

Philosophy: An Introduction, Hodder & Stoughton (London, England), 1979.

The Politics of Procrustes (philosophical essays), Temple Smith, 1981.

Thinking about Social Thinking, Basil Blackwell (New York, NY), 1985.

Darwinian Evolution, Granada Paladin (London, England), 1985, republished with a new introduction, Transaction (New Brunswick, NJ), 1997.

David Hume: Philosopher of Moral Science, Basil Blackwell (Oxford, England), 1986.

(With Godfrey Vesey) *Agency and Necessity,* Basil Blackwell (Oxford, England), 1987.

The Logic of Mortality, Basil Blackwell (Oxford, England), 1987, republished with a new introduction as *Merely Mortal?: Can You Survive Your Own Death?,* Prometheus (Amherst, NY), 2001.

Power to the Parents: Reversing Educational Decline, Sherwood (London, England), 1987.

Equality in Liberty and Justice, Routledge (New York, NY), 1989.

(With Terry Miethe) *Does God Exist?: A Believer and an Atheist Debate,* HarperSanFrancisco (San Francisco, CA), 1991.

Aetheistic Humanism, Prometheus Books (Buffalo, NY), 1993.

Shephard's Warning: Setting Schools Back on Course, Adam Smith Institute (London, England), 1994.

How to Think Straight: An Introduction to Critical Reasoning, Prometheus Books (Amherst, NY), 1998.

Philosophical Essays, Rowman & Littlefield Publishers (Lanham, MD), 1998.

(With William Lane Craig and Terry Miethe) *Does God Exist?: The Craig-Flew Debate,* Ashgate (Burlington, VT), 2003.

Social Life and Moral Judgement, Transaction (New Brunswick, NJ), 2003.

EDITOR

(And author of introduction) *Logic and Language,* Humanities (New York, NY), Volume 1, 1951, Volume 2, 1953.

(With A. C. MacIntyre) *New Essays in Philosophical Theology,* Macmillan (London, England), 1955.

Essays in Conceptual Analysis, Macmillan (London, England), 1956.

(And author of introduction) *Hume on Human Nature and Understanding,* Collier, 1962.

(And author of introduction) *Body, Mind and Death,* Macmillan (London, England), 1964.

(And author of introduction) *Malthus: An Essay on the Principle of Population,* Penguin (Harmondsworth, England), 1971.

(And contributor) *A Dictionary of Philosophy,* Macmillan (London, England), 1979.

Philosophical Problems of Parapsychology, Prometheus Books (Buffalo, NY), 1987.

(And author of introduction) *Hume's Inquiry Concerning Human Understanding,* Open Court (La Salle, IL), 1988.

(And author of introduction) *Hume's Writings on Religion,* Open Court (La Salle, IL), 1992.

Contributor to books, including *Religious Belief and Philosophical Thought,* edited by W. P. Alston, Harcourt (New York, NY), 1963; *Philosophy and*

Parapsychology, edited by J. K. Ludwig, Prometheus Books (Buffalo, NY), 1977; *Sidney Hook: Philosopher of Democracy and Humanism,* edited by P. Kurtz, Prometheus Books (Buffalo, NY), 1983; *Philosophy in the United Kingdom Today,* edited by S. Shanker, Croom Helm, 1986; and *Reincarnation: Fact or Fable,* edited by A. Berger and J. Berger, HarperCollins (New York, NY), 1991.

Flew's works have been translated into other languages, including Spanish, Portuguese, Italian, German, Welsh, Danish, Hebrew, and Japanese.

Contributor to encyclopedias, including *Encyclopaedia of Philosophy, Encyclopaedia Britannica,* and *Collier's Encyclopaedia.* Also contributor to professional journals in England, Germany, Australia, and the United States. Member of editorial board, *Sociological Review,* 1954-71; past member of editorial advisory board, *Question;* consulting editor, *Humanist,* 1972—, *Journal of Critical Analysis,* beginning 1974, *Hume Studies,* 1976-1995, and *Journal of Libertarian Studies,* 1976—.

SIDELIGHTS: Antony Flew is a widely recognized British philosopher. His father was a clergyman, and Flew developed a strong interest in religion at a young age. Many of his books and writings center on religious philosophy, though he also writes about psychoanalysis, psychical research, crime and evolutionary ethics. As a newly graduated scholar from Oxford University, Flew became involved with what was widely described and denounced as "Oxford linguistic philosophy." This was supposed to be merely verbal and therefore trivializing. But that it was not, at least in his case, can be seen from the fact that he began work there on what later became his Gifford Lectures on the question of a future life.

Flew calls himself a secular humanist, which means that he looks for facts to support religious, political or social ideas and rejects the notion of "just having faith." In 1993, his collection of essays, *Atheistic Humanism,* looked at religious beliefs and the human condition within this framework. The book also covers topics such as mental illness, racism, and communism. A critic for *Free Inquiry* found it to have "penetrating insights" which gave readers "an opportunity to ponder and enjoy the wisdom of one of the major secular thinkers of our time."

His 2000 book *Merely Mortal? Can You Survive Your Own Death?* is a reprint of a 1987 work, *The Logic of Mortality,* in which Flew addresses the question of a future life. A reviewer for *Atheism.com* found Flew's argument to be neither "easy (nor) simple to understand" and Joseph Shaw of the *Times Literary Supplement* thought that the author's reasoning "is rarely made sufficiently clear." However, a critic for *Secweb.org* felt Flew did a fine job of analyzing the various ways philosophers have tried to explain life after death. The reviewer called *Merely Mortal* "a profoundly thoughtful book" that highlights a "complex issue with logical rigor and engaging wit."

BIOGRAPHICAL AND CRITICAL SOURCES:

PERIODICALS

Capital Times, February 23, 1998, Todd R. Svanoe, "What Happened to Make the God Debate So Godawful?," p. 2A.
Free Inquiry, summer, 1994, review of *Aetheistic Humanism,* p. 64.
Religious Studies, June, 1993, Peter Byrne, review of *David Hume: Philosopher of Moral Science,* p. 274.
Times Literary Supplement, November 23, 2001, Joseph Shaw, "Soul Survivor," p. 32.

ONLINE

Agnosticism/Atheism, http://atheism.about.com/ (June 21, 2002), "Surviving Death."
Ludwig von Mises Institute Web Site, http://www.mises.org/ (June 21, 2002), "Antony G. N. Flew, 2001 Schlarbaum Laureate."
Secular Web, http://www.secweb.org/ (July 23, 2002), review of *Merely Mortal?: Can You Survive Your Own Death?*
Theology Today, http://theologytoday.ptsem.edu/ (July 23, 2002), review of *Does God Exist?: The Craig-Flew Debate.*

FRATIANNI, Michele (Ugo) 1941-

PERSONAL: Born March 7, 1941, in Florence, Italy; immigrated to the United States, 1964; son of Giuseppe and Nannina (Pistilli) Fratianni; married Linda Kubiac, September 29, 1963; children: John, Paul, Claudia. *Education:* Duca d'Aosta (Florence, Italy), graduated, 1961; Ohio State University, B.A. (cum laude) and M.A., both 1967, Ph.D., 1971. *Hobbies and other interests:* Running, swimming, hiking, skiing, music, travel.

ADDRESSES: Home—4593 North Maple Grove Rd., Bloomington, IN 47401. *Office*—Department of Business Economics and Public Policy, Kelley School of Business, Indiana University—Bloomington, 10th and Fee Lane, Bloomington, IN 47405; fax: 812-855-3354. *E-mail*—fratiann@indiana.edu.

CAREER: Indiana University—Bloomington, assistant professor, 1971-75, associate professor of business economics and public policy, 1975-76; Commission of the European Communities, Brussels, Belgium, economic advisor, 1976-79; Indiana University—Bloomington, professor, 1979-93, AMOCO faculty fellow, 1993-97, W. George Pinnell Professor of Business Economics and Public Policy, 1998—, department chair, 1997—, director of business program at University of Maastricht, 2001. Catholic University of Louvain, visiting professor, 1973—; Catholic University of Milan, visiting professor, 1985-86; University of Rome, Università Sapienza, visiting professor, 1991; Free University of Berlin, Bundesbank Professor of International Monetary Economics, 1995; Marquette University, Allis-Chalmers Distinguished Professor of International Economics, 1995; University of Brescia, member of finance faculty, 2002; guest speaker at many other institutions, including Carnegie-Mellon University, Claremont Graduate School, Erasmus University, Harvard University, Johns Hopkins University, London School of Economics and Political Science, London, University of Aberdeen, University of Athens, and University of Bucharest. International Economic Center, Rome, Italy, founding member, 1988—; UniversEd, president, 1999; Center for Economics and Policy Studies, Turin, Italy, member of board of directors. *Open Economies Review,* founder and managing editor, 1990—. Argus Research Corp., affiliate, 1974-76; Confindustria, member of scientific board, 1976-79; President's Council of Economic Advisors, senior staff economist, 1981-82; International Baltic Economic Commission, head of Monetary and Fiscal Policy Committee, 1991-92; Nemetria of Foligno, member of scientific board, 1997—; consultant to governments of Italy, Estonia, Latvia, Lithuania, and Vietnam, and to banks, corporations, educational institutions, and foundations.

MEMBER: International Trade and Finance Association (member of board of directors), American Economic Association, Mont Pelerin Society, Phi Beta Kappa, Beta Gamma Sigma.

AWARDS, HONORS: Awards from International Business Research Institute, 1971, 1972, 1973, and Comitato Nazionale delle Ricerche, 1972; Medal of the President of the Italian Republic, 1982; named ufficiale della Repubblica italiana, 1982; Gold Medal, Pio Manzu' Center, 1982; senior Fulbright fellow, 1985-86; fellow, Indiana Center for Global Business, 1989; Scanno Prize for economics, 1991; grants from Center for German and European Studies, University of California—Berkeley, 1991-92, 1993-94; St. Vincent Prize for economics, 1992; fellow, Fondo Interbancario di Tutela dei Depositi, Rome, 1993; British Academy visiting professor, 1994.

WRITINGS:

(With Paolo Savona) *La Liquidita' internazionale* (title means "International Liquidity"), Il Mulino (Bologna, Italy), 1972.

Inflazione, produzione e politica economica in Italia (title means "Inflation, Output, and Economic Policy in Italy"), Franco Angeli (Milan, Italy), 1975.

(With G. LaMalfa and B. Trezza) *L'economia italiana, 1974-1975* (title means "The Italian Economy, 1974-1975"), Franco Angeli (Milan, Italy), 1975.

(With P. Armani, M. DeCecco, and G. LaMalfa) *L'economia italiana, 1975-1977* (title means "The Italian Economy, 1975-1977"), Franco Angeli (Milan, Italy), 1976.

(With John C. Pattison) *Le organizzazioni economiche internazionali* (title means "International Economic Organizations"), Franco Angeli (Milan, Italy), 1977.

(With G. Basevi, M. DeCecco, and G. LaMalfa) *L'economic italiana, 1976-1978* (title means "The Italian Economy, 1976-1978"), Franco Angeli (Milan, Italy), 1977.

(With others) *L'economic italiana, 1977-1979* (title means "The Italian Economy, 1977-1979"), Franco Angeli (Milan, Italy), 1978.

(Editor) *One Money for Europe,* Macmillan (London, England), 1978.

(With Paul DeGrauwe and Mustapha Nabli) *Money, Output, and Exchange Rates: The European Experience,* Macmillan (London, England), 1985.

(With Franco Spinelli) *La storia monetaria d'Italia, 1860-1980,* Mondadori (Milan, Italy), 1991, revised translation published as *A Monetary History of Italy,* Cambridge University Press (New York, NY), 1997.

(Editor, with C. Wilborg and T. D. Willett) *Financial Regulation and Monetary Arrangements after 1992,* North-Holland Publishing (New York, NY), 1991.

(Editor, with Dominick Salvatore) *Handbook of Monetary Policy,* Greenwood Press (Westport, CT), 1992.

(With Jürgen von Hagen) *The European Monetary System and European Monetary Union,* Westview Press (Boulder, CO), 1992.

(With Jürgen von Hagen and Christopher Waller) *The Maastricht Way to EMU,* International Finance Section, Department of Economics, Princeton University (Princeton, NJ), 1992.

(Editor, with Dominick Salvatore) *Monetary Policy in Developed Economies,* Greenwood Press (Westport, CT), 1993.

(Editor, with Dominick Salvatore and Jürgen von Hagen) *Macroeconomic Policy in Open Economies,* Greenwood Press (Westport, CT), 1997.

(Acting editor) Horst Entorf, editor, *Mismatch Explanations of European Unemployment: A Critical Evaluation,* Springer (New York, NY), 1998.

(Editor, with Dominick Salvatore and Paolo Savona) *Ideas for the Future of the International Monetary System,* Kluwer Academic (Boston, MA), 1999.

(With Franco Spinelli) *Storia monetaria d'Italia: Lira e politica monetaria dall'unitá all'Unione europea,* ETAS (Milan, Italy), 2001.

(Editor, with Paolo Savona and John J. Kirton) *Governing Global Finance: New Challenges, G7 and IMF Contributions,* Ashgate Publishing (Burlington, VT), 2002.

(Editor, with Paolo Savona and John J. Kirton) *Sustaining Global Growth and Development: G7 and IMF Governance,* Ashgate Publishing (Burlington, VT), 2003.

Coeditor of the series "Global Finance," Ashgate Publishing (Burlington, VT), 2002—. Contributor of several dozen articles to economics and finance journals. Member of review board, *Rivista di diritto valutario e di economic internazionale,* until 1992, *Mondo bancario,* 2000—, *Rivista di sistemi finanziari, Political Economy of Global Interdependence,* and *International Trade Journal;* member of editorial advisory board, *Sviluppo economico.*

SIDELIGHTS: Michele Fratianni once told *CA:* "I studied economics because I wanted to understand the world and change it. Perhaps I was naive, as young people can be. Today, many years after I made that decision, my professional work becomes most gratifying when I can sense that it may have an impact on the way economic policy is formulated and implemented."

BIOGRAPHICAL AND CRITICAL SOURCES:

PERIODICALS

Choice, October, 1997, D. Mitch, review of *A Monetary History of Italy,* p. 341.

De Economist, December, 1998, Henriette Prast, review of *A Monetary History of Italy,* p. 642.

Economic History Review, August, 1998, Francesca Carnevali, review of *A Monetary History of Italy,* p. 626.

Economic Journal, May, 1998, Geoffrey E. Wood, review of *A Monetary History of Italy,* p. 885.

Journal of Common Market Studies, March, 1995, Andrew J. Hughes Hallett, review of *The European Monetary System and European Monetary Union,* p. 166.

Journal of Economic History, March, 1999, review of *A Monetary History of Italy,* p. 218.

Journal of Economic Literature, March, 1994, review of *Monetary Policy in Developed Economies,* p. 208; December, 1997, review of *A Monetary History of Italy,* p. 2168; March, 1998, review of *Macroeconomic Policy in Open Economies,* p. 330; March, 1999, Gianni Toniolo, review of *A Monetary History of Italy,* p. 211; September, 1999, review of *Ideas for the Future of the International Monetary System,* p. 1252.

Kyklos, winter, 1997, Carsten Hefeker, review of *A Monetary History of Italy,* p. 599.

Reference and Research Book News, November, 1997, review of *Macroeconomic Policy in Open Economies,* p. 54.

Weltwirtschaftliches Archiv, fall, 1998, Michael Carlberg, review of *Macroeconomic Policy in Open Economies,* p. 743.

ONLINE

Michele Fratianni Home Page, http://www.bus. indiana.edu/fratiann/bio.htm (September 16, 2004).*

G

GEMMETT, Robert J(ames) 1936-

PERSONAL: Born March 11, 1936, in Schenectady, NY; son of A. James and Dorothy (MacFarlane) Gemmett; married Kendra Baxter, January 25, 1964; children: Stephen, Scott, David, Kerry. *Education:* Siena College, B.A. (cum laude), 1959; University of Massachusetts, M.A., 1962; Syracuse University, Ph.D., 1967.

ADDRESSES: Office—Department of English, State University of New York—College at Brockport, Hartwell 202B, 350 New Campus Dr., Brockport, NY 14420-2914. *E-mail*—Rgemmet@po.brockport.edu.

CAREER: Clarkson College of Technology, Potsdam, NY, instructor in English, 1964-65; State University of New York—College at Brockport, Brockport, NY, associate professor, 1967-70, professor of English, 1970-92, department chair, 1975-79, dean of humanities, 1979-82, dean of letters and sciences, 1982-92; State University of New York—College at Buffalo, Buffalo, NY, provost and vice president for academic affairs, 1992-97; State University of New York—College at Brockport, Brockport, NY, professor of English, 1997—. *Military service:* U.S. Army, 1959; became second lieutenant.

AWARDS, HONORS: Outstanding Educators in America recognition of merit, 1975.

WRITINGS:

William Beckford, Twayne, 1977.
Beckford's Fonthill: The Rise of a Romantic Icon, Michael Russell (Wilby, Norwich, England), 2003.

Author of introduction, *Men of Letters,* Volume III, Mansell Information Publishing (London, England), 1972; and *Vathek,* 1786 and 1787 editions, by William Beckford, Scholars Facsimiles and Reprints, 1972. Contributor of essays to *Nineteenth-Century Literary Criticism,* Thomson Gale (Detroit, MI), 1987, and *Classic Fantasy Writers,* edited by Howard Bloom, Chelsea House (New York, NY), 1994. Contributor of articles to *English Miscellany, Philological Quarterly, Gazette des Beaux Arts, Papers of the Bibliographical Society of America, Library Chronicle, American Book Collector, Etudes Anglaises,* and other English journals.

EDITOR

William Beckford, *Biographical Memoirs of Extraordinary Painters,* Fairleigh Dickinson University Press, 1969.
William Beckford, *Dreams, Waking Thoughts and Incidents,* Fairleigh Dickinson University Press, 1971.
William Beckford, *Episodes of Vathek,* Fairleigh Dickinson University Press, 1975.
(And author of introduction and notes) *The Consummate Collector: William Beckford's Letters to His Bookseller,* Michael Russell (Wilby, Norwich, England), 2000.

Associate editor, *English Record,* 1967-69.

SIDELIGHTS: Robert J. Gemmett's edition of William Beckford's letters, *The Consummate Collector,* was well received by *Times Literary Supplement* reviewer

Anthony Hobson. He claimed that "Robert Gemmett has succeeded most creditably in deciphering Beckford's difficult hand, which frequently baffled Bentley's clerk in the 1890s." Gemmett's 2003 book, *Beckford's Fonthhill: The Rise of a Romantic Icon,* focuses on the history of Fonthill Abbey.

BIOGRAPHICAL AND CRITICAL SOURCES:

BOOKS

Spector, Robert Donald, *The English Gothic: A Bibliographic Guide to Writers from Horace Walpole to Mary Shelley,* Greenwood Press (Westport, CT), 1984.

PERIODICALS

Times Literary Supplement, July 20, 2001, Anthony Hobson, review of *The Consummate Collector: William Beckford's Letters to His Bookseller,* p. 36.

*　　*　　*

GEORGE, Kristine O'Connell 1954-

PERSONAL: Born May 6, 1954, in Denver, CO. *Education:* Colorado State University, B.S., 1976.

ADDRESSES: Agent—c/o Author Mail, Clarion Books, 215 Park Ave., New York, NY 10003. *E-mail*—kristine@kristinegeorge.com.

CAREER: Writer. Conference speaker and visiting author in schools; poetry consultant for *Storytime* television program, produced by Public Broadcasting System; University of California-Los Angeles Writers' Program, writing instructor for children's poetry, beginning 1999.

AWARDS, HONORS: Lee Bennett Hopkins Promising Poet Award, International Reading Association (IRA), 1998; Lee Bennett Hopkins Poetry Award, 1998; American Booksellers Association (ABA) Pick of the Lists designation, National Council of Teachers of English (NCTE) Notable Book in the Language Arts designation, and *School Library Journal* Best Books designation, all 1998, all for *The Great Frog Race and Other Poems;* New York Public Library's 100 Titles for Reading and Sharing listee, 1998, for *The Great Frog Race* and *Old Elm Speaks: Tree Poems,* and 2001, for *Book!;* Chicago Public Library Best of the Best listee, 1998, for *Old Elm Speaks;* Golden Kite Award, Society of Children's Book Writers and Illustrators, 1999; Myra Cohn Livingston Award for Excellence in Children's Poetry, Southern California Council on Literature for Children and Young People, 1999, and 2002, for *Toasting Marshmallows: Camping Poems;* Oppenheimer Toy Portfolio Gold Award, 2001, for *Book!;* Bank Street College Claudia Lewis Poetry Award, and South Dakota Prairie Bud Award nomination, both 2002, both for *Little Dog and Duncan;* IRA/Children's Book Council Choice designation, William Alllen White Book Award nomination, and South Carolina Junior Book Award nomination, all 2003, all for *Swimming Upstream: Middle School Poems;* Texas Bluebonnet Master List nomination, 2005, for *Hummingbird Nest: A Journal of Poems.*

WRITINGS:

The Great Frog Race and Other Poems, illustrated by Kate Kiesler, introduction by Myra Cohn Livingston, Clarion Books (New York, NY), 1997.

Old Elm Speaks: Tree Poems, illustrated by Kate Kiesler, Clarion Books (New York, NY), 1998.

Little Dog Poems, illustrated by June Otani, Clarion Books (New York, NY), 1999.

Toasting Marshmallows: Camping Poems, illustrated by Kay Kiesler, Clarion Books (New York, NY), 2001.

Book!, illustrated by Maggie Smith, Clarion Books (New York, NY), 2001.

Swimming Upstream: Middle School Poems, illustrated by Debbie Tilley, Clarion Books (New York, NY), 2002.

Little Dog and Duncan, illustrated by June Otani, Clarion Books (New York, NY), 2002.

One Mitten, illustrated by Maggie Smith, Clarion Books (New York, NY), 2004.

Hummingbird Nest: A Journal of Poems, illustrated by Barry Moser, Harcourt (Orlando, FL), 2004.

Up!, illustrated by Hiroe Nakata, Clarion Books (New York, NY), 2005.

Fold Me a Poem, illustrated by Lauren Stringer, Harcourt (Orlando, FL), 2005.

Contributor of stories and poems to anthologies and to periodicals, including *Cricket* and *Spider.* Contributor to *Children's Writers and Illustrators Market,* Writer's Digest Books, 2000.

SIDELIGHTS: Kristine O'Connell George is the author of several well-received collections of poetry for young people. In her introduction to George's debut work, *The Great Frog Race and Other Poems,* Myra Cohn Livingston wrote that it "is not only refreshing but urgent that our children hear poetry resonating with music, keen observation, fresh metaphor and personification, and meaningful flights of imagination. . . . George promises us that!" Other works by George include the collections *Swimming Upstream: Middle School Poems* and *Toasting Marsh-mallows: Camping Poems,* as well as several picture books that contain a rhyming text. Praising George's picture book *Little Dog and Duncan,* about a small pup who has to compete for the attention of his young owner when a rambunctious Irish wolfhound comes to play, Joy Fleishhacker noted in *School Library Journal* that the author possesses a talent for focusing on "ordinary moments and describing them in accessible yet lyrical language, transforming the mundane into the magical."

Born and raised in Colorado, George began her career as a poet to the young after a 1989 writing class taught by author Myra Cohn Livingston. Her first published work was 1997's *The Great Frog Race and Other Poems,* which a *Publishers Weekly* reviewer characterized as "an invitation to experience joy and wonder." Many of George's poems reflect her love of the natural world, and everything from tadpoles and wild birds to horses and trees appear throughout her books. Margaret Bush remarked in *School Library Journal* on the many poetic forms George employs: "Haiku, blank verse, bits of rhyme, and some lovely little bundles of words are sprinkled along in pieces that are descriptive and engaging." Deborah Stevenson likened some of George's "quiet and observant" poems to those of William Carlos Williams in her review for the *Bulletin of the Center for Children's Books,* adding: "The phraseology is fresh and apt, employing tactile as well as visual conceits, and the subjects are kid-appealing ones indeed."

George uses several poetic forms to celebrate the natural world in her second collection, *Old Elm Speaks: Tree Poems,* which Tunie Munson-Benson in the *Riverbank Review* described as "beckoning as irresistibly as a basketful of polished stones." Here George's playful use of language makes music of her observations of the knotholes in a wooden fence, squirrels playing in a tree, a tree branch that juts out in such a way as to make it a perfect imaginary horse for a small child, and a fisherman who catches a pine tree rather than a fish. A critic for *Kirkus Reviews* dubbed the book "a lovely, often luminous, collection," while a *Publishers Weekly* contributor described *Old Elm Speaks* as "just the right gift for nature lovers."

"Writing the poems for *Old Elm Speaks* was such a joy!" George noted on her Web site, reflecting the personal connection her writing has for her. "I have always loved trees—their diversity, quiet dignity, and the places they hold in the landscape of my memories. I was the type of child who always noticed trees and I still remember specific trees from homes in Colorado, Texas, Oregon, Ohio, and Idaho. . . . Many of these poems represent special memories not only of trees, but also places I love."

George also draws from her personal experiences in *Hummingbird Nest: A Journal of Poems.* The book follows the author's family as they watch a pair of hummingbirds hatch youngsters and grow them to maturity in a nest the mother bird built in a potted tree on the patio of the George family's home. After nest-building, tiny eggs hatch, and suddenly every waking hour is spent feeding the tiny hatchlings. It is not long until the tiny birds are old enough to take their first flight, and suddenly, they are gone. In addition to poems describing each stage of the family's observations, George includes notes about the hummingbird, making *Hummingbird Nest* useful as a reference tool for budding naturalists. "As in the best nature writing, the excitement here is in the particulars that bring readers close up to a universe," noted Hazel Rochman in *Booklist,* while a *Kirkus Reviews* critic praised the book as a "smooth, easy-reading glimpse into the natural world," enhanced by realistic water-color illustrations by Barry Moser.

In the books *Little Dog Poems* and *Little Dog and Duncan,* George depicts the life of a small puppy. *Little Dog Poems* follows dog and owner on their round of daily activities, including a war between the pup and the vacuum cleaner, watching with hopeful fascination as Mom cooks in the kitchen, and playing a game of catch with his young owner. *Booklist* contributor Stephanie Zvirin viewed the volume as "a charming way to introduce little ones to the form and feeling of poetry," while Joanna Rudge Long, writing in *Horn Book,* asserted that *Little Dog Poems* is especially distinguished by "the author's true understanding of canine behavior and her insight into the happy relationship between dog and child."

BIOGRAPHICAL AND CRITICAL SOURCES:

BOOKS

George, Kristine O'Connell, *The Great Frog Race and Other Poems,* introduction by Myra Cohn Livingston, Clarion Books (New York, NY), 1997.

PERIODICALS

Appraisal, spring, 1999, pp. 17-18.
Booklist, March 15, 1997, p. 1238; January 1, 1999, review of *Old Elm Speaks: Tree Poems,* p. 784; March 15, 1999 Stephanie Zvirin, review of *Little Dog Poems;* March 15, 2001, Gillian Engberg, review of *Toasting Marshallows: Camping Poems,* p. 1394; January 1, 2003, GraceAnne A. DeCandido, review of *Swimming Upstream: Middle School Poems,* p. 878; February 1, 2004, Hazel Rochman, review of *Hummingbird Nest: A Journal of Poems,* p. 974; November 15, 2004, Ilene Cooper, review of *One Mitten,* p. 590.
Bulletin of the Center for Children's Books, June, 1997, Deborah Stevenson, review of *The Great Frog Race and Other Poems,* p. 358.
Creative Classroom, March-April, 1999, p. 36.
Horn Book, March-April, 1999, Joanna Rudge Long, review of *Little Dog Poems,* p. 216; July-August, 2002, Roger Sutton, review of *Little Dog and Duncan,* p. 478; January-February, 2003, Martha V. Parravano, review of *Swimming Upstream,* p. 89.
Kirkus Reviews, February 15, 1997, p. 299; August 1, 1998, review of *Old Elm Speaks,* p. 1116; September 15, 2001, review of *Book!,* p. 1358; August 1, 2002, review of *Swimming Upstream,* p. 1129; March 1, 2004, review of *Hummingbird Nest,* p. 222.
Publishers Weekly, January 27, 1997, review of *The Great Frog Race and Other Poems,* p. 107: September 14, 1998, review of *Old Elm Speaks,*

p. 68; February 22, 1999, review of *Little Dog Poems,* p. 94; March 12, 2001, review of *Toasting Marshmallows,* p. 90; October 1, 2001, review of *Book!,* p. 60; March 11, 2002, review of *Swimming Upstream,* p. 74.
Riverbank Review, fall, 1996, Tunie Munson-Benson, review of *Old Elm Speaks,* p. 41.
School Library Journal, April, 1997, Margaret Bush, review of *The Great Frog Race and Other Poems,* p. 124; September, 1998, pp. 190-191; May, 1999, p. 106; July, 2001, Luann Toth, review of *Toasting Marshmallows,* p. 93; March, 2002, Joy Fleishhacker, review of *Little Dog and Duncan,* p. 212; September, 2002, Kristen Oravec, review of *Swimming Upstream,* p. 244; April, 2004, Susan Scheps, review of *Hummingbird Nest,* p. 111; December, 2004, Laura Scott, review of *One Mitten,* p. 109.

ONLINE

Kristine O'Connell George Web site, http://www. kristinegeorge.com/ (December 2, 2004).*

*   *   *

GILBERT, Sister Mary
See DEFREES, Madeline

*   *   *

GLEITZMAN, Morris 1953-

PERSONAL: First syllable of surname rhymes with "light"; born January 9, 1953, in Sleaford, Lincolnshire, England; immigrated to Australia, 1969; son of Phillip (an auditor) and Pamela (Bates) Gleitzman; married Christine McCaul (a film editor), February 9, 1978 (separated January, 1994); children: Sophie, Ben. *Education:* Canberra College of Advanced Education, B.A., 1974. *Hobbies and other interests:* Travel, reading, making lists.

ADDRESSES: Home—Victoria, Australia. *Agent*—Anthony Williams, 50 Oxford St., Paddington, Sydney, New South Wales 2021, Australia. *E-mail*—morris@ morrisgleitzman.com.

CAREER: Australian Broadcasting Corporation, Sydney, New South Wales, television promotions director, 1973-75, television entertainment script editor and producer, 1975-76, and writer for *The Norman Gunston Show,* 1976-78; Seven Network, Sydney, writer for *The Norman Gunston Show,* 1978-81; freelance writer, 1981—.

AWARDS, HONORS: Awgie Award, Australian Writers Guild, 1985, for television film *The Other Facts of Life;* Family Award, 1990, for *Two Weeks with the Queen;* Book of the Year Younger Honour, Children's Book Council of Australia, 1992, for *Misery Guts,* and 1993, for *Blabber Mouth;* COOL Award (Australia Capital Territory), BILBY Award (Queensland), YABBA Award (Victoria), and KOALA Award shortlist (New South Wales), and *Guardian* Children's Fiction Award shortlist, all 1999, all for *Bumface;* Dymocks Booksellers Children's Choice Awards Favorite Australian Author designation, 1999.

WRITINGS:

NOVELS; FOR CHILDREN

The Other Facts of Life (adapted from author's television screenplay of the same title; also see below), Penguin (Ringwood, Victoria, Australia), 1985, reprinted, 2004.

Second Childhood (adapted from author's television screenplay), Puffin (Ringwood, Victoria, Australia), 1990.

Misery Guts, Piper (Sydney, New South Wales, Australia), 1991, Harcourt (San Diego, CA), 1993.

Worry Warts, Pan Macmillan (Sydney, New South Wales, Australia), 1992, Harcourt (San Diego, CA), 1993.

Puppy Fat, Pan Macmillan (Sydney, New South Wales, Australia), 1992, Harcourt (San Diego, CA), 1995.

Blabber Mouth, Pan Macmillan (Sydney, New South Wales, Australia), 1992, Harcourt (San Diego, CA), 1995.

Sticky Beak, Pan Macmillan (Sydney, New South Wales, Australia), 1993, Harcourt (San Diego, CA), 1995.

Belly Flop, Pan Macmillan (Sydney, New South Wales, Australia), 1996.

Water Wings, Pan Macmillan (Sydney, New South Wales, Australia), 1996.

Bumface, Puffin (Ringwood, Victoria, Australia), 1998.

Gift of the Gab, Puffin (Ringwood, Victoria, Australia), 1999.

Toad Rage, Puffin (Ringwood, Victoria, Australia), 1999, Random House (New York, NY), 2004.

Adults Only, Puffin (Ringwood, Victoria, Australia), 2001.

Toad Heaven, Puffin (Ringwood, Victoria, Australia), 2001, Random House (New York, NY), 2005.

Boy Overboard, Puffin (Camberwell, Victoria, Australia), 2002.

Teachers's Pet, Puffin (Camberwell, Victoria, Australia), 2003.

Toad Away, Puffin (Camberwell, Victoria, Australia), 2003.

Girl Underground, Puffin (Camberwell, Victoria, Australia), 2004.

Worm Story, Puffin (Camberwell, Victoria, Australia), 2004.

Gleitzman's books have been translated into French, Japanese, German, Italian, and Spanish.

"WICKED!" SERIES; NOVELS

(With Paul Jennings) *The Slobberers,* Puffin (Ringwood, Victoria, Australia), 1997.

(With Paul Jennings) *Battering Rams,* Puffin (Ringwood, Victoria, Australia), 1997.

(With Paul Jennings) *Croaked,* Puffin (Ringwood, Victoria, Australia), 1997.

(With Paul Jennings) *Dead Ringer,* Puffin (Ringwood, Victoria, Australia), 1997.

(With Paul Jennings) *The Creeper,* Puffin (Ringwood, Victoria, Australia), 1997.

(With Paul Jennings) *Till Death Us Do Part,* Puffin (Ringwood, Victoria, Australia), 1997.

(With Paul Jennings) *Wicked!* (includes all six volumes), Puffin (Ringwood, Victoria, Australia), 1998.

"DEADLY!" SERIES; NOVELS

(With Paul Jennings) *Nude,* Puffin (Ringwood, Victoria, Australia), 2000.

(With Paul Jennings) *Brats,* Puffin (Ringwood, Victoria, Australia), 2000.

(With Paul Jennings) *Stiff,* Puffin (Ringwood, Victoria, Australia), 2000.

(With Paul Jennings) *Hunt,* Puffin (Ringwood, Victoria, Australia), 2001.

(With Paul Jennings) *Grope,* Puffin (Ringwood, Victoria, Australia), 2001.

(With Paul Jennings) *Pluck,* Puffin (Ringwood, Victoria, Australia), 2001.

(With Paul Jennings) *Deadly!* (includes all six volumes), Puffin (Ringwood, Victoria, Australia), 2002.

OTHER

Doctors and Nurses (screenplay), Universal Entertainment, 1981.

Melvin Son of Alvin (screenplay), Roadshow, 1984.

The Other Facts of Life (television film), Ten Network, 1985.

Skin Free (two-act play), produced in Sydney, New South Wales, 1986.

(With Trevor Farrant) *Not a Papal Tour* (stage show), produced in Canberra, Australian Capital Territory, at Canberra Theatre, 1987.

Two Weeks with the Queen (adult novel), Blackie & Son, 1989, Putnam (New York, NY), 1991.

Harbour Beat (screenplay), Palm Beach Pictures/ Zenith Productions, 1990.

Just Looking: Gleitzman on Television (collected columns), Sun Books (Chippendale, New South Wales, Australia), 1992.

Gleitzman on Saturday (collected columns), Macmillan, 1993.

SelfHelpLess: Fifty-seven Pieces of Crucial Advice for People Who Need a Bit More Time to Get It Right, Penguin (Ringwood, Victoria, Australia), 2000.

Writer of scripts for television series, including *Second Childhood, Crossroads, Bust, Instant TV,* and *The Daryl Somers Show.* Author of weekly television column in *Sydney Morning Herald,* 1987-92; columnist for *Good Weekend* (magazine supplement to *Sydney Morning Herald* and *Melbourne Age*), beginning 1990.

ADAPTATIONS: Gleitzman's novel *Two Weeks with the Queen* was adapted as a play by Mary Morris, Piper, 1994.

SIDELIGHTS: Although he started out his writing career as a television scriptwriter, Morris Gleitzman has earned a reputation in his adopted home of Australia for creating humorous, evocative young-adult novels as well as penning entertaining novel series such as *Wicked!* and *Deadly!* with fellow writer Paul Jennings. The "cheeky brand of humor" and "sensible, tolerant attitude" toward family life that a *Publishers Weekly* reviewer noticed in Gleitzman's early novels, has continued to be honed by the author, and his dry humor continues to find an appreciative audience with children and critics alike. "One looks forward to a Gleitzman title," wrote Trevor Carey in *Magpies;* and according to *Horn Book* critic Karen Jameyson, the award-winning writer's name "has been steadily edging its way into cult territory." By 1999 Gleitzman was considered one of the most popular children's writers in Australia, and the majority of his books have been translated into several languages.

The secret of Gleitzman's success, according to some critics, is his ability to couch highly sensitive topics and conflicts in chaotic situations peppered with amusing dialogues. Readers may find themselves laughing through stories about divorce, alienation, and physical challenges as these crises are encountered by the author's young protagonists. In his book *Boy Overboard* he addresses a broader concern facing young people while still employing his trademark humor, creating a likeable protagonist who lives in Afghanistan with his family and must face intolerance and the problems faced by refugees when his family is forced to flee to Australia. Gleitzman once explained that, when writing for a young audience, he uses "humor to explore the big subjects. I like characters who find themselves face to face with The Biggies unequipped with the adult armory of evasion, rationalization, and red wine."

Born and raised in the south of London, Gleitzman immigrated to Australia at age sixteen and quickly decided to become a writer. "I thought I'd better do some of those colorful jobs writers always seem to have done," he once commented. "I worked for a bit as a frozen-chicken thawer, a department store Santa Claus, an assistant to a fashion designer, and a rolling-stock unhooker in a sugar mill. I applied for whaling, but they rejected me because I said I'd only do it if I could throw the whales back." After enrolling in a college program in professional writing, Gleitzman established himself as a writer in the film and television industry in Australia. He worked as a promotions director and script editor and producer for the Australian Broadcasting Corporation, and wrote for

The Norman Gunston Show for several years before becoming a freelance writer.

Gleitzman's first two books were adapted from his screenplays, and these projects gave him the confidence to make the career move from playwright to novelist. His most widely known novel, the award-winning *Two Weeks with the Queen,* was conceived as a novel "in a flash," as the writer once explained. "As I was writing it, I realized it was, in part, a story about the tendency of loving parents to overprotect their kids from difficult realities, both domestic and global. I was pleased to discover this, as I do it all the time myself."

"The things that happen in my books are almost all made up," Gleitzman admitted in a question-and-answer on his Web site. "For me, imagination makes much better stories than memory. Specially as my memory isn't very good. I can't remember many of the adventures of my childhood, so it's easier for me to make them up. Occasionally, though, a bit of my real life creeps into a story. I emigrated from England with my folks when I was sixteen, and that experience helped me write *Misery Guts.*"

Misery Guts and its sequel, *Worry Warts,* Gleitzman's two novels about nervous teen Keith Shipley, describe the effects of parents' attempts to protect their children, and also of children's efforts to protect their parents. Keith is troubled by his worried parents, a couple of "misery guts." His attempt to pick up their business—as well as their spirits—by painting their shop in the south of London a glossy mango color fails. Keith's parents show no interest in his plans for a tropical vacation or a move to Australia. When Keith finally persuades them to take a day trip to the beach, he forgets to turn the fryer at the fish-and-chips shop off. As a result, the shop burns down, and the family's business is ruined. To Keith's delight, his parents decide to begin another business in sunny Australia. As *Misery Guts* closes, readers find Keith content and the misery guts hopeful.

The Shipley family drama continues in *Worry Warts,* as money problems keep Keith's parents quarreling. Keith paints their car to cheer them up but it doesn't help; they announce that they want to divorce. Thinking that money will keep his parents together, Keith runs away to the opal fields. Although he manages to find an opal, he becomes trapped in a mine and his

parents are forced into a costly rescue effort to bring their son home safely. While Keith eventually convinces his parents to stay together for him, he eventually puts his own desires aside for the good of all. While Ilene Cooper noted in *Booklist* that the conclusion of *Worry Warts* may be "unsatisfying" for those who applauded the boy's "efforts to keep his family together," a *Kirkus Reviews* critic found the same conclusion "surprising but appropriate."

Keith and his family return in several more novels by Gleitzman, including *Puppy Fat,* which finds Keith still at work solving his separated and now-single parents' problems for them. Worried that, in their mid-thirties, they have both become overweight and doddery and need to find new partners, he channels his artistic talents into finding ways to advertise their availability for dating. However, painting them in skimpy bathing suits on a wall in his South London neighborhood proves unsuccessful, so he calls in help, with predictably humorous results. A *Publishers Weekly* contributor wrote that Gleitzman's "punchy narrative, droll characters, and original plot" make *Puppy Fat* a "real page-turner," while in *Booklist* Ilene Cooper noted that the author characteristically "turns everyday situations upside down with his humor and off-the-wall take on life."

Blabber Mouth, Sticky Beak, and *Gift of the Gab* all feature Rowena Batts, a girl who was born without the ability to speak. Although she is dumb, Rowena manages to express her opinion with signs, written words, and actions. While in *Blabber Mouth* the central problems revolve around Rowena's relationship with her flamboyant father, his decision to remarry causes new problems in *Sticky Beak,* In this novel Rowena expands her communication tools, throwing a Jelly Custard Surprise during a party for her teacher, who has married Rowena's father and is pregnant with Rowena's half-sibling. Despite Rowena's speech problem and sometimes-outlandish behavior, she is a resilient protagonist. By the end of *Sticky Beak,* for example, she has learned new ways of coping with her outrageous yet loving father, her new stepmother, the new baby, and even the class bully. *Gift of the Gab* finds her reconciling with her father while attempting to uncover the reason for her speech problem, which takes the family to France in search of answers. According to *Magpies* contributor Cathryn Crowe, Gleitzman "wraps" themes involving rejection and insecurity into "a tight bundle with plenty of zany humour."

In an unusual step for Gleitzman, he takes on an animal protagonist in *Toad Rage* and its sequels, *Toad Heaven* and *Toad Away*. In *Toad Rage* readers meet Australian cane toad Limpy, who is angered over the number of relatives who have ended up as road kill. In an effort to end the needless slaughter of amphibians, Limpy begins a public relations campaign, trying to sell humans on the notion that cane toads are truly man's best friend and ultimately hoping to become the next Olympic mascot. *Toad Away* finds Limpy still searching for a safe haven for cane toads, and joining with two friends to travel to the mythical Amazon, which is rumored to be such a place. Praising *Toad Rage* as a "hilarous dark comedy," a *Publishers Weekly* writer noted that Gleitzman originally wrote the novel for the 2000 Sydney Olympics as a tongue-in-cheek commentary on the country's animal-mascot selection process. Whatever its origins, the novel works on its own merits; as Ed Sullivan wrote in *Booklist*, Gleitzman's saga of "one toad's bold quest to reach out to another species will give readers plenty of laughs." "This toad's-eye view of human society provides both solid entertainment and a barbed commentary on the importance of looks," added a *Kirkus Reviews* contributor.

BIOGRAPHICAL AND CRITICAL SOURCES:

PERIODICALS

Booklist, July, 1993, Ilene Cooper, review of *Worry Warts*, p. 1958; May 1, 1995, Mary Harris Veeder, review of *Blabber Mouth*, p. 1561; June 1, 1995, Mary Harris Veeder, review of *Sticky Beak*, p. 1770; June 1, 1996, Ilene Cooper, review of *Puppy Fat*, p. 171; March 1, 2004, Ed Sullivan, review of *Toad Rage*, p. 1188.

Horn Book, July, 1993, Karen Jameyson, "News from down Under," pp. 496-498; July-August, 1995, Elizabeth S. Watson, review of *Blabber Mouth*, p. 458.

Junior Bookshelf, November, 1993, review of *Sticky Beak*, pp. 65-66.

Kirkus Reviews, February 1, 1993, review of *Misery Guts*, p. 146; April 1, 2004, review of *Toad Rage*, p. 329.

Magpies, November, 1991, p. 29; November, 1992, Trevor Carey, review of *Blabber Mouth*, p. 30; November, 1993, Cathryn Crowe, review of *Sticky Beak*, p. 32.

Publishers Weekly, January 11, 1991, review of *Two Weeks with the Queen*, p. 105; February 8, 1993, review of *Misery Guts* and *Worry Warts*, p. 87; May 6, 1996, review of *Puppy Fat*, p. 8; March 22, 2004, review of *Toad Rage*, p. 86.

School Library Journal, May, 1993, pp. 104-105.

ONLINE

Morris Gleitzman Web site, http://www.morris gleitzman.com (January 17, 2005).*

* * *

GORDON, Amy 1949-
(Amy Lawson)

PERSONAL: Born January 22, 1949, in Boston, MA; daughter of Lincoln (a professor, diplomat, and economist) and Allison (an artist, writer, and mother; maiden name, Wright), Gordon; married Richard Lawson (divorced, 1995); children: Nicholas Lawson, Hugh Lawson. *Education:* Bard College, graduated, 1972. *Politics:* "Eclectic." *Religion:* "Eclectic." *Hobbies and other interests:* Writing, reading, mountain climbing, sailing, "spending time with people I like," traveling.

ADDRESSES: Home—P.O. Box 186, 2 Old Sunderland Rd., Montague, MA 01351. *Agent*—George Nicholson, Sterling Lord Literistic, 65 Bleecker St., New York, NY 10012.

CAREER: Bement School (K-9 boarding school), Deerfield, MA, drama teacher and director, chair of fine arts program, 1980—.

AWARDS, HONORS: Texas Blue Bonnet Award nomination, 2004, and Missouri Association of Librarians award, both for *The Gorillas of Gill Park*.

WRITINGS:

(Under name Amy Lawson) *The Talking Bird and the Story Pouch*, illustrated by Craig McFarland Brown, Harper (New York, NY), 1983.

(Under name Amy Lawson) *Star Baby,* illustrated by Margot Apple, Harcourt Brace Jovanovich (San Diego, CA), 1991.

Midnight Magic, illustrated by Judy Clifford, Bridge-Water (Mahwah, NJ), 1995.

When JFK Was My Father, Houghton Mifflin (Boston, MA), 1999.

The Gorillas of Gill Park, Holiday House (New York, NY), 2003.

The Secret Life of a Boarding School Brat, Holiday House (New York, NY), 2004.

WORK IN PROGRESS: The Blue Gang of Gill Park, for Holiday House.

SIDELIGHTS: Amy Gordon's books for young people reflect their author's belief in the positive power of imagination. While her 1995 chapter book *Midnight Magic* extols the value and fun of imagination for beginning readers, Gordon's teen novel *When JFK Was My Father* asserts the power of a fantasy life for adolescents. Harnessing imagination through the creative act of writing is at the core of Gordon's 2004 novel, *The Secret Life of a Boarding School Brat,* a book that had its basis in the author's own experiences. As Gordon recalled, after two years living in Rio de Janeiro, Brazil, with her family, "I was sent back to the United States for a more serious education at a girls' boarding school. I went there for five years—five years of a blue uniform skirt, a white blouse, sensible shoes, and crazy housemothers. In the fall of my first year, John F. Kennedy was shot; in the spring of my last year, Bobby Kennedy was shot." After attending Bard College "during the turbulent years of the late '60s and early '70s," Gordon explained: "I found my way to teaching; I was a camp counselor for many years and knew that I loved working with kids. Now I teach drama and put on plays with kids and write as much as I can between teaching and raising my two sons."

Midnight Magic finds Uncle Harry babysitting Jake and Sam during a weekend of crises: Sam has lost a tooth and Jake's pet hamsters are missing. Uncle Harry distracts the children by enacting their favorite story, "Puss in Boots," and when they wake up on Saturday morning, Sam finds a golden key left under his pillow by the Tooth Fairy. When Sam and Jake begin a search for the evil ogre of the "Puss in Boots" story, hoping

to return the golden key to him, they somehow end up on the hamster's trail. *School Library Journal* reviewer Mary Jo Drungil singled out Gordon's "utterly realistic" portrait of two likeable young boys, as well as their "ideal" uncle, for special praise, and predicted that *Midnight Magic* is "certain to be appreciated by young fairy-tale fans."

Geared for middle-grade readers, *The Gorillas of Gill Park* is a humorous novel that focuses on Willy, a lonely middle-schooler who finds a world of new friends while spending the summer with his widowed aunt. The practical-minded Willy is instantly set at ease by his quirky Aunt Bridget, whose job as a costume designer now keeps her busy sewing gorilla costumes in her small urban apartment. Nearby, Willy discovers a small park run by an equally eccentric wealthy musician, and when the park is threatened by land developers the boy's practical sense helps win the day. In *Booklist* Gillian Engberg praised *The Gorillas of Gill Park* as a "suspenseful, winning story" in which "delicious words, clever dialogue, and endearing characters" retain reader attention. Noting that Gordon draws her cast of characters from among "folk of varying degrees of eccentricity," a *Publishers Weekly* critic added that the young protagonist's "gradual discovery of his own worth is satisfying" and the storyline "often funny."

Taking place in the 1960s, Gordon's novel *When JFK Was My Father* centers on fourteen-year-old Georgia Hughes, who lives in Brazil with her emotionally remote parents. When her parents get divorced, Georgia and her mother move back to the United States, and Georgia is deposited in a boarding school. The highly inventive Georgia feels abandoned by both parents, particularly her father, and she compensates for her loneliness as she did in Brazil: by pretending that recently assassinated U.S. president John F. Kennedy is her real father. When Tim, a friend from Brazil who has run away from his boarding school, invites Georgia to hit the road with him, she suddenly realizes that her school, and the friends she has made there, may have filled an important void in her life. "Georgia's account of her virtual abandonment at school by her parents and her barely conscious search for a home is both poignant and gently funny," contended Lauren Adams, reviewing *When JFK Was My Father* for *Horn Book.* Praising Gordon's novel as "well paced with moments of dramatic tension," the critic added that "Georgia's refreshing narrative" ably reveals the cast of interesting secondary characters. "Gordon writes in a vivid, defining style that allows Georgia to emerge as a fresh, fully realized character," attested Ilene Cooper in *Booklist,* while Connie Tyrrell Burns wrote in *School Library Journal* that the success of *When JFK Was My Father* rests on Gordon's creation of a "likable and well-drawn character" with whom readers can identify.

The gift of a diary by her grandmother proves to be Lydia's salvation in *The Secret Life of a Boarding School Brat.* Also taking place in the 1960s, the novel follows Lydia Rice, a seventh-grader who feels isolated, not only because of her parents' divorce and their decision to ship her off to boarding school, but also because of the recent death of a beloved grandmother. Written in the form of the diary Lydia starts while at Miss Pocket's Boarding School, the novel follows the girl's efforts to solve a puzzle from the past, a task put to the lonely girl by the school's kind-hearted maintenance man. Noting the novel's "lively pacing and appealing if improbable . . . characters," a *Publishers Weekly* contributor predicted that "many readers will be caught up in the mystery" like Lydia. In *Horn Book* Susan Dove Lempke had special praise for the young protagonist's "lively personality" and Gordon's depiction of "the intergenerational friendship she forms" with the school handyman, while a *Kirkus Reviews* critic dubbed *The Secret Life of a Boarding School Brat* a "pleasant read."

Gordon once explained: "When I was young, I was a shy person in a verbal, intellectual, talkative family. I discovered that if I *wrote* entertaining stories as Christmas presents, then I could get the entire family to stop talking and pay attention to me. The written word allowed me to have a voice.

"I loved to read when I was young, and spent quite a lot of time pretending. I loved the world of childhood and left it reluctantly. In my adult life, I am very lucky to have a career (teaching drama and directing plays with 6th-9th graders) which allows me to encourage pretending. The creative problem-solving involved in teaching helps my writing, and the kids I teach, also, of course, inspire me. I am a lot less shy, now, but I still feel the written word is my best tool for expressing and sharing my real self."

BIOGRAPHICAL AND CRITICAL SOURCES:

PERIODICALS

Booklist, June 1, 1999, Ilene Cooper, review of *When JFK Was My Father,* p. 1813; June 1, 2003, Gillian Engberg, review of *The Gorillas of Gill Park,* p. 1776.

Horn Book, July-August, 1999, Lauren Adams, review of *When JFK Was My Father,* pp. 463-464; July-August, 2004, Susan Dove Lempke, review of *The Secret Life of a Boarding School Brat,* p. 452.

Kirkus Reviews, April 15, 2004, review of *The Secret Life of a Boarding School Brat,* p. 394.

New York Times Book Review, October 17, 1999, Patricia McCormick, review of *When JFK Was My Father,* p. 31.

Publishers Weekly, May 26, 2003, review of *The Gorillas of Gill Park,* p. 70; March 22, 2004, review of *The Secret Life of a Boarding School Brat,* p. 86.

School Library Journal, December, 1995, Mary Jo Drungil, review of *Midnight Magic,* pp. 80-81; April, 1999, Connie Tyrrell Burns, review of *When JFK Was My Father,* p. 134.

*   *   *

GOTTESMAN, S. D.
See POHL, Frederik

*   *   *

GRAY, Alasdair (James) 1934-

PERSONAL: Born December 28, 1934, in Glasgow, Scotland; son of Alex Gray (a machine operator) and Amy (Fleming) Gray (a homemaker); children: Andrew. *Education:* Glasgow School of Art, diploma (design and printmaking), 1957. *Politics:* "Socialist. Supporter of Scottish Home Rule and Campaign for Nuclear Disarmament." *Religion:* "Rational pantheism."

ADDRESSES: Home—2 Marchmont Terrace, Glasgow G12 9LT, Scotland. *Agent*—Giles Gordon, 6 Ann St., Edinburgh EH 4 1PJ, Scotland.

Alasdair Gray

CAREER: Part-time art teacher in Lanarkshire and Glasgow, Scotland, 1958-62; theatrical scene painter in Glasgow, 1962-63; freelance playwright and painter in Glasgow, 1963-75; People's Palace (local history museum), Glasgow, artist-recorder, 1976-77; University of Glasgow, writer-in-residence, 1977-79, professor of creative writing, 2001—; freelance painter and maker of books in Glasgow, 1979-2001.

MEMBER: Society of Authors, Glasgow Print Workshop, various organizations supporting trade unions and nuclear disarmament.

AWARDS, HONORS: Bellahouston Travelling Scholarship, 1957; Three grants from Scottish Arts Council, between 1968 and 1981; Booker Prize nomination, Book Trust (England), 1981, award from Saltire Society, 1982, and Niven Novel Award, all for *Lanark: A Life in Four Books;* award from Cheltenham Literary Festival, 1983, for *Unlikely Stories, Mostly;* award from Scottish branch of PEN, 1986; Whitbread Prize, and Guardian Fiction Prize, both 1992, both for *Poor Things.*

WRITINGS:

(And illustrator) *Lanark: A Life in Four Books* (novel), Harper (New York, NY), 1981, revised edition, Braziller (New York, NY), 1985.

(And illustrator) *Unlikely Stories, Mostly* (short stories; includes "The Star," "The Spread of Ian Nicol," and "Five Letters from an Eastern Empire"), Canongate Books (Edinburgh, Scotland), 1983, revised edition, Penguin (London, England), 1984.

1982 Janine (novel), J. Cape (London, England), 1984, revised edition, Penguin (New York, NY), 1985.

The Fall of Kelvin Walker: A Fable of the Sixties (novel; adapted from his television play of the same title; also see below), Canongate Books (Edinburgh, Scotland), 1985, Braziller (New York, NY), 1986.

(With James Kelman and Agnes Owens) *Lean Tales* (short-story anthology), J. Cape, (London, England), 1985.

Saltire Self-Portrait 4, Saltire Society Publications (Edinburgh, Scotland), 1988.

(And illustrator) *McGrotty and Ludmilla; or, The Harbinger Report: A Romance of the Eighties,* Dog and Bone Press (Glasgow, Scotland), 1989.

(And illustrator) *Old Negatives: Four Verse Sequences,* J. Cape (London, England), 1989.

Something Leather (novel), Random House (New York, NY), 1990.

Poor Things: Episodes from the Early Life of Archibald McCandless, M.D., Scottish Public Health Officer (novel), Harcourt (New York, NY), 1992.

Why Scots Should Rule Scotland, Canongate Books (Edinburgh, Scotland), 1992.

(And illustrator) *Ten Tales Tall and True: Social Realism, Sexual Comedy, Science Fiction, and Satire,* Harcourt (New York, NY), 1993.

(And illustrator) *A History Maker,* Canongate Books (Edinburgh, Scotland), 1994, Harcourt (New York, NY), 1996.

(And illustrator) *Mavis Belfrage: A Romantic Novel with Five Shorter Tales,* Bloomsbury (London, England), 1996.

The Artist in His World: Prints, 1986-1997 (poetry; prints by Ian McCulloch), Argyll (Gelndaruel, Argyll, Scotland), 1998.

(And illustrator) *The Book of Prefaces,* Bloomsbury (London, England), 2000.

Sixteen Occasional Poems, Morag McAlpine (Glasgow, Scotland), 2000.

A Short Survey of Classical Scottish Writing, Canongate Books (Edinburgh, Scotland), 2001.

The British Book of Popular Political Songs, Bloomsbury (London, England), 2002.

Ends of Our Tethers: 13 Sorry Stories, includes "Big Pockets with Buttoned Flaps, Swan burial," and "No Bluebeard," Canongate Books (Edinburg, Scotland), 2003.

STAGE PLAYS

Dialogue (one-act; first produced in Edinburgh, Scotland, at Gateway Theatre, 1971), Scottish Theatre (Kirknewton, Scotland), 1971.

The Fall of Kelvin Walker (two-act; adapted from his television play of the same title; also see below), first produced in Stirling, Scotland, at McRoberts Centre, University of Stirling, 1972.

The Loss of the Golden Silence (one-act), first produced in Edinburgh, Scotland, at Pool Theatre, 1973.

Homeward Bound (one-act), first produced in Edinburgh, Scotland, at Pool Theatre, 1973.

(With Tom Leonard and Liz Lochhead) *Tickly Mince* (two-act), first produced in Glasgow, Scotland, at Tron Theatre, 1982.

(With Liz Lochhead, Tom Leonard, and James Kelman) *The Pie of Damocles* (two-act; also see below), first produced in Glasgow, Scotland, at Tron Theatre, 1983.

McGrotty and Ludmilla, first produced in Glasgow, Scotland, at Tron Theatre, 1987.

(And illustrator) *Working Legs: A Play for People without Them* (first produced by Birds of Paradise Company, 1998), Dog and Bone Press (Glasgow, Scotland), 1997.

RADIO PLAYS

Quiet People, British Broadcasting Corporation (BBC), 1968.

The Night Off, British Broadcasting Corporation (BBC), 1969.

Thomas Muir of Huntershill, British Broadcasting Corporation (BBC), 1970.

The Loss of the Golden Silence, British Broadcasting Corporation (BBC), 1974.

McGrotty and Ludmilla, British Broadcasting Corporation (BBC), 1976.

The Vital Witness (documentary), British Broadcasting Corporation (BBC), 1979.

Near the Driver, translation into German by Berndt Rullkotter broadcast by Westdeutsche Rundfunk, 1983, original text broadcast by British Broadcasting Corporation (BBC), 1988.

TELEVISION PLAYS

The Fall of Kelvin Walker, British Broadcasting Corporation (BBC), 1968.

Dialogue, British Broadcasting Corporation (BBC), 1972.

Triangles, Granada, 1972.

The Man Who Knew about Electricity, British Broadcasting Corporation (BBC), 1973.

Honesty (educational documentary), British Broadcasting Corporation (BBC), 1974.

Today and Yesterday (series of three twenty-minute educational documentaries), British Broadcasting Corporation (BBC), 1975.

Beloved, Granada, 1976.

The Gadfly, Granada, 1977.

The Story of a Recluse, British Broadcasting Corporation (BBC), 1987.

OTHER

(Designer and illustrator) Wilma Paterson, *Songs of Scotland,* Mainstream, 1995.

Author and reader of *Some Unlikely Stories* (audiocassette), Canongate Audio, 1994, and *Scenes from Lanark, Volume 1* (audiocassette), Canongate Audio, 1995.

WORK IN PROGRESS: A Life in Pictures: Paintings, Murals, and Graphic Work, for Canongate Books.

SIDELIGHTS: After more than twenty years as a painter, and a scriptwriter for radio and television, Alasdair Gray rose to literary prominence with the publication of several of his books in the 1980s. His works have been noted for their mixture of realistic social commentary and vivid fantasy augmented by the author's own evocative illustrations. Jonathan Baumbach wrote in the *New York Times Book Review* that Gray's work "has a verbal energy, an intensity of vision, that has been mostly missing from the English novel since D. H. Lawrence." David Lodge of the *New Republic* said that Gray "is that rather rare bird among contemporary British writers—a genuine experimentalist, transgressing the rules of formal English prose . . . boldly and imaginatively."

In his writing, Gray often draws upon his Scottish background, and he is regarded as a major force in the literature of his homeland. Author Anthony Burgess, for instance, said in the London *Observer* that he considered Gray the best Scottish novelist since Sir Walter Scott became popular in the early nineteenth century. Unlike Scott, who made his country a setting for historical romance, Gray focuses on contemporary Scotland where the industrial economy is deteriorating and many citizens fear that their social and economic destiny has been surrendered to England. Critics praised Gray for putting such themes as Scotland's decline and powerlessness into a larger context that any reader could appreciate. "Using Glasgow as his undeniable starting point," Douglas Gifford wrote in *Studies in Scottish Literature,* "Gray . . . transforms local and hitherto restricting images, which limited [other] novelists of real ability. . . . into symbols of universal prophetic relevance." As noted above, Gray became prominent as a writer only after several years of working as an artist and illustrator. Gray traces his own literary and artistic development to the early years of his life, once explaining that "as soon as I could draw and tell stories, which was around the age of four or five, I spent a lot of time doing these or planning to do them. My parents were friendly to my childish efforts, as were most of my teachers, though they also told me I was unlikely to make a living by either of these jobs. . . . I was delighted to go to art school, because I was a maturer draftsman and painter than writer. My writings while at art school were attempts to prepare something I knew would take long to finish: though I didn't know how long."

Gray went on to say that although his first novel took years to complete, the story line of what would become his now acclaimed first novel, *Lanark: A Life in Four Books,* had essentially been worked out in his mind by the time he was eighteen. A long and complex work that some reviewers considered partly autobiographical, *Lanark* opens in Unthank, an ugly, declining city explained in reviews as a comment on Glasgow and other Western industrial centers. As in George Orwell's *Nineteen Eighty-four,* citizens of Unthank are ruled by a domineering and intrusive bureaucracy. Lanark is a lonely young man unable to remember his past. Along with many of his fellow-citizens, he is plagued with "dragonhide," an insidious, scaly skin infection seen as symbolic of his emotional isolation. Cured of his affliction by doctors at a scientific institute below the surface of the Earth, Lanark realizes to his disgust that the staff is as arrogant and manipulative as the ruling elite on the surface. Before escaping from this underworld, Lanark has a vision in which he sees the life story of a young man who mysteriously resembles him—Duncan Thaw, an aspiring artist who lives in twentieth-century Glasgow.

Thaw's story, which comprises nearly half the book, is virtually a novel within a novel. It echoes the story of Lanark while displaying a markedly different literary technique. As William Boyd explained in the *Times Literary Supplement,* "The narration of Thaw's life turns out to be a brilliant and moving evocation of a talented and imaginative child growing up in working-class Glasgow. The style is limpid and classically elegant, the detail solidly documentary and in marked contrast to the fantastical and surrealistic accoutrements of the first 100 pages." Like Gray, Thaw attends art school in Glasgow, and, as with Lanark, Thaw's loneliness and isolation are expressed outwardly in a skin disease, eczema. With increasing desperation, Thaw seeks fulfillment in love and art, and his disappointment culminates in a violent outburst with tragic consequences. Boyd considered Thaw's story "a minor classic of the literature of adolescence," and Gifford likened it to James Joyce's novel *A Portrait of the Artist As a Young Man.* The last part of Gray's book focuses once more on Lanark, depicting his futile struggle to improve the world around him. Readers have often remarked on the various diseases the characters in *Lanark's* Unthank suffer from: dragonhide, mouths, twittering rigor, softs. When asked if these diseases had allegorical significance, Gray once commented: "Probably, but I came to that conclusion after, not before, I imagined and described them. And it would limit the reader's enjoyment and understanding of my stories to fix on one 'allegorical significance' and say 'This is it.'" While some critics felt *Lanark* to be hampered by its size and intricacy, it rapidly achieved critical recognition in Britain, and Burgess featured it in his book *Ninety-nine Novels: The Best in English since 1939—A Personal Choice,* declaring, "It was time Scotland produced a shattering work of fiction in the modern idiom. This is it."

Although *Lanark* rapidly achieved critical recognition in Britain, it was Gray's second novel, *1982 Janine,* that was the first to be widely known in the United States. When asked why his work had finally attained critical notice in the United States, Gray once commented: "*Lanark* was the first novel I had published in the U.S.A., by Harper & Row in 1981. It was speedily remaindered, because Harper & Row classified it as science fiction, only sent it to sci-fi magazines for review, and the sci-fi reviewers were not amused. . . . I suppose my books have been published in the United States because they sold well in Britain, and were praised by authors of *A Clockwork Orange* [Anthony Burgess] and *The History Man* [Malcolm Bradbury]."

1982 Janine records the thoughts of Jock McLeish, a disappointed, middle-aged Scottish businessman, during a long night of heavy drinking. In his mind, Jock plays and replays fantasies in which he sexually tortures helpless women, and he gives names and identities to his victims, including Janine of the title. Burgess expressed the opinion of several reviewers when he wrote in the *Observer* that such material was offensive and unneeded. But admirers of the novel, such as Richard Eder of the *Los Angeles Times,* felt that Jock's sexual fantasies were a valid metaphor for the character's own sense of helplessness. Jock, who rose to a managerial post from a working-class background, now hates himself because he is financially dependent on the ruling classes he once hoped to change. Eder observed that Jock's powerlessness is in its turn a metaphor for the subjugation of Scotland. Jock expounds on the sorry state of his homeland in the course of his drunken railings. Scotland's economy, he charges, has been starved in order to strengthen the country's political master, England; what is more, if war with the Soviet Union breaks out, Jock expects the English to use Scotland as a nuclear battlefield. As the novel ends, Jock resolves to quit his job and change his life for the better. Eder commended Gray for conveying a portrait of helplessness and the search for self-realization "in a flamboyantly comic narrator whose verbal blue streak is given depth by a winning impulse to self-discovery, and some alarming insight."

Gray's short-story collection, *Unlikely Stories, Mostly,* is "if anything more idiosyncratic" than *1982 Janine,* according to Jonathan Baumbach of the *New York Times Book Review.* Many reviewers praised the imaginativeness of the stories while acknowledging that the collection, which includes work dating back to Gray's teenage years, is uneven in quality. Gary Marmorstein observed in the *Los Angeles Times Book*

Review, some of the stories are "slight but fun," including "The Star," in which a boy catches a star and swallows it, and "The Spread of Ian Nicol," in which a man slowly splits in two like a microbe reproducing itself. By contrast, "Five Letters from an Eastern Empire" is one of several more complex tales that received special praise. Set in the capital of a powerful empire, the story focuses on a talented poet. Gradually readers learn the source of the poet's artistic inspiration: the emperor murdered the boy's parents by razing the city in which they lived, then ordered him to write about the destruction. "The tone of the story remains under perfect control as it darkens and deepens," according to Adam Mar-Jones in the *Times Literary Supplement,* "until an apparently reckless comedy has become a cruel parable about power and meaning." While responding to a question about *Lanark* and the possible allegorical significance of its characters, Gray related an anecdote about the story "Five Letters from an Eastern Empire": "I wrote [the story] when [I was] writer-in-residence at Glasgow University. When I finished, it occurred to me that the Eastern Empire was an allegory of modern Britain viewed from Glasgow University by a writer-in-residence. A year ago I met someone just returned from Tokyo, who said he had heard a Chinese and a Japanese academic having an argument about my Eastern Empire story. The Chinese was quite sure the empire was meant to be China, the Japanese that it was Japan. My only knowledge of these lands is from a few color prints, Arthur Waley's translation of the novel *Monkey* [by Wu Ch'eng-en] and some translated poems."

Gray's third novel, *The Fall of Kelvin Walker: A Fable of the Sixties,* was inspired by personal experience. Still struggling to establish his career several years after his graduation from art school, Gray was tapped as the subject of a documentary by a successful friend at the British Broadcasting Corporation (BBC). Gray, who had been living on welfare, suddenly found himself treated to airline flights and limousine rides at the BBC's expense. In *The Fall of Kelvin Walker* the title character, a young Scotsman with a burning desire for power, has a similar chance to use the communications media to fulfill his wildest fantasies. Though Kelvin arrives in London with little besides self-confidence and a fast-talking manner, his persistence and good luck soon win him a national following as an interviewer on a television show. But in his pride and ambition, Walker forgets that he exercises such influence only at the whims of his corporate bosses, and when he displeases them, his fall from grace is as abrupt as his rise.

The Fall of Kelvin Walker, which Gray adapted from his 1968 teleplay of the same title ("I sent it to a [BBC] director I know. He gave it to a producer who liked it"), is shorter and less surrealistic than his previous novels. The *Observer*'s Hermione Lee, though she stressed that Gray "is always worth attending to," felt that this novel "doesn't allow him the big scope he thrives on." By contrast, Larry McCaffery of the *New York Times Book Review* praised *The Fall of Kelvin Walker* for its "economy of means and exquisite control of detail." Gray "is now fully in command of his virtuoso abilities as a stylist and storyteller," McCaffery said, asserting that Gray's first four books—"each of which impresses in very different ways—indicate that he is emerging as the most vibrant and original new voice in English fiction."

As reviewers became familiar with Gray's work, they noticed several recurring features: illustrations by the author, typographical eccentricities, and an emphasis on the city of Glasgow. When asked about the illustrations, Gray explained a little about the process of creating this kind of manuscript: "The illustrations and cover designs of my books are not essential to them, being thought of after the text is complete. I add them because they make the book more enjoyable. The queer typography, in the three stories which use it, was devised in the act of writing, not added after, like sugar to porridge."

As Gray continued to write, critical reception of his work varied widely. Many reviewers acknowledged his genius in such works as *Lanark,* while books such as *Something Leather* and *McGrotty and Ludmilla; or, The Harbinger Report: A Romance of the Eighties* were criticized for lacking the intensity of his earlier work. Gray himself was remarkably candid about the quality and intent of some of these efforts. For example, he described *McGrotty and Ludmilla; or, The Harbinger Report* as an Aladdin story set in modern Whitehall, "with the hero a junior civil servant, wicked uncle Abanizir a senior one, and the magic lamp a secret government paper which gave whoever held it unlimited powers of blackmail." And works such as *Something Leather,* said Gerald Mangan in the *Times Literary Supplement,* placed Gray in "an unfortunate tradition in Scottish fiction, whereby novelists have tended to exhaust their inspiration in

the effort of a single major achievement." That *Lanark* was a major achievement Mangan had no doubt. "*Lanark* is now so monumental a Scottish landmark," he wrote, "that few readers would have reproached him if a decade of silence had followed it." Instead, Gray brought out "a good deal of inferior material that had evidently subsidized or distracted him during the composition of his epic." A *New York Times Book Review* article by John Kenny Crane further explained the circumstances under which Gray composed *Something Leather.* According to Crane, a publisher had been pushing Gray for years to produce a new novel. Getting nowhere and needing money, Gray shuffled around in his rejected short-story manuscripts and came up with one about a conventional working woman in Glasgow who decides to shave off her hair and begin dressing in leather clothing. The publisher sent Gray a substantial advance, and the tale of the bald, leather-clad Glaswegian woman became his first chapter, "One for the Album." Other unpublished stories, unstaged plays, and early radio and TV scripts were also pressed into service and ultimately published as *Something Leather.* Crane commented in his review: "Gray, who has published some very creditable works of fiction, shamelessly admits to absolutely everything in his epilogue." Yet, the critic added, "Taken on their own, some of the interior chapters have artistry and merit. I particularly liked the reflections on war in one titled 'In the Boiler Room' and the comical friction caused by the divergent life styles of boarders in 'Quiet People.' As short stories, some are quite fine. I would recommend the reader take them as such, even though Mr. Gray insists they are part of a novel." And despite his own criticism of *Something Leather,* Mangan said that in the five stories that comprise the work, Gray's "prose is generally notable for its refusal of second-hand definitions; and it is not surprising to find, among other consolations, a divertingly cynical diatribe on Glasgow's current status as culture-capital."

With the publication of *Poor Things: Episodes from the Early Life of Archibald McCandless, M.D., Scottish Public Health Officer,* purportedly edited by Gray, the author returns to form, suggested Philip Hensher in the *Spectator,* "after a rather sticky patch." The work drew comparisons to such authors as Daniel Defoe and Laurence Sterne, partly because of its eccentric humor and setting and partly because of Gray's skillful use of the traditions of Victorian novels, which, according to Barbara Hardy in the *Times Literary Supplement,* "embodied their liberal notions of providence and progress in realistic narratives which often surge into optimistic or melioristic visions on the last page."

Set in Glasgow during the 1880s, the novel is narrated by Archie McCandless, a young medical student, who befriends the eccentric Godwin Baxter, another medical student. Baxter has been experimenting on the body of a beautiful and pregnant young woman who committed suicide to escape her abusive husband, and has created "Bella" by transplanting the brain of the fetus into its mother's skull. Bella is sexually mature and wholly amoral, and McCandless wants to marry her. She, however, runs off with a wicked playboy whom she soon drives to insanity and death. A clever final twist produces a book that Hensher described as "a great deal more than entertaining only on finishing it. Then your strongest urge is to start reading it again."

Gray uses his visual and writing talents in *Ten Tall Tales and True: Social Realism, Sexual Comedy, Science Fiction, and Satire*. He illustrates the cover with ten animal tails, then showing each animal in its entirety within the covers. A critic for the *Review of Contemporary Fiction* asked: "Is Gray suggesting perhaps the fragmented and nonhuman character of our life when we do not exist in a state of wholeness?" Set in present-day Scotland, the stories explore human relationships with humor and feeling. "[Gray's] stories most often dramatize those symbioses of oppression in which people find just the right partner, family or group to dominate or be dominated by," wrote Ron Loewinsohn in the *New York Times Book Review*. Observed Christopher Bray in the *Spectator*, "Stories and characters like these ought to make you downcast, and they would, were it not for the pithy intensity with which Gray sketches things in."

Gray expresses his concern for modern society in *A History Maker*, a political allegory set in a twenty-third-century Scotland that seems reminiscent of more ancient times. Society has become matriarchal, and men have little to do but kill each other; their war games are televised as entertainment. "Gray's touch is light and wry, and there is enough strangeness in his future to whet conventional SF appetites. But there is no mistaking the relevance of his allegory to the situation of nation-states in today's uneasy post-Cold War peace," maintained a *Village Voice Literary Supplement* reviewer. A *Publishers Weekly* reviewer stated that *A History Maker* succeeds on "all of its many levels" and is a fine work of social satire: "The wit is sharp, the social commentary on target and, most important, the quirky, arch-voiced storytelling is unfailingly entertaining."

The Book of Prefaces is an unusual volume, which took Gray years to compile and edit. It is, as the title suggests, a collection of what he considers the greatest prefaces in works of literature written in English. It begins with the seventh-century author Caedmon and progresses through the twentieth century. Michael Kerrigan in the *Times Literary Supplement* had mixed feelings about *The Book of Prefaces;* while crediting Gray with choosing "prefaces that motivate the reader to seek out in their entirety the works they introduce, and to acknowledge the alternative futures that past achievements have made," he criticized the book for adhering too closely to a "rigid and restrictive" selection of works, and called it "striking in its portentousness." A very different point of view was expressed by Peter Dollard in *Library Journal* who found *The Book of Prefaces* to be "a delightfully original, ironic, and humorous compilation," a genuine "work of literature" in its own right, thanks to the "fascinating and often idiosyncratic commentary" by Gray.

When Sam Phipps reviewed *The Ends of our Tethers: 13 Sorry Stories,* for the *Spectator,* he remarked that Gray's first fiction in seven years "confirms that at the age of sixty-eight he is in rude, wry and irascible health, compellingly inventive and perceptive—and never afraid to send himself up. Indeed an ambivalent mood of defiance and self-ridicule runs through the collection, beginning with the jacket, which as always Gray has designed himself: a naked, athletic, bearded man bearing a close resemblance to the author." The entire collection is dedicated to Agnes Owens, an excellent although little-known Scottish author, and, in it, Gray's characters develop largely as what Irvine Welsh, reviewing the book for the *Guardian*, called "disappointed idealists, saddened by setbacks both political and personal, the latter usually of a romantic nature, and their progress charts more than the customary replacement of youthful idealism with the cynicism of old age." Welsh commented that Gray's "new collection of short stories contains almost everything we have come to associate with its author. The pages glow with keen and incisive wit, are stuffed with quirky and downright weird occurrences, while the philosophical ruminations make us pause for thought, and the sad, flawed, often cowardly, but ultimately humane and decent protagonists are back with a vengeance. Once again, the book is beautifully illustrated by the author's own hand, and in the appendix the critics are playfully baited in advance."

BIOGRAPHICAL AND CRITICAL SOURCES:

BOOKS

Bernstein, Stephen, *Alasdair Gray,* Associated University Presses (Cranbury, NJ), 1999.

Burgess, Anthony, *Ninety-nine Novels: The Best in English since 1939—A Personal Choice,* Allison & Busby (London, England), 1984.

Contemporary Literary Criticism, Volume 41, Thomson Gale (Detroit, MI), 1987.

Crawford, R., and T. Naim, editors, *The Arts of Alasdair Gray,* Edinburgh University Press (Edinburgh, Scotland), 1991.

Dictionary of Literary Biography, Volume 194: *British Novelists since 1960, Second Series,* Thomson Gale (Detroit, MI), 1998.

Moore, Phil, editor, *Alasdair Gray: Critical Appreciations and Bibliography,* British Library (London, England), 2001.

PERIODICALS

Booklist, March 1, 1994, Gilbert Taylor, review of *Ten Tales Tall and True: Social Realism, Sexual Comedy, Science Fiction, and Satire,* p. 1180; October 1, 2000, Mary Ellen Quinn, review of *The Book of Prefaces,* p. 374.

Books, September, 1993, p. 9.

Christian Science Monitor, October 5, 1984.

Daily Telegraph, August 30, 1992, Kate Chisholm, review of *Poor Things: Episodes from the Early Life of Archibald McCandless, M.D., Scottish Public Health Officer;* December 17, 1994, David Profumo, review of *A History Maker;* November 11, 1995, Candida Clark and Jason Thompson, review of *A History Maker;* January 18, 1997, Miranda France, interview with Alasdair Gray.

Guardian, September 2, 1992, Francis Spufford, interview with Alasdair Gray; June 18, 1998, Jonathan Jones, interview with Alasdair Gray; October 11, 2003, Irvine Welsh, review of *The Ends of our Tethers: 13 Sorry Stories,* p. 26.

Kirkus Reviews, February 1, 1994, review of *Ten Tales Tall and True,* p. 87; February 15, 1996, review of *A History Maker,* p. 247.

Library Journal, May 1, 1991, Francis Poole, review of *Library Journal,* p. 108; August, 2000, Peter Dollard, review of *The Book of Prefaces,* p. 102.

Los Angeles Times, November 21, 1984, Richard Eder, review of *1982 Janine.*

Los Angeles Times Book Review, December 9, 1984, Gary Marmorstein, review of *Unlikely Stories, Mostly.*

New Republic, November 12, 1984.

New Statesman, November 25, 1994, p. 48.

New Statesman & Society, September 11, 1992, Christopher Harvie, review of *Poor Things,* p. 38; November 25, 1994, Boyd Tonkin, review of *A History Maker,* p. 48.

Newsweek, March 22, 1993, Malcolm Jones, Jr., review of *Poor Things,* p. 70.

New York, March 8, 1993, Rhoda Koenig, review of *Poor Things,* p. 84.

New Yorker, April 12, 1993, review of *Poor Things,* p. 121.

New York Review of Books, April 25, 1991.

New York Times Book Review, October 28, 1984, Jonathan Baumbach, review of *Unlikely Stories, Mostly,* p. 9; May 5, 1985; December 21, 1986, Larry McCaffery, review of *The Fall of Kelvin Walker: A Fable of the Sixties,* p. 7; August 4, 1991, John Kenny Crane, review of *Something Leather,* p. 15; March 28, 1993, review of *Poor Things,* p. 8; March 6, 1994, Ron Loewinsohn, review of *Ten Tales Tall and True,* p. 11; August 18, 1996, Nicholas Birns, review of *A History Maker,* p. 18.

Observer (London, England), April 15, 1984; March 31, 1985; September 27, 1994, p. 21; December 10, 1995, p. 15.

Publishers Weekly, April 19, 1991, Sybil Steinberg, review of *Something Leather,* p. 58; January 25, 1993, review of *Poor Things,* p. 78; January 31, 1994, review of *Ten Tales Tall and True,* p. 76; March 4, 1996, review of *A History Maker,* p. 61.

Review of Contemporary Fiction, fall, 1994, Lynne Diamond-Nigh, review of *Poor Things* and *Ten Tales Tall and True,* p. 204.

Spectator, February 28, 1981; September 5, 1992; October 30, 1993, p. 35; October 18, 2003, Sam Phipps, review of *The Ends of Our Tethers,* p. 61.

Stage, November 30, 1972.

Studies in Scottish Literature, Volume 18, 1983, article by Douglas Gifford.

Sunday Times (London, Engalnd), December 11, 1994, Andro Linklater, review of *A History Maker.*

Times (London, England), April 1, 1986.

Times Literary Supplement, February 27, 1981; March 18, 1983; April 13, 1984; March 29, 1985; May 10, 1985; July 6-12, 1990, Gerald Mangan,

"Lucrative Lines," p. 731; April 3, 1992; August 28, 1992; December 9, 1994, p. 22; August 11, 2000, Michael Kerrigan, review of *A Book of Prefaces,* p. 10.

Village Voice Literary Supplement, December, 1984; April, 1996, p. 8.

Washington Post Book World, December 16, 1984; August 31, 1986; June 16, 1991.

Whole Earth Review, December 22, 1995, James Donnely, review of *Ten Tales Tall and True.* *

*   *   *

GREER, Richard
   See SILVERBERG, Robert

*   *   *

GREGOR, Lee
   See POHL, Frederik

*   *   *

GROSSBACH, Robert 1941-

PERSONAL: Born December 31, 1941, in Bronx, NY; son of Herman and Mollie Grossbach; married Sylvia Cohen; children: Mitchell, Elliot, Jennifer. *Education:* Cooper Union, B.S.E.E., 1962; Columbia University, M.E.E., 1965.

ADDRESSES: Agent—c/o Author Mail, St. Martin's Press, 175 5th Ave., New York, NY 10010.

CAREER: Wheeler Laboratories, Long Island, NY, engineer, 1962-65; Loral Corp., Bronx, NY, senior engineer, 1965-68; Narda Microwaves, Plainview, NY, section head, 1970-77; freelance writer and engineering consultant, 1977—.

MEMBER: Authors Guild, Authors League of America, Screenwriters Guild of America, Institute of Electrical and Electronics Engineers.

AWARDS, HONORS: Isaacson Award for best short story, New School for Social Research, 1969, for "The Abolition of Surveying at Camp Green."

WRITINGS:

Someone Great, Harper's Magazine Press (New York, NY), 1971.

Easy and Hard Ways Out, Harper's Magazine Press (New York, NY), 1975, published as *Best Defense,* Carroll & Graf (New York, NY), 1984.

Never Say Die: An Autonecrographical Novel, Harper (New York, NY), 1979.

A Shortage of Engineers (humorous novel), St. Martin's Press (New York, NY), 2001.

Also author of a novel, *Round Trip.* Contributor to books, including *Laughing Space* (short-story anthology), edited by Isaac Asimov, Houghton Mifflin (Boston, MA), 1982. Contributor of short stories and technical articles to periodicals, including *Transatlantic Review,Magazine of Fantasy and Science Fiction, Creative Computing, Microwave Journal,* and Institute of Electrical and Electronic Engineers *Proceedings.*

NOVELIZATIONS OF SCREENPLAYS

The Goodbye Girl (based on screenplay by Neil Simon), Warner Books (New York, NY), 1977.

The Cheap Detective (based on screenplay by Neil Simon), Warner Books (New York, NY), 1978.

California Suite (based on screenplay by Neil Simon), Warner Books (New York, NY), 1978.

The Frisco Kid (based on screenplay by Michael Elias), Warner Books (New York, NY), 1979.

. . . And Justice for All (based on screenplay by Barry Levinson), Ballantine (New York, NY), 1979.

Going in Style (based on screenplay by Martin Brest), Warner Books (New York, NY), 1979.

Chapter Two (based on screenplay by Neil Simon), Warner Books (New York, NY), 1980.

The Devil and Max Devlin (based on screenplay by Steve Tesich), Ballantine (New York, NY), 1981.

ADAPTATIONS: Easy and Hard Ways Out was filmed as a motion picture titled *Best Defense,* starring Dudley Moore and Eddie Murphy.

BIOGRAPHICAL AND CRITICAL SOURCES:

PERIODICALS

Kirkus Reviews, May 15, 2001, review of *A Shortage of Engineers,* p. 684.

Publishers Weekly, June 25, 2001, review of *A Shortage of Engineers,* p. 48.

ONLINE

BookReporter.com, http://www.bookreporter.com/ (March 31, 2003), Roz Shea, review of *A Shortage of Engineers.**

*   *   *

GUNESEKERA, Romesh 1954-

PERSONAL: Born 1954, in Colombo, Sri Lanka; raised in Sri Lanka, the Philippines, and England; children: two daughters.

ADDRESSES: Home—London, England. *Agent*—c/o Author Mail, Bloomsbury Publishing, 38 Soho Square, London W1D 3HB, England.

CAREER: Novelist and short-story writer.

AWARDS, HONORS: Arts Council Writers' Bursary, 1991; finalist, David Higham Prize, 1992, Commonwealth Writers' Regional Prize, 1993, and Notable Book of the Year, *New York Times,* 1993, all for *Monkfish Moon;* finalist for Booker Prize and *Guardian Fiction Prize,* both 1994, for *Reef;* Best First Work award, *Yorkshire Post,* 1994, for *Reef;* Premio Mondello, 1997, for *Reef;* nominated for New Voice Award; BBC Asia Award for Achievement in Writing and Literature, 1998.

WRITINGS:

Monkfish Moon (short stories), Granta Books (London, England), 1992, New Press (New York, NY), 1992.
Reef (novel), New Press (New York, NY), 1995.
The Sandglass (novel), Granta Books (London, England), 1998, Riverhead Books (New York, NY), 1999.
Heaven's Edge (novel), Grove Press (New York, NY), 2002.

SIDELIGHTS: In his highly acclaimed stories and novels, Romesh Gunesekera sets his native Sri Lanka at the center of action. On the strength of his first

Romesh Gunesekera

volume of short stories, 1992's *Monkfish Moon,* and his first novel, 1994's *Reef,* Gunesekera was placed by critics in the select company of the most promising young British writers; D. C. R. A. Goonetilleke declared him "arguably one of the top twenty young British novelists" in *Contemporary Novelists,* and poet-diplomat Guy Amirthanayagam, writing for the *Washington Post Book World,* informed readers, "He bids fair to join the likes of V. S. Naipaul, Salman Rushdie, Timothy Mo and Kazuo Ishiguro." *Monkfish Moon* was less than 140 pages long—Suzanne Berne, in the *New York Times Book Review,* called it a "slender, evocative book"—but as Goonetilleke pointed out, "each story is distinct in spite of a common motif of refurbishing dilapidated interiors and . . . an ironic theme of severance, parting, fracture, and failure." With further novels, including 1998's *Sandglass* and 2002's *Heaven's Edge,* Gunesekera has consolidated those early appraisals of his literary potential, eliciting praise from critics and fellow writers alike.

Though several of the stories in *Monkfish Moon* are set in London, Sri Lankan life, and especially the civil war between Tamil and Sinhala forces, makes itself felt from across the sea. D. J. Taylor, reviewing the book for the *New Statesman and Society,* felt that the stories were strongest when politics emerged quietly from the background as in "Batik" and "A House in the Country," rather than being placed in the foreground of the narration as in "Storm Petrel." Taylor felt that "Gunesekera's forte is atmosphere: tiny intimations of disquiet, sudden adjustments to the psychological thermostat against a background of political turmoil. . . . [he] achieves his best effects in stories where character resists the thraldom imposed on it by environment." Taylor further named the title story and "Carapace" as examples of this strength.

The novel *Reef* solidified Gunesekera's growing reputation. A coming-of-age story about a young domestic servant named Triton, it is set mainly in the 1960s but is narrated in flashback from the vantage point of thirty years later. As a boy, Triton is brought into the house of Salgado, a marine biologist obsessed with saving a local reef. Triton acquires the skills of cookery, and, within the limits of the experiences available to him, grows in sophistication. A worldly Sri Lankan woman, Nili, enters the household as Salgado's lover. The lovers part on bitter terms, after which Salgado and Triton move to London. In that city, Triton achieves a degree of independence as owner of a prosperous snack bar and eventually a restaurant. In the end, Salgado returns to the ravaged land of Sri Lanka to rejoin Nili, who has been psychologically maimed and rendered homeless by the communal violence.

Critics received *Reef* enthusiastically, praising in particular its language and characters. "The strength of the novel lies in its treatment of individual lives and personal relations and in its characteristic use of language," wrote Goonetilleke. "Gunesekera's style is sensuous and impassioned, almost incandescent," proclaimed Amirthanayagam. Travel writer Pico Iyer, in the *New York Review of Books,* was also impressed by the subtle beauties of Gunesekera's apparently simple prose, calling the book an "unusual prose-poem." Referring to the novel's "exquisitely sensuous surface," Iyer elaborated that the book was "lush" with descriptions of flora and fauna, of scents and sights: "The strength of *Reef,* in fact, lies in its unforced and convincing depiction of a self-contained

universe." Iyer added praise for the novelist's supple technique: "The remarkable thing about this novel, indeed, is that it achieves nearly all of its effects silently, as it were, through almost imperceptible shadings of language and texture. . . . *Reef* proceeds so gently and lyrically—whispering around us like a murmurous sea—that it is easy to overlook just how subversive the book is." The subversiveness and "singular courage" of the book, Iyer commented, lay in its presentation of social corruption as deeper than ideology or fashion. All in all, *Reef* was, for that reviewer, "the best novel from the subcontinent since Rohinton Mistry's *Such a Long Journey. . . .* Calmly, it gives us a new and unexpected world, and gradually it makes it feel like home."

Neil Gordon, in the *Boston Review,* compared the central Christmas-dinner scene in *Reef* to James Joyce's novella *The Dead,* and called the young author "one of the two or three best writers I've encountered among my contemporaries." Like other critics, Gordon loved what he termed Gunesekera's "wholly original, very ambitious language," and applied the epithet "exquisite." Gordon doubted whether the novel succeeded in weaving topical political concerns organically into Triton's first-person narrative; however, he clarified, "emotional realities are what this book, in its perceptive, quiet voice, is most convincingly about." Aamer Hussein, a *Times Literary Supplement* reviewer, also commented on the short-storylike nature of the novel, surmising that "the author . . . has cunningly contrived to compose his novel of fragments structured like complete stories; but each story is deliberately deprived of an essential element, which is later revealed at the right moment."

Another aspect of Gunesekera's achievement that came in for praise was his creation of character, particularly that of Salgado. Richard Eder, in the *Los Angeles Times Book Review,* called Salgado "a wonderful mix of abstraction and urgency." Eder praised Gunesekera for saying so much within the deliberately confined scope of a first-person tale about a servant: "[He] has taken the risk of telling a large story in the tiny, almost cloying constriction of meals, recipes, furniture polishing and a boy's besotted reverence for the figure for whom he performed these tasks." The risk paid off, Eder implied, thus meriting its author respect both for courage and for achievement.

Gordon, a novelist himself, wrote of Gunesekera's work in the *Boston Review* concluding: "The perceptive, thrilling dram of his narration seems to burst the limits of his framing device, a tribute to the power of his story. I look forward to reading every word he writes . . . in the hopes of seeing his stories escape his rather tendentious narrative bias toward literary relevance and speak more simply and dramatically for themselves."

Similar themes are presented in Gunesekera's second novel, *The Sandglass,* which "addresses the search for a personal and national sense of belonging," according to Akash Kapur in the *New York Times Book Review.* In this novel, the author indirectly tells the story of Sri Lanka's bloody civil war in the tale of a long-standing feud between two families, the Ducals and the Vatunases. The feud, like the country's war, involves contested land, in this case a house bought by Jason Ducal in Colombo that was once a part of the Vatunas estate. Set in London, the book is filtered through the thoughts of an expatriate from Sir Lanka, Chip, whose memories are spurred by the death of Pearl Ducal and the arrival from Colombo of her son, Prins Ducal, for his mother's funeral. The reader is introduced to four generations of conflict between the Ducal and Vatunas families via bits and pieces of diaries and anecdotes as the novel moves back and forth in time and place.

This book elicited more praise from the critics. Bonnie Johnston, writing in *Booklist,* called it a "touching drama" that is "part murder mystery, part historical fiction." Iyer, reviewing the novel in *Time,* commended the author's "exquisite, jeweled miniatures" that give the book depth and resonance. For Janet Ingraham Dwyer in *Library Journal,* it was a "tender, accomplished novel." Similarly, a reviewer for *Publishers Weekly* called it a "poignant tale." Not all reviewers were full of praise, however. Nisid Hajari, writing in *Time International,* faulted the novel for its characters who "speak with inconsistent voices—formal one moment, almost incomprehensively colloquial the next." Eder, writing in the *Los Angeles Times Book Review,* also found problems with the narrative structure. Noting that the book "evokes a miasma of familial and national evil," Eder further observed that the "author's indirection and cloudiness and the paralyzed destinies of his characters . . . produce narrative confusion and bog it down." For Hugo Barnacle, writing in the *Sunday Times,* however, "the anecdotal retrospection of the narrative is a good way to catch the atmosphere created by a death in the family." Christina Koning of the London *Times*

thought that the author was "adept at conveying an elegiac mood, and there are passages of great poignancy in his book." And more praise came from Maya Jaggi in the *Guardian,* who concluded that "this novel reaffirms Gunesekera's strengths in illuminating intimate truths through a minimal plot."

In Gunesekera's 2002 novel, *Heaven's Edge,* the protagonist, Marc, returns to an unnamed island, much like the author's native Sri Lanka, in an "almost epic quest to discover and understand both his homeland and himself," according to *Library Journal*'s Caroline Hallsworth. Back in his environmentally despoiled island, Marc meets Uva, an ecological activist, who introduces him to her world of resistance against the repressive regime. Here to find his father, Marc instead finds love, and then loses it when government troops set out after Uva. Marc, too, becomes an enemy of the regime and is incarcerated in a government camp until he manages to escape, and then sets out on a journey to find Uva. As a reviewer for *Publishers Weekly* commented, this search "has moments of both breathtaking suspense . . . and quiet introspection." For the same reviewer, the "compelling romance [between Marc and Uva] makes this one of [Gunesekera's] best efforts." A critic for *Kirkus Reviews* called the book "strange [and] lyrical," while *Booklist*'s Michele Leber observed that the author "writes lyrically and with feeling," combining "elements of fable and magic realism."

Other critics found fault with the characterization and more fanciful elements, however. Phil Baker, for example, writing in the *Sunday Times,* felt the book was "ambitious but unsatisfying," and Peter Bien noted in *World Literature Today* that the "novel's artistry fails to match the promise of its theme." Though despairing of the "fair amount of eco-babble" in the book, the *Sunday Telegraph*'s David Robson found that "the novel is also, at its best, an engaging adventure story set in an unusual landscape, exquisitely described." Similar praise came from other reviewers. Kapur commended the "spare and muscular" prose in the book and further observed that the "story may be dreamlike, but [Gunesekera's] prose is resolutely grounded." *Heaven's Edge* is, for Kapur, a "story that uses realism to transcend reality, to hint at deeper mysteries and more profound truths." And Abdulrazak Gurnah, writing in the *Times Literary Supplement,* called it a "gripping novel written with an unforced poetic assurance."

BIOGRAPHICAL AND CRITICAL SOURCES:

BOOKS

Contemporary Literary Criticism, Volume 91: *Yearbook 1995,* Thomson Gale (Detroit, MI), 1996, pp. 33-44.
Contemporary Novelists, 6th edition, St. James Press (Detroit, MI), 1996, pp. 423-424.

PERIODICALS

Booklist, September 15, 1998, Bonnie Johnston, review of *The Sandglass,* p. 199; January 1, 2003, Michele Leber, review of *Heaven's Edge,* p. 847.
Boston Globe, March 16, 2003, Amanda Heller, review of *Heaven's Edge,* p. D7.
Boston Review, April, 1995, Neil Gordon, review of *Reef,* pp. 31-32.
Christian Science Monitor, March 30, 1995, Rubin Merle, review of *Reef,* p. B2.
Globe & Mail (Toronto, Ontario, Canada), July 5, 2003, Martin Levin, review of *Heaven's Edge,* p. D13.
Guardian (London, England), February 26, 1998, Maya Jaggi, review of *The Sandglass,* p. 14; May 11, 2002, Jaggi, review of *Heaven's Edge,* p. 9.
Kirkus Reviews, November 1, 2002, review of *Heaven's Edge,* p. 1553.
Library Journal, September 1, 1998, Janet Ingraham Dwyer, review of *The Sandglass,* p. 213; February 15, 2003, Caroline Hallsworth, review of *Heaven's Edge,* p. 168.
Los Angeles Times Book Review, February 19, 1995, Richard Eder, review of *Reef,* pp. 3, 11; November 1, 1998, Eder, review of *The Sandglass,* p. 2; March 10, 2003, Merle Rubin, review of *Heaven's Edge,* p. E13.
New Internationalist, May, 2002, Peter Whittaker, review of *Heaven's Edge,* pp. 31-32.
New Statesman and Society, February 28, 1992, D. J. Taylor, review of *Monkfish Moon,* p. 47; September 2, 1994, p. 38; February 20, 1998, Jason Cowley, review of *The Sandglass,* p. 49.
New York Review of Books, June 22, 1995, Pico Iyer, review of *Reef,* pp. 30-31.
New York Times Book Review, August 1, 1993, Suzanne Berne, review of *Monkfish Moon,* p. 10; January 17, 1999, Jacqueline Carey, review of *The Sandglass,* p. 17; February 23, 2003, Akash Kapur, review of *Heaven's Edge,* p. 6.

Paradise Experience, February 13, 1998, review of *The Sandglass.*
Publishers Weekly, August 3, 1998, review of *The Sandglass,* p. 71; January 27, 2003, review of *Heaven's Edge,* pp. 237-238.
Spectator, May 25, 2002, Gabriele Annan, review of *Heaven's Edge,* pp. 45-46.
Sunday Telegraph (London, England), April 14, 2002, David Robson, review of *Heaven's Edge.*
Sunday Times (London, England), February 15, 1998, Hugo Barnacle, review of *The Sandglass,* p. 9; April 14, 2002, Phil Baker, review of *Heaven's Edge,* p. 43.
Time, September 7, 1998, Pico Iyer, review of *The Sandglass,* p. 80.
Time International, April 13, 1998, Nisid Hajari, review of *The Sandglass,* p. 130.
Times (London, England), January 29, 1998, Christina Koning, review of *The Sandglass,* p. 39; April 24, 2002, Anthea Lawson, review of *Heaven's Edge,* p. 20.
Times Literary Supplement, June 24, 1994, Aamer Hussein, review of *Reef,* p. 23; April 12, 2002, Abdulrazak Gurnah, review of *Heaven's Edge,* p. 10.
Washington Post Book World, June 25, 1995, Guy Amirthanayagam, review of *Reef,* p. 5.
World Literature Today, April-June, 2003, Peter Bien, review of *Heaven's Edge,* p. 91.

ONLINE

Romesh Gunesekera Official Web site, www.romeshgunesekera.com (February 4, 2004).*

* * *

GUSSOW, Joan Dye 1928-

PERSONAL: Born October 4, 1928, in Alhambra, CA; daughter of Chester H. (a civil engineer) and M. Joyce (Fisher) Dye; married Alan M. Gussow (an artist and conservationist), October 21, 1956 (deceased); children: Adam Stefan, Seth James. *Education:* Pomona College, B.A., 1950; Yeshiva University, graduate study, 1965-67; Columbia University, M.Ed., 1974, Ed.D., 1975. *Politics:* "Democrat-liberal."

ADDRESSES: Home—563 Piermont Ave., Piermont, NY 10968.

CAREER: Time, Inc., New York, NY, researcher, 1950-56; freelance writer, 1956-58; Yeshiva University, New York, NY, editorial and research assistant, 1964-66, editorial and research assistant at Albert Einstein College of Medicine, Bronx, NY, 1966-69; Columbia University, Teachers College, New York, New York, instructor in nutrition, 1970-75, assistant professor of nutrition and education and chairperson of nutrition program, beginning 1975, professor emeritus, 1994—. National Organic Standards Board, member, 1996—.

MEMBER: American Association for the Advancement of Science, American Dietetic Association (member of board of directors), Community Nutrition Institute (vice president and member of board of directors), Society for Nutrition Education, Consumer Action Now.

WRITINGS:

(With Herbert G. Birch) *Disadvantaged Children: Health, Nutrition and School Failure,* Grune & Stratton (New York, NY), 1970.
(Compiler) *The Feeding Web: Issues in Nutritional Ecology,* Full Publishing (Palo Alto, CA), 1978.
(Compiler, with Paul R. Thomas) *The Nutrition Debate: Sorting Out Some Answers,* Bull Publishing (Palo Alto, CA), 1986.
Chicken Little, Tomato Sauce, and Agriculture: Who Will Produce Tomorrow's Food?, Bootstrap Press (New York, NY), 1991.
This Organic Life: Confessions of a Suburban Homesteader, Chelsea Green Publishing (White River Junction, VT), 2001.

Contributor of articles to professional journals.

SIDELIGHTS: Joan Dye Gussow once told *CA:* "My principal area of specialization so far as subject matter is concerned is nutrition; however, my overall focus of interest is in bringing about social and economic change before it is too late. I question the value of writing 'just another book' in pursuing this end—but have concluded that books influence opinion leaders and opinion leaders *may* influence the course of events. I continue to be interested in the 'massest' of the mass media—television."

BIOGRAPHICAL AND CRITICAL SOURCES:

PERIODICALS

Booklist, December 15, 1978, review of *The Feeding Web: Issues in Nutritional Ecology,* p. 669; January 15, 1987, review of *The Nutrition Debate: Sorting Out Some Answers,* p. 740.
Choice, April, 1992, H. W. Ockerman, review of *Chicken Little, Tomato Sauce, and Agriculture: Who Will Produce Tomorrow's Foods?,* p. 1246.
Food Technology, February, 1993, John B. Allred, review of *Chicken Little, Tomato Sauce, and Agriculture,* p. 135.
Human Behavior, November, 1978, review of *The Feeding Web,* p. 73.
Journal of Home Economics, winter, 1979, review of *The Feeding Web,* p. 8.
Journal of Nutrition Education, November-December, 1992, Carol C. Giesecke, review of *Chicken Little, Tomato Sauce, and Agriculture,* p. 323.
Kirkus Reviews, March 1, 1987, review of *The Nutrition Debate,* p. 367.
Library Journal, May 15, 2001, Ilse Heidmann, review of *This Organic Life: Confessions of a Suburban Homesteader,* p. 152.
New York Times Book Review, June 3, 2001, Verlyn Klinkenborg, review of *This Organic Life,* p. 8; November 17, 2002, Scott Veale, review of *This Organic Life,* p. 60.
Nutrition Action Healthletter, September, 1991, Bonnie Liebman, "A Chicken Little in Our Future?" (interview), p. 1.
Reference and Research Book News, August, 2001, review of *This Organic Life,* p. 250.
Utne Reader, September, 2001, review of *This Organic Life,* p. 100.
Workbook, spring, 1992, review of *Chicken Little, Tomato Sauce, and Agriculture,* p. 24.*

H

HAMILTON, Franklin
See SILVERBERG, Robert

*   *   *

HAMPTON, Wilborn

PERSONAL: Born in Dallas, TX; married an editor. *Education:* University of Texas at Austin, B.A., c. 1963.

ADDRESSES: Home—New York, NY. *Agent*—c/o Author Mail, Candlewick Press, 2067 Massachusetts Ave., 5th Floor, Cambridge, MA 02140.

CAREER: Journalist and author. United Press International (UPI), cub reporter in Dallas, TX, 1963, then foreign correspondent; *New York Times,* New York, NY, editor.

AWARDS, HONORS: Blue Ribbon Award, 1997, Young Adult Library Services Association Editor's Picks for Reluctant Readers designation, 1998, and Texas Bluebonnet Award nomination, 1999, all for *Kennedy Assassinated!*

WRITINGS:

Kennedy Assassinated!: The World Mourns: A Reporter's Story, Candlewick Press (Cambridge, MA), 1997.

Meltdown: A Race against Nuclear Disaster at Three Mile Island: A Reporter's Story, Candlewick Press (Cambridge, MA), 2001.
September 11, 2001: Attack on New York City, Candlewick Press (Cambridge, MA), 2003.

SIDELIGHTS: In *Kennedy Assassinated!: The World Mourns: A Reporter's Story,* journalist Wilborn Hampton tells the story of how, as a rookie reporter, he happened to be the first employee at United Press International's Dallas, Texas, offices to receive an incoming telephone call reporting that President John F. Kennedy had just been shot. Ironically, the 1963 assassination launched Hampton's career in a new direction: an English literature major, he proved that he had journalistic savvy and fortitude in the hours that ensued as he covered the unfolding story. With what reviewer Elizabeth Bush, writing in the *Bulletin of the Center for Children's Books,* called "journalistic flair and raw, edge-of-the-seat urgency," Hampton describes the pandemonium in covering the breaking story of the successful assassination attempt, as reporters attempted to out-scoop each other for the latest developments and wrestle for use of the press phone. In one case, Hampton tells of purposefully tying up a hospital phone line so that UPI could have direct and instant access to ongoing events. He also moves beyond the assassination and describes related historical events, such as the inauguration of Vice President Lyndon Johnson and the murder of Lee Harvey Oswald at the hands of Jack Ruby, highlighting his text with photos that lend historical perspective. A reviewer for *Publishers Weekly* claimed that the journalist's "taut narrative is absorbing enough to keep pages turning." Hampton does not neglect the emotional impact of the event either, and describes breaking down and crying at Kennedy's death.

During his career as a reporter, Hampton has come face to face with other momentous turns of fate. In *Meltdown: A Race against Nuclear Disaster at Three Mile Island,* he describes one of the worst nuclear power plant accidents in the United States, narrating the story in hour-by-hour chronology. In what a *Publishers Weekly* reviewer described as an "engaging, personal, behind-the-scenes viewpoint," Hampton moves from a discussion of Hiroshima, Japan, as it came under nuclear attack during World War II through the development of nuclear energy to the problems of the Three Mile Island nuclear plant in Harrisburg, Pennsylvania, in 1979. By ending his book with a discussion of the nuclear tragedy at the Soviet plant at Chernobyl in the mid-1980s, Hampton encourages readers to consider "weighty ethical questions about the future of atomic power," the *Publishers Weekly* reviewer added. *Meltdown* provides information regarding the basic operation of a nuclear plant and how the U.S. government dealt with the tragedy as well as presenting readers with "a glimpse into the workings of an experienced journalist," according to *Horn Book* contributor Betty Carter, who praised the book as a "dramatic narrative."

Hampton was living and working in New York City the day the United States came under attack by terrorists, and his book *September 11, 2001: Attack on New York City* presents his experiences. His book takes the form of a collection of vignettes that focus on the way individual people—including those who lost family members, those who lived through the ordeal, and those who helped in clean-up efforts—coped with tragedy. "Without sentimentalizing or sensationalizing, Hampton connects all these stories into a cohesive narrative," noted *Horn Book* contributor Betty Carter, praising the book as "accessible and informative." A *Publishers Weekly* reviewer noted that Hampton's "strong, and occasionally rawly emotional, reporting" is compelling, while in *Booklist* GraceAnne A. DeCandido dubbed *September 11, 2001* "one of the best" books written to explain that fateful day to younger readers.

BIOGRAPHICAL AND CRITICAL SOURCES:

PERIODICALS

Booklist, September 15, 1997, Ilene Cooper, review of *Kennedy Assassinated!: The World Mourns: A Reporter's Story,* p. 230; January 1, 2002, Randy

Meyer, review of *Meltdown: A Race against Nuclear Disaster at Three Mile Island: A Reporter's Story,* p. 835; July, 2003, GraceAnne A. DeCandido, review of *September 11, 2001: Attack on New York City,* p. 1878.

Bulletin of the Center for Children's Books, October, 1997, pp. 52-53.

Horn Book, January-February, 2003, Betty Carter, review of *Meltdown,* p. 98; September-October, 2003, Betty Carter, review of *September 11, 2001,* p. 629.

New York Times Book Review, November 16, 1997, p. 28.

Publishers Weekly, July 28, 1997, review of *Kennedy Assassinated!,* p. 75; November 3, 1997, p. 60; October 15, 2001, review of *Meltdown,* p. 73; August 18, 2003, review of *September 11, 2001,* p. 81.

School Library Journal, October, 1997, review of *Kennedy Assassinated!,* p. 147; July, 2003, Wendy Lukehart, review of *September 11, 2001,* p. 141.

ONLINE

Candlewick Press Web site, http://www.candlewick.com/ (January 23, 2005), "Wilborn Hampton."*

*   *   *

HARTMANN, William K(enneth) 1939-

PERSONAL: Born June 6, 1939, in New Kensington, PA; son of Ernest C. (an engineer) and Erdys C. (Carmichael) Hartmann; married Gayle G. Harrison (an editor), March 22, 1970; children: Amy. *Education:* Pennsylvania State University, B.S., 1961; University of Arizona, M.S., 1965, Ph.D., 1966.

ADDRESSES: Home—2224 East 4th St., Tucson, AZ 85719. *Office*—Planetary Science Institute, 620 North 6th Ave., Tucson, AZ 85705-8331. *E-mail*—hartmann@psi.edu.

CAREER: University of Arizona, Tucson, assistant professor of astronomy, 1966-70; IIT Research Institute, Tucson, AZ, research scientist, 1969-71, senior scientist, 1971-72; Science Applications International Corp., Tucson, senior scientist at

Planetary Science Institute, 1972-95; Planetary Science Institute, Tucson, senior scientist at San Juan Research Institute, 1995—. University of Hawaii, visiting associate professor, 1975; member of affiliated faculty, University of Hawaii—Hilo, 1990, and University of Arizona, 1993. National Aeronautics and Space Administration, investigator for 1971 Mariner 9 Mars Mission, 1971-72, and Mars Observer Mission, 1991, member of imaging team for U.S. Mars Global Surveyor Mission, 1996, and investigator for Russian Mars 96 Mission; National Research Council, member of committee on planetary exploration, 1984-87; consultant to Smithsonian Air and Space Museum and House Select Committee on Assassinations. Painter of astronomical scenes, with work represented in books and exhibitions. Member of Tucson Advisory Committee on Air Pollution, 1970-71, and Pima County Air Pollution Advisory Committee, beginning 1975.

MEMBER: American Astronomical Society, American Association for the Advancement of Science (fellow), Society of Southwestern Authors.

AWARDS, HONORS: Nininger Meteorite Award, Arizona State University, 1965, for research on meteorites and the early history of the solar system; Carl Sagan Memorial Award, American Astronomical Society, 1998; cowinner of Rucorn-Florensky Medal, European Geophysical Society, 2002; Asteroid 3341 was named Hartmann in honor of the author's research on the evolution of the solar system.

WRITINGS:

Moon and Planets, Wadsworth (New York, NY), 1972, 4th edition, 1998.

(With Odell Raper) *The New Mars,* U.S. Government Printing Office (Washington, DC), 1974.

Astronomy: The Cosmic Journey, Wadsworth (New York, NY), 1977, 6th edition, 2002.

(With Daid F. Tver and Lloyd Motz) *Dictionary of Astronomy, Space, and Atmospheric Phenomena,* Van Nostrand Reinhold, (New York, NY), 1979.

(And illustrator; with Ron Miller) *The Grand Tour: A Traveler's Guide to the Solar System,* Workman Publishing (New York, NY), 1981.

(Editor, with R. J. Phillips and G. J. Taylor) *Origin of the Moon,* Lunar and Planetary Institute (Houston, TX), 1986.

Out of the Cradle: Exploring the Frontiers beyond Earth, illustrated by Hartmann, Ron Miller, and Pamela Lee, Workman Publishing (New York, NY), 1984.

Cycles of Fire: Stars, Galaxies, and the Wonder of Deep Space, illustrated by Hartmann, Ron Miller, Pamela Lee, and Tom Miller, Workman Publishing (New York, NY), 1987.

(And photographer) *Desert Heart: Chronicles of the Sonoran Desert,* Fischer Books (Tucson, AZ), 1989.

(Coeditor) *In the Stream of Stars: The Soviet/American Space Art Book,* Workman Publishing (New York, NY), 1990.

The Cosmic Voyage: Through Time and Space, Wadsworth (Belmont, CA), 1990.

The History of Earth: An Illustrated Chronicle of an Evolving Planet, illustrated by Hartmann and Ron Miller, Workman Publishing (New York, NY), 1991.

The American Desert, Crown Publishers (New York, NY), 1991.

Mars Underground (novel), Tor Books (New York, NY), 1997.

(With Chris Impey) *The Universe Revealed,* Brooks/Cole (Pacific Grove, CA), 2000.

(Editor, with R. Kellenbach and J. Geiss) *Chronology and Evolution of Mars,* Kluwer Academic (Boston, MA), 2001.

Cities of Gold: A Novel of the Ancient and Modern Southwest, Forge (New York, NY), 2002.

A Traveler's Guide to Mars, Workman Publishing (New York, NY), 2003.

Contributor of articles and paintings to astronomy journals and other magazines, including *Scientific American* and *Natural History.* Associate editor, *Journal of Geophysical Research,* 1974-77; member of editorial advisory board, *Astronomy.*

SIDELIGHTS: William K. Hartmann once wrote: "By background I am an astronomer with research interests in the origin and early evolution of the planets, and the possibility of planets and life elsewhere in the universe. In my writing, I have tried to communicate some of the excitement of current space exploration to the public. This is important because many scientists are not motivated to do it at all, and because we live in an age that threatens to exchange exploration and discovery for mysticism and magic. My writings stress the reflection of space discovery back onto a new perception of earth's environment."

BIOGRAPHICAL AND CRITICAL SOURCES:

PERIODICALS

Kirkus Reviews, October 15, 2002, review of *Cities of Gold: A Novel of the Ancient and Modern Southwest,* p. 1495.
Odyssey, December, 1999, Stephen James O'Meara, "Five Steps Beyond: An Interview with Carl Sagan Memorial Award Winner William K. Hartmann," p. 20.
SciTech Book News, March, 2002, review of *The Cosmic Journey,* p. 49.

ONLINE

Planetary Science Institute: Bill Hartmann's Home Page, http://www.psi.edu/hartmann (November 15, 2004).*

*　　　*　　　*

HASSRICK, Peter H(eyl) 1941-

PERSONAL: Born April 27, 1941, in Philadelphia, PA; son of Royal Brown (a writer) and E. Barbara (Morgan) Hassrick; married Elizabeth Drake, June 14, 1963; children: Philip Heyl, Charles Royal. *Education:* Attended Harvard University, 1962; University of Colorado, B.A., 1963; University of Denver, M.A., 1969.

ADDRESSES: Office—520 Parrington Oval, Room 202, University of Oklahoma, Norman, OK 73019. *E-mail*—hassrick@ou.edu.

CAREER: Lone Star Ranch, Elizabeth, CO, rancher and assistant foreman, summers, 1960-63; high school teacher of history, Spanish, and art history in Steamboat Springs, CO, 1963-67; Amon Carter Museum, Fort Worth, TX, curator of collections, 1969-75; Whitney Gallery of Western Art, Cody, WY, curator and director of Buffalo Bill Historical Center, 1976-96; Georgia O'Keeffe Museum, Santa Fe, NM, director, 1996-97; University of Oklahoma, Norman, Charles Marion Russell Professor of Art History and director of Charles M. Russell Center for the Study of Art of

the American West, 1998—. Texas Christian University, instructor in history, 1974-75; Rancher in Colorado, summers, 1963-65.

MEMBER: American Association of Museums.

AWARDS, HONORS: Leadership Award, Yellowstone National Park, 1989; Wyoming Governor's Art award, 1989.

WRITINGS:

Birger Sandzen, Amon Carter Museum (Fort Worth, TX), 1970.
Frederic Remington: An Essay and Catalogue to Accompany a Retrospective Exhibition, Amon Carter Museum (Fort Worth, TX), 1972.
Frederic Remington: Paintings, Drawings, and Sculpture in the Amon Carter Museum and the Sid W. Richardson Foundation Collections, Harry N. Abrams (New York, NY), 1973.
(Editor) *Amon Carter Museum of Western Art: Catalogue of the Collection, 1972,* Amon Carter Museum (Fort Worth, TX), 1973.
(With Ron Tyler) *The American West,* U.S. Information Agency (Washington, DC), 1974.
The Way West, Harry N. Abrams (New York, NY), 1977.
The Artists, Buffalo Bill, and the Wild West, Brooklyn Museum (Brooklyn, NY), 1981.
(With Patricia Trenton) *The Rocky Mountains: A Vision for Artists in the Nineteenth Century,* University of Oklahoma Press (Norman, OK), 1983.
Treasures of the Old West: Paintings and Sculpture from the Thomas Gilcrease Institute of American History and Art, Harry N. Abrams (New York, NY), 1984.
George Catlin: Drawings of the North American Indians, Doubleday (New York, NY), 1984.
(With Michael Edward Shapiro and others) *Frederic Remington: The Masterworks,* Harry N. Abrams (New York, NY), 1988.
American Frontier Life: Early Western Painting and Prints, Crown Publishing Group (New York, NY), 1989.
Charles M. Russell, Harry N. Abrams (New York, NY), 1989, University of Oklahoma Press (Norman, OK), 1999.

The Frederic Remington Studio, Buffalo Bill Histori-
cal Center (Cody, WY), 1994.
(With Melissa J. Webster) *Frederic Remington: A
Catalogue Raisonne of Paintings, Watercolors,
and Drawings,* two volumes, with CD-ROM, Buf-
falo Bill Historical Center (Cody, WY), 1996.
(General editor) *The Georgia O'Keeffe Museum,* Harry
N. Abrams (New York, NY), 1997.
(Editor and author of introduction) *The American West:
Out of Myth, into Reality,* Trust for Museum
Exhibitions (Washington, DC), 2000.
*Drawn to Yellowstone: Artists in America's First
National Park,* Autry Museum of Western Heritage
(Los Angeles), 2002.
*Wildlife and Western Heroes: Alexander Phimister
Proctor, Sculptor,* Amon Carter Museum (Fort
Worth, TX), 2003.

Author of introduction for several art books, including
Unending Frontier: Art of the West, Charles M. Rus-
sell Center for the Study of Art of the American West
(Norman, OK), 2000; and *After the Hunt: The Art
Collection of William B. Ruger,* Stackpole Books
(Mechanicsburg, PA), 2003. Contributor to *American
Art Review, Southwestern Historical Quarterly, Ameri-
can Art Review,Antiques, American West,Montana,* and
other periodicals.

BIOGRAPHICAL AND CRITICAL SOURCES:

PERIODICALS

American Artist, September, 1988, Mary Carroll
Nelson, review of *Frederic Remington: The
Masterworks,* p. 12; September, 1989, Mary Car-
roll Nelson, review of *Charles M. Russell,* p. 118.
American West, May-June, 1988, review of *Frederic
Remington: The Masterworks,* p. 60.
Art Journal, fall, 1997, Roberta K. Tarbell review of
*Frederic Remington: A Catalogue Raisonne of
Paintings, Watercolors, and Drawings,* p. 84.
Booklist, August, 1989, review of *Charles M. Russell,*
p. 1935; September 1, 1997, Donna Seaman,
review of *The Georgia O'Keeffe Museum,* p. 47;
November 15, 2002, Gilbert Taylor, review of
*Drawn to Yellowstone: Artists in America's First
National Park,* pp. 559-560.
Choice, December, 1989, review of *Charles M.
Russell,* p. 621; March, 2003, P. D. Thomas,
review of *Drawn to Yellowstone,* p. 1171.

Library Journal, August 20, 1987, Raymond L.
Wilson, review of *American Frontier Life: Early
Western Painting and Prints,* p. 117; June 15,
1988, Raymond L. Wilson, review of *Frederic
Remington: The Masterworks,* p. 54; June 15,
1989, Russell T. Clement, review of *Charles M.
Russell,* p. 56; September 15, 1997, Kathryn
Wekselman, review of *The Georgia O'Keeffe
Museum,* p. 68.
Parade, December 28, 1997, Herbert Kupferberg,
review of *The Georgia O'Keeffe Museum,* p. 21.
People, April 25, 1988, Harriet Shapiro, review of
Frederic Remington: The Masterworks, p. 27.
Publishers Weekly, February 5, 1988, Genevieve
Stuttaford, review of *Frederic Remington: The
Masterworks,* p. 78.
Southwestern Historical Quarterly, October, 1997, Al
Lowman, review of *Frederic Remington: A
Catalogue Raisonne of Paintings, Watercolors,
and Drawings,* p. 261; April, 2001, William H.
Goetzmann, review of *The American West: Out of
Myth, into Reality,* p. 609.
Western Historical Quarterly, autumn, 1998, review of
*Frederic Remington: A Catalogue Raisonne of
Paintings, Watercolors, and Drawings,* p. 364.*

*   *   *

HAUGELAND, John (Christian) 1945-

PERSONAL: Born March 13, 1945, in Harrisburg, IL;
son of John (an engineer) and Carol (a teacher) Haugeland; married Joan Wellman (a philosopher), 1999;
children: John. *Education:* Harvey Mudd College,
B.S., 1966; University of California, Berkeley, Ph.D.,
1976.

ADDRESSES: Office—Department of Philosophy,
University of Chicago, 1010 E. 59th St., Chicago, IL
60637.

CAREER: U.S. Peace Corps, volunteer in Tonga, 1967-
69; University of Pittsburgh, Pittsburgh, PA, assistant
professor, 1974-81, associate professor, 1981-86,
professor of philosophy, beginning 1986; currently
professor of philosophy and member of Committee on
Conceptual and Historical Studies of Science, University of Chicago. Fellow at Center for Advanced Study
in the Behavioral Sciences, Palo Alto, CA, 1979-80.

MEMBER: American Philosophical Association.

WRITINGS:

(Editor) *Mind Design,* MIT Press (Cambridge, MA), 1981.
Artificial Intelligence: The Very Idea, MIT Press (Cambridge, MA), 1985.
(Editor) *Mind Design II: Philosophy, Psychology, Artificial Intelligence,* MIT Press (Cambridge, MA), 1997.
Having Thought: Essays in the Metaphysics of Mind, Harvard University Press (Cambridge, MA), 1998.
(Editor, with James Conant) Thomas S. Kuhn, *The Road since Structure: Philosophical Essays, 1970-1993, with an Autobiographical Interview,* University of Chicago Press (Chicago, IL), 2000.

Contributor to periodicals, including *Behavior and Brain Science, Journal of Philosophy, Philosophical Topics, Nous, Southern Journal of Philosophy,* and *Philosophical Perspectives.*

WORK IN PROGRESS: Heidegger Disclosed, "an interpretation of Being and Time."

SIDELIGHTS: John Haugeland is a philosopher whose interests range across a spectrum of issues, including the problems of objectivity, truth, and materialism, the implications of artificial intelligence, the origins of understanding, intentionality, and thought, and the relationship between personality and intelligence. Haugeland's work is specialist in nature and appeals primarily to students and teachers of philosophy and those engaged in explorations of artificial intelligence. Nevertheless, his work can be appreciated by dedicated general readers. *MAA Online* contributor Keith Devlin, reviewing *Having Thought: Essays in the Metaphysics of Mind* wrote: "Despite the difficult prose . . . I found the book made me think, which is surely the author's main intention. . . . Many of the issues Haugeland addresses are undoubtedly going to occupy a central place in the science of the next millennium."

BIOGRAPHICAL AND CRITICAL SOURCES:

PERIODICALS

Choice, February 1999, R. M. Stewart, review of *Having Thought: Essays in the Metaphysics of Mind,* p. 1072.

Computers and the Humanities, October, 1991, review of *Artificial Intelligence: The Very Idea,* p. 331.
History of Political Economy, winter, 2001, Mark Blaug, review of *The Road since Structure: Philosophical Essays, 1970-1993, with an Autobiographical Interview,* p. 855.
Journal of Philosophy, August, 1999, Daniel C. Dennett, review of *Having Thought,* p. 430.
London Review of Books, July 19, 2001, Peter Lipton, "Kant on Wheels," p. 30.
Philosophy, October, 1999, Michael Morris, review of *Having Thought,* p. 606.
Philosophy in Review, June, 1999, review of *Having Thought,* p. 188.
Philosophy of Science, September, 1999, Lynne Rudder Baker, review of *Having Thought,* p. 494.
Physics Today, March, 2001, Gilles De Gennes, review of *The Road since Structure,* p. 53.
Reference & Research Book News, November, 1998, review of *Having Thought,* p. 7.
Times Literary Supplement, August 1, 2000.

ONLINE

Harvard University Press Web site, http://www.hup.harvard.edu/ (January 27, 2002), review of *Having Thought.*
MAA Online, http://www.maa.org/ (August, 1998), Keith Devlin, "Mathematicians and Philosophers— Chalk and Cheese?"
Stanford University Web site, http://www-formal.stanford.edu/jmc/reviews/ (April 18, 2002), review of *Artificial Intelligence: The Very Idea.*

*   *   *

HEFFERNAN, Thomas Farel 1933-

PERSONAL: Born May 29, 1933, in Buffalo, NY; son of Thomas Andrew (in sales) and Katherine (a technical librarian; maiden name, Gallagher) Heffernan; married Carol Falvo (a professor of English), March 21, 1970; children: Geoffrey. *Education:* Fordham University, B.A., 1956, M.A., 1959; Columbia University, Ph.D., 1970.

ADDRESSES: Home—148 Kildare Rd., Garden City, NY 11530. *Office*—Department of English, Harvey Hall, Room 208, Adelphi University, Garden City, NY 11530.

CAREER: Adelphi University, Garden City, NY, professor of English.

MEMBER: Modern Language Association of America, Melville Society.

WRITINGS:

Stove by a Whale: Owen Chase and the Essex, Wesleyan University Press (Middletown, CT), 1981.
Wood Quay: The Clash over Dublin's Viking Past, University of Texas Press (Austin, TX), 1988.
The Richest Vein: Literary and Historical Surprises in Aurora, New York, Tallcot Bookshop, 1992.
Mutiny on the Globe: The Fatal Voyage of Samuel Comstock, W. W. Norton (New York, NY), 2002.

SIDELIGHTS: For ninety-three days during 1819 and 1820 a whaleship, the *Essex* out of Nantucket, was attacked and ultimately defeated by a whale in the Pacific Ocean, killing all but seven of the twenty men aboard. The surviving first mate, Owen Chase, produced a narrative account of the sufferings experienced by the crew during the ordeal, including details of their cannibalism in order to survive. In *Stove by a Whale,* Heffernan studies Chase's writings, questions some of the actions of the crew, and details Chase's life after the tragedy.

In *Mutiny on the Globe: The Fatal Voyage of Samuel Comstock,* Heffernan relates the events surrounding the violent mutiny aboard the whaleship *Globe,* and the role of Thomas Comstock, who led the revolt. A *Publishers Weekly* reviewer called the book a "dynamic, tightly edited record" of the event.

BIOGRAPHICAL AND CRITICAL SOURCES:

PERIODICALS

Kliatt, April, 1991, review of *Stove by a Whale: Owen Chase and the Essex,* p. 24.
Library Journal, May 15, 2002, review of *Mutiny on the Globe: The Fatal Voyage of Samuel Comstock,* p. 109.
Modern Language Review, January, 1985, review of *Stove by a Whale,* p. 131.
Natural History, November, 1988, John R. Alden, review of *Wood Quay: The Clash over Dublin's Viking Past,* p. 92.

New Yorker, June 10, 2002, Leo Carey, review of *Mutiny on the Globe.*
New York Times Book Review, October 4, 1981; May 19, 2002, review of *Mutiny on the Globe,* p. 11.
Oceans, July-August, 1983, review of *Stove by a Whale,* p. 62.
Publishers Weekly, April 1, 2002, review of *Mutiny on the Globe,* p. 66.*

*   *   *

HENLEY, Beth
    See HENLEY, Elizabeth Becker

*   *   *

HENLEY, Elizabeth Becker 1952-
(Beth Henley)

PERSONAL: Born May 8, 1952, in Jackson, MS; daughter of Charles Boyce (an attorney) and Elizabeth Josephine (an actress; maiden name, Becker) Henley. *Education:* Southern Methodist University, B.F.A., 1974; attended University of Illinois, 1975-76.

ADDRESSES: Home—Los Angeles, CA. *Agent*—Gilbert Parker, William Morris Agency, 1350 Avenue of the Americas, New York, NY 10019.

CAREER: Actress and playwright. Theatre Three, Dallas, TX, actress, 1972-73; Southern Methodist University, Directors Colloquium, Dallas, member of acting ensemble, 1973; Dallas Minority Repertory Theatre, teacher of creative dramatics, 1974-75; University of Illinois, Urbana, teacher of beginning acting, Lessac voice technique, and playwriting, 1975-76. Actress, Great American People Show, summer, 1976; producer, Loretta Theatre, a production company.

AWARDS, HONORS: Cowinner of Great American Playwriting Contest, Actor's Theatre of Louisville, 1978, Susan Smith Blackburn Award nomination, 1979, New York Drama Critics Circle Award for best new American play, from *Newsday,* 1981, Pulitzer Prize for drama, 1981, and Antoinette Perry ("Tony") Award nomination for best play, 1981, all for *Crimes of the Heart;* Academy Award nomination for best adapted screenplay, 1986, for movie version of *Crimes of the Heart.*

Elizabeth Becker Henley

WRITINGS:

ALL UNDER NAME BETH HENLEY

Am I Blue (one-act play; first produced in Dallas, Texas, at Southern Methodist University Margo Jones Theatre, 1973), Dramatists Play Service (New York, NY), 1982.

Crimes of the Heart (three-act play; first produced in Louisville, KY, 1979; produced on Broadway at John Golden Theatre, November 4, 1981; revived in New York, NY, 2001; also see below), Dramatists Play Service (New York, NY), 1981.

Morgan's Daughters (script for television pilot), Paramount, 1979.

The Miss Firecracker Contest (two-act play; first produced in Los Angeles, CA, 1980; produced off-Broadway at Manhattan Theatre Club, June, 1980; also see below), Dramatists Play Service (New York, NY), 1985.

The Wake of Jamey Foster (two-act play; first produced in Hartford, CT, 1982; produced on Broadway at Eugene O'Neill Theatre, October 14, 1982), Dramatists Play Service (New York, NY), 1985.

The Debutante Ball (play, first produced in Costa Mesa, CA, 1985), University Press of Mississippi (Jackson, MS), 1991.

(With Budge Threlkeld) *Survival Guides* (television script), Public Broadcasting System (Alexandria, VA), 1985.

Crimes of the Heart (screenplay; based on author's play of the same title), De Laurentiis Entertainment, 1986.

Nobody's Fool (screenplay), Island Pictures, 1986.

(With David Byrne and Stephen Tobolowsky) *True Stories* (screenplay), Warner Bros., 1986.

The Lucky Spot (play; first produced in Williamstown, MA, 1986; produced on Broadway at City Center Theatre, April, 1987), Dramatists Play Service (New York, NY), 1987.

Miss Firecracker (screenplay; based on her play), Corsair Pictures, 1988.

Abundance (play; produced in Los Angeles, CA, 1989), Dramatists Play Service (New York, NY), 1990.

Monologues for Women (play), Dramaline Publications (Rancho Mirage, CA), 1992.

(And director) *Control Freaks* (one-act play; produced in Los Angeles, CA, at Met Theater, 1993.

Beth Henley: Four Plays, Heinemann/Methuen (Portsmouth, NH), 1994.

L-Play (play), produced in Stockbridge, MA, 1996.

Come West with Me (screenplay; based on author's play *Abundance*), Twentieth Century-Fox, 1998.

Collected Plays, Volume I: *1980-1989,* Smith & Kraus (Lyme, NH), 2000.

Collected Plays, Volume II: *1990-1999,* Smith & Kraus (Lyme, NH), 2000.

Impossible Marriage (play), Dramatists Play Service (New York, NY), 1999.

Three Plays by Beth Henley, Dramatists Play Service (New York, NY), 2002.

Family Week (play), produced Off-Broadway, 2000.

Sisters of the Winter Madrigal (play), Dramatists Play Service (New York, NY), 2001.

Signature (play), Dramatists Play Service (New York, NY), 2003.

Revelers (play), Dramatists Play Service (New York, NY), 2003.

Ridiculous Fraud (play), produced at Sundance Institute Theatre Lab, Sundance, UT, 2004.

Tight Pants (play), produced in Los Angeles, CA, at the MET Theater, 2004.

SIDELIGHTS: Elizabeth Becker Henley—better known to theatregoers as Beth Henley—is a member of the new breed of American playwrights dedicated to preserving regional voices on the stage. In Henley's case, her Mississippi upbringing provides the background for a host of Southern-accented plays, one of which, the black comedy *Crimes of the Heart,* went on to win her a Pulitzer Prize when she was twenty-nine years of age. Like many playwrights before her, Henley originally set her sights on being an actress, but ventured into writing after deciding there were not many good contemporary roles for Southern women. A graduate of Southern Methodist University, Henley got her first play produced there, a one-act work titled *Am I Blue.* In 1976, she moved to Los Angeles to live with actor/director Stephen Tobolowsky, with whom she would later collaborate on the screenplay *True Stories.* Three years later Henley submitted a three-act play to the Great American Play Contest sponsored by Actors Theatre of Louisville, Kentucky. Henley's play, *Crimes of the Heart,* won the contest and there began the first of its many successful stagings.

Set in Hazlehurst, Mississippi, a few years after Hurricane Camille, passed through the area, the story centers on three eccentric sisters who converge in the home of the youngest, Babe, after she has shot her well-to-do husband because, as Babe puts it, "I didn't like his looks." The other sisters include Meg, a would-be singer who has struck out in Hollywood; and Lenny, single and desperate at age thirty. These sisters, according to Edith Oliver in a *New Yorker* review, the "walking wounded, who are in tears at one moment and giggling and hugging at the next, . . . are very much of the South, of Mississippi, and [novelist] Eudora Welty has prepared us for them." John Simon, reviewing the production for *New York* magazine, stated that "the play is an essence, *the* essence of provincial living." Simon further called *Crimes of the Heart* a "loving and teasing look back at deep-southern, small-town life, at the effect of constricted living and confined thinking on three different yet not wholly unalike sisters amid Chekhovian boredom in honeysuckle country, and, above all, at the sorely tried but resilient affection and loyalty of these sisters for one another."

Some critics took exception to Henley's use of ironic black humor in *Crimes of the Heart.* Michael Feingold, writing in the *Village Voice,* for instance, thought the playwright's attitude toward her three main characters, with its "pity and mockery aimed at them in laser-gun bursts," has "no organic connection and no deep roots.

The play gives the impression of gossiping about its characters rather than presenting them, and [Henley's] voice, though both individual and skillful, is the voice of a small-town southern spinster yattering away on the phone, oozing pretended sympathy and real malice for her unfortunate subjects, and never at any point coming close to the truth of their lives." *New Leader* reviewer Leo Sauvage discovered "nothing enthralling in spending an evening with three badly adjusted, if not mentally retarded sisters, who are given free rein to exhibit their individual eccentricities," and dubbed Henley's humor "sick, not black."

Other reviewers saw more to value in Henley's work. *Crimes of the Heart* may be "overlong, occasionally cliched and annoyingly frivolous at moments," noted *Daily News* critic Don Nelson, "but Henley keeps intriguing us with a delightfully wacky humor plus a series of little mysteries played out by characters we can never dismiss as superficial on a set that absorbs us into their lives." "The physical modesty of her play belies the bounty of plot, peculiarity, and comedy within it," concluded *Saturday Review* writer Scot Haller of Henley's effort. "Like Flannery O'Connor, Henley creates ridiculous characters but doesn't ridicule them. Like Lanford Wilson, she examines ordinary people with extraordinary compassion. Treating the eccentricities of her characters with empathy, [Henley] manages to render strange turns of events not only believable but affecting."

Crimes of the Heart was nominated for a Tony award when first produced and subsequently adapted by its author into movie form, the screenplay of which was nominated for an Academy award. In a review of the movie adaptation for the *New Republic,* Stanley Kauffmann wrote, "Comic Beth Henley has adapted her play for the screen with careful balance. . . maintain[ing] the poise of her exceptionally good play. . . keep[ing] the braided deception and truth of the original." A review by Peter Travers for *People* was less flattering: "The seams in Henley's play . . . show up more glaringly when blown up to wide screen size," Travers maintained, adding that "Henley's saving grace is her antic humor." In 2001, a revival of *Crimes of the Heart* opened at the Second Stage Theater in New York City. The play starred Amy Ryan, Mary Catherine Garrison, and Enid Graham, and was directed by Garry Hynes.

Henley's screenplay *True Stories* takes a look at "the petty bourgeois customs, the media hype, the bloated vulgarities of American small-town life," according to Kauffmann in another review for the *New Republic.* In the film, director and cowriter David Byrne, the lead singer of the Talking Heads, serves as a tour guide to this mythical Texas town, driving around in a red convertible showing viewers the oh-so-local sites and scenery. According to Kauffmann, "The result has the shape, designed yet seemingly casual, of Monty Python scripts but very little of their incisive wit. . . . The catalog of cartoons along the way is trite and not often funny." A *People* critic called *True Stories* one of 1986's "most notable and offbeat films," and Henley, "one of the 25 Most Intriguing People of '86. . . . She earned her 1986 merit badge by wielding a wicked wit."

In other work for film in addition to *True Stories* and *Crimes of the Heart,* Henley adapted her play *The Miss Firecracker Contest* into a screenplay, and also wrote an original screenplay, *Nobody's Fool.* In *The Miss Firecracker Contest,* a ne'er-do-well young woman, Carnelle Scott, seeks to uplift her station in her small Mississippi town; in hopes of gaining respect she hopes to win the "Miss Firecracker" beauty contest, a rather cheesy local affair. To that end, Carnelle enlists other outcasts in her town to aid in her quest. As the play version opens, Carnelle is seen on a bare stage dressed in a leotard and draped in an American flag, tap-dancing and baton-twirling her way through the "Star-Spangled Banner." "Though [the playwright's] territory looks superficially like the contemporary American South," wrote *Time*'s Richard Schickel, "it is really a country of the mind: one of Tennessee Williams' provinces that has surrendered to a Chekhovian raiding party, perhaps. Her strength is a wild anecdotal inventiveness, but her people, lost in the ramshackle dreams and tumble-down ambitions with which she invests them, often seem to be metaphors waywardly adrift. They are blown this way and that by the gales of laughter they provoke, and they frequently fail to find a solid connection with clear and generally relevant meaning." Unfortunately for Henley, *The Miss Firecracker Contest* did not last long on the boards.

Nobody's Fool focuses on a frustrated young Arizona woman working as a waitress and trying to allow a new love into her life while living with the memories of a past one. According to Kauffmann, *Nobody's Fool* is "about helplessness and its counterfeit armor, about a young woman in the grip of a destructive sexual at-

traction who is ultimately saved by another lover—who may or may not turn out to be equally hurtful." In Kauffmann's words, the screenplay for *Nobody's Fool* is "authentic, unique [and] rounded." Henley "writes with a unique voice, quiet, comic, even whimsical, but with hidden venom." In an interview with Mark Lee for *Written By,* Henley said of *Nobody's Fool:* "It's very different to create something from scratch than having the great mercy of having source material. Over the years I've learned how to think more visually and let go of dialogue and visualize the movement of the film."

Henley's other screenplays, for both film and television, include the draft of the screenplay for the film version of Annie Proulx's novel *The Shipping News,* coauthoring the television script *Survival Guides* for public television, and penning the teleplay *Ruby McCullough,* based on a true story of a Southern black woman. Henley also wrote the script for the televison pilot *Morgan's Daughters,* served as a writer for the Public Broadcasting Service special *Trying Times,* and wrote a CBS television movie titled *Meant to Be,* that starred actors Ted Danson and Mary Steenburgen.

Other early plays by Henley include *The Wake of Jamey Foster, The Debutante Ball, The Lucky Spot, Monologues for Women,* and *L-Plays* which were produced at venues across the country, from New England and New York, to Chicago and California. More popular have been her longer works, among them *Impossible Marriage, Signature,* and *Sisters of the Winter Madrigal,* while other plays have been less successful. Keeping with her Southern theme, Henley sets *Impossible Marriage* in Savannah, Georgia, and relates the story of a young woman whose upcoming marriage is opposed by her older, and very pregnant, sister, as well as by others. A *TheaterMania.com* reviewer called *Impossible Marriage* "a surprisingly—for Henley, at least—upbeat family saga that served as a reminder of the power of her distinctive, theatrical voice," while in the *Long Island Business News,* Richard Scholem commented: "It's impossible to keep a straight face watching Beth Henley's *Impossible Marriage. . . .* Its . . . bigger-than-life . . . characters are deliciously overwrought, over dramatic, over magnified and over the edge."

In *Signature,* another successful venture for Henley, the playwright takes a "high-tech, sci-fi, bizarrely futuristic look at Hollywood, where marriage is a career choice and everyone is desperate to make his or her mark on an indifferent world," according to Terri Roberts, in a review for *Back Stage West.* Citing a *New York Times* review, Roberts added that "Henley is on a word high. Those words dizzyingly play, collide, enlighten, ceaselessly question, and even give answers with wit and without avoidance." As Roberts quoted Henley herself, the playwright noted: "I was fascinated that Los Angeles is really about people who have come out here to make a signature, to make a mark, to not live and have a family and do a job and die in the place where they were born. . . . Everything seems so new and dangerous. . . . I like that notion for the play—that all these people are just on the edge and don't really know how to behave at all." In another *Back Stage West* review, Dany Margolies commented that the play's "characters range from unsettlingly slightly off-kilter personalities to the outrageously psychotic ones that seem comfortingly familiar."

Sisters of the Winter Madrigal is a one-act play that could have been longer, according to Laura Weinert in her review for *Back Stage West.* The play, Weinert asserted, seems to "yearn for expansion into [a] full-length play. . . . Rarely do we leave the theatre wishing the playwright had written more words." Henley's play, set in a rural town in a time long ago, focuses on two orphaned sisters, the town whore, and a betrothed cowhearder who is trying to wiggle out of a marriage in favor of a better offer. "One can't help but wonder what heights [the actors] might reach if [the play was] given an entire evening to fill and . . . able to build to more meaningful denouements," summarized the critic.

Diverting from her prominent theme of female bonding, Henley's *Ridiculous Fraud* is a comedy set in New Orleans about the relationship among three adult brothers, each trying to cope with the fact that their father is serving time for committing a "ridiculous fraud." Henley had the opportunity to develop this play, which was commissioned by the McCarter Theater Center of the Performing Arts in Princeton, New Jersey, at the Sundance Institute Theater Laboratory, in Sundance, Utah. *Tight Pants* is a one-act play exploring an erotic triangle. Daryl Miller, writing in the *Los Angeles Times,* noted in a review of the play's production that Henley's "deft writing is matched by spot-on acting and sharp directing." A contributor to the *Maestro Theatre* Web site called the farce "as odd as it is funny."

Many of Henley's plays have been incorporated into collections, including two volumes that together comprise much of her oeuvre, the two-volume *Collected Plays.* In a review for *Library Journal,* Thomas Luddy hailed the appearance of the work, noting that it "reveals a consistently excellent body of work from a distinctive voice of the American theater. . . . As this set reveals, Henley's most important contribution to the theater is her memorable gallery of women characters, which has kept her plays alive on stages across the country." Jack Helbig agreed, stating in *Booklist* that both volumes are "most welcome. . . . Henley wittily introduces each play and, as she does, sprinkles fascinating recollections of actors and directors involved in the premiere productions."

Henley's plays continue to be produced across the United States and internationally and have been translated into over ten languages. Her stage, movie, and television productions have starred a host of well-known actors, among them, Rosanna Arquette, Ted Danson, Holly Hunter, Diane Keaton, Jessica Lange, Carol Kane, Swoosie Kurtz, Laraine Newman, Tim Robbins, Sam Shepard, and Sissy Spacek. As actor Hunter told an online interviewer for *TheaterMania. com,* Henley "is an original observer. . . . And she is not really swayed by what other people think in terms of how she navigates her own life. . . . Beth keeps her unique point of view solidly intact."

In an interview with Mark Lee for *Written By,* Henley explained that in writing for both stage and film, she has had to bring different considerations to bear, particularly in adapting works from one medium to another. "The impulse of the theater will always be something about being there. And the fact that you can laugh and the person will react or not react. Or you can shout at them to stop, and they will hear you. The vitality of that is something I find overwhelming. Film is so different. I love that you can send that film out, and people can see it in countries that you've never been to, and you can touch people's hearts that can't get out of their village. They're being given a new perspective on the world. The influence of film is amazing. It can make your stories even more powerful."

BIOGRAPHICAL AND CRITICAL SOURCES:

BOOKS

Contemporary Literary Criticism, Thomson Gale (Detroit, MI), Volume 23, 1983.
Dictionary of Literary Biography Yearbook: 1986, Thomson Gale (Detroit, MI), 1987.

PERIODICALS

Back Stage, August 6, 1993, Rob Kendt, review of *Control Freaks,* p. 8.

Back Stage West, October 12, 2000, review of *Signature,* p. 18; July 19, 2001, Laura Weinert, review of *Sisters of the Winter Madrigal,* p. 12.

Booklist, June 1, 2000, Jack Helbig, review of *Collected Plays,* Volume I: *1980-1989* and *Collected Plays,* Volume II: *1990-1999,* p. 1836.

Chicago Sun-Times, April 28, 1989, Roger Ebert, review of *Miss Firecracker.*

Daily News (New York, NY), November 5, 1981.

Library Journal, October 15, 1991.

Long Island Business News, November 6, 1998, Benjamin Scholem, review of *Impossible Marriage,* p. 38.

Los Angeles Times, April 16, 1983; May 7, 2004, Daryl H. Miller, review of *Tight Pants.*

New Leader, November 30, 1981.

New Republic, November 10, 1986, Stanley Kauffmann, review of *True Stories,* p. 26; December 15, 1986, Stanley Kauffmann, review of *Nobody's Fool,* p. 22; February 2, 1987, Stanley Kauffmann, review of *Crimes of the Heart,* p. 26; December 17, 1990, Robert Brustein, review of *Abundance,* p. 28.

Newsday, August 27, 1996.

Newsweek, December 22, 1986; May 1, 1989.

New York, November 16, 1981; May 11, 1987; May 15, 1989; November 12, 1990.

New Yorker, January 12, 1981; May 11, 1987; May 29, 1989; November 12, 1990.

New York Times, June 8, 1979; December 22, 1980; February 15, 1981; April 14, 1981; June 10, 1981; June 11, 1981; October 25, 1981; November 5, 1981; December 28, 1981; April 14, 1982; May 28, 1984; November 2, 1986.

New York Times Magazine, May 1, 1983.

People, December 15, 1986, Peter Travers, review of *Crimes of the Heart* (movie), p. 12; December 22, 1986, "The 25 Most Intriguing People of '86," p. 91.

Playbill, July 5, 2004, Kenneth Jones, "Beth Henley, Joe Hortua, Tectonic Theatre, Stephen Dillane Work in 2004 Sundance Theatre Lab July 5-25."

Saturday Review, November, 1981; January, 1982.

Time, June 11, 1984; December 22, 1986; May 1, 1989.

Variety, May 10, 1989; August 9, 1993; April 17, 2000, Charles Isherwood, review of *Family Week,* p. 34.

Village Voice, November 18, 1981.

Washington Post, December 12, 1986.

Written By, June-July 2000, Mark Lee, interview with Henley.

ONLINE

Maestro Web site, http://www.maestro.ws/arts/ (April, 2004), "Beth Henley."

Met Theater Web site, http://www.7metshorts.com/ (July 31, 2004), review of *Tight Pants.*

TheaterMania.com, http://www.theatermania.com/ (April 11, 2000), Kathy Henderson, review of *Family Week.*

Univerity of Mississippi, Department of English Web site, http://www.olemiss.edu/depts/english/ (July 29, 2004), "Beth Henley."*

*   *   *

HEPPENHEIMER, T(homas) A(dolph) 1947-

PERSONAL: Born January 1, 1947, in New York, NY; son of Henry Gunther (a toolmaker) and Betty Lorraine (a secretary; maiden name, Amitin) Heppenheimer; married Phyllis Marcia Safdy, December 9, 1967 (divorced May 9, 1977); married Beverley Brownlee, June 8, 1998; children: (first marriage) Laurie, Alex, Connie. *Education:* Michigan State University, B.S.M.E., 1967, M.S.M.E., 1968; University of Michigan, Ph.D., 1972. *Politics:* Republican.

ADDRESSES: Home and office—11040 Blue Allium Ave., Fountain Valley, CA 92708. *E-mail*—taheppenheimer@yahoo.com.

CAREER: Science Applications, Inc., Schiller Park, IL, scientist, 1972-73; Rockwell International Corp., Downey, CA, member of technical staff in systems engineering, 1973-74; California Institute of Technology, Pasadena, research fellow in planetary science, 1974-75; Max Planck Institute for Nuclear

Physics, Heidelberg, West Germany, Alexander von Humboldt Research Fellow, 1976-78; K.R.G., Inc., Palos Verdes Peninsula, CA, vice president, 1978-82; full-time writer, 1982—. University of California—Irvine, instructor, 1988-90. Forum for the Advancement of Students in Science and Technology, technical vice president, 1971-73.

MEMBER: American Institute of Aeronautics and Astronautics (associate fellow), American Association for the Advancement of Science, American Astronomical Society (Division of Dynamical Astronomy), British Interplanetary Society (fellow), Sigma Xi, Tau Beta Pi, Pi Tau Sigma, Phi Kappa Phi, Phi Eta Sigma.

WRITINGS:

Colonies in Space (Book-of-the-Month Club alternate selection), introduction by Ray Bradbury, Stackpole (Mechanicsburg, PA), 1977.
Toward Distant Suns (Book-of-the-Month Club alternate selection), Stackpole (Mechanicsburg, PA), 1979.
The Real Future, Doubleday (Garden City, NY), 1983.
The Man-Made Sun: The Quest for Fusion Power (Book-of-the-Month Club alternate science selection), Little, Brown (Boston, MA), 1984.
The Coming Quake: Science and Trembling on the California Earthquake Frontier, Times Books (New York, NY), 1988.
Superconductivity: Research, Applications and Potential Markets, Pasha Publications (Arlington, VA), 1988.
(Editor and contributor) *Anti-Submarine Warfare: The Threat, the Strategy, the Solution,* Pasha Publications (Arlington, VA), 1989.
Hypersonic Technologies and the National Aerospace Plane, Pasha Publications (Arlington, VA), 1990.
Turbulent Skies: The History of Commercial Aviation, J. Wiley (New York, NY), 1995.
Countdown: A History of Space Flight, John Wiley (New York, NY), 1997.
The Space Shuttle Decision: NASA's Search for a Reusable Space Vehicle, History Office, Office of Policy and Plans, National Aeronautics and Space Administration (Washington, DC), 1999.
A Brief History of Flight: From Balloons to Mach 3 and Beyond, John Wiley (New York, NY), 2001.
History of the Space Shuttle, Volume 1: *Development of the Space Shuttle, 1965-1972,* Volume 2: *Development of the Space Shuttle, 1972-1981,* Smithsonian Institution Press (Washington, DC), 2002.
First Flight: The Wright Brothers and the Invention of the Airplane, John Wiley (Hoboken, NJ), 2003.

Contributor to books, including *Space Manufacturing Facilities: Space Colonies,* edited by Jerry Grey, American Institute of Aeronautics and Astronautics, Volumes 1-2, 1977, Volume 3, 1979, Volume 4, 1981; *The Origin of the Solar System,* by S. F. Dermott, Wiley-Interscience (New York, NY), 1978; *Universe,* by Don Dixon, Houghton Mifflin (Boston, MA), 1981; *The Real Future,* Doubleday (New York, NY), 1983; and *Robotics,* edited by Marvin Minsky, Doubleday (New York, NY), 1985. Contributor of numerous articles to scientific journals and popular science magazines, including *Yearbook of Science and the Future, Popular Science, Discover, American Heritage, Omni, Science Digest, Mosaic,* and *High Technology.* Book review editor, *Journal of the Astronautical Sciences,* 1979-86.

ADAPTATIONS: Turbulent Skies was adapted as a television documentary titled *Chasing the Sun: Heroes and Daredevils,* aired by Public Broadcasting Service.

SIDELIGHTS: T. A. Heppenheimer once told *CA:* "I spent several years as a working scientist before I discovered that being an author and freelance writer is more fun and more lucrative. Nevertheless, my background in science is with me every time I do an interview or sit at my typewriter. This continues to give me unique sources of material to write about, and helps me greatly in keeping current on the most significant insights and critical thinking in my areas of interest. It is especially helpful when I go to conferences—or to colleagues' offices, who welcome me as one who knows their world intimately. Science writing is a career in its own right; any scientist who deals with an editor or agent will soon find he needs more than a knowledge of his field. Yet it will not do to have simply a good writing style; one must have technical knowledge, too. It is by going forward in this fashion, by spending time at seminars and keeping up with the journals, that I maintain the flow of new, significant ideas that contribute to the standard of quality I seek in my work. And there is more. I find true science to be more imaginative, more stimulating, more exciting than all but the very best in science fiction. There is a pleasure in actually doing science, in wrestling with nature and in seeking to make discoveries, which to me is quite thrilling; and I try to convey this excitement in my writings."

BIOGRAPHICAL AND CRITICAL SOURCES:

PERIODICALS

Air and Space/Smithsonian, December, 1995, review of *Turbulent Skies: The History of Commercial Aviation,* p. 90.

American Scientist, May-June, 1998, Alexander Gurshtein, review of *Countdown: A History of Space Flight,* p. 294; May, 2001, review of *A Brief History of Flight: From Balloons to Mach 3 and Beyond,* p. 267.

Astronomy, April, 1998, review of *Countdown,* p. 106.

Booklist, September 1, 1988, review of *The Coming Quake: Science and Trembling on the California Earthquake Frontier,* p. 15; September 1, 1995, David Rouse, review of *Turbulent Skies,* p. 22; May 15, 1997, Roland Green, review of *Countdown,* p. 1546.

Book Report, November-December, 1997, Steven M. Baule, review of *Countdown,* p. 54.

Choice, February, 1989, review of *The Coming Quake,* p. 966; September, 1996, review of *Turbulent Skies,* p. 149; October, 1997, A. M. Strauss, review of *Countdown,* p. 316; October, 2001, R. E. Bilstein, review of *A Brief History of Flight,* p. 331.

History: Review of New Books, spring, 1998, John A. Heitmann, review of *Countdown,* p. 153.

Isis, June, 1999, Robert G. Ferguson, review of *Turbulent Skies,* p. 399; December, 1999, review of *Countdown,* p. 856.

Journal of American History, June, 1998, Martin J. Collins, review of *Countdown,* p. 307.

Journal of Government Information, November, 2000, review of *The Space Shuttle Decision: NASA's Search for a Reusable Space Vehicle,* p. 703.

Kirkus Reviews, August 1, 1988, review of *The Coming Quake,* p. 1123; July 1, 1995, review of *Turbulent Skies,* p. 919; April 1, 1997, review of *Countdown,* p. 521.

Library Journal, August, 1995, review of *Turbulent Skies,* p. 88; May 15, 1997, Thomas J. Frieling, review of *Countdown,* p. 97; February 15, 2003, John Carver Edwards, review of *First Flight: The Wright Brothers and the Invention of the Airplane,* p. 150.

London Review of Books, March 5, 1998, review of *Countdown,* p. 13.

Los Angeles Times Book Review, March 18, 1984; October 2, 1988, review of *The Coming Quake,* p. 1.

Nature, March 12, 1998, Alex Roland, review of *Countdown,* p. 143.

New Scientist, June 28, 1997, review of *Countdown,* p. 40.

New York Times Book Review, April 1, 1984; January 1, 1989, K. C. Cole, review of *The Coming Quake,* p. 11.

Observer (London, England), May 25, 1997, review of *Countdown,* p. 17.

Publishers Weekly, August 5, 1988, Genevieve Stuttaford, review of *The Coming Quake,* p. 75; July 31, 1995, review of *Turbulent Skies,* p. 88; April 14, 1997, review of *Countdown,* p. 65; January 6, 2003, review of *First Flight,* p. 52.

Reference and Research Book News, August, 1997, review of *Countdown,* p. 176.

Science Books and Films, January, 1989, review of *The Coming Quake,* p. 156; November, 1997, review of *Countdown,* p. 235.

Scientific American, January, 1998, John M. Logsdon, review of *Countdown,* p. 108.

SciTech Book News, September, 2001, review of *A Brief History of Flight,*

Space Policy, November, 1998, Jeff Kingwell, review of *Countdown,* p. 255.

Space World, April, 1988, John Rhea, review of *Hypersonic Technologies and the National Aerospace Plane,* p. 36.

Technology and Culture, April, 1987, Bruce R. Wheaton, review of *The Man-Made Sun: The Quest for Fusion Power,* p. 394; April, 2001, Alex Roland, review of *The Space Shuttle Decision,* p. 386.

Times Literary Supplement, February 27, 1998, review of *Countdown,* p. 30.

Transportation Journal, spring, 1996, Richard R. Young, review of *Turbulent Skies,* p. 55.*

*   *   *

HOGG, Enderby
See MEADES, Jonathan (Turner)

*   *   *

HOLLANDER, Paul
See SILVERBERG, Robert

HOLTE, James Craig 1949-

PERSONAL: Born July 9, 1949, in Staten Island, NY; son of Fred (an engineer) and Marie (a homemaker; maiden name, Hunt) Holte; children: Molly Amanda Hilburn-Holte. *Education:* Columbia University, B.A., 1971; University of Cincinnati, M.A. (with highest honors), 1973, Ph.D. (with highest honors), 1978. *Politics:* Democrat.

ADDRESSES: Home—102 Cherrywood Dr., Greenville, NC 27858. *Office*—Department of English, 2211 Bate Bldg., East Carolina University, Greenville, NC 27858-4353; fax: 252-328-4889. *E-mail*—holtcj@ mail.ecu.edu.

CAREER: University of Cincinnati, Cincinnati, OH, instructor in English, 1976; University of New Orleans, New Orleans, LA, instructor in English, 1976-81; East Carolina University, Greenville, began as associate professor, became professor of English and director of graduate studies in English, 1981—. WWNO-Radio, film critic.

MEMBER: International Association for the Fantastic in the Arts, Modern Language Association of America, Popular Culture Association, MELUS.

WRITINGS:

The Ethnic I, Greenwood Press (Westport, CT), 1988.
The Conversion Experience in America, Greenwood Press (Westport, CT), 1992.
Dracula in the Dark: The Dracula Film Adaptations, Greenwood Press (Westport, CT), 1997.
(Editor and contributor) *The Fantastic Vampire: Studies in the Children of the Night,* Greenwood Press (Westport, CT), 2002.

Contributor of articles and more than 300 reviews to periodicals. Editor, *Ruthven Literary Bulletin;* special editor, *Journal of the Fantastic in the Arts.*

SIDELIGHTS: James Craig Holte once told *CA:* "The major theme running through my work is the influence of popular culture on American history and literature. My studies of American ethnic and religious autobiography demonstrate the personal and popular nature of much American writing, and they are indicative of my interest in the influence of ethnicity and religion in American culture.

"My writing on film, especially the work on film adaptations of Bram Stoker's *Dracula,* illustrates my belief in the significance of popular forms of culture. I am interested in the study of popular genres and movements, and I see the millennial celebrations as occasions of great popular and critical interest."

BIOGRAPHICAL AND CRITICAL SOURCES:

PERIODICALS

Church History, June, 1996, review of *The Conversion Experience in America,* p. 315.
Extrapolation, summer, 1998, review of *Dracula in the Dark: The Dracula Film Adaptations,* p. 172.
Science-Fiction Studies, November, 1997, review of *Dracula in the Dark,* p. 518.

ONLINE

East Carolina University Web site, http://www.ecu. edu/english/profiles/holte.htm/ (November 15, 2004).*

*   *   *

HOUELLEBECQ, Michel 1958-

PERSONAL: Born 1958.

ADDRESSES: Agent—c/o Author Mail, Flammarion, 26 rue Racine, F-75278, Paris, Cedex 06, France.

CAREER: Author. Former National Assembly computer programmer.

AWARDS, HONORS: Prix Flore, 1995, for *Extension du domaine de la lutte;* Prix Novembre, 1998, for *Les Particules Elementaires;* International IMPAC Dublin Literary Award, 2002, for *Atomised.*

Michel Houellebecq

WRITINGS:

H. P. Lovecraft: contre le monde, contre la vie, Editions du Rocher (Monaco), 1991.

La Poursuite du bonheur: poemes, Editions de la Difference (Paris, France), 1991.

Rester vivant: methode, Editions de la Difference (Paris, France), 1991.

Extension du domaine de la lutte, Nadeau (Paris, France), 1994, translation by Paul Hammond published as *Whatever,* Serpent's Tail (London, England), 1999.

Le sens du combat, Flammarion (Paris, France), 1996.

Les Particules Elementaires, Flammarion (Paris, France), 1998, translation by Frank Wynne published as *The Elementary Particles,* Knopf (New York, NY), 2000, also published as *Atomised,* Heinemann (London, England), 2000.

Plateforme, Flammarion (Paris, France), 2001, translation by Frank Wynne published as *Platform: A Novel,* Knopf (New York, NY), 2003.

(Author of text) Michel Houellebecq, *Nudes* (photography), Harry N. Abrams (New York, NY), 2003.

Lanzarote, translated from the French by Frank Wynne, William Heinemann (London, England), 2003.

ADAPTATIONS: Film rights to *Les Particules Elementaires* have been sold.

SIDELIGHTS: Michel Houellebecq is a best-selling French author who has a growing English-speaking audience as his work is translated. His two well-known and controversial works, the 1994 short novel *Extension du domaine de la lutte* (published in 1999 as *Whatever*) and the novel *Les Particules Elementaires* (title means "Elementary Particles"), earned him a Prix Flore and a Prix Novembre respectively. In his works, Houellebecq relates his concerns regarding various societal problems, including those affecting the United States.

Houellebecq's *Extension du domaine de la lutte* is a story of alienation in the computer age. The unnamed narrator is a computer engineer without friends or purpose who withdraws rather than adapt to the world around him. He has had no romantic life since breaking up with his girlfriend two years earlier. Even more deprived than the narrator is Bernard, who is still seeking his first encounter. The two men are sent by their company on a consulting job. Bernard is described as having a very unattractive appearance, and the inappropriate advances he makes to several women are rejected. "That both men see women only in terms of their sexual features makes their impotence even more pathetic," wrote a *Publishers Weekly* reviewer. The more the narrator tries to define love, the less able he is to experience it. "The topic of sexual misery emerges, and the narrator interpolates two miniessays," wrote Maria Green, who reviewed the French version of the novel in *World Literature Today.* "The first deals with inequality, as pitiless on the sexual as on the economic level. The second is a virulent attack on psychoanalysis, another form of alienation."

The story has a tragic ending. The narrator has a nervous breakdown, and Bernard is killed in an automobile accident. While in a mental hospital, the narrator concludes that none of the patients are really ill—they are actually suffering from lack of physical contact. The narrator feels that, although technology keeps us informed and in touch, our lives are devoid of real interpersonal communication. In a *Booklist* review, Bonnie Johnston said, "Houellebecq captures precisely the cynical disillusionment of disaffected youth."

Houellebecq's novel *Les Particules Elementaires* sold over two hundred thousand copies in the four months following its publication. There are plans to produce a movie adaptation. An *Economist* reviewer said that the "remarkable best-seller is France's biggest literary sensation since Francoise Sagan, people are saying, or since Albert Camus even. It was not so much published as detonated in Paris . . . and the rows it provoked burst at once out of the review sections on to front pages." Houellebecq shows his contempt for the Socialist establishment that rose from the student protest movements, slams French universities for bowing to bureaucracy, and criticizes feminism.

The theme of *Les Particules Elementaires* (published in English as *The Elementary Particles* and as *Atomised*) claims that since 1968 sexual liberation and materialism have corrupted society, leading to despair and violence. Bruno and his half-brother Michel are the forty-something sons of a promiscuous and unloving mother. Bruno has failed at everything he has touched—marriage, fatherhood, writing, and teaching, and he "writes sadistic pornography," according to a reviewer writing in the *Economist*. Michel is a geneticist who despises humanity and envisions a world of engineered, sexless humans. The *Economist* contributor wrote that "the pairing of these two antiheroes—one literary and stuck in the past; the other scientific and future-mad—gives a clue to the book's ambition to be a novel of ideas." Adam Gopnik wrote in the *New Yorker* that the book "is less a novel than a kind of eighteenth-century *conte moral,* at once a narrative and a philosophical essay, in which an obsession with oral sex oscillates strangely with fatuous ideological posturing, as in a story by Sade or in the proceedings of an American congressional committee. It is obscene, hateful, pretentious, half educated, funny, ambitious, and oddly moving."

Bruno is obsessed by sex. He has his penis surgically enlarged, divorces his wife, and begins a relationship with a woman named Christine. During a group orgy, Christine's back is broken, and she then commits suicide. Bruno is institutionalized after going mad. Michel takes a position in Ireland to work in genetic research and creates a sexless and immortal humanoid. Gopnik wrote that "though the book's bitter tone and its readiness to say the unsayable recall Genet, and even Celine, its literary, dystopian feel brings it much closer to Burroughs (who anticipated the sexless clone years ago), or to J. G. Ballard." In spite of the book's

disdain for American culture, Gopnik called this "a very 'American' book. If anything, Houellebecq envies the land of Bill Gates and Snoop Doggy Dogg for its nearness to the real infernal machines; the whole Western world is going straight to hell anyway, but at least Americans get the window seat." *Les Particules Elementaires* has been condemned for its language, scenes about masturbation, and antiliberal sentiments. Gopnik pointed out that what is termed liberalism in France is what is considered conservatism in the United States. "To the French left, 'liberalism' (or, as it is often called, 'wild' or 'savage' liberalism, a quaint and comic thought in American terms) has also come to mean, essentially, American civilization, in all its McDonald's, 'Friends,' and Exxon aspects." Being antiliberal in France means being for big government.

Gopnik concluded: "What is memorable in Houellebecq's book is not the pseudoscientific incantations, or the potted 'theories,' but the depth of feeling, the authentic disgust with *fin-de-siecle* liberal materialism. The scathing, sarcastic loathing for consumer society and its rituals—for women's magazines, gyms, night clubs, Club Med—gives real pathos to the book."

Houellebecq's 2001 book *Plateforme* was published in English as *Platform: A Novel* in 2003. The author tells the tale of Michel Renault, a disaffected Parisian bureaucrat who works for the Ministry of Culture and whose father has been murdered by a Muslim. Renault takes his inheritance, travels to Thailand with a tour group, and falls for a fellow tourist named Valerie. When the group returns to Paris, Michel and Valerie move in together and act out their sexual obsessions. Michel subsequently convinces Valerie, who works for a hotel chain, and her boss to turn various third-world hotels into sex resorts. A *Publishers Weekly* contributor noted that for Houellebecq hedonism is the only true thing of value in a culture that is spiritually bankrupt and, as a result, "only the sensations of the body have any worth—hence, the utopian value of sex tourism." As the novel progress, the plan appears to be going forward smoothly until one of the hotels is attacked by an Islamic terrorist group. The incident destroys Michel's love and ultimately his life. Calling *Platform* Houellebecq's "most controversial novel yet," *Harper's* contributor Cristina Nehring noted that "Houellebecq does, in fact, go after the big quarry, the big quandaries, the big issues of his age. But he goes after these issues in so individual and honest and blithely self-centered a way that it is almost impossible for him to offer a consistent statement about them." Nehring, who found the depiction of the constant coupling of the major characters to be "drab," also commented, "But if he is frequently incoherent in his general pronouncements, he is ingenious in his local insights. Houellebecq's fiction is full of jarringly honest microreflections; fascinating fragments, glittering shards that cut us to the quick." Richard Lacayo, writing in *Time,* noted that the author "has a gift for sleepy invective" and added, "But he's like a bad date—brimming with rank charm but few useful judgments." A *Publishers Weekly* reviewer commented, "This is an important book, a rare must-read for anyone who wants to take the measure of contemporary European discontents."

In *Lanzarote* Houellebecq continues his exploration of the disillusioned and bored who find that the promises of materialism leave them empty. This time, the narrator seeks to dispel his ennui by going on a vacation trip to Lanzarote, part of the Canary Islands. He then meets two bisexual women and, in typical Houellebecq style, engages in vigorous sex with them. Another character, a Belgian police inspector, disdains such decadence but later becomes suspect in a pedophile scandal. In addition to writing the book, Houellebecq includes his own photographs of the island, which plays an important symbolic role in the novel. As pointed out by Philip Horne in the Manchester *Guardian,* "The doings of the Eurotourists take place against an alienating waste land, 'a barren desert' in which vast geologic forces dwarf human effort." *New Statesman* contributor Jason Cowley commented, "Lanzarote is a peculiar book. It is not quite an unconventional travelogue, nor is it fiction in any recognisable form. It reads more like random diary observations, or perhaps a long, hastily written e-mail to a close friend." Cowley also commented that readers should not expect realism in the author's works because "he is a programmatic writer, a thinker who begins with a thesis and ideas, and then seeks to dramatise them in a series of increasingly unreal situations. You read him, therefore, not to be drugged by narrative, but to be exhilarated by his insight into, and understanding of, the defining conflicts and tensions of the present."

BIOGRAPHICAL AND CRITICAL SOURCES:

PERIODICALS

Booklist, January 1, 1999, Bonnie Johnston, review of *Extension du domaine de la lutte* (translated as *Whatever*), p. 832.

Economist, February 13, 1999, review of *Les Particules Elementaires* (translated as *The Elementary Particles*).

Entertainment Weekly, July 18, 2003, Troy Patterson, review of *Platform,* p. 80.

French Review, December, 1997, p. 316.

Guardian, November 28, 1998, p. S10.

Harper's, August, 2003, Cristina Nehring, review of *Platform,* p. 75.

Independent, January 2, 1999, p.WR9.

Library Journal, July, 2003, Barbara Hoffert, review of *Platform,* p. 122.

New Statesman, July 28, 2003, Jason Cowley, review of *Lanzarote,* p. 37.

New Yorker, December 28, 1998, Adam Gopnik, review of *Les Particules Elementaires* (translated as *The Elementary Particles*), pp. 61, 64-67; July 7, 2003, Julian Barrnes, review of *Platfrom,* p. 072.

People, August 25, 2003, review of *Platform,* p. 43.

Print, July-August, 2004, review of *Nude,* p. 28.

Publishers Weekly, November 23, 1998, review of *Extension du domaine de la lutte* (translated as *Whatever*), p. 58; June 9, 2003, review of *Platform,* p. 34.

Report, November 18, 2002, review of *Platform,* pp. 58-59.

Time, July 14, 2003, Richard Lacayo, review of *Platform,* p. 72.

World Literature Today, summer, 1995, Maria Green, review of *Extension du domaine de la lutte,* p. 550.

ONLINE

Guardian (Manchester England), http://books.guardian.co.uk/ (August 9, 2003), Philip Horne, "Dust to Dust," review of *Lanzarote.**

*   *   *

HOWARD, Maureen 1930-

PERSONAL: Born June 28, 1930, Bridgeport, CT; daughter of William L. (a county detective) and Loretta (Burns) Kearns; married Daniel F. Howard (a professor of English), August 28, 1954 (divorced, 1967); married David J. Gordon (a professor), April 2, 1968 (divorced); married Mark Probst (a financial advisor

Maureen Howard

and novelist); children: (first marriage) Loretta Howard. *Education:* Smith College, B.A., 1952. *Hobbies and other interests:* Gardening, cooking.

ADDRESSES: Home—New York, NY. *Agent*—Gloria Loomis, Watkins, Loomis Agency, 150 East 35th St., Ste. 530, New York, NY 10016.

CAREER: Author of novels, literary criticism, and book reviews; editor. Worked in publishing and advertising, 1952-54; University of California, Santa Barbara, lecturer in English and drama, 1968-69; New School for Social Research, New York, NY, lecturer in English and creative writing, 1967-68, 1970-71, 1974—; currently professor of writing, Columbia University, New York, NY; member of English Department Yale University, 1991—. Instructor at Amherst College and Brooklyn College.

AWARDS, HONORS: Guggenheim fellowship, 1967-68; fellow of Radcliffe Institute, 1967-68; National Book Critics Circle Award in general nonfiction, 1980, and American Book Award nomination in autobio-

graphy/biography, 1981, both for *Facts of Life;* PEN/ Faulkner Award for Fiction nominations, 1983, for *Grace Abounding,* and 1987, for *Expensive Habits;* also for *Natural History;* Ingram Merrill fellow, National Endowment for the Arts, 1988; Literary Lion Award, New York Public Library, 1993; recipient of an Academy Award in Literature from the American Academy of Arts and Letters.

WRITINGS:

NOVELS

Not a Word about Nightingales, Atheneum (New York, NY), 1961.
Bridgeport Bus, Harcourt (New York, NY), 1966.
Before My Time, Little, Brown (Boston, MA), 1975.
Grace Abounding, Little, Brown (Boston, MA), 1982.
Expensive Habits, Summit Books (New York, NY), 1986.
(Coauthor) *Mrs. Dalloway,* Harcourt Brace (New York, NY), 1990.
Natural History, Norton (New York, NY), 1992.
A Lover's Almanac, Viking (New York, NY), 1998.
(Author of introduction) *Three Novels: "O Pioneers!," "The Song of the Lark," and "My Antonia,"* Carroll & Graf (New York, NY), 1998.
Big As Life: Three Tales for Spring (novellas), Viking (New York, NY), 2001.
The Silver Screen, Viking (New York, NY), 2004.

OTHER

(Editor) *Seven American Women Writers of the Twentieth Century,* University of Minnesota Press, 1977.
Facts of Life (autobiography), Little, Brown (Boston, MA), 1978, reprinted, with new afterword by the author, Penguin Books (New York, NY), 1999.
(Editor) *Contemporary American Essays,* Viking (New York, NY), 1984, published as *The Penguin Book of Contemporary American Essays,* Penguin Books (New York, NY), 1985.
(Coeditor) *Cabbage and Bones: An Anthology of Irish-American Women's Fiction,* Henry Holt, 1997.

Also author of a produced play and of screenplays. Works included in numerous anthologies, including *The Best American Short Stories, 1965,* edited by Martha Foley and David Burnett, Houghton Mifflin, 1965, and *Statements,* edited by Jonathan Baumbach, Braziller, 1975. Contributor to various periodicals, including *New York Times Book Review, New Republic, New Yorker, Hudson Review, Yale Review,* and *Vogue.*

SIDELIGHTS: Maureen Howard's literary talents are considered by many to be expansive. She is recognized as a thoroughly professional, perceptive, and sensitive literary critic and editor and a much-admired lecturer who shares her experience and thoughts on creative writing. Her novels are also praised for their clarity, linguistic precision, and character development. Peter S. Prescott declared in *Newsweek* that Howard is "a grand writer of English prose; she's witty and (a rarer quality in novelists) she's intelligent as well." Often compared to the writings of Henry James and Virginia Woolf, Howard's novels, in addition to her autobiography, have been described as brilliantly sensitive commentaries on contemporary American society.

Howard's first novel, *Not a Word about Nightingales,* portrays a family's unsuccessful attempt to achieve happiness and personal fulfillment. While on a research trip to Perugia, Italy, college professor Albert Sedgely discards his respected and secure middle-class life and family and decides to remain in the small village. After completely changing his priorities and his lifestyle, Sedgely takes a mistress and strives to find inner peace and happiness. Meanwhile, his wife sends their eighteen-year-old daughter, Rosemary, to convince Sedgely to return home. While Rosemary quickly becomes enchanted with the colorful Italian life, Sedgely becomes increasingly disenchanted. Back in the United States, Sedgely's wife is beginning to enjoy her newfound independence. Rosemary's attraction to her new lifestyle, too, is short-lived. Doris Grumbach explained in the *New York Times Book Review* that Howard's intent in *Not a Word about Nightingales* is to write "about the deadly continuity of the marital condition," a condition from which "there is no permanent exit, only acceptance and repetition of marriage's inexorable routine."

Not a Word about Nightingales perfectly highlights a recurring theme found in most of Howard's works of fiction—that the individual must accept the fact that the events that make up and shape his or her life are predetermined. While none of us can change our destiny, each one of us is free to grow, develop, and make choices within the limits our character allows. Remarked David M. Taylor in the *Directory of Literary Biography Yearbook: 1983,* Howard's protagonists "have limited control of their fates, but the exercise of will to effect change is championed rather than discouraged. It appears that the author believes that things will generally turn out badly, but the attempt at change is worthwhile."

In *Bridgeport Bus,* Howard's second novel, a major life change comes for thirty-five-year-old Mary Agnes Keely, an aspiring writer who after an argument with her stifling widowed mother leaves the home they both share and moves to New York City. Obtaining employment as a copywriter and showing real talent as a fledgling author, Mary Agnes takes in a troubled roommate, begins an affair with an advertising-agency artist, and keeps company with a group of Bohemian artists. Toward the end of the book, she finds herself pregnant and totally alone. While Elaine Ruben described *Bridgeport Bus* in the *New Republic* as "a funny, sad work some readers were fortunate to discover and then eager to pass on to friends," Daniel Stern wrote in the *Saturday Review,* "that such a diverse and sensitized imagination should exist in the captive body of an Irish Catholic spinster in fruitless rebellion against the paucity of experience to which she appears to be condemned is merely the cream of the irony." Stern continued that, by the time Howard's protagonist arrives at the "concluding insight that 'it was no great sin to be, at last, alone,' the reader has been rewarded for his attention in a thousand subtle but tangible ways."

Writing novels populated with solid characters such as Mary Agnes in *Bridgeport Bus* and other strong-willed women such as Laura Quinn in *Before My Time,* Maud Dowd in *Grace Abounding,* and Margaret Flood in *Expensive Habits,* in addition to the powerful cast found in her autobiography, *Facts of Life,* Howard is referred to by some critics as a "woman's writer." These reviewers remarked that her novels systematically revolve around women who are searching for their identity and their place within society's accepted boundaries. These female characters often work hard to grow and strive towards self-awareness, even against seemingly very difficult odds. A reviewer for the *Washington Post Book World* described Howard's novels as "meticulously observed and beautifully written short studies of women caught in the world of men, lost to themselves, and finding little meaning in what they do."

Most critics seemed to express a similar opinion to Paul Gray in his *Time* review of *Before My Time* when he commented that one of Howard's most identifiable and admired talents lies in her ability to successfully shape and structure the language in each of her books. This task is accomplished without distracting attention from her novel's other elements. "Certainly Miss Howard's stylistic virtuosity cannot be disputed," stated Pearl K. Bell in the *New Leader*. "Every inch of her prose . . . is trimmed and polished with meticulous skill." Sybil S. Steinberg of *Publishers Weekly* observed that the fact that "critics have generally praised Howard's impeccable command of language, her exact and tartly humorous prose, somewhat surprises [Howard.]" Howard explained to Steinberg: "Of course I am fascinated with language, but I don't think that is so unusual. I should think all writers who are serious about what they're doing *would* care a lot about language. I think it's very odd when I pick up a novel and see that language has not been honored or used well, or played with."

In her award-winning autobiography, *Facts of Life,* Howard recounts her life as the daughter of Irish-Catholic parents, a college professor's wife, and the experiences that have shaped her life. "Howard is a talented novelist who has never written anything so concentrated and properly disturbing as this memoir," stated Alfred Kazin in the *New Republic*. "The style is very, very bright; the other characters are wonderfully alive; the suffering and resentment out of which the book was written stick to it like a burr. . . . A painfully strong, good book." And Walter Clemons wrote in *Newsweek* that *Facts of Life* "is brief, witty and utterly original. Its candor and conspicuous reticences are exciting and puzzling. . . . It exemplifies Howard's unsettling combination of elegance and earthiness."

In her fourth novel, *Grace Abounding,* Howard follows the path of Maud Dowd's life beginning with her very colorless and spiritless existence as a forty-three-year-old widow and mother of a teenage daughter, Elizabeth. Maud spends much of her time spying on her neighbors—a pair of spinster sisters—and visiting her dying mother. Maud's life dramatically changes after her mother dies and, after ending a brief and dreadful relationship with an unworthy man, she moves to New York City to pursue vocal training for the talented Elizabeth. Maud remarries a successful and loving man, earns a Ph.D. in psychology, and

becomes a children's therapist. Elizabeth, in turn, happily gives up her promising singing career to marry and have children. Life for Maud is not entirely golden however, as she copes with the death of a three-year-old patient and wrestles with her own mortality.

Robert Dawidoff wrote in the *Los Angeles Times* that *Grace Abounding* "conveys a shrewd feeling for how life changes, how things affect and happen to people, how some stories have endings and meanings and some do not, staying, rather, unresolved in several memories—and how, where faith had best be, grace had better be." "It does give a sense of lives as they are really lived such as only a small minority of novelists in each generation can or even want to manage," remarked Noel Perrin in the *New York Times Book Review*. "Howard . . . is a writer to read. Here the sensibility. There the intelligence." Diane M. Ross commented in the *Chicago Tribune* that "meant to involve us in the irregular rhythms of particular lives, the structure of [*Grace Abounding*] allows for shifting points of view and for chronological gaps in the narrative. . . [*Grace Abounding*] depends upon an accumulation of detail and a pattering of scenes rather than a straightforward plot. . . . Howard crosscuts between characters and locations, and blithely elides large chunks of time. . . . Her details are epiphanies, and they range from the ridiculous to the graceful."

At the beginning of Howard's 1986 novel, *Expensive Habits,* seemingly successful and well-known writer Margaret Flood lies in a hospital room after learning she has a deteriorating heart disease. The forty-five-year-old returns to her Manhattan apartment and, through a sequence of flashback scenes, the reader sees Margaret's life as a continual series of episodes—many involving loyalty and betrayal—that leave her searching for her true identity and self-worth. Margaret hopes this search will bring her the peace and contentment she so desperately desires. Jonathan Yardley suggested in the *Washington Post Book World* that Howard's *Expensive Habits* "is a serious and accomplished piece of work . . . certainly a book rich in integrity and elegance, by a writer who matters." Nora Johnson of the *Los Angeles times Book Review* wrote: "Maureen Howard's fine fifth novel attempts more, and accomplishes more, than all the others, marking her steady progress toward the highest rank of American fiction writers. . . . It's dazzling to see how deftly she wields her author's tools." And Gray commented in *Time:* "The author smuggles more subjects into a book than its length seems to allow. . . . [Howard] has skills that do not comfortably translate into screaming paperback covers and megabuck reprints. She is one of those rare contemporaries whose work demands, and deserves, rereadings."

Natural History broke with the author's characteristic focus. Taking place in Connecticut's affluent Fairfield County, *Natural History* follows the Bray family whose patriarch, Billy Bray, is county detective. The aftermath of a murder investigation Bray undertakes in 1945 leaves the family shadowed by the murdered man's brother who seeks revenge for what he feels was a botched job by Bray in bringing his brother's killer to justice. Meanwhile, the Bray children, Cathy and James, grow up and leave Bridgeport for promising careers only to return in disillusionment. Critical of what he terms the novel's "unreadability," *Washington Post Book World* reviewer Noel Perrin contended that "the real character in this book is the city of Bridgeport [where the author was raised] and the author's purpose is to say goodbye. . . . That city has turned to slums and depression and homeless people in parks, and the book is a kind of wake." Also commenting on the novel's unconventionality, *Women's Review of Books* writer Gail Pool found *Natural History* to be "something of a stew. Though [Howard] juxtaposes strands of natural, social and personal history, patterns of American hopes and familiarities, she fails to weave these threads together into an enlightening or moving whole." *New Republic* reviewer Marc Robinson, however, praised Howard as "linguistically acrobatic, imaginatively daring," and maintained that "Howard's refreshing distrust of psychological consistency and ultimate 'meaning' informs . . . *Natural History,* making its emotional appeal indirect, unassuming, yet all the more satisfying once found."

A Lover's Almanac, described by Lorna Sage in the *New York Times Book Review* as a "strange bundle of a novel," tells the story of a Generation X couple who struggle with conventional impulses toward love and marriage on the eve of the millennium. An elderly couple also begin a romance, and the novel alternates between these parallel tales of lovers, with bits of wisdom from Benjamin Franklin, Thomas Edison, and many others thrown in, in the style of the *Old Farmer's Almanac,* leading Sage to call the novel "rich propaganda for whatever's real, though it looks fanciful on

the surface." A *Kirkus Reviews* critic described this novel as a work "as expansive as an almanac, with a bit of everything in it," while a reviewer for *Booklist* asserted that Howard's improvisations on the almanac form, including bits of astrology and faux psychic predictions, explore "the often unexpected consequences of acts both creative and destructive."

In Howard's 2004 novel *The Silver Screen,* silent movie actress Isabel Maher must deal with the advent of the talkies and retires in Providence, Rhode Island, to care for her disabled husband and two children who, as they mature, have difficulty dealing with their mother's exotic past. Then, as they age themselves, they must deal with their mother's illness and death and the influence her life has had on theirs. While Ann H. Fisher commented in *Library Journal* that Howard's "prose is a bit languid and the story sometimes convoluted," a *Publishers Weekly* reviewer commented that Howard fleshes out the four primary characters "in lovely and precise prose and by the complexities of communication and disconnection." Donna Seaman, reviewing the novel for *Booklist,* stated: "*The Silver Screen* extends Howard's penetrating inquiry into love, art, and spirituality, and places her in accord with A. S. Byatt and Iris Murdoch."

BIOGRAPHICAL AND CRITICAL SOURCES:

BOOKS

Contemporary Literary Criticism, Thomson Gale (Detroit, MI), Volume 5, 1976, Volume 14, 1980, Volume 46, 1988.
Dictionary of Literary Biography Yearbook: 1983, Thomson Gale (Detroit, MI), 1984.

PERIODICALS

Booklist, September 1, 1997, review of *A Lover's Almanac;* May 15, 2004, Donna Seaman, review of *The Silver Screen,* p. 1580.
Chicago Tribune, November 14, 1982, Diane M. Ross, review of *Grace Abounding.*
Critics, February 1, 1979.
Harper's, November, 1978.
Kirkus Reviews, October 15, 1997, review of *A Lover's Almanac.*

Library Journal, June 15, 2004, Ann H. Fisher, review of *The Silver Screen,* p. 58.

Los Angeles Times, December 7, 1982, David Dawidoff, review of *Grace Abounding.*

Los Angeles Times Book Review, May 18, 1986.

Nation, December 21, 1992, p. 777.

New Leader, January 20, 1975, Pearl K. Bell, review of *Before My Time;* December 14, 1992, Hope Hale Davis, review of *Natural History,* p. 24.

New Republic, February 8, 1975, Alfred Kazin, review of *Facts of Life;* September 9, 1978, Elaine Ruben, review of *Bridgeport Bus;* October 4, 1982, Anne Tyler, review of *Grace Abounding,* p. 35; November 9, 1992, Marc Robinson, review of *Natural History,* p. 46.

Newsweek, January 20, 1975, Walter Clemons, review of *Facts of Life;* October 11, 1982, Peter S. Prescott, review of *Grace Abounding,* p. 109.

New York, June 19, 1995, p. 37.

New York Review of Books, December 3, 1992, p. 30.

New York Times, October 2, 1982, Anatole Broyard, review of *Grace Abounding,* p. 21; May 24, 1986, Michiko Kakutani, review of *Expensive Habits,* p. 11.

New York Times Book Review, January 19, 1975; September 26, 1982, Noel Perrin, review of *Grace Abounding,* p. 7; December 5, 1982, review of *Grace Abounding,* p. 40; June 8, 1986, Laurie Miller, review of *Careless about our Lives,* p. 9; October 18, 1992, Sean O'Casey, review of *Natural History,* p. 1; January 18, 1998, Lorna Sage, review of *A Lover's Almanac,* p. 6.

Partisan Review, Volume 56, number 1, 1987.

Publishers Weekly, August 24, 1992, review of *Natural History,* p. 58; May 17, 2004, review of *The Silver Screen,* p. 31.

Saturday Review, October 28, 1978, Daniel Stern, review of *Bridgeport Bus.*

Sewanee Review, winter, 1974-75.

Spectator, November 8, 1986.

Time, January 27, 1975, Paul Gray, review of *Before My Time;* May 26, 1986, Paul Gray, review of *Expensive Habits,* p. 78.

Washington Post Book World, October 10, 1982; May 11, 1986; November 22, 1992, p. 6.

Women's Review of Books, December 1992, Gail Pool, review of *Natural History,* p. 20.*

*   *   *

HOWARD, Warren F.
See POHL, Frederik

HUBER, Jeffrey T(odd) 1960-

PERSONAL: Born August 6, 1960, in Louisville, KY; son of James Bennett and Joyce Ann (Schaeftlein) Huber. *Education:* Fashion Institute of Technology of the State University of New York, A.A.S., 1981, B.S., 1983; University of Kentucky, M.L.S., 1987; University of Pittsburgh, Ph.D., 1991. *Hobbies and other interests:* Cooking, antiques, travel.

ADDRESSES: Office—Active Digital Library, Eskind Biomedical Library, Medical Center, Vanderbilt University, P.O. Box 22905, Nashville, TN 37232-8340.

CAREER: Huber Electric Co., Inc., administrative assistant, 1983-86; New York Public Library, New York, NY, serials cataloger in Research Division, 1987-88; Brookdale Hospital Medical Center, assistant librarian at Marie Smith Schwartz Medical Library, 1988-89; Whitman-Walker Clinic, AIDS information specialist intern, 1990; Pennsylvania AIDS Education and Training Center, AIDS information specialist intern, 1990; University of Pittsburgh, Pittsburgh, PA, library specialist on Pneumonia Patient Outcomes Research Team, 1991-92, fellow of Section of Medical Informatics, Department of Medicine, 1992-93, visiting lecturer in library science, 1992-93; Texas Woman's University, Denton, assistant professor of library and information studies and cochair of Task Force on HIV/AIDS, 1993-95; Vanderbilt University, Medical Center, Nashville, TN, research information scientist in Active Digital Library, Eskind Biomedical Library, 1995—. National Clearinghouse for Mental Health Pamphlets, member of advisory committee, 1992-93. Member of National Lesbian and Gay Health Foundation, 1990—, and Global AIDS Information Network, 1993—.

MEMBER: International Society for AIDS Education, American Library Association, Special Libraries Association, Medical Library Association, American Culture Association, Association for Death Education and Counseling, Texas Library Association, Beta Phi Mu.

WRITINGS:

(Editor) *How to Find Information about AIDS,* 2nd edition, Haworth Press (Binghamton, NY), 1992.

(Editor) *A Dictionary of AIDS Related Terminology,* Neal-Schuman (New York, NY), 1993, 2nd edition (with Mary L. Gillaspy) published as *Encyclopedic Dictionary of AIDS-Related Terminology,* Haworth Information Press (New York, NY), 2000.

(With Mary L. Gillaspy) *HIV/AIDS and HIV/AIDS-Related Terminology: A Means of Organizing the Body of Knowledge,* Haworth Press (New York, NY), 1996.

HIV/AIDS Community Information Services: Experiences in Serving Both At-Risk and HIV-Infected Populations, Haworth Press (New York, NY), 1996.

(Editor) *HIV/AIDS Internet Information Sources and Resources,* Harrington Park Press (Binghamton, NY), 1998.

(With Kris Riddlesperger) *Eating Positive: A Nutrition Guide and Recipe Book for People with HIV/AIDS,* Haworth Press (Binghamton, NY), 1998.

Work represented in books, including *The African American Community in the State of New York and the Impact of AIDS (Acquired Immunodeficiency Syndrome): A Preliminary Report,* New York African American Institute, State University of New York, 1991. Contributor of articles and reviews to periodicals.

SIDELIGHTS: Jeffrey T. Huber once told *CA:* "I began writing because of my personal and professional interest in HIV and AIDS. My intention and motivation has been to influence the body of information concerning the epidemic. I compiled and edited my dictionary because I knew that many individuals affected by HIV and AIDS did not understand the technical terms often used in discussing the illness, and to include population-specific vocabulary that has been incorporated into discussions concerning the pandemic."

BIOGRAPHICAL AND CRITICAL SOURCES:

PERIODICALS

American Reference Books Annual, 1994, review of *A Dictionary of AIDS-Related Terminology,* p. 751; 1997, review of *HIV/AIDS and HIV/AIDS-Related Terminology: A Means of Organizing the Body of Knowledge,* p. 241; 1999, review of *IIIV/AIDS*

Internet Sources and Resources, p. 610; 2001, review of *Encyclopedic Dictionary of AIDS-Related Terminology,* p. 676.

Australian Academic and Research Libraries, December, 1997, Stephen Michael Barnett, review of *HIV/AIDS Community Information Services: Experiences in Serving Both At-Risk and HIV-Infected Populations,* p. 322.

Booklist, October 1, 1996, review of *HIV/AIDS and HIV/AIDS-Related Terminology,* p. 370; February 15, 2001, review of *Encyclopedic Dictionary of AIDS-Related Terminology,* p. 1178.

Bulletin of the Medical Library Association, January, 1993, pp. 83-84.

Choice, November, 1996, review of *HIV/AIDS Community Information Services,* p. 492; January, 1997, review of *HIV/AIDS and HIV/AIDS-Related Terminology,* p. 828; May, 1999, review of *HIV/AIDS Internet Information Sources and Resources,* p. HS4; May, 1999, review of *Eating Positive: A Nutrition Guide and Recipe Book for People with HIV/AIDS,* p. HS29; June, 2001, review of *Encyclopedic Dictionary of AIDS-Related Terminology,* p. 1772.

Indexer, April, 1997, review of *HIV/AIDS and HIV/AIDS-Related Terminology,*

Library Association Record, June, 1999, review of *HIV/AIDS Internet Information Sources and Resources,* p. 360.

Reference and Research Book News, May, 1998, review of *Eating Positive,* p. 180.

School Library Media Quarterly, fall, 1996, review of *HIV/AIDS Community Information Sources* and *HIV/AIDS and HIV/AIDS-Related Terminology,* p. 64.

SciTech Book News, September, 1996, review of *HIV/AIDS Community Information Services,* p. 28; June, 1998, review of *Eating Positive,* p. 82; March, 2001, review of *Encyclopedic Dictionary of AIDS-Related Terminology,* p. 98.*

*   *   *

HUEBNER, Fredrick D. 1955-

PERSONAL: Surname is pronounced "*heeb*-ner"; born December 31, 1955, in Harvey, IL; son of Darell K. (a marketing manager and chemical engineer) and Betty Jean (a homemaker; maiden name, Davis) Huebner; married Christine M. Skemp (a public relations executive), April 21, 1979; children: Katherine Marie. *Education:* Macalester College, B.A. (magna cum laude), 1978; University of Washington, Seattle, J.D. (with honors), 1982. *Politics:* Democrat.

ADDRESSES: Home—Seattle, WA. *Office*—Helsell, Fetterman, Martin, Todd & Hokanson, 1500 Puget Sound Plaza, Seattle, WA 98111. *Agent*—Clyde Taylor, Curtis Brown Ltd., 10 Astor Pl., New York, NY 10003.

CAREER: Admitted to the Bar of Washington State; Helsell, Fetterman, Martin, Todd & Hokanson (law firm), Seattle, WA, partner, beginning 1982.

MEMBER: American Bar Association, King County Bar Association, Washington Lawyers for the Arts.

WRITINGS:

"MATT RIORDAN" NOVELS

The Joshua Sequence, Fawcett (New York, NY), 1986.
The Black Rose, Fawcett (New York, NY), 1987.
Judgment by Fire, Fawcett (New York, NY), 1988.
Picture Postcard, Fawcett/Columbine (New York, NY), 1990.
Methods of Execution, Simon & Schuster (New York, NY), 1994.

OTHER

Shades of Justice (novel), Simon & Schuster (New York, NY), 2001.

Contributor to *Washington Law Review* and *Washington State Bar News.*

SIDELIGHTS: Fredrick D. Huebner once told *CA:* "I use crime and detective fiction to explore legal issues and to present a contemporary description of the Pacific Northwest."

BIOGRAPHICAL AND CRITICAL SOURCES:

PERIODICALS

Armchair Detective, fall, 1991, review of *Picture Postcard,* p. 507; fall, 1994, review of *Methods of Execution,* p. 491; winter, 1995, review of *Methods of Execution,* p. 80; spring, 1995, review of *Picture Postcard,* p. 137.
Booklist, March 15, 1994, review of *Methods of Execution,* p. 1330; June 1, 2001, review of *Shades of Justice,* p. 1852.
Federal Bar News and Journal, November-December, 1994, Barbara Clay, review of *Methods of Execution,* pp. 707-708.
Kirkus Reviews, March 1, 1994, review of *Methods of Execution,* p. 250; May 1, 2001, review of *Shades of Justice,* p. 2001.
Library Journal, April 1, 1994, review of *Methods of Execution,* p. 137.
Los Angeles Times Book Review, December 23, 2001, review of *Shades of Justice,* p. 9.
Publishers Weekly, February 21, 1994, review of *Methods of Execution,* p. 236; June 25, 2001, review of *Shades of Justice,* p. 51.
Trial, July, 1994, review of *Methods of Execution,* p. 88.
Tribune Books (Chicago, IL), June 5, 1994, review of *Methods of Execution,* p. 9.*

I-J

IBBOTSON, Eva 1925-

PERSONAL: Born January 21, 1925, in Vienna, Austria; daughter of B. P. (a physiologist) and Anna (a writer; maiden name, Gmeyner) Wiesner; married Alan Ibbotson (a university lecturer), June 21, 1948; children: Lalage Ann, Tobias John, Piers David, Justin Paul. *Education:* Bedford College, London, B.Sc., 1945; attended Cambridge University, 1946-47; University of Durham, diploma in education, 1965. *Hobbies and other interests:* Ecology and environmental preservation, music, continental literature, history ("My favorite period is 1904!").

ADDRESSES: Home—2 Collingwood Terrace, Jesmond, Newcastle upon Tyne NE2 2JP, England. *Agent*—Curtis Brown, 162-168 Regent St., London W1R 5TA, England; John Cushman Associates Inc., 25 West 42nd St., New York, NY 10036.

CAREER: Full-time writer. Former research worker, university teacher, and schoolteacher.

AWARDS, HONORS: Carnegie Medal shortlist, British Library Association, 1979, for *Which Witch?,* and 2001, for *Journey to the River Sea;* Best Romantic Novel of the Year Published in England, Romantic Novelists Association, 1983, for *Magic Flutes;* Smarties Prize Shortlist, and Best Books designation, *School Library Journal,* 1998, for *The Secret of Platform 13; Guardian* Children's Fiction Award runner-up, and Whitbread Children's Book of the Year award shortlist, and Smarties Prize shortlist, all 2001, all for *Journey to the River Sea.*

WRITINGS:

FOR CHILDREN

The Great Ghost Rescue, illustrated by Simon Stern, Macmillan (London, England), 1975, illustrated by Giulio Maestro, Walck, 1975, illustrated by Kevin Hawkes, Dutton (New York, NY), 2002.

Which Witch?, illustrated by Annabel Large, Macmillan (London, England), 1979, Scholastic (New York, NY), 1988.

The Worm and the Toffee-nosed Princess, and Other Stories of Monsters (folklore), illustrated by Margaret Chamberlain, Macmillan (London, England), 1983, illustrated by Russell Ayto, Hodder Children's (London, England), 1997.

The Haunting of Hiram C. Hopgood, Macmillan (London, England), 1987, published as *The Haunting of Granite Falls,* Dutton (New York, NY), 2004.

Not Just a Witch, illustrated by Alice Englander, Macmillan (London, England), 1989, Chivers North America, 1992.

The Secret of Platform 13, illustrated by Sue Porter, Macmillan (London, England), 1994, Dutton (New York, NY), 1998.

Dial-a-Ghost, illustrated by Kirsten Meyer, Macmillan (London, England), 1996, illustrated by Kevin Hawkes, Dutton (New York, NY), 2001.

Monster Mission, illustrated by Teresa Sdralevich, Macmillan (London, England), 1999, published as *Island of the Aunts,* illustrated by Kevin Hawkes, Dutton (New York, NY), 2000.

Journey to the River Sea, illustrated by Kevin Hawkes, Dutton (New York, NY), 2001.

The Star of Kazan, illustrated by Kevin Hawkes, Dutton (New York, NY), 2004.

ROMANCE NOVELS

A Countess below Stairs, MacDonald (London, England), 1981, Avon (New York, NY), 1982.

Magic Flutes, St. Martin's Press (New York, NY), 1982.

A Glove Shop in Vienna and Other Stories, Century (London, England), 1984, St. Martin's Press (New York, NY), 1992.

A Company of Swans, St. Martin's Press (New York, NY), 1985.

Madensky Square, St. Martin's Press (New York, NY), 1988.

The Morning Gift, St. Martin's Press (New York, NY), 1993.

A Song for Summer, Arrow (London, England), 1997, St. Martin's Press (New York, NY), 1998.

OTHER

Linda Came Today (television drama), ATV, 1965.

Contributor of hundreds of articles and stories to periodicals. Works have been anthologized in books, including *Yearbook of the American Short Story.*

ADAPTATIONS: Dial-a-Ghost, The Great Ghost Rescue, The Haunting of Hiram C. Hopgood, Not Just a Witch, The Secret of Platform 13, and *Which Witch?* have all been released on audiocassette.

SIDELIGHTS: Vienna-born British writer Eva Ibbotson works in two markedly different areas of fiction: tongue-in-cheek ghost stories for a young-adult audience; and adult romances that are frequently set in her hometown during the early part of the twentieth century. Of this dual career, she herself once said, "After years of writing magazine stories and books for children, I am trying hard to break down the barrier between 'romantic novels' and 'serious novels' which are respectfully reviewed." Certainly no one would accuse her of being too serious in her ghost stories, which are written in a "spirit" of great fun. As *Horn Book* reviewer Kitty Flynn explained, "Ibbotson's vivid descriptions of the gruesome and grotesque will delight readers, and even the ghastliest of her spectral characters manages to be likable." Still, the smooth, easy flow of her supernatural tales, which has won Ib-

botson praise from many critics, fits well with the second half of her stated desires as a novelist: "My aim is to produce books that are light, humorous, even a little erudite, but secure in their happy endings. One could call it an attempt to write, in words, a good Viennese waltz!"

Growing up in Austria, Ibbotson moved with her family to England after the Nazis took power during the 1940s. She got her degree at the University of London and intended to become a physiologist, although the amount of animal experimentation required of this career path soon caused her to change her mind. Instead, she got married and raised a family. She returned to school and earned a degree in education in the mid-1960s. One of her first written works was the television play *Linda Came Today,* produced by ATV in 1965; her first children's book, *The Great Ghost Rescue,* was published a decade later, in 1975, and she has been writing ever since.

Ibbotson's books for younger readers have gained her a large following among both British and American readers due to her imaginative plots and clever dialogue. Reviewing *The Great Ghost Rescue,* a critic noted in *Growing Point* that the author develops "a gloriously improbable situation with an inexhaustible provision of verbal wit." Noting Ibbotson's penchant for flouting "political correctness," the contributor also noted that she pokes fun at "some of the more lumbering conservation-sermons disguised as fiction which are currently being offered to young readers." The novel focuses on Rick Henderson, a serious-minded boarding-school student concerned about the environment, who sees the ghosts in the story as something of an endangered species and sets about to help them. Humphrey the Horrible, in particular, needs help, because he lacks the ability to frighten the students at Rick's boarding school, and he is joined in seeking Rick's help by family members Headless Aunt Hortensia and George the Screaming Skull, among others. Noting that the story has "considerable appeal," *School Library Journal* contributor Steven Engelfried added that the novel benefits from Ibbotson's "deliciously consistent macabre humor and the entertaining ensemble of ghosts" she conjures up with her pen. According to Ann A. Flowers in *Horn Book,* "The delightfully horrid details and the richly comic assortment of ghosts make [*The Great Ghost Rescue*] an amusing and satisfying story."

Which Witch? is the story of a competition between witches eager to become the bride of the wicked wizard of the North, Arridian. A reviewer in *Junior Bookshelf* praised the novel, noting that Ibbotson's writing is so visual and evocative that, "With all respect to [illustrator] Annabel Large, illustrations are superfluous." *Dial-a-Ghost* finds Ibbotson on similar ground as it relates the activities surrounding a ghost placement agency. "There are plenty of bloodstains and creepy crawlies," promised a reviewer in *Junior Bookshelf,* "and many rather grotesque humans who help to make the ghosts seem normal."

Ghosts faced the problem of relocation in *The Great Ghost Rescue* and they encounter a similar situation in *The Haunting of Hiram C. Hopgood,* published in the United States as *The Haunting of Granite Falls.* Hopgood, a Texas oil magnate, wants to buy an English castle and bring it home with him, and twelve-year-old Alex MacBuff, an orphan who can no longer afford to keep up his ancestral home, is happy to sell it. The only problem is that Hopgood demands that the castle arrive in Texas ghost-free, and Alex has to figure out a way to negotiate with the ghosts, which include a Viking warrior, a toothless vampire named Stanislaus, and a hell-hound. Along the way, he has an innocent romance with Hopgood's ten-year-old daughter Helen, whom the ghosts assist when she is kidnapped. "This combination of farce and fantasy," wrote Elizabeth Finlayson in *School Librarian,* "has much to offer besides a thoroughly enjoyable story." Noting that the story "gives new meaning to the term 'blended family,'" *Horn Book* contributor Kristi Elle Jemtegaard praised the author's "knack for vivid detail" and noted that in *The Haunting of Granite Falls* "the comfort of a happy ending is never in doubt."

Not Just a Witch, like *Which Witch?,* concerns a competition between witches, but this time the rivalry is between two former friends who have a silly falling out over a hat. Dora and Heckie—short for Hecate—compete with each other to see who can rid a town of the most evil. Employing a classic remedy, Dora turns problem personalities into stone, but Heckie is more imaginative: she transforms her town's evildoers into caged zoo animals. When their private competition is discovered by an entrepreneurial furrier named Lionel Knapsack, the battle between the witches is cooperated: wooing Heckie with chocolate, Lionel plans to turn a whole prison full of inmates into snow leopards, a creature whose fur is highly marketable. Noting that *Not Just a Witch* deals with the perennial battle between good and evil, a *Publishers Weekly* contribu-

tor wrote that "Ibbotson again blends hilarious social commentary . . . into a potent recipe for fun."

Most of Ibbotson's early supernatural tales involve ghosts or witches, but *The Secret of Platform 13* constitutes somewhat of a departure. Next to Platform 13, in an old subway station—or Tube station, as they are called in London—is a gate into a mythic underworld of wizards and fairies. The gate only opens once every nine years, and a spoiled, selfish woman named Larina Trottle takes advantage of this opportunity to kidnap the child prince from the other world and bring him back to London. The denizens of the underworld have to come up to the surface and find their boy and rescue him, which they do with the help of Larina's son Ben. Ben, as it turns out, is lovable and kind, whereas Raymond, the boy they are searching for, has become a little tyrant under Larina's care. Praising the book as "fast, fun," and "full of bizarre characters and ideas," a reviewer in *Books for Keeps* dubbed *The Secret of Platform 13* "a real imagination tickler" with a surprise ending.

In contrast to Ibbotson's ghost stories, her adult novels, such as *Magic Flutes, Madensky Square,* and *The Morning Gift,* are much "quieter" books, though nonetheless imbued with the author's good humor and wit. *Madensky Square,* like most of the others, takes place in Vienna—in this case, the Vienna of 1911, which is yet unsullied by World War I. The story of Susanna, a dressmaker whose shop opens onto the quiet square, is told through her diary, in which she reveals a number of surprising details, including an ongoing affair with a nobleman. "This refreshing novel in which the heroine overcomes hardship [and] sticks to her ideals, [is] carried off without sticky sentimentality," wrote a critic in *Publishers Weekly.*

In a similar vein, Ibbotson's children's book *Journey to the River Sea* takes place in 1910 and focuses on a young girl who is un-haunted by ghosts of any kind. Instead of spectres, orphaned Maia Fielding is troubled by her new guardians, the Carters, who bring her to live with them on their poorly run rubber plantation in Brazil, where they live while pretending they are back in England. Escaping the confines of the Carters' home, Maia meets new friends and discovers a new world in the exotic Amazon rainforest around her. In addition to becoming enmeshed in the investigations of a pair of British detectives, Maia also discovers her life's calling: to be an explorer. Noting that the author "does a wonderful job of turning genre themes topsy-turvy," *Booklist* contributor Jean Franklin praised Ibbotson's "plucky" protagonist and her "delightfully humorous style." *Journey to the River Sea* is a novel "rich in drama, suspense, hints of romance, and a sense of justice," added Jean Gaffney in a review for *School Library Journal,* the critic going on to praise Ibbotson for bringing Brazil's "natural beauty and the time period . . . to life."

In addition to humor and a fast-moving story, all of Ibbotson's books are united by her creation of spirited protagonists, many of whom have talents that are overlooked by those around them. "Every kid wants to believe that he or she is special and hopes that someone out there will recognize their hidden talents and uniqueness, qualities that, too often, adults do fail to see," commented Jeannette Hulick in a profile of Ibbotson for the *Bulletin of the Center for Children's Books Online.* "In the words of Aunt Etta of *Island of the Aunts,* 'You'd be surprised. There are children all over the place whose parents don't know how lucky they are.' Fortunately, in Ibbotson's worlds, kids do find confirmation that they are, in fact, extraordinary people."

BIOGRAPHICAL AND CRITICAL SOURCES:

BOOKS

Ibbotson, Eva, *Island of the Aunts,* Dutton (New York, NY), 2000.

PERIODICALS

Booklist, January 1, 1985, p. 620; June 15, 1985, p. 1435; September 15, 1988, p. 120; August, 1993, p. 2036; December 15, 2001, Jean Franklin, review of *Journey to the River Sea,* p. 727; May 1, 2004, Kay Weisman, review of *The Haunting of Granite Falls,* p. 1559.
Books for Keeps, November, 1995, review of *The Secret of Platform 13,* p. 11.
Growing Point, November, 1979, p. 3598; April, 1975, review of *The Great Ghost Rescue,* p. 2599.
Horn Book, December, 1975, Ann A. Flowers, review of *The Great Ghost Rescue,* pp. 593-594; January-February, 2002, Christine M. Heppermann, review

of *Journey to the River Sea,* p. 78; September-October, 2002, Kitty Flynn, review of *The Great Ghost Rescue,* p. 574; July-August, 2004, Kristi Elle Jemtegaard, review of *The Haunting of Granite Falls,* p. 453.
Junior Bookshelf, October, 1979, review of *Which Witch?,* p. 279; October, 1987, p. 235; February, 1990, review of *Not Just a Witch,* p. 27; October, 1996, review of *Dial-a-Ghost,* pp. 202-203.
Kirkus Reviews, June 1, 1985, p. 492; June 1, 1993, pp. 678-679; January 1, 1998, p. 57; June 15, 2003, review of *Not Just a Witch,* p. 859.
Publishers Weekly, October 13, 1975, p. 111; October 26, 1984, p. 96; May 31, 1985, p. 46; September 2, 1988, review of *Madensky Square,* p. 86; July 19, 1993, p. 238; July 21, 2003, review of *Not Just a Witch,* p. 195.
School Librarian, September, 1980, p. 266; February, 1988, Elizabeth Finlayson, review of *The Haunting of Hiram C. Hopgood,* p. 28.
School Library Journal, May, 1975, p. 70; January, 2002, Jean Gaffney, review of *Journey to the River Sea,* p. 132; August, 2002, Steven Engelfried, review of *The Great Ghost Rescue,* p. 189.

ONLINE

Bulletin of the Center for Children's Books Online, http://www.lis.uiuc.edu/puboff/bccb/ (March 1, 2002), Jeannette Hulick, "Eva Ibbotson."
Penguin Putnam Web site, http://www.penguinputnam.com/ (December 2, 2004).*

*   *   *

JARVIS, E. K.
    See SILVERBERG, Robert

*   *   *

JINKS, Catherine 1963-

PERSONAL: Born November 17, 1963, in Brisbane, Queensland, Australia; daughter of Brian and Rhonda (Dickings) Jinks; married Peter Dockrill (November 22, 1992); children: one daughter. *Education:* University of Sydney, B.A. (with honors), 1986. *Politics:* "Left."

Catherine Jinks

ADDRESSES: Home—Sydney, New South Wales, Australia. *Agent*—Margaret Connolly, 16 Winton St., Warrawee, Sydney, New South Wales 2074, Australia.

CAREER: Author and illustrator. Westpac Banking Corp., Sydney, New South Wales, Australia, journalist, 1986-93; full-time writer. Lecturer, workshop presenter, and writer-in-residence at Australian schools.

AWARDS, HONORS: Australian Children's Book of the Year Award shortlist, Children's Book Council of Australia (CBC), 1993, for *Pagan's Crusade,* 1997, for *Pagan's Scribe,* and 2001, for *You'll Wake the Baby!;* Victoria Premier's Award shortlist, 1993, for *Pagan's Crusade;* Adelaide Festival Award shortlist, 1996, for *Pagan's Vows;* Australian Children's Book of the Year Award in older readers category, 1996, for *Pagan's Vows,* and 1998, for *Eye to Eye;* Fantasy, Sci-Fi, Horror award in young-adult division, 1997, and CROW Award shortlist, 1998, both for *Eye to Eye;* New South Wales State Literary Award shortlist, 1999, for *Eye to Eye,* and 2000, for *The Stinking Great Lie;* Family Award for Children's Book in picture-book category, 2001, and Young Australian Best Book Award shortlist, and Kids Own Australian Literature Award shortlist, both 2002, all for *You'll Wake the*

Baby!; Aurealis Award for fantasy shortlist, and CBC notable book designation, both for *Eglantine.*

WRITINGS:

This Way Out, Omnibus (Sydney, New South Wales, Australia), 1991.
Pagan's Crusade, Oxford University Press (Melbourne, Victoria, Australia), 1992, Candlewick Press (Cambridge, MA), 2003.
The Future Trap, Omnibus (Sydney, New South Wales, Australia), 1993, new edition, Puffin (Ringwood, Victoria, Australia), 1999.
Pagan in Exile, Omnibus (Sydney, New South Wales, Australia), 1994, Candlewick Press (Cambridge, MA), 2004.
Witch Bank, Puffin (Ringwood, Victoria, Australia), 1995.
Pagan's Vows, Omnibus (Sydney, New South Wales, Australia), 1995, Candlewick Press (Cambridge, MA), 2004.
Pagan's Scribe, Omnibus (Sydney, New South Wales, Australia), 1996.
An Evening with the Messiah (adult novel), Penguin (Camberwell, Victoria, Australia), 1996.
Eye to Eye, Puffin (Ringwood, Victoria, Australia), 1997.
Little White Secrets (adult novel), Penguin (Ringwood, Victoria, Australia), 1997.
(And illustrator) *The Bone Quest Saga,* Volume I: *The Secret of Hermitage Isle* (comic book), ABC Books (Sydney, New South Wales, Australia), 1997.
Piggy in the Middle, Penguin (Ringwood, Victoria, Australia), 1998.
(And illustrator) *The Horrible Holiday,* Puffin (Ringwood, Victoria, Australia), 1998.
The Inquisitor, Pan Macmillan (Sydney, New South Wales, Australia), 1999, St. Martin's Minotaur (New York, NY), 2002.
The Stinking Great Lie, Puffin (Ringwood, Victoria, Australia), 1999.
The Notary (adult mystery), Pan Macmillan (Sydney, New South Wales, Australia), 2000.
You'll Wake the Baby! (picture book), illustrated by Andrew McLean, Viking (Ringwood, Victoria, Australia), 2000.
What's Hector McKerrow Doing These Days?, Pan Macmillan (Sydney, New South Wales, Australia), 2000.

Bella Vista (adult story collection), Putnam (New York, NY), 2001.

The Rapture, Pan Macmillan (Sydney, New South Wales, Australia), 2001.

The Gentleman's Garden, Allen & Unwin (Crows Nest, New South Wales, Australia), 2002.

(And illustrator) *Daryl's Dinner,* Puffin (Camberwell, Victoria, Australia), 2002.

Eglantine: A Ghost Story, Allen & Unwin (Crows Nest, New South Wales, Australia), 2002.

Eloise: A Ghost Story, Allen & Unwin (Crows Nest, New South Wales, Australia), 2003.

Eustace: A Ghost Story, Allen & Unwin (Crows Nest, New South Wales, Australia), 2003.

Elysium: A Ghost Story, Allen & Unwin (Crows Nest, New South Wales, Australia), 2004.

The Road, Allen & Unwin (Crows Nest, New South Wales, Australia), 2004.

Spinning Around (adult novel), Allen & Unwin (Crows Nest, New South Wales, Australia), 2004.

Evil Genius, Allen & Unwin (Crows Nest, New South Wales, Australia), 2005.

Jinks's novels have been translated into German.

SIDELIGHTS: Australian author Catherine Jinks is best known for her "Pagan" series, which draws readers into the medieval world. The series, which includes the books *Pagan's Crusade, Pagan in Exile, Pagan's Vows,* and *Pagan's Scribe,* grew out of Jinks's interest in medieval history and focus on sixteen-year-old Christian Arab Pagan Kidrouk, who works as a squire for Templar Knight Lord Roland Roucy de Bram during the Crusades. During a tour of Jerusalem and then back through Europe during a period of religious unrest, the "Pagan" books combine Jinks's wide-ranging knowledge of the medieval period with her engaging writing style and quirky sense of humor. Other books that draw readers into the medieval past include the murder mystery *The Inquisitor,* while Jinks returns to the present for several picture books and self-illustrated middle-grade novels, novels for adults, and the novels comprising her popular "Ghost Story" series.

Jinks was born in Australia in 1963 and grew up amid a book-loving family in Papua, New Guinea. An avid writer since childhood, she once recalled: "I've always wanted to produce books, and sent my first 'novel' off to a publisher when I was twelve." The novel's title was *I Want to Be a Jungle Girl;* due to the lack of foresight of the receiving publisher, it was never printed. After moving to Australia and graduating from the University of Sydney with a degree in medieval history, she married and relocated with her Canadian husband to Nova Scotia from 1993 to 1994, before returning to Australia with her family.

Jinks's first book for young adults, *This Way Out,* was published in 1991, after its author had spent several years working as a journalist. This novel is a contemporary story that focuses on a fifteen-year-old girl's dissatisfaction with her life and her search for a job that will pay for the photographs she hopes will begin her modeling career. "*This Way Out* reveals the author's awareness of some of the frustrations and longings of youth," remarked Cathryn Crowe in *Magpies.*

For her second book, Jinks introduces her twelfth-century ragamuffin character, Pagan, as he attempts to rise above a childhood on the streets of Jerusalem by finding a place with the Knights Templar. The novel, which takes place in 1187, focuses on the relationship between the streetwise Pagan and Templar Knight Lord Roland, who as a member of the order charged with protecting travelers, is the epitome of upper-class strength and valor. Touring the Middle East to advance the cause of Christianity, the pair are forced to enter battle to defend the city of Jerusalem and the Christian pilgrims visiting the Holy City from the Muslim warlord Saladin, who is attempting to recapture the city for Islam. "The aristocratic Templar and his scruffy squire make an unlikely partnership and it is a measure of the success of Ms. Jinks's story that we accept the mutual respect that grows up between the partners under the stress of violent action," continued Marcus Crouch in *Junior Bookshelf.*

Pagan's Crusade was described as "a curious, and curiously fascinating, novel" by Marcus Crouch in his review for *Junior Bookshelf.* Critics have noted the author's unusual choice of modern vernacular speech for her medieval characters, a choice that yields "a style which is elliptical and abrupt and, at times, wildly funny," according to a reviewer for *Magpies.* Praising Jinks's characters as "lively and engaging," *Horn Book* contributor Anita L. Burkam added that the irreverent squire's "sarcastic first-person narration, while faithful to the details of medieval life, contains more than a touch of irony." Comparing Jinks's humor to that of

British comedy troupe Monty Python, a *Publishers Weekly* reviewer wrote that the "alternately hilarious, often poignant novel . . . turns medieval history into fodder for both high comedy and allegory." Also praising *Pagan's Crusade*, a *Kirkus Reviews* critic maintained that the book's "orphan's-eye view" helps readers visualize "the overripe streets of twelfth-century Jerusalem" and also "introduces a character as lovable, stubbornly loyal, and smart-mouthed as any Disney film sidekick."

In the first sequel to *Pagan's Crusade, Pagan in Exile,* Lord Roland takes Pagan back to his estate in Languedoc, France, where the knight becomes involved in the domestic wars among the twelfth-century landed aristocracy while trying to summon others to help the Order retake Jerusalem. Like Jinks's first volume, *Pagan in Exile* was praised for its young protagonist's humorous first-person narration, although its plot contains a darker focus due to its depiction of the brutality and squalor of medieval life. Noting that the author successfully brings to life an epoch "that was particularly dark and dirty," *Booklist* contributor Ilene Cooper added that followers of the "Pagan" series would likely "find other books set in the Middle Ages pallid" by comparison.

Other books in the "Pagan" series include *Pagan's Vows* and *Pagan's Scribe. Pagan's Vows* finds Pagan and Lord Roland serving as novices at the Abbey of Saint Martin as a way of avoiding the brutality of medieval French society. While Roland quickly accepts the way of life at the Benedictine monastery, Pagan sees the dishonesty and hypocrisy running rampant in this house of God. Rejecting the blind obedience demanded of him and the discomfort, he is determined to unveil the corruption in the monastic hierarchy, even if it angers Lord Roland. Jinks concludes her series with *Pagan's Scribe,* in which Isadore recounts Pagan's rise to become an archdeacon of the Catholic Church in France. *Pagan's Vows* won the Australian Children's Book of the Year Award for the older readers category from the Children's Book Council of Australia, one of several awards accorded the series. In her acceptance speech published in *Reading Time,* Jinks noted, "In a funny sort of way I see the award as more of a tribute to Pagan than to me." "He's been through a lot," she added of her popular fictional character, "yet he's kept his humour and his courage and his loving heart."

Like the "Pagan" books, *The Inquisitor* is another novel by Jinks that has found its way into the hands of U.S. readers. Taking place in fourteenth-century France during the Inquisition, the novel focuses on the efforts of Inquisitor Father Bernard Peyre to track down the person who murdered and dismembered the corpse of the priest's supervisor, Father Augustin. As his search uncovers corruption in the church hierarchy, Bernard finds his reputation sullied—and his life threatened—by charges of heresy in what *Booklist* reviewer Carrie Bissey dubbed a "smart page-turner that paints a convincing portrait of the struggle to live in the shadow of a . . . [corrupt] institution." Citing Bernard as a "sympathetic and engaging narrator," a *Publishers Weekly* reviewer also praised Jinks for her creation of a "gripping escape sequence" to crown the novel's plot.

A prolific writer at home in a variety of genres, Jinks continues to author stand-alone titles for children of several ages, and has also embarked on a second series with *Eglantine: A Ghost Story.* As the first of the "Ghost Story" books, *Eglantine* introduces Allie Gebhardt, junior ghost hunter. In this book, as well as its sequels *Eustace, Eloise,* and *Elysium,* Allie gradually gains the tools of the ghost-hunting trade—seances, dealing with emanations, and how to put a spirit to rest—as various unearthly spectres cross her path. "I feel shocking if I'm not working on a book and have no problem applying myself to their creation—no writer's block for me. I love creating stories; if I didn't, I wouldn't be doing it. It's the best job in the world (I just wish it paid more!)."

BIOGRAPHICAL AND CRITICAL SOURCES:

PERIODICALS

Booklist, October 1, 2002, Carrie Bissey, review of *The Inquisitor,* p. 304; January 1, 2004, Ilene Cooper, review of *Pagan in Exile,* p. 844.
Horn Book, July, 1993, Karen Jameyson, review of *Pagan's Crusade,* p. 498; September-October, 2003, Anita L. Burkam, review of *Pagan's Crusade,* p. 611; May-June, 2004, Anita L. Burkam, review of *Pagan in Exile,* p. 328.
Junior Bookshelf, December, 1993, Marcus Crouch, review of *Pagan's Crusade,* pp. 246-247.
Kirkus Reviews, September 15, 2002, review of *The Inquisitor,* p. 1355; October 14, 2003, review of *Pagan's Crusade,* p. 1272; December 15, 2003, review of *Pagan in Exile,* p. 1450.
Kliatt, January, 2004, Paula Rohrlick, review of *Pagan's Crusade* and *Pagan in Exile,* p. 8.

Magpies, November, 1992, review of *Pagan's Crusade,* p. 14; March, 1993, Cathryn Crowe, review of *This Way Out,* p. 32; May, 1993, Joan Zahnleiter, review of *Pagan's Crusade,* p. 24; July, 1995, review of *Pagan in Exile,* p. 24.

Publishers Weekly, September 30, 2002, review of *The Inquisitor,* p. 53; November 10, 2003, review of *Pagan's Crusade,* p. 63.

Reading Time, November, 1996, Catherine Jinks, acceptance speech for Australian Children's Book of the Year Award, pp. 7-8.

School Library Journal, December, 2003, Douglas P. Davey, review of *Pagan's Crusade,* p. 153.

ONLINE

Allen & Unwin Web site, http://www.allenandunwin.com/ (October 20, 2004), "Catherine Jinks."

Aussie Reviews Online, http://www.aussiereviews.com/ (October 24, 2004), review of *Eglantine: A Ghost Story.*

January Online, http://www.januarymagazine.com/ (October, 2003), Sue Bursztynski, review of *Eloise: A Ghost Story.*

Lateral Learning Speakers' Agency Web site, http://www.laterallearning.com/ (October 21, 2004), "Catherine Jinks."

Penguin Books Web site, http://www.penguin.com.au/ (June 20, 2001), "Catherine Jinks."*

*   *   *

JORGENSON, Ivar
See SILVERBERG, Robert

*   *   *

JUDD, Cyril
See POHL, Frederik

K

KASTEL, Warren
See SILVERBERG, Robert

*   *   *

KAZANTZIS, Judith 1940-

PERSONAL: Born August 14, 1940, in Oxford, England; daughter of Francis (a writer and politician) and Elizabeth (a biographer; maiden name, Harman) Pakenham; married Alec Kazantzis (a barrister), 1982 (divorced); children: Miranda, Arthur. *Education:* Somerville College, Oxford, B.A., 1961. *Politics:* Socialist (British Labour Party).

ADDRESSES: Home—32 St. Anne's Cres., Lewes, East Sussex BN7 1SB, England. *E-mail*—judithkazantzis@writersartists.net.

CAREER: Poet, artist, and reviewer. Home tutor for Inner London Education Authority, London, England, 1970s. South-East Arts, committee member and panelist, 1978-79; gives readings from her works in England and abroad. *Exhibitions:* Individual art shows have been conducted at Poetry Society Gallery, London, 1987, and Combined Harvest Gallery, London, 1989.

WRITINGS:

POETRY

Minefield, Sidgwick & Jackson (London, England), 1977.
The Wicked Queen, Sidgwick & Jackson (London, England), 1980.

(With Michèle Roberts and Michelene Wandor) *Touch Papers,* Allison & Busby (London, England), 1982.
Let's Pretend, Virago (London, England), 1984.
Flame Tree, Methuen (London, England), 1988.
The Rabbit Magician Plate, Sinclair-Stevenson (London, England), 1992.
Selected Poems, 1977-1992, Sinclair-Stevenson (London, England), 1995.
Swimming through the Grand Hotel: Poems 1993-1996, Dufour (Chester Springs, PA), 1997.
The Odysseus Poems: Fictions on the Odyssey of Homer, illustrated by Jacqueline Morreau, Cargo Press (Manaccan, Cornwall, England), 1999.

Shorter works include the pamphlets "A Poem for Guatemala," Bedlam Press (Leamington Spa, Yorkshire, England), 1986; "Judith Kazantzis," Leamington Poetry Society (Leamington Spa, Yorkshire, England), 1987; and "The Florida Swamps," Oasis Press (London, England), 1990. Work represented in anthologies, including *A Celebration of Wilfred Owen,* Interpreters House; *A Ring of Words,* 1998; *Poems on the Underground,* Cassell, 2001; *Parents,* Enitharmon Press, 2000; and *Red Sky at Night,* 2003. Contributor of poetry to periodicals, including *London, Stand, Ambit, Agenda, Poetry Review, Poetry Wales, Honest Ulsterman, Poetry Ireland, Red Pepper,* and *New Statesman.*

OTHER

(Editor) *The Gordon Riots: A Collection of Contemporary Documents,* Jonathan Cape (London, England), 1966.
(Editor) *Women in Revolt: The Fight for Emancipation; A Collection of Contemporary Documents,* Jonathan Cape (London, England), 1968.

Of Love and Terror (novel), Saqi Press (London, England), 2002.
(Translator) *In Cyclops Cave,* 2002.

Also contributor of short stories to *Critical Quarterly, Aquarius, London,* and other periodicals; poetry reviewer for periodicals, including *Spare Rib, Times Literary Supplement,* and *Agenda.* Poetry editor, *PEN Broadsheet.*

SIDELIGHTS: Judith Kazantzis, the author of numerous volumes of poetry, published *Minefield* in 1977, a collection which caused *Times Literary Supplement* reviewer D. M. Thomas to comment that "if a minefield could write poetry, this is the poetry it would write." Thomas admired the poet's "nervous energy, bitter wit, and keen eye for striking visual detail." In *Contemporary Review,* Derek Stanford likewise remarked on Kazantzis's "exclamatory imagism," as he termed it, feeling that the poet "explodes like a bomb in her small collection."

A later collection, *Flame Tree,* drew an approving review from Clair Wills in the *Times Literary Supplement.* Wills cited "Finally: Ethiopia" as especially impressive for its skill in contrasting "the detached language of a radio news bulletin with personal horror." The reviewer also praised the title poem, "Flame Tree," which deplores the destruction of the rain forests, for its "formal and emotional complexity" and its successful welding of a feminist message with broader social concerns.

The Rabbit Magician Plate contains poems set in England, Ireland, and America and presents settings as varied as the swamps of ·Florida, the mountains of Central America, and the tree-lined roads of New England. Peter Finch in the *New Welsh Review* called the collection "work which excites as much by its fresh subject matter . . . as by its surprising use of language." And John Firth in *London* magazine noted that *The Rabbit Magician Plate* "is a longish trip with varied stations: always vibrant, often moving, and never pedestrian."

BIOGRAPHICAL AND CRITICAL SOURCES:

BOOKS

Contemporary Poets, 7th edition, St. James Press (Detroit, MI), 2001.
Contemporary Women Poets, St. James Press (Detroit, MI), 1998.

PERIODICALS

Agenda, spring, 1997, review of *Selected Poems, 1977-1992,* p. 128; summer, 1999, review of *Swimming through the Grand Hotel: Poems 1993-1996,* p. 93.
Contemporary Review, February, 1978, Derek Stanford, review of *Minefield.*
London, April-May, 1993, John Firth, review of *The Rabbit Magician Plate,* pp. 128-129.
New Welsh Review, winter, 1992, Peter Finch, review of *The Rabbit Magician Plate.*
Observer (London, England), November 25, 1984.
Poetry Review, winter, 1992.
Times Literary Supplement, January 20, 1978, D. M. Thomas, review of *Minefield;* October 17, 1980; June 24, 1988, Clair Wills, review of *Flame Tree;* January 5, 1996, review of *Selected Poems, 1977-1992,* p. 28; January 2, 1998, review of *Swimming through the Grand Hotel,* p. 21.

ONLINE

Cargo Press Web site: Our Authors, Judith Kazantzis, http://www.cargo-press.co.uk/kazantzis/ (February 10, 2003).
Enitharmon Press Web site, http://www.enitharmon.co. uk/ (February 10, 2003).
Writers Artists Web site, http://www.writersartists.net/ (February 10, 2003).*

*   *   *

KELLER, Suzanne 1930-

PERSONAL: Born April 16, 1930, in Vienna, Austria; came to United States in 1939, naturalized citizen, 1944. *Education:* Hunter College (now of the City University of New York), A.B., 1948; Columbia University, M.A., 1950, Ph.D., 1953. *Hobbies and other interests:* Travel.

ADDRESSES: Office—c/o Department of Sociology, Princeton University, Princeton, NJ 08540.

CAREER: Interpreter and translator in Paris, France, 1952-53; Massachusetts Institute of Technology, Center for International Studies, Cambridge, research associate in international relations, 1954-57; Brandeis University, Waltham, MA, assistant professor of sociology, 1957-60; New York Medical College, New York, NY, research associate in psychiatry, 1961-62; Vassar College, Poughkeepsie, NY, associate professor of sociology, 1962-63; Fulbright lecturer in Athens, Greece, 1963-65; Athens Center of Ekistics, Athens, lecturer and research analyst, 1965-67; Princeton University, Princeton, NJ, professor of sociology, beginning 1968. Princeton University, visiting professor, 1966.

MEMBER: World Society for Ekistics, World Future Society, American Sociological Association (vice president, 1975-77).

AWARDS, HONORS: Guggenheim Foundation fellow, 1972.

WRITINGS:

Beyond the Ruling Class, Random House (New York, NY), 1963.
The Urban Neighborhood, Random House (New York, NY), 1968.
(With Donald Light, Jr.) *Sociology,* Random House (New York, NY), 1975.
(Editor) *Building for Women,* Lexington Books (Lexington, MA), 1981.
(Consulting editor) *Marriage and Family Today,* Random House (New York, NY), 1983.
(With Craig Calhoun and Donald Light) *Understanding Sociology,* photographs by Douglas Harper, McGraw-Hill (New York, NY), 1995.
Community: Pursuing the Dream, Living the Reality, Princeton University Press (Princeton, NJ), 2002.

Contributor to sociology journals and other periodicals.

BIOGRAPHICAL AND CRITICAL SOURCES:

PERIODICALS

Library Journal, January, 2003, M. C. Duhig, review of *Community: Pursuing the Dream, Living the Reality,* p. 139.*

KILLINGER, John 1933-

PERSONAL: Born June 12, 1933, in Germantown, KY; son of John Raymond and Jessie Frances Killinger; married Anne Katherine Waddle (a composer), June 12, 1952; children: John Eric, Paul Krister. *Education:* Baylor University, A.B., 1953; University of Kentucky, M.A., 1954, Ph.D., 1957; Harvard University, S.T.B., 1959; Princeton Theological Seminary, Th.D., 1963. *Politics:* Democrat. *Hobbies and other interests:* Art, theater.

ADDRESSES: Agent—c/o Author Mail, Abingdon Press, 201 8th Ave. S., P.O. Box 801, Nashville, TN 37202-0801.

CAREER: Ordained Baptist minister, 1952; pastor of Baptist church in North Reading, MA, 1957-59; Georgetown College, Georgetown, KY, associate professor English, 1959-61; Princeton Theological Seminary, Princeton, NJ, instructor in homiletics, 1961-63; Kentucky Southern College, Louisville, academic dean, 1963-65; Vanderbilt University, Nashville, TN, professor of preaching, worship, and literature, beginning 1965. University of Chicago, visiting professor, 1965. American Church in Paris, theologian in residence, 1967-68; also served as Presbyterian minister. Ecumenical Council on Drama and the Other Arts, member, vice president, 1976-77.

MEMBER: American Academy of Religion, American Academy of Homiletics, Societas Liturgica.

WRITINGS:

Hemingway and the Dead Gods, University Press of Kentucky (Lexington, KY), 1960.
The Failure of Theology in Modern Literature, Abingdon Press (Nashville, TN), 1963.
The Thickness of Glory, Abingdon Press (Nashville, TN), 1965.
The Word Not Bound: A One-Act Play, Word Books (Waco, TX), 1968.
The Centrality of Preaching in the Total Task of the Ministry, Word Books (Waco, TX), 1969.
For God's Sake, Be Human, Word Books (Waco, TX), 1970.
Leave It to the Spirit, Harper (New York, NY), 1971.

World in Collapse: The Vision of Absurd Drama, Dell (New York, NY), 1971.

The Salvation Tree, Harper (New York, NY), 1973.

The Fragile Presence: Transcendence in Modern Literature, Fortress Press (Philadelphia, PA), 1973.

(Editor) *Experimental Preaching,* Abingdon Press (Nashville, TN), 1973.

All You Lonely People, All You Lonely People, Word Books (Waco, TX), 1973.

The Second Coming of the Church, Abingdon Press (Nashville, TN), 1974.

(Editor) *The Eleven o'Clock News and Other Sermons,* Abingdon Press (Nashville, TN), 1975.

Bread for the Wilderness, Wine for the Journey, Word Books (Waco, TX), 1976.

A Sense of His Presence, Doubleday (New York, NY), 1977, published in *A Devotional Guide to the Gospels: 336 Meditations,* Word Books (Waco, TX), 1984.

His Power in You, Doubleday (New York, NY), 1978, published in *A Devotional Guide to the Gospels: 336 Meditations,* Word Books (Waco, TX), 1984.

A Little Primer on Prayer, Word Books (Waco, TX), 1979.

A Devotional Guide to Luke: The Gospel of Contagious Joy, Word Books (Waco, TX), 1980, published in *A Devotional Guide to the Gospels: 336 Meditations,* Word Books (Waco, TX), 1984.

The Loneliness of Children, Vanguard Press (New York, NY), 1980.

A Devotional Guide to John: The Gospel of Eternal Life, Word Books (Waco, TX), 1981, published in *A Devotional Guide to the Gospels: 336 Meditations,* Word Books (Waco, TX), 1984.

Prayer, the Act of Being with God, Word Books (Waco, TX), 1981, published as *Beginning Prayer,* Upper Room Books (Nashville, TN), 1993.

Christ in the Seasons of Ministry, Word Books (Waco, TX), 1983.

The Cup and the Waterfall: The Adventure of Living in the Present Moment, Paulist Press (New York, NY), 1983.

A Devotional Guide to the Gospels: 336 Meditations (contains *A Sense of His Presence, His Power in You, A Devotional Guide to Luke: The Gospel of Contagious Joy,* and *A Devotional Guide to John: The Gospel of Eternal Life*), Word Books (Waco, TX), 1984.

Fundamentals of Preaching, Fortress Press (Philadelphia, PA), 1985.

Parables for Christmas, Abingdon Press (Nashville, TN), 1985.

Sea Breezes: Thoughts of God from a Summer Beach, Abingdon Press (Nashville, TN), 1985.

The Tender Shepherd, Abingdon Press (Nashville, TN), 1985.

Contemporary Wedding Services, Abingdon Press (Nashville, TN), 1986.

Christ and the Seasons of Marriage, Broadman Press (Nashville, TN), 1987.

The God Named Hallowed: The Lord's Prayer for Today, Abingdon Press (Nashville, TN), 1988.

To My People with Love: The Ten Commandments for Today, Abingdon Press (Nashville, TN), 1988.

Christmas Spoken Here, Broadman Press (Nashville, TN), 1989.

(With Jack Hayford and Howard Stevenson) *Mastering Worship,* Multnomah Press (Portland, OR), 1990.

You Are What You Believe: The Apostles' Creed for Today, Abingdon Press (Nashville, TN), 1990.

Letting God Bless You: The Beatitudes for Today, Abingdon Press (Nashville, TN), 1992.

The Greatest Teachings of Jesus, Abingdon Press (Nashville, TN), 1993.

Jessie (novel), McCracken Press, 1993.

Day by Day with Jesus: 365 Meditations on the Gospels, Abingdon Press (Nashville, TN), 1994.

Preaching to a Church in Crisis: A Homiletic for the Last Days of the Mainline Church, CSS (Lima, OH), 1995.

Fundamentals of Preaching, Fortress Press (Minneapolis, MN), 1996.

Raising Your Spiritual Awareness through 365 Simple Gifts from God, Dimensions for Living (Nashville, TN), 1998.

Preaching the New Millennium, Abingdon Press (Nashville, TN), 1999.

Lost in Wonder, Love, and Praise: Prayers for Christian Worship, Abingdon Press (Nashville, TN), 2001.

God, the Devil, and Harry Potter: A Christian Minister's Defense of the Beloved Novels, Thomas Dunne Books (New York, NY), 2002.

Ten Things I Learned Wrong from a Conservative Church, Crossroad Publishing (New York, NY), 2002.

Enter Every Trembling Heart: Prayers for Christian Worship, Abingdon Press (Nashville, TN), 2003.

Also author of *Jesus, the Greatest Teacher in the World.*

BIOGRAPHICAL AND CRITICAL SOURCES:

PERIODICALS

America, June 12, 1982, A. Robert Casey, review of *Prayer, the Act of Being with God,* p. 465.

Best Sellers, July, 1980, review of *The Loneliness of Children,* p. 144.

Booklist, September 1, 1980, review of *The Loneliness of Children,* p. 8.

Childhood Education, May, 1981, review of *The Loneliness of Children,* p. 308.

Choice, April, 1981, review of *The Loneliness of Children,* p. 1165.

Christian Century, March 11, 1981, David J. Ernsberger, review of *The Loneliness of Children,* p. 274; May 21, 1985, David B. Watermulder, review of *A Devotional Guide to the Gospels: 336 Meditations* and *Fundamentals of Preaching,* p. 527.

Christian Herald, December, 1985, David Kucharsky, review of *Parables for Christmas,* p. 61.

Kirkus Reviews, June 15, 1980, review of *The Loneliness of Children,* p. 819.

Library Journal, July, 1980, Susan B. Hagloch, review of *The Loneliness of Children,* p. 1524; November 1, 1993, Joanna M. Thompson, review of *Jessie,* p. 148; January, 2003, Graham Christian, review of *God, the Devil, and Harry Potter: A Christian Minister's Defense of the Beloved Novels,* p. 122.

Publishers Weekly, June 27, 1980, review of *The Loneliness of Children,* p. 72; October 4, 1993, review of *Jessie,* p. 66; November 11, 2002, review of *God, the Devil, and Harry Potter,* p. 58.

Science Books and Films, September, 1981, review of *The Loneliness of Children,* p. 3.

Theology Today, January, 1986, review of *Fundamentals of Preaching,* p. 562.*

*   *   *

KILPATRICK, Nancy 1946-
(Amarantha Knight)

PERSONAL: Born May 6, 1946, in Philadelphia, PA; daughter of George Christopoulos and Viola Hopkins; married Len Kirschner, October 30, 1964 (marriage ended, 1975); married Michael Kilpatrick, June 22, 1984 (marriage ended). *Education:* Attended Temple University, 1964. *Religion:* "No particular." *Hobbies and other interests:* Jungian psychology, music, dance, masks.

ADDRESSES: Home and office—1077 Bathurst St., Toronto, Ontario M5R 3G8, Canada; fax: 416-535-4270. *Agent*—Ricia Mainhardt, 612 Argyle St., Ste. L5, Brooklyn, NY 11230. *E-mail*—n.kilpatrick@genie.com; nkilpatr@gbrownc.on.ca.

CAREER: George Brown College, Toronto, Ontario, Canada, writing teacher, 1985-95; freelance writer for newspapers and magazines. C. G. Jung Foundation, member. Guest on television and radio programs in Canada and the United States; gives readings from her works.

MEMBER: Horror Writers Association (member of board of trustees), Science Fiction and Fantasy Writers of America, Crime Writers of Canada, Editors Association of Canada, Speculative Fiction Writers of Canada, Transylvanian Society of Dracula (Canadian chapter), Thee Vampire Guild (England), Burnaby Writers' Society, Gothic Society, Toronto HYDRA, Count Dracula Fan Club.

AWARDS, HONORS: Arthur Ellis Award for Best Canadian Mystery, 1992, for the story "Mantrap"; winner of *Standing Stone* short-story contest, horror category; five grants from Ontario Arts Council; finalist, Bram Stoker Award and Aurora Award, 1993, for "Farm Wife," and 1995, for *Near Death.*

WRITINGS:

NOVELS

(With Don Bassingwaithe) *As One Dead* (adapted from the game *Vampire: The Masquerade*), White Wolf (Atlanta, GA), 1993.

Near Death (horror), Pocket Books (New York, NY), 1994.

Child of the Night, Raven (London, England), 1996, Pumpkin Books (Eureka, CA), 1999.

Dracul: An Eternal Love Story, Lucard Publishing (San Diego, CA), 1998.

Reborn, 1999.

Bloodlover, Baskerville Books (Toronto, Ontario, Canada), 2000.

The Vampire Stories of Nancy Kilpatrick, Mosaic Press (Oakville, Ontario, Canada), 2000.

(With Michael Kilpatrick) *Eternal City,* Five Star (Waterville, ME), 2003.

"DARKER PASSIONS" SERIES; UNDER PSEUDONYM AMARANTHA KNIGHT

Dracula (adapted from Bram Stoker's novel), Masquerade Books (New York, NY), 1993.

Dr. Jekyll and Mr. Hyde (adapted from Robert Louis Stevenson's story), Masquerade Books (New York, NY), 1995.

Frankenstein (adapted from Mary Shelley's novel), Masquerade Books (New York, NY), 1995.

The Fall of the House of Usher (adapted from Edgar Allan Poe's short story), Masquerade Books (New York, NY), 1995.

The Portrait of Dorian Gray (adapted from Oscar Wilde's novel), Masquerade Books (New York, NY), 1996.

The Amarantha Knight Reader (excerpts from "Darker Passions" novels), Masquerade Books (New York, NY), 1996.

Also author of *Carmille.*

EDITOR, UNDER PSEUDONYM AMARANTHA KNIGHT, AND CONTRIBUTOR, AS NANCY KILPATRICK

Love Bites, Masquerade Books (New York, NY), 1994.

Flesh Fantastic, Masquerade Books (New York, NY), 1995.

Seductive Spectres, Masquerade Books (New York, NY), 1996.

Sex Macabre, Masquerade Books (New York, NY), 1996.

OTHER

Sex and the Single Vampire (short stories; part of *The Vampire Trilogies*), Tal Publications (Leesburg, VA), 1994.

(Editor, with Thomas S. Roche) *In the Shadow of the Gargoyle,* Ace Books (New York, NY), 1998.

The Vampire Stories of Nancy Kilpatrick, Mosaic Press (Oakville, Ontario, Canada), 2000.

Cold Comfort (short stories), Dark Tales (Grandview, MO), 2001.

(Editor, with Thomas S. Roche) *Graven Images,* Ace Books (New York, NY), 2001.

Goth Bible: A Compendium for the Darkly Inclined, St. Martin's (New York, NY), 2004.

Work represented in anthologies, including *Bizarre Sex and Other Crimes of Passion—The Book,* edited by Stan Tal, Masquerade Books (New York, NY), 1994; *One Hundred Vicious Little Vampires,* edited by Weinberg and Dziemianowicz, Barnes & Noble (New York, NY), 1995; and *A Horror a Day,* edited by Weinberg, Greenberg, and Dziemianowicz, Barnes & Noble (New York, NY), 1996. Contributor to *VampErotica,* Brainstorm Comics. Contributor to magazines and newspapers, including *Midnight Zoo, Metropolis, Toronto Life, International Vampire, Crimson,* and *Horror.*

SIDELIGHTS: Nancy Kilpatrick is known for her various writings—under both her own name and under the pseudonym Amarantha Knight—in the horror fiction genre. Her most prominent publications under her own name are probably the novels *Near Death* and *Child of the Night,* both of which relate the various escapades of three vampires: the sensual Andre, the spiritual David, and the intellectual Karl. *Near Death,* the first volume featuring this unlikely trinity, relates their exploits in contemporary times. Like the vampires of many other tales, Kilpatrick's trio crave blood and possess extraordinary physical strength. In addition, they show the usual, fatal vulnerability to sunlight. But they also conduct sexual relations with living beings, and they may even enter into monogamous relationships with their sexual partners after having transformed them into like-minded bloodsuckers. The action in *Near Death* is triggered by the trio's apprehension of a drug-addicted woman who unknowingly accepted the task of exterminating one of them. While Andre, David, and Karl search for their unknown enemy, the woman accepts one of the heroes as her lover and, thus, joins them in vampirism. She even manages to overcome her drug addiction. *Child of the Night,* the second volume of what was projected to be a trilogy, details the adventures of Andre, David, and Karl prior to the events of *Near Death.* Tom Winstead, writing in the *St. James Guide to Horror, Ghost, and Gothic Writers,* ranked *Near Death* and *Child of the Night* as Kilpatrick's "best novels." *Reborn* was planned to conclude the trilogy.

Vampires are also the central figures in *As One Dead,* Kilpatrick's collaboration with Don Bassingthwaite. In the novel, which is derived from the role-playing game *Vampire: The Masquerade,* a half-breed vampire tries to undermine the class distinctions between two vampire sects in Toronto, Canada.

In addition to writing novels, Kilpatrick has produced dozens of short stories in various collections and periodicals. Among her many tales are "Metal Fatigue," about a hopeless worker who fantasizes about sex with aliens; and "Heartbeat," which concerns ethnicity's influence on perspective. Kilpatrick has also published various works under the pseudonym Amarantha Knight. Notable among these works are the "Darker Passions" series of volumes providing erotic perspectives on classic horror tales such as *Dracula* and *The Fall of the House of Usher.*

Kilpatrick once told *CA:* "I began as a literary writer, but found that my interests veered toward the dark side of life. I still loved plot and storytelling, even when minimalism became the norm in the literary world. The genres of horror, dark fantasy, and mystery have given me the room I've needed to tell a dark story and to work with the negative side of archetypes. I am keenly interested in the process of transformation, and that seems to be a major theme in my work."

BIOGRAPHICAL AND CRITICAL SOURCES:

BOOKS

St. James Guide to Horror, Ghost, and Gothic Writers, St. James Press (Detroit, MI), 1998.

PERIODICALS

Booklist, October 15, 2001, Kristine Huntley, review of *Cold Comfort,* p. 387.
Books in Canada, February, 1995.
Eye, September 1, 1994.

Fantasy and Science Fiction, October-November, 1994.
International Vampire, October, 1994.
Kliatt, March, 2001, review of *Graven Images,* p. 26.
Kliatt Young Adult Paperback Book Guide, March, 1999, review of *In the Shadow of the Gargoyle,* p. 23.
Locus, May, 2001, review of *Bloodlover,* p. 31.
Ottawa Citizen, August, 1995.
Publishers Weekly, January 25, 1999, review of *Near Death, Child of the Night* and *Reborn,* p. 77; September 10, 2001, review of *Cold Comfort,* p. 66; January 6, 2003, review of *Eternal City,* p. 45.
Romantic Times, October, 1994.
Science Fiction Chronicle, August, 1999, review of *In the Shadow of the Gargoyle,* p. 45.
Toronto Star, September 12, 1992; October 30, 1994; December 3, 1994; December 17, 1994.
Voice of Youth Advocates, April, 2001, review of *Graven Images,* p. 52.
Writer's Block, spring, 1995.*

*   *   *

KIMMELMAN, Leslie (Grodinsky) 1958-

PERSONAL: Born April 19, 1958, in Philadelphia, PA; married Ray Kimmelman, 1984; children: Natalie, Gregory. *Education:* Middlebury College, B.A. (magna cum laude), 1980. *Religion:* Jewish.

ADDRESSES: Home—Ardsley, NY. *Agent*—c/o Author Mail, HarperCollins Children's Books, 1350 Avenue of the Americas, New York, NY 10019.

CAREER: William Morrow Publishers, New York, NY, editorial assistant for children's books, 1980-82; Taft Corp., Washington, DC, marketing associate, 1982-83; Harper & Row Publishers, New York, NY, children's book editor, 1983-89; writer and freelance editor, 1989–.

AWARDS, HONORS: Pick of the List citation, American Booksellers Association, and Notable Book in the Field of Social Studies designation, American Library Association, both 1989, both for *Frannie's Fruits.*

WRITINGS:

PICTURE BOOKS

Frannie's Fruits, illustrated by Petra Mathers, Harper (New York, NY), 1989.

Me and Nana, illustrated by Marilee Robin Burton, Harper (New York, NY), 1990.

Hanukkah Lights, Hanukkah Nights, illustrated by John Himmelman, HarperCollins (New York, NY), 1992.

Hooray! It's Passover!, illustrated by John Himmelman, HarperCollins (New York, NY), 1996.

Sound the Shofar! A Story of Rosh Hashanah and Yom Kippur, illustrated by John Himmelman, Harper-Collins (New York, NY), 1998.

Dance, Sing, Remember: A Celebration of Jewish Holidays, illustrated by Ora Eitan, HarperCollins (New York, NY), 2000.

The Runaway Latkes, illustrated by Paul Yalowitz, Albert Whitman (Morton Grove, IL), 2000.

Round the Turkey: A Grateful Thanksgiving, illustrated by Nancy Cote, Albert Whitman (Morton Grove, IL), 2002.

Happy Fourth of July, Jenny Sweeney!, illustrated by Nancy Cote, Albert Whitman (Morton Grove, IL), 2003.

Emily and Bo, Best Friends, illustrated by True Kelley, Holiday House (New York, NY), 2005.

How Do I Love You?, illustrated by Lisa McCue, HarperCollins (New York, NY), in press.

SIDELIGHTS: In her children's books author Leslie Kimmelman focuses on strong family relationships. Whether working together, enjoying special outings, or sharing the special joy of a holiday season, loving families wherein young children are nurtured and allowed to participate are portrayed in Kimmelman's books. In *Frannie's Fruits,* her first picture book, parents and children work side by side at the bustling, seasonal fruit-and-vegetable stand named for the family dog. There is much to be done, as the fresh produce must be washed, polished, and piled high, the flowers trimmed and freshened, and merchandise shelved and priced. Told through the eyes of the family's youngest daughter, the book chronicles the day's events and each customer's purchases and eccentricities, including, as Hanna B. Zeiger noted in *Horn Book,* everyone from "the sour woman who wants a dozen

lemons to the romantic couple buying the biggest bouquet of flowers." The critic praised *Frannie's Fruits* as "a welcome addition to stories about people working and enjoying their work."

Me and Nana, revolves around the special bond between young Natalie and her sprightly, slightly unusual grandmother, a woman with whom the girl enjoys spending time. Writing in *Booklist,* Ellen Mandel remarked that Kimmelman and illustrator Marilee Robin Burton "invite readers to be part of the warm and loving twosome's perfect relationship."

Happy Fourth of July, Jenny Sweeney! finds a young girl caught up in the excitement of her town's Independence Day celebration. Jenny decides to take part in the bustle by washing her family dog, and the book recounts the preparations of the girl's family and neighbors in getting ready for the parade. Kimmelman describes the festivities in rhyming couplets enhanced by illustrations that *School Library Journal* reviewer Linda M. Kenton noted "honor America's melting pot" through the inclusion of an ethnically diverse neighborhood. Reflecting pride in the heritage the holiday represents, Kimmelman closes her book with a page detailing information regarding the flag, the Liberty Bell, and the signers of the Declaration of Independence.

Many of Kimmelman's books focus on the traditions of the Jewish faith. In *Hanukkah Lights, Hanukkah Nights* the "warmth of family love and joy of holiday celebration light up" what a *School Library Journal* reviewer called a "simple narrative." Each of the eight nights of Hanukkah is described by Kimmelman in two sentences on a double-page spread. The rituals and activities associated with the holiday are illustrated by various family members as they engage in lighting candles, flipping latkes, and giving holiday blessings. Eleven Jewish holidays are given broader coverage in Kimmelman's *Dance, Sing, Remember: A Celebration of Jewish Holidays,* which covers not only the well-known Rosh Hashanah and Hanukkah but also includes Shavot, Shabbat, and Yom Hashoah. In *School Library Journal,* Teri Markson noted that Kimmelman's text is "wonderfully written, simple yet informative," while Stephanie Zvirin added in *Booklist* that the author introduces the holidays "in a lively, dramatic way, limiting details so as not to overwhelm [the] very young." Praising the book as "valuable for its inclusion of several holidays rarely (if ever) mentioned in secular children's literature," *Horn Book* reviewer Lauren Adams added that *Dance, Sing, Remember,* with illustrations by Ora Eitan, "is truly an invitation to celebrate."

BIOGRAPHICAL AND CRITICAL SOURCES:

PERIODICALS

Booklist, October 15, 1990, Ellen Mandel, review of *Me and Nana,* p. 447; September 1, 1992, p. 63; March 15, 1996, Ellen Mandel, review of *Hooray! It's Passover,* p. 1266; October 1, 2000, Stephanie Zvirin, review of *Dance, Sing, Remember: A Celebration of Jewish Holidays,* p. 356; May 15, 2003, Karen Hutt, review of *Happy Fourth of July, Jenny Sweeney!,* p. 1672.

Horn Book, May-June, 1989, Hanna B. Zeiger, review of *Frannie's Fruits,* pp. 359-360; July, 1990, p. 39; November, 2000, Lauren Adams, review of *Dance, Sing, Remember,* p. 769.

Kirkus Reviews, February 1, 1989, p. 210; March 15, 2003, review of *Happy Fourth of July, Jenny Sweeney!,* p. 470.

New York Times Book Review, September 10, 1989, p. 32; November 11, 1990, p. 57.

Publishers Weekly, February 24, 1989, p. 230; September 7, 1992, review of *Hanukkah Lights, Hanukkah Nights,* p. 62; February 12, 1996, review of *Hooray! It's Passover,* p. 72; July 27, 1998, review of *Sound the Shofar,* p. 70; September 15, 2000, review of *The Runaway Latkes,* p. 66.

School Library Journal, June, 1989, p. 90; November, 1990, p. 94; October, 1992, review of *Hanukkah Lights, Hanukkah Nights,* p. 42; October, 2000, review of *The Runaway Latkes,* p. 65, and Teri Markson, review of *Dance, Sing, Remember,* p. 148; September, 2002, Genevieve Gallagher, review of *Round the Turkey: A Grateful Thanksgiving,* p. 195; July, 2003, Linda M. Kenton, review of *Happy Fourth of July, Jenny Sweeney!,* p. 100.*

*   *   *

KINSELLA, James 1959-

PERSONAL: Born October 10, 1959, in St. Louis, MO; son of Robert and Dolores (Guzy) Kinsella. *Education:* Haverford College, B.A. (with honors), 1982.

ADDRESSES: Office—Interoute Headquarters, Walbrook Bldg., 195 Marsh Wall, London E14 9SG, England.

CAREER: Pennsylvania Journal-Reporter, Philadelphia, reporter, 1980-82; *California Lawyer,* San Francisco, reporter, 1982-83; *Santa Cruz's Weekly,* Santa Cruz, CA, assistant editor, 1983, managing editor, 1983-84; *Sacramento,* Sacramento, CA, managing editor of news, 1983-85, senior editor, 1984-85; *Los Angeles Herald Examiner,* Los Angeles, CA, editorial page editor, 1985-89; *American Report* (Tokyo, Japan), correspondent, beginning 1989; *Mercury News,* San Jose, CA, assistant foreign and national editor, beginning 1990. Gannett Center for Media Studies, Columbia University, fellow, 1987-88; East-West Center, University of Hawaii at Manoa, Jefferson fellow, 1990; Time Warner's Pathfinder, founding editor; MSNBC.com, general manager, 1996-99; MSNBC on the Net, CEO, 1999-2000; World Online, chairman, 2000-01; Interoute, executive chairman, 2002—; guest on Canadian television program *The Editors.* University of California, Berkeley, member of interdisciplinary panel on public policy; Greater Los Angeles Partnership for the Homeless, executive volunteer; consultant to Robert Woods Johnson Foundation and New York City Commission on acquired immunodeficiency syndrome (AIDS).

AWARDS, HONORS: Award for best editorial page in the state, California Newspaper Publishers Association, 1987; award for best editorial series, California-Nevada Associated Press, 1987; Gustavus Myers Award, Gustavus Myers Center for the Study of Bigotry and Human Rights, 1989, for *Covering the Plague: AIDS and the American Media.*

WRITINGS:

Covering the Plague: AIDS and the American Media, Rutgers University Press (East Brunswick, NJ), 1990.

Also contributor to books on the media.

SIDELIGHTS: James Kinsella is a celebrated media mogul, having earned a name for himself as the chairman of major media corporations such as Time Warner and MSNBC.com. He has held senior positions at other technology and media organizations such as World Online and Interoute. Kinsella drew on his decades of experience in the media to author and contribute to four books. His most recognized book, *Covering the Plague: AIDS and the American Media,* looks at the way the AIDS epidemic in the United States has been covered by the American media. Kinsella is often critical of the media, claiming that the AIDS issue can be trivialized, or even ignored, by the mainstream press until it somehow affects the general heterosexual population. A reviewer in *Publishers Weekly* maintained that Kinsella "shows how the media and medical experts fumbled in the AIDS story." Writing for *Library Journal,* James E. Van Buskirk noted that "Kinsella's inclusion of a historical time line, extensive notes, and an index contribute to this fascinating exposé's importance for journalism and general interest collections."

BIOGRAPHICAL AND CRITICAL SOURCES:

PERIODICALS

Journalism Quarterly, autumn, 1990, James K. Hertog, review of *Covering the Plague,* pp. 623-624.

Journal of Health, Politics, Policy, and Law, spring, 1991, David C. Colby, review of *Covering the Plague: AIDS and the American Media,* pp. 176-181.

Library Journal, February 1, 1990, James E. Van Buskirk, review of *Covering the Plague,* p. 91.

Los Angeles Times Book Review, April 8, 1990, p. 5.

Nature, August 9, 1990, Don C. Des, review of *Covering the Plague,* p. 521.

New York Times Book Review, May 6, 1990, H. Jack Geiger, review of *Covering the Plague,* p. 23.

Publishers Weekly, January 19, 1990, Genevieve Stuttaford, review of *Covering the Plague,* pp. 92-93.

Washington Post Journalism Review, July-August 1990, Timothy Cook, review of *Covering the Plague,* p. 39.*

*   *   *

KNIGHT, Amarantha
   See KILPATRICK, Nancy

KNOX, Calvin M.
   See SILVERBERG, Robert

*   *   *

KRAMER, Jane 1938-

PERSONAL: Born August 7, 1938, in Providence, RI; daughter of Louis (a physician) and Jessica (Shore) Kramer; married Vincent Crapanzano (an anthropologist, professor, and writer), April 30, 1967; children: Aleksandra. *Education:* Vassar College, B.A. (with honors), 1959; Columbia University, M.A., 1961.

ADDRESSES: Home—New York, NY. *Office*—New Yorker, 25 W. 43rd St., New York, NY 10036. *Agent*—Lynn Nesbit, International Creative Management, 40 W. 57th St., New York, NY 10019.

CAREER: Morningsider, New York, NY, founder and writer, 1961-62; *Village Voice,* New York, NY, writer, 1962-63; *New Yorker,* New York, NY, writer, including the regular feature "Letter from Europe," 1963—. City University of New York—Bernard M. Baruch College, Sidney Harmon writer in residence, 1999; University of California—Berkeley, Regents Professor; Princeton University, visiting professor. Member of Council on Foreign Relations and New York Institute for the Humanities; Journalists Human Rights Committee (also known as Committee to Protect Journalists), founding board member; associate of Environmental Defense Fund; consultant to German Marshall Fund, 1981.

MEMBER: Writers Guild of America East (board member, 1963-65), Authors League of America, Authors Guild, PEN, American Academy of Arts and Sciences (fellow), Book Critics Circle, Phi Beta Kappa.

AWARDS, HONORS: Emmy Award, National Academy of Television Arts and Sciences, 1966, for documentary, "This Is Edward Steichen"; named woman of the year, *Mademoiselle,* 1968; Front Page Award, best magazine feature, *New Yorker,* 1977, for "The Invandrare"; award from Overseas Press Club of America, 1979; American Book Award, 1981, for *Unsettling Europe;* National Book Awards, best paperback nonfiction book, 1981, for *The Last Cowboy,* and feature writing category, 1993, for *Whose Art Is It?;* Prix Européen de l'Essai Charles Veillon, for German edition of *Europeans;* President's Medal, Vassar College; Mary McCarthy Award, Bard College.

WRITINGS:

Off Washington Square: A Reporter Looks at Greenwich Village, Duell, Sloan & Pearce (New York, NY), 1963.
Allen Ginsberg in America, Random House (New York, NY), 1969, published as *Paterfamilias,* Gollancz (London, England), 1970.
Honor to the Bride Like the Pigeon That Guards Its Grain under the Clove Tree, Farrar, Straus & Giroux (New York, NY), 1970.
The Last Cowboy, Harper (New York, NY), 1978.
Unsettling Europe, Random House (New York, NY), 1980.
Europeans, Farrar, Straus & Giroux (New York, NY), 1988.
Whose Art Is It?, Duke University Press (Durham, NC), 1994.
The Politics of Memory: Looking for Germany in the New Germany, Random House (New York, NY), 1996.
Lone Patriot: The Short Career of an American Militiaman, Pantheon Books (New York, NY), 2002.

Contributor to periodicals, including the *New Yorker,New York Times Book Review,* and *New York Review of Books.*

The book *Europeans* was published in German.

SIDELIGHTS: "In her thirty years at the *New Yorker* Jane Kramer has written shrewd profiles of Italian peasants, Moroccan teenagers, Texas cowboys, German skinheads, New York City artists, and European heads of state," wrote John J. Pauly in the *Dictionary of Literary Biography.* "Reviews of her books in popular magazines and newspapers have praised the grace and clarity of her writing. Yet this cosmopolitan body of work, with an intellectual depth unmatched in contemporary journalism, has received almost no scholarly attention. Such recognition is long overdue,

for Kramer has written eloquently about the politics of cultural identity . . . that have characterized the late twentieth century."

Kramer's first widely reviewed book, *Allen Ginsberg in America,* met with a mixed reception. Some critics observed that Kramer's biographical portrait was too sketchy and admiring. Malcolm Muggeridge in the *Observer* called the author "sentimental, whimsical, sprawling" and explained that what the book "is lacking is any serious critical estimate of Ginsberg and his work." Similarly, Steve Lerner of the *Village Voice* observed "that while the book is an up, easy-flowing, often informative narrative about a colorful man, it lacks the tension and deep, often uncomfortable probing that a good biography requires in order to adequately depict a public figure." Lerner added, however, that even though Kramer "is repetitious of the flower-bedecked caricature we all know and love, she also manages to present enough new information, describe enough scenes that the television cameras missed, and hear enough good words that were inaudible to the masses to piece together a living Ginsberg. This, in itself, is enough of a recommendation to make the book worth reading for an audience of post beat-early hip generation who have missed the real article in person."

Honor to the Bride Like the Pigeon That Guards Its Grain under the Clove Tree is about the kidnapping and violation of a thirteen-year-old girl from her Arab family living in Meknes, Morocco. She is the family's most valuable asset, for her virginal state will bring in a substantial bride price. Therefore, when she is returned to her relatives, her family comically endeavors to legally reestablish her virginity. Martha Duffy of *Time* praised *Honor to the Bride.* It "is an excellent example of the 'nonfiction novel,'" she commented. "Beyond its entertainment value, the book offers a remarkable glimpse into . . . Arab attitudes toward justice, money and women. . . . Thanks to the author's effortless narrative, the reader hurtles through an exotic world, not realizing until the end that he has been taken on a fascinating trip through the Arab mind."

The Last Cowboy is the story of Henry Blanton, a cowboy who lives and works on a ranch in the Texas panhandle. With motion picture star Glenn Ford as his model, Blanton has embodied the image of the proud cowboy to such a degree that he has become a caricature. Henry McDonald of the *Washington Post* explained that Blanton is seen "as an anomaly, not so much because he seems bigoted, chauvinistic and unpredictably violent. Rather, his oddity stems from his determination to live out a fantasy of himself as a rugged and heroic cowboy in a land which devalues such qualities." In the *New York Times,* John Leonard complimented the author on her portrait of Blanton and remarked: "It is a measure of Jane Kramer's immense skill that we come to like Henry almost in spite of himself. . . . We aren't poked in the tearducts; we merely watch and eavesdrop. . . . She [Kramer] is incapable of contempt, although the sadness has spurs." McDonald described *The Last Cowboy* as an "insightful, unsentimental and handsomely crafted work."

Unsettling Europe also received favorable reviews from critics. Irving Howe in the *New York Times Book Review* explained that "this accomplished book consists of four social-historical sketches—suavely but sturdily composed—about people in Europe who have been uprooted from their natural communities and thrust into alien, sometimes hostile settings." Featured are a Yugoslav family living in Sweden, French Algerians living in Provence, Ugandan Muslims dwelling in a London ghetto, and Italian Communists who feel their Party has forsaken them and the revolution. In the *Nation,* Thomas Flanagan assessed that "Kramer's intention is to break down the exhausted, conventional categories in which sociology and journalism solicit us to consider contemporary Europe, by creating for us the bitter, absurd, fractured lives of 'people who fell into the cracks of history.'" James N. Baker of *Newsweek* noted that Kramer's "is no-nonsense journalism at its best: direct, finely detailed portraits of four troubled families . . . by a writer who combines the skills of a social historian with those of a novelist."

Kramer deepened her portrait of Europe and its people in her book *Europeans,* which is made up of *New Yorker* pieces written between 1978 and 1988. It includes sketches of cities, descriptions of ordinary people, long stories about controversial news events, obituaries and sketches of famous citizens, and comic and serious reflections. "Reviewers reported that *Europeans* was a superb piece of writing," reported Pauly. "They called it 'masterful,' 'exquisite,' 'polished,' 'distinguished,' and 'brilliant.'" Pauly wrote that "*Europeans* interprets politics of cultural identity as it is

played out in national policy, cultural mythology, news coverage, local prejudice, and family history. Kramer understands European politics as a symbolic drama and treats political events as cultural texts. Particularly new and notable are the book's ambitious profiles of five major cities—Hamburg, Paris, Zurich, London, and West Berlin. These city essays are among the most accomplished and opinionated pieces Kramer has ever written."

For *Whose Art Is It?,* Kramer turned her attention back to the United States. The book, originally published as a long article in the *New Yorker,* details a conflict that arose over publicly funded sculpture in the Bronx. Internationally known sculptor John Ahearn was awarded a commission from New York City's Percent for Art Program to install three statues in front of a police station. He chose to depict a man with a pit bull, a man with a basketball and a boom box, and a girl on roller skates. Protests arose on the grounds that the figures were stereotypes, demeaning to Bronx residents, and Ahearn voluntarily removed the statues less than a week after they were installed. Pauly called it "a stylistic tour de force . . . [that] displays the dense, graceful, complex narrative that Kramer has spent years perfecting." He further commented that "ultimately, *Whose Art Is It?* examines the social conflicts often referenced by shorthand terms such as *multiculturalism* and *political correctness.*"

In appreciation of Kramer's body of work, Pauly declared: "Over three decades she has developed one of the most elegant and distinctive voices in American literary journalism. She has written with depth and sophistication about an extraordinary range of topics. She has earned the admiration of careful readers and other professional writers. She has refused to traffic in celebrity, speculation, or shallow controversy. She writes eloquently of her subjects' virtues and vices, regardless of their social standing. Yet for all the praise of her beautiful writing style, Kramer remains underappreciated as a reporter and analyst." Pauly conjectured that if Kramer were a man, if she wrote "in a more ponderously theoretical style . . . if she promoted herself as shamelessly as others do, she would find herself being heralded by the newsweeklies as a 'public intellectual.'"

Pauly concluded: "The profession of journalism is mythically devoted, in equal measure, to objectivity and publicity, to detachment and fame, and journalists, like women, struggle to make themselves visible. The worst journalists settle for notoriety, serving as television pundits, currying favor with the powerful, surfing the tides of public opinion. The best, like Kramer, cherish their independence but want something more. They seek to make their presence felt, to serve as witnesses rather than remain just observers."

BIOGRAPHICAL AND CRITICAL SOURCES:

BOOKS

Dictionary of Literary Biography, Volume 185: *American Literary Journalists, 1945-1995, First Series,* Thomson Gale (Detroit, MI), 1997.
McAuliffe, Kevin M., *The Great American Newspaper: The Rise and Fall of the Village Voice,* Scribner (New York, NY), 1978, pp. 71-73.

PERIODICALS

Booklist, May 15, 2002, Bryce Christensen, review of *Lone Patriot: The Short Career of an American Militiaman,* p. 1559.
Books and Culture, January, 1998, review of *The Politics of Memory: Looking for Germany in the New Century,* p. 45.
Christian Science Monitor, July 17, 1969.
Nation, May 31, 1980.
New Statesman, August 13, 1971.
Newsweek, June 9, 1980, James N. Baker, review of *Unsettling Europe.*
New York Review of Books, August 14, 1980.
New York Times, May 17, 1969; January 24, 1978, John Leonard, review of *The Last Cowboy;* June 16, 2002, Timothy Egan, review of *Lone Patriot,* pp. 7-6.
New York Times Book Review, May 11, 1969; May 18, 1980, Irving Howe, review of *Unsettling Europe.*
Observer, February 8, 1970, Malcolm Muggeridge, review of *Allen Ginsberg in America.*
Publishers Weekly, May 27, 2002, review of *Lone Patriot,* p. 48.
Time, August 8, 1969; January 4, 1971, Martha Duffy review of *Honor to the Bride Like the Pigeon That Guards Its Grain under the Clove Tree.*
Village Voice, September 4, 1969, Steve Lerner, review of *Allen Ginsberg in America.*
Washington Post, April 1, 1978, Henry McDonald, review of *The Last Cowboy.*

ONLINE

Bernard M. Baruch College Web site, http://www.baruch.cuny.edu/ (August 16, 2002).
Killing the Buddha.com, http://www.killingthebuddha.com/ (August 16, 2002), Jeff Sharlet, review of *Lone Patriot.*
Seattle Post-Intelligencer Online, http://seattlepi.nwsource.com/ (June 19, 2002), Joel Connelly, review of *Lone Patriot.*
USA Today Online, http://www.usatoday.com/ (June 20, 2002), Stephen J. Lyons, review of *Lone Patriot.* *

*   *   *

KUMIN, Maxine (Winokur) 1925-

PERSONAL: Born June 6, 1925, in Philadelphia, PA; daughter of Peter (a pawnbroker) and Doll (Simon) Winokur; married Victor Montwid Kumin (an engineering consultant), June 29, 1946; children: Jane Simon, Judith Montwid, Daniel David. *Education:* Radcliffe College, A.B., 1946, M.A., 1948.

ADDRESSES: Home—40 Harriman Lane, Warner, NH 03278. *Agent*—Curtis Brown, 10 Astor Place, New York, NY 10003.

CAREER: Poet, children's author, and fiction writer. Tufts University, Medford, MA, instructor, 1958-61, lecturer in English, 1965-68; Radcliffe College, Cambridge, MA, scholar of Radcliffe Institute for Independent Study (now called The Bunting Institute), 1961-63. University of Massachusetts—Amherst, visiting lecturer in English, 1973; Columbia University, New York, NY, adjunct professor of writing, 1975; Brandeis University, Waltham, MA, Fannie Hurst Professor of Literature, 1975; Princeton University, Princeton, NJ, visiting senior fellow and lecturer, 1977; Washington University, St. Louis, MO, Fannie Hurst Professor of Literature, 1977; Randolph-Macon Woman's College, Lynchburg, VA, Carolyn Wilkerson Bell Visiting Scholar, 1978; Woodrow Wilson Visiting Fellow, 1979; Princeton University, visiting lecturer, 1979, 1981-82; Bucknell University, Lewisburg, PA, poet-in-residence, 1983; Massachusetts Institute of Technology, Cambridge, MA, visiting professor, 1984;

Maxine Kumin

Atlantic Center for the Arts, New Smyrna Beach, FL, master artist, 1984; University of Miami, Miami, FL, visiting professor, 1995; Pitzer College, Claremont, CA, visiting professor, 1996; Davidson College, Davidson, NC, McGee Professor of Writing, 1997; Florida International University, Miami, visiting professor, 1998-99. Member of staff, Bread Loaf Writers' Conference, 1969-71, 1973, 1975, 1977, and Sewanee Writers' Conference, 1993-94. Traveled with the United States Information Agency's Arts America Tour, 1983. Poetry consultant to Library of Congress, 1981-82. Elector, The Poet's Corner, Cathedral of St. John the Divine, 1990—; Chancellor, Academy of American Poets, 1995—.

MEMBER: Poetry Society of America, PEN, Authors Guild, Writers Union, Radcliffe Alumnae Association.

AWARDS, HONORS: Lowell Mason Palmer Award, 1960; National Endowment for the Arts grant, 1966; National Council on the Arts and Humanities fellow, 1967-68; William Marion Reedy Award, 1968; Eunice Tietjens Memorial Prize, *Poetry,* 1972; Pulitzer Prize for poetry, 1973, for *Up Country: Poems of New England;* Borestone Mountain Award, 1976; Radcliffe College Alumnae Recognition Award, 1978; Woodrow Wilson fellowship, 1979-80, 1991-93; American Academy and Institute of Arts and Letters award, 1980, for excellence in literature; Academy of American Poets fellowship, 1985; Levison award, *Poetry,* 1986; named Poet Laureate of the state of New Hampshire, 1989-94; Sarah Joseph Hale Award, Richards Library (Newport, NH), 1992; Poets' Prize, 1994, and Aiken Taylor Poetry Prize, 1995, both for *Looking for Luck;* Harvard Graduate School of Arts and Sciences Centennial Award, 1996; D.H.L., Centre College, 1976, Davis and Elkins College, 1977, Regis College, 1979, New England College, 1982, Claremont Graduate School, 1983, University of New Hampshire, 1984, and Keene State College, 1995.

WRITINGS:

POETRY

Halfway, Holt (New York, NY), 1961.

The Privilege, Harper (New York, NY), 1965.

The Nightmare Factory, Harper (New York, NY), 1970.

Up Country: Poems of New England, New and Selected, illustrated by Barbara Swan, Harper (New York, NY), 1972.

House, Bridge, Fountain, Gate, Viking (New York, NY), 1975.

Progress Report (sound recording), Watershed, 1976.

The Retrieval System, Viking (New York, NY), 1978.

Our Ground Time Here Will Be Brief: New and Selected Poems, Viking (New York, NY), 1982.

Closing the Ring: Selected Poems, Press of Appletree Alley, Bucknell University (Lewisburg, PA), 1984.

The Long Approach, Viking (New York, NY), 1985.

Nurture, Viking Penguin (New York, NY), 1989.

Looking for Luck, W. W. Norton (New York, NY), 1992.

Connecting the Dots: Poems, W. W. Norton (New York, NY), 1996.

Selected Poems, 1960-1990, W. W. Norton (New York, NY), 1997.

The Long Marriage, W. W. Norton (New York, NY), 2001.

Bringing Together: Uncollected Early Poems, 1958-1988, W. W. Norton (New York, NY), 2003.

FICTION

Through Dooms of Love (novel), Harper (New York, NY), 1965, published as *A Daughter and Her Loves,* Gollancz (London, England), 1965.

The Passions of Uxport (novel), Harper (New York, NY), 1968.

The Abduction (novel), Harper (New York, NY), 1971.

The Designated Heir (novel), Viking (New York, NY), 1974.

Why Can't We Live Together Like Civilized Human Beings? (short stories), Viking (New York, NY), 1982.

Quit Monks or Die! (mystery novel), Story Line (Ashland, OR), 1999.

FOR CHILDREN

Sebastian and the Dragon, Putnam (New York, NY), 1960.

Spring Things, Putnam (New York, NY), 1961.

A Summer Story, Putnam (New York, NY), 1961.

Follow the Fall, Putnam (New York, NY), 1961.

A Winter Friend, Putnam (New York, NY), 1961.

Mittens in May, Putnam (New York, NY), 1962.

No One Writes a Letter to the Snail, Putnam (New York, NY), 1962.

(With Anne Sexton) *Eggs of Things,* Putnam (New York, NY), 1963.

Archibald the Traveling Poodle, Putnam (New York, NY), 1963.

(With Anne Sexton) *More Eggs of Things,* Putnam (New York, NY), 1964.

Speedy Digs Downside Up, Putnam (New York, NY), 1964.

The Beach before Breakfast, Putnam (New York, NY), 1964.

Paul Bunyan, Putnam (New York, NY), 1966.

Faraway Farm, W. W. Norton (New York, NY), 1967.

The Wonderful Babies of 1809 and Other Years, Putnam (New York, NY), 1968.

When Grandmother Was Young, Putnam (New York, NY), 1969.

When Mother Was Young, Putnam (New York, NY), 1970.

When Great-Grandmother Was Young, illustrated by Don Almquist, Putnam (New York, NY), 1971.

(With Anne Sexton) *Joey and the Birthday Present,* illustrated by Evaline Ness, McGraw-Hill (New York, NY), 1971.

(With Anne Sexton) *The Wizard's Tears,* McGraw-Hill (New York, NY), 1975.

What Color Is Caesar?, illustrated by Evaline Ness, McGraw-Hill (New York, NY), 1978.

The Microscope, illustrated by Arnold Lobel, Harper (New York, NY), 1984.

OTHER

(Author of introduction) Carole Oles, *The Loneliness Factor,* Texas Tech University Press (Lubbock, TX), 1979.

To Make a Prairie: Essays on Poets, Poetry, and Country Living, University of Michigan Press (Ann Arbor, MI), 1980.

(Editor) William Carpenter, *Rain,* Northeastern University Press (Boston, MA), 1985.

In Deep: Country Essays, Viking (New York, NY), 1987.

Women, Animals, and Vegetables: Essays and Stories, W. W. Norton (New York, NY), 1994.

Diane Ackerman and Maxine Kumin Reading from Their Work (sound recording), Archive of Recorded Poetry and Literature, Library of Congress (Washington, DC), 1994.

Always Beginning: Essays on a Life in Poetry, Copper Canyon (Port Townsend, WA), 2000.

Inside the Halo and Beyond: The Anatomy of a Recovery, W. W. Norton (New York, NY), 2000.

Former columnist, *Writer.* Contributor of poetry to *New Yorker, Atlantic, Poetry, Saturday Review,* and other periodicals. Kumin's manuscripts are held at the Bienecke Library, Yale University.

SIDELIGHTS: Even though the awards she has received for her work have included the prestigious Pulitzer Prize, Maxine Kumin's works have yet to be the subject of serious study by academics. A former poetry consultant for the Library of Congress and a staff member of the Bread Loaf Writers' Conference, Kumin has remained active in teaching and writing during a career that has spanned over three decades. Despite the necessity of traveling away from home to lecture at schools and universities around the United States, Kumin has retained close ties with her farmhouse in rural New Hampshire; in an interview with Joan Norris published in *Crazy Horse,* the poet disclosed, "Practically all of [my poems] have come out of this geography and this state of mind."

Kumin is often referred to as a regional pastoral poet as her verse is deeply rooted to her native New England. "I have been twitted with the epithet 'Roberta Frost,' which is not a bad thing to be," Kumin told interviewer Karla Hammond in the *Western Humanities Review.* In other efforts to classify her work, critics have also described her as a transcendentalist, like Henry David Thoreau, or a confessional poet, like Kumin's friend and coauthor, the late Anne Sexton. But *New York Times* reviewer Michiko Kakutani found her most like Galway Kinnell, since both are "concerned with human mortality, with the love shared between parents and their children, with the seasonal patterns of nature and the possibility of retrieving and preserving the past." In many ways, critics also point out, Kumin is not like other poets. "In a period when most contemporary poetry reflects a chaotic and meaningless universe, Kumin is one of a handful of poets who insist upon order," Susan Ludvigson elaborated in the *Dictionary of Literary Biography.* Whatever her link to other poets may be, Philip Booth maintained in the *American Poetry Review* that "what is remarkable . . . is the extent to which poets like Maxine Kumin can survive and outdistance both their peers and themselves by increasingly trusting those elements of their work which are most strongly individual." For Kumin, Booth noted, these elements include "the dailiness of farm life and farm death."

Her "well-made poems and stories are two ways of coming at the same immemorial preoccupations: aging and mortality," wrote Clara Claiborne Park in the *Nation,* and deemed Kumin's work "the fiction and poetry of maturity." Her poems are also mature for another reason: Kumin did not begin to write and publish until mid-life, though she had shown an inclination to write poetry much earlier. During high school, she wrote what she considered to be very poor poetry of a late adolescent. And later, as a freshman at Radcliffe, Kumin presented a sheaf of poems to the instructor for his comments. Kumin told Norris, "He had written on the front: 'Say it with flowers, but for God's sake don't try to write poems.' That just closed me off. I didn't try to write another poem for about six years." By that time she had become the wife of an engineer, the mother of three children, a resident of a Boston suburb, and was acutely miserable. When Kumin began writing again as a kind of therapy, she at last found encouragement in workshops at the Boston Center for Adult Education.

The poems Kumin began to compose during the early period in her writing career recall her childhood in a home on a hill "between a convent and a madhouse." In these poems, wrote Ludvigson, Kumin displays "an early mastery of technique" and "deals skillfully with subjects that she continues to explore throughout her career: religious and cultural identity, the fragility of human life, loss and the ever-present threat of loss, the relation of man to nature." Many of these early works were collected in Kumin's first book of poems, *Halfway,* which was published in 1961 when she was thirty-six. Another outgrowth of the Boston workshops Kumin attended was her friendship with Anne Sexton. Both homemakers with children when they began their literary careers, they wrote four children's books together and in general contributed to each other's development. "Maxine, a Radcliffe graduate, possessed a technical expertise and an analytical detachment that balanced Anne's mercurial brilliance," explained Linda Gray Sexton and Lois Ames, editors of *Anne Sexton: A Self-Portrait in Letters.* The two poets "often communicated daily, by letter if separated by oceans, otherwise by telephone. They supervised each other's poetry and prose, 'workshopping' line by line for hours." Consequently, critics tried to trace a strong mutual influence, but both poets denied one. Ludvigson noted, "In a 1974 interview in *Women's Studies,* each claimed she never tampered with the other's voice, and each offered, according to Sexton, 'to think how to shape, how to make better, but not, how to make like me.'" Nonetheless, there were some significant exchanges. As Kumin related in the chapter she contributed to *Anne Sexton: The Artist and Her Critics,* Sexton had written several poems based on fairy tales that later became part of her Pulitzer Prize-winning book, *Transformations.* Sexton "had no thought of a collection at first," said Kumin. "I urged and bullied her to go on after the first few poems to think in terms of a whole book of them." Kumin also suggested the title. "We had been talking about the way many contemporary poets translated from languages they did not themselves read, but used trots or had the poems filtered through an interpreter, and that these poems were *adaptations.* It struck me then that Anne's poems about the fairy tales went one step further and were *transformations.*" Sexton reciprocated by suggesting the title for the book that was to become Kumin's Pulitzer Prize winner. "In that same conversation Annie was urging me to collect the 'pastoral' poems I'd written, and I said, 'but what would I call it?' and she said, '*Up Country,* of course.'"

"It is the tie between Kumin and Sexton that fascinates many readers," Ludvigson noted, and the public's interest peaked when Sexton committed suicide in 1974. . . .. Yet, despite her connection to Sexton, Kumin's work shows little signs of being included in the confessional school. Rather, observed Monroe K. Spears in the *Washington Post Book World,* "much of her poetry throughout is openly autobiographical, and the reader becomes acquainted with her family. . ., her Frostian New Hampshire neighbor Henry Manley, . . . and so on." The "loss of the parent" and the "relinquishment of the child" are two central themes Kumin identified in a lecture on her work given at Princeton in 1977 and reprinted in *To Make a Prairie: Essays on Poets, Poetry, and Country Living.* Booth explained the presence of these themes in Kumin's 1978 book, *The Retrieval System,* by noting that the poet "is familiar (in every sense) with how one's parents depart toward death at nearly the same time one's children leave to find lives of their own. Inevitable as such desertions may be, their coincidence . . . is the shock which these seismographic poems record and try to recover from." Booth believed Kumin's poems "amply show that suffering doesn't require confession to validate pain," and that her "mode is memorial rather than confessional."

"Transcendental" is another label sometimes applied to Kumin but in a modified sense; while Kumin's poetry may call up images of Thoreau and "insist on man's affinity with the natural world," Ludvigson noted that it falls short of suggesting the "merging of the self with nature" that transcendentalism requires. Joyce Carol Oates wrote in the *New York Times Book Review* that Kumin's 1972 work *Up Country* "acknowledges its debt to Thoreau" but provides "a sharp-edged, unflinching and occasionally nightmarish subjectivity exasperatingly absent in Thoreau." Ludvigson suggested that "her unsentimental relationship with nature . . . allows Kumin to write poems . . . which are ostensibly 'about' the necessary killing of woodchucks and mysterious tracks in the snow, but which chill us with her portrayal of man's capacity for brutality." Brad Crenshaw considered it "a major plus" that Kumin "is not much addicted to transcendental escapes." Rather, as he elaborated in a *Parnassus* review of 1982's *Our Ground Time Here Will Be Brief: New and Selected Poems,* "the voice of the poems is that of a strong woman. In an unforgiving environment, Kumin neither flinches at the strenuous physical labors that comprise her usual responsibilities, nor quails before her emotional disappointments. She's mentally tough. Her poetry records how she stands up to the disasters of weather, disease, difficult births and

lamentable deaths, and how she's confident she'll remain standing until the very end."

Whereas critics debate Kumin's similarity to Thoreau, they unanimously recognize how her work resembles that of Robert Frost. The works of both poets show a close attention to the details of New England rural life. The poet told Hammond, "I particularly observe things in nature because they interest me, but I don't think of it as observing. What I'm always after is to get the facts: to be true to the actuality." Attention to nature provides Kumin with images well-suited to her themes of loss and survival. Oates explained, "Any group of poems that deals with nature is more or less committed to the honoring of cycles, the birth/death/birth wheel, the phenomenon of creatures giving way to creatures." Booth expressed a similar opinion when he commented: "The distinctive nature of Maxine Kumin's present poems derives from the primary fact that she lives in, and writes from, a world where constant (if partial) recovery of what's 'lost' is as sure as the procession of the equinoxes, or as familiar as mucking-out the horses' daily dung."

Kumin's preference for traditional verse forms is also what causes critics to liken her to Frost. Not only is there an order "to be discovered . . . in the natural world," she told Martha George Meek in a *Massachusetts Review* interview, "there is also an order that a human can impose on the chaos of his emotions and the chaos of events." Kumin achieves this order by structuring her poetry, controlling the most emotional subjects by fitting them to exacting patterns of syllable count and rhyme. As she told Hammond, "The harder—that is, the more psychically difficult— the poem is to write, the more likely I am to choose a difficult pattern to pound it into. This is true because, paradoxically, the difficulty frees me to be more honest and more direct."

When Kumin finds she has more to say than a poem's structure will accommodate, she approaches her subject again in fiction. "I tend to steal from myself," she said in an interview published in *To Make a Prairie.* "The compass of the poem is so small and so demanding, you have to be so selective, and there are so many things that get left out that you feel cheated. So you take all those things . . . and they get into fiction." Comparing Kumin's work in both genres, *Tribune Books* contributor Catherine Petroski commented, "Kumin's practice of poetry buttresses her practice of short fiction: The turns of phrase and points of view come from a poet, not a recorder of events. Similarly, the concerns of fiction—the chains of cause and effect, the explorations of character, the sense of scene—have much to do with the power of Kumin's best poems." Spears summed up his review by commenting: "One of the pleasures of reading Kumin is to see the same experience appear differently in the different forms of poems, stories, and novels."

If there is one experience that Kumin confronts in all her works, it is loss. The poet talked about her obsession with mortality in the conclusion of a *Country Journal* article in which she reflected on the death of a foal: "A horse-friend from New York state writes me her condolences. She too has lost not one foal, but twin Thoroughbreds. . . . According to some astrological prognosticatory chart, we are both sixes on the scale. Sixes, Mary Beth writes, practice all their lives to die well, 'act as Morticians of All Life and hold private burying rituals in their hearts.'" Accordingly, Kumin wrote, she believes "very strongly that poetry is essentially elegiac in its nature, and that all poems are in one sense or another elegies." She explained to Hammond, "Love poems, particularly, are elegies because if we were not informed with a sense of dying we wouldn't be moved to write love poems."

"Kumin writes as well as ever in her customary modes," Robert B. Shaw said in *Poetry* of *The Long Approach,* Kumin's eighth book of poems. Many critics concurred with Shaw's assessment, yet some criticized those poems that examine such world problems as pollution, religious persecution, nuclear holocaust, and famine. These poems "are aimed resolutely outward," wrote *Washington Post Book World* contributor Wendy Lesser, who believed that Kumin's "issue" poems "founder on their opinion making." Holly Prado, writing in the *Los Angeles Times Book Review,* similarly said that the poet "doesn't arrive at her best work until . . . she arrives at her farm in New Hampshire." In this part of the book, Kumin "reverts . . . to what is close, ordinary, . . . [upon] which she can meditate with X-ray gaze," Harold Beaver explained in the *New York Times Book Review.* In his analysis of *The Long Approach* in *Poetry,* Shaw suggested: "If Kumin wishes to venture into public terrain, perhaps her voice, which is essentially private, needs to adjust itself to the new and very different demands she is now placing on it. This will no doubt take some time. It can be assumed, at any rate, that a

poet of her intelligence stands an even chance of solving the problems involved."

Of *Nurture,* Kumin's next collection of poems, *New York Times Book Review* contributor Carol Muske remarked, "Maxine Kumin sounds weary . . . and with good reason. These poems are exhaustive in their sorrow: they are predominantly short, brutal elegies for the natural world." The poems in this 1989 collection reflect the author's trademark environmental consciousness and her anger at the devastation wrought by humans on the natural world; Diane Wakoski, writing in the *Women's Review of Books,* criticized these poems as "bitter, overstated, trivial." But Wakoski praised the more personal poems in the collection, noting that in these pieces "the goddess voice and stance returns." Kumin's 1992 verse collection, *Looking for Luck,* leaves behind some of the bitterness and anger apparent in her previous collection in exchange for "cheerful, chatty bulletins from the New Hampshire farm where she gardens and raises horses," commented Lisa Zeidner in the *New York Times Book Review.* And in her 1996 work, *Connecting the Dots: Poems,* the poet similarly "reexamines the familiar materials of her previous books with her far-ranging eye and technical skill," according to Fay Weldon, who reviewed the volume in the *Boston Book Review.* As with other Kumin collections, some criticism arose regarding the insubstantial theme and tone of some of the poems included in these volumes. "Sometimes the emotions seem too politely underplayed," declared Zeidner. However, reviewers commended Kumin's better poetry, praising her "linguistic brilliance and formal excellence," in the words of Weldon. Weldon concluded that Kumin "commands the nuances and music of rhyme and slant-rhyme as powerfully as any living poet."

In 1997, Kumin published *Selected Poems, 1960-1990.* Extending from her first volume, *Halfway,* through 1989's *Nurture, Selected Poems* was praised by Judy Clarence in *Library Journal* for allowing the reader the opportunity to "move slowly, meanderingly, deliciously through the stages of Kumin's poetic life." Noting that the poet's "unsentimental affinity for animals has been her divining rod for locating and observing the natural world's seemingly inexhaustible beauty and mankind's terrifying willingness to destroy it," a *Publishers Weekly* reviewer praised the collection for illustrating this through Kumin's "plain style," "surprising imagery . . . and recurring reflections."

Praising Kumin's collection for its accessibility by the average reader, Richard Tillinghast commented in his review for the *New York Times Book Review* that "her poems bracingly remind us of several enduring virtues valued by anyone who reads verse for pleasure. . . . She has the versatility to build an orderly, measured structure in rhyme and meter, or to adopt the easier virtues of free verse for a more transient, informal effect." Furthermore, the critic maintained, Kumin's poems are *about* something; they tell a story that carries the reader into the world Kumin creates and leads to a satisfying conclusion.

Kumin followed *Selected Poems* with *The Long Marriage,* which celebrates her five-decade marriage to her husband, their life together in New Hampshire, and nature. Donna Seaman, writing in *Booklist,* stated that Kumin's observations are "crisp" and added that "Kumin moves surefootedly" in her work. *New York Times Book Review* contributor Megan Harland similarly called Kumin's observations "earthy" and "practical," and she declared that "Kumin's tonal clarity is transformative."

Kumin's 1994 prose collection, *Women, Animals, and Vegetables,* offers insight into the author's pastoral life on her farm in New Hampshire. In essays and short stories, she "describes the pleasures of raising and riding horses, of gardening and mushrooming, of learning how in the country 'things have a way of balancing out,'" explained Christopher Merrill in the *Los Angeles Times Book Review.* Anne Raver, writing in the *New York Times Book Review,* averred that some of the material in the book pales in comparison to Kumin's poetry, which covers many of the same themes and issues "more brilliantly." She continued, "It is a Pulitzer Prize-winning poet's misfortune, perhaps, to be judged harshly by the standards she herself has set." But Merrill concluded of the collection: "This is a book many readers will find companionable."

In 1999 Kumin published a mystery novel reflecting her commitment and concern for animals. *Quit Monks or Die!* is an unusual tale centering around the disappearance of a pair of monkeys at a testing lab and a murder of the lab director. A reviewer for *Publishers Weekly* called the plot for *Quit Monks or Die!* a "masterpiece of construction" and declared the book "one of the best mysteries of the year." *New York Times Book Review* critic Laura Jamison commented

that Kumin's character sketches were "effective" and that she is "a capable stylist." And while Jamison was disappointed in the mystery's outcome, she commended Kumin for her "highly original prose" and was captivated by "her provocative analysis of human nature."

When Kumin was seventy-three she suffered an accident while preparing a horse for competition. In the accident, she broke her neck and received serious internal injuries, injuries that kill ninety-five percent of those who receive similar ones. She was able to make a successful recovery, however, and her book *Inside the Halo and Beyond: The Anatomy of a Recovery* describes her road to recovery. Anne Roiphe, writing for the *New York Times Book Review,* described the language Kumin used in *Inside the Halo and Beyond* as "precise and spare." As her poetry deals with everyday life, so does the book. Roiphe noted that although Kumin is a poet, this book "is rarely poetic in the usual sense of heightened metaphor or compacted image." She did not write an autobiographical tell-all, but simply wrote about the specific experience of her time in recovery and people and feelings she encountered along the way. Roiphe likened the tenet "to a dignified prayer of thanks" that resonates "wisdom while announcing a triumph of body and soul." A reviewer for *Publishers Weekly* commented, however, that the book was "uneven and overlong," but believed that Kumin's fans would find *Inside the Halo and Beyond* "irresistible."

The same year that *Inside the Halo and Beyond* was released, Kumin also published *Always Beginning: Essays on a Life in Poetry,* a collection of essays and poems describing Kumin's daily life as a poet. She includes interviews, diary entries, and keynote addresses, as well as poetry. A reviewer for *Publishers Weekly* called Kumin's life as presented "wonderful[ly] poetic." Although *New York Times Book Review* reviewer Sunil Iyengar was less impressed, calling the book "bland" and "haphazard," *Library Journal* contributor Doris Lynch asserted that the essays encapsulate "a kind of grace."

Reviewing Kumin's multidecade career, Booth commented that the poet "has simply gotten better and better at what she has always been good at: a resonant language, an autobiographical immediacy, unsystematized intelligence, and radical compassion. One does not learn compassion without having suffered." Crenshaw noted that "Americans traditionally have pre-ferred their women poets to be depressed and victimized," but he claimed that Kumin's "posture regarding despair" sets her apart from "the sweet in-nocents who have been driven to insane passions and flamboyant destructions." And Wakoski wrote in *Contemporary Women Poets:* "The one thing that is clear throughout [Kumin's] substantial body of work is that she believes survival is possible, if only through the proper use of the imagination to retrieve those things which are loved well enough."

BIOGRAPHICAL AND CRITICAL SOURCES:

BOOKS

Authors in the News, Volume 2, Thomson Gale (Detroit, MI), 1976.

Contemporary Literary Criticism, Thomson Gale (Detroit, MI), Volume 5, 1976, Volume 13, 1980, Volume 28, 1984.

Contemporary Women Poets, St. James Press (Detroit, MI), 1997.

Dictionary of Literary Biography, Volume 5: *American Poets since World War II,* Thomson Gale (Detroit, MI), 1980.

Grosholz, Emily, *Telling the Barn Swallow: Poets on the Poetry of Maxine Kumin,* University Press of New England (Boston, MA), 1997.

Kumin, Maxine, *Halfway,* Holt (New York, NY), 1961.

Kumin, Maxine, *To Make a Prairie: Essays on Poets, Poetry, and Country Living,* University of Michigan Press (Ann Arbor, MI), 1980.

McClatchy, J. D., editor, *Anne Sexton: The Artist and Her Critics,* Indiana University Press (Bloomington, IN), 1978.

Sexton, Anne, Linda Gray, and Lois Ames, editors, *Anne Sexton: A Self-Portrait in Letters,* Houghton Mifflin (New York, NY), 1977.

PERIODICALS

America, February 28, 1976.

American Poetry Review, March, 1976; November, 1978.

Atlantic, October, 1971.

Belles Lettres, fall, 1992, p. 51.

Booklist, August, 1999, Donna Seaman and Emily Melton, review of *Quit Monks or Die!,* p. 2035; May 1, 2000, Donna Seaman, review of *Inside the Halo and Beyond: The Anatomy of a Recovery* and *Always Beginning: Essays on a Life in Poetry,* p. 1639; November 15, 2001, Donna Seaman, review of *The Long Marriage,* p. 542.

Boston Book Review, July 1, 1996, Fay Weldon, review of *Connecting the Dots: Poems.*

Boston Herald, April 30, 2000, Elizabeth Hand, "Pain Purged on *Journey;* Kumin Heals from Horse Accident," p. O62; May 18, 2000, Stephanie Schorow, "Inside the *Halo* Justice," p. O59.

Choice, January, 1966.

Christian Science Monitor, August 9, 1961; February 28, 1973.

Country Journal, spring, 1979, article by Maxine Kumin.

Crazy Horse, summer, 1975, Joan Norris, interview with Maxine Kumin.

Hudson Review, summer, 2001, R. S. Gwynn, review of *Always Beginning,* p. 341.

Kirkus Reviews, May 1, 1994, p. 609; July, 1999, Margaret A. Smith, review of *Quit Monks or Die!,* p. 142; August 1, 1999, review of *Quit Monks or Die!,* p. 1176.

Library Journal, June 15, 1997, Judy Clarence, review of *Selected Poems, 1960-1990,* p. 74; July, 1999, review of *Quit Monks or Die!,* p. 142; June 1, 2000, Doris Lynch, review of *Always Beginning,* p. 124; September 1, 2001, Judy Clarence, review of *The Long Marriage,* p. 184.

Los Angeles Times Book Review, June 13, 1982; December 1, 1985; June 26, 1988, p. 14; November 6, 1994, p. 13.

Massachusetts Review, spring, 1975, Martha George Meek.

Nation, July 24, 1982, Clara Claiborne Park, review of *Why Can't We Live Together Like Civilized Human Beings?,* p. 89.

New Leader, January 22, 1973.

New Letters, summer, 2000, Jeffrey S. Cramer, "Peaceable Island," p. 61.

New Republic, August 10, 1974.

New Yorker, December 4, 1971.

New York Times, June 26, 1974, review by Michiko Kakutani.

New York Times Book Review, March 28, 1965; May 5, 1968; November 19, 1972; June 23, 1974; September 7, 1975; April 23, 1978; August 8, 1982, Alicia Ostriker, review of *Our Ground Time Here Will Be Brief: New and Selected Poems,*

p. 10; March 2, 1986, Harold Beaver, review of *The Long Approach,* p. 14; August 30, 1987, Adrienne S. Barnes, review of *In Deep: Country Essays,* p. 21; November 5, 1989, Carol Muske, review of *Nurture,* p. 32; March 21, 1993, Lisa Zeider, review of *Looking for Luck,* p. 14; August 28, 1994, Anne Raver, review of *Women, Animals, and Vegetables: Essays and Stories,* p. 12; August 3, 1997, Richard Tillinghast, review of *Selected Poems, 1960-1990,* p. 10; September 26, 1999, Laura Jamison, review of *Quit Monks or Die!,* p. 15; July 30, 2000, Anne Roiphe, review of *Inside the Halo and Beyond,* p. 15; September 3, 2000, Sunil Iyengar, review of *Always Beginning,* p. 15; December 9, 2001, Megan Harlan, review of *The Long Marriage,* p. 33.

Parnassus, spring-summer, 1973; spring, 1985, Brad Crenshaw, review of *Our Ground Time Here Will Be Brief.*

Poetry, January, 1979; April, 1990, p. 48; November, 1992; June, 1999, p. 181.

Prairie Schooner, spring, 1976.

Publishers Weekly, May 30, 1994, review of *Women, Animals, and Vegetables,* p. 41; June 3, 1996, review of *Connecting the Dots,* p. 73; January 6, 1997, "Telling the Barnswallow: Poets on the Poetry of Maxine Kumin," p. 58; April 28, 1997, review of *Selected Poems, 1960-1990,* p. 70; August 23, 1999, review of *Quit Monks or Die!,* p. 50; May 15, 2000, review of *Inside the Halo and Beyond,* p. 100; August 14, 2000, review of *Always Beginning,* p. 349; August 27, 2001, review of *The Long Marriage,* p. 75.

Saturday Review, May 6, 1961; December 25, 1965; May 9, 1970; March 25, 1972.

Sewanee Review, spring, 1974; winter, 1995, p. 141.

Shenandoah, spring, 1976.

Smithsonian, November, 1987.

Times Literary Supplement, May 9, 1975.

Tribune Books August 29, 1982; February 2, 1986; July 9, 1989, p. 6.

Village Voice, September 5, 1974; July 20, 1982.

Virginia Quarterly Review, spring, 1971.

Washington Post, May 6, 1980.

Washington Post Book World, May 5, 1968; October 10, 1971; June 22, 1982; February 2, 1986; November 22, 1992, p. 8.

Western Humanities Review, spring, 1979, Karla Hammond, interview with Maxine Kumin.

Women's Review of Books, October, 1989, Diane Wakowski, review of *Nurture,* p. 20; April, 2001,

Judith Barrington, review of *Always Beginning* and *Inside the Halo and Beyond,* p. 6.

Yale Review, autumn, 1968.

ONLINE

Atlantic Unbound, http://www.theatlantic.com/ (February 2, 2002), Erin Rogers, "The Art of Living."*

*   *   *

KWAKYE, Benjamin 1967-

PERSONAL: Born January 7, 1967, in Accra, Ghana; son of B. S. K. (a police officer) and Victoria (in business; maiden name, Mensah) Kwakye. *Ethnicity:* "Ashanti." *Education:* Dartmouth University, B.A., 1990, Harvard University Law School, J.D., 1993. *Hobbies and other interests:* Soccer.

ADDRESSES: Home—1509 Dobson St., No. 2, Evanston, IL 60202. *Office*—Hospira, Inc., 275 N. Field Dr., Lake Forest, IL 60045. *E-mail*—bkkwakye@ yahoo.com.

CAREER: Writer. Porter, Wright, Morris & Arthur, associate attorney, 1993-97; Abbott Laboratories, Abbott Park, IL, counsel, 1997-2004; Hospira, Inc., Lake Forest, IL, senior counsel, 2004—.

AWARDS, HONORS: Commonwealth Writers Prize, regional prize (Africa), best first book, for *The Clothes of Nakedness.*

WRITINGS:

The Clothes of Nakedness (novel), Heinemann (Portsmouth, NH), 1998.

The Sun by Night, Africa World Press (Trenton, NJ), in press.

ADAPTATIONS: The novel *The Clothes of Nakedness* was adapted as a play of the week by the British Broadcasting Corporation.

SIDELIGHTS: Ghanaian author Benjamin Kwakye's debut book, *The Clothes of Nakedness,* takes place in Accra, Ghana. This award-winning novel examines the dichotomies of wealth and poverty and of integrity and evil. The main character, who goes by the name Mystique Mysterious, introduces evil to a suburb of Accra and brings pain and suffering into people's lives. Mystique can create havoc and turbulence and cause the most well-intentioned people to commit evil deeds. A *Publishers Weekly* contributor deemed *The Clothes of Nakedness* a "cautionary tale of greed and excess," noting that while the setting could hold promise of exotic events, it contains "an unsatisfying and forced conclusion."

Kwakye once told *CA:* "I am afraid that the *Publishers Weekly* reviewer had a rather narrow and simplistic approach to the book. As a 'Western' reviewer, he or she probably expected a certain genre of book for an African novel. I wonder why a setting must yield a certain expected result. Please note that the book has won the Commonwealth Writers Prize for best first book for the Africa region."

BIOGRAPHICAL AND CRITICAL SOURCES:

PERIODICALS

Publishers Weekly, April 20, 1998, review of *The Clothes of Nakedness,* p. 49.

*   *   *

KYGER, Joanne (Elizabeth) 1934-

PERSONAL: Born November 19, 1934, in Vallejo, CA; daughter of Jacob Holmes (a career navy officer) and Anne (Lamont) Kyger; married Gary Snyder (a poet), February 23, 1960 (divorced, 1964); married John Boyce (a painter), 1966 (separated, 1970; died, 1972). *Education:* Attended Santa Barbara College (now University of California, Santa Barbara), 1952-56.

ADDRESSES: Home—Box 688, Bolinas, CA 94924.

CAREER: Poet. Teaches at Naropa Institute, Boulder, CO, and at New College, San Francisco, CA. Performer and poet in an experimental television project, 1967-68.

Joanne Kyger

AWARDS, HONORS: Grant from National Endowment for the Arts, 1968; Bay Area Book Reviewers Awards (BABRA) nominee, poetry, 2003, for *As Ever: Selected Poems.*

WRITINGS:

POETRY

The Tapestry and the Web, Four Seasons Foundation (San Francisco, CA), 1965.
The Fool in April: A Poem, Coyote Books (San Francisco, CA), 1966.
Places to Go, Black Sparrow Press (Los Angeles, CA), 1970.
Joanne, Angel Hair Books (New York, NY), 1970.
Desecheo Notebook, Arif Press (Berkeley, CA), 1971.
Trip Out and Fall Back, Arif Press (Berkeley, CA), 1974.
All This Every Day, Big Sky (Berkeley, CA), 1975.
(With Larry Fagin) *Lettre de Paris,* Poltroon Press (Berkeley, CA), 1977.

Up My Coast, Floating Island (Point Reyes, CA), 1979.

The Wonderful Focus of You, Z Press (Calais, VT), 1980.

The Japan-India Journals, Tombouctou Books (Bolinas, CA), 1981, published as *Strange Big Moon: The Japan and India Journals, 1960-1964,* North Atlantic Books (Berkeley, CA), 2000.

Mexico Blonde, Evergreen Press (Bolinas, CA), 1981.

Going On: Selected Poems, 1958-1980, selected by Robert Creeley, Dutton (New York, NY), 1983.

The Dharma Committee, Smithereens Press (Bolinas, CA), 1986.

Phenomenological: A Curriculum of the Soul, Institute of Further Studies (Canton, NY), 1989.

Just Space: Poems, 1979-1989, Black Sparrow Press (Santa Rosa, CA), 1991.

Some Sketches from the Life of Helena Petrovna Blavatsky, Rodent Press (Boulder, CO), 1996.

Some Life, Post-Apollo Press (Sausalito, CA), 2000.

Again: Poems, 1980-2000, La Alameda Press (Albuquerque, NM), 2001.

As Ever: Selected Poems, edited with a foreword by Michael Rothenberg, introduction by David Meltzer, Penguin Poets (New York, NY), 2002.

10 Shines, Larry Fagin Press, 2003.

The Distressed Look, Coyote Books (Salinas, CA), 2004.

God Never Dies, Blue Press, 2004.

Contributor to books, including *Rising Tides,* edited by Laura Chester and Sharon Barba, Pocket Books, 1973. Contributor to anthologies, including *The American Literary Anthology,* edited by George Plimpton and Peter Ardery, Random House, 1969; and *The World Anthology,* edited by Anne Waldman, Bobbs-Merrill, 1969. Contributor to numerous periodicals, including *Paris Review, Poetry, Coyote's Journal, Peninsula, Intent, Rockey Ledge,* and *World.* Contributor to anthologies, including *A Book of Luminous Things: An International Anthology of Poets,* edited by Czeslaw Milosz, Harcourt Brace, 1999; *American Poets Say Goodbye to the 20th Century,* edited by Andrei Codrescu, Eight Windows Press, 1999; *Meeting the Buddha: On Pilgrimage in Buddhist India,* edited by Molly Emma Aitken, River Head Books (New York, NY); *What Book: Buddha Poems from Beat to Hip Hop,* edited by Garch Gach, Parallax Press, 1999; *San Franciso Beat: Talking with Poets* (interviews), edited by David Meltzer, City Lights Books, 2001; and *Beat Poets,* edited by Carmel Ciuraru, Knopf (New York, NY), 2002.

Kyger's papers are deposited at the Archive for New Poetry, University of California, San Diego.

WORK IN PROGRESS: Collected Poems.

SIDELIGHTS: A leading figure in San Francisco poetry circles, Joanne Kyger was a member of some of the groups that formed around senior poets Robert Duncan and Jack Spicer in the late 1950s and fostered such writers as Richard Brautigan, Michael McClure, and George Stanley.

From 1970 on, noted Bill Berkson in the *Dictionary of Literary Biography,* "Kyger's poems have dealt with a number of set themes: Buddhist and American Indian figures and myths, the relationship of the individual psyche to the social-political life of the town, love and marriage, and travel." According to Berkson, during a 1974 panel discussion at Kent State University, Kyger "spoke of her change from what she termed 'the linear line': 'at this point the kind of space that interests me is the kind of space that vibrates its meaning. It's the one-liner or the sampler on the wall. . . . It just stays there for a long time. You can go back into the one line and it will keep giving off overtones.'"

Kyger lived and traveled extensively in Japan during her late twenties. *Strange Big Moon: The Japan and India Journals, 1960-1964,* first published in 1981 as *The Japan-India Journals,* chronicles four eventful years in Kyger's life in Japan. There, in the company of Allen Ginsberg, Peter Orlovsky, and her new husband, Gary Snyder, she began to study Zen and develop her poetic voice. In prose and photographs, Kyger recounts her early Buddhist practice, her meeting with the young Dalai Lama, and her observations of her own and her companions' experiences with drugs, with literature, and with a different culture. "Her journals are witty, amusing, razor-incisive, and at times touching and sad," remarked a writer on the *North Atlantic Books* Web site.

In *Some Sketches from the Life of Helena Petrovna Blavatsky,* Kyger presents a collection of a dozen brief scenes culled from biographies of Blavatsky, the founder of Theosophy and an early pioneer in bringing Buddhist thought and practice to America. "Blavatsky's theosophy, along with associated movements of figures such as Krishnamurti, helped to form the spiritual ethos of the West Coast in the 1960s, fostering both Buddhism and New Ageism," commented Devin Johnston in the *Chicago Review.* "In turn, this religious climate contributed to shaping the San Francisco poetry community in which Kyger has long played an active role." Kyger approaches Blavatsky with seriousness and respect, despite the severe criticism, sometimes even ridicule, that Blavatsky and Theosophy have faced over the years. The biographical material adheres closely to accounts written by Blavatsky herself. The work "is written in the clean, flowing free verse which is typical of the poet, and provides for pleasurable reading in its sense of spontaneity," Johnston remarked.

"Kyger's gifts as a narrator are extraordinary," wrote a biographer in *Contemporary Women Poets.* "In fact, it is this technique that characterizes almost all her poems—a pattern marked by sudden cuts of consciousness, the narrative abruptly shifting in flight, not relying on startling imagery to signal changes of direction." A *Publishers Weekly* critic, in a review of Kyger's short poetry collection *Some Life,* remarked that the poet "inhabits a singular verbal space as engaging and essential as it is offhand and self-questioning."

As Ever: Selected Poems collects works from nearly four decades of Kyger's career, spanning the late 1950s to 2001. Many of the poems are infused with Buddhist and Zen sensibilities. Others are reminiscent of Beat poetry, observed a reviewer on the *Shambhala Sun* Web site. However, "there is absolutely no agenda here: it's fun and frolicking and heartfelt," the reviewer commented.

"Kyger's images are few: puns not essential; devices, tricks, syncopations unintended; diction comfortable," wrote the *Contemporary Women Poets* biographer. "Her poems are attentive to a spirit's needs, a deep-drawn aim within aimlessness."

BIOGRAPHICAL AND CRITICAL SOURCES:

BOOKS

Contemporary Women Poets, St. James Press (Detroit, MI), 1998.
Dictionary of Literary Biography, Volume 16: *The Beats: Literary Bohemians in Postwar America,* Thomson Gale (Detroit, MI), 1983.

PERIODICALS

Book, September-October, 2002, Stephen Whited, review of *As Ever: Selected Poems,* pp. 79-80.
Chicago Review, winter, 1997, Devin Johnston, review of *Some Sketches from the Life of Helena Petrovna Blavatsky,* pp. 114-116.
Publishers Weekly, June 26, 2000, review of *Some Life,* p. 72; June 17, 2002, review of *As Ever,* pp. 57-58.

ONLINE

Crooked Cucumber Web site, http://www.cuke.com/ (February 24, 2004), interview with Joanne Kyger.
North Atlantic Books Web site, http://www. northatlanticbooks.com/ (December, 2000).
Poetry Daily Web site, http://www.poems.com/ (February 24, 2004), profile of Joanne Kyger.
University of California, San Diego Web site, http:// www.ucsd.edu/ (February 24, 2004), biography of Joanne Kyger.
Shambhala Sun Web site, http://www.shambhalasun. com/ (November, 2002), review of *As Ever.*

*   *   *

KYLE, Susan (Spaeth) 1946-
(Diana Blayne, Katy Currie, Diana Palmer)

PERSONAL: Born December 12, 1946, in Cuthbert, GA; daughter of William Olin Spaeth (a college professor) and Maggie Eloise Cliatt Spaeth (a nurse and journalist); married James Edward Kyle (a computer consultant), October 9, 1972; children: Blayne Edward. *Education:* Piedmont College, B.A. (summa cum laude), 1995; graduate work at California State University. *Politics:* Republican. *Religion:* Presbyterian. *Hobbies and other interests:* Archaeology, anthropology, herpetology (iguanas, monitor lizards), gardening, blues piano, astronomy, music.

ADDRESSES: Home and office—P.O. Box 844, Cornelia, GA 30531-0844. *Agent*—Maureen Walters, Curtis Brown Ltd., 10 Astor Place, New York, NY 10003. *E-mail*—diana@dianapalmer.com.

CAREER: Times, Gainesville, GA, district staff reporter, 1969-84; *Tri-County Advertiser,* Clarkesville, GA, staff reporter, 1972-82; *Atlanta Constitution,* district staff member, late 1970s. American Heart Association, member of board of directors of Habersham County chapter, late 1970s-early 1980s, county publicity chair, early 1980s; American Cancer Society, member of board of directors of Habersham County chapter, late 1970-early 1980s. Novelist, 1979—.

MEMBER: Authors Guild, National Geographic Society, Cousteau Society, American Museum of Natural History, Custer Battlefield Preservation Society, National Cattleman's Association, Smithsonian Institution, American Archaeological Association, Metropolitan Opera Guild, American Federation of Herptoculturalists, Lionel Railroaders Club, Star Trek Fan Club, Piedmont College Anthropology Club.

AWARDS, HONORS: Awards include numerous bestseller awards; Reviewer's Choice Award, *Romantic Times,* 1985, for *The Tender Stranger;* three Silver Pen Awards, *Affaire de Coeur,* 1985, 1988, and 1989; silver certificate, *Affaire de Coeur,* 1988, for *Tyler;* gold certificate, *Affaire de Coeur,* 1988, for *Diamond Spur* and *Fire Brand;* regional Maggie Awards, Romance Writers of American, for *Soldier of Fortune* and *Diamond Spur;* Series Romance Storyteller award, *Romantic Times,* 1988-89.

WRITINGS:

NOVELS; UNDER NAME SUSAN KYLE, EXCEPT WHERE INDICATED

(As Susan S. Kyle) *The Morcai Battalion* (science fiction), Manor Books (New York, NY), 1980.
(Under pseudonym Katy Currie) *Blind Promises,* Silhouette Inspirational (New York, NY), 1984.
Diamond Spur, Warner Popular Library (New York, NY), 1988.
Fire Brand, Warner Popular Library (New York, NY), 1989.
Night Fever, Warner Popular Library (New York, NY), 1990.
True Colors, Warner Popular Library (New York, NY), 1991.
Escapade, Warner Popular Library (New York, NY), 1992.
After Midnight, Warner Popular Library (New York, NY), 1993.

NOVELS; UNDER PSEUDONYM DIANA PALMER

Now and Forever, MacFadden Romances (New York, NY), 1979.
Storm over the Lake, MacFadden Romances (New York, NY), 1979.
To Have and to Hold, MacFadden Romances (New York, NY), 1979.
Sweet Enemy, MacFadden Romances (New York, NY), 1980.
Bound by a Promise, MacFadden Romances (New York, NY), 1980.
Love on Trial, MacFadden Romances (New York, NY), 1980.
To Love and Cherish, MacFadden Romances (New York, NY), 1980.
Dream's End, MacFadden Romances (New York, NY), 1980.
If Winter Comes, MacFadden Romances (New York, NY), 1981.
At Winter's End, MacFadden Romances (New York, NY), 1981.
Heather's Song, MacFadden Romances (New York, NY), 1982.
The Cowboy and the Lady, Silhouette Books (New York, NY), 1982.
Friends and Lovers, Silhouette Books (New York, NY), 1983.
Fire and Ice, Silhouette Books (New York, NY), 1983.
Snow Kisses, Silhouette Books (New York, NY), 1983.
Darling Enemy, Silhouette Romance (New York, NY), 1983.
Diamond Girl, Silhouette Books (New York, NY), 1984.
The Rawhide Man, Silhouette Books (New York, NY), 1984.
Lady Love, Silhouette Books (New York, NY), 1984.
Roomful of Roses, Silhouette Romance (New York, NY), 1984.
Heart of Ice, Silhouette Romance (New York, NY), 1984.
Passion Flower, Silhouette Romance (New York, NY), 1984.
Cattleman's Choice, Silhouette Books (New York, NY), 1985.
Love by Proxy, Silhouette Books (New York, NY), 1985.
The Australian, MacFadden Romances (New York, NY), 1985.
Eye of the Tiger, Silhouette Books (New York, NY), 1986.

Loveplay, Silhouette Books (New York, NY), 1986.

Rawhide and Lace, Silhouette Books (New York, NY), 1986.

After the Music, Silhouette Romance (New York, NY), 1986.

Champagne Girl, Silhouette Romance (New York, NY), 1986.

Unlikely Lover, Silhouette Romance (New York, NY), 1986.

Rage of Passion, Silhouette Books (New York, NY), 1987.

Fit for a King, Silhouette Books (New York, NY), 1987.

Betrayed by Love, Silhouette Books (New York, NY), 1987.

Woman Hater, Silhouette Romance (New York, NY), 1987.

Hoodwinked, Silhouette Books (New York, NY), 1989.

His Girl Friday, Silhouette Books (New York, NY), 1989.

Lacy (historical novel), Ivy Books (New York, NY), 1991.

Trilby (historical novel), Ivy Books (New York, NY), 1993.

Amelia (historical novel), Ivy Books (New York, NY), 1993.

King's Ransom, Silhouette Romance (New York, NY), 1993.

Calamity Mom, Silhouette Books (New York, NY), 1993.

Secret Agent Man, Silhouette Books (New York, NY), 1994.

The Savage Heart, Fawcett (New York, NY), 1997.

Once in Paris, Mira (New York, NY), 1998.

Paper Rose, Mira (New York, NY), 1999.

The Texas Ranger, Mira (New York, NY), 2001.

Desperado, Mira (New York, NY), 2002.

(With Lenora Worth and Loree Lough) *Blessings in Disguise,* Steeple Hill Books (New York, NY), 2003.

(Author of foreword) *The Black Moth,* by Georgette Heyer, Harlequin Books (New York, NY), 2003.

Also coauthor, under pseudonym Diana Palmer, with Debbie Macomber and Judith Duncan, of the story collection *To Mother with Love;* and with Jennifer Blake and Heather Graham, of the story collection *With a Southern Touch,* Mira Books (Don Mills, Ontario, Canada), 2002.

"DIANA PALMER DUETS" SERIES; UNDER PSEUDONYM DIANA PALMER

Sweet Enemy [and] *Love on Trial,* Silhouette Books (New York, NY), 1990.

Storm over the Lake [and] *To Love and Cherish,* Silhouette Books (New York, NY), 1990.

If Winter Comes [and] *Now and Forever,* Silhouette Books (New York, NY), 1990.

After the Music [and] *Dream's End,* Silhouette Books (New York, NY), 1990.

Bound by a Promise [and] *Passion Flower,* Silhouette Books (New York, NY), 1990.

To Have and Hold [and] *The Cowboy and the Lady,* Silhouette Books (New York, NY), 1990.

"MERCENARY" SERIES; UNDER PSEUDONYM DIANA PALMER

The Tender Stranger, Silhouette Books (New York, NY), 1985.

Soldier of Fortune, Silhouette Romance (New York, NY), 1985.

Enamored, Silhouette Books (New York, NY), 1988.

"LONG TALL TEXAN" SERIES; UNDER PSEUDNYM DIANA PALMER

Calhoun, Silhouette Romance (New York, NY), 1988.

Justin, Silhouette Romance (New York, NY), 1988.

Tyler, Silhouette Romance (New York, NY), 1988.

Sutton's Way, Silhouette Romance (New York, NY), 1989.

Ethan, Silhouette Romance (New York, NY), 1990.

Connal, Silhouette Romance (New York, NY), 1990.

Harden, Silhouette Romance (New York, NY), 1991.

Evan, Silhouette Romance (New York, NY), 1991.

Donovan, Silhouette Romance (New York, NY), 1992.

Emmett, Silhouette Romance (New York, NY), 1993.

"MAN OF THE MONTH" SERIES; UNDER PSEUDONYM DIANA PALMER

Reluctant Father, Silhouette Books (New York, NY), 1989.

Hunter, Silhouette Books (New York, NY), 1990.

Nelson's Brand, Silhouette Books (New York, NY), 1991.

The Best Is Yet to Come, Silhouette Books (New York, NY), 1991.

Night of Love, Silhouette Books (New York, NY), 1993.

"MOST WANTED" TRILOGY; UNDER PSEUDONYM DIANA PALMER

(And part of the "Man of the Month" series) *The Case of the Mesmerizing Boss,* Silhouette Books (New York, NY), 1992.

The Case of the Confirmed Bachelor, Silhouette Books (New York, NY), 1992.

The Case of the Missing Secretary, Silhouette Books (New York, NY), 1992.

NOVELS; UNDER PSEUDONYM DIANA BLAYNE

Color Love Blue, Dell (New York, NY), 1984.
Tangled Destinies, Dell (New York, NY), 1986.
Denim and Lace, Dell (New York, NY), 1990.

"CANDLELIGHT ECSTASY" SERIES; UNDER PSEUDONYM DIANA BLAYNE

A Waiting Game, Dell (New York, NY), 1982.
A Loving Arrangement, Dell (New York, NY), 1983.
White Sand Wild Sea, Dell (New York, NY), 1983.
Dark Surrender, Dell (New York, NY), 1983.

Contributor of short stories to anthologies published by Silhouette, including *Silhouette Christmas Stories,* 1987, and *Silhouette Summer Sizzlers,* with Sherryl Woods and Patricia Coughlin, 1991.

WORK IN PROGRESS: A mainstream novel set in the South, for Warner; a historical novel which takes place during the first part of the twentieth century in east Texas, for Fawcett; research on different historical time periods.

SIDELIGHTS: Susan Kyle has penned numerous novels in several genres under her own name and using several pseudonyms. She is best known, however, for her many romance novels as Diana Palmer. As a writer for *Twentieth-Century Romance and Historical Writers* observed, "Palmer has a special talent for developing disagreeable heroes, then letting them be changed by love. Although her novels are generally short, she manages to make this reversal of character believable."

Though, as Palmer, she has published under the auspices of Silhouette, Fawcett, and Ivy, as the twenty-first century approached she began putting novels out with Mira. Among these is 1998's *Once in Paris.* Brianne, its young heroine, gets sent to Paris to study by her stepfather. While there, she falls in love with a much older man—a man who is involved in undercover espionage. A *Publishers Weekly* reviewer, discussing *Once in Paris,* commented that "the dialogue is charming, the characters likable and the sex sizzling." In 2001, Palmer's *The Texas Ranger* became available to her fans. As in many of Palmer's romances, the hero and heroine have had a more or less disastrous encounter earlier in their lives, and circumstances bring them back together. In this case, Texas Ranger Matt has testified against Josette during the trial of a man who assaulted her, but now they must work together to investigate a murder that may be linked to organized crime. The following year, Palmer published *Desperado.* In this tale, the couple is a man and his foster sister. According to another *Publishers Weekly* critic, "Palmer's compelling suspense and beautiful visuals keep the reader interested."

Kyle once told *CA:*"I was born in Cuthbert, a small rural southwestern Georgia town where the majority of the people were farmers. For the first five years of my life, while my parents completed their college degrees in Atlanta, I lived with my mother's parents on their tenant farm in Calhoun County, Georgia. It was while following my grandfather's plow across the fields that I collected arrowheads and developed an interest in prehistoric indigenous Americans.

"As a young girl, I was privileged to experience a way of life which is now found only in history books. We had no modern amenities on the farm, which meant that we had to draw water from a well, cook food on a wood stove, and go to bed by kerosene lantern. This glimpse of the past gave me a wonderful background in the hardships of nineteenth-century life. I have used it to great advantage in my writing.

"From the time I was thirteen years old, I wanted to be a writer. I joined the staff of two newspapers when I graduated from high school, hoping to improve my style and learn more about gathering information. After I married in 1972, my husband John never minded helping me with housework and with our son, Blayne, so that I had enough time to write while working full time as a reporter every day. There were editors who taught me to polish my style, librarians and friends and a loving sister who encouraged me. Later when I was published, I found myself with a wonderful following of loyal readers whose kindness and loyalty helped me through some very hard times. They are my family, and they come in a rainbow of colors, religions, backgrounds, and viewpoints. I love them all.

"God willing, I hope I can keep writing books for a long, long time. If, through my work, I can bring joy to one heavy heart, or surprise a laugh from a throat tight with pain or grief, then I will feel that my life has been worthwhile."

BIOGRAPHICAL AND CRITICAL SOURCES:

BOOKS

Twentieth-Century Romance and Historical Writers, 3rd edition, St. James Press (Detroit, MI), 1994.

PERIODICALS

Kirkus Reviews, May 15, 2002, review of *Desperado,* p. 694.
Publishers Weekly, November 2, 1992, review of *Escapade,* p. 66; December 14, 1992, review of *Trilby,* p. 54; November 2, 1998, review of *Once in Paris,* p. 79; July 2, 2001, review of *The Texas Ranger,* p. 57; May 13, 2002, review of *With a Southern Touch,* p. 57; June 17, 2002, review of *Desperado,* pp. 43-44; June 16, 2003, review of *Lawless,* p. 50.

ONLINE

Diana Palmer Home Page, http://www.dianapalmer. com (July 17, 2002).*

L

LAVOND, Paul Dennis
See POHL, Frederik

* * *

LAWSON, Amy
See GORDON, Amy

* * *

LEE, R(oy) Alton 1931-

PERSONAL: Born May 24, 1931, in White City, KS; son of Ralph A. (a farmer) and Alice (Butts) Lee; married Marilyn J. Kurzava, October 19, 1963; children: Michael Alton (deceased), Edward Alan, Deborah Ann. *Education:* Kansas State Teachers College, B.S., 1955, M.S., 1958; University of Oklahoma, Ph.D., 1962. *Politics:* Democrat. *Religion:* Roman Catholic.

ADDRESSES: Home—976 Crestview, Vermillion, SD 57069. *Office*—Department of History, University of South Dakota, Vermillion, SD 57069.

CAREER: Central State College (now University), Edmond, OK, 1961-66, began as assistant professor, became associate professor of history; University of South Dakota, Vermillion, associate professor, 1966-70, from professor of history to professor emeritus, 1970—, chair of department, 1970-73.

MEMBER: Organization of American Historians, Phi Alpha Theta.

AWARDS, HONORS: Harry S. Truman Library research grant, 1961.

WRITINGS:

Pasquale Paoli: Fighter for Freedom, Kansas State Teachers College (Emporia, KS), 1961.
Truman and Taft-Hartley: A Question of Mandate, University of Kentucky Press (Lexington, KY), 1966.
A History of Regulatory Taxation, University Press of Kentucky (Lexington, KY), 1973.
Dwight D. Eisenhower, Soldier and Statesman, Nelson-Hall (Chicago, IL), 1981.
(Editor, with Archie P. McDonald and Donald W. Whisenhunt) *Encyclopedia USA: The Encyclopedia of the United States of America Past and Present,* thirty-one volumes, Academic International Press (Gulf Breeze, FL), 1983–2003.
(Editor) *Agricultural Legacies: Essays in Honor of Gilbert C. Fite,* University of South Dakota Press (Vermillion, SD), 1986.
Eisenhower and Landrum-Griffin: A Study in Labor-Management Politics, University Press of Kentucky (Lexington, KY), 1990.
(Compiler) *Dwight D. Eisenhower: A Bibliography of His Times and Presidency,* Scholarly Resources (Wilmington, DE), 1991.
Harry S. Truman: Where Did the Buck Stop?, P. Lang (New York, NY), 1991.
T-Town on the Plains, Sunflower University Press (Manhattan, KS), 1999.
The Bizarre Careers of John R. Brinkley, University Press of Kentucky (Lexington, KY), 2002.

Contributor to historical journals.

SIDELIGHTS: In a career that has spanned more than three decades, R. Alton Lee, a professor emeritus of American history at the University of South Dakota, has written books on a number of subjects, including labor relations, regulatory taxation, Presidents Truman and Eisenhower, and the con man John R. Brinkley.

Among Lee's works, *Truman and Taft-Hartley: A Question of Mandate* and the follow-up volume, *Eisenhower and Landrum-Griffin: A Study in Labor-Management Politics,* combine to create a discussion of a complex topic. The former title, a reworking of Lee's doctoral dissertation, deals with the political implications of the Taft-Hartley Act of 1947, while the later, published a quarter-century later, deals with the enactment of the Landrum-Griffin Act. *Truman and Taft-Hartley* "is a careful study of the reexamination of national labor policy in the Truman years," according to David R. Mayhew of the *Journal of American History.* In it Lee focuses, as he himself explained, on "the struggle between the agricultural and industrial groups that dominated Congress and the laboring elements that, through the President, controlled the executive branch of government." Mayhew acknowledged that detecting public mandates is "uncertain science" and that in this area Lee "is on less secure ground" than in other discussions. *Industrial and Labor Relations Review* critic Emily Clark Brown likewise remarked that readers "may be put off . . . by broad and unqualified assumptions and, at points, by generalizations based more on these assumptions than on presentations of evidence." Yet Brown found the work valuable for its factual content, remarking that "materials presented in this book are of greater interest and value than its assumptions and conclusions." Acknowledging that the study would have been stronger if Lee had considered such social issues as civil rights, housing, and inflation as they affected voters was Richard O. Davies, who nevertheless wrote in the *Journal of Southern History* that "Lee's best chapters are those which demonstrate how Truman manipulated the labor issue to his political advantage in 1948."

Despite any perceived errors in political analysis, the study has filled a gap in the historical literature. "Anyone interested in the life cycle of this national controversy will wish to consult Lee's book," Mayhew

predicted. This proved to be true, for in a 1991 review of Lee's follow-up work, Duane Tananbaum noted in the *Journal of American History* that *Truman and Taft-Hartley* "still stands as the definitive work on the Taft-Hartley Act." In *Eisenhower and Landrum-Griffin,* Lee conducted interviews, surveyed the existing literature, and "worked closely with the sources," noted Herbert S. Parmet in the *American Historical Review.* This work, which Parmet judged "equals in importance his earlier study of the Taft-Hartley Act," probes how the Eisenhower administration proposed bills to restrict the power of organized labor, including providing "a clear analysis of the workings of the conservative coalition." As Christopher L. Tomlins noted in the *Journal of Economic History,* "Lee's very readable book . . . written more or less by the same formula [as *Truman and Taft-Hartley*] is informative, insightful, and downright entertaining. . . . A political historian of traditional stripe, Lee is particularly acute on the details of partisan warfare, Congressional procedure, and lobbying." Yet, in Tomlins's view "Lee is much less successful when it comes to placing it [the act] in any structural or historical context. As a result, his conclusions are mundane and disappointing. In particular Lee makes no serious attempt to assess the impact of labor law on the organized labor movement." Even within its narrow focus, *Choice* reviewer D. Lindstrom predicted that, like its predecessor, *Eisenhower and Landrum-Griffin* "will be the definitive work" on the topic.

With *Dwight D. Eisenhower: Soldier and Statesman* and *Dwight D. Eisenhower: A Bibliography of His Times and Presidency,* Lee contributed to the literature on our thirty-fourth president. Lee paints the picture of Eisenhower as a product of his age, one who brought about calm after the chaos of the Korean War. Yet Lee criticizes Eisenhower for not stopping Joseph McCarthy from witch-hunting and for not supporting the efforts of the Supreme Court to end segregation. "By giving readers a concise account of Eisenhower's entire career, Lee fills an important gap in the existing literature," wrote Robert A. Divine in a collective review of books on Eisenhower for the *Journal of American History.* The work's enthusiasts included *American Historical Review* critic Parmet, who described the biography as "a smooth, useful synthesis of more than a decade of scholarship," and *History Teacher* contributor Gerald Horne, who wrote: "Professor Lee has accomplished his purpose of producing a comprehensive view of the life of Eisenhower that is a worthy addition to the historian's bookshelf."

After writing *T-Town on the Plains,* a history of his hometown of White City, Kansas, Lee penned the biography of an unusual man. John R. Brinkley was a con man, advertiser, and entrepreneur, who was known in the Plains states during the 1920s as "The Goat Doctor." Born and raised in poverty in Appalachian North Carolina, Brinkley was determined to make his fortune, which he did by studying medicine and making a career of male fertility treatments. He transplanted the gonads of goats into impotent men and earned a great following. He created a radio station that featured country music and his medical advice, becoming a target of the American Medical Association for his questionable medical practices. Drawing on archival material, Lee chronicles Brinkley's colorful career in "a lively manner" noted *Booklist* reviewer William Beatty. *Journal of American History* writer Angus McLaren also suggested that "readers with a penchant for the 'lives of the rich and famous' approach to biography should enjoy this study," for Lee details the extravagant manner in which Brinkley squandered his fortune, dying in poverty. Another enthusiast of the work was Garna L. Christian, who wrote in the *Journal of Southern History* that Brinkley created "a readable and insightful story of an individual more complex than his detractors knew or acknowledged," and that "the saga of this flawed genius is told with good humor, grudging respect, and considerable detail. Lee couches every issue in historical detail."

BIOGRAPHICAL AND CRITICAL SOURCES:

PERIODICALS

Agricultural History, fall, 2000, Virgil W. Dean, review of *T-Town on the Plains,* pp. 835-836.

American Historical Review, July, 1967, review of *Truman and Taft-Hartley: A Question of Mandate,* pp. 1518-1519; February, 1983, Herbert S. Parmet, review of *Dwight D. Eisenhower, Soldier and Statesman,* p. 215; April, 1991, Herbert S. Parmet, review of *Eisenhower and Landrum-Griffin: A Study in Labor-Management Politics,* p. 636.

American Political Science Review, September, 1976, Clara Penniman, review of *A History of Regulatory Taxation,* pp. 978-979.

Best Sellers, April, 1982, review of *Dwight D. Eisenhower, Soldier and Statesman,* p. 19.

Bloomsbury Review, July-August, 2002, Kim Long, review of *The Bizarre Careers of John R. Brinkley.*

Booklist, April 1, 2002, William Beatty, review of *The Bizarre Careers of John R. Brinkley,* pp. 1299-1300.

Business History Review, summer, 1990, review of *Eisenhower and Landrum-Griffin,* p. 343.

Choice, June, 1982, review of *Dwight D. Eisenhower, Soldier and Statesman,* p. 1480; June, 1990, D. Lindstrom, review of *Eisenhower and Landrum-Griffin;* March, 1991; October, 2002, review of *The Bizarre Careers of John R. Brinkley.*

Historian, August, 1983, review of *Dwight D. Eisenhower, Soldier and Statesman,* p. 598; May, 1998, review of *Agricultural Legacies: Essays in Honor of Gilbert C. Fite,* p. 449; summer, 1991, review of *Eisenhower and Landrum-Griffin,* p. 830.

History, spring, 1991, review of *Eisenhower and Landrum-Griffin,* p. 140.

History Teacher May, 1983, Gerald Horne, review of *Dwight D. Eisenhower, Soldier and Statesman,* pp. 442-443.

Industrial and Labor Relations Review, July, 1967, Emily Clark Brown, review of *Truman and Taft-Hartley,* pp. 715-716.

Journal of American Culture, winter, 1997, review of *Encyclopedia USA: The Encyclopedia of the United States of America Past and Present,* p. 114.

Journal of American History, June, 1967, David R. Mayhew, review of *Truman and Taft-Hartley,* pp. 197-198; March, 1975, Thomas K. McCraw, review of *A History of Regulatory Taxation,* pp. 1129-1130; December, 1982, Robert A. Divine, review of *Dwight D. Eisenhower, Soldier and Statesman,* pp. 768-770; December, 1987, Robert A. McGuire, review of *Agricultural Legacies,* pp. 1037-1038; March, 1991, Duane Tananbaum, review of *Eisenhower and Landrum-Griffen,* pp. 1422-1423; March, 1993, James N. Giglio, review of *Dwight D. Eisenhower: A Bibliography of His Times and Presidency,* pp. 1714-1717; February, 2004, Angus McLaren, review of *The Bizarre Careers of John R. Brinkley.*

Journal of Economic History, September, 1991, Christopher L. Tomlins, review of *Eisenhower and Landrum-Griffin,* pp. 741-743.

Journal of Southern History, August, 1967, Richard O. Davies, review of *Truman and Traft-Hartley,* pp. 430-431; May, 1988, John T. Schlebecker, review of *Agricultural Legacies,* pp. 372-374; November, 2003, Garna L. Christian, review of *The Bizarre Careers of John R. Brinkley,* pp. 971-972.

Presidential Studies Quarterly, fall, 1991, review of *Eisenhower and Landrum-Griffin,* p. 781; fall,

1992, review of *Dwight D. Eisenhower: A Bibliography of His Times and Presidency,* pp. 821-822.

Publishers Weekly, March 11, 2002, review of *The Bizarre Careers of John R. Brinkley,* p. 63.

Reference & Research Book News, February, 1992, review of *Dwight D. Eisenhower: A Bibliography of His Times and Presidency,* p. 9.

RQ, summer, 1993, review of *Dwight D. Eisenhower: A Bibliography of His Times and Presidency,* pp. 492-493.

Sun (Baltimore, MD), April 21, 2002, Michael Pakenham, review of *The Bizarre Careers of John R. Brinkley,* p. 10E.

University Press Book News, March, 1990, review of *Eisenhower and Landrum-Griffin,* p. 16.

Virginia Quarterly Review, winter, 1991, review of *Eisenhower and Landrum-Griffin,* p. 24.

Wall Street Journal, May 24, 2002, review of *The Bizarre Careers of John R. Brinkley,* p. W11.

Western Historical Quarterly, October, 1987, review of *Agricultural Legacies,* p. 438.

Wilson Library Bulletin, December, 1991, review of *Dwight D. Eisenhower: A Bibliography of His Times and Presidency,* p. 123.*

* * *

LEONARD, Hugh
See BYRNE, John Keyes

* * *

LEONARD, Kathy S. 1952-

PERSONAL: Born December 20, 1952, in CA; daughter of Jerome C. and Kathleen M. Leonard. *Ethnicity:* "Caucasian." *Education:* Attended University of Madrid, Spain, 1972-73; University of California, Riverside, B.A. (Spanish), 1974; California Standard Elementary Teaching Credential, 1975; Bilingual Cross-Cultural Specialist Credential, 1978; Santa Clara University, M.A. (bilingual education), 1979; California Community College, Credential (basic education), 1979; University of Nevada, Reno, B.A. (fine arts), 1983; University of Arizona, Tucson, studied at Institute of Court Interpreting, 1983; California Community College, Credential (Spanish), 1985; University of California, Davis, Ph.D. (Hispanic linguistics), 1991. Studied and conducted research in Bolivia, Argentina, Mexico, Italy, Guatemala, and Spain.

ADDRESSES: Home—2103 Prairie View E., Ames, IA 50010. *Office*—Iowa State University, 300 Pearson Hall, Ames, IA 50010. *E-mail*—kleonard@iastate.edu.

CAREER: Hollister Unified School District, CA, first- and second-grade teacher of bilingual students, 1975-78; Washoe County Municipal Court, Reno, NV, court interpreter on call, 1979-83; Yolo County Municipal Court, Woodland, CA, court interpreter on call, 1979-83; University of Reno, Reno, NV, lecturer, 1981-83; University of California, Davis, associate instructor, 1983-90, instructor, summers of 1985-89; Dixon High School, Dixon, CA, high school teacher of advanced Spanish, 1984; Yuba Community College, Woodland, CA, instructor, 1986-91; Universidad de la Plata, Buenos Aires, Argentina, instructor of English as a second language, 1990; Holmes Junior High School, Davis, Spanish teacher for seventh-and eighth-grade students, 1991; Iowa State University, Ames, assistant professor, 1991-97, associate professor of Spanish, Hispanic linguistics, and Latin American literature, 1997-2002, professor of Spanish, 2002—. Participant in conferences and workshops. Volunteer teacher of disadvantaged children and volunteer interpreter for Central American refugees.

MEMBER: American Literary Translators Association, Modern Language Association, Midwest Modern Language Association, Iowa Foreign Language Association, Association of Teachers of Spanish and Portuguese.

AWARDS, HONORS: Rotary International fellow, 1990; LASRI summer salary grant, Iowa State University, 1992; visiting scholar, National Endowment for the Humanities summer seminar at University of Texas, Austin, and University of the Americas, Cholula, Mexico, 1992; foreign travel grant and university research grant, Iowa State University, 1992-93; incentive grant for curriculum internationalization, Iowa State University, 1993-94; instructional development grant, Iowa State University, 1994-95, 1996; research fellow and visiting scholar in Latin American studies, Cornell/Pittsburgh Consortium, Cornell University, 1995; Text and Academic Authors Association grant, 1995; travel grant, Iowa State University, 1995; special research initiation grant, Iowa State University, 1995; faculty improvement leave, 1995-96; Iowa State University Foundation Award, 1996, for early achievement in undergraduate teaching; travel grants and special opportunity grant, Center for Teaching Excellence, 1997; Wakonse fellow, 1997; Fulbright-Hays grant, 1998; Culture Corps grant, 1998, 1999, 2003, 2003-04, 2005; grant, Council on Scholarship in the Humanities, 1999; Casa Hispànica Learning Community grant, 1999, 2001-02; Council on Scholarship in the Humanities grant, 2000-03; travel grant, 2000-02; National Endowment for the Humanities grant, 2001-02, 2003; named honorary member, Uniòn Cultural Palas Atenea, 2002; Phillip G. Hubbard Award for Educational Excellence nomination, Iowa State University, 2002; designated Master Teacher for experiential learning abroad, LAS College and Center for Teaching Excellence, 2002-03.

WRITINGS:

EDITOR

(And translator) *Cruel Fictions, Cruel Realities: Short Stories by Latin-American Women Writers,* foreword by Aria Maria Shua, Latin American Literary Review Press (Pittsburgh, PA), 1997.
Index to Translated Short Fiction by Latin-American Women in English-Language Anthologies, Greenwood Press (Westport, CT), 1997.
(And translator with Susan E. Benner) *Fire from the Andes: Short Fiction by Women from Bolivia, Ecuador, and Peru,* University of New Mexico Press (Albuquerque, NM), 1998.

TRANSLATOR

Giancarla de Quiroga, *Aurora* (translation of novel *La flor de "la candelaria"*), Women in Translation (Seattle, WA), 1999.

Contributor of translations to books, including *Language and Culture in Learning: Teaching Spanish to Native Speakers of Spanish,* edited by Barbara J. Merino, Henry R. Trueba, and Fabian Samaniego, Falmer Press (Washington, DC), 1993; *Conversations with Susan Sontag,* edited by Leland Poague, University Press of Mississippi (Jackson, MS), 1995; and *The Movies: Texts, Receptions, Exposures,* edited by Laurence Goldstein and Ira Konigsberg, University of Michigan Press (Ann Arbor, MI), 1996. Translations of short stories have appeared in periodicals, including *American Voice, Antigonish Review, Calyx, Critical Matrix, Feminist Studies, Flyway, Michigan Quarterly Review, Puerto del Sol,* and *Xavier Review.*

OTHER

Una revelacion desde la escritura. Entrevistas a poetas bolivianas (title means "A Literary Revelation: Interviews with Bolivian Women Authors"), Peter Lang (New York, NY), 2001.

Sentir lo oscuro, La Hoguera Editorial (Santa Cruz, Bolivia), 2002.
Bibliographic Guide to Chicana and Latina Narrative, Praeger (Westport, CT), 2003.

Contributor to books, including *Visions and Reality in Foreign-Language Teaching: Where We Are, Where We Are Going. Report of Central States Conference on the Teaching of Foreign Languages,* National Textbook Company (Chicago, IL), 1993; and *Geography del cuerpo: Aproximaciones a la obra de Marjorie Agosin,* edited by Emma Sepulveda, Cuarto Propio (Santiago, Chile), 1997. Contributor to periodicals, including *Americas Review, Chasqui, Hispamerica: Revista de Literatura 75, Hispania, ERIC Digest, Innovations Abstracts, Modern Language Journal,* and Dartmouth College *Ram's Horn.*

SIDELIGHTS: Kathy S. Leonard is an associate professor of Spanish, Hispanic linguistics, and literature at Iowa State University. She has taught at the elementary school, junior high, and high school levels and has worked as a volunteer teacher of disadvantaged children and as a volunteer interpreter for Central American refugees. In addition to her other writing, Leonard has translated short stories and essays from English into Spanish and from Spanish into English.

Leonard has traveled the world researching the writings of Latin-American women. She edited and translated *Cruel Fictions, Cruel Realities: Short Stories by Latin-American Women Writers,* a collection of nineteen stories by twelve women from South American countries. "These short stories are superbly written," observed Lisa Rohrbaugh in *Library Journal.* Each of the stories deals with cruelty, and most are "marked by heavy doses of magic realism or black humor," explained Nancy Pearl in a review for *Booklist.* The stories include "The Sailor's Wife," by Silvia Diaz Fierro, a tale of a man who loves a mermaid, and a story by Ines Fernandez Moreno about a mother whose children's needs deprive her of her body parts. *World Literature Today* contributor Naomi Lindstrom noted that the works in *Cruel Fictions* "are well written," commenting that the volume "succeeds in being different and surprising," and advising that "anyone whose familiarity with Spanish American women's writing is through translation should take a look at Leonard's anthology."

The growth of women's studies programs has also led to an increased interest in the writings of Latin-American women. Leonard edited *Index to Translated Short Fiction by Latin-American Women in English-Language Anthologies,* a guide to Spanish and Portuguese fiction published in over one hundred anthologies from 1918 to 1996. With Susan E. Benner, Leonard also edited and translated *Fire from the Andes: Short Fiction by Women from Bolivia, Ecuador, and Peru. Fire from the Andes* features short stories by twenty-four contemporary female writers from the three countries referenced in the book's title. It includes biographical information about the authors, bibliographies featuring literature from Bolivia, Ecuador, and Peru, and "an excellent bibliography" listing short stories written in Spanish, according to *Library Journal* contributor Mary Margaret Benson. Benson commented that "the stories, for the most part dark, center on women's interior lives." *Fire from the Andes* contains Ecuadorian Monica Bravo's story of an old woman who knits memories of her past into a shroud, Bolivian Marcella Gutierrez's contemporary account of the biblical figures of Adam, Eve, and Lilith, and Peruvian Pilar Dughi's tale of a woman who becomes a terrorist.

BIOGRAPHICAL AND CRITICAL SOURCES:

PERIODICALS

Americas, April, 2000, Barbara Mujica, review of *Aurora,* p. 62.

Booklist, August, 1997, Nancy Pearl, review of *Cruel Fictions, Cruel Realities: Short Stories by Latin-American Women Writers,* p. 1876.

Library Journal, September 15, 1997, Lisa Rohrbaugh, review of *Cruel Fictions, Cruel Realities,* p. 105; February 1, 1998, Mary Margaret Benson, review of *Fire from the Andes: Short Fiction by Women from Bolivia, Ecuador, and Peru,* p. 114.

Review of Contemporary Fiction, spring, 1998, Robert Headley, review of *Cruel Fictions, Cruel Realities,* p. 252.

World Literature Today, spring, 1998, Naomi Lindstrom, review of *Cruel Fictions, Cruel Realities,* pp. 345-346.

LEVINSON, Barry 1942-

PERSONAL: Born April 6, 1942, in Baltimore, MD; son of Irv (in appliance business) and Vi (Krichinsky) Levinson; married Valerie Curtin (a screenwriter and actress; divorced, 1982); married Diana Mona (an artist); children: Jack, Sam, Patrick Mona, Michelle Mona. *Education:* Attended Community College of Baltimore and American University. *Politics:* Democrat.

ADDRESSES: Office—Baltimore Pictures, 5555 Melrose Ave., Los Angeles, CA 90038. *Agent*—Creative Artists Agency, 9830 Wilshire Blvd., Beverly Hills, CA 90212.

CAREER: Actor, producer, director, and writer. Member of standup comedy and writing team with actor Craig T. Nelson, c. 1969-72; actor in television shows, including *The Lohman and Barkley Show,* 1969, *The Tim Conway Comedy Hour,* 1970, and *The Carol Burnett Show,* 1974-75. Actor in motion pictures, including *Silent Movie,* 1976, *High Anxiety,* 1978, and *History of the World, Part I,* 1981. Director of motion pictures, including *The Natural,* 1984, *Young Sherlock Holmes,* 1985, *Good Morning, Vietnam,* 1987, *Rain Man,* 1988, *Bugsy,* 1991, *Disclosure,* 1994, *Wag the Dog,* 1997, and *Bandits,* 2001. Director and producer of television productions, including *Homicide: Life on the Street,* NBC, beginning 1993. Baltimore Pictures (production company), Hollywood, CA, founder and president, beginning 1989.

MEMBER: Directors Guild of America, Writers Guild of America, Screen Actors Guild.

AWARDS, HONORS: Emmy Awards, Academy of Television Arts and Sciences, best writing in a variety or music program, 1974 and 1975, and outstanding achievement in a comedy, variety, or music series, 1976, all for *The Carol Burnett Show;* Academy of Motion Picture Arts and Sciences, Academy Award nominations, best original screenplay, 1979, for . . . *And Justice for All,* and 1982, for *Diner,* Academy Award, best director, 1988, for *Rain Man,* Academy Award nomination, best original screenplay, 1990, for *Avalon,* and Academy Award nomination, best director, 1991, for *Bugsy;* award for outstanding achievement, Directors Guild of America, 1988, for *Rain Man.*

Barry Levinson

WRITINGS:

Sixty-Six (novel), Broadway Books (New York, NY), 2003.

SCREENPLAYS

(With Mel Brooks, Ron Clark, and Rudy DeLuca) *Silent Movie,* Twentieth Century-Fox, 1976.

(With Mel Brooks, Ron Clark, and Rudy DeLuca) *High Anxiety,* Twentieth Century-Fox, 1978.

(With Valerie Curtin) *. . . And Justice for All,* Columbia, 1979.

(With Valerie Curtin) *Inside Moves,* Associated Film Distributors, 1980.

(With Valerie Curtin) *Best Friends,* Warner Bros., 1982.

(And director) *Diner,* Metro-Goldwyn-Mayer/United Artists, 1982.

(With Valerie Curtin and Robert Klane) *Unfaithfully Yours* (adapted from Preston Sturges's film of the same title), Twentieth Century-Fox, 1984.

(And director) *Tin Men,* Buena Vista, 1987.

(And director) *Avalon,* TriStar, 1990.

(With Valerie Curtin; and producer and director) *Toys,* Twentieth Century-Fox, 1992.

(And producer and director) *Jimmy Hollywood,* Paramount, 1994.

(And director) *Sleepers* (based on a book by Lorenzo Carcaterra), Warner Bros., 1996.

(And director) *Liberty Heights,* Baltimore Pictures (Hollywood, CA), 1999.

TELEVISION SERIES

(With Craig T. Nelson and others) *The Lohman and Barkley Show,* NBC-TV, 1969.

(With Craig T. Nelson and others) *The Tim Conway Comedy Hour,* CBS-TV, 1970.

(With Craig T. Nelson and others) *The Marty Feldman Comedy Machine,* ABC-TV, 1972.

(With Craig T. Nelson and others) *The John Byner Comedy Hour,* CBS-TV, 1972.

(With others) *The Carol Burnett Show,* CBS-TV, 1974–75.

SIDELIGHTS: Barry Levinson is a prominent film-maker who emerged at the forefront of American cinema in the 1980s. He began his show business career in the late 1960s as a comedian partnered with Craig T. Nelson, who later went on to considerable ac-claim as a motion picture and television actor (most notably with the popular sitcom *Coach*). That stint led, in turn, to work as a writer for the television series *The Lohman and Barkley Show.* Throughout the early 1970s Levinson remained active in television as a writer on such shows as *The Tim Conway Comedy Hour* and *The Marty Feldman Comedy Machine.* In 1974 Levinson became a writer for *The Carol Burnett Show,* which later won an Emmy Award as the medium's best comedy program.

While writing for *The Carol Burnett Show* Levinson also began working as a screenwriter. He first col-laborated on the script for Mel Brooks's 1976 comedy *Silent Movie,* a broad farce about a band of bungling filmmakers, then he contributed to the screenplay for Brooks's *High Anxiety,* a spoof of film director Alfred Hitchcock's many celebrated thrillers, including *Vertigo, The Birds,* and *Psycho.*

Levinson followed these films with a series of screenplays written with his wife at the time, Valerie Curtin. The couple's first joint effort as screenwriters,

. . . *And Justice for All,* was a broad, but essentially black, comedy about America's legal system. This film, directed by Norman Jewison, features a suicidal judge (who lunches while sitting on an upper-story window ledge and performs bodily functions while holding a shotgun to his mouth), a criminal judge (who gleefully confesses his guilt in committing rape), and a good-hearted, somewhat beleaguered attorney (who is compelled, against his better judgment, to defend the despicable judge). The movie was not without its detractors, some of whom decried its seemingly overwhelming nature. *Washington Post* contributor Gary Arnold, for example, proclaimed the comedy "grotesque." But the film did have its supporters within the Hollywood film community, members of which saw fit to accord . . . *And Justice for All* an Academy Award nomination for best original screenplay.

Levinson and Curtin continued with *Inside Moves,* an ultimately inspirational film—directed by Richard Donner—about the denizens of a blue-collar bar. This film, with principal characters such as a survivor of a suicide attempt, an aspiring basketball player, and a prostitute, was described by *New York Times* contributor Janet Maslin as "modest and sentimental."

In 1982 Levinson made his debut as writer-director with *Diner,* a comedy about a band of five misfits in Baltimore in the 1950s. Each of the men in this group is somewhat inept socially. Eddie, for instance, is a football fanatic who is so ambivalent about his wedding engagement that he subjects his fiance to an extended series of sports questions; if she fails to answer correctly, the marriage plans end. The gangly Shrevie is already married, but relations with his wife are dull and unstimulating, and he finds himself longing for a time when sex was mysterious and exciting. Boogie, a sexually rambunctious beautician, is the most worldly of the five protagonists but the least inclined to succeed. Similarly, the relatively rich Fenwick possesses a sardonic wit that only occasionally conceals a bent for self-destruction, but he also shows himself—in a particularly funny sequence—to be surprisingly informed. Rounding out the group is Billy, a good-natured fellow frustrated by his inability to persuade his pregnant girlfriend into marriage. All the main characters in *Diner* are still maturing, and that process itself constitutes the action of the film. As Gene Siskel wrote in the *Chicago Tribune,* "There's a lot more growing to be done, and that growing—or failure to grow—is what *Diner* is made of."

Best Friends is a Levinson-Curtin comedy (also directed by Norman Jewison) about a screenwriting couple who undermine their loving relationship by getting married. Despite the presence of popular box-office performers Goldie Hawn and Burt Reynolds, *Best Friends* proved only intermittently funny to many critics.

Levinson and Curtin teamed up again for *Unfaithfully Yours,* an updating of director Preston Sturges's classic comedy about an orchestra conductor who mistakenly suspects his wife of infidelity. Some reviewers objected to the new film's slower pacing and streamlined narrative. In the *Chicago Tribune,* Siskel, for example, accused the film's director, Howard Zieff, of trying "to top a reasonably good film by simplifying it, by removing some of its story." *Time* critic Richard Schickel, however, proclaimed that the Levinson-Curtin version "scores a narrow but clean win over one's nostalgic sentiment for [Sturges's] original." He added that the remake "reminds you of Hollywood's good old days without making you mourn for them."

In 1984 Levinson resumed his directorial career with *The Natural,* screenwriter Robert Towne's adaptation of Bernard Malamud's acclaimed baseball novel. The film features Robert Redford as Roy Hobbs, a once promising pitcher who is slowly making a comeback as a slugger. Hobbs had been a major-league candidate when his career suddenly ended after he was wounded by a deranged woman. But sixteen years later he appears again as the major league's oldest rookie. With his hand-carved bat, Hobbs produces several dramatic hits and soon has his team contending for the championship.

The Natural, a significant success with the moviegoing public, marked something of a comeback—or rather, a return to activity—for Redford, who had worked only sporadically in Hollywood after winning an Academy Award for his directorial debut, *Ordinary People. The Natural* confirmed to reviewers Levinson's status as a director with a particular flair for characterization and peculiarly American subject matter.

Following the success of *The Natural,* Levinson was engaged to direct *Young Sherlock Holmes,* which features writer Arthur Conan Doyle's legendary sleuth as a schoolboy determined to undo an evil band inhabiting a temple beneath London. Although *Young*

Sherlock Holmes bears little in common with Levinson's previous works, it nonetheless proved an appealing and accomplished work and a substantial favorite with filmgoers.

Levinson returned to his native Baltimore for *Tin Men,* his second film as writer-director. This comedy concerns the rivalry between two aluminum-siding con artists during the summer of 1963. The principals, Bill Babowsky and Ernest Tilley, quickly become mutual antagonists after meeting in an automobile accident: Tilley has damaged Babowsky's car, and Babowsky vows revenge against his fellow home-improvement hustler. He steals the affections of Tilley's attractive wife, Nora, and thereupon proclaims himself triumphant. But when Tilley learns of the affair he confesses himself glad to be rid of his wife, whereupon Babowsky finds himself in an emotional quagmire. While this rivalry ensues, both men see their profession threatened by the Maryland Home Improvement Commission, which is conducting an investigation of unethical practices.

Reviewers found *Tin Men* an inventive, well-made comedy. *Newsweek* contributor David Ansen deemed the film "a very American comedy" and "a solid, smart piece of work," and he concluded that "its evocatively mixed moods seem a response to life—not just to some old movie formula." A *Nation* reviewer noted its "middle-aged wisdom." Another enthusiastic reviewer, Sheila Benson of the *Los Angeles Times* called *Tin Men* one of the year's "most insightful and human American comedies."

In 1987 Levinson directed *Good Morning, Vietnam,* an offbeat comedy-drama about a comic radio broadcaster's experiences during the Vietnam war. This film, written by Mitch Markowitze, depicts the wartime exploits of Adrian Cronauer (based on an actual figure of the same name), who is expelled from Saigon after providing broadcasts too critical of America's wartime policies and activities. Cronauer is played by Robin Williams, a frequently manic comic who gained increasing acclaim in the 1980s as an actor. *Maclean's* reviewer Lawrence O'Toole noted that with "the wild-spirited Cronauer, Williams finds a role around which he can wrap his prodigious comic talents." O'Toole also reported that director Levinson "deftly meshes the comic and dramatic tones."

After completing *Good Morning, Vietnam,* Levinson directed *Rain Man,* an often funny film written by Barry Morrow and Ronald Bass about two brothers,

one of whom is autistic, as they travel from Cincinnati to Los Angeles. The older brother, Raymond, is an autistic savant: he is incapable of emotionally connecting with others, but he is in possession of computer-like recall and near-instantaneous mathematical capability. Charlie, Raymond's younger brother, is a cynical opportunist who intends to parlay Raymond's extraordinary mathematical flair into quick riches in Las Vegas's gambling casinos. *Nation* contributor Stuart Klawans described *Rain Man* as "a buddy picture with one buddy missing, a road movie without much to see along the way." But during their travels together Charlie comes to love his autistic brother, and Raymond, in return, seems to realize a simple affection—or, at least, a comfortable familiarity—for Charlie.

In 1990 Levinson returned again to Baltimore with *Avalon,* the story of an immigrant family from 1914 to the mid-1960s, which Levinson wrote and directed. This film, which Levinson based on memories related by his grandfather, was found by some reviewers to be heartwarming, even somewhat inspirational, in its depiction of immigrant life during much of the twentieth century. *Avalon* proved only lukewarm at theater box-offices, however, and although it received an Academy Award nomination for best original screenplay, it remains one of Levinson's lesser-appreciated works.

After the commercial disappointment of *Avalon,* Levinson agreed to direct *Bugsy,* which showcases Warren Beatty as the quirky Bugsy Siegel, a gangster who ingratiated—or intimidated—his way into Hollywood and, eventually, Las Vegas, before meeting an untimely, violent demise. *Bugsy* gained a fair measure of acclaim, impressing reviewers with Beatty's uncharacteristically unsettling portrayal, and earned Levinson an Academy Award nomination for best director.

Less successful for Levinson was *Toys,* his next venture as writer-director. This special-effects-rich film—written by Levinson with Curtin (the pair had divorced ten years earlier)—concerns a naive toy lover's efforts to wrestle management of a family-owned toy factory from a cynical, opportunistic relative. Despite the presence of popular comic actor Robin Williams, *Toys* failed to find substantial favor with critics or the public. The costly film was the realization of a longtime goal, however.

The movie *Jimmy Hollywood,* scripted and directed by Levinson, evokes qualities of the filmmaker's earlier, most-heralded efforts. In telling the story of a Hollywood lowlife and aspiring actor turned vigilante, Levinson "is back in the small, low-budget, personal mode of *Diner* and *Tin Men,*" according to Ansen in *Newsweek. New Yorker* contributor Anthony Lane also made this observation, noting Levinson's return to a previous style of "rough edges and loose tongues." Ansen remarked that *Jimmy Hollywood* "has the bittersweet, unexpected flavors of a personal vision."

In 1994, Levinson lent his directorial skills to *Disclosure,* the film adaptation of author Michael Crichton's best-selling novel. Set in the high-tech world of a major computer software corporation, the film pits its male protagonist against a scheming female executive. Wrapped into the multileveled story are elements of corporate espionage, virtual reality technology, and accusations of sexual harassment—with a twist. A success at the box-office, *Disclosure* further confirmed Levinson's credentials as a director of major feature films.

Levinson then wrote and directed the film *Sleepers,* which is adapted from the memoirs of Lorenzo Carcaterra. The story centers around four friends who are members of a youth gang in Hell's Kitchen. When their troublesome exploits land them in a reform school, they are subjected to repeated humiliation and sexual abuse from the guards. The bulk of the film takes place after the boys have grown to adulthood. Two of them, having chosen crime as their vocation, track down the guards and murder them. When they are placed on trial for the act, a third member of the gang, now an assistant district attorney, is assigned to try the case.

BIOGRAPHICAL AND CRITICAL SOURCES:

PERIODICALS

American Film, June, 1982.

Chicago Tribune, October 19, 1979; July 2, 1982, Gene Siskel, review of *Diner;* February 10, 1984, Gene Siskel, review of *Unfaithfully Yours;* March 15, 1987.
Chicago Tribune Arts, October 21, 1990, p. 8.
Detroit Free Press, March 13, 1987.
Entertainment Weekly, May 5, 1995, p. 54.
Esquire Film Quarterly, October, 1982.
Los Angeles Times, May 7, 1982; December 16, 1982; February 10, 1984; March 6, 1987, Sheila Benson, review of *Tin Men.*
Maclean's, January 4, 1988, Lawrence O'Toole, review of *Good Morning, Vietnam,* p. 61.
Nation, April 4, 1987, review of *Tin Men;* January 9, 1989, Stuart Klawans, review of *Rain Man.*
New Republic, January 9, 1989, pp. 24-25.
Newsweek, March 2, 1987, David Ansen, review of *Tin Men,* p. 78; January 4, 1988, pp. 50-51; December 19, 1988, p. 57; January 16, 1989, pp. 52-56; April 11, 1994, David Ansen, review of *Jimmy Hollywood,* p. 74.
New Yorker, January 11, 1988; April 4, 1994, Anthony Lane, review of *Jimmy Hollywood,* pp. 97-98.
New York Times, December 19, 1980, Janet Maslin, review of *Inside Moves;* April 2, 1982; December 17, 1982; February 10, 1984; March 6, 1987; March 15, 1987; September 15, 1989.
New York Times Magazine, March 11, 1990.
Rolling Stone, May 13, 1982; January 12, 1989; April 21, 1994, p. 95.
Time, February 20, 1984, Richard Schickel, review of *Unfaithfully Yours;* May 14, 1987.
Washington Post, October 19, 1979, Gary Arnold, review of *. . . And Justice for All;* May 14, 1982; February 15, 1984; March 13, 1987.*

*   *   *

LINN, Margot
See ZIEFERT, Harriet

*   *   *

LLOSA, (Jorge) Mario (Pedro) Vargas
See VARGAS LLOSA, (Jorge) Mario (Pedro)

M

MacKINNON, Catharine A. 1946-

PERSONAL: Born October 7, 1946; daughter of George E. and Elizabeth V. (Davis) MacKinnon. *Education:* Smith College, B.A. (magna cum laude), 1969; Yale University, J.D., 1977, Ph.D., 1987.

ADDRESSES: Office—c/o Sandy Springer, University of Michigan Law School, 625 South State Street, Ann Arbor, MI 48109-1215.

CAREER: Lawyer, legal scholar, educator, author, consultant to committees writing civil laws against pornography and other forms of sexual abuse and inequality, and political activist. Admitted to the bar of Connecticut State, 1978; visiting professor of law at Yale University, Harvard University, Stanford University, University of California, Los Angeles, and University of Chicago—Columbia, 1980-2002; assistant professor of law at University of Minnesota, 1982-84; professor of law at York University, Toronto, Ontario, Canada, 1988-90; University of Michigan School of Law, Ann Arbor, MI, professor of law then Elizabeth A. Long Professor of Law, 1989—.

Catharine A. MacKinnon

WRITINGS:

Sexual Harassment of Working Women: A Case of Sex Discrimination, Yale University Press (New Haven, CT), 1979.

Feminism Unmodified: Discourses on Life and Law, Harvard University Press (Cambridge MA), 1987.

(With Andrea Dworkin) *Pornography and Civil Rights: A New Day for Women's Equality,* Organizing against Pornography (Minneapolis, MN), 1988.

Toward a Feminist Theory of the State, Harvard University Press (Cambridge, MA), 1989.

Only Words, Harvard University Press (Cambridge, MA), 1993.

(With Andrea Dworkin) *In Harm's Way: The Pornography Civil Rights Hearings,* Harvard University Press (Cambridge, MA), 1997.

Sex Equality, Foundation Press (New York, NY), 2001.

(Editor, with Reva B. Siegel) *Directions in Sexual Harassment Law,* Yale University Press (New Haven, CT), 2004.

Women's Lives, Men's Laws, Belknap Press of Harvard University (Cambridge, MA), 2005.

Author has contributed numerous articles to academic journals and popular magazines and newspapers, including the *Encyclopedia of the American Constitution, Tocqueville Review,* and the *New York Times.* Also contributor to numerous legal books, including *Law and Language,* edited by T. Morawetz, Ashgate, 2000; *Theorizing Feminism: Parallel Trends in the Humanities and Social Sciences,* 2nd edition, edited by A. C. Herrmann and A. J. Stewart, Westview Press, 2001; and *Animal Rights: Current Debates and New Directions,* edited by C. R. Sunstein and M. C. Nussbaum, Oxford University Press, 2004.

SIDELIGHTS: Catharine A. MacKinnon, a feminist author, activist, and legal scholar, ranks among the most original and controversial social theorists in the United States. MacKinnon broke new legal ground in the late 1970s by arguing that the sexual harassment of women in the workplace constitutes a form of sex discrimination in violation of existing civil rights statutes. MacKinnon's thesis, elaborated fully in her 1979 book *Sexual Harassment of Working Women: A Case of Sex Discrimination,* has won wide acceptance in the courtroom and become an important weapon in fighting the mistreatment of working women.

MacKinnon subsequently directed her efforts toward combating pornography. In 1983, she and her colleague, author Andrea Dworkin, helped draft an antipornography ordinance for the city of Indianapolis, Indiana. The ordinance made it possible for people who could prove harm to sue for the sexually explicit subordination of women through pictures or words as a form of sex discrimination. The ordinance was supported politically and in litigation by women and men of many political persuasions, as well as by grassroots feminist organizations, scholars, civil rights activists, lawyers, and survivors of sexual assault. The Indianapolis ordinance (and a similar law MacKinnon and Dworkin drafted for Minneapolis, Minnesota, and

passed twice by the city council) was opposed, however, by some legal scholars, civil libertarians, and a few feminists, who argued that it amounted to state censorship. A federal appeals court struck down the ordinance as an unconstitutional violation of free speech, a result upheld without opinion by the U.S. Supreme Court.

MacKinnon outlines her views on the pornography issue and responds to opponents in *Pornography and Civil Rights,* which she wrote with Dworkin, in *Feminism Unmodified: Discourses on Life and Law,* a collection of speeches delivered from 1981 to 1986, and in *Only Words,* in 1993. In brief, the author defines pornography as the sexual subordination of women to men; argues that it constitutes, reinforces, and perpetuates male dominance throughout society and is thus a form of sex-based discrimination. MacKinnon observes that much pornography requires for its making—and produces through its use—rape and other acts of sexual sadism and aggression against women as well as bigotry and hatred toward women throughout society. Recognizing the human rights violations caused by pornography is thus not an issue of art or morality, but one of treating women as equals.

This thesis has drawn both criticism and support across the political spectrum. Some conservatives have opposed MacKinnon's attacks on male social and sexual dominance. Among liberals are those who question a causal link between pornography and the abuse of women. MacKinnon argues that the link between pornography and sexual inequality is indisputable and refers to overwhelming empirical support. She asserts in *Feminism Unmodified* that pornographers act as the shock troops for male domination by making the female body into a thing for sexual use. Dehumanized and humiliated in a way that is sexualized, women also become targets of violence and discrimination, both in pornography and in other aspects of life. Hence, MacKinnon wrote, pornography—by subordinating women—is "more act-like than thought-like" and free speech concerns are misplaced. "Pornography isn't protected by the First Amendment any more than sexual harassment is," the author remarked to *New York Times* interviewer Tamar Lewin. "It's not a question of free speech or ideas. Pornography is a form of action."

Feminism Unmodified received varying critical responses. *Nation* contributor Maureen Mullarkey, for example, criticized *Feminism Unmodified* as relying on "slogans, false premises, half-information, sinister innuendo and ad-hoc reasoning." Expressing a highly favorable opinion in the *New York Times Book Review* was political philosopher Alison Jaggar, who described the book as "an unorthodox but relentlessly consistent perspective on issues fundamental to feminism" and praised it as "passionate, brilliant, [and] polemical."

MacKinnon's contributions to feminist and social theory have by no means been limited to her opposition to pornography. The speeches in *Feminism Unmodified* also address issues of abortion, rape, women's athletics, sexual harassment, and the rights of Native American women; and *Toward a Feminist Theory of the State,* published in 1989, outlines a unified political/social/sexual theory of male domination. MacKinnon reconceptualizes equality from its traditional approach focusing on sameness and difference to an analysis of dominance and subordination.

In *Only Words,* MacKinnon tackles the issue of circumstances in which forms of expression (specifically sexually explicit words or photographs that subordinate men or women) can be considered active. She makes her case through three passionate and exceptionally well-researched essays. The essays criticize the legal protection of pornography compared with sexual harassment and with racial discrimination and other forms of abuse that are not protected as speech, despite being words. A *Kirkus Reviews* critic describes MacKinnon's essays as "passionate [and] intellectually fascinating." The reviewer goes on to say that though MacKinnon's conviction sometimes causes her ideas to elide, "the ideas are original and gripping, her references are wide-ranging, her legal logic is provocative."

In Harm's Way: The Pornography Civil Rights Hearings compiles the oral testimony of victims of pornography. Cass Sunstein, reviewing this volume for *Law and Philosophy,* summarized its value as "an important addition for academics and for others to the pornography debate." *In Harm's Way,* Sunstein noted, presents both sides of the debate, including pornography opponents, social science experts, and authorities on abuse and prostitution, as well as advocates of unfettered freedom of speech.

Throughout her writings, MacKinnon attacks "liberal feminism" for limiting its objectives to helping a few women "succeed" in male terms instead of addressing

the roots of male domination. She is more concerned with subverting the male-biased definitions of gender and social realities of inequality that she believes permeate society and perpetuate male supremacy in a way that damages all women and some men. MacKinnon considers issues of race and class as integral to the social/sexual equation. As a tenured professor at the University of Michigan Law School, MacKinnon is expected by observers to remain at the forefront of legal scholarship.

In 2001, MacKinnon's law school casebook *Sex Equality* was published. The book focuses on sexual harassment both in the work place and in education. Beginning with an examination of conventional sex equality law and theory, MacKinnon goes on to analyze the problem in context of the social and cultural environment and issues not generally encompassed within the laws concerning sex discrimination. From a discussion of the Western standards for equality based on the philosophy of Aristotle to a movement of international law away from this standard, MacKinnon probes a wide range of social and legal issues. For example, she discusses how rape is sometimes looked at as a type of torture or genocide in international law. Writing in *off our backs,* Carol Anne Douglas said she "was mistakenly daunted" when she saw that the publication was a casebook that included court decisions and comments. However, she noted that the author "has produced an astounding book on sex equality." Douglas also said, "This book is fascinating and incredibly valuable, a crowning achievement in MacKinnon's brilliant career as well as a great resource for the feminist movement. It should be widely read for many years, until sex equality is a reality." MacKinnon also served as coeditor with Reva B. Siegel of *Directions in Sexual Harassment Law,* which contains thirty-seven essays from various experts in the field of sexual harassment law and litigation. Philip Y. Blue, writing in *Library Journal,* noted, "As much an overview of the psychological construction of women's resistance to sexual harassment as its legal counterpart, this book forms an excellent compilation of the latest thought and research."

BIOGRAPHICAL AND CRITICAL SOURCES:

BOOKS

MacKinnon, Catharine A., *Feminism Unmodified: Discourses on Life and Law,* Harvard University Press (Cambridge MA), 1987.

PERIODICALS

Commentary, September, 1993, Carol Iannone, review of *Only Words,* p. 51.

Detroit Free Press, March 1, 1989.

Globe and Mail (Toronto, Ontario, Canada), December 9, 1989.

Kirkus Reviews, July 15, 1993, review of *Only Words.*

Law and Philosophy, 1997, Cass Sunstein, review of *In Harms Way: The Pornography Civil Rights Hearings,* p. 177.

Library Journal, February 15, 2004, Philip Y. Blue, review of *Directions in Sexual Harassment Law,* p. 143.

Nation, May 30, 1987, Maureen Mullarkey, review of *Feminism Unmodified: Discourses on Life and Law;* November 15, 1993, Carlin Romano, review of *Only Words,* p. 563.

New Republic, June 29, 1998, review of *In Harm's Way,* p. 25.

New Statesman & Society, June 3, 1994, Sue Golding, review of *Only Words,* p. 45.

New York Times, February 24, 1989, Tamar Lewin, "Job Offer to Feminist Scholar May Mark Turn," section B, p. 5.

New York Times Book Review, May 3, 1987, Alison Jaggar, review of *Feminism Unmodified: Discourses on Life and Law,* p. 3.

off our backs, January-February, 2004, Carol Anne Douglas, review of *Sex Equality,* p. 53.

Psychology Today, September, 1987.

Publishers Weekly, August 2, 1993, review of *Only Words,* p. 69.

Reason, February, 1994, Cathy Young, review of *Only Words,* p. 57.

Time, March 10, 1986; April 17, 1989.

*   *   *

MALCOLM, Dan
  See SILVERBERG, Robert

*   *   *

MARCHANT, Catherine
  See COOKSON, Catherine (McMullen)

MARGOLIN, Harriet
  See ZIEFERT, Harriet

*   *   *

MARINER, Scott
  See POHL, Frederik

*   *   *

MARTIN, Steve 1945-

PERSONAL: Born August 14, 1945, Waco, TX; son of Glenn (a realtor) and Mary (Lee) Martin; married Victoria Tennant (an actress), 1986 (divorced, 1994). *Education:* Attended Cal State University at Long Beach and University of California at Los Angeles. *Hobbies and other interests:* Reading old magic books, art books, museum catalogs, and the *New Yorker* magazine; playing horseshoes; skiing.

ADDRESSES: Home—Beverly Hills, CA *Office*—P.O. Box 929, Beverly Hills, CA 90213. *Agent*—c/o Ed Limato, International Creative Management, 8942 Wilshire Blvd., Beverly Hills, CA 90211.

CAREER: Comedian, actor, and writer. Partner in the Aspen Film Society and 40 Share Productions. Worked at Disneyland and Knott's Berry Farm in the early 1960s; performer in coffeehouses, c. 1963; comedy writer for television programs, including *The Smothers Brothers Comedy Hour,* 1968, *The John Denver Rocky Mountain Christmas Show,* 1975, and *Van Dyke and Company,* 1975, and for performers, including Glen Campbell, Ray Stevens, Pat Paulsen, John Denver, and Sonny and Cher; has made numerous guest appearances on television programs, including *The Tonight Show Starring Johnny Carson, Dinah!, The Merv Griffin Show, The Dick Cavett Show,* and *Saturday Night Live;* executive producer, *Domestic Life* (television series), Columbia Broadcasting System (CBS), 1984; actor in motion pictures, including *The Absent-Minded Waiter,* 1977, *The Jerk,* 1979, *Pennies from Heaven,* 1981, *Dead Men Don't Wear Plaid,* 1982, *The Man with Two Brains,* 1983, *The Lonely Guy,* 1984, *All of Me,* 1984, *Little Shop of Horrors,* 1986, *Three Amigos!,* 1986, *Roxanne,* 1987, *Planes, Trains, and Automobiles,* 1987, *Dirty Rotten*

Steve Martin

Scoundrels, 1988, *Parenthood,* 1989, *My Blue Heaven,* 1990, *Father of the Bride,* 1991, *Grand Canyon,* 1991, *L. A. Story,* 1991, *Housesitter,* 1992, *Leap of Faith,* 1993, *Mixed Nuts,* 1994, *A Simple Twist of Fate,* 1994, *Father of the Bride Part II,* 1995, *Sgt. Bilko,* 1996, *Bowfinger,* 1999, *The Out of Towners,* 1999, *Joe Gould's Secret,* 2000, *Novocaine,* 2001, and *Bringing Down the House,* 2003; also actor in (theater) *Waiting for Godot,* 1988, and (television) *And the Band Played On,* 1993.

MEMBER: Screen Actors Guild, American Guild of Variety Artists, American Federation of Television and Radio Artists.

AWARDS, HONORS: Emmy Award, National Academy of Television Arts and Sciences, 1969, for best achievement in comedy, variety, or music for *The Smothers Brothers Comedy Hour;* Emmy Award nomination, 1975, for best writing in a comedy, variety, or music special for *Van Dyke and Company;* Georgie Award, American Guild of Variety Artists, 1977; Academy Award nomination, Academy of Motion Picture Arts and Sciences, 1977, for *The Absent-Minded Waiter;* Jack Benny Award, University of

California at Los Angeles, 1978, for entertainment excellence; Grammy Award, National Academy of Recording Arts and Sciences, 1978, for *Let's Get Small,* and 1979, for *A Wild and Crazy Guy;* National Society of Film Critics Award and New York Film Critics Circle Award, both 1984, both for role in *All of Me;* best actor award from Los Angeles Film Critics Association and best screenplay award from Writers Guild of America, both 1987, both for *Roxanne;* two New York Critics Outer Circle Awards, for best play and best playwright, 1996, for *Picasso at the Lapin Agile;* Boston Film Excellence Award, 2001.

WRITINGS:

Cruel Shoes (humorous sketches; Literary Guild alternate selection; Playboy Book Club featured alternate), Press of the Pegacycle Lady, 1977, revised and enlarged edition, Putnam (New York, NY), 1979.

The Absent-Minded Waiter (screenplay), Paramount (Los Angeles, CA), 1977.

Let's Get Small (recording), Warner Bros. (Los Angeles, CA), 1977.

Steve Martin: A Wild and Crazy Guy (television special), National Broadcasting Corporation (NBC), 1978.

A Wild and Crazy Guy (recording), Warner Bros. (Los Angeles, CA), 1978.

King Tut (recording), Warner Bros. (Los Angeles, CA), 1978.

Comedy Is Not Pretty (recording; also see below), Warner Bros. (Los Angeles, CA), 1979.

(With Carl Reiner) *The Jerk* (screenplay), Universal (Los Angeles, CA), 1979.

Comedy Is Not Pretty (television special), NBC, 1980.

Steve Martin's Best Show Ever (television special), NBC, 1981.

The Steve Martin Brothers (recording), Warner Bros. (Los Angeles, CA), 1982.

(With Carl Reiner and George Gipe) *Dead Men Don't Wear Plaid* (screenplay), Universal (Los Angeles, CA), 1982.

(Cowriter) *The Man with Two Brains* (screenplay), Warner Bros. (Los Angeles, CA), 1983.

(With Lorne Michaels and Randy Newman; and executive producer) *Three Amigos!* (screenplay), Orion (Los Angeles, CA), 1986.

(And executive producer) *Roxanne* (screenplay; based on *Cyrano de Bergerac* by Edmond Rostand), Columbia (Los Angeles, CA), 1987.

L. A. Story, Tri-Star (Los Angeles, CA), 1991.

Picasso at the Lapin Agile (play; also see below), first produced in Chicago by Steppenwolf Theater Co., 1993.

A Simple Twist of Fate (screenplay), Buena Vista Pictures (Los Angeles, CA), 1994.

WASP (play; also see below), first produced in New York City at the Public Theater, 1995.

Picasso at the Lapin Agile and Other Plays, Grove Press (New York, NY), 1996.

L. A. Story; and, Roxanne: Two Screenplays, Grove Press (New York, NY), 1997.

Meteor Shower (play), first produced in Los Angeles, 1997.

Pure Drivel, Hyperion (New York, NY), 1998.

WASP and Other Plays, Samuel French (New York, NY), 1998.

Bowfinger, Universal (Los Angeles, CA), 1999.

Shopgirl (novella), Hyperion (New York, NY), 2000.

The Pleasure of My Company, Hyperion (New York, NY), 2003.

Contributor of essays to *New Yorker, Rolling Stone,* and *New York Times.* Also adapted Carl Sternheim's play *The Underpants* for a production by the Classic Stage Company in New York, April, 2002.

ADAPTATIONS: Shopgirl is to appear as a film; *Picasso at the Lapin Agile,* adapted and directed by Fred Schepisi, was produced in 2003.

SIDELIGHTS: "Well, EXCUUUUSE MEEEE!!!" Steve Martin would roar during his stand-up comedy routine, his entire body shaking with indignation, and the audience, many sporting giant bunny ears or a fake arrow through the head, erupting with howls, cheers, and an ovation comparable to those heard at rock concerts. The bizarre incongruity of a junior-executive type wearing balloons on his head, latex nose and glasses, and a white, custom-tailored, three-piece suit struck the perfect chord with American audiences in the 1970s. Martin's sudden attacks of "happy feet" took him lurching across the stage; he twisted balloons into absurd shapes, then named them "Puppy dog! Venereal disease! The Sistine Chapel!" He performed magic tricks that did not quite work. But most of all, Martin parodied the whole idea of a comedian standing on stage telling jokes. Playing the part of a "wild and crazy guy," Martin became one of the most notable stand-up comics of the decade. His

first two comedy albums won Grammy Awards and sold millions of copies; he scored a hit single with the absurd song, "King Tut"; and the book, *Cruel Shoes,* his collection of humorous sketches, was a national best-seller. By 1979 Martin had graduated to films, making the box-office smash, *The Jerk,* and following with a string of other films throughout the 1980s. His performance in 1984's *All of Me* earned popular acclaim as well as awards from the National Society of Film Critics and the New York Film Critics Circle. *Roxanne* showed him capable of touching character portrayals, while *Planes, Trains, and Automobiles* gave Martin the chance to play the straight man. Over the course of two decades, Martin "evolved from a coolly absurdist stand-up comic to a fully formed, amazingly nimble comic actor," noted Janet Maslin in the *New York Times.*

In the 1990s Martin's evolution continued, this time in unexpected directions. He began to write pieces for the *New Yorker,* and these reflected not only his comedic talents but a literary bent as well. He also began to write plays, including the popular *Picasso at the Lapin Agile.* The dawn of the twenty-first century has found Martin to be less engaged in television and film comedy and more engaged in serious creative endeavors, including his well-received novellas, *Shopgirl* and *The Pleasure of My Company.* Reflecting on his move into fiction-writing, Martin told *Time* magazine: "'A lot of people think that celebrities are isolated. But the truth is that every minute of their lives is as melodramatic as every minute of everybody else's. So you can extrapolate from your own experience into almost anything. The emotions are no different.'"

Martin's fascination with the entertainment world stems back to his childhood. He was stage-struck at the age of three and grew up idolizing such comedians as Laurel and Hardy, Jerry Lewis, and Red Skelton. "The first day I saw a movie," he told *Newsweek*'s Tony Schwartz, "I knew that's what I wanted to do." By the age of five, he was memorizing Red Skelton's television skits and performing them at school show-and-tells. When his family moved to California, he hiked over to the new Disneyland amusement park and got a part-time job selling guidebooks, magic tricks, and Frontierland rodeo ropes. "I had mystical summer nights there," he recalled. "Fireworks, lights in the trees, a dance band playing music from the '40s."

During working hours he would sneak away to watch an old vaudevillian comic, Wally Boag, at Disneyland's Golden Horseshoe Revue. The comedian performed a routine of songs, jokes, and balloon tricks that Martin committed to memory. Soon Martin was performing the tricks he sold, twirling a lasso, playing the banjo, and appearing in a Boag production called "It's Vaudeville Again." After eight years at the Magic Kingdom, Martin left for nearby Knott's Berry Farm to act in melodrama at the Birdcage Theatre and perform his own fifteen-minute routines of comedy, magic, and banjo music.

Martin's budding career was cut short by his discovery of education. He fell in love with Stormy, an actress in the Birdcage company, who persuaded him to read Somerset Maugham's *The Razor's Edge.* "It was all about a person who questions life," Martin told Schwartz. "I read it and I can remember afterward sitting in a park and Stormy saying, 'Knowledge is the most important thing there is.'" Convinced, Martin enrolled at Long Beach State College where he studied philosophy for the next three years. But when he came across the arguments of Ludwig Wittgenstein concerning semantics, and the philosopher's contention that nothing was absolutely true, his interest in philosophy waned. Martin concluded that "the only logical thing was comedy because you don't have to explain it or justify it." He transferred to the University of California and changed his major to theatre.

Martin's first big break in show business came when he submitted some of his written material to Mason Williams, the head writer for CBS-TV's *The Smothers Brothers Comedy Hour.* At the time, Martin was broke, living in a maid's quarters in Bel Air, struggling as a performer at small clubs and coffeehouses, and studying television writing at UCLA. Williams invited him to join the writing staff of the show, one of the highest-rated on television at the time. "I didn't have any *idea* what I was doing there," he admitted. "So young and inexperienced in such a big-league job. But I was too busy repressing it all to deal with it." CBS cancelled the show in 1968, but Martin and the show's ten other writers won an Emmy for their work. The award tripled Martin's value as a writer, and he was soon making $1,500 a week writing for entertainers like Glen Campbell, Ray Stevens, Pat Paulsen, John Denver, and Sonny and Cher. Still, his ambition was to work onstage: "I decided to stop writing for other people and perform full-time again," he told Kathy

Lowry of *New Times.* "I was bored with writing all that formula stuff. I wanted to deal directly with the audience."

The early 1970s proved to be a dismal period in Martin's career. He took his stand-up act on the road, playing every small club he could find and opening for rock groups whose drugged, impatient audiences shouted him off the stage. "Back then they didn't know what a comedian was," Martin told Janet Coleman in *New York.* He later satirized the period in one of his routines: a marijuana-smoking hippie is watching Martin perform, nods slowly, then drawls, "These guys are *good.*" Coleman noted that Martin is "still annoyed by the ritual sloppiness and inattention of the 'love generation' audience."

Success as a stand-up comedian came when Martin developed a distinctive stage persona. He was a pioneer of postmodernist comedy, or comedy poking fun at the entertainment industry itself. When doing his act, Martin became a parody of a comedian. His character was shallow and slick, desperate for acceptance, full of insincere show-business asides to the audience, and unaware of his own stupidity. Balloon gags, juggling, banjo playing, and rabbit ears were all used in a deliberately hokey attempt to get laughs. Pauline Kael described Martin's stand-up act in the *New Yorker:* "Onstage, he puts across the idea that he's going to do some cornball routine, and then when he does it, it has quotation marks around it, and that's what makes it hilarious. He does the routine straight, yet he's totally facetious."

His usual performance would begin with Martin walking out in his six-hundred-dollar white suit, an expensive banjo slung over his shoulder, and announcing: "Hi, I'm Steve Martin, and I'll be out in *just* a minute!" For a few moments, he would goof in the spotlight, hum to himself, look around aimlessly. He was "waiting for the drugs to take effect," he would explain. Then, "Okay, you paid the money, you're expecting to see a professional show, so let's not waste any more time, here we go with Professional Show Business, let's go, hey!" He steps back, starts tuning the banjo, plucking one string then another, turning a peg or two, then moves up and smashes his nose into the microphone. "Okay, we're moving now, eh folks? Yes, these are the good times and we're having them, ah ha ha ha."

"I mean," David Felton wondered in *Rolling Stone,* "what *is* this shit? Here's one of the hottest comedians in the business . . . and he's standing up there like a *jerk,* an *idiot,* a f——-ing *asshole!* And that's the whole point." Lowry explained: "Steve Martin just wants to get a laugh; he doesn't much care about being profound or pricking society's conscience."Tony Schwartz in *Newsweek* claimed that Martin's style "is a pie in the faces of Lenny Bruce, Dick Gregory, Mort Sahl and all the iconoclastic comics who dominated the stand-up scene in the '60s." Martin agreed. Speaking to *U.S. News & World Report,* he revealed: "The '60s was a time of humorlessness in America. Everybody was so dead earnest. . . . During this time, the cheapest way to get a laugh was to make a political joke. . . . When I made my breakthrough in comedy in the early 1970s, politics was very much on everybody's mind. I saw it as my job to take it off their minds and so left politics out of my comedy. I think that was a big part of my success. There was no moralizing, no left, no right; it was just about a human being."

Martin transferred his stage persona to the screen in 1979's *The Jerk,* a film that grossed over seventy million dollars at the box office. Playing the white son in a poor black family (obviously an adopted son, but Martin doesn't realize it), he goes on to win and lose a fortune with a crazy invention. Audiences loved the movie, but critics found it wanting, expecting it to be somehow more "relevant" or provocative. Martin's next few efforts were also met with critical coolness. Audience appeal was also limited. *Pennies from Heaven,* a lush musical set in the 1930s, lost money; *Dead Men Don't Wear Plaid,* a spoof of the hard-boiled detective genre that incorporated scenes from vintage movies, was a box-office disappointment. Speaking of this period to Kenneth Turan in *Rolling Stone,* Martin said, "It was like a dog scratching around to find a place to sit, getting up and down, walking around five or six times, before finally settling somewhere. That's the way I kept walking, trying to find the right screen persona to sit in. Something I like playing. Something I can do again."

It was only with *All of Me,* in which Martin costarred with Lily Tomlin, that he discovered a comfortable screen character. Ironically for the comic who had made his reputation as a "wild man," Martin's new character was a normal fellow who is beset with unusual problems. In the film, Martin plays a lawyer who becomes possessed by the spirit of a dead woman. One side of his body is controlled by the woman, the other side by him. Martin's amazing ability to portray this absurd physical condition—half male and half female—drew widespread critical praise and won him two major film awards as well. "To see his physical contortions in *All of Me,*" wrote Turan, "to watch him trying to play both sexes simultaneously . . . is so boggling that audiences are often far too flabbergasted to laugh at all. Had he been born in another century, Martin might have been burned at the stake for witchcraft or demonic possession." In addition to the film's physical humor, Jack Barth maintained in *Film Comment:* "*All of Me* is Martin's first comedy to subjugate gags to story and characterization. . . . [It] is also the first Martin film to deliver a satisfying ending." The result pleased the filmgoing public as well as the critics. "*All of Me,*" noted Turan, was "the number one film in America, with reviews to match."

Martin further developed his new screen character in subsequent films, particularly in *Roxanne,* a gentle, updated version of the classic *Cyrano de Bergerac.* Martin plays a small-town fireman with an absurdly long nose. Called upon to assist a friend woo the new woman in town, Martin falls in love with her himself. Writing in the *Chicago Tribune,* Dave Kehr called the film "a romantic comedy of grace, buoyancy and surprising emotional depth, filled with civilized pleasures." Tom Shales in the *Washington Post* reported that "critics have adored the writing, but have also likened Martin's comedic agility onscreen to Charlie Chaplin's. There have been references to things like 'comic genius' bursting forth." In her review for the *Los Angeles Times,* Sheila Benson stated, "I can't think of a current movie in which every element is in such balance: Martin seems unfettered, expansive, utterly at ease, capable of any physical feat. . . . There's a tenderness to him that's magnetic." David Ansen in *Newsweek* concluded: "*Roxanne* is a charmer. Sweet-spirited, relaxed, it's a sun-dappled romantic comedy. . . . This is the culmination of a long quest to exorcise [Martin's] stage persona as a wild and crazy guy."

By the late 1980s Martin had left his stand-up "wild and crazy" image behind him. He had become, in the words of Richard Corliss of *Time,* "this decade's most charming and resourceful comic actor." A wide variety of film comedy roles were suddenly available to him. In *Planes, Trains, and Automobiles* Martin played the straight man to John Candy, in *Dirty Rotten Scoundrels* he played a con man with Michael Caine, and in

Parenthood he was a middle-class father. And all three films, in pleasant contrast to several earlier Martin efforts, were solid box-office hits.

Martin's fame as a film star has overshadowed the considerable efforts he has put into writing over the years. He created his own stand-up comedy routines and has screenplay credits in many of his films, including *Dead Men Don't Wear Plaid, L. A. Story, Roxanne,* and *Bowfinger.* It was therefore a natural progression for him to move into other genres as a creative writer, and he has enjoyed some significant successes with plays, essays, and fiction. In 1993 his play *Picasso at the Lapin Agile* had its premiere in Chicago at the Steppenwolf Theater Company, and the show has since been performed on national tour and in London. The play provides a whimsical look at what might have happened if Albert Einstein, Pablo Picasso, and Elvis Presley all met at a celebrated Parisian bar circa 1910. *WASP,* another Martin theater piece, made its debut at New York City's Public Theater.

Another breakthrough for Martin occurred when the *New Yorker* began to publish his humorous essays. These pieces, collected in the book *Pure Drivel,* demonstrate his facility with wordplay as well as his talent as a satirist. "Twenty years ago you wouldn't have thought of Steve in the tradition of James Thurber and S. J. Perelman, but now he's really established himself as a prose writer," noted publisher David Ebershoff in *Yahoo! News.* Ebershoff added: "Steve is a rare figure in American humor because these days, rightly or wrongly, humor is thought of in terms of performance and not writing." In her *New York Times Book Review* critique of *Pure Drivel,* Susan Shapiro praised the work for its "chameleon quality," noting that the tone "ranges from parody to irony to just plain silliness." *Booklist* correspondent Donna Seaman commended *Pure Drivel* for its "intelligent, innovative, and self-conscious humor." Seaman also observed that Martin crafts prose "as notable for its meticulousness as for its drollery." A *Kirkus Reviews* critic deemed the pieces "lighter-than-air mockery. Often ingenious."

Shopgirl, Martin's first novella, shows the artist working a different vein of material. While not completely lacking in humor, the tale of a young store clerk and her affair with a noncommittal middle-aged businessman is an earnest exploration of mismanaged relationships and thwarted ambitions. "The funny thing about Steve Martin's first work of extended fiction, *Shopgirl,*

is that it's not funny," wrote Richard Corliss in *Time.* "*Shopgirl . . .* offers quieter pleasures: a delicate portrait of people inflicting subtle pain on others and themselves, and an appeal to the intelligent heart." In the *New York Times Book Review,* John Lanchester described the novella as "elegant, bleak, desolatingly sad," adding that the work "has an edge to it, and a deep unassuageable loneliness. Steve Martin's most achieved work to date may well have the strange effect of making people glad not to be Steve Martin." A *Publishers Weekly* reviewer was impressed by Martin's ability to write serious fiction, concluding that *Shopgirl* is "yet another of this intelligent performer's attempts to expand his range." Bonnie Smothers made a similar observation in *Booklist* when she suggested that the novella "may mark a new direction in a noteworthy writer's career."

Martin's second novella, *The Pleasure of My Company,* is about a somewhat neurotic, obsessive-compulsive man, Daniel Pecan Cambridge, who lives alone in a rundown Santa Monica, California, apartment. Cambridge cannot hold a job and passes his dull, lonely days imagining romances and awaiting visits from his social worker. He is also driven to keep exactly 1,125 watts of lightbulbs burning at all times in his apartment, and he relies on driveways when walking around his neighborhood since he cannot bring himself to step over curbs. A *Publishers Weekly* reviewer found the book to be "funnier than *Shopgirl* but put together just as smartly," adding, "What's most remarkable about it, though, is its tenderness, a complex mix of wit, poignancy and Martin's clear, great affection for his characters." A reviewer in *Kirkus Reviews* agreed that *The Pleasure of My Company* is "a joy. . . . Although Martin succumbs to a banal plot choice later on, when his neurotic goes on a road trip, this is a genuinely funny and surprisingly touching tale."

While Martin docs not intend to retire from films, he is encouraged by the new direction his career has taken and by what serious writing has taught him. He told the *Detroit Free Press:* "It was time to focus on a more narrow range of interest. I talk to my friend Marty Short about this conscious withdrawal from competing in the Hollywood world. It would be embarrassing if we didn't. I know a little bit more about myself now, enough to write. I know now that other people exist." Asked by the *Knight-Ridder/Tribune News Service* about his methods, he said: "I'm lazy. I do most of my writing when I'm on my bicycle in the park, and I come home and type it up. So when I get a line, I always remember where I was when I wrote it. It's sort of nice actually—like remembering where you were when you first met someone."

BIOGRAPHICAL AND CRITICAL SOURCES:

BOOKS

Contemporary Literary Criticism, Volume 30, Thomson Gale (Detroit, MI), 1984.
Lenburg, Greg, Randy Skretvedt, and Jeff Lenburg, *Steve Martin: The Unauthorized Biography,* St. Martin's Press (New York, NY), 1980.

PERIODICALS

American Film, June, 1982; November, 1988; August, 1989.
Booklist, September 1, 1998, Donna Seaman, review of *Pure Drivel;* July, 2000, Bonnie Smothers, review of *Shopgirl,* p. 1974.
Chicago Tribune, June 19, 1987; July 13, 1987.
Detroit Free Press, November 1, 2000, Bruce Weber, "Actor Branches Out to Book Writing," p. D9.
Esquire, March 27, 1979; April, 1996, p. 66.
Film Comment, January, 1979.
Films in Review, February, 1988.
Gentlemen's Quarterly, July, 1990, p. 116.
Kirkus Reviews, September 1, 1998, review of *Pure Drivel;* August 1, 2003, review of *The Pleasure of My Company,* p. 982.
Knight-Ridder/Tribune News Service, December 6, 1995, Chris Hewitt, "Steve Martin Downplays His Contribution to *Father of the Bride* Sequel," p. K2855; April 11, 1997, Lynn Carey, "Probing the Agile Comic Mind behind *Picasso at the Lapin Agile,*" p. K6300; October 18, 2000, John Mark Eberhart, "More Writers Find Solace in the Novella," p. K4898.
Life, March, 1992, p. 46.
Los Angeles Times, December 27, 1984; June 19, 1987; June 28, 1987; June 30, 1987.
New Republic, March 11, 1991, Stanley Kauffmann, review of *L. A. Story,* p. 28.
Newsweek, January 31, 1977; April 3, 1978; June 22, 1987.
New Times, September 2, 1977.
New York, August 22, 1977.
New Yorker, June 27, 1983; November 29, 1993, p. 98.
New York Times, January 14, 1980; May 21, 1982; June 19, 1987; July 12, 1987; May 31, 1992, p. 28; October 17, 2000, Bruce Weber, "Arrow out of the Head and into a Shy Heroine's Heart," p. B1.
New York Times Book Review, September 13, 1998, Susan Shapiro, review of *Pure Drivel;* October 29, 2000, John Lanchester, "The Counter Life."
People, May 1, 1978; July 6, 1987; February 25, 1991, Ralph Novak, review of *L. A. Story,* p. 11; October 16, 2000, Kyle Smith, review of *Shopgirl,* p. 55.
Publishers Weekly, August 7, 2000, review of *Shopgirl,* p. 72; September 15, 2003, review of *The Pleasure of My Company,* p. 44.
Rolling Stone, December 1, 1977; July 27, 1978; November 30, 1978; April 5, 1979; November 8, 1984.
Saturday Evening Post, November-December, 1989, p. 52.
Time, October 31, 1977; June 15, 1987; August 24, 1987; October 16, 2000, Richard Corliss, "But Seriously, Folks: Steve Martin Talks about His First Novella, a Delicate, Poignant Modern Romance about a Shy Shopgirl," p. 113.
U.S. News & World Report, June 17, 1985.
Washington Post, September 15, 1977; June 3, 1979; June 23, 1979; June 19, 1987.

ONLINE

ABC News.com, http://abcnews.go.com/ (October 19, 2000), Buck Wolf, "Steve Martin, Renaissance Clown."
Steve Martin Web site, http://www.stevemartin.com/ (October 19, 2000).
Yahoo! News, http://dailynews.yahoo.com/ (October 4, 2000), Hillel Italie, "Steve Martin Gets Literary."*

*   *   *

MARTIN, Webber
See SILVERBERG, Robert

*   *   *

MASON, Ernst
See POHL, Frederik

MAWER, Simon 1948-

PERSONAL: Born 1948, in England; married; wife's name Connie; children: Matthew, Julia. *Education:* Attended Brasenose College, Oxford.

ADDRESSES: Home—Rome, Italy. *Agent*—Charles Walker, Peters Fraser & Dunlop, Drury House, 34-43 Russell St., London WC2B 5HA, England. *E-mail*—author@simonmawer.com.

CAREER: Writer and educator. Former biology teacher in Guernsey, Channel Islands, as well as in Malta and Italy; St. George's English School, Rome, Italy.

AWARDS, HONORS: McKitterick Prize, 1989, for *Chimera;* Boardman Tasker Prize for mountain literature, 2003, for *The Fall.*

WRITINGS:

NOVELS

Chimera, Penguin (New York, NY), 1989.
The Bitter Cross, Sinclair-Stevenson (London, England), 1992.
A Jealous God, Andre Deutsch (London, England), 1996.
Mendel's Dwarf, Transworld, 1997, Harmony Books (New York, NY), 1998.
The Gospel of Judas, Little, Brown (Boston, MA), 2001.
The Fall, Little, Brown (Boston, MA), 2003.

Mendel's Dwarf has been translated into German, French, Italian, Dutch, Hebrew and Portuguese; *The Gospel of Judas* has been translated into French, Italian, Dutch, and Portuguese.

NONFICTION

A Place in Italy, Sinclair-Stevenson (London, England), 1992.

WORK IN PROGRESS: Becoming Absent, working title.

SIDELIGHTS: After a nomadic childhood spent in England and the Mediterranean, Simon Mawer has spent more than twenty years teaching biology in Rome, Italy. Simultaneously, he has been writing novels that incorporate a variety of personal interests—mountain climbing, scientific exploration, the events of World War II, religious realignment—into graceful, complex narratives. Introduced to American readers with his fourth novel, *Mendel's Dwarf,* Mawer has become a notable name in British fiction. In the *Atlantic Monthly,* Michael Upchurch said that Mawer should be ranked alongside Iris Murdoch, William Boyd, and Michael Frayn, and explained: "Mawer's prose is admirably lyrical, playful, and precise. His greatest strength, however, is in crafting probing, puzzlelike narratives that yield compelling dramas of the mind and heart." In a review of *The Gospel of Judas* for the *Christian Science Monitor,* Thomas D'Evelyn called Mawer a "world-class novelist" and added, "Mawer's use of the novel to explore social, political, intimate, and religious history reveals the power of this genre to redeem the present."

Chimera, Mawer's first novel, is the story of half-Italian British agent David Hewison, formerly an archeologist, who parachutes into Italy during World War II. It is also the story of Hewison's nephew Anthony, who becomes curious about his uncle's past and visits him forty years later in Italy, where Hewison has settled in a villa and is engaged in an archeological dig of an ancient Etruscan settlement. The novel, like an archeology dig, intricately layers memories and events.

A Place in Italy is Mawer's account of several months he and his wife spent in Avea, a small Italian village. Living in a house that consists of two rooms and a cave carved out of the hillside, they become part of the village, part of its gossip and relationships. He and his wife savor the local food and customs and their connection to the villagers. Eventually they move on, but as Caroline Moorehead wrote in the *Times Literary Supplement,* "The good-humored book that has come out of their time in Avea is an evocative reminder of how successfully the Italians have been at hanging on to the pleasures of the passing seasons."

The Bitter Cross is a historical novel set in a time of religious conflict: the sixteenth-century Protestant revolution of northern Europe and the Turkish/Islamic onslaught in Italy and other Mediterranean countries.

Set in Malta, between the two regions, the book is a complicated story of love and war featuring Gerald Paulet, a Knight of St. John in Malta. Betty Abel, writing for the *Contemporary Review,* noted that the book is "exciting and imaginative. Simon Mawer has vividly described his impressive characters and their exotic setting." Brian Morton of the *Times Educational Supplement* similarly stated, "Mawer writes the kind of historical fiction that convinces because it doesn't strive too hard to establish extraneous detail."

A Jealous God tells the story of Helen Hardin and her quest to find out whether or not her father, Andrew, a British intelligence agent who was rumored to have been killed in 1946 in the Palestinian bombing of the King David Hotel in Jerusalem, is actually dead. A *Publishers Weekly* reviewer described Mawer as "a poetic, masterful explorer of hidden motives, erotic desires, divided loyalties." In this book Mawer interweaves Helen's search for the truth with her illicit affair with her stepbrother and her guilty relationship with her mother. Simon Louvish wrote in the *New Statesman,* "The novel twists and turns between these narratives, allowing us a kind of God-like eye to see the connections that Helen, kept from the truth by her dying mother Lorna, may never find out."

Mawer's fourth novel, *Mendel's Dwarf,* stars brilliant geneticist Benedict Lambert, a descendant of the famous early geneticist and monk Gregor Mendel. Lambert is a dwarf, suffering from the genetic mutation of achondroplasia, and is obsessed with finding the genetic basis for his condition. The book is a dual biography, interweaving the story of Lambert's life with that of Mendel, but plot is secondary to sensibility in this imaginative novel. As Francine Prose wrote in the *New York Times,* "Far more interesting is the breadth and depth of the narrator's sensibility—his mix of seriousness and grace, the charm and lack of pedantry with which he touches on a range of weighty ideas. . . . [The book is] an odd and affecting literary experiment that keeps pushing itself and its readers to think harder, go deeper." A reviewer in *Library Journal* agreed, calling the book "a wonderfully crafted, thought-provoking tale in which the science never gets in the way of the story."

In *The Gospel of Judas,* Mawer imagines the impact of a newly discovered ancient scroll refuting accounts of Jesus' resurrection. Father Leo Newman is a scholar in Rome who is asked to translate the scroll and reveal its message to the world. Already troubled by his relationship with a diplomat's wife and shaken in his faith, he worries about the potential effect of the manuscript on all Christians. Writing for *Publishers Weekly,* Jeff Zaleski deemed that "discerning readers will relish Mawer's excellent writing and subtle treatment of potentially over-the-top subject matter." *Newsweek* reviewer Andrew Nagorski relished the challenge of Mawer's hypothetical situation: "In a book based on the premise that Jesus didn't rise from the dead, resurrection is a recurring theme. A factual history would never have imbued these personal struggles with the same emotional resonance."

The twin thrills of mountain climbing—the pure beauty of the surroundings and flirtation with danger—are the centerpieces of *The Fall,* a novel set in North Wales. When Jamie, an expert climber, is killed under mysterious circumstances on a dangerous rock face, his widow is visited by an old climbing partner, Rob. Relationships between these three, as well as between the men's mothers, prove to be complex. Questions arise about Rob and Jamie's paternity, reaching back into events of the post-World War II period. Critics repeatedly relished Mawer's prose and clear intimacy with the subject of climbing, but sometimes found his characters rendered with less skill. In the *The Saturday Review,* D. J. Taylor gave "all credit to Mawer for writing a book whose real theme . . . is the sheer insignificance of puny humanity when set against environmental splendour." He also said, "One could wish that the human entanglements lurking in the mountains' shadow were worked out with something more than a kind of emotional algebra." Others cast the novel as Mawer's finest work. "*The Fall* is the most meticulously plotted of all Mawer's books," said Mark Crees in the *Times Literary Supplement;* "yet it also stands as his most unrestrained and direct achievement." James Hopkin remarked in the *New Statesman* that this was Mawer's "ideal subject" and that the novel "becomes an elegy for a life of lost opportunity and love, a meditation on ageing and regret that gently supersedes the eulogy to the thrill of the climb."

BIOGRAPHICAL AND CRITICAL SOURCES:

PERIODICALS

Atlantic Monthly, June, 2001, Michael Upchurch, review of *The Gospel of Judas,* p. 106.

Christian Science Monitor, July 26, 2001, Thomas D'Evelyn, "Personal and World Faith Shaken," p. 20.

Contemporary Review, July, 1992, Betty Abel, review of *The Bitter Cross,* p. 44.

Library Journal, November 15, 1997, David W. Henderson and Barbara Hoffert, review of *Mendel's Dwarf,* p. 77.

New Statesman, February 9, 1996, Simon Louvish, review of *A Jealous God,* p. 137; March 10, 2003, James Hopkin, "Novel of the Week: *The Fall,*" p. 53.

Newsweek, June 18, 2001, Andrew Nagorski, "If Judas Told His Story. . .," p. 62.

New York Times, March 22, 1998, Francine Prose, "Get Out the Chromosomal Map," p. 13.

Publishers Weekly, July 8, 1996, review of *A Jealous God,* p. 76; November 3, 1997, review of *Mendel's Dwarf,* p. 64; April 9, 2001, Jeff Zaleski, review of *The Gospel of Judas,* p. 48; December 23, 2002, Jeff Zaleski, review of *The Fall,* p. 249.

Saturday Review, February 15, 2003, D. J. Taylor, review of *The Fall,* p. 29.

Times Educational Supplement, June 5, 1992, Brian Morton, review of *The Bitter Cross,* p. 32.

Times Literary Supplement, November 27, 1992, Caroline Moorehead, review of *A Place in Italy,* p. 10; February 28, 2003, Mark Crees, "Don't Look Down," p. 23.

Washington Post, January 26, 2003, Richard Byrne, "Down We Go," p. T7.

The World & I, June, 2003, Joseph Sullivan, review of *The Fall,* pp. 218-223.

ONLINE

Simon Mawer Home Page, http://www.simonmawer.com/ (November 15, 2003).

*   *   *

MCCANN, Edson
  See POHL, Frederik

*   *   *

MCCREIGH, James
  See POHL, Frederik

McPHERSON, James Alan 1943-

PERSONAL: Born September 16, 1943, in Savannah, GA; son of James Allen and Mable (Smalls) McPherson. *Education:* Attended Morgan State University, 1963-64; Morris Brown College, B.A., 1965; Harvard University, LL.B., 1968; University of Iowa, M.F.A., 1969.

ADDRESSES: Office—Department of English, University of Iowa, Iowa City, IA 52242.

CAREER: University of Iowa, Iowa City, instructor in writing at Law School, 1968-69, instructor in Afro-American literature, 1969; University of California, Santa Cruz, faculty member, 1969-70; Morgan State University, Baltimore, MD, faculty member, 1975-76; University of Virginia, Charlottesville, faculty member, 1976-81; University of Iowa, Writers Workshop, Iowa City, professor, 1981—; *Double Take* magazine, editor, 1995—; Stanford University, Palo Alto, CA, behavioral studies fellow, 1997—.

MEMBER: Authors League of America, PEN, American Academy of Arts and Sciences, National Association for the Advancement of Colored People, American Civil Liberties Union.

AWARDS, HONORS: First prize, *Atlantic* short story contest, 1965, for "Gold Coast"; grant from Atlantic Monthly Press and Little, Brown, 1969; National Institute of Arts and Letters award in literature, 1970; Guggenheim fellow, 1972-73; Pulitzer Prize, 1978, for *Elbow Room: Stories;* MacArthur fellowship, 1981; Excellence in Technology award, University of Iowa, 1991; Best American Essays, 1990, 1993, 1994, 1995; Pushcart Prize, 1995.

WRITINGS:

Hue and Cry: Short Stories, Atlantic-Little, Brown (Boston, MA), 1969, reprinted, Ecco Press (New York, NY), 2001.

(Editor, with Miller Williams) *Railroad: Trains and Train People in American Culture,* Random House (New York, NY), 1976.

Elbow Room: Stories, Atlantic-Little, Brown (Boston, MA), 1977.

James Alan McPherson

(Author of foreword) Breece D'J Pancake, *The Stories of Breece D'J Pancake,* Atlantic-Little, Brown (Boston, MA), 1983, reprinted, Little, Brown (Boston, MA), 2002.

Crabcakes: A Memoir, Simon & Schuster (New York, NY), 1998.

(Editor, with DeWitt Henry) *Fathering Daughters: Reflections by Men,* Beacon Press (Boston, MA), 1998.

A Region Not Home: Reflections from Exile, Simon & Schuster (New York, NY), 2000.

Work has been anthologized in books, including *Cutting Edges,* edited by J. Hicks, Holt (New York, NY), 1973; *Black Insights: Significant Literature by Afro-Americans, 1760 to the Present,* edited by Nick A. Ford, Wiley (New York, NY), 1976; *Book for Boston,* edited by Llewellyn Howland and Isabelle Storey, David Godine (Boston, MA), 1980; *Speaking for You,* edited by Kimberly W. Benson, Howard University Press, 1987; *A World Unsuspected,* edited by Alex Harris, Hill, NC], 1987; and *New Black Voices,* New American Library. Contributor to periodicals, including *Atlantic, Esquire, New York Times Magazine,* *Playboy, Reader's Digest,* and *Callaloo.* Contributing editor, *Atlantic,* beginning 1969; editor of special issue, *Iowa Review,* winter, 1984.

SIDELIGHTS: James Alan McPherson's stories of ordinary, working-class people, though often concerning African-American characters, are noted for their ability to confront universal human problems. "His standpoint," Robie Macauley explained in the *New York Times Book Review,* "[is] that of a writer and a black, but not that of a black writer. [McPherson] refused to let his fiction fall into any color-code or ethnic code." Because of this stance, McPherson's characters are more fully rounded than are those of more racially conscious writers. As Paul Bailey wrote in the *Observer Review* and quoted in *Contemporary Literary Criticism,* "The Negroes and whites [McPherson] describes always remain individual people—he never allows himself the luxury of turning them into Problems." Explaining his approach to the characters in his stories, McPherson was quoted by Patsy B. Perry of the *Dictionary of Literary Biography* as saying: "Certain of these people [my characters] happen to be black, and certain of them happen to be white; but I have tried to keep the color part of most of them far in the background, where these things should rightly be kept." McPherson has published two collections of short stories, *Hue and Cry: Short Stories* and *Elbow Room: Stories.* In 1978 he was awarded the Pulitzer Prize for fiction.

McPherson was born and raised in Savannah, Georgia, a city in which several cultures—including the French, Spanish, and Indian—have been uniquely blended. He cites this rich cultural heritage as a determining factor in his own ability to transcend racial barriers. The McPherson family also influenced his development of values. The author's father, at one time the only licensed black master electrician in Georgia, and his mother, a domestic in a white household, had important contacts in both the white and black communities. Through their efforts, McPherson obtained work as a grocery boy in a local supermarket and as a waiter on a train. These experiences formed the basis for several later stories. McPherson's train employment also allowed him to travel across the country. Perry noted that McPherson "affirms the importance of both white and black communities in his development as an individual and as a writer of humanistic ideas."

McPherson's writing career began in the 1960s while he was still attending law school. His story "Gold

Coast" won first prize in a contest sponsored by the *Atlantic* magazine, which has gone on to play a pivotal role in McPherson's career. After earning a bachelor's degree, a law degree, and a master's degree in creative writing, McPherson became a contributing editor of the *Atlantic* in 1969. And the magazine, in conjunction with Little, Brown, also published his two collections of short stories.

McPherson's first collection, *Hue and Cry,* deals with characters whose lives are so desperate that they can only rage impotently against their situations. "The fact that these characters . . . ," wrote Perry, "know nothing else to do except to sink slowly into madness, scream unintelligibly, or seek refuge . . . provides reason enough for McPherson's hue and cry." A *Times Literary Supplement* critic pointed to the book's "mostly desperate, mostly black, mostly lost figures in the urban nightmare of violence, rage and bewilderment that is currently America."

Despite the grim nature of his stories, McPherson manages to depict the lives of his characters with sympathy and grace. Bailey allows that McPherson's "powers of observation and character-drawing are remarkable, displaying a mature novelist's understanding of the vagaries and inconsistencies of human affairs." Writing in *Harper's,* Irving Howe maintained that McPherson "possesses an ability some writers take decades to acquire, the ability to keep the right distance from the creatures of his imagination, not to get murkily involved and blot out his figures with vanity and fuss." Granville Hicks in the *Saturday Review* noted that McPherson "is acutely aware of the misery and injustice in the world, and he sympathizes deeply with the victims whether they are black or white."

Elbow Room, McPherson's second collection, won even more critical praise than its predecessor. Again concerned with characters in desperate situations, the stories of *Elbow Room* are nonetheless more optimistic than McPherson's earlier works, the characters more willing to struggle for some measure of success. They "engage in life's battles with integrity of mind and spirit," as Perry explains. This optimism is noted by several critics. Robert Phillips, reviewing the book for *Commonweal,* found the stories in *Elbow Room* to be "difficult struggles for survival, yet [McPherson's] sense of humor allows him to dwell on moments which otherwise might prove unbearable." Writing in *Newsweek,* Margo Jefferson called McPherson "an astute realist who knows how to turn the conflicts between individual personalities and the surrounding culture into artful and highly serious comedies of manners."

McPherson's ability to create believable characters, and his focus on the underlying humanity of all his characters, has been praised by such critics as Phillips. McPherson's stories, Phillips maintained, "ultimately become not so much about the black condition as the human condition. . . . *Elbow Room* is a book of singular achievement." Macauley explained that McPherson has been able "to look beneath skin color and cliches of attitude into the hearts of his characters. . . . This is a fairly rare ability in American fiction." A *New Yorker* reviewer listed several other characteristics of McPherson's stories that are worthy of attention, calling him "one of those rare writers who can tell a story, describe shadings of character, and make sociological observations with equal subtlety."

McPherson broke a silence of nearly twenty years in 1998 with publication of *Crabcakes: A Memoir,* "a profoundly personal tale of displacement and discovery that is poetic and universal," according to a writer for *Kirkus Reviews.* Roy Hoffman in the *New York Times Book Review* reported that the book, "part lilting memoir, part anxious meditation," deals elliptically with McPherson's long struggle with writer's block, his travels in Japan, and his slow recovery of a sense of connection with his past and present. Hoffman faulted the author for being "far more elusive than the protagonists in his short fiction. . . . When McPherson writes fiction, he insists that his characters reveal whether they've been abandoned by a lover, frozen out by a child. Why should he, as a memoirist, reveal far less?" Conversely, a reviewer for *Black Studies* deemed the book "richly rewarding," and a *Publishers Weekly* reviewer dubbed *Crabcakes* an "intense mosaic" that "combines James Baldwin's moral compulsion to testify and Ishmael Reed's iconoclastic experimentalism."

McPherson followed up *Crabcakes* with *A Region Not Home: Reflections from Exile,* another collection of personal and cultural essays. *Booklist* reviewer Mary Carroll wrote that in this work "McPherson offers flashes of unexpected insight; his path often twists and turns, but his side trips are well worth the time and effort." In *Publishers Weekly* a reviewer added of *A*

Region Not Home that, "Throughout, there's an easy kitchentable quality to McPherson's style that invites the reader. . . . these are essays on how to live."

Speaking of the obstacles and opportunities facing black writers in the late twentieth century, McPherson once wrote in the *Atlantic:* "It seems to me much of our writing has been, and continues to be, sociological because black writers have been concerned with protesting black humanity and racial injustice to the larger society in those terms most easily understood by nonblack people. It also seems to me that we can correct this limitation either by defining and affirming the values and cultural institutions of our people for their education or by employing our own sense of reality and our own conception of what human life should be to explore, and perhaps help define, the cultural realities of contemporary American life."

BIOGRAPHICAL AND CRITICAL SOURCES:

BOOKS

Beavers, Herman, *Wrestling Angels into Song: The Fictions of Ernest J. Faines and James Alan McPherson,* University of Pennsylvania Press, 1995.
Contemporary Literary Criticism, Volume 19, Thomson Gale (Detroit, MI), 1981.
Dictionary of Literary Biography, Volume 38: *Afro-American Writers after 1955: Dramatists and Prose Writers,* Thomson Gale (Detroit, MI), 1985.
Wallace, Jon, *The Politics of Style: Language As Theme in the Fiction of Berger, McGuane, and McPherson,* Hollowbrook, 1992.

PERIODICALS

Antioch Review, winter, 1978.
Atlantic, December, 1970; February, 1977, review of *Elbow Room: Stories.*
Black Studies, February 1, 1998.
Booklist, June 1, 1998, review of *Crabcakes: A Memoir,* p. 1682; February 15, 2000, Mary Carroll, review of *A Region Not Home,* p. 1073.
Chicago Tribune Book World, May 25, 1969, review of *Hue and Cry.*
Christian Science Monitor, July 31, 1969, review of *Hue and Cry.*
CLA Journal, June, 1979.
Commonweal, September 19, 1969; September 15, 1978, Robert Phillips, review of *Elbow Room.*
Critique, summer, 1996, p. 314.
Ebony, December, 1981.
Essence, January, 1998, p. 61.
Guardian Weekly, April 16, 1989.
Harper's, December, 1969, Irving Howe, review of *Hue and Cry.*
Kirkus Reviews, November 15, 1997.
Library Journal, January, 1998, p. 100; June 15, 1998, review of *Crabcakes,* p. 96; January, 2000, review of *A Region Not Home,* p. 106.
Nation, December 16, 1978.
Negro Digest, October, 1969; November, 1969.
Newsweek, June 16, 1969; October 17, 1977.
New Yorker, November 21, 1977, review of *Elbow Room.*
New York Review of Books, November 10, 1977.
New York Times Book Review, June 1, 1969, review of *Hue and Cry;* September 25, 1977, review of *Elbow Room;* September 2, 1979; February 13, 1983; May 13, 1984; February 15, 1998, Roy Hoffman, review of *Crabcakes,* p. 15.
People, March 30, 1998, p. 39.
Publishers Weekly, November 17, 1997, p. 44; December 15, 1997, p. 36; May 4, 1998, p. 196; January 24, 2000, review of *A Region Not Home,* p. 302.
Saturday Review, May 24, 1969, review of *Hue and Cry.*
Spectator, November 22, 1969.
Studies in American Fiction, autumn, 1973.
Times Literary Supplement, December 25, 1969.
Washington Post Book World, October 30, 1977; March 6, 1983.

ONLINE

Inertia Online, http://www.inertiamagazine.com/ (August 23, 2004), interview with MacPherson.*

*   *   *

McTAGGART, Lynne (Ann) 1951-

PERSONAL: Born January 23, 1951, in Yonkers, NY; daughter of Robert Charles and Olga Cecelia (Gargiullo) McTaggart; married Bryan Hubbard (an executive). *Education:* Attended Northwestern University, 1969-71; Bennington College, B.A., 1973.

ADDRESSES: Home—London, England.

CAREER: Affiliated with *Playboy* magazine, Chicago, IL, 1971-72, and with *Atlantic Monthly,* Boston, MA, 1972-73; *Saturday Review/World,* New York, NY, assistant editor, 1973-74; *Chicago Tribune*/New York News Syndicate, New York, NY, associate editor, 1974-75, managing editor, 1975-77; freelance writer and editor, beginning 1977. Publisher, *What Doctors Don't Tell You* (newsletter), founder and editor.

MEMBER: Alpha Lambda Delta.

AWARDS, HONORS: Merit Award, New York City Women's Press Club, 1976.

WRITINGS:

The Baby Brokers: The Marketing of White Babies in America, Dial (New York, NY), 1980.
Kathleen Kennedy: Her Life and Times, Dial (New York, NY), 1983, published as *Kathleen Kennedy: The Untold Story of Jack Kennedy's Favourite Sister,* Weidenfeld & Nicolson (London, England), 1984.
What Doctors Don't Tell You: The Truth about the Dangers of Modern Medicine, Avon Books (New York, NY), 1998.
The Field: The Quests for the Secret Force of the Universe, HarperCollins (London, England), 2001.

Editor in chief, *Silo* (literary magazine of Bennington College), 1971-73. Contributor of articles to periodicals, including *New York Times.*

ADAPTATIONS: The Baby Brokers: The Marketing of White Babies in America was adapted into a television film titled *Born to Be Sold,* broadcast by the National Broadcasting Corporation, 1981.

SIDELIGHTS: Lynne McTaggart, a long-time journalist who has served on the staff of such periodicals as the *Atlantic Monthly* and *Chicago Tribune,* gained fame for her articles uncovering the malpractices related to private adoptions. Conducting her own undercover investigations, McTaggart first posed as a pregnant college student then later as a woman looking to adopt a child. A few years later, she expanded

on these experiences to write a full-length book on the subject. Titled *The Baby Brokers: The Marketing of White Babies,* the volume appeared in 1980.

In the course of her investigations, McTaggart had unearthed the seamier side of the private adoption business—young, impoverished women who were virtually selling their unborn children for a hefty price to couples unable to have children of their own. Unwilling to suffer the bureaucratic difficulties involved in dealing with a government-sanctioned agency, these couples would retain lawyers and private operations to enable them to adopt a child. McTaggart's book relates the tale, using pseudonyms, of an actual unwed mother and childless couple who are brought together by an adoption attorney. Although *The Baby Brokers* does not condemn private adoption itself, it reveals that the intermediary army of lawyers and agents who arrange these deals profit handsomely for their services. The lawyer for the couple in *The Baby Brokers* is openly identified, as are other key players in the independent adoption agency business.

As McTaggart points out, studies show that children adopted outside the usual rigorous parameters of state-affiliated agencies fare just as well as privately-placed youths. *The Baby Brokers* points an accusing finger, however, at those who treat human lives as a commodity. Although McTaggart's original articles on the subject had triggered a national regulatory movement aimed at curbing abuse related to the private adoption business, a review of *The Baby Brokers* by *Washington Post* contributor Barbara Joe noted that McTaggart's claims were somewhat dated at the time the book was published.

McTaggart's next work chronicles the dramatic but brief life of Kathleen Kennedy, sister of John F. Kennedy, former president of the United States. Nicknamed "Kick" by her friends and relatives, Kennedy was the eldest daughter of staunch Irish-Catholic parents. Her father, Joseph Kennedy, was a successful businessman and also served as ambassador of the United States to England in the 1930s. Her mother, Rose, was a devout Catholic, and Kennedy herself was brought up to believe in strict notions of propriety; when she married William Hartington, Marquis and Duke of Hartington—and member of the Church of England—her family was upset.

McTaggart's book traces events following the wedding, shortly after which Kennedy was widowed when Hartington was killed in action during the war. Kennedy refused to return to America and her family, staying in England after the tragedy. A few years later, she became involved with another English nobleman, Earl Peter Fitzwilliam. Although the earl was still married, the couple planned a wedding contingent upon the earl's intended divorce. They were, however, killed when their plane crashed during a heavy storm in France in 1948 (Kennedy was only twenty-eight years old at the time). Although newspapers carried the news of her death, the details of the event were not disclosed by the family for fear of harming the political careers of Kennedy's brothers, John and Robert.

While praising the author's insights into the interfamilial drama of the Kennedy household, *New York Times Book Review* contributor Anna Shapiro commented that the "most revealing part" of the book were McTaggart's disclosures about the events surrounding Kennedy's death. Elizabeth Mehren of the *Los Angeles Times* described *Kathleen Kennedy: Her Life and Times* as "a feast for savorers of Kennediana. Chatty, chockfull of anecdotes and seemingly convincing conversations, this obviously well-researched volume reveals as much about the Kennedy family as a whole as it does about its most spirited sister."

BIOGRAPHICAL AND CRITICAL SOURCES:

PERIODICALS

Books, September, 1996, review of *What Doctors Don't Tell You: The Truth about the Dangers of Modern Medicine,* p. 21.
Chicago Tribune Book World, November 20, 1983.
Los Angeles Times, January 1, 1984, Elizabeth Mehren, review of *Kathleen Kennedy: Her Life and Times,* p. 4.
New York Times, November 1, 1981.
Newsweek, November 21, 1983, p. 89.
New York Times Book Review, November 20, 1983, Anna Shapiro, review of *Kathleen Kennedy,* p. 16; February 3, 1985, p. 34.
Publishers Weekly, June 10, 2002, review of *The Field: The Quest for the Secret Force of the Universe,* p. 53.
Spectator, March 24, 1984, p. 21.
Washington Post, February 22, 1980, Barbara Joe, review of *The Baby Brokers: The Marketing of White Babies,* p. D7.

ONLINE

Channelling-Online, http://channelling-online.com/ (October 7, 2004), Tony Neate, review of *The Field.*
Ultimate QXCI Resource Centre Web site, http://www.theqxci.com/ (June, 2002), review of *The Field.*
What Doctors Don't Tell You Web site, http://www.wddty.co.uk/ (October 25, 2004).*

*   *   *

MEADES, Jonathan (Turner) 1947-
    (Enderby Hogg, Russell Russell, John Tee, Eddie Tyde)

PERSONAL: Born January 21, 1947, in Salisbury, England; son of John William (a soldier) and Margery Agnes (a teacher; maiden name, Hogg) Meades; married Sally Dorothy Renee Brown, September 15, 1980 (divorced, March, 1984); married Frances Anne Bentley, January 6, 1988; children: four; (first marriage) Holly and Rose (twins); (second marriage) Eleanor Lily. *Education:* Attended University of Bordeaux, 1965-66, and Royal Academy of Dramatic Art, 1967-69.

ADDRESSES: Home—Borough, London, England. *Agent*—Pat Kavanagh, A. D. Peters & Co. Ltd., 10 Buckingham St., London WC2N 6BU, England.

CAREER: Freelance designer and copywriter, 1969-72; freelance journalist, 1971-75; lecturer in liberal studies, 1975-76; staff writer for *Time Out* magazine, 1976-78; *Observer,* London, England, staff writer, 1978-79; staff writer for *Architectural Review,* 1979-80; editor of *Event,* 1981-82; *Tattler,* London, features editor, 1982-87; *Times* (London), restaurant critic, 1986-2001; freelance writer, 1987—. Presenter and writer for television programs and documentaries on food, architecture, and culture, including *Meades Eats, Travels with Pevsner, Abroad with Jonathan Meades, Further Abroad with Jonathan Meades,* and *Even Further Abroad with Jonathan Meades.*

AWARDS, HONORS: Glenfiddich Award for best food journalist, 1999.

WRITINGS:

This Is Their Life (television biographies), Salamander (London, England), 1979.

(With Philip Bagenal) *An Illustrated Atlas of the World's Great Buildings,* Salamander (London, England), 1980.

Filthy English (stories), J. Cape (London, England), 1984.

(With Deyan Sudjic and Peter Cook) *English Extremists: The Architecture of Campbell Zogolovitch Wilkinson Gough* (essays), Fourth Estate (London, England), 1988.

Peter Knows What Dick Likes (stories, prose, and a screenplay), Paladin Grafton (London, England), 1989.

Pompey (novel), Grafton (London, England), 1993.

Incest and Morris Dancing (food essays), Cassell (London, England), 2002.

The Fowler Family Business (novel), Fourth Estate (London, England), 2002.

Author of a weekly restaurant column in the *Times* (London). Contributor to periodicals, including *Curious, Harpers and Queen, Craft, Literary Review, Granta, Vogue, Books and Bookmen,* and *Dial,* sometimes under the pseudonyms John Tee, Eddie Tyde, Russell Russell, and Enderby Hogg.

SIDELIGHTS: Irascible, erudite, and disdainful of the mediocre, Jonathan Meades is a novelist, food critic, journalist, cultural gadfly, and connoisseur of architecture. Best known throughout Britain as the black-clad presenter and commentator on such television fare as *Meades Eats* and *Abroad with Jonathan Meades,* Meades combines the refinement of a gourmand's Epicurean tastes with the acerbic commentary and poison pen of a gonzo journalist. "Jonathan Meades has been compared, favorably, to Rabelais and, flatteringly, to Swift," remarked Henry Hitchings in the *Times Literary Supplement.* "The truth is that he outstrips both in the gaudiness of his imagination." Meades, wrote Lloyd Evans in the *Daily Mail,* "is a snob—let's not mince our words here—an outstanding, world-class snob. A gifted scorner, and a passionate eulogist." When a participant in the *You Ask the Questions* feature in the *Independent* asked Meades if he was a snob, Meades replied, "Everyone is snobbish about something or other. Snobbishness is merely a deprecatory synonym of discrimination."

His first novel, *Pompey,* concerns Ray Butt, a reformed stand-up comedian turned church leader in the southern English coastal town of Pompey—a setting based in large part on Meades's "adopted spiritual home of Portsmouth," wrote Jenny Turner in the *Guardian.* In his former life in the pubs and comedy clubs, Butt spewed off-color jokes and lewd stories as easily as if they were prayers. But a drunken-driving accident shattered his body, killed his wife, and led him to religious transformation. As the head of the Church of the Best Ever Redemption, Butt presides over the functions and needs of his congregation. Still, Butt lives for the day when another automobile accident makes available another donated organ or dollop of living flesh that can be stitched into his body to prolong his life, as though he himself were a neomodern Prometheus.

Butt shares Pompey with the Vallender family, an assortment of depraved characters who operate a fireworks factory—one is eaten by a crocodile in the Belgian Congo, another chokes on his own waste while wearing a latex bondage outfit, and another brings a fatal virus to Pompey, contracted after eating a pygmy in the Belgian Congo. "Although it sounds chaotic, *Pompey* actually has a weirdly elegant architectonic to it, a sense of its own shape that is best got at by reading long and fast," Turner commented. "And although it may sound cold and cynical, *Pompey*'s dominant mood is rather dreamy, sad, and puzzled, a feeling partly created by having Meades himself appear in his narrative as a heartlessly normal suburban middle-class thug." Susan Jeffreys, writing in *New Statesman & Society,* called *Pompey* "an extraordinary work, peopled by the repellent, dwelling on the vile and yet done with so deft and brilliant a touch; a picnic in the heart of darkness." Jeffreys concluded, "What a dark pleasure it is to come across writing that is both luminous and bilious."

Meades served as the food critic for the London *Times* for fifteen years, finally laying down his fork and pen in 2001. "Purveyors of the bland, the unauthentic, and the mediocre will have been sleeping easier since last December, when Britain's most vitriolic, knowledgeable, and literate restaurant critic handed in his napkin" for the final time, wrote Christopher Hirst in the *Independent.* More than 200 of his best reviews are collected in *Incest and Morris Dancing,* published in 2002. The title of the book derives from a quote by Sir Arnold Bax, a British author and composer, who advised, "Try everything once except incest and folk dancing" (switched by Meades to morris dancing).

Chief among reasons for Meades's longevity as a food critic were his ability to focus on topics beyond the merely gastronomic, and "his near-limitless reservoir of bile," Hirst remarked. "The twin passions propelling this book are a profound appreciation of top-notch cuisine, preferably French in origin and visceral in content, and a Swiftian disdain for the tastes of the mass of the populace," Hirst commented. The book is "good fun to read and terrific fun to hate," Evans observed.

In Meades's 2002 novel, *The Fowler Family Business,* the "family business" of the title is Henry Fowler's inheritance—a mortuary in south London. And it is a legacy that Henry takes seriously, having twice been named Young Funeral Director of the Year. Henry accepts his station in life, but there are dark secrets and lies that line the rocky path from Henry's youth as a doted-upon and cherubic boy, to respected adult professional, to ruined and morally bankrupt middle-aged man. As a boy, Henry pushes his friend Stanley off a high railroad bridge; the death is ruled an accident, and Henry doesn't reveal otherwise. Afterward, Henry and Stanley's younger brother Curly become inseparable. As adults, Curly discovers he is impotent, and asks Henry to impregnate his wife, as a favor. Henry gladly obliges, but discovers in the process that he is also sterile—which brings up questions of his own children's paternity. "Meades's novel is what is generally described as a romp," Hitchings commented. "His characters blunder around insanely, and new ones turn up without much warning."

Filthy English, first published in 1984 and reprinted in 1994, was noted for its use of language. "Meades's linguistic games, together with a frequent lack of coherent narrative, often lead to incomprehensibility, but you'd be hard pushed to find a more invigorating use of English, filthy or otherwise," observed reviewers in the *Times.*

Jonathan Meades told *CA:* "I am quite incapable of explaining *why* I write what I write. My writing has been described as 'gruesome,' 'enticingly repellent,' 'intended to deprave and corrupt,' 'odd and gorgeous,' 'haunting,' and 'relentlessly tasteless.' My characters are base, corrupt, and hugely unpleasant. I fondly suppose that I am none of these. My interests are called civilized: buildings, food, and so on. In fiction I like high style and low incidents—plenty of both. I also like intense concentration, distillation: epics in miniature."

BIOGRAPHICAL AND CRITICAL SOURCES:

PERIODICALS

Books, January, 1990, review of *Peters Knows What Dick Likes,* p. 5.

Building Design, September 6, 2002, Alan Powers, "The Centre Ground (The Opinions of Jonathan Meades on the Picturesque)," p. 10.

Daily Mail (London, England), May 31, 2002, Lloyd Evans, "Snob a la Carte," review of *Incest and Morris Dancing,* p. 58.

Guardian (London, England), May 4, 1993, Jenny Turner, review of *Pompey;* February 9, 2002, Alex Clark, "Poison Pen," review of *The Fowler Family Business;* June 8, 2002, Tom Jaine, "Where's the Beef? Tom Jaine Is Left Feeling Hungry," review of *Incest and Morris Dancing,* p. 15.

Guardian Weekly, January 30, 1994, review of *Pompey,* p. 28.

Independent (London, England), January 30, 2002, Brian Jones, "You Ask the Questions: Jonathan Meades," interview with Meades, p. 7; May 30, 2002, Christopher Hirst, "The Thursday Book: Truly and Legend in His Own Lunchtime," review of *Incest and Morris Dancing,* p. 18.

New Statesman, February 11, 2002, Hugo Barnacle, review of *The Fowler Family Business,* p. 53.

New Statesman & Society, April 23, 1993, Susan Jeffreys, review of *Pompey,* pp. 30-31.

Observer (London, England), April 25, 1993, review of *Pompey,* p. 63; September 18, 1994, review of *Filthy English,* p. 20.

Spectator, May 1, 1993, review of *Pompey,* p. 35.

Times (London, England), May 2, 1993, Tom Shone, "Expletives Deleted?," review of *Filthy English;* October 2, 1994, Ned Balfe, Phil Baker, Pam Barrett, Ian Critchley, Joanna Duckworth, Ivan Hill, Edward Platt, and Roger Williams, review of *Filthy English;* August 14, 2002, Iain Finlayson, review of *Incest and Morris Dancing,* p. 18.

Times Literary Supplement, April 9, 1993, review of *Pompey,* p. 20; February 15, 2002, Henry Hitchings, "English Vices," review of *The Fowler Family Business;* August 2, 2002, Paul Levy, "Off the Menu," review of *Incest and Morris Dancing.*

ONLINE

BBC Television Web site, http://www.bbc.co.uk/ (March, 2003), transcript of online chat with Jonathan Meades; (February 6, 2004), *Meades Eats* Web site.

Guardian Unlimited Web site, http://www.guardian.co.uk/ (February 9, 2002), review of *The Fowler Family Business.*

Telegraph (London, England) Web site, http://www.telegraph.co.uk/ (February 22, 2003), Harry Mount, "Portrait of a Driver: Jonathan Meades," interview with Meades.*

*   *   *

MEDWED, Mameve

PERSONAL: Given name is pronounced "mame-eve"; born in Bangor, ME; daughter of Harry (a lawyer) and Mimi (a teacher) Stern; married Howard Medwed (a lawyer), August 9, 1964; children: Daniel, Jonathan. *Education:* Simmons College, B.A. (with honors), 1964; attended writing workshops at Brandeis University and Radcliffe. *Politics:* Democrat. *Hobbies and other interests:* Art, literature, movies, food.

ADDRESSES: Office—58 Washington Ave., Cambridge, MA 02140. *Agent*—Lisa Bankoff, International Creative Management, 40 West 57th St., New York, NY 10019. *E-mail*—mameve@comcast.net.

CAREER: Cambridge Center for Adult Education, Cambridge, MA, instructor for fiction writing workshops, 1979—. Lesley College, mentor for master's degree in fine arts program, 1986-88; Simmons College, Robert M. Gay Memorial Lecturer, 1996. Advanced fiction workshop, teacher, 1985-86; Company of Writers, teacher of advanced creative writing workshop, 1994-95; panelist and member, Virginia Center for the Book; board member, Cambridge Center for Adult Education; gives readings and public lectures; participant on library panels and at book festivals.

MEMBER: Authors Guild, PEN New England.

AWARDS, HONORS: Finalist, Massachusetts Artists Foundation Award, 1985; honored author, Library Lover's Annual Dinner, 2003.

WRITINGS:

Mail (novel), Warner Books (New York, NY), 1997.
Host Family, Warner Books (New York, NY), 2000.
The End of an Error (novel), Warner Books (New York, NY), 2003.

The Celebrity Register, researcher and writer, 1963; contributor of stories, articles, and reviews to periodicals, including *Newsday, Kirkus Reviews, Playgirl, Redbook, Nantucket Review, Boston Globe, Missouri Review, Yankee, Readerville Journal, Ascent,* and *Confrontation.*

ADAPTATIONS: Mail was adapted for audio cassette, 1997, and has been optioned as a motion picture by Archer Street Films, directed by Sharon Maguire and screenplay written by Wendy Wasserstein.

SIDELIGHTS: Described by a *New York Times Book Review* critic as a "wacky, funny . . . off-the-wall send-up of the take-charge-of-your-life novel," Mameve Medwed's first novel, *Mail,* "was enjoyed by many," observed Beth Gibbs in a *Library Journal* report, "and she does not disappoint with her second, engaging book." Gibbs was referring to *Host Family,* a comedy of manners set in the academic whirl of Cambridge, Massachusetts. After twenty years of marriage, fortyish Henry and Daisy Lewis seem to have a charmed future in store. Their grown son, Sam, is about to attend Harvard; the couple is looking forward to hosting yet another foreign-exchange student, the French beauty Giselle. But something is different this year. Henry develops a Francophile obsession, which turns to passion for Giselle. Meanwhile, Daisy is noticed by Truman Wolff, "a parasitologist whose studies of 'virus-host relationships' seem particularly apt," according to a *Publishers Weekly* contributor. In another twist to the story, Sam has grown enamored of Truman's teenage daughter, Phoebe, but loses her to the dashing Andrea, an Italian exchange student.

"Throughout this novel," stated Roisin Fagan in *Bookreporter,* "Medwed weaves metaphors comparing relationships to parasites of every sort: lice, tapeworms, even computer viruses." It wasn't the metaphors that gave Christopher Atamian pause, but rather the characterization. In a *New York Times Book Review* piece, Atamian assessed *Host Family* as a novel "meant to be a study of community and family," but found that "you don't empathize with [Medwed's] characters, who seem to lack vision and will." Harriet Klausner, on the other hand, told *BookBrowser* that those same key characters "are fully developed so that the audience can moan and groan in tune to their actions and reactions." To the *Publishers Weekly* critic, the book is "a cuttingly funny and heartwarming tale."

In her third book, *The End of an Error*, Medwed follows a middle-aged woman as she tries to determine if she should remain with the devoted, but routine husband she married or attempt to reunite with her first love, an English boy she met while a teen. Of *The End of an Error*, a *Booklist* critic thought, "This witty and diverting and even enchanting look at middle age should make Medwed a household name," while a *Boston Globe* critic found that Medwed "has a gift for descriptive detail, finding pathos and humor in the stuff of everyday life."

In an essay for *Author! Author!*, Medwed revealed that the impetus for Host Family came from her own background: "For twenty-five years, my husband and I have been hosting international students who come to study at Harvard," she wrote. "We've faced thousands of challenging meals, experienced dozens of instances of culture shock, . . . and displayed not always tasteful or even recognizable souvenirs on our table tops."

BIOGRAPHICAL AND CRITICAL SOURCES:

PERIODICALS

Booklist, April 1, 1997, review of *Mail*, p. 1282; May 15, 2003, Patty Engelmann, review of *The End of an Error*, p. 1644.
Books, December, 1997, review of *Mail*, p. 20.
Bookwatch, July, 1997, review of *Mail*, p. 11.
Boston Globe, July 21, 2003, review of *The End of an Error*, and "Between the Lines with Mameve Medwed."
Kirkus Reviews, March 15, 1997, review of *Mail*, p. 410; December 1, 1999, review of *Host Family*, p. 1834.
Library Journal, June 15, 1997, review of *Mail*, p. 98; September 15, 1997, review of *Mail*, p. 128; October 1, 1997, review of *Mail*, p. 50; January,

2000, Beth Gibbs, review of *Host Family*, p. 161; May 15, 2003, Nancy Pearl, review of *The End of an Error*, p. 126.
New York Times Book Review, July 13, 1997, review of *Mail*, p. 18; February 13, 2000, Christopher Atamian, review of *Host Family*.
Publishers Weekly, March 3, 1997, review of *Mail*, p. 62; July 7, 1997, review of *Mail* (audio version), p. 33; November, 22, 1999, review of *Host Family*, p. 40; May 5, 2003, review of *The End of an Error*, p. 195.
Rapport, number 2, 1997, review of *Mail*, p. 22.

ONLINE

Author! Author!, http://www.twbookmark.com/ (July 17, 2002), Mameve Medwed, "How I Came to Write *Host Family*."
BookBrowser, http://www.bookbrowser.com/, February 18, 2000, Harriet Klausner, review of *Host Family*.
Bookreporter, http://www.bookreporter.com/ (July 17, 2002), Roisin Fagan, review of *Host Family*.

*   *   *

MEGGED, Aharon 1920-

PERSONAL: Name is sometimes spelled Aron Meged or Aharon Meged; born August 10, 1920, in Wloçlavek, Poland; immigrated to Palestine (now Israel), c. 1925; son of Moshe (a teacher) and Leah (Reichgot) Megged; married Eda Zirlin (a writer and painter), May 11, 1944; children: Eyal, Amos. *Education:* Attended high school in Palestine (now Israel), 1933-37. *Politics:* Labour. *Religion:* Jewish.

ADDRESSES: Home—26 Rupin St., Tel-Aviv, Israel. *Agent*—Gloria Stern Literary Agency, 1230 Park Ave., New York, NY 10028.

CAREER: Member of a kibbutz in Sdot-Yam, Israel, 1938-50; *Massa* (biweekly newspaper), Tel-Aviv, Israel, editor, 1952-55; *Lamerchav* (daily newspaper), Tel-Aviv, literary editor, 1955-68; Israeli Embassy, London, England, cultural attache, 1968-71; *Davar* (daily newspaper), Tel-Aviv, columnist, 1971-c. 1983; author, 1983—. Writer in residence, University of

Haifa, 1974, and Oxford University, 1978. Zionist missionary in the United States, 1946-48; participant in several lecture tours in the United States.

MEMBER: International PEN (president of Israel center, 1980-88), Israeli Writer's Association (member of central committee, 1954-60), National Arts Council (member of central committee, 1962-67), Hebrew Academy, Israeli Journalist's Association.

AWARDS, HONORS: Ussishkin Prize, 1955, for *Hedvah ve-ani: u-farashat korotenu ba-`ir Tel-Aviv,* and 1966, for *ha-Hai `al ha-met;* Brenner Prize, 1957, for *Yisrael haverim;* Shlonsky Prize, 1963, for *ha-Berihah: sheloshah masa`ot;* Israeli Prime Minister's Award, 1973; Bialik Prize, 1973, for *Mahberot Evyatar* and *'Al etsim ve-avanim;* Fichman Prize, 1973, for *`A´sahel;* Kenneth B. Smilen Literature Award, 1983; Present Tense Prize, 1983, for *`A´sahel* in English translation; Gatmon Prize, 1987; Rockefeller Foundation fellow in Bellagio, Italy, 1988; Polak Prize, 1989; Newman Prize, 1991.

WRITINGS:

El ha-yeladim be-Teman (juvenile; title means "To the Children in Yemen"), United Synagogues of America (New York, NY), 1948.

Ruah yamin (short stories; title means "Spirit of the Seas"), Hotsa'at ha-Kibutz ha-me'uhad (Tel-Aviv, Israel), 1950.

Hedvah ve-ani: u-farashat korotenu ba-`ir Tel-Aviv (novel; produced as a two-act play in Tel-Aviv, Israel, at Habimah Theater, 1955), ha-Kibutz ha-me'uhad (Tel-Aviv, Israel), 1954, reprinted, 1993, translation of stage version published as *Hedva and I: A Play in Two Acts,* Youth and Hechalutz Department of the Zionist Organization (Jerusalem, Israel), 1957.

Yisrael haverim (short stories; title means "Israeli Folk"), ha-Kibutz ha-me'uhad (Tel-Aviv, Israel), 1955.

Mikreh ha-kesil (novel), ha-Kibutz ha-me'uhad (Tel-Aviv, Israel), 1959, translation by Aubrey Hodes published as *Fortunes of a Fool,* Victor Gollancz (London, England), 1962, Random House (New York, NY), 1963.

ha-Berihah: sheloshah masa`ot (three novellas; title means "The Escape"), ha-Kibutz ha-me'uhad (Tel-Aviv, Israel), 1962.

*Mi-sipure ha-yom ha-sheni: Geshem nedavot; Ma`a'seh bilti ragil; Yad va-shem,* Ketsin hinukh rashi, `Anaf ha'skalah (Tel-Aviv, Israel), 1965.

*ha-Hai `al ha-met* (novel), `Am `oved (Tel-Aviv, Israel), 1965, translation by Misha Louvish published as *Living on the Dead,* Jonathan Cape (London, England), 1970, McCall Publishing (New York, NY), 1971.

*`Avel* (title means "Iniquity"), `Am `oved (Tel-Aviv, Israel), 1966.

ha-Yom ha-Sheni (short stories; title means "The Second Day"), Tarmil (Tel-Aviv, Israel), 1967.

ha-Hayim ha-ketsarim (novel), ha-Kibutz ha-me'uhad (Tel-Aviv, Israel), 1972, translation by Miriam Arad published as *The Short Life,* Taplinger Publishing (New York, NY), 1980.

Sheloshah sipurim, 1972.

Hatsot ha-yom (title means "Midday"), ha-Kibutz ha-me'uhad (Tel-Aviv, Israel), 1973.

Mahberot Evyatar (title means "Evyatar's Notebooks"), ha-Kibutz ha-me'uhad (Tel-Aviv, Israel), 1973.

*`Al etsim ve-avanim* (title means "Of Trees and Stones"), `Am `oved (Tel-Aviv, Israel), 1973.

ha-'Ataleph (novel; title means "The Bat"), `Am `oved (Tel-Aviv, Israel), 1975.

*Haints u-veno veha-ruah ha-ra`ah* (novella; title means "Heinz, His Son and the Evil Spirit"), `Am `oved (Tel-Aviv, Israel), 1976.

*`A´sahel* (novel), `Am `oved (Tel-Aviv, Israel), 1978, translation by Robert Whitehill and Susan C. Lilly published as *Asahel,* Taplinger Publishing (New York, NY), 1982.

Ahavat ne`urim (juvenile; title means "Young Love"), Dvir (Tel-Aviv, Israel), 1979.

Massa be-av (novel; title means "Journey in the Month of Av"), `Am `oved (Tel-Aviv, Israel), 1981.

*ha-Gamal ha-me `ofef ve-dabeshet ha-zahav* (novel; title means "The Flying Camel and the Golden Hump"), `Am `oved (Tel-Aviv, Israel), 1982.

*Masa` ha-yeladim el ha-Arets ha-Muvtahat: parshat yalde Selvino,* `Am `oved (Tel-Aviv, Israel), 1984, translation by Vivian Eden published as *The Story of the Selvino Children: Journey to the Promised Land,* Vallentine Mitchell (Portland, OR), 2002.

Ezor ha-ra`ash (collected newspaper columns; title means "The Turbulent Zone"), ha-Kibutz ha-me'uhad (Tel-Aviv, Israel), c. 1985.

*Ma`a'seh meguneh: sheloshah Sipurim* (three novellas; title means "Indecent Act"), `Am `oved (Tel-Aviv, Israel), 1986.

Foiglman (novel), `Am `oved (Tel-Aviv, Israel), 1987, translation by Marganet Weinberger-Rotman, Toby Press (New Milford, CT), 2003.

*Shulhan ha-ketivah: kovets ma'amarim be-`inyene sifrut* (criticism; title means "The Writing Desk"), `Am `oved (Tel-Aviv, Israel), 1989.

Mivhar sipurim (short stories), Zemorah-Bitan (Tel-Aviv, Israel), 1989.

*Nadav ve-imo: sipur li-vene-ha-ne`urim* (young adult novel; title means "Nadav and His Mother"), Devir be-shituf `im Amkor (Tel-Aviv, Israel), 1989.

*Yom ha-or shel `Anat* (title means "Anat's Day of Illumination"), `Am `oved (Tel-Aviv, Israel), 1992.

Ga`gu`im le-Olgah (title means "Longing for Olga"), `Am `oved (Tel-Aviv, Israel), 1994.

Duda'im min ha-arets ha-kedoshah (title means "Mandrakes from the Holy Land"), `Am `oved (Tel-Aviv, Israel), 1998.

Persefoneh zokheret (title means "Persephone Remembers"), Zemorah-Bitan (Tel-Aviv, Israel), 2000.

`Ad ha-`erev (title means "Till Evening Falls"), Zemorah-Bitan (Tel-Aviv, Israel), 2001.

Nikmat Yotam (title means "Yotam's Vengeance"), Zemorah-Bitan (Tel-Aviv, Israel), 2003.

Work represented in anthologies, including *A Whole Loaf,* edited by S. J. Kahn, 1957; *Yisrael* edited by J. Leftwich, 1963; *Hebrew Short Stories 2,* edited by S. Y. Penueli and A. Ukhmani, 1965; and *The New Israeli Writers,* edited by D. Rabikovitz, 1969. Contributor to journals and newspapers, often under pseudonym A. M., including *Encounter, Midstream,Listener, Moment, Partisan Review,* and *Atlantic Monthly.*

Megged's books have been published in Romanian, Russian, Spanish, German, Italian, Portuguese, Yiddish, and French.

PLAYS

Inkubator al Hassels (three-act; title means "Incubator on the Rocks"), first produced in Tel-Aviv, Israel, at Ohel Theater, 1950.

Harhek ba-`arava: mahazeh be-shalosh ma`arakhot (title means "Far in the Wasteland"), Sifriyat po`alim (Merhavyah, Israel), 1951.

Baderech Le-Eilat (two-act; title means "The Way to Eylat"; first produced in Tel-Aviv, Israel, at Habimah Theater, 1955), Sifriat po`alom (Merhavyah, Israel), 1955.

I Like Mike (three-act; first produced in Tel-Aviv, Israel, at Habimah Theater, 1960), ha-Kibutz ha-me'uhad (Tel-Aviv, Israel) 1960.

Hamesh hamesh (two-act; title means "Tit for Tat"), first produced in Tel-Aviv, Israel, at Ohel Theater, 1960.

*Hanah Senesh: mahazeh bi-shete ma`arakhot* (two-act; first produced in Tel-Aviv, Israel, at Habimah Theater, 1962), ha-Kibutz ha-me'uhad (Tel-Aviv, Israel), 1954, reprinted, Or-`am (Tel-Aviv, Israel), 1989.

Be-reshit (three act; title means "Genesis;" first produced in Tel-Aviv, Israel, at Habimah Theater, 1965), Or Am (Tel-Aviv, Israel), 1965, published as *The First Sin,* Centre Hongrois De l'I.I.T. (Budapest, Hungary), 1982.

*ha-`Onah ha-bo`eret: mahazeh bi-shete ma`arakhot* (two-act; title means "The High Season"; first produced in Tel-Aviv, Israel, at Habimah Theater, 1968), `Amikam (Tel-Aviv, Israel), 1967.

El hatzippor (title means "To the Bird"), produced in Haifa, Israel, at Haifa Theater, 1974.

Megged's plays have also produced in the United States, Argentina, Sweden, Switzerland, and other locations.

ADAPTATIONS: The stage play *I Like Mike* was adapted as a screenplay.

SIDELIGHTS: Jacob Kabakoff, in a *World Literature Today* review, called Aharon Megged "one of the leading short story writers and novelists of the generation of Israel's War of Independence" and noted that the author has depicted "the varied aspects of life in the new state, from war themes to the kibbutz and urban life." In his novel *Living on the Dead,* Megged tells the story of a young Israeli writer who has signed a contract with a publishing house to write a biography of one of the country's Zionist pioneers. Even though he collects an advance from the publisher and receives monthly checks on which he is able to live and conduct research, the writer is unable to finish the project. Stephen G. Kellman of *Modern Fiction Studies* explained that "examples of necrophagia, of living on the dead, are scattered throughout this novel, from poets who seem to cultivate experiences in order to convert them into inert stanzas to a nation fond of worshipping its heroes dead. Jonas [the protagonist] is consumed by the realization that he himself is the most voracious necrophage in the drama. . . . [Like] those scholars who bide their time until such lives as Stravinsky, Pound, or Picasso are completed before rushing out with the definitive study, Jonas, beneficiary of the publisher's monthly check, is in a real sense feeding himself from a dead man."

Megged once told *CA:* "Life in the country, first, in childhood, in a small village, and then in a Kibbutz, had a great effect on my work. In later years I traveled much in Europe in search of Jewish medieval mysticism, especially in Spain and France. European writers, such as Kafka, Svevo, Gogol, Chekhov, had influence on my work."

BIOGRAPHICAL AND CRITICAL SOURCES:

BOOKS

Contemporary Literary Criticism, Volume 9, Thomson Gale (Detroit, MI), 1979.

PERIODICALS

Choice, March, 1983, review of *Asahel,* p. 997.
Commentary, August, 1972, Harold Fisch, review of *Living on the Dead,* pp. 74-75.
Kirkus Reviews, November 1, 1981, review of *Asahel,* p. 1366.
Library Journal, March 1, 1982, review of *Asahel,* p. 563.
Modern Fiction Studies, summer, 1976, Stephen G. Kellman, review of *Living on the Dead,* pp. 231-237.
New York Times Book Review, January 11, 1981, review of *The Short Life,* p. 10.
Publishers Weekly, November 20, 1981, review of *Asahel,* p. 44.
World Literature Today, spring, 1977, review by Jacob Kabakoff; spring, 1981, review of *The Short Life,* p. 369; summer, 1983, review of *Asahel,* p. 507; autumn, 1995, review of *Ga`gu`im le-Olgah,* p. 862.*

*   *   *

MERRIMAN, Alex
    See SILVERBERG, Robert

MERWIN, W(illiam) S(tanley) 1927-

PERSONAL: Born September 30, 1927, in New York, NY; son of a Presbyterian minister; married Dorothy Jeanne Ferry (divorced); married Dido Milroy (divorced); married Paula Schwartz. *Education:* Princeton University, A.B., 1947; attended one year of graduate study in modern languages.

ADDRESSES: Home—Haiku, HI. *Agent*—c/o Author Mail, Atheneum Publishers, 866 3rd Ave., New York, NY 10022-6221.

CAREER: Poet. Tutor in France and Portugal, 1949; tutor of Robert Graves's son in Majorca, 1950; lived in London, England, 1951-54, supporting himself largely by doing translations of Spanish and French classics for British Broadcasting Corporation (BBC) *Third Programme;* playwright for Poets' Theatre, Cambridge, MA, 1956; lived in New York, NY, 1961-63; associated with Roger Planchon's Theatre de la Cite, Lyon, France, ten months during 1964-65; moved to Hawaii in the late 1970s. In 1999, Merwin was named Poetry Consultant to the Library of Congress for a jointly-held position with poets Rita Dove and Louise Glück.

MEMBER: National Institute of Arts and Letters.

AWARDS, HONORS: Kenyon Review fellowship in poetry, 1954; Rockefeller fellowship, 1956; National Institute of Arts and Letters grant, 1957; Arts Council of Great Britain playwriting bursary, 1957; Rabinowitz Foundation grant, 1961; Bess Hokin Prize, *Poetry,* 1962; Ford Foundation grant, 1964-65; fellowship from Chapelbrook Foundation, 1966; Harriet Monroe Memorial Prize, *Poetry,* 1967; Rockefeller Foundation grant, 1969; Pulitzer Prize for poetry, 1971, for *The Carrier of Ladders;* fellowship from the Academy of American Poets, 1973; Guggenheim fellowship, 1973, 1983; Shelley Memorial Award, 1974; Bollingen Prize for poetry, Yale University Library, 1979; Lenore Marshall Poetry Prize, 1994, for *Travels;* Tanning Prize for poetry, 1994; Lila Wallace *Reader's Digest* fellowship, 1994.

WRITINGS:

POETRY, EXCEPT AS INDICATED

A Mask for Janus (also see below), Yale University Press (New Haven, CT), 1952.

W. S. Merwin

The Dancing Bears (also see below), Yale University Press (New Haven, CT), 1954.

Green with Beasts (also see below), Knopf (New York, NY), 1956.

The Drunk in the Furnace (also see below), Macmillan (New York, NY), 1960.

(Editor) *West Wind: Supplement of American Poetry,* Poetry Book Society (London, England), 1961.

The Moving Target, Atheneum (New York, NY), 1963.

Collected Poems, Atheneum (New York, NY), 1966.

The Lice, Atheneum (New York, NY), 1969.

Animae, Kayak (San Francisco, CA), 1969.

The Miner's Pale Children (prose), Atheneum (New York, NY), 1970, reprinted, Holt (New York, NY), 1994.

The Carrier of Ladders, Atheneum (New York, NY), 1970.

(With A. D. Moore) *Signs,* Stone Wall Press (Iowa City, IA), 1970.

Asian Figures, Atheneum (New York, NY), 1973.

Writings to an Unfinished Accompaniment, Atheneum (New York, NY), 1973.

The First Four Books of Poems (contains *A Mask for Janus, The Dancing Bears, Green with Beasts,* and *The Drunk in the Furnace*), Atheneum (New York, NY), 1975.

The Compass Flower, Atheneum (New York, NY), 1977.

Houses and Travellers (prose), Atheneum (New York, NY), 1977, reprinted, Holt (New York, NY), 1994.

Feathers from the Hill, Windhover (Iowa City, IA), 1978.

Finding the Islands, North Point Press (San Francisco, CA), 1982.

Unframed Originals: Recollections (prose), Atheneum (New York, NY), 1982.

Opening the Hand, Atheneum (New York, NY), 1983.

The Rain in the Trees: Poems, Knopf (New York, NY), 1988.

Selected Poems, Atheneum (New York, NY), 1988.

The Lost Upland (prose), Knopf (New York, NY), 1992.

Travels: Poems, Knopf (New York, NY), 1993.

The Vixen: Poems, Knopf (New York, NY), 1996.

(Compiler) *Lament for the Makers: A Memorial Anthology,* Counterpoint (Washington, DC), 1996.

Flower and Hand: Poems, 1977-1983, Copper Canyon Press (Port Townsend, WA), 1996.

The Folding Cliffs: A Narrative (prose), Knopf (New York, NY), 1998.

East Window: The Asian Poems, Copper Canyon Press (Port Townsend, WA), 1998.

The River Sound: Poems, Knopf (New York, NY), 1999.

The Pupil, Knopf (New York, NY), 2001.

The Mays of Ventadorn (prose, National Geographic Direction Series), National Geographic (Washington, DC), 2002.

The Ends of the Earth (essays), Shoemaker & Hoard (Washington, DC), 2004.

Migration: New and Selected Poems, Copper Canyon Press (Port Townsend, WA), 2005.

Present Company, Copper Canyon Press (Port Townsend, WA), 2005.

Contributor to numerous anthologies. Merwin's poems have been recorded for the Archive of Recorded Poetry and Literature, 1994.

Contributor to magazines, including *Nation, Harper's, Poetry, New Yorker, Atlantic, Kenyon Review,* and *Evergreen Review.* Poetry editor, *Nation,* 1962.

A reader, with others, on sound recordings, including *Poetry and the American People: Reading, Voice, and Publication in the 19th and 20th Centuries,* Library of Congress Bicentennial Symposium, 2000; *Poetry in America: Favorite Poems: An Evening of Readings and a Special Favorite Poem Audio and Video Presentation,* Library of Congress (Washington, DC), 2000; *An Evening of Dante in English Translation,* Library of Congress (Washington, DC), 2000.

The W. S. Merwin Archive in the Rare Book Room of the University Library of the University of Illinois at Urbana-Champaign contains notes, drafts, and manuscripts of published and unpublished work by Merwin from the mid-1940s to the early 1980s.

TRANSLATOR

The Poem of the Cid, Dent (London, England), 1959, New American Library (New York, NY), 1962.

(Contributor) Eric Bentley, editor, *The Classic Theatre,* Doubleday (New York, NY), 1961.

The Satires of Persius, Indiana University Press (Bloomington, IN), 1961.

Some Spanish Ballads, Abelard (London, England), 1961, published as *Spanish Ballads,* Doubleday Anchor (New York, NY), 1961.

*The Life of Lazarillo de Tormes: His Fortunes and Adversities,*Doubleday Anchor (New York, NY), 1962.

(Contributor) *Medieval Epics,* Modern Library (New York, NY), 1963.

(With Denise Levertov, William Carlos Williams, and others) Nicanor Parra, *Poems and Antipoems,* New Directions (New York, NY), 1968.

Jean Follain, *Transparence of the World,* Atheneum (New York, NY), 1969, reprinted, Copper Canyon Press (Port Townsend, WA), 2003.

W. S. Merwin: Selected Translations, 1948-1968, Atheneum (New York, NY), 1969.

(And author of introduction) S. Chamfort, *Products of the Perfected Civilization: Selected Writings of Chamfort,* Macmillan (New York, NY), 1969.

Porchia, *Voices: Selected Writings of Antonio Porchia,* Follett (Chicago, IL), 1969, reprinted, Copper Canyon Press (Port Townsend, WA), 2003.

Pablo Neruda, *Twenty Poems and a Song of Despair,* Cape (London, England), 1969, reprinted, with introduction by Christina García, illustrations by Pablo Picasso, Penguin Books (New York, NY), 2004.

(With others) Pablo Neruda, *Selected Poems,* Dell (New York, NY), 1970.

(With Clarence Brown) Osip Mandelstam, *Selected Poems,* Oxford University Press (New York, NY), 1973, reprinted as *The Selected Poems of Osip Mandelstam,* New York Review of Books (New York, NY), 2004.

(With J. Moussaieff Mason) *Sanskrit Love Poetry,* Columbia University Press (New York, NY), 1977, published as *Peacock's Egg: Love Poems from Ancient India,* North Point Press (San Francisco, CA), 1981.

Roberto Juarroz, *Vertical Poems,* Kayak (San Francisco, CA), 1977.

(With George E. Dimock, Jr.) Euripides, *Iphigenia at Aulius,* Oxford University Press (New York, NY), 1978.

Selected Translations, 1968-78, Atheneum (New York, NY), 1979.

Robert the Devil, Windhover (Iowa City, IA), 1981.

Four French Plays, Atheneum (New York, NY), 1984.

From the Spanish Morning, Atheneum (New York, NY), 1984.

Dante Alighieri, *Purgatorio,* Knopf (New York, NY), 2000.

Gawain and the Green Knight, a New Verse Translation, Knopf (New York, NY), 2002.

Also translator of Lope de Rueda, "Eufemia," in *Tulane Drama Review,* December, 1958; Lesage, "Crispin," in *Tulane Drama Review;* Lope Felix de Vega Carpio, *Punishment without Vengeance,*1958; Federico García Lorca, "Yerma" and "Blood," 1969.

PLAYS

(With Dido Milroy) *Darkling Child,* produced, 1956.

Favor Island, produced at Poets' Theatre, Cambridge, MA, 1957, and on British Broadcasting Corporation *Third Programme,* 1958.

The Gilded West, produced at Belgrade Theatre, Coventry, England, 1961.

SIDELIGHTS: W. S. Merwin is a major American writer whose poetry, translations, and prose have won praise from literary critics since the publication of his first book. The spare, hard verse comprising the body of Merwin's work has been characterized by many as very difficult reading. However, it is generally agreed that this poetry is worth whatever extra effort may be required to appreciate it. In a *Yale Review* article, Laurence Lieberman stated, "This poetry, at its best—and at our best as readers—is able to meet us and engage our wills as never before in the thresholds between waking and sleeping, past and future, self and anti-self, men and gods, the living and the dead." Although Merwin's writing has undergone many stylistic changes through the course of his career, it is unified by the recurring theme of man's separation from nature. The poet sees the consequences of that alienation as disastrous, both for the human race and for the rest of the world.

Merwin, who feels strongly about ecological issues, once commented: "It makes me angry to feel that the natural world is taken to have so little importance." He gave an example from his own life: "The Pennsylvania that I grew up in and loved as a child isn't there . . . it's been strip-mined: it really is literally not there. This happens to a lot of people, but I don't see why one has to express indifference about it. It matters . . . It's like being told that you can't possibly be mentally healthy." As an illustration of the poet's commitment to environmental concerns, he has lived since the late 1970s on an old pineapple plantation in Hawaii, which he has been painstakingly restoring to its original rainforest state.

Merwin's despair over the desecration of nature is strongly expressed in his collection *The Lice.* Lieberman commented: "To read these poems is an act of self-purification. Every poem in the book pronounces a judgement against modern men—the gravest sentence the poetic imagination can conceive for man's withered and wasted conscience: our sweep of history adds up to one thing only, a moral vacuity that is absolute and irrevocable. This book is a testament of betrayals; we have betrayed all beings that had power to save us: the forest, the animals, the gods, the dead, the spirit in us, the words. Now, in our last moments alive, they return to haunt us." Published in 1969, *The Lice* remains one of Merwin's best-known volumes of poetry. Throughout his subsequent work, Merwin has continued to produce striking poems using nature as a backdrop. *The Vixen,* for instance, is an exploration of the rural forest in southwestern France that Merwin called home for many years. *New Yorker* critic J. D. McClatchy remarked that "the book is suffused with details of country life—solitary walks and garden work, woodsmoke, birdsong, lightfall." In his poem "Leviathan," published in the 1956 collection *Green*

with Beasts, Merwin writes of time and nature through the specific examples of the whale as narrated in myth, legend, and observation. In this poem it is nature, represented by sea and whale, that is strong. Conversely, humanity is weak. Chris Semansky in *Poetry for Students* noted: "In his poem 'Leviathan,' W. S. Merwin describes the multiple ways in which the whale has historically served as a symbol to human culture and the ways in which the image of the whale has served as a receptacle for human hopes and fears."

His obsession with the meaning of America and its values makes Merwin like the great nineteenth-century poet Walt Whitman, L. Edwin Folsom noted in *Shenandoah.* "His poetry . . . often implicitly and sometimes explicitly responds to Whitman; his twentieth-century sparsity and soberness—his doubts about the value of America—answer, temper, Whitman's nineteenth-century expansiveness and exuberance—his enthusiasm over the American creation." Folsom summarized his comparison by saying, "Whitman's self sought to contain all, to embody past, present, and future; Merwin's self seeks to contain nothing, to empty itself of a dead past. . . . [Having taken a journey in the past,] Merwin does not return to the present replenished with the native ways: he returns only with an affirmation of man's stupidity and inhumanity, and of an irreplaceable emptiness lying beneath this continent. Having re-taken the Whitmanesque American journey, having relived the creation of the country via the medium of poetry, Merwin finds the American creation to be not a creation at all, but a destruction, an imposed obliteration that he believes will be repaid in kind."

The poetic forms of many eras and societies are the foundation for a great deal of Merwin's poetry. His first books contained many pieces inspired by classical models. According to Vernon Young in the *American Poetry Review,* the poems are traceable to "Biblical tales, Classical myth, love songs from the Age of Chivalry, Renaissance retellings; they comprise carols, roundels, odes, ballads, sestinas, and they contrive golden equivalents of emblematic models: the masque, the Zodiac, the Dance of Death." Merwin's versions are so perfectly rendered, stated Young, that "were you to redistribute these poems, unsigned, among collections of translated material or of English Poetry Down the Ages, any but the most erudite reader would heedlessly accept them as renderings of Theocritus,

Catullus, Ronsard. . . . One thing is certain. Before embarking on the narratives published in 1956 and after, Merwin was in secure formal command. Shape and duration, melody, vocal inflection, were under superb control. No stanzaic model was alien to him; no line length was beyond his dexterity." Eric Hartley also commented on the importance of Merwin's background in the *Dictionary of Literary Biography:* "From the first of his career as a poet, Merwin has steeped himself in other cultures and other literary traditions, and he has been praised as a translator. This eclectic background has given him a sense of the presence of the past, of timelessness in time, that comes across emphatically in his poetry. Without some understanding of this background the reader cannot fully appreciate Merwin's poetry. Moreover, without such appreciation one cannot comprehend the thrust of Merwin's poetic and philosophical development."

However, John Vernon pointed out in a *Western Humanities Review* article that Merwin's poems are not difficult in a scholarly sense. The problem is the jaded ear of the modern reader. "These are some of the most unacademic poems I have ever read, in the sense that they could never be discussed in a university classroom, since they have no 'meaning' in any usual sense. . . . I think of what Samuel Beckett said about *Finnegans Wake:* we are too decadent to read this. That is, we are so used to a language that is flattened out and hollowed out, that is slavishly descriptive, that when we encounter a language as delicately modulated and as finely sensual as this, it is like trying to read Braille with boxing gloves on."

Some literary critics have identified Merwin with the group known as the oracular poets, but Merwin himself once commented: "I have not evolved an abstract aesthetic theory and am not aware of belonging to any particular group of writers. I neither read nor write much criticism, and think of its current vast proliferation chiefly as a symptom, inseparable from other technological substitutions. . . . I imagine that a society whose triumphs one after the other emerge as new symbols of death, and that feeds itself by poisoning the earth, may be expected, even while it grows in strength and statistics, to soothe its fears with trumpery hopes, refer to nihilism as progress, dismiss the private authority of the senses as it has cashiered belief, and of course find the arts exploitable but unsatisfying." The essayist for *Contemporary Poets* admitted that "Merwin has been associated with the tradition of

contemporary poets known as the oracular poets, and if his surrealistic style has been compared to that of Roethke, Bly, Wright, Dickey, Plath, Olson, and even Lowell, his apocalyptic vision is entirely his own."

Of his development as a writer, Merwin once said, "I started writing hymns for my father almost as soon as I could write at all, illustrating them. I recall some rather stern little pieces addressed, in a manner I was familiar with, to backsliders, but I can remember too wondering whether there might not be some more liberating mode. In Scranton there was an anthology of *Best Loved Poems of the American People* in the house, which seemed for a time to afford some clues. But the first real writers that held me were not poets: Conrad first, and then Tolstoy, and it was not until I had received a scholarship and gone away to the university that I began to read poetry steadily and try incessantly, and with abiding desperation, to write it. I was not a satisfactory student; . . . I spent most of my time either in the university library, or riding in the country: I had discovered that the polo and ROTC stables were full of horses with no one to exercise them. I believe I was not noticeably respectful either of the curriculum and its evident purposes, nor of several of its professors, and I was saved from the thoroughly justified impatience of the administration, as I later learned, by the intercessions of R. P. Blackmur, who thought I needed a few years at the place to pick up what education I might be capable of assimilating, and I did in fact gain a limited but invaluable acquaintance with a few modern languages. While I was there, John Berryman, Herman Broch, and Blackmur himself, helped me, by example as much as by design, to find out some things about writing; of course it was years before I began to realize just what I had learned, and from whom. . . . Writing is something I know little about; less at some times than at others. I think, though, that so far as it is poetry it is a matter of correspondences: one glimpses them, pieces of an order, or thinks one does, and tries to convey the sense of what one has seen to those to whom it may matter, including, if possible, one's self."

The success of Merwin's attempts to convey his vision was summed up by Stephen Spender in the *New York Review of Books:* "These poems communicate a sense of someone watching and waiting, surrounding himself with silence, so that he can see minute particles, listen to infinitesimal sounds, with a passivity of attention, a refusal to disturb with his own observing consciousness the object observed. It is as though things write their own poems through Merwin. At their best they are poems of total attention and as such they protest against our world of total distraction."

Merwin was once asked what social role a poet plays—if any—in America. He commented: "I think there's a kind of desperate hope built into poetry now that one really wants, hopelessly, to save the world. One is trying to say everything that can be said for the things that one loves while there's still time. I think that's a social role, don't you? . . . We keep expressing our anger and our love, and we hope, hopelessly perhaps, that it will have some effect. But I certainly have moved beyond the despair, or the searing, dumb vision that I felt after writing *The Lice;* one can't live only in despair and anger without eventually destroying the thing one is angry in defense of. The world is still here, and there are aspects of human life that are *not* purely destructive, and there is a need to pay attention to the things around us while they are still around us. And you know, in a way, if you don't pay that attention, the anger is just bitterness."

BIOGRAPHICAL AND CRITICAL SOURCES:

BOOKS

Brunner, Edward J., *Poetry As Labor and Privilege: The Writings of W. S. Merwin,* University of Illinois Press (Urbana, IL), 1991.

Christhilf, Mark, *W. S. Merwin the Mythmaker,* University of Missouri Press (Columbia, MO), 1986.

Contemporary Literary Criticism, Thomson Gale (Detroit, MI), Volume 1, 1973, Volume 2, 1974, Volume 3, 1975, Volume 5, 1976, Volume 8, 1978, Volume 13, 1980, Volume 18, 1981.

Contemporary Poets, 6th edition, St. James Press (Detroit, MI), 1996.

Davis, Cheri, *W. S. Merwin,* Twayne (Boston, MA), 1981.

Dickey, James, *Babel to Byzantium,* Farrar, Straus (New York, NY), 1968.

Dictionary of Literary Biography, Volume 5: *American Poets since World War II,* Thomson Gale (Detroit, MI), 1980.

Hix, H. L., *Understanding W. S. Merwin,* University of South Carolina Press (Columbia, SC), 1997.

Hoeppner, Edward Haworth, *Echoes and Moving Fields: Structure and Subjectivity in the Poetry of W. S. Merwin and John Ashbery,* Associated University Presses (Cranberry, NJ), 1994.

Howard, Richard, *Alone with America: Essays on the Art of Poetry in the United States since 1950,* Atheneum (New York, NY), 1969.

Hungerford, Edward, *Poets in Progress,* Northwestern University Press (Evanston, IL), 1962.

Nelson, Cary, and Ed Folsom, editors, *W. S. Merwin: Essays on the Poetry,* University of Illinois Press (Urbana, IL), 1987.

Poetry for Students, Volume 5, Thomson Gale (Detroit, MI), 1999.

Rexroth, Kenneth, *With Eye and Ear,* Herder (New York, NY), 1970.

Rexroth, Kenneth, *American Poetry in the Twentieth Century,* Herder (New York, NY), 1971.

Rosenthal, M. L., *The Modern Poets: A Critical Introduction,* Oxford University Press (New York, NY), 1960.

Shaw, Robert B., editor, *American Poetry since 1960: Some Critical Perspectives,* Dufour (Chester Springs, PA), 1974.

Stepanchev, Stephen, *American Poetry since 1945,* Harper (New York, NY), 1965.

PERIODICALS

American Poetry Review, January-February, 1978.

Booklist, November 1, 1996, review of *Lament for the Makers: A Memorial Anthology,* p. 476; January 1, 1999, review of *The Folding Cliffs: A Narrative,* p. 777; March 15, 1999, review of *The Folding Cliffs,* p. 1276.

Chicago Tribune Book World, December 26, 1982.

Commonweal, June 18, 1999, review of *The Folding Cliffs,* p. 24.

Concerning Poetry, spring, 1975.

Furioso, spring, 1953.

Hudson Review, winter, 1967-68; summer, 1973; spring, 1999, review of *The Folding Cliffs,* p. 141.

Iowa Review, winter, 1982, Cary Nelson and Ed Folsom, "Fact Has Two Faces: An Interview with W. S. Merwin," pp. 30-66.

Library Journal, January, 1996, p. 104; October 15, 1998, review of *The Folding Cliffs,* p. 74; November 1, 1996, review of *Lament for the Makers,* p. 71.

Los Angeles Times, August 21, 1983.

Los Angeles Times Book Review, August 21, 1983.

Modern Language Quarterly, March, 1983, pp. 65-79; September, 1988, pp. 262-284.

Modern Poetry Studies, winter, 1975.

Nation, December 14, 1970; December 12, 1994, Gerald Stern, "The Lenore Marshall Poetry Prize-1994," p. 733.

New Leader, January 13, 1997, review of *Lament for the Makers,* p. 15; December 14, 1998, review of *The Folding Cliffs,* p. 23.

New Mexico Quarterly, autumn, 1964.

New Republic, March 22, 1999, review of *The River Sound: Poems* and *The Folding Cliffs,* p. 40.

New Yorker, June 3, 1996, J. D. McClatchy, review of *The Vixen: Poems,* p. 92; December, 7, 1998, review of *The Folding Cliffs,* p. 200.

New York Review of Books, May 6, 1971; September 20, 1973; March 27, 1997, review of *The Vixen* and *Lament for the Makers,* p. 18.

New York Times Book Review, October 18, 1970; June 19, 1977; August 1, 1982; October 9, 1983; April 4, 1999, Melanie Rehak, "Poetic Justice"; June 6, 1999, review of *The River Sound,* p. 37; December 5, 1999, review of *The River Sound,* p. 78.

New York Times Magazine, February 19, 1995, p. 39.

Ontario Review, fall-winter, 1977-78.

Partisan Review, summer, 1958; winter, 1971-72.

Poet and Critic, spring, 1990, pp. 37-40.

Poetry, May, 1953; May, 1961; February, 1963; June, 1964; August, 1974.

Prairie Schooner, fall, 1957; fall, 1962; winter, 1962-63; fall, 1968; winter, 1971-72.

Publishers Weekly, November, 27, 1995, p. 65; February 24, 1997, review of *Flower and Hand: Poems, 1977-1983,* p. 86.

Sewanee Review, spring, 1974.

Shenandoah, spring, 1968; winter, 1970; spring, 1978.

Southern Review, April, 1980.

Village Voice, July 4, 1974.

Virginia Quarterly Review, summer, 1973; spring, 1997, review of *Lament for the Makers,* p. 48; spring, 1999, review of *The Folding Cliffs,* p. 67; autumn, 1999, review of *The River Sound,* p. 136.

Voices, January-April, 1953; May-August, 1957; September-December, 1961.

Washington Post Book World, August 31, 1975; September 18, 1977; August 15, 1982; June 3, 1984.

Western Humanities Review, spring, 1970; spring, 1971.

Western Review, spring, 1955.

World Literature Today, autumn, 1996, review of *The Vixen,* p. 964; spring, 1997, review of *Lament for the Makers,* p. 391; autumn, 2000, review of *The River Sound,* p. 820.

Yale Review, summer, 1961; summer, 1968; summer, 1973; July, 1999, review of *The River Sound,* p. 167.

ONLINE

Steven Barclay Agency Web site, http://www.barclay agency.com/ (August 4, 2004), "William S. Merwin."*

*   *   *

MITCHELL, Clyde
See SILVERBERG, Robert

*   *   *

MORRIS, Mary (Joan) McGarry 1943-

PERSONAL: Born 1943, in Meriden, CT; daughter of John and Margaret (Chiriaco) McGarry; married Michael Morris (an attorney), 1962; children: Mary Margaret, Sarah, Melissa, Michael, Amy. *Education:* Attended University of Vermont, 1960-62, and University of Massachusetts, 1962-63.

ADDRESSES: Home—Andover, MA. *Agent*—Naggar Literary Agency, 216 E. 75th St., New York, NY 10021.

CAREER: Massachusetts Department of Welfare, Lawrence, financial assistance social worker, 1980-86; writer.

AWARDS, HONORS: National Book Award nomination, 1988, and PEN/Faulkner Award nomination, 1989, both for *Vanished.*

WRITINGS:

NOVELS

Vanished, Viking (New York, NY), 1988.
A Dangerous Woman, Viking (New York, NY), 1991.

Mary McGarry Morris

Songs in Ordinary Time, Viking (New York, NY), 1995.

Fiona Range, Viking (New York, NY), 2000.

A Hole in the Universe, Viking (New York, NY), 2004.

The Lost Mother, Viking (New York, NY), 2005.

Also contributor of book reviews to periodicals, including *New York Times Book Review.*

ADAPTATIONS: A Dangerous Woman was adapted as a feature film starring Deborah Winger.

SIDELIGHTS: As the author of several novels, Mary McGarry Morris has received considerable attention from critics and readers, as well as from prestigious awards panels. Her books are noted for their depictions of mentally and emotionally impaired individuals who have difficulty coping with an inhospitable world. As *New York Times Book Review* contributor Alice McDermott put it, "Morris does not devise plots, but traps: steel-toothed, inescapable traps of circumstance and personality against which her characters struggle . . . and then fail." Ultimately, Morris suggests that

these individuals are incapable of surviving their surroundings. Her books typically conclude with violent murders, death apparently being all that is left for characters who have exhausted their other possibilities.

Such grim subjects seem odd coming from Morris, a mother of five children who, following college, went on to live what *Los Angeles Times* writer Elizabeth Mehren described as a "stunningly balanced life." The disorder Morris depicts in her books may stem, in part, from her own childhood. Her parents separated when she was very young and, though her father continued to live separately, he, along with Morris and her mother, moved to Rutland, Vermont, when the author was six years old. It was in Rutland that Morris came to know the small New England communities that she features in her novels. When her mother and stepfather began employing retarded and emotionally disturbed men in their restaurant, she was exposed to another important influence. As she once told *People* magazine writer Kim Hubbard, her mother "believed everyone deserved a chance." The author would later manifest the same concern for society's outsiders by featuring mentally handicapped individuals in her fiction.

After marrying, Morris settled in Andover, Massachusetts, and was soon involved with raising a family and writing. Not surprisingly, her family obligations often took her away from her fiction and poetry. "With five children there couldn't be a set schedule for much," she told *Washington Post* writer Judith Weinraub. "It was always hard to find the time." Morris's writing regimen was also interrupted when she took a job as a social worker in order to help pay the children's college tuition. Consequently, her early attempts at novels remained unfinished, and the work that would eventually prove successful was painfully slow in coming. Her first novel, *Vanished,* took nearly eight years to write, and was then rejected twenty-seven times by publishers and agents. Without a publication to substantiate her abilities, Morris kept her writing a secret from everyone but her family. Despite this isolation, she continued to work on her fiction. "Writing was just *in* me," she told Weinraub. "I even began to think I probably would never be published. And I was accepting of that."

In 1986 Morris finally achieved a partial affirmation of her talents when she placed *Vanished* with noted literary agent Jean V. Naggar; two years later it was published. *Vanished* centers on Aubrey Wallace, a man whose socialization is so severely limited, most consider him retarded. Though he is functional to a certain degree—he has a job, a wife, and children—Aubrey is unquestioning and utterly passive. These qualities lead to trouble when Aubrey crosses paths with Dotty Johnson, a disturbed teenager who has recently killed her sexually abusive father. Dotty attempts to steal Aubrey's pickup, and Aubrey jumps into the cab. Unable to take any action to stop her, Aubrey just rides along, and this beginning is typical of their time together. Whatever Dotty wants, she takes, and whatever Aubrey encounters, he accepts. The next day Dotty kidnaps a baby, and the child becomes part of the roving, maladjusted family, crisscrossing the country from Massachusetts to Florida. They survive by finding work as migrant laborers, by stealing, and by prostitution. Five years after the kidnaping, they move in with a violent ex-convict named Jiggy Huller and his family. When Huller discovers the truth about the kidnaping, he hatches a plan to collect a 25,000 dollar reward for the child that ultimately brings about the novel's bloody conclusion.

Several critics commented that Morris's style and technique in *Vanished* are of an exceptionally high caliber for a first novelist. *New York Times Book Review* contributor Harry Crews noted that "her language is precise, concrete, and sensual. Her eye for telling detail is good, and her ear for the way people talk is tone-perfect." Opinions were divided, however, regarding Morris's handling of the novel's story elements. Some critics suggested that her emotionally charged topics—rape, murder, incest, kidnaping, prostitution, and adultery—run the risk of overwhelming the rest of the book. Richard Eder, writing in the *Los Angeles Times Book Review,* found that the novel, unable to transform its negative subject matter into a meaningful message, "sinks into its chamber of horrors." *New York Times* reviewer Michiko Kakutani also focused on the novel's preoccupation with ugly and sinister elements, but reached a different judgment. "Melodramatic as these events sound," Kakutani wrote, "they are presented with such authority by Ms. Morris that they hum with both the authenticity of real life and the mythic power of fable. This is a startling and powerful debut."

A Dangerous Woman, Morris's second novel, features another emotionally impaired protagonist, Martha Horgan, who is in many ways the counterpart to

Aubrey Wallace in *Vanished.* Like Aubrey, Martha Horgan is an outcast, characterized as disturbed by the residents of her Vermont town. She is plagued by physical tics and is unable to interact with others in a mature manner. Sometimes her brutal honesty offends those around her; sometimes she explodes into childish rages. At other times, however, Martha almost becomes a functioning part of her community. Early in the book she gets a job at a dry cleaners and earns a degree of independence. She moves out of her aunt's home and forges a tenuous friendship with a coworker, Birdy. These gains are lost, however, due in part to Martha's insistence on exposing Birdy's lover as a thief. Martha's honesty costs her both the job and the friendship, and she is forced to return to her Aunt Frances's home. There an alcoholic handyman employed by Aunt Frances takes Martha as a temporary lover, then abandons her in favor of Frances. When she is forced to leave her aunt's home, Martha has few options, and tragedy is imminent.

Morris chose to relay much of the novel's action through Martha's disturbed perceptions, and this unconventional approach impressed several reviewers. Richard Eder of the *Los Angeles Times Book Review* wrote that *A Dangerous Woman* "is powerfully and dangerously written. To cast a blinding light on her protagonist, Morris has sacrificed subtleties or shadings. The balance of the outsider as both victim and helpless instigator is difficult to maintain." Jaimy Gordon, writing in the *Washington Post,* maintained that some of the story elements—including Martha's near rape at the age of sixteen—are unnecessary. Gordon also criticized some occasionally clumsy prose in the novel, but praised Morris's "remarkable portrait of a disturbed woman." This judgment was echoed by *Vogue* contributor Michael Upchurch, who emphasized the author's ability to "draw the reader so completely into Martha's world that it becomes impossible not to sympathize with her."

New York Times Book Review contributor Alice McDermott, comparing Morris's two novels, summarized: "*A Dangerous Woman* is not, finally, as convincing or as compelling . . . as was Ms. Morris's first book, nor is the prose quite so striking." Despite these reservations, the critic commended the powerful vision Morris puts forth in both of the novels. "The bleakness of her landscape remains pervasive," McDermott wrote. "This makes all the more remarkable those instants of frail light—a simple man's love for a child, a lost woman's recollection of affection—that she so deftly, so briefly, calls forth from the darkness."

Morris proved with her first two novels that she "can depict society's outsiders—people with bleak presents and no futures—with rare understanding and compassion," noted a *Publishers Weekly* critic. Her third novel, *Songs in Ordinary Time* evidences this as well. The novel revolves around the Fermoyles, a family living in a small town in Vermont in 1960. Marie Fermoyle has struggled for years to support and raise her three children despite the lack of support from her alcoholic ex-husband. Enter Omar Duvall, a con man who convinces Marie to invest in one of his scams. The novel involves numerous subplots involving various friends and neighbors who "each in his or her own way is necessary to the town's ecosystem," commented Vanessa V. Friedman in *Entertainment Weekly*.

Critical reviews of *Songs in Ordinary Time* were mixed. "This novel becomes more powerful as one reads, building to a heart stopping denouement," noted a critic for *Publishers Weekly*. Michiko Kakutani, on the other hand, wrote in the *New York Times Book Review* that the author's protagonists "lack the emotional chiaroscuro that Ms. Morris has lavished on her creations in the past." However, in *USA Today* Susan Kelly argued that *Songs in Ordinary Time* is "beautifully written." Kelly observed, "There is grace and poetry in Morris's prose. She opens the door to these people's souls, showing all their fears and flaws without making them seem ridiculous or unworthy."

In Morris's 2000 novel, *Fiona Range,* the title character is "smart, beautiful, and haunted by a past she cannot live down," according to Carolyn Kubisz in *Booklist*. Abandoned by her unwed mother as a baby, Fiona was raised by her aunt and uncle. Her relationships roll along, disaster after disaster. After her cousin Elizabeth returns from New York City with her fiancé, Fiona ends up sleeping both with him and with one of Elizabeth's former boyfriends. "Fiona knows she needs to reclaim her life, but each step she takes is closer to the abyss," found Harriet Klausner in *BookBrowser.*

Critics were again largely positive in their assessment of *Fiona Range*. "How these characters interact, what they say, and what they hide, makes for entertaining, suspenseful reading," opined Yvette Weller Olson in *Library Journal.* Olson found the work "compelling and satisfying." A *Publishers Weekly* critic's review was mixed, maintaining that the plot tends to "go in circles" and that Fiona's self-destructive nature distances the character from reader sympathy. Nonetheless, the critic went on to praise the "sustained tension in the narrative," and found that "the denouement packs a thriller's excitement." Kubisz found the narrative "slow moving at times," but concluded that Morris's ending, "with its twist of plot and hidden secrets revealed, makes this a worthy read."

In *A Hole in the Universe* Morris tells the story of outcast Gordon Loomis, who comes home after serving a twenty-five-year sentence for a murder he may not have committed. Struggling to cope with life outside prison, the gloomy Gordon just wants to be left alone; instead, he must fend off the intrusive attention of people. He spurns his brother's help in finding him a job, and feels helpless when the spinsterish Delores wants to help him become the "normal" man he wants to be. He tries to avoid the needy teenage daughter of the junkie across the street. Unfortunately, Gordon is unable to keep his life at a safe distance for long. His basic integrity draws him toward the people he seeks to protect, even though he is punished for his good deeds. When new accusations whirl around Gordon for a second crime he did not commit, the tale moves to its fitful conclusion and Gordon emerges as the novel's pathetic but winning hero.

Reviews of *A Hole in the Universe* were predominately enthusiastic. *Booklist* contributor Deborah Donovan found Morris's "empathy for Gordon . . . palpable, leaving the reader in awe of her uncanny ability to capture and convey each personality's unique essence." *New York Times* contributor John Hartl was more reserved in his assessment, writing, "What keeps this borderline potboiler simmering is the sense that the characters really are evolving." On the other hand, *Boston Globe* reviewer Caroline Leavitt applauded the novel's "topnotch suspense" and "expert plotting that make Morris such a superb storyteller," and was especially impressed with the author's inclusion of those "small heroics that resonate and break your heart."

BIOGRAPHICAL AND CRITICAL SOURCES:

PERIODICALS

Booklist, July, 1995, Donna Seaman, review of *Songs in Ordinary Time,* p. 1860; February 15, 2000,

Carolyn Kubisz, review of *Fiona Range,* p. 1052; February 1, 2004, Deborah Donovan, review of *A Hole in the Universe,* p. 993.

Chicago Tribune, March 7, 2004, Jessica Treadway, review of *A Hole in the Universe,* p. 4.

Detroit Free Press, February 3, 1991.

Entertainment Weekly, July 28, 1995, Vanessa V. Friedman, review of *Songs in Ordinary Time,* p. 57.

Library Journal, March 15, 2000, Yvette Weller Olson, review of *Fiona Range,* p. 128.

Los Angeles Times, March 7, 1991, pp. E1, E6.

Los Angeles Times Book Review, June 26, 1988, p. 3; January 20, 1991; April 25, 2004, Francie Lin, review of *A Hole in the Universe,* p. 6.

Newsweek, April 8, 1991, David Gates, review of *A Dangerous Woman,* pp. 61, 63.

New York, January 14, 1991, Rhoda Koenig, review of *A Dangerous Woman,* p. 67.

New Yorker, August 8, 1988, pp. 84-85.

New York Times, June 4, 1988, Michiko Kakutani, review of *Vanished,* p. 14.

New York Times Book Review, July 3, 1988, Harry Crews, "On the Lam with Dotty," p. 5; January 13, 1991, Alice McDermott, "The Loneliness of an Ogre," p. 9; August 4, 1995, Michiko Kakutani, review of *Songs in Ordinary Time;* March 21, 2004, John Hartl, review of *A Hole in the Universe,* p. 16.

People, April 15, 1991, Kim Hubbard, review of *A Dangerous Woman,* pp. 93-94.

Publishers Weekly, May 15, 1995, review of *Songs in Ordinary Times,* p. 53; March 13, 2000, review of *Fiona Range,* p. 59; January 26, 2004, review of *A Hole in the Universe,* p. 227.

Time, July 4, 1988, review of *Vanished,* p. 71; January 28, 1991, Mary Carlson, review of *A Dangerous Woman,* pp. 89-90.

USA Today, December 2, 1999, Susan Kelly, "*Songs* No Ordinary Novel"; May 10, 2000, Susan Kelly, "Teen Never Feels at Home in *Range.*"

Vogue, January, 1991, pp. 112-113.

Washington Post, January 8, 1991; March 26, 1991, p. B1, B4; March 7, 2004, Caroline Leavitt, review of *A Hole in the Universe,* p. T6.

ONLINE

BookBrowser.com, http://www.bookbrowser.com/ (May, 2000), Harriet Klausner, review of *Fiona Range.**

MURSTEIN, Bernard I(rving) 1929-

PERSONAL: Born April 29, 1929, in Vilna, Lithuania; immigrated to the United States, 1930; naturalized U.S. citizen; son of Leon (a taxi fleet owner) and Martha (Schalachman) Murstein; married Nelly Kashy (a professor of French and Italian at Connecticut College), August 27, 1954; children: S. Danielle, Colette Anne. *Education:* City College (now of the City University of New York), B.S.S., 1950; University of Miami, Coral Gables, FL, M.S., 1951; University of Texas, Ph.D., 1955. *Politics:* "Liberal-independent." *Religion:* Jewish. *Hobbies and other interests:* Stock analysis and research.

ADDRESSES: Home—46 Beacon Hill Dr., Waterford, CT 06385-4110. *Office*—c/o Box 5581, Connecticut College, 270 Mohegan Ave., New London, CT 06320-4196. *E-mail*—bimur@conncoll.edu.

CAREER: Louisville Child Guidance Center, Louisville, KY, psychotherapy intern, 1953-54; University of Texas, Main University (now University of Texas—Austin), Austin, Hogg Foundation research fellow at M. D. Anderson Hospital, 1955-56; Louisiana State University, Baton Rouge, assistant professor of psychology and director of psychology clinic, 1956-58; University of Portland, Portland, OR, associate professor of psychology and coordinator of research, 1958-60; National Institute of Mental Health, Portland, director of research and principal investigator at Interfaith Counseling Center, 1960-62; University of Connecticut, Storrs, associate professor of family relations, 1962-63; Connecticut College, New London, associate professor, 1963-65, professor of psychology, 1965-99, May Buckley Sadowski Professor, 1994-99, professor emeritus, 1999—, department chair, 1976-79, 1990-91. University of Louvain, Fulbright professor, 1968-69. Private practice of psychology, beginning 1979.

MEMBER: International Council of Psychologists, International Society for the Study of Interpersonal Relationships, American Psychological Association (fellow), Society for Personality Assessment (fellow; president, 1973-74), National Council on Family Relations.

AWARDS, HONORS: U.S. Public Health Service fellowship, 1954; grants from National Institute of Mental Health, 1960-63, 1964-68, National Science Foundation, 1970-71, Mellon Foundation, 1978, 1980, and George I. Alden Trust, 1982.

WRITINGS:

Theory and Research in Projective Techniques, Emphasizing the Thematic Apperception Test, Wiley (New York, NY), 1963.

(Editor) *Handbook of Projective Techniques,* Basic Books (New York, NY), 1965.

Theories of Attraction and Love, Springer Publishing (New York, NY), 1971.

Love, Sex, and Marriage through the Ages, Springer Publishing (New York, NY), 1974.

Who Will Marry Whom: Theories and Research in Marital Choice, Springer Publishing (New York, NY), 1976.

(Editor) *Exploring Intimate Life Styles,* Springer Publishing (New York, NY), 1978.

Paths to Marriage, Sage Publications (Beverly Hills, CA), 1986.

Getting Psyched for Wall Street: A Rational Approach to an Irrational Market, Cypress Publishing Group, 2002.

Contributor to books, including *Contemporary Issues in Thematic Apperceptive Methods,* 1961; and *Projective Techniques,* 1964. Contributor of more than 100 articles to periodicals, including *Psychological Reports, Journal of Projective Psychology and Mental Health, International Journal of Psychology, Journal of Social and Personal Relationships,* and *Journal of Abnormal Psychology.* Associate editor, *Journal of Marriage and the Family,* 1975-80.

WORK IN PROGRESS: Memoirs of a Septuagenerian.

SIDELIGHTS: Bernard I. Murstein once told *CA:* "Some years ago I made a statement after dealing with the contents of our dull, plodding psychological journals. I jocularly referred to it as Murstein's Law: 'The amount of research devoted to a topic on human behavior is inversely related to its importance and interest to mankind.' My research and writing efforts devoted to investigating attraction, love, marital choice, and marital functioning have attempted to change the veridicality of that statement and to study what I perceive to be the most important factor in most lives—the quantity and quality of our intimate relationships."

More recently, he added: "Around 1980 I discovered the concept of 'inter-spousal deafness,' a condition in which, if one member of a couple is in conversation with a third party, the attempt of the spouse to communicate is useless, because a person's ears shut down selectively as soon as spouse's voice is recognized. The ears open immediately for non-spousal sounds.

"In my old age, my libido has switched its focus from the study of love to that of the psychology of money; hence, my 2002 book."

N

NASH, Gary B. 1933-

PERSONAL: Born July 27, 1933, in Philadelphia, PA; son of Ralph C. and Edith (Baring) Nash; married Mary Workum, December 20, 1955 (divorced); children: Brooke, Robin, Jennifer, David. *Education:* Princeton University, B.A., 1955, Ph.D., 1964.

ADDRESSES: Home—16174 Alcima Ave., Pacific Palisades, CA 90272. *Office*—Department of History, University of California, Box 951473, 6265 Bunche Hall, 405 Hilgard Ave., Los Angeles, CA 90095-1473. *E-mail*—gnash@ucla.edu.

CAREER: Princeton University, Princeton, NJ, assistant professor of history, 1964-66; University of California, Los Angeles, associate professor, 1968-72, professor of history, beginning 1972, became professor emeritus, director of National Center for History in the Schools, 1994—, also served as dean of undergraduate and inter-college curricular development and of council on educational development. Guest historian, Historical Society of Pennsylvania permanent exhibit, 1989-97; founding member and member of board of trustees, National Council for History Education, beginning 1990, vice chair, 1992-96; primary history consultant, Schlessinger Production series in United States history, 1996-97; historical consultant and writer for "Lights of Liberty" tour, Philadelphia, PA, 1999—; supervisor of history curriculum for online education service EduLink, Inc., 2000—. Has served on numerous prize and nominating committees, as well as faculty advisory committees. *Military service:* U.S. Navy, 1955-58; became lieutenant junior grade.

MEMBER: American Historical Association, Society of American Historians, American Academy of Arts and Sciences, American Antiquarian Society, Organization of American Historians (president, 1994-95).

AWARDS, HONORS: Guggenheim fellow, 1969-70; best book prize, Society for the History of the Early American Republic, 1989, for *Forging Freedom: The Formation of Philadelphia's Black Community, 1720-1840;* Distinguished Award in Research and Teaching, University of California, 1996, for history; prize for best book in American history, American Historical Association (Pacific Coast Branch), for *Quakers and Politics: Pennsylvania, 1681-1726;* Pulitzer Prize finalist and Silver Prize in Literature from the Commonwealth Club of California, both for *The Urban Crucible: Social Change, Political Consciousness and the Origins of the American Revolution;* Defense of Academic Freedom Award, National Council for Social Studies; has also received research grants from the American Council of Learned Societies, the American Philosophical Society, and the University of California Institute of Humanities.

WRITINGS:

Quakers and Politics: Pennsylvania, 1681-1726, Princeton University Press (Princeton, NJ), 1968, new edition, Northeastern University Press (Boston, MA), 1993.
Class and Society in Early America, Prentice-Hall (Englewood Cliffs, NJ), 1970.
Red, White, and Black: The Peoples of Early America, Princeton-Hall (Englewood Cliffs, NJ), 1974, 4th edition, 2000.

The Urban Crucible: Social Change, Political Consciousness, and the Origins and the American Revolution, Harvard University Press (Cambridge, MA), 1979, abridged edition published as *The Urban Crucible: The Northern Seaports and the Origins of the American Revolution,* 1986.

Race, Class, and Politics: Essays on American Colonial and Revolutionary Society, foreword by Richard S. Dunn, University of Illinois Press (Urbana, IL), 1986.

Forging Freedom: The Formation of Philadelphia's Black Community, 1720-1840, Harvard University Press (Cambridge, MA), 1988.

Race and Revolution: The Inaugural Merrill Jensen Lectures, Madison House (Madison, WI), 1990.

American Odyssey: The United States in the Twentieth Century, Glencoe (Lake Forest, IL), 1991, teacher's wraparound edition, 1994.

(With Jean R. Soderlund) *Freedom by Degrees: Emancipation in Pennsylvania and Its Aftermath,* Oxford University Press (New York, NY), 1991.

(With Charlotte Crabtree and Ross E. Dunn) *History on Trial: National Identity, Culture Wars and the Teaching of the Past,* Knopf (New York, NY), 1997.

America's Hidden Mestizo Histo, Owl Publishing, 1998.

Forbidden Love: The Secret History of Mixed-Race America (young adult nonfiction), Holt (New York, NY), 1999.

(With Richard S. Dunn) *Sugar and Slaves: The Rise of the Planter Class in the English West Indies, 1624-1713,* University of North Carolina Press (Chapel Hill, NC), 2000.

First City: Philadelphia and the Forging of Historical Memory, University of Pennsylvania Press (Philadelphia, PA), 2002.

Landmarks of the American Revolution (young adult nonfiction), Oxford University Press (New York, NY), 2003.

Author of introduction, *The Negro in the American Revolution,* by Benjamin Quarles, University of North Carolina Press, 1996. Contributor to over twenty books, including *America Will Be: Houghton Mifflin Social Studies,* Houghton Mifflin, 1997; *American Will Be—Level 5,* Houghton Mifflin, 1999; and *A Message of Ancient Days,* McDougal Littell, 2001. Contributor to periodicals, including *William and Mary Quarterly.* General editor, with Julie Roy Jeffrey and others, of *The American People: Creating a Nation and a Society*

(includes study guide), Harper (New York, NY), 1986, 6th edition, Longman (New York, NY), 2004, brief edition, Harper (New York, NY), 1992, brief 4th edition, Longman (New York, NY), 2003; general editor of *Encyclopedia of American History,* Facts on File (New York, NY), 2003. Has served on editorial advisory boards.

EDITOR

(With Richard Weiss) *The Great Fear: Race in the Mind of America,* Holt (New York, NY), 1970.

The Private Side of American History: Readings in Everyday Life, since 1865, Harcourt (New York, NY), 1975, 5th edition, International Thomson, 2004.

(With David G. Sweet) *Struggle and Survival in Colonial America,* University of California Press (Berkeley, CA), 1981.

Retracing the Past: Readings in the History of the American People, Harper (New York, NY), 1986, 5th edition, edited with Ronald Schultz, Longman (New York, NY), 2003.

(Coeditor) *Lessons from History: Essential Understandings and Historical Perspectives Students Should Acquire,* 1992.

(With Charlotte Crabtree) *National Standards for World History: Exploring Paths to the Present,* National Center for History in the Schools (Los Angeles, CA), 1994.

(With Charlotte Crabtree) *National Standards for History for Grades K-4: Expanding Children's World in Time and Space,* revised edition, DIANE Publishing (Collingdale, PA), 1994.

(With Kirk Ankeney, Richard Del Rio, and David Vigilante) *Bring History Alive: A Sourcebook for Teaching United States History,* National Council for the Social Studies (Washington, DC), 1996.

(Coeditor) *Empire, Society, and Labor: Essays in Honor of Richard S. Dunn,* 1997.

SIDELIGHTS: Although Gary B. Nash has been writing history books for decades in which he has tried to bring to light the multicultural aspects of history to Americans, he did not gain a great deal of attention for his efforts until the mid-1990s, when he helped develop a curriculum for students that would show them a wider world than previous textbooks that he believed had a distinctly white-male-Protestant outlook. With the input of dozens of educational and historical organizations around the country, and with government funding initiated in 1991, Nash and Charlotte Crabtree compiled the *National Standards for World History: Exploring Paths to the Present* in 1994 at the University of California at Los Angeles. The curriculum they recommended for students became highly controversial, with some saying that it takes political correctness too far by putting a negative spin on Western civilization; others went so far as to call it racist, if perhaps unintentionally so. As *Washington Post* contributor Guy Gugliotta reported, former National Endowment for the Humanities chair Lynne V. Cheney, who had approved of the grants for the project when it began, said that by "deciding not to give any emphasis to Western civilization, they lost any organizing principle," asserting that an emphasis on the West is essential for the understanding of "the rise of democratic standards."

Harsher criticism came from various minority scholars who complained of the way the suggested curriculum has what they feel are slanted views of Jews, Native Americans, Arabic peoples, blacks, and other minorities. In his defense, Nash told Doug Cumming in an *Atlanta Journal and Constitution* interview that the final product he and Crabtree edited was "produced collaboratively by scores of teachers at every level of history education" and that the new curriculum is important for showing students that American history is not one dimensional. "I think a more inclusive, balanced history based on modern scholarship is more affirming and creates a firmer basis for unum along with the pluribus."

When Nash, the son of a General Electric employee, was a high school student growing up in a white, middle-class Merion, Pennsylvania, he received the traditional American history teachings in which America began with the English pilgrims, was founded by white men with noble ideals, and was defended through several wars for just causes. Attending Princeton University challenged that viewpoint for him, however, and Nash was introduced to the exciting field of social history by one of his professors, Eric Goldman, the author of *Rendezvous with Destiny*. From Goldman's lectures, Nash found out that there was a lot about American history that was not so glorious and that was even disturbing. Becoming a social activist, he joined a Unitarian civil rights group after earning his B.A. and helped migrant farm workers as a carpenter. A stint in the U.S. Navy brought him into

contact with people in other countries who had very different views on America. "His foreign hosts brought him face-to-face with a less forgiving view of American racism, its segregation, and its history of slavery," according to Kenneth Finkel in a Philly.com article. Returning to Princeton, Nash became one of a new group of academics who delved into church records, tax documents, wills, and other obscure papers to dig up little reported historical views that were important to America's social and cultural evolution.

One of his early works in the area of social history, *Red, White, and Black: The Peoples of Early America*, treads new ground in discussing how Native Americans, African Americans, and European Americans interacted with each other during the seventeenth and eighteenth centuries. The aim of the book is to show that there was much more going on at this time than what the white settlers were accomplishing. Although finding merit in this approach, Allen W. Trelease commented in the *American Historical Review* that "sometimes . . . this leads all too easily to a new imbalance, with the polarity reversed." As the critic noted, Nash seems to emphasize the brutality of European colonizers while downplaying the weaknesses of New World civilizations, such as the Aztec's lack of a written language, or overstating their accomplishments, such as the political union of the Iroquois tribes.

A number of Nash's books concern the issues of slavery in America and of white-black relations, especially during the Revolutionary War era. Nash plays the iconoclast here by publishing the real stories behind the American myths that have built up over time. For instance, in his *Freedom by Degrees: Emancipation in Philadelphia and Its Aftermath*, Nash and coauthor Jean R. Soderland reveal that, contrary to commonly held beliefs, slavery in Pennsylvania was abolished first among New England states not because of any noble idealism on the part of Quakers or other Europeans, but rather by various economic realities, including "the high death rate among urban slaves, a decline in slave imports, and an increase in runaway slaves," according to Philip D. Thomas in the *Historian*. An emancipation law in the state did put a final end to slavery, the authors admit, but the practice probably would have died out anyway.

Race and Revolution: The Inaugural Merrill Jensen Lectures contains three essays and reproduces documentary evidence that "argues convincingly" that

America's founding fathers understood that their ownership of slaves was contrary to "their equalitarian ideology," as David Szatmary explained in a *Library Journal* review. Many Americans know these days that Thomas Jefferson was a slave owner, but it might surprise some who are not historians that other much-admired figures, including George Washington and Benjamin Franklin, also owned slaves. Nash further sets the record straight that political leaders in the North were just as much to blame as plantation owners in the South for not taking the opportunity when the country was founded to end institutionalized slavery when America established its first laws. Nash, said *Village Voice* critic Tom Frank, "is well qualified to offer this bold perspective. His coverage of the free black community's vigorous efforts to achieve justice in white supremacist society in the northern states is particularly illuminating."

In his Pulitzer-nominated *The Urban Crucible: Social Change, Political Consciousness, and the Origins and the American Revolution,* Nash analyzes the economic development of three U.S. cities: Boston, Philadelphia, and New York. Focusing on the distribution of wealth, he illuminates the lives of labor and other lower-class Americans during the Revolutionary War, showing that there was not just one lower class but many, and that each social strata had its own characteristics, problems, and complaints that helped bring about the birth of the nation. Calling this "an important work," *Library Journal* critic Milton Cantor praised *The Urban Crucible* as a "pioneering study" that displays Nash's "meticulous research." Although Jack P. Greene, writing in the *American Historical Review,* felt that Nash's analysis of how economic conditions changed the social strata, which led to political upheavals, is "two-dimensional" because it neglects such areas as "material conditions and styles of life," the reviewer praised the author for uncovering "significant displays of lower-class consciousness. More important, he has linked them successfully with lower-class behavior and thereby enriched our understanding of the complexity of the American Revolution."

A native of Philadelphia, although he now resides in southern California, Nash has focused on the history of this city in several of his books, including *Forging Freedom: The Formation of Philadelphia's Black Community, 1720-1840* and *First City: Philadelphia and the Forging of Historical Memory.* As with his other history books, the author endeavors to cover aspects of his topic previously missed by other historians. Toward this end, the former book closely examines the contributions blacks made in the past to Philadelphia, while the latter Nash uncovers what Finkel called "long-lost stories about everyday heroes so compelling and resonant that we can now retire Philadelphia's threadbare, simplistic tales of times past." A number of reviewers, furthermore, were grateful for the author's *Forging Freedom,* which "provides a new, more complex understanding of white racial attitudes and policies in the city that viewed itself the anti-slavery capital of the world," stated Ira Berlin in the *Journal of American Ethnic History.*

While most of Nash's books are intended for adult audiences, in recent years he has also penned books that are appropriate for younger readers, including *Forbidden Love: The Secret History of Mixed-Race America* and *Landmarks of the American Revolution.* His *Landmarks* book goes beyond the usual important sites of the American Revolution to also include landmarks that are important for the religious and political battles they memorialize. Also, as is typical of Nash, he provides information representing other viewpoints from the war, including those of the loyalists and Native Americans who sided with the British during the Revolution. *Forbidden Love* details the stories of various European Americans who married or had children with minorities of black, Asian, or Native American descent, putting these events within their historical, political, and social context. Included are the historical facts about such people as Thomas Jefferson and Sally Hemings, John Rolfe and Pocahontas, and, more recently, Phil Gramm and his Japanese-American wife. But the author also includes a number of lesser-known cases neglected by history books that help highlight his points on the harm that stereotypes and prejudices cause. *Booklist*'s Hazel Rochman felt that Nash's book will provide "connections and context" for students learning about the history of America's racially mixed society, while Michelle Martin wrote in *Horn Book* that "Nash's text gives young adults a detailed overview of the history of racism and segregation in America, beginning with the fact that racial definitions 'lack any objective foundation.'"

Nash's devotion to educating Americans on the complex history of this country is seen not only in the books discussed above but also in his ongoing work in reference books, such as his work as general editor of the *Encyclopedia of American History* and his coeditorship of *Bring History Alive: A Sourcebook for Teaching United States History.* Through his work, Nash has been credited by many for helping to change the direction of history education for the better by broadening students' views of just what it means to be an American. The gains that he and other educators have made, however, have not been without their controversy, especially with regard to curriculum changes, a battle that he documents with Charlotte Crabtree and Ross E. Dunn in 1997's *History on Trial: National Identity, Culture Wars and the Teaching of the Past.* The typical accusation that critics have made against Nash's approach is that it undervalues the contributions of European Americans and overstresses those made by the people who have typically been marginalized in the history books. As Keith Windschuttle noted in a *New Criterion* review, "All voices should be heard, but in their proper context." Cheney, as noted above, excoriated the authors of the revised curriculum, and conservatives such as radio host Rush Limbaugh "accused the authors of the standards of seeking to indoctrinate students with their radical message of hate America," reported Edward H. Shapiro in the *World and I.* Shapiro continued, "*History on Trial* claims that the opposition to the National History Standards was simply the latest attempt in the continuing effort by right-wing elements to stifle criticism of American political and economic institutions." Although not taking up the right-wing's position, Shapiro, who is a history professor at Seton Hall, commented that to ask typical high school students to grasp the incredible scope and detail of Nash and company's standards is simply not realistic in an era in which half of the country's college students are taking remedial English.

Despite the controversy and possible flaws in these history standards, the proposal and defense of revised standards for teaching history has been a valuable chapter in the evolution of the American educational system, maintained some critics. As Michael Berube concluded in a *Nation* review, "*History on Trial* is a necessary book. With its colorful cast of characters and ambitious historical sweep, it could perhaps have been a riveting book as well. But like the standards of which it is a belated and eloquent defense, it's a service to the nation's history teachers and a very serviceable document—altogether a worthy, thorough, commendable effort. Almost, I imagine, enough to make one believe in historical progress after all."

BIOGRAPHICAL AND CRITICAL SOURCES:

PERIODICALS

American Historical Review, June, 1969, Philip S. Klein, review of *Quakers and Politics: Pennsylvania, 1681-1726,* pp. 1704-1705; December, 1975, Allen W. Trelease, review of *Red, White, and Black: The Peoples of Early America,* p. 1379; February, 1981, Jack P. Greene, review of *The Urban Crucible: Social Change, Political Consciousness, and the Origins and the American Revolution,* p. 200; December, 1989, Eric Foner, review of *Forging Freedom: The Formation of Philadelphia's Black Community, 1720-1840,* p. 1470; April, 1992, R. S. Dunn, review of *Freedom by Degrees: Emancipation in Pennsylvania and Its Aftermath,* p. 611; April, 2003, Eric Sandweiss, review of *First City: Philadelphia and the Forging of Historical Memory,* p. 515.

American Journal of Education, August, 1999, Chad Gaffield, review of *History on Trial: Culture Wars and the Teaching of the Past,* p. 344.

American Journal of Sociology, January, 1972, Elijah Anderson, review of *The Great Fear: Race in the Mind of America,* pp. 789-790.

American Quarterly, summer, 1969, Lloyd N. Dendinger, review of *Quakers and Politics,* p. 389.

American Sociological Review, December, 1971, Suzanne Keller, review of *Class and Society in Early America,* p. 1134.

Atlanta Journal and Constitution, January 6, 1996, Doug Cumming, "University of California History Professor Gary B. Nash, Who Helped Write Proposed National Standards for Teaching History, Has Been Accused by Conservatives of Trashing American History," p. A2.

Booklist, September 15, 1997, Mary Carroll, review of *History on Trial,* p. 204; May 15, 1999, Hazel Rochman, review of *Forbidden Love: The Secret History of Mixed-Race America,* p. 1687; May 15, 2003, James Rettig, "Double Dose of History," p. 1690.

Book Report, March-April, 1998, Ron Marinucci, "Reviews: Nonfiction."

Bulletin—Society for the Study of Labour History, spring, 1988, Edward Countryman, review of *Race, Class, and Politics: Essays on American Colonial and Revolutionary Society,* p. 111.

Business History Review, autumn, 1971, Alan Tully, review of *Class and Society in Early America,* pp. 372-374.

Business Wire, February 14, 2000, "EduLink, Inc. Announces Agreement with Premier Authority on Historical Content Curriculum," p. 1.

Canadian Journal of History, December, 1999, Christopher Kent, review of *History on Trial,* p. 386.

Christian Science Monitor, October 6, 1997, Gregory M. Lamb, "In Teaching History, No Single View of the Past Prevails."

Contemporary Sociology, September, 1972, James M. Fendrich, review of *The Great Fear,* pp. 465-466.

Education Digest, February, 1998, Dudley Barlow, "Education Resources"; April, 1999, Dudley Barlow, "Education Resources."

Ethnohistory, spring, 1983, John K. Chance, review of *Struggle and Survival in Colonial America,* p. 127.

History of Education, June, 1999, Kevin J. Brehony, review of *History on Trial.*

History Teacher, January, 1971, William M. Fowler Jr., review of *Class and Society in Early America,* pp. 77-78.

History Today, June, 1980, Geoffrey Seed, review of *The Urban Crucible,* p. 53.

Horn Book, July, 1999, Michelle Martin, review of *Forbidden Love,* p. 482.

International Migration Review, winter, 1971, Pierre L. van den Berghe, review of *The Great Fear,* pp. 514-515.

International Review of Education, Volume 44, issue 5-6, 1998, review of *History on Trial,* p. 601.

Journal of American Ethnic History, spring, 1991, Ira Berlin, "Reviews."

Journal of American History, September, 1969, James LaVerne Anderson, review of *Quakers and Politics,* pp. 348-349.

Journal of Social History, fall, 1981, Christopher Clar, review of *The Urban Crucible;* fall, 1992, G. S. Rowe, "Reviews."

Knight Ridder Tribune News Service, May 28, 2002, Jerry Large, "Nation's History Lies Buried under Ignorance," p. 1.

Labor History, spring, 1992, Thomas Joseph Davis, review of *Freedom by Degrees,* p. 294.

Library Journal, January 15, 1980, Milton Cantor, review of *The Urban Crucible,* p. 200; April 15, 1986, Roy H. Tryon, review of *Race, Class, and Politics,* p. 79; May 1, 1988, Thomas J. Davis, review of *Forging Freedom,* p. 79; October 1, 1990, David Szatmary, review of *Race and Revolution,* p. 101; March 1, 2003, Nathan Ward, review of *Encyclopedia of American History,* p. 78; April 1, 2003, Nathan Ward, "A New Historical Literacy?"

Los Angeles Times Book Review, December 14, 1997, "Nonfiction," p. 6.

Nation, December, 1997, Michael Berube, review of *History on Trial,* p. 25.

National Review, November 10, 1997, John Fonte, review of *History on Trial,* p. 56.

New Criterion, June, 1998, Keith Windschuttle, "The Problem of Democratic History," p. 22.

New York Times Book Review, November 30, 1997, Sean Wilentz, "Don't Know Much about History," p. 28; September 12, 1999, Brent Staples, "Children's Books," p. 36.

Phylon, Volume 32, number 4, Francesco Cordasco, review of *The Sources of Racism in America,* pp. 420-421.

Public Historian, summer, 2002, Michael Kammen, review of *First City,* p. 53.

Publishers Weekly, September 1, 1997, review of *History on Trial,* p. 91; June 28, 1999, "Not a Black or White Issue," p. 81.

Reference & User Services Quarterly, fall, 2003, David A. Lincove, review of *Encyclopedia of American History,* p. 78.

San Francisco Chronicle, October 27, 1991, Robert Reinhold, "California Rewrites History," p. 7Z1.

School Library Journal, April, 2003, Linda Greengrass, review of *Encyclopedia of American History,* p. 99; August, 2003, Lana Miles, review of *Landmarks of the American Revolution,* p. 184.

Social Studies, May-June, 1998, John J. Chiodo, review of *History on Trial,* p. 140.

Teacher Magazine, May-June, 1998, David Ruenzel, "History in the Making."

Village Voice, November 11, 1997, Tom Frank, "History Clash," p. 59.

Virginia—Pilot (Norfolk, VA), December 14, 1997, Tom Robotham, "Teaching History: Glorify Our Past or Show Ugly Side," p. J2.

Virginia Quarterly Review, spring, 1969.

Washington Post, November 11, 1994, Guy Gugliotta, "World History Teaching Standards Draw Critics," p. A4.

Washington Times, November 16, 1997, Martin Morse Wooster, "Perilous Path to Reform," p. B6.

William and Mary Quarterly, April, 1969, Joseph E. Illick, review of *Quakers and Politics,* pp. 292-295.

World & I, March, 1998, Edward S. Shapiro, review of *History on Trial,* p. 279.

ONLINE

Philly.com, http://www.philly.com/ (May 10, 2004), Kenneth Finkel, "A Colorful Past."*

O

O'BRIEN, Timothy (Brian) 1929-

PERSONAL: Born March 8, 1929, in Shillong, Assam, India; son of Brian Palliser Tiegue (a soldier) and Elinor Laura (Mackenzie) O'Brien; married Jenny Jones (a designer), November 22, 1997. *Education:* Attended Wellington College, Crowthorne, Berkshire, 1942-47; attended Corpus Christi College, Cambridge, 1952; studied stage design under Donald Oenslager at Yale University, 1952-53. *Hobbies and other interests:* Sailing.

ADDRESSES: Office—Flat 3, 97 Cambridge St., London SW1V 4PY, England; and Garstons Gatcombe, Newport, Isle of Wight O30 3EQ, England. *E-mail*—all@highwaterjones.com.

CAREER: Stage and exhibition designer. British Broadcasting Corporation (BBC-TV), London, England, design assistant, 1954-55; Associated Rediffusion Television, London, designer, 1955-56; ABC Television, London, head of design, 1956-65; partnership in stage design with Tazeena Firth, 1961-79; Royal Shakespeare Company, Stratford-upon-Avon, Warwickshire, England, associate designer, 1966-88, honorary associate artist, 1988—; National Theatre, London, designer, 1974-77. Lecturer, Royal College of Art, London, 1966-67.

Stage work as scenic designer includes productions of *The Bald Primadonna,* London, 1956, *The New Tenant,* London, 1956, *Hunter's Moon,* London, 1958, *Five Finger Exercise,* London, 1958, *The Daring Buds of May,* London, 1959, *Don't Shoot, We're English,* London, 1960, *Henry IV, Part I,* London, 1961, *Progress to the Park,* London, 1961, *The Bartered Bride,* 1962, *The Girl of the Golden West,* 1962, *Next Time I'll Sing to You,* London, 1963, *License to Murder,* London, 1963, *Luv,* London, 1963, *Poor Bitos,* London, 1963, New York, NY, 1964, *Hedda Gabler,* London, 1964, *Entertaining Mr. Sloane,* London, 1964, *A Scent of Flowers,* London, 1964, *Waiting for Godot,* London, 1964, *Traveling Light,* London, 1965, *A Scent of Flowers,* Stuttgart, Germany, 1965, *Tango,* Royal Shakespeare Company, 1966, *Days in the Trees,* Royal Shakespeare Company, 1966, *Joey Joey,* Royal Shakespeare Company, 1966, *Staircase,* Royal Shakespeare Company, 1966, *All's Well That Ends Well,* Royal Shakespeare Company, 1967, *As You Like It,* Royal Shakespeare Company, 1967, *Romeo and Juliet,* Royal Shakespeare Company, 1967, *The Merry Wives of Windsor,* Royal Shakespeare Company, 1968, *Troilus and Cressida,* Royal Shakespeare Company, 1968, *The Latent Heterosexual,* Royal Shakespeare Company, 1968, *Pericles,* Royal Shakespeare Company, 1969, *Women Beware Women,* Royal Shakespeare Company, 1969, *Bartholomew Fair,* Royal Shakespeare Company, 1969, *The Knot Garden,* Royal Opera, 1970, *Measure for Measure,* Royal Shakespeare Company, 1970, *The Merchant of Venice,* Royal Shakespeare Company, 1971, *Enemies,* Royal Shakespeare Company, 1971, (with Tazeena Firth) *The Man of Mode,* Royal Shakespeare Company, 1971, *La Cenerentola,* Oslo, Norway, 1972, *Lower Depths, The Island of the Mighty,* Royal Shakespeare Company, 1972, *As You Like It,* OC Shakespeare Company, 1972, *Richard II,* Royal Shakespeare Company, 1973, *Love's Labour's Lost,* Royal Shakespeare Company, 1973, *Next of Kin,* National Theater of Great Britain, London, 1974, *The Bassarids,* English National Opera, 1974, *Summerfolk,* Royal Shakespeare Company, 1974, *Pericles,* Comedie

Française, Paris, 1974, *The Merry Wives of Windsor,* Royal Shakespeare Company, 1975, *The Marrying of Ann Leete,* Royal Shakespeare Company, 1975, *Peter Grimes,* Royal Opera, London, 1975, *John Gabriel Borkman,* National Theater, 1975, *The Bassarids,* Frankfurt, 1975, *Wozzeck,* Adelaide Festival, 1976, *The Zykovs,* Royal Shakespeare Company, 1976, *Troilus and Cressida,* National Theater, 1976, *The Force of Habit,* National Theater, 1976, *Falstaff,* Berlin Opera, 1977, *Tales from the Vienna Woods,* National Theater, 1977, *Bedroom Farce,* National Theater, 1977, *The Cunning Little Vixen,* Goteborg, Sweden, 1978, *A Midsummer Night's Dream,* Sydney Opera House, Australia, 1978, *Evita,* National Theater, 1978, then New York, NY, 1979, *The Rake's Progress,* Royal Opera, 1979, *Peter Grimes,* Goteborg, Sweden, 1979, *Lulu,* Royal Opera, London, 1981, *La Ronde,* Royal Shakespeare Company, 1982, *A Doll's Life,* New York, NY, 1982, *Le Grand Macabre,* English National Opera, London, 1982, *Turandot,* Vienna State Opera, 1983, *Tannhauser,* Royal Opera, London, 1984, *The Mastersingers of Nuremberg,* English National Opera, 1984, *Tramway Road,* Lyric Theatre-Hammersmith, London, 1984, *Samson,* Royal Opera, 1985, *Sicilian Vespers,* Grande Theatre, Geneva, 1985, *Old Times,* Theatre Royal, Haymarket, London, 1985, *Lucia di Lammermoor,* Cologne Opera, 1985, *The Threepenny Opera,* National Theatre, 1986, *Die Meistersinger von Nurnberg,* Netherlands Opera, 1986, *The American Clock,* National Theatre, 1986, *Otello,* Royal Opera, 1987, revived 1990, *Die Entfuhrung aus dem Serail,* Royal Opera, 1987, *Three Sisters,* Royal Shakespeare Company, 1988, *Cymbeline,* Royal Shakespeare Company, 1989, *Exclusive,* Strand Theatre, London, 1989, *King,* Piccadilly Theatre, London, 1990, *Love's Labour's Lost,* Royal Shakespeare Company, 1990, *Twelfth Night,* Playhouse, 1991, *Tartuffe,* Playhouse, 1991, *War and Peace,* Kirov, Leningrad, 1991, *Beauty and the Beast,* City of Birmingham Touring Opera, 1991, *Columbus and the Discovery of Japan,* Royal Shakespeare Company, 1992, *Eugene Onegin,* Royal Opera, 1993, *Misha's Party,* Royal Shakespeare Company, 1993, *On Approval,* Playhouse, 1994, *The Clandestine Marriage,* Queen's Theatre, London, 1994, *The Merry Wives of Windsor,* National Theatre, 1995, *The Master Builder,* Royal Haymarket, London, 1995, *Outis,* La Scala, Milan, 1996, *A Christmas Carol,* Theatr Clwyd, 1997, *Twelfth Night,* 1999, *Macbeth,* Chichester Festival, 2000, *Macbeth,* Theatre Clwyd, 2002, *Bedroom Farce,* San Carlos, Lisbon, 2000, and *Werther.* Film work as scenic designer includes *Night Must Fall,* 1964. Television work as scenic designer includes *The Flying Dutchman,* 1958. Exhibitions include *British Theatre Design '83-87,* Riverside Studios, London, 1988. Member of international jury, Prague Quadriennale, 1999. *Military service:* British Army Intelligence Corps, Austria, sergeant, 1948-49.

MEMBER: Society of British Theatre Designers (co-founder, 1971; chairperson, 1984-91).

AWARDS, HONORS: Prague Quadriennale Gold Medal Award for best set design, 1975; Golden Triga for best national exhibit, 1991; elected Royal Designer for Industry, 1991; elected Master of Faculty, 1999-2001.

WRITINGS:

(With David Fingleton) *British Theatre Design '83-87,* [London, England], 1988.

Contributor to *British Theatre Design, the Modern Age,* edited by John Goodwin, 1989.

SIDELIGHTS: Commenting in *Contemporary Designers,* British stage and exhibition designer Timothy O'Brien described his work as the creation of "a world, its people and their circumstances, in the service of a production and its ideas." Design must be "relevant" and easy to understand in order "to persuade the freshly arrived audience to clear their minds." It should help "to remove stale associations," but the work of the designer fails "if fashion obscures content."

Relating his ideas to his work on the 1975 production of *John Gabriel Borkman,* staged by Great Britain's National Theater, O'Brien laid the scene thus in *Contemporary Designers:* "Things connect. Borkman stands, self-imprisoned in his upstairs room. A hidden door in a faded tapestry of a nymph and her shepherd opens to admit the woman he loved and then forsook when he married her sister for worldly advantage. The audience shivers afresh at the consequences."

Born the son of British parents in India in 1929, O'Brien spent two years just after World War II as an army sergeant stationed in Austria. He began to work as a scenic designer for the London stage in 1956, with the production of *The Bald Primadonna.* There followed numerous productions that included works of Shakespeare ranging from a 1961 staging of *Henry IV, Part I,* 1967's *All's Well That Ends Well,* and the following year's *The Merry Wives of Windsor* to 1970's *Measure for Measure* and 1971's *The Merchant of Venice.* O'Brien also started to design for more modern classics, such as Henrik Ibsen's *Hedda Gabler* and Samuel Beckett's *Waiting for Godot,* both in 1964, as well as Ibsen's *The Master Builder* in 1995. He also participated in the production of musical works that included a 1984 production of Richard Wagner's opera *Tannhauser,* Bertolt Brecht and Kurt Weill's *Threepenny Opera* in 1986, and a 1993 production of Tchaikovsky's *Eugene Onegin.* To U.S. audiences perhaps the most notable of O'Brien's designs were those he did for the premiere of Andrew Lloyd Webber's *Evita* in 1978.

Writing in the *Hartford Courant,* Malcolm Johnson suggested that O'Brien's "stage-spanning bridge" designed for *Evita*—the place from which the title character addressed the Argentine throngs—has become a defining structure in Lloyd Webber's more recent work. "*Evita* and its breathtaking look, both harshly mechanistic and redolent of revolutionary Latin murals," wrote Johnson, "inaugurated a new era for Lloyd Webber, and for musical theater. Thereafter, even if Lloyd Webber originally conceived of a new work as intimate, as in the case of both *Cats* and *Starlight Express,* the urge toward spectacle proved irresistible."

Though it may be true, as Shakespeare wrote, that "the play's the thing," O'Brien's work has attracted plenty of notice by theatre reviewers. L. Potter, writing in the *Times Literary Supplement* regarding a production of *Love's Labour's Lost* staged at the Royal Shakespeare Theatre in Stratford-on-Avon, called O'Brien's sets "exceptionally beautiful." Benedict Nightingale of the London *Times* reviewed the Royal Shakespeare Company's presentation of the same play in London a year later, a production whose cast included an actor then little known to U.S. audiences, Ralph Fiennes. Having returned to "its main London home," Nightingale suggested, "as if to apologise for being so long away," it appeared that the company, and specifically O'Brien, had given "its stage a disarmingly luxuriant look. Timothy O'Brien might have collaborated with Monet and Renoir in creating the lush foliage of reds, yellows, purples, and greens that towers above Shakespeare's lords as they loll on cushions

enjoying their *dejeuner sur l'herbe* [a reference to *Lunch on the Grass,* a famous Monet painting] in the dappled light."

O'Brien once told *CA:* "When Graham Vick, the director, and I went to visit Luciano Berio about his new opera *Outis,* of which the premiere was imminent but the music incomplete, I asked him what it was, to which he replied: 'A musical action in five cycles. A network of expectations. No outcome, however. No premise either.' So I set happily to work in a black space designing scenography containing a sixty-foot revolving stage, secret walls springing up from the floor, a sale of childhood myths by an auctioneer who grew to twenty-five feet and was pricked to death, a Golden Calf made of sixty-eight television sets, a brothel of glass barriers, a dream-laden supermarket, a forest, a child's Trojan horse, a cruise liner, an airport lounge and a concert platform which saw the death of music. Outis—the Greek word for nobody—is the name Odysseus gives himself in the cave of Polyphemus. When Polyphemus cries out that 'Nobody' has blinded him, the other Cyclops do not come to his aid and Outis escapes. Outis's journey does not end in this opera. Berio confronts his own life at the end of the twentieth century, during which he feels conviction has died."

BIOGRAPHICAL AND CRITICAL SOURCES:

BOOKS

Contemporary Designers, 3rd edition, St. James Press (Detroit, MI), 1990.

PERIODICALS

Hartford Courant, August 20, 1995, p. G1.
Theatre Crafts International, February, 1996, p. 16.
Times (London, England), March 28, 1991.
Times Literary Supplement, September 14, 1990, p. 975; November 1, 1991, p. 18; July 31, 1992, p. 18.

*   *   *

ORMSBY, Eric (Linn) 1941-

PERSONAL: Born October 16, 1941, in Atlanta, GA; son of Robert Linn (a college professor) and Virginia (an author and teacher; maiden name, Haire) Ormsby; married Dorothy Louise Hoffmann, July 22, 1967 (divorced, 1995); married Irena Murray (an architectural historian), September 30, 1995; children: (first marriage) Daniel Paul, Charles Martin. *Education:* Attended Columbia University, 1959-60, 1963-64; University of Pennsylvania, B.A. (summa cum laude), 1971; Princeton University, M.A., 1973, Ph.D., 1981; Rutgers University, M.L.S., 1978; also attended University of Tübingen, 1973-74. *Religion:* Roman Catholic. *Hobbies and other interests:* Natural history, cooking, photography.

ADDRESSES: Home—2600 Ave. Pierre Dupuy, Apt. 207, Montreal, Quebec H3C 3R6, Canada. *Office*—Institute of Islamic Studies, McGill University, 3485 McTavish St., Montreal, Quebec H3A 1Y1, Canada. *E-mail*—eric.ormsby@mcgill.ca.

CAREER: Writer. Princeton University, Princeton, NJ, Near East bibliographer, 1975-1977, lecturer in Near Eastern studies, 1981, 1983, curator of Near East Collections, 1977-83; Catholic University of America, Washington, DC, director of libraries, 1983-86; McGill University, Montreal, Quebec, Canada, director of libraries, 1986-96, associate professor, 1986-96, professor at Institute of Islamic Studies, 1996—. Princeton Adult School, instructor, 1978-80; Washington Consortium, chair of continuing education committee, 1983-86; Sous-Comité des Bibliothèques, president, 1989-91; Center for Research Libraries, Chicago, IL, board member, 1989-95; member of Canadian Centre for Architecture and Conseil des recteurs et des principaux des univs. du Québec; former consultant to New York University Al Akhawayn University, and Saudi Arabian Monetary Agency.

MEMBER: Canadian Association of Research Libraries (vice president, 1988-89), Middle Eastern Libraries Association (vice president, 1981-82, president, 1982-83), Hölderlin Gesellschaft, Association pour l'Avancement des Sciences et des Techniques de la Documentation, Société des Amis de Jean de La Fontaine, Phi Beta Kappa.

AWARDS, HONORS: Fellow of German Academic Exchange Service in Tübingen, Germany, 1973-74; citation for "outstanding academic book," *Choice,* 1984, for *Theodicy in Islamic Thought: The Dispute over al-Ghazali's "Best of All Possible Worlds"*; QSPELL Award for Poetry, 1991, for *Bavarian Shrine and Other Poems;* Ingram Merrill Award, 1993.

WRITINGS:

POETRY

Bavarian Shrine and Other Poems, ECW Press (Toronto, Ontario, Canada), 1990.
Coastlines, ECW Press (Toronto, Ontario, Canada), 1992.
For a Modest God: New and Selected Poems, Grove Press (New York, NY), 1997.
Araby, Signal Editions (Montreal, Quebec, Canada), 2001.
Daybreak at the Straits, Zoo Press (Lincoln, NE), 2004.

Work represented in anthologies, including *The Arvon International Poetry Competition Anthology,* 1987; *Narcopolis and Other Poems,* Hell's Kitchen (New York, NY), 1989; *The Priory Book of Christian Poetry,* Collins (London, England), 1990; *Literature: The Human Experience,* 7th edition, St. Martin's Press (New York, NY), 1998; and *The Best American Poetry 1998,* edited by John Hollander, Scribner (New York, NY), 1998. Contributor of poetry to periodicals, including *Acumen, New Criterion, Literary Imagination, America, Gastronomica, Descant, Fiddlehead, Malahat Review, Poetry Canada,* and *Salmagundi.*

NONFICTION

Theodicy in Islamic Thought: The Dispute over al-Ghazali's "Best of All Possible Worlds," Princeton University Press (Princeton, NJ), 1984.
(With R. Mach) *Handlist of Arabic Manuscripts in the Princeton University Library,* Princeton University Press (Princeton, NJ), 1986.
(Editor) *Moses Maimonides and His Time,* Catholic University of America Press (Washington, DC), 1989.
Facsimiles of Time: Essays on Poetry and Translation, Porcupine's Quill (Erin, Ontario, Canada), 2001.

Contributor to books, including *God and Creation,* edited by David Burrell and Bernard McGinn, University of Notre Dame Press (Notre Dame, IN), 1990; *Islamic Studies Presented to Charles J. Adams,* E. J. Brill (Leiden, Netherlands), 1991; *From Africa to Zen: An Introduction to World Philosophy,* edited by Robert

C. Solomon and Kathleen Higgins, Rowman & Little-field (Lanham, MD), 1993; *Readings in World Philosophy,* edited by Robert C. Solomon and Kathleen Higgins, McGraw-Hill (New York, NY), 1995; and *The Cambridge History of Arabic Literature: The Literature of Al-Andalus,* edited by M. R. Menocal and others, Cambridge University Press (New York, NY), 2000. Contributor of articles and reviews to periodicals, including *New Republic, New Yorker, Shenandoah, Journal of Islamic Law and Society, Middle East Journal, Catholic Historical Review, Journal of Religion, Essays in Canadian Writing, Southwest Review,* and *Yale Review.*

Some of Ormsby's writings have been translated into Czech and Serbian.

SIDELIGHTS: Religious scholar and poet Eric Ormsby combines the many facets of his experience and scholarship in his collection of poetry titled *For a Modest God: New and Selected Poems.* The poetry, according to *Library Journal* contributor Thomas F. Merrill, takes a look at ordinary items and draws deeper impressions about the broad universal order that we all occupy. The author succeeds, according to Merrill, and uses an abundance of detail and description. While a *Publishers Weekly* reviewer responded negatively to Ormsby's frequent switches from esoteric to very ordinary language, the critic noted the author's ability to "render detail richly and in the language of decay." Ormsby manages to depict "rot" poetically, employing such images as Lazarus "dressed in delicate ruffles of fungus," observed that reviewer, adding that it is the author's ability to describe decay that gives the collection its strength.

Ormsby demonstrated his comfort with both Christian and Islamic religion and history in *Theodicy in Islamic Thought: The Dispute over al-Ghazali's "Best of All Possible Worlds."* The book examines a little-known Islamic theological argument of the twelfth century that originated with the theologian al-Ghazali, who maintained that "this is the best of all possible worlds." The argument was proposed as a parameter for belief in God and suggested that such trust in God included acceptance of this world as the best place possible. The remainder of the book lays out the historical arguments presented to this point of view. W. Montgomery Watt of *Religious Studies* credited Ormsby for his "logical" approach to the argument, rather than a chronological or historical viewpoint. Montgomery also cited Ormsby's efforts in uncovering the subject matter, and looked forward to future works. Gerhard Boewering of the *Catholic Historical Review,* although noting that the analysis by the author was not as sharp as he desired, complimented Ormsby on the source material presented which had been previously unavailable. B. B. Lawrence of *Choice* called *Theodicy in Islamic Thought* "intellectual history at its best."

Ormsby also edited a collection of essays titled *Moses Maimonides and His Time,* which surveys the life of this unique and multifaceted personality significant in religious history. Maimonides lived between A.D. 1138 and 1204 and performed a variety of roles, including political activist, court physician, author, and codifier of Jewish law. According to Gad Freudenthal in *Isis,* understanding Maimonides is akin to understanding the shaping forces in Jewish culture, especially before the nineteenth century. Freudenthal observed that a historical interpretation of Maimonides is difficult since much of the information about him is contradictory. At least one essay in the collection tries to unearth the essence of the man and attempts to answer the question of whether Maimonides was able to put his values and beliefs into everyday practice. An essay in the collection describes Maimonides as "a committed religionist and a committed philosopher," an example of his all-encompassing approach to thought. Freudenthal found it "striking" that the remaining records of Maimonides's thinking reflect little of then-contemporary social happenings, such as politics or war. Freudenthal found it positive that students of Muslim culture and history were able to contribute their viewpoints to the collection. David R. Lachterman of the *Review of Metaphysics* called the collection "well-conceived and well-executed" and appreciated the inclusion of names and topics indexes.

BIOGRAPHICAL AND CRITICAL SOURCES:

BOOKS

Hollander, John, editor, *Best American Poetry 1998,* Scribner (New York, NY), 1998.
The Norton Anthology of Poetry, 4th edition, W. W. Norton (New York, NY), 1996.
The Norton Introduction to Literature, 5th edition, W. W. Norton (New York, NY), 1991.

PERIODICALS

Books in Canada, May, 1998, pp. 8-11.

Boston Review, October-November, 1998, p. 53.

Catholic Historical Review, April, 1987, Gerhard Boewering, review of *Theodicy in Islamic Thought: The Dispute over al-Ghazali's "Best of All Possible Worlds,"* pp. 296-297.

Choice, January, 1985, B. B. Lawrence, review of *Theodicy in Islamic Thought,* p. 700.

Isis, March, 1993, Gad Freudenthal, review of *Moses Maimonides and His Time,* pp. 139-141.

Library Journal, April 1, 1997, Thomas F. Merrill, review of *For a Modest God: New and Selected Poems,* p. 98.

Montreal Gazette, May 3, 1997, pp. 13-15.

New Criterion, September, 1998, pp. 65-67.

Publishers Weekly, March 31, 1997, review of *For a Modest God,* p. 70.

Religious Studies, March, 1986, W. Montgomery Watt, review of *Theodicy in Islamic Thought,* pp. 153-154.

Religious Studies Review, July, 1985, p. 312.

Review of Metaphysics, September, 1990, David R. Lachterman, review of *Moses Maimonides and His Time,* pp. 157-160.

*   *   *

OSBORNE, David
  See SILVERBERG, Robert

*   *   *

OSBORNE, George
  See SILVERBERG, Robert

P

PALAHNIUK, Chuck 1962-

PERSONAL: Surname is pronounced "paul-ah-nik"; born February 21, 1962, in Pasco, WA; son of Fred (a railroad brakeman) and Carol (an office manager at a nuclear power plant) Palahniuk. *Education:* University of Oregon, received journalism degree, 1986.

ADDRESSES: Home—Portland, OR. *Agent*—Edward Hibbert, Donadio and Olson, Inc., 121 West 27th St., Ste. 704, New York, NY 10001.

CAREER: Novelist. Briefly worked for a newspaper in Gresham, OR; worked for Freightliner as a service documentation specialist for thirteen years; appeared as rapper "Chucky P." on BBC Radio.

MEMBER: National Cacophony Society.

AWARDS, HONORS: Oregon Book Award, and Pacific Northwest Booksellers Award, both for *Fight Club;* Bram Stoker Award nomination for best novel, Horror Writers Association, 2002, for *Lullaby.*

WRITINGS:

NOVELS

Fight Club, W. W. Norton (New York, NY), 1996.
Invisible Monsters, W. W. Norton (New York, NY), 1999.
Survivor, Norton (New York, NY), 1999.

Chuck Palahniuk

Choke, Doubleday (New York, NY), 2001.
Lullaby (first in a trilogy), Doubleday (New York, NY), 2002.
Diary, Doubleday (New York, NY), 2003.

NONFICTION

Fugitives and Refugees: A Walk in Portland, Oregon, Crown (New York, NY), 2003.
Stranger Than Fiction, Doubleday (New York, NY), 2004.

Contributor to periodicals, including *Gear, Playboy, Portland Mercury, Independent, L. A. Weekly,* and *Black Book.*

ADAPTATIONS: Fight Club was released as a film in 1999.

WORK IN PROGRESS: Two more novels to complete the trilogy begun with *Lullaby.*

SIDELIGHTS: The author of several unconventional novels as well as a quirky hometown travelogue and a collection of essays on Hollywood cult figures, Chuck Palahniuk began his writing career with the apocalyptic novel *Fight Club,* which became a cult classic and the basis of the 1999 Hollywood film by the same name. It features a secret fight club in which men beat each other bloody and whose members eventually develop into an anarchist army that is funded by selling soap made of liposuctioned human fat. Palahniuk's subsequent works have featured equally shocking and bizarre premises, and are also sustained by the author's black humor and cynical viewpoint. On the heels of the film, Palahniuk quickly published three more novels, *Invisible Monsters, Survivor,* and *Choke.* These works were also reportedly considered to be serious candidates for screen adaptations.

In the wake of *Fight Club,* Palahniuk has repeatedly been called on to tell his own story, in which he once despaired of ever becoming a novelist. His job documenting diesel service procedures left little time for writing. He thought about waiting to write until he retired, but came to the conclusion that he might die before that happened. So Palahniuk snatched moments in waiting rooms, laundromats, and traffic jams, squeezing in the work whenever he could. He sent a manuscript to a publisher and it was rejected, presumably because of its rather shocking content. Instead of feeling discouraged, Palahniuk got mad and decided to send the publisher an even more outrageous story. The novel *Fight Club* was the result.

Palahniuk has also related how life experiences have inspired his novels. *Fight Club* was born of Palahniuk's own fights, and of the lack of response his bruised and bloody face got from coworkers. He told *Salon.com* writer Sarah Tomlinson that he realized "you could really do anything you wanted in your personal life, as long as you looked so bad that people would not want to know the details. I started thinking of a fight club as a really structured, controlled way of just going nuts in a really safe situation." However, in *Fight Club* this "safe" pastime has frightening consequences. The unnamed narrator has a bland, unhappy life, and has been seeking solace, however undeserved, by faking terminal illness at support-group meetings. He befriends Tyler Durden, an unpredictable young man who suggests starting the fight club. It is Durden who starts having an affair with Marla, a woman the narrator met at a meeting where he claimed to have testicular cancer. The fight club inspires countless others and it turns out that Durden has larger, destructive plans for his army of thousands of nihilists. He unveils Project Mayhem, a plan to terrorize corporate America by attacking the world's tallest building.

Critics described *Fight Club* as both disturbing and fascinating. A *Publishers Weekly* writer warned that almost any reader was likely to find something offensive. The reviewer called the book "caustic, outrageous, bleakly funny, violent and always unsettling" as well as "utterly original." In a *Booklist* review, Thomas Gaughan described *Fight Club* as "gen X's most articulate assault yet on baby-boomer sensibilities" and a work sure to disturb young readers' parents. He concluded that it was "powerful, and possibly brilliant."

A *Guardian Unlimited* article by Stuart Jeffries considered the literary and social relevance of *Fight Club.* Jeffries called the novel "the 90s reply to *American Psycho,* Bret Easton Ellis's satire on youthful white-collar greed and banality in Wall Street in the 80s." His interview with Palahniuk revealed that the author has read Kierkegaard, Sartre, and Camus; and Jeffries felt that "it shows in his nihilistic insistence on destroying lifestyles that serve nobody well, and recognizing the importance of mortality." The reviewer also remarked that the book "has proven appealing to men of a certain age. At times it seems to be exclusively about men whose fathers were absent during their childhoods." Moreover, Jeffries surmised that at several points the novel "suggests that all-male clubs are the only way men can re-establish their male potency."

Concern about the impact of *Fight Club* increased with the release of the feature film. The emergence of copycat clubs did not disturb Palahniuk, who believes their members were probably already expressing their violent impulses in other, more dangerous ways. However, a rumor emerged that Twentieth Century-Fox delayed the film's release following the tragic shootings at Columbine High School. In an interview for the *Orlando Weekly Movies,* Palahniuk indirectly commented on the possibility of links between his writing and such acts of violence. He called the fight club experience "an honest, consensual violence. . . . It's not victimizing violence. It's not a chickenshit walking into a crowded place full of helpless people with a gun."

The author's second novel, *Survivor,* is also a violent, darkly comic, bitter picture of American life. Its chapters proceed in reverse chronological order, beginning with forty-seven, and the pages begin with number 289 and end with one. Thus, the reader is introduced to the protagonist Tender Branson moments before his death, as his plane is about to crash into the Australian desert. Branson is telling his story into the jet's black box, explaining how he came to be the last living member of the Creedish Death Cult. His story is outrageous: as a Creedalist, he became an unpaid servant in exchange for donations to the church; slave labor charges and an FBI raid on the Creedish compound resulted in a mass suicide; media interest in Branson turned him into a celebrity and book-selling, self-help guru. But it is also revealed that the cult suicides may in fact be murders, and that Branson's brother Adam may be a survivor and a serial killer.

Reviews of *Survivor* were enthusiastic, although *Fight Club* sometimes cast a shadow over the new novel. A *Kirkus Reviews* writer called the book "brilliant, engrossing, substantial, and fun" and asserted that "Palahniuk carves out credible, moving dramas from situations that seemed simply outlandish and sad on the evening news." In the *Oregonian,* Frank Bures suggested that with *Survivor* Palahniuk "demonstrates his ranges as a writer." Bures compared *Fight Club*'s "twisted carpe diem" to this novel's "ironic laments." The reviewer concluded, "If there is a central theme to *Survivor,* it is . . . disgust at superficiality and sameness. Yet it gets lost among the other questions raised about free will, fate, mindless following, religious hypocrisy, death and other existential, if tangential, matters." *Village Voice* writer Lily Burana was disappointed by what followed a fascinating open: "Problem is, once it is revealed that Tender is the last surviving Creedish, the book becomes predictable."

The narrative swerves from the deft, carefully imagined satire of a tiny, workaday life and plunges straight into a 'Toontown-like hyperbolic broadcast of living large before the masses." At the review's end, she also pondered whether "many young-adult readers—hungry kids trapped in suburban and rural America . . . might make a cult hero of Palahniuk."

The original manuscript for Palahniuk's third novel, *Invisible Monsters,* was the story that publishers rejected prior to *Fight Club.* Palahniuk was glad to have had the chance to improve the novel, and rewrote over three-quarters of the book before submitting it. In part a satirical stab at the fashion industry, the novel was conceived after its author sat reading fashion magazines at his local laundromat. Commenting on the novel in the *Village Voice,* Palahniuk called *Invisible Monsters* "a *Valley of the Dolls* book, a summer beach book. . . . Don't take it very seriously." However, he also noted it was inspired by his reading of French philosopher Michael Foucault and Foucault's exploration of identity.

Like *Survivor, Invisible Monsters* begins at its story's end; however, it then reveals episodes in Shannon McFarland's life in a random sequence. Shannon is a former model who lost the lower half of her face in a shooting. She is left without a career and is filled with anger at her ex-boyfriend Manus and her ex-girlfriend Evie, who had an affair after the shooting. Convinced that the pair may be responsible for her wounds, Shannon goes on a cross-country road trip with a new friend, the transgendered Brandy Alexander. Their goal is to confront Evie in Texas, where she is about to be married. In the process, Shannon and Brandy kidnap Manus and start secretly feeding him female hormone pills. In the process, it is revealed that Brandy is Shannon's brother, whom she had believed was dead of AIDS.

The plot's twists and jumps left many reviewers on the fence about *Invisible Monsters.* In the *San Francisco Chronicle,* James Sullivan said, "All this roughhousing will make readers punch-drunk by the book's climax. It's Palahniuk's least successful effort to date, yet there are more than enough moments of insight to recommend" the novel. A *Kirkus Reviews* writer called it "too clever by half: a Chinese box of a novel fascinating in its intricacies but pretty hard to get a grip on whole." A reviewer for *Publishers Weekly* tired of the flashbacks and use of "a fashion photographers commands . . . to signpost the narrator's epiphanies," but acknowledged that the book "does have fun moments when campy banter tops the heroine's flat, whiny bathos." Writing for *Booklist,* George Needham concluded, "By the end, most readers will be both exhausted and exhilarated."

Palahniuk's fourth novel, *Choke,* firmly cemented his reputation as a skilled writer who continues to keep his readers uncomfortable. In this novel, the central character is Victor Mancini, a young man who supplements his paycheck in an unusual way: he fakes choking in a different restaurant every night, confident that someone will volunteer to save him and, upon hearing his hard-luck story, send him cash on a regular basis. Victor is a medical school dropout, works a menial job at a historical village, and is a sex addict who indulges himself mid-flight in airplane bathrooms. Flashbacks show that Victor's mother, now a senile woman in a nursing home, gave him a miserable childhood. However, he still wants to help her. A mysterious doctor at the nursing home reveals that his mother believes he was conceived by her contact with a holy relic, which would make him the son of Jesus.

In a review for the *New York Times* Janet Maslin was both frustrated and impressed by elements in *Choke.* She introduced the story line with the comment that "Palahniuk is hard to beat if you'd like a working definition of the adolescent male state of mind." And she named him among Irvine Welsh and J. G. Ballard as "writers equally devoted to bizarre circumstances and the bleakest of humor." Yet Maslin admired "the sheer, anarchic fierceness of imagination that fuels [the novel's] wildest individual vignettes," and dubbed *Choke* "an uneven but still raw and vital book, punctuated with outrageous, off-the-wall moments that work as often as not."

In the *Oregonian* John Foyston confessed that the novel contains several details he could not openly discuss in "a family newspaper." Foyston came to the conclusion that "With this, his fourth novel, Palahniuk's strengths and weaknesses are plain enough. His most endearing trait—the thing that keeps me reading—is that marvelous quicksilver voice of his. *Choke* also benefits from Palahniuk's taste for obscure and obsessive erudition, which shows up in the ongoing internal monologue of an AWOL med student." The reviewer was left wanting more plot and more agreeable characters, yet he felt that "the exuber-

ance" of the author's "language makes it still worthwhile to brave these often chilly and dark waters."

Palahniuk's more recent project is a horror trilogy that begins with the novel *Lullaby.* In this bizarre tale, newspaper reporter Carl Streator is writing a story about Sudden Infant Death Syndrome (SIDS) when he discovers a macabre connection with a book of poetry. In each of the five cases of SIDS he investigates he finds the same edition of the book in which an ancient African tribal poem has been reprinted. The poem was originally intended as a way to decrease the tribes' population in desperate times when there was not enough food to go around. Now it has been carelessly reprinted in a book, and the dilemma the reporter faces is that he does not know how many copies of the book are extant and how to get rid of them before it is too late. Teaming up with a real estate agent, Helen Hoover Boyle, who also knows the "culling song," Streator sets out to destroy all known copies of the book. Two more strange characters join in this eerie quest, Mona, Helen's assistant, and her boyfriend, Oyster.

Maslin, writing in the *New York Times,* was again both fascinated and repelled by Palahniuk's "tireless pursuit of the outrageous" in *Lullaby.* Like Kurt Vonnegut, he "juggles nihilism and idealism with fluid, funny ease, and he repeats and rephrases word patterns until they take on an almost mystical aspect." Virginia Heffernan, reviewing *Lullaby* for the *New York Times Book Review,* was less impressed, dubbing the novel a "nauseating picaresque" with "less than zero sacred." A *Kirkus Reviews* contributor saw more to like in the novel, calling it the kind of "outrageous, darkly comic fun . . . you'd expect from Palahniuk." And *Booklist* reviewer John Green felt that what separates *Lullaby* from Palahniuk's earlier work "is its emotional depth, its ability to explore the unbearable pain of losing a child just as richly as it laments our consume-or-die worldview."

Palahniuk's sixth novel, *Diary,* is told in the form of a diary that Misty Marie Kleinman writes for her carpenter husband, Peter Wilmot, who lies in a coma following a suicide attempt. Misty is an artist who prefers the blandly pictorial to edgy modern art; she was attracted to Peter originally because of the picturesque island he took her to live on. However, she wound up working as a waitress to support her daughter and mother-in-law, while Peter's carpentry work became an outlet for his mental instability, as he started engineering hidden rooms in which he plastered obscenities. Misty has now become consumed with her painting, and her friends and acquaintances mysteriously want her to paint more and more; if she stops, she gets excruciating headaches. The force that drives her somehow seems to be controlled by members of her family, whose intentions are unclear.

Typically, reviews of *Diary* were mixed. A *Publishers Weekly* contributor noted that the author "captures the reader hook, line and sinker" from the first page, and then spins a "twisted tale [that is] one of his most memorable works to date." *Booklist*'s John Green similarly found that the book's "fantastically grotesque premise propels the story," but also found fault with the writing, which "lacks the satirical precision" of Palahniuk's other works. In contrast, *Book* contributor James Sullivan praised *Diary* as a "deft meditation on great art and the toll it takes." David Wright, reviewing the novel in *Library Journal*, called *Diary* a "blend of paranoiac horror along the lines of *Rosemary's Baby*," while Flynn, in *Entertainment Weekly*, dubbed the work "pretty stunning, funky stuff."

BIOGRAPHICAL AND CRITICAL SOURCES:

PERIODICALS

Book, September-October, 2002, Michael Kaplan, interview with Palahniuk, p. 13; September-October, 2003, James Sullivan, review of *Diary,* p. 92.

Booklist, July, 1996, Thomas Gaughan, review of *Fight Club,* p. 1804; September 15, 1999, George Needham, review of *Invisible Monsters,* p. 233; August, 2002, John Green, review of *Lullaby,* p. 1887; July, 2003, John Green, review of *Diary,* p. 1846; July, 2003, Bill Ott, review of *Fugitives and Refugees,* p. 1858; December 15, 2003, Ted Hipple, review of *Diary,* p. 762.

Entertainment Weekly, May 25, 2001, Troy Patterson, "Hard to Swallow: In Choke, the Latest from the Author of *Fight Club,* Chuck Palahniuk's Hip Nihilism Comes to Naught," p. 72; July 18, 2003, Noah Robischon, review of *Fugitives and Refugees,* p. 80; September 5, 2003, Gillian Flynn, review of *Diary,* p. 79; September 26, 2003, Karen Valby, "Chuck Palahniuk Does Not Attend Fight Club," p. 62; September 26, 2003, Noah Robischon, "Joining the Club," p. 67.

Kirkus Reviews, December 15, 1998, review of *Survivor,* p. 1755; August 1, 1999, review of *Invisible Monsters,* p. 1160; June 15, 2002, review of *Lullaby,* p. 834; May 1, 2003, review of *Fugitives and Refugees,* pp. 663.

Kliatt, September, 2003, Jacqueline Edwards, review of *Diary,* pp. 54-55.

Library Journal, March 1, 2001, Heath Madom, review of *Choke,* p. 132; August, 2002, Andrea Kempf, review of *Lullaby,* p. 144; July, 2003, John McCormick, review of *Fugitives and Refugees,* p. 112; July, 2003, David Wright, review of *Diary,* p. 125.

Los Angeles Times, October 15, 1999, review of *Fight Club,* p. 1; October 6, 2002, Susan Salter Reynolds, review of *Lullaby,* p. E1; August 10, 2003, Christopher Reynolds, review of *Fugitives and Refugees,* p. L9.

Newsweek, September 1, 2003, Andrew Phillips, interview with Palahniuk, p. 10.

New York Times, May 24, 2001, Janet Maslin, "An Immature Con Man with a Mom Problem"; September 12, 2002, Janet Maslin, review of *Lullaby,* p. E9; August 31, 2003, Taylor Antrim, review of *Fugitives and Refugees,* and *Diary,* p. 5.

New York Times Book Review, May 27, 2001, Jennifer Reese, review of *Choke,* p. 16; October 20, 2002, Virginia Heffernan, review of *Lullaby,* p. 17.

New York Times Magazine, September 29, 2002, John Glassie, "The Pugilist Novelist" (interview), p. 21.

Oregonian, March 10, 1999, Frank Bures, "*Survivor* Stews over Superficiality of Society"; May 13, 2001, John Foyston, review of *Choke.*

Publishers Weekly, June 3, 1996, review of *Fight Club,* p. 60; July 5, 1999, review of *Invisible Monsters,* p. 56; March 20, 2000, John F. Baker, "*Fight Club* Author to Broadway," p. 15; April 2, 2001, review of *Choke,* p. 37; July 1, 2002, review of *Lullaby,* pp. 46-47; July 8, 2002, John F. Baker, "No D-day Choke for Chuck," p. 12; September 2, 2002, interview with Palahniuk, p. 49; September 30, 2002, Daisy Maryles, "Not a Sleeper," p. 18; May 12, 2003, review of *Fugitives and Refugees,* pp. 51-52; July 7, 2003, review of *Choke,* pp. 26-27; July 7, 2003, review of *Diary,* pp. 50-51; September 8, 2003, Daisy Maryles, "Dear Diary," p. 18; December 1, 2003, review of *Diary,* p. 20.

San Francisco Chronicle, September 12, 1999, James Sullivan, "Model Misbehavior."

Time, September 23, 2002, Richard Lacayo, review of *Lullaby,* p. 76.

Village Voice, February 24, Lily Burana, "Cult Club; October 13-19," Emily Jenkins, "Extreme Sport."

Washington Post Book World, May 27, 2001, review of *Choke,* p. 6; August 31, 2003, Marc Nesbitt, review of *Diary,* p. p.

Western Journal of Medicine, May, 2002, Shahin Chandrasoma, interview with Palahniuk, pp. 200-202.

ONLINE

Chuck Palahniuk Home Page, http://www.chuck palahniuk.net/ (March 4, 2004).

Guardian Unlimited, http://www.film.guardian.co.uk/ (May 12, 2000), Stuart Jeffries, "Bruise Control."

Oregonian Online, http://www.oregonlive.com/ (December 12, 2003), Shawn Levy, review of *Postcards from the Future;* (December 19, 2003) "We Barely Saw Ye, Chuck."

Powells.com, http://www.powells.com/ (September 4, 2003), C. P. Farley, "Author Interviews: Chuck Palahniuk."

Salon.com, http://www.salon.com/ (October 13, 1999), Sarah Tomlinson, "Is It Fistfighting, or Just Multi-tasking?"

Telegraph Online, http://www.telegraph.co.uk/ (October 21, 2003), William Leith, "A Writer's Life: Chuck Palahniuk."

OTHER

Widmyer, Dennis, Kevin Kolsch, and Josh Chaplinsky, *Postcards from the Future: The Chuck Palahniuk Documentary* (film), ChuckPalahniuk.net, 2003.*

*   *   *

PALMER, Diana
   See KYLE, Susan (Spaeth)

*   *   *

PARK, Jordan
   See POHL, Frederik

*   *   *

PHILLIPS, Caryl 1958-

PERSONAL: Born March 13, 1958, in St. Kitts, West Indies; immigrated to England, 1958. *Education:* Queen's College, Oxford, B.A. (honours), 1979.

Caryl Phillips

ADDRESSES: Home—New York, NY. *Office*—Department of English, Barnard College, New York, NY 10027-6598. *Agent*—(literary) Georgia Garrett, A. P. Watt Ltd., 20 John St., London WC1N 2DR, England; (dramatic) Judy Daish, Judy Daish Associates, 2 St. Charles Place, London W10 6EQ, England.

CAREER: Writer. *Observer* Festival of Theatre, Oxford, founding chairman, 1978, artistic director, 1979; writer-in-residence, Factory Arts Center (Arts Council of Great Britain), London, England, 1980-82, University of Mysore, Mysore, India, 1987, University of Stockholm, Stockholm, Sweden, 1989, and National Institute of Education, Singapore, summer, 1994; Arvon Foundation, England, writing instructor, summers, 1983—; visiting lecturer, University of Ghana, 1990, and University of Poznan, Poland, 1991; Amherst College, Amherst, MA, visiting writer, 1990-92, co-director of Creative Writing Center, 1992-97, writer-in-residence, 1992-97, professor of English, 1997-98; Humber College, Toronto, Ontario, Canada, visiting writer, August 1992 and 1993; New York University, visiting professor of English, fall, 1993; Barnard College, Columbia University, New York, NY, professor of English, Henry R. Luce Professor of Migration and Social Order, 1998—, director of Initiatives in the Humanities, 2003—, director of Barnard Forum on Migration. Heartland Productions, director, 1994-2000; University of West Indies, Barbados, visiting professor of humanities, summer 1999-2000. Faber & Faber, Boston, MA, consultant editor, 1992-94, London, England, series editor, 1996-2000. British Council, senior advisor for literature, 2002—; visiting writer at schools, including Yale University, 2004. Coordinator, speaker, and participant of international conferences, seminars and festivals, 1986—. Member, Arts Council of Great Britain drama panel, 1982-85; British Film Institute Production Board, 1985-88; Bush Theater board, 1985-89; and "The Caribbean Writer" board, United States Virgin Islands, 1989—; University of Kent, honorary senior member, beginning 1988; *World Literature Written in English,* member of advisory board, beginning 1998; British Council, member of arts advisory committee; *Belgian Journal of English Language and Literatures,* member of advisory board, 2003—.

AWARDS, HONORS: British Arts Council bursary, 1984; fiftieth anniversary fellowship, British Council, 1984; Giles Cooper Award, British Broadcasting Corp. (BBC), 1984, for *The Wasted Years;* Malcolm X Prize for Literature, 1985, for *The Final Passage;* Martin Luther King Memorial Prize, 1987, for *The European Tribe;* Young Writer of the Year Award, London *Sunday Times,* 1992; Guggenheim fellowship, 1992; Booker Prize nomination, 1993, and James Tait Black Memorial Prize, 1994, both for *Crossing the River;* included on *Granta* list of Best Young British Writers, 1993; Lannan Literary Award for fiction, 1994, for oeuvre; Rockefeller Foundation Bellagio residency, 1994; A.M. Hon., Amherst College, 1995; Hon. D., Leeds Metropolitan University, 1997; University of West Indies Humanities Scholar of the Year, 1999; fellow, Royal Society of Literature, 2000; Silver Ombu award for best screenplay, Mar del Plata Film Festival (Argentina), 2002, for *The Mystic Masseur;* Mel and Lois Tukman Fellow, New York Public Library's Dorothy and Lewis B. Cullman Center for Scholars and Writers, 2002-03; Hon.D., University of York, 2003; Hon.D. Letters, University of Leeds, 2003; National Book Critics Circle Award finalist for fiction, 2003, and PEN/Faulkner Award for Fiction nomination, and Commonwealth Writers Prize for Best Book, both 2004, all for *A Distant Shore.*

WRITINGS:

FICTION

The Final Passage, Penguin (New York, NY), 1985.

A State of Independence, Farrar, Straus (New York, NY), 1986.
Higher Ground, Viking (London, England), 1989, Viking (New York, NY), 1990.
Cambridge, Bloomsbury (London, England), 1991, Knopf (New York, NY), 1992.
Crossing the River, Bloomsbury (London, England), 1993, Knopf (New York, NY), 1994.
The Nature of Blood, Knopf (New York, NY), 1997.
A Distant Shore, Knopf (New York, NY), 2003.

PLAYS

Strange Fruit (first produced at Crucible Theatre, Sheffield, England, 1980), Amber Lane Press, 1981.
Where There Is Darkness (produced at Lyric Hammersmith Theatre, London, England, 1982), Amber Lane Press, 1982.
The Shelter (first produced at Lyric Hammersmith Theatre, 1983), Amber Lane Press, 1984.

Also author of *The Hotel Cristobel.*

SCREENPLAYS

Welcome to Birmingham (documentary), Central TV, 1983.
"The Hope and Glory," aired on *Play for Today,* British Broadcasting Corporation (BBC), 1984.
"Lost in Music," aired on *Global Report,* BBC, 1984.
The Record, Channel 4, 1985.
Playing Away (aired on *Film on 4,* Channel 4, 1986), Faber & Faber (London, England), 1987.
(And coproducer) *The Final Passage,* Channel 4, 1996.
The Mystic Masseur, Merchant Ivory Productions, 2001.

RADIO PLAYS

The Wasted Years (produced for BBC Radio 4, 1984), Methuen (London, England), 1985.
Crossing the River, BBC Radio 3, 1985.
The Prince of Africa, BBC Radio 3, 1987.
Writing Fiction, BBC Radio 4, 1991.
A Kind of Home: James Baldwin in Paris, BBC Radio 4, 2004.

RADIO DOCUMENTARIES

St. Kitts Independence (Pride of Place), BBC Radio 4, 1983.
Sport and the Black Community, BBC Radio 4, 1984.
No Complaints: James Baldwin at Sixty, BBC Radio 4, 1985.
The Spirit of America, BBC Radio 4, 1995.
These Islands Now: Transformations in British Culture, BBC Radio 3, 1995.
(Editor) *Extravagant Strangers: The "Other" Voice in English Literature* (produced for BBC Radio 3, 1997), published as *Extravagant Strangers: A Literature of Belonging,* Vintage (New York, NY), 1997.
"I Too Am America," aired on *Archive Hour,* BBC Radio 4, 2004.

OTHER

The European Tribe (nonfiction), Farrar, Straus (New York, NY), 1987.
(Editor) *The Right Set: A Tennis Anthology,* Vintage (New York, NY), 1999.
The Atlantic Sound (nonfiction), Knopf (New York, NY), 2000.
A New World Order, Secker & Warburg (London, England), 2001, Vintage (New York, NY), 2002.

Contributor of articles to periodicals, including London *Times* and *Sunday Times, Caribbean Review of Books, Guardian, Financial Times, New York Times, New Republic, New York Times Book Review, Washington Post Book World, Daily Telegraph, Los Angeles Times Book Review, Race Today Review,* and *Bomb.* Contributor of articles to anthologies, including *Lost Classics,* edited by Michael Ondaatje and others, Knopf Canada (Toronto, Ontario, Canada), 2000; and *How Novelists Work,* edited by Maura Dooley, Seren Press, 2000. *Bomb* magazine, New York, NY, contributing editor, 1993—; Graywolf Press, Minneapolis, MN, consulting editor, 1994—; *Wasifiri* magazine, London, England, advisory editor, 1995—.

Some of the author's works have been translated into French, Swedish, Dutch, German, Portuguese, Spanish, Polish, Greek, Finnish, Japanese, and Turkish.

Phillips's manuscripts are housed at the Beinecke Library, Yale University, New Haven, CT.

SIDELIGHTS: The compromised identity of the black West Indian, their African roots, and their displacement to other reaches is the common thread that links the writings of author and educator Caryl Phillips. A prolific writer of novels, television and movie scripts, radio dramas, and nonfiction pieces, Phillips focuses on "migration, belonging, discovery and hope," as quoted in a Barnard College Web site summary. As Phillips added on the online site, "It is the same story rewritten in many ways. I feel it is my duty to tell the story and I can't stop telling it. As long as I feel I have something to say I have the obligation of saying it and I will keep on writing."

Phillips's work is a reflection of his own roots and multinational existence in three cultures: Caribbean, British, and American. He was born in the West Indies, on the Island of St. Kitts, although his family migrated to Leeds, England, when he was only a few months old. He was raised in a working-class neighborhood where his parents instilled in him the importance of education. Teaching by example, both parents eventually earned college degrees. Although participating in sports gave him self-confidence, Phillips took academics to heart and was the first person from his school to be accepted into Oxford University. First studying theater and directing a number of plays, Phillips switched to studying English literature and language and graduated after three years with honors.

In addition to writing, Phillips has traveled the globe teaching and participating in seminars. Since graduating from college in 1979, Phillips has been a visiting professor, lecturer, and writer-in-residence at a dozen universities on almost every continent and has participated in over sixty seminars in over twenty countries, serving as the keynote speaker at many events. In the introduction to his book of essays, *The European Tribe,* Phillips acknowledges that early in his career he "felt like a transplanted tree that had failed to take root in foreign soil." *The European Tribe* is the result of Phillips's journeys throughout the world to examine racism and define his own place in a white-dominated society. This book won the Martin Luther King Memorial Prize.

In novels such as *The Final Passage* and *A State of Independence,* Phillips's main characters wander without firm roots between their native West Indies and England. *Higher Ground,* a trilogy of stories that encompasses a period of 200 years, examines, through multiple points of view, the lingering consequences of being uprooted from one's homeland. Each story concerns the survival of individuals adrift in a hostile culture, but the author extends his outlook to include the perspective of a white European female. Phillips again uses contrasting points of view in his historical novels *Cambridge* and *Crossing the River.*

In *The Final Passage,* Phillips's first novel and winner of the Malcom X Prize for Literature, protagonist Leila Preston intends to emigrate with her baby from their Caribbean island home to England. Although Leila is fleeing from the emotional pain of a bad marriage to Michael, a lazy and unfaithful drunk, she ends up traveling with him after a last-minute reconciliation. Not surprisingly, "the new start proves to be a resumption of the old pain," wrote David Montrose in the *Times Literary Supplement.* Despite Michael's promise to reform, he backslides into his old habits. Also, Leila's mother, who had already immigrated to England, is dying in a hospital. "England itself administers further hurts," Montrose pointed out. "Walls carry racist slogans, landlords' signs stipulate 'no coloureds.'" After five months, Leila leaves Michael for good and returns home to the West Indies. "Her prospects of serenity remain uncertain, but the outlook at least seems promising," Montrose commented in the *Times Literary Supplement,* adding later that Phillips's writing "sustains an atmosphere of emotional adversity." Calvin Forbes, a critic for the *Washington Post Book World,* noticed that Phillips "is one of the few black writers considering the cross-Atlantic relationship."

John Sutherland summed up Phillips's second novel, *A State of Independence,* in the *London Review of Books* as a work that thematically "deals with the contradictions inherent in being a 'British West Indian.'" The narrative takes place on an island modeled closely after St. Kitts; Bertram Francis, the main character, arrives home after twenty years spent in England as a scholarship student who failed to reach many of his goals. The island is about to become an independent nation, and, like his homeland, Bertram would like to cast off the last vestiges of his Britishness. However, he soon discovers that his brother has died, his mother bitterly resents his long absence, and an old friend who has risen to the position of deputy prime minister of the new regime thinks little of his scheme to start up a local business. This highly placed friend reminds Bertram that this "is no longer the island he left,"

observed a reviewer in *Best Sellers,* who commented further that "Bertram's own independence has estranged him from the people and the island he once knew." Perceiving the book as a discussion on "the national tensions of post-imperialism," Sutherland stated in the *London Review of Books* that *A State of Independence* "is both a promising and an accomplished work."

The opening story of Phillips's novella trilogy, *Higher Ground,* is titled "Heartland" and is, in the words of Charles Johnson of the *Los Angeles Times Book Review,* "a chilling, Kafkaesque parable about the slave trade." The narrator, a shepherd on the West African coast, is taken captive by British traders and sold to one of their associates, who teaches him English as well as the fundamentals of slave trading. Eventually, this nameless narrator cooperates with the British, betraying his fellow Africans. "He is half-slave and half-free, poised in a nightmarish limbo between two cultures," Johnson remarked. When the narrator does finally defy his captors—unable to tolerate the abuse of a black teenage girl he himself helped to enslave—his dubious freedom is ended for good and he is sold on the auction block. Critic Adam Lively, in a review for the *Times Literary Supplement,* singled out "Heartland" as being "a particularly impressive single sweep of narrative," and commented that it "owes its immediacy to [the] strength of visual imagination."

The second story in *Higher Ground* is "The Cargo Rap," which is told by convict Rudi Williams in letters he writes from prison during the late 1960s. A self-proclaimed Marxist-Leninist and an adherent of the Black Power movement, Rudi sends home letters full of politics and polemic. "Ironically, Rudi's black nationalist tirades to his family against 'race-mixing' and integration are at odds with his uncritical acceptance of (white) Marx and Lenin," Johnson remarked in the *Los Angeles Times Book Review,* complimenting Phillips for "a fine job of showing the contradictions in Rudi's character."

Higher Ground closes with the title novella, a story about Irina, a Jewish refugee from Poland, who encounters England in much the same way as do Phillips's black Caribbean characters. The story is set in the 1950s when, according to Penelope Lively in the *Times Literary Supplement,* "the backlash against postwar immigration is beginning to be felt." Irina marries, but attempts to commit suicide after the marriage deteriorates, and is sent to a hospital, where she develops an aversion to further emotional attachments. Upon her release from the hospital, Irina meets a West Indian named Louis, and they share a sexual encounter, although "their friendship across the gulf of cultures falters," according to Johnson in the *Los Angeles Times Book Review*. Johnson appreciated that the author's "ever growing skill . . . does allow us to know Irina and the suffering of the dispossessed, the forgotten."

In *Cambridge,* Phillips not only employs another white woman as a major character, he also writes from her perspective. The diary of Emily Cartwright, the British daughter of a West Indies plantation owner, comprises the bulk of the novel and provides a feminine perspective on the institution of slavery. Although she might be considered as liberal for her era because she is revolted by conditions on the plantation, Emily nonetheless believes that Africans—an inferior race in her opinion—were intended by God to work for whites. "Unable to comprehend the negative effects of slavery on both slave and slaveholder, she is convinced it is [the slaveholder's] contact with the slaves that causes the otherwise good Christian white man to behave in repulsive ways," summed up Clarence Major in the *Washington Post Book World.*

Emily's commentary is countered by the journal of an elderly slave known as Cambridge, who has been thrown in jail for defying his captors. As a teenager, he had been Olumide, an African kidnapped by slave traders and intended for sale in America. The captain, however, "renames him Tom, like a pet, and keeps him," according to Major in the *Washington Post Book World.* Tom becomes an educated Christian, renames himself David Henderson, and marries. When his wife dies, he decides to embark on a journey to Africa as a Christian proselytizer, but is kidnapped by the ship's captain and again enslaved, at a plantation in the West Indies. Olumide ultimately receives the name Cambridge—a reference to his fluency in English—from the slave overseer at the plantation. Cambridge has spent many years in hard servitude by the time Emily makes her visit. When she encounters Cambridge, she resents his attitude and is "offended by his speaking the King's English with much flourish, his arrogance in addressing her without permission in terms that suggest an equal standing," stated Calvin Forbes in the Chicago *Tribune Books.*

In his devotion to Christianity, Cambridge resembles other characters from Phillips's fiction—for example,

the shepherd in "Heartland," and Bertram in *A State of Independence*—whose identities are split between two irreconcilable worlds. He "is enslaved twice—first in England . . . and secondly upon his return as a 'free man of color' to Africa," Forbes commented. The author's deft handling of his characters elicited praise from reviewers, including Forbes, who remarked that "One of the marvels of . . . *Cambridge* is how artfully [Phillips] manages to convey in a relatively few pages the frailties of many of the people caught in slavery's web." Major, writing in the *Washington Post Book World,* was particularly impressed with the character of Emily, declaring that "her nineteenth-century white racist mentality becomes a black author's allegorical and ironic means of making one of the subtlest, but most insistent, statements ever about the troubled and urgent relationships between a particular past and the present, Africa and Europe, justice and injustice."

"*Crossing the River* consists of four separate stories bound together by a central theme—slavery and its legacy," commented Lucasta Miller in a review of the novel for the *New Statesman & Society*. In "The Pagan Coast," Phillips offers the story of a freed slave, Nash, and his liberal, well-meaning former owner, Edward. Nash travels to Africa as a missionary, but when his correspondence home to Edward abruptly ceases, Edward himself travels to Africa in search of Nash. Once in Liberia, Edward discovers that Nash has died. "West" features Martha Randolph, an elderly black woman longing to reach California in the late nineteenth century, as well as other black pioneers who ventured west during this period. "Crossing the River" features journal entries by a slave-ship owner in the mid-1700s. The final piece, "Somewhere in England," is set in Yorkshire during World War II and concerns a white English woman's affair with a black soldier. The four narrative pieces are framed by the words of an anonymous African father who despairs at having sold his children into slavery after his crops failed. "Gradually, as the stories in the main text unfold, we realize that this father has taken on the mythic proportions of the continent of Africa, that his abandonment represents the irreversible history of entire peoples," noted Janet Burroway in the *New York Times Book Review.*

Critics responded enthusiastically to *Crossing the River,* and the book was awarded several prizes. Commenting on the author's use of myriad historical sources in fashioning the novel, *Times Literary Supplement* reviewer Oliver Reynolds averred, "One of Phillips's gifts is his ability to transform his sources into the felt life of fiction." In her review of the work, Miller also praised Phillips's use of historical elements: "His deep awareness of the historical process is combined with an exceptionally intelligent prose style—clear, unencumbered, and compassionate." Nicholas Lezard, writing in the *London Review of Books,* commended the author's ability to evoke the language and tone of previous eras and places. Lezard contended, "Phillips's talent has developed along the lines of accomplished ventriloquism." Burroway concluded in her review of the work that it "presents a brilliantly coherent vision of two and half centuries of the African diaspora." The novel was a finalist for Britain's prestigious Booker Prize for literature.

The dichotomies Major mentioned in reviewing *Cambridge*—"Africa and Europe, justice and injustice"— are discussed by Phillips as present-day concerns in *The European Tribe.* As Ashok Bery explained in a review of the work for the *Times Literary Supplement,* Phillips "travelled around Europe for nearly a year in an attempt to understand the forces that had helped to shape him; [*The European Tribe*] comes out of that period." Phillips attempts to reconcile "his divided Afro-British self by examining the Europeans as a Pan-Africanist anthropologist might, treating the French, British, Soviets, and Spanish as a single white tribe determined to keep people of color . . . down," Charles R. Johnson remarked in the *Los Angeles Times Book Review.* From visits to countries around the world, Phillips records incidents of racism and intolerance, including the actions of France's National Front party to put a halt on African immigration. In Oslo he was detained by suspicious customs officials; in Detroit he was harassed by police. *The European Tribe,* Johnson concluded, "comprised partly of personal odyssey, partly of political indictment, is too important a book to be ignored."

Phillips examines the slave trade again in *The Atlantic Sound,* a narrative tracing the busy slave trading route from Liverpool, England, to Accra, Ghana, to Charleston, South Carolina. In three stories featuring historical characters, Phillips contrasts his own observations of the three cities with a character whose life was bound up in the slave trade. He writes of John Ocansey, a nineteenth-century trader based in Liverpool, Philip Quaque, an African priest of the eighteenth century who lived in Ghana, and J. Waites Waring, a Charleston judge of the 1940s. "The book's central theme," Edward G. McCormack remarked in *Library Journal,* "is the exploitation of blacks by the Western world since 1553." A critic for *Publishers Weekly* praised Phillips for his "keen intelligence, careful research and well-expressed truths," while Victoria Bond and Kelly Ellis, wrote in the *Black Issues Book Review* that the author possesses "penetrating, proactive insight and a historian's careful and acute eye."

Phillips's seventh novel, the widely acclaimed *A Distant Shore,* won the Commonwealth Writers Prize for Best Book of 2004, was a finalist for the National Book Critics Circle Award for Fiction, and was nominated for the PEN/Faulkner Award for Fiction. Like other novels by the author, *A Distant Shore* brings to life the struggles of two displaced people of conflicting races and cultures. Unlike Phillips's other works, however, this book takes place in the present. One main character is Dorothy, a white teacher in her fifties who, amidst scandal, was forced to retire early and then relocated to the town where her family has roots. The other main character is Gabrial, a black African who fled the violence of his country and the pain of his lost life there, starting a new one in the same British town as Dorothy. The story tells, sometimes in reverse chronology, of an anxious relationship between the two that is scrutinized by the local, somewhat mistrustful townspeople. Discussing his decision to address the present in his fiction, Phillips told Morrison: "It seems odd that it's taken me until now to set a novel in the present. The rest have been historical. I had to describe my own roots before I could deal with contemporary events."

Many reviews of *A Distant Shore* were positive. As a *Publishers Weekly* review noted, Phillips depicts his protagonists "with a faithful eye that reveals their inner beauty as clearly as their defects. A true master of form, he manipulates narrative time . . . and perspective to create a disjointed sense of place that mirrors the tortured, fractured inner lives of his characters." In the *Black Issues Book Review,* Denolyn Carroll remarked, "The author's clever pacing of the novel, through sudden shifts in thought and time sequences, keeps the story intriguing. His use of descriptive detail and subtle symbolism is achingly on point." And Morrison commented that *A Distant Shore* "neatly dissects what [Dorothy] . . . sees as a decline in civility and standards in modern Britain—a situation her less punctilious neighbors blame on immigration." Writing in *Library Journal,* Kellie Gillespie added that "Phillips has created a poignant and quietly powerful portrait of contemporary alienation," while in *Entertainment Weekly* Lori L. Tharps summarized *A Distant Shore* as a "Greek tragedy set in modern England" that, "while critiquing Britain's current racial climate, offers storytelling both raw and heartbreaking."

Although he has found success as a novelist, Phillips was initially known as a playwright. In plays such as *Strange Fruit* and *A Kind of Home: James Baldwin in Paris,* his characters struggle with the same doubts over identity and rootlessness that define the protagonists in his novels. The two brothers in *Strange Fruit,* living in England, typify this crisis—one "rejects all non-black values," the other is "torn between 'white' and 'black' values," according to Diana Devlin in *Drama.* However, as the novelist/playwright remains aware, a simple rejection of "white values" will not resolve the conflict of identity that concerns his protagonist. In the radio play *A Kind of Home* Phillips tells the story of a man he knew personally and views as another displaced soul, creating a work that follows Baldwin from Harlem to exile in Paris and his development as a major twentieth-century writer.

Phillips noted of his work, as quoted in the *Africa News Service:* "Why do I write? Because it is a way of organizing my feelings about myself and the world around me. . . . Writing provides a means by which I can sit in judgement upon myself and reach conclusions (however temporary) that enable me to shuffle towards the next day and another crisis. And then, of course, there is the technical challenge of writing. To say what I have to say, and to hope to say it in the most incisive manner. To strive towards this goal, and fail honestly, yet continue to strive. To aspire to purify the language; to desire to sharpen the blade of narrative clarity, and then strike quick unseen blows. For me, writing is all of this."

Capturing the essence of Phillips's contribution to contemporary literature, Ledent remarked that the writer's "compassionate engagement with lonely, marginalized characters helps us to transgress such artificial boundaries as race, gender, and nation, and calls into question the myths of homogeneity that all too often underlie conquistadorial impulses, both personal and collective. This is why Phillips's work affords an uncompromising, yet eminently humane,

reflection on the composite societies in which we live." And Morrison summarized, "Not only is [Phillips] one of the most accomplished black novelists writing in English, but he is fast becoming known as one of the most productive all-around men of letters anywhere."

BIOGRAPHICAL AND CRITICAL SOURCES:

BOOKS

Black Writers, 2nd edition, Thomson Gale (Detroit, MI), 1996.

Contemporary Dramatists, 6th edition, St. James Press (Detroit, MI), 1999.

Contemporary Novelists, 7th edition, St. James Press (Detroit, MI), 2001.

Dictionary of Literary Biography, Volume 157: *Twentieth-Century Caribbean and Black African Writers, Third Series,* Thomson Gale (Detroit, MI), 1995.

Phillips, Caryl, *The European Tribe* (nonfiction), Farrar, Straus (New York, NY), 1987.

PERIODICALS

Africa News Service, January 22, 2004, "Caryl Phillips 'Crossing Borders' at British Council."

Best Sellers, October, 1986, p. 252.

Black Issues Book Review, November, 2000, Victoria Bond and Kelly Ellis, review of *The Atlantic Sound,* p. 49; March-April, 2004, Donolyn Carroll, review of *A Distant Shore,* p. 51.

Booklist, February 15, 1998, Brad Hooper, reviews of *Crossing the River* and *Cambridge,* p. 979; December 15, 1998, Vanessa Bush, review of *Extravagant Strangers: A Literature of Belonging,* p. 721; September 1, 2003, Donna Seaman, review of *A Distant Shore,* p. 7.

Drama, summer, 1982, p. 52.

Economist, June 17, 2000, "Ethnic Identity: A Novel Eye," p. 12.

Entertainment Weekly, October 24, 2003, Lori L. Tharps, review of *A Distant Shore,* p. 112.

Essence, December, 1987, p. 26; November, 1989, p. 32.

Kirkus Reviews, August 15, 2003, review of *A Distant Shore,* p. 1041.

Library Journal, December, 1998, Mary Paumier Jones, review of *Extravagant Strangers,* p. 105; October 1, 2000, Edward G. McCormack, review of *The Atlantic Sound,* p. 122; October 15, 2003, Kellie Gillespie, review of *A Distant Shore,* p. 99.

London Review of Books, April 3, 1986, p. 5; September 23, 1993, p. 21.

Los Angeles Times Book Review, July 19, 1987, pp. 3, 11; October 1, 1989, pp. 2, 11.

M2 Best Books, May 18, 2004, "2004 Commonwealth Writers Prize Winners Announced."

New Republic, June 13, 1994, p. 40; October 24, 1994, p. 34.

New Statesman & Society, May 23, 1993, p. 34; March 17, 2003, Benjamin Markovits, review of *A Distant Shore,* p. 54.

Newsweek International, May 10, 1999, Rana Dogar, "A Citizen of the World," p. 63.

New Yorker, August 10, 1992, p. 76.

New York Review of Books, April 26, 2001, Pankaj Mishra, review of *The Atlantic Sound,* p. 49.

New York Times Book Review, August 9, 1987, p. 7; September 24, 1989, p. 27; April 29, 1990, p. 38; February 16, 1992, p. 1; January 30, 1994, p. 10; October 29, 2000, Geoffrey Moorhouse, "African Connection," p. 12.

Publishers Weekly, May 22, 1987, p. 62; June 23, 1989, p. 50; January 19, 1990, p. 103; December 13, 1991, p. 44; November 22, 1993, p. 49; November 16, 1998, review of *Extravagant Strangers,* p. 55; September 18, 2000, review of *The Atlantic Sound,* p. 95; September 29, 2003, review of *A Distant Shore,* p. 44.

Time International, May 19, 2003, Donald Morrison, "A Writer of Wrongs: British Novelist Caryl Phillips Takes on History's Worst Injustices, and Still Has Time for Golf," p. 62.

Times Literary Supplement, March 8, 1985, p. 266; April 10, 1987, p. 396; June 2, 1989, p. 619; May 14, 1993, p. 22.

Tribune Books (Chicago, IL), March 1, 1992, section 14, p. 6.

Washington Post Book World, March 4, 1990, p. 8; February 9, 1992, pp. 4, 10.

ONLINE

Caryl Phillips Web site, http://www.carylphillips.com (August 6, 2004).

Contemporary Writers in the UK Web site, http://www.contemporarywriters.com/authors/ (August 6, 2004).

Guardian Online, http://books.guardian.co.uk/ (May 15, 2004), "The Silenced Minority"; (July 17, 2004) "Kingdom of the Blind."

University of Liège English Department Web site, http://www.ulg.ac.be/facphl/ (August 6, 2004) "Caryl Phillips."

Yale Daily News Online, http://www.yaledailynews.com/ (February 10, 2004), Dan Adler, "Novelist Emphasizes Human Aspect of Books."*

*   *   *

PICCIRILLI, Thomas Edward 1965-
(Tom Piccirilli)

PERSONAL: Born May 27, 1965, in New York, NY; married Michelle Scalise, June 12, 2004. *Education:* Suffolk Community College, A.A., 1985; Hofstra University, B.A., 1987.

ADDRESSES: Home—1529 Baldwin Blvd., Bay Shore, NY 11706. *E-mail*—picself1@aol.com.

CAREER: Reader for various publishers, including Baen Books; coeditor for *Pirate Writings* magazine; fiction editor for *Epitaph* and *Space & Time* magazines. Has also worked part-time for a moving company.

AWARDS, HONORS: Bram Stoker Award nominations, Horror Writers Association, 1990, for best first novel *Dark Father,* 1999, for best short story collection *Deep into That Darkness Peering,* 1999, for novel *Hexes,* 2000, for novel *The Deceased,* 2003, for best poetry collection *This Cape Is Red because I've Been Bleeding,* 2003, for best short fiction for "The Misfit Child Grows Fat on Despair," 2004, for best novel *A Choir of Ill Children,* and 2004, for best long fiction "Fuckin' Lie Down Already"; *Deathrealm* award for best collection, 1995; Bram Stoker Awards, Horror Writers Association, 2000, for poetry collection *A Student of Hell,* 2002, for novel *The Night Class;* World Fantasy Award nomination, 2000, for *Deep into That Darkness Peering. A Choir of Ill Children* was named one of the year's best fantasy novels by *Locus* magazine, 2003.

WRITINGS:

FICTION

Dark Father (horror novel), Pocket Books (New York, NY), 1990.

Pentacle (short stories), introduction by Jack Cady, Pirate Writings (Bridgewaters, NY), 1995.

Shards (mystery novel), Write Way (Aurora, CO), 1996.

The Hanging Man & Other Strange Suspensions (short stories), Wilder (Greenfield, MA), 1996.

(With Edward Lee and Gerard Houarner) *Inside the Works* (short stories), Necro Publications (Orlando, FL), 1997.

The Dog Syndrome & Other Sick Puppies (short stories), Dark Dixie (Marietta, GA), 1997.

The Dead Past ("Felicity Grove" mystery series), Write Way (Aurora, CO), 1997.

Sorrow's Crown ("Felicity Grove" mystery series), Write Way (Aurora, CO), 1998.

Hexes (horror novel), Leisure Books (New York, NY), 1999.

Deep into That Darkness Peering (short stories), illustrated by Chad Savage, introduction by Poppy Z. Brite, afterword by Richard Laymon, Terminal Fright Press, 1999.

Epitaphs, Mystery Guild (New York, NY), 1999.

The Deceased, Leisure Books (New York, NY), 2000.

The Night Class (mystery novel), Shadowlands Press (Centreville, VA), 2001.

A Lower Deep (novel), Leisure Books (New York, NY), 2001.

Grave Men (novel), Leisure Books (New York, NY), 2002.

(With Gerard Houarner) *Bastards of Alchemy* (short story chapbook), Necro Publications (Orlando, FL), 2002.

(With Ed Gorman and Keith Minnion) *Cast in Dark Waters* (novella), Cemetery Dance (Baltimore, MD), 2002.

A Choir of Ill Children, Nightshade (New York, NY), 2003.

(With Bentley Little, Douglas Clegg, and Christopher Golden) *Four Dark Nights,* Leisure Books (New York, NY), 2003.

Mean Sheep (horror stories), Delirium Books (North Webster, IN), 2003.

Fuckin' Lie Down Already (limited edition novella), Endeavor Press (Annapolis, MD), 2003.

Coffin Blues, Leisure Books (New York, NY), 2004.

OTHER

A Student of Hell (poetry), Skull Job Productions, 2000.

Welcome to Hell: A Working Guide for the Beginning Writer, Fairwood Press (Auburn, WA), 2000.

This Cape Is Red because I've Been Bleeding (poetry), illustrated by Caniglia, Catalyst Press (New York, NY), 2002.

(Editor) *The Devil's Wine,* Cemetery Dance (Baltimore, MD), 2004.

Contributor of short stories to books, including *Hot Blood: Stranger by Night,* edited by Jeff Gelb and Michael Garrett, Pocket Books, 1995; *Hot Blood: Fear the Fever,* edited by Jeff Gelb and Michael Garrett, Pocket Books, 1996; *White House Horrors,* edited by Martin H. Greenberg, DAW, 1996; *Hot Blood: Crimes of Passion,* edited by Jeff Gelb and Michael Garrett, Pocket Books, 1997; *The Conspiracy Files,* edited by Martin H. Greenberg and Scott Urban, DAW, 1998; *Best of the American West II,* edited by Ed Gorman and Martin H. Greenberg, Berkley, 1999; *Future Crimes,* edited by Martin H. Greenberg and John Helfers, DAW, 1999; *Star Colonies,* edited by Ed Gorman, Martin H. Greenberg, and John Helfers, DAW, 2000; *October Dreams,* edited by Richard Chizmar and Robert Morrish, Cemetery Dance, 2000; *Bad News,* edited by Richard Laymon, Cemetery Dance, 2000; *Songs of Cthulhu,* edited by Stephen Mark Rainey, Chaosium, 2001; *Desperadoes,* edited by Ed Gorman and Martin H. Greenberg, Berkley, 2001; *Museum of Horrors,* edited by Dennis Etchison, Leisure Books, 2001; *New Mythos Legends,* edited by Bruce R. Gehweiler, Marietta Publishing, 2002; *Dead Cats Bouncing,* edited by Gerard Houarner, Necro Publications, 2002; *The 2nd Coming: The Best of Pirate Writings,* edited by Edward J. McFadden, Padwolf, 2003; and *Deconstructing Tolkien: A Fundamental Anaylsis of the Lord of the Rings,* edited by Edward J. McFadden, Padwolf, 2004. Also contributor of short stories to periodicals, including *Cemetery Dance, Deathrealm, Talebones, Pirate Writings, Terminal Fright, Lore, TransVersions, Silver Web, Not One of Us,* and *Hardboiled.* Author of introduction, *Deadliest of the Species,* by Michael Oliveri, illustrated by Kenneth Waters, Vox13 Publishing, 2001. Book reviewer for *Mystery News, Horror, New York Review of Science Fiction* and the Barnes & Noble Web site.

WORK IN PROGRESS: A novel, *November Mourns,* for Bantam.

SIDELIGHTS: Thomas Edward Piccirilli writes novels in the noir mystery and horror genres under the name Tom Piccirilli. Mostly publishing through small presses, he has not yet achieved best-seller status, though he has received wide critical acclaim and several awards, including Bram Stoker Awards for his poetry collection *A Student of Hell* and the novel *The*

Night Class. "I'm a big fan of bad horror movies, Beat poetry, and Fifties noir, especially the Gold Medal books," he related on the Nightshade Books Web site. Piccirilli has turned his love of things creepy and bizarre into a successful writing career.

In his debut novel, a horror tale titled *Dark Father,* Piccirilli recounts the story of two brothers, Samuel and Daniel, bastard children who do not know the identity of their father. The brothers grow closer following the demise of their mother, a fearful woman who had been keeping a terrible secret. The brothers' strange psychic powers come to a head after a bitter quarrel over a young woman. When their father returns, the brothers learn the facts about their birth.

Piccirilli has also been widely praised for his short horror stories. A series character in the genre emerged with the author's first collection, *Pentacle.* While an essayist for the *St. James Guide to Horror, Ghost and Gothic Writers* felt that the author was too heavy-handed in addressing themes of "religion, morality, and the afterlife" in *Dark Father,* the critic felt that Piccirilli had found a better format for addressing his ideas in the short stories of *Pentacle.* The main character in all the tales collected here is an unnamed necromancer whose companion is a familiar called Self. Together, this unusual team faces witches, monsters, and death. In the last story of the collection, "Eyebiting and Other Displays of Affection," the challenges the necromancer faces almost kill him, and "he knows that Self is the only one who can save him," related the *St. James Guide* contributor. "Suddenly, however, he realizes that their relationship has changed: he can no longer define who is the master and who is the servant, just as it's impossible to pinpoint which of them is good and which is evil." The critic admired Piccirilli's blend of suspense and horror in stories that are described as "both lyrical and lean." The necromancer and Self return in the novel *A Lower Deep,* in which he faces the greatest challenge of all: temptation. Confronting a coven of witches who plan to interfere with the second coming of Christ, the necromancer is tempted to help them when he is promised the return of the woman he loves from the dead if he cooperates. "This tale is not for the fainthearted," warned Brianna Yamashita and Jeff Zaleski in *Publishers Weekly;* "there's enough bloodletting and hellish savagery here to give even the most hardened horror fans the creeps."

More recently, Piccirilli received plaudits for his twisted tale *A Choir of Ill Children,* a bizarre story of horror that features conjoined triplets who share a frontal lobe and speak with one voice as if they were an oracle of some kind. Dodi Coots, the daughter of a conjurer, takes care of the triplets' physical needs, while their older brother, Thomas, manages the expensive antebellum estate in the swampy Pott County where they live. To this strange mix the author adds Thomas's friend Drabbs Bibbler, an African American who speaks in tongues, has epileptic fits, and likes to walk around in the nude, and film student Sarah, who arrives to make a movie about the triplets and ends up falling in love with one of them. Plenty of supernatural goings on occur among the strange cast of characters, including the mystery of the fate of Thomas's supposedly dead father. Peter Cannon and Jeff Zaleski, writing in *Publishers Weekly,* praised *A Choir of Ill Children* for the author's ability to create "a world where what happens on the outside is a pale reflection of what goes on inside." And a *Kirkus Reviews* contributor called the novel "lyrical, ghastly, first-class horror."

Besides his many horror stories, the author has written a number of noir mysteries that have also garnered praise. *Shards,* his first, is the story of a New York crime novelist named Nathaniel, who is in turmoil over the suicide of a disturbed young woman named Susan. When Nathaniel learns that there may be some link between her suicide and his brother, who is serving prison time for murder, he feels he must probe Susan's death. Rex E. Klett, writing in *Library Journal,* recommended *Shards* based on its convoluted plot, emotional intensity, and "memorably detailed" writing. Piccarelli's award-winning *The Night Class* blends mystery with horror. Here, student Call Prentiss, after returning to college from Christmas break, learns that a young woman has been murdered in his room. Deciding to investigate the death on his own, he discovers that the victim faked her transcripts. As he digs deeper, grotesque secrets at the university are revealed; and as he gets closer and closer to the truth he begins to suffer the wounds of the stigmata.

BIOGRAPHICAL AND CRITICAL SOURCES:

BOOKS

Reginald, Robert, *Science Fiction and Fantasy Literature, 1975-1991,* Thomson Gale (Detroit, MI), 1992.
St. James Guide to Horror, Ghost and Gothic Writers, St. James Press (Detroit, MI), 1998.

PERIODICALS

Fantasy & Science Fiction, May, 2003, Charles De Lint, review of *This Cape Is Red because I've Been Bleeding.*

Kirkus Reviews, April 15, 2003, review of *A Choir of Ill Children.*

Library Journal, August, 1996, Rex E. Klett, review of *Shards,* p. 117.

Publishers Weekly, August 30,1999, review of *Deep into That Darkness Peering;* December 18, 2000, review of *The Night Class;* September 17, 2001, Brianna Yamashita and Jeff Zaleski, review of *A Lower Deep;* September 30, 2002, Peter Cannon and Jeff Zaleski, review of *Four Dark Nights;* June 30, 2003, Peter Cannon and Jeff Zaleski, review of *A Choir of Children.*

Science Fiction Chronicle, October-November, 2000, Don D'Ammassa, review of *Deceased,* p. 61.

ONLINE

Nightshade Books, http://www.nightshadebooks.com/ (May 4, 2004).*

*   *   *

PICCIRILLI, Tom
     See PICCIRILLI, Thomas Edward

*   *   *

POHL, Frederik 1919-

(Elton V. Andrews, Paul Fleur, S. D. Gottesman, Lee Gregor, Warren F. Howard, Cyril Judd, a joint pseudonym, Paul Dennis Lavond, Scott Mariner, Ernst Mason, Edson McCann, a joint pseudonym, James McCreigh, Jordan Park, a joint pseudonym, Charles Satterfield, Donald Stacy, Dirk Wilson)

PERSONAL: Born November 26, 1919, in New York, NY; son of Fred George (a salesman) and Anna Jane (Mason) Pohl; married Doris Baumgardt, 1940 (divorced, 1944); married Dorothy LesTina, August, 1945 (divorced, 1947); married Judith Merril, 1948 (divorced, 1952); married Carol M. Ulf Stanton,

Frederik Pohl

September 15, 1952 (divorced, 1983); married Elizabeth Anne Hull (a professor of English), July, 1984; children: Ann (Mrs. Walter Weary), Karen (Mrs. Robert Dixon), Frederik III (deceased), Frederik IV, Kathy. *Education:* Attended public schools in Brooklyn, NY, "dropped out in senior year." *Politics:* Democrat. *Religion:* Unitarian.

ADDRESSES: Home and office—855 S. Harvard Dr., Palatine, IL 60067.

CAREER: Writer. Popular Publications, New York, NY, editor, 1939-43; Popular Science Publishing Co., New York, NY, editor in book department and assistant circulation manager, 1946-49; literary agent, 1946-53; freelance writer 1953-60; *Galaxy* magazine, New York, NY, editor, 1961-69; Ace Books, New York, NY, executive editor, 1971-72; Bantam Books, New York, NY, science fiction editor, 1973-79. Staff lecturer, American Management Association, 1966-69; cultural exchange lecturer in science fiction for U.S. Department of State in Yugoslavia, Romania, and the Soviet Union, 1974; also lecturer at more than two hundred colleges in the United States, Canada, and abroad;

represented United States at international literary conferences in England, Italy, Brazil, Canada, and Japan. Has appeared on more than four hundred radio and television programs in nine countries. County committeeman, Democratic Party, Monmouth City, NJ, 1956-69; trustee, The Harbour School, Red Bank, NJ, 1972-75, and First Unitarian Church of Monmouth City, 1973-75. *Military service:* U.S. Army Air Forces, 1943-45; received seven battle stars.

MEMBER: Science Fiction Writers of America (president, 1974-76), Authors Guild (Midwest area representative; member of council, 1975—), British Interplanetary Society (fellow), American Astronautical Society, World Science Fiction (president, 1980-82), American Association for the Advancement of Science (fellow), World Future Society, American Civil Liberties Union (trustee, Monmouth County, NJ, 1968-71), New York Academy of Sciences.

AWARDS, HONORS: Edward E. Smith Award, 1966; Hugo Award, World Science Fiction Convention, 1966, 1967, and 1968, for best editor, 1974, for short story, "The Meeting," 1978, for best novel, *Gateway,* and 1986, for story "Fermi and Frost"; H. G. Wells Award, 1975; Nebula Award, Science Fiction Writers of America, 1977, for best novel, *Man Plus,* and 1978, for best novel, *Gateway;* John W. Campbell Award, Center for the Study of Science Fiction, 1978, for *Gateway,* and 1986, for *The Years of the City;* National Book Award, 1980, for *JEM;* Popular Culture Association annual award, 1982; guest of honor at science fiction convention in Katowice, Poland, 1987; Grand Master Award, Science Fiction Writers of America, 1993; Milford award, 1995; Gallun award, 1998; Prix Utopia, 2000; Hubbard Lifetime Achievement, 2000.

WRITINGS:

(Under pseudonym James McCreigh) *Danger Moon,* American Science Fiction (Sydney, Australia), 1953.

(With Lester del Rey, under joint pseudonym Edson McCann) *Preferred Risk,* Simon & Schuster (New York, NY), 1955.

Alternating Currents (short stories), Ballantine (New York, NY), 1956.

(Under pseudonym Donald Stacy) *The God of Channel 1,* Ballantine (New York, NY), 1956.

(With Walter Lasly) *Turn the Tigers Loose,* Ballantine (New York, NY), 1956.

Edge of the City (novel; based on screenplay by Robert Alan Aurthur), Ballantine (New York, NY), 1957.

The Case against Tomorrow, Ballantine (New York, NY), 1957.

Slave Ship, Ballantine (New York, NY), 1957.

Tomorrow Times Seven: Science Fiction Stories, Ballantine (New York, NY), 1959.

The Man Who Ate the World, Ballantine (New York, NY), 1960.

Drunkard's Walk (also see below), Ballantine (New York, NY), 1960.

(Under pseudonym Ernst Mason) *Tiberius* (biography), Ballantine (New York, NY), 1960.

Turn Left at Thursday: Three Novelettes and Three Stories, Ballantine (New York, NY), 1961.

The Expert Dreamers, Doubleday (New York, NY), 1962.

The Abominable Earthman, Ballantine (New York, NY), 1963.

The Case against Tomorrow: Science Fiction Short Stories, Ballantine (New York, NY), 1965.

A Plague of Pythons, Ballantine (New York, NY), 1965.

The Frederik Pohl Omnibus, Gollancz (London, England), 1966, portions published as *Survival Kit,* Panther (London, England), 1979.

Drunkard's Walk, Penguin (Harmondsworth, England), 1966.

Digits and Dastards, Ballantine (New York, NY), 1968.

The Age of the Pussyfoot (also see below), Ballantine (New York, NY), 1969.

Day Million (short stories), Ballantine (New York, NY), 1970.

Practical Politics, 1972 (nonfiction), Ballantine (New York, NY), 1971.

The Gold at the Starbow's End, Ballantine (New York, NY), 1972.

(With Carol Pohl) *Jupiter,* Ballantine (New York, NY), 1973.

The Best of Frederik Pohl, introduction by Lester del Rey, Doubleday (New York, NY), 1975.

The Early Pohl, Doubleday (New York, NY), 1976.

In the Problem Pit, Bantam (New York, NY), 1976.

Man Plus, Random House (New York, NY), 1976.

Gateway, St. Martin's Press (New York, NY), 1977.

The Way the Future Was: A Memoir, Ballantine (New York, NY), 1978.

JEM: The Making of a Utopia, St. Martin's Press (New York, NY), 1979.

Beyond the Blue Event Horizon, Ballantine (New York, NY), 1980.

Syzygy, Bantam (New York, NY), 1981.

The Cool War, Ballantine (New York, NY), 1981.

Planets Three, Berkley (New York, NY), 1982.

Bilpohl, Two Novels: Drunkard's Walk and The Age of the Pussyfoot, Ballantine (New York, NY), 1982.

Starburst, Ballantine (New York, NY), 1982.

Starbow, Ballantine (New York, NY), 1982.

(Author of introduction) *New Visions: A Collection of Modern Science Fiction Art,* Doubleday (New York, NY), 1982.

Midas World, St. Martin's Press (New York, NY), 1983.

Heechee Rendezvous, Ballantine (New York, NY), 1984.

The Years of the City, Simon & Schuster (New York, NY), 1984.

The Merchant's War, St. Martin's Press (New York, NY), 1984.

Pohlstars, Ballantine (New York, NY), 1984.

Black Star Rising, Ballantine (New York, NY), 1985.

The Coming of the Quantum Cats, Bantam (New York, NY), 1986.

Terror, Berkley (New York, NY), 1986.

Chernobyl, Bantam (New York, NY), l987.

The Annals of the Heechee, Ballantine (New York, NY), 1987.

Narabedla Ltd., Del Rey (New York, NY), 1988.

The Day the Martians Came, St. Martin's Press (New York, NY), 1988.

Homegoing, Del Rey (New York, NY), 1989.

The Gateway Trip: Tales and Vignettes of the Heechee, illustrated by Frank Kelly Freas, Easton Press (Norwalk, CT), 1990.

The World at the End of Time, Ballantine (New York, NY), 1990.

Outnumbering the Dead, illustrated by Steve Crisp, Century, 1990.

(With Isaac Asimov) *Our Angry Earth,* Tor (New York, NY), 1991.

Stopping at Slowyear, illustrated by Rob Alexander, Axolotl Press (Seattle, WA), 1991.

Mining the Oort, Ballantine (New York, NY), 1992.

(With Thomas T. Thomas) *Mars Plus,* Baen (New York, NY), 1994.

The Voices of Heaven, Tor (New York, NY), 1994.

The Other End of Time, Tor (New York, NY), 1996.

The Siege of Eternity, Tor (New York, NY), 1997.

O Pioneer!, Tor (New York, NY), 1998.

The Far Shore of Time, Tor (New York, NY), 1999.

Chasing Science: Science As a Spectator Sport (nonfiction), Tor (New York, NY), 2000.

The Boy Who Would Live Forever: A Novel of Gateway, Tor (New York, NY), 2004.

Also coauthor, with Marion Zimmer Bradley, of *Elbow Room.* Contributor, sometimes under pseudonyms, to *Galaxy, Worlds of Fantasy, Science Fiction Quarterly, Rogue, Impulse, Astonishing, Imagination, If, Beyond, Playboy, Infinity,* and other magazines.

WITH CYRIL M. KORNBLUTH

(Under joint pseudonym Cyril Judd) *Gunner Cade,* Simon & Schuster, 1952.

(Under joint pseudonym Cyril Judd) *Outpost Mars,* Abelard Press (New York, NY), 1952.

The Space Merchants (also see below), Ballantine (New York, NY), 1953, 2nd edition, 1981.

Search the Sky, Ballantine (New York, NY), 1954.

Gladiator-at-Law, Ballantine (New York, NY), 1955.

A Town Is Drowning, Ballantine (New York, NY), 1955.

Presidential Year, Ballantine (New York, NY), 1956.

(Under joint pseudonym Jordan Park) *Sorority House,* Lion Press (New York, NY), 1956.

(Under joint pseudonym Jordan Park) *The Man of Cold Raaes,* Pyramid Publications (New York, NY), 1958.

Wolfbane, Ballantine (New York, NY), 1959.

The Wonder Effect (short stories), Ballantine (New York, NY), 1962, revised edition published as *Critical Mass,* Bantam (New York, NY), 1977.

Before the Universe and Other Stories: The Best of the Early Work of Science Fiction's Most Famous Team of Collaborators, Bantam (New York, NY), 1980.

Venus, Inc., (includes *The Space Merchants* and *The Merchants' War*), Doubleday (New York, NY), 1985.

Our Best: The Best of Frederik Pohl and C. M. Kornbluth, Baen (New York, NY), 1987.

WITH JACK WILLIAMSON

Undersea Quest (also see below), Gnome Press (New York, NY), 1954.

Undersea Fleet (also see below), Gnome Press (New York, NY), 1956.

Undersea City (also see below), Gnome Press (New York, NY), 1958.

The Reefs of Space (also see below), Ballantine (New York, NY), 1963.

Starchild (also see below), Ballantine (New York, NY), 1965.

Rogue Star (also see below), Ballantine (New York, NY), 1969.

Farthest Star: The Saga of Cuckoo, Ballantine (New York, NY), 1975.

The Starchild Trilogy: The Reefs of Space, Starchild, and Rogue Star, Doubleday, 1977.

Wall around a Star, Ballantine (New York, NY), 1983.

Land's End, St. Martin's Press (New York, NY), 1988.

The Singers of Time, Doubleday (New York, NY), 1991.

The Undersea Trilogy (contains *Undersea Quest, Undersea Fleet,* and *Undersea City*), Baen (New York, NY), 1992.

EDITOR

Beyond the End of Time, Permabooks (Garden City, NY), 1952.

Star Science Fiction Stories, six volumes, Ballantine (New York, NY), 1953–1959.

Shadow of Tomorrow, Permabooks (Garden City, NY), 1953.

Star Short Novels, Ballantine (New York, NY), 1954.

(And author of introduction) *Assignment in Tomorrow: An Anthology,* Hanover House (Garden City, NY), 1954.

Star of Stars, Doubleday (New York, NY), 1960, published as *Star Fourteen,* Whiting & Wheaton (London, England), 1966.

The Expert Dreamer, Doubleday (New York, NY), 1962.

Time Waits for Winthrop and Four Other Short Novels from "Galaxy," Doubleday (New York, NY), 1962.

The Best Science Fiction from "Worlds of If" Magazine, Galaxy Publishing, 1964.

The Seventh Galaxy Reader, Doubleday (New York, NY), 1964.

The Eighth Galaxy Reader, Doubleday (New York, NY), 1965, published as *Final Encounter,* Curtis Books (New York, NY), 1965.

The If Reader of Science Fiction, Doubleday (New York, NY), 1966.

The Ninth Galaxy Reader, Doubleday (New York, NY), 1966.

The Tenth Galaxy Reader, Doubleday (New York, NY), 1967, published as *Door to Anywhere,* Curtis Books (New York, NY), 1967.

The Second If Reader of Science Fiction, Doubleday (New York, NY), 1968.

The Eleventh Galaxy Reader, Doubleday (New York, NY), 1969.

Nightmare Age, Ballantine (New York, NY), 1970.

Best Science Fiction for 1972, Ace Books (New York, NY), 1973.

(With Carol Pohl) *Jupiter,* Ballantine (New York, NY), 1973.

(With wife, Carol Pohl) *Science Fiction: The Great Years,* Ace Books (New York, NY), Volume 1, 1973, Volume 2, 1976.

The Science Fiction Roll of Honor: An Anthology of Fiction and Nonfiction by Guests of Honor at World Science Fiction Conventions, Random House (New York, NY), 1975.

(And author of introduction) *The Best of C. M. Kornbluth,* Doubleday (New York, NY), 1976.

(With Carol Pohl) *Science Fiction Discoveries,* Bantam (New York, NY), 1976.

The Best of C. M. Kornbluth, Doubleday (New York, NY), 1976.

(With Martin H. Greenberg and Joseph D. Olander) *Science Fiction of the Forties,* Avon (New York, NY), 1978.

(With Martin H. Greenberg and Joseph D. Olander) *Galaxy: Thirty Years of Innovative Science Fiction,* Playboy Press (Chicago, IL), 1980.

Nebula Winners Fourteen, Harper (New York, NY), 1980.

(With Martin H. Greenberg and Joseph D. Olander) *The Great Science Fiction Series: Stories from the Best of the Series from 1944 to 1980,* Harper (New York, NY), 1980.

(With son, Frederik Pohl IV) *Science Fiction: Studies in Film,* Ace Books (New York, NY), 1981.

Yesterday's Tomorrows: Favorite Stories from Forty Years As a Science Fiction Editor, Berkley (New York, NY), 1982.

(With wife, Elizabeth Anne Hill) *Tales from the Planet Earth,* St. Martin's Press (New York, NY), 1986.

(With others) *Worlds of If: A Retrospective Anthology,* Bluejay Books, 1986.

Asimov, Isaac, *Our Angry Earth,* Tor (New York, NY), 1991.

The SFWA Grand Masters, Volume 1, Tor (New York, NY), 1999.

The SFWA Grand Masters, Volume 2, Tor (New York, NY), 2000.

The SFWA Grand Masters, Volume 3, Tor (New York, NY), 2001.

SIDELIGHTS: "Like all the other great men in SF," wrote Algis Budrys in the *Magazine of Fantasy and Science Fiction,* "Frederik Pohl is idiosyncratic, essentially self-made, and brilliant. Unlike many of the others, he has an extremely broad range of interests and education." In addition to his obvious affinity for science and writing, Pohl has also shown a lively interest in music and politics. During the course of his long career, which spans more than sixty years, he has made his mark as a writer, editor, literary agent, and enthusiastic promoter of science fiction. He is, Robert Scholes and Eric S. Rabkin asserted in *Science Fiction: History, Science, Vision,* "one of the few men to make a genuine impact on the science fiction field."

Pohl attended school sporadically as a child, and dropped out completely "as soon as it was legal," as he once commented. The library fed his hunger for knowledge, and he read voraciously. "'Catholic' is the word for my tastes," he explained. "There were days when I would take out a book at random and go home to see what I had found. A lot of what I read was so profoundly trashy that I no longer remember it at all, but in among the volumes of trash were precious insights and inspirations. Somewhere in my mid-teens I discovered the Russians—Tolstoi, Gogol, Pushkin, Dostoevski—and the weirder Americans like Thorne Smith and James Branch Cabell. Before I was old enough to vote I came across the French decadents— Proust and Huysmans in particular, as well as Baudelaire and Anatole France." Visits to museums, movies, and bookstores rounded out his education.

During the 1930s, he became involved with several groups devoted to the new field of science fiction, where he met many writers who would be his fellow pioneers in the field: C. M. Kornbluth, Isaac Asimov, and James Blish, among others. By the 1950s, he had written a number of influential books with Kornbluth, which "pioneered and excelled in a completely new kind of science fiction," wrote Charles Platt in *Dream Makers: The Uncommon People Who Write Science Fiction.* "They invented and played with 'Sociological SF'—alternate futures here on Earth, exaggerating and satirizing real-life social forces and trends." The best

of these collaborations was *The Space Merchants,* a satirical look at a world ruled by advertising; the book was inspired by Pohl's own short stint in an advertising agency. In this world, "exploitation of resources, pollution of environment, and overpopulation are all rampant," Scholes and Rabkin pointed out, "while the advertisers use every device of behavior control including addictive substances in the products. The beauty of [the book] is that it manages to be absurd and at the same time frighteningly close to the way that many people actually think. The lightness of touch and consistency of imagination make it a true classic of science fiction." "This novel is the single work most mentioned when Pohl's fiction is discussed," Stephen H. Goldman of the *Dictionary of Literary Biography* explained. "It is on every critic's list of science fiction classics and has never been out of print since its first appearance. While Pohl and Kornbluth produced other highly readable novels *The Space Merchants* remains their single greatest achievement." The book has been translated into over fifteen languages, including Japanese, Hebrew, Serbo-Croatian, Dutch, and Latvian.

As editor of *Galaxy* and later with Bantam Books, Pohl was a strong supporter of the "new wave" writers in science fiction—writers who borrowed literary techniques from mainstream literature to use in their science fiction, while eliminating what they saw as the genre's clichés. Ironically, Pohl came under fire from some of these writers for being too conservative. "I published the majority of 'new-wave' writers," Pohl told Platt. "It wasn't the stories I objected to, it was the snottiness of the proponents. . . . The thing that the 'new wave' did that I treasure was to shake up old dinosaurs, like Isaac [Asimov], and for that matter me . . . , and show them that you do not really have to construct a story according to the 1930s pulp or Hollywood standards."

Some of the new wave's influence can be seen in Pohl's prize-winning novel *Gateway.* The author has said he considers it his best novel, and many commentators agree with that assessment. *Gateway* is the story of the discovery of an ancient spaceport of the Heechee, a long-dead civilization. Each spaceship found at the port is operable, but so highly advanced that the propulsion system and the destination for which it is programmed are incomprehensible to humans. A few brave adventurers dare to travel in the ships in a kind of lottery system. "Occasionally," wrote

Goldman, "one of the Heechee ships lands at a site that is filled with undiscovered artifacts, and the human riders share in the financial rewards these discoveries can bring." At other times, the adventurers never return, or return dead. The story, Mark Rose of the *New Republic* found, "conveys a vivid sense of the pathos and absurdity of human ignorance in attempting to exploit a barely understood universe." Patrick Parrinder of the *Times Literary Supplement* agreed: "The novel is remarkable for its portrayal of human explorers rushing into space in a mood of abject fear and greed, in machines they cannot understand or control."

The story of the spaceport and its hazardous explorations is interspersed with seriocomic scenes involving a guilt-ridden adventurer—an adventurer who made a fortune during a trip on which he was forced to abandon the woman he loves—and his computer psychoanalyst. "Pohl's touch is always light and sure," Rose commented, "and, indeed parts of the novel are extremely funny." Goldman noted that in *Gateway* "Pohl has finally balanced the demands of an imaginative world and the presentation of a highly complex character. . . . This balance has led to his most successful novel thus far." In *Gateway,* Roz Kaveney of *Books and Bookmen* believed, Pohl "successfully combined wit and humanity in a novel of character. [The result is] a highly competent, darkly witty entertainment." Other critics found the computer psychoanalyst a particularly believable character. "What makes this book so intriguing," Peter Ackroyd wrote in the *Spectator,* "is not its occasional satire and consistent good humor, but the fact that Pohl has managed to convey the insistent presence of the non-human, a presence which may indeed haunt our future."

Pohl's next novel, *JEM: The Making of a Utopia,* also won critical praise, including the National Book Award in 1980. Set in the near future when the Earth has been divided into three camps—People, Fuel, and Food—the novel tells the story of three bands of human colonists on another planet. When there is a war and a resulting social breakdown on Earth, the colony is suddenly independent and "must then find a way to reconcile its divisions, both among the colonists and between the colonists and the three excellently depicted native sapient species, if it is to survive," wrote Tom Easton of the *Magazine of Fantasy and Science Fiction.* Gerald Jonas of the *New York Times*

Book Review compared *JEM* to *The Space Merchants* because "*JEM* is also social satire—but without the humor." "It is essentially a political allegory," Alex de Jonge of the *Spectator* observed, "describing the struggle between the world's three blocs . . . each attempting to colonize a planet."

The colonization of Jem repeats some mistakes made on Earth. "With systematic, undeviating logic," wrote Budrys, "Pohl depicts the consequent rape of Jem. As each of the expeditions struggles to do its best, there are moments of hope, and moments of triumph. But they are all no more than peaks on a downhill slope. The ending of it all is so genuinely sad that one realizes abruptly how rarely SF evokes pure sorrow, and how profound Pohl's vision was in conceiving of this story." Russell Lord of the *Christian Science Monitor* found it is Pohl's "basically poetic imagination that elevates this novel to a high position among the author's works."

Pohl's 1982 novel, *Starburst,* was a sequel to one he had written a decade earlier, *The Gold at Starbow's End. Starburst* concerns four American couples, all perfect physical specimens and geniuses to boot. They are tricked into undertaking a space mission to a nonexistent planet by a scientist who wants to give them limitless time to expand their human knowledge. Their transmissions back to Earth eventually overload the planet's computers, bringing about catastrophe for the planet. A *Publishers Weekly* writer commented, "This novel is Pohl at his best, blending science, speculation and satire to fascinate us from first page to last." And a contributor to *Voice of Youth Advocates* called *Starburst* a "creatively cryptic blending of narrative, scientific, and mythological description. Speculation at its best by the master of the genre!"

In *The Voices of Heaven,* published in 1994, Pohl features Barry di Hoa, who is hijacked from his comfortable perch on the Moon and forcibly placed on a ship bound for the planet Pava. Once here, he discovers a society of humans in the grips of a fundamentalist religion, whose leaders are prone to instigating mass suicide. He also meets the Lepsnative Pavan creatures that take the form of giant caterpillars early in their life form before evolving into butterflies. Pohl uses the narrative to expound on familiar questions of religion, state, and human behavior. A contributor to the *Washington Post Book World* remarked that the author created "as chilling an ending as you'll find in modern science fiction" and averred that *The Voices of Heaven* is "perhaps the most perfectly constructed of all Pohl's books."

During the 1990s, Pohl made another significant contribution to the science fiction genre with a trio of novels known as the Eschaton Sequence: *The Other End of Time, The Siege of Eternity,* and *The Far Shore of Time.* The story concerns a war over Earth, fought between two alien races: the scarecrow-like Others and the Horch, who are reminiscent of dinosaurs. The Others have implanted transmitters into the brains of many people so that they could monitor key thoughts and senses. The Others promise to protect humans from the Horch, but they also plan to turn them into slaves. "In this war against Ultimate Evil, [human beings] are the hobbits, but without the cuteness, and only the sourest of comic relief," commented Russell Letson in *Locus.* He went on to say that the irony that pervades *The Far Shore of Time* made it "the strongest book of the three and a real keeper." *Kirkus Reviews* contributor Paul M. Lamey rated *The Far Shore of Time* "solidly engrossing and professionally rendered," and a *Publishers Weekly* writer found that "Pohl's fertile imagination and subtle characterizations are as evident as ever. The book's densely packed action and impressive world-building make it a gratifying wrap-up to an entertaining series."

Although his work as a science fiction writer has brought him an international reputation, Pohl has also played a large role in science fiction publishing, having served stints as the editor of *Galaxy* magazine, and as editor with the paperback publishing firms of Ballantine, Ace Books, and Bantam. In these positions, he has helped to develop new talent in the genre and publish daring or experimental work by more experienced writers. Among the books Pohl has brought into print are Joanna Russ's *The Female Man,* a controversial feminist novel, and Samuel Delany's *Dhalgren,* a novel that had been seeking a publisher for many years before Pohl took a chance on it. *Dhalgren* went on to sell over one million copies.

For every promising new talent Pohl has nurtured, there have been many instances of frustration, however. In a 1970 interview with Paul Walker for *Speaking of Science Fiction,* Pohl remarked that the economic demands of the sci-fi industry led to a plethora of overwritten manuscripts. Even those submissions he has read that have some good qualities,

he said, "are fat, bloated, stretched out, milked. The reason for this is the pressure of the market; there is little market for short stories and novelettes, an insatiable market for novels. So if you are a writer of moderate talent and standing, what do you do with your short story ideas? Why, you do what everybody else does: you pad them out to 60,000 words, whether they can stand it or not."

Joseph McClellan of the *Washington Post Book World* offered an insight into what has made Pohl's writing among the best in twentieth-century science fiction. "Pohl's work," McClellan wrote, "offers science fiction at its best: basic human problems . . . woven deftly into an intricate plot; pure adventure happening to believable (if not deeply drawn) characters in surroundings almost beyond the borders of imagination; and at the end, when other questions have been laid to rest, the posing of a new question as unfathomable as time and space themselves."

Offering a different view, essayist David N. Samuelson noted in *Bookvoices for the Future* that Pohl's reputation as a master of his craft does not preclude criticism of his work. While the author "is at the top of American SF writers who are 'fan oriented,'" wrote Samuelson, Pohl still "shows significant defects" as an artist. "Even the best of his fiction is sometimes marred by the intrusion of melodrama, sentimentality, unrationalized fantasy, and other features more or less calculated to appeal to an addicted audience. For the most part, his work seems to lack depth, density, an authentic personal voice, and a sense of style as anything more than a serviceable medium." In Samuelson's opinion, Pohl's shortcomings as a writer stem in part from his commercial instincts as an editor. Years of producing marketable fiction has "no doubt limited him at times to what he though his known audience was willing to accept. If it was narrow and provincial, so were his stories prior to 1952. When satire and social criticism were in, he still felt constrained to gild them with snappy patter, melodramatic plots and irrelevant aliens. His Hugos as editor were won for a magazine committed largely to adventure stories and essentially lightweight material." For his part, Pohl has said that he has schooled himself "to disregard criticism, or at least to discount nine-tenths of it."

Criticism notwithstanding, Pohl remains a "star among stars," according to Robert Wilcox in the *St. James Guide to Science Fiction Writers,* who added that the author has "shaped and seasoned the literature of science fiction as almost no one else has. His kaleidoscopic background has equipped him with skills and values possessed by few if any rivals." In *Locus* Pohl shared his thoughts on what a friend, John Rackham, once termed the 'science fiction method': "The science fiction method is dissection and reconstruction. You look at the world around you, and you take it apart into all its components. Then you take some of those components, throw them away, and plug in different ones, start it up and see what happens."

BIOGRAPHICAL AND CRITICAL SOURCES:

BOOKS

Aldiss, Brian, *Billion Year Spree: The History of Science Fiction,* Doubleday (New York, NY), 1973.

Amis, Kingsley, *New Maps of Hell: A Survey of Science Fiction,* Harcourt (New York, NY), 1960.

Carter, Paul A., *The Creation of Tomorrow: Fifty Years of Magazine Science-Fiction,* Columbia University Press (New York, NY), 1977.

Clareson, Thomas D., and Thomas L. Wymer, editors, *Voices for the Future,* Volume 3, Bowling Green University (Bowling Green, OH), 1984.

Clareson, Thomas D., *Frederik Pohl,* Borgo Press (San Bernardino, CA), 1987.

Contemporary Literary Criticism, Volume 18, Thomson Gale (Detroit, MI) 1981.

Dictionary of Literary Biography, Volume 8: *Twentieth-Century American Science-Fiction Writers,* Thomson Gale (Detroit, MI) 1981.

Platt, Charles, *Dream Makers: The Uncommon People Who Write Science Fiction,* Berkley (New York, NY), 1980.

Pohl, Frederik, *The Way the Future Was: A Memoir,* Ballantine (New York, NY), 1978.

St. James Guide to Science-Fiction Writers, St. James Press (Detroit, MI), 1996.

Scholes, Robert, and Eric S. Rabkin, *Science Fiction: History, Science, Vision,* Oxford University Press (New York, NY), 1977.

Short Story Criticism, Volume 25, Thomson Gale (Detroit, MI) 1997.

Vision, Oxford University Press (New York, NY), 1977.

Walker, Paul, *Speaking of Science Fiction: The Paul Walker Interviews,* Luna Press, 1978.

PERIODICALS

Analog, February, 1977; January, 1979; December, 1979; May, 1980; December, 1999, Tom Easton, review of *The Far Shore of Time,* p. 135.

Booklist, May 1, 1999, Roland Green, review of *The SFWA Grand Masters,* Volume 1, p. 1582; August, 1999, Roberta Johnson review of *The Far Shore of Time,* p. 2038; March 1, 2000, Roland Green, review of *The SFWA Grand Masters,* Volume 2, p. 1200.

Books and Bookmen, November, 1979.

Christian Science Monitor, June 20, 1979.

Kirkus Reviews, April 1, 1999, Paul M. Lamey, review of *The SFWA Grand Masters,* Volume 1, p. 496; June 15, 1999, Paul M. Lamey, review of *The Far Shore of Time,* p. 928.

Library Journal, May 15, 1998, review of *O Pioneer!;* April 15, 1999, Devon Thomas, review of *The SFWA Grand Masters,* Volume 1, p. 149; August 1, 1999, Jackie Cassada, review of *The Far Shore of Time,* p. 148.

Locus, August, 1999, Russell Letson, review of *The Far Shore of Time,* p. 25; October, 2000, "Frederik Pohl: Chasing Science," pp. 6, 71-72.

Los Angeles Times, December 11, 1986.

Magazine of Fantasy and Science Fiction, March, 1978; September, 1979.

New Republic, November 26, 1977.

New Statesman, April 15, 1977.

New York Times, September 7, 1983.

New York Times Book Review, March 27, 1977; May 20, 1979; November 15, 1987; April 24, 1988; July 2, 1989; July 10, 1994, p. 30.

Publishers Weekly, July 31, 1978; October 19, 1990, review of *The Gateway Trip: Tales and Vignettes of the Heechee;* September 27, 1991, review of *Our Angry Earth;* April 6, 1992, review of *Outnumbering the Dead;* May 23, 1994, p. 82; September 22, 1997, review of *The Siege of Eternity,* May 25, 1998, review of *O Pioneer!;* May 24, 1999, review of *The SFWA Grand Masters,* Volume 1, p. 74; July 26, 1999, review of *The Far Shore of Time,* p. 67; November 27, 2000, review of *Chasing Science,* p. 68.

Rapport, November 2, 1994, p. 26.

Science Fiction Chronicle, August, 1999, Don D'Ammassa, review of *The SFWA Grand Masters,* Volume 1, p. 44.

Spectator, January 28, 1978.

Times (London, England), November 24, 1983; August 8, 1985; January 16, 1988; January 17, 1991.

Times Literary Supplement, January 14, 1977; January 27, 1978; May 14, 1983.

Tribune Books (Chicago, IL), March 15, 1987; August 16, 1987; August 21, 1988; July 15, 1990; December 30, 1990.

USA Today Magazine, December, 1999, Frederik Pohl, "Goodbye Traffic Jams and Mega-Airports?," p. 5.

Voice of Youth Advocates, April, 1984; December, 1986, p. 240; April, 1987, p. 40; February, 1991, p. 366; April, 1991, pp. 46-47.

Washington Post, October 4, 1987.

Washington Post Book World, March 14, 1980; November 23, 1980; July 25, 1982; February 28, 1988; April 30, 1989; June 26, 1994, p. ll.*

R

RANDALL, Robert
    See SILVERBERG, Robert

*   *   *

RATHMELL, George W(esley) 1931-

PERSONAL: Born March 14, 1931, in Berkeley, CA; son of George H. and Grace Wagner (Muenks) Rathmell; married Margaret Montgomery, December 21, 1958 (died, 1998); partner of Janet Lee Gage, beginning August 9, 2004. *Education:* University of California at Berkeley, B.A., 1956; California State University at San Francisco, M.A., 1970; Sorbonne, University of Paris, Certificat de Langue Superieur. *Politics:* Democrat. *Religion:* Protestant.

ADDRESSES: Home—Box 98, Sea Ranch, CA 95497. *E-mail*—gwr@mcn.org.

CAREER: Oakland Unified School District, Oakland, CA, teacher of English, 1958-87; University of California Extension Department, Berkeley, instructor in education, 1967-86; Santa Rosa Junior College, Santa Rosa, CA, instructor in English, 1988-2000. *Military service:* U.S. Army, 1949-52, Corps of Engineers; became corporal; received Korean Service Medal, U.N. Service Medal, and National Defense Service Medal.

MEMBER: California Writers' Club, Sea Ranch Foundation.

AWARDS, HONORS: First prize, California Writers' Club short-story contest, 1996.

WRITINGS:

Bench Marks in Reading: A Guide to Reading Instruction in the Second-Language Classroom, Alemany Press (San Francisco), 1984.
Realms of Gold: The Colorful Writers of San Francisco, 1850-1950, Creative Arts Press (Berkeley, CA), 1998.
A Passport to Hell: The Mystery of Richard Realf, Authors Choice Press (San Jose, CA), 2002.

Contributor to *The Californians, Gualala Arts Bulletin, Independent Coast Observer, Sea Ranch Soundings,* and *Coast;* also author of monthly column on California history for *Nob Hill Gazette.*

WORK IN PROGRESS: A biographical novel on Richard Realf.

SIDELIGHTS: A teacher of writing for many years and a member of the faculty of Santa Rosa Junior College from 1988 to 2000, George W. Rathmell is also an enthusiast of the study of California history and literature. He has written numerous short stories and articles for California publications, and several in the latter category—on Bret Harte, on Frank Norris, and on California literary history in general—would serve as a springboard for his first general-interest book, *Realms of Gold: The Colorful Writers of San*

Francisco, 1850-1950, published in 1998. Rathmell is also the author of a guide to reading instruction for educational professionals.

Realms of Gold chronicles San Francisco's long history of providing a favorable climate to renegades and iconoclasts of all stripes, but especially those of a literary bent, and the volume presents a wealth of anecdotes that have accumulated along the way. Together with glimpses into the life and work of Harte and Norris, Rathmell weaves in tales about Richard Henry Dana, Mark Twain, Ina Coolbrith, Ambrose Bierce, Jack London, and John Steinbeck—just a few of the stellar names in American letters who either hailed from the Bay area or lived and wrote there during a significant period in their careers. Harte was the founder of one of San Francisco's outstanding literary journals, while Twain worked as a journalist under his real name of Samuel Clemens, became familiar with the city jail's drunk tank, and adopted his nom de plume. After they had left San Francisco, Harte and Twain were made honorary members of the Bohemian Club, and Rathmell writes in detail about this exclusive lodge's long period of influence. *Realms of Gold* also devotes space to the post-World War II literary developments that would later give birth to the Beat Generation. A contributor to *Publishers Weekly* praised Rathmell for presenting "a breezy, accessible, entertaining portrait" of not just the assemblage of literary stars large and small who once called the city home, "but also a glimpse at the radically changed world that spawned them."

Of his book *A Passport to Hell: The Mystery of Richard Realf,* Rathmell called the work an "unconventional biography, told in the words of the people who knew the subject, those who loved him and those who despised him."

Rathmell told *CA:* "I was born in the San Francisco Bay Area and have lived there all my life, and over the years I have developed an interest in and a deep affection for the area's literary history. Numerous trips to France have given me an appreciation of the respect that the French accord to their writers, both past and contemporary. I hope to encourage similar respect among my fellow Californians. My work, fiction and nonfiction, has been particularly influenced by Gerald Haslam and Michelle Cliff."

BIOGRAPHICAL AND CRITICAL SOURCES:

PERIODICALS

Press Democrat, March 29, 1998, review of *Realms of Gold: The Colorful Writers of San Francisco, 1850-1950.*
Publishers Weekly, March 23, 1998, review of *Realms of Gold,* p. 91.
Sea Ranch Soundings, spring, 1998, review of *Realms of Gold,* p. 12.

*   *   *

REED, James Wesley 1944-

PERSONAL: Born October 17, 1944, in New Orleans, LA.; son of James Horace (an engineer) and Mary (an accountant; maiden name, Reid) Reed; married Diane Spitzfaden (a college administrator), 1962; children: two. *Education:* Louisiana State University in New Orleans (now University of New Orleans), B.A., 1967; Harvard University, A.M., 1968, Ph.D., 1974.

ADDRESSES: Office—Department of History, Rutgers University, New Brunswick, NJ 08901. *E-mail*—jwr@ rci.rutgers.edu.

CAREER: Schlesinger Library, Cambridge, MA, research fellow in history, 1973-75; Rutgers University, New Brunswick, NJ, assistant professor, 1975-78, associate professor, beginning 1978, now professor of history, acting dean, 1985-94.

WRITINGS:

From Private Vice to Public Virtue: The Birth Control Movement and American Society since 1830, Basic Books (New York, NY), 1978, published as *The Birth Control Movement and American Society: From Private Vice to Public Virtue,* Princeton University Press, 1983.

SIDELIGHTS: James Wesley Reed once told *CA:* "I believe that most of the issues that concern us can better be understood in historical perspective. Thus, I have written a book on the birth control movement, and I am working on the history of mental testing and primatology."*

*   *   *

RENSIE, Willis
     See EISNER, Will(iam Erwin)

*   *   *

ROBERTSON, Ellis
     See SILVERBERG, Robert

*   *   *

ROBINSON, Lloyd
     See SILVERBERG, Robert

*   *   *

ROBINSON, Marilynne 1944(?)-

PERSONAL: Born c. 1944, in Sandpoint, ID; married; children: two sons. *Education:* Brown University, B.A.; University of Washington, M.A., Ph.D.

ADDRESSES: Home—Massachusetts. *Agent*—c/o Author Mail, Farrar, Straus, and Giroux, 19 Union Square W., New York, NY 10003.

CAREER: Writer.

AWARDS, HONORS: Ernest Hemingway Foundation award for best first novel, PEN American Center, Richard and Hinda Rosenthal Award, American Academy and Institute of Arts and Letters, PEN/Faulkner fiction award nomination, and Pulitzer Prize nomination, all 1982, all for *Housekeeping;* National Book Critics Circle Award, 2004, PEN/Faulkner Award nomination, 2005, and Pulitzer Prize for Fiction, 2005, all for *Gilead.*

WRITINGS:

Housekeeping (novel), Farrar, Straus (New York, NY), 1981.
Mother Country: Britain, the Nuclear State, and Nuclear Pollution, Farrar, Straus (New York, NY), 1989.

Marilynne Robinson

The Death of Adam: Essays on Modern Thought, Houghton Mifflin (Boston, MA), 1998.
Puritans and Prigs, Holt (New York, NY), 1999.
(Author of introduction) Kate Chopin, *The Awakening and Selected Short Stories,* Bantam (New York, NY), 2003.
Gilead (novel), Farrar, Straus (New York, NY), 2004.

Contributor to books, including *Christian Scholarship for What?,* Calvin College Alumni and Public Relations (Grand Rapids, MI), 2003. Contributor of stories and articles to periodicals, including the *New York Times Book Review, Quarto,* and *Harper's.*

ADAPTATIONS: Housekeeping was adapted by Bill Forsyth into a film and released by Columbia in 1987.

SIDELIGHTS: Marilynne Robinson's debut novel *Housekeeping* earned its author the 1982 Ernest Hemingway Foundation award for best first novel, a 1982 Richard and Hinda Rosenthal Award, and a nomination for the Pulitzer Prize. It also earned praise from numerous literary critics, such as Marc Granetz, who in the *New Republic* deemed *Housekeeping* "a beautiful and unusual novel about transience and durability [that] revolves around familiar objects, details of everyday." Paul Gray in *Time* remarked of *Housekeeping,* "This first novel does much more than show promise; it brilliantly portrays the impermanence of all things, especially beauty and happiness, and the struggle to keep what can never be owned." And, in Anatole Broyard's assessment in the *New York Times, Housekeeping* is "a first novel that sounds as if the author has been treasuring it up all her life, waiting for it to form itself. . . . You can feel in the book a gathering voluptuous release of confidence, a delighted surprise at the unexpected capacities of language, a close, careful fondness for people that we thought only saints felt. . . . Robinson works with light, dark, water, heat, cold, textures, sounds and smells. . . . Though her ambition is tall, she remains down to earth, where the best novels happen."

In *Housekeeping,* Robinson follows the lives of two adolescent girls through several guardianship changes. The story begins as a woman named Helen returns to her childhood home in Fingerbone, a small community isolated in the mountains of Idaho. With her, she brings her two daughters, Ruth and Lucille, and leaves the girls on the porch of their grandmother's home. Helen then drives her car into the nearby lake, taking her own life in the same place her father drowned years before. After Helen's suicide, Ruth and Lucille fall under the care of their grandmother, who attempts to restore normalcy to their lives through daily routine. As Ruth explains in *Housekeeping,* "She whited shoes and braided hair and turned back bedclothes as if reenacting the commonplace would make it merely commonplace again." After Ruth and Lucille's grandmother dies, the girls are cared for by two maiden great-aunts who move in and also try to use unchanging daily routine to provide reassurance and stability in the sisters' lives. But the aunts, set in their habits, cannot adapt to the changing needs of children and so, leaving the girls, they ultimately return to their former residence and the orderly lifestyle that they prefer.

The girls' next guardian is their mother's sister Sylvie, an eccentric drifter whose idea of housekeeping is "a merging of love and squalor," explained Julie Kavanagh in her *Times Literary Supplement* review of *Housekeeping.* Characteristic of this merging are Sylvie's collection of scraps, newspapers, and emptied food containers and her willingness to allow the outside to come inside the house in the form of animals and dead leaves. According to Kavanagh, Sylvie's housekeeping habits signify the novel's main theme—"an acceptance of transience, an acceptance which Sylvie embodies."

This acceptance of transience is tied to the idea that "memory and loss can paradoxically be a reminder of an eternal reunion to come," Kavanagh commented. *Housekeeping* shows one of the girls, Ruth, discovering and adopting Sylvie's way of viewing life and death. She comes to feel, like Sylvie, what she calls "the life of perished things" and to believe that "what perished need not be lost." Suzanne O'Malley reaffirmed this interpretation of Sylvie's perspective in *Ms.* magazine, stating that the woman's "peculiar brand of housekeeping included letting leaves gather in the corners. Ruth speculates that Sylvie actually took care not to disturb the leaves. . . . The point is not that Sylvie and her nieces lived in squalor—though that may be true enough—but that those who expect the past to leap to life at any minute consider 'accumulation to be the essence of housekeeping.'"

While Ruth accompanies Sylvie in her nighttime boat excursions on the lake where Sylvie's sister and father drowned and watches her strange aunt meditate in the dark on the past and come to terms with change, the other girl, Lucille, becomes increasingly alienated from her sister and aunt. Lucille dislikes being different from other adolescents, wants to fit in, be a part of Fingerbone society, and live a normal life. So she leaves her sister with Sylvie and moves in with one of her school teachers. From this point on, noted Art Seidenbaum in the *Los Angeles Times,* Sylvie and Ruth become "more like each other, . . . less like their immediate neighbors [and] less like any people who must do rather than drift."

Eventually the residents of Fingerbone decide that Ruth's living with Sylvie is detrimental to the girl, and that they must take Ruth away from her aunt. To prevent this, Ruth and Sylvie burn down their house, leave Fingerbone via the railway bridge over the lake, and take up a life of drifting. The novel's narrative begins to reflect this drifting, mingling the thoughts, dreams, and perceptions of Ruth, the narrator of *Housekeeping.* As Ruth herself remarks: "I have never distinguished readily between thinking and dreaming." And, according to Le Anne Schreiber in the *New York Times Book Review,* "these distinctions break down utterly" as Ruth feels the pressure from the town to conform or split from Sylvie. "The controlled lyricism of Ruth's language, which had been anchored in sensuous detail, becomes unmoored." The novel, like Ruth, then becomes "fevered and hallucinatory," concluded Schreiber. Kavanagh similarly noted the change in *Housekeeping*'s style once Ruth and Sylvie decide to leave home: "The previously realistic narrative now begins to mirror the drifters' new freedom and to take the form of arcane, meandering reflections. That the pair have symbolically transcended the mundane by crossing the bridge is reiterated by a free . . . prose-style." Anne Morddel, a contributor to *Contemporary Novelists,* observed that "Robinson's style itself is evocative of drifting and drifters' tales, with long, often poetic descriptions that suddenly snap back to the original point or deflect to a new, unrelated one."

Several critics considered *Housekeeping* to be a sort of long prose poem. According to Schreiber, the novel "reads as slowly as poetry—and for the same reason: The language is so precise, so distilled, so beautiful that one doesn't want to miss any pleasure it might yield up to patience." Kavanagh likewise remarked, "It is a complex work, and as such should be read slowly and carefully." But, Kavanagh concluded, "this is not to say that it is impenetrable or over-intense. The author's control of plot, her eye for eccentricity, her clarity, quiet humour and delicate touch, invest the book with a lightness that successfully counterbalances the density of thought." Morddel saw some faults in the novel, such as some angry outbursts from Ruth that seem out of character. However, she emphasized that "these are small flaws in a book that is so rich with thought and feeling that it compels the reader to slow down and truly read."

After *Housekeeping* Robinson published a couple of nonfiction works, *Mother Country: Britain, the Nuclear State, and Nuclear Pollution,* and *The Death of Adam: Essays on Modern Thought.* The former is a passionate denunciation of the British government's management of the Sellafield nuclear processing plant. "The documentation behind the essay is exhaustive; the selective bibliography takes up twenty-two pages," noted Thomas Schaub in a *Contemporary Literature* profile of Robinson. "Throughout, Robinson's analysis of Sellafield is driven by a twin outrage: not only at

the tons of nuclear waste being dumped into the sea each day, but also at the fact that a government which makes claims for the moralism of its acts is superintending this degradation of the earth." Robinson told Schaub the Sellafield situation represents "a profound abuse of the environment in an enormously, densely populated part of the world. And unless everything they've told us about radioactive contamination was some kind of a malicious fairy tale, there can only be very grievous consequences, and nothing was done to make us aware of this at all." She does not spare environmental organizations from her criticism; in her interview with Schaub, she asserted that they have "an enormous amount of information . . . that is never, ever communicated to people in this country." *New York Times Book Review* contributor Len Ackland, however, found a shortage of useful information in Robinson's book. Her "clear and justified passion unfortunately exceeds the evidence she brings to bear," he wrote, maintaining that "the reader will search in vain for facts" that back up Robinson's arguments. He also thought the author spent too much time on other subjects before dealing with Sellafield; he wished for "a rigorous short essay instead of this lengthy polemic."

Numerous essays on a plethora of topics are collected in Robinson's *The Death of Adam.* Subjects include theologian John Calvin, the relationship of the McGuffey reader to nineteenth-century American social reform movements, and Charles Darwin's theory of evolution. Robinson calls the essays "contrarian in method and spirit," and defines contrarians as those who realize that both "the prevailing view of things" and the opposite point of view "can be assumed to be wrong." Therefore, "they undertake to demonstrate that there are other ways of thinking, for which better arguments can be made." In a review for the *Christian Century,* Kathleen Norris described the collection as "rigorous but invigorating" and "a bracing book of truly contrarian essays." As Norris observed, "With a novelist's sharp eye, Robinson exposes our bland acceptance of capitalist brutalities, our addiction to anxiety, our idolization of success, and our attendant loss of the ability to comprehend the significance of events. . . . While Robinson sometimes rants, as a contrarian is wont to do, her book is large in spirit." Norris particularly praised Robinson's handling of religion: "A rigorous thinker, blessedly conscious of history, Robinson makes a frontal assault on the easy, dismissive stereotypes of religion that abound in our culture." Similarly, Roger Kimball commented in the *New York Times Book Review,* "One would have to search far and wide to find another contemporary novelist writing articulate essays defending the theology of John Calvin or the moral and social lives of the Puritans. We all know that Puritans were dour, sex-hating, joy-abominating folk—except that, as Robinson shows, this widely embraced caricature is a calumny." A *Publishers Weekly* reviewer noted the large role Robinson's essays give to morality and reported that "for the most part her moral integrity is accompanied by an equally rigorous intellectual integrity." Kimball perceived a "current of high moral seriousness" in the book and averred that "one of Robinson's great merits as an essayist is her refusal to take her opinions secondhand. Her book is a goad to renewed curiosity." Norris concluded, "Ideologues of all stripes are likely to be enraged by this book—which seems like poetic justice to me. But if readers are willing to engage a book that may chip away at their ignorance and challenge their most dearly held assumptions and stereotypes, then Robinson's book will do its work."

Robinson's second novel, *Gilead,* explores the impact of family and generational relationships, somewhat as she does in *Housekeeping.* As a *Library Journal* contributor noted, "As his life winds down, Rev. John Adams relates the story of his own father and grandfather, both preachers but one a pacifist and one a gun-toting abolitionist." Robinson carries out her theme in the form of a letter written by seventy-year-old Ames to his own son, and to his namesake, his son's best friend, speaking with wisdom of the holy and mystical links that are forged between fathers and sons. Praising Robinson's long-awaited second novel, *Booklist* contributor Donna Seaman dubbed *Gilead* "wonderful, a work of profound beauty and wonder," and added, "Millennia of philosophical musings and a century of American history are refracted through the prism of Robinson's exquisite and uplifting" tale.

BIOGRAPHICAL AND CRITICAL SOURCES:

BOOKS

Contemporary Literary Criticism, Volume 25, Thomson Gale (Detroit, MI), 1983.

Contemporary Novelists, St. James (Detroit, MI), 1996.

Robinson, Marilynne, *Housekeeping,* Farrar, Straus (New York, NY), 1981.

PERIODICALS

American Scholar, winter 1999, review of *The Death of Adam: Essays on Modern Thought,* p. 147.
Booklist, August, 2004, Donna Seaman, review of *Gilead,* p. 1874.
Chicago Tribune Book World, March 15, 1981.
Christian Century, November 18, 1998, p. 1101.
Commonweal, May 22, 1981.
Contemporary Literature, summer, 1994, p. VI.
Critique, spring 1999, "Sheltered Vagrancy in Marilynne Robinson's *Housekeeping,*" p. 2.
Encounter, May, 1981.
Library Journal, July 15, 2004.
Los Angeles Times, January 14, 1981.
Ms., April, 1981.
Nation, February 7, 1981.
New Republic, February 21, 1981.
New Statesman, March 20, 1981.
New York Times, January 7, 1981; April 6, 1982.
New York Times Book Review, February 8, 1981; February 28, 1982; July 16, 1989, p. 7; February 7, 1999.
Observer (London, England), March 1, 1981.
Publishers Weekly, July 27, 1998, p. 60.
Time, February 2, 1981.
Times Literary Supplement, April 3, 1981; August 13, 1982.*

*　　*　　*

RODMAN, Eric
    See SILVERBERG, Robert

*　　*　　*

ROUSE, Mary A(mes) 1934-

PERSONAL: Born July 31, 1934, in De Soto, MO; daughter of Horace Walker (a postmaster) and Edith Blanche (a schoolteacher; maiden name, Farley) Ames; married Richard Hunter Rouse (a medieval historian and writer), September 7, 1959; children: Thomas

Richard, Andrew Hunter, Jonathan Joseph. *Education:* Southeast Missouri State College (now University), B.A. (summa cum laude), 1955, B.S. (summa cum laude), 1957; Cornell University, M.A., 1961. *Politics:* "Jeffersonian Democrat." *Religion:* "Atheist."

ADDRESSES: Home—11444 Berwick St., Los Angeles, CA 90049. *Office*—Center for Medieval and Renaissance Studies, University of California—Los Angeles, Los Angeles, CA 90024-1485.

CAREER: Teacher at public elementary schools in De Soto, MO, 1955-56; high school teacher of history, government, and Spanish, De Soto, 1957-58; junior high school teacher of American history in Trummansburg, NY, 1960-61; University of California—Los Angeles, managing editor of *Viator: Medieval and Renaissance Studies* at Center for Medieval and Renaissance Studies, 1976—.

MEMBER: Mediaeval Academy of America, Medieval Association of the Pacific (member of council, 1982-84, 1993-95).

AWARDS, HONORS: Woodrow Wilson fellow, 1958-60.

WRITINGS:

(Editor, with W. M. Newman) *Charters of St-Fursy of Péronne,* Mediaeval Academy of America (Cambridge, MA), 1977.

(With husband, R. H. Rouse) *Preachers, Florilegia, and Sermons: Studies on the Manipulus Florum of Thomas of Ireland,* Pontifical Institute of Medieval Studies (Toronto, Ontario, Canada), 1979.

(With R. H. Rouse) *Cartolai, Illuminators, and Printers in Fifteenth-Century Italy: The Evidence of the Ripoli Press,* Department of Special Collections, University of California—Los Angeles, (Los Angeles, CA), 1988.

(Editor, with R. H. Rouse, and coauthor of introduction and notes) R. A. B. Mynors, *Registrum Anglie de libris doctorum et auctorum veterum,* British Library (London, England), 1991.

(With R. H. Rouse) *Authentic Witnesses: Approaches to Medieval Texts and Manuscripts,* University of Notre Dame Press (Notre Dame, IN), 1991.

(With R. H. Rouse) *Manuscripts and Their Makers: Commercial Book Producers in Medieval Paris, 1200-1500,* two volumes, Harvey Miller (Turnhout, Belgium), 2000.

Work represented in anthologies, including *The Classics in the Middle Ages,* edited by A. S. Bernardo and S. Levin, [Binghamton, NY], 1990; *Medieval Book Production: Assessing the Evidence,* edited by L. L. Brownrigg, [Los Altos Hills, CA], 1990; and *Intellectual Life in the Middle Ages: Essays Presented to Margaret Gibson,* edited by L. Smith and B. Ward, [London, England], 1992. Contributor to scholarly journals. Editor, *MAP Newsletter* and *Chronica* (annual), Medieval Association of the Pacific, 1992—.

SIDELIGHTS: Mary A. Rouse once told *CA:* "My husband and I are medieval historians who specialize in the culture that surrounds the handwritten books—the manuscripts—that served European readers from the beginning of history until the spread of the printing press in the late fifteenth century. From the beginning of our marriage, we have collaborated in the writing of everything we have produced. We are unique among our medievalist colleagues in working in this fashion and, surprisingly enough, we still remain rather good friends after all these years of trampling each other's egos."

BIOGRAPHICAL AND CRITICAL SOURCES:

PERIODICALS

Book Collector, summer, 1992, review of *Registrum Anglie de libris doctorum et auctorum veterum,* p. 161.

Catholic Historical Review, April, 1982, review of *Preachers, Florilegia, and Sermons: Studies on the Manipulus Florum of Thomas of Ireland,* p. 308.

Libraries and Culture, fall, 1993, review of *Registrum Anglie de libris doctorum et auctorum veterum,* p. 476; winter, 1995, review of *Authentic Witnesses: Approaches to Medieval Texts and Manuscripts,* p. 115.

Library, December, 1994, review of *Registrum Anglie de libris doctorum et auctorum veterum,* p. 335.

Library Quarterly, April, 1994, review of *Authentic Witnesses,* p. 216.

Modern Language Review, April, 1995, review of *Authentic Witnesses,* p. 339.

Religious Studies Review, July, 1987, review of *Preachers, Florilegia, and Sermons,* p. 267.

Speculum, January, 1982, review of *Preachers, Florilegia, and Sermons,* p. 220; January, 1994, review of *Registrum Anglie de libris doctorum et auctorum veterum,* p. 248.

Times Literary Supplement, August 14, 1992, review of *Registrum Anglie de libris doctorum et auctorum veterum,* p. 24; December 21, 2001, John Lowden, review of *Manuscripts and Their Makers: Commercial Book Producers in Medieval Paris, 1200-1500,* p. 29.*

*   *   *

ROUSE, Richard H(unter) 1933-

PERSONAL: Born August 14, 1933, in Boston, MA; son of Hunter and Dorothy (Husmert) Rouse; married Mary Ames (a medieval historian and writer), September 7, 1959; children: Thomas Richard, Andrew Hunter, Jonathan Joseph. *Education:* University of Iowa, B.A., 1955; University of Chicago, M.A., 1957; Cornell University, Ph.D., 1963.

ADDRESSES: Home—11444 Berwick St., Los Angeles, CA 90049. *Office*—Department of History, University of California—Los Angeles, Los Angeles, CA 90024-1485.

CAREER: Cornell University, Ithaca, NY, reference librarian, 1957-58; Harvard University, Cambridge, MA, assistant curator of manuscripts for Houghton Library, 1962-63; University of California—Los Angeles, assistant professor, 1963-69, associate professor, 1969-75, professor of history, 1975—, associate director of Center for Medieval and Renaissance Studies, 1967-68. University of Pennsylvania, Rosenback Lecturer, 1975; Oxford University, visiting fellow of All Souls College, 1978-79. St. John's University, member of advisory board for Monastic Manuscript Microfilm Library, 1970—. Comité International de Paleographie, member, beginning c. 1973.

MEMBER: International Society for the Study of Mediaeval Philosophy, Mediaeval Academy of America (fellow), Medieval Association of the Pacific (president, 1968-72).

AWARDS, HONORS: Fellow, American Council of Learned Societies, 1972-73; Guggenheim fellow, 1975-76; fellow, National Endowment for the Humanities, 1981-83.

WRITINGS:

Guide to Serial Bibliographies for Medieval Studies, University of California Press (Berkeley, CA), 1969.

(Coeditor) *Viator: Medieval and Renaissance Studies,* seven volumes, beginning 1970.

(With wife, M. A. Rouse) *Preachers, Florilegia and Sermons: Studies on the Manipuluo Florum of Thomas of Ireland,* Pontifical Institute of Medieval Studies (Toronto, Ontario, Canada) 1979.

(Member of editorial board, with C. W. Dutschke and D. J. Dutschke) *Medieval and Renaissance Manuscripts in the Claremont Libraries,* University of California Press (Berkeley, CA), 1986.

(With M. A. Rouse) *Cartolai, Illuminators, and Printers in Fifteenth-Century Italy: The Evidence of the Ripoli Press,* Department of Special Collections, University of California—Los Angeles (Los Angeles, CA), 1988.

(Editor, with Louis J. Bataillon and Bertrand G. Guyot) *La production du livre universitaire au Moyen Age: exemplar et pecia,* Editions du Centre national de la recherche scientifique (Paris, France), 1988.

(Editor, with C. W. Dutschke and Sara S. Hodson) *Guide to Medieval and Renaissance Manuscripts in the Huntington Library,* two volumes, Huntington Library (San Marino, CA), 1989.

(Editor, with M. A. Rouse, and coauthor of introduction and notes) *Registrum Anglie de libris doctorum et auctorum veterum,* British Library (London, England), 1991.

(With M. A. Rouse) *Authentic Witnesses: Approaches to Medieval Texts and Manuscripts,* University of Notre Dame Press (Notre Dame, IN), 1991.

(Editor) *Medieval and Renaissance Manuscripts at the University of California, Los Angeles,* University of California Press (Berkeley, CA), 1991.

(With M. A. Rouse) *Manuscripts and Their Makers: Commercial Book Producers in Medieval Paris, 1200-1500,* two volumes, Harvey Miller (Turnhout, Belgium), 2000.

Contributor to books, including *Medieval Learning and Literature: Essays Presented to R. W. Hunt,*

Oxford University Press (Oxford, England), 1975. Contributor to periodicals, including *Studies in Cistercian History* and *Speculum.*

BIOGRAPHICAL AND CRITICAL SOURCES:

PERIODICALS

Book Collector, summer, 1992, review of *Registrum Anglie de libris doctorum et auctorum veterum,* p. 161.
Catholic Historical Review, April, 1982, review of *Preachers, Florilegia, and Sermons: Studies on the Manipulus Florum of Thomas of Ireland,* p. 308.
Libraries and Culture, fall, 1993, review of *Registrum Anglie de libris doctorum et auctorum veterum,* p. 476; winter, 1995, review of *Authentic Witnesses: Approaches to Medieval Texts and Manuscripts,* p. 115.
Library, December, 1994, review of *Registrum Anglie de libris doctorum et auctorum veterum,* p. 335.
Library Quarterly, April, 1994, review of *Authentic Witnesses,* p. 216.
Modern Language Review, April, 1995, review of *Authentic Witnesses,* p. 339.
Religious Studies Review, July, 1987, review of *Preachers, Florilegia, and Sermons,* p. 267.
Speculum, January, 1982, review of *Preachers, Florilegia, and Sermons,* p. 220; January, 1994, review of *Registrum Anglie de libris doctorum et auctorum veterum,* p. 248.
Times Literary Supplement, August 14, 1992, review of *Registrum Anglie de libris doctorum et auctorum veterum,* p. 24; December 21, 2001, John Lowden, review of *Manuscripts and Their Makers: Commercial Book Producers in Medieval Paris, 1200-1500,* p. 29.*

*   *   *

RULE, Ann 1935-
    (Andy Stack)

PERSONAL: Born October 22, 1935, in Lowell, MI; daughter of Chester R. (an athletics coach) and Sophie (a teacher) Stackhouse; married Bill Rule (a teacher and technical writer; divorced, 1972); children: Laura,

Ann Rule

Leslie, Andy, Mike, Bruce. *Education:* University of Washington, B.A., 1954; graduate study at University of Washington; received degree in police science. *Hobbies and other interests:* Gardening, walking, pets, collecting "way too many things."

ADDRESSES: Home—Box 98846, Seattle, WA 98198. *Agent*—The Foley Agency, 34 East 38th St., New York, NY 10016. *E-mail*—annier37@aol.com.

CAREER: Writer. Has worked as a police officer in Seattle, WA, and as a caseworker for the Washington State Department of Public Assistance.

AWARDS, HONORS: Achievement Award, Pacific Northwest Writers Conference, 1991; two Anthony Awards, from Bouchercon; Peabody Award for miniseries *Small Sacrifices;* Readers' Choice Awards, *Reader's Digest,* 2003.

WRITINGS:

NONFICTION

Beautiful Seattle, Beautiful America (Woodburn, OR), 1979, published as *Beautiful America's Seattle,* Beautiful America (Woodburn, OR), 1989.

The Stranger beside Me, Norton (New York, NY), 1980, revised twentieth anniversary edition, Norton (New York, NY), 2000.

Small Sacrifices: A True Story of Passion and Murder, New American Library (New York, NY), 1987.

If You Really Loved Me: A True Story of Desire and Murder, Simon & Schuster (New York, NY), 1991.

Everything She Ever Wanted: A True Story of Obsessive Love, Murder, and Betrayal, Simon & Schuster (New York, NY), 1992.

Dead by Sunset: Perfect Husband, Perfect Killer?, Simon & Schuster (New York, NY), 1995.

Bitter Harvest: A Woman's Fury, a Mother's Sacrifice, Simon & Schuster (New York, NY), 1997.

. . . And Never Let Her Go: Thomas Capano, the Deadly Seducer, Simon & Schuster (New York, NY), 1999.

Every Breath You Take: A True Story of Obsessive Revenge and Murder, Free Press (New York, NY), 2001.

Heart Full of Lies: A True Story of Desire and Death, Free Press (New York, NY), 2003.

Without Pity: Ann Rule's Most Dangerous Killers, Pocket Books (New York, NY), 2003.

Green River, Running Red: The Real Story of the Green River Killer, America's Deadliest Serial Murderer, Free Press (New York, NY), 2004.

"ANN RULE'S CRIME FILES" SERIES

A Rose for Her Grave and Other True Cases (also see below), Pocket Books (New York, NY), 1993.

You Belong to Me and Other True Cases, Pocket Books (New York, NY), 1994.

A Fever in the Heart and Other True Cases, Pocket Books (New York, NY), 1996.

In the Name of Love and Other True Cases, Pocket Books (New York, NY), 1998.

The End of the Dream: The Golden Boy Who Never Grew Up and Other True Cases, Pocket Books (New York, NY), 1999.

A Rage to Kill and Other True Cases, Pocket Books (New York, NY), 1999.

Empty Promises and Other True Cases, Pocket Books (New York, NY), 2001.

Last Dance, Last Chance and Other True Cases, Pocket Books (New York, NY), 2003.

Kiss Me, Kill Me, and Other True Cases, Pocket Books (New York, NY), 2004.

Also author of *Ann Rule's Omnibus* (contains *A Rose for Her Grave, You Belong to Me,* and *A Fever in the Heart*).

"TRUE CRIME ANNALS" SERIES; UNDER PSEUDONYM ANDY STACK

Lust Killer, New American Library (New York, NY), 1983.

Want-Ad Killer, New American Library (New York, NY), 1983.

The I-Five Killer, New American Library (New York, NY), 1984.

OTHER

Possession (novel), Norton (New York, NY), 1983.

Contributor to various periodicals, including *Cosmopolitan, Good Housekeeping, Ladies' Home Journal, Seattle Times, True Confessions,* and *True Detective.*

ADAPTATIONS: An adaptation of *Small Sacrifices: A True Story of Passion and Murder* was broadcast on ABC-TV, 1989; *Dead by Sunset, . . . And Never Let Her Go,* and *Small Sacrifices* have been produced as television miniseries; *Ann Rule Presents: The Stranger beside Me,* a docudrama produced by the USA Network and based on Rule's book *The Stranger beside Me,* aired on March 21, 2003.

SIDELIGHTS: Ann Rule's writing has earned her a reputation as an expert on criminal behavior. She is the author of such best-selling books as *The Stranger beside Me, Small Sacrifices: A True Story of Passion and Murder,* and numerous other books which discuss the lives of notorious killers. In addition to lecturing on the subject of crime, she has provided testimony in court cases and has lent her expertise in order to help police agencies understand the behavior of psychopathic murderers. Although she has earned respect for the books published under her own name, some of her early work was done under the pseudonym Andy Stack. In the *New York Times,* Rule stated that publishers at the time "thought nobody would want to read a crime story written by a female."

Rule's interest in crime developed from a very early age. As a child, she spent time with her grandfather, a sheriff in Stanton, Michigan. "It fascinated me how grandpa could take a broken button or a blood drop and figure out who done it," she remarked in an interview with *People.* Rule attended the University of Washington, where she studied creative writing and criminology, and later became a police officer in Seattle. She lost her position on the force, however, when people found out about her extreme nearsightedness.

After her husband suspended his professional career to resume his education, Rule decided to provide for her family by writing stories about actual crimes. Through researching her pieces, Rule spent time with arson and homicide divisions of the police department, attended specialty classes in police science, and built a network of contacts with people involved in law enforcement throughout the Northwest.

In the early 1970s Rule worked on a suicide hot-line at the Seattle Crisis Center with a student intern named Ted Bundy. Of Bundy, Rule told *People,* "I used to think that if I were younger or my daughters were older, this would be the perfect man." Bundy was convicted of murder in 1978 and was ultimately implicated in the slaying of more than thirty-five women. Before Bundy's arrest and conviction, Rule was commissioned to write a book on a string of murders committed in the Northwest. The work was eventually published as *The Stranger beside Me,* an account of Bundy that earned critical acclaim due in part to Rule's association with the killer. In the *New York Times Book Review* Thomas Thompson remarked that the author "does have an extraordinary angle that makes *The Stranger beside Me* dramatic and, occasionally, as chilling as a bedroom window shattering at midnight."

During the initial investigation into the Seattle-area murders, as information about the killer became known, Rule became increasingly suspicious about Bundy's possible involvement and provided investigators with a tip that her associate might be the killer, but was relieved when the police did not follow up on her lead. Rule felt in some way duped by Bundy, however, when his guilt was confirmed; Bundy did not share the negative character traits associated with such notorious serial killers as Charles Manson, Richard Speck, and John Gacy. He was a handsome,

educated, and charismatic individual with political aspirations. In *The Stranger beside Me,* Rule reports how Bundy moved to Salt Lake City, where he became a Mormon and studied to become a lawyer, then to Colorado and Florida. In each state, law enforcement officials were faced with investigations into gruesome murders that Bundy allegedly committed.

After Bundy was arrested for the murder of two members of the Chi Omega sorority at Florida State University, he chose to act as his own lawyer. Although he was given the opportunity to accept a seventy-five-year term of imprisonment, he chose to defend himself in a trial and was subsequently given the death penalty. Throughout *The Stranger beside Me,* Rule reports on how she and others were fooled by Bundy because he was successful at displaying the positive aspects of his character while hiding his negative traits. Of the time that she spent with Bundy at the crisis center, she wrote, as quoted by Thompson, "If, as many people believe today, Ted Bundy took lives, he also saved lives. I know he did, because I was there when he did it."

In *Small Sacrifices,* published in 1987, Rule relates the story of Diane Downs, a mother of three who claimed that she stopped her car on the highway to assist a "bushy-haired stranger" who had flagged her down. According to Downs, the stranger then proceeded to shoot her and her children. One of her children died, one was paralyzed, and one survived after having a stroke. In her book, Rule shows how police were wary about Downs's story from the time they first heard it. In the emergency room, Downs seemed more concerned about whether there were holes in her new car than she was about the condition of her children. Also, when one police officer heard that Downs had been shot, he predicted the location of her wound—in an area that would not cause fatal injury, indicating that the injury was self-inflicted. Rule also notes that authorities are usually suspicious when they hear victims speak of a bushy-haired stranger, identified by the police as a "BHS." Rule writes, as quoted by Carolyn Banks in the *Washington Post:* "The BHS is the guy who isn't there, the man the defendant claims is *really* responsible. . . . Of course, the BHS can never be produced in court." Downs was eventually tried and convicted of the crimes committed against her children.

Rule delves into Downs's past in *Small Sacrifices,* noting how Downs was the victim of considerable sexual abuse as a child. As a teenager, she slit her wrists in a failed suicide attempt. Rule relates that Downs entered into a destructive marital relationship in order to extricate herself from her difficult family situation and achieved happiness only after giving birth to a child. Downs later gave birth to a second infant, but then had an abortion to terminate a third pregnancy. Feeling guilty about the abortion, Downs decided to atone for her action by conceiving a fourth child. Instead of choosing her husband to father the child, though, she selected a coworker. "I picked somebody that was attractive . . . healthy . . . not abusive of drugs and alcohol, strong—bone structure—you know, the whole bit: a *good specimen*. It was really clinical," Downs said, as recorded in *Small Sacrifices*.

After watching a television show that focused on surrogate parenting, Downs convinced herself that she could make a living by providing other couples with babies. According to Rule, Downs had plans to begin a surrogate-parenting clinic of her own. Later, she entered into an affair with Lew Lewiston, a married man who was averse to the idea of fathering children. The prosecution charged that after Lewiston ended his relationship with Downs, she tried to kill her offspring to appease her former lover. Downs was convicted of the crime and sentenced to life plus fifty years of imprisonment. She escaped from jail in the early 1990s and was found ten days later at the home of Wayne Seifer, a psychiatric assistant and the spouse of one of Downs's fellow convicts. At the time of the breakout, Rule predicted that, based on her subject's pattern of behavior, Downs would seek out a suitable mate with the intention of getting pregnant during her time away from prison.

At the time of the escape, Rule knew that Downs had read *Small Sacrifices* and was not pleased with the way the author had portrayed her. In an interview with *Publishers Weekly* the author stated, "I'm not paranoid about my safety, but there are some people I won't write about: drug dealers, cults, motorcycle gangs and organized crime. I don't want someone I don't even know coming back at me." In *People* she revealed that she supports the death penalty in cases that involve serial killers, because too many of them are released from prison and end up repeating their pattern of crime.

Upon its release, *Small Sacrifices* was praised by several reviewers. Banks, for instance, noted that "Ann Rule is able to relate Diane Downs's crimes—as she

did Ted Bundy's in her earlier *The Stranger beside Me*—with high tension. Rule has an instinct for suspense, knowing just what information to leak to the reader and when." And Eileen Ogintz of the *Chicago Tribune* acknowledged that "the book is superbly researched. It succeeds because Rule knew what details, eyewitness accounts and evidence to include— and what not to."

As she began to earn a living through her crime writing, Rule started to feel guilty about deriving an income from reporting on the misfortunes of others. A psychologist, however, convinced her that "what matters is how you feel about people," as recounted in her *Publishers Weekly* interview. His advice contributed to Rule's approach toward reporting on crime. "I get to know the victim so well that I can see and feel the pain that these people go through: the victim, the victim's family and the family of the perpetrator. Out of consideration for them, I often leave out as much as I include." In the *New York Times,* Rule also remarked to Robert Lindsey on how she has assisted authorities at the United States Justice Department in implementing a plan for tracking seemingly unrelated murders. Such work, she noted, "is kind of my vindication for profiting from other people's tragedies. I'd like to put myself out of the business of being a crime writer and go on to other things. Sadly, the serial murder keeps going on."

In the early 1990s Rule released *If You Really Loved Me,* which tells about the murder of Linda Brown, the fifth wife of David Arnold Brown, a man who amassed considerable wealth in the field of data retrieval. The Browns lived in Orange County, California, with their infant daughter, Krystal, Linda's seventeen-year-old sister, Patricia Bailey, and David's fourteen-year-old daughter from a previous marriage, Cinnamon. At the beginning of her book, Rule describes the homicide as it was originally interpreted by the police. According to Patricia Bailey, Cinnamon shot Linda and then fled from the house. Investigating officer Fred McLean discovered Cinnamon in a doghouse in the backyard, wearing a vomit-and urine-stained sweat suit—an indication that she had tried to commit suicide by swallowing pills. She also had a note: "Dear God, please forgive me. I didn't mean to hurt her," as quoted in the *New York Times Book Review* by critic Maggie Paley.

Cinnamon confessed to the murder but later admitted that she did not remember committing the crime. She was sentenced to a minimum of twenty-seven years of imprisonment, beginning in a juvenile detention facility. In the second section of the book, Rule presents facts concerning the investigation of the case. Authorities discovered that before the murder, David Brown continually manipulated family members by pretending to be gravely ill and seeking medical attention for bouts of depression. In order to win the devotion of his wife, daughters, and sister-in-law, he fed them promises, threatened them, and provided them with gifts. On a number of occasions, he also coerced the women who lived with him into having sexual relations with him.

Authorities became concerned upon discovering that Brown received more than $800,000 in insurance settlements after his wife's death. Additionally, he continued to share a residence with his sister-in-law, whom he married in 1986. Rule noted that as time passed, Brown visited Cinnamon less frequently. Cinnamon, meanwhile, was refused the opportunity to be paroled because she continued to attest that she had no memory of committing the murder. After hearing a secretly taped session between Brown and his daughter, as well as Cinnamon's own testimony as to what occurred on the day that her stepmother was murdered, authorities brought David Brown to trial, convicted him of the crime, and sentenced him to life in prison.

Robert Campbell of the *Los Angeles Times Book Review* felt that *If You Really Loved Me* could have been structured in order to provide readers with a greater sense of suspense. He did, however, praise Rule for her handling of the second half of her four-part book. Campbell felt that "Part Three, 'The Arrest and the Death List,' presents as gripping a plot and as complicated an investigation of a complex character as any imagined in fiction, and Part Four, 'The Trial,' wraps up the whole affair with a great deal of energy and skill." And Paley, although she wanted Rule to provide more insight into David Brown, remarked that Rule "writes of detectives, their procedures and temperaments in a flat, just-the-facts style that has quiet authority. She spins a narrative with the skill of these detectives, who must hold in their minds contradictory statements, observations and assessments and make sense—and a good case—out of them all." In the Toronto *Globe and Mail* Margaret Cannon called *If You Really Loved Me* "a harrowing story of how [investigators] were able to sift through the lies and tears of two teen-aged girls to bring a vicious killer to

justice. Rule has a clear prose style that seldom slips into wordiness. . . . and she has a deft sense of humor."

Rule probes the case of another murderous husband in *Dead by Sunset: Perfect Husband, Perfect Killer?* Brad Cunningham was handsome, charismatic, successful, and violent with women. After the birth of three sons, Cunningham's fourth wife, Cheryl Keeton, a lawyer, left the abusive marriage and would not allow Cunningham to see the boys. Although Cunningham was the prime suspect in Keeton's murder when her badly beaten body was found in 1986, police could not connect him with the crime. Eventually Keeton's law firm hired an attorney so her estate could bring a wrongful death lawsuit against Cunningham. By the time the civil case began, Cunningham was married to his fifth wife. The jury returned a guilty verdict and assessed a huge judgment. The verdict in the civil case compelled the district attorney's office to indict Cunningham two years later—seven years after Keeton's murder; he was convicted in 1994 and sentenced to a minimum of twenty-two years in prison.

In *Bitter Harvest: A Woman's Fury, a Mother's Sacrifice,* Rule probed the case of Dr. Debora Green, a brilliant, well-to-do woman who was apparently devoted to her three children. When her husband left her for another woman, however, Green took her revenge in an unspeakable fashion: she set fire to their home, starting a blaze that resulted in the deaths of two of their three children. Arson investigators even believed that she had deliberately planned the blaze in such a way that would block the children's escape routes. Rule chronicles the unhappy marriage and the other failures that lurked beneath Green's apparent successes. Despite her formidable intellect, she had failed at her medical practice and become addicted to alcohol and drugs, as well as struggling with a serious weight problem. Before murdering her children, she had attempted to poison her husband. *Bitter Harvest* is an "outstanding chronicle of a crime investigation," according to Christine A. Moesch in *Library Journal,* and it is also a "riveting profile of a brilliant mind and empty soul." The reviewer for *Publishers Weekly* stated that *Bitter Harvest* is "another tension-filled, page-turning chronology and analysis of a psychopath in action."

Another apparently successful, respectable person who committed foul crimes is exposed in . . . *And Never Let Her Go: Thomas Capano, the Deadly Seducer.*

Thomas Capano was an attorney with prestigious connections. He came from a respected family in Delaware, was married, and appeared to be leading an enviable life. In reality, he had numerous mistresses. One of them was Anne Marie Fahey, a secretary to the state's governor and a woman seventeen years his junior. This troubled, anorexic woman with a history of being abused became one of Capano's obsessions. Eventually she tried to end their relationship, but soon after that she was reported missing. In the investigation that followed, it was shown that Capano had murdered her and, with the help of his brothers, stuffed her body into a large cooler which he dumped into the Atlantic. He later tried to pin the blame for his crime on one of his other mistresses. . . . *And Never Let Her Go* is a "compassionate portrayal of the victim and a chilling portrayal of her killer," according to a *Booklist* reviewer, who went on to call the book a "true page-turner, a compelling rendering of a crime committed by a deeply troubled, egotistical sociopath." The disturbing story is, "in Rule's capable hands, the raw material for a modern-day tragedy," remarked a *Publishers Weekly* contributor.

Every Breath You Take: A True Story of Obsessive Revenge and Murder concerns the murder of Sheila Bellush, a wife and mother of six children. As a young woman, Bellush met and married Allen Blackthorne, a charming yet violent sociopath, but she left the marriage after enduring years of abuse. Though Blackthorne and Bellush both remarried, Blackthorne developed an obsessive need to punish his ex-wife for divorcing him. Having told her sister that she feared for her life, Bellush was later found murdered, surrounded by her young children. Police quickly arrested the killers-for-hire, and Blackthorne was prosecuted for the murder. "Rule presents the facts of a murder case with all the intrigue, suspense and characterization of an accomplished novelist," according to a *Publishers Weekly* critic. In *Booklist* Brad Hooper stated, "Rule excels at painting psychologically perceptive portraits of all the characters in this stranger-than-fiction but nevertheless real-life drama."

In *Heart Full of Lies: A True Story of Desire and Death*, Rule "meticulously documents the case of a woman who used domestic abuse as an excuse to kill her husband," wrote *New York Times Book Review* critic John D. Thomas. Rule examines the murder of Chris Northon, whose wife, Liysa Northon, claimed that she shot at and accidentally killed her abusive husband to protect herself from attack. Police investigating the crime found Norton's body wrapped up in a sleeping bag, with a well-placed bullet wound to the head. In *Heart Full of Lies* the author informs readers "about Northon and her desire to control the lives of those around her and about Chris, who worked desperately to keep his marriage afloat," observed *Library Journal* critic Danna Bell-Russel. "You can still see the cop in Rule: she interrogates witnesses, tracks down inconsistencies in stories, slogs through victims' letters and e-mails, analyzes forensic evidence, attends trials," wrote *Booklist* contributor Connie Fletcher.

In her interview with *Publishers Weekly,* Rule explained the appeal of her work to many readers. "Whenever I'm signing books, invariably someone comes up to me, usually a young mother trailing a small child or a grandmotherly looking woman, and says, 'Why do I love the books you write? What's wrong with me?' I always ask them what they would do if they found a spider in the bathtub. Nine times out of ten they tell me that they would remove the spider with a tissue and put it outside. I believe that the gentlest among us are the most fascinated by the cruelest. We simply cannot believe that anyone would hurt someone else."

BIOGRAPHICAL AND CRITICAL SOURCES:

BOOKS

Bestsellers 90, Volume 2, Thomson Gale (Detroit, MI), 1990.

Contemporary Popular Writers, St. James Press (Detroit, MI), 1997.

Rule, Ann, *Small Sacrifices: A True Story of Passion and Murder,* New American Library (New York, NY), 1987.

Rule, Ann, *The Stranger beside Me,* Norton (New York, NY), 1980.

PERIODICALS

Booklist, September 1, 1995, Sue-Ellen Beauregard, review of *Dead by Sunset: Perfect Husband, Perfect Killer?,* p. 4; Sue-Ellen Beauregard, review of *Bitter Harvest: A Woman's Fury, a Mother's*

Sacrifice, p. 666; October 1, 1999, review of . . . *And Never Let Her Go: Thomas Capano, the Deadly Seducer,* p. 307; December 15, 2000, David Pitt, review of *Empty Promises and Other True Cases,* p. 766; September 15, 2001, Brad Hooper, review of *Every Breath You Take: A True Story of Obsession, Revenge and Murder,* p. 163; October 1, 2003, Connie Fletcher, review of *Heart Full of Lies: A True Story of Desire and Death,* p. 274.

Chicago Tribune, May 11, 1987.

Globe and Mail (Toronto, Ontario, Canada), May 25, 1991, p. C7.

Good Housekeeping, September, 1991, p. 42.

Houston Chronicle, March 31, 2001, Ann Hodges, review of . . . *And Never Let Her Go* (miniseries), p. 9.

Kirkus Reviews, August 15, 1995, p. 1172; January 1, 1998, review of *Bitter Harvest,* p. 41.

Kliatt, November, 1993, p. 36; November, 1994, p. 38; September, 1998, review of *Bitter Harvest* (audio version), p. 67.

Law Institute Journal, July, 1996, Morgana Keast, review of *A Rose for Her Grave and Other True Cases,* p. 78.

Library Journal, October 1, 1995, Christine A. Moesch, review of *Dead by Sunset,* p. 101; November 1, 1996, Sandra K. Lindheimer, review of *A Fever in the Heart and Other True Cases,* p. 91; February 1, 1998, Christine A. Moesch, review of *Bitter Harvest,* p. 100; March 15, 1998, Denise A. Garofalo, review of *Bitter Harvest* (audio version), p. 109; April 1, 2000, Gordon Blackwell, review of . . . *And Never Let Her Go,* p. 149; October 1, 2000, Michael Rogers, review of *The Stranger beside Me,* p. 153; February 1, 2004, Danna Bell-Russel, review of *Heart Full of Lies* (audiobook), p. 140.

Los Angeles Times, May 7, 1987.

Los Angeles Times Book Review, May 8, 1983; October 30, 1983; April 29, 1984; August 18, 1991, p. 9.

New Law Journal, May 31, 1996, review of *Dead by Sunset,* p. 811.

New Republic, March 28, 1981.

New York Times, February 21, 1984; July 11, 2001, Maureen Dowd, "The Lost Girls," p. A21.

New York Times Book Review, August 24, 1980; June 14, 1987; May 26, 1991, p. 12; January 3, 1993, p. 5; October 22, 1995, Walter Walker, review of *Dead by Sunset,* p. 38; March 15, 1998, Carolyn T. Hughes, review of *Bitter Harvest,* p. 26;

December 21, 2003, John D. Thomas, "Books in Brief: Nonfiction," p. 20.

People, September 14, 1987; November 20, 1995, David Hiltbrand, review of *Dead by Sunset* (television miniseries), p. 17; January 26, 1998, J. D. Reed, review of *Bitter Harvest,* p. 35; January 1, 2000, review of . . . *And Never Let Her Go,* p. 41.

Publishers Weekly, May 3, 1991; October 25, 1993, p. 59; August 8, 1994, p. 418; September 4, 1995, review of *Dead by Sunset,* p. 56; December 22, 1997, review of *Bitter Harvest,* p. 49; August 9, 1999; September 20, 1999, review of . . . *And Never Let Her Go,* p. 66; April 1, 2002, review of *Every Breath You Take* (audiobook review), p. 31.

Saturday Review, August, 1980.

Savvy, August, 1987, p. 13.

Time, June 28, 2004, Andrea Sachs, "The Rule of Law," p. A10.

Virginian Pilot-Ledger Star, March 3, 1998, Charlene Cason, review of *Bitter Harvest,* p. E5.

Washington Post, May 13, 1987; March 12, 1998, Carolyn Banks, review of *Bitter Harvest,* p. C2; November 1, 1999, Jonathan Groner, "In Delaware, a Murder under the Microscope," p. C4.

Washington Post Book World, August 17, 1980; January 24, 1999, review of *The End of the Dream: The Golden Boy Who Never Grew Up and Other True Cases,* p. 12; September 5, 1999, review of . . . *And Never Let Her Go,* p. 5; October 17, 1999, Marie Arana, "Ann Rule: A Career in True Crime," p. 8, Ann Rule, "The Writing Life," p. 8; November 1, 1999, Jonathan Groner, review of . . . *And Never Let Her Go,* p. C4.

Women's Review of Books, June, 1998, Jeffrey Ann Goudie, review of *Bitter Harvest,* p. 26.

Writer, December, 2001, p. 66.

Writer's Digest, December, 1992, p. 27.

ONLINE

Ann Rule's Official Home Page, http://www.annrules.com/ (August 10, 2004).

Celebrity Café, http://www.thecelebritycafe.com/ (October 1, 2001), Dominick A. Miserandino, interview with Ann Rule.

Writers Review, http://www.writersreview.com/ (October 1, 2001), interview with Ann Rule.*

*   *   *

RUSSELL, Russell
See MEADES, Jonathan (Turner)

RYLANT, Cynthia 1954-

PERSONAL: Surname is pronounced "rye-*lunt*"; born June 6, 1954, in Hopewell, VA; daughter of John Tune (an army sergeant) and Leatrel (a nurse; maiden name, Rylant) Smith; twice married and divorced; children: Nathaniel; companion of Dav Pilkey (an author/illustrator). *Education:* Morris Harvey College (now University of Charleston), B.A., 1975; Marshall University, M.A., 1976; Kent State University, M.L.S., 1982. *Politics:* Democrat. *Religion:* "Christian, no denomination."

ADDRESSES: Home—Eugene, OR. *Agent*—Sarah Maizes, William Morris Agency, 151 El Camino Dr., Beverly Hills, CA 90212.

CAREER: Writer. Marshall University, Huntington, WV, part-time English instructor, 1979-80; Akron Public Library, Akron, OH, children's librarian, 1983; University of Akron, Akron, part-time English lecturer, 1983-84; Northeastern Ohio Universities College of Medicine, Rootstown, part-time lecturer, 1991—.

AWARDS, HONORS: When I Was Young in the Mountains was named a *Booklist* reviewer's choice, 1982, Caldecott Honor Book, American Library Association (ALA) notable book, and Reading Rainbow selection, all 1983; American Book Award nomination, 1983, and English-Speaking Union Book-across-the-Sea Ambassador of Honor Award, 1984, both for *When I Was Young in the Mountains; Waiting to Waltz . . . a Childhood* was named an ALA notable book, a *School Library Journal* best book of 1984, a National Council for Social Studies best book, 1984, and a Society of Midland Authors best children's book, 1985; *The Relatives Came* was named a *New York Times* best illustrated book, a *Horn Book* honor book, a Child Study Association of America's children's book of the year, all 1985, and a Caldecott Honor Book, 1986; *A Blue-eyed Daisy* was named a Child Study Association of America's children's book of the year, 1985; *Every Living Thing* was named a *School Library Journal* best book, 1985; *New York Times* best illustrated book for, *The Relatives Came,* 1985; *A Fine White Dust* was named a *Parents' Choice* selection, 1986, a *Horn Book* honor book, and a Newbery Honor Book, all 1987; American Library Association best book for young adults citation, 1988, for *A Kindness;* Ohioana Award, 1990, for *But I'll Be Back Again; Appalachia: The*

Voices of Sleeping Birds was named a *Boston Globe/Horn Book* honor book for nonfiction, 1991, and received the Ohioana Award, 1992; *Henry and Mudge Get the Cold Shivers* was named a Garden State Children's Book award recipient by the Children's Services Section of the New Jersey Library Association, 1992; Parents' Choice Award, 1992, *Boston Globe/Horn Book* award winner, Newbery Medal, Reading Magic Award, and Hungry Mind Award, all 1993, all for *Missing May;* American Library Association best book for young adults citation, for *A Couple of Kooks and other Stories about Love; School Library Journal,* best book of the year citation, for *Children of Christmas.* Books in the "Henry and Mudge" series have received child-selected awards, including the Garden State Children's Book Award, Children's Services Section of the New Jersey Library Association, and the Children's Choice Award, Association of Booksellers for Children.

WRITINGS:

CHILDREN'S BOOKS

When I Was Young in the Mountains, illustrated by Diane Goode, Dutton (New York, NY), 1982.

Miss Maggie, illustrated by Thomas DiGrazia, Dutton (New York, NY), 1983.

This Year's Garden, illustrated by Mary Szilagyi, Bradbury (New York, NY), 1984.

The Relatives Came, illustrated by Stephen Gammell, Bradbury (New York, NY), 1985.

Night in the Country, illustrated by Mary Szilagyi, Bradbury (New York, NY), 1986.

Birthday Presents, illustrated by Sucie Stevenson, Orchard Books (New York, NY), 1987.

All I See, illustrated by Peter Catalanotto, Orchard Books (New York, NY), 1988.

Mr. Griggs' Work, illustrated by Julie Downing, Orchard Books (New York, NY), 1989.

An Angel for Solomon Singer, illustrated by Peter Catalanotto, Orchard Books (New York, NY), 1992.

Best Wishes, photographs by Carlo Ontal, R. C. Owen Publishers (Katonah, NY), 1992.

The Dreamer, illustrated by Barry Moser, Blue Sky Press (New York, NY), 1993.

Dog Heaven, Blue Sky Press (New York, NY), 1995.

The Van Gogh Caé, Harcourt Brace (San Diego, CA), 1995.

Gooseberry Park, illustrated by Arthur Howard, Harcourt Brace (San Diego, CA), 1995.

The Whales, Blue Sky Press (New York, NY), 1996.

The Old Woman Who Named Things, illustrated by Kathryn Brown, Harcourt Brace (San Diego, CA), 1996.

The Bookshop Dog, Blue Sky Press (New York, NY), 1996.

Cat Heaven, Blue Sky Press (New York, NY), 1997.

Silver Packages: An Appalachian Christmas Story, illustrated by Chris K. Soentpiet, Orchard Books (New York, NY), 1997.

An Everyday Book, Simon & Schuster (New York, NY), 1997.

Scarecrow, illustrated by Lauren Stringer, Harcourt Brace (San Diego, CA), 1997.

Bear Day, illustrated by Jennifer Selby, Harcourt Brace (San Diego, CA), 1998.

The Bird House, illustrated by Barry Moser, Blue Sky Press (New York, NY), 1998.

Tulip Sees America, illustrated by Lisa Desimini, Blue Sky Press (New York, NY), 1998.

Bunny Bungalow, illustrated by Nancy Hayashi, Harcourt Brace (San Diego, CA), 1999.

The Cookie-Store Cat, Blue Sky Press (New York, NY), 1999.

The Heavenly Village, Blue Sky Press (New York, NY), 1999.

Let's Go Home: The Wonderful Things about a House, illustrated by Wendy Anderson Halperin, Simon & Schuster (New York, NY), 2000.

In November, illustrated by Jill Kastner, Harcourt Brace (San Diego, CA), 2000.

Thimbleberry Stories, illustrated by Maggie Kneen, Harcourt Brace (San Diego, CA), 2000.

The Wonderful Happens, illustrated by Coco Dowley, Simon & Schuster (New York, NY), 2000.

The Ticky-Tacky Doll, illustrated by Harvey Stevenson, Harcourt Brace (San Diego, CA), 2000.

The Great Gracie Chase, illustrated by Mark Teague, Blue Sky Press (New York, NY), 2001.

Old Town in the Green Groves, HarperCollins (New York, NY), in press.

Good Morning, Sweetie Pie and Other Poems for Little Children, illustrated by Jane Dyer, Simon & Schuster (New York, NY), 2001.

"HENRY AND MUDGE" SERIES, ILLUSTRATED BY SUCIE STEVENSON, UNLESS OTHERWISE NOTED

Henry and Mudge: The First Book of Their Adventures, illustrated by James Stevenson, Bradbury (New York, NY), 1987.

Henry and Mudge in Puddle Trouble: The Second Book of Their Adventures, Bradbury (New York, NY), 1987.

Henry and Mudge in the Green Time: The Third Book of Their Adventures, Bradbury (New York, NY), 1987.

Henry and Mudge under the Yellow Moon: The Fourth Book of Their Adventures, Bradbury (New York, NY), 1987.

Henry and Mudge in the Sparkle Days: The Fifth Book of Their Adventures, Bradbury (New York, NY), 1988.

Henry and Mudge and the Forever Sea: The Sixth Book of Their Adventures, Bradbury (New York, NY), 1989.

Henry and Mudge Get the Cold Shivers: The Seventh Book of Their Adventures, Bradbury (New York, NY), 1989.

Henry and Mudge and the Happy Cat: The Eighth Book of Their Adventures, Bradbury (New York, NY), 1990.

Henry and Mudge and the Bedtime Thumps: The Ninth Book of Their Adventures, Bradbury (New York, NY), 1991.

Henry and Mudge Take the Big Test: The Tenth Book of Their Adventures, Bradbury (New York, NY), 1991.

Henry and Mudge and the Long Weekend: The Eleventh Book of Their Adventures, Bradbury (New York, NY), 1992.

Henry and Mudge and the Wild Wind: The Twelfth Book of Their Adventures, Bradbury (New York, NY), 1993.

Henry and Mudge and the Careful Cousin: The Thirteenth Book of Their Adventures, Bradbury (New York, NY), 1994.

Henry and Mudge and the Best Day of All: The Fourteenth Book of Their Adventures, Bradbury (New York, NY), 1995.

Henry and Mudge in the Family Trees: The Fifteenth Book of Their Adventures, Simon & Schuster (New York, NY), 1997.

Henry and Mudge and the Sneaky Crackers: The Sixteenth Book of Their Adventures, Simon & Schuster (New York, NY), 1998.

Henry and Mudge and the Starry Night: The Seventeenth Book of Their Adventures, Simon & Schuster (New York, NY), 1998.

Henry and Mudge and Annie's Good Move: The Eighteenth Book of Their Adventures, Simon & Schuster (New York, NY), 1998.

Henry and Mudge and the Snowman Plan: The Nineteenth Book of Their Adventures, Simon & Schuster (New York, NY), 1999.

Henry and Mudge and the Funny Lunch: The Twentieth Book of Their Adventures, Simon & Schuster (New York, NY), 1999.

Henry and Mudge and the Tall Tree House: The Twenty-first Book of Their Adventures, illustrated by Carolyn Bracken, Simon & Schuster (New York, NY), 1999.

Henry and Mudge and Mrs. Hopper's House: The Twenty-second Book of Their Adventures, illustrated by Carolyn Bracken, Simon & Schuster (New York, NY), 1999.

Henry and Mudge and the Great Grandpas: The Twenty-third Book of Their Adventures, Simon & Schuster (New York, NY), 1999.

Henry and Mudge and a Very Special Merry Christmas: The Twenty-fourth Book of Their Adventures, Simon & Schuster (New York, NY), 1999.

Henry and Mudge and the Snowman Plan: The Twenty-fifth Book of Their Adventures, Simon & Schuster (New York, NY), 1999.

Henry and Mudge and the Wild Goose Chase: The Twenty-sixth Book of Their Adventures, illustrated by Carolyn Bracken, Simon & Schuster (New York, NY), 1999.

Henry and Mudge and the Big Sleepover: The Twenty-seventh Book of Their Adventures, Simon & Schuster (New York, NY), 1999.

Henry and Mudge and the Tumbling Trip: The Twenty-eighth Book of Their Adventures, Simon & Schuster (New York, NY), 1999.

Henry and Mudge and Annie's Perfect Pet: The Twenty-ninth Book of Their Adventures, Simon & Schuster (New York, NY), 2000.

Puppy Mudge Takes a Bath, illustrated by Isidre Mones, Simon & Schuster (New York, NY), 2002.

Puppy Mudge Has a Snack, illustrated by Isidre Mones Simon & Schuster (New York, NY), 2003.

"MR. PUTTER AND TABBY" SERIES

Mr. Putter and Tabby Walk the Dog, illustrated by Arthur Howard, Harcourt Brace (San Diego, CA), 1994.

Mr. Putter and Tabby Bake the Cake, illustrated by Arthur Howard, Harcourt Brace (San Diego, CA), 1994.

Mr. Putter and Tabby Pour the Tea, illustrated by Arthur Howard, Harcourt Brace (San Diego, CA), 1994.

Mr. Putter and Tabby Pick the Pears, illustrated by Arthur Howard, Harcourt Brace (San Diego, CA), 1995.

Mr. Putter and Tabby Row the Boat, illustrated by Arthur Howard, Harcourt Brace (San Diego, CA), 1997.

Mr. Putter and Tabby Fly the Plane, illustrated by Arthur Howard, Harcourt Brace (San Diego, CA), 1997.

Mr. Putter & Tabby Take the Train, illustrated by Arthur Howard, Harcourt Brace (San Diego, CA), 1998.

Mr. Putter & Tabby Toot the Horn, illustrated by Arthur Howard, Harcourt Brace (San Diego, CA), 1998.

Mr. Putter & Tabby Paint the Porch, illustrated by Arthur Howard, Harcourt Brace (San Diego, CA), 2000.

Mr. Putter & Tabby Feed the Fish, illustrated by Arthur Howard, Harcourt Brace (San Diego, CA), 2001.

Mr. Putter & Tabby Catch the Cold, illustrated by Arthur Howard, Harcourt Brace (San Diego, CA), 2002.

Mr. Putter & Tabby Stir the Soup, illustrated by Arthur Howard, Harcourt Brace (San Diego, CA), 2003.

Mr. Putter & Tabby Write the Book, illustrated by Arthur Howard, Harcourt Brace (San Diego, CA), 2004.

"EVERYDAY BOOKS" SERIES

The Everyday Garden, Bradbury (New York), 1993.

The Everyday Town, Bradbury (New York, NY), 1993.

The Everyday Children, Bradbury (New York, NY), 1993.

The Everyday Pets, Bradbury (New York, NY), 1993.

The Everyday House, Bradbury (New York, NY), 1993.

"HIGH-RISE PRIVATE EYES" SERIES

The Case of the Missing Monkey, illustrated by G. Brian Karas, Greenwillow Books (New York, NY), 2000.

The Case of the Climbing Cat, illustrated by G. Brian Karas, Greenwillow Books (New York, NY), 2000.

The Case of the Puzzling Possum, illustrated by G. Brian Karas, Greenwillow Books (New York, NY), 2001.

The Case of the Troublesome Turtle, illustrated by G. Brian Karas, Greenwillow Books (New York, NY), 2001.

The Case of the Sleepy Sloth, illustrated by G. Brian Karas, Greenwillow Books (New York, NY), 2002.

The Case of the Fidgety Fox, illustrated by G. Brian Karas, Greenwillow Books (New York, NY), 2003.

The Case of the Baffled Bear, illustrated by G. Brian Karas, Greenwill Books (New York, NY), 2004.

"POPPLETON" SERIES

Poppleton, illustrated by Mark Teague, Blue Sky Press (New York, NY), 1997.

Poppleton and Friends, illustrated by Mark Teague, Blue Sky Press (New York, NY), 1997.

Poppleton Everyday, illustrated by Mark Teague, Blue Sky Press (New York, NY), 1998.

Poppleton Forever, illustrated by Mark Teague, Blue Sky Press (New York, NY), 1998.

Poppleton in Fall, illustrated by Mark Teague, Blue Sky Press (New York, NY), 1999.

Poppleton in Spring, illustrated by Mark Teague, Scholastic (New York, NY), 1999.

Poppleton Has Fun, illustrated by Mark Teague, Blue Sky Press (New York, NY), 2000.

Poppleton in Winter, illustrated by Mark Teague, Blue Sky Press (New York, NY), 2001.

"COBBLE STREET COUSINS" SERIES

In Aunt Lucy's Kitchen, illustrated by Wendy Anderson Halperin, Simon & Schuster (New York, NY), 1998.

A Little Shopping, illustrated by Wendy Anderson Halperin, Simon & Schuster (New York, NY), 1998.

Some Good News, illustrated by Wendy Anderson Halperin, Simon & Schuster (New York, NY), 1999.

Special Gifts, illustrated by Wendy Anderson Halperin, Simon & Schuster (New York, NY), 1999.

Summer Party, illustrated by Wendy Anderson Halperin, Simon & Schuster (New York, NY), 2001.

Wedding Flowers, illustrated by Wendy Anderson Halperin, Simon & Schuster (New York, NY), 2002.

"LITTLE WHISTLE" SERIES

Little Whistle's Dinner Party, illustrated by Tim Bowers, Harcourt Brace (San Diego, CA), 2001.

Little Whistle, illustrated by Tim Bowers, Harcourt Brace (San Diego, CA), 2001.

Little Whistle's Medicine, illustrated by Tim Bowers, Harcourt Brace (San Diego, CA), 2002.

Little Whistle's Christmas, illustrated by Tim Bowers, Harcourt Brace (San Diego, CA), 2003.

"BLUE HILL MEADOWS" SERIES

The Blue Hill Meadows and the Much-loved Dog, illustrated by Ellen Beier, Harcourt Brace (San Diego, CA), 1997.

The Blue Hill Meadows, illustrated by Ellen Beier, Harcourt Brace (San Diego, CA), 1997.

"LIGHTHOUSE FAMILY" SERIES

The Storm, illustrated by Preston McDaniels, Simon & Schuster (New York, NY), 2002.

The Whale, illustrated by Preston McDaniels, Simon & Schuster (New York, NY), 2003.

The Eagle, illustrated by Preston McDaniels, Simon & Schuster (New York, NY), 2004.

YOUNG ADULT FICTION

A Blue-eyed Daisy (novel), Bradbury (New York, NY), 1985, published as *Some Year for Ellie,* illustrated by Kate Rogers, Viking Kestrel (New York, NY), 1986.

Every Living Thing (stories), Bradbury (New York, NY), 1985.

A Fine White Dust (novel), Bradbury (New York, NY), 1986.

Children of Christmas: Stories for the Season, illustrated by S. D. Schindler, Orchard Books (New York, NY), 1987, published as *Silver Packages and Other Stories,* 1987.

A Kindness (novel), Orchard Books (New York, NY), 1989.

A Couple of Kooks, And Other Stories about Love, Orchard Books (New York, NY), 1990.

Missing May, Orchard Books (New York, NY), 1992.

I Had Seen Castles, Harcourt Brace (San Diego, CA), 1993.
The Islander (novel), DK Ink (New York, NY), 1998.

YOUNG ADULT POETRY

Waiting to Waltz . . . a Childhood (poetry), illustrated by Stephen Gammell, Bradbury (New York, NY), 1984.
Soda Jerk (poetry), illustrated by Peter Catalanotto, Orchard Books (New York, NY), 1990.
Something Permanent, photographs by Walker Evans, Harcourt Brace (San Diego, CA), 1994.

YOUNG ADULT NONFICTION

But I'll Be Back Again: An Album (autobiography), Orchard Books (New York, NY), 1989.
Appalachia: The Voices of Sleeping Birds, illustrated by Barry Moser, Harcourt Brace (San Diego, CA), 1991.
Margaret, Frank, and Andy: Three Writers' Stories, Harcourt Brace (San Diego, CA), 1996.
Bless Us All: A Child's Yearbook of Blessings, Simon & Schuster (New York, NY), 1998.
Give Me Grace: A Child's Daybook of Prayers, Simon & Schuster (New York, NY), 1999.

OTHER

Christmas in the Country, illustrated by Diane Goode, Blue Sky Press (New York, NY), 2002.
Old Town in the Green Groves: The Lost Little House Years, illustrated by Jim LaMarche, HarperCollins (New York, NY), 2002.
God Went to Beauty School, HarperCollins (New York, NY), 2003.
Moonlight: The Halloween Cat, HarperCollins (New York, NY), 2003.
Long Night Moon, illustrated by Mark Siegel, Simon & Schuster (New York, NY), 2004.
If You'll Be My Valentine, HarperCollins (New York, NY), 2005.

ADAPTATIONS: *When I Was Young in the Mountains,* 1983, *This Year's Garden,* 1983, and *The Relatives Came,* 1986, were adapted as filmstrips by Random House. Many of her works are available on audiocassette. Several of her books are available on film through American School Publishers. Rylant is the subject of the video *Meet the Author: Cynthia Rylant.*

SIDELIGHTS: Cynthia Rylant is an award-winning children's and young adult author whose work includes picture books, poetry, short stories, and novels. With a writing style that has been described as unadorned, clear, and lyrical, the author presents young people's experiences with sensitivity and perceptiveness, branding her protagonists' concerns as legitimate and equally important as those of adults. Rylant's characters tend to be contemplative and set apart from their peers by their situations. Explaining her leaning toward such subjects, the author remarked in *Horn Book,* "I get a lot of personal gratification thinking of those people who don't get any attention in the world and making them really valuable in my fiction—making them absolutely shine with their beauty." She continued, "I don't ever quite write really happy novels; I don't want to deal with the people who have what they want. I want to deal with people who don't have what they want, to show their lives too."

Critics suggest that Rylant appears sympathetic to her characters' plights because she also faced uncommon hardships as a child. In her autobiography *But I'll Be Back Again: An Album,* the author stated, "They say that to be a writer you must first have an unhappy childhood. I don't know if unhappiness is necessary, but I think maybe some children who have suffered a loss too great for words grow up into writers who are always trying to find those words, trying to find a meaning for the way they have lived."

Rylant's parents had a stormy marriage and separated when the author was four years old; she admits that she naively blamed herself for their troubles. The author and her mother moved to West Virginia where Rylant was left in her grandparents' care while her mother earned a nursing degree. Her father wrote occasionally when she first moved, but the letters eventually stopped. Because none of her relatives spoke about her father, she was afraid to ask questions about him. After years of silence, however, he contacted Rylant. The author dreamed of their reunion, but before it could take place her father, a Korean War veteran who suffered from hepatitis and alcoholism, succumbed to these diseases. He died when she was thirteen. In *But*

I'll Be Back Again, the author stated, "I did not have a chance to know him or to say goodbye to him, and that is all the loss I needed to become a writer."

Unhappiness, however, did not dominate the author's childhood. Rylant enjoyed the rustic West Virginia environment while living with her grandparents in a mountain town where many houses had neither electricity nor running water. The lack of amenities did not bother young Rylant; she felt secure surrounded by equally poor yet friendly, church-going neighbors. When the author was eight years old, she and her mother moved to another West Virginia town named Beaver. Judging in retrospect for *CA,* she called this new location "without a doubt a small, sparkling universe that gave me a lifetime's worth of material for my writing."

As an adolescent in this rural setting, though, Rylant began to recognize and become envious of the fact that other people had more material possessions than she and her mother did. In addition, Beaver—which had at first offered adventure—now appeared backward and dull compared to larger cities. Reflecting in her autobiography, *But I'll Be Back Again,* Rylant remarked, "As long as I stayed in Beaver, I felt I was somebody important. . . . But as soon as I left town to go anywhere else, my sense of being somebody special evaporated into nothing and I became dull and ugly and poor." She continued, "I wanted to be someone else, and that turned out to be the worst curse and the best gift of my life. I would finish out my childhood forgetting who I really was and what I really thought, and I would listen to other people and repeat their ideas instead of finding my own. That was the curse. The gift was that I would be willing to try to write books when I grew up."

The first book Rylant produced was *When I Was Young in the Mountains,* a picture book reminiscing about life in West Virginia's Appalachian Mountains which was praised for its simple, yet evocative text and was named a Caldecott honor book. With subsequent picture books, including *The Relatives Came, This Year's Garden,* and her "Henry and Mudge" series, Rylant has received considerable recognition and awards. The author told *CA:* "I like writing picture books because that medium gives me a chance to capture in a brief space what I consider life's profound experiences—grandmother crying at a swimming hole baptism, a family planting a garden together, relatives

coming for a visit. There is a poignancy and beauty in these events, and I don't want to write adult poetry about them because then I'll have to layer it with some adult disillusionment."

Rylant continued her use of poetry in books for older readers. In *Waiting to Waltz . . . a Childhood,* the author offers an autobiographical collection of thirty free-verse poems which record her coming-of-age. These events include embarrassment because her mother was too busy to join school committees and reckoning with the deaths of both an absent father and a beloved pet. One passage documents the surprising transformation from child to young adult: "Forgetting when / I was last time / a child. / Never knowing / when it / ended." *Waiting to Waltz* also weaves in events and symbols of the 1960s to produce what critics deemed a vivid recreation of the era.

Another book of verse, *Soda Jerk,* combines illustrations by Peter Catalanotto with twenty-eight related poems by Rylant to present the thoughts of a nameless protagonist who works as an attendant at a soda fountain. The title of this work is the slang term for the job. The jerk, as the narrator calls himself, offers commentary on issues ranging from his customers' lives to his fears about the future. Valerie Sayers, writing in the *New York Times Book Review,* remarked that with her short poems, "Rylant manages to shape enough action to fill several short stories and to create a protagonist who is not only likable but charming and engaging." *Soda Jerk,* the critic concluded, "is full of respect for a boy's powers of observation, and its images, both written and painted, are striking."

In 1985 Rylant published her first novel, *A Blue-eyed Daisy.* Set in Appalachia, the episodic work is told by eleven-year-old Ellie Farley during the course of a year. The youngest of five daughters, Ellie contends with her apprehensions and conflicting emotions about growing up. For example, she overcomes her fear of contracting epilepsy after witnessing a classmate's seizure; copes with her unemployed, alcoholic father's imperfections and the possibility of his death after an accident; and battles the nervous anticipation of her first co-ed party. A reviewer for *Publishers Weekly* proclaimed *A Blue-eyed Daisy* an "exquisite novel, written with love."

Rylant's novel, *A Fine White Dust,* was named a Newbery Honor Book. In this work, a deeply religious seventh-grader named Pete believes he has found a human incarnation of God in a roving preacher named Carson. When attending a revival meeting, Pete is mesmerized by Carson's charismatic presence and, after being "saved," agrees to become his disciple. Despite his hesitance to leave his family and friends, Pete reasons that such a sacrifice is needed to fully embrace the holy life. Pete's mission is never fulfilled, however, because the preacher unexpectedly runs off with a young woman. Although he initially feels betrayed, Pete develops a more mature understanding of love and faith. *Wilson Library Bulletin* contributor Frances Bradburn praised, "The careful crafting of delicate subjects is . . . beautifully illustrated" in *A Fine White Dust.*

Another of Rylant's works, *A Couple of Kooks, and Other Stories about Love,* offers various examples of the emotion. In "A Crush," a mentally handicapped man secretly leaves flowers for a female hardware-store worker. An older woman finds love with a man ten years her junior in "Clematis." And in the title story, two teenagers use the nine months of the girl's pregnancy to try to instill their hopes, love, and food preferences in the baby that they will be forced to give up for adoption. Critics commended Rylant for her honest, compassionate portrayal of her subjects' feelings.

Rylant has authored a number of series for children and young adults, including the "Henry and Mudge," "Little Whistle," "Poppleton," "High-Rise Private Eyes," "Mr. Putter and Tabby," "The Lighthouse Family," and "Everyday" books. Each series features sensitive characters, who have special relationships with a friend, a pet, or a family member. This theme of warmth, love, and comfort runs throughout many of Rylant's series and individual books. In *Let's Go Home: The Wonderful Things about a House,* Rylant takes the reader on a tour throughout a house, vividly describing each room. "In a quiet, warm mood, the narrative delineates the gestures and activities of a multigenerational household," noted Blair Christolon in *School Library Journal.* In the same publication, Lauralyn Persson commended another of Rylant's books, *Good Morning, Sweetie Pie and other Poems for Little Children,* for its "fluid, relaxed, and unabashedly sweet" poems. Persson believed that children who read the poems will be "surrounded by love, security, and attention." Also in *School Library Journal,* reviewer Beth Tegart remarked that *The Great Gracie Chase: Stop That Dog!* is filled with "charm,

humor, and joy," and Barbara Buckley noted that Rylant's *Thimbleberry Stories* are "sweet and contain messages on the meaning of friendship."

Some of Rylant's books also deal with spirituality. Her novel *The Heavenly Village* is a series of vignettes told by people who aren't quite ready to enter Heaven. They stop off on their way to finish telling their stories. Each chapter begins with a quotation from the Bible. A *Publishers Weekly* reviewer noted, "Rylant's precise language and deeply comforting vision are her strong suits." *God Went to Beauty School* is a book of poems that focus on the question, "What if God was one of us?" Throughout the poems, God does things that normal, everyday people do. He goes to beauty school because He likes hands and wants to learn how to do nails. He gets arrested, climbs a mountain, and goes to the doctor. John Green noted in *Booklist* that the poems "play on Christian tradition without disrespect, ultimately celebrating God's kindness and love." Jennifer M. Brabander wrote in *Horn Book,* "In these compelling poems, Rylant puts to exceptionally good use her folksy storytelling skills, her spare and direct writing style, and her ability to sincerely extol life's simple, everyday pleasure and painful losses."

With her works for children and young adults, Rylant has earned a loyal readership as well as positive critical response. Yet, when facing the future of her career, Rylant admits to insecurities. In *Horn Book* she explained, "I get afraid of what I am going to do for the next fifty years. Surely, I think to myself, I can't keep this up. I am just going to run dry—or worse, get boring and predictable." Nonetheless, the author does feel a sense of accomplishment beyond the recognition and awards her works have received. In *Horn Book* Rylant confided that writing "has given me a sense of self-worth that I didn't have my whole childhood. I am really proud of that. The [books] . . . have carried me through some troubled times and have made me feel that I am worthy of having a place on this earth."

BIOGRAPHICAL AND CRITICAL SOURCES:

BOOKS

Authors and Artists for Young Adults, Volume 45, Thomson Gale (Detroit, MI), 2002.
Children's Literature Review, Volume 15, Thomson Gale (Detroit, MI), 1988.

Continuum Encyclopedia of Children's Literature, Continuum (New York, NY), 2001.

Rylant, Cynthia, *But I'll Be Back Again: An Album,* Orchard Books (New York, NY), 1989.

Rylant, Cynthia, *Waiting to Waltz . . . a Childhood,* Bradbury (New York, NY), 1984.

St. James Guide to Children's Writers, 5th edition, St. James Press (Detroit, MI), 1999.

St. James Guide to Young Adult Writers, 2nd edition, St. James Press (Detroit, MI), 1999.

Something about the Author Autobiography Series, Volume 13, Thomson Gale (Detroit, MI), 1991.

Writers for Young Adults, Supplement 1, Scribner (New York, NY), 2000.

PERIODICALS

Bloomsbury Review, July, 1992, p. 22.

Book, September, 1999, review of *The Heavenly Village,* p. 92.

Booklist, February 15, 1992, p. 1105; January 1, 1997, p. 854; February 1, 1997, p. 950; April 1, 1997, p. 1334; April 15, 1997, p. 1437; August, 1997, pp. 1910-11; September 1, 1997, pp. 126, 135, 140-41; January 1, 1999, Linda Perkins, review of *In Aunt Lucy's Kitchen,* p. 879, review of *A Little Shopping,* p. 879; April 15, 1999, review of *Bunny Bungalow,* p. 1537; May 15, 1999, review of *The Cookie-Store Cat,* p. 1703; June 1, 1999, review of *Special Gifts,* p. 1832, review of *Some Good News,* p. 1832; October 1, 1999, review of *Henry and Mudge and the Snowman Plan,* p. 366, review of *Give Me Grace,* p. 375; October 15, 1999, review of *Poppleton in Fall,* p. 456; November 1, 1999, review of *The Van Gogh Café,* p. 549; December 1, 1999, review of *Henry and Mudge and Annie's Perfect Pet,* p. 716, review of *The Heavenly Village,* p. 706; April 15, 2000, Stephanie Zvirin, review of *Mr. Putter and Tabby Paint the Porch,* p. 1542; October 1, 2000, Carolyn Phelan, review of *The Case of the Climbing Cat,* p. 352; November, 15, 2000, Ellen Mandel, review of *Poppleton Has Fun,* p. 650; December 1, 2003, review of *The Case of the Puzzling Possum,* p. 708; February 15, 2001, review of *Little Whistle,* p. 1142, review of *The Great Gracie Chase,* p. 1142; May 1, 2001, review of *Mr. Putter and Tabby Feed the Fish,* p. 1684; May 15, 2001, review of *The Case of the Troublesome Turtle,* p. 1753; May, 2001, review of *The Case of the*

Climbing Cat, p. 826; June 1, 2001, review of *Summer Party,* p. 1884; September 15, 2001, review of *Good Morning, Sweetie Pie and other Poems for Little Children,* p. 229; October 1, 2001, review of *Little Whistle's Dinner Party,* p. 326; February 15, 2002, review of *Wedding Flowers,* p. 1015; March 1, 2002, review of *Little Whistle's Medicine,* p. 1144; April 15, 2002, review of *Let's Go Home: The Wonderful Things about a House,* p. 1399; September 1, 2002, Ilene Cooper, review of *The Ticky-Tacky Doll,* p. 137; November 1, 2002, Ilene Cooper, review of *Mr. Putter and Tabby Catch the Cold,* p. 509; November 15, 2002, Karin Snelson, review of *The Lighthouse Family: The Storm,* p. 612; January 1, 2003, Connie Fletcher, review of *The Case of the Sleepy Sloth,* p. 893; March 15, 2003, Gillian Engberg, review of *Henry and Mudge and Mrs. Hopper's House,* p. 1333; July, 2003, Gillian Engberg, review of *Henry and Mudge and the Snowman Plan,* p. 1900, Stephanie Zvirin, review of *Mr. Putter and Tabby Stir the Soup,* p. 1903; August, 2003, John Green, review of *God Went to Beauty School,* p. 1983; September 1, 2003, Kay Weisman, review of *The Lighthouse Family: The Whale,* p. 121; September 15, 2003, Karin Snelson, review of *Moonlight: The Halloween Cat,* p. 248; October 1, 2003, Carolyn Phelan, review of *Herny and Mudge and the Wild Goose Chase,* p. 329.

Bulletin of the Center for Children's Books, January, 1999, review of *In Aunt Lucy's Kitchen,* p. 181, review of *A Little Shopping,* p. 181; February, 1999, review of *Bless Us All,* p. 216; March, 2001, review of *The Great Gracie Chase,* p. 278; May, 2001, review of *Little Whistle,* p. 351; December, 2001, review of *Poppleton in Winter,* p. 152.

Children's Book and Play Review, January, 2001, review of *Mr. Putter and Tabby Paint the Porch,* p. 26; March, 2001, review of *In November,* p. 20; May, 2001, review of *The Old Woman Who Named Things,* p. 25.

Children's Book Review Service, January, 1999, review of *Bear Day,* p. 52; May, 1999, review of *Bunny Bungalow,* p. 112; July, 1999, review of *The Cookie-Store Cat,* p. 149.

Children's Bookwatch, February, 1999, review of *The Islander,* p. 4; March, 1999, review of *A Little Shopping,* p. 1, review of *In Aunt Lucy's Kitchen,* p. 1, review of *Poppleton in Spring,* p. 4, review of *The Cookie-Store Cat,* p. 4, review of *Bunny Bungalow,* p. 3; April, 2001, review of *Little Whistle,* p. 4; June, 2001, review of *The*

Great Gracie Chase, p. 4; September, 2001, review of *Little Whistle's Dinner Party,* p. 6; January, 2002, review of *Poppleton in Winter,* p. 5.

Detroit Free Press, July 1, 2001, review of *The Great Gracie Chase,* p. 5E; March 31, 2002, review of *Good Morning, Sweetie Pie and other Poems for Little Children,* p. 5E.

Early Childhood Education Journal, summer, 2001, review of *The Old Woman Who Named Things,* p. 237.

Horn Book, November-December, 1987, pp. 695-703; March, 2001, review of *The Case of the Puzzling Possum,* p. 212; May, 2001, review of *The Case of the Troublesome Turtle,* p. 337; July-August, 2003, Jennifer M. Brabander, review of *God Went to Beauty School,* p. 474.

Instructor, May, 1999, review of *Henry and Mudge and the Happy Cat,* p. 12.

Journal of Adolescent and Adult Literacy, April, 1999, review of *The Islander,* p. 592.

Kirkus Reviews, January 15, 1992, p. 120; April 1, 1999, review of *Bunny Bungalow,* p. 537; May 1, 1999, review of *The Cookie-Store Cat,* p. 726; July 15, 1999, review of *Poppleton in Fall,* p. 1139; February 1, 2001, review of *The Great Gracie Chase,* p. 188; February 15, 2001, review of *The Case of the Puzzling Possum,* p. 264; September 1, 2001, review of *Poppleton in Winter,* p. 1300, review of *Little Whistle's Dinner Party,* p. 1300; September 15, 2001, review of *Good Morning, Sweetie Pie and other Poems for Little Children,* p. 1367; January 15, 2002, review of *Little Whistle's Medicine,* p. 108; April 15, 2002, review of *Let's Go Home,* p. 577; March 1, 2003, review of *The Case of the Fidgety Fox,* p. 397; June 15, 2003, review of *God Went to Beauty School,* p. 864; July 1, 2003, review of *Moonlight: The Halloween Cat,* p. 914.

Kliatt, July, 1999, review of *Missing May,* p. 4; September, 1999, review of *The Van Gogh Café,* p. 60, review of *The Heavenly Village,* p. 12.

New York Times Book Review, November 10, 1985, p. 37; June 30, 1990, p. 24; January 17, 1999, review of *A Little Shopping,* p. 26; August 12, 2001, review of *Little Whistle,* p. 25.

Publishers Weekly, March 8, 1985, p. 91; February 3, 1992, p. 82; June 16, 1997, pp. 58, 59-60; July 21, 1997, pp. 178-179; March 15, 1999, review of *Bunny Bungalow,* p. 56; May 24, 1999, review of *The Cookie-Store Cat,* p. 77; June 7, 1999, review of *Special Gifts,* p. 85, review of *Some Good News,* p. 85; October 25, 1999, review of *The Heavenly Village,* p. 74, review of *Give Me Grace,* p. 73; November 29, 1999, review of *The Islander,* p. 73; April 17, 2000, review of *Thimbleberry Stories,* p. 81; August 7, 2000, review of *The Case of the Missing Monkey,* p. 95; April 2, 2001, review of *Little Whistle,* p. 63; April 30, 2001, review of *Scarecrow,* p. 80; June 18, 2001, review of *The Blue Hill Meadows,* p. 83, review of *A Blue-eyed Daisy,* p. 83; September 3, 2001, review of *Good Morning, Sweetie Pie and other Poems for Little Children,* p. 86; December 24, 2001, review of *Little Whistle's Dinner Party,* p. 67, review of *Bunny Bungalow,* p. 67; March 18, 2002, review of *Little Whistle's Medicine,* p. 105; April 1, 2002, review of *The Heavenly Village,* p. 86; April 15, 2002, review of *Wedding Flowers,* p. 66; April 22, 2002, review of *Let's Go Home,* p. 68; April 29, 2002, review of *When I Was Young in the Mountains,* p. 73; June 9, 2003, review of *God Went to Beauty School,* p. 53; August 4, 2003, review of *Moonlight: The Halloween Cat,* p. 77; September 29, 2003, review of *Little Whistle,* p. 67.

Reading Teacher, September, 1999, review of *Poppleton Forever,* p. 84; November, 2001, review of *In November,* p. 307.

School Library Journal, March, 1992, p. 241; March, 1997, p. 165; April, 1997, p. 116; October, 1997, p. 43; September, 1997, p. 193; January, 1999, review of *Bear Day,* p. 101; February, 1999, review of *In Aunt Lucy's Kitchen,* p. 88, review of *Henry and Mudge under the Yellow Moon,* p. 69, review of *A Little Shopping,* p. 88; March, 1999, review of *Poppleton in Spring,* p. 184; April, 1999, review of *The Cookie-Store Cat,* p. 108; June, 1999, review of *Special Gifts,* p. 106, review of *Some Good News,* p. 106, review of *Henry and Mudge in the Sparkle Days,* p. 77, review of *Bunny Bungalow,* p. 106; July, 1999, review of *Henry and Mudge in the Green Time,* p. 53; September, 1999, review of *Poppleton in Fall,* p. 203; December, 1999, review of *Give Me Grace,* p. 125; March, 2000, Selene S. Vasquez, review of *Henry and Mudge and the Snowman Plan,* p. 212, Elaine Fort Weischedel, review of *The Heavenly Village,* p. 242; April, 2000, Diane Janoff, review of *Henry and Mudge and Annie's Perfect Pet,* p. 113; May, 2000, Barbara Buckley, review of *Thimbleberry Stories,* p. 154; August, 2000, Blair Christolson, review of *The Case of the Climbing Cat,* p. 164; April, 2001, Karen Land, review of *The Case of the Puzzling Possum,* p. 121, Beth

Tegart, review of *The Great Gracie Chase!*, p. 121; May, 2001, Anne Knickerbocker, review of *Mr. Putter and Tabby Feed the Fish*, p. 134, review of *Summer Party*, p. 134, review of *Little Whistle*, p. 134; July, 2001, review of *The Case of the Troublesome Turtle*, p. 88; October, 2001, Sharon McNeil, review of *Little Whistle's Dinner Party*, p. 130, review of *Poppleton in Winter*, p. 130; December, 2001, Lauralyn Persson, review of *Good Morning, Sweetie Pie and Other Poems for Little Children*, p. 128; April, 2002, Heather E. Miller, review of *Little Whistle's Medicine*, p. 122, review of *Old Town in the Green Groves*, p. 156; June, 2002, Blair Christolon, review of *Let's Go Home*, p. 124; February, 2003, Lee Bock, review of *The Old Woman Who Named Things*, p. 97, Lisa Smith, review of *Henry and Mudge and the Tall Tree House*, p. 120; March, 2003, Mary Burkey, audio book review of *Henry and Mudge and the Starry Night*, p. 90; April, 2003, Marilyn Taniguchi, review of *Puppy Mudge Takes a Bath*, p. 137; May, 2003, Sherrie Davidson, audio book review of *Henry and Mudge and Annie's Good Move*, p. 76, Doris Losey, review of *The Case of the Fidgety Fox*, p. 129; July, 2003, Maura Smith, audio book review of *Henry and Mudge and the Snowman Plan*, p. 69; September, 2003, Sherrie Davidson, audio book review of *The Case of the Climbing Cat*, p. 72, Mercedes Smith, audio book review of *The Case of the Missing Monkey*, p. 73,

Karen Scott, audio book review of *The Case of the Puzzling Possum*, p. 73, James K. Irwin, review of *Moonlight: The Halloween Cat*, p. 190.

Social Studies, January, 2001, review of *Mr. Griggs' Work*, p. 39.

Teacher Librarian, March, 1999, review of *A Little Shopping*, p. 40; October, 1999, review of *The Cookie-Store Cat*, p. 57.

Tribune Books (Chicago, IL), March 25, 2001, review of *Mr. Putter and Tabby Feed the Fish*, p. 5.

Voice of Youth Advocates, April, 1992, p. 34.

Washington Post, December 24, 1990.

ONLINE

About.com, http://childrensbooks.about.com/ (June 2, 2003), "Spotlight on Cynthia Rylant."

Cynthia Rylant Web site, http://www.cynthiarylant.com/ (June 2, 2003).

Houghton Mifflin Web site, http://www.eduplace.com/kids/ (November 17, 2003), "Meet the Author: Cynthia Rylant."

Newport This Week Online, http://www.newportthisweek.com/news/ (June 2, 2003), review of *Poppleton*.

Pittsburgh Post-Gazette Online, http://www.postgazette.com/ (November 17, 2003), Lisa Dennis, "Cynthia Rylant's 60-plus Books Conquer a World of Subjects."*

S

SARRANTONIO, Al 1952-

PERSONAL: Born May 25, 1952, in Queens, NY; married; children: two sons. *Education:* Manhattan College, B.A., 1974.

ADDRESSES: Home—Putnam Valley, NY. *Agent*—Sharon Jarvis and Co., 260 Willard Ave., Staten Island, NY 10314.

CAREER: Doubleday and Co., Inc., New York City, editorial assistant, 1975-82; writer, 1982—.

MEMBER: Science Fiction Writers of America, Horror Writers of America.

WRITINGS:

NOVELS

The Worms, Doubleday (Garden City, NY), 1985.
Totentanz, Tor Books (New York City), 1985.
Campbell Wood, Doubleday (Garden City, NY), 1986.
The Boy with Penny Eyes, Tor Books (New York, NY), 1987.
Cold Night, Tor Books (New York, NY), 1987.
Moonbane, Bantam (New York, NY), 1989.
October, Bantam (New York, NY), 1990.
House Haunted, Bantam (New York, NY), 1991.
Skeletons, Bantam (New York, NY), 1992.
Summer Cool, Walker (New York, NY), 1993.
Kitt Peak, M. Evans (New York, NY), 1993.

Exile, New American Library (New York, NY), 1996.
Journey, New American Library (New York, NY), 1997.
Personal Agendas, Dell (New York, NY), 1997.
Return, New American Library (New York, NY), 1998.
Orangefield, Cemetery Dance (Forest Hill, MD), 2002.

EDITOR

The Fireside Treasury of Great Humor, Simon & Schuster (New York, NY), 1987.
The Fireside Treasury of New Humor, Simon & Schuster (New York, NY), 1989.
The National Lampoon Treasury of Humor, Simon & Schuster (New York, NY), 1991.
(With Martin H. Greenberg) *100 Hair-Raising Little Horror Stories,* Barnes & Noble (New York, NY), 1993.
999: New Stories of Horror and Suspense, Avon Books (New York, NY), 1999.
Redshift: Extreme Visions of Speculative Fiction, Roc (New York, NY), 2001.
Flights: Extreme Visions of Fantasy, Roc (New York, NY), 2004.

OTHER

Toybox (short stories), Cemetery Dance (Forest Hill, MD), 2000.

Also author of *West Texas,* M. Evans (New York, NY). Work represented in anthologies, including *The Year's Best Horror Stories,* Volumes XI and XII; *Great Ghost*

Stories;Laughing Space; Ghosts; and *Shadows,* Volumes 4, 5, 6, and 8. Contributor of short stories to magazines, including *Heavy Metal, Twilight Zone, Isaac Asimov's Science Fiction, Night Cry,* and *Mystery Scene.*

SIDELIGHTS: Al Sarrantonio wrote two novels featuring private investigator Jack Blaine, a retired cop who operates in the community of Yonkers, New York. In *Cold Night* and *Summer Cool,* Blaine investigates police chicanery. Blaine is eased from the police force in *Cold Night,* due to the machinations of corrupt officers. In *Summer Cool,* he is asked to find an officer who has abandoned his family, left town, and seems to be murdering his drug-dealing colleagues. A critic for *Publishers Weekly* wrote: "Drugs, betrayal and corruption at the highest levels figure in a story that stretches the bounds of credibility but provides a satisfying, even shocking, climax."

Sarrantonio has also written a number of horror thrillers, science fiction novels, and short stories for magazines. Writing in the *St. James Guide to Horror, Ghost and Gothic Writers,* Don D'Ammassa cited Sarrantonio's novel *Totentanz* as "a powerful, controlled work, unusually so for a first novel. . . . *The Boy with Penny Eyes* is Sarrantonio's most restrained and successful horror novel. The boy of the title appears to be autistic, never shows joy or sorrow, never speaks, and the adults who shuffle him from one home to another despair of ever reaching him. But he isn't entirely unaware. His eyes are always moving, watching, searching for another child, the other half of his personality from whom he has been supernaturally severed. . . . The most interesting and in some ways the best-written of Sarrantonio's horror novels is *Skeletons,* which also contains a great deal of dark humour. Through some unexplained device, all of the skeletons on Earth have been restored to life, and each of them is determined to pursue his or her former career. . . . Despite the obvious satire, the mood of the novel is distinctly that of horror, because the armies of the undead intend to supplant the living and wrest from them control of the Earth. . . . This one's a bizarre twist on the *Night of the Living Dead* films."

D'Ammassa concluded: "In general Sarrantonio's short fiction seems more controlled and thoughtful than his novels, which often rely so much on physical action that the characters never achieve any depth. At the

same time *The Boy with Penny Eyes* and *Skeletons* in particular indicate that Sarrantonio possesses the skills to be a successful novelist when he sets his mind to it."

BIOGRAPHICAL AND CRITICAL SOURCES:

BOOKS

St. James Guide to Horror, Ghost and Gothic Writers, St. James Press (Detroit, MI), 1998.

PERIODICALS

Booklist, September 1, 1999, Ray Olson, review of *999: New Stories of Horror and Suspense,* p. 67; November 1, 2001, Regina Schroeder, review of *Redshift: Extreme Visions of Speculative Fiction,* p. 463.
Bookwatch, January, 2002, review of *Redshift,* p. 10.
Kirkus Reviews, July 15, 1999, review of *999,* p. 1077.
Library Journal, September 15, 1999, Jackie Cassada, review of *999,* p. 115; December, 2001, Jackie Cassada, review of *Redshift,* p. 181.
Locus, October, 1999, review of *999,* pp. 21, 25.
Publishers Weekly, July 12, 1993, review of *Summer Cool,* p. 72; August 9, 1999, review of *999,* p. 348; January 17, 2000, review of *Toybox,* p. 48; November 5, 2001, review of *Redshift,* p. 45; November 4, 2002, review of *Orangefield,* p. 68.
Science Fiction Chronicle, March, 2002, review of *Redshift,* p. 34.

ONLINE

DarkEcho Horror Online, http://www.darkecho.com/ (August, 1999), Paula Guran, review of *999.**

*   *   *

SATTERFIELD, Charles
See POHL, Frederik

*   *   *

SCOTT, Willard H., Jr. 1934-

PERSONAL: Born March 7, 1934, in Alexandria, VA; son of Herman (in insurance sales) and Thelma (a telephone operator; maiden name, Phillips) Scott; married Mary Dwyer, August 7, 1959; children: Mary, Sally. *Education:* American University, B.A., 1955.

ADDRESSES: Home—Route 710, Delaplane, VA 22025. *Office*—NBC, 30 Rockefeller Plaza, Room 701A, New York, NY 10020. *Agent*—Bill Adler, 551 5th Ave., New York, NY 10020.

CAREER: National Broadcasting Co. (NBC), New York, NY, page with WRC-TV in Washington, DC, 1950, broadcaster (with Ed Walker—"The Joy Boys") for WOL-Radio in Washington, DC, 1950-53, for WRC-AM in Washington, DC, 1953-72, for Station WWDC in Washington, DC, 1972-74, weather reporter on *Today* show, 1980—. Weekend disc jockey for Station WINX, 1950. Weather reporter at WRC-AM, 1959-72, and WRC-TV, beginning in 1967. Appeared frequently on television as Ronald MacDonald and Bozo the Clown during the 1960s; announcer on commercials.

AWARDS, HONORS: Named Humanitarian-in-Residence, National Society of Fund Raisers, 1975; named Washingtonian-of-the-Year, *Washingtonian* magazine, 1979; inducted into Newspaper Carrier Hall of Fame, Newspaper Association of America, 2001.

WRITINGS:

Willard Scott's The Joy of Living, Coward (New York, NY), 1982.

Willard Scott's Down Home Stories, Bobbs-Merrill (Indianapolis, IN), 1984.

Willard Scott's All-American Cookbook, Macmillan (New York, NY), 1986.

(With Daniel Paisner) *America Is My Neighborhood,* Simon & Schuster (New York, NY), 1987.

(With Robert Shosteck) *Robert Shosteck's Weekenders Guide to the Four Seasons,* revised edition, edited by Susan C. Dore, Pelican, 1988.

Not Guilty: Detective Stories from the Strand (audio recording), narrated by Edward Raleigh, DH Audio, 1995.

(With Bill Crider) *Murder under Blue Skies* (mystery novel), Dutton (New York, NY), 1998.

(With Bill Crider) *Murder in the Mist: A Stanley Waters Mystery,* Dutton (New York, NY), 1999.

(With Robert Shosteck) *Weekend Getaways around Washington, D.C.: Including Virginia, Maryland, Delaware, Pennsylvania, New Jersey, West Virginia, and North Carolina,* 9th edition, edited by Victoria J. Heland, Pelican, 2000.

(With others) *The Older the Fiddle, the Better the Tune: The Joys of Reaching a Certain Age,* Hyperion (New York, NY), 2003.

(With others) *If I Knew It Was Going to Be This Much Fun, I Would Have Become a Grandparent First,* Hyperion (New York, NY), 2004.

Also author of introduction to *The Thanksgiving Book: An Illustrated Treasury of Lore, Tales, Poems, Prayers, and the Best in Holiday Feasting,* edited by Jerome Agel and Melinda Corey, Smithmark Publishing, 1995; contributor to *The Christmas Tree at Rockefeller Center,* by Carla Torcilieri Dagostino, Lickle Publishing, 1997.

SIDELIGHTS: Willard Scott began reporting the weather on NBC's *Today* show on March 10, 1980. Already renowned as a radio and television personality in Washington, D.C., the broadcaster's zany approach to reporting the weather initially drew negative responses from many *Today* viewers. Clearly, Scott was not adverse to blowing kisses to fans or doffing his wig while on the air. Yet within the year, Scott was being favorably received by the majority of his viewers. In his autobiography *Willard Scott's The Joy of Living,* the broadcaster spoke about his national television success. "I'm a mutation," he wrote, "If you put me on an audience tape, everything is wrong. . . . If you were to look at my resume, you'd see that I'm 48 years old, I'm bald, I'm overweight, I don't make all the smooth moves, and I dress like a slob. . . . I'd never come out of the computer as being a hit . . . yet . . . I take tremendous pride in the fact that I beat the system." After appearing for more than twenty years on *Today,* Scott is now a fixture on the NBC television network, wishing centenarians happy birthday two mornings a week and serving as substitute weatherman. His corny, folksy appeal has also translated to the printed page in books ranging from autobiography to humor and fiction.

Scott attributes his lifelong success to a happy and secure childhood with a loving mother and father. *The Joy of Living* contains many fond anecdotes concerning his parents; Vic Sussman noted in the *Washington Post Book World* that "Scott's account of [his mother] Thelma's long battle with Alzheimer's Disease and [his father] Herman's slow wasting away are particularly moving." The critic also remarked that the chapter on the "Joy Boys," the radio comedy team that Scott created with Ed Walker, was one of the best in the volume. *The Joy of Living* would have been a better book had Scott treated us to more anecdotes about those years," Sussman determined. "Unfortunately, as do many who achieve national fame, [he] casts himself as a pundit, advising his readers on . . . marriage, divorce, child-rearing, human relations and religion. . . . Still, Scott is a superb performer and many of his fans will welcome this book."

With the assistance of coauthor Bill Crider, Scott has also turned his hand to mystery writing. *Murder under Blue Skies* introduces a rather familiar protagonist, the widowed and retired weatherman Stanley Waters, who is opening a B & B in his Virginia hometown. When a guest is poisoned by the cook's salsa, Waters learns that the police chief is someone he dated in high school. The relationship heats up again when the two work together to solve the murder. *Booklist* reviewer Emily Melton deemed that the novel has "a fair degree of flair and charm" and that it overcomes "smarmy" moments by being "more often gently humorous." A *Publishers Weekly* reviewer advised that it was likely Crider's help that made "this slow-paced jaunt read like a story told from a front-porch rocker." A wide variety of humor in the mystery appealed to *School Library Journal* critic Pam Johnson, who said that "the mystery itself unfolds carefully, allowing for plenty of speculation and red-herring clues."

Scott and Crider teamed up again to write *Murder in the Mist: A Stanley Waters Mystery,* in which Waters escapes serious harm from a bullet at a Civil War reenactment, but a local businessman near him is killed. Of this novel, *Booklist*'s Wes Lukowsky suggested that the story is "as enjoyable an exercise in mayhem as one is likely to find." And a *Publishers Weekly* writer called the novel "entertaining, if lightweight" and described Waters as "an intriguing mixture of innocence and guile."

Among Scott's other writings are *Willard Scott's Down Home Stories,* a collection of old, puny humor; *Willard Scott's All-American Cookbook,* which includes recipes from restaurants he has visited; and *America Is My Neighborhood,* a patriotic collection that sketches people met during his broadcasting career. Two books by Scott collect the writings of others: *The Older the Fiddle, the Better the Tune: The Joys of Reaching a Certain Age* offers comments by older famous and

not-so-famous individuals, and *If I Knew It Was Going to Be This Much Fun, I Would Have Become a Grandparent First* groups humorous essays by well-known figures with incidentals by Scott about being a grandparent.

BIOGRAPHICAL AND CRITICAL SOURCES:

PERIODICALS

Booklist, January 1, 1998, Emily Melton, review of *Murder under Blue Skies,* p. 784; January 1, 1999, Wes Lukowsky, review of *Murder in the Mist: A Stanley Waters Mystery,* p. 840.

Knight Ridder/Tribune News Service, June 20, 2003, Michael Kilian, "With a Name Like Willard Scott, This Has to Be Good," p. K7838.

Library Journal, November 1, 1982, Randall Rafferty, review of *Willard Scott's The Joy of Living,* p. 2092; November 15, 1986, Ruth Diebold, review of *Willard Scott's All-American Cookbook,* p. 97; October 1, 1987, Boyd Childress and Janet Fletcher, review of *America Is My Neighborhood,* p. 103.

People, January 28, 1985, Campbell Geeslin, review of *Willard Scott's Down Home Stories,* p. 15.

PR Newswire, July 23, 2001, "Today Show's Willard Scott Inducted into NAA's Newspaper Carrier Hall of Fame."

Publishers Weekly, November 3, 1997, review of *Murder under Blue Skies,* p. 68; December 14, 1998, review of *Murder in the Mist,* p. 60; February 24, 2003, review of *The Older the Fiddle, the Better the Tune: The Joys of Reaching a Certain Age,* p. 59; March 1, 2004, review of *If I Knew It Was Going to Be This Much Fun, I Would Have Become a Grandparent First,* p. 61.

Saturday Evening Post, November-December, 2003, review of *The Older the Fiddle, the Better the Tune.*

School Library Journal September, 1998, Pam Johnson, review of *Murder under Blue Skies.*

Washington Post Book World, September 23, 1982, Vic Sussman, review of *Willard Scott's The Joy of Living.**

*   *   *

SEBASTIAN, Lee
    See SILVERBERG, Robert

SHAPIRO, Mel 1937-

PERSONAL: Born December 16, 1937, in Brooklyn, NY; son of Benjamin and Lillian Shapiro; married Jeanne Paynter (in advertising), January 26, 1963; children: Joshua, Benjamin. *Education:* Carnegie Institute of Technology, B.F.A., 1961, M.F.A., 1961.

ADDRESSES: Agent—Frank Weissberg, 505 Park Ave., New York, NY 10016. *E-mail*—mshapiro@tft. ucla.edu.

CAREER: Writer and director of Broadway and Off-Broadway shows, plays, films, and television shows. School of Theatre, New York University, New York, NY, cofounder; Carnegie-Mellon University (formerly Carnegie Institute of Technology), Pittsburgh, PA, head of drama department, 1980; University of California at Los Angeles, head of directing program, 1992—. Director of films and plays including *Heart Break House,* produced 1965 at Arena Stage, Washington, DC; *Long Day's Journey into Night,* 1965, *Merton of the Movies,* 1968, *Serjeant Musgrave's Dance,* 1968, and *Mourning Becomes Electra,* 1969, all at Guthrie Theatre, Minneapolis, MN; *The House of Blue Leaves,* 1971, Truck and Warehouse Theatre, New York, NY; *Two Gentlemen of Verona,* 1971, St. James Theatre, Broadway, New York, NY; *The Karl Marx Play,* 1973, American Place Theatre, New York, NY; *The Gin Game,* 1977, Stratford Theatre, Ontario, Canada; *Stop the World—I Want to Get Off,* 1978, New York State Theater, Broadway; *Bosoms and Neglect,* 1979, Longacre Theatre, Broadway; *Road Show,* 1987, Circle Repertory Theatre, New York, NY; *Marco Polo Sings a Solo,* 1998, Signature Theater Company, New York, NY; *Ellenor,* 1990, and *Speed the Plow,* 1991, both at Hazlett Jr. Theatre, Pittsburgh; *Taming of the Shrew,* 1999, Shakespeare in the Park, Public Theatre, Delacorte Theater, New York, NY; *Big Love,* 2002, Pacific Resident Theatre, Los Angeles, CA. Director of plays for New York Shakespeare Festival, including *Richard III, Rich and Famous,* and *Older People;* director of films, including *Sammy Stops the World,* based on Broadway play, *Stop the World—I Want to Get Off,* 1978; director of television shows, including *Phyllis,* 1977, *Doc,* 1977, and *On Our Own,* 1978. *Military service:* U.S. Army, 1954-57; served as Korean interpreter.

MEMBER: Society of Stage Directors and Choreographers (member of executive board).

AWARDS, HONORS: New York Drama Critics Circle Award, 1971, for *House of Blue Leaves,* and 1972, for *Two Gentlemen of Verona;* Antoinette Perry Award (Tony), 1972, for *Two Gentlemen of Verona;* Obie Award from *Village Voice,* 1972, for direction of *Two Gentlemen of Verona;* Drama Desk Award, 1972, for direction of *Older People* and *Two Gentlemen of Verona.*

WRITINGS:

(With John Guare; also director) *Two Gentlemen of Verona* (musical libretto; adaptation of the play by Shakespeare; first produced in New York City at Delacorte Theatre, August, 1971; produced on Broadway at St. James Theatre, December 1, 1971), Holt (New York, NY), 1972.
An Actor Performs, Harcourt Brace (Fort Worth, TX), 1997.
The Lay of the Land (screenplay), produced by Northern Arts Entertainment, 1997.
The Director's Companion, Harcourt Brace (Fort Worth, TX), 1998.

Founder of *Journal* of Society of Stage Directors and Choreographers, 1979.

SIDELIGHTS: With two books and close to forty theatrical productions to his credit, Mel Shapiro is an accomplished author, playwright, educator, and director. In a panel discussion moderated by Michael Bloom and published in *American Theatre,* Shapiro credits his success to the training he received at Carnegie Mellon and the invaluable help of his mentor, Ted Hoffman. "He got me my first job at Arena [Stage in Washington, DC], and when I was fired from Arena, he got me into the Guthrie [Theatre in Minneapolis]. It was an extraordinary blessing to have someone like that, so when I started teaching, I tried to repay that by helping students whom I thought were talented," explained Shapiro. His work in the theatre has earned him a Tony, an Obie, and two New York Drama Club Awards. In 1992, after a long career of directing and writing, Shapiro joined the staff of the University of California at Los Angeles (UCLA). A reviewer in *LA Weekly* said Shapiro's "professional achievements have been matched by his dedication to teaching the craft of acting."

Shapiro once told *CA:* "I began directing plays while in service in Japan. I was a Korean interpreter and my friend across the hall was a Chinese linguist. He was directing an English language production of *Blithe Spirit* and needed an assistant. His lead got sick and he had to play the part, so I ended up as director. This was in 1955. The bug bit. I went to Carnegie after the army and then on to the regional theatre: Arena Stage, Tyrone Guthrie, Center Theatre Group, Eugene O'Neill. I am now very interested in the training and development of new American writing for the theatre and hope Carnegie will be a good place for that to happen."

After a succession of small productions, Shapiro's first major success as both director and playwright was with a radical adaptation from Shakespeare's *Two Gentlemen of Verona.* First produced by Joseph Papp at the Delacorte Theatre for the free New York Shakespeare Festival in Central Park, this version of Shakespeare's first comedy mixes music, humor, and a multinational cast to produce "a wacky and wonderfully funny pastiche," remarked *Cue*'s Marilyn Stasio. The critic also noted that Shapiro and Guare said they aimed for "a true Americanization of Shakespearean comedy by combining our various musical traditions with their motley comic heritage and bouncing it all off the richness of our ethnic pattern." *Two Gentlemen of Verona* was so successful that it was produced on Broadway in the same year, receiving equally enthusiastic reviews. A *Newsweek* critic praised that rarely has Broadway "breathed such an air of joyous skylarking as this show whooshes in." The same critic theorized that Guare and Shapiro's adaptation reintroduced New York City "to its own piebald, polyglot dramatis personae."

Following its eighteen-month run on Broadway in the early 1970s, the play has not seen widespread performance. "No major revivals, no movie, no CD soundtrack: Even the cockiest of musical theatre buffs have trouble remembering *Two Gentlemen of Verona*," observed Charles McNulty in a review for *American Theatre* of the New Jersey Shakespeare Festival (NJSF)'s remake of this production. "The recent NJSF production, a triumph of hot pinks, minis, and soulful go-go, proved there is nothing anachronistic about the show's energy," McNulty concluded. Shapiro and Guare's adaptation of Shakespeare's work continues to be performed, albeit sparsely, and enjoyed by audiences and critics alike.

In Shapiro's first book, *An Actor Performs,* he recounts his vast experience in the theater for readers. In the book, Shapiro cites techniques he has used to improve his own performance and the performances of actors he has directed. *The Director's Companion,* Shapiro's second book, has been well received among critics and readers. A number of educational programs that teach directing, including those at San Jose State University, George Mason University, and Monash University, have adopted the book as part of their curriculum. "I wanted the book to cover the material technically," Shapiro explained in an interview published on the University of California, Los Angeles Web site, "but I wanted it to be casual, the way I talk in class and the way I feel students today like to listen." In *Director's Companion,* Shapiro echoes his classroom experience, presenting problems to the reader that are commonly faced by his students. He talks his reader through the problem and identifies solutions.

On the University of California, Los Angeles Web site, Shapiro gave students what he considers to be his best advice: "Follow your instincts. It's so intuitive, this business of directing; you really have to use your instincts and your life, your experiences, what you know, to dip into the work."

BIOGRAPHICAL AND CRITICAL SOURCES:

PERIODICALS

American Theatre, September, 1996, Charles McNulty, "Just Diversions," p. 11; January, 2002, Michael Bloom, "So You Want to Be a Director: Approaches to Theatre Training," (panel discussion), p. 27.
Back Stage, July 16, 1999, David Sheward, theatre review of *The Taming of the Shrew,* p. 29.
Cue, August 7, 1971.
Entertainment Weekly, July 9, 1999, Lisa Schwarzbaum and others, "Now Playing," theatre review of *The Taming of the Shew,* p. 64.
Maclean's, June 30, 1980, Mark Czarnecki, theatre review of *The Gin Game,* p. 55; August 4, 1980, Mark Czarnecki, theatre review of *Bosoms and Neglect,* p. 46.
Nation, June 20, 1987, Thomas M. Disch, theatre review of *Road Show,* p. 860.
Newsweek, December 13, 1971.
New York, October 12, 1998, John Simon, theatre review of *Marco Polo Sings a Solo,* p. 86.

New Yorker, June 1, 1987, Edith Oliver, theatre review of *Road Show,* p. 94; October 12, 1998, John Lahr, theatre review of *Marco Polo Sings a Solo,* p. 97.

New York Times, December 2, 1971, Clive Barnes, "*Two Gentlemen of Verona:* Musical Is Adaptation by Guare and Shapiro;" August 8, 1971, Peter Schjeldahl, "An Up-to-Date and Sexy *Verona*"; May 8, 1980, Judith Cummings and Albin Krebs, "Still Close to Broadway," (interview) p. A28; May 22, 1987, Mel Gussow, theatre review of *Road Show,* p. C3; September 26, 1987, Lawrence Ven Gelder, movie review of *The Lay of the Land,* p. B18.

Variety, December 8, 1971; May 27, 1987, theatre review of *Road Show,* p. 110; June 13, 1990, theatre review of *Eleanor,* p. 82; September 27, 1997, Howard Feinstein, movie review of *The Lay of the Land,* p. 67; October 5, 1998, Charles Isherwood, theatre review of *Marco Polo Sings a Solo,* p. 80; July 12, 1999, Charles Isherwood, theatre review of *The Taming of the Shrew,* p. 46.

ONLINE

iclassics.com, http://www.iclassics.com/ (November 19, 2003), Ron Spivak, "*Two Gentlemen of Verona:* Excerpts from the Liner Notes."

Playbill Online, http://www.playbill.com/ (June 2, 2002), Steven Suskin, "On the Record: Two Gents, of Verona and Dogpatch."

University of California, Los Angeles Web site, http://www.ucla.edu/ (February 26, 2004), interview with Shapiro.*

*   *   *

SHEPARD, Sam 1943-

PERSONAL: Original name, Samuel Shepard Rogers VII; born November 5, 1943, in Fort Sheridan, IL; son of Samuel Shepard (a teacher and farmer) and Elaine (Schook) Rogers; married O-Lan Johnson Dark (an actress), November 9, 1969 (divorced); currently living with Jessica Lange (an actress and film producer); children: (first marriage) Jesse Mojo; (with Lange) Hannah Jane, Samuel Walker. *Education:* Attended Mount Antonio Junior College, California, 1960-61. *Hobbies and other interests:* Polo, rodeo.

Sam Shepard

ADDRESSES: Office—Sam Shepard, International Creative Management, 8942 Wilshire Blvd., Beverly Hills, California, CA 90211-1934. *Agent*—Toby Cole, 234 W. 44th St., New York, NY 10036.

CAREER: Writer, 1964—. Conley Arabian Horse Ranch, Chino, CA, stable hand, 1958-60; Bishop's Company Repertory Players (touring theatre group), actor, 1962-63; Village Gate, New York, NY, busboy, 1963-64. Rock musician (drums and guitar) with Holy Modal Rounders, 1968-71; playwright in residence at Magic Theatre, San Francisco, CA, 1974-84; actor in feature films, including *Days of Heaven,* 1978, *Resurrection,* 1980, *Raggedy Man,* 1981, *Frances,* 1982, *The Right Stuff,* 1983, *Country,* 1984, *Fool for Love,* 1985, and *Crimes of the Heart,* 1986, *Baby Boom,* 1987, *Steel Magnolias,* 1989, *The Hot Spot,* 1990, *Defenseless,* 1991, *Voyager,* 1991, *Thunderheart,* 1992, *The Pelican Brief,* 1993, *Silent Tongue,* 1994, *Safe Passage,* 1994, and *Black Hawk Down,* 2002; director of feature film *Far North,* 1988.

MEMBER: American Academy and Institute of Arts and Letters, 1992.

AWARDS, HONORS: Obie Awards from *Village Voice* for best plays of the Off-Broadway season, 1966, for

Chicago, Icarus's Mother, and *Red Cross,* 1967, for *La Turista,* 1968, for *Forensic and the Navigators* and *Melodrama Play,* 1973, for *The Tooth of Crime,* 1975, for *Action,* 1977, for *Curse of the Starving Class,* 1979, for *Buried Child,* and 1984, for *Fool for Love;* grant from University of Minnesota, 1966; Rockefeller foundation grant and Yale University fellowship, 1967; Guggenheim foundation memorial fellowships, 1968 and 1971; National Institute and American Academy award for literature, 1974; Brandeis University creative arts award, 1975-76; Pulitzer Prize for drama, 1979, for *Buried Child;* Academy Award for best supporting actor nomination from Academy of Motion Picture Arts and Sciences, 1984, for *The Right Stuff;* Golden Palm Award from Cannes Film Festival, 1984, for *Paris, Texas;* New York Drama Critics' Circle Award, 1986, for *A Lie of the Mind;* American Academy of Arts and Letters Gold Medal for Drama, 1992; Theater Hall of Fame, 1994; Antoinette Perry Award Nomination for best play, 1996, for *Buried Child;* revised version of *True West,* first produced off-Broadway in 1980, nominated for a Tony Award for best play, 2000.

WRITINGS:

PLAYS

Cowboys (one-act), first produced Off-Off-Broadway at St. Mark Church in-the-Bowery, October 16, 1964.

The Rock Garden (one-act; also see below), first produced Off-Off-Broadway at St. Mark Church in-the-Bowery, October 16, 1964.

4-H Club (one act; also see below), first produced Off-Broadway at Cherry Lane Theatre, 1965.

Up to Thursday (one-act), first produced Off-Broadway at Cherry Lane Theatre, February 10, 1965.

Dog (one-act), first produced Off-Broadway at La Mama Experimental Theatre Club, February 10, 1965.

Chicago (one-act; also see below), first produced Off-Off-Broadway at St. Mark Church in-the-Bowery, April 16, 1965.

Icarus's Mother (one-act; also see below), first produced Off-Off-Broadway at Caffe Cino, November 16, 1965.

Fourteen Hundred Thousand (one-act; also see below), first produced at Firehouse Theater, Minneapolis, MN, 1966.

Red Cross (one-act; also see below), first produced Off-Broadway at Martinique Theatre, April 12, 1966.

La Turista (two-act; first produced Off-Broadway at American Place Theatre, March 4, 1967; also see below), Bobbs-Merrill (Indianapolis, IN), 1968.

Cowboys #2 (one-act; also see below), first produced Off-Broadway at Old Reliable, August 12, 1967.

Forensic and the Navigators (one-act; also see below), first produced Off-Off-Broadway at St. Mark Church in-the-Bowery, December 29, 1967.

(Contributor) *Oh! Calcutta!,* first produced on Broadway at Eden Theatre, 1969.

The Unseen Hand (one-act; also see below), first produced Off-Broadway at La Mama Experimental Theatre Club, December 26, 1969.

Holy Ghostly (one-act; also see below), first produced in New York, NY, 1970.

Operation Sidewinder (two-act; first produced Off-Broadway at Vivian Beaumont Theatre, March 12, 1970; also see below), Bobbs-Merrill, 1970.

Shaved Splits (also see below), first produced Off-Broadway at La Mama Experimental Theatre Club, July 29, 1970.

Mad Dog Blues (one-act; also see below), first produced Off-Off-Broadway at St. Mark Church in-the-Bowery, March 4, 1971.

(With Patti Smith) *Cowboy Mouth* (also see below), first produced at Transverse Theatre, Edinburgh, Scotland, April 2, 1971, produced Off-Broadway at American Place Theatre, April 29, 1971.

Back Bog Beast Bait (one-act; also see below), first produced Off-Broadway at American Place Theatre, April 29, 1971.

The Tooth of Crime (two-act; also see below), first produced at McCarter Theatre, Princeton, NJ, 1972, produced Off-Off-Broadway at Performing Garage, March 7, 1973.

Blue Bitch (also see below), first produced Off-Off-Broadway at Theatre Genesis, February, 1973.

(With Megan Terry and Jean-Claude van Itallie) *Nightwalk* (also see below), first produced Off-Off-Broadway at St. Clement's Church, September 8, 1973.

Geography of a Horse Dreamer (two-act; also see below), first produced at Theatre Upstairs, London, England, February 2, 1974.

Little Ocean, first produced at Hampstead Theatre Club, London, England, March 25, 1974.

Action (one-act; also see below), first produced Off-Broadway at American Place Theatre, April 4, 1975.

Killer's Head (one-act; also see below), first produced Off-Broadway at American Place Theatre, April 4, 1975.

Angel City (also see below), first produced at Magic Theatre, San Francisco, CA, 1976.

Curse of the Starving Class (two-act; also see below), first produced Off-Broadway at Newman/Public Theatre, March, 1978.

Buried Child (two-act; also see below), first produced Off-Broadway at Theatre of the New City, November, 1978.

Seduced (also see below), first produced Off-Broadway at American Place Theatre, February 1, 1979.

Suicide in B-flat (also see below), first produced Off-Off-Broadway at Impossible Ragtime Theatre, March 14, 1979.

Tongues, first produced at Eureka Theatre Festival, CA, 1979, produced Off-Off-Broadway at The Other Stage, November 6, 1979.

Savage/Love, first produced at Eureka Theater Festival, CA, 1979, produced Off-Off-Broadway at The Other Stage, November 6, 1979.

True West (two-act; first produced Off-Broadway at Public Theatre, December 23, 1980), Doubleday, 1981.

(Also director of original production) *Fool for Love* (one-act; also see below), first produced at Magic Theatre, San Francisco, 1983, produced Off-Broadway by Circle Repertory Company, May 27, 1983.

The Sad Lament of Pecos Bill on the Eve of Killing His Wife (one-act; also see below), first produced Off-Broadway at La Mama Experimental Theatre Club, September 25, 1983.

Superstitions (one-act), first produced Off-Broadway at La Mama Experimental Theatre Club, September 25, 1983.

(Also director of original production) *A Lie of the Mind* (three-act; first produced Off-Broadway at Promenade Theatre, December, 1985), published with *The War in Heaven* (also see below), New American Library (New York, NY), 1987.

Hawk Moon, produced in London, England, 1989.

States of Shock, produced in New York, NY, 1991.

Simpatico, Dramatists Play Service (New York, NY), 1995.

Curse of the Starving Class, Dramatists Play Service (New York, NY), 1997.

Eyes for Consuela, from the story "The Blue Bouquet" by Octavio Paz, Dramatists Play Service (New York, NY), 1999.

The Late Henry Moss, produced at the Signature Theater in New York, NY, 2001.

(And director) *The God of Hell,* produced Off-Broadway at the New School University in New York, NY, 2004.

PLAY COLLECTIONS

Five Plays by Sam Shepard (contains *Icarus's Mother, Chicago, Melodrama Play, Red Cross,* and *Fourteen Hundred Thousand*), Bobbs-Merrill (Indianapolis, IN), 1967.

The Unseen Hand and Other Plays (contains *The Unseen Hand, 4-H Club, Shaved Splits, Forensic and the Navigators, Holy Ghostly,* and *Back Bog Beast Bait*), Bobbs-Merrill (Indianapolis, IN), 1971.

Mad Dog Blues and Other Plays (includes *Mad Dog Blues, The Rock Garden, Cowboys #2, Cowboy Mouth, Blue Bitch,* and *Nightwalk*), Winter House (New York, NY), 1972.

The Tooth of Crime [and] *Geography of a Horse Dreamer,* Grove (New York, NY), 1974.

Angel City, Curse of the Starving Class and Other Plays (includes *Angel City, Curse of the Starving Class, Killer's Head,* and *Action*), Urizen Books (New York, NY), 1976.

Buried Child, Seduced, Suicide in B-flat, Urizen Books (New York, NY), 1979.

Four Two-Act Plays by Sam Shepard (contains *La Turista, The Tooth of Crime, Geography of a Horse Dreamer,* and *Operation Sidewinder*), Urizen Books (New York, NY), 1980.

Chicago and Other Plays, Urizen Books (New York, NY), 1981.

The Unseen Hand and Other Plays, Urizen Books (New York, NY), 1981.

Seven Plays by Sam Shepard, Bantam (New York, NY), 1981.

Fool for Love [and] *The Sad Lament of Pecos Bill on the Eve of Killing His Wife,* City Lights Books (San Francisco, CA), 1983.

Fool for Love and Other Plays, Bantam (New York, NY), 1984.

The Unseen Hand and Other Plays, Bantam (New York, NY), 1986.

States of Shock, Far North, [and] *Silent Tongue,* Vintage (New York, NY), 1993.

The Late Henry Moss, Eyes for Consuela, [and] *When the World Was Green,* Vintage (New York, NY), 2002.

SCREENPLAYS

(With Michelangelo Antonioni, Tonino Guerra, Fred Graham, and Clare Peploe) *Zabriskie Point* (produced by Metro-Goldwyn-Mayer, 1970), Cappelli (Bologna, Italy), 1970, published with Antonioni's *Red Desert,* Simon & Schuster (New York, NY), 1972.
(With L. M. Kit Carson) *Paris, Texas,* Twentieth Century-Fox, 1984.
Fool for Love (based on Shepard's play of the same title), Golan Globus, 1985.
Far North, Alive, 1988.
Silent Tongue, Trimark, 1992.

OTHER

Hawk Moon: A Book of Short Stories, Poems, and Monologues, Black Sparrow Press (Santa Barbara, CA), 1973.
Rolling Thunder Logbook, Viking (New York, NY), 1977, Da Capo Press (Cambridge, MA), 2004.
Motel Chronicles, City Lights Books (San Francisco, CA), 1982.
(With Joseph Chaikin) *The War in Heaven* (radio drama; first broadcast over WBAI in January, 1985), published with *A Lie of the Mind,* New American Library (New York, NY), 1987.
Joseph Chaikin and Sam Shepard: Letters and Texts, 1972-1984, edited by Barry V. Daniels, New American Library (New York, NY), 1989.
Cruising Paradise: Tales, Knopf (New York, NY), 1996.
Great Dream of Heaven: Stories, Knopf (New York, NY), 2002.

Also author, with Robert Frank, of *Me and My Brother,* and with Murray Mednick, of *Ringaleerio.*

ADAPTATIONS: *Fourteen Hundred Thousand* was filmed for NET *Playhouse,* 1969; *Blue Bitch* was filmed by the British Broadcasting Corporation (BBC), 1973; *True West* was filmed for the Public Broadcasting Service (PBS) series *American Playhouse.*

SIDELIGHTS: Sam Shepard has devoted more than two decades to a highly eclectic—and critically acclaimed—career in the performing arts. He is consid-

ered the preeminent literary playwright of his generation. Shepard has also directed plays of his authorship, played drums and guitar in rock bands and jazz ensembles, and acted in major feature films. His movie appearances include leading roles in *The Right Stuff* and *Country,* but acting is a sideline for the man *Newsweek*'s Jack Kroll called "the poet laureate of America's emotional Badlands." Despite his success in Hollywood, Shepard is primarily a playwright whose dramas explore mythic images of modern America in the nation's own eccentric vernacular.

Shepard established himself by writing numerous one-act plays and vignettes for the Off-Off-Broadway experimental theatre. Although his audiences have grown and his plays have been widely produced in America and abroad, he has yet to stage a production on Broadway. *New Republic* contributor Robert Brustein, who found Shepard "one of our most celebrated writers," contends that the lack of attention from Broadway "has not limited Shepard's powers." Brustein added: "Unlike those predecessors who wilted under such conditions, Shepard has flourished in a state of marginality. . . . Shepard's work has been a model of growth and variety." From his early surreal one-acts to his more realistic two-and three-act plays, Shepard has stressed artistic integrity rather than marketability. As a result, Kroll contended, Shepard plays have "overturned theatrical conventions and created a new kind of drama filled with violence, lyricism and an intensely American compound of comic and tragic power."

Shepard has won eleven Obie Awards for best Off-Broadway plays, a Pulitzer Prize for *Buried Child,* and a New York Drama Critics' Circle Award in 1986 for *A Lie of the Mind.* Richard A. Davis wrote in *Plays and Players* magazine that Shepard has both "a tremendous ability to make words bring the imagination of an audience to life" and "a talent for creating with words alone extremely believable emotional experiences." According to *Village Voice* correspondent Michael Feingold, Shepard "has the real playwright's gift of habitually transposing his feelings and visions into drama as a mere matter of praxis. He speaks through the theatre as naturally as most of us speak through the telephone." Shepard's plays use modern idiomatic language as well as such prevailing themes of American popular culture, particularly the American West, Hollywood and the rock-and-roll industry. "No one knows better than Sam Shepard that the true

American West is gone forever," wrote Frank Rich in the *New York Times,* "but there may be no writer alive more gifted at reinventing it out of pure literary air."

Shepard's modern cowboys, drifters, farmers, and other offspring of the frontier era yearn for a purer past that may never have existed as they quarrel with family members. *Journal of Popular Culture* contributor George Stambolian maintained that, like many of his fellow playwrights, Shepard "knows that the old frontier myths of America's youth are no longer a valid expression of our modern anxieties, even though they continue to influence our thoughts." Stambolian said Shepard seeks "a new mythology that will encompass all the diverse figures of our cultural history together with the psychological and social conditions they represent. . . . Shepard's greatest contribution to a new American mythology may well be his elaboration of a new myth of the modern artist."

Sam Shepard's theater is marked by "a spirit of comedy that tosses and turns in a bed of revulsion," as Richard Eder wrote in the *New York Times.* Malicious mischief and comic mayhem intensify Shepard's tragic vision; in many of his plays, inventive dialogue supplements vigorous action. As David Richards wrote in the *Washington Post,* actors and directors "respond to the slam-bang potential in [Shepard's] scripts, which allows them to go for broke, trash the furniture, and generally shred the scenery. Whatever else you've got, you've got a wild and wooly fight on your hands." The theatrical fisticuffs, sometimes physical, sometimes verbal, is on the overriding American musical rhythms. *New York Times* theatre critic Clive Barnes said: "Mr. Shepard writes mythic plays in American jazz-poetry. . . . He is trying to express truths wrapped up in legends and with the kind of symbolism you often find nowadays in pop music. His command of language is daring and inventive—some of the words sound new, and quite a few of them actually are." Richard L. Homan made a similar point in the *Critical Quarterly:* "Shepard's vivid use of language and flair for fantasy have suggested something less like drama and more like poetry in some unfamiliar oral tradition."

While Shepard's subjects—nostalgia, power struggles, family tensions—may seem simple at first, his plays remain "extraordinarily resistant to thematic exegesis," Richard Gilman wrote in his introduction to *Seven Plays by Sam Shepard.* Gilman added that standard criticism of Shepard is inadequate because the dramatist "slips out of all the categories" and seems to have come "out of no literary or theatrical tradition at all but precisely for the breakdown or absence—on the level of art if not of commerce—of all such traditions in America." Gilman added that several of the plays "seem like fragments, chunks of various sizes thrown out from some mother lode of urgent and heterogeneous imagination in which [Shepard] has scrabbled with pick, shovel, gun-butt and hands. The reason so many of them seem incomplete is that they lack the clear boundaries as artifact, the internal order, the progress toward a denouement . . . and the consistency of tone and procedure that ordinarily characterize good drama."

In *American Dreams: The Imagination of Sam Shepard,* Michael Earley said Shepard "seems to have forged a whole new kind of American play that has yet to receive adequate reckoning." Earley called the playwright "a true American primitive, a literary naif coursing the stage of American drama as if for the first time" who brings to his work "a liberating interplay of word, theme and image that has always been the hallmark of the romantic impulse. His plays don't work like plays in the traditional sense but more like romances, where the imaginary landscape (his version of America) is so remote and open that it allows for the depiction of legend, adventure, and even the supernatural." *Partisan Review* contributor Ross Wetzsteon contended that viewers respond to Shepard's plays "not by interpreting their plots or analyzing their characters or dissecting their themes, but simply by experiencing their resonance. . . . Shepard's arias seek to soar into a disembodied freedom, to create emotions beyond rational structure, to induce in both player and audience a trance like state of grace." Shepard, born in Fort Sheridan, Illinois, was given the name his forebears had used for six generations— Samuel Shepard Rogers. His father was a career army officer, so as a youngster Shepard moved from base to base in the United States and even spent some time in Guam. When Shepard's father retired from the service, the family settled on a ranch in Duarte, California, where they grew avocados and raised sheep. Although the livelihood was precarious, Shepard enjoyed the atmosphere on the ranch and liked working with horses and other animals. Influenced by his father's interest in Dixieland jazz, Shepard gravitated to music; he began to play the drums and started what *Dictionary of Literary Biography* contributor David W. Engel called "his lifelong involvement with rock-and-roll music and its subculture." He graduated from Duarte High School in 1960 and spent one year studying agricultural science at the local junior college, but his family situation deteriorated as his father began drinking excessively. Shepard fled by joining a touring theatrical group called the Bishop's Company Repertory Players. At age nineteen, he found himself in New York, determined to seek his fortune with only a few months' acting experience.

By chance Shepard encountered a high school friend in New York, Charles Mingus, Jr., son of the renowned jazz musician. Mingus found Shepard a job at The Village Gate, a jazz club, and the two young men became roommates. While working at The Village Gate, Shepard met Ralph Cook, founder of the Off-Off-Broadway company Theatre Genesis. Cook encouraged Shepard to write plays, and Shepard produced *Cowboys* and *The Rock Garden,* two one-acts that became part of the first Theatre Genesis show at St. Mark Church in-the-Bowery. Though Engel noted that most of the critics regarded Shepard's first two works as "bad imitations of Beckett," the *Village Voice* columnist "gave the plays a rave review." Shepard began to rapidly turn out one-act pieces, many performed Off-Off-Broadway; they attracted a cult following within that theatrical circuit. Shepard also continued his association with jazz and rock music, incorporating the rhythms into his dialogue and including musical riffs in the scripts. He reminisced about his early career in *New York* magazine: "When I arrived in New York there was this environment of *art* going on. I mean, it was really tangible. And you were right *in* the thing, especially on the Lower East Side. La Mama, Theatre Genesis, . . . all those theaters were just starting. So that was a great coincidence. I had a place to go and put something on without having to go through a producer or go through the commercial network. All of that was in response to the tightness of Broadway and Off-Broadway, where you couldn't get a play done."

Shepard told *New York* he did his early work hastily. "There wasn't much rewriting done," he said. "I had this whole attitude toward that work that it was somehow violating it to go back and rework it. . . . Why spend the time rewriting when there was another one to do?" Kroll said: "The true artist starts with his obsessions, then makes them ours as well. The very young Sam Shepard exploded his obsessions like firecrackers; in his crazy, brilliant early plays he was

escaping his demons, not speaking to ours." *New York Times* correspondent Mel Gussow, who has monitored Shepard's career, called the playwright's early works "a series of mystical epics (on both a large and small scale) mixing figures from folklore with visitors from the outer space of fantasy fiction." The Shepard one-acts, still frequently performed at theatre festivals and universities, juxtapose visual and verbal images with dramatic collage. Stambolian said the technique "forces the spectator to view the surface, so to speak, from behind, from within the imagination that conceived it."

"Shepard draws much of his material from popular culture sources such as B-grade westerns, sci-fi and horror films, popular folklore, country and rock music and murder-mysteries," *Modern Drama* critic Charles R. Bachman wrote. "In his best work he transforms the original stereotyped characters and situations into an imaginative, linguistically brilliant, quasi-surrealistic chemistry of text and stage presentation which is original and authentically his own." According to Stanley Kauffmann in the *New Republic,* the deliberate use of movie types "is part of Shepard's general method: the language and music of rock, spaceman fantasies, Wild West fantasies, gangster fantasies—pop-culture forms that he uses as building blocks, rituals of contemporary religion to heighten communion."

Some critics have dismissed Shepard's early work as undisciplined and obscure. *Massachusetts Review* essayist David Madden found the plays "mired in swampy attitudes toward Mom and Dad. Their main line of reasoning seems to be that if Mom and Dad's middle-class values are false, that if they and the institutions they uphold are complacent and indifferent, the only alternative is some form of outlaw behavior or ideology." Other national drama critics have evaluated the one-act plays quite differently. In the *New York Review of Books,* Robert Mazzocco wrote: "If one is content to follow this hard-nosed, drug-induced, pop-flavored style, this perpetual retuning of old genres and old myths, one encounters, finally, a profuse and unique panorama of where we are now and where we have been." Stambolian said that Shepard "is in fact showing to what extent the mind, and particularly the modern American mind, can become and has become entrapped by its own verbal and imaginative creations." And, according to Barnes, Shepard "is so sweetly unserious about his plays, and so desperately serious about what he is saying. . . . There is more in them than meets the mind. They are very easy to be funny about, yet they linger oddly in the imagination." In his own assessment of his first plays, Shepard told *New York* he thinks of them as "survival kits, in a way. They were explosions that were coming out of some kind of inner turmoil in me that I didn't understand at all. There are areas in some of them that are still mysterious to me." Shepard's first major production, *Operation Sidewinder*, premiered at the Vivian Beaumont Theatre in 1970. Engel described the two-act play as "an excellent example of how [Shepard] combines the roles of poet, musician, and playwright." Set in the Hopi Indian country of the American Southwest, *Operation Sidewinder* follows the attempts to control a huge, mechanical rattlesnake originally designed to trace unidentified flying objects. Air force commandos, Hopi snake-worshippers, black power activists, and even a beautiful but foolish blonde named Honey try to use the computerized sidewinder for their own ends. Engel noted that the "playful and satiric action is amplified by Shepard's production techniques. He assaults the senses of the audience by the use of intense sound and lights, and by various chants and songs." Shepard himself performed music in the play with a rock band, the Holy Modal Rounders. Although Engel said "the psychological resonance of stylized production, and not its sociological satire, is Shepard's aim," some critics called the work overly moralistic and stylistically confusing. "The difficulty of the play is in the writing," Barnes said. "The symbolic progression, while clearly charting the progress to atomic holocaust, is altogether too symbolic." Kroll maintained that the play's energy "has congealed in a half-slick pop machine with the feel of celluloid and the clackey sound of doctrinaire contemporaneity." Martin Gottfried viewed the play differently in *Women's Wear Daily*. "Everything about Sam Shepard's *Operation Sidewinder* is important to our theatre," Gottfried wrote. "More than any recent major production, it is built upon exactly the style and the mentality energizing the youth movement in America today."

In 1971 Shepard took his wife and infant son and moved to England. Having long experimented with drugs, the playwright sought escape from the abusive patterns he saw destroying fellow artists in New York. He also hoped to become more involved with rock music, still a central obsession. He did not accomplish that goal, but as Engel noted, he did "write and produce some of his finest works" while living in London. Gussow wrote: "As the author became recognized as an artist and found himself courted by such unearthly powers as Hollywood, he went through a Faustian phase. The result was a series of plays about art and the seduction of the artist." Plays such as *Angel City, Geography of a Horse Dreamer,* and *The Tooth of Crime* explore various aspects of the artist/visionary's dilemma when faced with public tastes or corporate profit-taking. Mazzocco felt that at this stage in his career Shepard chose to examine "not so much in political or economic parallels as in those of domination and submission, the nature of power in America. Or, more precisely, the duplicitous nature of 'success' and 'failure,' where it's implied that a failure of nerve and not that of a 'life' is at the basis of both." The playwright also discovered, as Richard A. Davis wrote, that "it is only within the individual mind that one finds his 'shelter' from the world; and even this shelter is not permanent, for the mind and body are tied together. To a great extent, Shepard's dramas have all been caught in this continual exploration of the same human problem."

The Tooth of Crime further strengthened Shepard's literary reputation. A two-act study of rock-and-roll stars who fight to gain status and "turf," the play "depicts a society which worships raw power," in Engel's words. London *Times* reviewer Irving Wardle wrote: "Its central battle to the death between an aging superstar and a young pretender to his throne is as timeless as a myth . . . and . . . has proved a durably amazing reflection of the West Coast scene. If any classic has emerged from the last twenty years of the American experimental theatre, this is it."

"Moving freely from gangster movies of the 40's to punk rock of the 70's, Mr. Shepard speaks in a language that is vividly idiomatic," Gussow wrote. Mazzocco called *The Tooth of Crime* "undoubtedly the quintessential Shepard play" and "a dazzlingly corrosive work . . . one of the most original achievements in contemporary theater. It is also the play that best illustrates the various facets—at once highly eclectic and highly singular—of [Shepard's] genius."

The Tooth of Crime represented a stylistic departure for Shepard. Bachman contended that the work "utilizes . . . the traditional dramatic values of taut, disciplined structure, vivid and consistent characterization, and crescendo of suspense." The transition, however, from modernist to traditional style has hardly been smooth. According to Richard L. Homan in the *Critical Quarterly,* Shepard has learned "to express the outrage, which gave rise to the experimental theatre, in plays which work through realistic conventions to challenge our everyday sense of reality." Shepard told *New York* that he sees a growing emphasis on character in his plays since 1972. "When I started writing," he said, "I wasn't interested in character at all. In fact, I thought it was useless, old-fashioned, stuck in a certain way. . . . I preferred a character that was constantly unidentifiable, shifting through the actor, so that the actor could almost play anything, and the audience was never expected to identify with the character. . . . But I had broken away from the idea of character without understanding it." Shepard's more recent plays explore characters—especially idiosyncratic and eccentric ones—for dramatic effect.

Gussow believed Shepard's new phase of writing reflects the changes in his own life. The playwright increasingly seeks to expose "the erosion and the conflagration of the ill-American family," Gussow said. Mazzocco said Shepard has "turned from the game to the trap, from the trail back to the hearth, from warfare in a 'buddy culture' to warfare among kith and kin." Four of Shepard's plays, *Buried Child, Curse of the Starving Class, True West,* and *A Lie of the Mind,* document in scenes of black humor the peculiar savagery of modern American family life. *New York Times* contributor Benedict Nightingale found these plays peopled by a "legion of the lost," whose "essential tragedy . . . seems . . . to be that they are simultaneously searching for things that are incompatible and possibly not attainable anyway: excitement and security, the exhilaration of self-fulfillment and a sense of belonging, freedom and roots."

Buried Child and *A Lie of the Mind,* separated by seven years, examine disturbed families. In *Buried Child,* David Richards wrote in the *Washington Post,* Shepard "delivers a requiem for America, land of the surreal and home of the crazed. . . . Beyond the white frame farmhouse that contains the evening's action, the amber waves of grain mask a dark secret. The fruited plain is rotting and the purple mountain's majesty is like a bad bruise on the landscape." In *Buried Child,* son Vince arrives at his midwestern farm home after a long absence. A dangerous cast of relatives confronts him, harboring secrets of incest and

murder. Richard Christiansen, in the *Chicago Tribune,* called the Pulitzer Prize-winning play "a Norman Rockwell portrait created for *Mad Magazine,* a scene from America's heartland that reeks with 'the stench of sin.'" Similarly, *A Lie of the Mind* presents a tale of "interior domestic violence, the damage that one does to filial, fraternal and marital bonds—and the love that lingers in the air after the havoc has run its natural course," Gussow wrote. In that work, two families are galvanized into violence when a jealous husband beats his wife, almost fatally. *A Lie of the Mind* won the New York Drama Critics' Circle Award for best new Off-Broadway play of 1985, and Shepard himself directed the original production.

Fool for Love, which Shepard also directed, is probably his best-known work. The one-act piece has been produced for the stage and has also been made into a feature film in which Shepard starred. *Fool for Love* alternates submission and rejection between two lovers who may also be half-brother and half-sister. New York *Daily News* critic Douglas Watt said the ninety-minute, nonstop drama "is Sam Shepard's purest and most beautiful play. An aching love story of classical symmetry, it is . . . like watching the division of an amoeba in reverse, ending with a perfect whole." *Fool for Love,* wrote *New York Times* reviewer Frank Rich, "is a western for our time. We watch a pair of figurative gunslingers fight to the finish—not with bullets, but with piercing words that give ballast to the weight of a nation's buried dreams. . . . As Shepard's people race verbally through the debris of the West, they search for the identities and familial roots that have disappeared with the landscape of legend." In the *New Republic,* Brustein found "nothing very thick or complicated about either the characters or the plot" and a lack of resolution to the play's ending. Still, the critic concluded that *Fool for Love* is "not so much a text as a legend, not so much a play as a scenario for stage choreography, and under the miraculous direction of the playwright, each moment is rich with balletic nuances."

Since 1978 Shepard has taken a major movie role each year, and was nominated for an Academy Award for his performance in *The Right Stuff.* He has, despite his discomfort with the image, assumed a certain matinee idol status. "Shepard did not become famous by writing plays," Stephen Fay wrote in *Vogue.* "Like it or not, acting [has] made him a celebrity." Shepard does *not* like to be considered a screen celebrity; his attitude toward film work is ambivalent, and public scrutiny has made him a recluse. He told *New York:* "There's a definite fear about being diminished through film. It's very easy to do too much of it, to a point where you're lost. Image-making is really what film acting is about. It's image-making, as opposed to character-making, and in some cases it's not true." But *Film Comment* essayist David Thomson contended that Shepard's long-standing fascination with movies lures him into that sort of work. "His sternness wants to be tested against their decadence," Thomson wrote. "His restraint struggles to reconcile a simultaneous contempt and need for movies. The uneasiness hovers between passion and foolishness, between the lack of skill and a monolith of intractability."

Shepard has often contradicted his own persona. In *Country,* for instance, he portrays a farmer who wilts under pressure when threatened with foreclosure, and in *Fool for Love* he appears as a womanizing, luckless rodeo rider. According to Thomson, Shepard brings the same sort of integrity to his movie roles that he brings to his writing. "For five years or so," Thomson wrote, "he has been prowling around the house of cinema, coming in a little way, armored with disdain, slipping out, but coming back, as if it intrigued and tempted his large talent. And movies need him. . . . But as with all prowlers, there remains a doubt as to whether this roaming, wolfen, mongrel lurcher wants to live in the house or tear it to pieces with his jaws and then howl at the desert moon, queen of dead worlds." Shepard told *New York:* "I'm a writer. The more I act, the more resistance I have to it. Now it seems to me that being an actor in films is like being sentenced to a trailer for twelve weeks."

In 1983, German director Wim Wenders commissioned Shepard to write a screenplay based loosely on the playwright's book *Motel Chronicles.* The resulting work, *Paris, Texas,* was a unanimous winner of the Golden Palm Award at the 1984 Cannes Film Festival. The film recasts many of Shepard's central concerns— broken families, the myth of the loner, and the elegy for the old West—in a story of reunion between a father and a son. In *People* magazine, Peter Travers called *Paris, Texas* the "most disturbing film ever about the roots of family relationships. Shepard's words and Wenders' images blend in a magical poetry." *New York* reviewer David Denby found the film "a lifeless art-world hallucination—a movie composed entirely of self-conscious flourishes," but most other critics praised the work.

For all his work in other media, Shepard is still most highly regarded for his playwriting. "He is indeed an original," wrote Edith Oliver in the *New Yorker,* "but it might be pointed out that the qualities that make him so valuable are the enduring ones—good writing, wit, dramatic invention, and the ability to create characters." Stambolian added, "It is certain that in a society drifting rapidly into the escapism of a permanent, and often instant, nostalgia, Shepard's plays are a sign of artistic health and awareness, and are, therefore, worthy of our attention." John Lahr elaborated on this idea in *Plays and Players:* "Shepard, who has put himself outside the killing commercial climate of American life and theatre for the last few years, seems to be saying . . . that the only real geography is internal." And, as *New York Times* correspondent Walter Kerr concluded, "everyone's got to admire [Shepard's] steadfast insistence on pursuing the vision in his head."

Shepard himself sees room for growth in his writing. "I guess I'm always hoping for one play that will end my need to write plays," he told *Vogue.* "Sort of the definitive piece, but it never happens. There's always disappointment, something missing, some level that hasn't been touched, and the more you write the more you struggle, even if you are riding a wave of inspiration. And if the piece does touch something, you always know you haven't got to the depths of certain emotional territory. So you go out and try another one." According to *New Statesman* reviewer Benedict Nightingale, "We can rely on [Shepard] to continue bringing a distinctively American eye, ear and intelligence to the diagnosis of what are, if you think about it, universal anxieties."

The playwright told the *New York Times* that he has no plans to stop. "I want to do the work that fascinates me," he said.

BIOGRAPHICAL AND CRITICAL SOURCES:

BOOKS

Almanac of Famous People, 6th edition, Thomson Gale (Detroit, MI), 1998.
Auerbach, Doris, *Sam Shepard, Arthur Kopit, and the Off Broadway Theater,* Twayne (Boston, MA), 1982.

Banham, Martin, editor, *The Cambridge Guide to World Theatre,* Cambridge University Press (New York, NY), 1988.

Bowman, John S., editor, *Cambridge Dictionary of American Biography,* Cambridge University Press (New York, NY), 1996.

Contemporary Dramatists, 6th edition, St. James Press (Detroit, MI), 1999.

Contemporary Literary Criticism, Thomson Gale (Detroit, MI), Volume 4, 1975, Volume 6, 1976, Volume 17, 1981, Volume 34, 1985, Volume 41, 1987, Volume 44, 1987.

Contemporary Theatre, Film, and Television, Volume 25, Thomson Gale (Detroit, MI), 2000.

Dictionary of Literary Biography, Thomson Gale (Detroit, MI), Volume 8: *Twentieth-Century American Dramatists,* 1981, Volume 212: *Twentieth-Century American Western Writers, Second Series,* 1999.

Drabble, Margaret, editor, *The Oxford Companion to English Literature,* 6th edition, Oxford University Press (New York, NY), 2000.

Drama Criticism, Volume 5, Thomson Gale (Detroit, MI), 1995.

Drama for Students, Volume 14, Greg Barnhisel, "Critical Essay on *Curse of the Starving Class,*" Thomson Gale (Detroit, MI), 2002.

Earl Blackwell's Celebrity Register 1990, Thomson Gale (Detroit, MI), 1990.

Encyclopedia of World Biography, 2nd edition, Thomson Gale (Detroit, MI), 1998.

Encyclopedia of World Literature in the Twentieth Century, Volume 4, St. James Press (Detroit, MI), 1999.

Graham, Laura, *Sam Shepard: Theme, Image, and the Director,* Lang (New York, NY), 1995.

Greasley, Philip, editor, *Dictionary of Midwestern Literature,* Volume 1: *The Authors,* Indiana University Press (Bloomington, IN), 2001.

Harmon, Justin, et al, *American Cultural Leaders from Colonial Times to the Present,* ABC-Clio (Santa Barbara, CA), 1993.

Hart, James D., editor, *The Oxford Companion to American Literature,* 6th edition, Oxford University Press (New York, NY), 1995.

Hart, Lynda, *Sam Shepard's Metaphorical Stages,* Greenwood Press (Westport, CT), 1987.

International Dictionary of Films and Filmmakers, Volume 3: *Actors and Actresses,* St. James Press (Detroit, MI), 1996.

International Dictionary of Theatre, Volume 2: *Playwrights,* St. James Press (Detroit, MI), 1993.

King, Kimball, *Ten Modern American Playwrights,* Garland (New York, NY), 1982.

King, Kimball, *Sam Shepard: A Case Book,* Garland (New York, NY), 1988.

Magill, Frank N., editor, *Critical Survey of Drama,* revised edition, Volume 6, Salem Press (Pasadena, CA), 1994.

Magill, Frank N., editor, *Cyclopedia of World Authors,* revised 3rd edition, Volume 5, Salem Press (Pasadena, CA), 1997.

Magill, Frank N., editor, *Magill's Survey of American Literature,* Volume 5, Marshall Cavendish (New York, NY), 1991.

Marranca, Bonnie, editor, *American Dreams: The Imagination of Sam Shepard,* Performing Arts Journal Publications (New York, NY), 1981.

Mottram, Ron, *Inner Landscapes: The Theater of Sam Shepard,* University of Missouri Press (Columbia, MO), 1984.

Newsmakers 1996, Issue 4, Thomson Gale (Detroit, MI), 1996.

New York Times Theatre Reviews, New York Times Company (New York, NY), 1971.

Oumano, Ellen, *Sam Shepard: The Life and Work of an American Dreamer,* St. Martin's Press (New York, NY), 1986.

Parker, Peter, editor, *A Reader's Guide to Twentieth-Century Writers,* Oxford University Press (New York, NY), 1996.

Patraka, Vivian M., and Siegel, Mark, *Sam Shepard,* Boise State University (Boise, ID), 1985.

Peck, David, editor, *Identities and Issues in Literature,* Volume 3, Salem Press (Pasadena, CA), 1997.

Riggs, Thomas, editor, *Reference Guide to American Literature,* 4th edition, St. James Press (Detroit, MI), 2000.

St. James Encyclopedia of Popular Culture, St. James Press (Detroit, MI), 2000.

Schlueter, Paul and June, editors, *Modern American Literature,* Volume 5, second supplement to the 4th edition, *A Library of Literary Criticism,* Continuum (New York, NY), 1985.

Serafin, Steven R., editor, *Encyclopedia of American Literature,* Continuum (New York, NY), 1999.

Shepard, Sam, *Five Plays by Sam Shepard,* Bobbs-Merrill (Indianapolis, IN), 1967.

Shepard, Sam, *Mad Dog Blues and Other Plays,* Winter House, 1972.

Shepard, Sam, *Seven Plays by Sam Shepard,* Bantam (New York, NY), 1981.

Shewey, Don, *Sam Shepard,* Dell (New York, NY), 1985.

Trussler, Simon, *File on Shepard,* Methuen (London, England), 1989.

Tucker, Martin, editor, *Modern American Literature,* Volume 6, supplement to the 4th edition, *A Library of Literary Criticism,* Continuum (New York, NY), 1985.

Tucker, Martin, editor, *Literary Exile in the Twentieth Century: An Analysis and Biographical Dictionary,* Greenwood (New York, NY), 1991.

Wallflower Critical Guide to Contemporary North American Directors, Columbia University Press (New York, NY), 2001.

Weales, Gerald, *The Jumping-Off Place: American Drama in the 1960's,* Macmillan (New York, NY), 1969.

PERIODICALS

After Dark, June, 1975.

America, November 5, 1983.

American Film, October, 1984.

American Theatre, October, 2000, "Alma Pater," p. 40.

Back Stage, May 3, 1996, Daniel Sheward, review of *Buried Child,* p. 48; May 16, 1997, Peter Shaughnessy, review of *Curse of the Starving Class,* p. 64; March 24, 2000, Eric Grode, review of *True West,* p. 64; October 26, 2001, David Sheward, review of *The Late Henry Moss,* p. 56.

Back Stage West, September 28, 2000, Kristina Mannion, review of *Simpatico,* p. 18; January 18, 2001, Michael Green, review of *Fool for Love,* p. 14.

Booklist, April 15, 1996, Donna Seaman, review of *Cruising Paradise,* p. 1422.

Books, December, 1997, review of *Cruising Paradise,* p. 20.

Canadian Forum, March, 1985.

Chicago Tribune, December 15, 1978; December 7, 1979; July 2, 1980; April 23, 1982; December 16, 1985; December 18, 1985.

Christian Century, November 21, 1984.

Christian Science Monitor, June 9, 1983.

Commonweal, June 14, 1968; May 8, 1970; November 30, 1984; July 12, 1991.

Cosmopolitan, January, 1985.

Critical Quarterly, spring, 1982.

Cue, April 11, 1970; July 18, 1970; February 17, 1973; March 31, 1973; March 18, 1978.

Daily News (New York, NY), May 27, 1983.

Drama, winter, 1965; spring, 1969; autumn, 1973; summer, 1976.

Educational Theatre Journal, October, 1977.

Entertainment Weekly, May 31, 1996, Margot Mifflin, review of *Cruising Paradise,* p. 54.

Esquire, February, 1980; November, 1988.

Film Comment, November-December, 1983; June, 1984.

Globe and Mail (Toronto, Ontario, Canada), December 21, 1985.

Guardian, February 20, 1974.

Harper's Bazaar, September, 1985; November, 1994, p. 98.

Hollywood Reporter, August 12, 2002, Barry Garron, review of *True West,* pp. 33-34.

Hudson Review, spring, 1979; spring, 1984.

Interview, September, 1988.

Journal of Popular Culture, spring, 1974.

Kirkus Reviews, March 15, 1996, review of *Cruising Paradise,* p. 403; August 1, 2002, review of *Great Dream of Heaven,* p. 1071.

Kliatt, November, 1996, review of *Cruising Paradise* (audio recording), p. 47.

Library Journal, May 15, 1996, review of *Cruising Paradise* (audio recording), p. 100; June 15, 1996, review of *Cruising Paradise,* p. 95, reviews of *Simpatico* and *The Unseen Hand and Other Plays,* p. 97.

Listener, September 26, 1974.

London Magazine, December, 1968.

Los Angeles Magazine, March, 1988.

Los Angeles Times, May 12, 1982; February 12, 1983; October 1, 1983; December 12, 1983; March 14, 1984; November 16, 1984; September 25, 1985; December 6, 1985; January 25, 1986; April 11, 1986; August 11, 1986.

Los Angeles Times Book Review, July 28, 1996, review of *Cruising Paradise,* p. 6.

Maclean's, October 29, 1984; December 24, 1984; January 13, 1986; January 18, 1988; November 21, 1988; October 2, 2000, "Actor, Playwright, Cowboy," p. 74.

Mademoiselle, March, 1985.

Massachusetts Review, autumn, 1967.

Modern Drama, December, 1976, March, 1979; March, 1981.

Ms., November, 1984.

Nation, February 21, 1966; April 4, 1966; March 30, 1970; March 26, 1973; May 3, 1975; January 10, 1976; February 24, 1979; January 31, 1981; October 27, 1984; December 29, 1984; January 5, 1985; January 11, 1986; February 22, 1986.

New Leader, April 10, 1967.

New Republic, April 21, 1973; April 8, 1978; January 31, 1981; June 27, 1983; October 29, 1984; December 3, 1984; December 23, 1985; September 29, 1986; February 2, 1987; November 28, 1988, Stanley Kauffmann, review of *Far North,* pp. 22-23; July 15, 1995, p. 27.

New Statesman, August 24, 1984; October 12, 1984; March 1, 1985; July 4, 1986; October 30, 1987; February 9, 1990; September 6, 1991; July 23, 2001, Katherine Duncan-Jones, "A Little Legend about Love," review of *A Lie of the Mind,* p. 45.

Newsweek, March 23, 1970; January 5, 1981; June 6, 1983; October 1, 1984; November 19, 1984; November 11, 1985; December 16, 1985.

New York, November 27, 1978; February 19, 1979; June 13, 1983; December 5, 1983; October 15, 1984; November 19, 1984; December 9, 1985; May 27, 1991; May 13, 1996, p. 64.

New Yorker, May 11, 1968; March 21, 1970; March 17, 1973; May 5, 1975; December 22, 1975; November 29, 1982; October 1, 1984; September 2, 1985; January 27, 1986; December 15, 1986; June 3, 1991; April 22, 1996, p. 84; May 27, 1996, p. 138.

New York Post, May 27, 1983.

New York Review of Books, April 6, 1967; May 9, 1985.

New York Times, February 11, 1965; April 13, 1966; May 28, 1968; April 13, 1969; March 15, 1970; April 2, 1970; March 8, 1971; June 28, 1971; March 7, 1973; September 17, 1977; March 3, 1978; April 28, 1978; November 7, 1978; December 10, 1978; February 2, 1979; March 4, 1979; March 14, 1979; April 17, 1979; June 3, 1979; February 7, 1980; March 12, 1980; December 24, 1980; November 9, 1981; January 6, 1982; October 18, 1982; March 2, 1983; May 27, 1983; June 5, 1983; September 20, 1983; September 25, 1983; January 29, 1984; September 28, 1984; September 30, 1984; November 9, 1984; November 14, 1984; November 18, 1984; November 22, 1984; November 29, 1984; November 30, 1984; August 15, 1985; October 1, 1985; October 4, 1985; November 14, 1985; December 1, 1985; December 15, 1985; January 12, 1986; January 21, 1986; April 13, 1986; May 17, 1996, review of *Cruising Paradise,* p. B12; June 16, 1996, review of *Buried Child,* p. H5.

New York Times Book Review, June 23, 1996, review of *Cruising Paradise,* p. 23; September 7, 1997, review of *Cruising Paradise,* p. 40.

Partisan Review, Volume XLI, number 2, 1974; Volume XLIX, number 2, 1982.

People, December 26, 1983; January 2, 1984; October 15, 1984; November 5, 1984; December 9, 1985; January 6, 1986; June 10, 1996, p. 15; November 14, 1988, Peter Travers, review of *Far North,* p. 24.

Plays and Players, June, 1970; October-November, 1971; April, 1974; May, 1974; November, 1974; April, 1979.

Publishers Weekly, April 1, 1996, review of *Cruising Paradise,* p. 38; April 15, 1996, review of *Cruising Paradise,* p. 48; September 9, 2002, review of *Great Dream of Heaven,* pp. 40-41.

Quill & Quire, February, 1980.

Rolling Stone, August 11, 1977; December 18, 1986; February 24, 1994.

Saturday Review, December, 1984.

Spectator, November 16, 1996, review of *Cruising Paradise,* p. 51.

Theatre Journal, March, 1984.

Theatre Quarterly, August, 1974.

Time, November 27, 1972; June 6, 1983; October 8, 1984; August 12, 1985; December 2, 1985; December 16, 1985; November 7, 1988, Richard Corliss, review of *Far North,* pp. 108-109; May 20, 1996, Richard Zoglin, review of *Buried Child,* p. 77.

Times (London, England), September 24, 1983; September 26, 1983; October 6, 1984; January 7, 1986.

Times Literary Supplement, November 24, 1978; March 1, 1985; November 22, 1996, review of *Cruising Paradise,* p. 22.

Variety, September 14, 1988; May 20, 1991; February 8, 1993; September 19, 1994; May 5, 1997, Robert L. Daniels, review of *Curse of the Starving Class,* p. 213; February 16, 1998, Greg Evans, review of *Eyes for Consuela,* p. 68; July 16, 2001, Matt Wolf, review of *A Lie of the Mind,* p. 25.

Village Voice, April 4, 1977; August 15, 1977; February 12, 1979.

Vogue, February, 1984; February, 1985.

Washington Post, January 14, 1979; June 2, 1979; March 5, 1983; April 22, 1983; October 23, 1983; April 12, 1985; October 15, 1985; May 1, 1986; September 12, 1986.

Western American Literature, fall, 1989, review of *True West,* p. 225.

Women's Wear Daily, March 13, 1970; May 27, 1983.

World Literature Today, winter, 1997, review of *Cruising Paradise,* p. 152.

ONLINE

Moonstruck Drama Bookstore Web site, http://www. imagi-nation.com/moonstruck/ (March 5, 2003), biography of Sam Shepard.

Pegasos Web site, http://www.kirjasto.sci.fi/ (March 5, 2003), biography of Sam Shepard.

Thespian Net Web site, http://www.thespiannet.com/ (March 5, 2003), biography of Sam Shepard.*

*   *   *

SHRIVER, Lionel 1957-

PERSONAL: Born May 18, 1957, in Gastonia, NC; daughter of Donald W. (an ethicist and seminary president) and Peggy (an administrator; maiden name, Leu) Shriver. *Education:* Columbia University, B.A., 1978, M.F.A., 1982.

ADDRESSES: Home—19 Notting Hill, Belfast BT9 5NS, Northern Ireland. *Agent*—Kathy Anderson—Scovil, Chichak, Galen, 12 W. 19th St., New York, NY 10016. *E-mail*—theshrive@aol.com.

CAREER: Radio and print journalist; English and writing instructor at various colleges.

MEMBER: PEN, Authors Guild, Authors League of America.

AWARDS, HONORS: Aer Lingus travel award, 1993; Northern Ireland Arts Council literature grants, 1993 and 1996; Sheldon & Stewart Solicitors "Anonymous Donor" grant, 1995; Orange Prize for Fiction, 2005, for *We Need to Talk about Kevin.*

WRITINGS:

The Female of the Species, Farrar, Straus (New York, NY), 1987.

(And illustrator) *Checker and the Derailleurs,* Farrar, Straus (New York, NY), 1988.

The Bleeding Heart, Farrar, Straus (New York, NY), 1990, published as *Ordinary Decent Criminals,* HarperCollins (London, England), 1992.

Game Control, Faber & Faber (London, England), 1994.

A Perfectly Good Family, Faber & Faber (London, England), 1996.

Double Fault, Doubleday (New York, NY), 1997.

We Need to Talk about Kevin, Counterpoint (New York, NY), 2003.

Also contributor to *Wall Street Journal, Belfast Telegraph, Irish News, Tennis, Philadelphia Inquirer,* and *Fortnight.*

SIDELIGHTS: Lionel Shriver's first three novels, *The Female of the Species, Checker and the Derailleurs,* and *The Bleeding Heart,* have generated high praise for their energy, imagination, wit, and originality, but are particularly noted for their uncompromisingly lucid, if not at times cynical, perception of human interaction. With a singular emphasis on the charismatic personality, Shriver, who once studied under the renowned anthropologist Margaret Mead at Columbia University, shows a "keen eye for the archetypal characters common to human tribes everywhere," according to *People* contributor Kim Hubbard. Through her focus on charisma and its accompanying power structures, Shriver exposes what she sees as some of the primitive social dynamics—domination and subordination in academic hierarchy, the "groupie" syndrome in modern music, and thrill-seeking masochism in political activism—that comprise modern civilization. Indeed, Shriver applies her unflinching perspective to her own craft in which, she says, persuasiveness is often taken for truth. "Fiction writers are fakers—it's a trade secret," Shriver said in *Interview* magazine. "The whole idea of novels, in fact, is a conceit, however seductive—as if anyone knows what it's like to be other people. And one of the dangers of all text is that 'truth,' awkwardly put, can seem like a lie, but the dubious assertion will carry because it sounds right." Each of her novels investigates a world in which the powerful but often irrational forces of persuasion rule.

The Female of the Species is the story of highly regarded fifty-nine-year-old anthropologist Gray Kaiser, who is, in her own words, "very tall, and very strong and very brilliant," as quoted from the novel in Ralph Novak's *People* review. Kaiser rose to fame in the 1940s, when she studied a long-lost tribe in Kenya that was under the influence of American pilot Charles

Corgie. Corgie, having convinced the tribe that he was a god, briefly shared his power with Kaiser. After a fiasco leading to Corgie's death, however, Kaiser fled back to a more comfortably deified position in the academic world. She returns to Kenya many years later with her longtime platonic living partner and devotee, Errol McEchern, and a young graduate student, Raphael, who is, coincidentally, identical to Corgie in looks and character. In the romantic triangle that arises, the formerly predominant Kaiser subjugates herself to the twenty-five-year-old Raphael, revealing some tortured aspects of human relations.

Critical reaction to *The Female of the Species* was mixed. Chicago *Tribune Books* contributor Celia Hilliard found the novel "convincing, both as a power struggle and a love triangle," but contended that Shriver is "heavy-handed." "Every encounter these characters share is in some way brutal, confused, and painful," she complained. Paul Kincaid, in his *Times Literary Supplement* review, suggested that although the novel "sparkles with ideas," Shriver's literary inexperience deters her from answering the provoking questions her work raises. But many critics praised *The Female of the Species* for its accurate, if bleak, representation of life. Novak, calling the work a "terrific first novel," remarked that though disturbing, "it all too often seems all too true."

The world of rock music and a more upbeat protagonist lighten the tone of Shriver's second novel, *Checker and the Derailleurs.* Checker Secretti is a nineteen-year-old drummer in a New York bar band. He possesses such a strong natural charm that people follow him simply to share his joy in life. Checker's magnetism, free of the need and manipulation connected with charisma in *The Female of the Species,* is nevertheless a significant social force that almost magically organizes his followers into harmonious roles around him. In fact, some critics suggested that Checker's appeal beguiles not only the other characters but readers as well. The mysteries that surround Checker's romance with Syria Pyramus, his periodic disappearances, and, most importantly, his unflagging cheerfulness, "keep readers guessing to the end," according to Hubbard. The novel has "adolescent energy and raw appeal," *New York Times Book Review* contributor Margot Mifflin raved. The critic added that "with psychological depth and wry humor" Shriver succeeded in "pulling off a novel that not only works, but rocks."

Shriver's third novel, *The Bleeding Heart,* set in 1988 Northern Ireland, explores the social dynamics of a country perennially at war. The main character, Estrin Lancaster, is a thirty-two-year-old American woman who has spent the last ten years moving from one politically distressed area to another. Living in a bombed-out house on the border between warring Catholic and Protestant neighborhoods in Belfast, she becomes romantically involved with Farrell O'Phelan, a political activist, bomb disposer, and, in the words of Michael Upchurch in his *Washington Post Book World* review, "the most troubled, charismatic character in the place." Even in the danger and self-sacrifice of political rebellion, Shriver portrays power as a function of "dubious assertion" rather than heroism. Although Farrell is working tirelessly to unify Catholics and Protestants, he is manipulative, cynical, and masochistic. Like Estrin, he is unwilling or unable to make a commitment and is addicted to the social violence that is a part of everyday existence in Belfast—an atmosphere depicted by Shriver, according to Upchurch, as "partylike." Through the turbulent love affair between Estrin and Farrell in this violent background, the novel explores some frightening manifestations of life in a state of constant crisis.

Shriver's cynicism and an unexpected twist in plot at the end of *The Bleeding Heart* both unnerved and impressed critics. Upchurch observed that "the bracing, acid wit and rich hyperbole are constant and a little terrifying. Who can be this cynical about horrors?" The critic consequently answered: "Shriver can—and for a purpose." Reviewers agreed that Shriver's relentlessly penetrating outlook is gripping and effective in *The Bleeding Heart,* whether or not the reader is comfortable with the picture it paints of human nature. Upchurch hailed this "shrewdly caustic and unexpectedly moving novel" as "challenging, disturbing fiction," which "quivers with enticing energy, seduces you with its nervy amoral appeal."

Game Control, Shriver's fourth novel, is "a sardonic, sexy, salutary novel about, of all things, population control," according to Jonathan Stevenson in the *New Scientist.* The book "mixes dark comedy, intellectual sparring, doomsday thrills and psychological scrutiny in a bold and bracing cocktail," remarked *New Statesman and Society* critic Boyd Tonkin. Even though it is set in Africa, Giles Foden rewarded *Game Control* in the *Times Literary Supplement* for "neither trad[ing] on the continent as 'exotica' nor piously making literary capital out of human misery." Stevenson commented that the book "indulges neither the props of the techno-thriller nor the emotional exploitation of the genre suspense yarn," arguing that "Shriver's characters and their aura of feigned sacrifice while living in the Third World simply strike too true a chord." Faulting the novel's characters, *Guardian* contributor Sylvia Brownrigg criticized the novel: "The three [main characters] are not so much people as opportunities for argument. . . . A novel needs an emotional centre, however, not just a line of argument. . . . Shriver . . . is capable of enlivening her stories with slices of vivid prose or surprising description. Ultimately, though, the main characters remain bloodless." Some critics, including Brownrigg, Tonkin, and Stevenson, positively remarked on the appearance of Shriver's intelligence and the true-to-life aspects woven into her story. "Playing with genres," said Foden, "Shriver encourages the reader to consider serious matters, without serving up tedious ethical fiction, making us aware of shifting issues by shifting our perspective on the action itself."

Shriver's fifth and sixth novels, *A Perfectly Good Family* and *Double Fault,* received many positive reviews from critics. *A Perfectly Good Family* explores the reactions and feelings of three adults with negative memories of their childhood after their mother's death. "Shriver evinces a far sharper sense of irony than, say, Anne Tyler," remarked Jonathan Stevenson in a *Scotsman* review, "but much greater subtlety than, say, Jane Smiley." In the *New Statesman and Society* a reviewer described *A Perfectly Good Family* as "typically clever and astringent." However, "the plot moves between detached scenes, and sometimes feels slow," stated Sarah Rigby in the *Times Literary Supplement.* She continued, "The characters are believable, but they conform to extreme models." Rigby noted that even though the novel is "inconsistent, Lionel Shriver is clearly a competent writer, and one of her most unambiguous successes is her portrayal of feeling—of the odd, inconstant emotions and the sense of distorted guilt that accompany bereavement."

Double Fault, called an "earnest narrative" and a "didactic novel" in *Publishers Weekly,* and "an eye-opening and authentic look at the cutthroat world of pro tennis" in *Booklist,* is centered on two professional tennis players, their marriage, and the negative effect of ambitions, competition, and work within the same occupation. "An interesting idea," wrote Jonathan

Yardley in the *Washington Post,* but "undone by an artless novel." Yardley elaborated that Shriver "writes well, but she is insufficiently confident of her characters, her plot and her storytelling powers. Her narrative is littered with gratuitous analysis that merely serves to get in the story's way, and toward the end she reaches the novelist's avenue of last resort: She brings a psychologist onto the scene." In contrast, a *Publishers Weekly* critic believed that Shriver is successful with *Double Fault*'s theme, and "all too well" presents "a cautionary tale about the fatal mix of love and ambition." In the *New York Times Book Review* Michael Mewshaw also lauded *Double Fault,* noting that "Shriver shows in a masterstroke why character is fate and how sport reveals it." *Library Journal* contributor Nancy Pearl concluded: "Shriver is a talented enough writer to win over some readers, but many will lose patience with Willy," the story's main female character.

In the late 1990s a series of school killings across the United States frightened students and parents. At that time Shriver was thinking about becoming a mother and the shootings both gave her pause and sparked the idea for her epistolary novel *We Need to Talk about Kevin.* "The idea of writing a book in which my son or the narrator's son became one of those killers was an interesting exercise for me in sorting out what I was afraid of, and why I had put off childbearing as long as I had," Shriver said on National Public Radio's *Weekend Edition Sunday.* In the first part of the book, Shriver reflects on the ambivalence that many women feel about childbearing and in particular her own experiences as the daughter of a mother who admonished her that having children would ruin her life. Shriver used the Internet to research the topic, reading essays and interviews about teenage killers, and told the story through letters from Eva, the mother of teenage killer Kevin, to the divorced father of Kevin. In the first half of the book the letter writer reflects on Kevin's childhood, during which the boy consistently showed signs of being a monster, while in the latter she writes of present-day concerns.

Dealing with such a current topic, *We Need to Talk about Kevin* garnered many reviews, some of which varied diametrically. Several critics took Shriver to task about stylistic matters, such as what they felt was the weak characterization of the husband, and what *New York Times* critic Matthew Flamm called "Shriver's tendency to overwrite." Noting that "the plot drags," Susan Balee suggested in the *Philadelphia Inquirer* that Shriver "cut much of the first half of the book in order to make a tauter novel." "Despite its early flaws and slow start, the book drives home its chilling point in the final pages," wrote Patti Hartigan in the *Boston Globe.* Among the work's enthusiasts was a *Publishers Weekly* contributor, who dubbed the work "a harrowing, psychologically astute, sometimes even darkly humorous novel," and *Library Journal* critic Karen Fauls-Traynor, who praised its "compelling writing" and "never stale" plot.

Feminist readers made much of the author's ambivalence about motherhood, some viewing it as satire or criticism of the supposedly natural maternal instinct women should feel. For example, *Guardian* reviewer Rachel Cusk reported that *We Need to Talk about Kevin,* which "can almost be read as a blackly comic fable in which modern feminist fears are made flesh," has "unexpectedly become an underground feminist hit." As such, Cusk concluded, "Shriver's satire on child-centred families captained by adult buffoons whose intellectual, not to mention erotic, life is in pieces, could not be more timely." As for Shriver's consideration of possible motherhood for herself, she told Cusk that writing the novel made her realize something: "My reservations about having children were stolid in my character and not a passing thing I needed to get over."

BIOGRAPHICAL AND CRITICAL SOURCES:

PERIODICALS

Belfast Telegraph, March 16, 1996, review of *A Perfectly Good Family.*

Booklist, August, 1997, Emily Melton, review of *Double Fault,* p. 1881; May 1, 2003, Deborah Donovan, review of *We Need to Talk about Kevin* pp. 1582-1583.

Boston Globe, July 15, 2003, Patti Hartigan, review of *We Need to Talk about Kevin,* p. C6.

Glamour, June, 1988, Laura Mathews, review of *Checker and the Derailleurs,* p. 180.

Guardian (Manchester, England), May 3, 1994, Sylvia Brownrigg, review of *Game Control,* section 2, p. 13; March 29, 1996, review of *A Perfectly Good Family;* October 4, 2003, Rachel Cusk, review of *We Need to Talk about Kevin,* p. 44; November 15, 2003, Sarah A. Smith, review of *We Need to Talk about Kevin,* p. 26.

Independent, May 5, 1996, review of *A Perfectly Good Family.*

Interview, July, 1987, "Lionel Shriver," p. 209.

Kirkus Reviews, June 15, 1997, review of *Double Fault,* p. 907; March 1, 2003, review of *We Need to Talk about Kevin,* pp. 342-343.

Library Journal, February 15, 1987, Ann H. Fisher, review of *The Female of the Species,* p. 163; May 15, 1988, Ethan Bumas, review of *Checker and the Derailleurs,* p. 94; September 1, 1990, Ann H. Fisher, review of *The Bleeding Heart,* p. 258; July, 1997, Nancy Pearl, review of *Double Fault,* p. 128; May 1, 2003, Karen Fauls-Traynor, review of *We Need to Talk about Kevin,* p 157.

New Scientist, April 30, 1994, Jonathan Stevenson, review of *Game Control,* p. 43.

New Statesman and Society, April 29, 1994, Boyd Tonkin, review of *Game Control;* March 15, 1996, review of *A Perfectly Good Family.*

New York, March 30, 1987, Rhoda Koenig and Celia McGee, review of *The Female of the Species,* p. 98.

New York Newsday, August 24, 1997, review of *Double Fault.*

New York Post, July 27, 1997, review of *Double Fault,.*

New York Times, August 3, 2003, Matthew Flamm, review of *We Need to Talk about Kevin,* section 7, p. 16.

New York Times Book Review, July 19, 1987, Katherine Bouton, review of *The Female of the Species;* July 24, 1988, Margot Mifflin, review of *Checker and the Derailleurs;* September 14, 1997, Michael Mewshaw, review of *Double Fault,* p. 19; August 3, 2003, Matthew Flamm, review of *We Need to Talk about Kevin,* p. 16.

People, April 27, 1987, Ralph Novak, review of *The Female of the Species,* p. 10; July 4, 1988, Kim Hubbard, review of *Checker and the Derailleurs,* p. 25; August 29, 1988, review of *The Female of the Species,* p. 33; July 21, 1989, review of *Checker and the Derailluers,* p. 56; November 12, 1990, Michael Neill, review of *The Bleeding Heart,* p. 32.

Philadelphia Inquirer, October 19, 1997, review of *Double Fault;* July 30, 2003, Susan Balee, review of *We Need to Talk about Kevin.*

Publishers Weekly, February 13, 1987, Sybil Steinberg, review of *The Female of the Species,* p. 82; April 22, 1988, Sybil Steinberg, review of *Checker and the Derailleurs,* p. 64; July 20, 1990, Sybil Steinberg, review of *The Bleeding Heart,* p. 52; June 30, 1997, review of *Double Fault,* p. 65;

March 24, 2003, review of *We Need to Talk about Kevin,* p. 55.

Scotsman, June 22, 1996, Jonathan Stevenson, review of *A Perfectly Good Family,* p. 22.

Spectator, August 8, 1992, Brian Inglis, review of *Ordinary Decent Criminals,* p. 24.

Tennis, October, 1997, review of *Double Fault,* p. 82.

Times Literary Supplement, March 18, 1988, Paul Kincaid, review of *The Female of the Species,* p. 302; June 12, 1992, Keith Jeffery, review of *Ordinary Descent Criminals,* p. 20; April 15, 1994, Giles Foden, review of *Game Control,* p. 23; April 19, 1996, Sarah Rigby, review of *A Perfectly Good Family,* p. 24.

Tribune Books (Chicago, IL), April 19, 1987, Celia Hilliard, review of *The Female of the Species.*

Washington Post, August 6, 1997, Jonathan Yardley, review of *A Perfectly Good Family,* p. C4.

Washington Post Book World, November 20, 1990, Michael Upchurch, review of *The Bleeding Heart.*

ONLINE

Identity Theory, http://www.identitytheory.com/ (July 24, 2003), Robert Birnbaum, "Author of *We Need to Talk about Kevin* Talks with Robert Birnbaum."

OTHER

Weekend Edition Sunday, National Public Radio, "Interview: Lionel Shriver," July 13, 2003.*

*   *   *

SILVERBERG, Robert 1935-

(Gordon Aghill, a joint pseudonym, Robert Arnette, a house pseudonym, T. D. Bethlen, Alexander Blade, a house pseudonym, Ralph Burke, a joint pseudonym, Walker Chapman, Dirk Clinton, Roy Cook, Walter Drummond, Dan Eliot, Don Elliott, Richard Greer, a house pseudonym, Franklin Hamilton, Paul Hollander, E. K. Jarvis, a house pseudonym, Ivar Jorgenson, Warren Kastel, a house pseudonym, Calvin M. Knox, Dan Malcolm, Webber Martin, Alex Merriman, Clyde Mitchell, a house pseudonym, David Osborne, George Osborne, Robert Randall, a joint pseudonym, Ellis Robertson, a

Robert Silverberg

joint pseudonym, Lloyd Robinson, Eric Rodman, Lee Sebastian, Leonard G. Spencer, a house pseudonym, S. M. Tenneshaw, a house pseudonym, Hall Thornton, Gerald Vance, a house pseudonym, Richard F. Watson)

PERSONAL: Born January 15, 1935, in New York, NY; son of Michael (an accountant) and Helen (Baim) Silverberg; married Barbara H. Brown (an engineer), August 26, 1956 (separated, 1976; divorced, 1986); married Karen L. Haber, 1987. *Education:* Columbia University, B.A., 1956.

ADDRESSES: Home—P.O. Box 13160, Station E, Oakland, CA 94661-0160. *Agent*—Ralph Vicinanza, 111 8th Ave., No. 1501, New York, NY 10011. *E-mail*—ragberg@attglobal.net.

CAREER: Writer, 1956—; president, Agberg Ltd., beginning 1981.

MEMBER: Science Fiction Writers of America (president, 1967-68), Hydra Club (chair, 1958-61).

AWARDS, HONORS: Hugo Awards, World Science Fiction Convention, for best new author, 1956, best novella, 1969, for *Nightwings,* best novella, 1987, for *Gilgamesh in the Outback,* and best novelette, 1990, for *Enter a Soldier. Later: Enter Another; New York*

Times best hundred children's books citation, 1960, for *Lost Race of Mars;* Spring Book Festival Awards, *New York Herald Tribune,* 1962, for *Lost Cities and Vanished Civilizations,* and 1967, for *The Auk, the Dodo, and the Oryx: Vanished and Vanishing Creatures;* National Association of Independent Schools award, 1966, for *The Old Ones: Indians of the American Southwest;* Nebula Award nominations, Science Fiction Writers of America, best novel, 1967, for *Thorns,* best novella, 1967, for *Hawksbill Station,* best novella, 1968, for *Nightwings,* best novel, 1969, for *Up the Line,* best novella, 1969, for *To Jorslem,* best novel, 1970, for *Tower of Glass,* best novel, 1972, for *The Book of Skulls,* best novel, 1972, for *Dying Inside,* best novel, 1975, for *The Stochastic Man,* best novel, 1976, for *Shadrach in the Furnace,* best short story, 1982, for "The Pope of Chimps," best novella, 1983, for *Homefaring,* best novella, 1986, for *Gilgamesh in the Outback,* best novella, 1987, for *The Secret Sharer,* and best novelette, 1989, for *Enter a Soldier. Later: Enter Another;* Hugo Award nominations, best novel, 1968, for *Thorns,* best novella, 1968, for *Hawksbill Station,* best novel, 1970, for *Up the Line,* best short story, 1970, for "Passengers," best novella, 1970, for *To Jorslem,* best novel, 1971, for *Tower of Glass,* best short story, 1971, for "The World Outside," best novel, 1972, for *A Time of Changes,* best novel, 1972, for *The World Inside,* best novel, 1973, for *The Book of Skulls,* best novel, 1973, for *Dying Inside,* best short story, 1973, for "When We Went to See the End of the World," best novella, 1975, for *Born with the Dead,* best short story, 1975, for "Schwartz between Galaxies," best novel, 1976, for *The Stochastic Man,* best novel, 1977, for *Shadrach in the Furnace,* best novel, 1981, for *Lord Valentine's Castle,* best short story, 1981, for "Our Lady of the Sauropods," best novella, 1986, for *Sailing to Byzantium,* best novella, 1988, for *The Secret Sharer,* best novella, 1993, for *Thebes of the Hundred Gates,* best short story, 1995, for "Via Roma," and best short story, 1996, for "Hot Times in Magma City"; Guest of Honor, World Science Fiction Convention, 1970; Nebula Awards, Science Fiction Writers of America, best short story, 1970, for "Passengers," best short story, 1972, for "Good News from the Vatican," best novel, 1972, for *A Time of Changes,* best novella, 1975, for *Born with the Dead,* and best novella, 1986, for *Sailing to Byzantium;* John W. Campbell Memorial Award, 1973, for excellence in writing; Jupiter Award, best novella, 1973, for *The Feast of St. Dionysus;* Prix Apollo, novel, 1976, for *Nightwings;* Milford Award, 1981, for editing; *Locus* Awards, best fantasy novel, 1982, for *Lord Valentine's Castle,* and best anthology, 1999, for

Legends: Short Novels by the Masters of Modern Fantasy; Grand Master Nebula Award, 2004, for body of work.

WRITINGS:

SCIENCE FICTION

Master of Life and Death (also see below), Ace Books (New York, NY), 1957.

The Thirteenth Immortal (bound with *This Fortress World* by J. E. Gunn), Ace Books (New York, NY), 1957.

Invaders from Earth (bound with *Across Time* by D. Grinnell), Ace Books (New York, NY), 1958, published separately, Avon (New York, NY), 1968, published as *We, the Marauders* (bound with *Giants in the Earth* by James Blish under joint title *A Pair in Space*), Belmont (New York, NY), 1965.

Stepsons of Terra (bound with *A Man Called Destiny* by L. Wright), Ace Books (New York, NY), 1958, published separately, 1977.

The Planet Killers (bound with *We Claim These Stars!* by Poul Anderson), Ace Books (New York, NY), 1959.

Collision Course, Avalon (New York, NY), 1961.

Next Stop the Stars (story collection) [and] *The Seed of Earth* (novel), Ace Books (New York, NY), 1962, published separately, 1977.

Recalled to Life, Lancer Books (New York, NY), 1962.

The Silent Invaders (bound with *Battle on Venus* by William F. Temple), Ace Books (New York, NY), 1963, published separately, 1973.

Godling, Go Home! (story collection), Belmont (New York, NY), 1964.

Conquerors from the Darkness, Holt (New York, NY), 1965.

To Worlds Beyond: Stories of Science Fiction, Chilton, 1965.

Needle in a Timestack (story collection), Ballantine (New York, NY), 1966, revised edition, Ace Books (New York, NY), 1985.

Planet of Death, Holt (New York, NY), 1967.

Thorns, Ballantine (New York, NY), 1967.

Those Who Watch, New American Library (New York, NY), 1967.

The Time-Hoppers, Doubleday (New York, NY), 1967.

To Open the Sky (story collection), Ballantine (New York, NY), 1967.

Hawksbill Station, Doubleday (New York, NY), 1968, published as *The Anvil of Time,* Sidgwick & Jackson (London, England), 1968.

The Masks of Time, Ballantine (New York, NY), 1968, published as *Vornan-19,* Sidgwick & Jackson (London, England), 1970.

Dimension Thirteen (story collection), Ballantine (New York, NY), 1969.

The Man in the Maze, Avon (New York, NY), 1969.

Nightwings, Avon (New York, NY), 1969.

(With others) *Three for Tomorrow: Three Original Novellas of Science Fiction,* Meredith Press, 1969.

Three Survived, Holt (New York, NY), 1969.

To Live Again, Doubleday (New York, NY), 1969.

Up the Line, Ballantine (New York, NY), 1969, revised edition, 1978.

The Cube Root of Uncertainty (story collection), Macmillan (New York, NY), 1970.

Downward to the Earth, Doubleday (New York, NY), 1970.

Parsecs and Parables: Ten Science Fiction Stories, Doubleday (New York, NY), 1970.

A Robert Silverberg Omnibus (contains *Master of Life and Death, Invaders from Earth,* and *The Time-Hoppers*), Sidgwick & Jackson (London, England), 1970.

Tower of Glass, Scribner (New York, NY), 1970.

Moonferns and Starsongs (story collection), Ballantine (New York, NY), 1971.

Son of Man, Ballantine (New York, NY), 1971.

A Time of Changes, New American Library (New York, NY), 1971.

The World Inside, Doubleday (New York, NY), 1971.

The Book of Skulls, Scribner (New York, NY), 1972.

Dying Inside, Scribner (New York, NY), 1972, recorded by the author, Caedmon, 1979.

The Reality Trip and Other Implausibilities (story collection), Ballantine (New York, NY), 1972.

The Second Trip, Doubleday (New York, NY), 1972.

Earth's Other Shadow: Nine Science Fiction Stories, New American Library (New York, NY), 1973.

(With others) *No Mind of Man: Three Original Novellas of Science Fiction,* Hawthorn, 1973.

Unfamiliar Territory (story collection), Scribner (New York, NY), 1973.

Valley beyond Time (story collection), Dell (New York, NY), 1973.

Born with the Dead: Three Novellas about the Spirit of Man, Random House (New York, NY), 1974.

Sundance and Other Science Fiction Stories, Thomas Nelson (Nashville, TN), 1974.

The Feast of St. Dionysus: Five Science Fiction Stories, Scribner (New York, NY), 1975.

The Stochastic Man, Harper (New York, NY), 1975.

The Best of Robert Silverberg, Volume 1, Pocket Books (New York, NY), 1976, Volume 2, Gregg, 1978.

Capricorn Games (story collection), Random House (New York, NY), 1976.

Shadrach in the Furnace, Bobbs-Merrill (Indianapolis, IN), 1976.

The Shores of Tomorrow (story collection), Thomas Nelson, 1976.

The Songs of Summer and Other Stories, Gollancz (London, England), 1979.

Lord Valentine's Castle, Harper (New York, NY), 1980.

The Desert of Stolen Dreams, Underwood-Miller, 1981.

A Robert Silverberg Omnibus (contains *Downward to the Earth, The Man in the Maze,* and *Nightwings*), Harper (New York, NY), 1981.

Majipoor Chronicles, Arbor House (New York, NY), 1982.

World of a Thousand Colors (story collection), Arbor House (New York, NY), 1982.

Valentine Pontifex (sequel to *Lord Valentine's Castle*), Arbor House (New York, NY), 1983.

The Conglomeroid Cocktail Party (story collection), Arbor House (New York, NY), 1984.

Sailing to Byzantium, Underwood-Miller, 1985.

Tom O'Bedlam, Donald I. Fine, 1985.

Beyond the Safe Zone: Collected Short Fiction of Robert Silverberg, Donald I. Fine, 1986.

Star of Gypsies, Donald I. Fine, 1986.

At Winter's End, Warner (New York, NY), 1988.

Born with the Dead (bound with *The Saliva Tree* by Brian W. Aldiss), Tor Books (New York, NY), 1988.

To the Land of the Living, Gollancz (London, England), 1989.

(With wife, Karen Haber) *The Mutant Season,* Foundation/Doubleday (New York, NY), 1989.

The New Springtime, Warner (New York, NY), 1990.

In Another Country: Vintage Season, Tor Books (New York, NY), 1990.

(With Isaac Asimov) *Nightfall,* Doubleday (New York, NY), 1990.

Time Gate II, Baen Books (San Bernardino, CA), 1990.

The Face of the Waters, Bantam (New York, NY), 1991.

(With Isaac Asimov) *Child of Time,* Gollancz (London, England), 1991.

(With Isaac Asimov) *The Ugly Little Boy,* Doubleday (New York, NY), 1992.

Thebes of the Hundred Gates, Pulphouse, 1992.

The Collected Stories of Robert Silverberg, Volume 1: Secret Sharers, Bantam (New York, NY), 1992, published in two volumes, Grafton (London, Englan), 1992.

(With Isaac Asimov) *The Positronic Man,* Doubleday (New York, NY), 1993.

Kingdoms of the Wall, Bantam (New York, NY), 1993.

Hot Sky at Midnight, Bantam (New York, NY), 1994.

The Mountains of Majipoor, Bantam (New York, NY), 1995.

Sorcerers of Majipoor, HarperPrism (New York, NY), 1996.

Starborne, Bantam (New York, NY), 1996.

The Alien Years, HarperPrism (New York, NY), 1998.

Lord Prestimion, HarperPrism (New York, NY), 1999.

Roma Eterna, HarperCollins/Eos (New York, NY), 2003.

Also author of short story "Passengers," published in *Orbit 4,* edited by Damon Knight, 1969; of novella *To Jorslem,* published in the periodical *Galaxy,* February, 1969; of short story "The World Outside," published in *Galaxy,* October, 1970; of short story "Good News from the Vatican," published in *Universe 1,* edited by Terry Carr, 1971; of short story "When We Went to See the End of the World," published in *Universe 2,* edited by Terry Carr, 1972; of short story "Schwartz between the Galaxies," published in *Stellar 1,* edited by Judy Lynn del Rey, 1973; of short story "Our Lady of the Sauropods," published in the periodical *Omni,* September, 1980; of short story "The Pope of Chimps," published in *Perpetual Light,* edited by Alan Ryan, 1982; of novella *Homefaring,* published in the periodical *Amazing Stories,* November, 1983; of novella *Gilgamesh in the Outback,* published in the periodical *Asimov's Science Fiction,* July, 1986; of novella *The Secret Sharer,* published in *Asimov's Science Fiction,* September, 1987; of novella *Enter a Soldier. Later: Enter Another,* published in *Asimov's Science Fiction,* June, 1989; of short story "Via Roma," published in *Asimov's Science Fiction,* April, 1994; of short story "Hot Times in Magma City," published in *Asimov's Science Fiction,* December, 1995. Contributor to books, including *The Day the Sun Stood Still,* Thomas Nelson (Nashville, TN), 1972; and *An Exaltation of Stars: Transcendental Adventures in Science Fiction,* edited by Terry Carr, Simon & Schuster (New York, NY), 1973.

JUVENILE FICTION

Revolt on Alpha C, Crowell, 1955.

Starman's Quest, Gnome Press, 1959.

Lost Race of Mars, Winston, 1960.

Regan's Planet, Pyramid Books, 1964, revised edition published as *World's Fair, 1992,* Follett, 1970.

Time of the Great Freeze, Holt (New York, NY), 1964.

The Mask of Akhnaten, Macmillan (New York, NY), 1965.

The Gate of Worlds, Holt (New York, NY), 1967.

The Calibrated Alligator and Other Science Fiction Stories, Holt (New York, NY), 1969.

Across a Billion Years, Dial (New York, NY), 1969.

Sunrise on Mercury and Other Science Fiction Stories, Thomas Nelson (Nashville, TN), 1975.

(Editor, with Charles G. Waugh and Martin H. Greenberg) *The Science Fictional Dinosaur,* Avon (New York, NY), 1982.

Project Pendulum, Walker (New York, NY), 1987.

Letters from Atlantis, Macmillan (New York, NY), 1990.

NONFICTION

First American into Space, Monarch, 1961.

Lost Cities and Vanished Civilizations, Chilton, 1962.

Empires in the Dust: Ancient Civilizations Brought to Light, Chilton, 1963.

The Fabulous Rockefellers: A Compelling, Personalized Account of One of America's First Families, Monarch, 1963.

Akhnaten: The Rebel Pharaoh, Chilton, 1964.

(Editor) *Great Adventures in Archaeology,* Dial (New York, NY), 1964.

Man before Adam: The Story of Man in Search of His Origins, Macrae Smith, 1964.

The Great Wall of China, Chilton, 1965, published as *The Long Rampart: The Story of the Great Wall of China,* 1966.

Scientists and Scoundrels: A Book of Hoaxes, Crowell, 1965.

Bridges, Macrae Smith, 1966.

Frontiers in Archaeology, Chilton, 1966.

The Auk, the Dodo, and the Oryx: Vanished and Vanishing Creatures, Crowell, 1967.

Light for the World: Edison and the Power Industry, Van Nostrand (New York, NY), 1967.

Men against Time: Salvage Archaeology in the United States, Macmillan (New York, NY), 1967.

Mound Builders of Ancient America: The Archaeology of a Myth, New York Graphic Society (New York, NY), 1968.

The Challenge of Climate: Man and His Environment, Meredith Press, 1969.

The World of Space, Meredith Press, 1969.

If I Forget Thee, O Jerusalem: American Jews and the State of Israel, Morrow (New York, NY), 1970.

The Pueblo Revolt, Weybright & Talley, 1970.

Before the Sphinx: Early Egypt, Thomas Nelson (Nashville, TN), 1971.

Clocks for the Ages: How Scientists Date the Past, Macmillan (New York, NY), 1971.

To the Western Shore: Growth of the United States, 1776-1853, Doubleday (New York, NY), 1971.

The Longest Voyage: Circumnavigators in the Age of Discovery, Bobbs-Merrill, 1972.

The Realm of Prester John, Doubleday (New York, NY), 1972.

Drug Themes in Science Fiction, National Institute on Drug Abuse, 1974.

Contributor to nonfiction books, including *Those Who Can,* New American Library (New York, NY), 1973; and *Hell's Cartographers: Some Personal Histories of Science Fiction Writers,* Harper (New York, NY), 1975.

JUVENILE NONFICTION

Treasures beneath the Sea, Whitman Publishing, 1960.

Fifteen Battles That Changed the World, Putnam (New York, NY), 1963.

Home of the Red Man: Indian North America before Columbus, New York Graphic Society (New York, NY), 1963.

Sunken History: The Story of Underwater Archaeology, Chilton, 1963.

The Great Doctors, Putnam (New York, NY), 1964.

The Man Who Found Nineveh: The Story of Austen Henry Layard, Holt (New York, NY), 1964.

Men Who Mastered the Atom, Putnam (New York, NY), 1965.

Niels Bohr: The Man Who Mapped the Atom, Macrae Smith, 1965.

The Old Ones: Indians of the American Southwest, New York Graphic Society (New York, NY), 1965.

Socrates, Putnam (New York, NY), 1965.

The World of Coral, Duell (London, England), 1965.

Forgotten by Time: A Book of Living Fossils, Crowell, 1966.

To the Rock of Darius: The Story of Henry Rawlinson, Holt (New York, NY), 1966.

The Adventures of Nat Palmer: Antarctic Explorer and Clipper Ship Pioneer, McGraw-Hill (New York, NY), 1967.

The Dawn of Medicine, Putnam (New York, NY), 1967.

The Morning of Mankind: Prehistoric Man in Europe, New York Graphic Society (New York, NY), 1967.

The World of the Rain Forest, Meredith Press, 1967.

Four Men Who Changed the Universe, Putnam (New York, NY), 1968.

Ghost Towns of the American West, Crowell (New York, NY), 1968.

Stormy Voyager: The Story of Charles Wilkes, Lippincott (Philadelphia, PA), 1968.

The World of the Ocean Depths, Meredith Press, 1968.

Bruce of the Blue Nile, Holt (New York, NY), 1969.

Vanishing Giants: The Story of the Sequoias, Simon & Schuster (New York, NY), 1969.

Wonders of Ancient Chinese Science, Hawthorn, 1969.

Mammoths, Mastodons, and Man, McGraw-Hill (New York, NY), 1970.

The Seven Wonders of the Ancient World, Crowell-Collier, 1970.

(With Arthur C. Clarke) *Into Space: A Young Person's Guide to Space,* Harper (New York, NY), revised edition, 1971.

John Muir: Prophet among the Glaciers, Putnam (New York, NY), 1972.

The World within the Ocean Wave, Weybright & Talley, 1972.

The World within the Tide Pool, Weybright & Talley, 1972.

EDITOR; SCIENCE FICTION

Earthmen and Strangers: Nine Stories of Science Fiction, Duell (London, England), 1966.

Voyagers in Time: Twelve Stories of Science Fiction, Meredith Press, 1967.

Men and Machines: Ten Stories of Science Fiction, Meredith Press, 1968.

Dark Stars, Ballantine (New York, NY), 1969.

Tomorrow's Worlds: Ten Stories of Science Fiction, Meredith Press, 1969.

The Ends of Time: Eight Stories of Science Fiction, Hawthorn, 1970.

Great Short Novels of Science Fiction, Ballantine (New York, NY), 1970.

The Mirror of Infinity: A Critics' Anthology of Science Fiction, Harper (New York, NY), 1970.

The Science Fiction Hall of Fame, Doubleday (New York, NY), Volume 1, 1970, published in two volumes, Sphere (London, England), 1972.

Worlds of Maybe: Seven Stories of Science Fiction, Thomas Nelson (Nashville, TN), 1970.

Alpha, Volumes 1-6, Ballantine (New York, NY), 1970–76, Volumes 7-9, Berkley (New York, NY), 1977–78.

Four Futures, Hawthorn, 1971.

Mind to Mind: Nine Stories of Science Fiction, Thomas Nelson (Nashville, TN), 1971.

The Science Fiction Bestiary: Nine Stories of Science Fiction, Thomas Nelson (Nashville, TN), 1971.

To the Stars: Eight Stories of Science Fiction, Hawthorn, 1971.

Beyond Control: Seven Stories of Science Fiction, Thomas Nelson (Nashville, TN), 1972.

Invaders from Space: Ten Stories of Science Fiction, Hawthorn, 1972.

Chains of the Sea: Three Original Novellas of Science Fiction, Thomas Nelson (Nashville, TN), 1973.

Deep Space: Eight Stories of Science Fiction, Thomas Nelson (Nashville, TN), 1973.

Other Dimensions: Ten Stories of Science Fiction, Hawthorn, 1973.

Three Trips in Time and Space, Hawthorn, 1973.

Infinite Jests: The Lighter Side of Science Fiction, Chilton, 1974.

Mutants: Eleven Stories of Science Fiction, Thomas Nelson (Nashville, TN), 1974.

Threads of Time: Three Original Novellas of Science Fiction, Thomas Nelson (Nashville, TN), 1974.

Windows into Tomorrow: Nine Stories of Science Fiction, Hawthorn, 1974.

(With Roger Elwood) *Epoch,* Berkley (New York, NY), 1975.

Explorers of Space: Eight Stories of Science Fiction, Thomas Nelson (Nashville, TN), 1975.

The New Atlantis and Other Novellas of Science Fiction, Warner Books (New York, NY), 1975.

Strange Gifts: Eight Stories of Science Fiction, Thomas Nelson (Nashville, TN), 1975.

The Aliens: Seven Stories of Science Fiction, Thomas Nelson (Nashville, TN), 1976.

The Crystal Ship: Three Original Novellas of Science Fiction, Thomas Nelson (Nashville, TN), 1976.

Earth Is the Strangest Planet: Ten Stories of Science Fiction, Thomas Nelson (Nashville, TN), 1977.

Galactic Dreamers: Science Fiction As Visionary Literature, Random House (New York, NY), 1977.

The Infinite Web: Eight Stories of Science Fiction, Dial (New York, NY), 1977.

Triax: Three Original Novellas, Pinnacle, 1977.

Trips in Time: Nine Stories of Science Fiction, Thomas Nelson (Nashville, TN), 1977.

Lost Worlds, Unknown Horizons: Nine Stories of Science Fiction, Thomas Nelson (Nashville, TN), 1978.

The Androids Are Coming: Seven Stories of Science Fiction, Elsevier-Nelson (Nashville, TN), 1979.

(With Martin H. Greenberg and Joseph D. Olander) *Car Sinister,* Avon (New York, NY), 1979.

(With Martin H. Greenberg and Joseph D. Olander) *Dawn of Time: Prehistory through Science Fiction,* Elsevier-Nelson (Nashville, TN), 1979.

The Edge of Space: Three Original Novellas of Science Fiction, Elsevier-Nelson (Nashville, TN), 1979.

(With Martin H. Greenberg) *The Arbor House Treasury of Great Science Fiction Short Novels,* Arbor House (New York, NY), 1980.

(With Martin H. Greenberg) *The Arbor House Treasury of Modern Science Fiction,* Arbor House (New York, NY), 1980.

Randall Garrett, *The Best of Randall Garrett,* Pocket Books (New York, NY), 1982.

The Nebula Awards, Arbor House (New York, NY), 1983.

(With Martin H. Greenberg) *The Arbor House Treasury of Science Fiction Masterpieces,* Arbor House (New York, NY), 1983.

(With Martin H. Greenberg) *The Fantasy Hall of Fame,* Arbor House (New York, NY), 1983.

(With Martin H. Greenberg) *The Time Travelers: A Science Fiction Quartet,* Donald I. Fine, 1985.

(With Martin H. Greenberg) *Neanderthals,* New American Library (New York, NY), 1987.

Robert Silverberg's Worlds of Wonder, Warner (New York, NY), 1987.

(With Martin H. Greenberg) *The Mammoth Book of Fantasy All-Time Greats,* Robinson, 1988.

Worlds Imagined: Fifteen Short Stories, Crown (New York, NY), 1989.

(With Haber) *Universe 1,* Foundation/Doubleday (New York, NY), 1990.

(With Haber) *Universe 2,* Bantam Books (New York, NY), 1992.

Murasaki: A Novel in Six Parts, Bantam/Spectra, 1993.

Alfred Bester, *Virtual Unrealities: The Short Fiction of Alfred Bester,* Vintage (New York, NY), 1997.

Legends: Short Novels by the Masters of Modern Fantasy, Tor Books (New York, NY), 1997.
Legends II: Short Novels by the Masters of Modern Fantasy, Ballantine (New York, NY), 1997.
A Century of Fantasy, 1980-1989, MJF Books, 1997.
A Century of Science Fiction, 1950-1959, MJF Books, 1997.
Far Horizons: All New Tales from the Greatest Worlds of Science Fiction, Avon Eos (New York, NY), 1999.
Phases of the Moon: Stories of Six Decades, SubterraneanTor Books (New York, NY), 1997.

EDITOR; "NEW DIMENSIONS" SERIES

New Dimensions, Volumes 1-5, Doubleday (New York, NY), 1971–75, Volumes 6-10, Harper, (New York, NY) 1976–80, (with Marta Randall) Volumes 11-12, Pocket Books (New York, NY), 1980–81.
The Best of New Dimensions, Pocket Books (New York, NY), 1979.

UNDER PSEUDONYM WALKER CHAPMAN

The Loneliest Continent: The Story of Antarctic Discovery, New York Graphic Society (New York, NY), 1964.
(Editor) *Antarctic Conquest: The Great Explorers in Their Own Words,* Bobbs-Merrill, 1966.
Kublai Khan: Lord of Xanadu, Bobbs-Merrill, 1966.
The Golden Dream: Seekers of El Dorado, Bobbs-Merrill 1967, published as *The Search for El Dorado,* 1967.

UNDER PSEUDONYM DON ELLIOTT

Flesh Peddlers, Nightstand, 1960.
Passion Trap, Nightstand, 1960.
Backstage Sinner, Nightstand, 1961.
Lust Goddess, Nightstand, 1961.
Sin Cruise, Nightstand, 1961.
Kept Man, Midnight, 1962.
Shame House, Midnight, 1962.
Sin Hellion, Ember, 1963.
Sin Servant, Nightstand, 1963.
Beatnik Wanton, Evening, 1964.
Flesh Bride, Evening, 1964.
Flesh Prize, Leisure, 1964.

Flesh Taker, Ember, 1964.
Sin Warped, Leisure, 1964.
Switch Trap, Evening, 1964.
Nudie Packet, Idle Hour, 1965.
The Young Wanton, Sundown, 1965.
Depravity Town, Reed, 1973.
Jungle Street, Reed, 1973.
Summertime Affair, Reed, 1973.

Also author of eighty other novels, 1959-65, under pseudonyms Dan Eliot and Don Elliott.

OTHER

(With Randall Garrett, under joint pseudonym Robert Randall) *The Shrouded Planet,* Gnome Press, 1957, published under names Robert Silverberg and Randall Garrett, Donning, 1980.
(Under pseudonym Calvin M. Knox) *Lest We Forget Thee, Earth,* Ace Books (New York, NY), 1958.
(Under pseudonym David Osborne) *Aliens from Space,* Avalon, 1958.
(Under pseudonym Ivar Jorgenson) *Starhaven,* Avalon, 1958.
(Under pseudonym David Osborne) *Invisible Barriers,* Avalon, 1958.
(With Randall Garrett, under joint pseudonym Robert Randall) *The Dawning Light,* Gnome Press, 1959, published under names Robert Silverberg and Randall Garrett, Donning, 1981.
(Under pseudonym Calvin M. Knox) *The Plot against Earth,* Ace Books (New York, NY), 1959.
(Under pseudonym Walter Drummond) *Philosopher of Evil,* Regency Books, 1962.
(Under pseudonym Walter Drummond) *How to Spend Money,* Regency Books, 1963.
(Under pseudonym Franklin Hamilton) *1066,* Dial (New York, NY), 1963.
(Under pseudonym Calvin M. Knox) *One of Our Asteroids Is Missing,* Ace Books (New York, NY), 1964.
(Under pseudonym Paul Hollander) *The Labors of Hercules,* Putnam (New York, NY), 1965.
(Under pseudonym Franklin Hamilton) *The Crusades,* Dial (New York, NY), 1965.
(Under pseudonym Lloyd Robinson) *The Hopefuls: Ten Presidential Candidates,* Doubleday (New York, NY), 1966.
(Under pseudonym Roy Cook) *Leaders of Labor,* Lippincott (Philadelphia, PA), 1966.

(Under pseudonym Lee Sebastian) *Rivers,* Holt (New York, NY), 1966.

(Under pseudonym Franklin Hamilton) *Challenge for a Throne: The Wars of the Roses,* Dial (New York, NY), 1967.

(Under pseudonym Lloyd Robinson) *The Stolen Election: Hayes versus Tilden,* Doubleday (New York, NY), 1968.

(Under pseudonym Paul Hollander) *Sam Houston,* Putnam (New York, NY), 1968.

(Under pseudonym Lee Sebastian) *The South Pole,* Holt (New York, NY), 1968.

Robert Silverberg Reads "To See the Invisible Man" and "Passengers" (recording), Pelican Records, 1979.

Lord of Darkness (fiction), Arbor House (New York, NY), 1983.

Gilgamesh the King (fiction), Arbor House (New York, NY), 1984.

Reflections and Refractions: Thoughts on Science-Fiction, Science, and Other Matters, Underwood Books (Grass Valley, CA), 1997.

Contributor, sometimes under pseudonyms, to *Omni, Playboy, Amazing Stories Science Fiction, Fantastic Stories Science Fiction, Magazine of Fantasy and Science Fiction,* and other publications.

SIDELIGHTS: Robert Silverberg is among the best-known contemporary science-fiction writers in the United States. A prolific author, he has won the field's prestigious Grand Master Nebula Award as well as the Nebula and Hugo awards and has received more award nominations for his work than any other writer in the genre. Interestingly, despite his prominence in the field, Silverberg's science fiction makes up only a portion of his total production—indeed, he has even left the field entirely to work in other genres on two separate occasions. Much of Silverberg's work has been nonfiction, reflecting his interests in such varied topics as archaeology, conservation, history, and the natural sciences. He has received awards for several of these nonfiction books; in fact, his *Mound Builders of Ancient America: The Archaeology of a Myth* has been hailed as one of the standard works on the subject. Still, this considerable success in the nonfiction field has been largely overshadowed by his continuing popularity among science-fiction fans. As George R. R. Martin, writing in the *Washington Post Book World,* admitted, Silverberg "is best known and best regarded for his work within science fiction."

Silverberg began his writing career while still a student at Columbia University in the 1950s. He had decided to become a science-fiction writer because of his own reaction to the genre as a boy. As he once told Jeffrey M. Elliot in *Science Fiction Voices #2:* "When I was a boy, I read science fiction and it did wonderful things for me. It opened the universe to me. I feel a sense of obligation to science fiction to replace what I had taken from it, to add to the shelf, to put something there for someone else that would do for them what other writers had done for me." Silverberg's first sales were to the science-fiction magazines of the 1950s, and his first book, 1955's *Revolt on Alpha C,* was a juvenile science-fiction novel. Upon graduation from Columbia in 1956, he became a full-time freelance writer. His work was already so popular that the World Science Fiction Convention, a gathering of the genre's devotees, voted him the Hugo Award as the best new writer of 1956. At the time, Silverberg was only twenty-one years old.

During the 1950s Silverberg produced hundreds of stories for science-fiction magazines, and his production was so voluminous that he was obliged to publish much of this work under a host of pseudonyms. Silverberg recalled that time to Charles Platt in *Dream Makers: The Uncommon People Who Write Science Fiction:* "I was courted by editors considerably back then, because I was so dependable; if they said, 'Give me a story by next Thursday,' I would." Essayist George W. Tuma characterized these early stories in the *Dictionary of Literary Biography* as "conform[ing] closely to the conventions of science fiction: alien beings, technological gadgetry, standard plot devices, confrontations between [Earthlings] and extraterrestrial beings, and so forth."

In 1959 a downturn in sales forced many science-fiction magazines out of business. No longer able to support himself by writing for the genre—and somewhat disillusioned by the formulaic nature of the work desired by publishers—Silverberg instead turned to writing articles for popular magazines, maintaining his high level of production by turning out two pieces every working day. By the early 1960s he began writing juvenile nonfiction, a career transition he once recalled with some relief, noting: "I severed my connections with my sleazy magazine outlets and ascended into this new, astoundingly respectable and rewarding career." In a few years Silverberg established himself as one of the most successful nonfiction writers in the country, publishing books about Antarctica, ancient Egypt, the U.S. space program, medical history, and a host of other topics for young readers. "I was considered one of the most skilled popularizers of the sciences in the United States," the author remembered.

During the 1960s Silverberg maintained a rapid writing pace, publishing nearly two million words per year, not only juvenile nonfiction works but science-fiction novels, such as the highly praised *Collision Course,* 1963's *The Silent Invaders,* sci-fi short stories, and rewrites of many of his earlier novels. He told Elliot that he managed to write prolifically due to intense concentration. "I concentrated on a point source and the words just came out right," the author recalled. Barry M. Malzberg in the *Magazine of Fantasy and Science Fiction* allowed that "the man is prolific. Indeed, the man may be, in terms of accumulation of work per working year, the most prolific writer who ever lived."

However, the years of prolific writing finally ended in the mid-1960s. Silverberg later cited two factors for the slowdown in his production at that time. The first was a hyperactive thyroid gland, brought on by prolonged overwork, which forced him in 1966 to slow his working pace considerably. The second factor was a fire in early 1968 at Silverberg's New York City home. This fire "drained from me, evidently forever, much of the bizarre energy that had allowed me to write a dozen or more significant books in a single year," the author once commented.

Despite the drop in production, the late 1960s found the author embarking on more experimental science-fiction writing. In fact, it is the work from this period that most observers have credited as the beginning of his serious fiction in the genre. Thomas D. Clareson, although noting in his book *Robert Silverberg* that "from the beginning, he was a skilled storyteller," marked 1969 to 1976 as the period when Silverberg "conducted his most deliberate experiments and attained the most consistent command of his material." Malzberg claimed that "in or around 1965 Silverberg put his toys away and began to write literature." *Thorns* has been cited as the author's transitional work through its focus on not only the physical universe, but the inner, psychic universe as reflected by philosophical, psychological, and social elements. In the novel, human protagonist Minner Burris has been physically altered to conform to beings on the planet Manipol.

On Manipol, while now accepted for his appearance, Burris is emotionally isolated from native Manipolians due to his social, cultural, and psychological differences. Eventually returning to Earth, he finds himself rejected due to his unusual appearance. Burris's resulting alienation from human society is contrasted with that of other characters, whose circumstances have set them apart while their inner natures continue to need the contact of fellow humans.

In part, the change in Silverberg's science fiction of the late 1960s reflected shifts in the field as a whole. The New Wave, a movement of writers—including Silverberg—trying to break out of the pulp formulas of science fiction and utilize the techniques of modernist literature, had a powerful influence on many writers in the field. New subjects and approaches were suddenly suitable for commercial science fiction. Referring to such novels as 1969's *Nightwings* and 1968's *Hawksbill Station, New York Times Book Review* contributor Theodore Sturgeon maintained that Silverberg "changed into something quite new and different—his own man, saying his own things his own way, and doing it with richness and diversity." Tuma also saw a transformation in Silverberg's work, stating that the author finally "found his unique approach to science fiction, in terms of both content and writing style." And Russell Letson, writing in *Extrapolation,* found Silverberg's more recent fiction "pursued the modernist themes of anxiety and alienation" while he "shaped science fiction materials to deal with themes that were not previously part of the American sf mainstream." Speaking of the novels *Thorns* and *Hawksbill Station,* as well as of the story "To See the Invisible Man," Brian M. Stableford in *Masters of Science Fiction* saw Silverberg as using "science fictional ideas to dramatize situations of extreme alienation."

As Silverberg sought to extend the range of science fiction, his experiments with style and narrative structure continued into the 1970s. "Having already proved that he could write every kind of s.f. story at least as well as anyone else," Gerald Jonas commented in the *New York Times Book Review,* "Silverberg set out . . . to stretch both the genre and himself." In 1971's *Son of Man,* for example, he writes of a series of bizarre adventure sequences set on "not the physical planet Earth but the Earth of human perception—the model world of the mind," as Stableford related. Clay, the novel's aptly named protagonist, time-shifts to the future, where he meets several species of humanoids that have evolved in differing directions. In this future world, communication between beings involves sexual contact, and Clay eventually experiences unity and transcendence through understanding the heightened significance of physical union. Sandra Miesel, writing in *Extrapolation,* called *Son of Man* a "sensuous, didactic, and witty novel" in which "the dream fantasy is stretched to the breaking point."

Despite the fact that his new approach in his work put Silverberg in the forefront of the science-fiction field—"By the 1970s Silverberg was writing science fiction much as such of his contemporaries as Barth, Reed, Bartheleme, and Coover were presenting their renditions of everyday American life," Clareson noted in *Voices for the Future: Essays on Major Science-Fiction Writers*—Silverberg was dissatisfied with the response to his work. His books won awards, but their sales were poor and they often met with uninformed critical comments from science-fiction purists. "I was at first bewildered by the response I was getting from the audience," Silverberg told Platt. "There are passages in *Dying Inside* or in *Nightwings* which I think are sheer ecstatic song, but people would come up to me and say, Why do you write such depressing books? Something was wrong." By 1975 all of Silverberg's more serious books, upon which he had placed such importance, were out of print. At that point he announced his retirement from science fiction.

For the next four years Silverberg wrote no new science fiction. Instead, he devoted his time to the garden of his California home. But in 1978 he was pushed back into the field after he and his first wife separated and she required a house of her own. To raise the necessary money, Silverberg decided to write "one last book." The result, *Lord Valentine's Castle,* is a massive novel that set a record for its time when it was offered to publishers at auction. Harper & Row paid the largest sum ever offered for a science-fiction novel: 127,500 dollars. Silverberg was a writer again.

In *Lord Valentine's Castle* Silverberg mixes elements from science fiction and heroic fantasy. The science-fiction elements include a far-future setting, the imaginary planet of Majipoor, and a host of exotic alien life forms. However, the plot is common to the fantasy genre. It involves a quest by the exiled prince of a distant planet to regain the throne of Majipoor, right the ancient wrong of dispossession committed against the planet's original inhabitants, the primitive

Metamorph peoples, and rejuvenate his own self-confidence. The clever combination of genre elements was praised by Jack Sullivan in the *New York Times Book Review.* Sullivan described *Lord Valentine's Castle* as "an imaginative fusion of action, sorcery and science fiction, with visionary adventure scenes undergirded by scientific explanations." In his book *Robert Silverberg,* Clareson stated, "whatever else it does, *Lord Valentine's Castle* demands that its readers re-examine the relationship between science fiction and fantasy, for in this narrative Silverberg has fused the two together."

The rich diversity of the planet Majipoor was remarked upon by several reviewers, including Patrick Parrinder, reviewing for the *Times Literary Supplement.* "Silverberg's invention," Parrinder wrote, "is prodigious throughout. The early sections . . . are a near-encyclopaedia of unnatural wonders and weird ecosystems. I suspect this book breaks all records in the coinage of new species." John Charnay of the *Los Angeles Times Book Review,* although believing the book "lacks depth of dialogue and emotion to match the grandeur of scenery and plot," still found that "Silverberg's inventiveness is intriguing."

The success of *Lord Valentine's Castle* drew Silverberg back into the writing life. He began to write stories for *Omni* magazine, where several old friends were working. In 1982 he published *Majipoor Chronicles,* a novel fashioned from several short stories set on the planet introduced in *Lord Valentine's Castle.* Each story is an episode from Majipoor's history, which has been stored on an experience-record. By using a futuristic reading machine, a young boy is able to relive these historical events. "As a result," Michael Bishop commented in the *Washington Post Book World,* "the stories become something more than stories—vivid initiation experiences in the boy's struggle to manhood. A neat trick, this." Sturgeon, in his review of the novel for the *Los Angeles Times Book Review,* expressed "absolute awe at Silverberg's capacity for creating images—wonder upon wonder, marvel upon marvel, all with verisimilitude. . . . This is a beautiful book."

With the novel *Valentine Pontifex,* Silverberg did what he had once vowed he would never do: write a sequel to *Lord Valentine's Castle.* Colin Greenland, of the *Times Literary Supplement,* who had found *Lord Valentine's Castle* to be a weak novel that "satisfied readers' wishes for a great big safe world where nice things flourish and evil succumbs to forgiveness," saw Silverberg's sequel as an "act of conscience for *Lord Valentine's Castle*." In *Valentine Pontifex*, Lord Valentine, now restored to his position as ruler of Majipoor, faces opposition from the Piurivars, an aboriginal race dispossessed years before by Earthling colonists. The Piurivars release plagues and deadly bio-engineered creatures upon the humans. Finding that "the lazy pace through time and space" found in *Lord Valentine's Castle* gives way in this novel "to a dance of conflicting emotions and political intrigue," a reviewer for the *Voice Literary Supplement* regarded *Lord Valentine's Castle, Majipoor Chronicles*, and *Valentine Pontifex* as related works forming a loose trilogy that "becomes a whole in a way that the form rarely achieves."

Silverberg continued the "Majipoor" series with *The Mountains of Majipoor, Sorcerers of Majipoor*, and *Lord Prestimion. The Mountains of Majipoor* "is a modest story," recounted Roland Green in *Booklist*, "but the marvelously well-realized world of Majipoor and Silverberg's graceful prose carry it along in a fashion that most lovers of Majipoor will find highly satisfying." *Lord Prestimion*, published in 1999, was also well received by critics. Jackie Cassada in *Library Journal* wrote: "Silverberg excels at balancing strong characters and complex plotting to achieve a rare example of epic fantasy told with a scientist's eye for detail."

In the years since his return from self-imposed "early retirement," Silverberg has continued his work in the genre with both novels and short stories that expand upon his view of future worlds. Among those are 1988's *At Winter's End*, the following year's *To the Land of the Living*, and *Kingdoms of the Wall*, which Silverberg published in 1993. Compared by one reviewer to the works of nineteenth-century British fantasy writer Lord Dunsany, *Kingdoms of the Wall* follows the pilgrimage of a group of young alien beings to the summit of a daunting mountain range called Kosa Saag, or "the Wall." The purpose of the pilgrimage was to learn from the gods who live at that great height. Traditionally, few pilgrims ever returned from this annual trip, and none had ever returned sane. On the way, the group passes through numerous "worlds" at different levels of the mountains' ascent, at one point coming across a space traveler, an "Irtiman"—Earthman—who has been stranded on their planet. He

is weak from hunger and eventually dies. Finally, nearing the summit, the surviving members of the group are tempted to end their quest when they discover a land of magic where they can remain perpetually young. *Analog* reviewer Tom Easton viewed Silverberg's tale as social allegory: "He is . . . hinting that those who persevere despite all the pressures upon them to conform do not find the satisfaction they crave. In fact, if they ever reach the goal of their quest, they are crashingly disillusioned." In contrast, *New York Times Book Review* critic Gerald Jonas viewed the work as a religious parable "about the dangers of seeking more intimate contact with the powers that control the universe." Disregarding both social and spiritual implications, Paul Di-Filippo lauded *Kingdoms of the Wall* in his *Washington Post Book World* review "for its first two-thirds, pure witchery, a Bosch-like canvas of strange creatures and places. . . . *Kingdoms of the Wall* proves once more, if it needed proving, that scaling and comprehending Robert Silverberg is just as exciting as tackling Kosa Saag."

Many of Silverberg's works have been supplemented in bookstores by reprints and limited editions of earlier, often unpublished works. In addition, several collections have drawn together some of his best short fiction from the 1970s and 1980s. *The Conglomeroid Cocktail Party*, released in 1984, collects several short stories from the early 1980s that a *Sci-Fi Review* critic termed "very slick, very polished, and often [focusing on] substantial matters, but at the same time . . . perfunctory." However, Stan Gebler Davies disagreed in *Punch*, praising Silverberg's ability to portray time-travel realistically. Citing included works, such as "Needles in a Timestack" and "Jennifer's Lover," Davies noted that "Silverberg is hooked on time-travel and comes as near as any writer to getting away with it."

With the publication of the first part of *The Collected Stories of Robert Silverberg* in 1992, Silverberg devotees were able to sample twenty-four of his most critically acclaimed short stories of the 1980s. In addition to the novella *Sailing to Byzantium*, winner of the Nebula Award, and *Enter a Soldier. Later: Enter Another*, a Hugo winner, are lesser-known but equally well-written works, each prefaced by the author's own introduction putting the story into the context of the author's total oeuvre. "The end result," noted Gary K. Wolfe in *Locus*, "is not only a good lesson in craft and style, but a clear picture of a highly professional writer who knows exactly what he's doing—even when he plays it safe." James Sallis agreed in a *Los Angeles Times Book Review* piece, "This man who speaks so insistently of simple craftsmanship again and again delivers, surreptitiously and a little abashedly, it seems, a rare kind of art."

Over a writing career spanning several decades, Silverberg has produced an immense body of original fiction in several genres, authored numerous nonfiction works, and edited several highly praised collections, such as 1993's shared-world anthology titles *Murasaki*, featuring work by writers Frederik Pohl, Nancy Kress, and Pou Anderson. Commenting on Silverberg's diversity, Martin reflected that "few writers, past or present, have had careers quite as varied, dramatic, and contradictory as that of Robert Silverberg." He is, Elliot declared, "a titan in the science fiction field." Silverberg's contributions to the field, Clareson added in the *Magazine of Fantasy and Science Fiction,* are of predictably high quality: "He will tell a good story, he will fuse together content and form, and he will add to our perception of the human condition." In his introduction to *Galactic Dreamers: Science Fiction As Visionary Literature,* Silverberg explained what he has strived to attain in his work: "To show the reader something he has never been able to see with his own eyes, something strange and unique, beautiful and troubling, which draws him for a moment out of himself, places him in contact with the vastness of the universe, gives him for a sizzling moment a communion with the fabric of space and time, and leaves him forever transformed, forever enlarged."

BIOGRAPHICAL AND CRITICAL SOURCES:

BOOKS

Aldiss, Brian, and Harry Harrison, editors, *Hell's Cartographers: Some Personal Histories of Science-Fiction Writers,* Harper (New York, NY), 1975.

Chapman, Edgar L., *The Road to Castle Mount: The Science Fiction of Robert Silverberg,* Greenwood Press (New York, NY), 1999.

Children's Literature Review, Volume 59, Thomson Gale (Detroit, MI), 2000.

Clareson, Thomas D., editor, *Voices for the Future: Essays on Major Science Fiction Writers,* Volume 2, Bowling Green State University Popular Press, 1979.

Clareson, Thomas D., *Robert Silverberg,* Starmont House, 1983.

Clareson, Thomas D., *Robert Silverberg: A Primary and Secondary Bibliography,* G. K. Hall (Boston, MA), 1983.

Contemporary Literary Criticism, Volume 7, Thomson Gale (Detroit, MI), 1977.

Dictionary of Literary Biography, Volume 8: *Twentieth-Century American Science Fiction Writers,* Thomson Gale (Detroit, MI), 1981.

Elliot, Jeffrey M., *Science Fiction Voices #2,* Borgo Press (San Bernardino, CA), 1979.

Magill, Frank N., editor, *Survey of Science Fiction,* Salem Press, 1979.

Platt, Charles, *Dream Makers: The Uncommon People Who Write Science Fiction,* Berkley (New York, NY), 1980.

Rabkin, Eric S., and others, editors, *No Place Else,* Southern Illinois University Press (Carbondale, IL), 1983.

Schweitzer, Darrell, editor, *Exploring Fantasy Worlds: Essays on Fantastic Literature,* Borgo Press (San Bernardino, CA), 1985.

Silverberg, Robert, editor, *Galactic Dreamers: Science Fiction As Visionary Literature,* Random House (New York, NY), 1977.

Stableford, Brian M., *Masters of Science Fiction,* Borgo Press (San Bernardino, CA), 1981.

Staircar, Tom, editor, *Critical Encounters II,* Ungar, 1982.

Walker, Paul, *Speaking of Science Fiction: The Paul Walker Interviews,* Luna Press, 1978.

PERIODICALS

Analog Science Fiction/Science Fact, November, 1979; December, 1990; August, 1993, p. 162; July, 1994, p. 306.

Atlantic, April, 1972.

Booklist, September 1, 1992; February 1, 1995, p. 993; May 15, 1996, p. 1573; April 1, 1997, p. 1277; August, 1998, p. 1924; May 15, 1999, p. 1676; May 1, 2003, p. 1586.

Essays in Arts and Sciences, August, 1980.

Extrapolation, summer, 1979; winter, 1980; winter, 1982.

Fantasy Newsletter, June-July, 1983.

Library Journal, June 15, 1997, p. 101; August, 1998, p. 139; August, 1999, p. 147.

Locus, March, 1992, p. 60; April, 1992, p. 15; October, 1992, p. 33; January, 1993, pp. 22-23; February, 1994, p. 27.

Los Angeles Times Book Review, May 18, 1980; April 18, 1986; September 13, 1987; January 10, 1993.

Magazine of Fantasy and Science Fiction, April, 1971; April, 1974; May, 1988.

Megavore, March, 1981.

National Review, November 3, 1970.

New Statesman, June 18, 1976.

New York Times Book Review, May 9, 1965; November 3, 1968; March 5, 1972; August 24, 1975; August 3, 1980; August 4, 1985; November 23, 1986; July 24, 1988; December 31, 1989; May 13, 1990; December 9, 1990; May 3, 1992, p. 38; March 14, 1993; November 14, 1993; March 13, 1994, p. 30; June 30, 1996, p. 28.

Publishers Weekly, December 20, 1993, p. 54; January 16, 1995, p. 444; May 27, 1996, p. 69; January 27, 1997, p. 86; June 16, 1997, p. 49; June 29, 1998, p. 40; September 21, 1998, p. 78; April 12, 1999, p. 58; July 26, 1999, p. 68; May 3, 2004, p. 176.

Punch, March 6, 1985, p. 54.

Rapport, Volume 18, number 2, 1994, p. 19.

Science Fiction: A Review of Speculative Literature, September, 1983.

Science Fiction Chronicle, January, 1985; May, 1985.

Sci-Fi Review, February, 1985, pp. 51-52.

Starship, November, 1982.

Times (London, England), November 19, 1988; August 2, 1990.

Times Literary Supplement, June 12, 1969; March 15, 1974; November 7, 1980; August 3, 1984; January 2, 1987.

Tribune Books (Chicago, IL), December 30, 1990.

Voice Literary Supplement, December, 1983.

Voice of Youth Advocates, August, 1993, pp. 170-171; June, 1993, p. 104.

Washington Post Book World, February 28, 1982; May 8, 1983; September 28, 1986; September 27, 1987; May 27, 1990; March 28, 1993, p. 9.

Writer, November, 1977.*

*   *   *

SIMIC, Charles 1938-

PERSONAL: Born May 9, 1938, in Belgrade, Yugoslavia; immigrated to the United States, 1954, naturalized citizen, 1971; son of George (an engineer) and Helen (Matijevic) Simic; married Helene Dubin (a designer),

Charles Simic

October 25, 1965; children: Anna, Philip. *Education:* New York University, B.A., 1967. *Religion:* Eastern Orthodox.

ADDRESSES: Home—P.O. Box 192, Strafford, NH 03884-0192. *Office*—Department of English, University of New Hampshire, Durham, NH 03824.

CAREER: Poet and educator. *Aperture* (photography magazine), New York, NY, editorial assistant, 1966-69; University of New Hampshire, Durham, associate professor of English, 1973—. Visiting assistant professor of English, State University of California, Hayward, 1970-73, Boston University, 1975, and Columbia University, 1979. *Military service:* U.S. Army, 1961-63.

AWARDS, HONORS: PEN International Award for translation, 1970; Guggenheim fellowship, 1972-73; National Endowment for the Arts fellowship, 1974-75, and 1979-80; Edgar Allan Poe Award from American Academy of Poets, 1975; National Institute of Arts and Letters and American Academy of Arts and Letters Award, 1976; National Book Award nomination, 1978, for *Charon's Cosmology;* Harriet Monroe Poetry Award from University of Chicago, Di Castignola Award from Poetry Society of America, 1980, and PEN translation award, all 1980; Fulbright traveling fellowship, 1982; Ingram Merrill fellowship, 1983-84; MacArthur Foundation fellowship, 1984-89; Pulitzer Prize nominations, 1986 and 1987; Pulitzer Prize, 1990, for *The World Doesn't End;* National Book Award finalist in poetry, 1996, for *Walking the Black Cat;* nominated for the National Book Award for poetry and for the *Los Angeles Times* Book Award for poetry, both 2003, both for *The Voice at 3:00 a.m.: Selected Late and New Poems.*

WRITINGS:

POETRY

What the Grass Says, Kayak (San Francisco, CA), 1967.

Somewhere among Us a Stone Is Taking Notes, Kayak (San Francisco, CA), 1969.

Dismantling the Silence, Braziller (New York, NY), 1971.

White, New Rivers Press, 1972, revised edition, Logbridge Rhodes (Durango, CO), 1980.

Return to a Place Lit by a Glass of Milk, Braziller (New York, NY), 1974.

Biography and a Lament, Bartholemew's Cobble (Hartford, CT), 1976.

Charon's Cosmology, Braziller (New York, NY), 1977.

Brooms: Selected Poems, Edge Press (Christchurch, NZ), 1978.

School for Dark Thoughts, Banyan Press (Pawlet, VT), 1978, sound recording of same title published by Watershed Tapes (Washington, DC), 1978.

Classic Ballroom Dances, Braziller (New York, NY), 1980.

Austerities, Braziller (New York, NY), 1982.

Weather Forecast for Utopia and Vicinity, Station Hill Press (Barrytown, NY), 1983.

Selected Poems, 1963-1983, Braziller (New York, NY), 1985.

Unending Blues, Harcourt (New York, NY), 1986.

Nine Poems, Exact Change (Cambridge, MA), 1989.

The World Doesn't End, Harcourt (New York, NY), 1989.

The Book of Gods and Devils, Harcourt (New York, NY), 1990.

Hotel Insomnia, Harcourt (New York, NY), 1992.

A Wedding in Hell: Poems, Harcourt (New York, NY), 1994.

Frightening Toys, Faber & Faber (New York, NY), 1995.

Walking the Black Cat: Poems, Harcourt (New York, NY), 1996.

Jackstraws: Poems, Harcourt (New York, NY), 1999, revised edition, Faber & Faber (New York, NY), 2000.

Selected Early Poems, Braziller (New York, NY), 2000.

Night Picnic, Harcourt (New York, NY), 2001.

The Voice at 3:00 a.m.: Selected Late and New Poems, Harcourt (New York, NY), 2003.

Aunt Lettuce, I Want to Peek under Your Skirt, Bloomsbury USA (New York, NY), 2005.

Contributor of poetry to more than one hundred magazines, including *New Yorker, Poetry, Nation, Kayak, Atlantic, Esquire, Chicago Review, New Republic, American Poetry Review, Paris Review,* and *Harvard Magazine.*

TRANSLATOR

Ivan V. Lalic, *Fire Gardens,* New Rivers Press (Moorhead, MN), 1970.

Vasko Popa, *The Little Box: Poems,* Charioteer Press (Washington, DC), 1970.

Four Modern Yugoslav Poets: Ivan V. Lalic, Branko Miljkovic, Milorad Pavic, Ljubomir Simovic, Lillabulero (Ithaca, NY), 1970.

(And editor, with Mark Strand) *Another Republic: Seventeen European and South American Writers,* Viking (New York, NY), 1976.

Vasko Popa, *Homage to the Lame Wolf: Selected Poems,* Field (Oberlin, OH), 1979.

(With Peter Kastmiler) Slavko Mihalic, *Atlantis,* Greenfield Review Press (Greenfield Center, NY), 1983.

Tomaz Salamun, *Selected Poems,* Viking (New York, NY), 1987.

Ivan V. Lalic, *Roll Call of Mirrors,* Wesleyan University Press, 1987.

Aleksandar Ristovic, *Some Other Wine or Light,* Charioteer Press (Washington, DC), 1989.

Stavko Janevski, *Bandit Wind,* Dryad Press (College Park, MD), 1991.

Novica Tadic, *Night Mail: Selected Poems,* Oberlin College Press (Oberlin, OH), 1992.

Horse Has Six Legs: Contemporary Serbian Poetry, Graywolf Press (Saint Paul, MN), 1992.

Aleksander Ristovic, *Devil's Lunch,* Faber & Faber (New York, NY), 1999.

Radmila Lazic, *A Wake for the Living,* Graywolf Press (Saint Paul, MN), 2003.

Gunter Grass, *The Gunter Grass Reader,* Harcourt (New York, NY), 2004.

OTHER

The Uncertain Certainty: Interviews, Essays, and Notes on Poetry, University of Michigan Press (Ann Arbor, MI), 1985.

Wonderful Words, Silent Truth, University of Michigan Press (Ann Arbor, MI), 1990.

Dime-Store Alchemy: The Art of Joseph Cornell, Ecco (New York, NY), 1992.

The Unemployed Fortune-Teller: Essays and Memoirs, University of Michigan Press (Ann Arbor, MI), 1994.

Orphan Factory: Essays and Memoirs, University of Michigan Press (Ann Arbor, MI), 1997.

A Fly in the Soup: Memoirs, University of Michigan Press (Ann Arbor, MI), 2000.

Metaphysician in the Dark (essays), University of Michigan Press (Ann Arbor, MI), 2003.

(Editor, with Don Paterson) *New British Poetry,* Graywolf Press (Saint Paul, MN), 2004.

Simic's works have been translated into several languages, including French, Dutch, Macedonian, Norwegian, Polish, Spanish, and German.

Contributor to anthologies, including *Young American Poets,* Follett, 1968; *Contemporary American Poets,* World Publishing, 1969; *Major Young American Poets,* World Publishing, 1971; *America a Prophesy,* Random House, 1973; *Shake the Kaleidoscope: A New Anthology of Modern Poetry,* Pocket Books, 1973; *The New Naked Poetry,* Bobbs-Merrill, 1976; *The American Poetry Anthology,* Avon, 1976; *A Geography of Poets,* Bantam, 1979; *Contemporary American Poetry, 1950-1980,* Longman, 1983; *The Norton Anthology of Poetry,* Norton, 1983; *Harvard Book of American Poetry,* Harvard University Press, 1985; and *The Harper American Literature,* Volume 2, Harper, 1987. Author of introductions, *Homage to a Cat: As It Were: Logscapes of the Lost Ages,* by Vernon Newton, Northern Lights, 1991, and *Prisoners of Freedom: Contemporary Slovenian Poetry,* edited by Ales Debeljak, Pedernal, 1992.

SIDELIGHTS: Charles Simic, a native of Yugoslavia who immigrated to the United States during his teens, has been hailed as one of his adopted homeland's finest poets. Simic's work, which includes *Unending Blues, Walking the Black Cat,* and *Hotel Insomnia,* has won numerous awards, among them the 1990 Pulitzer Prize and the coveted MacArthur Foundation "genius grant." Although he writes in English, Simic draws upon his own experiences of war-torn Belgrade to compose poems about the physical and spiritual poverty of modern life. *Hudson Review* contributor Liam Rector noted that the author's work "has about it a purity, an originality unmatched by many of his contemporaries."

The receipt of a Pulitzer Prize for *The World Doesn't End* may have widened Simic's audience, but the poet has never lacked admirers in the community of creative writers. In the *Chicago Review,* Victor Contoski characterized Simic's work as "some of the most strikingly original poetry of our time, a poetry shockingly stark in its concepts, imagery, and language." *Georgia Review* correspondent Peter Stitt wrote: "The fact that [Simic] spent his first eleven years surviving World War II as a resident of Eastern Europe makes him a going-away-from-home writer in an especially profound way. . . . He is one of the wisest poets of his generation, and one of the best." In a piece for the *New Boston Review,* Robert Shaw concluded that Simic "is remarkably successful at drawing the reader into his own creative moment."

Simic spent his formative years in Belgrade. His early childhood coincided with World War II; several times his family evacuated their home to escape indiscriminate bombing—or as he put it in an online interview for *Cortland Review,* "My travel agents were Hitler and Stalin." The atmosphere of violence and desperation continued after the war. Simic's father left the country for work in Italy, and his mother tried several times to follow, only to be turned back by authorities.

In the meantime, young Simic was growing up in Belgrade, where he was considered a below-average student and a minor troublemaker.

When Simic was fifteen, his mother finally arranged for the family to travel to Paris. After a year spent studying English in night school and attending French public schools during the day, Simic sailed for America and a reunion with his father. He entered the United States at New York City and then moved with his family to Chicago, where he enrolled in high school. In a suburban school with caring teachers and motivated students, Simic began to take new interest in his courses, especially literature.

Simic also began to take a serious interest in poetry, though he admits that one reason he began exploring the art form was to meet girls. Talking on the *Artful Dodge* home page, Simic compared his nascent interest in poetry to another early passion, jazz: "It's a music I've loved from the first time I heard it. . . . There was an American Armed Forces station in Italy and you could pick it up. And I remember my mother and I had a terrific, old German radio; it was a huge thing and I was playing with the dial, and I heard something and I wanted to figure out what the hell it was. It was Big Band music, a kind of bluesy thing. . . . I remember instantly liking it. I had no idea what it was."

Simic's first poems were published in 1959, when he was twenty-one. He also confesses that he started a novel at age twenty, a decision he has lived to regret: "You've got to be really stupid to start writing a novel at twenty," he told *Artful Dodge*. "I remember I wrote out a plot, to page 55. Then I ran out of ideas."

Between that year and 1961, when he entered the service, he churned out a number of poems, most of which he has since destroyed. Simic finally earned his bachelor's degree in 1966. His first full-length collection of poems, *What the Grass Says,* was published the following year. In a very short time, Simic's work, including both original poetry in English and translations of important Yugoslavian poets, began to attract critical attention. In *The American Moment: American Poetry in the Mid-Century,* Geoffrey Thurley noted that the substance of Simic's earliest verse—its material referents—"are European and rural rather than American and urban. . . . The world his poetry cre-

ates—or rather with its brilliant semantic evacuation decreates—is that of central Europe—woods, ponds, peasant furniture." *Voice Literary Supplement* reviewer Matthew Flamm also contended that Simic was writing "about bewilderment, about being part of history's comedy act, in which he grew up half-abandoned in Belgrade and then became, with his Slavic accent, an American poet."

Simic's work defies easy categorization. Some poems reflect a surreal, metaphysical bent and others offer grimly realistic portraits of violence and despair. *Hudson Review* contributor Vernon Young maintained that memory—a taproot deep into European folklore—is the common source of all of Simic's poetry. "Simic, a graduate of NYU, married and a father in pragmatic America, turns, when he composes poems, to his unconscious and to earlier pools of memory," the critic wrote. "Within microcosmic verses which may be impish, sardonic, quasirealistic or utterly outrageous, he succinctly implies an historical montage." Young elaborated: "His Yugoslavia is a peninsula of the mind. . . . He speaks by the fable; his method is to transpose historical actuality into a surreal key. . . . [Simic] feels the European yesterday on his pulses."

Some of Simic's best-known works challenge the dividing line between the ordinary and extraordinary. He gives substance and even life to inanimate objects, discerning the strangeness in household items as ordinary as a knife or a spoon. Shaw wrote in the *New Republic* that the most striking perception of the author's early poems was that "inanimate objects pursue a life of their own and present, at times, a dark parody of human existence." *Chicago Review* contributor Victor Contoski concluded: "Simic's efforts to interpret the relationship between the animate and inanimate have led to some of the most strikingly original poetry of our time, a poetry shockingly stark in its concepts, imagery, and language." As Anthony Libby put it in the *New York Times Book Review,* Simic "takes us to his mysterious target, the other world concealed in this one."

Childhood experiences of war, poverty, and hunger lie behind a number of Simic's poems. *Georgia Review* correspondent Peter Stitt claimed that the poet's most persistent concern "is with the effect of cruel political structures upon ordinary human life. . . . The world of Simic's poems is frightening, mysterious, hostile, dangerous." Thurley also declared that Simic "creates a world of silence, waiting for the unspeakable to happen, or subsisting in the limbo left afterwards. . . . The dimension of menace in Simic becomes metaphysics in itself." Simic tempers this perception of horror with gallows humor and an ironic self-awareness. Stitt averred: "Even the most somber poems . . . exhibit a liveliness of style and imagination that seems to re-create, before our eyes, the possibility of light upon the earth. Perhaps a better way of expressing this would be to say that Simic counters the darkness of political structures with the sanctifying light of art."

Critics find Simic's style particularly accessible, a substantial achievement for an author for whom English is a second language. According to Shaw, the "exile's consciousness still colors [Simic's] language as well as his view of existence. Having mastered a second language, Simic is especially aware of the power of words, and of the limits which words grope to overcome. His diction is resolutely plain: as with the everyday objects he writes about, he uncovers unexpected depth in apparently commonplace language." In the *New Letters Review of Books*, Michael Milburn remarked: "Charles Simic is a poet of original vision. . . . Simic practically taunts the reader with a familiarity bordering on cliche. He seems to challenge himself to write as plainly as possible, while still producing works of freshness and originality. [His works] literally beckon us off the street and into a world that at first looks indistinguishable from our own. . . . But a brilliant method lies behind Simic's plainness. . . . Casual, unobtrusive language expresses the most fantastic images." Milburn added that the poet "mines ingredients of language and experience that readers may take for granted, and fuses them in a singular music."

Since 1973 Simic has taught English, creative writing, and criticism at the University of New Hampshire. He describes the New England environment as ripe for producing original thinkers because, as he said on *Artful Dodge*, "[there] are these states like Maine and New Hampshire filled with little out-of-the-way places which have winter for nine months. You discover that these poor children in these places have inner lives, an inwardness, because there is nothing else to do but scrutinize the self. Introspection is a big thing, even though now cable TV has come into New England."

At the same time, Simic has reached out to students in urban settings, places where poetry isn't assumed to be part of daily life. But the students in New York City slums, he says, "had absolutely no difficulty understanding poetry. . . . I was reading them Whitman. I was reading them Emily Dickinson. And this happened repeatedly. I found that these kids understood poetry much better than the kids in [upscale] Westchester." As opposed to the inner-city youths who accepted the poetry on its own terms, Simic notes, the suburban students, "if you gave them the simplest poem, would want to know what it 'means'. . . . They did not know how to read poetry."

In 1996 Simic published another poetry collection, *Walking the Black Cat*. In this work, a *Publishers Weekly* reviewer found the poet's "short, taut lines" carve "dark-edged images" in passages that present the black cat—a traditional symbol of bad luck—as a "constant, even loved, companion." On the other hand, Paul Breslin of *Poetry* had more to criticize: While the best passages in *Black Cat* "won't submit to their own glibness altogether . . . on the whole I have the sense of a style running on automatic pilot, the urgencies that once called it into existence largely forgotten." (Responding to such criticism, the poet remarked to J. M. Spalding in the *Cortland Review*: "I would consider myself a total failure in life if Paul Breslin admired my work. Everything I have ever done as a poet was done in contempt of what he regards as 'good' poetry.")

In addition to poetry and prose poems, Simic has also written several works of prose nonfiction, including 1992's *Dime-Store Alchemy: The Art of Joseph Cornell*. A literary paean to one of the most innovative visual artists of the twentieth century, Simic's book highlights Cornell's work, which included minimalist sculptures using found objects to create intriguing surrealist collages, by creating verbal collages that are themselves composed of still smaller units of prose. "As in his poems, Simic's style in *Dime-Store Alchemy* is deceptively offhand and playful," noted Edward Hirsch in the *New Yorker*, "moving fluently between the frontal statement and the indirect suggestion, the ordinary and the metaphysical." Among Simic's essay collections is *Orphan Factory*. According to a *Publishers Weekly* reviewer, these essays and brief memoirs are at their best "when fragmentary and spontaneous ideas and images combine." The reviewer also praised the work for its "wisdom and humor."

The poetry collection *The Voice at 3:00 a.m.: Selected Late and New Poems* offers "oblique self-perceptions, metaphysical musings, inexplicable intimations and—

not least—amorous affection," according to John Taylor of the *Antioch Review*. Donna Seaman of *Booklist* declared Simic a "unique and necessary voice in American poetry" whose "brooding lyrics are eloquently spare."

Diana Engelmann of the *Antioch Review* commented at length about Simic's poetry as being a dual voice that speaks both as an American and as an exile. She observed, "While it is true that the experiences of Charles Simic, the 'American poet,' provide a uniquely cohesive force in his verse, it is also true that the voices of the foreign and of the mother tongue memory still echo in many poems." Engelmann concluded, "Simic's poems convey the characteristic duality of exile: they are at once authentic statements of the contemporary American sensibility and vessels of internal translation, offering a passage to what is silent and foreign." Discussing his creative process, Simic commented on *Artful Dodge*: "When you start putting words on the page, an associative process takes over. And, all of a sudden, there are surprises. All of a sudden you say to yourself, 'My God, how did this come into your head? Why is this on the page?' I just simply go where it takes me."

BIOGRAPHICAL AND CRITICAL SOURCES:

BOOKS

Contemporary Authors Autobiography Series, Volume 4, Thomson Gale (Detroit, MI), 1986.
Contemporary Literary Criticism, Thomson Gale (Detroit, MI), Volume 6, 1976, Volume 9, 1978, Volume 22, 1982, Volume 49, 1988, Volume 68, 1991.
Thurley, Geoffrey, *The American Moment: American Poetry in the Mid-Century,* St. Martin's Press (New York, NY), 1978.
Weigl, Bruce, editor, *Charles Simic: Essays on the Poetry,* University of Michigan Press (Ann Arbor, MI), 1996.

PERIODICALS

America, January 13, 1996, p. 18.
Antioch Review, spring, 1977; John Taylor, review of *The Voice at 3:00 a.m.: Selected Late and New Poems;* winter, 2004, p. 176; winter, 2004, Diana Engelmann, "Speaking in Tongues: Exile and Internal Translation in the Poetry of Charles Simic," p. 44.

Booklist, October 1, 1997, review of *Walking the Black Cat,* p. 317; April 1, 2003, Donna Seaman, review of *The Voice at 3:00 a.m.,* p. 1370.
Boston Review, March-April, 1981; April, 1986.
Chicago Review, Volume 48, number 4, 1977.
Choice, March, 1975.
Gargoyle, number 22-23, 1983.
Georgia Review, winter, 1976; summer, 1986.
Hudson Review, spring, 1981; autumn, 1986.
Los Angeles Times Book Review, March 16, 1986; December 7, 1986; December 27, 1992, pp. 1, 8.
New Boston Review, March-April, 1981.
New Letters Review of Books, spring, 1987.
New Republic, January 24, 1976; March 1, 1993, p. 28.
New Yorker, December 21, 1992, pp. 130-135; June 28, 1993, p. 74.
New York Times, May 28, 1990.
New York Times Book Review, March 5, 1978; October 12, 1980; May 1, 1983; January 12, 1986; October 18, 1987; March 21, 1993, pp. 14, 16; April 16, 2000, review of *Selected Early Poems,* p. 23.
People, May 5, 1997, review of *Walking the Black Cat,* p. 40.
Ploughshares, Volume 7, number 1, 1981.
Poet and Critic, Volume 9, number 1, 1975.
Poetry, December, 1968; September, 1971; March, 1972; February, 1975; November, 1978; July, 1981; October, 1983; July, 1987; April, 1996, p. 33; July, 1997, review of *Walking the Black Cat,* p. 226.
Poetry Review, June, 1983.
Publishers Weekly, November 2, 1990; September 21, 1992, p. 78; August 25, 1997, review of *Orphan Factory,* p. 54.
Stand, summer, 1984.
Tribune Books (Chicago, IL), June 12, 1983.
Village Voice, April 4, 1974; February 28, 1984.
Virginia Quarterly Review, spring, 1975.
Voice Literary Supplement, December, 1986.
Washington Post, April 13, 1990.
Washington Post Book World, November 2, 1980; April 13, 1986; May 7, 1989; January 3, 1993, pp. 9-10.

ONLINE

Artful Dodge, http://www.wooster.edu/ (August 24, 2000).
Cortland Review, http://www.cortlandreview.com/ (August 24, 2000).*

SIMPSON, Louis (Aston Marantz) 1923-

PERSONAL: Born March 27, 1923, in Kingston, Jamaica, British West Indies; United States citizen; son of Aston and Rosalind (Marantz) Simpson; married Jeanne Rogers, 1949 (divorced, 1954); married Dorothy Roochvarg, 1955 (divorced, 1979); married Miriam Butensky Bachner, 1985; children: (first marriage) Matthew; (second marriage) Anne, Anthony. *Education:* Columbia University, B.S., 1948, A.M., 1950, Ph.D., 1959.

ADDRESSES: Home—186 Old Field Rd., Setauket, New York, NY 11733-1636.

CAREER: Bobbs-Merrill Publishing Co., New York, NY, editor, 1950-55; Columbia University, New York, NY, instructor in English, 1953-59; New School for Social Research, instructor in English, 1955-59; University of California, Berkeley, 1959-67, began as assistant professor, became professor of English; State University of New York at Stony Brook, professor of English and comparative literature, 1967-91, distinguished professor, 1991-93, professor emeritus, 1993—. Has given poetry readings at colleges and poetry centers throughout the United States and Europe and on television and radio programs in New York, San Francisco, and London. *Military service:* U.S. Army, 1943-46; became sergeant; awarded Bronze Star with oak leaf cluster, Purple Heart (twice), Presidential Unit Citation.

MEMBER: American Academy in Rome.

AWARDS, HONORS: Fellowship in literature (Prix de Rome) at American Academy in Rome, 1957; *Hudson Review* fellowship, 1957; Columbia University, distinguished alumni award, 1960, Medal for Excellence, 1965; Edna St. Vincent Millay Award, 1960; Guggenheim fellowship, 1962, 1970; American Council of Learned Societies grant, 1963; Pulitzer Prize for poetry, 1964, for *At the End of the Open Road;* Medal for Excellence, Columbia University, 1965; Commonwealth Club of California poetry award, 1965; American Academy of Arts and Letters award in literature, 1976; D.H.L., Eastern Michigan University, 1977; Institute of Jamaica, Centenary Medal, 1980; Jewish Book Council, Award for Poetry, 1981; Elmer Holmes Bobst Award, 1987; Academy of

Louis Simpson

American Poets, Harold Morton Landon Translation Award, 1998, for *Modern Poets of France;* Hampden Sydney College, D.Litt., 1990; nominated for the National Book Award for poetry, 2003, for *The Owner of the House: New Collected Poems;* Griffin Poetry Prize, 2004 for *The Owner of the House.*

WRITINGS:

The Arrivistes: Poems, 1940-49, Fine Editions, 1949.
Good News of Death and Other Poems, Scribner (New York, NY), 1955.
(Editor, with Donald Hall and Robert Pack) *The New Poets of England and America,* Meridian, 1957.
A Dream of Governors (poems), Wesleyan University Press (Middletown, CT), 1959.
Riverside Drive (novel), Atheneum, 1962.
James Hogg: A Critical Study, St. Martin's Press (New York, NY), 1962.
At the End of the Open Road (poems), Wesleyan University Press (Middletown, CT), 1963.
(Contributor) Thom Gunn and Ted Hughes, editors, *Five American Poets,* Faber (London, England), 1963.

Selected Poems, Harcourt (New York, NY), 1965.

(Editor) *An Introduction to Poetry,* St. Martin's Press (New York, NY), 1967, 2nd edition, 1972.

Adventures of the Letter I (poems), Harper (New York, NY), 1971.

North of Jamaica (autobiography), Harper (New York, NY), 1972, published as *Air with Armed Men,* London Magazine Editions, 1972.

Three on the Tower: The Lives and Works of Ezra Pound, T. S. Eliot and William Carlos Williams (literary criticism), Morrow, 1975.

Searching for the Ox (poems), Morrow, 1976.

A Revolution in Taste: Studies of Dylan Thomas, Allen Ginsberg, Sylvia Plath and Robert Lowell (literary criticism), Macmillan, 1978, published in England as *Studies of Dylan Thomas, Allen Ginsberg, Sylvia Plath and Robert Lowell,* Macmillan (New York, NY), 1979.

Armidale (poems), BOA Editions, 1979.

Out of Season (poems), Deerfield Press, 1979.

Caviare at the Funeral (poems), Franklin Watts, 1980.

A Company of Poets (literary criticism), University of Michigan (Ann Arbor, MI), 1981.

The Best Hour of the Night (poems), Ticknor & Fields, 1983.

People Live Here: Selected Poems, 1949-1983, BOA Editions, 1983.

The Character of the Poet (literary criticism), University of Michigan (Ann Arbor, MI), 1986.

An Introduction to Poetry, St. Martin's Press (New York, NY), 1986.

Collected Poems, Paragon House (New York, NY), 1988.

Selected Prose, Paragon House (New York, NY), 1988.

Selected Prose, Paragon House (New York, NY), 1989.

Wei Wei and Other Friends (poems), Typographeum, 1990.

In the Room We Share (poems), Paragon House (New York, NY), 1990.

Jamaica Poems, Press of Appletree Alley, 1993.

Ships Going into the Blue: Essays and Notes on Poetry, University of Michigan Press (Ann Arbor, MI), 1994.

The King My Father's Wreck (memoir), Story Line Press, 1994.

There You Are: Poems, Story Line (Brownsville, OR), 1995.

Modern Poets of France: A Bilingual Anthology (poems), Story Line Press, 1997.

(Translator) *The Legacy & The Testament,* Story Line Press, 2000.

The Owner of the House: New Collected Poems, BOA Editions, 2003.

Contributor of poems, plays, and articles to literary periodicals, including *American Poetry Review, Listener, Hudson Review, Paris Review,* and *Critical Quarterly.* Sound recordings include: *Louis Simpson Reading His Poems with Comment in New York City, Mar. 19, 1959,* 1959; *Louis Aston Marantz Simpson and James Wright Reading and Discussing Their Poetry in the Coolidge Auditorium, Dec. 5, 1966,* 1966.

SIDELIGHTS: Jamaican-born poet and educator Louis Simpson, author of poetry collections that include the Pulitzer Prize-winning *At the End of the Open Road, Searching for the Ox,* and *There You Are,* is noted for simple, controlled verses that reveal hidden layers of meaning. Critic Yohma Gray wrote in praise of the poet's ability to make his readers heed that which usually passes undiscerned. "Even in the most mundane experience there is a vast area of unperceived reality," the critic noted, "and it is Louis Simpson's kind of poetry which brings it to our notice. It enables us to see things which are ordinarily all about us but which we do not ordinarily see; it adds a new dimension to our sensational perception, making us hear with our eyes and see with our ears." Gray maintained in "The Poetry of Louis Simpson" in *Poets in Progress* that poetry seeks the same goal as religious belief: "to formulate a coherent and significant meaning for life. The poetry of Louis Simpson offers us that meaning."

In a discussion of Simpson's early poetry, Gray commented that the author "never departs from traditional form and structure and yet he never departs from contemporary themes and concerns." Gray described one poem, for example, in which Simpson "handles a modern psychological situation in the delicate cadence of seventeenth-century verse." Ronald Moran in *Louis Simpson* made a similar comment in regard to *The Arrivistes,* Simpson's first book. Moran found that Simpson often sounds "like an Elizabethan song-maker or like a Cavalier poet." Gray argued that this juxtaposition of traditional form (ordered meter and rhyme) and modern subjects emphasizes, particularly in the poems about the world wars, the chaotic quality and the tensions of contemporary life. Gray found that Simpson neither complains nor moralizes about modern problems; rather he clarifies difficulties and presents rational insights.

After 1959, the publication date of *A Dream of Governors,* there was a perceived change in Simpson's work; reviewer Stephen Stepanchev contended in

American Poetry since 1945 that it changed for the better. Notes Stepanchev: "The prosaism of his early work—which required metrics and rhyme in order to give it character as verse—now gave way to rich, fresh, haunting imagery. His philosophical and political speculations achieved a distinction and brilliance that they had lacked before." A *Chicago Review* critic had more cautious praise for the shift in Simpson's poetry, writing that, "*A Dream of Governors* has wit, sophistication, perceptiveness, intelligence, variety, and knowingness, but it comes perilously close to being a poetry of chic." The reviewer went on to say that this early work lacks a depth of feeling.

However, he continued, "*At the End of the Open Road* . . . is a different story entirely. Simpson has found the secret of releasing the meaning and power of his themes. . . . It is not that his stanzas . . . are becoming more flexible and experimental: this in itself does not mean very much. . . . What is more fundamental, it seems to me, is that greater stylistic flexibility should be the sign of growth in the character and thought of the speaker. Simpson is becoming more able to be a part of what he writes about, and to make what he writes about more a part of him." *New York Time Book Review*'s Edward Hirsch agreed that the Pulitzer Prize-winning *At the End of the Open Road* indicates a growth and finesse in Simpson's poetry, opining, "It is not only a major breakthrough in his own work; it is also one of the tours de force of American poetry in the 60's." Hirsch described *At the End of the Open Road* as "a sustained meditation on the American character," noting, "The moral genius of this book is that it traverses the open road of American mythology and brings us back to ourselves; it sees us not as we wish to be but as we are."

Not all critics appreciated the change in Simpson's verse. In a review of 1965's *Selected Poems,* which contains twelve new poems in addition to selections of earlier work, Harry Morris stated that "Simpson's first three volumes are better" than his new poetry. Morris believed that Simpson's "new freedoms" have not helped him convey his themes more effectively. T. O'Hara, in a critique of *Adventures of the Letter I,* also questioned Simpson's new manner: "What has happened to Louis Simpson's energy? . . . It almost appears that success has mellowed the tough poetic instinct that once propelled him, for this present collection barely flexes a muscle." Yet Marie Borroff, speaking of the same book, avowed, "When the

remaining decades of the twentieth century have passed ignominiously into history along with the 1960's, these stanzas and other gifts will remain to us." And Christopher Hope deemed *Adventures* "a work of pure, brilliant invention."

A mix of criticism continued in reviews of *Searching for the Ox.* Derwent May found the quiet, reflective mood of the poems attractive. Nikki Stiller, on the other hand, felt that "Louis Simpson's work now suggests too much comfort: emotional, physical, intellectual. He has stopped struggling, it seems, for words, for rhythms, for his own deepest self." Yet in contrast to this, Peter Stitt remarked that *Searching for the Ox* "is a tremendously refreshing book. . . . The style in which [the poems] are written presents us with no barriers—it is plain, direct and relaxed. Moreover, the poems tell a story, or stories, in which we can take a real interest."

Simpson's ability to have his poems relate stories of interest is evident as well in *Collected Poems.* Selections from his poetry created from 1940 through the 1980s, *Collected Poems* focuses on the lives of everyday citizens. "For the last two decades [Simpson's] appetite has increasingly been for re-creating quintessentially American stories of ordinary people . . . living out lives of quiet desperation," found Hirsch, noting, "He has turned his ardor and ingenuity to uncovering the secret and public lives of people stripped of their expectations and bewildered by their fates." "Simpson takes part in the existence of other people, and pecks or picks about the shopping mall with them, or the redwoods and the Golden Gate, or Paris, or the battlefields of the Second World War which so nearly unmade him," observed the *Times Literary Supplement*'s William Scammell, adding, "And he manages to do this without relinquishing his own firm sense of identity, or slumping into a reverent pantheistic incoherence." Scammell concluded with praise for *Collected Poems* as "a master-class for reader and writer alike, alive on every page." "But mastery is not the right metaphor to end on," he surmised, "for Simpson is someone who stands outside aestheticism, outside schools and movements."

In *There You Are: Poems,* the poet again "send[s] us into the lives of people and their stories," commented Mark Jarman in the *Hudson Review.* A *Publishers Weekly* contributor stated that in *There You Are* while "combining straightforward diction with oblique insights, Simpson limns people and stories with an irony tempered by compassion." Jarman hailed Simpson as "a poet of the American character and vernacular." Praising Simpson's storytelling skill and style, Jarman claimed "that no one writing today has a better understanding of narrative as a figure of speech. Each of his stories is like a piece standing for life as a whole, existing in a kind of chaste simplicity and yet, to paraphrase Simpson himself, giving off vibrations."

Simpson occasionally ventures from verse into other genres: novel, autobiography, and literary critical study. Robert Massie wrote of the poet's 1962 novel *Riverside Drive* in the *New York Times Book Review:* "Into fragments of dialogue, [Simpson] packs more meaning and drama than many novelists can bring off in a chapter. . . . As novels go, *Riverside Drive* is not a tragedy to shake the Gods—but it should stir most of its readers. From the first chapter to the last, it has the ring of truth." Concerning Simpson's literary critical study *A Revolution in Taste,* Paul Zweig commented that the author "has provided a series of engaging portraits of poets whom he presents less as cultural exemplars than as individuals struggling, as Baudelaire wrote, to absolve the pain of their lives with the grace of an enduring poem. It is the life narrowing intensely and heatedly into the act of writing that interests Simpson, the life pared to the poem. And this has enabled him to write a series of compact literary biographies that have the pithiness of a seventeenth-century 'character' and a literary good sense that reminds me of [Samuel] Johnson's *Lives of the Poets.*"

Simpson has also written several volumes of autobiography, including 1972's *North of Jamaica* and *The King My Father's Wreck,* published in 1994. The latter work recounts the poet's early years in Jamaica and his transition to adulthood and literary maturity through a selection of essays. Focusing on specific images from his past—his mother's disappearance from home when he was a young boy, his excitement at the prospect of becoming a U.S. citizen, a dissatisfying job working as an editor for a publishing house, the experiences he encountered in the armed forces during World War II that led to later protestations over the conflict in Vietnam, returning a book to his Jamaican school sixty years after borrowing it—*The King My Father's Wreck* is written in the same spare style that is characteristic of Simpson's verse. The poet's "insistent voice" imbues his reminiscences with "more dramatic emotional topography than most," com-

mented a *Publishers Weekly* reviewer, thereby "rewarding adventurous readers."

His much-acclaimed anthology *The Owner of the House: New Collected Poems* represents a sixty-year career, in which Simpson has chosen to represent himself as a sociologist of suburbia's banalities. Although in poems like "Shoe-Fly Pie," he revisits the West Indies of his childhood, he always keeps one foot in his adopted country, never slipping into sentimentality. The outsider's perspective allows him to confront "the terror and beauty of life with a wry sense of humor and a mysterious sense of fate," wrote Edward Hirsch of the *Washington Post.* In his recent poems, there is a sense of an acceptance of life "here, on this street / where the houses from the outside / are all alike, and so are the people." In his review, David Orr of the *New York Times* stated, "If there's little Louis Simpson 'could learn from anyone' at this point, that's only because he's worked so hard and so long—and successfully—to learn it for himself."

BIOGRAPHICAL AND CRITICAL SOURCES:

BOOKS

Contemporary Literary Criticism, Thomson Gale (Detroit, MI), Volume 4, 1975, Volume 7, 1977, Volume 9, 1978, Volume 32, 1985.

Hungerford, Edward, editor, *Poets in Progress: Critical Prefaces to Thirteen Modern American Poets,* Northwestern University Press, 1967.

Lazer, Hank, editor, *On Louis Simpson: Depths beyond Happiness,* University of Michigan, 1988.

Lensing, George S., and Ronald Moran, *Four Poets and the Emotive Imagination,* Louisiana State University Press (Baton Rouge, LA), 1976.

Moran, Ronald, *Louis Simpson,* Twayne, 1972.

Roberson, William H., *Louis Simpson: A Reference Guide,* G. K. Hall, 1980.

Stepanchev, Stephen, *American Poetry since 1945,* Harper (New York, NY), 1965.

Stitt, Peter, *The World's Hieroglyphic Beauty: Five American Poets,* University of Georgia, 1985.

PERIODICALS

American Poetry Review, January-February, 1979.

Best Sellers, June 15, 1972.

Chicago Review, Volume XIX, number 1, 1966.

Christian Science Monitor, November 18, 2003, p. 17.
Harper's, October, 1965.
Hudson Review, autumn, 1996.
Listener, November 25, 1976.
London Magazine, February-March, 1977.
Los Angeles Times Book Review, April 30, 1995, p. 13.
Midstream, December, 1976.
New Statesman, January 31, 1964.
New York Herald Tribune Book Review, November 15, 1959; May 13, 1962.
New York Times Book Review, September 27, 1959; May 13, 1962; May 9, 1976; December 17, 1978; January 29, 1984; November 13, 1988; September 21, 2003, p. 17.
New York Times Magazine, May 2, 1965.
Parnassus, Volume 21, pp. 138-145.
Poetry, April, 1960.
Publishers Weekly, October 24, 1994, p. 58; July 31, 1995.
Saturday Review, May 21, 1960.
Saturday Review/World, April 3, 1976.
Sewanee Review, spring, 1969.
Time, May 18, 1962.
Times Literary Supplement, June 9, 1966; January 4, 1980; July 4, 1986; May 5, 1989.
Washington Post Book World, March 5, 1995, p. 12; October 26, 2003, article by Edward Hirsch, p. T12.
Yale Review, March, 1964; October, 1972.

*   *   *

SMITH, Roger 1953-

PERSONAL: Born April 15, 1953, in Billings, MT; son of Arthur F. (a high school teacher) and Dorothy (a homemaker; maiden name, Crambert) Smith; married Cherie Herman (divorced, June, 1987); married Sandra Wilborn (a physician), May 9, 1990; children: Shea, Maren. *Ethnicity:* "Caucasian." *Education:* Attended Reed College, 1971-72; University of Nevada, Reno, B.A., M.A., 1980; Stanford University, Ph.D., 1987. *Politics:* Democrat. *Hobbies and other interests:* Tin whistle, dragon boating.

ADDRESSES: Home—2644 N.E. 24th Ave., Portland, OR 97212. *E-mail*—irtnogebw@msn.com.

CAREER: Writer. *Nevada* (magazine), Carson City, associate editor, 1981-82; Associated Press, Carson City, legislative correspondent, 1986; Fairleigh Dickin-

son University, Teaneck, NJ, assistant professor of English, 1987-89; writer, 1989—. Adjunct instructor at Linfield College, Willamette University, and Concordia College, all in Oregon, between 1989 and 1994. *Military service:* U.S. Marine Corps, 1973-77.

MEMBER: Planetary Society, Nature Conservancy.

AWARDS, HONORS: Fulbright grant for Denmark, 1985-86.

WRITINGS:

(With Phil Allen and Alastair Bearne) *Energy, Matter, and Form: Toward a Science of Consciousness,* University of the Trees Press (Boulder Creek, CA), 1977.
Popular Physics and Astronomy: An Annotated Bibliography, Scarecrow Press (Lanham, MD), 1996.
(Editor) *The Solar System,* Salem Press (Englewood Cliffs, NJ), 1998.
(Associate editor) *The Biographical Encyclopedia of Scientists,* Marshall Cavendish (Freeport, NY), 1998.
Biographies of Scientists: An Annotated Bibliography, Scarecrow Press (Lanham, MD), 1998.
Inventions and Inventors, Salem Press (Pasadena, CA), 2002.

SIDELIGHTS: Roger Smith once told *CA:* "I write to supply readers with clear explanations of natural phenomena, technology, and the methods of science."

*   *   *

SPENCER, Leonard G.
See SILVERBERG, Robert

*   *   *

STACK, Andy
See RULE, Ann

*   *   *

STACY, Donald
See POHL, Frederik

STEVENSON, Randall 1953-

PERSONAL: Born June 25, 1953, in Banff, Scotland; son of William (a teacher) and Helen (a teacher; maiden name, Martin) Stevenson; married Sarah Carpenter (a lecturer), September 18, 1981; children: Andrew John, Matthew William, Anna Jane. *Education:* University of Edinburgh, M.A. (with first-class honors), 1975; Oxford University, M.Litt., 1978. *Hobbies and other interests:* Watching and playing tennis, football, and badminton, hill walking, astronomy.

ADDRESSES: Home—134 Craiglea Dr., Edinburgh EH10 5PR, Scotland. *Office*—Department of English Literature, University of Edinburgh, Edinburgh EH9 8JX, Scotland. *E-mail*—randall.stevenson@ed.ac.uk.

CAREER: Writer. Women Teachers' College, Birnin Kebbi, Nigeria, principal teacher of English, 1975-76; University of Edinburgh, Edinburgh, Scotland, lecturer, 1978-92, senior lecturer, 1992-97, reader in English literature, 1997—. Scottish Universities' International Summer School, director, 1981-82; British Council visiting lecturer in Yugoslavia, Portugal, Poland, Bulgaria, Spain, Belgium, Romania, Hungary, Korea, Israel, Nigeria, and Egypt.

WRITINGS:

York Notes on "David Copperfield," Longman (London, England), 1980.
(With Colin Nicholson) *York Notes on "The Sound and the Fury,"* Longman (London, England), 1983.
(With Colin Nicholson) *York Notes on "The Crying of Lot 49,"* Longman (London, England), 1984.
The British Novel since the Thirties, Batsford (London, England), 1986.
The British Novel in the Twentieth Century: An Introduction, British Council (London, England), 1988.
Modernist Fiction, Harvester Wheatsheaf (New York, NY), 1992, revised edition, Longman (London, England) 1998.
A Reader's Guide to the Twentieth-Century Novel in Britain, Harvester Wheatsheaf (New York, NY), 1993.
(Editor, with Gavin Wallace) *The Scottish Novel since the Seventies,* Edinburgh University Press (Edinburgh, Scotland), 1993.

(Editor, with Gavin Wallace) *Scottish Theatre since the Seventies,* Edinburgh University Press (Edinburgh, Scotland), 1996.
(Editor, with Cairns Craig) *Twentieth-Century Scottish Drama: An Anthology,* Canongate (Edinburgh, Scotland), 2001.
Oxford English Literary History, Volume 12: *1960-2000: The Last of England?,* Oxford University Press (New York, NY), 2004.
(Editor, with Brian McHale, and contributor) *The Edinburgh Companion to Twentieth-Century Literatures in English,* Edinburgh University Press (Edinburgh, Scotland), 2005.

Contributor to books, including *The History of Scottish Literature,* edited by Cairns Craig, Aberdeen University Press (Aberdeen, Scotland), 1987; *Twentieth Century Scottish Theatre,* edited by Margaret Rose, Unicopli (Milan, Italy), 2000; *Beyond Scotland,* edited by David Goldie and others, Rodopi Press, 2004; *The Cambridge Companion to E. M. Forster,* edited by David Bradshaw, Cambridge University Press (New York, NY), 2004; and *Frae Ither Tongues: Essays on Modern Translation into Scots,* edited by Bill Findlay, Multilingual (Clevedon, England), 2004. Theater reviewer for BBC-Radio, British Broadcasting Corporation. Contributor of articles and reviews to magazines, including *International Journal of Scottish Theatre* and *Guardian Review.*

*   *   *

STILLWELL, Paul (Lewis) 1944-

PERSONAL: Born April 22, 1944, in Dayton, OH; son of Carl Neller (a minister) and Vera Pauline (a homemaker; maiden name, Limper) Stillwell; married Karen Lee McKenzie (a homemaker), August 12, 1970; children: Joseph Paul, Robert Carl, James Lee. *Education:* Drury College, A.B., 1966; University of Missouri—Columbia, M.A., 1978. *Religion:* United Church of Christ.

ADDRESSES: Home—262 Waycross Way, Arnold, MD 21021. *Office*—U.S. Naval Institute, 118 Maryland Ave., Annapolis, MD 21402.

CAREER: St. Louis Cardinals (professional baseball team), St. Louis, MO, assistant public relations director, 1972; St. Louis Cardinals (professional football team), St. Louis, assistant public relations director, 1972-74; U.S. Naval Institute, Annapolis, MD, member of editorial staff of *Proceedings,* 1974-81, editor of *Naval Review,* 1981-87, director of oral history, 1982-92, editor in chief of *Naval History,* 1987-92, director of history division, beginning 1993. *Military service:* U.S. Naval Reserve, 1962-92, active duty, 1966-69; served in Pacific theater; became commander; received Navy Commendation Medal with combat "V."

MEMBER: Naval Reserve Association.

AWARDS, HONORS: Selection as "notable history book," *New York Times,* 1993, for *The Golden Thirteen: Recollections of the First Black Naval Officers;* named author of the year, Naval Institute Press, 1993; Alfred Thayer Mahan Award for literary achievement, Navy League of the United States, 1994.

WRITINGS:

Battleship New Jersey: An Illustrated History, Naval Institute Press (Annapolis, MD), 1986.
Battleship Arizona: An Illustrated History, U.S. Naval Institute (Annapolis, MD), 1991.
(With Yogi Kaufman) *Sharks of Steel,* photographs by Steve and Yogi Kaufman, Naval Institute Press (Annapolis, MD), 1993.
Battleship Missouri: An Illustrated History, U.S. Naval Institute (Annapolis, MD), 1996.
Battleships, MetroBooks (New York, NY), 2001.
Carrier War: Aviation Art of World War II, Friedman/Fairfax (New York, NY), 2002.

Contributor to *Encyclopedia Americana.* Contributor to periodicals, including *Sea Power* and *Marine Corps Gazette.*

EDITOR

Air Raid: Pearl Harbor! Recollections of a Day of Infamy, Naval Institute Press (Annapolis, MD), 1981.
(Editor) *The Golden Thirteen: Recollections of the First Black Naval Officers,* foreword by Colin L. Powell, Naval Institute Press (Annapolis, MD), 1993.

Assault on Normandy: First-Person Accounts from the Sea Services, Naval Institute Press (Annapolis, MD), 1994.

INTERVIEWER

The Reminiscences of Mr. George C. Cooper, Member of the Golden Thirteen, U.S. Naval Institute (Annapolis, MD), 1989.
Reminiscences of Mr. Graham E. Martin, Member of the Golden Thirteen, U.S. Naval Institute (Annapolis, MD), 1989.
Reminiscences of Rear Admiral Elliott B. Strauss, U.S. Navy (Retired), Oral History Department, U.S. Naval Institute (Annapolis, MD), 1989.
Howard T. Kerr, W. Lewis Glenn, and Worth H. Bagley, *Reminiscences of Admiral Zumwalt,* U.S. Naval Institute (Annapolis, MD), 1989.
The Reminiscences of Captain Frederick A. Edwards, Sr., U. S. Navy (Retired), U.S. Naval Institute (Annapolis, MD), 1992.
The Reminiscences of Dr. Samuel E. Barnes, Member of the Golden Thirteen, U.S. Naval Institute (Annapolis, MD), 1993.
(With John T. Mason, Jr.) *The Reminiscences of Rear Admiral Odale D. Waters, Jr., U.S. Navy (Retired),* U. S. Naval Institute (Annapolis, MD), 1994.
The Reminiscences of Lieutenant Commander John Wesley Lee, Jr., U.S. Navy (Retired), U.S. Naval Institute (Annapolis, MD), 1994.
The Reminiscences of Commander Paul H. Backus, U.S. Navy (Retired), U.S. Naval Institute (Annapolis, MD), 1995.
The Reminiscences of Roger L. Bond, U.S. Naval Institute (Annapolis, MD), 1995.
The Reminiscences of Admiral Robert L. J. Long, U.S. Navy (Retired), U.S. Naval Institute (Annapolis, MD), 1995.
(With Barrett Tillman) *The Reminiscences of Captain Daniel Webb Tomlinson IV, U.S. Naval Reserve (Retired),* U.S. Naval Institute (Annapolis, MD), 1995.
Reminiscences of Vice Admiral Thomas R. Weschler, U.S. Navy (Retired), U.S. Naval Institute (Annapolis, MD), 1995.
The Reminiscences of Captain Arthur R. Hawkins, U.S. Navy (Retired), U.S. Naval Institute (Annapolis, MD), 1996.
The Reminiscences of Dr. Leo M. Karpeles, U.S. Naval Institute (Annapolis, MD), 1996.

The Reminiscences of Vice Admiral Robert Taylor Scott Keith, U.S. Navy (Retired), U.S. Naval Institute (Annapolis, MD), 1996.

The Reminiscences of Captain Paul Richard Schratz, U.S. Navy (Retired), U.S. Naval Institute (Annapolis, MD), 1996.

The Reminiscences of Rear Admiral Norvell G. Ward, U.S. Navy (Retired), U.S. Naval Institute (Annapolis, MD), 1996.

The Reminiscences of Captain Grayson Merrill, U.S. Navy (Retired), U.S. Naval Institute (Annapolis, MD), 1997.

The Reminiscences of Admiral Harold Edson Shear, U.S. Navy (Retired), U.S. Naval Institute (Annapolis, MD), 1997.

The Reminiscences of Admiral Harry D. Train II, U.S. Navy (Retired), U.S. Naval Institute (Annapolis, MD), 1997.

The Reminiscences of Master Chief Boatswain's Mate Carl M. Brashear, U.S. Navy (Retired), U.S. Naval Institute (Annapolis, MD), 1998.

The Reminiscences of Rear Admiral Neil M. Stevenson, Chaplain Corps, U.S. Navy (Retired), U.S. Naval Institute (Annapolis, MD), 1998.

The Reminiscences of Captain Wilma Leona Jackson, Nurse Corps, U.S. Navy (Retired), U.S. Naval Institute (Annapolis, MD), 1999.

The Reminiscences of Vice Admiral Jerome H. King, Jr., U.S. Navy (Retired), U.S. Naval Institute (Annapolis, MD), 1999.

The Reminiscences of Elda Elwood Logue, U.S. Naval Institute (Annapolis, MD), 1999.

The Reminiscences of Lieutenant Commander Richard A. Harralson, U.S. Navy (Retired), U.S. Naval Institute (Annapolis, MD), 2000.

The Reminiscences of Rear Admiral Albert G. Mumma, U.S. Navy (Retired), U.S. Naval Institute (Annapolis, MD), 2001.

The Reminiscences of Vice Admiral Joe Williams, Jr., U.S. Navy (Retired), U.S. Naval Institute (Annapolis, MD), 2002.

The Reminiscences of Rear Admiral Oakley E. Osborn, U.S. Navy (Retired), U.S. Naval Institute (Annapolis, MD), 2002.

The Reminiscences of Rear Admiral Robert W. McNitt, U.S. Navy (Retired), U.S. Naval Institute (Annapolis, MD), 2002.

The Reminiscences of Rear Admiral Almon C. Wilson, Medical Corps, U.S. Navy (Retired), U.S. Naval Institute (Annapolis, MD), 2002.

The Reminiscences of Rear Admiral Doniphan B. Shelton, U.S. Navy (Retired), U.S. Naval Institute (Annapolis, MD), 2003.

The Reminiscences of Captain Franklin F. Shellenbarger, U.S. Maritime Service (Retired), U.S. Naval Institute (Annapolis, MD), 2003.

The Reminiscences of Captain Herbert E. Hetu, U.S. Navy (Retired), U.S. Naval Institute (Annapolis, MD), 2003.

The Reminiscences of Rear Admiral Julian T. Burke, Jr., U.S. Navy (Retired), U.S. Naval Institute (Annapolis, MD), 2003.

The Reminiscences of Rear Admiral Joseph C. Wylie, Jr., U.S. Navy (Retired), U.S. Naval Institute (Annapolis, MD), 2003.

SIDELIGHTS: Paul Stillwell's *Air Raid: Pearl Harbor!* is a collection of forty-seven memoirs. The book includes an article by the Japanese pilot who led the attack in 1945. Other contributors are American and Japanese officers and enlisted personnel, civilians, both men and women, and professional journalists. The work is heavily illustrated with photographs, which were described thus in the *Washington Post Book World* by Roger Pineau: "Some [are] familiar, some rare, but all well chosen and arranged. Finding Pearl Harbor-vintage photographs of all forty-seven authors was a nice touch and no mean task." Clay Blair of the *Chicago Tribune* found *Air Raid* to be "provocative, informative, nicely balanced between Big and Little Picture. In its own highly personal and subjective way it gives a full account of what happened."

Stillwell once told *CA:* "My service in the crew of the USS *New Jersey* in 1969 led to an interest in battleships and their history. This was reflected in *Battleship New Jersey: An Illustrated History.* I did a great deal of documentary research to form the factual skeleton for the story, but the real flesh and blood came in the words of other former crew members. I conducted oral history interviews with more than 100 of them and thus was able to tell the human side of the story of this great ship. I planned a similar approach in writing about the battleship *Arizona.* Because of her loss at the hands of the Japanese on December 7, 1941, she became one of the most famous U.S. Navy ships. Curiously, though, little has been written about her twenty-five years of active service prior to World War II. By interviewing former *Arizona* men, I wanted to bring her story to life, as I did with the *New Jersey.*"

BIOGRAPHICAL AND CRITICAL SOURCES:

PERIODICALS

AB Bookman's Weekly, July 1, 1996, review of *Battleship Missouri: An Illustrated History,* p. 28.

American History, June, 1994, review of *Assault on Normandy: First-Person Accounts from the Sea Services,* p. 20.

Armed Forces and Society, winter, 1994, review of *The Golden Thirteen: Recollections of the First Black Naval Officers,* p. 330.

Black Scholar, fall, 1994, review of *The Golden Thirteen,* p. 63.

Booklist, January 15, 1992, review of *Battleship Arizona: An Illustrated History,* pp. 894, 921; January 15, 1993, review of *The Golden Thirteen,* p. 858; June 1, 2002, Roland Green, review of *Carrier War: Aviation Art of World War II,* p. 1674.

Bookwatch, April, 1993, review of *The Golden Thirteen,* p. 5.

Book World, November 10, 1991, review of *Battleship Arizona,* p. 11.

Chicago Tribune, December 6, 1981, Clay Blair, review of *Air Raid: Pearl Harbor!*

Choice, July, 1993, review of *The Golden Thirteen,* p. 1832;

Journal of American History, June, 1994, review of *The Golden Thirteen,* p. 332.

Kliatt Young Adult Paperback Book Guide, March, 1995, review of *The Golden Thirteen,* p. 28.

Library Journal, September 1, 1991, review of *Battleship Arizona,* p. 206; December, 1991, review of *Battleship Arizona,* p. 168; March 1, 1993, review of *The Golden Thirteen,* p. 92.

Naval War College Review, summer, 1993, review of *Battleship Arizona,* p. 141; summer, 1997, review of *Assault on Normandy,* p. 155.

New Technical Books, July, 1992, review of *Battleship Arizona,* p. 834.

New York Times Book Review, April 18, 1993, review of *The Golden Thirteen,* p. 21; October 9, 1994, review of *The Golden Thirteen,* p. 32.

Oral History Review, winter, 1996, Charles J. Lang, review of *The Golden Thirteen,* p. 113.

Public Historian, spring, 1994, review of *The Golden Thirteen,* p. 83; spring, 1995, review of *Battleship Arizona,* p. 96.

Publishers Weekly, January 4, 1993, review of *The Golden Thirteen,* p. 63.

Rapport: West Coast Review of Books, Art, and Entertainment, May, 1992, review of *Battleship Arizona,* p. 63.

Reference and Research Book News, September, 1996, review of *Battleship Missouri,* p. 62.

Sea History, summer, 1993, review of *The Golden Thirteen,* p. 28.

Washington Post Book World, November 22, 1981, Roger Pineau, review of *Air Raid.*

ONLINE

Battleshop.org, http://www.battleship.org/ (August 21, 2002), John DiGiantomasso, review of *Battleship Missouri.**

*   *   *

STRUM, Philippa 1938-

PERSONAL: Born December 14, 1938, in New York, NY; daughter of Joseph B. and Ida P. Strum; children: David Strum Weiss. *Education:* Brandeis University, B.A., 1959; Harvard University, Ed.M., 1960; New School for Social Research, Ph.D., 1964.

ADDRESSES: Home—124 W. 79th St., New York, NY 10024-6446. *Office*—Department of Political Science, Brooklyn College of the City University of New York, Brooklyn, NY 11210. *E-mail*—pstrum@mindspring.com.

CAREER: Brooklyn College of the City University of New York, Brooklyn, NY, lecturer in political science, 1962-64; Rutgers University, Newark, NJ, instructor, 1964-65, assistant professor, 1965-72, associate professor of political science, 1972-73; Brooklyn College of the City University of New York, associate professor of political science, 1972-75; City University of New York, Brooklyn College and the Graduate Center, professor, 1976-99; Dubach Visiting Distinguished Professor, Oregon State University, Corvallis, OR, April, 1988; Virginia Commonwealth University, Richmond, VA, Lyons Distinguished Visiting Professor, April, 1997; Wayne State University Law School, Detroit, MI, Walter Gibbs Visiting Professor of Constitutional Law, winter, 2000, winter, 2001; Brooklyn College, New York, NY, Broeklundian Professor of Political Science, 1998-99, Broeklundian Professor of Political Science Emerita, 1999—. Instructor at New School for Social Research, summers, 1962-64; visiting professor, Barnard College, 1978-79; visiting associate professor at Brooklyn College of the City University of New York, 1972-73; member, CUNY Graduate Center Faculty, 1963-99.

MEMBER: American Political Science Association, American Association of University Professors, Caucus for a New Political Science, American Civil Liberties Union, New York Civil Liberties Union.

AWARDS, HONORS: Research fellow, Harvard University, summer, 1960; Fulbright Senior Lecturer, fellow, Truman Institute of Hebrew University, 1985-86; City University of New York Faculty Resident Award Program, 1994-95, 1999-2000; Fulbright senior lecturer, Bogazici Universitesi, Istanbul, spring, 1995; fellow, Woodrow Wilson International Center for Scholars, 1997-98; Honorable mention, American Bar Association Silver Gavel Award, 2000, for *When the Nazis Came to Skokie: Freedom for Speech We Hate.*

WRITINGS:

(With Michael Shmidman) *On Studying Political Science,* Goodyear Publishing (Santa Monica, CA), 1969.

Presidential Power and American Democracy, Goodyear Publishing (Santa Monica, CA), 1972, 2nd edition, 1979.

The Supreme Court and "Political Questions," University of Alabama Press (University, AL), 1974.

Louis D. Brandeis: Justice for the People, Harvard University Press, (Cambridge, MA), 1984.

The Women Are Marching: The Second Sex and the Palestinian Revolution, Lawrence Hill Books, (Chicago, IL), 1992.

Brandeis: Beyond Progressivism, University Press of Kansas, (Lawrence, KS), 1993.

(Editor) *Brandeis on Democracy,* University Press of Kansas, (Lawrence, KS), 1995.

Privacy, the Debate in the United States since 1945, under the general editorship of Gerald W. Nash and Richard W. Etulain, Harcourt Brace College Publishers, (Fort Worth, TX), 1998.

When the Nazis Came to Skokie: Freedom for Speech We Hate, University Press of Kansas, (Lawrence, KS), 1999.

Women in the Barracks: The VMI Case and Equal Rights, University Press of Kansas, (Lawrence, KS), 2002.

(Editor, with Danielle Tarantolo) *Women Immigrants in the United States: Proceedings of a Conference Sponsored by the Woodrow Wilson International Center for Scholars and the Migration Policy Institute, September 9, 2002,* Woodrow Wilson International Center for Scholars (Washington, DC), 2003.

Contributor to many professional journals and to *New Republic.*

SIDELIGHTS: Philippa Strum is a political scientist, human rights activist, and a foremost authority on former Supreme Court Justice Louis Brandeis. Brandeis was known as the "People's Attorney" for his work on behalf of the public and for his tenure as Supreme Court Justice (1916-1938). After publishing her critically acclaimed biography *Louis P. Brandeis: Justice for the People,* Strum penned *Brandeis: Beyond Progressivism,* in which she uncovers Brandeis's political values. "This latest work is particularly significant, since Brandeis was not a systematic thinker who derived ideas from books," noted Kermit L. Hall in *The Historian.* Hall went on to say, "Perhaps only a biographer of Strum's insight could tease from Brandeis's life anything like a complete understanding of his ideas. Nevertheless, she does exactly that."

Hall explains that Brandeis believed political and economic liberty complemented and reinforced each other. In *Brandeis: Beyond Progressivism,* Strum reveals Brandeis's aversions to big government and big business because they threaten individual liberty. "In defining the basic elements of Brandeis's political views, Strum offers interesting contrasts between Brandeis and Dewey, and Brandeis and the Progressive tradition, in order to demonstrate the uniqueness of his thought," observed David Schultz in the *Law and Politics Book Review.* In *Brandeis on Democracy,* Strum's third book about Brandeis, Strum presents selections from Brandeis's speeches and letters to family and colleagues as well as newspaper interviews and judicial opinions.

The Women Are Marching: The Second Sex and the Palestinian Revolution recounts the Palestinian uprising known as the intifada, which erupted in the Gaza Strip and spread to the West Bank. Intifada's commercial strikes and mass demonstrations resulted in political and economic change and also stimulated reform in the lives of Palestinian women, who had been largely confined to the home. Intifada prompted Palestinian women to take to the streets to challenge religion and social traditions, particularly those related to women's rights. Strum traveled to the West Bank in July, 1989, to observe the Palestinian women's movement and interview women involved. A *Publisher's Weekly* reviewer maintained that in *The Women Are Marching* Strum presents a "fresh, in-depth perspective on the changing sexual and social roles of Palestinian women" and "raises disturbing questions about the growing influence of Islamic fundamentalism on West Bank women's lives and about whether women's advances will outlive the occupation."

Strum argues the need for personal space in *Privacy: The Debate in the United States since 1945.* She concludes privacy is essential for the psychological well-being of individuals and the proper function of democracy. Strum expresses her concern that technological advances may lead to an infringement on the right to privacy. "Strum's new book on privacy is an absolute delight," remarked Bill Weaver in the *Law and Politics Book Review.* Weaver observed that Strum "uses examples not merely meant to shock or dismay but also to make clear the underlying policy considerations and estimations of convenience that lead to incursions on privacy."

In a review of *When the Nazis Came to Skokie: Freedom for Speech We Hate,* Jerold S. Auerbach noted, "Strum is alert to the paradox of extending free speech to those who would then destroy it for others." Strum contemplates whether racists and anti-Semites should be afforded free speech under the protection of the First Amendment in her analysis of *Skokie v. Collin,* in which the National Socialist Party of America, a neo-Nazi group, sued for the right to hold an anti-Jewish demonstration in Skokie, a Chicago suburb heavily populated with Holocaust survivors. The Nazis eventually won the case, but ironically never held the demonstration. Wrote Temple Lentz in a review published on the *Centerstage Chicago* Web site, "Strum's book is as much social history as legal, as much political science as critical theory, and all of it is written gracefully, intelligently, and simply." Lentz went on to say, "The lives and voices of the people involved leap from the page as if to tell their own stories aloud, and let readers make the final decision." *Library Journal*'s Philip Young noted that Strum "carefully and methodically traces the history and issues of the case all the way to the United States Supreme Court."

In *Women in the Barracks: The VMI Case and Equal Rights,* Strum examines the integration of women into military institutions. The book discusses the landmark case of *United States v. Virginia,* the 1996 U.S. Supreme Court Case that forced Virginia Military Institute (VMI) to end its 157-year tradition as an all-male institution and admit women. Strum explores the impact of the case on the men and women at VMI,

dubbed the "West Point of the South." Writing in *History: Review of New Books,* Lance Janda considered the book "a rare gem" that combines "rigorous primary and secondary research with graceful prose." Strum analyzes both viewpoints in the book and includes interviews with opposing lawyers as well as VMI administrators and faculty. She discusses what led Justice Ginsburg to conclude that while VMI's rigorous and harsh training methods deter some women from applying, they also deter some men, and that women should have the right to attend the school if they are qualified to do so. Janda observed that "Strum does overreach a bit when assessing the importance of the VMI case," noting that America's federal service academies admitted women in 1976, two decades before VMI. However, Janda maintained that his criticism is "entirely minor" and described the book as "a balanced and very satisfying work overall" that appeals to a wide audience including scholars and anyone interested in the history of VMI.

BIOGRAPHICAL AND CRITICAL SOURCES:

BOOKS

Directory of American Scholars, Thomson Gale (Detroit, MI), 2001.

PERIODICALS

American Academy of Political and Social Science, March, 1985, review of *Louis D. Brandeis: Justice for the People,* p. 203; July, 1995, review of *Brandeis: Beyond Progressivism,* p. 177.

American Historical Review, April, 1985, review of *Louis D. Brandeis,* p. 510; December, 1994, review of *Brandeis: Beyond Progressivism,* p. 1766.

American Jewish History, March, 2000, Jerold S. Auerbach, review of *When the Nazis Came to Skokie: Freedom for Speech We Hate,* p. 147.

American Political Science Review, June, 1977, review of *The Supreme Court and "Political Questions,"* p. 744; March, 1985, review of *Louis D. Brandeis,* p. 228.

American Spectator, April, 1995, review of *Brandeis: Beyond Progressivism,* p. 685.

Bookwatch, October, 1992, review of *The Women Are Marching,* p. 5.

Book World, January 2, 1994, review of *Brandeis: Beyond Progressivism,* p. 4.

Choice, September, 1984, review of *Louis D. Brandeis,* p. 193; January, 1993, review of *The Women Are Marching,* p. 865; January, 1994, review of *Brandeis: Beyond Progressivism,* p. 870; June, 1995, review of *Brandeis on Democracy,* p. 1672.

Harvard Law Review, December, 1996, review of *Brandeis on Democracy,* p. 561.

Historian, summer, 1994, Kermit L. Hall, review of *Brandeis: Beyond Progressivism,* pp. 761-762.

History: Reviews of New Books, winter, 1995, review of *Brandeis: Beyond Progressivism,* p. 57; summer, 2002, Lance Janda, review of *Women in the Barracks: The VMI Case and Equal Rights,* pp. 140-142.

Journal of American History, September, 1985, review of *Louis D. Brandeis,* p. 438; December, 1994, review of *Brandeis: Beyond Progressivism,* p. 1350.

Journal of American Studies, December, 1985, review of *Louis D. Brandeis,* p. 464.

Journal of Politics, May, 1985, review of *Louis D. Brandeis,* p. 754.

Kirkus Reviews, March 15, 1984, review of *Louis D. Brandeis,* p. 302.

Law and Politics Book Review, October, 1994, review of *Brandeis: Beyond Progressivism,* pp. 136-139; July, 1998, review of *Privacy: The Debate in the United States since 1945,* pp. 289-291.

Library Journal, May 1, 1984, review of *Louis D. Brandeis,* p. 894; June 15, 1992, review of *The Women Are Marching,* p. 91; March 1, 1999, Philip Young, review of *When the Nazis Came to Skokie,* p. 98.

Middle East, December, 1992, review of *The Women Are Marching,* p. 42.

Ms., July, 1992, review of *The Women Are Marching,* p. 66.

Multicultural Review, December, 1993, review of *The Women Are Marching,* p. 17.

National Civic Review, November, 1980, review of *Presidential Power and American Democracy,* p. 592; December, 1984, review of *Louis D. Brandeis,* p. 590.

Perspectives on Political Science, summer, 1994, review of *Brandeis: Beyond Progressivism,* p. 144.

Political Science Quarterly, spring, 1985, review of *Louis D. Brandeis,* p. 155.

Presidential Studies Quarterly, summer, 1994, review of *Brandeis: Beyond Progressivism,* p. 655.

Publishers Weekly, April 6, 1984, review of *Louis D. Brandeis,* p. 64; June 8, 1992, review of *The Women Are Marching,* p. 59; July 26, 1993, review of *Brandeis: Beyond Progressivism,* pp. 50-52.

Religious Studies Review, April, 1985, review of *Louis D. Brandeis,* p. 203.

Review of Politics, summer, 1994, review of *Brandeis: Beyond Progressivism,* p. 602.

Reviews in American History, March, 1985, review of *Louis D. Brandeis,* p. 94.

San Francisco Review of Books, review of *The Women Are Marching,* p. 26.

Small Press, review of *The Women Are Marching,* p. 59.

Times Literary Supplement, April 5, 1985, review of *Louis D. Brandeis,* p. 373.

Virginia Quarterly Review, autumn, 1984, review of *Louis D. Brandeis,* p. 734.

Yale Law Journal, November, 1985, review of *Louis D. Brandeis,* p. 195.

ONLINE

American Jewish Archives Journal Web site, http://www.huc.edu/aja/97-r4.htm/ (November 25, 2002), Arthur Gross-Schaefer, review of *Brandeis: Beyond Progressivism.*

Centerstage Online, http://search.centerstage.net/literature/articles/strum.html/ (November 25, 2002), Temple Lentz, review of *When the Nazis Came to Skokie.*

New York Times Online, http://www.nytimes.com/ (July 7, 2002), Paula Friedman review of *Women in the Barracks.**

T

TEACHOUT, Terry 1956-

PERSONAL: Born February 6, 1956, in Cape Girardeau, MO; son of H. H. (a hardware salesman) and Evelyn (a typist; maiden name, Crosno) Teachout; married Elizabeth Cullers (an opera coach), 1980. *Education:* Attended St. John's College, 1974; William Jewell College, B.S., 1979; attended University of Illinois—Urbana-Champaign, 1983-85. *Hobbies and other interests:* Reading, playing the piano, listening to classical music and jazz, watching movies, collecting animated cartoons from the forties and fifties, attending performances by the New York City Ballet, American Ballet Theater, Paul Taylor Dance Company, and Merce Cunningham Dance Company.

ADDRESSES: Home and office—205 West 84th St., Apt. B, New York, NY 10024-4660. *Agent*—Glen Hartley, Writers' Representatives, Inc., 25 West 19th St., New York, NY 10011. *E-mail*—76753.1225@ compuserve.com.

CAREER: Music critic, author, and editor. *Star and Times,* Kansas City, MO, music critic, 1977-83; *Harper's,* New York, NY, assistant editor, 1985-86, senior editor, 1986-87; *New York Daily News,* New York, NY, editorial writer, 1987-93, classical music and dance critic, 1993-2000; *Commentary,* music critic, 1995—; *Washington Post,* arts columnist, 1999—. Country and bluegrass bassist in southeast Missouri, 1972-74; jazz bassist in Kansas City, 1977-83. Founder of Vile Body (gatherings continue under the name, The Fabiani Society), a salon for young New York conservatives.

WRITINGS:

(Editor) Whittaker Chambers, *Ghosts on the Roof: Selected Journalism of Whittaker Chambers, 1931-1959,* Regnery Gateway (Washington, DC), 1989, republished, with a new introduction by Milton Hindus, as *Ghosts on the Roof: Selected Essays,* Transaction Publishers (New Brunswick, NJ), 1996.
(Editor) *Beyond the Boom: New Voices on American Life, Culture, and Politics,* introduction by Tom Wolfe, Poseidon (New York, NY), 1990.
City Limits: Memories of a Small-Town Boy, Poseidon (New York, NY), 1991.
(Editor and author of introduction) H. L. Mencken, *A Second Mencken Chrestomathy,* Knopf (New York, NY), 1995.
The Skeptic: A Life of H. L. Mencken, HarperCollins (New York, NY), 2002.
A Terry Teachout Reader, Yale University Press (New Haven, CT), 2004.
All in the Dances: A Brief Life of George Balanchine, Harcourt (Orlando, FL), 2004.

Contributor to periodicals, including *American Scholar, American Spectator, Commentary, National Review, New Criterion, Time,* and *New Dance Review.* Contributing editor, *Musical America.*

SIDELIGHTS: Terry Teachout has had a long and varied career as a writer, editor, and critic for such prominent publications as *Harper's, New York Daily News, Commentary, Time,* and the *Washington Post.* Working as both a writer and an editor for such publications prepared Teachout to publish his own books.

Teachout's *Ghosts on the Roof: Selected Journalism of Whittaker Chambers, 1931-1959* is a collection of magazine articles written by Chambers and published in periodicals, such as *New Masses, Time,* and *National Review.* Chambers, formerly a member of the Communist party, appeared before the House of Un-American Activities Committee in 1948 and accused Alger Hiss, an official in the U.S. State Department, of being a Communist. These accusations eventually led to a conviction on perjury charges and jail time for Hiss, and ruined Chambers's career as a journalist. According to Joseph Sobran of the *National Review,* in *Ghosts on the Roof,* "we finally meet Chambers alone, without the shadow of the Hiss case." The articles in the book introduce readers to a writer who "combined depth of mind with an elegant popular touch" and wrote "intelligently about serious things without writing 'down' to his readers," voiced Sobran. "In its way, this book of fragments rounds out the record of a shattered life," he concluded.

Teachout is also the founder of Vile Body, a salon for right-leaning, conservative writers and thinkers that later changed its name to The Fabiani Society. *Beyond the Boom: New Voices on American Life, Culture, and Politics* is a group of essays penned by Vile Body authors such as Andrew Ferguson, Bruce Bawer, and Maggie Gallagher. Born at the latter end of the Baby Boom generation, these authors question and criticize the generation of free-loving, authority-questioning hippies that preceded them. *Beyond the Boom* examines an array of topics, including politics, movies, books, and decades of art. Priscilla L. Buckley of the *National Review* called the book "the nearest thing yet to that serious book that cries out to be written on a generation—the Woodstock generation—whose unexpunged sins have poisoned America's cultural and spiritual landscape for the successor generation, and the rest of us." James Wolcott of the *New Republic,* on the other hand, felt that the Vile Body essayists "can't imagine anything better than what they've already had. The only future they want belongs to the past."

City Limits: Memories of a Small-Town Boy is an autobiographical account of Teachout's boyhood in a Missouri town, his education and early career, and his move to New York City. A *Publishers Weekly* contributor noted that Teachout explains "how he eventually had to lift himself out of his comfortable and secure Midwestern life" and move to New York if he ever hoped to make a career out of writing. "Mr. Teachout's

remembrances are presented with charm and wit," wrote *National Review* critic Brad Miner, "and they provide a passage into one's own past."

While working on a biography of the controversial journalist and critic H. L. Mencken, Teachout edited and published *A Second Mencken Chrestomathy,* an anthology of Mencken's works. Teachout discovered the unfinished work, a gathering of excerpts collected by Mencken himself, while researching the noted author's life. A *Publishers Weekly* reviewer considered the most impressive aspect of the anthology to be the variety of topics Mencken discussed, which ranged from politics to music.

The Skeptic: A Life of H. L. Mencken is the result of a decade's worth of research and writing. In an interview with Kathryn Jean Lopez on the *National Review* Web site, Teachout explained his interest in writing Mencken's biography: "Not only did I find Mencken hugely interesting, but I was also struck by the fact that our careers had followed similar paths." Both Teachout and Mencken worked variously as writers and editors for several different periodicals, often switching between political topics and critiques of the arts. In *The Skeptic,* the author explores the personal and professional life of the infamous Mencken.

Mencken was known for hurling insults at anyone and everyone who would read them. Documents published before and after his death established his reputation as an anti-Semite and showed his admiration for Germany. Teachout reveals that Mencken's bold, brash writing style differed greatly from the cautious lifestyle he led in private. Writing in *Commentary,* John Gross pointed out that *The Skeptic* provides "a rounded personal portrait rather than an intellectual one." Mencken "remains a difficult case, but in addition to telling a very good story very engagingly, Terry Teachout's book makes it much easier for us to achieve a balanced judgment," concluded Gross. A *Publishers Weekly* critic observed that Teachout "simplifies" Mencken's life for readers and provides "a tidy, fascinating biography that has much of the neat phrasing and sly wit that the rancorous writer displayed himself."

In his *National Review* interview, Teachout told Lopez that while he admired Mencken's "ability to get himself—his personality—onto the printed page," he disliked Mencken's "coldness." A *Kirkus Reviews* critic praised Teachout's objectivity, stating that the biography is a "balanced portrait of the muckraking newsman, and an excursion into American intellectual history and journalism."

BIOGRAPHICAL AND CRITICAL SOURCES:

PERIODICALS

American Spectator, March, 1990, review of *Ghosts on the Roof: Selected Journalism of Whittaker Chambers, 1931-1959,* p. 36; January, 1991, review of *Beyond the Boom: New Voices on American Life, Culture, and Politics,* p. 37; January, 1992, review of *City Limits: Memories of a Small-Town Boy,* p. 70.

Biography, spring, 2003, review of *The Skeptic: A Life of H. L. Mencken,* p. 374.

Book World, October 13, 1991, review of *City Limits,* p. 4.

Christian Century, March 6, 1991, review of *Beyond the Boom,* p. 271; April 5, 2003, David Stewart, review of *The Skeptic,* p. 41.

Commentary, March 6, 1991, review of *Beyond the Boom,* p. 63; November, 2002, John Gross, "Bane of the Booboisie," review of *The Skeptic,* p. 70.

Commonweal, April 5, 1991, review of *Beyond the Boom,* p. 234.

Economist, November 2, 2002, "A Good Hater; H. L. Mencken," review of *The Skeptic.*

Hudson Review, summer, 1991, review of *Beyond the Boom,* p. 326.

Kirkus Reviews, September 1, 1991, review of *City Limits,* p. 1150; August 15, 2002, review of *The Skeptic,* p. 1208.

Nation, November 25, 2002, Carlin Romano, "The Scourge of Baltimore," review of *The Skeptic,* p. 25.

National Review, June 2, 1989, Joseph Sobran, review of *Ghosts on the Roof,* p. 48; October 15, 1990, Priscilla L. Buckley, review of *Beyond the Boom,* p. 70; October 21, 1991, Brad Miner, review of *City Limits,* p. 40.

New Republic, December 3, 1990, James Wolcott, review of *Beyond the Boom,* p. 34.

Newsday, November 14, 2002, Dan Cryer, "The Work and Not-So-Wonderful Life of Mencken."

New Yorker, December 25, 1995, review of *A Second Mencken Chrestomathy,* p. 144.

New York Observer, November 25, 2002, Adam Kirsch, "The Scourge of the 'Booboisie,' Briskly, Judiciously Measured."

New York Times, November 17, 2002, Christopher Hitchens, "*The Skeptic:* Mencken, a Smart Set of One."

New York Times Book Review, November 10, 1991, review of *City Limits,* p. 14.

Publishers Weekly, August 30, 1991, review of *City Limits,* p. 74; December 12, 1994, review of *A Second Mencken Chrestomathy,* p. 57; August 19, 2002, review of *The Skeptic,* p. 74; March 1, 2004, review of *A Terry Teachout Reader,* p. 57.

Reason, April, 1991, review of *Beyond the Boom,* p. 51.

Time, December 3, 1990.

Washington Post Book World, April 8, 1990.

World and I, April, 2003, Charles A. Fecher, "A Partial Portrait—Critic Terry Teachout Has Done an Impressive Job of Bringing Together in One Unified Narrative the Many Distinct Faces of H. L. Mencken's Life," p. 230.

ONLINE

National Review Online Web site, http://www.nationalreview.com/ (November 25, 2002), "Writing Mencken," interview with Terry Teachout.

Ruthless Reviews Web site, http://www.ruthlessreviews.com/ (November 25, 2002), review of *A Second Mencken Chrestomathy.**

*   *   *

TEE, John
See MEADES, Jonathan (Turner)

*   *   *

TENNESHAW, S. M.
See SILVERBERG, Robert

*   *   *

THORNTON, Hall
See SILVERBERG, Robert

TULCHINSKY, Karen X.

PERSONAL: Born in Toronto, Ontario, Canada; daughter of Jack (a businessman) and Marion (a homemaker; maiden name, Jacobson) Tully; companion of Terrie Hamazaki, 1995. *Ethnicity:* "Jewish-Russian." *Education:* Banff School of Fine Arts, 1981; York University, B.F.A., 1982; Canadian Film Center, received degree. *Religion:* Jewish.

ADDRESSES: Agent—c/o Author Mail, Raincoast Books, 9050 Shaughnessy St., Vancouver, British Columbia V6P 6E5, Canada.

CAREER: Freelance author and editor. Has taught creative writing at the Kootenay School of Writing, Langara College, Stonewall Writers Retreat, and elsewhere; producer of short films and videos, including *Straight in the Face, A Sign,* and *Love Inside;* writer for television drama series *Keys Cut Here,* CTV, and researcher for television program *Weird Homes, Weird Weddings,* Yaletown Entertainment. Has also been an extra in three films.

MEMBER: Writers Union of Canada, Federation of British Columbia Writers, Praxis Center for Screenwriters.

AWARDS, HONORS: Van City Book Prize, 1996, for *In Her Nature; Love Ruins Everything* was named a top ten book of 1998 by *Bay Area Reporter;* finalist for Lambda Literary Award, for *To Be Continued;* American Library Association Literary Award shortlist, for *Love Ruins Everything;* British Columbia Arts Council Fiction Writer's grant; British Columbia Film Professional Development grant; finalist, Chesterfield Writers Film Project; Praxis Screenwriting Competition shortlist.

WRITINGS:

In Her Nature (short fiction), Women's Press (Toronto, Ontario, Canada), 1995.
Love Ruins Everything (novel), Press Gang Publishers (Vancouver, British Columbia, Canada), 1998.
Love and Other Ruins (novel; sequel to *Love Ruins Everything*), Polestar (Berkeley, CA, and San Diego, CA), 2002.
The Five Books of Moses Lapinsky (novel), Polestar (Vancouver, British Columbia, Canada), 2003.

Writer and director of short video *Contractions of the Heart,* Canadian Film Centre; author of scripts for *Love Ruins Everything,* based on her book, and of

Sticks and Stones and *One Thousand Cranes.* Contributor of books reviews and articles to periodicals, including *Vancouver Sun, Quill & Quire, Lambda Book Report, Girlfriends, Curve,* and *DIVA. Love Ruins Everything* has been translated into German.

EDITOR

(With James C. Johnstone) *Queer View Mirror,* Arsenal Pulp Press (Vancouver, British Columbia, Canada), 1995.
(With Rosamund Elwin) *Tangled Sheets: Stories and Poems of Lesbian Lust,* Women's Press (Toronto, Ontario, Canada), 1995.
(With James C. Johnstone) *Queer View Mirror 2: Lesbian and Gay Short Fiction,* Arsenal Pulp Press (Vancouver, British Columbia, Canada), 1997.
Friday the Rabbi Wore Lace: Jewish Lesbian Erotica, Cleis Press (San Francisco, CA), 1998.
(With Michele Karlsberg) *To Be Continued . . . ,* Firebrand Books (Ithaca, NY), 1998.
Hot & Bothered: Short Short Fiction on Lesbian Desire, Arsenal Pulp Press (Vancouver, British Columbia, Canada), 1998.
(With Michele Karlsberg) *To Be Continued: Take Two,* Firebrand Books (Ithaca, NY), 1999.
Hot and Bothered 2: Short Short Fiction on Lesbian Desire, Arsenal Pulp Press (Vancouver, British Columbia, Canada), 1999.
Hot and Bothered 3: Short Short Fiction on Lesbian Desire, Arsenal Pulp Press (Vancouver, British Columbia, Canada), 2001.
Hot and Bothered 4: Short Short Fiction on Lesbian Desire, Arsenal Pulp Press (Vancouver, British Columbia, Canada), 2003.

WORK IN PROGRESS: A screenplay version of *The Five Books of Moses Lapinsky.*

SIDELIGHTS: Karen X. Tulchinsky writes from the unique perspective of a Canadian lesbian Jew. Often praised for her characterizations, especially in such novels as *Love Ruins Everything* and its sequel, *Love and Other Ruins,* Tulchinsky has also written short stories and has edited or coedited numerous collections of lesbian erotica. The daughter of Jewish immigrants who changed their name to Tully when they came to Canada, Tulchinsky changed her surname back to the original to reassert her ethnic identity. But not only did she have to deal with the identity crisis of being Jewish in a predominantly Christian landscape, she also had to deal with her family's reaction to her sexual preferences as a lesbian. Describing her background of growing up gay and Jewish in Toronto, she told Mordecai Richler in a *Saturday Night* article: "I was raised to become a nice Jewish girl who would grow up to marry a nice Jewish boy, preferably a doctor. Imagine my parents' surprise when I came out as a lesbian and they watched helplessly as year after year I became more and more butch, and their hopes and dreams for their second daughter fizzled and died. (Well, I didn't marry one, but I look like a nice Jewish boy. My parents' consolation prize)." Both the Jewish and the lesbian perspective are underrepresented in literature, Tulchinsky feels, a lapse that she has tried to address in her fiction, her editing, and in the short films and videos she has more recently been writing and producing in Canada.

Tulchinsky's first novel, *Love Ruins Everything,* was termed "earnest and gutsy" by reviewer Sharon Abron Drache in the Toronto *Globe and Mail.* The story features Nomi Rabinovitch, a lesbian Jew originally born in Toronto who is living and working illegally in San Francisco. She stays with her lover, Sapphire, until Sapphire falls in love with and leaves Nomi for a "burly buzzcut man." Nomi mopes, rants, and suffers from heartbreak until a family disruption is provided—Nomi's mother, Faygie, is getting married. Going back to Toronto for the wedding, Nomi reunites with many family characters. *Toronto Star* critic Judith Fitzgerald called the novel a "tragicomic tale," noting that Tulchinsky combines "a lush and light-hearted romance" with "a searing blow-by-blow of the gruesome devastation [of] AIDS" in the life of the family.

According to a *Publishers Weekly* critic, the novel is infused with a comic edge, as well, through Tulchinsky's in-depth and entertaining look at some of Nomi's diverse relatives. Against the backdrop of a lively Jewish family affair the reader is introduced to relatives such as Nomi's brothers, Josh and Izzy; Bubbi, Faygie's future mother-in-law, who hears only what she wants to hear and complains loudly of the upcoming marriage; Uncle Solly, who spends time in and out of jail and belongs to the Jewish Mafia; and Henry, Nomi's gay cousin. Henry and his activist partner Albert are convinced that the U.S. government has introduced the AIDS virus as a biological weapon and is helping to spread it. Through Albert and Henry, Nomi also meets and falls in love with Julie Sakamoto, who is also involved in efforts to expose the suspected U.S. government plot. While the *Publishers Weekly*

reviewer found the governmental intrigue aspect of the plot slightly disruptive and "too neatly resolved" for a comic love story such as this, the reviewer called the story "spirited" and the heroine likable and "original." Drache concluded in the *Globe and Mail* that "Tulchinsky not only writes well, she has something important to say."

Nomi and Henry return in the sequel to *Love Ruins Everything* titled *Love and Other Ruins.* The story picks up where the first novel left off, though it is not necessary to have read the first installment to understand what is going on in the second book. Nomi is working as a waitress in a San Francisco lesbian bar, getting over her first love, and trying to work out a long-distance relationship with Julie, who still lives in Toronto. Meanwhile, Henry continues his mission with his friends to expose the government plot they believe is conspiring to spread AIDS among homosexuals. But while critics enjoyed the story line of the novel, what mainly impressed them were Tulchinsky's talents for dialogue and characterization. The author "has a superb ear for dialogue," stated Martha E. Stone in *Gay & Lesbian Review Worldwide,* adding that she especially enjoyed the Jewish characters of the older generation: "These Borscht Belt characters are perhaps a little too broad, but they're charming in their cluelessness." While noting that there are many humorous moments in *Love and Other Ruins, Booklist* critic Whitney Scott added that Tulchinsky "opts less for guffaws than poignant sighs this time" but that her portrayals of Nomi, Henry and the supporting cast leave readers "eager for more." Her descriptions of lovers, friends and family "has a way of making it all seem so familiar and comfortable and just plain wonderful," concluded Joy Parks in *Herizons.*

Tulchinsky's more ambitious novel *The Five Books of Moses Lapinsky* is a multigenerational saga about a Toronto Jewish family that begins in the 1930s. The author was inspired to write the story after hearing about the Christie Pits park riot of 1933 in which Jews and Nazi-sympathizing Protestants clashed during a baseball game one hot summer afternoon. Though nobody was killed in the ensuing violence, many were hurt, and Tulchinsky thought that this moment in history would be a good jumping-off point for her tale. In her fictionalized version, several members of the Lapinsky family get involved in the melee, and the youngest member, five-year-old Izzy, is hurt so badly that he suffers brain damage. The author then follows the tales of Izzy's brothers, parents, and other family who are wracked by guilt over failing to protect young Izzy. Sonny gets his frustrations out of his system by becoming a professional boxer, though his chosen career path puts him in conflict with his parents. Meanwhile, brother Lenny goes off to war and becomes a hero, while the brothers' father, Yacov, struggles to open his own business. The tension in the troubled family is punctuated by the author's descriptions of boxing and battlefield scenes.

A critic for the *Toronto Star* particularly found Tulchinsky's recounting of the battle at Dieppe beach to be a "powerful scene." The novel ends with the family members slowly coming to terms with what happened to Izzy, and the author readdresses the tragic moment at Christie Pitts. It was this part that the *Toronto Star* reviewer felt "jar[red] the narrative flow"; however, the critic praised Tulchinsky for avoiding any preachy moments about racial or religious prejudice. "It's a novel," the writer concluded, "and a good one, a lovingly written, sweeping drama that is all the more surprising because its twenty-something, Vancouver author is better known for her modern fiction and racy gay porn." "Though rooted in a specific community," said another *Toronto Star* contributor, "Tulchinsky's novel is about a universal phenomenon. *The Five Books of Moses Lapinsky* emerges as a study of the different attitudes of first- and second-generation immigrants—the father Yacov, intent on being inconspicuous, and his Canadian-born sons, who fight fiercely for their rights."

In addition to her fiction, Tulchinsky has edited numerous collections of homoerotic fiction. As with her portrayals of Jewish Canadians, the author feels that lesbian and erotic literature are legitimate genres that deserve publication, and she makes no apologies for helping to publish such stories. "I think lesbians are still starved for sexual imagery reflecting our lives," she declared in a *Lambda Book Report* interview. "Even with the progress we've made with gay and lesbian characters appearing on prime-time television, in our day-to-day lives we are still bombarded with representations of heterosexual sexuality. I think we need to see reflections of our lives and our sexuality in fiction. It's healing. It's fun. It's entertaining. No matter what else is going on in the world, sex is popular."

BIOGRAPHICAL AND CRITICAL SOURCES:

PERIODICALS

Booklist, June 1, 1999, Whitney Scott, review of *To Be Continued: Take Two,* p. 1787; April 15, 2003, Whitney Scott, review of *Love and Other Ruins,* p. 1451.

Canadian Book Reviewer Annual, 1995, Britta Santowski, review of *In Her Nature,* p. 202.

Curve, October, 2003, Rachel Pepper, "Mapping the Source," p. 44.

Gay & Lesbian Review Worldwide, May-June, 2003, Martha E. Stone, "Tale and True from Canada," p. 43.

Globe and Mail (Toronto, Ontario, Canada), March 21, 1998, Sharon Abron Drache, review of *Love Ruins Everything.*

Herizons, summer, 2000, review of *Hot and Bothered 2: Short Short Fiction on Lesbian Desire,* pp. 37-38; fall, 2002, Danette Dooley, review of *Hot and Bothered 3: Short Short Fiction on Lesbian Desire,* p. 46; spring, 2003, Joy Parks, review of *Love and Other Ruins.*

Lambda Book Report, October, 1997, Simon Jordan, review of *Queer View Mirror 2: Lesbian and Gay Short Fiction,* p. 13; August, 1998, Jyl Lynn Felman, review of *Hot and Bothered: Short Short Fiction on Lesbian Desire;* December, 1998, Paula Martinac, review of *To Be Continued. . . ,* p. 29; February, 2000, Katherine Gleason, review of *Hot and Bothered 2,* p. 24.

Lesbian Review of Books, winter, 1999-2000, review of *To Be Continued: Take Two;* winter, 2000-2001, Donna Allegra, "Tickling Your Fance."

Library Journal, January, 1999, Ina Rimpau, review of *To Be Continued. . . ,* p. 162.

Publishers Weekly, October 30, 1995, Maria Simson, "Forecasts: Paperbacks," p. 57; February 2, 1998, review of *Love Ruins Everything,* p. 82; October 19, 1998, review of *To Be Continued. . . ,* p. 57.

Saturday Night, October, 1999, Mordecai Richler, "The Oy of Sex," p. 41.

Toronto Star, March 21, 1998, Judith Fitzgerald, review of *Love Ruins Everything;* August 16, 2003, "Novel Marks Bleak Anniversary of Christie Pits Riot," p. H11; November 9, 2003, "Family Drama in Old Toronto," p. D14.

ONLINE

Karen X. Tulchinsky Home Page, http://www.karenx tulchinsky.com (May 17, 2004).*

*   *   *

TYDE, Eddie
See MEADES, Jonathan (Turner)

V

VANCE, Gerald
  See SILVERBERG, Robert

*   *   *

VARGAS LLOSA, (Jorge) Mario (Pedro) 1936-
  (Mario Vargas Llosa)

PERSONAL: Born March 28, 1936, in Arequipa, Peru; became Spanish citizen, 1994; son of Ernesto Vargas Maldonaldo and Dora Llosa Ureta; married Julia Urquidi, 1955 (divorced); married Patricia Llosa, 1965; children: (second marriage) Alvaro, Gonzalo, Morgana. *Education:* Attended University of San Marcos; University of Madrid, Ph.D., 1959. *Politics:* Liberal. *Religion:* Agnostic. *Hobbies and other interests:* Films, jogging, football.

ADDRESSES: Home—Spain. *Agent*—Agencia Carmen Balcells, Diagonal 580, 08021 Barcelona, Spain.

CAREER: Writer. Journalist with *La Industria,* Piura, Peru, and with Radio Panamericana and *La Cronica,* both in Lima, Peru, c. 1950s; worked in Paris, France, as a journalist with Agence France-Presse, as a broadcaster with the radio-television network ORTF, and as a language teacher; Queen Mary College and Kings College, London, England, faculty member, 1966-68; Washington State University, Seattle, writer-in-residence, 1968; University of Puerto Rico, visiting professor, 1969; *Libre,* Paris, France, cofounder, 1971; Columbia University, New York, NY, Edward Laroque

Mario Vargas Llosa

Tinker Visiting Professor, 1975; former fellow, Woodrow Wilson Center, Washington, DC; former host of Peruvian television program *The Tower of Babel;* Peruvian presidential candidate, Liberty Movement, 1990.

MEMBER: PEN (president 1976-79), Academy Peruana de la Lengua.

403

AWARDS, HONORS: Premio Leopoldo Alas, 1959, for *Los jefes;* Premio Biblioteca Breve, 1962, for *La ciudad y los perros;* Premio de la Critica Española, 1963, for *La ciudad y los perros,* and 1967, for *La casa verde;* Premio Nacional de la Novela, and Premio Internacional Literatura Romulo Gallegos, both 1967, both for *La casa verde;* annual prize for theater (Argentina), 1981; Congressional Medal of Honour (Peru), 1981; Instituo Italo Latinoamericano Iila prize (Italy), 1982; Ritz Paris Hemingway Award, 1985, for *The War of the End of the World;* Legion d'honneur (France), 1985; Principe de Asturias Prize for Letters, 1986; named Chevalier de l'Ordre des Arts et des Lettres (France), 1993; Cervantes prize for literature, 1994; Jerusalem prize, 1995; National Book Critics Circle Award for Criticism, 1997, for *Making Waves.*

WRITINGS:

FICTION

Los jefes (story collection; title means "The Leaders"; also see below), Rocas (Barcelona, Spain), 1959, translation by Ronald Christ and Gregory Kolovakos published in *The Cubs and Other Stories,* Harper (New York, NY), 1979.

La ciudad y los perros (novel), Seix Barral (Barcelona, Spain), 1963, translation by Lysander Kemp published as *The Time of the Hero,* Grove (New York, NY), 1966, 2nd edition, Alfaguara (Madrid, Spain), 1999.

La casa verde (novel), Seix Barral (Barcelona, Spain), 1966, translation by Gregory Rabassa published as *The Green House,* Harper (New York, NY), 1968.

Los cachorros (novella; title means "The Cubs"; also see below), Lumen (Barcelona, Spain), 1967.

Conversacion en la catedral (novel), two volumes, Seix Barral (Barcelona, Spain), 1969, translation by Gregory Rabassa published as *Conversation in the Cathedral,* Harper (New York, NY), 1975.

Los cachorros; Los jefes, Peisa (Lima, Peru), 1973.

Pantaleon y las visitadoras (novel), Seix Barral (Barcelona, Spain), 1973, translation by Ronald Christ and Gregory Kolovakos published as *Captain Pantoja and the Special Service,* Harper (New York, NY), 1978.

La tia Julia y el escribidor (novel), Seix Barral (Barcelona, Spain), 1977, translation by Helen Lane published as *Aunt Julia and the Scriptwriter,* Farrar, Straus (New York, NY), 1982.

The Cubs and Other Stories, translations by Ronald Christ and Gregory Kolovakos, Harper (New York, NY), 1979.

La guerra del fin del mundo (novel), Seix Barral (Barcelona, Spain), 1981, translation by Helen Lane published as *The War of the End of the World,* Farrar, Straus (New York, NY), 1984.

Historia de Mayta (novel), Seix Barral (Barcelona, Spain), 1985, translation by Alfred MacAdam published as *The Real Life of Alejandro Mayta,* Farrar, Straus (New York, NY), 1986.

Quien mato a Palomino Molero? (novel), Seix Barral (Barcelona, Spain), 1986, translation by Alfred MacAdam published as *Who Killed Palomino Molero?,* Farrar, Straus (New York, NY), 1987.

El hablador (novel), Seix Barral (Barcelona, Spain), 1987, translation by Helen Lane published as *The Storyteller,* Farrar, Straus (New York, NY), 1989.

Elogio de la madrastra (novel), Tusquets (Barcelona, Spain), 1988, translation by Helen Lane published as *In Praise of the Stepmother,* Farrar, Straus (New York, NY), 1990.

Lituma en los Andes (novel), Planeta (Barcelona, Spain), 1993, translation by Edith Grossman published as *Death in the Andes,* Farrar, Straus (New York, NY), 1996.

Los cuadernos de don Rigoberto, Alfaguara (Madrid, Spain), 1997, translation by Edith Grossman published as *The Notebooks of Don Rigoberto,* Farrar, Straus (New York, NY), 1998.

La fiesta del chivo, Alfaguara (Madrid, Spain), 2000, translation by Edith Grossman published as *The Feast of the Goat,* Farrar, Straus (New York, NY), 2002.

El paraíso en la otra esquina, Alfaguara (Lima, Peru), 2003, translation by Natasha Wimmer published as *The Way to Paradise,* Farrar, Straus (New York, NY), 2003.

PLAYS

La senorita de Tacna (produced as *Senorita from Tacna* in New York, NY, 1983; produced as *The Young Lady from Tacna* in Los Angeles, 1985), Seix Barral (Barcelona, Spain), 1981, translation by David Graham-Young published as *The Young Lady from Tacna* in *Mario Vargas Llosa: Three Plays* (also see below), 1990.

Kathie y el hipopotamo: Comedia en dos actos (translation by Kerry McKenny and Anthony Oliver-Smith produced as *Kathie and the Hip-*

popotamus in Edinburgh, Scotland, 1986), Seix Barral (Barcelona, Spain), 1983, translation by David Graham-Young published in *Mario Vargas Llosa: Three Plays* (also see below), 1990.

La chunga (translation by Joanne Pottlitzer first produced in New York, NY, 1986), Seix Barral (Barcelona, Spain), 1986, translation by David Graham-Young published in *Mario Vargas Llosa: Three Plays* (also see below), 1990.

Mario Vargas Llosa: Three Plays (contains *The Young Lady from Tacna, Kathie and the Hippopotamus,* and *La chunga*), Hill & Wang (New York, NY), 1990.

El señor de los balcones (title means "Lord of the Balconies"), Seix Barral (Barcelona, Spain), 1993.

Also author of *Le Huida* (title means "The Escape"), produced in Piura, Peru.

OTHER

La novela, Fundacion de Cultura Universitaria (Montevideo, Uruguay), 1968.

(With Gabriel García Márquez) *La novela en America Latina,* Milla Batres (Lima, Peru), 1968.

(Editor, with G. Brotherston) *Seven Stories from Spanish America,* Elsevier Science, 1968.

Antologia minima de M. Vargas Llosa, Tiempo Contemporaneo (Buenos Aires, Argentina), 1969.

Letra de batalla per "Tirant lo Blanc," Edicions 62, 1969, published as *Carta de batalla por Tirant lo Blanc,* Seix Barral (Barcelona, Spain), 1991.

(With Oscar Collazos and Julio Cortazar) *Literatura en la revolucion y revolucion en la literatura,* Siglo Veintiuno (Mexico City, Mexico), 1970.

Los cachorros; El desafio; Dia domingo, Salvat (Barcelona, Spain), 1970, *Dia domingo* published separately, Amadis (Buenos Aires, Argentina), 1971.

García Márquez: Historia de un deicidio (title means "García Márquez: The Story of a Deicide"), Seix Barral (Barcelona, Spain), 1971.

La historia secreta de una novela, Tusquets (Madrid, Spain), 1971.

(With Martin de Riquer) *El combate imaginario: Las cartas de batalla de Joanot Martorell,* Seix Barral (Barcelona, Spain), 1972.

(With Angel Rama) *García Márquez y la problematica de la novela,* Corregidor-Marcha (Buenos Aires, Argentina), 1973.

Obras escogidas: novelas y cuentos, Aguilar (Madrid, Spain), 1973.

La orgia perpetua: Flaubert y "Madame Bovary," Taurus (Madrid, Spain), 1975, translation by Helen Lane published as *The Perpetual Orgy: Flaubert and "Madame Bovary,"* Farrar, Straus (New York, NY), 1986.

Conversacion en la catedral; La orgia perpetua; Pantaleon y las visitadoras, Aguilar (Madrid, Spain), 1978.

Jose Maria Arguedas, entre sapos y halcones, Ediciones Cultura Hispanica del Centro Iberoamericano de Cooperacion (Madrid, Spain), 1978.

La utopia arcaica, Centre of Latin American Studies, University of Cambridge (Cambridge, England), 1978.

The Genesis and Evolution of "Pantaleon y las visitadoras," City College (New York, NY), 1979.

Art, Authenticity, and Latin-American Culture, Wilson Center (Washington, DC), 1981.

Entre Sartre y Camus, Huracan (Rio Piedras, Puerto Rico), 1981.

Contra viento y marea (journalism; title means "Against All Odds"), three volumes, Seix Barral (Barcelona, Spain), 1983–1990.

La cultura de la libertad, la libertad de la cultura, Fundacion Eduardo Frei (Santiago, Chile), 1985.

El debate, Universidad del Pacifico, Centro de Investigacion (Lima, Peru), 1990.

La verdad de las mentiras (essays; title means "The Truth of Lies"), Seix Barral (Barcelona, Spain), 1990.

A Writer's Reality, Syracuse University Press (Syracuse, NY), 1991.

El pez en el agua: Memorias, Seix Barral (Barcelona, Spain), 1993, translation by Helen Lane published as *A Fish in the Water: A Memoir,* Farrar, Straus (New York, NY), 1994.

Desafios a la libertad, Aguilar (Madrid, Spain), 1994.

Ojos bonitos, cuadros feos, Peisa (Lima, Peru), 1996.

Making Waves, edited and translated by John King, Farrar, Straus (New York, NY), 1997.

Una historia no oficial, Espasa Calpe (Madrid, Spain), 1997.

(With Paul Bowles) *Claudio Bravo: Paintings and Drawings,* Abbeville Press (New York, NY), 1997.

Cartas a un joven novelista (title means "Letters to a Young Novelist"), Ariel/Planeta (Barcelona, Spain), 1997.

Obra reunida. Narrativa breve (short stories), Alfaguara (Madrid, Spain), 1999.

(With others) *Los desafios a la socieda abierta: A fines del siglo XX* (title means "Challenges to the Open Society: At the End of the Twentieth Century"), Ameghino (Buenos Aires, Argentina), 1999.

(Author of introduction) Plinio Apuleyo Mendoza, and Carlos Alberto Montaner, *Guide to the Perfect Latin-American Idiot*, translation by Michaela Lajda Ames, Madison Books, distributed by National Book Network (Lanham, MD), 2000.

El lenguaje de la pasion, El Pais (Madrid, Spain), 2001, translation by Natasha Wimmer published as *The Language of Passion*, Farrar, Straus (New York, NY), 2003.

(Author of text) *Andes,* photographs by Pablo Corral Vega, National Geographic Society (Washington, DC), 2001.

Literatura y politica (transcription of conferences), Technical School of Monterrey (Monterrey, Mexico), 2001.

Palma, Valor nacional (speech given October 6, 1956), Universidad Ricardo Palma (Lima, Peru), 2003.

(Author of text) *Diario de Irak,* photographs by daughter, Morgana Vargas Llosa, Aguilar (Buenos Aires, Argentina), 2003.

Contributor to *The Eye of the Heart,* 1973; contributor to periodicals, including *Commentary, Harper's, National Review, New Perspectives Quarterly, New York Times Book Review, New York Times Magazine, UNESCO Courier,* and *World Press Review.* Selected works have been recorded by the Library of Congress Archive of Recorded Poetry and Literature.

ADAPTATIONS: The Cubs was filmed in 1971; *Captain Pantoja and the Special Service* was filmed in 1976 (Vargas Llosa directed the film, which was banned in Peru); *Aunt Julia and the Scriptwriter* was adapted as a television series in Peru, as a screenplay written by William Boyd and directed by Jon Amiel in 1989, and as a motion picture titled *Tune in Tomorrow,* c. 1990; *The Feast of the Goat* was adapted for the stage by Veronia Triana and Jorge Ali Triana and directed by Jorge Ali Triana at the Gramercy Arts Theater in New York in 2003.

SIDELIGHTS: Peruvian writer Mario Vargas Llosa often draws from his personal experiences to write of the injustices and corruption of contemporary Latin America. At one time an admirer of communist Cuba,

since the early 1970s Vargas Llosa has been opposed to tyrannies of both the political left and right. He advocates democracy, a free market, and individual liberty and cautions against extreme or violent political action, instead calling for peaceful democratic reforms. In 1989 Vargas Llosa was chosen to be the presidential candidate of Fredemo, a political coalition in Peru; though at one point he held a large lead in election polls, in the end he lost the election to Alberto Fujimori. Through his novels—marked by complex structures and an innovative merging of dialogue and description in an attempt to recreate the actual feeling of life—Vargas Llosa has established himself as one of the most important of contemporary writers in the Spanish language.

As a young man, Vargas Llosa spent two years at the Leoncio Prado Military Academy. Sent there by his father, who had discovered that his son wrote poetry and was therefore fearful for the boy's masculinity, Vargas Llosa found the school, with its "restrictions, the military discipline and the brutal, bullying atmosphere, unbearable," he later recalled in the *New York Times Magazine.* His years at the school inspired his first novel, *The Time of the Hero,* first published in Spanish as *La ciudad y los perros.* The book is, R. Z. Sheppard stated in *Time,* "a brutal slab of naturalism about life and violent death." The novel's success was ensured when the school's officials objected to Vargas Llosa's portrayal of their institution. "One thousand copies were ceremoniously burned in the patio of the school and several generals attacked it bitterly. One of them said that the book was the work of a 'degenerate mind,' and another, who was more imaginative, claimed that I had undoubtedly been paid by Ecuador to undermine the prestige of the Peruvian Army," Vargas Llosa recalled in his *New York Times Magazine* article.

Vargas Llosa wrote *The Time of the Hero* after leaving Peru for Europe in 1958, when he was twenty-two. In embracing Europe and entering into self-imposed exile from his native land, Vargas Llosa was following in the footsteps of numerous Latin-American writers, including Jorge Luis Borges, Julio Cortazar, and Carlos Fuentes. Vargas Llosa was to stay in Europe for thirty years, not returning to Peru until the late 1980s after the country had slipped into political chaos and economic impoverishment. These conditions prompted Vargas Llosa's decision to seek the presidency of Peru. During his three decades in Europe, Vargas Llosa became an internationally celebrated author.

Though Vargas Llosa had attracted widespread attention with his first novel, it was his second novel that cemented his status as a major novelist. In the award-winning *La casa verde* (*The Green House*), Vargas Llosa draws upon another period from his childhood for inspiration. For several years his family lived in the Peruvian jungle town of Piura, and his memories of the gaudy local brothel, known to everyone as the Green House, form the basis of his novel. The book's several stories are interwoven in a nonlinear narrative revolving around the brothel and the family that owns it, the military that runs the town, a dealer in stolen rubber in the nearby jungle, and a prostitute who was raised in a convent. "Scenes overlap, different times and places overrun each other . . . echoes precede voices, and disembodied consciences dissolve almost before they can be identified," Luis Harss and Barbara Dohmann wrote in *Into the Mainstream: Conversations with Latin-American Writers.* Gregory Rabassa, writing in *World Literature Today,* noted that the novel's title "is the connective theme that links the primitive world of the jungle to the primal lusts of 'civilization' which are enclosed by the green walls of the whorehouse." Rabassa saw, too, that Vargas Llosa's narrative style "has not reduced time to a device of measurement or location, a practical tool, but has conjoined it with space, so that the characters carry their space with them too . . . inseparable from their time." Harss and Dohmann found that *The Green House* "is probably the most accomplished work of fiction ever to come out of Latin America. It has sweep, beauty, imaginative scope, and a sustained eruptive power that carries the reader from first page to last like a fish in a bloodstream."

With *Conversacion en la catedral,* translated as *Conversation in the Cathedral,* Vargas Llosa widened his scope. Whereas in previous novels he had sought to recreate the repression and corruption of a particular place, in *Conversation in the Cathedral* he attempts to provide a panoramic view of his native country. As John M. Kirk stated in the *International Fiction Review,* this novel "presents a wider, more encompassing view of Peruvian society. . . . [Vargas Llosa's] gaze extends further afield in a determined effort to incorporate as many representative regions of Peru as possible." Set during the dictatorship of Manuel Odria in the late 1940s and 1950s, the society depicted in the novel "is one of corruption in virtually all the shapes and spheres you can imagine," Wolfgang A. Luchting wrote in the *Review of the Center for Inter-American Relations.* Penny Leroux, in a review of the book for the *Nation,* called it "one of the most scathing denunciations ever written on the corruption and immorality of Latin America's ruling classes."

The nonlinear writing of *Conversation in the Cathedral* was seen by several critics to be the culmination of Vargas Llosa's narrative experimentation. Writing in the *Review of the Center for Inter-American Relations,* Ronald Christ called the novel "a masterpiece of montage" and "a massive assault on simultanity." Christ argued that Vargas Llosa links fragments of prose together to achieve a montage effect that "promotes a linking of actions and words, speech and description, image and image, point of view and point of view." Kirk explained that in *Conversation in the Cathedral,* Vargas Llosa is "attempting the ambitious and obviously impossible plan of conveying to the reader all aspects of the reality of [Peruvian] society, of writing the 'total' novel." By interweaving five different narratives, Vargas Llosa forces the reader to study the text closely, making the reader an "accomplice of the writer [which] undoubtedly helps the reader to a more profound understanding of the work." Kirk concluded that *Conversation in the Cathedral* is "both a perfect showcase for all the structural techniques and thematic obsessions found in [Vargas Llosa's] . . . other work, as well as being the true culmination of his personal anguish for Peru."

Speaking of these early novels in *Modern Latin American Literature,* D. P. Gallagher argued that one effect of their complex nonlinear structures is to "re-enact the complexity of the situations described in them." By juxtaposing unrelated elements, cutting off dialogue at critical moments, and breaking the narration, Vargas Llosa suggests the disparate geological conditions of Peru, recreates the difficulties involved in living in that country, and re-enacts "the very nature of conversation and of communication in general, particularly in a society devoted to the concealment of truth and to the flaunting of deceptive images," Gallagher believed. Ronald de Feo pointed out in the *New Republic* that these early novels all explore "with a near-savage seriousness and single-mindedness themes of social and political corruption." But in *Captain Pantoja and the Special Service* "a new unexpected element entered Vargas Llosa's work: an unrestrained sense of humor," de Feo reported.

A farcical novel involving a military officer's assignment to provide prostitutes for troops in the Peruvian jungle, *Captain Pantoja and the Special Service* is "told through an artful combination of dry military dispatches, juicy personal letters, verbose radio rhetoric, and lurid sensationalist news reports," Gene Bell-Villada wrote in *Commonweal*. Vargas Llosa also mixes conversations from different places and times, as he did in previous novels. And like these earlier works, *Captain Pantoja and the Special Service* "sniffs out corruption in high places, but it also presents something of a break, Vargas Llosa here shedding his high seriousness and adopting a humorous ribald tone," Bell-Villada concluded. The novel's satirical attack is aimed not at the military, a *Times Literary Supplement* reviewer wrote, but at "any institution which channels instincts into a socially acceptable ritual. The humor of the narrative derives less from this serious underlying motive, however, than from the various linguistic codes into which people channel the darker forces."

The humorous tone of *Captain Pantoja and the Special Service* is also found in *Aunt Julia and the Scriptwriter.* The novel concerns two characters based on people in Vargas Llosa's own life: his first wife, Julia, who was his aunt by marriage, and a writer of radio soap opera whom Vargas Llosa names Pedro Camacho in the novel. The eighteen-year-old narrator, Mario, has a love affair with the thirty-two-year-old Julia. Their story is interrupted in alternate chapters by Camacho's wildly complicated soap opera scripts. As Camacho goes mad, his daily scripts for ten different soap operas become more and more entangled, with characters from one serial appearing in others and all of his plots converging into a single unlikely story. The scripts display "fissures through which are revealed secret obsessions, aversions and perversions that allow us to view his soap operas as the story of his disturbed mind," Jose Miguel Oviedo wrote in *World Literature Today*. "The result," explained Nicholas Shakespeare in the *Times Literary Supplement*, "is that Camacho ends up in an asylum, while Mario concludes his real-life soap opera by running off to marry Aunt Julia."

Although *Aunt Julia and the Scriptwriter* is as humorous as *Captain Pantoja and the Special Service*, "it has a thematic richness and density the other book lacked," de Feo believed. This richness is found in the novel's exploration of the writer's life and of the relationship between a creative work and its inspiration. In the contrasting of soap opera plots with the real-life romance of Mario and Julia, the novel raises questions about the distinctions between fiction

and fact. In a review for *New York,* Carolyn Clay called *Aunt Julia and the Scriptwriter* "a treatise on the art of writing, on the relationship of stimuli to imagination." It is, de Feo observed, "a multilayered, high-spirited, and in the end terribly affecting text about the interplay of fiction and reality, the transformation of life into art, and life seen and sometimes even lived as fiction."

In *The War of the End of the World,* Vargas Llosa for the first time sets his story outside of his native Peru. He turns instead to Brazil and bases his story on an apocalyptic religious movement that gained momentum toward the end of the nineteenth century. Convinced that the year 1900 marked the end of the world, these zealots, led by a man named the Counselor, set up the community of Canudos. Because of the Counselor's continued denunciations of the Brazilian government, which he called the "antichrist" for its legal separation of church and state, the national government sent in troops to break up this religious community. The first military assault was repulsed, as were the second and third, but the fourth expedition involved a force of some 4,000 soldiers. They laid waste to the entire area and killed nearly 40,000 people.

Vargas Llosa told Wendy Smith in *Publishers Weekly* that he was drawn to write of this bloody episode because he felt the fanaticism of both sides in this conflict is exemplary of late-twentieth-century Latin America. "Fanaticism is the root of violence in Latin America," he explained. In the Brazilian war, he believes, is a microcosm of Latin America. "Canudos presents a limited situation in which you can see clearly. Everything is there: a society in which on the one hand people are living a very old-fashioned life and have an archaic way of thinking, and on the other hand progressives want to impose modernism on society with guns. This creates a total lack of communication, of dialogue, and when there is no communication, war or repression or upheaval comes immediately," he told Smith. In an article for the *Washington Post,* Vargas Llosa explained to Curt Suplee that "in the history of the Canudos war you could really see something that has been happening in Latin American history over the nineteenth and twentieth centuries—the total lack of communication between two sections of a society which kill each other fighting *ghosts,* no? Fighting fictional enemies who are invented out of fanaticism. This kind of reciprocal incapacity of understanding is probably the main problem we have to overcome in Latin America."

Not only is *The War of the End of the World* set in the nineteenth century, but its length and approach are also of that time. A writer for the London *Times* called it "a massive novel in the nineteenth-century tradition: massive in content, in its ambitions, in its technical achievement." Gordon Brotherston of the *Times Literary Supplement* described the book as being "on the grand scale of the nineteenth century," while Salman Rushdie in the *New Republic* similarly defined the novel as "a modern tragedy on the grand scale." Richard Locke wrote in the *Washington Post Book World* that *The War of the End of the World* "overshadows the majority of novels published . . . in the past few years. Indeed, it makes most recent American fiction seem very small, very private, very gray, and very timid."

Vargas Llosa's political perspective in *The War of the End of the World* exhibited a marked change from his earlier works. He does not attack a corrupt society, instead treating both sides in the Canudos war ironically. The novel ends with a character from either side locked in a fight to the death. As Rushdie observed, "This image would seem to crystallize Vargas Llosa's political vision." This condemnation of both sides in the Canudos conflict reflects Vargas Llosa's view of the contemporary Latin-American scene, where rightist dictatorships often battle communist guerrillas. Suplee described Vargas Llosa as "a humanist who reviles with equal vigor tyrannies of the right or left (is there really a difference, he asks, between 'good tortures and bad tortures'?)."

Although his political views have changed during the course of his career, taking him from a leftist supporter of communist Cuba to a strong advocate of democracy, Vargas Llosa's abhorrence of dictatorship, violence, and corruption has remained constant. He sees Latin-American intellectuals as participants in a continuing cycle of "repression, chaos, and subversion," he told Philip Bennett in the *Washington Post*. Many of these intellectuals, Vargas Llosa explained further, "are seduced by rigidly dogmatic stands. Although they are not accustomed to pick up a rifle or throw bombs from their studies, they foment and defend the violence." Speaking of the late-twentieth-century conflict in Peru between the government and the Maoist guerrilla movement the Shining Path, Vargas Llosa clarified to Suplee that "the struggle between the guerrillas and the armed forces is really a settling of accounts between privileged sectors of society, and the peasant masses are used cynically and brutally by those who say they want to 'liberate' them."

Vargas Llosa believes that a Latin-American writer is obligated to speak out on political matters. "If you're a writer in a country like Peru," he told Suplee, "you're a privileged person because you know how to read and write, you have an audience, you are respected. It is a moral obligation of a writer in Latin America to be involved in civic activities." This belief led Vargas Llosa in 1987 to speak out when the Peruvian government proposed to nationalize the country's banks. His protest quickly led to a mass movement in opposition to the plan, and the government was forced to back down. Vargas Llosa's supporters went on to create Fredemo, a political party calling for democracy, a free market, and individual liberty. Together with two other political parties, Fredemo established a coalition group called the Liberty Movement. In June of 1989 Vargas Llosa was chosen to be the coalition's presidential candidate for Peru's 1990 elections. Visiting small rural towns, the urban strongholds of his Marxist opponents, and the jungle villages of the country's Indians, Vargas Llosa campaigned on what he believes is Peru's foremost problem: "We have to defend democracy against the military and against the extreme Left." Opinion polls in late summer of 1988 showed him to be the leading contender for the presidency, with a 44-to-19-percent lead over his nearest opponent. By the time of the election, however, Vargas Llosa's lead had eroded, and he ended up losing the election to Alberto Fujimori.

Vargas Llosa chronicles his experience as a presidential candidate in *A Fish in the Water.* In addition to discussing the campaign, however, the author also offers a memoir of his early years in Peru. Noted Rockwell Gray in Chicago's *Tribune Books,* "One string of alternating chapters in the book ends with the young writer's departure for France in 1958; the other recreates the exhausting and dangerous [presidential] campaign that carried him to every corner of Peru." Alan Riding in the *New York Times Book Review* added that the book "serves as [Vargas Llosa's] . . . mea culpa: he explains why the aspiring writer of the 1950's became a politician in the late 1980's and why, in the end, this was a terrible mistake." Vargas Llosa's account of his childhood and young adulthood includes his ambivalent relationship with his father, whom he met for the first time at age eleven and toward whom he had an intense dislike. Mark Falcoff, writing in the *Times Literary Supplement,* declared, "The pages of this book dealing with the father-son relationship are among the most violent and passionate Vargas Llosa has ever written." The author also covers his years at a military prep school and his university years in Lima.

In discussing his failed presidential campaign in *A Fish in the Water,* Vargas Llosa portrays the political backstabbing, unavoidable compromises, and character attacks that characterized the campaign against Fujimori. He also writes about his alienation from the majority of Peruvians: as a white, wealthy, educated, expatriate intellectual, he had little in common with poor Peruvians of Indian descent, many of whom do not speak Spanish. Commented Riding, "Tall, white and well dressed, he invariably looked out of place." Falcoff explained that "the chapters dealing with the presidential campaign suggest an impressive knowledge of Peruvian society at all levels and in the several regions, particularly the needs of its humblest groups." Gray, however, remarked, "Much of this book is engaging and informative, but it becomes at times slack, even gossipy, and assumes an interest in the nuances of Peruvian political and literary life shared by very few American readers."

After losing the campaign, Vargas Llosa returned to Europe—this time to Spain, where he assumed Spanish citizenship. His first novel after running for president, *Death in the Andes,* is set in his homeland amid the modern political and social strife evidenced by the rebellion of the Shining Path guerrilla movement. In part a murder mystery, the novel follows Corporal Lituma as he ventures from his home in Peru's coastal region to a mountain village to investigate the disappearance of three men. In addition to the story line of the missing men, Vargas Llosa intersperses tales of violence committed by the Shining Path as well as a romantic story involving Tomas Carreño, Lituma's guide and partner. Critics praised Vargas Llosa's skill in creating a technically ambitious novel, although some reviewers remarked that the author failed to integrate the various plot lines into a coherent story line. *New York Times Book Review* contributor Madison Smartt Bell, for instance, commented that "amid this multiplicity of plot potential, the reader may share Lituma's difficulty in finding any central focus, or even in identifying a single continuous thread." Similarly, Rockwell Gray, again writing in Chicago's *Tribune Books,* averred that "for all the

author's adroit weaving of shifts in viewpoint, voice and time—his attempt to grasp Peru's dilemma from many angles—this technically interesting novel is not on a par with his best work." In contrast, *Washington Post Book World* contributor Marie Arana-Ward wrote, "This is well-knit social criticism as trenchant as any by [Honore] Balzac or [Gustave] Flaubert—an ingenious patchwork of the conflicting mythologies that have shaped the New World psyche since the big bang of Columbus's first step on shore." And Bell admitted, "The individual vignettes are often brilliant."

Vargas Llosa's next novel, *The Notebooks of Don Rigoberto,* is also set in Peru. In this dream-like narrative, Don Rigoberto has separated from his beautiful wife, Doña Lucrecia, because of a sexual encounter between her and her stepson, Fonchito, a precocious boy who has yet to reach puberty. Don Rigoberto misses his wife terribly, and to appease his loneliness he imagines, and writes about, Lucrecia's erotic life—with him as well as with other lovers. It is unclear how much of the narrative is meant to be true and how much is a fantasy. This book lacks the political overtones of much of Vargas Llosa's work, but it does provide "grand, sexy reading for sophisticated audiences," reflected Barbara Hoffert in *Library Journal.* A *Publishers Weekly* writer remarked, "As in much of his writing, Vargas Llosa creates a certain timelessness, a dream-like play on the present. The more he leaves sex to the imagination, the more erotic and beautifully suggestive it becomes."

The author mixes fiction and fact in his novel *The Feast of the Goat,* concerning Dominican dictator Rafael Trujillo. Trujillo was assassinated in 1961, and his death remains a cause for celebration in the Dominican Republic. Despite his cruelty and perversions, Trujillo was supported by the U.S. government since he was seen as being strongly against communism. Vargas Llosa tells the story of Urania Cabral, a successful New York City lawyer who was victimized by her father and Trujillo shortly before the dictator's death. Moving forward and back in time, in the author's trademark style, the novel gives a detailed portrait of Trujillo and his frustration with the one enemy he could not conquer: his own advancing age. Obsessive about his habits and grooming, he is unable to do a thing about his increasing incontinence and sexual impotence. The methods he used to victimize individuals and, in fact, his entire country are laid out here, while the stories of Urania, her father, and the men who killed Trujillo are also presented with empathy. "This is an impressively crafted novel," commented Sebastian Shakespeare in the *New Statesman*. "The set pieces are magnificent . . . but it's the small details that you recall: the smell of cheap perfume sprayed on to electric chairs to conceal the stench of urine, excrement and charred flesh." Noting that the Trujillista era was noted for its vileness, Liliana Wendorff added in *Library Journal* that Vargas Llosa "skillfully uses language to demystify subjects that could easily offend." Concluded Jonathan Heawood in the *Guardian Unlimited*, "*The Feast of the Goat* is as dark and complicated as a Jacobean revenge tragedy; but it is also rich and humane."

"A major figure in contemporary Latin American letters," as Locke explained, and "the man whom many describe as the national conscience of his native Peru," as George de Lama wrote in the *Chicago Tribune*, Vargas Llosa is usually ranked with Jorgé Luis Borges, Gabriel García Márquez, and other writers in what has been called the Latin American "Boom" of the 1960s. His body of work set in his native Peru, Suzanne Jill Levine explained in the *New York Times Book Review*, is "one of the largest narrative efforts in contemporary Latin American letters. . . . [He] has begun a complete inventory of the political, social, economic and cultural reality of Peru. . . . Very deliberately, Vargas Llosa has chosen to be his country's conscience." But Vargas Llosa warns that a writer's role is limited. "Even great writers can be totally blind on political matters and can put their prestige and their imagination and fantasy at the service of a policy, which, if it materialized, would be destruction of what they do," Sheppard quoted Vargas Llosa as telling a PEN conference. "To be in the situation of Poland is no better than to be in the situation of Chile. I feel perplexed by these questions. I want to fight for societies where perplexity is still permitted."

BIOGRAPHICAL AND CRITICAL SOURCES:

BOOKS

Acosta, Oscar, and others, *Las honduras de Mario Vargas Llosa*, Universidad Pedagógica Nacional Francisco Morazán (Tegucigalpa, Honduras), 2003.

A Marxist Reading of Fuentes, Vargas Llosa, and Puig, University Press of America (Lanham, MD), 1994.

Booker, Keith M., *Vargas Llosa among the Postmodernists*, University Press of Florida (Gainesville, FL), 1994.

Cano Gaviria, Ricardo, *El buitre y el ave fenix: Conversaciones con Mario Vargas Llosa*, Anagrama (Barcelona, Spain), 1972.

Castro-Klarén, Sara, *Mario Vargas Llosa: análisis introductorio*, Latinoamericana Editores, 1988.

Contemporary Literary Criticism, Thomson Gale (Detroit, MI), Volume 3, 1975, Volume 6, 1976, Volume 9, 1978, Volume 10, 1979, Volume 15, 1980, Volume 31, 1985, Volume 42, 1987, Volume 85, 1995.

Dictionary of Literary Biography, Volume 145: *Modern Latin-American Fiction Writers, Second Series*, Thomson Gale (Detroit, MI), 1994.

El autor y su obra: Mario Vargas Llosa, Universidad Computense de Madrid (Madrid, Spain), 1990.

Encyclopedia of World Biography, 2nd edition, Thomson Gale (Detroit, MI), 1998.

Encyclopedia of World Literature in the Twentieth Century, St. James Press (Detroit, MI), 1999.

Establier Pérez, Helene, *Mario Vargas Llosa y el nuevo arte de hacer novelas*, Universidad de Alicante, 1998.

Feal, Rosemary Geisdorfer, *Novel Lives: The Fictional Autobiographies of Guillermo Cabrera Infante and Mario Vargas Llosa*, University of North Carolina Press (Chapel Hill, NC), 1986.

Gallagher, D. P., *Modern Latin-American Literature*, Oxford University Press (New York, NY), 1973.

Gerdes, Dick, *Mario Vargas Llosa*, Twayne (Boston, MA), 1985.

Gladieu, Marie-Madeleine, *Mario Vargas Llosa*, L'Harmattan (Paris, France), 1989.

Gnutzmann, Rita, *Cómo leer a Mario Vargas Llosa*, Ediciones Júcar, 1992.

Harss, Luis, and Barbara Dohmann, *Into the Mainstream: Conversations with Latin-American Writers*, Harper (New York, NY), 1967.

Hernández de López, Ana María, *Mario Vargas Llosa: opera omnia*, Editorial Pliegos (Madrid, Spain), 1994.

Hispanic Literature Criticism, Thomson Gale (Detroit, MI), 1994.

Köllman, Sabine, *Vargas Llosa's Fiction and the Demons of Politics*, P. Lang (New York, NY), 2002.

Kristal, Efrain, *Temptation of the Word: The Novels of Mario Vargas Llosa*, Vanderbilt University Press (Nashville, TN), 1998.

Lewis, Marvin A., *From Lime to Leticia: The Peruvian Novels of Mario Vargas Llosa,* University Press of America (Lanham, MD), 1983.

Moses, Michael Valdez, *The Novel and the Globalization of Culture,* Oxford University Press (New York, NY), 1995.

Muñoz, Braulio, *A Storyteller: Mario Vargas Llosa between Civilization and Barbarism,* Rowman & Littlefield Publishers (Lanham, MD), 2000.

Oviedo, Jose Miguel, editor, *Mario Vargas Llosa: el escritor y la critica,* Taurus (Madrid, Spain), 1981.

Oviedo, Jose Miguel, *Mario Vargas Llosa: La invencion de una realidad,* Seix Barral (Barcelona, Spain), 1982.

Pereira, Antonio, *La concepcion literaria de Mario Vargas Llosa,* Universidad Nacional Autonoma de Mexico (Mexico City, Mexico), 1981.

Reference Guide to World Literature, 2nd edition, Thomson Gale (Detroit, MI), 1995.

Requejo, Nestor Tenorio, editor, *Mario Vargas Llosa, el fuego de la literatura: textos básicos de aproximación a la narrativa vargasllosiana,* Arteidea Editores (Lima, Peru), 2001.

Rodriguez Elizondo, José, *Vargas Llosa: historia de un doble parricidio,* La Noria (Santiago, Chile), 1993.

Rodriguez Rea, Miguel Angel, *Tras las huellas de un crítico: Mario Vargas Llosa,* Fonda Editorial (Lima, Peru), 1998.

Rossmann, Charles, and Alan Warren Friedman, editors, *Mario Vargas Llosa: A Collection of Critical Essays,* University of Texas Press (Austin, TX), 1978.

Standish, Peter, *Vargas Llosa: La ciudad y los perros,* Grant & Cutler (London, England), 1983.

Williams, Raymond L., *Vargas Llosa: otra historia de un decidio,* Universidad Nacional Autónoma de México (Mexico, DF), 2001.

Williams, Raymond Leslie, *Mario Vargas Llosa,* Ungar (New York, NY), 1986.

PERIODICALS

Americas, March-April, 1989, p. 22; March-April, 1995, p. 62; January, 2001, p. 63.

Atlantic Monthly, March, 1936, pp. 122-124.

Book, November-December, 2003, pp. 9-10.

Bookletter, April 28, 1975.

Booklist, March 15, 1994, p. 1299; March 1, 1998, review of *The Notebooks of Don Rigoberto,* p. 1097; August, 1998, review of *Los cuadernos de Don Rigoberto,* p. 1980; September 1, 1998, review of *Los cuadernos de Don Rigoberto,* p. 74; January 1, 2002, review of *The Feast of the Goat,* p. 762; June 1, 2003, p. 1730; September 15, 2003, p. 181.

Bulletin of Bibliography, December, 1986.

Chicago Tribune, January 3, 1989; June 23, 1989; August 3, 1989.

Commonweal, June 8, 1979.

Esquire, April, 1990, p. 103.

Globe & Mail (Toronto, Ontario, Canada), July 17, 1999, review of *The Notebooks of Don Rigoberto,* p. D16.

Harper's, June, 1987, p. 15.

Hispamerica, Volume 63, 1992, pp. 33-41.

Hispania, March, 1976.

Hudson Review, winter, 1976.

International Fiction Review, January, 1977.

Interview, September, 1988, p. 86.

Kirkus Reviews, March 15, 1998, review of *The Notebooks of Don Rigoberto,* p. 363; March 1, 2003, p. 371; October 1, 2003, p. 1200.

Latin American Literary Review, Volume 11, number 22, 1983, pp. 15-25; January-June, 1987, pp. 121-131, 201-206.

Library Journal, March 15, 1994, p. 116; May 1, 1994, p. 114; April 15, 1997, pp. 82-83; April 1, 1998, Barbara Hoffert, review of *The Notebooks of Don Rigoberto,* p. 126; July, 1998, review of *Cartas a un novelista,* p. 77; January, 1999, review of *The Notebooks of Don Rigoberto,* p. 57; June 1, 2001, Liliana Wendorff, review of *The Feast of the Goat,* p. S31; January, 2002, review of *The Feast of the Goat,* p. 52; April 1, 2003, pp. 99-100; October 15, 2003, p. 100.

London Review of Books, September 17, 1998, review of *The Notebooks of Don Rigoberto,* p. 30.

Los Angeles Times, May 20, 1985; December 18, 1988.

Los Angeles Times Book Review, February 2, 1986.

Maclean's, April 9, 1990, p. 32.

Modern Language Notes, March, 1990, pp. 351-366.

Mother Jones, January, 1989, p. 22.

Nation, November 22, 1975; February 12, 1996, p. 28.

National Review, December 10, 1982; May 16, 1994, p. 65; April 17, 1995, p. 53.

New Leader, March 17, 1975; November 15, 1982; June 6, 1994, pp. 5-6.

New Perspectives Quarterly, fall, 1993, p. 53.

New Republic, August 16-23, 1982; October 8, 1984, pp. 25-27; June 8, 1987, p. 54; February 12, 1990, p. 20.

New Scientist, October 24, 1998, review of *Death in the Andes,* p. 50.

New Statesman, June 21, 1996, pp. 46-47; March 25, 2002, Sebastian Shakespeare, review of *The Feast of the Goat,* p. 57; November 24, 2003, Jonathan Heawood, review of *The Way to Paradise,* p. 55.

Newsweek, February 10, 1986; April 9, 1990, p. 33; October 1, 1990, p. 67.

New York, August 23, 1982.

New Yorker, February 24, 1986, pp. 98, 101-104; August 24, 1987, p. 83; December 25, 1989, p. 103; October 1, 1990, pp. 107-110; April 15, 1996, p. 84; June 17, 2002.

New York Review of Books, March 20, 1975; January 24, 1980; July 16, 1987, p. 35; October 11, 1990, p. 17; May 26, 1994, p. 19; May 9, 1996, p. 16; July 16, 1998, review of *The Notebooks of Don Rigoberto,* p. 31; July 4, 1999, review of *The Notebooks of Don Rigoberto,* p. 20.

New York Times, March 30, 1985; January 8, 1986; February 9, 1986; February 12, 1986; September 10, 1989; December 6, 1998, review of *Making Waves,* p. 97.

New York Times Book Review, March 23, 1975; April 9, 1978; September 23, 1979; August 1, 1982; December 2, 1984; February 2, 1986; May 31, 1987, p. 13; October 29, 1989, p. 1; October 14, 1990, p. 11; March 10, 1991, p. 13; May 15, 1994, p. 10; February 18, 1996, p. 7; August 3, 1997, Jay Parini, review of *Making Waves,* p. 8; December 6, 1998, review of *The Notebooks of Don Rigoberto,* p. 71; September 13, 1998, review of *Making Waves, The Real Life of Alejandro Mayta,* and *Who Killed Palomino Molero?,* p. 44; June 28, 1998, review of *The Notebooks of Don Rigoberto,* p. 10; November 25, 2001, Walter Kirn, review of *The Feast of the Goat,* p. 10.

New York Times Magazine, November 20, 1983; November 5, 1989, p. 44.

Observer (London, England), June 28, 1998, review of *The Notebooks of Don Rigoberto,* p. 17; August 15, 1999, review of *The Notebooks of Don Rigoberto,* p. 14.

Paris Review, fall, 1990, pp. 47-72.

Partisan Review, Volume 46, number 4, 1979.

People, April 9, 1990, p. 71.

PMLA, Volume 106, number 1, 1991, pp. 46-59.

Publishers Weekly, October 5, 1984; April 11, 1994, p.49; November 20, 1995, p. 65; April 21, 1997 p. 49; March 23, 1998, review of *The Notebooks of Don Rigoberto,* p. 76; April 22, 2002. p. 57; September 29, 2003, p. 40.

Review of Contemporary Fiction, spring, 1997, pp. 15-24; spring, 1997, pp. 58-69; spring, 1997, pp. 70-75; spring, 1997 pp. 76-77; spring, 1998, pp. 231-232; spring 2003, p. 165.

Review of the Center for Inter-American Relations, spring, 1975.

Saturday Review, January 11, 1975.

School Library Journal, June, 2003, pp. 45-46.

Spectator, May 14, 1983; July 25, 1998, review of *The Notebooks of Don Rigoberto,* p. 32; November 15, 2003, Sebastian Smee, "Gaugin and His Gritty Granny," p. 54.

Time, February 17, 1975; August 9, 1982; January 27, 1986; March 10, 1986; July 27, 1987, p. 64; September 7, 1987; November 13, 1989, p. 110; April 9, 1990, p. 56; October 22, 1990, p. 89; June 13, 1994, p. 75; February 12, 1996, p. 75.

Times (London, England), May 13, 1985; August 5, 1986; June 29, 1998, review of *The Notebooks of Don Rigoberto,* p. 74.

Times Literary Supplement, October 12, 1973; May 20, 1983; March 8, 1985; May 17, 1985; July 1, 1988; June 17, 1994, p. 11; August 7, 1998, review of *The Notebooks of Don Rigoberto,* p. 7.

Tribune Books (Chicago, IL), October 7, 1979; January 12, 1986, October 29, 1989; September 11, 1994, p. 7; March 3, 1996, p. 6.

U.S. News and World Report, May 9, 1988, p. 69; November 5, 1990, p. 15.

Virginia Quarterly Review, autumn, 1998, review of *Making Waves,* p. 121.

Vital Speeches, October 1, 1992, p. 755.

Vogue, October, 1990, p. 254.

Wall Street Journal, June 12, 1998, review of *The Notebooks of Don Rigoberto,* p. W12.

Washington Post, August 29, 1983; October 1, 1984; March 26, 1989.

Washington Post Book World, August 26, 1984; February 9, 1986; May 22, 1994, p. 5; February 25, 1996, p. 1; July 26, 1998, review of *The Notebooks of Don Rigoberto,* p. 8.

Wilson Quarterly, summer, 2002, p. 105.

World Literature Today, winter, 1978 (special issue on Vargas Llosa); spring, 1978; winter, 1999, review of *Los cuadernos de Don Rigoberto,* p. 120; summer, 2000, review of *La fiesta del chivo,* p. 676; April-June, 2003, p. 79.

ONLINE

Guardian Unlimited, http://books.guardian.co.uk/ (May 1, 2002), review of *The Feast of the Goat.*

January Magazine Web Site, http://www.january magazine.com/ (August 16, 2004), Heidi Johnson-Wright, interview with Mario Vargas Llosa.

Mario Vargas Llosa Home Page, http://www.mvargas llosa.com/ (August 16, 2004).

OTHER

Sklodowska, Elzbieta, *An Interview with Mario Vargas Llosa,* American Audio Prose Library, 1994.*

*   *   *

VOGEL, Paula A(nne) 1951-

PERSONAL: Born November 16, 1951, in Washington, DC; daughter of Donald S. (in advertising) and Phyllis (Bremerman) Vogel. *Education:* Catholic University of America, B.A., 1974; Cornell University, A.B.D., 1977.

ADDRESSES: Home—42 Grove St., No. 13, New York, NY 10014. *Agent*—c/o Peter Franklin, William Morris Agency, 1325 Avenue of the Americas, New York, NY 10019.

CAREER: American Place Theatre, New York, NY, member of staff, 1978-79; Cornell University, Ithaca, NY, member of faculty of theatre arts, 1979-82; Brown University, head of M.F.A. writing program, 1985—. Executive member of Women's Studies, 1977-78. Playwriting instructor, 1981, and consultant at Perseverance Theatre, Juneau, AK; resident playwright at the Signature Theatre, 2004-05. Consultant to Central Casting Theatre, Ithaca; board member, Saratoga International Theatre Institute. Conductor of playwriting workshops at McGill University and at St. Elizabeth's Hospital; has taught at the Maximum Security Center for women at the Adult Corrections Institute in Rhode Island.

MEMBER: Bryn Mawr Drop-out Society (founder), Dramatists Guild, Circle Repertory, Writers Guild of America East.

AWARDS, HONORS: Heerbes-McCalmon Playwriting Award, 1975 and 1976; American College Theatre Festival Award for best new play, 1977, for *Meg;*

Paula A. Vogel

American National Theatre and Academy—West Award, 1978; playwriting fellowship from National Endowment for the Arts, 1979-80; Pew/TCG senior residency award, 1995-97; Guggenheim Award, 1995; Fund for New American Plays award, 1995, for *Hot 'n' Throbbing;* New York Drama Critics Award for best new play, Drama Desk Award for outstanding play, and Off-Broadway Award, *Village Voice,* all 1997, and Pulitzer Prize for Drama, 1998, all for *How I Learned to Drive;* also recipient of a Bunting fellowship, a McKnight fellowship at the Playwright's Center, two National Endowment for the Arts fellowships, and a residency at the Rockefeller Foundation's Bellagio Center.

WRITINGS:

PLAYS

Meg, (three-act; first produced in Washington, DC, at Kennedy Center, 1977), Samuel French (New York, NY), 1977.

Apple-Brown Betty, (one-act) first produced in Louisville, KY, February, 1979.

Desdemona: A Play about a Handkerchief, (two-act; first produced at State University of New York at Binghamton, April, 1980), Dramatists Play Service (New York, NY), 1994.

The Oldest Profession, (one-act), first produced in New York, NY, at Hudson Guild Theatre, December, 1981.

Bertha in Blue, (one-act), first produced in New York, NY, at Hudson Guild Theatre, December, 1981.

The Last Pat Epstein Show before the Reruns (two-act), first produced in Ithaca, NY, February, 1982.

The Baltimore Waltz (also see below), Dramatists Play Service (New York, NY), 1992.

And Baby Makes Seven, first produced in San Francisco, CA, 1992.

Hot 'n' Throbbing, produced in New York, NY, 1992.

The Baltimore Waltz and Other Plays, Theatre Communications Group (New York, NY), 1996.

The Mineola Twins (also see below), first produced in Juneau, AK, 1996.

How I Learned to Drive (also see below), Dramatists Play Service (New York, NY), 1997.

The Mammary Plays (includes *How I Learned to Drive* and *The Mineola Twins*), Theatre Communications Group (New York, NY), 1998.

The Long Christmas Ride Home, Theatre Communications Group (New York, NY), 2004.

OTHER

(With William M. Hoffman and others) *The Way We Live Now: American Plays and the AIDS Crisis,* Theatre Communications Group (New York, NY), 1990.

(With Terrence McNally and Harvey Fierstein) *On Common Ground* (screenplay), Showtime, 2000.

WORK IN PROGRESS: *The Castrato Play,* a five-character play about castrati in seventeenth-century Italy; *Method Acting,* a novel about academia and the violation of acting.

SIDELIGHTS: Paula A. Vogel is not one to shy away from often highly politicized, commonly taboo topics . . . she faces them head on with eloquence and compassion. Throughout her career Vogel, an award-winning playwright, has delved into an assortment of topics from the nontraditional family to AIDS to domestic violence to pedophilia. As she explained to the Minneapolis *Star Tribune,* "I always feel that I'm

writing the script and my audience is writing the play. The fact that 200 people can go in there and come out to have arguments in the car and lobby, and that everyone is always right: That makes it an ideal platform for democracy." Vogel had her first big success with *The Baltimore Waltz* in 1992, then won the Pulitzer Prize for drama in 1998 for *How I Learned to Drive.*

In 1986, Vogel's brother Carl, to whom she was very close, contracted HIV, the virus that causes AIDS. Eventually, Carl became ill and Vogel cared for him. During this time she developed the idea for *The Baltimore Waltz.* "I wrote this play in my head while in the hospital, waiting for the doctors," Vogel remarked to Pamela Sommers in the *Washington Post.* The play concerns a woman, Anna, who comes down with Acquired Toilet Disease (ATD), an affliction of single, female elementary school teachers, and Anna's brother, Carl, a gay library employee. Vogel uses the fictional ATD to force the audience to re-examine their views on AIDS, which is the real subject of the play. Her characters lament that no one is aggressively seeking a cure for the disease ATD because it afflicts a segment of the population that is relatively powerless. Later in the play, the audience discovers that the story is actually taking place in Anna's mind as she tends to her dying brother Carl in a Baltimore hospital.

How I Learned to Drive was inspired by one of Vogel's favorite novels, Vladimir Nabokov's *Lolita.* Dick Scanlan in the *Advocate* praised the author's "flair for poetic dialogue in an era when a television style of naturalism has seeped its way into the theater." Stefan Kanfer in the *New Leader* also applauded Vogel's writing, stating, "Neither her plot nor her people are predictable; in the middle of the saddest scene she evokes a laugh, and just when a moment seems to be edging on hilarity she introduces a wistful note that leaves the smiles frozen on the audience's faces." *How I Learned to Drive* was an off-Broadway hit and earned the 1998 Pulitzer Prize for drama.

In conjunction with *How I Learned to Drive,* Vogel wrote *The Mineola Twins,* which was published with *How I Learned to Drive* as *The Mammary Plays.* Ben Brantley, commenting on *The Mineola Twins* in the *New York Times,* noted, "Those who know this dramatist only from . . . *How I Learned to Drive* . . . may have difficulty recognizing her voice here." *The Mineola Twins* is a comedy about the political schism that divides people, as well as the confining roles prescribed for women.

Vogel's *The Long Christmas Ride Home* tells of a family spinning out of control, as does their car on the way home from an unhappy holiday meal. In a clash of past and present, the play's flash-forward reveals how which each individual is eventually shaped by the prejudice and intolerance demonstrated at the family gathering. Gerard Raymond commented in the *Advocate* that *The Christmas Ride Home* "bears all the Vogel hallmarks: humor, compassion, unflinching honesty, and a political voice filtered through a family drama."

As Vogel once commented of her career: "The playwright is in an unenviable position. On the one hand, as a practitioner interested in writing crafted, intelligent, forward-looking plays, she (or he) is at the same time unable to find permanent financial support from academic communities which espouse high theatrical standards. One can only bite the bullet, write, and live as a VISTA volunteer for the arts."

BIOGRAPHICAL AND CRITICAL SOURCES:

BOOKS

Contemporary Dramatists, 6th edition, St. James Press (Detroit, MI), 1999.
Newsmakers 1999, Issue 2, Thomson Gale (Detroit, MI), 1999.

PERIODICALS

Advocate, June 10, 1997, p. 61; January 20, 1998, p. 99; February 2, 1999, Dick Scanlan, review of *How I Learned to Drive,* p. 42.
American Theater, February 1997, p. 24.
Dallas Morning News, May 27, 1997, p. A 21; April 15, 1998, p. A33; October 25, 1998, p. C1.
Independent on Sunday, June 21, 1998, p. 7.
Jewish Exponent, July 17, 1997.
Los Angeles Times, April 15, 1998, p. A14.
Nation, July 28, 1997, p. 24.
New Leader, June 30, 1997, Stefan Kanfer, review of *How I Learned to Drive,* p. 21
New Republic, July 7, 1997, p. 28.
Newsday, July 29, 1993, p. 67; November 12, 1993, p. 73; March 17, 1997, p. B5.
New York, April 7, 1997, p. 46.
New York Times, May 7, 1993, p. C5; November 12, 1993, p. C20; March 16, 1997, sec, 2, p. 6; March 17, 1997, p. C11; February 19, 1999, Ben Brantley, review of *The Mammary Plays,* p. B1.
Reuters, April 14, 1998.
Star Tribune (Minneapolis, MN), May 15, 1998, p. E1; May 19, 1998, p. E4.
Variety, April 20, 1998, p. 57.
Washington Post, May 22, 1994, p. G14.*

W

WABER, Bernard 1924-

PERSONAL: Born September 27, 1924, in Philadelphia, PA; son of Henry and Pauline (Fleishman) Waber; married Ethel Bernstein, 1952; children: Paulis, Kim, Jan Gary. *Education:* Attended University of Pennsylvania, Philadelphia College of Art, 1946-50, and Pennsylvania Academy of Fine Arts, 1950-51. *Hobbies and other interests:* Playing piano, cooking, Broadway theatre.

ADDRESSES: Home—3653 Bertha Dr., Baldwin Harbor, NY 11510.

CAREER: Commercial artist for Condé Nast Publications, New York, NY, and *Seventeen,* New York, NY, 1952-54; graphic designer for *Life,* New York, NY, 1955-72, and *People,* New York, NY, 1974-88; author and illustrator of children's books, beginning 1961. *Military service:* U.S. Army, 1942-45; became staff sergeant.

AWARDS, HONORS: Children's Spring Book Festival picture book honor, *New York Herald Tribune,* 1962, for *The House on East 88th Street; An Anteater Named Arthur* selected among American Institute of Graphic Arts Children's Books, 1967-68; Notable Book designation, American Library Association, 1970, and named *Boston Globe-Horn Book* honor book for illustration, 1971, both for *A Firefly Named Torchy; Ira Sleeps Over* included in Children's Book Council Children's Book Showcase, 1973; *But Names Will*

Bernard Waber

Never Hurt Me selected among Child Study Association's Children's Books of the Year, 1976; Lewis Carroll Shelf Award, 1979, for *Lyle, Lyle, Crocodile;* International Reading Association's Children's Choice designation, 1979, for *The Snake: A Very Long Story.*

WRITINGS:

SELF-ILLUSTRATED

Lorenzo, Houghton Mifflin (Boston, MA), 1961.

How to Go about Laying an Egg, Houghton Mifflin (Boston, MA), 1963.

Rich Cat, Poor Cat, Houghton Mifflin (Boston, MA), 1963.

Just Like Abraham Lincoln, Houghton Mifflin (Boston, MA), 1964.

"You Look Ridiculous," Said the Rhinoceros to the Hippopotamus, Houghton Mifflin (Boston, MA), 1966.

Cheese, Houghton Mifflin (Boston, MA), 1967.

An Anteater Named Arthur, Houghton Mifflin (Boston, MA), 1967.

A Rose for Mr. Bloom, Houghton Mifflin (Boston, MA), 1968.

A Firefly Named Torchy, Houghton Mifflin (Boston, MA), 1970.

Nobody Is Perfick (collection of short stories), Houghton Mifflin (Boston, MA), 1971.

Ira Sleeps Over, Houghton Mifflin (Boston, MA), 1972.

I Was All Thumbs, Houghton Mifflin (Boston, MA), 1975.

But Names Will Never Hurt Me, Houghton Mifflin (Boston, MA), 1976.

Good-bye, Funny Dumpy-Lumpy, Houghton Mifflin (Boston, MA), 1977.

Mice on My Mind, Houghton Mifflin (Boston, MA), 1977.

The Snake: A Very Long Story, Houghton Mifflin (Boston, MA), 1978.

Dear Hildegarde, Houghton Mifflin (Boston, MA), 1980.

You're a Little Kid with a Big Heart, Houghton Mifflin (Boston, MA), 1980.

Bernard, Houghton Mifflin (Boston, MA), 1982.

Ira Says Goodbye, Houghton Mifflin (Boston, MA), 1988.

Do You See a Mouse?, Houghton Mifflin (Boston, MA), 1995.

Gina, Houghton Mifflin (Boston, MA), 1995.

A Lion Named Shirley Williamson, Houghton Mifflin (Boston, MA), 1996.

Bearsie Bear and the Surprise Sleepover Party, Houghton Mifflin (Boston, MA), 1997.

The Mouse That Snored, Houghton Mifflin (Boston, MA), 2000.

Fast Food! Gulp! Gulp!, Houghton Mifflin (Boston, MA), 2001.

Courage, Houghton Mifflin (Boston, MA), 2002.

Evie and Margie, Houghton Mifflin (Boston, MA), 2003.

Betty's Day Off, Houghton Mifflin (Boston, MA), 2005.

Waber's manuscripts are included in the Kerlan Collection, University of Minnesota.

"LYLE" SERIES

The House on East 88th Street, Houghton Mifflin (Boston, MA), 1962, published as *Welcome, Lyle,* Chatto, Boyd & Oliver (London, England), 1969.

Lyle, Lyle, Crocodile, Houghton Mifflin (Boston, MA), 1965.

Lyle and the Birthday Party, Houghton Mifflin (Boston, MA), 1966.

Lovable Lyle, Houghton Mifflin (Boston, MA), 1969.

Lyle Finds His Mother, Houghton Mifflin (Boston, MA), 1974.

Funny, Funny Lyle, Houghton Mifflin (Boston, MA), 1987.

Lyle at the Office, Houghton Mifflin (Boston, MA), 1994.

Lyle at Christmas, Houghton Mifflin (Boston, MA), 1998.

ADAPTATIONS: The House on East 88th Street, Lovable Lyle, Lyle, Lyle, Crocodile, and *Lyle and the Birthday Party* were adapted as filmstrips with record or cassette by Miller-Brody; *Lyle* was adapted as a stage play and produced at the McAlpin Rooftop Theatre, 1970; *Ira Sleeps Over* was filmed by Phoenix/ BFA Films; *Ira Sleeps Over* and *Ira Says Goodbye* were adapted as a filmstrip with cassette by Live Oak Media, 1984 and 1989 respectively; *Lyle, the Musical,* an animated film, was televised by Home Box Office, 1987; *Lyle,* a musical stage production, was produced in Chicago, IL, 1989; *Lyle, Lyle, Crocodile,* was adapted from *The House on East 88th Street* and was produced as a stage play by Michael Slade and recorded on videotape by Hi-Tops Video.

SIDELIGHTS: Noted for the quirkily titled *The Mouse That Snored, A Lion Named Shirley Williamson,* and *Fast Food! Gulp! Gulp!,* popular picture-book author and illustrator Bernard Waber is perhaps best known for his books about a crocodile named Lyle. The humorous and endearing cartoon reptile appears for the first time in *The House on East 88th Street,* where he is discovered in the Primm family's bathtub. "With aplomb and dazzling showmanship, Lyle entertains and enchants" the Primms, according to *Twentieth-Century Children's Writers* contributor Martha J. Fick. Along with the Primms, a host of young readers have responded with enthusiasm to Waber's other picture books featuring Lyle. "It's hard to go wrong with Lyle," asserted *Booklist* reviewer Ilene Cooper after reading *Lyle at the Office.* Cooper's sentiment was echoed by a *Kirkus Reviews* critic, who maintained that "most would follow the lovable Lyle anywhere." "The croc is so darn . . . lovable, and Waber's pictures are so much fun to look at" that each new installment in the "Lyle" series is eagerly awaited, explained Michael Cart in his *Booklist* review of *Lyle at Christmas.*

Featuring the author's penchant for rhymes and wordplay together with his characteristically droll, understated wit, many of Waber's stand-alone stories for primary graders have been similarly well received. "Armed with a clear understanding of the anxieties, taunts, and humor that go hand in hand with childhood," as *Children's Books and Their Creators* contributor Lynn Sygiel noted, "Waber provides the readers of his . . . books with a mirror of their childhood experiences." Fick similarly asserted that in the "Lyle" books, "text and illustrations merge dynamically to balance fantasy with the exploration of feelings and relationships" that are central to the lives of younger children.

Born in Philadelphia, Pennsylvania, in 1924, Waber credits an early interest in motion pictures with his evolution as an author and illustrator. "When I was about eight years of age," he once recalled, "I had the astonishing good fortune to obtain after-school employment in a neighborhood movie theater. It was my job to raise seats and pick up discarded candy wrappers after daily matinee performances. Admission to a movie theater free of charge was living and breathing my own fantasy. It was also my first experience doing work I enjoyed." "Each day," he continued, "I raced from school to theater . . . and caught the final ten or fifteen minutes of . . . a daily new feature film. Following the performance, having seen only the ending, I would try to reconstruct what I imagined to

be the middle and beginning. It occurs to me that this was my earliest attempt at plotting, which may or may not account for the frequency with which endings to my own stories come to me before I have realized earlier developments."

During Waber's childhood, his family moved frequently because of business failures. The author once commented: "Each time relocation was necessary, I sought assurance from my parents that a neighborhood library and a motion picture theater existed within rollerskating distance. Availability of prospective playmates was a serious matter too, of course, but by my reasoning the library and cinema were life-giving urgencies, a survival kit for any new neighborhood."

Although he started a degree in finance at the University of Pennsylvania, when World War II began he left school to serve his country. After the war he returned to college, this time to study art, and earned his degree in 1951. Waber began his career as a commercial artist, but was nudged into the illustrating of children's books by encouragement from his colleagues. "My involvement with children's books originated with some illustrations of children I carried in my art portfolio," he wrote in *Twentieth-Century Children's Writers.* "Several art directors suggested that my drawings seemed suited for children's books. At the same time, I was also having read-aloud sessions with my own three children. I am afraid my enthusiasm for 'their' books began, in fact, to cause them occasional discomfort. 'Daddy, why don't you look at the grown-ups' books,' they once chided as I trailed after them into the children's room of our local library. Before long I was mailing out stories and ideas to publishers."

In the spirit of his highly regarded "Lyle" books, Waber has written a number of comical fantasies for children revolving around the adventures of a variety of other endearing anthropomorphic animals. A showcase for his whimsical, cartoon-style art, such works as *Do You See a Mouse?, Evie and Margie,* and *A Lion Named Shirley Williamson* have been praised for their ability to capture the imagination of beginning readers. In *Do You See a Mouse?* a complaint has been registered at the elegant Park Snoot Hotel: someone has seen a mouse. "Do you see a mouse? I do not see a mouse" is the common refrain throughout, as employees and other guests find it difficult to imagine a rodent at Park Snoot. "Delighted youngsters, however, will squeal 'Yes!' as they spy the mouse on the subsequent pages of this predictable yet engaging tale," noted a *Publishers Weekly* reviewer. Hanna B. Zeiger of *Horn Book* asserted: "Waber's characterizations are full of sly humor, and readers of all ages will have to smile at the antics of the little rascally rodent who successfully bamboozles one and all in this comic adventure."

Rodents again make an appearance in *The Mouse That Snored,* the title a play on the novel *The Mouse That Roared* by Leonard Wibberly. Into a hushed household where a husband and wife live in silence, quieting their footfalls with slippers and sharing their home with a silent cat and a parrot whose muffled caw is "Hush! Be still" comes a mouse. While by day the newcomer masters the ability to live up to the traditional adage "Quiet as a mouse," when sleep takes over, his snores shake the roof. Praising Waber as a "master humorist," Susan P. Bloom noted in *Horn Book* that the author's illustrations bolster "the drama between a roaring, snoring city mouse and the silent country home he disrupts." "Hilarious banter builds up noisily," Bloom added of Waber's easy-to-read tale.

A Lion Named Shirley Williamson begins with the odd naming of a new lion at the public zoo due to a miscommunication between the zoo director and a representative of the Wildlife Trading Company. Shirley joins the zoo's other lions—Goobah, Poobah, and Aroobah—and is an instant hit with the public and with the zookeeper, who gives her special treatment. However, the jealousy of the other lions and the firing of the zookeeper, along with the humiliation of the zoo director's renaming her "Bongo," causes Shirley to run away. "Waber is back in full form with a story that is both hysterical and poignant," enthused Ilene Cooper in a review for *Booklist.* Cooper added that the book "succeeds at every level," citing its lively plot, "characters that show the inevitable tangle of emotions life elicits," and artwork that appeals to both children and adults.

A pair of hippos is the focus of *Evie and Margie,* which sheds a humorous light on the ups and downs of being best friends. Evie and Margie know they will always be friends, even when they both grow up and become famous actors. However, a casting decision for a school production of *Cinderella* threatens their connection: Margie gets the role and Evie is assigned to be Margie's understudy, as well as being cast in the

role of a talking tree. Any tensions between the two hippos is resolved on the day of the play, in a book that a *Publishers Weekly* contributor dubbed "an entertaining and subtly edifying portrait of a robust friendship." Ilene Cooper in *Booklist* described *Evie and Margie* as a "satisfying, well-plotted picture book" and commended Waber for his sense of humor and including the "lessons about friendship and jealousy [that] are an important part of the story." Calling the work "vintage Waber," *School Library Journal* reviewer Bina Williams praised the illustrations for their "great facial expressions and humorous, child-friendly images," and added that the story "gets to the heart of what is important to children."

Although he opts for animal characters more often than not, humans also figure in books by Waber. *Ira Sleeps Over* tells the story of a young boy who, chided by his older siblings, struggles to determine whether he really should leave his teddy bear behind for an overnight visit to his friend Reggie's house. Ira makes a second appearance in *Ira Says Goodbye,* which explores a somewhat similar dilemma: best friend Reggie is moving away, and his initial excitement over the move hurts Ira's feelings. "The author's portrayals of the confusing array of emotions are wryly accurate," maintained a *Publishers Weekly* reviewer, describing the book as "warm, wise, and ultimately reassuring." Elizabeth S. Watson noted in *Horn Book* that Waber "uses an understated style that is perfect for suggesting the grief of parting with a best friend, without putting a burden on the story."

Gina is another of Waber's books for very young children dealing with moving and friendships—in this case, creating new friends. Gina has just moved into a new apartment building in Queens, and to her dismay there are no other girls in the building but only "boys, boys, boys galore . . . on every floor." After tiring of playing alone, the spunky young protagonist gains new friends by demonstrating her skills in such important particulars as baseball, tree climbing, and biking. "Another winner from the redoubtable Waber," exclaimed *School Library Journal* contributor Virginia Opocensky, while a *Publishers Weekly* reviewer praised "the domesticated daffiness of [Waber's] action-packed watercolors."

On a more serious note, Waber responded to the terrorists attacks of September 11, 2001, and their aftermath with *Courage.* A "simple book with a complex message," as it was described by *Booklist* reviewer GraceAnn A. DeCandido, *Courage* begins with the statement "There are many kinds of courage," and then goes on to illustrate the courage that people can exhibit in their everyday lives. From riding a two-wheel bicycle for the first time and taking that first jump off the high diving board to trying a new kind of food, Waber shows children that a hero can be hiding in almost anyone. Calling *Courage* "poignant yet entertaining," a *Publishers Weekly* reviewer added that the volume "is a natural read-aloud likely to spark valuable adult-child dialogue and to help youngsters conquer their own fears." Despite the seriousness of the message, Waber's characteristic "wobbly-lined cartoons add touches of humor," noted a *Kirkus Reviews* critic, while DeCandido concluded that the author/illustrator successfully depicts "an abstraction in concrete ways that will resonate with children."

As he explained in an interview posted on the Houghton Mifflin Web site, Waber was inspired about courage not only by September 11th, but by memories of growing up during the Great Depression of the 1930s. As he noted, courage is "the summoning of core strengths, faith, and idealism in confrontation with life's challenges. My parents' bracing themselves against all odds during the Great Depression taught me valuable lessons in this regard. However, because we are humans with frailties, courage can also mean asking for help and support in the face of overwhelming circumstances." While Waber had begun writing the book *Courage* prior to the fall of 2001, "that tragic day was so deeply affecting, and so defining of courage for us all, it influenced the book's inclusion of firefighters and a police officer."

BIOGRAPHICAL AND CRITICAL SOURCES:

BOOKS

Children's Books and Their Creators, edited by Anita Silvey, Houghton Mifflin (Boston, MA), 1995, pp. 666-668.
Kingman, Lee, and others, compilers, *Illustrators of Children's Books: 1967-1976,* Horn Book, 1978.
Twentieth-Century Children's Writers, 4th edition, St. James Press (Detroit, MI), 1994, pp. 987-988.
Waber, Bernard, *Gina,* Houghton Mifflin (Boston, MA), 1995.
Waber, Bernard, *Courage,* Houghton Mifflin (Boston, MA), 2002.

PERIODICALS

Booklist, August, 1987, p. 1753; June 1, 1994, Ilene Cooper, review of *Lyle at the Office,* p. 1846; September 1, 1996, Ilene Cooper, review of *A Lion Named Shirley Williamson,* p. 128; September 1, 1998, Michael Cart, review of *Lyle at Christmas,* p. 135; August, 2000, Tim Arnold, review of *The Mouse That Snored,* p. 2150; December 15, 2002, GraceAnn A. DeCandido, review of *Courage,* p. 765; October 15, 2003, Ilene Cooper, review of *Evie and Margie,* p. 409.
Horn Book, September-October, 1987, p. 604; November-December, 1988, Elizabeth S. Watson, review of *Ira Says Goodbye,* p. 779; July-August, 1995, Hanna B. Zeiger, review of *Do You See a Mouse?,* pp. 454-455; September-October, 1997, Ann A. Flowers, review of *Bearsie Bear and the Surprise Sleepover Party,* p. 565; November, 1998, Ann A. Flowers, review of *Lyle at Christmas,* p. 721; November, 2000, Susan P. Bloom, review of *The Mouse That Snored,* p. 750; September-October, 2003, Betty Carter, review of *Evie and Margie,* p. 604.
Kirkus Reviews, August 15, 1987, p. 1246; July 15, 1994, review of *Lyle at the Office,* p. 997; October 1, 2001, review of *Fast Food! Gulp! Gulp!,* p. 1435; October 15, 2002, review of *Courage,* p. 1539; October 15, 2003, review of *Evie and Margie,* p. 1227.
New York Times Book Review, March 5, 1989, p. 31.
Publishers Weekly, July 8, 1988, review of *Ira Says Goodbye,* p. 54; January 23, 1995, review of *Do You See a Mouse?,* p. 70; August 14, 1995, review of *Gina,* p. 83; September 15, 1997, review of *Bearsie Bear and the Surprise Sleepover Party,* p. 75; August 7, 2000, review of *The Mouse That Snored,* p. 94; October 15, 2001, review of *Fast Food! Gulp! Gulp!,* p. 70; October 7, 2002, review of *Courage,* p. 72; December 1, 2003, review of *Evie and Margie,* p. 55.
Reading Today, December, 2001, Lynne T. Burke, review of *Fast Food! Gulp! Gulp!,* p. 32.
School Library Journal, September, 1995, p. 188; October, 1995, Virginia Opocensky, review of *Gina,* p. 123; December, 1996, pp. 108-109; October, 2000, Kathie Meizner, review of *The Mouse That Snored,* p. 140; September, 2001, Joyce Adams Burner, review of *Fast Food! Gulp! Gulp!,* p. 208; December, 2002, Jessica Snow, review of *Courage,* p. 131; October, 2003, Bina Williams, review of *Evie and Margie,* p. 140.

Houghton Mifflin Web site, http://www.houghtonmifflin books.com/ (October 26, 2004), "Bernard Waber, Author/Illustrator."*

*   *   *

WALTERS, Eric (Robert) 1957-

PERSONAL: Born March 3, 1957, in Toronto, Ontario, Canada; son of Eric (a woodworker) and Christina (a homemaker) Walters; married, December 28, 1984; wife's name Anita (a social worker); children: Christina, Nicholas, Julia. *Education:* York University, B.A., 1979, B.S.W., 1983, M.S.W., 1985; University of Toronto, B.Ed., 1989. *Politics:* Liberal. *Religion:* United Church of Canada. *Hobbies and other interests:* Playing and coaching basketball and soccer, music, playing the saxophone.

ADDRESSES: Home—Mississauga, Ontario, Canada. *Office*—c/o Author Mail, Orca Book Publishers, P.O. Box 468, Custer, WA 98240. *E-mail*—ewalters@ interlog.com.

CAREER: Writer and educator. Affiliated with Children's Aid Society, Simcoe County, Ontario, Canada, 1979-81, Region of Peel, 1981-85; Strothers Treatment Centre, social worker, 1986-89; Emergency Department, Credit Valley Hospital, Mississauga, Ontario, crisis social worker, 1989—; Peel Region Board of Education, teacher, beginning 1989; writer, 1991—.

MEMBER: Canadian Society of Children's Authors, Illustrators, and Performers, Writers' Union of Canada, Ontario Public School Teachers' Federation.

AWARDS, HONORS: Silver Birch Award, Ontario Library Association, 1997, Blue Heron Book Award, Blue Heron Books, 1997, and Children's Choice Award, Canadian Children's Book Centre (CBC), all for *STARS;* Silver Birch Award, CBC Choice Award, and Ruth Schwartz Award nomination, all 1997, all for *Trapped in Ice;* Ruth Schwartz Award, CBC Choice Award, New York Public Library Books for the Teen

Eric Walters

Age designation, and Canadian Library Book of the Year Honor selection, all 1998, all for *War of the Eagles;* CBC Choice Award, and Red Cedar Award nomination, both 1998, both for *Diamonds in the Rough;* Canadian Library Association (CLA) Honour Book designation, 1998, for *The Hydrofoil Mystery;* CLA Book of the Year shortlist, 2000, and UNESCO Honor Selection designation, 2003, both for *Caged Eagles;* Red Maple Award, and Snow Willow Award, both 2002, both for *Rebound;* CBC Choice Award, and Red Maple Award finalist, both 2002, both for *The Bully Boys;* Silver Birch Award, 2003, and Arthur Ellis Award shortlist, both 2003, both for *Camp X;* Torgi Award, 2003, for *Run.*

WRITINGS:

(With Norm Rippon) *Improve Your Child's Spelling 1,* Momentum Publishing, 1991.
(With Norm Rippon) *Improve Your Child's Spelling 2,* Momentum Publishing, 1993.

Stand Your Ground, Stoddart (Toronto, Ontario, Canada), 1994.

STARS, Stoddart (Toronto, Ontario, Canada), 1996.

Trapped in Ice, Viking, 1997.

Diamonds in the Rough, Stoddart (Buffalo, NY), 1998.

War of the Eagles, Orca (Custer, WA), 1998.

Stranded, HarperCollins (Toronto, Ontario, Canada), 1998.

The Hydrofoil Mystery, Puffin (Toronto, Ontario, Canada), 1998.

Visions, 1999.

Tiger by the Tail, 1999.

The Money Pit Mystery, HarperCollins (Toronto, Ontario, Canada), 1999.

Caged Eagles (sequel to *War of the Eagles*), Orca (Custer, WA), 2000.

The Bully Boys, Viking (Toronto, Ontario, Canada), 2000.

Rebound, Stoddart (Buffalo, NY), 2001.

Northern Exposures, HarperCollins (Toronto, Ontario, Canada), 2001.

Tiger in Trouble, Beach Holme (Vancouver, British Columbia, Canada), 2001.

Camp X, Penguin Canada (Toronto, Ontario, Canada), 2002.

Ricky, HarperCollins (Toronto, Ontario, Canada), 2002.

Tiger Town, Beach Holme (Vancouver, British Columbia, Canada), 2002.

Royal Ransom, Puffin Canada (Toronto, Ontario, Canada), 2003.

Run, Puffin (Toronto Ontario, Canada), 2003.

Grind, Orca (Custer, WA), 2004.

Overdrive, Orca (Custer, WA), 2004.

I've Got an Idea, HarperCollins (Toronto, Ontario, Canada), 2004.

Camp 30 (sequel to *Camp X*), Penguin Canada (Toronto, Ontario, Canada), 2004.

Death by Exposure, 2004.

(With daughter, Christina Walters) *The True Story of Santa Claus,* Chestnut Publishing (Toronto, Ontario, Canada), 2004.

Author's works have been translated into French, Dutch, Japanese, and Chinese.

"BASKETBALL" SERIES

Three on Three, Orca (Custer, WA), 1999.

Full Court Press, Orca (Custer, WA), 2000.

Hoop Crazy, Orca (Custer, WA), 2001.

Long Shot, Orca (Custer, WA), 2001.

Road Trip, Orca (Custer, WA), 2002.

Off Season, Orca (Victoria, British Columbia, Canada), 2003.

Underdog, Orca (Victoria, British Columbia, Canada), 2004.

(With Jerome "Junk Yard Dog" Williams) *Triple Threat,* Orca (Custer, WA), 2005.

WORK IN PROGRESS: Tiger Trap, Elixir, Black and White, Sketches, Juice, The Falls, They All Fall Down, and *Shattered,* all novels for teen readers.

SIDELIGHTS: The novels of Canadian author Eric Walters have been compared by critics to the work of well-known YA writers Gary Paulsen and Will Hobbs. As *Resource Links* contributor Gillian Richardson noted of the author's 2003 novel *Royal Ransom,* Walters "excels at seizing the reader's attention with rapid-fire action scenes, often involving survival against nature." His first novel, *Stand Your Ground,* sold out instantly, while *STARS,* Walters's second novel, won both the Silver Birch Award and the Blue Heron Book Award. Books nominated for these awards are selected by juries of young adults, a testament to Walters's success at writing stories with which his audience can identify. His books have also proved popular because his teen protagonists invariably succeed despite the hurdles they face. This message—that obstacles can be overcome—is, in fact, what initially attracted Walters to writing for young adults. "I prefer writing children's novels because they are like morality plays," the prolific novelist once asserted. "There is much more right and wrong in them. In adult novels, it's almost as if you have to emphasize the bad or wrong, and I don't want the wrong people to win. I like happy endings."

Walters originally pursued a career as a social worker, but went on to become a teacher while continuing to work part-time as a crisis social worker in an emergency department. In 1991, inspired by the books he read aloud to his fifth-grade students, he decided to try his hand at writing his own books for children. His creative writing classes now became a sharing process for both Walters and his students; they took turns reading one another's writing, and he expected the students to give his work the same critical appraisal he gave theirs. In fact, it was his students' enthusiasm after hearing the first draft of *Stand Your Ground* that convinced Walters to send the completed draft to a publisher.

"The underlying theme of many of my books is about a sense of belonging," Walters once commented, "and about how you sometimes have to work to get to that place." His protagonists are frequently gifted teens to whom life has dealt a severe blow. Their stories revolve around the challenges they experience when they are suddenly offered an opportunity they had previously lacked. Will they recognize and accept it—or turn their backs? In both *Stand Your Ground* and *STARS,* seizing an opportunity involves rejecting the thrill of living outside the law and recognizing the value of the ordinary. In *Stand Your Ground,* for example, the protagonist comes to realize that he prefers living with his old-fashioned Dutch grandparents to wheeling deals with his con-artist father. In *STARS,* a city boy spends his time planning his escape from a Northern Ontario camp for young offenders before he realizes how much he has come to love the wilderness.

Walters's street-smart but sensitive protagonists are based on children he remembers from growing up with in a troubled neighborhood in west-end Toronto. His mother died when he was four years old, and he and his older sister ended up raising themselves. For much of his youth, Walters ran wild, playing in neighboring stockyards, running through sewers, and fleeing the police. His world was populated by "smart people pushed in the wrong directions," as he once recalled, and these same people provide his stories with much of their drama. Like his protagonists, Walters managed to escape this world, a cultural move he once compared to immigrating to a new country: "You leave things behind and there's a sense of loss."

Walters's 2003 novel *Run* focuses on a true story: the 1980 effort of Canadian athlete Terry Fox to run across Canada following a leg amputation. The novel weaves Fox's story into the fictional story of Winston MacDonald, Jr., a student whose drinking and truancy have caused him to be sent to live with his journalist father. When Winston's father is sent to cover Fox's Marathon of Hope, the teen has the chance to travel in Fox's support van and even runs alongside Fox, learning a lesson about perseverance and character. "It is a testament to Walters's talents that he manages to depict Terry as both a hero and a human," noted *Resource Links* reviewer Nadine d'Entremont, praising *Run* as an "excellent novel" that "skillfully explores a range of themes, including family, friendship, determination, and heroism." In writing *Run* Walters had the support

of Fox's family, and he donated all royalties from the sale of the book to the Terry Fox Foundation to fund cancer research.

Several of Walters's novels focus on the World War II period. In *War of the Eagles* Jed, a Native American teen of the Tsimshian nation, learns about prejudice firsthand as he watches the attitudes of his fellow townspeople change toward their Japanese neighbors as the war progresses and tensions mount in Jed's small Canadian fishing village. In the sequel to *War of the Eagles, Caged Eagles,* Walters focuses on the experiences of Jed's friend, fourteen-year-old Tadashi Fukushima, who together with his Japanese-Canadian family and others of similar heritage from the village, is forced into an internment camp for the duration of the war. The boy does not understand his parents' fatalistic attitude in dealing with this humiliation; he grows angry as their possessions are taken from them and he must live with the women in a makeshift hovel while his father lives elsewhere in the camp with the men. Together with a new friend, Tadashi finds a way to leave the camp undetected, and in an act of defiance he sinks the family's fishing boat—the source of their livelihood—to prevent it from being sold. Praising *Caged Eagles, Booklist* reviewer Chris Sherman noted that Walters "admirably succeeds" in helping readers understand the "humiliation, anger, and depression" of Tadashi's family, while also weaving an element of adventure into the boy's story. In a *School Library Journal* review, Kathleen Isaacs called the book "a disturbing and convincing story that needs to be told," while in *Booklist* John Peters hailed *War of the Eagles* as "a multifaceted, well-knit story" that is enhanced by Walters's "fluent storytelling."

In *Camp X* twelve-year-old George and his older brother Jack are left alone when their father leaves to fight in World War II and their mother gets a job in a munitions factory. Exploring their new town of Whitby, Ontario, the boys stumble upon a secret military installation: a British-run camp to train Allied spies. As they learn more about the camp, they gain the confidence of the presiding director, and are ultimately asked to assist camp command in making deliveries to the munitions factory nearby. During their delivery run, George and Jack discover a plot to undermine the camp, and realize that not everyone they know can be trusted. Noting that *Camp X* is based on an actual military installation, *Resource Links* contributor Victoria Pennell praised the novel for containing "fast-moving action" that will appeal to upper-elementary-aged readers who enjoy military history. Fans of the novel will also appreciate *Camp 30,* a sequel in which George and Jack move to another town and discover a different type of camp: a prisoner-of-war camp that houses German soldiers. Like *Camp X, Camp 30* is also based on Canadian history; the actual camp was located in Bowmanville, Ontario, and served as a temporary home for some of the highest-ranking German officers to be captured by Allied troops during the war.

In addition to writing problem novels featuring older teens, Walters is the author of a popular series of books for young basketball fans. Beginning with *Three on Three,* the series includes the chapter books *Full Court Press, Long Shot, Hoop Crazy, Off Season,* and *Road Trip* among its titles. *Off Season* focuses on third-grade friends and basketball team members Nick and Kia, who travel to British Columbia to visit Nick's cousin Ned during summer vacation. Although the three spend some time shooting hoops on a rustic basketball court Ned's father has built, the city pair also learn to appreciate learning about the ways of the wild when they become trapped, ringed in by forest fires. In *Road Trip,* the boys hit the road, traveling to compete in a high-pressure tournament where the stakes are even higher for their coach. Praising the series' writing style as "easy and fast paced," *Resource Links* reviewer Stephanie Olson added that "basketball fans will love the excitement" generated by the young team's competitive spirit. The eighth book in the series, *Triple Threat,* was cowritten by NBA star Jerome "Junk Yard Dog" Williams. Williams is also a character in the book and helps Nick and Kia overcome bullies.

Walters credits the popularity of his fiction to his realistic plots and vivid details. As he once explained, "I do a lot of personal research. I've hung out at a tough biker bar, white water rafted, rock climbed, played with people's pet lions and tigers and bears, spent days in a wheelchair, and stood outside in a blizzard in a T-shirt and shorts to find out what it was like to freeze to death."

Walters's own experiences as a youth, combined with things he has seen while working as a social worker, family therapist, and teacher, have convinced him that many good people caught in a dead end "don't get out alive." As a result, he has found writing about

characters who *do* manage to escape to be a form of catharsis. He identifies so closely with his characters that he worries about them even after a book is finished. Recalling what people said of him when he was a youth, he acknowledges, "A lot of my life has been dedicated to proving people wrong."

BIOGRAPHICAL AND CRITICAL SOURCES:

PERIODICALS

Booklist, December 15, 1998, John Peters, review of *War of the Eagles,* p. 752; June 1, 2000, Tim Arnold, review of *Three on Three,* p. 1898; December 1, 2000, Chris Sherman, review of *Caged Eagles,* p. 702; April 1, 2001, Roger Leslie, review of *Full Court Press,* p. 1473.
Journal of Adolescent and Adult Literacy, October, 1996, p. 158.
Quill & Quire, February, 1995, p. 39; May, 1996, p. 35.
Resource Links, February, 1998, review of *Trapped in Ice,* p. 113; October, 1998, review of *War of the Eagles,* p. 21; February, 2000, review of *Three on Three,* pp. 11-12, and review of *Stranded,* pp. 29-30; April, 2000, review of *The Bully Boys,* p. 12; October, 2000, review of *Caged Eagles,* p. 31; February, 2001, review of *Rebound,* p. 20; October, 2001, Shannon Danylko, review of *Hoop Crazy!,* and Johal Jinder, review of *Tiger in Trouble,* p. 20; December, 2001, Shannon Danylko, review of *Long Shot,* p. 23; April, 2002, Victoria Pennell, review of *Camp X,* p. 42; October, 2002, Stephanie Olson, review of *Road Trip,* p. 18; February, 2003, Gillian Richardson, review of *Royal Ransom,* p. 19; April, 2003, review of *Tiger Town,* p. 54; June, 2003, Teresa Hughes, review of *Ricky,* p. 36, and Elaine Rosepad, review of *Off Season,* p. 47; October, 2003, Nadine d'Entremont, review of *Run,* p. 37.
School Library Journal, November, 2000, Kathleen Isaacs, review of *Caged Eagles,* p. 164; October, 2001, Janice C. Hayes, review of *Rebound,* p. 174; July, 2002, Kate Kohlbeck, review of *Long Shot,* p. 127.
Teacher Librarian, March-April, 1999, review of *War of the Eagles,* p. 22.

ONLINE

Canadian Materials Online, http://www.umanitoba.ca/cm/ (September 26, 1998), Dave Jenkinson, interview with Walters.
Eric Walters Web site, http://www.interlog.com/~ewalters (December 24, 2004).

WATSON, Richard F.
   See SILVERBERG, Robert

         *   *   *

WELSH, Frank (Reeson) 1931-

PERSONAL: Born August 16, 1931, in Washington, England; son of Francis Cox Welsh (a banker) and Doris M. Ibbett (maiden name, Reeson); married Agnes Cowley (a county councilor), April 15, 1954; children: Jane Welsh Young, Sophie Welsh Rehmet, Ben, John. *Education:* Magdalene College, Cambridge, M.A., 1956. *Politics:* Labour. *Religion:* Church of England. *Hobbies and other interests:* Sailing.

ADDRESSES: Home—37 George St., Cambridge, England; and Le Vieux Logis de Lizant, 86400 Civray, France. *Agent*—Andrew Best, Curtis Brown, 162-168 Regent St., London W1R 5TA, England.

CAREER: Writer, 1982—. Affiliated with John Lewis Partnership, England, 1954-58, and CAS Group, England, 1958-64; William Brandt's Sons & Co. Ltd., England, managing director, 1965-72; Grindlays Bank, England, director, 1971-85. University of Tennessee, Knoxville, Alcoa distinguished visiting scholar and visiting lecturer, beginning 1979. Chair, Hadfields Ltd., 1967-79, Jensen Motors Ltd., 1968-72, and Cox & Kings, 1972-76; director, Henry Ansbacher & Co., 1976-82, and Trireme Trust, beginning 1983; member, British Waterways Board, 1975-81, Royal Commission on the National Health Service, 1976-79, and Health Education Council, 1978-80.

MEMBER: International Banker Association (member of general advisory council, 1976-80), N. British Industrial Association, London Industrial Association (chair, beginning 1984), Savile Club, United Oxford and Cambridge University Club.

WRITINGS:

The Profit of the State: Nationalised Industries and Public Enterprises, Temple Smith (London, England), 1982.

The Afflicted State: A Survey of Public Enterprise, Century (London, England), 1983.

First Blood: Tales of Horror from the Border Country, Constable (London, England), 1985.

(With George Ridley) *Bend'Or, Duke of Westminster: A Personal Memoir,* Clark (London, England), 1985.

Uneasy City: An Insider's View of the City of London, Weidenfeld & Nicolson (London, England), 1986.

Building the Trireme, Constable (London, England), 1988.

Companion Guide to the Lake District, Collins (London, England), 1989.

Hong Kong: A History, Collins (London, England), 1992, published as *A Borrowed Place: The History of Hong Kong,* Kodansha International (New York, NY), 1993, reprinted as *Hong Kong,* Harper-Collins (London, England), 1997.

Dangerous Deceits, HarperCollins (London, England), 1999.

South Africa: A Narrative History, Kodansha International (New York, NY), 1999.

The Four Nations: A History of the United Kingdom, Yale University Press (New Haven, CT), 2003.

A New History of Australia, Allen Lane (London, England), 2004.

Contributor to *Country Life.*

SIDELIGHTS: A self-confessed "historian by inclination and somewhat by training," British author Frank Welsh has found a niche, as he once explained, "between business history, social history, and political history, and I have a pronounced interest in nautical matters. My bias is that of a classically educated, unregenerate and unreconstructed, imperialist and traditionalist Englishman." As such, Welsh has written social histories and guides to England, including *Uneasy City: An Insider's View of the City of London, The Companion Guide to the Lake District,* and *The Four Nations: A History of the United Kingdom.* In addition, Welsh has penned histories of former colonies or dependencies of the British Empire, including *A Borrowed Place: The History of Hong Kong* and *South Africa: A Narrative History.*

In *A Borrowed Place,* Welsh traces the history of Hong Kong from its beginnings as an essentially barren island that was unwillingly ceded to the British by China in 1842. Hong Kong's growth happened initially because of the opium traders, who were looking for new materials to import. With the sale of the Kowloon Peninsula to England in 1859 and the leasing of the so-called New Territories, the British became overlords of the city and territory. Following Japanese occupation in World War II, Hong Kong emerged as one of the lions of the Asian economic region, with banking and investment concerns headquartering there; the city provided a window to mainland China when that country began to trade with the West. Welsh takes these aspects of Hong Kong into account in his "deeply researched" work, according to a contributor for *Publishers Weekly.* However, the same reviewer found *A Borrowed Place* to be a "sterile history." Andrew J. Nathan, reviewing the same work in the *New Republic,* commented that "Welsh has written a history not so much of Hong Kong as of British rule there, a study in colonial rather than Chinese history." Nathan further noted that Welsh "has used only a few Chinese sources, spelling Chinese personal and place names wrong almost as often as he spells them right." A writer for the *Economist,* however, had a better opinion of the book and its author: "Mr. Welsh tells the story well of the runt that became a champion."

Welsh delves into colonial history again with his *South Africa: A Narrative History.* Here he covers two hundred years of South African history "with bold strokes that some may find candid but others coarse," according to Thomas Davis in *Library Journal.* *Booklist*'s David Cline felt that Welsh "has created a precise account" of the country, from its earliest days of the bushmen, through the time of the early Dutch settlers and their decision to utilize slaves, to the establishment of the diamond mines, the takeover by the English in 1795, the 1910 establishment of the Union of South Africa, the days of apartheid, and on to South Africa's ultimate independence and the election of Nelson Mandela as its first black president. Cline also felt that Welsh's text was "comprehensive enough" for classroom use. A contributor for the *Journal of Negro History* found the work "particularly helpful" in contextualizing the country's modern condition into its historical tradition. A critic for *Publishers Weekly* had further praise for Welsh's history, calling it a "vivid narrative" and also noting that Welsh was both "outspoken and opinionated." And Stephen Taylor, reviewing the same work in the *New York Times Book Review,* found Welsh's narrative to be "refreshingly free of . . . polemics." According to Taylor, Welsh "stands squarely in the tradition of the liberal school: his assessments are judicious, his opinions fair."

With *The Four Nations,* Welsh turns his historian's eye to his own country, writing of the "creation, then the ongoing breakup, of the United Kingdom into its four component nations," as Robert Moore described the work in *Library Journal.* Starting his study with the Roman conquest of the island, Welsh traces the establishment of the modern boundaries of Wales, Scotland, England, and Ireland, paying special attention to the histories of the latter two countries. Emphasis is given to the Irish question, from the unsuccessful Rising of 1798, to the days of the Great Famine in mid-eighteenth century, the partition of the country in the early part of the twentieth century, and the ensuing religious conflict in Northern Ireland. Welsh also looks at the nationalistic movements in Wales and Scotland that have led to these regions' growing autonomy. According to a reviewer for *Publishers Weekly,* Welsh "has chosen breadth of coverage over depth" in this survey of 2,000 years of history. For Ronald Hutton, reviewing *The Four Nations* in the *Times Literary Supplement,* Welsh's work "is essentially a history of the English impact on the British Isles." Hutton further commented that this historical analysis is "a big, exciting, opinionated book that veers between the shrewd and the half-baked."

BIOGRAPHICAL AND CRITICAL SOURCES:

PERIODICALS

Booklist, November 15, 1998, David Cline, review of *South Africa: A Narrative History,* p. 564.

Economist (U.S.), September 4, 1993, review of *A Borrowed Place: The History of Hong Kong,* pp. 85-86.

Journal of Negro History, summer, 2000, review of *South Africa,* p. 141.

Library Journal, September 15, 1998, Thomas Davis, review of *South Africa,* p. 96; March 15, 2003, Robert Moore, review of *The Four Nations: A History of the United Kingdom,* p. 100.

New Republic, August 22, 1994, Andrew J. Nathan, review of *A Borrowed Place,* pp. 46-49.

New York Times Book Review, March 7, 1999, Stephan Taylor, review of *South Africa,* p. 30.

Publishers Weekly, August 16, 1993, review of *A Borrowed Place,* p. 95; December 7, 1998, review of *South Africa,* p. 43; March 3, 2003, review of *The Four Nations,* p. 64.

Times Literary Supplement, December 7, 2002, Ronald Hutton, review of *The Four Nations.**

WHITBOURN, John 1958-

PERSONAL: Born March 23, 1958, in Godalming, Surrey, England; married Elizabeth Caroline Gale, 1982; children: one son, two daughters. *Ethnicity:* "English." *Education:* University of Wales, University College, Cardiff, B.A., 1981.

ADDRESSES: Agent—Colin Smythe Ltd., P.O. Box 6, Gerrards Cross, Buckinghamshire SL9 8XA, England. *E-mail*—jaw@telinco.co.uk.

CAREER: Writer.

AWARDS, HONORS: British Broadcasting Corp./ Gollancz First Fantasy Novel Prize, 1991, for *A Dangerous Energy.*

WRITINGS:

FANTASY NOVELS

A Dangerous Energy, Victor Gollancz (London, England), 1992.
Popes and Phantoms, Victor Gollancz (London, England), 1993.
To Build Jerusalem, Victor Gollancz (London, England), 1994.
The Royal Changeling, Simon & Schuster (New York, NY), 1998.

Popes and Phantoms has been published in Russia.

"DOWNS-LORD TRIPTYCH"; FANTASY NOVELS

Downs-Lord Dawn, Simon & Schuster (New York, NY), 1999.
Downs-Lord Day, Simon & Schuster (New York, NY), 2000.
Downs-Lord Doomsday, Simon & Schuster (New York, NY), 2002.

SHORT STORIES

Binscombe Tales, Haunted Library (Chester, England), 1989.
Rollover Night, Haunted Library (Chester, England), 1990.

Popes and Phantoms, Haunted Library (Chester, England), 1993.
Binscombe Tales: Sinister Saxon Stories, Volume 1, Ash-Tree Press (Ashcroft, British Columbia, Canada), 1998.
Binscombe Tales: Sinister Sutangli Stories, Volume 2, Ash-Tree Press (Ashcroft, British Columbia, Canada), 1999.

BIOGRAPHICAL AND CRITICAL SOURCES:

BOOKS

St. James Guide to Fantasy Writers, St. James Press (Detroit, MI), 1996, pp. 604-605.

PERIODICALS

Necrofile, fall, 1998, review of *Binscombe Tales,* p. 8.

*   *   *

WIDEMAN, John Edgar 1941-

PERSONAL: Born June 14, 1941, in Washington, DC; son of Edgar and Bette (French) Wideman; married Judith Ann Goldman, 1965; children: Daniel Jerome, Jacob Edgar, Jamila Ann. *Education:* University of Pennsylvania, B.A., 1963; New College, Oxford, England, B.Phil., 1966.

ADDRESSES: Office—Department of English, University of Massachusetts, Amherst Campus, Bartlett Hall, Amherst, MA 01003. *E-mail*—jwhoops@english.umass.edu.

CAREER: Howard University, Washington, DC, teacher of American literature, summer, 1965; University of Pennsylvania, Philadelphia, PA, 1966-74, began as instructor, became professor of English, 1974, director of Afro-American studies program, 1971-73; University of Wyoming, Laramie, WY, professor of English, 1974-1986; University of Massachusetts—Amherst, Amherst, MA, professor of English, 1986—, named Distinguished Professor, 2001. Made U.S. Department of State lecture tour of Europe and the

John Edgar Wideman

Near East, 1976; Phi Beta Kappa lecturer, 1976; visiting writer and lecturer at numerous colleges and universities; has also served as administrator/teacher in a curriculum planning, teacher-training institute sponsored by National Defense Education Act. Assistant basketball coach, University of Pennsylvania, 1968-72. National Humanities Faculty consultant in numerous states; consultant to secondary schools across the country, 1968—.

MEMBER: Association of American Rhodes Scholars (member of board of directors and of state and national selection committees), American Studies Association (council, 1980-81), Modern Language Association, American Academy of Arts and Sciences, Phi Beta Kappa.

AWARDS, HONORS: Kent fellow, and Writers' Workshop, University of Iowa, 1966; named member of Philadelphia Big Five Basketball Hall of Fame, 1974; Young Humanist fellow, 1975—; PEN/Faulkner Award for fiction, 1984, for *Sent for You Yesterday;* National Book Award nomination, 1984, for *Brothers and Keepers;* D. Litt., University of Pennsylvania,

1985; Du Sable Museum Prize for Nonfiction, 1985; John Dos Passos Prize for Literature, Longwood College, 1986; National Magazine Editors Prize for Short Fiction, 1987; Lannan Literary fellowship for fiction, 1991; PEN/Faulkner Award and American Book Award, Before Columbus Foundation, 1991, both for *Philadelphia Fire;* MacArthur fellow, MacArthur Foundation, 1993; James Fenimore Cooper Prize for historical fiction, 1996, for *The Cattle Killing;* Rea Prize for short fiction, Dungannon Foundation, 1998; *Reader's Digest*/Lila Wallace grant, 1999; O. Henry Award for best short story of the year, 2000; New England Book Award for literary excellence, New England Booksellers Association, 2001, for *Hoop Roots: Basketball, Race, and Love;* Nonfiction Honor Book, Black Caucus Award, American Library Association, 2002, for *Hoop Roots: Basketball, Race, and Love;* grant, National Endowment Humanities; Chancellor's Medal, University of Massachusetts.

WRITINGS:

NOVELS

A Glance Away, Harcourt (New York, NY), 1967.
Hurry Home, Harcourt (New York, NY), 1970.
The Lynchers, Harcourt (New York, NY), 1973.
Hiding Place, Avon (New York, NY), 1981, Houghton Mifflin (Boston, MA), 1998.
Sent for You Yesterday, Avon (New York, NY), 1983.
Reuben, Henry Holt (New York, NY), 1987.
Philadelphia Fire, Henry Holt (New York, NY), 1990.
A Glance Away, Hurry Home, and The Lynchers: Three Early Novels by John Edgar Wideman, Henry Holt (New York, NY), 1994.
The Cattle Killing, Houghton Mifflin (Boston, MA), 1996.
Two Cities, Houghton Mifflin (Boston, MA), 1998.

COLLECTIONS

Damballah (short stories), Avon (New York, NY), 1981, Houghton Mifflin (Boston, MA), 1998.
The Homewood Trilogy (includes *Damballah, Hiding Place,* and *Sent for You Yesterday*), Avon (New York, NY), 1985.
Fever (short stories), Henry Holt (New York, NY), 1989.

The Stories of John Edgar Wideman, Pantheon Books (New York, NY), 1992, published as *All Stories Are True,* Vintage Books (New York, NY), 1993.

OTHER

Brothers and Keepers (memoirs), Henry Holt (New York, NY), 1984.

Fatheralong: A Meditation on Fathers and Sons, Race and Society, Pantheon (New York, NY), 1994.

(With Mumia Abu-Jamal) *Live from Death Row,* Addison Wesley (New York, NY), 1995.

(With Bonnie Tusmith) *Conversations with John Edgar Wideman,* University Press Of Mississippi (Jackson, MS), 1998.

Hoop Roots: Basketball, Race, and Love (memoir), Houghton Mifflin (Boston, MA), 2001.

(Editor) *My Soul Has Grown Deep: Classics of Early African-American Literature,* Running Press (Philadelphia, PA), 2001.

(Editor) *20: The Best of the Drue Heinz Literature Prize,* University of Pittsburgh Press (Pittsburgh, PA), 2001.

The Island Martinique, National Geographic (Washington, DC), 2003.

Contributor of articles, short stories, book reviews, and poetry to periodicals, including *American Poetry Review, Negro Digest, Black American Literature Forum,Black World, American Scholar,Gentleman's Quarterly, New York Times Book Review, North American Review,* and *Washington Post Book World.* Also author of introduction, *Every Tongue Got to Confess: Negro Folk-tales from the Gulf States,* edited by Zora Neale Hurston and Carla Kaplan, HarperCollins, 2001.

SIDELIGHTS: John Edgar Wideman has been hailed by Don Strachen in the *Los Angeles Times Book Review* as "the black Faulkner, the softcover Shakespeare." Such praise is not uncommon for this author, whose novel *Sent for You Yesterday* was selected as the 1984 PEN/Faulkner Award winner over works by Bernard Malamud, Cynthia Ozick, and William Kennedy. Wideman attended Oxford University in 1963 on a Rhodes scholarship, earned a degree in eighteenth-century literature, and later accepted a fellowship at the prestigious University of Iowa Writers' Workshop. Yet this "artist with whom any reader who admires ambitious fiction must sooner or later reckon,"

as a *New York Times* contributor called him, began his college career not as a writer, but as a basketball star. "I always wanted to play pro basketball—ever since I saw a ball and learned you could make money at it," he told Curt Suplee in the *Washington Post.* Recruited by the University of Pennsylvania, Wideman first studied psychology, attracted by the "mystical insight" that he told Suplee he thought the subject would yield. When his subjects of study instead "turned out to be rats" and clinical experiments, Wideman changed his major to English, while continuing to be mainly concerned with basketball. He played well enough to earn a place in the Philadelphia Big Five Basketball Hall of Fame but, he told Suplee, as his time at the university drew to a close, "I knew I wasn't going to be able to get into the NBA (National Basketball Association). What was left?"

The Rhodes scholarship answered that question. Wideman began to concentrate on his writing rather than sports and did so with such success that his first novel, *A Glance Away,* was published just a year after he earned his degree from Oxford. The story of a day in the life of a drug addict, *A Glance Away* reflects the harsh realities that Wideman saw and experienced during his youth in Homewood, Pittsburgh's ghetto. And, though the author later resided in other locales, including Wyoming, his novels continued to describe black urban experiences. He explained to Suplee, "My particular imagination has always worked well in a kind of exile. It fits the insider-outside view I've always had. It helps to write away from the center of the action."

Wideman's highly literate style is in sharp contrast to his gritty subject matter, and while reviews of his books have been generally favorable, some critics initially expressed the opinion that such a formal style was not appropriate for his stories of street life. Anatole Broyard praised *The Lynchers* in his *New York Times* review, stating: "Though we have heard the themes and variations of violence before in black writing, *The Lynchers* touches us in a more personal way, for John Edgar Wideman has a weapon more powerful than any knife or gun. His weapon is art. Eloquence is his arsenal, his arms cache. His prose, at its best, is a black panther, coiled to spring." But Broyard went on to say that the book is not flawless: "Far from it. Mr. Wideman ripples too many muscles in his writing, often cannot seem to decide whether to show or snow us. . . . [He] is wordy, and *The Lynchers* is as shaky in its structure as some of the buildings his characters inhabit. But he can *write,* and you come away from his book with the feeling that he is, as they say, very close to getting it all together." In the *New York Times,* John Leonard commented on the extensive use of literary devices in *The Lynchers:* "Flashback, flashforward, first person, third person, journals, identity exchange, interior monologue, dreams (historical and personal), puns, epiphanies. At times the devices seem a thicket through which one must hack one's weary way toward meanings arbitrarily obscure, a vegetable indulgence. But John Edgar Wideman is up to much more than storytelling. . . . He is capable of moving from ghetto language to [Irish writer James] Joyce with a flip of the page."

Saturday Review critic David Littlejohn agreed that Wideman's novels are very complex, and in his review of *Hurry Home* he criticized those who would judge this author as a storyteller: "Reviewers . . . are probably more responsible than anyone else for the common delusion that a novel is somehow contained in its discernible, realistic plot. . . . *Hurry Home* is primarily an experience, not a plot: an experience of words, dense, private, exploratory, and non-progressive." Littlejohn described *Hurry Home* as a retelling of an American myth, that of "the lonely search through the Old World" for a sense of cultural heritage, which "has been the pattern of a hundred thousand young Americans' lives and novels." According to Littlejohn, Wideman's version is "spare and eccentric, highly stylized, circling, allusive, antichronological, far more consciously symbolic than most versions, than the usual self-indulgent and romantic works of this genre—and hence both more rewarding and more difficult of access." Reviewing the same book in the *New York Times Book Review,* Joseph Goodman stated: "Many of its pages are packed with psychological insight, and nearly all reveal Mr. Wideman's formidable command of the techniques of fiction. Moreover, the theme is a profound one—the quest for a substantive sense of self. . . . The prose, paratactic and rich with puns, flows as freely as thought itself, giving us . . . Joycean echoes. . . . It is a dazzling display. . . . We can have nothing but admiration for Mr. Wideman's talent."

Enthusiastic reviews such as these established Wideman's reputation as a major talent in the literary world. When his fourth and fifth books—*Damballah,* a collection of short stories, and *Hiding Place,* a

novel—were issued originally as paperbacks, some critics, such as John Leonard and Mel Watkins, reacted with indignation. Leonard's *New York Times* review used extensive quotes from the books to demonstrate Wideman's virtuosity, and stated, "That [these] two new books will fall apart after a second reading is a scandal." Watkins's *New York Times Book Review* article on the two books, which were published simultaneously, had special praise for the short-story volume, and ended with a sentiment much like Leonard's on the books' binding. "In freeing his voice from the confines of the novel form," Watkins wrote, "[Wideman] has written what is possibly his most impressive work. . . . Each story moves far beyond the primary event on which it is focused. . . . Mr. Wideman has used a narrative laced with myth, superstition and dream sequences to create an elaborate poetic portrait of the lives of ordinary black people. . . . These books once again demonstrate that John Wideman is one of America's premier writers of fiction. That they were published originally in paperback perhaps suggests that he is also one of our most underrated writers." Actually, it was the author himself who had decided to bring the books out as original paperbacks. His reasons were philosophical and pragmatic. "I spend an enormous amount of time and energy writing and I want to write good books, but I also want people to read them," he explained to Edwin McDowell in the *New York Times.* Wideman's first three novels had been slow sellers "in spite of enormously positive reviews," he told Suplee, and it was his hope that the affordability of paperbacks would help give him a wider readership, particularly among "the people and the world I was writing about. A $15.95 novel had nothing to do with that world."

Damballah and *Hiding Place* were both set in Homewood, and in 1983 he published a third book with the same setting, titled *Sent for You Yesterday.* Critics were enthusiastic. "In this hypnotic and deeply lyrical novel, Mr. Wideman again returns to the ghetto where he was raised and transforms it into a magical location infused with poetry and pathos," wrote Alan Cheuse in the *New York Times Book Review.* "The narration here makes it clear that both as a molder of language and a builder of plots, Mr. Wideman has come into his full powers. He has the gift of making 'ordinary' folks memorable." Stated Garett Epps in the *Washington Post Book World,* "Wideman has a fluent command of the American language, written and spoken, and a fierce, loving vision of the people he writes about. Like the writing of William Faulkner,

Wideman's prose fiction is vivid and demanding—shuttling unpredictably between places, narrators and times, dwelling for a paragraph on the surface of things, then sneaking a key event into a clause that springs on the reader like a booby trap. . . . *Sent for You Yesterday* is a book to be savored, read slowly again and again."

When he ventured into nonfiction for the first time with his book *Brothers and Keepers,* Wideman continued to draw inspiration from the same source, Homewood. In this book, Wideman comes to terms with his brother Robby, younger by ten years, whose life was influenced by the street, its drugs, and its crime. The author wrote, "Even as I manufactured fiction from the events of my brother's life, from the history of the family that had nurtured us both, I knew something of a different order remained to be extricated. The fiction writer was a man with a real brother behind real bars [serving a life sentence in a Pennsylvania penitentiary]." In his review in the *Washington Post Book World,* Jonathan Yardley called *Brothers and Keepers* "the elder Wideman's effort to understand what happened, to confess and examine his own sense of guilt about his brother's fate (and his own)." The result, according to the reviewer, is "a depiction of the inexorably widening chasm that divides middle-class black Americans from the black underclass." Wideman's personal experience, added Yardley, also reveals that for the black person, "moving out of the ghetto into the white world is a process that requires excruciating compromises, sacrifices and denials, that leaves the person who makes the journey truly at home in neither the world he has entered nor the world he has left."

Wideman has, however, made a home for himself in literary circles, and at the same time has learned much about the nature of success. When *Sent for You Yesterday* won the PEN/Faulkner Award—the only major literary award in the United States to be judged, administered, and largely funded by writers—Wideman told Suplee he felt "warmth. That's what I felt. Starting at the toes and filling up. A gradual recognition that it could be real." The author maintained that if such an honor "doesn't happen again for a long time—or never happens again—it really doesn't matter," because he "learned more and more that the process itself was important, learned to take my satisfaction from the writing" during the years of comparative obscurity. "I'm an old jock," he explained.

"So I've kind of trained myself to be low-key. Sometimes the crowd screams, sometimes the crowd doesn't scream."

The narrator of Wideman's novel *Reuben* provides inexpensive legal aid to residents of Homewood. One of Reuben's clients is Kwansa, a young black prostitute whose husband, a recovering drug addict, kidnaps and seeks legal custody of their illegitimate child as revenge against her. Another customer is Wally, an assistant basketball coach at a local white university who seeks Reuben's counsel for two reasons, one being the killing of a white man in Chicago and the other being his fear that he will be blamed for the illegal recruiting practices of his department. Reviewing the book in the *Washington Post Book World,* Noel Perrin characterized Wideman's novels as myths. "In the end," Perrin wrote, "one sees that all the shocks—the murders, the fantasies, burnings, strong words—all of them amount to a kind of metaphor for the psychic damage that human beings do to each other and that is no less hurtful than spread-eagled beating, just less visible to the outer eye."

In *Philadelphia Fire,* Wideman brings together two stories, combining fact in fiction. In the first, he describes the events in Philadelphia when the police, under the direction of black mayor Wilson Goode, bombed the headquarters of an organization known as Move, a group that had defied city eviction notices and was armed with weapons. The police bombing killed six adults and five children, destroyed fifty-three homes, and left 262 people homeless. Wideman's novel begins with a quote by William Penn, the founder of Pennsylvania, stating his dream that the town would "never be burnt, and always be wholesome." As Chicago *Tribune Books* reviewer Paul Skenazy pointed out, *Philadelphia Fire* tries to make sense of the changes that have occurred since Penn's statement, changes that include poverty and racism, changes that resulted in the burning of the Philadelphia neighborhood. The other story being told in the book is that of Wideman's relationship with a son who has received a life sentence for murder. "Few pages of prose," Skenazy said, "carry as much pain as do Wideman's thoughts on his son, his words to him in prison, his feelings of confusion as a father." Skenazy concluded that *Philadelphia Fire* is "about a person, and a nation, losing its grip, destroying the very differences and dissonance that provide spirit, beauty, life." Rosemary L. Bray in the *New York Times Book Review* concurred; "the author takes his readers on a tour of urban America perched on the precipice of hell," Bray wrote, "a tour in which even his own personal tragedy is part of the view."

The Stories of John Edgar Wideman combined several earlier story collections, including *Damballah, Fever,* and *All Stories Are True.* Michael Harris wrote in the *Los Angeles Times Book Review* that a comparison between Wideman and Faulkner makes sense, "because of the scope of Wideman's project, his ear for voices, . . . and the way he shows the present as perpetually haunted by the past." *New York Times Book Review* contributor Michael Gorra also believed the Faulkner comparison is apt. "It is appropriate," Gorra wrote, "because both are concerned with the life of a community over time. It is appropriate because they both have a feel for the anecdotal folklore through which a community defines itself, because they both often choose to present their characters in the act of telling stories, and because in drawing on oral tradition they both write as their characters speak, in a language whose pith and vigor has not yet been worn into cliché." It is Gorra's conclusion that "the more you read John Edgar Wideman, the more impressive he seems."

Fatheralong: A Meditation on Fathers and Sons, Race and Society, like *Philadelphia Fire* and the Homewood stories, juxtaposes Wideman's personal life with larger issues. Mel Watkins in the *New York Times Book Review* referred to it as a hybrid of memoir and "a meditation on fatherhood, race, metaphysics, time and the afterlife." Wideman explores his strained relationship with his father and his troubles with his own son, and then frames them in the context of all father-son relationships as well as America's racist legacy. A *Village Voice* critic found the sections on Wideman's son, Jacob, to be his "most artful work. The Jacob sections overshadow simply because they're so much better written, their subject more emotionally grasped than any other." Mitchell Duneier in the *Los Angeles Times Book Review* called *Fatheralong* "a masterpiece of sociological speculation, constructed with such an abundance of wisdom as to compensate for its lack of evidence regarding questions to which there are no easy answers." In the Chicago *Tribune Books,* Michael Boynton, calling the work "part memoir, part manifesto," concluded that *Fatheralong* is an odd, sad book. Filled with flashes of insight told in Wideman's distinctive prose-poetry, it is at once personal and essentially opaque. . . . It leaves the

reader wanting to know more, hoping that its author will one day find the key he has been looking for."

Wideman returned to fiction with his novel, *The Cattle Killing.* In it, he weaves together memories from his narrator's childhood in Philadelphia with the plight of blacks in the city in the late eighteenth century, and the story of the South African Xhosa tribe, pulling together threads of history, religion, and race to form his story. The complex story met with somewhat mixed reviews, with critics finding flaws in the novel's coherence but praising Wideman's imaginative storytelling powers.

Sven Birkerts of the *New York Times Book Review* offered the negative point of view, claiming that the author "ventured beyond his readers" with *The Cattle Killing,* adding, "Filaments of story, of precious sense, are woven like bits of rag into a rug of shimmering but also perplexing suggestiveness." A more positive assessment came from Joyce Carol Oates in the *New York Review of Books,* who described the book as "purposefully framed by contemporary American black voices." She added, "*The Cattle Killing* juxtaposes lyrical, parable-like tales with presumably authentic historical accounts. . . . Boldly, the author indicates little distinction between voices, times, or settings." While "the result is a novel frequently difficult to assess," Oates recommended that readers approach the book "as a kind of music, an obsessive beat in the author's head, a nightmare from which he yearns . . . to be awakened. It is a work of operatic polyphony that strains to break free of linguistic constraints into theatrical spectacle."

An improvisational tone characterized the style of *Two Cities.* In this novel—set in the Philadelphia and Pittsburgh of the title—the author tells the story of Kassima, who has had her share of hard luck with men. As the story opens, she is tentatively stepping back into a social life after the grief of losing two sons to gang-related crime and an imprisoned husband to AIDS. She may have found happiness after meeting Robert Jones, a middle-aged man whose own difficult past has given him a rare wisdom. But after Robert nearly loses his life in a close call with a gun-wielding young man, "Kassima is so terrorized by the prospect of another loss that she abandons her nascent attachment and returns to protective mourning," according to Richard Bernstein, writing in the *New York Times.* Kassima finds a kindred spirit in Mr. Mallory, an elderly World War II veteran who boards at her home. When he dies, she turns to Robert for emotional help.

"This is the essential story," said Bernstein, "but Mr. Wideman weaves a tapestry of American life tightly around it, telling stories reminiscent of the Homewood trilogy." In his review, Bernstein found *Two Cities* to be as "angry and intemperate" as it was infused with "stylistic virtuosity."

My Soul Has Grown Deep: Classics of Early African American Literature, edited by Wideman, is a collection of twelve writings by well-known and lesser-known eighteenth-and nineteenth-century writers such as Phyllis Wheatley, Sojourner Truth, W. E. B. Dubois, and Booker T. Washington. *Library Journal* reviewer Karen S. E. Lempert praised Wideman for "providing a depth and breadth of content and editorial expertise rarely found" in this type of collection. Because of Wideman, wrote Donna Seamen in *Booklist,* "these eloquent and inspiring messages of hope will continue to be heard across the land and around the world."

Hoop Roots: Basketball, Race, and Love, said Wideman in an interview with Lisa Baker in the *African American Review,* is "really a study of race and culture—using sport as a way of getting people's attention." *Hoop Roots* follows Wideman's "lifelong love affair with basketball," commented David L. Ulin in the *Atlantic Monthly,* at times, "yielding to reflections on family, racial tension, memory, and the nebulous territory of storytelling itself." A *Publishers Weekly* called the book a "brilliant tribute to basketball, survival and families linked by blood, joy, and tragedy." This reviewer concluded that *Hoop Roots* "is as exhilarating as a few fast and furious hours on the court." Tracy Grant, a reviewer for *Black Issues Book Review,* found the book a challenge to read because of Wideman's "stream-of-consciousness writing style," but commented that "*Hoop Roots* demonstrates Wideman's unique voice and his true gift for capturing a slice of black life from the past."

"John Edgar Wideman is unafraid to experiment with many voices," declared Opal Palmer Adisa in the *Reference Guide to American Literature.* "He has pushed his fiction to embrace both European and African American aesthetic traditions. Some aspect of his life is at the center of all of his works. He probes, relentless in his attempt to understand the social machine that seems so controlling and leaves so many people feeling powerless." As Adisa concluded, while the author's experimental techniques "might not always provide clarity, his works nonetheless cause one to look beyond the surface."

BIOGRAPHICAL AND CRITICAL SOURCES:

BOOKS

African American Almanac, 8th edition, Thomson Gale (Detroit, MI), 2000.

Black Literature Criticism, Thomson Gale (Detroit, MI), 1992.

Contemporary Black Biography, Volume 5, Thomson Gale (Detroit, MI), 1994.

Contemporary Literary Criticism, Thomson Gale (Detroit, MI), Volume 5, 1976, Volume 34, 1985, Volume 36, 1986, Volume 67, 1992, Volume 122, 2000.

Dictionary of Literary Biography, Thomson Gale (Detroit, MI), Volume 33: *Afro-American Fiction Writers after 1955,* 1984, Volume 143: *American Novelists since World War II, Third Series,* 1994.

In Black and White: A Guide to Magazine Articles, Newspaper Articles, and Books concerning Black Individuals and Groups, 3rd edition, Thomson Gale (Detroit, MI), 1985.

Major Twentieth-Century Writers, 2nd edition, Thomson Gale (Detroit, MI), 1999.

Mbalia, Doreatha D., *John Edgar Wideman: Reclaiming the African Personality,* Associated University Presses (Cranbury, NJ), 1995.

Modern American Literature, Volume 3, 5th edition, St. James Press (Detroit, MI), 1999.

Modern Black Writers, St. James Press (Detroit, MI), 2000.

Notable Black American Men, Thomson Gale (Detroit, MI), 1999.

O'Brien, John, editor, *Interviews with Black Writers,* Liveright, 1973.

Reference Guide to American Literature, 4th edition, St. James Press (Detroit, MI), 2000.

Reference Guide to Short Fiction, 2nd edition, St. James Press (Detroit, MI), 1999.

Wideman, John Edgar, *Brothers and Keepers,* Henry Holt (New York, NY), 1984.

Wideman, John Edgar, *Philadelphia Fire,* Henry Holt (New York, NY), 1990.

PERIODICALS

African American Review, fall, 1992, Jessica Lustig, "Home: An Interview with John Edgar Wideman," pp. 453-457; summer, 1998, review of *The Cattle Killing,* p. 362; winter, 1998, Madhu Dubey, review of *Philadelphia Fire,* pp. 579-595; summer, 2000, Lisa Baker, "Storytelling and Democracy (in the Radical Sense): A Conversation with John Edgar Wideman," p. 263.

American Book Review, March-April, 1988, Harold Jaffe, "Rage," pp. 8-14; November, 1999, review of *Two Cities,* p. 4.

American Literature, March, 1999, "Conversation with John Edgar Wideman," p. 214.

American Scholar, autumn, 1967.

Atlantic Monthly, November, 2001, David L. Ulin, review of *Hoop Roots: Basketball, Race, and Love.*

Black American Literature Forum, spring-summer, 1986, John Bennion, "The Shape of Memory in John Edgar Wideman's *Sent for You Yesterday,*" pp. 143-150.

Black Issues Book Review, November-December 2001, Tracy Grant, review of *Hoop Roots,* p. 69.

Black Scholar, spring, 1998, Mumia Abu-Jamal, review of *Brothers and Keepers,* pp. 75-79.

Bloomsbury Review, January, 1999, review of *Two Cities,* p. 19.

Book, September, 2001, "John Edgar Wideman" (interview), p. 12.

Booklist, August, 1994, p. 1987; September 15, 1994, Joseph Keppler, review of *All Stories Are True,* p. 153; February 15, 1998, review of *The Cattle Killing,* p. 979; July, 1998, review of *Two Cities,* p. 1832; September 1, 2001, Wes Lukowsky, review of *Hoop Roots,* p. 38; September 15, 2001, Donna Seaman, review of *My Soul Has Grown Deep: Classics of Early African American Literature,* p. 180.

Callaloo, fall, 1985, Jacqueline Berben, "Beyond Discourse: The Unspoken versus Words in the Fiction of John Edgar Wideman," pp. 525-534; winter, 1990, author interview, pp. 47-61; summer, 1999, special issue devoted to Wideman, pp. 629-665.

Chicago Tribune Books, November 29, 1987, Gary Dretzka, "Haunting Novel of Rage and Love Packs a Punch," p. 6.

Christian Science Monitor, October 23, 1990, Shawn Smith, "Like Steam from a City Grate," p. 15; July 10, 1992.

CLA Journal, March, 1985, James Coleman, "Going Back Home: The Literary Development of John Edgar Wideman," pp. 326-343; March, 1990, Matthew Wilson, "The Circles of History in John Edgar Wideman's 'The Homewood Trilogy,'" pp. 239-259.

Contemporary Literature, fall, 1991, Ashraf H. A. Rushdy, "Fraternal Blues: John Edgar Wideman's *Homewood Trilogy,*" pp. 312-345.

Ebony, September, 2001, review of *Hoop Roots,* p. 22.

Esquire, September, 1998, review of *Two Cities,* p. 60.

Essence, October, 2001, Patrick Henry Bass, "Take Note," p. 70.

Hollins Critic, December, 1992, James Robert Saunders, "Exorcizing the Demons: John Edgar Wideman's Literary Response," pp. 1-10.

Interview, September, 2001, Patrick Giles, "Looking at Life from the Free Throw Line," p. 102.

Journal of Negro History, January, 1963.

Kenyon Review, spring, 1992, Jan Clausen, "Native Fathers," pp. 44-55.

Kirkus Reviews, August 1, 1996, p. 1092; July 15, 1998, review of *Two Cities,* p. 998.

Library Journal, March 1, 1994, Peter Joseph, review of *All Stories Are True,* p. 134; September 15, 1994, Michael A. Lutes, review of *Fatheralong: A Meditation on Fathers and Sons, Race and Society,* p. 85; July, 1996, Barbara Hoffert, review of *The Cattle Killing,* p. 164; November 1, 1998, review of *Two Cities,* p. 101; March 1, 1999, Michael Rogers, review of *Hiding Place* and *Damballah,* p. 116; October 15, 2001, Nathan Ward, review of *Hoop Roots,* p. 84; September 15, 2001, Karen E. S. Lempert, review of *My Soul Has Grown Deep,* p. 80; March 1, 2002, "ALA Awards at Midwinter," p. 18.

London Review of Books, November 27, 1997, Michael Wood, "Living in the Enemy's Dream," pp. 25-26.

Los Angeles Times, November 11, 1987.

Los Angeles Times Book Review, April 17, 1983; December 23, 1984, Ron Finney, "To Repair the Two Relations," p. 6; December 29, 1985; September 30, 1990; September 13, 1992; December 25, 1994, p. 2; September 27, 1998, review of *Two Cities,* p. 11.

Michigan Quarterly Review, winter, 1975.

Nation, January 1, 1990, Randall Kenan, review of *Fever,* pp. 25-27; October 28, 1996, Gene Seymour, "Dream Surgeon," pp. 58-60.

Negro Digest, May, 1963.

New Republic, July 13 and 20, 1992, Sven Birkerts, "The Art of Memory," pp. 42-44.

New Statesman, September 1, 1995, Ian Sansom, review of *Fatheralong,* p. 34.

Newsweek, May 7, 1970; October 1, 1990, Jack Kroll, review of *Philadelphia Fire,* p. 90.

New Yorker, October 1, 1998, review of *Two Cities,* p. 109.

New York Magazine, October 1, 1990, Rhoda Koenig, review of *Philadelphia Fire,* p. 66.

New York Review of Books, May 11, 1995, Darryl Pinckney, "Aristocrats," pp. 27-34; March 27, 1997, Joyce Carol Oates, "Troubles I've Seen," pp. 39-40.

New York Times, April 2, 1970; May 15, 1973; November 27, 1981; May 16, 1984; October 29, 1984; September 4, 1986; July 21, 1992; September 28, 1998, Richard Bernstein, "Finding Hope and Refuge on Bitter Urban Streets," p. E8.

New York Times Book Review, September 10, 1967; April 19, 1970; April 29, 1973; April 11, 1982, Mel Watkins, review of *Hiding Place,* pp. 6, 21; May 15, 1983, Alan Cheuse, review of *Sent for You Yesterday,* pp. 13, 41; November 4, 1984; January 13, 1985; December 15, 1985, C. Gerald Fraser, review of *A Glance Away,* p. 32; May 11, 1986, review of *Hurry Home,* p. 42; November 30, 1986, Patricia T. O'Conner, review of *The Lynchers,* p. 38; November 8, 1987, Walter Kendrick, review of *Reuben,* p. 3; October 16, 1988; December 10, 1989, Susan Fromberg Schaeffer, review of *Fever,* p. 1, and Rosemary L. Bray, "The Plague became the Fire," p. 30; September 30, 1990, Rosemary L. Bray, review of *Philadelphia Fire,* p. 7; October 14, 1990; November 17, 1991; June 14, 1992, Michael Gorra, "The Choral Voice of Homewood," p. 13; November 13, 1994, Mel Watkins, "A Son's Notes," p. 11; November 3, 1996, Sven Birkerts, "The Fever Days," p. 20; January 4, 1998, review of *The Cattle Killing,* p. 24; October 10, 1999, review of *Two Cities,* p. 36; December 5, 1999, review of *Two Cities,* p. 105; November 4, 2001, Will Blythe, "Benching Himself," p. 35; November 11, 2001, review of *Hoop Roots,* p. 30.

Progressive, July, 1999, Dean Bakopoulos, review of *Two Cities,* p. 44.

Publishers Weekly, August 12, 1996, p. 63; August 3, 1998, review of *Two Cities,* p. 72; June 8, 1998, "$30,000 Rea Prize to Wideman," p. 19; July 16, 2001, review of *Hoop Roots,* p. 167.

Revue française D'Etudes, April-June, 1991, Jacqueline Berben, "Promised Land and Wasteland in John Edgar Wideman's Recent Fiction," pp. 259-270.

Saturday Review, October 21, 1967; May 2, 1970.

Shenandoah, winter, 1974.

Sports Illustrated, November 19, 2001, Charles Hirshberg, "Books: A Basketball Tome That's Too Ambitious, Even for the Supposed Thinking Man," p. R3.

Tikkun, March-April, 1995, Mark Shechner, "Men Will Be Men," pp. 80-82.

Time, October 1, 1990; October 5, 1998, review of *Two Cities,* p. 88; November 19, 2001, "*Hoop Roots* by John Edgar Wideman," p. 143; October 1, 1990, R. T. Sheppard, review of *Philadelphia Fire,* p. 90.

Times (London, England), December 6, 1984.

Times Literary Supplement, December 21, 1984; January 16, 1987; August 5, 1988; August 23, 1991, "Cos I'm a So-o-oul Man," pp. 19-20.

Tribune Books (Chicago, IL), December 23, 1984; November 29, 1987; October 28, 1990; November 24, 1991; October 23, 1994, p. 8.

Village Voice, October 25, 1994.

Virginia Quarterly Review, spring, 1995, Sanford Pinsker, "The Moose on the Family Dinner Table," pp. 369-372.

Washington Post, May 10, 1984; May 12, 1984.

Washington Post Book World, July 3, 1983; September 29, 1996, Paul West, "Too Great a Sacrifice," p. 5; October 4, 1998, review of *Two Cities,* p. 5.

Whole Earth Review, summer, 1995, p. 78.

World Literature Today, winter, 1998, Jacqueline Brice-Finch, review of *The Cattle Killing,* p. 137.*

*   *   *

WILSON, Dirk
See POHL, Frederik

*   *   *

WULFFSON, Don (L.) 1943-

PERSONAL: Born August 21, 1943, in Los Angeles, CA; son of Charles Robin (an engineer) and Corinne (a real estate broker; maiden name, Lockwood) Wulffson; married Pamela Paisley (a teacher), June 29, 1969; children: Jennifer Sarah, Gwendolyn Stacy. *Education:* University of California, Los Angeles, B.A., 1965, teaching credential, 1967. *Politics:* "Confused

Don Wulffson

liberal." *Religion:* "Even more confused." *Hobbies and other interests:* Animals, sports, daydreaming.

ADDRESSES: Home—18718 Kirkcolm La., Northridge, CA 91326. *Agent*—Susan Cohen, Writers House, 21 West 26th St., New York, NY, 10010. *E-mail*—donpam@earthlink.net.

CAREER: Writer. Teacher of English, creative writing, and reading, 1967-94; full-time writer, beginning 1994.

MEMBER: Authors Guild, Authors League.

AWARDS, HONORS: Leather Medal, New Directions Publishing, 1971, for "You Too Can Be a Floorwax That Even Your Husband Could Apply" (poem); Outstanding Educator in America citation, 1980, 1981, 1983, 1985; Distinguished Achievement Award, Educational Press Association of America, 1981, for *Writing You'll Enjoy;* American Booksellers Pick of the List, 1997, for *The Kid Who Invented the Popsicle, and Other Surprising Stories about Inventions;* Christopher Award for Young-Adult Literature, 2001, for *Soldier X;* two Notable Social Studies Trade Book for Young People designations, National Council for the Social Studies/Children's Book Council, both 2002, for *Soldier X* and *The Kid Who Invented the Trampoline.*

WRITINGS:

Strange, Extraordinary Stories behind How Sports Came to Be, Lothrop (New York, NY), 1980.
True Stories You Won't Believe, Xerox Education Publications (Middletown, CT), 1980.
Extraordinary Stories behind the Invention of Ordinary Things, illustrated by Roy Doty, Lothrop (New York, NY), 1981.
Incredible True Adventures, Dodd, Mead (New York, NY), 1986.
Terror at Sea, Field Publications, 1988.
More Incredible True Adventures, Cobblehill Books (New York, NY), 1989.
Ordinary Things, Avon (New York, NY), 1990.
Amazing True Stories, illustrated by John R. Jones, Cobblehill Books (New York, NY), 1991.
(Coauthor and consultant) *Above and Beyond,* Time-Life Books (New York, NY), 1993.
The Kid Who Invented the Popsicle, and Other Surprising Stories about Inventions, Cobblehill Books (New York, NY), 1996.
When Human Heads Were Footballs: Surprising Stories of How Sports Began, illustrated by Mike Dietz, Aladdin (New York, NY), 1998.
Great Stories behind Famous Books, Alleyside Press (Ft. Atkinson, WI), 1999.
Pro Sports—How Did They Begin? Fun and Wacky Facts about Baseball, Basketball, and Football, Mondo Publishing (New York, NY), 2000.
Toys!: Amazing Stories behind Some Great Inventions, illustrated by Laurie Keller, Henry Holt (New York, NY), 2000.
The Kid Who Invented the Trampoline: More Surprising Stories about Inventions, Dutton (New York, NY), 2001.
Toybox Treasures, Dutton (New York, NY), 2003.
(With wife, Pam Wulffson) *Abracadabra to Zombie: More Than 500 Wacky Word Origins,* illustrated by Jared Lee, Dutton (New York, NY), 2003.

Contributor to *Discover How Things Work,* Publications International, 1996.

NOVELS; FOR CHILDREN

The Upside-down Ship, Albert Whitman (Morton Grove, IL), 1986.

Valley of the Screaming Statues ("Nightmares! How Will Yours End?" series), illustrated by Dominick Domingo, Putnam (New York, NY), 1994.

Castle of Horror ("Nightmares! How Will Yours End?" series), illustrated by Dominick Domingo, Price, Stern (Los Angeles, CA), 1994.

Planet of Terror ("Nightmares! How Will Yours End?" series), illustrated by Neal Yamamoto, Price, Stern (Los Angeles, CA), 1994.

Cave of Fear ("Nightmares! How Will Yours End?" series), illustrated by Neal Yamamoto, Price, Stern (Los Angeles, CA), 1995.

Soldier X, Viking Children's Books (New York, NY), 2001.

The Upside-Down Voyage, Mondo Publications (New York, NY), 2004.

STORIES; FOR CHILDREN

Eyebrowse (stories and nonfiction), Economy, 1976.

Visions (stories and nonfiction), Globe Book, 1980, published as *Facts and Fantasies,* 1982.

Time Fix and Other Tales of Terror, Cobblehill Books (New York, NY), 1993.

Screamers 1! The Fright Mask and Other Stories to Twist Your Mind, Troll Publication (Mahwah, NJ), 1994.

Screamers 2! The Trap Door and Other Stories to Twist Your Mind, Troll Publication (Mahwah, NJ), 1994.

Six-Minute Mysteries, illustrated by Laurel Long, Lowell House (Los Angeles, CA), 1994.

More Six-Minute Mysteries, illustrated by Laurel Long, Lowell House (Los Angeles, CA), 1995.

Future Fright: Tales of High-Tech Terror, Lowell House (Los Angeles, CA), 1996.

Mega Scary Stories for Sleep-overs, illustrated by Dwight Been, Price, Stern (Los Angeles, CA), 1996.

Aliens: Extraterrestrial Tales of Terror, Lowell House (Los Angeles, CA), 1996.

Fright Write, Contemporary Books (Chicago, IL), 1997.

Even More Scary Stories for Stormy Nights, illustrated by Eric Angeloch, Contemporary Books (Chicago, IL), 1997.

Contributor to anthologies, including *Bone-Chilling Tales of Fright* and *More Bone-Chilling Tales of Fright,* both 1994, and *Frantic: Lightning Strike, and Other Gripping Tales of Survival,* all published by Lowell House.

Author's works have been translated into Chinese.

OTHER

(Editor and contributor) *Themes and Writers* (literature series), four volumes, McGraw-Hill, 1973.

Building Vocabulary, Xerox Education Publications (Middletown, CT), 1976.

Writing You'll Enjoy, Xerox Education Publications (Middletown, CT), 1977.

The Touchstone Series, three volumes, Steck, 1977.

Punctuation Errors You Hate to Make (and How to Avoid Them), Xerox Education Publications (Middletown, CT), 1978.

The Wonderful Word Book, Xerox Education Publications (Middletown, CT), 1978.

Supergrammar, Pruett (Boulder, CO), 1980.

Mindgame: Experiences in Creative Writing, Xerox Education Publications (Middletown, CT), 1980.

The Basics of Writing, three volumes, Globe Book, 1985.

Bright and Beautiful, Scott, Foresman, 1985.

Point Blank (adult novel), Signet (New York, NY), 1987.

Contributor of articles, poems, and children's plays to journals, including *Boy's Life, Cricket, Child Life, Hyperion, Journal of Reading, Read,* and *Tangent Poetry Quarterly.* Contributor to anthologies, including *New Directions Twenty-three,* New Directions, 1971; *Words and Beyond,* Ginn, 1973; *National Poetry Anthology,* National Poetry Press, 1975; and *Isaac Asimov's Book of Facts,* Volume 2, Grossett & Dunlap, 1982. Also author of "Skillmaster" series, Xerox Education Publications.

SIDELIGHTS: California-based writer Don Wulffson is the author of numerous books for young readers—including *Time Fix and Other Tales of Terror, The Upside-down Ship, Soldier X,* and *Terror at Sea*—which have been praised by reviewers for their ability to lure even reluctant readers into turning the pages of a book. "I have always been intrigued by both the past and the future," Wulffson once commented. "With my readers, I greatly enjoy exploring how the world came to be, what it is today, and trying to anticipate what it might someday become."

"I think I knew how to write before I learned how to read," Wulffson also recalled. "Regardless, I've been writing ever since I was a little kid. My teachers never liked my writing (especially my sci-fi and adventure stories, which they thought were too wild and bizarre); but then again, I never liked any of my teachers, so I guess we're even.

"While in college I wanted to grow up to be [a noted poet like] Lawrence Ferlinghetti or a psychiatrist. Much to my dismay I ended up as an English teacher. In 1971 I published a surrealistic poem, 'You Too Can Be a Floorwax That Even Your Husband Could Apply.' It appeared in the New Directions annual that included works by Ferlinghetti. I was so impressed by my achievement that I decided to quit writing poetry."

While ceasing his poetry career, Wulffson continued teaching English language and composition on the high-school level. "All in all, I loved it. I miss it," the former poet later admitted. "I make up for it by writing full-time, writing the kinds of things I think that kids will like." As a writer for young readers, Wulffson has published hundreds of stories and poems, several plays, and more than thirty books. "I'm proud of that," he conceded, "but I'm only interested in what I'm writing now, not what I've written before. I've never even bothered reading any of my books."

From a hunter who ruthlessly kills a deer, only to be turned into a deer himself in "The Hunted," to a boy who dies from drowning after being haunted by a nightmare about the sea in "Dream World," Wulffson's popular story collection *Time Fix and Other Tales of Terror* runs the gauntlet from watery to weird. Equally imaginative are his other collections of scary stories, among them a series of make-your-own-nightmare novels that includes *Planet of Terror, Castle of Horror,* and *Valley of the Screaming Statues.* "I write because it's the only way I know of doing all the really interesting and strange things I know I'll never do," Wulffson said of his surprise endings and exciting plots, "and because it's the one way I have of being myself, as well as anybody else I feel like being." In *Valley of the Screaming Statues* a boy, the boy's brother, and his anthropologist father become separated in the jungles of Malaysia, while in *Castle of Horror* the young hero finds himself forced to wander the halls of a Scottish castle under the control of a fiendish magician.

A busy writer, Wulffson works "relentlessly, endlessly—usually on at least two or three books at the same time. I adhere to no schedule whatsoever. I write when I feel like it, which is most of the time." One of the longer works of fiction produced by such a dedication to his craft is *The Upside-down Ship,* published in 1986. The novel concerns a Scottish whaling captain named Bruce Gordon, whose ship is grounded by an iceberg in a northern sea. After several years of survival in this cold, forbidding region, he makes it back to civilization, only to find it equally forbidding. "It's about a man living alone in an empty, upside-down world," Wulffson explained. "He struggles year after year to get back to the 'real' world—and eventually does, only to discover he lost everything by leaving."

Wulffson counts the young-adult novel *Soldier X* as perhaps his best work. As he described it, *Soldier X* "is an antiwar novel. . . . about a boy who goes from being a German soldier on the Eastern Front to a patient in a Russian hospital." Reflecting on the book's theme, Wulffson added: "I think it was Faulkner who said that writing an antiwar novel is like trying to stop a bullet with a piece of paper. Maybe he's right. Maybe not. Perhaps someday an immense collective voice demanding peace will drown out the insipid bombast of those enamored of war. Perhaps someday all the armies of the world will wear the same uniform and will fight our collective enemies: hunger, disease, and poverty."

Based on an actual incident, *Soldier X* takes place during 1944, as sixteen-year-old Erik Brandt is drafted from the Hitler Youth into the German Army and sent, after only limited basic training, to the Russian Front where soldiers are desperately needed and few are likely to survive the brutality of trench warfare. Rendered unconscious during a Russian bombing, he awakens to discover that he has been separated from his regiment and is now stranded behind enemy lines. Drawing on his knowledge of Russian—Erik's mother was Russian, his father German—he steals the clothing off a Russian soldier's corpse and feigns amnesia, surviving the war in a soldier's hospital. A *Publishers Weekly* reviewer praised *Soldier X* for its "well-researched and meticulously recorded details of life under fire," while commending particularly Wulffson's central message: that one must "look past the outer trappings of the enemy to discover the human being inside the uniform." A *Horn Book* contributor also praised the novel for its "unusual perspective"; rather than dealing with the emotional issues surrounding betrayal of one's culture, *Soldier X* is far grittier:

Wulffson "records battlefield sequences with an unflinching—and occasionally numbing—brutality" as Erik focuses solely on survival.

In addition to his stories and novels, Wulffson has authored several language-arts programs for use at the secondary-school level, as well as numerous plays and short works of nonfiction for young adult readers. Among his best-known nonfiction works are *The Kid Who Invented the Popsicle, and Other Surprising Stories about Inventions* and its sequel, *The Kid Who Invented the Trampoline: More Surprising Stories about Inventions.* From the genesis of ice-cream treats to Post-It Notes and Zambonis, the books are written in a "conversational and humorous" style that *Booklist* contributor Shelley Townsend-Hudson praised as reflecting the author's "passion for his subject" and his "respect for the audience's intelligence." A similar approach is taken in *Toys!: Amazing Stories behind Some Great Inventions,* which discusses the creation of everything from Silly Putty and Play-Doh to Twister and Mr. Potato Head, as well as classics such as checkers, toy soldiers, Parcheesi, and other perennial favorites. Calling the book "intriguing," *Booklist* reviewer Carolyn Phelan added: "It's hard to say whether adults or kids will get a bigger kick" from *Toys!* Victoria Kidd also enjoyed the work, noting in *School Library Journal* that in his "engaging text" Wulffson also includes "a lesson in persistence, surprise outcomes, and creative thinking": toys such

as Slinky and Play-Doh were actually "invented" during failed efforts to create products to advance industry!

BIOGRAPHICAL AND CRITICAL SOURCES:

PERIODICALS

Booklist, May 15, 1986, p. 1389; July, 1994, Mary Harris Veeder, review of *Time Fix and Other Tales of Terror,* p. 1949; June 2, 2000, Carolyn Phelan, review of *Toys!: Amazing Stories behind Some Great Inventions,* p. 1890; May 1, 2001, Karen Simonetti, review of *Soldier X,* p. 1676; July, 2001, Shelley Townsend-Hudson, review of *The Kid Who Invented the Trampoline,* p. 2004.
Bulletin of the Center for Children's Books, November, 1986, p. 60; March, 1987, p. 139.
Horn Book, July, 2001, review of *Soldier X,* p. 463.
Publishers Weekly, June 19, 2000, review of *Toys!,* p. 82; January 29, 2001, review of *Soldier X,* p. 90; August 27, 2001, review of *The Kid Who Invented the Trampoline,* p. 87.
School Library Journal, October, 1986, p. 185; July, 1994; September, 2000, Victoria Kidd, review of *Toys!,* p. 257; March, 2001, Cheri Estes, review of *Soldier X,* p. 258; October, 2001, Carol Fazioli, review of *The Kid Who Invented the Trampoline,* p. 192; January, 2004, Linda Wadleigh, review of *Abracadabra to Zombie: More Than 500 Wacky Word Origins,* p. 162.*

Z

ZIEFERT, Harriet 1941-
(H. M. Ehrlich, Jane Fine, Margot Linn, Harriet Margolin)

PERSONAL: Born July 7, 1941, in North Bergen, NJ; *Education:* Smith College, B.A.; New York University, M.A.

ADDRESSES: Home—Lincoln, MA; Maplewood, NJ. *Agent*—c/o Author Mail, 515 South Valley St., Maplewood, NJ 07040. *E-mail*—hmziefinc@aol.com.

CAREER: Writer and book packager, 1983—. Former elementary school teacher; Scholastic, Inc., New York, NY, school materials developer.

AWARDS, HONORS: New Jersey Institute of Technology Award, 1987, for *Sarah's Question* and *The Small Potatoes' Busy Beach Day,* 1988, for *Good Night, Jessie!, Hurry Up, Jessie!, I Won't Go to Bed, Max and Diana and the Beach Day, Max and Diana and the Snowy Day, A New Coat for Anna, Pet Day, So Hungry!, Trip Day, Where's the Cat?, Where's the Dog?, Where's the Guinea Pig,* and *Worm Day,* and 1990, for *Where Babies Come From: Stories to Help Parents Answer Preschoolers' Questions about Sex;* Outstanding Science Trade Book for Children, National Science Teachers Association and the Children's Book Council, for *Let's Get a Pet.*

WRITINGS:

FOR CHILDREN

The Bath Book, Scholastic (New York, NY), 1981.
The Bed Book, Scholastic (New York, NY), 1981.

Baby Ben's Bow-Wow Book, Baby Ben's Busy Book, and *Baby Ben's Noisy Book,* illustrated by Norman Gorbaty, Random House (New York, NY), 1984.
Clappity Clap!, photos by Rudi Tesa, Viking (New York, NY), 1984.
Diggity Dig!, photos by Rudi Tesa, Viking (New York, NY), 1984.
Zippety Zip!, photos by Rudi Tesa, Viking (New York, NY), 1984.
Flip the Switch!, illustrated by Norman Gorbaty, Grosset (New York, NY), 1984.
Sleepy Dog, illustrated by Norman Gorbaty, Random House (New York, NY), 1984, republished, 2003.
Munchety Munch!, photos by Rudi Tesa, Viking (New York, NY), 1984.
Push the Button, illustrated by Norman Gorbaty, Grosset (New York, NY), 1984.
The Small Potatoes Club, illustrated by Richard Brown, Dell (New York, NY), 1984.
The Small Potatoes and the Magic Show, illustrated by Richard Brown, Dell (New York, NY), 1984.
Turn the Dial, illustrated by Norman Gorbaty, Grosset (New York, NY), 1984.
Turn the Key, illustrated by Norman Gorbaty, Grosset (New York, NY), 1984.
Where Is My Dinner?, Where Is My Family?, Where Is My Friend?, Where Is My House?, illustrated by Simms Taback, Grosset (New York, NY), 1984.
Baby Ben Gets Dressed, illustrated by Norman Gorbaty, Random House (New York, NY), 1985.
Birthday Card, Where Are You?, illustrated by Richard Brown, Puffin (New York, NY), 1985.
A Dozen Dogs, illustrated by Carol Nicklaus, Random House (New York, NY), 1985, republished, 2003.
Nicky's Christmas Surprise, illustrated by Richard Brown, Puffin (New York, NY), 1985.

On Our Way to the Barn, On Our Way to the Forest, On Our Way to the Water, On Our Way to the Zoo, illustrated by Simms Taback, Harper (New York, NY), 1985.

The Small Potatoes and the Birthday Party, illustrated by Richard Brown, Dell (New York, NY), 1985.

The Small Potatoes and the Sleep-Over, illustrated by Richard Brown, Dell (New York, NY), 1985.

So Sick!, illustrated by Carol Nicklaus, Random House (New York, NY), 1985.

Where's My Easter Egg?, illustrated by Richard Brown, Puffin (New York, NY), 1985.

Suppertime for Baby Ben, illustrated by Norman Gorbaty, Random House (New York, NY), 1985.

Baby Ben's Color Book, illustrated by Norman Gorbaty, Random House (New York, NY), 1985.

Where's the Halloween Treat?, illustrated by Richard Brown, Puffin (New York, NY), 1985.

All Clean!, illustrated by Henrik Drescher, Harper (New York, NY), 1986.

All Gone!, illustrated by Henrik Drescher, Harper (New York, NY), 1986.

Bear All Year, illustrated by Arnold Lobel, Viking (New York, NY), 1986.

Bear Gets Dressed, illustrated by Arnold Lobel, Viking (New York, NY), 1986.

Bear Goes Shopping, illustrated by Arnold Lobel, Viking (New York, NY), 1986.

Bear's Busy Morning, illustrated by Arnold Lobel, Viking (New York, NY), 1986.

Cock-a-Doodle-Doo!, illustrated by Henrik Drescher, Harper (New York, NY), 1986.

Dress Little Bunny, illustrated by Lisa Campbell Ernst, Viking (New York, NY), 1986.

Good Night, Lewis!, illustrated by Carol Nicklaus, Random House (New York, NY), 1986.

Harry Takes a Bath, illustrated by Mavis Smith, Viking (New York, NY), 1986.

Keeping Daddy Awake on the Way Home from the Beach, illustrated by Seymour Chwast, Harper (New York, NY), 1986.

Let's Go! Piggety Pig, illustrated by David Prebenna, Little, Brown (Boston, MA), 1986.

Let's Watch Nicky, illustrated by Richard Brown, Viking (New York, NY), 1986.

Lewis the Firefighter, illustrated by Carol Nicklaus, Random House (New York, NY), 1986.

Listen! Piggety Pig, illustrated by David Prebenna, Little, Brown (Boston, MA), 1986.

My Sister Says Nothing Ever Happens When We Go Sailing, illustrated by Seymour Chwast, Harper (New York, NY), 1986.

A New Coat for Anna, illustrated by Anita Lobel, Knopf (New York, NY), 1986.

Nicky's Friends, illustrated by Richard Brown, Viking (New York, NY), 1986.

Nicky's Noisy Night, illustrated by Richard Brown, Puffin (New York, NY), 1986.

Nicky's Picnic, illustrated by Richard Brown, Puffin (New York, NY), 1986.

No More! Piggety Pig, illustrated by David Prebenna, Little, Brown (Boston, MA), 1986.

No, No, Nicky, illustrated by Richard Brown, Viking (New York, NY), 1986.

Piggety Pig from Morning 'til Night, illustrated by David Prebenna, Little, Brown (Boston, MA), 1986.

Run! Run!, illustrated by Henrik Drescher, Harper (New York, NY), 1986.

Sarah's Questions, illustrated by Susan Bonners, Lothrop (New York, NY), 1986.

The Small Potatoes and the Snowball Fight, illustrated by Richard Brown, Dell (New York, NY), 1986.

The Small Potatoes' Busy Beach Day, illustrated by Richard Brown, Dell (New York, NY), 1986.

Play with Little Bunny, illustrated by Lisa Campbell Ernst, Viking (New York, NY), 1986.

Good Night, Jessie!, illustrated by Mavis Smith, Random House (New York, NY), 1987.

The Good-Day Bunnies, illustrated by Carol Nicklaus, Golden (New York, NY), 1987.

Harry Takes a Bath, illustrated by Mavis Smith, Viking (New York, NY), 1987.

Hurry Up, Jessie!, illustrated by Mavis Smith, Random House (New York, NY), 1987.

I Won't Go to Bed!, illustrated by Andrea Baruffi, Little, Brown (Boston, MA), 1987.

Jason's Bus Ride, illustrated by Simms Taback, Viking (New York, NY), 1987.

Lewis Said, Lewis Did, illustrated by Carol Nicklaus, Random House (New York, NY), 1987.

Max and Diana and the Beach Day, illustrated by Lonni Sue Johnson, Harper (New York, NY), 1987.

Max and Diana and the Birthday Present, illustrated by Lonni Sue Johnson, Harper (New York, NY), 1987.

Max and Diana and the Shopping Day, illustrated by Lonni Sue Johnson, Harper (New York, NY), 1987.

Max and Diana and the Snowy Day, illustrated by Lonni Sue Johnson, Harper (New York, NY), 1987.

Mike and Tony: Best Friends, illustrated by Catherine Siracusa, Viking (New York, NY), 1987.

A New House for Mole and Mouse, illustrated by David Prebenna, Puffin (New York, NY), 1987.

Nicky Upstairs and Down, illustrated by Richard Brown, Puffin (New York, NY), 1987.

Pet Day, illustrated by Richard Brown, Little, Brown (Boston, MA), 1987.

Say Good Night!, illustrated by Catherine Siracusa, Puffin (New York, NY), 1987.

So Big!, So Busy!, So Clean!, So Hungry!, [and] *So Little!,* illustrated by Mavis Smith, Random House (New York, NY), 1987.

Trip Day, illustrated by Richard Brown, Little, Brown (Boston, MA), 1987.

Where Is Nicky's Valentine?, illustrated by Richard Brown, Puffin (New York, NY), 1987.

Where's the Cat?, Where's the Dog, Where's the Turtle, [and] *Where's the Guinea Pig?,* illustrated by Simms Taback, Harper (New York, NY), 1987.

Worm Day, illustrated by Richard Brown, Little, Brown (Boston, MA), 1987.

(As Jane Fine) *Surprise!,* illustrated by Mary Morgan, Viking (New York, NY), 1988.

(As Margot Linn) *A Trip to the Dentist,* illustrated by Catherine Siracusa, Harper (New York, NY), 1988.

(As Margot Linn) *A Trip to the Doctor,* illustrated by Catherine Siracusa, Harper (New York, NY), 1988.

Andy Toots His Horn, illustrated by Sanford Hoffman, Viking (New York, NY), 1988.

Breakfast Time!, illustrated by Lisa Campbell Ernst, Simon & Schuster (New York, NY), 1988.

Bye-Bye, Daddy, illustrated by Lisa Campbell Ernst, Simon & Schuster (New York, NY), 1988.

Cat Games, illustrated by Claire Schumacher, Viking (New York, NY), 1988.

Chocolate Mud Cake, illustrated by Karen Gundersheimer, Harper (New York, NY), 1988.

A Clean House for Mole and Mouse, illustrated by David Prebenna, Viking (New York, NY), 1988.

Come out, Jessie!, illustrated by Mavis Smith, Random House (New York, NY), 1988.

Count with Little Bunny, illustrated by Lisa Campbell Ernst, Viking (New York, NY), 1988.

Daddy, Can You Play with Me?, illustrated by Emilie Boon, Viking (New York, NY), 1988.

Dark Night, Sleepy Night, illustrated by Andrea Baruffi, Viking (New York, NY), 1988.

Dinner's Ready, Jessie!, illustrated by Mavis Smith, Random House (New York, NY), 1988.

Don't Cry, Baby Sam, illustrated by Richard Brown, Viking (New York, NY), 1988.

Egg-Drop Day, illustrated by Richard Brown, Little, Brown (Boston, MA), 1988.

Feed Little Bunny, illustrated by Lisa Campbell Ernst, Viking (New York, NY), 1988.

Finding Robin Redbreast, illustrated by Mavis Smith, Puffin (New York, NY), 1988.

Good Morning, Sun!, illustrated by Lisa Campbell Ernst, Viking (New York, NY), 1988.

Good Night, Everyone!, illustrated by Andrea Baruffi, Little, Brown (Boston, MA), 1988.

Happy Birthday, Grandpa!, illustrated by Sidney Levitt, Harper (New York, NY), 1988.

Happy Easter, Grandma!, illustrated by Sidney Levitt, Harper (New York, NY), 1988.

Here Comes a Bus, illustrated by Richard Brown, Puffin (New York, NY), 1988.

Let's Get Dressed, illustrated by Lisa Campbell Ernst, Viking (New York, NY), 1988.

Me, Too! Me, Too!, illustrated by Karen Gundersheimer, Harper (New York, NY), 1988.

Mommy, Where Are You?, illustrated by Emilie Boon, Puffin (New York, NY), 1988.

Mystery Day, illustrated by Richard Brown, Little, Brown (Boston, MA), 1988.

Snow Magic, illustrated by Claire Schumacher, Viking (New York, NY), 1988.

Strike Four!, illustrated by Mavis Smith, Viking (New York, NY), 1988.

Thank You, Nicky, illustrated by Richard Brown, Puffin (New York, NY), 1988.

What Do I Hear?, What Do I See?, What Do I Smell?, What Do I Taste?, [and] *What Do I Touch?,* illustrated by Mavis Smith, Bantam (New York, NY), 1988.

Animal Count, Puffin (New York, NY), 1989.

Bears 1, 2, 3, Random House (New York, NY), 1989.

Before I Was Born, illustrated by Rufus Coes, Knopf (New York, NY), 1989.

The Best Castle Ever, illustrated by Carol Nicklaus, Random House (New York, NY), 1989.

The Big Birthday Box, illustrated by Laura Rader, Random House (New York, NY), 1989.

Boats, Puffin (New York, NY), 1989.

Can You Play?, Random House (New York, NY), 1989.

Dr. Cat, illustrated by Suzy Mandel, Viking (New York, NY), 1989.

Going on a Lion Hunt, illustrated by Mavis Smith, Puffin (New York, NY), 1989.

Harry Goes to Fun Land, Puffin (New York, NY), 1989.

Henry's Wrong Turn, illustrated by Andrea Baruffi, Little, Brown (Boston, MA), 1989.

How Big Is Big?, illustrated by Andrea Baruffi, Viking (New York, NY), 1989.

In a Scary Old House, illustrated by Mavis Smith, Puffin (New York, NY), 1989.

In My Kitchen, illustrated by Laura Rader, Random House (New York, NY), 1989.

Let's Trade, illustrated by Mary Morgan, Puffin (New York, NY), 1989.

My Getting-Ready-for-School Book, illustrated by Mavis Smith, Random House (New York, NY), 1989.

New Boots for Spring, illustrated by Deborah Kogan Ray, Viking (New York, NY), 1989.

No Ball Games Here, Puffin (New York, NY), 1989.

No More TV, Sleepy Dog, illustrated by Norman Gorbaty, Random House (New York, NY), 1989.

Please Let It Snow, illustrated by Amy Aitken, Viking (New York, NY), 1989.

The Prince Has a Boo-Boo!, illustrated by R. W. Alley, Random House (New York, NY), 1989.

Wait for Us!, illustrated by Amy Aitken, Random House (New York, NY), 1989.

When the TV Broke, illustrated by Mavis Smith, Viking (New York, NY), 1989.

(With Martin Silverman) *Where Babies Come From: Stories to Help Parents Answer Preschoolers' Questions about Sex,* illustrated by Claire Schumacher, Random House (New York, NY), 1989.

Wish for a Fish, illustrated by Argus Childers, Random House (New York, NY), 1989.

With Love from Grandma, illustrated by Deborah Kogan Ray, Viking (New York, NY), 1989.

Follow Me!, illustrated by Laura Rader, Puffin (New York, NY), 1990.

Getting Ready for the New Baby, illustrated by Laura Rader, Harper (New York, NY), 1990.

I Want to Sleep in Your Bed!, illustrated by Mavis Smith, Harper (New York, NY), 1990.

Let's Get a Pet, illustrated by Mavis Smith, Houghton Mifflin (Boston, MA), 1990.

Let's Swap, Puffin (New York, NY), 1990.

Little Bunny's Melon Patch, illustrated by Lisa Campbell Ernst, Puffin (New York, NY), 1990.

Little Bunny's Noisy Friends, illustrated by Lisa Campbell Ernst, Puffin (New York, NY), 1990.

My Getting-Ready-for-Christmas Book [and] *My Getting-Ready-for-Bed Book,* illustrated by Mavis Smith, Harper (New York, NY), 1990.

Noisy Barn!, illustrated by Simms Taback, Harper (New York, NY), 1990, republished, Blue Apple Books (Maplewood, NJ), 2003.

Parade, illustrated by Saul Mandel, Bantam (New York, NY), 1990.

Penny Goes to the Movies, illustrated by Laura Rader, Viking (New York, NY), 1990.

The Prince's Tooth Is Loose, illustrated by R. W. Alley, Random House (New York, NY), 1990.

Stitches, illustrated by Amy Aitken, Puffin (New York, NY), 1990.

Tim and Jim Take Off, illustrated by Suzy Mandel, Viking (New York, NY), 1990.

Under the Water, illustrated by Suzy Mandel, Puffin (New York, NY), 1990.

The Wheels on the Bus, illustrated by Andrea Baruffi, Random House (New York, NY), 1990.

Who Can Boo the Loudest?, Harper (New York, NY), 1990.

Zoo Parade!, illustrated by Simms Taback, Harper (New York, NY), 1990, republished, Blue Apple Books (Maplewood, NJ), 2003.

Big to Little, Little to Big, illustrated by Susan Baum, Simon & Schuster (New York, NY), 1991.

Bigger Than a Baby, illustrated by Laura Rader, HarperCollins (New York, NY), 1991.

Bob and Shirley: A Tale of Two Lobsters, illustrated by Mavis Smith, HarperCollins (New York, NY), 1991.

A Car Trip for Mole and Mouse, illustrated by David Prebenna, Puffin (New York, NY), 1991.

Dancing, illustrated by Laura Rader, HarperCollins (New York, NY), 1991.

Good Luck, Bad Luck, illustrated by Lillie James, Puffin (New York, NY), 1991.

Goody New Shoes, illustrated by Laura Rader, Puffin (New York, NY), 1991.

Harry Gets Ready for School, illustrated by Mavis Smith, Puffin (New York, NY), 1991.

Homes, Scholastic (New York, NY), 1991.

I Hate Boots!, illustrated by Laura Rader, HarperCollins (New York, NY), 1991.

Later, Rover, illustrated by David Jacobson, Puffin (New York, NY), 1991.

Measure Me: A Counting Book, HarperCollins (New York, NY), 1991.

Move Over, illustrated by Laura Rader, HarperCollins (New York, NY), 1991.

My Apple Tree, illustrated by Laura Rader, HarperCollins (New York, NY), 1991.

Sometimes I Share, illustrated by Carol Nicklaus, HarperCollins (New York, NY), 1991.

Take My Picture!, illustrated by Amy Aitken, HarperCollins (New York, NY), 1991.

Tommy the Winner, illustrated by Claire Schumacher, HarperCollins (New York, NY), 1991.

When Daddy Had the Chicken Pox, illustrated by Lionel Kalish, HarperCollins (New York, NY), 1991.

When Will Santa Come?, illustrated by Claire Schumacher, HarperCollins (New York, NY), 1991.

The Big, Red Blanket, illustrated by David Jacobson, HarperCollins (New York, NY), 1992.

Clothes on, Clothes Off, illustrated by Susan Baum, HarperCollins (New York, NY), 1992.

Come Visit My House!, illustrated by Mavis Smith, Viking (New York, NY), 1992.

Count up, Count Down, illustrated by Susan Baum, HarperCollins (New York, NY), 1992.

Empty to Full, Full to Empty, illustrated by Susan Baum, HarperCollins (New York, NY), 1992.

Halloween Parade, illustrated by Lillie James, Puffin (New York, NY), 1992.

Here Comes a Truck, illustrated by Richard Brown, Puffin (New York, NY), 1992.

Music Lessons, HarperCollins (New York, NY), 1992.

My Daddy, My Mommy, [and] *My Puppy,* Viking (New York, NY), 1992.

Oh No, Nicky!, illustrated by Richard Brown, Puffin (New York, NY), 1992.

The Princess Needs a Bath, HarperCollins (New York, NY), 1992.

Sam and Lucy, illustrated by Claire Schumacher, HarperCollins (New York, NY), 1992.

What Is Father's Day?, What Is Mother's Day?, What Is Halloween?, [and] *What Is Thanksgiving?,* illustrated by Claire Schumacher, HarperCollins (New York, NY), 1992.

Where's Daddy's Car? [and] *Where's Mommy's Truck?,* illustrated by Andrea Baruffi, HarperCollins (New York, NY), 1992.

Who Spilled the Milk?, HarperCollins (New York, NY), 1992.

Bear's Colors, Bear's Numbers, Bear's Shapes, [and] *Bear's Weather,* illustrated by Susan Baum, HarperCollins (New York, NY), 1993.

Clown Games, illustrated by Larry Stevens, Puffin (New York, NY), 1993.

My Camera, My Cassette Player, My Telephone, [and] *My Television,* illustrated by Laura Rader, Ziefert, Inc., 1993.

My Valentines, Harper (New York, NY), 1993.

What Is Valentine's Day?, illustrated by Claire Schumacher, HarperCollins (New York, NY), 1993.

Scooter's Christmas, illustrated by Richard Brown, Harper (New York, NY), 1993.

Three Wishes, illustrated by David Jacobson, Puffin (New York, NY), 1993.

What's a Birthday?, What's a Vacation?, [and] *What's a Wedding?,* illustrated by Claire Schumacher, HarperFestival (New York, NY), 1993.

Where's Bobo?, illustrated by Lillie James, Tambourine (New York, NY), 1993.

Halloween Parade, illustrated by Lillie James, Puffin (New York, NY), 1993.

(Reteller) *Goldilocks and the Three Bears,* illustrated by Laura Rader, Tambourine (New York, NY), 1994.

Pete's Chicken, illustrated by Laura Rader, Tambourine (New York, NY), 1994.

We Dare You!, illustrated by G. Brian Karas, Simon & Schuster (New York, NY), 1994.

(Reteller) *The Three Billy Goats Gruff,* illustrated by Laura Rader, Tambourine (New York, NY), 1994.

What Is Hanukkah? [and] *What Is Passover?,* illustrated by Lillie James, HarperFestival (New York, NY), 1994.

Where Is My Baby?, illustrated by Simms Taback, HarperFestival (New York, NY), 1994, republished, Handprint Books (Brooklyn, NY), 2002.

Animals of the Bible, illustrated by Letizia Galli, Doubleday (New York, NY), 1995.

The Best Smelling Alphabet Book, Little Simon (New York, NY), 1995.

(Reteller) *The Gingerbread Boy,* illustrated by Emily Bolam, Puffin (New York, NY), 1995.

Happy Birthday, Little Bear, illustrated by Susan Baum, Viking (New York, NY), 1995.

Little Mouse Meets Santa [and] *Little Mouse Meets the Easter Bunny,* HarperFestival (New York, NY), 1995.

The Little Red Hen, illustrated by Emily Bolam, Puffin (New York, NY), 1995.

Nicky, 1-2-3, Puffin (New York, NY), 1995.

Oh, What a Noisy Farm!, illustrated by Emily Bolam, Tambourine (New York, NY), 1995.

Scare the Moon, Candlewick (Cambridge, MA), 1995.

Take Care of Brown Bear, illustrated by Susan Baum, Viking (New York, NY), 1995.

(Reteller) *The Teeny-Tiny Woman,* illustrated by Laura Rader, Viking (New York, NY), 1995.

(Reteller) *The Three Little Pigs,* illustrated by Laura Rader, Viking (New York, NY), 1995.

What Rhymes with Eel?, Viking (New York, NY), 1995.

What's Polite? [and] *What's Pretend?,* Puffin (New York, NY), 1995.

Animal Play, DK Publishing (New York, NY), 1996.

Benjy Bear's Christmas [and] *Benjy Bear's Halloween,* illustrated by Emilie Boon, Candlewick (Cambridge, MA), 1996.

My Clothes [and] *My Food,* DK Publishing (New York, NY), 1996.

Play Colors [and] *Play Shapes,* DK Publishing (New York, NY), 1996.

Timothy's Shapes, illustrated by Emilie Boon, DK Publishing (New York, NY), 1996.

Timothy's Numbers, illustrated by Emilie Boon, DK Publishing (New York, NY), 1996.

The Wish Pillow, illustrated by Susan Baum, DK Publishing (New York, NY), 1996.

(Reteller) *The Princess and the Pea,* illustrated by Emily Bolam, Penguin (New York, NY), 1996.

Rosie Rabbit's Easter [and] *Rosie Rabbit's Valentine's Day,* Candlewick (Cambridge, MA), 1996.

Rosie's Red String, DK Publishing (New York, NY), 1996.

Sam's Boo-Boo, DK Publishing (New York, NY), 1996.

The Turnip, illustrated by Laura Rader, Puffin (New York, NY), 1996.

Two Little Witches, illustrated by Simms Taback, Candlewick (Cambridge, MA), 1996.

Who Said Moo?, illustrated by Simms Taback, Harper-Festival (New York, NY), 1996, republished, Handprint Books (Brooklyn, NY), 2002.

Baby Buggy, Buggy Baby, illustrated by Richard Brown, Houghton Mifflin (Boston, MA), 1997.

Bears Odd, Bears Even, illustrated by Andrea Baruffi, Viking (New York, NY), 1997.

The Cow in the House, illustrated by Emily Bolam, Puffin (New York, NY), 1997.

Eight Days of Hanukkah, illustrated by Melinda Levine, Viking (New York, NY), 1997.

(Reteller) *Henny-Penny,* illustrated by Emily Bolam, Viking (New York, NY), 1997.

Little Hippo and the New Baby, illustrated by Emilie Boon, DK Publishing (New York, NY), 1997.

The Magic Porridge Pot, illustrated by Emily Bolam, Viking (New York, NY), 1997.

Math Riddles, illustrated by Andrea Baruffi, Viking (New York, NY), 1997.

Mother Goose Math, illustrated by Emily Bolam, Viking (New York, NY), 1997.

Nicky Visits the Airport [and] *Nicky Visits the Fire Station,* illustrated by Richard Brown, Puffin (New York, NY), 1997.

Night, Knight, illustrated by Richard Brown, Houghton Mifflin (Boston, MA), 1997.

Sleepy-O!, illustrated by Laura Rader, Houghton Mifflin (Boston, MA), 1997.

No Bath Tonight!, illustrated by Emily Bolam, DK Publishing (New York, NY), 1997.

(Reteller) *The Ugly Duckling,* illustrated by Emily Bolam, Puffin (New York, NY), 1997.

Wee G., illustrated by Donald Saaf, Atheneum (New York, NY), 1997.

A Dozen Dozens, illustrated by Chris Demarest, Viking (New York, NY), 1998.

Elomenopeo, illustrated by Donald Saaf, Houghton Mifflin (Boston, MA), 1998.

I Swapped My Dog, illustrated by Emily Bolam, Houghton Mifflin (Boston, MA), 1998.

Little Hippo's New Friend, Little Hippo's New House, [and] *Little Hippo's New School,* illustrated by Emilie Boon, DK Publishing (New York, NY), 1998.

A Polar Bear Can Swim, illustrated by Emily Bolam, Viking (New York, NY), 1998.

Pushkin Meets the Bundle, illustrated by Donald Saaf, Atheneum (New York, NY), 1998.

Rabbit and Hare Divide an Apple, illustrated by Emily Bolam, Viking (New York, NY), 1998.

(Reteller) *When I First Came to This Land,* illustrated by Simms Taback, Putnam (New York, NY), 1998.

Bugs, Beetles, and Butterflies, illustrated by Lisa Flather, Viking (New York, NY), 1998.

Flip Flop Words, Dutton (New York, NY), 1998.

The Funny Red Christmas Stocking, illustrated by Laura Rader, Little Simon (New York, NY), 1998.

Waiting for Baby, illustrated by Emily Bolam, Henry Holt (New York, NY), 1998.

Who Walks on This Halloween Night?: A Lift-the-Flap Story, illustrated by Chris Demarest, Simon & Schuster, 1998.

Sara's Potty, DK Publishing (New York, NY), 1998.

Max's Potty, DK Publishing (New York, NY), 1999.

Daddies Are for Catching Fireflies, illustrated by Cynthia Jabar, Puffin (New York, NY), 1999.

Mommies Are for Counting Stars, illustrated by Cynthia Jabar, Puffin (New York, NY), 1999.

First Night, illustrated by S. D. Schindler, Putnam (New York, NY), 1999.

I Need a Valentine!, illustrated by Chris Demarest, Little Simon (New York, NY), 1999.

I Need an Easter Egg, illustrated by Laura Rader, Little Simon (New York, NY), 1999.

Clara Ann Cookie, illustrated by Emily Bolam, Houghton Mifflin (Boston, MA), 1999.

Talk, Baby!, illustrated by Emily Bolam, Henry Holt (New York, NY), 1999.

Animal Music, illustrated by Donald Saaf, Houghton Mifflin (Boston, MA), 1999.

Hats Off for the Fourth of July!, illustrated by Gustaf Miller, Viking (New York, NY), 2000.

(Reteller) *Little Red Riding Hood,* illustrated by Emily Bolam, Viking (New York, NY), 2000.

Presents for Santa, illustrated by Laura Rader, Viking (New York, NY), 2000.

Pumpkin Pie, paintings by Donald Dreifuss, Houghton Mifflin (Boston, MA), 2000.

Pushkin Minds the Bundle, paintings by Donald Saaf, Atheneum (New York, NY), 2000.

The Snow Child, illustrated by Julia Zanes, Viking (New York, NY), 2000.

Train Song, paintings by Donald Saaf, Orchard Books (New York, NY), 2000.

April Fool, illustrated by Chris Demarest, Viking/Puffin (New York, NY), 2000.

Clara Ann Cookie, Go to Bed!, illustrated by Emily Bolam, Houghton Mifflin (Boston, MA), 2000.

Moonride, illustrated by Seymour Chwast, Houghton Mifflin (Boston, MA), 2000.

First He Made the Sun, illustrated by Todd McKie, Putnam (New York, NY), 2000.

Grandmas Are for Tickles, illustrated by Jennifer Plecas, Puffin (New York, NY), 2000.

Grandpas Are for Finding Worms, illustrated by Jennifer Plecas, Puffin (New York, NY), 2000.

Ode to Humpty Dumpty, illustrated by Seymour Chwast, Houghton Mifflin (Boston, MA), 2001.

Birdhouse for Rent, illustrated by Donald Dreifuss, Houghton Mifflin (Boston, MA), 2001.

What Do Ducks Dream?, illustrated by Donald Saaf, Putnam (New York, NY), 2001.

No Kiss for Grandpa!, illustrated by Emilie Boon, Orchard Books (New York, NY), 2001.

Someday We'll Have Very Good Manners, illustrated by Chris Demarest, Putnam (New York, NY), 2001.

Thrity-nine Uses for a Friend, illustrated by Rebecca Doughty, Putnam (New York, NY), 2001.

Ding-Dong, Trick or Treat!, illustrated by Chris Demarest, Grosset (New York, NY), 2001.

Murphy Meets the Treadmill, illustrated by Emily Bolam, Houghton Mifflin (Boston, MA), 2001.

Squarehead, illustrated by Todd McKie, Houghton Mifflin (Boston, MA), 2001.

Cousins Are for Holiday Visits, illustrated by Emily Bolam, Puffin (New York, NY), 2002.

Egad, Alligator!, illustrated by Todd McKie, Houghton Mifflin (Boston, MA), 2002.

From Kalamazoo to Timbuktu, illustrated by Gustaf Miller, Putnam (New York, NY), 2002.

Teachers Are for Reading Stories, illustrated by Emily Bolam, Puffin (New York, NY), 2002.

Toes Have Wiggles, Kids Have Giggles, illustrated by Rebecca Doughty, Putnam (New York, NY), 2002.

You Can't Taste a Pickle with Your Ear: A Book about Your Five Senses, illustrated by Amanda Haley, Blue Apple Books (Maplewood, NJ), 2002.

Kitty Says Meow, illustrated by Santiago Cohen, Grosset (New York, NY), 2002.

My Funny Valentine: A Lift-the-Flap Book, illustrated by Emily Bolam, Puffin (New York, NY), 2002.

Lunchtime for a Purple Snake, illustrated by Todd McKie, Houghton Mifflin (Boston, MA), 2003.

Hey Irma!: This Is Halloween, illustrated by Barry Gott, Blue Apple Books (Maplewood, NJ), 2003.

Home for Navidad, illustrated by Santiago Cohen, Houghton Mifflin (Boston, MA), 2003.

Thrity-one Uses for a Mom, illustrated by Rebecca Doughty, Putnam (New York, NY), 2003.

A Dozen Ducklings Lost and Found: A Counting Story, illustrated by Donald Dreifuss, Houghton Mifflin (Boston, MA), 2003.

This Little Egg Went to Market, illustrated by Emily Bolam, Puffin (New York, NY), 2003.

You Can't Buy a Dinosaur with a Dime: Problem Solving in Dollars and Cents, illustrated by Amanda Haley, Blue Apple Books (Maplewood, NJ), 2003.

You Can't See Your Bones with Binoculars: A Guide to Your 206 Bones, illustrated by Amanda Haley, Blue Apple Books (Maplewood, NJ), 2003.

Rockheads, illustrated by Todd McKie, Houghton Mifflin (Boston, MA), 2004.

Forty-one Uses for a Cat, illustrated by Todd McKie, Barnes & Noble (New York, NY), 2004.

Forty-four Uses for a Dog, illustrated by Todd McKie, Barnes & Noble (New York, NY), 2004.

Noisy Forest, illustrated by Simms Taback, Blue Apple Books (Maplewood, NJ), 2004.

My Friend Grandpa, illustrated by Robert Wurzburg, Blue Apple Books (Maplewood, NJ), 2004.

Buzzy's Big Bedtime Book, illustrated by Emily Bolam, Blue Apple Books (Maplewood, NJ), 2004.

Buzzy's Birthday, illustrated by Emily Bolam, Blue Apple Books (Maplewood, NJ), 2004.

Schools Have Learn, illustrated by Amanda Haley, Blue Apple Books (Maplewood, NJ), 2004.

One Smart Skunk, illustrated by Santiago Cohen, Blue Apple Books (Maplewood, NJ), 2004.

Also the author of school readers and the text *The Literature Experience,* 1991. Ziefert's books have been translated into Spanish and French.

AS HARRIET MARGOLIN

Busy Bear's Closet, illustrated by Carol Nicklaus, Grosset (New York, NY), 1985.
Busy Bear's Cupboard, illustrated by Carol Nicklaus, Grosset (New York, NY), 1985.
Busy Bear's Refrigerator, illustrated by Carol Nicklaus, Grosset (New York, NY), 1985.
Busy Bear's Room, illustrated by Carol Nicklaus, Grosset (New York, NY), 1985.
The Good-Day Bunnies Shopping Day, illustrated by Carol Nicklaus, Golden (New York, NY), 1987.
The Good-Day Bunnies Swimming Day, illustrated by Carol Nicklaus, Golden (New York, NY), 1987.
The Good-Day Bunnies Tooth Day, illustrated by Carol Nicklaus, Golden (New York, NY), 1987.
The Good-Day Bunnies—The Great Spring Cookie Hunt, illustrated by Carol Nicklaus, Golden (New York, NY), 1987.

AS H. M. EHRLICH

Dr. Duck, illustrated by Laura Rader, Orchard Books (New York, NY), 2000.
Louie's Goose, illustrated by Laura Rader, Orchard Books (New York, NY), 2000.
Dancing Class, illustrated by Laura Rader, Orchard Books (New York, NY), 2001.
Gotcha, Louie!, illustrated by Laura Rader, Orchard Books (New York, NY), 2002.

ADAPTATIONS: A New Coat for Anna was adapted for filmstrip, Random House (New York, NY), 1988.

SIDELIGHTS: Harriet Ziefert is the prolific author and packager of scores of easy-to-read picture books for very young readers. Among her popular and award-winning titles are *Sleepy Dog, A New Coat for Anna, I Won't Go to Bed!, Sarah's Questions, Where Babies Come From: Stories to Help Parents Answer Preschoolers' Questions about Sex* (with Martin Silverman), and series books such as the "Max and Diana" and "Jessie" sets. A former teacher, Ziefert saw a need for more simplified texts at the first-grade

level and has applied herself to filling that need, creating books which tell a story in a mere fifty to seventy-five words. Ziefert writes her books quickly, as she has said, in under twelve hours, producing some twenty titles a year for which she then finds an illustrator, designer, and printer, delivering a completed package to the publisher.

Born in 1941, Ziefert grew up in North Bergen, New Jersey, studied at Smith College, and earned a master's degree in education from New York University. Subsequently, she worked for many years in elementary schools, teaching at various levels from kindergarten to the fifth grade. When she had her own children, Ziefert quit teaching; when her children reached school age, she decided to return to work, but in the field of publishing. At Scholastic, Ziefert produced materials for kindergarten language arts and social studies programs. She hoped to become an editor but was unsuccessful in finding a position and decided to write her own books instead.

Ziefert's resolve has spawned far more than a mere cottage industry. The list of her subsequent hundreds of titles includes concept books dealing with counting, the alphabet, rhyming, and questions, and titles for pure enjoyment featuring kittens, dogs, mice, chickens, and young boys and girls. Many of Ziefert's books are in series, and one of the most popular of these is "Mr. Rose's Class," a trilogy of books: *Pet Day, Trip Day,* and *Worm Day.* These books feature, according to a *Publishers Weekly* reviewer, "a smart, bespectacled teacher who asks questions, interferes gently and nudges kids in his class to think about the world around them." The class learns about pets, takes an outing to a pond, and discovers how worms mate in a series of books that "should appeal to beginning readers," according to *Booklist*'s Denise M. Wilms.

Ziefert created a series of pet recognition books with *Where's the Dog?, Where's the Cat?, Where's the Guinea Pig?,* and *Where's the Turtle?* These board books "encourage the toddler to observe familiar pets in the house and yard as they run, eat, drink and rest," noted a *Kirkus Reviews* critic. Rhymed sentences introduce each animal, and a "lift-the-flap" picture allows young readers to discover the hidden animal. Heide Piehler, in *School Library Journal,* felt that children "will enjoy the recognizable creatures, the hiding game, and . . . [the] illustrations."

Another board book series for toddlers is the group of titles featuring colorful animals enacting things children themselves do in their everyday lives. *So Big!, So Busy!, So Clean!, So Hungry!,* and *So Little!* demonstrate activities from getting dressed to playing with blocks and putting away toys. Sarah C. Vaughn, reviewing *So Hungry!* in *School Library Journal,* noted that an "added feature of this series is the note to parents that describes the various levels offered . . . and how best to use these books with children." Vaughn concluded that the title under review "would be a useful addition to most libraries."

More animals make an appearance in a quartet of books illustrated by Henrik Drescher, each of which describes—in two-word sentences—how animals eat, drink, move, and make noise. *All Clean!, All Gone!, Cock-a-Doodle-Doo!,* and *Run! Run!* practice word skills while at the same time providing enjoyable reading with their "lively" texts, according to a reviewer in *Publishers Weekly.* "This foursome is fast-paced and fun," concluded the reviewer. Another of Ziefert's signature reading series, "Hello Reading," includes *A New House for Mole and Mouse, Harry Takes a Bath, Jason's Bus Ride,* and *Mike and Tony: Best Friends.* The plotting for these stories is necessarily thin, "but illustrations are bold and bright," according to *Booklist*'s Ilene Cooper. A pair of animal friends happily move into a new house; a hippo named Harry takes a messy bath; a dog blocks the street, halting a boy's bus ride for a time; and two young boys learn to be friends, sharing lunch and sleeping over at each other's houses. Cooper concluded that "the short sentences, repetitive words, and colorful, childlike artwork invite beginning readers." Ziefert's "On Our Way" series also employs animals and short, rhyming sentences designed to build reading skills. Of *On Our Way to the Forest,* a *Publishers Weekly* reviewer commented that it is virtually "guaranteed to entertain its audience" with its "zippy text and amiable art."

Another of Ziefert's staples is the concept book. A series that employs a guessing game as its format also features a cheerful bear, with titles including *Bear All Year, Bear Gets Dressed, Bear Goes Shopping,* and *Bear's Busy Morning.* A *Kirkus Reviews* critic found these Bear stories to be a "delightful series of concept books, with stiff, glossy card stock to make them durable with young children," and useful in helping with the development of such concepts as sequencing, time, days of the week, and seasons. Marge Loch-Wouters, writing in *School Library Journal,* noted that these "playful books are good choices for preschool

story time and to put in the hands of young children who love the challenge of a guessing game." The "reason why" is at the heart of *Sarah's Questions,* the story of a young girl who asks her mother a variety of questions about the garden, the neighborhood animals, and other natural wonders. A contributor in *Publishers Weekly* felt that "the book's virtue is the quiet appreciation of everyday life," and a *Kirkus Reviews* critic dubbed this award-winning title a "summer idyll."

The concepts of friendship and safety are explored in some of the "Nicky" books, including *Nicky's Friends, Let's Watch Nicky,* and *No, No, Nicky.* The star of the books is a tiny, gray-striped kitten who makes friends with a boy and girl, mischievously goes after a goldfish, and stretches playfully. "These books are short, funny and very much to the point," noted a critic in *Publishers Weekly.* Reviewing *Nicky Upstairs and Down* for *Booklist,* Cooper maintained that this story of the kitten who runs all over the house is "just right for beginning readers." *Baby Buggy, Buggy Baby* and *Night, Knight* introduce homonyms, while sibling relations are dealt with in *Chocolate Mud Cake, Me Too! Me Too!,* and *Bigger Than a Baby.* Marge Loch-Wouters, in *School Library Journal,* called *Chocolate Mud Cake* and *Me Too! Me Too!* a "welcome change of pace from the many books on sibling rivalry." The sisters, Molly and Jenny, make mud pies and play dress-up on a rainy day. Molly, the older sister, generously includes her younger sibling in all the activities. *Booklist*'s Phillis Wilson concluded that "Jenny and Molly are a delight to meet." *Bigger Than a Baby* is a title "to help youngsters understand and appreciate their new siblings," according to Dorothy Evans in *School Library Journal.* This book compares the development of a baby to the growth of its older sister, and thus might "be useful for children adjusting to new siblings or for other children having trouble feeling comfortable with new abilities and responsibilities," observed Kay Weisman in *Booklist.*

Choosing a pet, bedtime, and counting absorb Ziefert's attention in, respectively, *Let's Get a Pet, I Won't Go to Bed!,* and *Two Little Witches: A Halloween Counting Story.* Picking out a pet is "serious" business, observed *Junior Bookshelf* reviewer Marcus Crouch. Noting the comic-strip format of *Let's Get a Pet,* Crouch concluded that Ziefert makes it "good fun too." *Books for Keeps* reviewer Liz Waterland recommended the book "for any family thinking about being joined by a furry, scaly or feathered friend." When Harry protests against bedtime in *I Won't Go to Bed!,* his father allows him to stay up and promptly goes to bed himself, leaving Harry to roam about the house. Finally Harry falls asleep on the floor, eventually to be retrieved by his father and put to bed. A *Publishers Weekly* reviewer commented that the book had a "traditional theme with a nontraditional treatment," while *Booklist*'s Cooper observed that Ziefert "catches the mood of children who fantasize about staying up all night." Counting is featured in *Two Little Witches,* in which little goblins learn to count to ten at Halloween. Ziefert also employs a counting format for an introduction to another holiday, *Eight Days of Hanukkah,* and treats holidays in general in several other series and nonseries titles.

Other popular and award-winning titles by Ziefert include *A New Coat for Anna, Pete's Chicken, Henry's Wrong Turn,* and *Oh, What a Noisy Farm!* With *A New Coat for Anna,* Ziefert developed a larger story line as well as a deeper thematic approach. In a book set just after World War II, Anna's mother trades a prized possession to create a new coat for her daughter. The coat is a year in the making as the wool is grown and spun, and the red dye extracted from berries. A critic in *Kirkus Reviews* deemed the book a "warmly satisfying variation on a familiar story," while *Horn Book* contributor Ethel R. Twichell noted that the "simple text, based on a true story, carries the narrative along effectively." Susan Scheps concluded in *School Library Journal* that "Ziefert's tale . . . will be understood and cherished by all ages." *Pete's Chicken* is another longer and more ambitious picture book, the story of "an artistic rabbit [who] celebrates the true spirit of originality," according to a critic in *Publishers Weekly.* When his art teacher tells the class to draw a chicken, Pete lets loose with a purple and orange masterpiece which initially brings laughter from his schoolmates. The *Publishers Weekly* reviewer concluded that "Ziefert's uncluttered, boisterous text practically sings, filled with Pete's happy proclamations of self-confidence," while *Booklist*'s Cooper observed that "some of Pete's self-assurance might rub off on readers."

A humpback whale wanders into the busy mouth of the Hudson River instead of staying safely out to sea in *Henry's Wrong Turn,* which was inspired by actual events. Ziefert's whale tours Staten Island and buzzes by some ships before being guided back out to sea in

a picture book "with simple prose that has a humorous edge," according to Wilms in *Booklist.* More humor is served up in *Oh, What a Noisy Farm!,* the story of a farmer's wife who yells at a bull chasing the farm's cow. The wife is joined by the husband and dog, all shouting and yapping at the bull, but when it and the cow become friends everybody settles down for a nap. Susan D. Lempke of the *Bulletin of the Center for Children's Books* noted that "children, who are fond of chasing each other and shouting, will particularly enjoy this simple, happy story (adults, on the other hand, may enjoy a grown-up giggle at the euphemistic 'friendship')."

Among Ziefert's other endeavors are retellings of well-known folk and fairy tales, including *The Teeny-Tiny Woman, The Little Red Hen, Goldilocks and the Three Bears,* and *Little Red Riding Hood. Little Red Riding Hood,* the classic don't-talk-to-strangers tale, finds a little girl dressed in a red, hooded sweatshirt making her way to Grandma's. Lisa Smith of *School Library Journal* commented that Ziefert "tells the story in a brisk, straightforward style." In *The Snow Child,* Ziefert retells an old Russian story about a man and a woman who wanted a child of their own. They mold a girl out of snow, and when the woman kisses the snow child, she comes to life and brings them great happiness. When spring arrives, the girl must leave and go to a cold place, and the couple is devastated. They are happy when winter arrives again, along with their beloved snow child.

Ziefert explores other important themes in her writings for children, such as respecting others' differences and learning to understand another person's perspective. *Squarehead* is Ziefert's tale of a boy named George who has a square head, lives in a square house, likes square buildings, and frowns at the sight of a circle. One night while dreaming, George is introduced to a whole new world of curves and circles, as he views the beautiful moon, sees a ringed planet, and spots Earth from outer space. *School Library Journal* critic Kathy M. Newby called *Squarehead* a "delightful read-aloud . . . about the value of appreciating differences." In *Egad Alligator!,* a young gator cannot understand why people run away yelling "Egad Alligator!" as he approaches them. At the end, the alligator finds himself perched upon a large snake, at which point he screams "Egad Python!" and runs away. Kathy Broderick of *Booklist* observed that the book's message is "about being able to understand the other fellow's point of view."

Ziefert's books often have a multicultural appeal. *Home for Navidad* tells the story of Rosa, a young girl living in Mexico who longs for her mother to return home from her housekeeping job in New York. Rosa lives a harsh life but, as a *Kirkus Reviews* contributor noted, Ziefert's book is "tender" and will give young readers a glimpse into a different world. Ziefert introduces Hanukkah to young children in *It's Hanukkah!* The book is filled with rhymes and explains Hanukkah traditions. *Booklist*'s Hazel Rochman wrote, "Adults will need to fill in some background; it's the joy that's paramount here." In *Thirty-nine Uses for a Friend*, Ziefert creates what *Booklist* reviewer Broderick called "a fine manual of friendship, celebrating the common experiences that friends share." The colorful illustrations that accompany each role a friend plays from "alarm clock" to "hairdresser" feature many races and ethnicities to make the book a universal read.

BIOGRAPHICAL AND CRITICAL SOURCES:

BOOKS

Cullinan, Bernice E., and Diane G. Person, editors, *Continuum Encyclopedia of Children's Literature*, Continuum (New York, NY), 2001.

PERIODICALS

Appraisal, winter, 1988, pp. 63-64.

Booklist, August, 1987, Ilene Cooper, review of "Hello Reading" series, p. 1754; September 1, 1987, Denise M. Wilms, review of *Pet Day* and others, pp. 75-76; November 15, 1987, Ilene Cooper, review of *I Won't Go to Bed,* p. 574; December 1, 1987, Ilene Cooper, review of *Nicky Upstairs and Down,* p. 640; November 15, 1988, Phillis Wilson, review of *Chocolate Mud Cake* and *Me Too! Me Too!,* p. 589; January 1, 1990, Denise M. Wilms, review of *Henry's Wrong Turn,* p. 922; May 15, 1991, p. 1806; December 15, 1991, Kay Weisman, review of *Bigger Than a Baby,* p. 768; September 15, 1994, Ilene Cooper, review of *Pete's Chicken,* p. 146; October 1, 1995, p. 329; September 1, 1996, p. 138; March 1, 1999, Stephanie Zvirin, review of *Clara Ann Cookie,* p. 1223; October 15, 1999, Stephanie Zvirin, review of *Animal Music,*

p. 457, GraceAnne DeCandido, review of *First Night,* p. 458; February 15, 2000, Hazel Rochman, review of *Little Red Riding Hood,* p. 1125, Carolyn Phelan, review of *April Fool!,* p. 1125; March 15, 2000, Marta Segal, review of *Moonride,* p. 1390; April 1, 2000, Carolyn Phelan, review of *Train Song,* p. 1472; April 15, 2000, Ellen Mandel, review of *First He Made the Sun,* p. 1555; December 1, 2000, Carolyn Phelan, review of *Presents for Santa,* p. 727, Gillian Engberg, review of *The Snow Child,* p. 727, Todd Morning, review of *Pumpkin Pie,* p. 724; February 15, 2001, Connie Fletcher, review of *Someday We'll Have Very Good Manners,* p. 1142; September 1, 2001, Ilene Cooper, review of *Murphy Meets the Treadmill,* p. 118; December 1, 2001, Kathy Broderick, review of *Thirty-nine Uses for a Friend,* p. 651; April 15, 2002, Kathy Broderick, review of *Egad Alligator!,* p. 1410; June 1, 2002, Ilene Cooper, review of *Toes Have Wiggles, Kids Have Giggles,* p. 1744; November 1, 2003, Hazel Rochman, review of *It's Hanukkah!,* p. 508; December 1, 2003, Gillian Engberg, review of *You Can't See Your Bones with Binoculars: A Guide to Your 206 Bones,* p. 681; March 1, 2004, Ilene Cooper, review of *Noisy Barn!,* p. 1199.

Books for Keeps, September, 1994, Liz Waterland, review of *Let's Get a Pet,* p. 7.

Book World, May 13, 2001, review of *Squarehead,* p. 9.

Bulletin of the Center for Children's Books, October, 1991, p. 53; May, 1995, Susan D. Lempke, review of *Oh, What a Noisy Farm,* p. 328; April, 1997, p. 302; May, 1998, p. 345; February, 2001, review of *Someday We'll Have Very Good Manners,* p. 242.

Children's Bookwatch, July, 2001, review of *What Do Ducks Dream?,* p. 6.

Horn Book, March, 1987, Edith Twichell, review of *A New Coat for Anna,* p. 204; July-August, 1998, p. 481.

Junior Bookshelf, October, 1994, Marcus Crouch, review of *Let's Get a Pet,* p. 167.

Kirkus Reviews, August 15, 1986, review of *Bear All Year* and others, p. 1293; September 15, 1986, review of *Sarah's Questions,* p. 1447; October 15, 1986, review of *A New Coat for Anna,* p. 1582; June 1, 1987, review of *Where's the Dog* and others, p. 864; August 15, 1994, p. 1141; June 15, 1995, p. 866; May 1, 1998, p. 666; December 15, 1999, review of *Little Red Riding Hood,* p. 1966;

April 1, 2001, review of *What Do Ducks Dream?*, p. 510; May 15, 2001, review of *No Kiss for Grandpa!*, p. 748; June 1, 2001, review of *Murphy Meets the Treadmill*, p. 808; August 15, 2001, review of *Birdhouse for Rent*, p. 1224; February 1, 2002, review of *Egad Alligator!*, p. 193; June 1, 2003, review of *You Can't Buy a Dinosaur with a Dime: Problem-Solving in Dollars and Cents*, p. 813; November 1, 2003, review of *Home for Navidad*, p. 1321; December 15, 2003, review of *You Can't See Your Bones with Binoculars*, p. 1455; April 1, 2004, review of *Rockheads*, p. 339; June 1, 2004, review of *Buzzy's Boo-Boo*, p. 543; June 15, 2004, review of *Thirty-three Uses for a Dad*, p. 583.

New York Times Book Review, November 21, 1999, Cynthia Zarin, review of *Talk, Baby!*, p. 54.

Publishers Weekly, August 22, 1986, review of *Run! Run!* and others, p. 92; October 31, 1986, review of *Sarah's Questions*, p. 64; November 28, 1986, review of *Nicky's Friends* and others, p. 72; June 26, 1987, review of *Pet Day* and others, p. 72; October 9, 1987, review of *I Won't Go to Bed*, p. 167; April 5, 1993, p. 74; June 21, 1993, review of *On Our Way to the Forest*, p. 103; June 27, 1994, review of *Pete's Chicken*, p. 78; April 17, 1995, p. 57; September 30, 1996, p. 85; March 9, 1998, p. 67; May 4, 1998, p. 212; April 5, 1999, review of *Clara Ann Cookie*, p. 239; September 20, 1999, review of *Talk, Baby!*, p. 90; June 5, 2000, review of *Hats Off for the Fourth of July!*, p. 93; March 26, 2001, review of *Ode to Humpty Dumpty*, p. 93; April 23, 2001, review of *Squarehead*, p. 77; June 4, 2001, review of *What Do Ducks Dream?*, p. 80; July 9, 2001, review of *Murphy Meets the Treadmill*, p. 67; March 4, 2002, reviews of *Where Is My Baby?* and *Who Said Moo?*, p. 81; November 4, 2002, review of *You Can't Taste a Pickle with Your Ear: A Book about Your Five Senses*, p. 83; February 3, 2003, reviews of *A Dozen Ducklings Lost and Found* and *Lunchtime for a Purple Snake*, p. 75; February 24, 2003, review of *Thirty-one Uses for a Mom*, p. 74; May 13, 2003, review of *Nicky's Noisy Night*, p. 68; September 22, 2003, review of *Home for Navidad*, p. 70.

Reading Teacher, May, 1999, review of *When I First Came to This Land*, p. 890.

Riverbank Review, summer, 2001, review of *What Do Ducks Dream?*, p. 34.

School Librarian, February, 1987, pp. 18-19; November, 1994, p. 148; February, 1997, p. 22;

spring, 1998, p. 22; autumn, 1999, review of *Waiting for Baby*, p. 134.

School Library Journal, December, 1986, Susan Scheps, review of *A New Coat for Anna*, p. 97; January, 1987, Marge Loch-Wouters, review of *Bear All Year* and others, p. 69; November, 1987, Heide Piehler, review of *Where's the Dog* and others, p. 98; March, 1988, Sarah C. Vaughn, review of *So Hungry!*, p. 180; December, 1988, Marge Loch-Wouters, review of *Chocolate Mud Cake* and *Me Too! Me Too!*, p. 96; January, 1992, Dorothy Evans, review of *Bigger Than a Baby*, p. 107; July, 1995, p. 71; September, 1995, p. 189; January, 1996, p. 99; July, 1997, p. 89; October, 1997, p. 39; May, 1998, p. 129; January, 1999, reviews of *Bugs, Beetles, and Butterflies* and *A Polar Bear Can Swim*, p. 123; April, 1999, review of *Clara Ann Cookie*, p. 110; May, 1999, review of *Waiting for Baby*, p. 102; August, 1999, reviews of *Daddies Are for Catching Fireflies* and *Mommies Are for Counting Stars*, p. 143; October, 1999, reviews of *Animal Music* and *Talk, Baby*, p. 130; December, 1999, review of *First Night*, p. 115; March, 2000, Diane Janoff, review of *April Fool!*, p. 220; April, 2000, Lisa Smith, review of *Little Red Riding Hood*, p. 128, Judith Constantinides, review of *Train Song*, p. 117; May, 2000, Kathy Piehl, review of *First He Made the Sun*, p. 159; July, 2000, Susan Garland, review of *Hats Off for the Fourth of July!*, p. 90; October, 2000, Piper L. Nyman, review of *Clara Ann Cookie, Go to Bed!*, p. 144; December, 2000, Corinne Camarata, review of *Moonride*, p. 128; February, 2001, Carolyn Jenks, review of *Someday We'll Have Very Good Manners*, p. 108; March, 2001, Anne Knickerbocker, review of *The Snow Child*, p. 244; May, 2001, Shara Alpern, review of *Ode to Humpty Dumpty*, p. 139, Kathy M. Newby, review of *Squarehead*, p. 139; June, 2001, Joy Fleishhacker, review of *What Do Ducks Dream?*, p. 132; September, 2001, Lauralyn Persson, review of *Birdhouse for Rent*, p. 210, Wanda Meyers-Hines, review of *On Halloween Night*, p. 210; October, 2001, Louie Lahana, review of *Murphy Meets the Treadmill*, p. 134; December, 2001, Alison Kastner, review of *Thirty-nine Uses for a Friend*, p. 116; April, 2002, Maryann H. Owen, review of *Egad Alligator!*, p. 128; June, 2002, Rosalyn Pierini, review of *Toes Have Wiggles, Kids Have Giggles*, p. 116; July, 2003, Leslie Barban, review of *You Can't Buy a Dinosaur with a Dime*, p. 120; October, 2003, Susan Patron, review of *Home for Navidad,* p. 69; January, 2004, Dona Ratterree, review of *You Can't See Your Bones with Binoculars,* p. 123; April, 2004, Donna Cardon, review of *Rockheads,* p. 144.

Social Education, May, 1999, review of *When I First Came to This Land,* p. 6.

Tribune Books (Chicago, IL), June 24, 2001, review of *What Do Ducks Dream?,* p. 5; October 21, 2001, review of *Birdhouse for Rent,* p. 4.

ONLINE

Educational Paperback Association Web site, http://www.edupaperback.org/ (November 25, 2002), "Ziefert, Harriet."

Readers Read Web site, http://www.readersread.com/ (November 25, 2002), review of *No Kiss for Grandpa!**